4-91

WALTER BREEN'S
COMPLETE ENCYCLOPEDIA
OF
U.S. AND COLONIAL
COINS

WALTER BREEN'S
COMPLETE ENCYCLOPEDIA
OF
U.S. AND COLONIAL
COINS

WALTER BREEN

F.C.I. PRESS, INC.

Doubleday

NEW YORK LONDON TORONTO SYDNEY AUCKLAND

Published by Doubleday, a division of
Bantam Doubleday Dell Publishing Group, Inc.,
666 Fifth Avenue, New York, New York 10103

Doubleday and the portrayal of an anchor with a dolphin
are trademarks of Doubleday, a division of
Bantam Doubleday Dell Publishing Group, Inc.

Designed by Elfriede Hueber

Library of Congress Cataloging in Publication Data

Breen, Walter H.
   Walter Breen's Complete encyclopedia of U.S. and colonial coins.

Bibliography: p.
   Includes index.
   1. Coins, American.   I. Title.
CJ1830.B69   1987   737.4973   79-6855
ISBN 0-385-14207-2

HOW TO USE THIS BOOK

What It Can Do for You. Whether you are totally unfamiliar with American coins beyond pocket change, or you are an advanced specialist, you can identify any major variety of United States coin, current or obsolete, familiar or unfamiliar; you can identify anything purporting to be an Early American Colonial coin; you can identify anything purporting to be a pioneer gold coin, a Confederate coin, or an authorized issue of the Kingdom of Hawaii.

What you can learn about it includes, among other things, historical circumstances of issue, physical characteristics, designer, engraver, mint of issue, quantity minted, and level of rarity. (Not all these classes of information have survived for every series.)

To the general public's favorite question, "How much is it worth?", only an approximate answer is possible. Price levels for any variety will depend on authenticity, condition, and various demand factors (including, often, positional die variety and even color). In some series they fluctuate from week to week with the gold bullion market; in others, with speculator and investor activity. For these reasons among many others, printed price levels in an encyclopedia would be obsolete before they reached the press. Many rarities reach the market so seldom that any price level would be guesswork. For some of these, auction prices are quoted in the main text; the year and circumstances can be determined from the auction's listing in the Bibliography. A coin's agreed-on value is of necessity based on what similar examples have brought at auction, where they were known to be genuine and correctly graded. *Auction prices quoted herein are part of the historical record; they are not to be taken as evidence of the resale value of any lower-grade example.*

For the rest, present plans are to compile annual price supplements, which will assign new numbers to all new issues and all verified discoveries. Price levels in each series will be the work of specialists.

For reasons of space, certain classes of collectible American metallic numismatic items are omitted. These include: 1) Minor (positional) varieties. 2) Most OMS's (off-metal strikings), including trial pieces of federal or pioneer issues; copper and other base-metal proofs 1863–85; coins struck on wrong planchets. 3) Mint errors in general. 4) Patterns and experimental pieces of unadopted designs. 5) Modern struck copies or imitations made for numismatic or souvenir trade. 6) Fractional California gold charms dated 1859–82 and later, struck for the jewelry trade, even those with dollar denominations imitating previous circulating issues. 7) Merchants' tokens and most other private issues made after the Philadelphia Mint began operations (1792). This includes the Lesher dollars, satirical Bryan money, and private circulating issues of Hawaii and Alaska. 8) Medals, gambling counters and other jetons, "model coins," play money, political medalets, etc. 9) Philippine, Cuban, and Puerto Rican issues. Most of these series are covered, not all adequately, by specialist works listed in the Bibliography.

How to Proceed. Every coin listed is preceded by a boldface number between **1** and **8035**. Your task is to find the correct number belonging to whichever coin you are looking up. If your coin has the words UNITED STATES OF AMERICA, it belongs to one of these groups: 1) Provisional mint issues of 1792, Chap. 16. 2) Federal issues, 1793–1984, Chaps. 17 through 39. 3) Gold issues of the San Francisco Provisional Branch Mint or "United States Assay Office of Gold," 1851–53, Chap. 40. Denomination and date will enable you to locate in the Contents the chapter and section in which your coin is described.

If your coin purports to be of prefederal (Early American Colonial) issue, look up its inscription in "Inscriptions on Colonial and Prefederal Coins: Translations and Index" (p. 4). This will yield the chapters and sections describing coins with these words. If none of your coin's inscriptions appear, it is probably foreign.

Pioneer gold issues are grouped by the state in which issued (Georgia, North Carolina, California, Utah, Oregon, Colorado). Confederate half dollars and cents, Alaska (Matanuska Valley) "bingles," and Kingdom of Hawaii issues follow those.

If your coin matches nothing in this Encyclopedia and yet purports to be American, it is likely to belong to one of the nine omitted classes above.

Warning: Once you have located your coin's boldface number, read the introductory text for the section containing that number, and the section heading which lists mint, designer, physical specifications, authorizing acts, grading standards. Many issues are individually discussed in these introductory texts at greater length than is feasible at their main listings. Failure to consult them may mean you are missing some of the most important information about the very item you were looking up. This includes pedigrees of known survivors of many of the extreme rarities.

Listings at each boldface number are necessarily condensed. Please familiarize yourself with the list under the heading "Bibliography, Abbreviations, Typographical Conventions." You will find, among other things, cross-references to other boldface numbers, and references to specialized works on positional varieties. A given boldface number may cover both rare and common varieties; you can lose nothing but a little time by looking these up, and you may find you have something better than you expected.

Happy hunting!
WALTER BREEN
Berkeley, California

ACKNOWLEDGMENTS

The following individuals, firms, and institutions generously furnished photographs used herein.   † = Deceased.

John W. Adams
†Kamal M. Ahwash
ANACS (Ed Fleischman)
American Numismatic Society
Philip E. Benedetti
Harry X Boosel
Q. David Bowers
Kenneth E. Bressett
The British Museum
Richard F. Buckley
Catherine E. Bullowa
Coin World
Jack Collins
David Davis
Tom DeLorey
†Homer K. Downing
†Louis Eliasberg, Sr.
Essex Numismatic Properties
First Coinvestors, Inc.
Bill Fivaz
John J. Ford, Jr.
Harry Forman
Lynn Glaser
Ken Goldman
George Gozan
William Grayson
Wade Hinderling
Johns Hopkins University
Steve Ivy
Krause Publications
Dana Linett
Manfra, Tordella & Brookes, Inc.
Dr. John R. McCloskey
Lester Merkin
Jay Miller
†Stuart Mosher
Tom Mulvaney
New England Rare Coin Galleries
Eric P. Newman
New Netherlands Coin Co., Inc.
†Sydney P. Noe
Paul Nugget
†Al Overton
†Richard Picker
Daniel Presburger
Rare Coin Company of America
  (RARCOA)
Jay Roe
H. Fred Simpson, Jr.
James C. Spilman

Frank M. Stirling
Superior Galleries
Anthony Swiatek
Anthony Terranova
Leroy C. Van Allen
Robert A. Vlack
Larry Whitlow
Whitman/Western Publishing Co.
Charles M. Wormser
Jerry Zelinka

The following individuals, firms, and institutions graciously furnished coins for photography:

John W. Adams
American Numismatic Society
Neil S. Berman
†Milford H. Bolender
†F. C. C. Boyd
W. L. Breisland
†Joseph Brobston
Mike Brownlee
Richard F. Buckley
Henry H. Clifford
Jerry Cohen
Jack Collins
†Theodore L. Craige
†Louis Eliasberg, Sr.
First Coinvestors, Inc.
Ronald J. Gillio
Henri Heller
Ed Hipps
Dr. Arthur Kahn
James D. King
Myron (Mike) Kliman
†A. Kosoff
Abner Kreisberg
Julian Leidman
Massachusetts Historical Society
Lester Merkin
R. E. Naftzger
†Mrs. R. Henry Norweb
†Richard Picker
†Wayte Raymond
Dr. Charles L. Ruby
Philip M. Showers
Smithsonian Institution
†Jacob N. Spiro
Anthony Terranova
Dr. George W. Vogt
William Wild

And over 20 other collectors and dealers requesting anonymity.

The following individuals and institutions have generously furnished technical information contributing to research incorporated herein:

Charles M. Adkins
†Kamal M. Ahwash
American Numismatic Society
Capt. Roy Ash
Richard August
Richard Bagg
Douglas Ball
†Robert Bashlow
Harry Bass
Jack H. Beymer
Michael Bobian
Harry X Boosel
Kenneth E. Bressett
Mike Brownlee
Richard F. Buckley
Carl W. A. Carlson
Ronnie Carr
†Dr. Vladimir Clain-Stefanelli
Ted Clark
Henry H. Clifford
Jack Collins
Alan D. Craig
†Theodore L. Craige
Mike Danish
John Dannreuther
David Davis
Tom DeLorey
Rev. Richard T. Deters, S.J.
Richard Doty
†Damon G. Douglas
Graham P. Dyer
Bill Fivaz
John J. Ford, Jr.
Harry Forman
John & Damia T. Francis
Dan Freidus
Melvin & George Fuld
Reed Hawn
Alan Herbert
Gene Hessler
Herbert P. Hicks
Robert W. Julian
Arthur M. Kagin
Donald Kagin
Alan Kessler
George Frederick Kolbe
†A. Kosoff
Myles Lambson
David Lange

Dr. Ivan B. Leaman
Julian Leidman
Denis W. Loring
A. George Mallis
Dr. John R. McCloskey
Alan Meghrig
Lester Merkin
Lee Minshull
†Lewis Moorman
†Stuart Mosher
John Herhold Murrell
R. E. Naftzger
Bernard Nagengast
The National Archives (Ms. Hope Hold-
    camper)
Eric P. Newman
†Sydney P. Noe
Dean Oakes
A. J. Ostheimer
†Al Overton
†Richard Picker
Andrew W. Pollock, III
Ken Potter

†Wayte Raymond
Jeff Rock
John Rowe
Philip Scott Rubin
Herbert A. Silberman
†David Sonderman
James C. Spilman
Anthony Swiatek
Don Taxay
Anthony Terranova
Marilyn Tiernan ("Collector's Clearing-
    house")
Gary A. Trudgen
Leroy C. Van Allen
Cornelius C. Vermeule
William Hallam Webber
Fritz Weber
Adolf Weiss
Randall E. Wiley
Robert C. Willey
Raymond H. Williamson
Douglas Winter
John Wright

I would also like specially to thank the
following individuals for other types of
help which came when it was most needed
—help without which this book would not
today be a reality:

†Kamal M. Ahwash
Stanley Apfelbaum
Marion Z. Bradley
Patrick R. Breen
Henry H. Clifford
Jack Collins
Dr. Alvin J. Glick
Anodea Judith
Donald Kagin
Pat MacGregor
Cindy McQuillin
Dr. Stephen Morin
†Stuart Mosher
Sterling Orser
†Wayte Raymond

CONTENTS

METROLOGY

The following tables reflect the common 17th–19th-century mint practice of reckoning coins at so many to the pound. Authorizing acts prior to 1792 did so; familiar instances include Virginia halfpence at 60 to the pound, Wood's halfpence at the same rate, FUGIO coppers at 44⁴/₉ to the pound. The reason for this type of reckoning was that bullion costs were charged at so many pence per pound, plus costs of dies, planchet preparation, and striking, while finished coins were delivered at an agreed-on (or sometimes statutory) figure of so many pieces to the pound. In some instances, weight standards have been deduced by weighing many examples and recording where figures cluster. Metric equivalents are provided for convenience. (Some coins in this table have not been assigned a figure for the number coined per pound.)

Nickel is included with the base metals, but when it was first used for coinage, mint authorities counted it as a precious metal and reckoned it in troy weight: Nickel 3¢ pieces were coined at 192 to the troy pound. French Régime coins were rated in royal edicts at so many to the marc = 244.753 grams (GD, p. 4). Here and in Chap. 5 we translate these figures directly into grains and grams. The conversion factors here used are 1 grain = 0.0647989 gram; 1 gram = 15.432356 grains; 1 troy pound = 12 troy ounces = 5,760 grains; 1 avoirdupois pound = 16 ounces avoir. = 7,000 grains.

TABLE I. WEIGHT STANDARDS (BASE METALS)

No. to the Pound Avoir.	Common Name	Grains	Grams
20	Clad Dollars (Eisenhower)	350.00	22.680
23	Tower Pence	304.34	19.721
25	ROSA AMERICANA 1733 Two-pence	280.00	18.144
	1792 Federal Cents	264.00	17.110
	1793 Federal Cents	208.00	13.480
35⁵/₇	Macclesfield (4,000 per cwt)	196.00	12.700
40	Heavy London; Clad 50¢	175.00	11.340
41²/₃	1796 Federal Cents	168.00	10.890
44⁴/₉	FUGIO (Federal 1787)	157.50	10.210
46	Tower Halfpence (1717–75)	152.17	9.861
46²/₃	Connecticut; New Jersey	150.00	9.720
50	Heavy Birmingham; Holt's Tin Halfpence	140.00	9.072
52	Irish Halfpence (1736–1823)	134.62	8.723
54	New Hampshire (June 1776)	129.63	8.400
56	Anthony Mini-Dollars	125.00	8.100
58¹/₃	Wood's Halfpence (First Sort)	120.00	7.776
60	Virginia; Birmingham Halfpence	116.67	7.560
63	Wood's Halfpence (Second Sort); Vermont	111.11	7.200
64	CONSTELLATIO NOVA (Second Sort)	109.38	7.087
	1793 Federal Half Cents	104.00	6.739

No. to the Pound Avoir.	Common Name	Grains	Grams
68	Wood's Halfpence (Third Sort)	102.94	6.670
70		100.00	6.480
72	CONSTELLATIO NOVA (Third Sort)	97.22	6.300
	Federal 2¢; Wood's (Fourth Sort)	96.00	6.221
80	Clad Quarters	87.50	5.670
83¹/₃	1796 Federal Half Cents	84.00	5.443
84		83.33	5.400
	Nickel 5¢	77.16	5.000
92	Tower ¼d; Morris's 5 Units	76.09	4.930
96		72.90	4.724
120	Wood's ¼d, Baltimore's Penny	58.33	3.780
145⁵/₆	Bronze Cents	48.00	3.110
	Steel Cents, Heavier	42.50	2.754
	Steel Cents, Lighter	41.50	2.689
200	Clad Dimes	35.00	2.268
233¹/₃	Nickel 3¢	30.00	1.944

TABLE II. WEIGHT STANDARDS (SILVER)

No. to the Pound Troy	Common Name	Fineness	Grains	Grams
13⁵/₇	Trade Dollars	900	420.00	27.216
	Dollar, Mexico or Seville (Mexico 1761–71 = 917; earlier, 931)	903	417.75	27.070
	Federal Dollar 1794–1836	892	416.00	26.956
	Federal Dollar 1837–1935	900	412.50	26.730
	Dollar, Peru 1760–1824 (1772–1824, 903 Fine. Wt. from SCWC)	917	385.81	25.000
	Silver Clad Eisenhower Dollar (Core .210 silver, clad with .800 silver)		379.51	24.592
21¹/₃	Morris's Mark, 1783	926	270.00	17.496
	French/Castorland ½ Écu	917	227.53	14.744
	Half Dollar 1794–1836	892	208.00	13.478
	Half Dollar 1837–53	900	206.25	13.365
	Half Dollar 1873–1964	900	192.90	12.500
30	Half Dollar 1853–73	900	192.00	12.441
	Silver Clad Kennedy Half Dollars (Core .210 silver, clad with .800 silver)		177.47	11.500
33	Tower Florin = 2 Shillings	925	174.55	11.310
42²/₃	Morris's Quint, 1783	926	135.00	8.748
	Quarter Dollar, 1796–1837	892	104.00	6.739
	Quarter Dollar, 1837–53	900	103.13	6.682
	Quarter Dollar, 1873–1964	900	96.45	6.250

No. to the Pound Troy	Common Name	Fineness	Grains	Grams
60	Quarter Dollar, 1853–73	900	96.00	6.221
62	Tower Shilling, 1662–1758	925	92.90	6.020
	Bicentennial Quarter (Core .210 silver, clad with .800 silver)		88.74	5.750
66	Tower Shilling, 1763–1919	925	87.27	5.655
	Twenty Cents	900	77.16	5.000
80	Boston Shilling, 1652–82	925	72.00	4.666
82½	Baltimore's Shilling	?	69.82	4.524
	Maryland Shilling, 1783	?	55.70	3.609
	Disme/Dime, 1792–1837	892	41.60	2.696
	Dime, 1837–53	900	41.25	2.673
	Dime, 1873–1964	900	38.58	2.500
150	Dime, 1853–73	900	38.40	2.488
160	Boston Sixpence, 1652–82	925	36.00	2.333
165	Baltimore's Sixpence	?	34.91	2.262
	Maryland Sixpence, 1783	?	27.85	1.805
213⅓	Morris's Bit, 1783	926	27.00	1.750
247½	Baltimore's Groat	?	23.27	1.508
	Half Disme/Dime, 1792–1837	892	20.80	1.348
	Half Dime, 1837–53	900	20.63	1.337
300	Half Dime, 1853–73	900	19.20	1.244
	Boston 3d, 1652–82	925	18.00	1.167
	Maryland 3d, 1783	?	13.92	0.902
	Billon Trime, 1851–53	750	12.38	0.802
480	Boston Twopence, 1662–82	925	12.00	0.777
500	Silver Trime, 1854–73	900	11.52	0.746

Finenesses are in parts silver per thousand, but were originally given as aliquot parts: $931 = {}^{67}/_{72}$; $926 = {}^{25}/_{27}$; $925 = \text{Sterling} = {}^{37}/_{40}$; $917 = {}^{11}/_{12}$; $903 = {}^{65}/_{72}$; $900 = {}^{9}/_{10}$; $892 = {}^{1,485}/_{1,664}$; $750 = {}^{3}/_{4}$. Further details are under individual issues.

TABLE III. WEIGHT STANDARDS (GOLD)

No. to the Pound Troy	Common Name	Fineness	Grains	Grams
	Californian 1850–53 (Fineness varies: See Chaps. 40, 43)		1,290.00	83.591
	Double Eagle	900	516.00	33.436
14	Brasher's Doubloon	?	411.43	26.660
21⅓	Eagle, 1795–1804	917	270.00	17.496
	Eagle, 1838–1933	900	258.00	16.718
28	Brasher's Half Doubloon	?	205.71	13.330
42⅔	Half Eagle, 1795–1834	917	135.00	8.748
43 11/15	Guinea, 1663–68	917	131.71	8.534
44½	Guinea, 1670–1813	917	129.44	8.387
	Half Eagle, 1834–1929 (Fineness 1834–37 = 899.225)	900	129.00	8.359
	Stella (Gold 60/70, Silver 3/70, Copper 7/70)	857	108.03	7.000
	Three Dollars	900	77.40	5.015
85⅓	Quarter Eagle, 1796–1834	917	67.50	4.374
	Quarter Eagle, 1834–1929 (Fineness 1834–37 = 899.225)	900	64.50	4.180
	Dollar, 1849–1917	900	25.80	1.672

To obtain weight of pure gold or silver in a coin of weight W and fineness F, multiply $W \times F/1{,}000$. To convert to decimal troy oz: If W is in grains, divide the product in step one by 480; if W is in grams, multiply by 0.0321507 and round off to not over three decimal places.

TABLE IV. ALIQUOT INCHES AND METRIC EQUIVALENTS

Diameters on all coins struck before the close collar was introduced (Boulton & Watt, 1788; Philadelphia, 1828–36) will vary slightly; especially in hammered coinages, blanks may be out of round. Directives and the rare laws specifying diameters sometimes used aliquot parts of inches in other units than American scale (sixteenths of an inch), but never metric units; the latter are included for convenience. In the main text, millimeters are often rounded off.

Aliquot Inches	American Scale	Decimal Inches	Millimeters
1 9/16	25	1.563	39.7
1 1/2	24	1.500	38.1
1 7/16	23	1.438	36.5
1 5/12		1.417	36.0
1 13/32	22.5	1.406	35.7
1 2/5		1.400	35.6
1 3/8	22	1.375	34.9
1 7/20		1.350	34.3
1 11/32	21.5	1.344	34.1
1 1/3		1.333	33.9
1 5/16	21	1.313	33.3
1 3/10		1.300	33.0
1 9/32	20.5	1.281	32.5
1 1/4	20	1.250	31.8
1 7/32	19.5	1.219	31.0
1 1/5		1.200	30.5
1 3/16	19	1.188	30.2
1 1/6		1.167	29.6
1 5/32	18.5	1.156	29.4
1 3/20		1.150	29.2
1 1/8	18	1.125	28.6
1 1/10		1.100	27.9
1 3/32	17.5	1.094	27.8
1 1/12		1.083	27.5
1 1/16	17	1.056	27.0
1 1/20		1.050	26.7
1 1/32	16.5	1.031	26.2
1	16	1.000	25.4
31/32	15.5	0.969	24.6
19/20		0.950	24.1
15/16	15	0.938	23.8
11/12		0.917	23.3
29/32	14.5	0.906	23.0
9/10		0.900	22.9
7/8	14	0.875	22.2
17/20		0.850	21.6
27/32	13.5	0.844	21.4
5/6		0.833	21.2
13/16	13	0.812	20.6
4/5		0.800	20.3
25/32	12.5	0.781	19.8
3/4	12	0.750	19.1
23/32	11.5	0.719	18.3
7/10		0.700	17.8
11/16	11	0.688	17.5
2/3		0.667	16.9
21/32	10.5	0.656	16.7
13/20		0.650	16.5
5/8	10	0.625	15.9
3/5		0.600	15.2
19/32	9.5	0.594	15.1
7/12		0.583	14.8
9/16	9	0.563	14.3
11/20		0.550	14.0
17/32	8.5	0.531	13.5
1/2	8	0.500	12.7
15/32	7.5	0.469	11.9
9/20		0.450	11.4
7/16	7	0.438	11.1
5/12		0.416	10.6
13/32	6.5	0.406	10.3
2/5		0.400	10.2
3/8	6	0.375	9.5

Part One

EARLY AMERICAN
COINS

COLONIAL, STATE, CONFEDERATION COINAGES, LOCAL TOKEN COINAGES, MERCHANTS' SPECULATIVE IMPORTS:

OVERVIEW

The history of the American colonies prior to the Revolution is largely the story of their struggles to achieve economic self-sufficiency in defiance of systematically hostile British policies. Economic self-sufficiency (which the colonists would later rename "liberty") meant the opportunity to market surplus produce at reasonable prices, using such income to buy necessities and even comforts, from whoever had them for sale, without unreasonable official interference by royal officials. Though to-day we take this for granted, in the 17th and 18th centuries the British Establishment interpreted it as little short of treason. Any colonial attempts at local coinage automatically connoted *lèse-majesté* punishable as treason.

The reasons for this peculiar view lie in economic theory then current in Europe, which theory (later called "mercantilism") the Establishment accepted without even momentary doubts. Unlike medieval theory, which had defined ownership of land as the ultimate source of wealth, or today's Gross National Product, mercantilism defined a nation's wealth as the amount of gold and silver physically held within national boundaries. An obvious consequence was that colonies existed for the sole purpose of increasing national wealth (not the colonists' own) by shipping raw materials to the home country: Colonial trade with foreign markets therefore had to be prevented at any cost (Ernst, pp. 18–24). This was accomplished by the following policies:

1. *Colonies must be kept on a barter economy as far as possible.* Until 1652, the Massachusetts Bay Colony used furs, grain, fish, musket balls, and (after 1627) Indian shell beads as money, at official valuations; the Maryland and Virginia colonies used tobacco, though in Virginia after 1727 warehouse receipts represented so many pounds of the leaf and circulated as a kind of money substitute (Crosby {1875}, pp. 19–21; Behrens {1923}, passim).

2. *Colonies must be paid in merchandise for their exports to Britain,* or at best in bills of exchange payable in London. When ships' traders bound for Britain bought colonists' exports, buyers naturally valued the merchandise as low as possible, whereas the British barter goods they pushed in exchange carried inflated prices. Use of bills of exchange (see ills., ANS {1976}, p. 101) meant that no gold or silver would be leaving Britain, though London manufacturers could cash them for gold and silver in payment for goods they shipped to the colo-

nies. Rarely, by royal concession, uncurrent base-metal coins unacceptable elsewhere (and in particular, on foreign trading ships) would be used in payments due the colonies. This is probably how Massachusetts Bay colonists found themselves as late as 1634 using worn-out and corroded farthing tokens; the Generall Court declared these coppers unacceptable in trade after March 1, 1634/35. (The date is O.S. = Julian Calendar; their year 1634 ended on March 24, their year 1635 began the next day.)

3. *All colonies must be supervised by Crown-appointed officials with royal warrants to suppress trade with foreign markets.* These warrants might also grant the power to manipulate exchange rates.

4. *Everything possible should be done to avoid paying for colonists' exports in Spanish or Mexican silver or gold, or in any other coinage with a known international trade value.*

5. *Taxes must be collected preferentially in gold and silver,* in case any bullion might have found its way to the colonists from local mines or traders. Otherwise they could be collected in produce before it reached the markets.

6. *Coining money is a royal prerogative, forbidden to colonists.* There were rare exceptions; the 1609 Virginia charter included the coining privilege, but it was unused until shortly before the Revolution. However, when Lord Baltimore ordered coins made for his Maryland colony in 1658 (reasoning that as no king occupied the throne, there was no *lèse-majesté),* the Clerke of Irons in the Tower Mint informed on him. Baltimore was summoned to Council (the equivalent of Star Chamber proceedings); he escaped execution only because the Commonwealth was then collapsing. Similarly, King James II revoked the Massachusetts Bay Colony's charter because he learned that the colonial Generall Court had continued for 30 years to authorize the manufacture and issue of silver coins—with the obsessive date 1652 to deceive royal spies by perpetuating the fiction that all these coins had been made during Cromwell's regime.

Despite all official attempts to prevent such trade (even to letters of marque and reprisal, i.e., royally sanctioned piracy), occasional merchant ships—largely from the West Indies—reached the harbors at Boston, New Haven, New York, Philadelphia, Baltimore Town, and Charleston, buying local produce in trade for rum, sugar, cloth, indigo and other dyes, utensils, muskets, and—despite all regulations—Spanish and Mexican silver dollars and occasional gold pieces. Royal officials needed the merchandise, too, even if bribery was not always a part of their decision to look the other way.

Needless to say, arbitrary and exploitive British policies produced hardship and created a climate of defiance, making active rebellion not only imaginable but sometimes inevitable (Ernst, passim). Massachusetts Bay colonists, for all their rigorist Puritan morality, remained scofflaws for the 30 years that John Hull's mint continued to make silver shillings and fractions. They saw official reprisals not as just punishment for sinful crime but as unjust overseas interference in the colonists' internal affairs. Loyalty to an unseen king 3,000 miles away (to whom they were hostile on religious grounds) became increasingly lip service, mere formality, without any emotional commitment to royal ministers' directives. After all, Crown authorities never familiarized themselves with the colonies' local problems, and therefore complacently shrugged off colonists' complaints.

Among later colonial acts of defiance may be named an increasing circulation of locally made paper currency, sometimes even in preference to officially authorized coins (Massachusetts authorized an issue of parchment pence in 1722 to avoid using William Wood's brass coins); increasing readiness to flout official policy by trading with non-British ships; and increasing acceptance of local mintages (Higley's coppers) or privately imported token coinages (Mark Newbie's "St. Patrick" coppers, Roche's VOCE POPULI coppers). Later still, the British coat of arms increasingly often vanished in favor of colonial arms on local paper currency, which notes said less and less and finally nothing about His Majesty George III. Eventually, for all that local public opinion ranged from fervent Toryism to equally fervent advocacy of armed insurrection and independence, medalets circulated as halfpence and farthings, jointly crediting the New York "Friends of Liberty and Trade" and the British statesman William Pitt for the repeal of the hated Stamp Act.

A few weeks before the Continental Congress adopted the Lee-Adams Resolution of Independence and promulgated the Declaration of Independence, the New Hampshire and Massachusetts authorities attempted autonomous state copper coinages. However, franchised state coppers became an effective circulating medium only after the Revolution. Two Maryland silversmiths circulated fractional silver pieces; the Massachusetts legislature set up a mint to make cents, and authorized coinage of gold and silver (which never materialized owing to lack of bullion); and three different state legislatures awarded contracts to private coiners to manufacture coppers, though eventually all these failed when the coppers' purchasing power depreciated. Part of the reason for this failure was mismanagement; part was competition from Machin's Mills (a Newburgh, N.Y., private mint run by the Revolutionary hero who had fortified West Point and stretched a chain across the Hudson River to stop invading British ships), which circulated large quantities of local imitations of state coins as well as of British halfpence (the notorious "Tory Coppers"); and part was competition from New York merchants, who imported kegs of tokens from private mints in Birmingham, England ("Bungtown Coppers").

In the meantime, the Continental Congress made several attempts at coinage on its own account, all frustrated by lack of silver bullion. The first, in 1776, led to the famous CONTINENTAL CURRENCY tin coins—apparently distributed only as samples and souvenirs. The second, in 1783, resulted in creation of the exceedingly rare silver CONSTELLATIO NOVA patterns, and in an informal agreement between Gouverneur Morris and Wyon's Mint (Birmingham, 1785) to make several tons of CONSTELLATIO NOVA coppers: a successful propaganda effort, spreading on both sides of the Atlantic the Confederation's "new constellation" device (the Original 13 Colonies under God, represented as 13 stars around the All-Seeing Eye) with the slogan translated as 'Liberty and Justice.' The third (1785) got no further than coinage of several series of

patterns at Wyon's Mint, some of the coppers (Decads) conforming to devices suggested by Robert Morris and Congress. The fourth (1786) led to defining a decimal coinage system, but no coinage. The fifth (1787) resulted in privately made patterns for coinage franchises, the project with the best chance of acceptance (Gen. Matthias Ogden's, represented by the 1787 IMMUNIS COLUMBIA coppers), being overridden by the reorganized Board of Treasury under the infamous Col. William Duer, who—persuaded by a $10,000 bribe—made sure that any coinage contract would be awarded instead to James Jarvis. Jarvis spent most of his time trying to persuade the British coiner Matthew Boulton to furnish planchets. In the meantime, Jarvis's assistants shipped the Treasury a token delivery of just under 400,000 FUGIO coppers (the amount originally called for being over 34 million), but they embezzled the remainder of the unpaid-for federal copper bullion intended for these coins to make some three million draped-bust Connecticut coppers instead, which passed at a higher nominal value though of lower weight. Congress unloaded the FUGIO coppers on Royal Flint, a hapless New York merchant who went bankrupt with them when their purchasing power collapsed. The sheriff hauled him off to debtor's prison after Flint had paid about 1/3 on account; Duer followed him there a few years later, but in the meantime the coppers had ceased to circulate at all.

Undaunted, Congress—after adoption of the Constitution—made still another attempt at a national decimal coinage, this one originally intended to portray George Washington, though the President objected to any such portrayal as "monarchical." In the meantime, the Birmingham coiner Obadiah Westwood, employing John Gregory Hancock as diesinker, made a variety of proposed coinages with Washington portraits. After the Philadelphia Mint began operations (fall 1792), local merchants continued to import quantities of Washington token coppers, from Westwood's and Kempson's mints. These coppers circulated as small change side by side with far smaller numbers of federal cents and half cents.

Every Early American Colonial coin—whether a local mintage or an import—has its own history, usually replete with local color and with its own details of skulduggery and scandal, side by side with honest attempts to provide an acceptable circulating medium. Though often crude in design and technology, these coins provide fascinating sidelights on the growth of free enterprise in the new nation, and on the state of native arts. Beyond doubt, the historical interest which crested during the national Bicentennial and is expected to crest again as we approach the bicentennial of the Constitution will enshrine Early American Colonial coins as precious historical relics comparable to Postmasters' Provisionals in stamps, Edison's earliest experimental cylinders in sound recordings, or the Wright Brothers' prototype planes.

INSCRIPTIONS ON COLONIAL AND PREFEDERAL COINS: TRANSLATIONS AND INDEX

With the following guide, you can at once locate any purported American colonial coin from any legible inscription. If your coin's inscription fails to appear below, the coin is excluded, and its claim to colonial status will be at best suspect. Warning: Noncolonial coins exist with some of these same inscriptions; these are marked "Also foreign." For certainty, see the chapters cited. Single quotation marks denote translations: Parenthesized capital letters supply parts of words omitted in the abbreviations found on the coins.

A

A:D (OM) = ANDOM
AMERICA Chap. 4, iv; 8, iv; 11, iii
AMERICANA Chap. 2, ii; 11, iii
AMERICAN CONGRESS Chaps. 9, 15
AMERICAN LIBERTY Chap. 6, ii
AM I NOT A MAN AND A BROTHER? Chap. 14, vii
ANDO or ANDOM = ANNO DOMINI 'In the year of the Lord' Chap. 1, ii
ANNAP(OLI)S Chap. 8, i
AN(N)O 'In the year' Chap. 1, ii
ANTIENT SCOTTISH WASHING Chap. 8, iv (Also foreign)
AT THE STORE OF TALBOT, ALLUM & LEE Chap. 8, iii
AUCTORI CONNEC or CONNECT = AUCTORITATE CONNECTICUTENSIS 'By authority of Connecticut' Chap. 6, iv
AUCTORI(TATE) PLEBIS 'By authority of the commoners' Chap. 12, iv
AUCTORI VERMON = AUCTORITATE VERMONTENSIUM 'By authority of the Green Mountain People = the Republic of Vermont' Chap. 6, iii

B

BALTIMORE TOWN Chap. 8, i
BARRY Chap. 8, i
BIRMINGHAM HALFPENNY Chap. 8, iii (Also foreign)
BLOFIELD CAVALRY Chap. 8, iii (Also foreign)
BRASHER Chap. 7, iii
BRITANNIA 'Britain' Chaps. 6, iii, iv, vii; 7, v, vi (Also foreign)
BRITISH SETTLEMENT KENTUCKY Chap. 8, vi

C

CAECILIVS D(OMI)N(V)S TERRAE-MARIAE & CT (= ET CAETERA) 'Cecil, Lord of Maryland and Other Domains' Chap. 1, iii
CARLOS III (or IV) D(EI) G(RATIA) HISPAN(IARVM) REX 'Charles III (or IV), by the Grace of God, King of the Spanish Lands' Chap. 8, vii (Also foreign)
CASTORLAND 'Beaverland' Chap. 8, v
CEORCIVS III REX diecutter's error for GEORGIVS III REX Chap. 7, v
CHALMERS Chap. 8, i
CHR(ISTV)S REGN(AT), (CHRISTVS) VINC(IT), (CHRISTVS) IMP(ERAT) 'Christ reigns, Christ conquers, Christ rules' Chap. 5, i (Also foreign, common on French coins for centuries; originally First Crusade battle cry, from Easter Lauds liturgy)
CHRONOMETERS Chap. 8, iii
CHURCH PENNY Chap. 13
COLONIES FRANÇOISES 'French Colonies' Chap. 5, i (Also foreign)
COLUMBIA 'Columbus's land' Chap 7, ii (Also foreign)
COMMERCE Chap. 12, ii (Also foreign)
COMMON WEALTH Chap. 6, vi
CONF(O)EDERATIO 'League, covenant, confederation' Chap. 11, iii, iv
CONNEC(TICUTENSIS) 'Of Connecticut' Chap. 6, iv
CONNECT, CONNFC, CONNLC = blunders for CONNEC
CONNECTICVT Chap. 4, ii
CONSTELLATIO NOVA 'The New Constellation' Chap. 10; 11, i, ii
CONTINENTAL CURRENCY (CURENCY, CURRENCEY) Chap. 9
CRESCITE ET MVLTIPLICAMINI 'Grow and multiply' (Gen. 1:28, 9:7) Chap. 1, iii
CUR(R)ENCY, CURRENCEY Chap. 9

D

DAWSON Chap. 4, i
D CHURCH PENNY Chap. 13
DE ADMIRAALS FLAG VAN ADMIRAAL HOWE 'Admiral Howe's flagship' Chap. 12, i
DEFENSOR LIBERTATIS 'Defender of Freedom' Chap. 6, i

DENARIVM (sc. AES) TERRAE-MARIAE 'Penny of Maryland' Chap. 1, iii (Properly, DENARIVM means 'tenfold' or 'decimal'; in context, AES, 'copper,' was understood.)
DOVBLE DE LA MERIQVE FRANCOISE '2-denier coin of French America' Chap. 5, i (LA MERIQVE is a blunder for L'AMÉRIQVE.)
D'VLUGTENDE AMERICAANEN VAN ROHDE YLAND 'The fleeing Americans of Rhode Island' Chap. 12, i

E

EARL HOWE Chap. 8, iii (Also foreign)
ECCE GREX 'Behold my flock' Chap. 3, ii
E PLURIBUS UNUM 'One (made up) of many' (from USA Great Seal) Chaps. 6, v; 7, ii; 11, iii, iv, v; 12, v. Federal coin motto since 1796 except 1838–72.
ET LIB INDE (= INDE ET LIB, q.v.), 'Independence and Liberty' Chap. 6, iii, iv
EXCELSIOR 'More excellent, more noble; Onward and Upward' (from New York State arms) Chap. 7, ii, iv

F

FLOREAT REX 'Prosper the King' Chap. 3, ii
FRANCO-AMERICANA COLONIA 'French-American Colony' Chap. 8, v
FRANKLIN PRESS Chap. 12, vi
FUCIO (blunder for FUGIO) Chap. 15
FUGIO 'I (Time) flee' Chaps. 9, 15 (Sundial motto, related to Horace, *Odes,* III, 29:48.)

G

GEN(ERA)L OF THE AMERICAN ARMIES Chap. 14, v, vii
GEN. WASHINGTON Chap. 11, iii, iv
GEORGE CLINTON Chap. 7, iv
GEORGEIVS WASHINGTON Chap. 14, viii
GEORGE WASHINGTON Chap. 14, vi, vii, viii
GEORGIVS III REX 'George III, King' Chap. 7, v (Also foreign)
GEORGIVS D(EI) G(RATIA) REX 'George, by the Grace of God, King' Chap. 2, ii, iii (Also foreign)
GEORGIVS D(EI) G(RATIA) MAG(NAE) BRI(TANNIAE) FRA(NCIAE) ET HIB (ERNIAE) REX 'George, by the grace of God, King of Great Britain, France, and Ireland' Chap. 2, ii (Also foreign)
GEORGIVS II D(EI) G(RATIA) REX 'George II, by the Grace of God, King' Chap. 2, ii, iii (Also foreign)
GEORGIVS II REX 'George II, King' Chap. 7, vi (Also foreign)
GEORGIVS III DEI GRATIA 'George III, by the Grace of God, (King)' Chaps. 2, iv; 14, iv (Also foreign)
GEORGIVS III REX 'George III, King' Chaps. 2, iv; 6, iii, vii; 7, v, vi (Also foreign)
GEORGIVS TRIUMPHO 'I, George, triumph' Chap. 14, i
GEO. WASHINGTON BORN VIRGINIA Chap. 14, v
GLORIAM REGNI TVI DICENT 'They shall speak of the glory of Thy Kingdom' Chap. 5, i (From Psalm 144(5):11, *Vulgate)*
GLOVCESTER COVRT HOVSE VIRGINIA Chap. 4, i
GODDESS LIBERTY Chap. 6, i
GOD PRESERVE CAROLINA AND THE LORDS PROPRIETORS Chap. 3, i
GOD PRESERVE LONDON Chap. 3, i
GOD PRESERVE NEW ENGLAND Chap. 3, i
G. WASHINGTON PRESIDENT. I. Chap. 16
G. WASHINGTON THE FIRM FRIEND Chap. 14, vii
G. W. PT. 'George Washington, President' Chap. 16

H

HIBERNIA 'Ireland' Chaps. 2, iii; 3, iii (Also foreign)
HISPANIOLA 'Little Spain' (= Haiti) Chap. 12, iv (Also foreign)
HONI SOIT QUI MAL Y PENSE 'Shame on whoever thinks ill of it' Chap. 8, iv (Also foreign) Motto of the Order of the Garter.

I

IACOBVS II D(EI) G(RATIA) MAG(NAE) BRI(TANNIAE) FRAN(CIAE) ET HIB(ERNIAE) REX 'James II, by the Grace of God, King of Great Britain, France, and Ireland' Chap. 2, i (Also foreign)

I AM GOOD COPPER Chap. 4, ii

I CHALMERS Chap. 8, i

I d LM 'One Penny Lawful Money' Chap. 6, i

IMMUNE COLUMBIA (Blunder for IMMUNIS COLUMBIA) Chaps. 7, v; 11, ii

IMMUNIS COLUMBIA 'Columbus's land (= America) is free' Chap. 11, iii, v

IND (or INDE) ET LIB = INDÉPENDANCE ET LIBERTÉ 'Independence and Liberty' Chaps. 6, iii, iv; 7, v (Not from Latin; the first word has no Latin counterpart.)

INDEP ET LIBER (see preceding) Chap. 12, iv

INDL ET LIB (Blunder for INDE ET LIB) Chap. 6, iv

INIMICA TYRANNIS AMERICA(NA) CONFEDERATIO '(The) America(n) Confederation is hostile to tyrants' Chap. 11, iii

IN NEW ENGLAND AN(N)O '. . . in the year' Chap. 1, ii

IOHN HOWARD PHILANTHROPIST Chap. 8, iii (Also foreign)

IRISH HALFPENNY Chap. 14, vii (Also foreign)

I S V C (Unknown meaning) Chap. 4, iii

J

J A G (= José Antonio Garza) Chap. 8, viii

J CUT MY WAY THROUGH Chap. 4, ii

JVAN ESTEVAN DE PENA FLORIDA Chap. 8, vii

L

LA FLOR(IDA) ORIENTAL PER ZESPED(E)S PROCLAM(ATUR) 'East Florida. (Coronation) proclaimed by (Gov.) Zespedes.' Chap. 8, vii

LIBER NATUS LIBERTATEM DEFENDO 'Born free, I defend freedom.' Chap. 7, iv, v

LIBERTAS (ET) JUSTITIA 'Liberty (and) Justice' Chaps. 10; 11, i

LIBERTY & COMMERCE Chap. 8, iii

LIBERTY & VIRTUE Chap. 6, i

LIBERTY & SECURITY Chap. 14, vii

LIB(ERTY) PAR(ENT) OF SCIENCE AND INDUSTRY Chap. 16

LIVERPOOL HALFPENNY Chap. 14, iv (Also foreign)

LON*DON* Chap. 3, i

LONDON GOD PRESERVE Chap. 3, i

LUD or LVD(OVICVS) XIII (or XIV, XV) D(EI) G(RATIA) FR(ANCIAE) ET N(AVARRAE) REX 'Louis XIII (XIV, XV), by the Grace of God, King of France and Navarre' Chap. 5, i, ii (Also foreign)

M

MASATHVSETS IN Chap. 1, ii

MASSACHUSETTS Chap. 6, vi

MASSACHUSETTS STATE Chap. 6, i

MAY COMMERCE FLOURISH Chap. 8, iv

MELBOURNE Chap. 14, iii (Also foreign)

MIND YOUR BUSINESS Chaps. 9, 15

MOTT'S N.Y. IMPORTERS, DEALERS, MANUFACTURERS Chap. 8, iii

N

NE 'New England' Chap. 1, ii

NEO-EBORACENSIS 'At New York' Chap. 7, i

NEO-EBORACUS 'New York' Chap. 7, iv

NEW ENGLAND Chaps. 1, ii; 4, iii

NEW YORKE IN AMERICA Chap. 4, iii

NON VI VIRTUTE VICI 'Not by violence, but by excellence, have I conquered.' Chaps. 7, i; 11, v

NORTH AMERICAN TOKEN Chap. 12, ii

NORTH WALES, Chap. 14, ix (Also foreign)

NORTH WEST COMPANY Chap. 8, ix

NO STAMPS Chap. 4, iv

NOVA CAESAREA 'New Jersey' Chap. 6, v

NOVA CONSTELLATIO 'The New Constellation' Chaps. 10; 11, i

NOVA EBORAC(A) 'New York' Chap. 7, ii, iii

N. YORK 1799 Chap. 13

O

OUR CAUSE IS JUST Chap. 12, v

P

PAYABLE AT THE FRANKLIN PRESS Chap. 12, vi

PAYABLE BY CLARK & HARRIS Chap. 14, vi

PAYABLE BY P.P.P. MYDDELTON Chap. 8, vi

PER ZESPED(E)S PROCLAM(ATUR) see LA FLORIDA

PIECE DE XXX (or XV) DENIERS 'Coin of 30 (or 15) Deniers' Chap. 5, i

PROMISSORY HALFPENNY Chap. 8, iii (Also foreign)

PROVINCE OF MASSA(CHUSETTS) Chap. 6, i

Q

QUARTA DECIMA STELLA 'The Fourteenth Star (of the New Constellation),' i.e., 'The Fourteenth State of the Union' = Vermont Chap. 6, iii

QVIESAT PLEBS Blunder for next. Chap. 3, ii

QVIESCAT PLEBS 'Let the commoners be quiet' Chap. 3, ii

R

REPUB(LICA) AMERI(CANA) 'The American Republic' Chap. 14, vii

RIGHAVLT DAWSON Chap. 4, i

ROSA AMERICANA 'The American (Royal) Rose' Chap. 2, ii

S

SALVE MAGNA PARENS FRUGUM 'Hail, Great Mother of Crops' Chap. 8, v

S I = Sommer Islands (Bermuda) Chap. 1, i

SIC ORITUR DOCTRINA SURGETQUE LIBERTAS 'Thus (= by the printing press) learning is disseminated and liberty shall arise.' Chap. 12, vi

SIT NOMEN DOM(INI) (or DNI) BENEDICT(UM) 'Blessed be the Name of the Lord' (Job 1:21 or Psalms 112(3):2, *Vulgate*) Chap. 5, i (Also foreign)

SOMMER I(S)LANDS = Bermuda Chap. 1, i

STANDISH BARRY Chap. 8, i

STATE OF MASSA(CHUSETTS) Chap. 6, i

STATES UNITED Chap. 15

STELLA QUARTA DECIMA see QUARTA above

SUCCESS TO THE UNITED STATES Chap. 14, viii

T

TALBOT, ALLUM & LEE Chap. 8, iii

THANKS TO THE FRIENDS OF LIBERTY AND TRADE Chap. 4, iv

THE RESTORER OF COMMERCE Chap. 4, iv

THE THEATRE AT NEW YORK Chap. 8, iv

THE VALUE OF THREE PENCE Chap. 4, ii

THE WHEELE GOES ROUND Chap. 4, ii

TOKEN 1820 Chap. 8, ix

TRIAL PIECE DESIGNED FOR U.S. CENT 1792 Chap. 16

U

UNANIMITY IS THE STRENGTH OF SOCIETY Chap. 12, v

UNITED STATES Chaps. 14, iii; 15

UNITED STATES OF AMERICA Chaps. 14, vi; 16

UNITY STATES OF AMERICA Chap. 14, iii

UNUM E PLURIBUS 'One (made up) out of many' Chap. 7, ii

U S Chaps. 10; 11, i, ii

U.S. CENT BY J. JARVIS 1787 Chap. 15

UTILE DULCI 'The useful with the sweet' = 'For business and pleasure' Chap 2, ii (From Horace, *Ars Poetica*, 343)

V

VAL(EO) 24 PART(EM) REAL HISPAN(IAE) '(I am) worth ¼ of the Spanish real' Chap. 2, i

VALUE (or VALVE) ME AS YOU PLEASE Chap. 4, ii

V E I C 4 (East India Company balemark) Chap. 12, vi (Also foreign)

VERMON(TENSIUM) AUCTORI(TATE) 'By authority of the Green Mountain People' (Vermont) Chap. 6, iii

VERMONTENSIUM (or VERMONT(I)S) RES PUBLICA 'The Republic of Vermont' Chap. 6, iii

VI DENIERS COLONIES '6 Deniers, (French) Colonies' Chap. 5, i

VIRGINIA Chap. 2, iv

VIRT(US) ET LIB(ERTAS) 'Strength and Freedom' Chap. 7, iii

VOCE POPOLI 'By the voice of the people' Chap. 14, i

VOCE POPULI 'By the voice of the people' Chap. 3, iii

VOOE POPULI (blunder for preceding) Chap. 3, iii

VTILE DVLCI = UTILE DULCI

W

WASHINGTON Chap. 14, iii

WASHINGTON & INDEPENDENCE Chap. 14, iii

WASHINGTON PRESIDENT Chap. 14, iv, v

WASHINGTON THE GREAT D: G: Chap. 14, ii

WE ARE ONE Chaps. 9, 15

W M (William Moulton) Chap. 6, ii

X

XII DENIERS COLONIES '12 Deniers, (French) Colonies' Chap. 5, i

Y

YORK. 1795. Chap. 8, iii (Also foreign)

Z

ZESPED(E)S Chap. 8, vii

CHAPTER 1

BRITISH COINAGES IN AMERICA: AUTONOMOUS ISSUES

i. SOMMER ISLANDS (Bermuda) (1615/16)

The earliest coinage for any English-speaking region in the New World was the so-called Hogge Money, made in 1615/16 in London on behalf of Gov. Daniel Tuckar by order of the "Governour and Company of the Citty of London for the Plantacioun of the Somer Ilands," after letters patent of James I dated 29 June 1615. This charter authorized coinage to pass current

> . . . betweene the Inhabitants there for the more easey [sic] of comerce and bargaining betweene them of such metall and in such manner and forme as the said Governour and Company in any of their said Generall Courts, shall limitt and appoint (Lefroy {1876}).

To understand better the "metall . . . manner and forme" of this crude coinage, we must first survey the early history of the Bermuda (or Sommer) Islands.

They were first sighted about 1505 by one Juan de Bermúdez, who stopped there en route to the West Indies, and who was shipwrecked there in 1532 en route to Cuba. On this latter voyage, his cargo contained numerous black hogs and sows; these swam ashore and ran wild, their descendants a century later furnishing ample meat for British colonists. In the meantime, the Islands acquired a fearful repute owing to the seasonal hurricanes and to their dangerous reefs, on which numerous French, Spanish, Dutch, and Flemish ships were wrecked. The ferocious hogs also inspired the sobriquet "Isle of Devills."

The first explorations occurred in 1609—unintentionally. On June 8, Sir Thomas Gates, Sir George Somers (or Sommers, or Summers—all these spellings recur), and Capt. Christopher Newport set sail from Plymouth, England, for the Virginia Colony in the *Sea Adventure,* with eight other ships and 500 men, only to be driven off by a hurricane on July 25, making landfall on the twenty-eighth. There they stayed to rebuild their ships, leaving Christopher Carter, Edward Chard, and Edward Waters to claim the Bermudas for England when they departed next May 10. This famous episode inspired Shakespeare's *The Tempest,* with its allusion to the Islands (Act I, Scene ii, Line 229) as the "still vex'd Bermoothes," the nearest he could come to a phonetic rendering of the Spanish name.

The Earl De La Ware (then Captain-General and Governor of the Virginia Colonies) persuaded Somers to return to Bermuda to bring back shiploads of provisions for England; but Somers died on the Islands in 1611 in what was later named (for him) Saint George Towne. His nephew and heir, Capt. Matthew Somers, brought the corpse back to England, where the authorities renamed the Bermoothes or Hogge Islands

"Somers Islands"—again after Sir George. Several shiploads of colonists followed Somers's route. The Virginia Company of London, under Sir Thomas Smith, Governor, on 25 Nov. 1612 (pursuant to Royal Statutes, 9 James I, 1612), bought the rights to Sir George's trading company, only to resign them in 1614 to the Crown. King James regranted them on 29 June 1615 to a new group of adventurers, the abovenamed "Governour and Company . . . for the Plantacioun of the Somer Ilands," alias the "Bermuda Company," which charter remained with their successors until Charles II's councillors recalled it in 1684. Master Richard Mo(o)re was named Governor of the "Iles and Colony," landing there July 11, 1612. In 1615, under the new charter, he was succeeded by a set of six rotating governors, each ruling for a month, which arrangement led only to forced labor, tyranny, hatred, rebellion, and desertion. In mid-May 1616, a new Governor, the Virginia planter Daniel Tuckar, arrived—only to prove a still worse tyrant. Tuckar is remembered today principally for introducing Hogge Money during his two years on the local throne.

Partly to minimize costs, partly so that the coins would not leave the colony on trading ships, the Company had the pieces of XII, VI, III, and II Pence privately made on the thinnest brassy planchets practicable, lightly silvered. Their unidentified private coiner used the ancient hammer method: The lower die was affixed to an anvil or tree stump, the coiner held the upper die (in a pair of tongs) atop the blank disk resting on the lower die, while a workman used a sledgehammer to force the designs into the blank. Though quick and easy, this method made uneven impressions; blanks are often not round. Arrival of the coins must have been sometime later in 1616, but there is no record of either date or quantity.

As all debts and taxes were payable in tobacco, the coins were a token issue representing the stated value in weights of leaf, and in quantity could represent a kind of warehouse receipt theoretically redeemable in tobacco. The Company's instructions to Gov.-designate Tuckar, Feb. 13, 1615/16, said, "You shall p.claime [= proclaim] the sayde Coyne to be currant to pass freely from man to man, only throughout the Islands, & not otherwise."

According to Capt. John Smith {1624}, their hog device commemorates "the abundance of Hogges (which) was found at their first landing." The full-rigged galleon probably represents the *Sea Adventure;* its cantoned flag, that of St. George. Original silvering is rarely visible, because exposure to salt spray in the Islands caused rapid corrosion. Chloride ions in salt spray combine with silver to form silver chloride; the spray, being an electrolyte, induces the dissimilar metals to gain or lose electrons, facilitating the chemical reaction and resulting in corrosion at the interface between brassy copper core and silvery coating. Unsurprisingly, later colony records ignore the coins; Smith spoke of them as already a thing of the past—presumably replaced by British farthing tokens and Spanish fractional silver coins, though we have no details of these. No more local coins were made for Bermuda until Boulton & Watt's 48,000 copper pennies of 1793.

The above account derives mostly from Crosby {1875}, Lefroy {1876, 1877, 1878, 1883}, and Bank of Bermuda {1972}.

The Hogge coins have always been rare. Crosby knew of only two Shillings (small sail rev.). Since 1972, at least 46 more (both vars.) have turned up in the Islands, probably thanks to metal detectors. Though most were in wretched condition, some few are sharp enough to enable complete die descriptions. The same remarks hold for the smaller denominations, except that fewer have turned up. Ancient rumors of a Groat (IV Pence coin) remain unconfirmed.

Dickeson's copy of the Shilling, made in Philadelphia in the 1850s and later muled with other dies, is not deceptive; its workmanship is modern, with beautiful sharp impressions on large round blanks, thick and thin, in various metals, with proof surfaces: Crosby, Pl. I, 18. The same comment holds for the fantasy "XX Shillings" pieces (cf. Garrett III: 1199), made in the 1880s by the New York City coin dealer A. Wuesthoff, and for a variety of later imitations of the Shilling—some of the latter grossly oversize. I have seen no deceptive forgeries of any denomination.

SOMMER ISLANDS COINAGES

Designer, Engraver, unknown. Mint, private, London? Composition, brassy copper, originally with thin silver (?) wash. Diameters, Weights, variable, below.

Grade range, POOR to VERY FINE. GOOD: Devices and inscriptions almost complete, major outlines of devices present. On Sixpence, size of portholes should be unmistakable. VERY GOOD: Partial water lines, partial rigging details. EXCEPTION: All denominations are weak, uneven strikings, usually much worn and corroded.

1 n.d. XII (Pence) = Shilling. Large sails. Ex. rare.
SOMMER * ILANDS * Pellet between forelegs and rear legs. Lower parts of hull normally weak. $^{19–22}/16'' = 30–35$ mm; 73.6–107 grs. = 4.77–6.96 gms. Discovered by Lorin G. Parmelee, 1875–90. Roper:2, $11,000.

2 n.d. XII (Pence). Small sails. Rare.
Same obv., rusted near letters. Always weak at lower l. and central obv., usually also below hull. Crosby {1875}, Pl. I, 1. Diameter as preceding; 63.5–177 grs. = 4.1–11.47 gms. Carnegie Inst.:1118, $12,000. Over 20 found in Bermuda ca. 1977. Discovered by Thomas Hollis before 1769.

3 n.d. VI (Pence) = Sixpence. Large portholes. Rare.
SOMMER + ILANDS + Group of 4 pellets between forelegs and rear legs, a fifth below grass. ANS {1914}, Pl. 11. $^{16–17}/16'' = 25–27$ mm; 33.6–58.5 grs. = 2.18–3.79 gms. Carnegie Inst.:1119, $13,000. Enl. ill.

Ex J. W. Garrett: 1197.
Courtesy Bowers & Ruddy
Galleries, Inc.

4 n.d. VI (Pence). Small portholes. Ex. rare.
Same obv. die. Rows of widely spaced studs on planking above and below portholes. Crosby, Pl. I, 2. Diameter as preceding; weight range, 36–63.1 grs. = 2.3–4.09 gms. Appleton, MHS, Roper:5, $8,800.

5 n.d. III (Pence) = Threepence. Ex. rare.
Quincunx (5 pellets in square array) before forefeet; S I (= Sommer Islands) flanking ship. $3/4'' = 19$ mm.   1) BM (ill.), 21.6 grs. = 1.4 gms.   2) E. Rodovan Bell.   3) Carnegie Inst.:1120, $40,000, Bank of Bermuda.   4) Parmelee, Brand, Newman.   5) Lauder:109, $36,000, ill. Yeoman Guide Book.   6), 7) Reported. Discovered by J. Kermack Ford in Bermuda before 1883: Lefroy {1883}.

6 n.d. II (Pence) = Twopence. Large star. Very rare.
Second I low. Star is between forelegs and rear legs. Row of 5 pellets below grass, a sixth below middle of the 5. S I flanking ship. $^{10–11}/16'' = 16–17.5$ mm; 16–21.2 grs. = 1.04–1.37 gms. Carnegie Inst.:1121.

7 n.d. II (Pence). Small star. Rare.

II about even. Same rev. ANS {1914}, Pl. 13; Clain-Stefanelli {1970}, fig. 14. Diameter as preceding; 19.5–26.9 grs. = 1.26–1.74 gms. Discovery coin was washed up on a South Shore beach near Port Royal (Bermuda), 1877, found by a child, thence to Gen. Lefroy {1878}. Byrne:67, $24,000; Roper:6.

ii. MASSACHUSETTS BAY COLONY SILVER, 1652–82
NE ISSUES (1652)

As the unrealistic British systematically tried to drain their colonies of hard cash through taxes and inflated prices for imported goods, while refusing to pay for colonial goods in any kind of specie or to allow them to make local coinage, by the late 1630s the Massachusetts Bay Colony was of necessity on a loosely regulated barter system. Its circulating media consisted largely of furs, dried fish, grain, musket balls, and (after 1627) *wanpanpiag*. The latter, now called "wampum," but then known mostly as "peage," consisted of strings of beads made by hand from certain types of shells; its value as a circulating medium among local Native Americans derived from the time spent making it. Typical valuations (1640): white, one farthing per bead; blue, one halfpenny per bead. By 1650 these had depreciated: white, two per farthing; black, one farthing per bead. Among the principal reasons for the lowered purchasing power was increased supply, largely of counterfeits made overseas: Bushnell {1859}.

The colonists had few coins, mostly British royal farthing tokens: presumably Lennox rounds and ovals of James I and Richmond rounds and ovals of Charles I (Peck, pp. 55–206, 228–85). These were then (ca. 1630–34) badly worn, corroded, and uncurrent in Britain. The Generall Court declared them no longer acceptable in Massachusetts after March 1, 1634/35 O.S. (Crosby, p. 26). Their general description: obv., two lys-headed scepters in saltire through a crown, IACO (or CARO) D G MAG BR(IT); rev., crowned harp, FRA ET HIB REX. 8.5–9 grs. = 0.55–0.58 gms.; 10–11/16″ = 16–17 mm. Copper, usually rough. Seaby {1961}, James I types 3, 4 = Peck, pp. 55–114; Charles I types 1, 4 = Peck, pp. 116–206, 228–85. They are not numbered in the present text for the same reason as Spanish, Mexican, and Peruvian 8 Reales coins: Their American circulation was only incidental.

However, after the execution of Charles I (Jan. 30, 1648/49 O.S.) and the defeat of royalist forces at Worcester (Sept. 3, 1651), there was no king on the throne, and the old royal regulations meant little. Colonists saw their fellow Puritans' regime as a relaxation of earlier restrictions. Foreign merchant ships and buccaneers increasingly made Boston a port of call, but many of the Spanish and Mexican dollars entering the colony from these sources proved lightweight, many others counterfeit: Snelling {1769}, p. 35. Accordingly, on May 26–27, 1652, an Act of the Generall Court of Massachusetts Bay Colony authorized John Hull and Robert Saunderson to fashion silver into disks of proper weight, to be stamped NE on one side and XII, VI, or III on the other, at the standard of 72 grs. (4.66 gms.) per XII Pence, or Shilling, and proportionately for lower denominations. This was enough below the British standard to prevent the coins from leaving the colony. These are the famous and

extremely rare NE (= New England) Shillings, Sixpences, and Threepences. Today, respectively, under 50, 6, and 2 (?) of these are traced. Two other Threepences vanished before 1900. All were made between June 11 and about Oct. 19, 1652, quantity unknown. Each piece required one or more sledgehammer blows to impart the design of one punch, being then flipped over and given the same treatment on the other side, orienting the punches at 12 and 6 o'clock (head-to-toe alignment)—a feature often neglected in the counterfeits. London mint assays (1684) showed that the genuine coins were of sterling fineness: Hocking {1906}, p. 299.

Authentication of any specimen offered is mandatory. Forgeries include both those made in the 1650s to spend and those made in the 1850s and later to sell to collectors. Most are pictured in Noe {1973}. Wyatt's (1856), with horizontal shading engraved in the dies, are also pictured in Crosby, Pl. I, 19–20.

NE ISSUES (June–Oct. 1652)

Designers, Engravers, John Hull and Robert Saunderson. Mint, Hull's, "The Great Street" (now Washington St. near Summer St.), Boston. Composition, silver, mostly sterling (925). Weight standard, Shilling, 72 grs. = 4.66 gms.; Sixpence, 36 grs. = 2.33 gms.; Threepence, 18 grs. = 1.17 gms. Diameters, Shilling, approx. 16–18/16″ = 25–28 mm; Sixpence, approx. 14/16″ = 22 mm; Threepence, approx. 3/4″ = 19 mm. Authorizing act, May 27, 1652.

Grade range, FAIR to VERY FINE. GOOD: NE and XII (or VI or III) fully legible, but less than half borders of punches clear; usually, coin will be much banged up. VERY GOOD: At least half of borders of punches clear. FINE: All or almost all of borders of punches clear. VERY FINE: Microscopic engravers' marks in protected areas.

8 n.d. XII (Pence) = Shilling. 6 vars. Very rare.
Crosby, Pl. I, 3.

9 n.d. VI (Pence). Ex. rare.
Crosby, Pl. I, 4. 1) ANS. 2) MHS. 3) BM. 4) Bushnell, Frossard, Garrett:1201, $75,000. 5) Eric P. Newman. 6) Roper:8, $56,100. 7) Lauder:114, $28,000.

10 n.d. (1652?) VI (Pence). Delicate letters. 2 or 3 known. Early circulating counterfeit?

11 n.d. III (Pence). Unique?

Crosby, Pl. I, 5. NE from same punch as in **9.** 1) MHS. Early circulating counterfeits have been seen on jewelry said to have been recovered from early graves.

14 1652 III (Pence). 3 known.

A D: in legend. 1) ANS. 2) Bushnell, Parmelee, W. P. Brown (1915), Brand, Boyd estate. 3) Ex Yale.

WILLOW TREE ISSUES (1653–60)

Anticipating the problem of clipping coins and passing them at full value, the Generall Court on Oct. 19, 1652, authorized coinage of the same XII, VI, and III (Pence) denominations, at the same weight standard, but of more sophisticated design. These were to bear the device of a tree (type unspecified) with MASATHVSETS IN around the coin, and on rev. NEW ENGLAND AN DOM around a circle containing date 1652 and denomination. Those struck in tiny quantities between winter 1652/53 and winter 1659/60 (all dated 1652) are the very rare Willow Tree issues. The trees are sketchy, no attempt being made to show separate branches. Most are badly worn; all are double- or triple-struck, obscuring some details. All were struck from hand-engraved cylindrical dies free to shift, rotate, or jiggle at successive sledgehammer blows, as Hull and Saunderson did not know the ancient moneyers' technique of fixing the lower die within an anvil. The obsessive date 1652 was specified in the Generall Court's original resolution, against a time when a restoration of the monarchy might entail severe sanctions against a colony which had arrogated to itself the royal prerogative of coinage. Crosby, pp. 32–44, quotes these documents at length.

As late as the Civil War the coins were known as "Palmetto Shillings" among coin dealers who failed to realize that most of the Massachusetts colonists would never have seen any such tree. We owe their present name of "Willow Tree" to Joseph J. Mickley of Philadelphia, "Father of American Coin Collecting": Noe {1943, 1973}. Survivors are in the same rarity class as the NE coins.

WILLOW TREE ISSUES

Designers, Engravers, Mint, Composition, Weights, Diameters, same as NE issues. Authorizing Act, Oct. 19, 1652.

No grade standards established. The coins are always double- or multiple-struck, some details obscured, others repeated.

12   1652 XII (Pence) = Shilling. 6 vars. Very rare.

Type of Crosby, Pl. I, 6. About 36–40 survive, some in museums.

13   1652 VI (Pence). Ex. rare.

Crosby, Pl. I, 7. A DOM in legend. About 13–15 known, some in museums.

OAK TREE ISSUES (1660–67)

Arrival of a screw press about 1660 coincided with a second seven-year contract between the Generall Court and coiner John Hull; they feared he was becoming too wealthy from the former contract! This resulted in the issue (1660–67) of "Oak Tree" coins, of the same denominations and standards as the earlier design, but better made. The dies were octagonal prisms, either wedged or vised into place in the screw press to prevent the multiple striking that had marred the Willow Tree coins. Steel suitable for making dies remained in very short supply; many varieties of all denominations (and all vars. of the Twopence) originated from repeated regrinding of the same dies to remove clash marks, rust, cracks, or other flaws, and by reengraving of letters, numerals, and branches thus weakened: Noe {1943, 1973}; Picker {1976}.

The "Oak Tree" designation dates back at least to 1662. In a stunning instance of political daring, Sir Thomas Temple in that year showed King Charles II one of these Shillings, identifying it to His Majesty as the oak tree at Boscobel in which the fugitive king had hidden from Cromwell's soldiers (Sept. 7–8, 1651), as in the old song "The Royal Oak it was the tree/That saved his Royal Majesty." At which the King, in good humor, called the colonists "a parcel of honest doggs" rather than ordering reprisals for treason (Crosby, pp. 49, 75).

On May 16, 1662, the Generall Court authorized coinage of twopenny pieces, of similar design and proportionate weight to the higher denominations, but dated 1662. These were to be coined for a period not to exceed seven years, in the proportion of "50 pounds in such smale money for euery hundred pounds by him [Hull] to be Coyned" (in higher denominations) during the first year, afterward in the proportion of "20 pounds in lik smale money Annually for euery hundred pounds that shall be Coyned." Accordingly, the 2d is much less rare than the 3d or 6d; only a single pair of dies was used, the rev. being repeatedly reground and reengraved to remove a crack. No mintage records survive, but dies of this size, so treated, might still have yielded 5,000 to 10,000 or more impressions.

The final issues of 1667 include **23,** a Shilling of transitional form (sometimes facetiously called "The Oak that got changed to a Pine"), and **28,** a Sixpence whose rev. remained in use after the shift to Pine Tree format later that year. At least five of these Sixpences **(29)** show evidence of being overstruck on worn or cut-down Shillings of the transitional type.

Many Shillings show teethmarks and attempted bendings as "witch pieces." During the 1692 Salem panic, carrying any bent silver coin was supposed a protection from witches. Noe {1952, 1973} suggests that the nursery rhyme about the crooked man who "found a crooked sixpence/against a crooked stile" may allude to this superstition. Specimens so treated have a historical interest far in excess of ordinary banged-up or worn-out examples, though they may look no better.

Authentication of all specimens is recommended. Forgeries include many made in the 1660s and '70s to spend, and others made ca. 1848–75 to sell to collectors. See Crosby, Pl. I, 21–23, II, 4, 25–28; Noe {1973} passim. The so-called "pattern" Sixpence, Crosby, fig. 18, Noe 15, is a unique private striking overstruck on a cut-down genuine Oak Tree Shilling; Garrett:1208 ($21,000), ex Bushnell, Mills, Ellsworth, 36.1 grs. = 2.34 gms. Its lettering style is altogether unlike the genuine. Many early struck forgeries are rarer than originals and command immense prices.

OAK TREE ISSUES

Designer, Engraver, Mint, Composition, Weight, Diameter, Authorizing Acts, as preceding, except that the Twopence was coined at 12 grs. = 0.78 gms., approx. $^{10}/_{16}'' = 16$ mm, per Act of May 16, 1662.

Grade range, POOR to UNC. GOOD: Full legends including date and XII. FINE: Inner circles of beads should be clear. Higher grades: Grade by surface. EXCEPTIONS: Many vars. have injured or buckled dies obscuring local details; 6d, 3d, and rev. of 2d may show blurred beaded circles even at VERY FINE. Outer beaded circles are often incomplete even in UNC.

15 1652 Shilling. Legends begin at 11:00 AN . DOM.
Noe 1; Crosby, Pl. I, 11.

16 1652 Shilling. Same; ANDO and rosette. About 7 known.
Noe 2.

17 1652 Shilling. Same; AN DO. without rosette. Very rare.
Noe 3. Usually weak at upper rev.

18 1652 Shilling. Legends begin at lower l.; shrubs, normal N's.
Noe 4, 5. The shrubs are hard to see. Only the one rev. Price for Noe 5 (ill.); Noe 4 (Crosby, Pl. I, 8) is scarcer.

19 1652 Shilling. Similar; no shrubs, normal N's.
Noe 6–9. Crosby, Pl. I, 9, 10.

20 1652 Shilling. Reversed obv. N; Delicate Tree. Very rare.
Noe 10, 12.5. Hair-thin weak branches.

21 1652 Shilling. Same; strong tree, double trunk.
Noe 11, 12. Reworked dies of preceding. See next 2.

22 1652 Shilling. Same; thin single trunk. Ex. rare.
Noe 13; Crosby, Pl. I, 12. Reworked dies of preceding. See next.

23 1652 Shilling. Transitional or "Spiny Tree."
Noe 13.3, 13.6, 13.9, 14; Crosby, fig. 7. Reworked dies of preceding. Trunk thicker, branches varyingly shaggy. Price for Noe 14 (ill.): Tip of 5 turns up; no die flaws r. of branches. Earlier states are rarer.

24 1652 Sixpence. IN on rev.
Noe 16. Usually weak at roots and E. Commands a premium with strong roots (ill.).

25 1652 Sixpence. Date high in field. Ex. rare.
Noe 17, 17.5; Crosby, Pl. I, 13. Dies reworked after severe clashing. Rev. always crosswise to obv. Possibly circulating counterfeits of the 1670s? MHS I:8, others. See next.

26 1652 Sixpence. 2 over reversed 2. Ex. rare.
Noe 18. ANS {1914}, Pl. 11. Reworked dies of last, sometimes called "1650"! Always in low grades. Rev. always crosswise to obv. MHS I:9.

27 1652 Sixpence. NEW ENGLAND . ANO. Reversed first S.
Noe 21.

28 1652 Sixpence. Same dies, S normal.
Noe 20, 22, and intermediate states, variously reworked. Rev. reappears on **47.** Probably issued 1666–67; see introduction.

29 1652 Sixpence. Nicknamed "6 over 12." 5 known.
As either of last 2 but overstruck on a cut-down Shilling. Cf. Garrett:1209, EF, $14,000. Publicized by William Wild {1966}. Enl. photo.

30 1652 Threepence. IN on obv.; 3 reversed S's. Very rare.
Noe 23; Crosby, Pl, I, 15. Style of tree is nearly as vague as on Willow Tree obvs.

31 1652 Threepence. Rosette altered from IN; first S reversed. Ex. rare.
Noe 24; Crosby, Pl. I, 14. Reworked dies of preceding.

32 165ᵲ Threepence. Normal S's; legends begin at 12:00.
Noe 25–27. Reworked dies of preceding; at least 5 states. Price for Noe 27 (ill.); earlier states are Ex. rare.

33 1652 Threepence. No IN; legends begin at 8:00. Very rare.
Noe 28, 28.5, and intermediate states of a single die-pair. Break develops at lower r. rev. Usually in low grades; crude flans.

Ex J. W. Garrett: 1211. Courtesy Bowers & Ruddy Galleries, Inc.

34 1652 Threepence. With IN; legends begin at 8:00. 2 known.
Noe-Newman 35. Reworked dies of preceding. Discovered by Breen, May 23, 1951. 1) Rumbel, 1952 ANA, Breisland:774, "Promised Lands":201 (ill.) Pictured in Newman {1959A}, Taxay {1971, 1976}. 2) McKean, Zug, Werner, Stack, Norweb. Pierced. Pictured in *SC* (1957).

35 1662 Twopence. Small 2.
Noe 29–32.5; Crosby, Pl. I, 16. At least 9 stages of reworking the single rev., to remove a flaw between 2 and edge. One die state, Noe-Newman 31.5, has date distorted, resembling "1672." Similar pieces dated 1652 are 19th-century forgeries by Wyatt and others.

36 1662 Twopence. Large 2.
Noe 33–34; Crosby, Pl. I, 17. At least 4 stages of reworked dies of preceding; same comment about "1652" coins.

LARGE PINE TREE ISSUES
(1667–74)

On Oct. 9, 1667, a third seven-year contract between the Generall Court and John Hull authorized issue of similar coins, still dated 1652, though with no renewal of the Twopence. These are the Large Pine Tree coins, far commoner than their predecessors, and famous for three centuries. Quantities issued were immense. The Large Shillings have AN DOM in rev. legend, as formerly, unlike the Small Shillings (below).

The Sixpence comes in two vars.: **47** has a spiny tree with a worn-out rev. left over from the Oak Tree series; **48** (much less rare) has pellets flanking the tree, like the first Shilling. These circumstances suggest that the Sixpences were contemporary with the earliest Shillings. Similar style considerations suggest that the four Threepence vars. were contemporary with the Sixpence; all fit better here than (as formerly listed) with the Small Shillings.

Die steel remained in short supply. Many Shilling vars. were therefore created in the same way as the Oak Tree coins, by regrinding and reengraving existing dies. This accounts for numerous vars. with differing trees but identical lettering, even to reversed N's Noe {1973}; Picker {1976}.

By the 1670s the colony's enemies in England had begun reminding King Charles II that the Massachusetts Puritans were continuing to strike coins on their own account, usurping royal prerogative. To placate the King, the colonists began shipping presents—in one instance a shipload of masts for the Royal Navy; but this at best delayed reprisals. Even continuing the obsessive 1652 date on the coins could hardly conceal evidence of ongoing manufacture after the Restoration.

Coinage of Large Shillings halted in Oct. 1674 on expiration of John Hull's contract, only to resume the following year with Small Shillings.

Many specimens show teethmarks and attempted bending. Like the Oak Tree pieces similarly treated, these are mementos of the Salem witchcraft delusion of 1692.

As with the Oak Tree issues, authentication is recommended to detect both the circulating counterfeits of the 1670s and more recent forgeries for collectors. The so-called "1652 Penny," similar to the 2d and 3d, belongs to the latter group. Some of these fakes are rarer than originals and command high prices: Noe {1950, 1973}; Newman {1959A}.

LARGE PINE TREE ISSUES
AN DOM in Rev. Legend

Designer, Engraver, Mint, Composition, Weight, Diameter, Authorizing Act, as preceding, except Shillings, $^{17-20}/_{16}'' = 27–31$ mm, and no Twopence.

Grade range, POOR to UNC. Grade standards as on Oak Tree coins.

37 1652 Shilling. Small tree, pellets flank trunk; date low.
Noe 1. Broadest flans of the series, often irregular.

38 1652 Shilling. Same obv.; date high. Unique?
Noe-Picker 1.5 Picker {1976}, p. 84. 73.9 grs. = 4.79 gms. Discovered by Richard Picker. Obv. reworked; rev. left over from Oak Tree period.

39 1652 Shilling. Straight branches.
Noe 2. Tree often weak.

40 1652 Shilling. Largest tree. Very rare.
Noe 3; Crosby, Pl. II, 2. Reworked dies of preceding.

41 1652 Shilling. Monogrammed NE.
Noe 8; Crosby, fig. 13. Rev. usually crumbling at letters.

42 1652 Shilling. One reversed N either side.
Noe 4–6, 9–10; Crosby, Pl. II, 1, 3. At least 7 successive reworked states of a single die-pair.

43   1652 Shilling. Legend begins below trunk. Very rare.
Noe 7. Uprights of M parallel to trunk. Rev. as preceding.

44   1652 Shilling. No H; no colons.
Noe 11; Crosby 2a-A1. Four reversed N's, from a miscut punch. Usually unevenly struck.

45   1652 Shilling. No H; rev. colons. Unique?
Noe-Picker 11.5, Crosby 2b-A2. Reworked dies of preceding. Picker {1976}, p. 86.   1) Parmelee, Jenning, Norweb.

46   1652 Shilling. "Nested bowls" branches. Very rare.
Noe 13, 14 (both ill., 13 supra); Noe 31 = Crosby, Pl. II, 5. Latter with heavy trunk and branches, thin numerals; Appleton, MHS I:48, unique, pierced. Always very worn and clipped; unknown with full inscriptions. Probably circulating counterfeits of the 1670s. Some are "witch pieces" (see introduction).

47   1652 (i.e., 1667?) Sixpence. Spiny tree. Very rare.
Noe 32; Crosby, Pl. II, 21. Rev. of **28.** Usually in low grades, always off center; obv. never shows any more of ETS IN, rev. always weak.

48   1652 Sixpence. Pellets flank trunk.
Noe 33, 33a (broken rev. die, ill.); Crosby, Pl. II, 20. Usually shows only bases of SATHVSE. Similar coins without pellets are 19th-century forgeries.

49   1652 Threepence. No pellets.
Noe 36–37; Crosby, Pl. II, 24. Tree altered from Oak type; rev. of Oak type. 4 stages of reworking obv. to eliminate a break above MA. Price for earliest state, Noe 36 (ill.); in later states tree is nearly stripped of leaves, M A distant, second A a blob, fewer beads in inner circle, only 7 beads in rosette.

50   1652 Threepence. Pellets flank trunk; NEW ENGLAND.:. Very rare.
Noe 34; Crosby, Pl. II, 23. Similar pieces without pellets at trunk are 19th-century forgeries.

51   1652 Threepence. Same but NEWENGLAND.ANO Ex. rare.
Noe 35; Crosby, Pl. II, 22. Reworked dies of preceding. D in ENGLAND rotated 180°. Enl. photo

Ex J. W. Garrett: 1227. Courtesy Bowers & Ruddy Galleries, Inc.

SMALL PINE TREE SHILLINGS
(1675–82)

The Generall Court renewed its contract with Hull and Saunderson May 12, 1675, for "this Seven yeares next to Come, if either of them liue so long," but for unknown reasons it remained unsigned until July 9. Coinage thereafter apparently consisted only of Small Pine Tree Shillings, still dated 1652. These were the coins most familiar in their own day as Boston or Bay Shillings. They were first publicly called Pine Tree Shillings in 1680, though the name was probably known earlier. Many went to pay troops in King Philip's War.

Issues were immense even compared with the Large Shillings. Noe {1950, 1973} has suggested that after negotiations with Crown authorities broke down and reprisals were certain

(1680–82), authorities ordered Hull to increase coinage to the limit of available silver bullion, on the principle "better be hanged for a sheep than a lamb," as the number of dies used greatly exceeded those for previous issues. Dies were smaller (permitting more impressions from each), and the final vars.—**61** and **62**—are among the most plentiful of all.

After Hull's contract expired, May 12, 1682, there was no talk of renewal. Hull died Oct. 1, 1683, and on Oct. 23, 1684, partly in reprisal for what Charles II's advisers had been characterizing as decades of treason, King James II revoked the Massachusetts Bay Colony's charter, leaving the colonists defenseless against further arbitrary exercises of royal power. He sent Col. Percie Kirke to establish a police state in the Province of Massachusetts, but Kirke died before he could begin his duties. His replacement, Sir Edmund Andros, arrived in Dec. 1686 with a warrant to value Spanish coins at the same rate as in other British colonies, but with instructions to restore the pre-1652 conditions, barter and all. Andros is best known for his futile visit to Hartford, Conn., where similar reprisals were in process: On Oct. 31, 1687, he arrived to seize that colony's charter, but during the proceedings someone blew out all the candles while others hid the document in an oak tree, later known as the Charter Oak. (This tree, then about 800 years old, stood until lightning felled it on Aug. 21, 1856; it is pictured on the Connecticut commemorative half dollar, **7514.**) As soon as word arrived of James II's ouster (1689), the colonists overthrew Andros and shipped him back to England in chains.

Genuine Bay Shillings became scarce, finally almost unobtainable. Many found their way to Canada, where they apparently passed as 12 Sols pieces. Maryland passed an enactment Nov. 19, 1686, that "New England Shillings and Sixpences" (Pine Tree coins) should pass as sterling (Bushnell {1859}). Counterfeit Shillings were numerous. Charles Pickering, Samuel Buckley, and Robert Fenton stood trial before Gov. William Penn and Council, Philadelphia, Oct. 1683, for forging Spanish "new Bitts" (1-real coins) and "Boston Money" or "New England Shillings"—evidently Oak or Pine Tree coins: *CNL* 51, pp. 628–29 (4/78). Spanish and Mexican dollars were seized for taxes. New England reverted to a barter economy.

Under orders to equip soldiers for action against Canada in King William's War (1690), Massachusetts authorities had to resort to paper currency, emulating the playing-card scrip the Canadians had been using since 1685 for similar purposes. The 1690 issue and its successors promptly depreciated, many being altered to simulate higher values, or imitated by counterfeiters undeterred by the death penalty: Newman {1976A}, pp. 144–48. Goods priced at a pound sterling were likely to cost five or six times that in Province notes, if merchants would accept paper payments at all. Bay Shillings remained a preferred medium of exchange throughout New England and nearby Canada, side by side with Mexican dollars, though few colonists had silver of any kind. No more silver would be coined locally for another century.

Clipped coins testify to early skulduggery; fraud artists filed or shaved off parts of the edges before spending the coins, thus over months accumulating enough silver free of charge to be worth selling or even turning over to Hull for coinage. The mere threat of clipping had induced the Generall Court to change from the adequate NE format to the Willow Tree design (above), no matter how poorly struck the resulting coins; but the Pine Tree Shillings, both Large and Small, suffered more from this practice than any previous issues. They are not so often seen bent and teethmarked for witch tokens, probably because the thicker flans used for the Small Shillings made bending much more difficult.

Authentication is recommended, for the same reasons as previous issues. Forgeries vary from hopelessly crude to deceptive; some are famous because pictured in Crosby, Noe {1952,

1973}, and Newman {1959A}, and these command high prices. That listed herein as **63** was in the Castine (Me.) hoard, buried in 1704 (Noe {1942}); later Woodward 10/1863:2467, and accepted as genuine by Crosby, Noe, and Newman. Richard Picker discovered a more obvious forgery punchlinked with **63** which led to exposure of the latter. Newman {1959A} finally established that the "Good Samaritan" Shillings are 19th-century forgeries, including the Bushnell piece long thought genuine (ill. ANS {1914}, Pl. 7).

Massachusetts silver coins are among the most historically important Colonial issues. Not only were they the first silver coins made within the continental United States, and the first international coins made within our national boundaries (circulating freely in Canada), they early became a cause célèbre, the occasion of the first major rebellion by any of the American colonies against British oppression, the beginning of that tradition of defiance which would later manifest itself in the 1722 parchment pence, the Boston Tea Party, the Sons of Liberty, and the Minutemen—a tradition focusing always on opposition to royal interference in the colonies' internal affairs. No wonder, then, that these coins have remained in continuous collector demand for over a century.

SMALL PINE TREE SHILLINGS
AN DO in Rev. Legend

Designer, Engraver, Mint, Composition, Weight, Authorizing Act as preceding; Diameter, $^{14-17}/_{16}$″ = 22–26 mm.

Grade range, POOR to UNC. GOOD: All legends legible; tree and some inner circle beads may be weak. FINE: All leaves boldly clear. Higher grades—grade by surface. Authentication always recommended.

52 1652 Shilling. Small letters; legends crowded l., spread r. Noe 15; Crosby, Pl. II, 8. Usually in low grades.

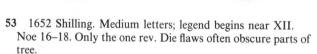

53 1652 Shilling. Medium letters; legend begins near XII. Noe 16–18. Only the one rev. Die flaws often obscure parts of tree.

54 1652 Shilling. Small obv. letters; same rev. Very rare. Noe 19–22. Price for Noe 19 (ill.); other vars. are Ex. rare.

55 1652 Shilling. Small obv. letters; medium rev. letters. Very rare.
  Noe 23. But compare **56–62.** Always in low grades.

56 1652 Shilling. Small obv. letters; large rev. letters. Ex. rare.
  Noe 27 and unlisted var. Letters as on **55.** Rev. reappears on **60.** Always in low grades. Discovery coin, William Summer Appleton, MHS I:40, "F."
57 1652 Shilling. Large tree; medium obv. and rev. letters. Ex. rare.
  Noe 24. Legends begin lower l., unlike **53.** Compare **59, 60.** Always in low grades.

58 1652 Shilling. Small obv. letters; NEVV. Very rare.
  Noe 25.

59 1652 Shilling. Medium obv. letters; NEVV. Rare.
  Noe 26.

60 1652 Shilling. Large letters, "cupid's bow" branches. Very rare.
  Noe 28; Crosby, Pl. II, 19. Severe die clashing weakens rev.

61 1652 Shilling. Quatrefoils. Rev. colons.
  Noe 29. Two die states, differing in top of tree. D in ENGLAND first rotated 180°, then corrected; traces of blunder fade out.

62 1652 Shilling. Quatrefoils. Rev., "Masonic" punctuation.
  Noe 30. Always on small polygonal flans. Probably issued through much of 1682.

63 1652 Shilling. MASASTHVSETS. Unique.
  Noe 12; Crosby, Pl. II, 6. 62 grs. = 4.02 gms. See introductory text.

iii. LORD BALTIMORE'S COINAGES (1658/59)

George Calvert (ca. 1580–1632), first Lord Baltimore, a member of the first London Company (which had colonized Virginia), established in 1632 a community in Newfoundland called "Avalon" to buy local fish and furs for resale to England. For this and his other services to the Crown, Charles I granted Calvert a charter making him sole Lord Proprietor of some 10 million acres in what was later called Maryland (named after Queen Henrietta Maria). As Calvert died April 13, 1632, during formalities connected with the grant, the charter was finally issued on June 20 to his son and heir Cecil Calvert, second Lord Baltimore (1609–75). Though the coining privilege was unmentioned, Cecil assumed it belonged to the grant because it had been included in the 1606 Virginia charter.

For decades afterward, Maryland's main crop and medium of exchange was tobacco. Unfortunately, the vast population and production increases lowered the leaf's purchasing power, so that while rents continued payable in fixed weights of tobacco, prices of everything else soared, including the musket balls and gunpowder used for small change. Many complaints reached Lord Baltimore, who in 1650 had to use his own cattle to pay soldiers in order to avert a mutiny: Crosby, p. 124. In 1658 Baltimore decided to exercise the coining privilege, directing that the colonial assembly pass ordinances authorizing the coins to be receivable for all rents, arrears, taxes, duties, and other obligations, and punishing counterfeiters. Gov. Fendall's abortive rebellion (March 13, 1659/60 O.S.) delayed enactment eight months until Lord Baltimore named his own brother Philip governor. The requested statutes followed, May 1, 1661. A further act of April 12, 1662, required every householder and freeman (in all at least 5,500 persons) to exchange 60 pounds of tobacco for 10 shillings in the new coins, throwing over £2,750 sterling into circulation. Implied ballpark figures: 20,000 or more Shillings, 35,200 or more Sixpences, and 52,800 or more Groats.

The coins were made in London, mint uncertain but possibly the Tower, in the winter of 1658/59. Richard (Thomas?) Pight, Clerke of Irons in the Tower, holder of a Puritan Commonwealth commission against false coiners, informed on the Cavalier Baltimore, and on Oct. 4, 1659, obtained a warrant for his arrest. Craig, p. 376, says that Pight seized Baltimore's "coins

and tools." The next day the Lord Proprietor was summoned to attend Council and give evidence. As Baltimore survived till 1675, presumably King Charles II interrupted any proceedings begun by the floundering Commonwealth.

These coins eventually vanished. Maryland reverted to barter economy. On Feb. 19, 1706, the colonial legislature passed an act making hemp (Cannabis sativa, alias marijuana), a staple crop, legal tender at sixpence per pound in payment of 25% of any debt: Bushnell {1859}. The rest would be payable in tobacco or other legally valued crops.

LORD BALTIMORE'S COINAGES

Designer, Engraver, uncertain. Mint, London (the Tower?). Composition, silver (sterling?); the Denarium is copper. Diameters: Shilling, about 17/16″ = 27 mm; Sixpence, 13.5/16″ = 21.4 mm; Groat, 11–12/16″ = 17.5–19.5 mm; Denarium, about 13/16″ = 19.9–20.4 mm. Weight standard believed 82½ Shillings to the troy lb., i.e., Shilling, 69.82 grs. = 4.524 gms.; Sixpence, 34.92 grs. = 2.262 gms.; Groat, 23.27 grs. = 1.508 gms.; Denarium, apparently 120 to the lb. avoir. = 58.33 grs. = 3.78 gms. Authorizing Act, May 1, 1661.

Grade range, POOR to nearly UNC. GOOD: Outlines of devices plain, few details of hair or drapery. VERY GOOD: Nearly half hair details. FINE: Over half hair details, partial drapery details. VERY FINE: Over 3/4 hair details, over half drapery details. Higher grades—grade by surfaces.

64 n.d. Shilling. Large head; MARIAE: Rare.
Crosby, Pl. III, 1. Base point at M. Usually, die injured below II; buckling weakens upper hair. 64.1–76 grs. = 4.15–4.92 gms. Enl. photos.

Jack Collins

65 n.d. Shilling. Small head; no colon after MARIAE. Unique?
V touches base point.   1) ANS, ex Downing.

66 n.d. Shilling. Same dies. Copper OMS. Ex. rare.
1) BM.   2) Glasgow Univ.   3) Ellsworth, Garrett:1231, $7,500, 72.4 grs. = 4.69 gms. (worn).   4) Ex Brand.   5) McLachlan.
67 n.d. Shilling. Cross botony quartered in arms. Unique. Crosby, p. 369. Shield matches current Maryland state arms as depicted on Maryland commemorative half dollar **7484**; the quartering is for Lady Baltimore.   1) European pvt. coll., ex Sir Frederick Morton Eden, baronet.
68 n.d. Sixpence. Small bust; no period after final I
Hyphen before M on obv. Crosby, Pl. III, 2. 33–44.2 grs. = 2.14–2.86 gms. Usually F to VF. Finest is possibly Robison:17, "AU," $5,000.

69 n.d. Sixpence. Same, no hyphen before M. Very rare. Apparently a reground state of same dies. Auction 81:4, others.

70 n.d. Sixpence. Small bust; period after final I. Ex. rare.
1) Wurtzbach, Brand.
71 n.d. Sixpence. Same dies. Copper OMS. Ex. rare.
Weight reported as 56.8 grs. = 3.68 gms.
72 n.d. Sixpence. Similar, MVLTILICAMINI. 2 known.
1) Parmelee, Brand, Norweb (ill.).   2) Newcomer, Garrett:1230, 44.2 grs. = 2.86 gms., VF, $13,500.

73 n.d. Sixpence. Large bust, period after final I. Ex. rare. 2 minor vars., both with correct spellings.

74 n.d. IV (Pence) = Groat. Large bust and shield. Rare. Crosby, Pl. III, 3. Hyphen in TERRAE-MARIAE; base point between VL. Later (rarely) with lumpy break joining shield to V of IV, e.g., Ellsworth, Garrett:1229, "EF," $15,000. Usually in low grades. 18.5–30 grs. = 1.2–1.94 gms.

75 n.d. IV (Pence). Small bust and shield. 2 known. Crosby, Pl. III, 4. No hyphen in TERRAE MARIAE; base point at M. 1) Clarke, Craige, Norweb. Enl. photos. 2) MHS.

76 n.d. Denarium = Penny. Copper. 5 known. Crosby, fig. 27. Obv., R in MARIAE first punched horizontal, then corrected. 1) Bindley, Miles, Dimsdale, Hodsol, Martin, Mickley, Bushnell, Parmelee, Brock, Univ. of Pa., Ward, Ford. Ill. *AJN* 1/1868, p. 93. 56.95 grs. = 3.69 gms. 2) SI, worn, corroded. 3) BMFA, worn, pierced. 4) Johnson-Meyer:1, worn, $28,000, Roper:46, $13,200. 66.25 grs. = 4.293 gms. Found by a Maryland college student using a metal detector. 5) Pvt. coll., worn, corroded. 2 types of numismatic forgeries: one deceptive with oldstyle lettering, the other (William Idler's) modern with mid-19th-century letters (vertical serifs to C's, S's, etc.), and, usually, Idler's advertisement in obv. field; this latter comes in various metals: Kenney {1952}. Neither has the corrected blunder in R.

CHAPTER 2

COINAGES AUTHORIZED BY ROYAL PATENT

i. HOLT'S TIN "PLANTATION" HALFPENCE (1688)

Though tin had been known since antiquity, and long since used for alloying copper in making bronze, the idea of tin coinage was seldom taken seriously because cold weather causes metallic tin (beta-tin) to crumble into powder (alpha-tin)—almost instantaneously at −40° C. or F., more slowly at temperatures even as high as 18° C. = 64.4° F., but more quickly if even a minute granule of alpha-tin is already present. Nevertheless, owners of tin mines in Devonshire and Cornwall, after a price collapse (1679–80), fell victim to the delusion that persuading royal authorities to order issues of tin coins would increase the market–and the current price–for their output. As a result, the Tower Mint struck tin farthings and halfpence for British domestic circulation 1684–92, and on Aug. 13, 1688, James II's secretary Henry Guy wrote to the mint officers asking them to name their objections, if any, to a similar coinage for the "American Plantations," as the colonies were then known.

Evidently no objections followed, as the Tower Mint struck the coins for Richard Holt & Co., representing the whole group of "Tynn ffarmers," during the last few weeks of James II's reign. Coinage was interrupted by the "Glorious Revolution" which ousted the King.

Newman {1955} published Henry Guy's letter, with a copy of Richard Holt's covering letter. This established that the coins were intended to be struck at 10 pence per lb. avoir. = 40 pieces to the pound = 175 grs. = 11.34 gms. each. None approach this weight; evidently the authorized standard was lowered before production began. Most originals weigh 138–142 grs. = 8.94–9.2 gms., evidently for 50 to the pound. There were at least six pairs of dies with a seventh rev. Available spectroscopic data indicate that the coins were at least 97.5% pure tin, the alloying elements principally antimony (naturally occurring), but no lead.

There is some doubt about the denomination. Domestic tin halfpence of James II (with small copper plugs) were coined at 40 to the pound; tin farthings of both Charles II and James II at 80 to the pound = 87.5 grs. = 5.67 gms. each. These "plantation" coins proclaim their value as 1/24 Spanish real = 1/192 Spanish dollar (8 Reales). In England, the Spanish dollar = 4s6d = 54 pence = 108 halfpence = 216 farthings; in Massachusetts Bay Colony, New York, and Virginia, the 8 Reales coin = 6s = 72d = 144 halfpence = 288 farthings: a rate later confirmed as "Proclamation Money." This would have made the tin pieces worth 1½ farthings each. But during this period,

any farthings passed in the colonies at double face, so that these may have passed at 1d or even 1½d each.

However, the coins proved unacceptable in America, especially after even brief exposure to New England and New York winters corroded them. Most original survivors show "tin pests"—areas of crumbling from exposure to cold; this is true even of the rare examples retaining original mint brilliance, i.e., without history of exposure to seawater or atmospheric contaminants such as smog. Many are virtually illegible; all are rare, especially the deviants with ET HB REX, with sidewise 4, or with transposed shields.

About 1828, the London coin dealer Matthew Young obtained two pairs of original dies (rusted and broken), with the ornamented parallel bars used for imparting the edge device (a line of about 90 beads). He struck a few hundred restrikes at 55 to the pound. These suffered the same fate as the originals, and they are now also rare, though a few more survive with mint brilliance. They show rust marks and often a long obv. break, absent on originals.

HOLT'S TIN "PLANTATION" HALFPENCE

Designer, Engraver, John Croker. Mint, Tower. Composition, tin (see introduction). Diameter, 17/16″ = 27 mm. Weight standard, 50 to the lb. = 140 grs. = 9.07 gms. Authorizing Act, Royal Patent, Aug. 13, 1688.

Grade range: POOR (corroded) to UNC., usually with "tin pests" (see introduction). No grade standard established; we suggest FINE: Part of saddle blanket shows; VERY FINE: Over half drapery details. Tin pests may obscure details even in UNCIRCULATED; grade as though without them, then mention them.

77 n.d. (1688) Halfpenny (?) Original.
   5 vars. 134.5–154 grs. = 8.72–9.98 gms. Unrusted dies. Pridmore III, 1, p. 269.

78 n.d. (1828) Restrike. Similar.
3 vars. 120–138.3 grs. = 7.78–8.96 gms. Head midway between G.B.; obv. rust and/or long break in field. See introductory text.

79 n.d. (1828) Copper OMS. Unique?
ANS. 149.6 grs. = 9.694 gms.

80 n.d. (1688) Halfpenny (?) ET.HB.REX. Original. Very rare. Newman 1-A. A spacing problem; probably the first die made. Pridmore III, 2, p. 269.

81 n.d. (1688) Halfpenny (?) Sidewise 4. Original. Very rare. Newman 3-C, 6-C. Latter Roper:71, $770.

82 n.d. (1688) Halfpenny (?) Transposed shields. Original. 6 known.
Harp nearest 24. Large fleurs de lys in French arms. Newman 2-G. Pridmore III, 3, p. 269. 1) BM. 2) Newman. 3, 4, 5) N.Y. dealers. 6) N.J. dealer.

ii. WOOD'S ROSA AMERICANA COINAGES (1722–33)

William Wood, of Wolverhampton (Staffordshire), owner of copper and tin mines in the West Country area of England, got the same idea that had deceived many other entrepreneurs in the 17th and 18th centuries, namely that one could make money by making coins. Accordingly, Wood exerted his considerable political clout until King George I was persuaded to sign a patent, July 12, 1722 (reproduced in Crosby, pp. 151–59).

This authorized Wood to issue some 100 tons of base-metal coins for the American Plantations. These were to be of twopenny, penny, and halfpenny denominations, and to be struck at 30 twopence = 60 pence = 120 halfpence to the pound (compared with the Tower Mint's 23 pence = 46 halfpence = 92 farthings to the pound), so that they could not pass current in England. The patent represented Wood as inventor of a new alloy in which the coins were to be struck. Wood's coinage metal (not to be confused with Wood's metal, i.e., fusible alloy) is a form of brass under the euphemism "Bath metal" = 75% copper, 24.7% "double refined linck [zinc: see Glossary], otherwise called Tutanaigne or Spelter," and 0.3% "fine virgin silver"—this last a purposeless waste.

The warrant proposed to throw into colonial circulation some £56,000 = 13,440,000 pence. If the amounts of the three denominations were equal in face value (a reasonable starting hypothesis), that would mean 2,240,000 Twopence, 4,480,000 Pennies, and 8,960,000 Halfpennies. Actual mintages were far smaller, though not precisely known.

Unfortunately for Wood's dreams of wealth, King George's avaricious mistress, Ehrengarde Melusina, Duchess of Munster and Kendal (commonly known as "The Maypole"), managed to get her hands on the warrant as soon as His Majesty had signed it. Wood could therefore not even gain entry to the Tower Mint to arrange for manufacture of original device punches and official supervision (let alone strike any coins) without first ransoming the document; and the Maypole's price was £10,000 sterling, or nearly $500,000 in modern purchasing power! As a result, Wood struck his coins at lower weight standards than those specified, and this circumstance stimulated protests and refusals; the role played by the "King's Whore" had made matters far worse.

Snelling's claim ({1769}, pp. 39–40) that local diesinkers Messrs. Lammas, Standbroke, and Harold "made the dies" may mean that they forged, turned, and hardened the working dies, and/or completed them by entering them with lettering and dates; it does not automatically mean that any of these individuals had anything to do with the designs. More likely John Croker, Engraver of the Tower Mint, designed and executed the original device punches, possibly with the aid of Samuel Bull, probationary engraver. Sir Isaac Newton, the illustrious mathematician/physicist/astrologer, then Master of the Mint, was appointed Royal Comptroller to test the coins for weight and malleability (then the only test for purity of copper, but completely inappropriate for Bath metal): Crosby, pp. 160, 153–54. Newton turned over this duty to his nephew, Mr. Barton.

According to Snelling (loc. cit.), coining went on in the French Change in Seven Dials (a ghastly industrial slum district in London), and supposedly also in Bristol, without the quality controls of the Tower Mint. Many of the coins show evidence of being struck on cast blanks instead of planchets properly cut from rolled strip. Snelling says that the blanks were heated before striking, presumably to soften them enough to minimize die breakage. This explains why many uncirculated survivors are discolored, showing local porosity and bulges from entrapped gas bubbles. Use of cast blanks also accounts for edges (especially on the Twopence) showing file marks that resulted from removal of rough areas or spurs. Wood's choice of alloy was metallurgically incompetent. When new the coins looked like brass; after brief circulation they became rough, suggesting cast counterfeits.

Their motto UTILE DULCI, idiomatically 'For business and pleasure,' is from Horace, *Ars Poetica,* 343: *Omne tulit punctum qui miscuit utile dulci*—'He took all the applause who blended sweet and useful.' The whole line appears on Massachusetts Codfish notes dated Oct. 18, 1776. The double Tudor rose found on all ROSA AMERICANA issues, which gave the coins their name, is in this context a cynical piece of flattery to the

King, falsely lauding him as the logical successor to the Plantagenets and Tudors, uniting in his own person the white and red roses of the Yorkists and Lancastrians. All knew that this petty German princeling insultingly refused even to learn to read English, and that he regarded the British Crown as of far less importance than his Hanoverian and Holy Roman Empire titles. The uncrowned rose of 1722 was originally on base pence of Edward VI (ca. 1551–53) and halfpence of Mary I ("Bloody" Mary) before and after her marriage to King Philip. The crowned rose of 1723 of Henry VIII first occurs as principal device on crowns and testoons.

The coins' arrival in New York and New England was most unwelcome, as royal authorities had not bothered to consult colonial assemblies. Worse still, sizes and weights were confusing: Wood's Twopence corresponded to no coin then in circulation; his Penny suggested a Tower halfpenny, his Halfpenny a farthing. New York merchants refused to accept them at all. The more rebellious Massachusetts patriots, bitterly remembering what had happened the last time a king tried to dictate money matters to them (over the Pine Tree Shillings), passed a law, in June 1722 (on first hearing of Wood's proposals, before the warrant was issued), authorizing manufacture and circulation of parchment pence, twopence, and threepence notes: Newman {1976A}, p. 153. This tactic resulted in storms of laughter at Wood's expense, culminating in 1724 with Jonathan Swift's *Drapier's Letters* smear campaign against Wood (below), and contributing to the Massachusetts tradition of defiance which led to the Revolution. W. C. Prime claims that these coins later circulated "in the South," probably from Maryland to Georgia: {1861}, Chap. VI.

Mass refusals of the coins led Wood to halt coinage early in 1724. Wood resigned his patent in exchange for a royal pension which yielded him more income than the coins had; he died in 1730.

The last of the ROSA AMERICANA issues were a few copper pattern Twopences dated 1733, struck at 25 to the pound. Their makers (Wood's heirs?) apparently intended to make a new coinage proposal to King George II, but nothing came of it. These Twopences are in very high relief, suitable more to medals than to coins (they will not stack); their designs have made them among the most coveted coins in the Early American series.

On the other hand, there is no evidence that the pattern Twopence, Pennies, and Halfpennies dated 1717 (Crosby, pp. 145–47, 372, and Pl. III, 10–13) represented any proposed coinage for the American colonies, nor that Wood had anything to do with them. Some students have pointed to alleged stylistic resemblances between the portraits of George I on these and on some of Wood's coins. To these eyes the resemblances are illusory; but even were they demonstrable, this could mean equally that they were made in the Tower Mint for some other would-be contract coiner. Their legends either repeat George I's Hanoverian titles (as Georg Ludwig, Duke of Brunswick and Lüneburg, Arch-Treasurer and Prince Elector of the Holy Roman Empire) or flatter him with the lie *Dat pacem et nouas* (sic: *novas) prebet et auget opes,* 'He gives us peace and benefits new (enterprises) and increases wealth.' These inscriptions fail to show any relevance to the American colonies. The coins' light weights prove that their makers intended them to circulate outside of England, but they may as easily have been meant for Scotland or Ireland as for any of the colonies. No official copper coinage had been made for either Scotland or Ireland for 20 years—a circumstance local authorities were unwilling to allow royal counselors to forget.

Much the same must be said of the 1724, 1727, and undated ROSA SINE SPINA ('Thornless Rose') pieces, speculatively listed as American since Crosby's day a century ago (Crosby, Pl, III, 16). Like their 1717 counterparts, the 1727's evidently

accompanied some unseen proposal connected in time with George II's coronation. It has been plausibly argued that the one large and two small roses on some of these coins were deliberately chosen as devices because they were ambiguously interpretable as meaning the island containing England, Scotland, and Wales, the smaller island of Ireland, and America; or as England, Ireland, and Scotland; or as George II, Queen Caroline, and Frederick Louis, Prince of Wales. But their ROSA SINE SPINA legend—found on domestic base coins from halfpence to half groats ever since Mary I's day almost 170 years earlier—was flattery to the Tudors.

Until their relevance to America can be documented, I prefer not to list either the 1717 "prepatent patterns" or the ROSA SINE SPINA among coins intended for the American colonies. All are pictured in Crosby, Nelson {1903, 1905}, and Taxay-Scott; all are of the highest rarity.

WOOD'S ROSA AMERICANA COINAGES

Designer, John Croker? Engravers, various. Mints, French Change, Hogg Lane, Seven Dials (London), and reportedly Bristol. Composition, "Bath metal" (75% copper, 24.7% zinc, 0.3% silver), except as noted. Diameters, variable: Twopence, 20–21/16" = 31.8–33.6 mm (except as noted); Penny, 16–18/16" = 25–29 mm; Halfpenny, 13–14/16" = 20.5–22 mm. Weight standard, 60 pence to the pound, i.e., Twopence, 233.33 grs. = 15.12 gms.; Penny, 116.67 grs. = 7.56 gms. Halfpenny, 58.33 grs. = 3.78 gms. (Observed weights often lighter.) Authorizing Act, Pat. 8, George I, Part 4, No. 1.

Grade range, FAIR to UNC. FINE: Over half hair details. VERY FINE: Over 3/4 hair details. EXTREMELY FINE: Only faintest rubbing on isolated central hair details, leaf tips, central beads of rose, and (on 1723 Crowned Rose coins) lys of crown, but in general individual strands or beads will not blur into one another. Even UNCIRCULATED pieces will sometimes show dark patina or porosity and edge file marks parallel to faces of coins.

83 n.d. (1722) First Prototype Twopence. Motto in field. Ex. rare.
Compare **84–87.** ANS's weighs 206.44 grs. = 13.777 gms. (worn).

84 n.d. (1722) Same dies. Penny flan. Ex. rare.
Always weak. 1) BM, 130.4 grs. = 8.45 gms. 2) Nelson {1959}, p. 26, and Pl. II, 1; Ryder, Boyd estate (ill.), 121 grs. = 7.83 gms. 3) Lauder:135, $1,400.

85 n.d. (1722) Same dies. Bath metal piedfort. Unique?
1) Ex Brand estate, double-struck.

86 n.d. (1722) Same dies. Jumbo copper piedfort. Unique.
1) Crosby, Parmelee, Mills, Garrett:1248, $4,250, 269.3 grs. = 17.45 gms. Crosby, Pl. III, 14. Known for over a century as the "Iron ROSA AMERICANA," possibly (on the guinea pig or *lucus a non lucendo* principle) because it contains no iron. Electrotype copies exist.

87 n.d. (1722) Second Prototype Twopence. Modified portrait. 2 known.
Same rev. Crosby, p. 372; in *SC* called "Very fine dies." Discovery coin, Parmelee:522. 1) Boyd estate. 2) Mrs. Norweb. Breen {1977}, p. 4.

88 n.d. (1722) Twopence. Motto on label. Very scarce.
Nelson 3 {1959}, p. 27, and Pl. II 2/3; Crosby, Pl. III. 15. Weight, 211.7–244 grs. = 13.72–15.81 gms. James D. King discovered a uniface lead trial striking of obv., 1970.

89 1722 Twopence. GEORGIUS. Stop after X. Rare.
Crosby, Pl. IV, 1; ANS {1914}, Pl. 3. 255–261.9 grs. = 16.52–16.97 gms. Stop = centered pellet unless noted. The GEORGIUS spelling continues through **105.**

90 1722 Twopence. No stop after X Rare.
Crosby, p. 162; ANS {1914}, Pl. 13.

91 1723 Prototype Twopence. Aged head. Proof. 2 known.
1) Dr. Hall, Brand estate, 223.3 grs. = 14.47 gms. 2) George J. Bauer, LM 11/68:26, Spink, 202.7 grs. = 13.135 gms. (ill.)

92 1723 Twopence. Stop after X., not 3
Crosby, p. 164, no. 3, and Pl. IV, 10; Nelson 14 {1959}, p. 30. 240 grs. = 15.6 gms. 14 vars., 3 ill. in Earle:1975–77. All Crowned Rose coins vary in size and elaboration of knobs.

93 1723 Twopence. Similar. Thin flan. Ex. rare.
1) Parsons, Ellsworth, Garrett:1251, $6,750, 142.7 grs. = 9.25 gms.

94 1723 Twopence. Stops after X. and 3. Rare.
2 vars., one ill. ANS {1914}, Pl. 14.

95 1723 Twopence. Stop after 3., not X Very rare.
Crosby, p. 164, no. 2, and Pl. IV, 9.

96 1723 Twopence. No stop after X or 3
5 vars. Crosby, p. 164, no. 1; ANS {1914}, Pl. 3.

97 1723 Twopence. Similar, UTILE DULI blunder. Unique?
1) Ex Newcomer coll., untraced.

98 1723 Twopence. "German silver" OMS. Unique?
Large knobs to scroll. Possibly tin or tutenag? 1) H. P. Smith:32.

99 1724 Prototype Twopence. MA. B. Bath metal. 4 known.
Nelson 17; Pl. II, 10. 1) Nelson, Ryder, Boyd estate, 200 grs. = 12.96 gms. 2) Newman. 3) Bauer, LM 11/68:33, Roper:93, $3,740, 202.8 grs. = 13.14 gms. 4) Lauder:148, flan chipped and cracked.

100 1724 Same dies. Copper. Ex. rare.
1) Australian pvt. coll., Robison:34, $4,600, 189.7 grs. = 12.29 gms.

101 1724 Same dies. Silver OMS. Unique.
Engraved WW (= William Wood?) below bust, VIII JVNE in l. field. Thought to have been Wood's pocket piece. Murdoch:438; Nelson {1959}, p. 31.

102 1724 Prototype Twopence, M B . FRA = Bath metal. Ex. rare.
Nelson {1959}, p. 31. 1) Boyd estate, silvered. 2) Bauer, LM 11/68:34, Spink. 3) Robison:35, thin flan, 139.4 grs. = 9.033 gms., $5,750.

103 1724 Same dies. Copper. 2 obv. vars. Ex. rare.
All seen to date are on penny flans, 139.4–159.3 grs. = 8.45–10.32 gms., for Tower halfpenny standard. A) Obv. as **102**. Nelson 17, p. 31. 1) Nelson, Ryder, Boyd estate, *NUM* 11/69, NN/Seaby 11/70, Robison, Roper:94, $2,860. B) M B FRA. 1) Mills, Jenks, Ellsworth, Garrett:1254, EF, $6,000. 2) Pvt. coll. (ill.)

104 1724 As preceding. Silver OMS. Unique.

105 1724 Obv. as last; rev. of 1723 halfpenny. Unique. Copper, penny flan. 1) Bushnell, Nelson, Ryder, Boyd estate.

106 1733 Pattern Twopence. GEORGIVS. Copper. Proof. 4 known.
$2^{1}/16'' = 33$ mm. Crosby, Pl. IV, 6; Nelson 20 and Pl. II, 11 {1959}, p. 32. 1) BM, 290 grs. = 18.9 gms. 2) Parmelee, Ellsworth, Garrett:1255, $22,500, Roper:196, 265.1 grs. = 17.18 gms. 3) Nelson, Ryder, Boyd estate. 4) Mrs. Norweb (ill.). Discovered by Thomas Hollis: Snelling {1769}, p. 40. Beware electrotype copies. Robinson's forgery (Crosby, Pl. IV, 17) has tall narrow letters, and the rose faces the wrong way; dies by Joseph Merriam ca. 1861. Silver [10], copper [45], brass [45], the copper occasionally rubbed down to simulate a worn genuine piece. See introductory text.

107 1733 Twopence. Same dies. Lead trial piece. Unique?
1) Ex a NYC transit policeman, Morton:462, $2,400 (impaired), Roper:97.

108 n.d. (1733) Same obv., uniface. Steel. 6 known.
1) BM, 245.6 grs. = 15.92 gms. 2) Garrett:1256, $1,700, cracked flan, 212 grs. = 13.74 gms. 3) Murdoch, Brand, Breisland:788, $3,200 (1973), blank rev. engraved HAWKINS JANY 1737.

109 1733 Twopence rev., uniface. Bath metal. Unique.
1) Boyd estate. Pierced; blank obv. engraved MR. JACKSON.

110 1722 First Prototype Penny. Bath metal. 2 known.
Tall narrow head; GEORGIVS./VTILE 1) Crosby, p. 162, Pl. IV, 2; Nelson 4, Pl. II, 5 (115 grs. = 7.45 gms.) {1959}, p. 27. 2) Roper:80, 116.5 grs. = 7.55 gms.

Ex J. W. Garrett: 1240. Courtesy Bowers & Ruddy Galleries, Inc.

111 1722 Same dies. Copper. 2 known.
1) Crosby, Nelson, Ryder, Boyd estate, 155 grs. = 10.04 gms. 2) Ellsworth, Garrett:1240, Proof, $5,500, 145.8 grs. = 9.448 gms.

112 1722 Second Prototype Penny. Copper. Unique?
Crosby, p. 162. Head as next but extra long hair ribbons. GEORGIVS/VTILE. Copper, broad flan. 1) Crosby:1305, Ryder, Boyd estate.

113 1722 Penny. GEORGIUS./VTILE. Short ribbons. Rare. Bath metal. Crosby, p. 162, Pl. IV, 3; Nelson 5 {1959}, p. 27. Struck at 60 to the lb. 3 minor vars.

114 1722 Penny. UTILE, no rev. rosettes. Very rare.
Crosby, p. 162, no. 1. Obv. of **146**. 125 grs. = 8.1 gms. Roper:84.

115 1722 Penny. UTILE., rosette after date only. Rare.
Crosby, p. 162, no. 2; Pl. IV, 5. 7 minor vars. James D. King found one with crudely reeded edge.

116 1722 Penny. UTILE., 2 rev. rosettes; centered stop after X.
Crosby, p. 162, no. 3; Pl. IV, 4. At least 10 vars.

117 1722 Penny. Same, stop after top of X. Ex. rare.
Parsons:56. Compare next and **123**.

118 1722 Penny. Same obv.; obvious double date. Ex. rare.
Date first entered well to l. of final position, then corrected; lower parts of extra digits plain. Discovered by Richard Picker.

119   1722 Penny. No stop after X Very rare.
Crosby, p. 162, no. 4.

120   1723 Prototype Penny. 24 pellets in center of rose. Ex.
rare.
Compare next.   1) Ex Yale, 1971. Discovered by Richard
Picker.
121   1723 Penny. No stop after large 3
This and all to follow have 17 pellets in center of rose (circles
of 10 and 6 round central one). At least 12 minor vars. Knobs
(finials on scroll) vary greatly in size and elaboration. Crosby,
Pl. IV, 12; Nelson 15, {1959}, p. 30. 115–148 grs. = 7.45–
9.59 gms.

122   1723 Penny. No stop after small 3
Crosby, Pl. IV, 11. Narrow 3 with short top. Same comments
about vars. and knobs.

123   1723 Penny. Stop after top of X. Very rare.
Discovered by Richard Picker. Compare **117**.
124   1723 Penny. Stop after large 3. Rare.
Wide 3, long top forming narrow acute angle with diagonal.
125   1723 Penny. Similar. Jumbo piedfort. Unique?
1) Crosby, Parmelee, Garrett:1245, $1,100, 198.2 grs. =
12.84 gms. (worn).

Ex J. W. Garrett: 1245. Courtesy Bowers & Ruddy Galleries, Inc.

126   1724/3 Prototype Penny. D. GRATIA. Bath metal. Ex.
rare.
Rev. as **128**. Nelson 18, {1959}, p. 31. 120 grs. = 7.78 gms.

127   1724/3 Same dies. Copper. Ex. rare.
Taxay-Scott C83, 93 grs. = 6 gms.

128   1724/3 Prototype Penny. DEI GRATIA Copper. Ex.
rare.
Crosby, p. 164, no. 1.
129   1724/3 Same, no stop after X Copper. Ex. rare.
Crosby, Pl. IV, 15, and p. 164, no. 2.   1) Bushnell, Mills,
Garrett:1246, 125.4 grs. = 8.125 gms. (worn), $2,600.
130   1724/3 Similar. Bath metal. Ex. rare, untraced.
Reported at 120 and 128 grs. = 7.78 and 8.3 gms. Uncertain
if obv. is same as **128** or **129**.
131   1724/3 Similar. Silver OMS. 2 known?
Scott C82.   1) Mickley, Bushnell, Parmelee:552.
132   1722 First Prototype Halfpenny. Bath metal. Ex. rare.
Legend DEI .GRATIA./ROSA.AMERI: VTILE.DVLCI.
links it in time with **107**. Crosby, p. 163, no. 1; Pl. IV, 6.
57.2–68.3 grs. = 3.71–4.43 gms.

133   1722 Second Prototype Halfpenny. Bath metal. Rare.
D : G : REX./ROSA.AMERI:UTILE.DULCI. U's corrected from V's. Crosby, p. 163, no. 2; Pl. IV, 7. 54.5–67.5
grs. = 3.53–4.37 gms. Often corroded. Dangerous counterfeits exist; authentication recommended. Proofs exist.

134 1722 Halfpenny. Legends in full.
Rosette after date only. 6 vars. Crosby, p. 163, no. 3; Pl. IV, 8.

Ex J. W. Garrett: 1235. Courtesy Bowers & Ruddy Galleries, Inc.

135 1722 Halfpenny. Similar, .17 over 172. Ex. rare.
Date first entered too close to DULCI without stop, then corrected; pellet punched over extra 1, 17 over 72. Discovered by this writer, 1953.

136 1723/2 Halfpenny. Uncrowned rose. Bath metal. Rare.
2 rev. rosettes. Usually in low grades and rough.

Ex J. W. Garrett: 1236. Courtesy Bowers & Ruddy Galleries, Inc.

137 1723/2 Halfpenny. Same. Copper. Very rare.
Same comment.

138 1723 Halfpenny. Same. Normal date. Bath metal. Very rare.
Crosby, p. 164; Pl. IV, 13. Nelson 13, {1959}, p. 30. 51–72.2 grs. = 3.3–4.68 gms. Usually in low grades and rough. 2 minor vars.

139 1723 Prototype Halfpenny. Silver OMS. Unique?
Crowned rose; large motto, small crown, GRATIA:1723: Taxay-Scott C76. 70 grs. = 4.54 gms.   1) Boyd estate.

140 1723 Halfpenny. No stop after 3 Bath metal.
Crosby, Pl. IV, 14 (small 3); SC (larger 3). These are hard to tell apart. Nelson 16 {1959}, p. 30. 61.4–66 grs. = 3.98–4.3 gms. Possibly 4 minor vars.

141 1723 Halfpenny. Stop after 3. Bath metal. Very rare.
142 1723 Similar. Silver OMS. Ex. rare.
1) Ex Nelson, 66 grs. = 4.3 gms.   2) Bushnell, Parmelee, Roper:92, 72.4 grs. = 4.69 gms., $9,900. Beware silverplated Bath-metal specimens. The ring test (see Glossary) will diagnose these.

iii. WOOD'S "HIBERNIA" COINAGES (1722–24)

A few weeks before George I signed the patent in favor of William Wood, authorizing the ROSA AMERICANA coins, he had signed a similar one (June 16, 1722) empowering Wood to make copper halfpence and farthings for Ireland, at 60 halfpence per pound. However, the King's mistress, "The Maypole," seized this document too (she had taken the patent for Wood's ROSA AMERICANA coinages), and Wood had to ransom it for reportedly the same amount—£10,000 sterling.

Sir Isaac Newton, appointed Royal Comptroller to supervise this coinage along with the ROSA AMERICANA issues, resigned in favor of his nephew, Mr. Barton. Hocking {1906}, p. 241, attributes the dies to "Old Harold," Tottenham Court Road, London. Mintage at Bristol (as well as at London) was authorized Aug. 23, 1722 (Craig {1953}, p. 370): Striking began Jan. 12, 1722/23 at Brown's Gardens, Phoenix St., Hogg Lane, Seven Dials (London), but no corresponding date is known for Bristol strikings (Nelson {1904, 1959}). Those struck in London were carted to Bristol for shipment to Ireland.

As the King had not bothered to consult the Irish Parliament before authorizing this coinage, the Irish took this as an insult, and refused to accept the new coins in payments, no matter how well designed and struck, no matter how much heavier they were than the decades-old, worn-out junk coppers then in circulation. On Sept. 27–28, 1723, both houses of the Irish Parliament vainly petitioned the Crown to revoke the authorization (Craig, loc. cit.). Irish indignation focused not only on the coins' light weight (60 halfpence to the pound instead of the Tower standard of 46) but on the role of "the King's Whore." Wood's furious reply in the Oct. 8, 1723, *Flying Post* worsened matters; thereafter almost nobody would accept the coins in payments. Coinage was suspended in March 1723/24: Craig {1953}, p. 371. Unaware of this halt, Jonathan Swift got into the act. This was the same Dean Swift who, cheated of a bishopric, revenged himself by writing outrageous political satires like *A Modest Proposal, Tale of a Tub,* and *Gulliver's Travels.* Adopting the pseudonym "M. B. Drapier," Swift published *The Drapier's Letters* (April–Dec. 1724) in a systematic smear campaign against Wood. The latter was heard to insist, unwisely, that he would "cram his brass down their throats"—leaving himself open to the Swift-ly following accusations of bribery, debasement, and fraud against the people of Ireland.

Nothing that Wood or the royal authorities could say or do thereafter about the coinage had the slightest effect. Royal assays (1724) showed the coins to be of honest copper but variable in weight: Nelson cites batches of halfpence coined at 58⅓, 63, and 68 to the lb. Despite prolonged efforts to unmask and imprison "Drapier," nobody revealed Swift as user of this *nom de guerre.* Wood resigned his patent (1725) in exchange for a pension, £3,000 per year for three years. The Irish had to make do without official copper coins until George II authorized a new issue of halfpence (1736). A year after the latter, royal orders withdrew Wood's coins from circulation. Profiteers promptly bought up the coppers for approximately bullion value, shipping out most of them to the American colonies as so many "Casks of Hard Ware" (the usual euphemism in ships' manifests for copper coins or tokens). They stayed in circulation over here until shortly before the Revolution; W. C. Prime said some were still current in 1861 ({1861}, Chap. VI)! Many worn examples have turned up in noncollector accumulations from New England, New York, New Jersey, and Pennsylvania, such groups (from internal evidence) dating to the mid-18th century; Wood's coins come with Roche's VOCE POPULI coppers, 1749 Tower halfpence (from the Crown shipment to New England), and counterfeit coppers of many kinds.

WOOD'S "HIBERNIA" COINAGES

Designer, John Croker? Engravers, various. Mints, Wood's, London, and Bristol (see introduction). Composition, copper. Diameters, Halfpence, $16-17/16'' = 25-27$ mm; Farthings, $13-14.5/16'' = 20.5-23$ mm (except as noted). Weight standard, 60 halfpence to the pound, i.e., Halfpence, 116.67 grs. = 7.56 gms.; Farthings, 58.33 grs. = 3.78 gms. Observed weights, Halfpence, 96–135.4 grs. = 6.2–8.78 gms. (see introductory text); Farthings, 51–65 grs. = 3.3–4.2 gms., for 130 to the lb.? Authorizing Act, Royal Warrant, June 16, 1722 = Pat. 8, Geo. I, Part 5, No. 5.

Grade range, GOOD to UNC. GOOD: Outlines of all devices show; all inscriptions and date legible. VERY GOOD: Partial hair and drapery details. FINE: About half hair and drapery details (centers often weak). VERY FINE: Over half hair and drapery. EXTREMELY FINE: Faintest rub on few isolated hair details, leg, breast, and female head; part of angel head on harp should show. EXCEPTIONS: Weak central striking is common.

143   1722 Prototype Halfpenny. Ex. rare.
Nelson 1, Pl. I, 1. Commonly, "Rocks Halfpenny." Some struck at 60 to the lb., others at 52. Garrett:1265, 133.1 grs. = 8.624 gms., F–VF, $2,000; Roper:98, 138.1 grs. = 8.94 gms. Usually in low grades. Coffey lists two proofs as in RIA, ex Dr. Aquilla Smith. {1911}, 1, 2.

144   1722 Halfpenny. Harp l.
Commonly "Type I." Nelson 3; Seaby {1961}, H 174, proofs H 175. At least 14 vars. Total, 1722–23, £15,481 = [7,430,880+], about 90% dated 1723.

Ex J. W. Garrett: 1266. Courtesy Bowers & Ruddy Galleries, Inc.

145   1722 Same. Silver OMS. Ex. rare, 2 reported.
Nelson 3, Pl. I, 2; Seaby H 176. 9 harp strings; 133 grs. = 8.62 gms. Beware silverplated copper strikings.

146   1722 Halfpenny. Harp r.
Commonly "Type II." Nelson 4, Pl. I, 3; Seaby H 177, proofs H 178. At least 14 vars. 116–135.4 grs. = 7.55–8.78 gms.

Ex J. W. Garrett: 1267. Courtesy Bowers & Ruddy Galleries, Inc.

147   1722 Halfpenny. Similar, DEII blunder. Very rare.
The 2 I's touch.   1) NN 60:268.

148   1722 Halfpenny. Similar. Silver OMS. Ex. rare.
Nelson {1959}, p. 20; Taxay-Scott C343. Beware silverplated copper strikings.

149   1723 First Prototype Halfpenny. Star before date. Ex. rare.
Nelson 9 {1959}, p. 22; Coffey 8; Seaby H 184. Discovered by Dr. Aquilla Smith.   1) RIA, 109 grs. = 7.06 gms. (for 64 to the lb.?).   2) Craige, pvt. coll., same weight.   3) NN, pvt. coll. (ill.)

150   1723 Second Prototype Halfpenny. Large head. Very rare.
Nelson 5 ("Pattern"); Coffey 12; Taxay-Scott C347. Large 3 and pellet before H (as on **152** only); 3 rev. vars., 10, 11, or 12 harp strings. Device punch taller than normal: 23 mm from bust point to highest curl atop head (normal is 21 mm). 29–30 mm = $17-19/16''$; 116–129.3 grs. = 7.56–8.38 gms. Parsons:80; Holmes:1261; Roper:107, $880.

151   1723 Similar. Silver OMS. Ex. rare.
Nelson 5 (as preceding), 123 grs. = 7.97 gms., metal unspecified; Seaby H 182 (?); Scott C347. Beware silverplated copper strikings.

152   1723/22 Halfpenny. Large 3 over 2.
Pellet before H. Seaby H 179. Roper:109. Compare **150**.

153   1723/22 Halfpenny. Small 3.
Pellet before H. Much of 2 shows r. of 3. 2 obv. vars. Roper:108.

154   1723 Halfpenny. Pellet before H; small 3.
20 minor vars.

155 1723 Halfpenny. No pellet before H; large 3.
23 minor vars.
156 1723 Halfpenny. Same. Silver OMS. Ex. rare.
No pellet before H, unlike **151**. Beware silverplated copper strikings.
157 1723 Halfpenny. No pellet before H; small 3.
At least 108 vars. including **158–161**. Proofs, Seaby H 181 (ill.); Roper:116, $3,630.

158 1723 Halfpenny. Similar, R's corrected from B's. Very rare.
Seaby H 183.
159 1723 Halfpenny. Similar. Beaded cincture. Very rare.
Spence:709. Several vars.; price for any with 5 or more clear beads at waist, almost in line with angel's nose. Those with only 1 or 2 beads price as **157**. Enl. photos

160 1723 Halfpenny. 2 stops after 1723. . Rare.
161 1723 Halfpenny. No stop after date. Rare.
Seaby H 185; Garrett:1272; others.
162 1724 First Prototype Halfpenny. Ex. rare.
HIBERNIA at l. 1) Richard Picker, discovery coin.

163 1724 Second Prototype Halfpenny. Silver OMS. Unique?
Close HIBERNIA. N above head, 4 touches harp. Taxay-Scott C357. 1) Nelson, Newcomer, Farouk:2352.
164 1724 Third Prototype Halfpenny. Farthing layout. Ex. rare.
DEI.GRATIA closely spaced. Seaby H 187. MacFarland:185; NYPL:2035, F, $412.
165 1724 Halfpenny. No stop after date.
5 vars. Nelson {1959}, p. 22. Total 1724 issue (both denominations), £40,000 or nearly 3 times the 1722–23 figures; but many of these are dated 1723, struck after 1724-dated coins with the same obvs.

166 1724 Halfpenny. With stop after date.
6 vars.

167 1724 Same. Silver OMS. Ex. rare.
Nelson {1959}, p. 22; Seaby H 188. Beware silverplated copper strikings.
168 1722 Prototype Farthing. .D:G :REX. Harp l. 8–10 known?
Nelson 2, Pl. I, 8; Seaby H 189; Scott C345. 51.7–60 grs. = 3.35–3.9 gms. Newcomer, Garrett:1257, $3,250; Roper:99.

169 1723 First Prototype Farthing. Same obv. Very rare.
Nelson 6 ("Pattern"); Seaby H 190. Weights as preceding. Usually with break through NIA. A tiny hoard (under 30?) turned up in England, 1978. Ellsworth, Garrett:1261, $3,500. Dangerous counterfeits exist.

170 1723 Second Prototype Farthing. Halfpenny layout. Very rare.

DEI . GRATIA far apart. 2 rev. vars. Robison:45, "UNC.," $725; Roper:114, 53.9 grs. = 3.49 gms.

171 1723 Same. Silver OMS. Ex. rare.
172 1723 Farthing. Normal legends.

DEI.GRATIA close. Seaby H 191; proof H 192. Many vars. All kinds, £1,086 = [1,042,560+].

173 1723 Same. Silver OMS. Very rare.

Nelson {1959}, p. 21; Seaby H 193; Taxay-Scott C355. Robison:40, $2,600, Proof; Roper:111, 71.1 grs. = 4.6 gms., $2,090. About 20 pieces turned up in England, 1971; 3 minor vars. Dangerous counterfeits exist.
174 1723 Farthing. Similar. GEORGIUS over GEORAIUS. Very rare.

Discovery coin, NN 60:279.

175 1724 Farthing. Stop after date. Very rare.

Mentioned at Nelson 10 {1959}, p. 22; Roper:122, UNC., $440.
176 1724 Same. Silver OMS. Ex. rare.

Mentioned at Nelson 10, loc. cit. Taxay-Scott C362. Beware silverplated copper strikings.
177 1724 Farthing. No stop after date. Very rare.

Mentioned at Nelson 10, loc. cit.; Roper:124, EF.
178 1724 Farthing. Jumbo piedfort. Ex. rare.

NN 60:287, 75.5 grs. = 4.89 gms.

iv. THE VIRGINIA HALFPENCE (1773)

Although the Virginia colony, alone among the Original 13, enjoyed a royal authorization to mint its own coins as part of its charter (1609), for reasons unknown nobody attempted to exercise that right for over 150 years. Tobacco was the standard medium of exchange. However, during the mid-18th century, with expanding population and trade, businessmen felt a need for some kind of coinage other than the unacceptable Birmingham coppers current in the northern colonies.

On May 20, 1773, the Virginia Assembly passed an act authorizing coinage of halfpence at the Tower Mint, pursuant to

the original charter, and the royal authorities approved. Accordingly, some five tons of halfpence arrived in Richmond aboard the *Virginia* (Craig {1953}; Newman {1956, 1962}).

The timorous Colonial Treasurer, Robert Carter Nicholas (whose signature is familiar on Virginia paper currency of the period), refused to release the coins into circulation until after a Royal Proclamation arrived specifically authorizing him to do so. Possibly Nicholas feared that issue without such written authority might have been construed as treasonous. When the proclamation reached Richmond, nearly a year later, the Revolution was on the verge of erupting into armed combat. Coins of all types were being hoarded.

Inevitably, as soon as Virginia halfpence began to circulate in succeeding years, they too were hoarded, and did little to alleviate the wartime need for hard money. Despite their royalist origin and designs, they did circulate during the 1780s when almost any coppers of suitable size and weight would pass at from 14 to 18 to the shilling. Despite their small size, they were actually no worse a proposition than most of the Birmingham coppers current in other colonies, being struck at the same weight standard (60 to the pound). Specimens have turned up in various grades from local archaeological digs, including Colonial Williamsburg.

Uncirculated survivors are almost all from a keg found in Richmond before the Civil War and long owned by Col. Mendes I. Cohen (1796–1879), of Baltimore, a famous coin collector of the 1870s. The keg went to his descendants, who sold the remainder (some 2,200 specimens) in 1929. Wayte Raymond handled most of these; they are mint red or partly red, the vast majority spotted or stained, and they represent most of the 20-odd pairs of dies used for the coinage (out of 40 obvs. and 30 revs. made): Breen {1952}; Newman {1956, 1962}.

Obv. and rev. matrixes and device punches remain in the Royal Mint coll., Llantrisant. Hocking {1910}, 119, nos. 2833, 2835 (matrixes), 2834 and 371 (punches): Dyer and Gaspar {1982}.

No documentation has surfaced about the 1774 proof pattern Shillings. Their obv. die, Hocking {1910}, 420, is identical to that of designer-engraver Pingo's proof Guinea, Fourth Issue; the rev. apparently has not survived. Recorded weights, 83.3–85 grs. = 5.4–5.51 gms., are close to the 1763–1919 Tower Shilling standard of 66 to the lb.

The Virginia halfpence occupy a unique place in American Colonial numismatics, being the sole copper coinage issued under royal authority for the only colony having the legal right to such coinage; the only issue whose circulation was actually interrupted by the Revolution; and the only one of which the average collector has a chance to obtain an uncirculated specimen.

THE VIRGINIA HALFPENCE

Designer, Engraver, Halfpenny, Richard Yeo; Shilling, Thomas Pingo. Mint, Tower. Composition, Halfpenny, pure copper; Shilling, silver 925 Fine. Diameter, about ³¹/₃₂″ = 25 mm (except as noted). Halfpenny weight standard, 60 to the pound = 116.67 grs. = 7.56 gms. (except as noted). Authorizing Act, May 20, 1773.

Grade range, FAIR to UNC. GOOD: All letters and date show. VERY GOOD: Partial hair details. FINE: Outlines of roll of hair above ear show. Over half hair details. VERY FINE: Over ¾ hair details. EXTREMELY FINE: Only very small isolated rubbed spots on hair and wreath. Mint-state examples from the Cohen hoard are normally spotted but retain original mint red.

179 1773 Prototype Halfpenny. Proof. Very rare.

Beaded borders, small 7's. Coined at Irish standard = 52 to

the lb. = 134.6 grs. = 8.72 gms.; observed, 130–137 grs. = 8.42–8.87 gms. ¹⁷/₁₆″ = 27 mm. Crosby, P1. IX, 10. Under 20 survive. Crosby, Garrett:1293, $7,000.

Ex J. W. Garrett: 1294. Courtesy Bowers & Ruddy Galleries, Inc.

180   1773 Halfpenny. [All kinds 672,000] Stop after S.
Serrated borders. 7 to 8 harp strings. Crosby, P1, IX, 12. Recent struck copies sold by the Colonial Williamsburg Foundation have CWF below bust, at first embossed, later incuse. Dangerous counterfeits exist.

181   1773 Halfpenny. No stop after S
Serrated borders. 6, 7, or 8 harp strings. Crosby, P1, IX, 11.

182   1774/3 Pattern Shilling. Proof. 6 known.
Crosby, P1. IX, 13. See introductory text.   1) Gschwend, Ellsworth, Garrett:1294, 83.3 grs. = 5.4 gms., $23,000.   2) Boyd estate.   3) Newman.   4) Norweb, SI.   5) Norweb.   6) Roper:131, 85 grs. = 5.51 gms., $14,300.

Ex J. W. Garrett: 1293. Courtesy Bowers & Ruddy Galleries, Inc.

183   1774/3 Same dies. Copper trial piece. Untraced.
Atkins {1889}, p. 25.

CHAPTER 3

PREREVOLUTIONARY IMPORTS

i. THE ELEPHANT HALFPENCE
(1666–94)

No documentation has turned up establishing their circumstances of issue. Peck ({1964}, pp. 137–39) and Taxay-Scott (p. 26) date them to about 1666, following Snelling's conjecture that the legend GOD PRESERVE LONDON alludes to the 1665–66 Great Plague and Fire. Peck ascribes them to the Royal African Company, claiming that they were struck from West African copper. This is oversimplified. The Duke of York (Charles II's brother) founded the Royal Company of Adventurers in 1662; it reorganized in 1672 as the Royal African Company, enjoying until 1697 a monopoly on African trade, specializing in gold, ivory, and slaves. Some British gold (1663–68) and silver (1666) coins, made from the Company's bullion, show the elephant wearing a howdah of turret shape, familiarly "Elephant and Castle." On these coins the ear is too poorly defined to identify the elephant unambiguously as African *(Loxodonta africana)* or Indian *(Elephas maximus),* though the historical context demands the former. On the coppers, the elephant—of different style—inaccurately attempts to depict the African species, giving Peck's attribution some credibility. Snelling said no available evidence supports—or refutes—the rumor Snelling quoted that these coppers were intended to circulate among the tiny group of British colonists in Tangier (1662–83). On the other hand, we can be certain that some of the regular GOD PRESERVE LONDON type reached the American colonies because specimens—associated with Mark Newbie's "St. Patrick" coppers—have been recovered from old noncollector accumulations in the New York and New Jersey areas, indicating that they passed here as halfpence when any copper of suitable size was acceptable.

The London Elephants may have been among the coins brought over from Bristol to Pennsylvania in 1682 by 40 Quaker refugee families. Edward R. Barnsley *(CNL* 16,2, p. 589, 7/77) quotes the *Loyal Impartial Mercury,* Oct. 3–6, 1682 (from a copy in Huntington Library, San Marino, Calif.), that the coppers the Quakers brought comprised £300 in "Half pence, and Farthings which in the colony go currant for twice their value."

The second Elephant die, found on the "Godless" and regular London halfpennies, reappeared in 1694 on the CAROLINA Elephants. On these latter, makers noticed the misspelling PROPRIETERS only after a few specimens had been struck. The corrected die (O punched over E) produced a larger quantity, but collapsed early; survivors are very rare, usually much worn, and often bulged in central rev. Circumstances of manufacture remain unknown.

Elephants from the first obv. (tusks far from border) with

GOD PRESERVE NEW ENGLAND 1694 are equally mysterious and of the highest rarity. Certainly few, if any, circulated in Massachusetts; in the 1690s, that colony's small-change needs were met—after a fashion—by barter. At least one of the survivors came from England (the Dr. Charles Clay coll., of Manchester).

THE ELEPHANT HALFPENCE

Designer, Engraver, John Roettier? Mint, Tower? Composition, copper. Diameter, about $18/16'' = 28.6$ mm. Weight standards, variable, as noted below.

Grade range, FAIR to UNC. GOOD: Full inscriptions. FINE: Some inner details of ear. VERY FINE: Some head details above eye and ear. EXTREMELY FINE: Few isolated rubbed spots on head, ear, and knee. EXCEPTIONS: Central die failure weakens inscription on the CAROLINA . . . PROPRIETORS pieces. Thick planchets on all vars. will often show splits and cracks.

184 n.d. (1666?) Halfpenny. Error in arms. Ex. rare.
Dagger in second quadrant. First obv., tusks away from border. Peck 502. Struck at 40 to the lb. = 175 grs. = 11.34 gms.; observed, 172.5–180.1 grs. = 11.18–11.67 gms. Jackman, Roper:140, $4,840.

185 n.d. (1666?) Halfpenny. Proper arms, central diagonals. Very rare.
Dagger in first quadrant; 5-pointed star below arms. First obv. Peck 501. Same weight standard; observed, 172–201 grs. = 11.1–13 gms.

186 n.d. (1672?) Halfpenny. No diagonals. Thick flan.
Second obv., tusks nearly touch border, as on all to follow
except **196**. Note 6-pointed star below arms. Peck 503; Betts
{1894} 81; Bell {1968} A1, pp. 235–36. Struck at 30 to the
lb. = 233.33 grs. = 15.12 gms.; observed, 224–253.7 grs. =
14.5–16.4 gms. Date 1672 is Peck's guess.

187 n.d. (1672?) Halfpenny. Same dies. Thin flan. Rare.
Peck 504. Struck at 60 to the lb. = 116.7 grs. = 7.56 gms.
188 n.d. (1672?) Halfpenny. Same dies. Overstrikes. Very rare.
Struck on cut-down pattern CAROLVS A CAROLO halfpence. NN 60:244; Robison:55, UNC., $3,400. 118.9–123
grs. = 7.705–8.08 gms.
189 n.d. (1672?) Halfpenny. Same dies. Brass. Untraced.
Peck 505, following Montagu, p. 72.
190 n.d. (1672?) "Godless" Halfpenny. Very rare.
Dickeson {1859}, p. 70; Betts 82; Peck 500. Struck at 46 to
the lb. = 152.174 grs. = 9.861 gms. Sometimes with un-
decipherable traces of undertype. Peck, Roper:141, UNC.,
$5,280. Enl. photo.

Jack Collins

191 1694 Halfpenny. PROPRIETERS error. Ex. rare.
Crosby, Pl. IX, 1; Betts 78. Struck at 46 to the lb., as preceding. 1) Ely, Parsons, Garrett:1315, UNC., $30,000, 141.6
grs. = 9.176 gms. 2) Appleton, MHS, 1976 ANA:87, UNC.,
$34,000. 3) Newman. 4) Mrs. Norweb. 5) Ryder, Boyd,
Roper:142, 140.6 grs. = 9.11 gms. 6) Robison:58, $4,200,
143.35 grs. = 9.289 gms. 7) Brand, Futter, gilt. 8) B&M,
UNC., 148.8 grs. = 9.642 gms.

Ex J. W. Garrett: 1316. Courtesy Bowers & Ruddy Galleries, Inc.

192 1694 Halfpenny. PROPRIETORS. Thick flan. Very rare.
Same dies, E corrected to O. Crosby, Pl. IX, 2. Struck at 40
to the lb.; observed, 176 grs. = 11.4 gms. 1976 ANA:88, EF,
$9,500. See note to **194.**

Ex J. W. Garrett: 1315. Courtesy Bowers & Ruddy Galleries, Inc.

193 1694 Halfpenny. Same dies. Medium flan. Rare.
Struck at 46 to the lb.; observed, 151.7–162 grs. = 9.83–10.5
gms. Usually in low grades. Roper:143, VF, $2,310. See note
to next.
194 1694 Halfpenny. Same dies. Thin flan. Very rare.
Struck at 60 to the lb.; observed, 108–130 grs. = 7–8.42 gms.
Bolen's forgeries (1869) lack the E within final O; normally
they come UNC. without central weakness. Silver [2], copper
[40], brass [5]; Crosby, Pl. IX, 28. Bolen's copper strikings
cluster around 164.3 grs. = 10.65 gms. One of the 2 silver
strikings is on an 1807 half dollar. Bolen also made 12 coppers with elephant on both sides: without inscription [2], with
ONLY TEN STRUCK [10]: Kenney {1952}.
195 1694 Halfpenny. Same dies? Brass. Thick flan. Untraced.
Cleveland:565. Represented as original, but is it a Bolen?
196 1694 Halfpenny. NEW ENGLAND. Thick flan. Ex. rare.
First obv., tusks away from border. Crosby, Pl. IX, 3; Betts
80. Struck at 30 to the lb. 1) Mickley, Appleton, MHS,
Roper:144 (ill.), 234.6 grs. = 15.2 gms. See note to next.

197 1694 Halfpenny. Same dies. Thinner flan. Ex. rare.
Struck at 52 to the lb. 1) Dr. Clay, Seavey, Parmelee,
Brand, Garrett:1317, $16,000, 132.4 grs. = 8.579 gms. 2)
Pvt. coll. Robinson's forgery (ca. 1861), from dies by Joseph
Merriam of Boston, has large modern letters; Crosby, Pl. IX,
29. Silver [3], copper [15], brass [15], nickel [15].

ii. NEWBIE'S "ST. PATRICK" COPPERS (1641–42)

The "St. Patrick" coins are numismatic Displaced Persons.
Originally they were struck at the Tower Mint (London), between 1641 and Aug. 1642 (when the Long Parliament seized
the mint), to pay Catholic royalist troops fighting Cromwell's
Protestant forces in the Ulster Rebellion. After the Puritans
executed Charles I and suppressed everything Catholic, these
coins went into hiding for decades. Their emblems would have
made possessing them evidence of sedition, spending them possibly treasonous.

After the restoration of Charles II and the 1662 Act of Uniformity, the coins reappeared in circulation, not in Protestant England, but in Catholic Ireland and the Isle of Man (1678). Tynwald (the Manx Parliament) declared them uncurrent after June 24, 1679: Grueber, p. 240. They still passed as halfpence and farthings in Ireland in 1724: Swift, *Drapier's Letters,* III; Smith {1854}. After the "St. Patrick" coppers were declared uncurrent, speculators offered them for sale at slightly above bullion value.

Mark Newbie (or Newby: Both spellings recur), a Northumberland Quaker, moved to Dublin, where he suffered religious persecution. He then moved to Ballicane, County Wicklow, where he was living in 1681 and planning to join fellow Quakers in their American settlement. Correctly guessing that small change would be in short supply in the colonies, Newbie brought along a cask containing £30 worth = 14,400 coppers. On Sept. 19, 1681, Newbie left Dublin for America, with 20 of his fellow Quakers, on the fishing boat *Owners Adventure.* They arrived on Nov. 18 at Salem, N.J. After wintering there, they bought a boat, sailed up Newton Creek, and settled in Old Gloucester County (near present-day Camden), where Newbie set up the first bank in the Province of New Jersey. He developed enough political clout to persuade the Provincial Assembly to declare his coppers legal tender, May 18, 1682; Newbie used at least 300 acres of his own lands as security for redemption of the coins. He died in fall 1682, but the coins continued to circulate, being known as Newbie's coppers or Newbie's halfpence. Both types apparently passed indiscriminately as halfpence. Dr. Edward Maris ({1881}, Introduction) testified that as late as the early 19th century—presumably during his own childhood—Newbie's coppers still turned up in change in Western New Jersey. I have also seen noncollector accumulations datable to the mid-18th century containing both denominations (mostly badly worn "farthings"), in association with Wood's coins and a variety of counterfeit halfpence, confirming Maris's report. Probably others were shipped from Ireland with Wood's coins after 1737. Cf. also Clement, Lang, Stewart {1947}, Gladfelter {1974}.

Proof that the obv. device portrays Charles I as King David is found on an uncirculated "halfpenny," ex Dr. Maris, Garrett colls., sharply enough struck that the portrait is unmistakable. It closely matches in workmanship Nicholas Briot's portrait of Charles I on an obscure British pattern (Peck 362). Don Taxay discovered that many of the "St. Patrick" coppers are punchlinked to some of Briot's Scottish pattern coins, which satisfactorily establishes their origin; Briot was then Engraver of the Tower Mint. The inscription FLOREAT REX, 'Prosper the King,' fits only a royalist Catholic circulation. Vlack var. numbers are from *Colonial Newsletter* 1/68, pp. 3–4; 4/68, pp. 18–19.

Rev. device on the "halfpennies" shows St. Patrick as bishop with crozier and congregation; the arms are those of the city of Dublin (three castles). This device and the legend ECCE GREX, 'Behold my flock,' again confirm an intended Irish Catholic circulation. "Farthings" show St. Patrick banishing a variety of beasts including the inevitable snakes—and a Pegasos, with QVIESCAT PLEBS, 'Let the commoners be quiet.' This is obviously a propaganda attempt to discourage further circulation of political songs, satirical verses, pasquinades, lampoons, etc.; Pegasos was then understood to refer less to paganism than to poetry. Both devices come from details of Gaultier's engraving (1619) on leaf opposite p. 1 in Messingham's folio *Florilegium* (1624): St. Patrick, with nimbus, cope, and miter, stands on dragons and snakes; his right hand blesses his kneeling followers, his left hand holds a staff topped by a double cross; in background is a cruciform church with steeple, in clouds a winged angel with scroll reading HAEC EST VOX HIBERNIGENARUM, 'This is the voice of the Irish.' Another scroll reads VENI ADJUVA NOS, 'Come help

us': Smith {1854}, who ascribes QVIESCAT PLEBS to "the trouble which followed the rebellion of 1641."

Both denominations are copper, with reeded edges, the brass splashers inserted into blanks before striking, and positioned so as to represent gold in the crown, exactly as on the Charles I rose farthing tokens of 1635–36. Occasional rare "farthings" show dolphins or other sea beasts, a martlet (legless bird) privymark (found also on other issues of the period), or a numeral 8, below the kneeling king; these may refer to provincial mints, to particular occasions, or to individual diesinkers. Workmanship is similar enough among all those with the martlet and/or 8, and again similar enough among all those with stars in legends, to suggest several discrete batches. As yet no collection available for study is large enough to provide evidence of punchlinked groups, nor does the preservation of most survivors permit this kind of study.

Issues were evidently very large, as over 120 die vars. exist of the "farthings." Judging by the resemblance of these issues to certain of the royal farthing tokens of Charles I, we may conjecture that at least some of Newbie's "farthings" may have been struck from roller dies, the coins being afterwards punched out of strips, and edges reeded by the Castaing machine. This process, then found in British and some Continental mints, made possible accurate positioning of the brass splashers on the strips. The splashers' irregularly variable contours, like their name, suggest that they began as droplets of molten metal on the strips, not solid flakes. Many catalogs list specimens without the brass at crown; usually, microscopic examination of examples genuinely lacking it shows that the brass was originally present but later either fell out or—perhaps more often—had been pried off in the mistaken belief that it was gold. Copper examples also come heavily enough patinated to obscure it, but close scrutiny will disclose the telltale difference in color or texture at the crown. Silver strikings show no splashers. High-grade survivors in any metal are rare and precious.

The name "farthings" is a misnomer, implying that they weighed half as much as the larger denomination, and passed at half the value. Weights of the smaller denomination are invariably too high compared with halfpence to make such theories tenable; the average "halfpenny" weighs much less than twice the lightest "farthing."

NEWBIE'S "ST. PATRICK" COPPERS

Designer, Nicholas Briot, after Gaultier. Engravers, Briot and others. Mint, Tower, others? Composition, copper with brass splasher at crown. Diameters, "Halfpenny," $^{17-20/16''}$ = 27–32 mm; "Farthing," $^{15-16/16''}$ = 24–25 mm. Weights, "Halfpenny," 120–149 grs. = 7.78–9.7 gms. (for 52 and 50 to the lb.?); "Farthing," 80–112.8 grs. (for 60, 72, and 80 to the lb.?). Reeded edges, except as noted.

Grade range, POOR to UNC., usually not above FINE. No standard established; we suggest GOOD: All legends legible. VERY GOOD: Partial drapery details. EXCEPTIONS: Uneven strikings are common; many show heavy patina or even corrosion.

198 n.d. "Halfpenny." FLORE AT REX Very large obv. letters. Very rare.
Crosby, p. 371. Crown divides FLORE AT. Vlack 3-C, 6-I.
199 n.d. "Halfpenny." FLORE AT REX. Medium obv. letters.
Crosby, Pl. III, 8; ANS {1914}, Pl. 9. Crown divides FLORE AT. Vlack 5-F, 5-D, 5-H.

200 n.d. "Halfpenny." FLOREAT .*. REX Large letters both sides.
Vlack 1-A, 1-B, 1-G. Compare next 4.

201 n.d. "Halfpenny." Similar but checkerboard floor. Very rare.
Crosby, Pl. III, 7. Vlack 2-C. Obv. die failure produces a bulge weakening king's head and drapery.

202 n.d. "Halfpenny." Similar. Plain edge. Ex. rare.
At least 3 vars.

203 n.d. "Halfpenny." FLOREAT. * .REX Small obv. letters. Large rev. letters. Vlack 4-B, 4-C, 4-G.

204 n.d. "Halfpenny." FLOREAT. * .REX Small letters both sides. Very rare.
Vlack 4-E; Coffey 4. Spence:695; Roper:53; Norweb, SI; RIA, 149 grs. = 9.71 gms.

205 n.d. Florin? Similar. Silver OMS. Ex. rare.
Crosby, p. 136; Coffey 1; Seaby {1961}, H 22. 176.5 grs. = 11.44 gms. Tower Shilling standard makes the Florin or 2 Shillings = 185.81 grs. = 12.04 gms. Discovery coin, John Putland, Dr. Aquilla Smith, RIA, worn, from one of the regular dies with star in obv. legend. Smith {1854}.

206 n.d. "Farthing." Nimbus around St. Patrick's head. Ex. rare.
Seaby H 25. 3 minor vars. Ellsworth, Garrett:1384, EF, $1,700, Roper:58, $742.50, 105 grs. = 6.8 gms.

207 n.d. Same. Shilling? Silver OMS. Ex. rare.
Seaby H 25a. 1) Caldecott, Parsons, Ellsworth, Garrett:1382, F, $7,250, 108.1 grs. = 7.01 gms. 2) Roper:57, $2,090, 89.8 grs. = 5.82 gms.

208 n.d. "Farthing." Nothing below king.
Over 70 vars., some punctuated with dots or colons variously combined. Letters vary in size.

209 n.d. Same. Gold OMS. Unique.
Seaby H 24b. No punctuation obv. or rev.; these dies not seen elsewhere, though similar unpunctuated dies occur in copper and silver. 1) Col. Green, Boyd, Ford, 1976 ANA:21, $46,000, 184.4 grs. = 11.95 gms.

210 n.d. Similar. Silver OMS. Very rare.
Seaby H 24a. At least 5 vars., variously punctuated. 77.8–123 grs. = 5.04–7.99 gms., some too light for shillings, others too heavy for 15 pence. Crosby, Mills, Garrett:1383, "AU," $13,000. Beware silverplated copper pieces. Authentication recommended.

211 n.d. "Farthing." Sea beasts below king.
Various punctuations; at least 16 vars. See next 7. Normally 3 or 4 beasts (dolphins?) in field below king, varying in size. Sometimes described as "ground below king."

212 n.d. "Farthing." Sea beasts, "Masonic" punctuation.
Several vars. The triangular group of dots may appear on obv. or rev. or both.

213 n.d. "Farthing." Sea beasts; stars in legends. Rare.
At least 8 vars., differing in distribution of stars. Usually those after REX dwindle in size. ANS has one with 2 stars vertical (like colon dots) after PLEBS; usually there is only one. See next.

214 n.d. "Farthing." Similar. REX* . . . ./QVIESAT blunder. Ex. rare.
1) Richard Picker, Roper:65, discovery coin. 2) 1984 Midwinter ANA:1548.

215 n.d. "Farthing." Small 8 below king, no martlet. Rare.
Seaby H 25c. The 8 is as in **217.** At least 3 vars. Sea beasts
not always visible.
216 n.d. "Farthing." Similar. Large 8 below king. Very rare.
Earle:1971. At least 2 vars. Sea beasts usually blurry.

217 n.d. "Farthing." Annulet, small 8 and martlet below king.
Very rare.

218 n.d. "Farthing." Martlet alone below king. Very rare.
Seaby H 25b. At least 3 vars. Appleton, MHS II:8, 1976
ANA:18, F–VF, $750.
219 n.d. Similar. Lead trial piece. Unique?
Crosby, p. 136, from Smith {1854}. Coffey 17. RIA.

iii. ROCHE'S VOCE POPULI
COPPERS (1760)

Grueber {1899} and Nelson {1904} attribute these to a Mr.
Roche or Roach, of South King St., Dublin, maker of army
buttons. The coppers' HIBERNIA legend indicates an intended
Irish circulation. Their 1760 date probably indicates a time of
initial issue after the death of George II and before the coronation of George III, comparable to papal *Sede Vacante* ('Vacant
Throne') coins.

Roche's coppers vary remarkably in portraiture, the halfpence depicting at least three different men, possibly five. Two
are dubiously identified as the Jacobite Pretenders: James Francis Edward Stuart (1688–1766), called "James III" by his partisans and "The Old Pretender" by others; and Charles Edward
Stuart (1720–88), called "Bonnie Prince Charlie" by his adher-
ents and "The Young Pretender" by others. Irish Catholics favored
either as an alternative to the Protestant Hanoverians
George II and III. A third portrait bust on these coins is still
more dubiously identified as John Hely-Hutchinson (1724–94),
eminent member of the Irish Parliament, later Irish Secretary of
State. Unfortunately, no portraits of Hely-Hutchinson are available in this country for verification, and most portraits of the
Stuart Pretenders are full face or were made when both were
much younger or older.

The letter P found either before face or below bust on one
series is another mystery. Nelson {1904} rendered it as
"Provost," but this is impossible: Hely-Hutchinson did not become Provost of Dublin College until 1774. The other interpretation, "Pretender," is equally out of the question, as partisans
of the Stuarts never used the term. Christmas II, pp. 11–12, and
Grueber, p. 246, suggested *Princeps,* 'Prince' or 'Head of the
Line,' the very term used by Octavius before he became Emperor Augustus: therefore obviously appropriate for a Stuart
pretender.

The coins come on cast blanks and rolled blanks; occasional

specimens are cast rather than struck, possibly made to fill an
order before new dies could be completed. More than one firm
may have made these coppers; there was no monopoly on either
design or inscription.

Those dated 1700 are mint errors. At least two dies were
originally misdated 1700, both being later corrected to 1760 by
adding an upper tail to the first zero, but a few specimens survive from an uncorrected die, having a distinct space between
first zero and exergual line. The "1760/00" coins have the loop
of the 6 identical in shape and size to the zero. Beware of specimens from which this tail has been removed to simulate the
rarer 1700.

Their legend VOCE POPULI, 'By the voice of the people,'
ambiguously alludes either to partisanship for the Stuart
pretenders or to the perpetual Irish quest for home rule. But
whatever its original purpose, it was later recognized as appropriate to the American colonists, whose struggles against Mad
King George echoed the centuries of Irish oppression by British
rulers to whom they were little more than pack animals. After
the new George III halfpence arrived from the Tower (1766),
Dublin speculators bought the VOCE POPULI coppers in
quantity and shipped them as "Casks of Hard Ware" to America. Though not originally intended for colonial circulation,
these coins passed in the Atlantic Seaboard colonies at least
until shortly before the Revolution and possibly later. They
have turned up in noncollector accumulations datable to the
early 1770s, along with Birmingham counterfeit halfpence of
George II and III, though not in post-Revolutionary groups.
The farthings must have formed at best a microscopic proportion of small change. Bressett {1960}.

ROCHE'S VOCE POPULI COPPERS

Designers, Engravers, various, unidentified. Mint, Roche's,
South King St., Dublin, others? Composition, copper (sometimes brassy). Diameters, Halfpence, about 17–$18/16'' = 27$–29
mm; Farthings, 13–$14/16'' = 20$–22 mm. Weight standards, Halfpence, 60 to the lb. = 116.67 grs. = 7.56 gms., less often 52 or
46 to the lb. = respectively 134.6 or 152.17 grs. = 8.723 or
9.861 gms.; Farthings, probably 120 to the lb. = 58.33 grs. =
3.78 gms.

Grade range, FAIR to UNC. No grade standards established.
Striking quality extremely variable; often on cast blanks, sometimes cast rather than struck. Grade by surface and by apparent
amount of wear on whichever details are well enough struck to
distinguish wear from weak striking. The Group I Halfpence
here ill. mostly qualify as EXTREMELY FINE or better; later
groups, VERY FINE up.

HALFPENCE

GROUP I: HIBER NIA + +
Head Divides R N

220 1760 Child's bust. Very rare.
NV (Nelson-Vlack) 1; DF (Dowle-Finn) 565; Z(elinka) 1-A.
Possibly after one of the childhood portraits of Bonnie Prince
Charlie?

221 1760 "Imperial" head.
Seaby (1961) H 221; NV 4; DF 566; Z. 2-A. Possibly portrays
Prince Charles Edward Stuart? Nelson {1904} claims that

this obv. comes with a rev. of Group III (below); unverified. Some struck at 52 to the lb. Roper:160, 136 grs. = 8.81 gms. Proofs reported: cf. Christmas II, pp. 11–12.

222 1760 Mature bust. Crosslet after VOCE. Very scarce.
Seaby H 222; NV 5, 8, 15. Various portraits; compare next 2. Slanting obv. border dentils, as in next 4. Enl. photos.

223 1760 Similar, crosslet almost midway E P.
NV 9; DF 571; Z. 6-C.

224 1760 No crosslet. Ex. rare.
NV 16; Z. 5-C. Obv. reappears on **229.**

GROUP II: HIBE RNIA + +
Head Divides E R

225 1760 No obv. punctuation. Very rare.
NV 7; DF 569; Z. 8-F. Repunched V. Later, die broken above HIB. Metropolitan FPL, n.d. (1962); 1981 ANA:361.

GROUP III: .HIBE RNIA.

226 1760/00 Crosslet after VOCE Scarce.
Seaby H 223; NV 2; DF 570; Z. 4-B. Tail added to first 0 to form a 6, touching exergue line.

227 1760 VOOE No punctuation
NV 3; DF 574; Z. 7-E. C corrected from O or reversed C? Nelson {1904} claimed that proofs exist; unconfirmed.

228 1760 VOCE Normal date, no punctuation. Ex. rare.
DF 573. "Corrected" (reground?) die of preceding. Untraced in USA.

229 1700 Blundered date; VOCE Ex. rare.
Seaby H 225; NV 6A; DF 568; Z. 5-Da. First 0 well away from exergue line. Struck on cast blanks. Beware specimens of **230** with tail of 6 scraped off to simulate 0.   1) Robison:64.   2) Roper:161, $632.50.

230 1760/00 VOCE. Rare.
Seaby H 224; NV 6; DF 567; Z. 5-D. Tail added to first 0 to make 6.

GROUP IV:
James III Portrait
Two Large Rosettes After A

231 1760 Portrait as next. Rare.
Seaby H 227; NV 10; DF 575; Z. 13-K. Discovered by Nelson about 1905. Roper:164, EF, $396, 160 grs. = 10.37 gms. Seaby H 226 (same rev., obv. of Group III) remains unconfirmed.

GROUP V:
James III Portrait; with Extra P
Two Large Rosettes After A

232 1760 P before face.
Grueber, 124; NV 12; DF 576; Z. 15-N. P = Princeps? See introductory text. Many struck at 52 to the lb.

233 1760 P below bust.
Seaby H 229; NV 11, 13, 14. Price for NV 11 or 13 (ill.), with double-punched P. NV 14 (Z. 16-O, Ex. rare) has normal P; branch lies along base of E. Many struck at 46 to the lb.

FARTHINGS

234 1760 Large letters. Rare.
Plain loop to truncation. Seaby H 230; NV 1. By maker of **220**. Always with heavy obv. clash marks. Miller, Garrett:1276, "F," $1,100; Roper:155, AU, $1,430. 56–64.6 grs. = 3.6–4.19 gms.

235 1760 Same. Setup trial on halfpenny flan. Unique?
Discovered in England, early 1982, later J. D. Parsons, B&R RCR 45 (8/82), p. 4.

236 1760 Small letters. Ex. rare.
No loop to truncation; rev. of **234**. Seaby H 231; NV 2.   1) Nelson, Breisland, Roper:156, EF, discovery coin, $2,200, 42.9 grs. = 2.78 gms.   2) Spence:713, UNC., $6,000. According to Rev. Henry Christmas, one of this or **234** exists in proof state. II, pp. 11–12.

CHAPTER 4

PREREVOLUTIONARY LOCAL ISSUES

About all pieces in this group, except for the Pitt tokens, two remarks apply: They are exceedingly rare, and they are swathed in mystery.

i. GLOUCESTER SHILLING TOKENS (1714)

Nothing more is known of these tokens than shows on their face; until 1981 that did not even include a complete inscription. Both survivors are so weakly and unevenly struck that the name Righault was not even guessed at from the discovery coin. No contemporaneous engravings show the original Gloucester Court House, so we cannot be certain if the inscription refers to the building, the village, or the firm name. Christopher Righault and Samuel Dawson were, respectively, landowners at Craney Creek and Ware Parish. (The Anglo-French name Righault originally must have rhymed with "We go.")

As Virginia's only legal currency then was tobacco, each token must have represented several oz. of the leaf, originally legally = 3 shillings per lb. (A wife in 1620 cost 100, later 150, lbs. of tobacco; such debts took precedence over all others: Bushnell {1859}. Tobacco warehouse receipts only began circulating as paper currency in 1727: Massey {1976}.)

The two survivors vary so much in weight that their original standard cannot be guessed at. That in the 1976 ANA auction (ex Dr. Charles Clay, G. F. Seavey, Woodward's 18th Sale (1874), William Bowdoin, W. S. Appleton, MHS) proved to be a cast copy of the Garrett coin.

A similar piece dated 1715 (Rulau-E VA 2), found by a metal detector in 1982, remains unconfirmed.

237 1714 Gloucester Shilling Token. 2 known.
GLOVCESTER COVRT.HOVSE. VIRGINIA. Rev., RIGHAVLT.DAWSON.ANNO.DOM.1714. Brass, 15/16″ = 24 mm. Rulau-E VA 1. 1) Mickley, Cram, Parmelee, Steigerwalt, Ten Eyck, Newcomer, Garrett:1318, $36,000, D. Kagin, Roper:147, $20,900, L.I. specialist, 61.1 grs. = 3.96

gms. Crosby, Pl. IX, 4.   2) Gerry Nelson:1, $3,250, Terranova, L.I. specialist, 43.44 grs. = 2.815 gms. *CW* 11/11/81, p. 1.

ii. HIGLEY'S COPPERS (1737–39)

Dr. Samuel Higley (ca. 1687–1737), born on the family farm near Tariffville, Conn., used his Yale degree to become first a schoolmaster, thereafter a surgeon, still later abandoning the professions to become a metallurgical pioneer. In 1727, he discovered and patented a process for making steel; later that year he bought a large land tract 1½ miles south of the "Copper Hill" (Simsbury) mines, discovered copper, and opened what was still known a century later as the Higley Mine, exporting large quantities of copper ore to England. In 1737 he began striking copper coins, which became so famous for their purity that jewelers melted down many for alloying gold and silver. In May 1737, Dr. Higley was aboard a ship lost at sea en route to England with some of his own copper ore. The "Copper Hill" mine served as a prison, 1773–1827. Cf. Johnson {1896}; Moore and Hawley; Phelps {1845}; Phelps {1860}, pp. 15–17, {1876}, pp. 19–21.

Though Dr. Samuel Higley presumably made the first 1737-dated coppers, the undated and 1739-dated pieces (and possibly some of the later 1737s) are attributed to his eldest brother John. This enterprise probably also included the Higleys' close friends Rev. Timothy Woodbridge and William Cradock. The last two were associated with Bostonian John Read's petition (Oct. 1739) for a franchise to make copper coins to pass current in Connecticut: Crosby, pp. 203–7.

Higley's copper issues must have been fairly extensive. At least eight obv. and five rev. dies were used, most not showing breakage. The first var. was apparently that showing deer and three hammers with legends THE VALVE OF THREE PENCE and CONNECTICVT 1737; later revs., perhaps to avoid the implication that these were officially authorized by the colonial assembly, read instead I AM GOOD COPPER. We may conjecture that the deer symbolizes freedom, the hammers malleability (then the only test for purity of copper) and/or the coining process itself. Later obvs. retain the III but read VALUE ME AS YOU PLEASE; later revs. show a broad axe with J CUT MY WAY THROUGH, suggesting that as the supply increased, the coins passed at decreasing rates, perhaps against increasing local resistance. Only the final axe die bears date 1739. Double striking (less extreme than on the Willow Tree silver) is normal on most vars., suggesting that the Higleys used the ancient hammer method rather than a screw press.

Survivors of all types are of extreme rarity. Despite an average grade of F to G, specimens auctioned in the last two decades

Ex J. W. Garrett: 1318. Courtesy Bowers & Ruddy Galleries, Inc.

have normally brought five-figure prices. However, over 99% of those offered at fixed prices, especially before the 1970s, have proved to be forgeries: casts, electrotypes, or worn-down Bolen imitations. Casts are porous and may show minute raised bubbles; electrotypes have lead cores and normally show edge seams. The ring test (see Glossary) elicits only a dull thud. Bolen's imitations are described below. Authentication is mandatory! No complete collection of Higley's coppers has yet been assembled.

HIGLEY'S COPPERS

Designer, Engraver, Dr. Samuel Higley and associates. Mint, Higley's, Granby, Conn. Composition, pure copper. Diameter, about $18/16'' = 28.6$ mm, rarely $19/16'' = 30$ mm. Weight, variable as noted.

Grade range, POOR to FINE. No grading standard established. We suggest GOOD: All inscriptions legible unless obscured by double striking.

238 1737 THE.VALVE.OF.THREE.PENCE./.CONNECTI-CVT. About 12 known.
Crosby, P1, VIII, 17, 18; Rulau-E Conn. 1. Three obv. vars. 119.8–151.1 grs. = 7.763–9.791 gms. Bolen's copies (Crosby, P1. VIII, 30) have a raised dot within C of PENCE, no die buckling, no multiple striking; silver [2], copper [40] (1864), latter 123.5–164.4 grs. = 8.003–10.65 gms. Dr. Frank Smith Edwards later bought Bolen's dies and made nickel and brass strikings; quantities unknown but very small.

239 1737 Same obv./I AM GOOD COPPER 2 known.
Crosby, P1. VIII, 19; Rulau-E Conn. 2.   1) John Allan, Mc-Coy:1666, Bushnell:190, Parmelee.
240 1737   VALVE . ME . AS . YOU . PLEASE ./I . AM . GOOD . COPPER. 3 known.
Crosby, P1. VIII, 20; Rulau-E Conn. 4.   1) Mitchelson, CSL.   2) Parmelee, B. G. Johnson, Newman. Ill. in Taxay {1971, 1976}.   3) Krugjohann:23, Roper:150, $2,420, 155.1 grs. = 10.05 gms., Ill. Compare next.

241 1737 VALUE . ME . AS . YOU . PLEASE/I . AM . GOOD . COPPER. 8 known.
Crosby, Pl. VIII, 21, 22; Rulau-E Conn. 3. Three obv. vars. Ellsworth, Garrett:1304, $8,000. 126.2–144.1 grs. = 8.178–9.338 gms.

242 n.d. (1738?) Same/Axe, J.CUT.MY.WAY.THROUGH. About 15 known.
Crosby, Pl. VIII, 23, 24, 25. Three obv. vars. Rulau-E Conn. 5. Axe handle points to Y, unlike the 1739. Miller, Garrett:1305, "EF," $45,000, 162.2 grs. = 10.51 gms. Others as light as 110 grs. = 7.13 gms.

Ex J. W. Garrett: 1307. Courtesy Bowers & Ruddy Galleries, Inc.

243 n.d. (1738?) THE.WHEELE.GOES.ROUND./As preceding. Unique.
Rulau-E Conn. 6. Discovered by Howland Wood, *NUM* 7/13. 151.9 grs. = 9.843 gms. Wood, Ellsworth, Garrett:1306, $75,000, Roper:154, $60,500, L.I. specialist.

Ex J. W. Garrett: 1305. Courtesy Bowers & Ruddy Galleries, Inc.

244 1739 Type of **242**. 10 known.
Crosby, Pl. VIII, 26; Rulau-E Conn. 7. Axe handle points to T. Two obv. dies, both earlier used on **242**. Ellsworth, Garrett:1307, $4,500, 119.5 grs. = 7.743 gms.; others as heavy as 178 grs. = 11.53 gms.

Ex J. W. Garrett: 1306. Courtesy Bowers & Ruddy Galleries, Inc.

iii. UNDATED APOCRYPHAL FARTHINGS

The NEW YORKE IN AMERICA farthing token first reached public attention in the *Historical Magazine* (Oct. 1861) through one of the lead strikings. Nothing is known of its origin or purpose. Its rev. device (Venus and Cupid under a palm tree) suggests propaganda for the colonies as a place to enjoy life. As the spelling YORKE with the final E occurs intermittently between 1664 and the 1770s, this does not permit a better guess about the token's date. Two brass strikings were found in Civil War token lots in the 1950s, which fact threw needless doubt on their age; almost anything of farthing size would have passed in the 1860s as a cent. Similar lots contained store cards datable to about 1834 and British farthing tokens of the 1820s. The lead discovery piece was at The Hague prior to 1850. Survivors occur in all grades, possibly 10 in brass, four in lead; but if they are indeed of 18th-century or earlier provenance, they could have only have represented farthings, which points to a prerevolutionary circulation. No grading standards are established.

The copper farthing token with two emaciated lions and I S V C, rev. in four lines NEW/ENGLA/ND/M (N's reversed, M inverted) is unique, its origin, purpose, and date unknown, its initials uninterpreted, its attribution to the 17th century or to New England unconfirmed, its present whereabouts unknown.

245 n.d. NEW YORKE Farthing token. Brass. Very rare.
Crosby, Pl. VIII, 14. 14/16″ = 22 mm. 36.02–55 grs. = 2.334–3.5 gms. Garrett:1322, "ABOUT FINE," $5,250; Jenks, Roper:145, $3,740.

246 n.d. Same dies. Lead trial piece. 4 or 5 known.
1) The Hague, 51 grs. = 3.3 gms. 2) SI. 3) Craige, Benedetti, Gore, Kensington, Roper:146, $3,960, 72.2 grs. = 4.68 gms. 4) Appleton, MHS, 1976 ANA:51.
247 n.d. I S V C Farthing token. Copper. Unique?
Crosby, Pl. VIII, 13. 1) Mickley, Seavey, Parmelee, DeWitt Smith, Brand, pvt. coll., 37 grs. = 2.38 gms.

iv. SMITHER'S PITT TOKENS
(1766)

When George Grenville, George III's Chancellor of the Exchequer, introduced the Stamp Act in Parliament early in 1765 (where it passed without debate), his ostensible purpose was to raise revenues to pay in part for the French and Indian Wars. Without consulting colonial assemblies, Parliament extended the British system of stamp duties into the American colonies. Neither Grenville nor the other royal advisers nor most members of Parliament had any idea that the Stamp Act would generate any opposition. Unfortunately for their plans, not only were the colonists chronically short of either British or Spanish silver to buy tax stamps (thanks to mercantilism: See Overview, above), but the text of the Stamp Act included several provisions which the colonists—except for the most fanatical Tories—saw as a threat. In particular, the Act required purchase of tax stamps not only for every sheet of paper or parchment for official use, but also for every newspaper, broadside, almanac, pamphlet, or other publication, and for every advertisement therein; unstamped papers were contraband. The implication: Not only were royal authorities trying to tax local publications out of existence, they were sabotaging publishers critical of government policy—an attack on freedom of the press.

When a copy of the Stamp Act arrived in New York late in summer 1765 (almost exactly 30 years after the John Peter Zenger affair), colonial assemblies began passing resolutions of protest. Massachusetts activists formed the radical secret societies known as Sons of Liberty; their milder New York City counterparts organized the Friends of Liberty and Trade. Delegates from all 13 colonies converged on New York's City Hall for the Stamp Act Congress, Oct. 7, 1765. Its major resolution declared that the Stamp Act and related measures extended "the jurisdiction of the Courts of Admiralty beyond its ancient limits" and that they had "a manifest tendency to subvert the Rights and Liberties of the Colonists." The congress further resolved that "it is inseparably essential to the Freedom of a People, and the undoubted rights of Englishmen, that no taxes be imposed on them but with their own consent, given personally or by their representatives," and that the colonists "are not, and from their local circumstances cannot be, represented in the House of Commons."

So intense and widespread was opposition to the Stamp Act that the expenses of collecting stamp duties far exceeded the revenues. Many local groups held parades where "liberty songs" (political protest songs) were sung, and royal governors and tax collectors were burned in effigy. The New York Sons of Liberty adopted a Non-Importation Agreement (the first of many), imposing a boycott against British trading ships. They also threatened loyalists who used the tax stamps with a boycott on their goods, and they banded together to protect nonusers from reprisals. While the Stamp Act Congress was still in session, Oct. 23, 1765, a British ship arrived loaded with stamps, and on Nov. 1 the Sons of Liberty hanged Gov. Colden in effigy on the door of Fort Amsterdam and then burned the houses of several pro-stamp officials.

This outrageous behavior became the subject of indignant denunciations in Parliament, where many of the more conservative members believed the colonists guilty of sedition verging on treason. But Sir William Pitt, the ablest speaker in Commons, the most popular statesman in England, the beloved "Great Commoner," defended the rebellious colonists and their opposition to the Stamp Act. He told Parliament in Jan. 1766 that "as subjects they are entitled to the common right of representation, and cannot be bound to pay taxes without their consent," demanding repeal—which followed on March 18. Even George III became so disgusted with the general reaction to his Chancellor's project that he dismissed Grenville.

The news caused general rejoicing on this side of the Atlantic. Colonial legislators and newspapers hailed Pitt as their savior. Medals and medalets struck on both sides of the ocean (according to Betts {1894}) lauded him as *Libertatis Vindex,* 'Defender of Liberty,' and as "The man who having saved the parent [England] pleaded with success for her children [the colonies]." On June 4, 1766, the New York Sons of Liberty erected a liberty pole in the "Fields" (now City Hall Park, where a replica still stands, forgotten), and organized celebrations. Among the medalets of this time are the Pitt Tokens, locally made on behalf of the Friends of Liberty and Trade from dies cut by James Smither (1741–97), allegedly after sketches furnished by Paul Revere. Both attributions appeared first in Dickeson {1859}, who called the engraver "Col. Smithers, of Philadelphia." Smither was a British gunsmith who had just emigrated to Philadelphia; he was in business there in 1768 and probably earlier. He is best known for his engraved plate elements for Pennsylvania currency (issues beginning April 3, 1772); during the Revolution he took part in Tory counterfeiting activities. Accused of high treason, June 2, 1778, by the Pennsylvania Supreme Executive Council, Smither left with British troops for New York, returning to Philadelphia in 1786: Newman {1976A}, pp. 19, 34, 298.

Nothing is known of why these tokens come in two sizes. Most likely the small type was an unsuccessful prototype; it comes crudely struck on cast blanks. Some of its letter punches reappear on the large type, proving their common origin. The large type comes in brass or copper, sometimes plated, on rolled blanks. The small final R in RESTORER is an awkward solution to a spacing problem; note also that STAMPS was first punched in small letters (as on the smaller token), then corrected to larger size, suggesting that these dies came later, the switch to larger letters following a false start with small.

Both sides come in all grades, indicating that they passed as money. It is unlikely that the smaller size circulated at a lower rate; farthings were seldom used in the colonies by the 1760s, and the small tokens weigh 2/3 of the large, whereas farthings were only half the weight of halfpence. More likely, both passed at par with Birmingham coppers, at 14 to the shilling—the standard rate since 1753. *CNL* 4/73, p. 401. Their circumstances of issue give the Pitt Tokens great historical interest.

SMITHER'S PITT TOKENS

Designer, Engraver, James Smither (after Revere?). Mint, private (NYC or Philadelphia?). Composition, brass, or copper. Diameters, "Farthing," $^{15.5-16.5}/16'' = 25$–26 mm; "Halfpenny," $^{17-18}/16'' = 27$–28.6 mm. Weights, "Farthing," 51.7–64.2 grs. = 3.35–4.16 gms. (for 120 to the pound?); "Halfpenny," 84.4–89 grs. = 5.47–5.8 gms. (for 80 to the lb.?).

Grade range, GOOD to UNC. FINE: Half the curls distinguishable; some part of planking visible. VERY FINE: At least 3/4 of curls clear; all planking and some portholes visible, poop deck may be flat. EXTREMELY FINE: Face on figurehead clear, some details of poop deck clear; few tiny isolated rubbed spots on curls, cheek.

248   1766 "Farthing." Brass. 6–8 known.
Betts 520. Edge plain or crudely reeded (by file?). Struck on cast blanks. Sometimes "silver-plated" (tin-plated?). The cop-

per piece mentioned by Betts is thought to be one of the dark, discolored brass ones. "Promised Lands," Laird Park:155, "F," \$8,250; Roper:169, EF, \$6,600.

249   1766 Same dies. Silver OMS. Reported.
250   1766 Same dies. Tin. Reported.
251   1766 "Halfpenny." Copper.
Betts 519. Often with traces of "silvering" (tin plating?). Robison:67, "AU," \$1,700.

252   1766 "Halfpenny." Same dies. Brass.
Same comments. Weights in same range as copper.
253   1766 Same dies. Silver OMS. Reported.
Betts 519.
254   1766 Same dies. Tin. Ex. rare.
Betts 519.   1) BM, 87.8 grs. = 5.69 gms.   2) Morgenthau 276:155 (Feb. 6, 1932), pvt. coll.

CHAPTER 5

ISSUES FOR CANADA AND LOUISIANA TERRITORY

i. THE FRENCH RÉGIME
(1640–1763)

We may take as a beginning neither Cabot's claim of New-foundland for the British (1497), nor Cartier's claim of the St. Lawrence River and Gulf regions for France (1534), but Champlain's colonization of Quebec in 1608, as only thereafter was any one area populous enough to develop local commerce and a need for coinage. British authorities set up several trading forts around the shores of Hudson's Bay beginning in 1670; France seized these in 1697 along with Newfoundland, but at her defeat in Queen Anne's War (1713) she lost these and Acadia (now Nova Scotia) to the British. Fifty years later she had to cede all of Canada to Britain pursuant to the Treaty of Paris ending the Seven Years' War.

During most of this period, official policy forced the *habitants* to remain primarily on a barter economy (see Overview above). Exceptions to this policy form the subject of this chapter; they fall into six classes, only the first three of which come within the scope of this study:

1. *Coins officially made for the French colonies in America.* (1670 silver 15 and 5 Sols; 1717 Perpignan coppers; 1721–22 Rochelle and Rouen coppers.)
2. *Ordinance of 1683 Countermarks.* (Spanish cob dollars countermarked with fleur de lys and Roman numerals according to weight.)
3. *Domestic coins officially exported to America.* (Billon issues of 1640–1756; copper sols of 1720; and the *Chameau* Treasure coins, 1725.)
4. *Domestic coins unofficially imported by merchants,* and included in official revaluations. (Willey 107–17, 125–33 = A through X below.)
5. *International trade coins unofficially imported by merchants.* (British guineas; Spanish and Mexican gold 8 Escudos and silver 8 Reales and fractions; Portuguese moidores and joes; Dutch lyon dollars; others. The list almost completely coincides with Solomon {1976}.)
6. *Lightweight British and Irish halfpence and tokens,* unofficially imported by merchants as "Casks of Hard Ware." These greatly outnumbered the genuine 1749 halfpence circulating in New England and Newfoundland.

We owe the Class 1 coins to the Compagnie des Indes Occidentales. Established by Edict of May 1664, dissolved Dec. 1677, and later reorganized, this group had a monopoly of trade and navigation in all French possessions in America and western Africa, and enough political clout to induce Louis XIV to issue the Edict of Feb. 19, 1670, authorizing a distinctive silver coinage for their use within the colonies: Shortt {1925} I, p. 27ff. These resembled the domestic coins except for their legend GLORIAM REGNI TVI DICENT—'They shall speak of the glory of Thy kingdom'—a singular piece of arrogance on the part of this most egotistical of all French kings: All knew that the Psalmist's verse, though originally addressed to God, would be readable as alluding instead to the kingdom of Louis XIV himself. The 15 and 5 Sols coins were struck in silver 11/12 = 916.67 Fine, respectively at 35 and 105 to the marc. (French coins' official weights were designated in aliquot parts of the marc, as British were of the pound troy or avoirdupois. As the marc = 3,777.114 grs. = 244.753 gms., a 15 Sols was to weigh 1/35 marc = 107.9 grs. = 6.993 gms., a 5 Sols proportionately 35.97 grs. = 2.331 gms. Similar calculations yield official weights for other coins in Classes 1–4 above.) Since 1662, Quebec authorities had officially valued domestic French coins at a 33 1/3% premium in a vain attempt to keep them from vanishing from circulation. The GLORIAM REGNI coins accordingly were to pass current respectively at 20 sols (= 1 livre) and 6 sols 8 deniers each, a value confirmed by order of the Conseil d'Estat (Council of State), Nov. 18, 1672. They vanished from circulation by 1680.

The same 1670 Edict authorized coinage of 2.4 million copper Doubles (2 Deniers coins). As the Paris Mint could find too little good copper for the purpose, the Conseil d'Estat on March 24, 1670, reopened the Nantes Mint and ordered melting there of nine long tons (37,500 marcs = 9,178.238 kg) of obsolete copper doubles tournois (1611–44 issues) to make up the necessary bullion. As the Nantes Mint's records perished in 1700, we may never learn why this order was not fulfilled. The unique Paris pattern is said to weigh 105 grs., for 35 to the marc; the Nantes coins were to be struck at 64 to the marc = 59.02 grs. = 3.824 gms. each. They would have resembled the Paris pattern **257**, except for mintmark T and corrected legend.

Acting in the name of the boy King Louis XV, the Duc d'Orléans in Dec. 1716 ordered the Perpignan Mint to strike coppers to pass current only in the colonies. There were to be 1.5 million XII Deniers and 3 million VI Deniers, respectively at 20 and 40 to the marc. However, available copper proved unusable; surviving sample coins of both denominations are on brassy flans showing cracks and cavitation. The Edict of June 1721 mentions the *mauvaise qualité,* 'wretched quality,' of this copper as aborting this mintage: Shortt I, pp. 500–3.

While the purchasing power of John Law's coppers was already dwindling in the colonies, the King issued the above-mentioned June 1721 Edict, ordering the mints of Rouen, La Rochelle, Bordeaux, and Nantes to make coppers for exclusively colonial circulation, replacing the Perpignan issue. There were to be three denominations, 18, 9, and 4½ deniers, respectively struck at 20, 40, and 80 to the marc; 30,000 marcs each from Rouen (mintmark B) and Bordeaux (K), 50,000 marcs from La Rochelle (H), and 40,000 from Nantes (T). Only the 9 Deniers denomination was made, and only with mintmarks B and H; they were coined at the same weight as the Perpignan 6 Deniers. The Compagnie des Indes imported copper in ready-made blanks from Stora Kopparbergs Bergslags AB, from ore mined at the "Copper Mountain" at Falun, 150 miles northwest of Stockholm—source of 2/3 of the copper European mints used since 1347: Shortt I, pp. 510–11; Tingstroem, p. 15. On June 11, 1722, authorities shipped to Quebec 10 casks of 9 Deniers coins (534,000 pieces in all, about 99% of them mintmarked H, the rest B), aboard the 600-ton, 133-foot royal pay and supply ship *Le Chameau*. This shipment was also to have included another 20,000 LT (livres tournois) in domestic silver coins (unidentified, possibly the "French ninepenny pieces" and 1720 Petit Louis d'argent, below, Class 4). The silver and gold coins were intended to pay troops to avert a threatened mutiny, to retire card money (playing cards marked with various denominations and signed by local officials), and to induce *habitants* to sell more beaver pelts to the Compagnie des Indes's company stores. As nobody had thought to register a copy of the June 1721 Edict with the Quebec Supreme Council, nobody was forced to accept the coppers. Colonists refused to receive them in payments for several reasons: Current price scales meant that no cash payments for anything involved any amount less than a sol marqué, while these coppers were to pass at only half that; and everyone feared another official devaluation—which followed two years later: Letter of Gov.-Gen. Vaudreuil and Intendant Begon to Comte de Maurepas, Nov. 2, 1724, quoted in Shortt I, pp. 536–37. Vaudreuil reported on Oct. 14, 1723, that the authorities had managed to pay out only 8,180 pieces: Shortt I, pp. 520–23. The rest cluttered the official warehouse until Sept. 26, 1726, when the Governor-General had his workmen load the 10 casks of coins onto *L'Éléphant,* bound for Rochefort, where they arrived Jan. 7, 1727: Shortt I, pp. 572–73. They were reshipped to Louisiana Territory at 6 deniers each (their older intrinsic value) instead of 9: Gadoury and Cousinie, no. 3.

During the century and a half preceding the British conquest of Canada, among the French on both sides of the Atlantic money's main name was *argent,* 'silver.' Primarily this meant Spanish dollars; ratings of all other coins depended on official valuations of the *piastre espagnole* ('Spanish piastre' or Peso of 8 Reales), and these valuations in turn depended on varying official or average weights of the latter—despite unenforceable regulations forbidding importation of these coins into Nouvelle France (Canada). Bowing to the inevitable, in 1681 the Superior Council authorized circulation of Spanish dollars of full weight at 3 livres, 19 sols, 1 denier each, with a discount for worn or lightweight pieces. This meant that each storekeeper had to weigh each Spanish dollar at the time of payment: an impossibly inconvenient situation. Accordingly, the Superior Council, Jan. 13, 1683, raised the current value of full-weight 8 Reales coins to 4 livres tournois, and ordered that these be countermarked with a fleur de lys. Pieces up to 6¼% lightweight would receive an additional countermark of I and pass at 3 livres 15 sols each; those up to 12½% lightweight would have II and lys, and pass at 3 livres 10 sols; those up to 18¾% deficient would have III and lys, passing at 3 livres 5 sols; those up to 25% lightweight, IIII and lys, passing at 3 livres each. Coins still lower in weight would be melted. This measure was successful, but the coins remained only briefly in circulation, and no survivors are traced today. Most likely some were exported; the rest lost enough weight in circulation to go to the melting pots. Any survivors are likely to be cob dollars of Car-

los II, 1667–83, Grove 373–386a: obv., crowned arms of Spain, flanked by o/M/G or o/M/L and 8, CAROLVS.II.DEI.G. and date around; rev., within 8-lobed tressure, cross cantoned with castles and lions, + HISPANIARVM.ET.INDIARVM.REX. Silver, 931 Fine, standard weight 418.7 grs. = 27.13 gms.

Coins of Class 3 primarily consisted of billon pieces which passed at a higher rate in Canada than in France. Immense quantities were struck for North American circulation. The first were the Paris Mint's counterstamps of 1640: Earlier billon pieces, some dating back to the Middle Ages, were recalled and countermarked with fleur de lys in beaded oval—the first Sols Marqués. When supplies of obsolete billon coins ran out, a similar 1641 issue followed, showing a device in the die resembling the countermark. These quickly vanished, as did a similar issue dated 1658. Several provincial mints made up new dies dated 1692 through 1700 to overstrike on the remaining obsolete billon coins (including some already countermarked); when supplies were exhausted, most French mints then in operation struck similar coins with dates from 1693–1705 on new blanks —the first billon-neuf sols.

Next came the billon "mousquetaires" of 1709–13, with crowned addorsed (back to back) LL, from mints in Lyon and Metz. Their name comes from the resemblance of their hollow Greek cross device to that on the tabards of royal musketeers. They were the first successful coinage for French colonies in America; later called "Old Sols," they circulated for generations. Mintages were immense, but survivors are few and mostly well worn; many were melted in 1738 and 1739, others were countermarked in 1763.

Only when exportable supplies of Old Sols ran out did King Louis XV authorize further billon issues. These were "Sous Marqués," properly Double Sols de 24 Deniers. Created by Edict of Sept. 1738, and prepared in secrecy during recall and melting of earlier copper and billon issues, these were made in unprecedented quantities by all 30 mints then in operation. Most are dated 1739, though most dates 1738–64 are known from Paris and many 1738–44, 1746–47, 1749–51 from provincial mints. Far fewer were made of the similar Demi Sous or Sols de 12 Deniers; most of the latter bear date 1740. Counterfeit Sous circulated indifferently side by side with the genuine, even as did British and American "Bungtown" coppers in the USA. Those most often seen are dated 1742 H, 1751 BB, 1755 A.

After the British conquered Canada, the Ordinance of Sept. 14, 1764, devalued the Sous down to a farthing apiece = 288 to the Spanish dollar = 320 to the Écu de 6 Livres. They retained their original higher value in Louisiana Territory. The present study supersedes Breen {1976A}.

John Law (1681–1729), the Scottish dreamer who managed to convince the Duc d'Orléans that inflated paper currency (backed by promises of wealth from the Mississippi and South Seas regions) would eliminate the French national debt as efficiently as silver and gold, was during part of 1720 in charge of both the French treasury and the mints. At his orders, the treasury shipped 1.6 million copper coins to Canada and 400,000 more to Isle Royale (now Cape Breton Island). Though the Edict of May 1719 called these *demi sols* (6 Deniers coins), Law's scheme included upward revaluation of all coins, so that these passed as sols until July 1720, when they acquired another 33⅓% premium; in 1721 they were devalued to 9 deniers, down to 6 in 1724.

The final group in Class 3 has acquired the collective name of *Chameau* Treasure coins. Royal authorities in May 1725 appointed Jean-Charles Percheron de Saint-James as master to take the ship *Le Chameau* to Canada; her cargo included among other things 82,010 livres tournois in gold and silver coins. A hurricane smashed her on what is still called Chameau Rock, in Kelpy Cove, off Cape Breton, Nova Scotia, early in the morning of Aug. 26, with all 316 aboard lost. During the late summer and early fall of 1965, Alex Storm's salvage team recovered about 900 gold Louis Mirlitons and 9,000 silver Écus aux 8 L, together with an undetermined quantity of smaller domestic silver, much of it too encrusted to be identifiable. Parke-Bernet Galleries auctioned 394 of the gold pieces, Dec. 10–11, 1971; some of these have reappeared at more recent auctions: Breen {1971B, 1976A}.

Coins of Class 4 (domestic French issues unofficially imported by merchants to pass in Canada at double face) have been occasionally sold as Canadian or even American colonials. The following coins are the best attested because they were found in Canadian hoards or mentioned in official revaluation orders.

Louis XIII Copper 1 and 2 Deniers (Demonetized, 1664):

A. *Denier tournois, young bust, plain collar.* Within circle, LOYS. XIII.R(OI).DE FRAN.ET.NAV. and mintmark A, D, E, G, K, O, or R (reportedly H) around. Rev., within circle, 2 fleurs de lys, mintmark below space between them; + DENIER .TOVRNOIS and date around, 1618–29 (date 1624 unverified). $2/3'' = 17$ mm; 24.2 grs. = 1.568 gms. = 156 to the marc. Plain edge, as all to follow unless noted. By Nicolas Briot. Ciani 1725; Willey 107; GD 2.

B. *Denier tournois, young bust in ruff.* Similar, but legend ends in FRAN.E.NA., mintmark A, D, E, G, K, or O (reportedly H) only on rev.; dates 1624–29, 1631–35 (1625 unverified). By Briot. Ciani 1726; Willey 107; GD 3.

C. *Double tournois, young armored bust.* As first Denier but LOVIS and NAVA, mintmark X; rev., 3 fleurs de lys, no mintmark, + DOVBLE.TOVRNOIS and dates 1614–16. $4/5'' = 20$ mm, 48.4 grs. = 3.136 gms. = 78 to the marc. By Briot. Ciani 1718; Willey 109; GD 7.

D. *Double tournois, child's bust, plain collar.* Legends and specifications as preceding but mintmarks A, D, G (1619), K, M (1611–12), S (1620), T, X (1614–16), &; dates 1610–20. By Briot, as next 2. Incl. in Willey 110; GD 5.

E. *Double tournois, child's bust in ruff.* Legends and specifications as last 2 but LVDOVIC XIII D G FRAN.ET NAV R; mintmarks A (1618), D (1611–13, 1615, 1617), O (1623–26); dates 1611–13, 1615, 1617–18, 1623–26. Incl. in Willey 110; GD 6.

F. *Double tournois, young bust, plain collar.* Device as first Denier above, legends and specifications as first Double but mintmarks A, D, F (1629), G, H (1619), K, O (1626), R, dates 1616–29 (1624 Ex. rare). Ciani 1722; Incl. in Willey 110; GD 8.

G. *Double tournois, young bust in ruff.* Device and legends as second Denier above, specifications as preceding Doubles. By Jean Warin. Mintmarks (obv. only) A, D, E (1631–35), F (1629, 1631), G, H (1631–32), K, R (1630, 1634); dates 1627–35. Incl. in Willey 110; GD 9.

H. *Double tournois, head l.* LVD.XIII.D:G.FR.ET NAV.REX Rev., 3 fleurs de lys, DOVBLE.TOVRNOIS (date) (mintmark above). Specifications as preceding Doubles. By Jean Warin. Various mintmarks; dates 1642–43. Ciani 1724; Willey 111; GD 12.

Louis XIV Copper Deniers and Doubles (Demonetized 1664):

I. *Denier tournois, child's head r.* LOVIS .XIIII. Rev., in circle, 2 fleurs de lys and mintmark A; around, + DENIER TOVRNOIS and dates (1648–49); 1655 I unverified. About $5/8'' = 15–16$ mm, 25 grs. = 1.62 gms. = 152 to the marc. By Jean Warin. Ciani 2006; Willey 108; GD 70. Vinchon 12/77:351.

J. *Double tournois, child's head r.* Similar but date below head; rev., large crowned fleur de lys, flanked by small crosses, mintmark A below, DOVBLE TOVRNOIS. Dates 1644, 1647,

both very rare, especially latter. About $4/5'' = 20$ mm; 50 grs. = 3.24 gms., for 76 to the marc. By Jean Warin. Ciani 2004; Willey 112; GD 71. Vinchon 12/77:349.

Louis XIV Copper Liards de France:

K. *Liard, crowned L.* Crowned draped young bust, LOVIS XIIII ROY DE FRAN.ET.NA. Rev., crowned L flanked by lys, LIARD.DE.FRANCE.; in exergue, mintmark A dividing date 16 54. About $9/10'' = 23$ mm; 62.95 grs. = 4.079 gms. = 60 to the marc. Very rare, possibly a pattern or prototype? By Jean Warin. Ciani 2011; Willey 113; GD 79. Vinchon 12/77:354.

L. *Liard, young bust, 3 lys.* Similar obv., L.XIIII.ROY.DE FR. ET DE NA. and dates (1655–58). Rev., LIARD/.DE./ FRANCE/mintmark, flanked by 2 lys, a third below. Specifications as preceding. By Jean Warin. Struck at special mints: A = Corbeil; B = Acquigny; B* = Pont de l'Arche; C = Caen; D = Vimy (Neuville); E = Meung sur Loire; G = Lusignan (rare, 1655–57); G: = Châtellerault (rare, Dec. 1657–58); I = Limoges; K = Bordeaux; R = Nîmes. Isaac Blandin had a special franchise to make these, in part from melted former issues, over objections of regular mintmasters; many of his coins proved underweight and there were riots at several of his special mints. The King forbade further coinage, devalued the liards first to 2 deniers (from 3), then a month later to 1 denier each. Many melted, 1692–1701, to make next. Ciani 2012; Willey 114; GD 80.

Louis XIV Later 3 and 6 Deniers:

M. *Liard, old bust, 3 lys.* Armored draped bust, long hair, similar legend but symbol above head, dates (1693–1702, 1707) after NAV. Rev. as preceding. Same specifications. By Joseph Roettier. Edict of June 9, 1693. Struck at over 20 regular mints. Ciani 2015; Willey 115; GD 81.

N. *Liard, old head.* Similar legend, bar symbol precedes L, dates (1707, 1713–15) after NAV. Rev. as preceding, mintmark W. Same specifications except 59.01 grs. = 3.824 gms. = 64 to the marc. By Norbert Roettier. Ciani 2016; Willey 116; GD 82.

O. *Dardennes 6 deniers.* Three pairs of addorsed L's, their legs forming an equilateral triangle, vertex down, fleur de lys at feet, mintmark (H, N, or &) within; LOVIS XIIII ROY DE FRANCE ET DE NAV. Rev., cross of scrolls, their knobbed ends forming heartshaped configurations holding lys; SIX DENIERS DE FRANCE and dates (1710–12). $15–18/16'' = 24–28$ mm (varies); 94.4 grs. = 6.118 gms. = 40 to the marc. By Norbert Roettier. Made from copper obtained by melting down old naval guns from Toulon and Rochefort. Ingots were rolled into strip and cut into planchets at the chateaux of Dardennes and Gold and shipped for coinage to the three mints of LaRochelle (H), Montpellier (N), and Aix (&); those struck at Dardennes have & mintmark and two points within center of rev. cross, the mark of the contractor Alain. Many proved lightweight. Willey says specimens have turned up in excavations at Louisbourg. Ciani 2019; Willey 117; GD 85.

Louis XIV Silver:

P. *2 Sols "des Traitants"* ('of the Contractors'). Draped laureate bust r. dividing LVD. .XIIII. Rev., 2 fleurs de lys, mintmark A (Paris) below; crown above dividing date (1674–77); D.G FR.ET.NAV.REX. By François Warin. 798.3 Fine, about $5/8'' = 15–16$ mm, 12.59 grs. = 0.816 gms. = 300 to the marc. This and next coined by private contractors, pursuant to Edict of April 8, 1674, at the instigation of the financier Jean-Baptiste Colbert, to raise funds for the King's wars in the Spanish Netherlands. Reduced to 1 sol 9 deniers, May 1679; demonetized and recalled for recoinage (Edict of Aug. 28, 1691). In the meantime, many circulated in Quebec at 2 sols 8 deniers, until reduced to 2 sols in 1705. All four dates are rare, especially 1677. Gadoury mentions a 1674 var. with "inverted" D in LVD (rotated 180°). Ciani 1958; Willey 125; GD 97.

Q. *4 Sols "des Traitants."* Draped laureate bust r., LVDOVICVS..XIIII.D.GRA. Rev., 4 lys, cruciform, mintmark A or D (Vimy) in center; above, crown dividing date (1674–77, 1679); FRAN. ET. NAVARRAE REX. By François Warin. Same fineness. $3/4'' = 19$ mm. 25.18 grs. = 1.631 gms. (GD says 1.809 gms.) = 150 to the marc. Same comments as to preceding, except that these circulated in Quebec at 5 sols 4 deniers. Date 1679 is very rare. Most were recalled and overstruck with dies of R below. Ciani 1957; Willey 126; GD 103.

R. *4 Sols aux 2 L.* Older draped laureate bust r., LVD. XIIII.D.G. (symbol) FR.ET NAV.REX., date below. Rev., 2 script L's interlaced and crowned, 3 fleurs de lys l., r., and between, mintmark below; around, DOMINE SALVVM FAC.REGEM (symbol). Weight and fineness as Q. Dates 1691–1700 (1695–1700 very rare), mintmarks A (1691–93), B (1691–92), C (1697), D, E (1691–94), H (1691–92, 1700), K (1691–93), Crowned L (1691), M (1691–94), Crowned M (1691), N, O (1691), P (1691–93), S (1691–92, 1694), Crowned S (1691, 1693), T (reported for 1698), V (1694–95, 1697), W, X (1691–92), Y, & (1692, 1696), 9 (1691, 1693–94). Overstruck on previous 4 Sols. Ciani 1959; Willey 127A; GD 106. Rev. device echoed in 1738–64 Sols Marqués. The similar 2 Sols (Ciani 1960, Willey 127, not in GD) remains untraced.

S. *5 Sols aux insignes.* Still older draped laureate bust r., no ribbon behind, L.XIIII D.G.FR.ET NA.REX around, date below. Rev., scepter and main de justice in saltire, cantoned with crown (above) and 3 fleurs de lys, mintmark below central lys; legend as R. Dates 1702–3 (many mints), 1704 BB, 1709 G (very rare). Overstruck on Q and R, as inflationary fund-raising measure for the War of the Spanish Succession, per Declaration of March 14, 1702. Passed in Canada at 6 sols 8 deniers, falling to 4 sols 8 deniers by 1709. Ciani 1965; Willey 128; GD 108.

T. *1/12 Écu aux palmes.* Old cuirassed draped bust r. with long hair, LVD.XIIII (soleil or radiant sun symbol) FR. ET NA.REX. Rev., crowned circular shield (3 fleurs de lys, 2 + 1) between 2 palm fronds, mintmark below, SIT NOMEN DOMINI BENEDICTVM around, date above, mintmark below. Silver, 917 = $11/12$ Fine, 108 to the marc = 2.26 gms., 19–21 mm. Overstruck weakly and unevenly on previous 1/12 Écus; rare choice. Dates 1694–1700 (1696–1700 rare); many mints. Officially valued at 6 sols in Quebec per order of Sept. 26, 1700. Ciani 1897; Willey 129; GD 119.

The next three were named in the British ordinance of Sept. 14, 1764, regulating currency after the conquest, as "French ninepenny pieces" because they had been circulating at 18 sols each = 9d Halifax currency. All are by Norbert Roettier.

U. *1/6 Écu = 20 Sols de Navarre.* Laureate-draped boy's bust r., LVD. XV. D.G. FR. ET. NAV. REX and symbol. Rev., crowned arms, quartered for France and Navarre, dividing XX S; legend as T above. Silver, 917 = $11/12$ Fine, 60 to the marc = 62.95 grs. = 4.079 gms., 23 mm. Dates 1719–20, many mintmarks. Many were recoined into W below. Ciani 2105; Willey 130; GD 295.

V. *Livre aux 2 L.* Similar obv., variant portrait (no ribbon behind head), same legend, symbol below. Rev., crowned addorsed LL, mintmark A below, SIT NOMEN, etc., around, date 1720 above. Pure silver, apparently $65 5/8$ to the marc = 58.55 grs. = 3.73 gms., 22 mm. [6,918,853] Many minor positional vars. Commonly misattributed to the Compagnie des Indes. John Law revalued it upward, at peak to double face (July 1720); later it sank to 18 sols, at which figure it circulated in Canada. Hoffman 84 (Pl. CXII); Ciani 2137; Willey 131; GD 296. Garrett:1299, EF, $600.

W. *1/6 Écu de France.* Laureate bust and legend similar to U, trefoil below bust. Rev., crowned arms of France (3 fleurs de lys), SIT NOMEN, etc., mintmark below, symbol and date

above. Silver, weight, and diameter as U, overstruck on latter. Dates 1720–23 (1723 is rare), many mintmarks. Issued at 30 sols (inflated), fell to 18. Ciani 2110; Willey 132; GD 296.

X. *1/3 Écu or "Petit Louis d'Argent."* Draped laureate bust r., same legend around as V above, date 1720 below. Rev., four pairs of addorsed L's form a cross, each arm crowned, cantoned with fleurs de lys, mintmark in center; CHRS. REGN. VINC. IMP and symbol around. Silver $11/12$ = 917 Fine, 30 to the marc = 125.9 grs. = 8.158 gms., 27 mm. Edge reeded with transverse line through reeds. Many mintmarks; most survivors are from Paris (A). Hoffman 33 (Pl. CIX); Ciani 2136; LeRoux 254c; GD 305, who mentions a 1720 W var. with REGNA.

The above have been listed in detail so that collectors encountering them will know their degree of relevance to colonial French America. Should documentation eventually demonstrate official shipments of any of these Class 4 coins (especially T through X), a later revision will number them in Class 3 below.

ISSUES FOR CANADA AND LOUISIANA TERRITORY

Designers, Engravers, Mints, Composition, Weights, Diameters, Authorizing Acts, see introductory text and notes to individual vars. No grade standards.

CLASS 1:
COINAGES INTENDED FOR FRENCH AMERICA

255 1670 A (= Paris) Louis de 15 sols. Silver. [40,000] Very rare.
Struck at 35 to the marc = 107.9 grs. = 6.99 gms.; approx. $18/16'' = 28$ mm; 917 = $11/12$ Fine. Plain edge. 12–14 known, without or with stop after TVI (latter rarer). Coined for the Compagnie des Indes Occidentales, per Royal Edict of Feb. 19, 1670. Above head, *soleil* or radiant sun face for mintmaster Pierre Cheval, in honor of the Sun King. Pellet below I is Paris Mint's secret mark. Above crown, a *tour* (castle or chess rook) for chief engraver Jean-Baptiste du Four. Beware electrotype copies. Crosby, p. 134; Ciani 2064; Breton 501; Willey 101. Ellsworth, Garrett:1297, VF, $29,000; Roper:181, F, $15,400.

256 1670 A Petit Louis de 5 sols. Silver. [200,000] Rare.
105 to the marc = 35.97 grs. = 2.331 gms.; fineness and symbols as last; about $14/16'' = 21$ mm. Plain edge. 7 minor vars. Crosby, p. 135; Ciani 2065; Breton 502; Willey 102.

257 1670 A Essai Double Denier. Copper. Unique.
Weight said to be 105 grs. = 6.8 gms., for 35 to the marc (but see introductory text); almost $15/16'' = 23.5$ mm. Legend is an error for DOVBLE DE L'AMERIQUE FRANÇOISE, '2-denier piece of French America.' Crosby, p. 134; Ciani

2066; Breton 503; Willey 103. Ex Bibliothèque Nationale, Count Ferrari, Virgil Brand, B. G. Johnson, Wayte Raymond, John J. Ford, Jr., Mrs. R. Henry Norweb. Beware electrotypes and counterfeits.

258 1717 Q (= Perpignan) Sol de 12 Deniers. Ex. rare.
Brassy copper, about $^{19}/_{16}'' = 30$ mm, struck at 20 to the marc = 188.9 grs. = 12.238 gms. 2 minor vars. Breton 504; LeRoux 252b; Craig 2; Willey 104. See introductory text. Beware electrotypes and counterfeits.

259 1717 Q Demi Sol de 6 Deniers. 3 or 4 reported.
As last but $^{15}/_{16}'' = 24$ mm; 40 to the marc = 94.43 grs. = 6.119 gms. Same comments. Cockleshell and flaming-heart symbols, respectively, are for mintmaster Christophe Bordeau, engraver Pierre Daquinot. Breton 505; LeRoux 252c; Craig 1; Willey 105. Beware electrotypes and counterfeits. A similar piece reported dated 1720 remains unconfirmed.

260 1721 B (= Rouen) Copper 9 Deniers. [1,200,000]
25–28 mm; weight as last. Edict of June 1721. Usually in low grades, dentilated borders weak or absent. Hunting horn and spade symbols are for mintmaster Pierre Duval and engraver Pierre de Roscherville, though the horn was traditional for Rouen coinage, honoring the vast royal game preserves. Breton 507; Willey 106.

261 1721 H (= Rochelle) 9 Deniers. Similar.
Authorized [2,000,000] for 1721–22; weight as last; 23.5–27 mm. Date 1721 comprises about ⅕ the total. Several minor vars., date wide or closer. Acorn and arrow symbols for

mintmaster Jean Donat, engraver Jean Lisard. Breton 506; Willey 106.

262 1722/21 H Similar. Scarce.
Lower part of 1 within 2. Discovered by this writer, Pittsburgh, June 1961. 3 vars.
263 1722 H Similar. Many vars.
Date varies in spacing. Usually on smaller blanks, 20–24 mm, not showing dentilated borders. Willey 106. Compare next 2.
264 1722 H Similar. FRANÇOISES over FRANIOISES. Rare.
265 1722 H Similar. Double date. Rare.

CLASS 2:
ORDINANCE OF 1683 COUNTERMARKS

266 n.d. 4 Livres. Unlocated.
Fleur de lys countermarked on Spanish or Mexican silver dollar of this or earlier date. At least 415 grs. = 26.3 gms. Most of these will be cob dollars of Carlos II, 1667–83: See introductory text.
267 n.d. 3 Livres 15 Sols. Unlocated.
Fleur de lys and I countermarked on similar dollar. At least 390 grs. = 25.3 gms. Same comments.
268 n.d. 3 Livres 10 Sols. Unlocated.
Fleur de lys and II countermarked on similar dollar. At least 365 grs. = 23.7 gms. Same comments.
269 n.d. 3 Livres 5 Sols. Unlocated.
Fleur de lys and III countermarked on similar dollar. At least 339 grs. = 22 gms. Same comments.
270 n.d. 3 Livres. Unlocated.
Fleur de lys and IIII countermarked on similar dollar. At least 313 grs. = 20.3 gms. Same comments.

CLASS 3:
DOMESTIC COINS OFFICIALLY EXPORTED

A. "Old Sols"

271 n.d. (1640) Countermarked billon douzain. Rare.
Fleur de lys in beaded oval, countermarked at Paris Mint on various older billon coins (24–26 mm), most often the issue of 1618 (GD 19 = Ciani 1903): crowned arms flanked by L's; cross cléchée cantoned by L's and crowns, SIT NOMEN, etc., mintmark A below). Other undertypes are rarer. Edict of June 1640. Nicknames included *monnaie grise,* 'gray coin,' "French sole mark," "sou mark," "black dogg." By Edict of Nov. 24, 1672, current in Canada at 20 deniers. Pridmore III, p. 10; Ciani 1709; Willey 19; GD 21, who failed to mention its colonial circulation.

272 1641 A Billon quinzain. Ex. rare.

Crowned arms flanked by L's, device imitating preceding countermark above crown; LVDOVICVS. XIII. A (mint-mark) FRAN.ET.NAV.REX Rev., cross cléchée cantoned by fleurs de lys, another lys in beaded oval in center; + SIT. NOMEN.DNI.BENEDICT.1641 around. Billon 24% silver, 26 mm, 100 to the marc = 37.78 grs. = 2.448 grs. By Jean Warin. Coined by the obsolescent hammer method. With-drawn in 1692. Hoffman 109; Ciani 1710; Willey 120; GD 22. 1), 2) European museum. 3) Pvt. coll. ex a hoard found in 1973. 4) Hinderling, Terranova (ill.).

273 1658 A Milled billon douzain. Ex. rare.

As preceding except L's crowned, date above shield, no imi-tations of countermark, and legend begins LVD.XIIII.; rev. legend ends in BENEDICTVM. Edict of July 18, 1658. Coined at 132 to the marc = 28.6 grs. = 1.85 gms. (Ciani says 1.275 gms. = 192 to the marc.) $^{15}/_{16}''$ = 24 mm. Billon 20% silver (Ciani says 23.5%). By Jean Warin. Raised to 15 deniers by Edict of Nov. 19, 1658; valued at 24 deniers in Canada; recalled in 1692. Hoffman 216; Ciani 1976; Willey 121; GD 86. Enl. photo

274 1658 A Same. Silver OMS. Ex. rare.

Ciani 1977. *Pièce de caprice?* Piedfort? Vinchon 12/77:338.

275 1658 A Milled billon sizain. Ex. rare.

As **273** except $^{7}/_{8}''$ = 22 mm. Coined at 264 to the marc = 14.3 grs. = 0.925 gms. Hoffman 217; Ciani 1978; GD 84. By Warin.

276 1692–1700 Recoined Billon Sol. Very rare.

Edict of Oct. 1692, raising values of previous sols to 15 de-niers; weights, diameters, as **273** (vary). Plain edges. By Jo-seph Roettier. Mintmark (many vars.) in center of cross of L's; price for 1693 A or 1695 A, others much rarer. Always with undertype. Ciani 1980; Willey 122; GD 91. A few are on sols with the 1640 countermark: GD 92a, 92b (ill.).

277 1693–1705 Billon-neuf Sol. Rare.

Same, without undertype. In all, [120,000,000] authorized of **276–77,** under half coined. A decree of Sept. 16, 1692 limited use to 100 or less in any single payment. Official values raised to 24, later lowered to 18 deniers. Weight as **273;** about 23 mm. Dates 1696–1705 very rare; many mints.

Billon "Mousquetaires"

278 1709 D (= Lyon) Double Sol de 30 Deniers. Ex. rare.

Edict of Sept. 1709. The nickname is from resemblance of the voided cross to that on musketeers' tabards. Replaced autho-rized but uncoined remainder of **276–77.** Coined at 100 to the marc = 37.77 grs. = 2.448 gms. $^{15}/_{16}''$ = about 24 mm; bil-lon of 20% silver. Plain edge. By Norbert Roettier. Ciani 1984; GD 102; Lafaurie {1968}. 1) Page {1931}. Ill. of **282.**

279 1709 AA (= Metz) Same. [465,238] 7 or 8 known.

The AA coins were soldiers' pay in the Ardennes; they passed at 33 deniers in Alsace, therefore few got to Canada or Louisiana Territory.

280 1710 D [All kinds 16,663,941]

Small or large roundels = disks at ends of cross arms.

281 1710 D Piedfort. Ex. rare.

Ciani 1985. 2.4 mm thick. 1) Ford. 2) Vinchon 12/77:342, 153.9 grs. = 9.97 gms. 3) Mike Ringo.

282 1710 AA [13,269,922]

With or without stop after LVD. Enl. photos above **278.** Mintage may include some dated 1709.

283 1710 AA Silver OMS piedfort. Unique?

Hoffman 223. 1) Banque du Canada.

284 1711 D [4,200,000+]

Mintage figure for Jan.–April; others delivered in 1712.

285 1711 AA [17,612,070] Very rare.

Minor positional vars. An early circulating counterfeit, found in Bordeaux in 1974, has reversed N in DENIERS; letters engraved, not punched. Copper, 31.3 grs. = 2.03 gms. ANS has another dated 1711 S.

286 1712 D [26,719,786–]

Minor positional vars. Mintage includes many dated 1711.

287 1712 AA [13,455,474] Ex. rare.

288 1713 D [all kinds 10,381,339] No star after date. Rare.

289 1713 D Star after date. Ex. rare.

290 1713 AA [all kinds 10,359,700] Pomegranate after date. Ex. rare.

291 1713 AA Star after date. Very rare.

"Demi Mousquetaires"

292 1711 AA Sol de 15 Deniers. Ex. rare.

Edict of May 5, 1711. Coined at Metz only, at 200 to the

marc = 18.89 grs. = 1.223 gms. Fineness as preceding. ³/₄″ = 19 mm (varies slightly). In all, [4,800,000] authorized to pay troops; few reached Canada or Louisiana Territory. GD 95. The 1710 AA coin—pictured (by line drawing) in Ciani, from Hoffman {1878}, Pl. CIII, 224—is untraced; if it exists it is a pattern. As most **292–96** survivors are in low grades, the date is in doubt.

293 1712/1 AA Only one seen.
294 1712 AA Very rare.
295 1713 AA [all kinds 1,706,400] Pomegranate after date. Very rare.
296 1713 AA Rosette after date. 4 or 5 seen.
Roper:183, UNC., $797.50.

B. John Law's Coppers

297 1719 BB (= Strasbourg) Copper Sol. Very rare.
Boy's head, long locks; LUDOVICVS.XV. DEI.GRATIA and symbol. Rev., crowned arms, top of crown dividing date, mintmark below base point of shield; FRANCIAE ET NAVARRAE REX and symbol. Edict of May 1719. Coined at 40 to the marc = 94.43 grs. = 6.119 gms. 1″ = 25 mm. Plain edge. By Norbert Roettier. Ciani 2142; GD 273. Other mintmarks may exist. See next.
298 1720 Copper Sol. Same type.
Mintmark A (Paris) rare; AA (Metz), BB (Strasbourg), and S (Reims) very rare. Others may exist. In all, [20,000,000] authorized, far fewer struck. John Law ordered 1.6 million shipped to Canada, to pass at 24 deniers each; they later fell in France to 9, then to 6 deniers. Dates 1721 S, 1722 K, 1723 Q are all rare, others 1721–24 Ex. rare or untraced; probably few or none reached America.

C. *Chameau* Treasure Coins

1. Gold "Louis Mirlitons"

The Edict of Aug. 1723 called these louis d'or de 27 livres, to be coined in gold of ¹¹/₁₂ or 917 fineness, at 37½ to the marc = 100.7 grs. = 5.527 gms. each, at all mints then operational. Diameter about ¹³/₁₆″ = 20–21 mm. Design by N. Roettier. Ciani 2083; Friedberg 205. "Type I" ("palmes courtes," GD 338) has short palm leaves, small crown; "Type II" ("grandes palmes," GD 339) has long palm leaves, larger crown, thick ends to interlaced L's. These may be collected by types, dates, or mints; listing below is by mints. Date 1723 most often comes in "Type I" with mintmark A, very rarely in "Type II" with mintmark A or H; 1724 is unconfirmed to exist in "Type I," but in "Type II" it most often shows mintmark A, K, N, or 9; 1725 is unconfirmed to exist in "Type I," but in "Type II" it least rarely shows mintmark A or N. Specimens salvaged from the 1725 wreck of *Le Chameau* (off Cape Breton, Nova Scotia) normally

come unworn but discolored or encrusted; see introductory text. The nickname Mirliton, 'reed flute,' possibly alludes to the refrain of a popular song ridiculing Cardinal Dubois, who had just become the Regent's prime minister (GD, p. 511).

A (Paris): Renard/Rose

299 1723 A "Type I." [1,729,200]
The renard or running fox is for mintmaster Mathieu Renard du Tasta; the rose for designer/ engraver Roettier. Ill. of **355.**

300 1723 A "Type II." Very rare.
Ill. of **310.**

301 1724 A [412,000]
All "Type II" coins have pellet between mintmark and VINC., unlike most "Type I's."
302 1725 A Rare.

B (Rouen): Spade Suit/Coiled Hunting Horn

303 1723 B "Type I." [103,200] Very rare.
For meanings of symbols see **260.**
304 1724 B "Type II." [27,200] Ex. rare.

C (Caen): Solid Molet/Anchor

305 1723 C "Type I." [40,000] Ex. rare.
A molet is a heraldic spur rowel, shaped like a 5-pointed star; usually voided (hollow center).
306 1724 C "Type II." [99,514] Very rare.
307 1725 C [35,407] Ex. rare, unlocated.
GD (p. 512) lists this as "Type I."

D (Lyon): Anchor/Eagle's Head Erased

308 1723 D [2,980] Pellets flank .VINC. Ex. rare.
"Erased" means with jagged truncation.
309 1724 D "Type II." [8,229] Ex. rare.
310 1725 D [3,119] Ex. rare, one reported.
Ill. at **300.**

E (Tours): Crescent/Molet

311 1723 E "Type I." [43,281] Very rare.
Large or small molet. Examples of both were in *Chameau* Treasure.
312 1724 E "Type II." [62,263] Very rare.
313 1725 E [68,684] Ex. rare, untraced.

G (Poitiers): Heart/Voided Greek Cross

314 1723 G [22,932] Ex. rare, untraced.
315 1724 G "Type II." [44,625] Very rare.
316 1725 G [16,784] Ex. rare, untraced.

H (La Rochelle): Arrow/Acorn

317 1723 H "Type I." [18,000] Pellets flank .VINC. Ex. rare.
For meanings of symbols see **261.**
318 1723 H "Type II." Ex. rare.
Mintage included in foregoing.
319 1724 H Very rare.
Groves:388, "AU," $2,400 (1974).

Molet/Acorn

320 1724 H "Type II." Ex. rare.
321 1725 H "Type II." Very rare.
GD (p. 512) lists a "Type I" as unconfirmed.

I (Limoges): Harp/Greek Cross

322 1723 I [2,400] Ex. rare, untraced.
323 1724/3 I "Type II." Ex. rare.
Discovered in the *Chameau* Treasure.
324 1724 I "Type II." Normal date. Ex. rare.
325 1725 I Ex. rare.

K (Bordeaux): Annulet/Lys

326 1723 K [10,400] Ex. rare.
Annulet = small ring.
327 1724 K "Type II." [291,600]
More of these were in the *Chameau* Treasure than any other
date-mintmark var. Groves:391, "AU," $2,300 (1974).
328 1725/4 K "Type II." Ex. rare.
Discovered in the *Chameau* Treasure.
329 1725 K Normal date, "Type II." Ex. rare.
Roper:193, $880. GD (p. 512) lists a "Type I" as uncon-
firmed.

L (Bayonne): Lozenge/Cinquefoil

330 1723 L "Type I." Ex. rare.
The lozenge is for mintmaster M. Lacroix; the cinquefoil for
engraver Léon Mousset.
331 1724 L "Type II." Ex. rare.
332 1725 L "Type II." Ex. rare.

M (Toulouse): Coronet (?)/Mask

333 1723 M "Type I." Pellets flank .VINC. Ex. rare.
Mintmaster's symbol is ambiguous in form, on some denominations looking more like a castle.
334 1724 M "Type II." Ex. rare.

N (Montpellier): Estoile/Crown

335 1723 N "Type I." [179,080] Very rare.
An estoile is a heraldic 6-pointed star, usually with curved
points. Compare next.

Molet/Crown

336 1723 N "Type I." Ex. rare.
Star has 5 points, not 6; the *Chameau* Treasure had vars.
with large or small molet.

Rooster/Crown

337 1724 N "Type II." [253,008] Rare.
338 1725 N "Type II." [185,064] Very rare.

O (Riom): Grape Leaf (?)/Trefoil

339 1723 O [33,601] Ex. rare, unlocated.
340 1724 O "Type II." [101,316] Very rare.
341 1725 O [36,479] Ex. rare, unlocated.

P (Dijon): Tree/Suspended Powder Horn

342 1723 P "Type I." [19,200] Ex. rare.
343 1724 P "Type II." Ex. rare.

Q (Perpignan): Spade Suit (?)/Plume

344 1723 Q "Type I." Ex. rare.

Cockleshell/Coronet

345 1724/3 Q "Type II." Ex. rare.
Discovered in the *Chameau* Treasure.
346 1724 Q Normal date, "Type II." Ex. rare.

R (Orleans): Tree/Griffin's Head Erased

347 1723 R "Type I." [70,137] Very rare.
348 1724 R "Type II." [125,456] Very rare.
349 1725 R [45,943] Ex. rare, unlocated.

S (Reims): Acorn/Ermine Tail (?)

350 1723 S "Type I." [6,800] Ex. rare.
S mintmark is usually accompanied by the Sainte Ampoule
or flask of Oil of Anointing used at royal coronations in
Reims Cathedral since A.D. 987. The acorn is for mintmaster
François Lagolle; the rev. symbol (which sometimes looks
like a lozenge) is for engraver Louis Guiquéro. Prieur
{1950}.
351 1724 S [36,000] Ex. rare, unlocated.
352 1725 S "Type II." [27,600] Ex. rare.

T (Nantes): Vertically Pierced Heart/Lion Passant Gardant

353 1723 T "Type I." [46,000] Ex. rare.
Heart pierced upward by phallic spearpoint.
354 1724 T "Type II." Ex. rare.

V (Troyes): Cross Fichée, Voided/Annulet

355 1723 "Type I." [51,764] Pellets flank .VINC. Ex. rare.
The ill. above **299** is of one from the *Chameau* Treasure.
356 1724 V [77,268] Ex. rare, unlocated.
357 1725 V "Type II." [21,259] Ex. rare.

W (Lille): Bar/Lozenge

358 1723 W "Type I." [58,758] Ex. rare.
359 1724 W "Type II." Ex. rare.
360 1725 W "Type II." Ex. rare.
1) Vinchon 3/81:218.

X (Amiens): Uncertain Symbols

361 1723 X "Type I." [44,800] Ex. rare.
362 1724 X "Type II." Ex. rare.
363 1725 X "Type II." Ex. rare.

Y (Bourges): Pierced Heart in Flames/Crescent

364 1723 Y [39,600] Ex. rare, unlocated.
365 1724 Y "Type II." Ex. rare.

Z (Grenoble): Tulip(?)/Pisces Symbol

366 1723 Z [48,070] Ex. rare, unlocated.
367 1724 Z "Type II." [96,917] Very rare.
The Pisces symbol = dolphins as in arms of Dauphiné.
368 1725 Z "Type II." [22,482] Ex. rare.

AA (Metz): Uncertain Symbols

369 1723 AA [3,200] Ex. rare, unlocated.
370 1724 AA [5,200] Ex. rare, unlocated.
371 1725 AA [23,200] Ex. rare, unlocated.

BB (Strasbourg): Uncertain Symbols

372 1723 BB "Type I." [8,400] Ex. rare.
373 1724 BB "Type II." Ex. rare.

Addorsed CC (Besançon): Uncertain Symbols

374 1723 Addorsed CC [14,400] Ex. rare, unlocated.
Rumored also to exist dated 1724.

& (Aix-en-Provence): Heart/Lozenge

375 1723 & "Type I." Ex. rare.
376 1724 & "Type II." Ex. rare.

9 (Rennes): Wheat sheaf/Bird

377 1723 9 "Type I." [71,200] Pellets flank .VINC. Very rare.
378 1724 9 "Type II." [233,223] Rare.

Baquette (Pau): Lion (?)/Maltese Cross

379 1724 Baquette "Type II." Ex. rare.
The baquette is a small standing cow, used as a mintmark for centuries; usually accompanied by monogram DBR = Domaines Béarnaises du Roi. GD 339a.

Lys/Maltese Cross

380 1725 Baquette [50,902] Ex. rare.
GD 339a. Other vars. of all the above are possible, as many coins were withheld from the *Chameau* Treasure auction. Breen {1971B}.

2. Silver Écu aux 8 L.

By Edict of Sept. 1724, these were to be coined at all operational mints, in silver $11/12 = 917$ Fine, at $10^3/8$ to the marc = 364.06 grs. = 23.59 gms. Edge lettered in relief DOMINE SALVUM FAC REGEM, 'God save the King.' 38.5 mm. By N. Roettier. Official valuation was 4 Livres = 80 Sols. The date 1724 comes with all mintmarks except L, M, Q, R, and Y; 1725 with all except P. Here we list only those date-mintmark combinations found in the *Chameau* Treasure for lack of evidence that any others were shipped to North America. This hoard included over 9,000 in various states of incrustation, many illegible in either date or mintmark or both. Sobin says fewer than 200 proved to be in collectible grade. GD 320.

381 1724 H Rare.
Ill. of **383**.

382 1724 K [144,212] Rare.
383 1724 T Rare.
Ill. above **381**. Other mints are possible.
384 1725 G [228,351] Rare.
385 1725 H
This date-mintmark combination comprised about 80% of identifiable survivors.
386 1725 I Rare.
387 1725 K Rare.
388 1725 O [415,146]
389 1725 T
Other mints are possible. Provenance from the *Chameau* Treasure would suffice to establish American relevance.

D. Sous Marqués

1. Double Sols de 24 Deniers

The Edict of Oct. 1, 1738 authorized manufacture of these in unlimited quantity from all operational mints, in billon of 25% silver, at 112 to the marc = 33.72 grs. = 2.185 gms. (Observed range, 28–41 grs. = 1.81–2.66 gms.) Diameter $7/8'' = 22.2$ mm. (varies). By J. C. Roettier. Pristine survivors show original silver wash. Those with pellet below D of LUD were made in the second semester or half year of date. Ciani 2138; Breton 508; Willey 124; GD 281. Many circulating counterfeits exist, ranging from grotesque to deceptive; these passed indifferently side by side with the genuine, and are collected today equally indifferently. Even official documents indiscriminately called the larger coins sous or sols, uniformly with the Old Sols, particularly the 30 Deniers coins of 1709–13. Preparation of the new ones took place in secrecy, and their explicit purposes included replacing exhausted colonial supplies of Old Sols. They therefore properly belong to Canada and Louisiana, though they also circulated in all overseas French territories, even long after the British conquest of Canada. They are collected by dates or by mints. The date 1738 comes with all mintmarks except D, L, N, Z, and Baquette; 1739, all; 1740, all except possibly X; 1741, all except S, T, X, and Baquette. Later dates come from fewer mints; 1753–62, only from A and BB. Coins dated 1757–64 were not shipped officially to Canada, but they reached New Orleans via trading ships. British occupation officials in Canada valued the coins at a farthing apiece, possibly from ignorance of their silver content, possibly to favor their export to other regions where they passed higher, unintentionally (?) creating a Canadian market for base Birmingham coppers. Both genuine and counterfeit Sous Marqués come with various official counterstamps indicating West Indian revaluations. Most of the circulating counterfeits price as commoner genuine Sous Marqués. Unlisted dates and mints exist, all very rare; we await publication of the new work by Robert A. Vlack.

A (Paris): Renard and Lozenge/Rosette.

390 1738 A [2,770,886]
Several minor vars. Circulating counterfeits exist.
391 1739 A [8,068,970]
Many minor vars.

392 1740/39 A Ex. rare.
393 1740 A [all kinds 1,089,942] Normal date. Very rare.
394 1741 A Very rare.
All seen are second semester. Circulating counterfeits exist, most often seen with BIT NOMEN error and unbarred A (inverted V) mintmark.
395 1742 A Very rare.
Circulating counterfeits exist.
396 1743 A [435,860] Rare.
Ill. in Wood {1914}. Divers in the 1950s recovered a small hoard from the wreck of the frigate *St. Geran,* sunk off Mauritius on the night of Aug. 17, 1744, en route from L'Orient since March 24. Hatie:101–2.
397 1744 A Ex. rare.
398 1745 A [293,130] Ex. rare.
Untraced in the USA.

399   1746 A [467,486] Ex. rare.
All seen to date are second semester.
400   1747 A [all kinds 327,160] Ex. rare.
Normal date. Untraced in the USA.
401   1747/6 A Second semester. Unique?
1) ANS coll.
402   1748 A Ex. rare.
403   1749 A Ex. rare.
All genuine examples seen to date are second semester. Circulating counterfeits are rare but less so than genuine.
404   1750 A [266,370] Very rare.
Most specimens offered are circulating counterfeits.
405   1751 A [234,070] Ex. rare.
406   1752 A [91,800] Ex. rare.
407   1753 A [114,620] Ex. rare.

Renard and Lozenge/Seeded Rose of 5 Petals

408   1754/3 A No pellet after NAV One seen.
Seeded rose is C. N. Roettier's tribute to his father J. C. Roettier.
409   1754 A Normal date. Ex. rare.
410   1755/4 A Ex. rare.
411   1755 A Very rare.
Most offered are circulating counterfeits; on these, letters are engraved (instead of punched), mintmark A is often barless (inverted V: ill.), and one var. has date 1755/3. The genuine are far rarer.

412   1756 A [128,600] Ex. rare.
413   1757 A Very rare.
Compare following.

Heron/Seeded Rose of 5 Petals

414   1757 A Very rare.
Heron is for new mintmaster Jean Dupeyron de la Corte. All seen to date are second semester; always weakly struck.

415   1758/4 A Ex. rare.
1) ANS.   2) Breen, first semester.   3) Rizzo, Pine Tree (9/78), second semester.
416   1758/7 A Ex. rare.
417   1758 A Normal date. Ex. rare.
Both semesters; first, Roper:188.
418   1759 A Ex. rare.

Heron/Croisette Potencée

419   1760/59 A Ex. rare.
All seen are second semester; date blurry. The croisette is for Charles Norbert Roettier. Of 1760 normal date, only circulating counterfeits are known.
420   1761 A Ex. rare.
Second semester only seen to date.

421   1762 A Ex. rare.
Both semesters.

Tree/Croisette Potencée

422   1762 A Ex. rare.
423   1763/2 A Ex. rare.
424   1763 A Rare.
425   1764 A
Plentiful from both semesters. Coins dated 1769 A are circulating counterfeits, but rarer than those of earlier dates. This may explain GD's listing of this date as reported but unconfirmed.

B (Rouen): Spade Suit/Coiled Hunting Horn

426   1738 B [366,777] Ex. rare.
Untraced in the USA.
427   1739 B [2,462,459] Very rare.
428   1740 B [all kinds 1,467,242] Very rare.
429   1740/39 B Ex. rare.
430   1741 B Ex. rare.
431   1742 B [all kinds 80,034] Ex. rare.
432   1742/39 B One seen.
1) John Jay Ford, Jr.
433   1742/1 B Ex. rare.
1) ANS.   2) R. Margolis. The 1762 B mentioned in GD as "reported, not confirmed" is possibly a typographical error for the common 1762 BB.

C (Caen): Estoile of 6/Urn?

434   1738 C [30,851] Ex. rare, untraced in USA.
Unpriced in GD. Estoile = heraldic 6-pointed star, normally emblazoned with curved points; in this small size, points are narrow straight wedges.
435   1739 C [1,580,526] Very rare.
436   1740 C [597,695] Ex. rare.
437   1741 C [310,034] Ex. rare.
438   1742 C [194,793] Ex. rare.
439   1743 C [167,554] Ex. rare.
440   1744 C [115,958] Ex. rare.
441   1745 C [99,950] Ex. rare, untraced in USA, as are next 7.
442   1746 C [98,430] Ex. rare.
443   1747 C [71,277] Ex. rare.
444   1748 C [79,385] Ex. rare.
445   1749 C [68,147] Ex. rare.
446   1750 C [82,467] Ex. rare.
447   1751 C [59,294] Ex. rare.
448   1752 C [5,439] Ex. rare.
Unpriced in GD.

D (Lyon): Estoile of 8/Bird (?)

449   1738 D Ex. rare.
1) R. Margolis.
450   1739 D [2,770,852] Very rare.
As in **434**, the estoile is a heraldic star, here with 8 points.
451   1740 D [678,136] Ex. rare.
452   1741 D [393,994] Ex. rare.
453   1742 D [49,070] Ex. rare, untraced in USA.
Unpriced in GD.

E (Tours): Heart/Molet

454   1738 E [20,798] Ex. rare.
Untraced in the USA. The molet or spur rowel looks like a 5-pointed star.
455   1739 E [1,029,400] Very rare.
456   1740 E [510,619] Ex. rare.
Circulating counterfeits show D G . FR and rev. rosette symbol.

457 1741 E [210,193] Ex. rare.
Untraced in the USA.
458 1742 E [87,782] Ex. rare.
459 1743 E [62,217] Ex. rare.
This and next 2 untraced in the USA.
460 1744 E [63,451] Ex. rare.
461 1745 E [26,311] Ex. rare.
462 1746 E [53,645] Ex. rare.
463 1747/6 E [31,386] Ex. rare.
Unpriced in GD, who ignores the overdate. No normal date
coin yet seen.
464 1748 E [31,483] Ex. rare.
This and next 2 untraced in the USA.
465 1749 E [28,240] Ex. rare.
Unpriced in GD.
466 1750 E [32,680] Ex. rare.
Unpriced in GD.

G (Poitiers): Uncertain Symbols

467 1738 G [115,084] Ex. rare.
468 1739 G [667,891] Ex. rare.
Always in low grades. Enl. photos

469 1740 G [169,864] Ex. rare.
Always in low grades.
470 1741 G Ex. rare.
471 1742 G [all kinds 76,187] Normal date. Ex. rare.
472 1742/1 G Only one seen.

H (La Rochelle): Solid Molet/Tower

473 1738 H [28,302] Ex. rare.
Untraced in the USA. Unpriced in GD. The molet is a solid
5-pointed star; the tower is for engraver Gilles Massenet.
474 1739 H [667,891] Ex. rare.
475 1740 H [217,927] Ex. rare.
476 1741 H Ex. rare.
477 1742 H [25,932] Ex. rare.
Genuine survivors have top of 4 open, and the proper symbols. Over 99% of those offered are (circulating?) counterfeits
(ill.): top of 4 closed; voided star between pellets, broad cross
pointée. 22–41 grs. = 1.43–2.66 gms.; sometimes coppery,
often UNC., plentiful in all grades.

478 1743 H [25,932] Ex. rare.
This and later dates untraced in the USA.
479 1744 H [23,057] Ex. rare.
480 1745 H [23,010] Ex. rare.
481 1746 H [27,546] Ex. rare.
482 1747 H [66,744] Ex. rare.
483 1748 H Ex. rare.

484 1749 H Ex. rare.
485 1750 H [600,800] Ex. rare.
486 1751 H [62,986] Ex. rare.
487 1752 H [27,070] Ex. rare.
Unpriced in GD.

I (Limoges): Lozenge and Aigrette/Staves in Saltire

488 1738 I [10,732] Ex. rare.
Untraced in the USA; unpriced in GD. Aigrette = ornamental plume; saltire = X-shaped formation.
489 1739 I [630,618] Very rare.
This and later dates always in low grades.

Lamp/Glaive (?)

490 1740 I [601,653] Very rare.
The glaive is a double-bladed weapon.
491 1741 I [150,800] Ex. rare.
492 1742 I [103,550] Ex. rare.
493 1743 I [52,460] Ex. rare.
Untraced in the USA; unpriced in GD.
494 1744 I [143,472] Ex. rare.
Same comments.

K (Bordeaux): Annulet/Plume

495 1738 K [14,384] Ex. rare.
Untraced in the USA; unpriced in GD. An annulet is a small
ring.
496 1739 K [1,282,512] Very rare.
497 1740 K [521,696] Ex. rare.
498 1741 K Ex. rare.
499 1742 K Ex. rare.
1) Fargeon coll.
500 1743 K [87,024] Ex. rare.
1) ANS, ex Boyd.
501 1744 K [all kinds 143,472] Ex. rare.
Normal date untraced in the USA.
502 1744/3 K Ex. rare.
1) Banque du Canada.

L (Bayonne): Leveret (?) Passant/Cinquefoil

503 1739 L [all kinds 239,400] Punctuated FR. Ex. rare.
Mintage may include coins dated 1738, reported to Gadoury
but unconfirmed.
504 1739 L Punctuated FR: Ex. rare.
505 1740 L [129,311] Ex. rare.
Dates 1740–50 untraced in the USA.
506 1741 L [75,066] Ex. rare.
507 1742 L [17,250] Ex. rare.
508 1743 L Ex. rare.
509 1744 L Ex. rare.
510 1745 L Ex. rare.
511 1746 L Ex. rare.
512 1747 L Ex. rare.
513 1748 L [51,300] Ex. rare.
514 1749 L [34,200] Ex. rare.
515 1750 L [34,200] Ex. rare.
516 1751 L [85,500] Ex. rare.
517 1752 L [74,100] Ex. rare.
Untraced in USA; unpriced in GD.

M (Toulouse): Voided Molet/Rose of 6

518 1738 M [185,285] Ex. rare.
Untraced in USA; unpriced in GD. The voided molet is a
hollow 5-pointed star; the rose has 6 petals.
519 1739 M [2,004,900] Very rare.
Banque du Canada.

520 1740 M [all kinds 665,408] Ex. rare.
Normal date untraced in the USA.
521 1740/39 M Only one seen.
Enl. photos.

522 1741 M [291,570] Ex. rare.
Untraced in the USA.
523 1742 M [all kinds 246,202] Ex. rare.
524 1743 M [131,224] Ex. rare.
Untraced in the USA; unpriced in GD.
525 1744 M [105,750] Ex. rare.
Same comments.

N (Montpellier): Anchor/Conch

526 1739 N [1,091,388] Rare.
527 1740 N [400,898] Ex. rare.
528 1741 N [102,557] Ex. rare.
529 1742/1 N Ex. rare.
Normal date probably exists.

O (Riom): Grape Leaf/Trefoil

530 1738 O [122,610] Ex. rare.
Unpriced in GD; only one seen in the USA. The trefoil may represent either the plant (clover) or the club suit.
531 1739 O [1,755,561] Very rare.
Several minor vars.
532 1740 O [419,182] Ex. rare.
533 1741 O [220,197] Ex. rare.
Untraced in the USA; unpriced in GD.
534 1742 O [135,522] Ex. rare.
Same comments.
535 1743 O [136,322] Ex. rare.
Untraced in the USA.
536 1744 O [35,378] Ex. rare.
Untraced in the USA; unpriced in GD.

P (Dijon): Anchor/Suspended Powder Horn

537 1738 P [211,879] Ex. rare.
Anchor is for mintmaster Pierre Nardot.
538 1738 P OMS silver piedfort. Unique?
Thick flan, reeded edge. Hoffman 69, Ciani 2139.   1) ANS, possibly ex Penchaud.
539 1739 P [1,382,522] Very rare.
540 1740 P [326,035] Ex. rare.
541 1741 P Ex. rare.
542 1743 P [129,666] Ex. rare.
Untraced in the USA.
543 1743 P [136,322] Ex. rare.
544 1744 P [167,898] Ex. rare.

Q (Perpignan): Uncertain Symbols

545 1738 Q [17,100] Ex. rare.
Untraced in the USA; unpriced in GD. Survivors should have obv. cockleshell symbol for mintmaster Christophe Bordeau.

546 1739 Q [22,800] Ex. rare.
Any coined through March 1739 should have cockleshell symbol as **545.**
547 1740 Q [328,897] Ex. rare.
Untraced in the USA.
548 1741 Q [113,527] Ex. rare.
Untraced in the USA; unpriced in GD.
549 1742 Q [91,522] Ex. rare.
Same comments.

R (Orleans): Glaive/Gargoyle

550 1738 R [22,438] Ex. rare.
The glaive is a double-bladed weapon.
551 1739 R [875,296] Ex. rare.
552 1740 R Ex. rare.
Untraced in the USA. Obv. may have glaive or molet symbol: See next.

Molet/Gargoyle

553 1741 R Ex. rare.
The molet here is a 5-pointed star.

S (Reims): Acorn/Fruit (?)

554 1738 S [285,156] Ex. rare.
The acorn is for mintmaster François Lagolle, the fruit (possibly meant for the Sainte Ampoule: See **350** above) for engraver Jérôme Savoye. If it does represent the Sainte Ampoule, it is stylized beyond certainty. Prieur {1950}.
555 1739 S [1,681,076] Ex. rare.
Prieur gives mintage as [1,731,096].
556 1740 S [165,061] Ex. rare.
Untraced in the USA. Issued before July 31, 1740. See next.

Key/Fruit (?)

557 1740 S [166,992] Ex. rare.
Untraced in the USA. Issued between Aug. 1 and Dec. 31. The key is a punning device for mintmaster Pierre Étienne Clay de Coincy: "Clay" sounds like French *clef,* 'key.' Mintage figures from Prieur; GD gives total of both as [408,433].

T (Nantes): Lion/Tower

558 1738 T [47,344] Ex. rare.
Untraced in the USA.
559 1739 T [442,282] Ex. rare.
560 1740 T [all kinds 257,642] Ex. rare.
All seen are in low grades, symbols uncertain.

Tree/Uncertain Symbol

561 1740 T Ex. rare.
All seen are in low grades.
562 1743 T Ex. rare.
Untraced in the USA.

V (Troyes en Champagne): Uncertain Symbols

563 1738 V [121,525] Ex. rare.
Beware confusing V with Y mintmark.
564 1739 V [986,587] Very rare.
Minor vars. exist. Circulating counterfeits exist.
565 1740 V [240,306] Ex. rare.
566 1741 V [92,010] Ex. rare.
567 1742 V [32,446] Ex. rare.
568 1755 V Ex. rare.
Untraced in the USA.

W (Lille): Bar/Lozenge

569   1738 W [339,610] Ex. rare.
The bar is a punning device for mintmaster P. F. Baret de Ferrand; the lozenge may represent the diamond suit.
570   1739 W [All kinds 6,475,088]
Several minor vars.
571   1739/8 W Only one seen.
1) David Laties coll.
572   1740 W [All kinds 404,693] Ex. rare.
573   1740/39 W Ex. rare.
574   1741 W Ex. rare.
575   1742 W Ex. rare.
Untraced in the USA.
576   1743 W [174,944] Ex. rare.
577   1744/3 W [Incl. in next] Only one seen.

Heron/Lozenge

578   1744 W [354,426] Rare.
579   1745 W [152,171] Ex. rare.
580   1746 W [119,472] Ex. rare.
Circulating counterfeits have obv. renard (fox) as though imitating Paris issue.
581   1747 W [168,960] Ex. rare.
582   1748 W Ex. rare.
Untraced in the USA.
583   1749 W Ex. rare.
Same comment.

X (Amiens): Boar's Head/Heart

584   1738 X [172,241] Ex. rare.
Untraced in the USA. The boar has apple in mouth.
585   1739 X [1,741,599] Ex. rare.
Dates 1740, 1741 remain known only to rumor.

Y (Bourges): Martlet/Crescent

586   1738 Y [100,443] Ex. rare.
Untraced in the USA; unpriced in GD.
587   1739 Y [684,618] Ex. rare.
Always in low grades. Beware confusing with V mintmark.
588   1740 Y [230,908] Ex. rare.
589   1742 Y [40,004] Ex. rare.
Untraced in the USA; unpriced in GD.

Z (Grenoble): Dolphin/Inverted Crown

590   1739 Z [269,299] Ex. rare.
Always in low grades. Dolphin alludes to Dauphiné arms.
591   1740 Z [149,328] Ex. rare.
Same comment.
592   1741 Z [96,271] Ex. rare.
Same comment.

AA (Metz): Cinquefoil Between Pellets/Ermine Tail

593   1738 AA [487,350] Ex. rare.
594   1739 AA [1,786,950] Very rare.
595   1740 AA [487,350] Ex. rare.
Untraced in the USA.
596   1741 AA [784,000] Ex. rare.
597   1742 AA [784,000] Ex. rare.
598   1743 AA [627,200] Ex. rare.
599   1744 AA [313,600] Ex. rare.
600   1745 AA [947,800] Ex. rare.
Untraced in the USA.
601   1746 AA [1,097,600] Ex. rare.
602   1747 AA [315,000] Ex. rare.
This and later dates untraced in the USA.
603   1748 AA [156,800] Ex. rare.

604   1749 AA Ex. rare.
605   1750 AA [156,800] Ex. rare.
606   1762 AA Ex. rare.

BB (Strasbourg): Heart/Voided Estoile of 6

607   1738 BB [441,882] Ex. rare.
The heart is for mintmaster Jean-Louis Bégerlé, the hollow 6-pointed star for engraver Pierre L'Écrivain.
608   1739 BB [911,038] Very rare.
Minor vars. exist. One in ANS has half the star missing (broken punch).
609   1740 BB [198,213] Ex. rare.
610   1741/38 BB Ex. rare.
611   1741/0 BB Ex. rare.
612   1741 BB Normal date. Ex. rare.
Minor vars. exist.
613   1742/1 BB Ex. rare.
614   1742 BB Normal date. Ex. rare.
615   1743 BB Ex. rare.
Untraced in the USA.
616   1744 BB [327,046] Ex. rare.
Several minor vars.
617   1745 BB Ex. rare.
Untraced in the USA.
618   1746 BB Ex. rare.
Same comment.
619   1747 BB Ex. rare.
620   1748 BB Ex. rare.
Dates 1748–55 untraced in the USA.
621   1749 BB Ex. rare.
622   1750 BB Ex. rare.
623   1751 BB Ex. rare.
All seen in the USA are circulating counterfeits; mintmark looks like HB, date small, letters engraved rather than punched. These price about as commoner genuine pieces.
624   1752 BB Ex. rare.
625   1753 BB Ex. rare.
626   1754 BB Ex. rare.
627   1755 BB Ex. rare.
628   1756/46 BB Very rare.
May exist with normal date. Rarer in France than in the USA.
629   1757 BB Ex. rare.
Untraced in the USA, as are next 4.
630   1758 BB Ex. rare.
631   1759 BB Ex. rare.
632   1760 BB Ex. rare.
633   1761 BB Ex. rare.
634   1762 BB Common.
Plentiful even UNC. One of the largest issues of all. Many minor vars.

Addorsed CC (Besançon): Eagle's Head Erased/Double Axe.

635   1738 CC [429,973] Ex. rare.
Untraced in the USA; unpriced in GD.
636   1739 CC [1,760,962] Ex. rare.
637   1740 CC [212,918] Ex. rare.
Several minor vars. Enl. photos.

638 1741 CC Ex. rare.

& (Aix-en-Provence): Anchor/Lozenge

639 1738 & [57,000] Ex. rare.
Untraced in the USA; unpriced in GD.
640 1739 & [581,400] Ex. rare.
641 1740 & [166,141] Ex. rare.
1) R. Margolis. Unpriced in GD.
642 1741 & [45,600] Ex. rare.
1) Breen coll. Unpriced in GD.
643 1743 & [32,160] Ex. rare.
Untraced in the USA; unpriced in GD.

9 (Rennes): Uncertain Symbols

644 1738 9 [2,536] Ex. rare.
Untraced in the USA; unpriced in GD.
645 1739 9 [606,993] Ex. rare.
646 1740 9 [801,090] Ex. rare.
647 1741 9 Ex. rare.
648 1742 9 [109,325] Ex. rare.
649 1743 9 [61,392] Ex. rare.
Untraced in the USA; unpriced in GD.
650 1744 9 [18,900] Ex. rare.
Same comments.

Baquette (Pau en Béarn): Various Symbols

651 1739 Baquette Unique?
Not in GD. Baquette = small stylized standing figure of a
cow, constant on Pau coins from 1610–1791. These also normally have monogram DBR = Domaines Béarnaises du
Roi. 1) Musée des Beaux Arts, Pau.
652 1740 Baquette [85,505] Ex. rare.
This and next untraced in the USA; unpriced in GD.
653 1742 Baquette [66,532] Ex. rare.
654 1743 Baquette [20,436] Ex. rare.
1) ANS, worn.
655 1744 Baquette [16,356] Ex. rare.
Dates 1744–52 untraced in the USA; unpriced in GD.
656 1745 Baquette [22,745] Ex. rare.
657 1746 Baquette [4,900] Ex. rare.
658 1749 Baquette [11,557] Ex. rare.
659 1751 Baquette [63,030] Ex. rare.
660 1752 Baquette [11,742] Ex. rare.

2. Sols de 12 Deniers, "Demi Sous"

The Edict of Oct. 1, 1738 authorized these at 224 to the
marc = 16.86 grs. = 1.093 gms., to be coined from all operational mints, at the same fineness as the Double Sols. Diameters
vary: 10–12/16″ = 16–19 mm. By J. C. Roettier. Breton 509;
Ciani 2139; Willey 124; GD 278. Devices and legends are as on
the Double Sols except that rev. legend ends in BENEDICT.
Mintmasters' and engravers' symbols are as on the Double Sols
except as noted. Quantities minted were far smaller. These circulated only briefly in Canada, where (in later years most of all)
almost no transactions involved any amount less than a Double
Sol. Others reached Louisiana Territory but we have no details
of their purchasing power. They are collected by date or mint:
The date 1738 is unobtainable, 1739 is exceedingly rare, as are
1741–48. Over 99% of survivors are dated 1740. For uniformity
with the Double Sols, they are here listed by mints. Almost all
are in low grades.

A (Paris): Renard/Voided Estoile of 6.

661 1738 A Unique.
1) Canadian pvt. coll. Unknown to GD.
662 1739 A 2 known.
1), 2) Canadian pvt. colls. Unseen by GD.

663 1740 A [49,280] Rare.
Minor vars. exist.
664 1746 A Ex. rare.
665 1748 A Rev. sixfoil. Very rare.
Enl. photo. GD values this higher than previous dates. One
dated 1764 A was rumored to be in the Paris Mint; this
remains unverified.

Jack Collins

B (Rouen): Spade Suit/Coiled Hunting Horn

666 1740 B [42,388] Ex. rare.
Several minor vars. Unpriced in GD.

C (Caen): Estoile of 6/Unidentified Symbol

667 1739 C [19,158] Ex. rare.
1) Banque du Canada.   2) Terranova.

D (Lyon): Estoile of 8/Bird?

668 1740 D [714,929] Very rare.
Minor vars. exist.

G (Poitiers): Uncertain Symbols

669 1740 G [85,580] Very rare.
Minor vars. exist.

I (Limoges): Lozenge and Aigrette/Staves in Saltire

670 1739 I Ex. rare.
Untraced in the USA.
671 1740 I [158,840] Ex. rare.
Untraced in the USA.

L (Bayonne): Uncertain Symbols

672 1740 L [119,354] Ex. rare.
Untraced in the USA; unpriced in GD.
673 1741 L [78,648] Ex. rare.
Same comments.

M (Toulouse): Voided Molet/Rose of 6

674 1740 M [66,593] 3 or 4 traced.
Unpriced in GD.

N (Montpellier): Anchor/Conch

675 1740 N Unique?
1) Reportedly in Banque du Canada. Unknown to GD.

O (Riom): Grape Leaf/Trefoil

676 1740 O [65,792] Ex. rare.

P (Dijon): Anchor/Suspended Powder Horn

677 1739 P [64,130] 3 or 4 traced.
Canadian pvt. colls.
678 1740 P [64,272] Ex. rare.

S (Reims): Acorn (?)/Fruit

679 1740 S [152,600] Untraced.
Data from Prieur. Unknown to GD.

T (Nantes): Uncertain Symbols

680 1739 T [19,158] Ex. rare.
Untraced in the USA; unpriced in GD.
681 1740 T [428,024] Very rare.
Minor vars. exist. Rarer than **683** despite larger mintage.

V (Troyes): Uncertain Symbols

682 1740 V [12,296] Ex. rare.
Untraced in the USA.

W (Lille): Bar/Lozenge

683 1740 W [394,044] Rare.
Minor vars. exist.

X (Amiens): Boar's Head/Heart

684 1740 X [32,125] Ex. rare.
1) Banque du Canada; others in pvt. colls.

Y (Bourges): Martlet/Crescent

685 1739 Y [13,220] Ex. rare.
Untraced in USA, unpriced in GD, as are next 2.
686 1740 Y [19,618] Ex. rare.
687 1742 Y [10,192] Ex. rare.

AA (Metz): Cinquefoil/Ermine Tail

688 1740 AA Normal punctuation. Rare.
Stops after FR. and CT.
689 1740 AA No stops after FR or CT Very rare.
Enl. photos.

BB (Strasbourg): Heart/Voided Estoile of 6

690 1740 BB Very scarce.
Several minor vars. Less rare in USA and Canada than 1740 D, T, or W, but rarer in France.

691 1746 BB Ex. rare.
Untraced in the USA.

Addorsed CC (Besançon): Eagle's Head Erased/Double Axe

692 1739 CC [14,560] Ex. rare.
1) R. Margolis.
693 1740 CC [24,192] Ex. rare.
Untraced in the USA; unpriced in GD.

& (Aix-en-Provence): Anchor/Lozenge

694 1740 & [37,225] Ex. rare.
1) Breen coll. Unpriced in GD. Enl. photo.

Jack Collins

9 (Rennes): Uncertain Symbols

695 1740 9 [14,442] Ex. rare.
Untraced in the USA; unpriced in GD.

ii. LOUISIANA TERRITORY AFTER THE CANADIAN RECONQUEST

In 1763, a Royal edict recalled all billon sous still circulating. These were to be returned to the Paris Mint for counterstamping, after which they would be shipped to the French Caribbean colonies, circulating there and in Louisiana Territory. Some 6 million received the official counterstamps, being thereafter internationally valued at 1/6 bitt or 1/6 escalin = 1½ pence = 1 black dogg each. The name Dogg or Black Dogg became practically official, though in both Louisiana and Caribbean Creole dialects the coins became known as sols tampés, promptly anglicized to stampees.

After the supply of older billon coins was exhausted, the Paris Mint (1779) made some 300,000 new billon blanks of about the same size and countermarked them similarly to pass as sols tampés in Cayenne (French Guiana); these "billon-neuf" sols circulated throughout the Caribbean and reached Louisiana along with older stampees.

In the meantime, the Paris Mint (1767) had issued 1.6 million copper Sols de 12 Deniers for the French Caribbean colonies. For unknown reasons, few circulated. Pursuant to a Decree of the Extraordinary Assembly of Guadeloupe, Sept. 28, 1793, the remainder (apparently over 98% of the original mintage) received a countermark of RF in oval, obliterating the three fleurs de lys rather than the crown. The countermarked pieces are properly known as Collots; they passed at 3 sols 9 deniers = 2¼ pence = ¼ escalin = ¼ bitt = 1½ stampees = 1½ doggs, according to locale. Later still, many of them reached the USA, where they passed as cents; they have turned up in noncollector accumulations with "1781" NORTH AMERICAN TOKEN and "1783" Birmingham Washington pieces, suggesting that East Coast circulation of all these derived from the same emergency: a coin shortage following the War of 1812. The 1767 coppers, with or without counterstamp, have long been accepted as colonially relevant. Pridmore III, pp. 228, 339–40.

All the above coins are herein included because many at least unofficially reached the New Orleans area. However, only **700–**

1 were formerly accepted as American colonials, owing to the common assumption that 18th-century America consisted solely of New England and the Atlantic Seaboard from New York through Georgia, which is manifest nonsense.

No grading standards are established for these coins.

696 n.d. (1763) Sol tampé, Stampee or Dogg, "Type I." [6,000,000+]

Crowned small C in depressed outline, 3 mm. Craig 7. Overstruck on almost any type of billon sou previously described; shipped to Cayenne and the French Antilles. Usually in low grades. Mintage figure includes next 2. Rarer undertypes bring higher prices.

697 n.d. (1763) Sol tampé, "Type II."

Crowned small C in relief, 3 mm. Craig 7A. Mintage included in **696.** Same comments. Undertypes sometimes counterfeit, often illegible. Ill. *SCWC,* p. 670.

698 n.d. (1763) Sol tampé, "Type III."

Crowned large C in relief, 5 mm. Craig 7B. Mintage included in **696.** Same comments.

699 n.d. (1779) Billon-neuf Sol tampé, "Type IV." [300,000]

As **698** but on billon blank, 23 mm, not overstruck on anything. Craig 10. Ill. *SCWC,* p. 670.

700 1767 Copper Sol de 12 Deniers [1,600,000]

Croisette potencée symbol is for chief engraver Charles Norbert Roettier. Device is properly described as lys-headed scepter and main de justice in saltire. Diameter 18/16″ = 28.6 mm. Coined at 20 to the marc = 188.89 grs. = 12.236 gms. Craig 4. Many minor vars. Over 98% were countermarked: See next. Uncountermarked specimens are rare in all grades, prohibitively rare choice.

701 1767 (i.e., 1793) Collot.

Various local valuations: See introductory text. Many minor vars. of both the copper and the countermark die.

Jack Collins

CHAPTER 6

STATE COINAGES: AUTHORIZED, PROPOSED, AND IMITATED

i. MASSACHUSETTS PATTERN COPPERS (1776)

Three different unique designs form this group. The first has for obv. a standing Indian with bow and arrow and PROVIN(CE OF) MASSA:, the legend beginning at 5 o'clock and proceeding counterclockwise. Rev. depicts the Goddess of Liberty, seated, with liberty pole (the lone survivor is too worn to show the traditional liberty cap, if any), globe behind her, watchdog at her feet; D(EFENSOR? LIB)ERTATIS around, reading normally. The single example is overstruck on a 1747 George II halfpenny, and pierced. Howland Wood announced discovery in *NUM* 6/11, p. 228. Use of the term "Province" rather than "State" proves that the die was made before July 4: After the Declaration of Independence, Massachusetts was no longer a royal province. No documentation survives about this or either of the next designs. Use of a British coin for a planchet permits no deductions about its intended weight standard.

The second is the "Three Heads" halfpenny, sometimes erroneously called the "Janus Copper." Its triple head device (facing l., full face forward, and r.) suggests watchfulness in every direction (against British redcoats?). Its legend STATE OF MASSA: indicates a time after July 4. On rev., the seated figure holds either an alarm bell (in reference to Paul Revere's ride?) or a liberty cap; beside her is a watchdog. The coin's weight of 81 grs. suggests a proposed coinage at 84 to the lb. (not much over half the Tower standard) and argues against its being an intended companion to the next.

The third and in many ways the most remarkable is the Pine Tree Penny. Its device alludes to the Sons of Liberty (Cambridge) flag, and that in turn to the Pine Tree Shillings of a century earlier (connoting the defiance of British authority these coins had embodied); the hill on which the tree stands would have reminded almost any local citizen of Bunker Hill. Flanking the trunk are letters 1d LM = One Penny Lawful Money. (Lawful Money was the local name for the exchange rate equating the Spanish dollar to 6 shillings; 1d LM = 1/12 shilling = 1/72 Spanish dollar = 1/9 bit. This Penny is the only known coin referring to this exchange rate, though much colonial paper currency specified LM rather than Proclamation Money.) Its weight of 198 grs. indicates a standard of 35 or 36 to the lb.: somewhat below the Birmingham standard (60 halfpence or 30 pence to the lb.) but proportionately far above the "Three Heads" coin, therefore proposed on a separate occasion from the latter.

Each of these coins shows enough stylistic resemblance to the others to justify attributing all three to the same diemaker. The

circumstances of discovery of the "Three Heads" pieces—with some of Paul Revere's plate proofs—convinced Matthew Adams Stickney before 1873 that Revere made it: Crosby, p. 304. But there are better reasons for following this attribution. Detailed comparisons of lettering peculiarities with those of both Paul Revere's 1775–76 currency and his securities plates show enough resemblances to assign all of these to him. Revere's inexperience as a diesinker, together with the limited supply of any copper other than base Birmingham imitations of British halfpence, may account for abandonment of this enterprise.

MASSACHUSETTS PATTERN COPPERS

Designer, Engraver, Paul Revere. Mint, private, Boston. Composition, copper. Diameters, Weight Standards, variable, as noted.

No grading standards established.

702 1776 Province Halfpenny. Unique.
See introductory text. About $^{17}/_{16}'' = 27$ mm = that of the 1747 halfpenny on which overstruck. 1) Howland Wood (1911), Parsons:98, ANS. Ill. ANS {1914}, Pl. 12.

703 1776 Three Heads Halfpenny. Unique.
See introductory text. Diameter $^{15}/_{16}'' = 23$ mm; 81.2 grs. = 5.26 gms. Crosby, Pl. VII, 8. 1) Matthew Adams Stickney (before 1873), Garrett:574, $40,000, pvt. coll. Modern forgeries exist from copy dies; they are not deceptive.

704   1776 State Penny. Unique.
   See introductory text. Diameter $20/16'' = 31.8$ mm; 198
   grs. $= 12.83$ gms. Crosby, Pl. VII, 7.   1) Edward Hooper (a
   schoolboy, 1852), Jeremiah Colburn, William Sumner Appleton, to MHS. Modern forgeries exist from copy dies; they are
   not deceptive.

ii. NEW HAMPSHIRE COPPERS
(1776)

On March 13, 1776, the New Hampshire House of Representatives and Council established a committee to inquire into "the
expediency of making Copper Coin." Members included
Wyseman Claggett (chairman), Capt. Pierce Long (who later
that year signed the Colony's paper currency), Jonathan Lovell,
Deacon Nahum Balden, and a Mr. Giles, this last name plus
the chairman being nominated by the Council. The committee
recommended that William Moulton be authorized to make
coppers weighing in all 100 lbs., to pass current at 108 to the
Spanish dollar (= 18 to the shilling, or three for twopence, the
usual rate for British coppers). These were to be of the standard
weight of British halfpence, and to bear such devices as the
General Assembly might approve: *AJN*, 8/1868, pp. 28–29;
Crosby, p. 175.

Assuming that these recommendations had the force of law,
and that Moulton followed his instructions to the letter, that
would mean 4,600 coppers averaging 152.17 grs. $= 9.86$ gms.
each. The actual number may have been slightly higher as nobody knew the actual British standard $= 46$ to the lb. (In 1785,
the Connecticut legislature thought it 150 grs. each; in 1787, the
New York legislature thought it 48 to the lb. $= 145.833$ grs.
each. As the last large shipment of Tower Mint halfpence had
reached New England in Sept. 1749, survivors from it were by
1776 mostly well worn.) Nevertheless, the survivors of the original Moulton batch weigh between 145 and 155 grs. apiece,
which is close enough. The latter conform to the design
sketched on the back of the legislative committee's report, reproduced in Crosby (loc. cit.). We may therefore take 4,600 as
very nearly the actual number coined. All were cast, steel dies
being unobtainable. Their harp device echoes less that of Irish
halfpence than the emblem found on the $7 Continental notes
then in circulation, with its motto *Majora minoribus consonant*,
'The bigger [strings or states] blend harmoniously with the
smaller.'

The Act of June 28, 1776 permitted any kind of coppers
locally made, with the same devices, and weighing 130 grs.
(8.42 gms. $= 54$ to the lb.) or more, to be received into the
Colony Treasury in exchange for New Hampshire paper currency at the same rate specified above. This may account for the
engraved imitations. It does not, however, explain the cast and
engraved pieces with tree, date, and WM; these, if genuine,
probably antedated the original March 1776 Committee report.
Their use of a pine tree device may allude to the Pine Tree
Shillings, or to New Hampshire's then immense forests: Com-

pare the earliest type of Vermont coppers, which feature ever-
green trees on a mountain range.

Many modern forgeries exist of all types of New Hampshire
coppers here shown, and they have obscured the whole subject.
Genuine examples are exceedingly rare; authentication is mandatory. No grading standards exist.

NEW HAMPSHIRE COPPERS

Designer, Engraver, William Moulton. Mint, Moulton's, location unknown. Composition, copper. Weight, Diameter, variable. Authorizing Acts, Committee Recommendations, March
1776; Act of June 28, 1776.
   No grading standards established.

705   1776 Pattern copper. Tree on straight ground. Ex. rare.
   Always cast. WM = William Moulton. Authentication mandatory. Enl. photos.

706   1776 Pattern copper. Tree on mound. 3 to 5 known.
   Always cast. Crosby, fig. 28A, p. 176. The Newcomer-Gar-
   rett example weighs 79.5 grs. $= 5.15$ gms.; it brought $7,500.
   Modern cast forgeries exist in quantity; these have occasioned doubt of all specimens offered. Authentication mandatory.

Ex J. W. Garrett: 1324. Courtesy Bowers & Ruddy Galleries, Inc.

707   1776 Engraved pattern copper. Similar. Ex. rare.
   Devices engraved directly onto blank. Genuineness doubted.
708   1776 Moulton's copper. [4,600] 8 or 9 known.
   Always cast. Issue of March 1776. Crosby, Pl. VI, 3. Note
   period after date 1776. No rev. legend. $18/16'' = 28.6$ mm
   (varies slightly); 145–155 grs. $= 9.4$–10 gms. That ill. is one
   of 2 or 3 finest. Stickney, Ellsworth, Garrett:1323 (worn, date
   illegible) brought $13,000. See introductory text. Authentica-
   tion mandatory.

709 1776 Local imitation copper. Engraved. Unique?
Intended to conform to Act of June 28? 127 grs. = 8.23 gms.: possibly engraved on an Irish halfpenny? 1) Hodge, Norweb, SI; Crosby, Pl. VI, 4 and fig. 28B, p. 176. See introductory text.

710 n.d. (1776?) Similar, die-struck. Unique?
1) R. R. Prann, 1947 ANA:593. Genuineness doubted. The fabric suggests wooden dies hammered into any available blank.

iii. VERMONT COPPERS
(1785–89)

On June 15, 1785, the Vermont legislature granted to Reuben Harmon, Jr., of Reuport (later Rupert), Bennington County, an exclusive franchise to make copper coins, no limit being set on amount. These were to weigh 160 grs. = 10.37 gms. apiece. As that figure exceeded even the Tower Mint halfpenny standard, far heavier than any other coppers then in circulation, the legislators reduced the mandatory weight on Oct. 27, 1785. Harmon's coppers thereafter needed to weigh only 111 grs. = 7.19 gms. = 63 to the pound. His bond (for £5,000) explicitly forbade him to coin any coppers of "Wait Mettle or Motto's contrary to said Act," i.e., to reduce weight further, to make coins of other than pure copper, or to change the designs or inscriptions.

Harmon set up his mint on Millbrook, a stream emptying into the Pawlet River, near the northeast boundary of Rupert. He hired as diemaker Col. William Coley, a New York City goldsmith, of Van Voorhis, Bailey and Coley, 27 Hanover Square. Coley's first design (probably fixed by the legislature, as the authorizing act specified) emulated two types of money then in circulation. Its device (Sun rising over the Green Mountains) alluded to Paul Revere's Massachusetts notes of 1779; its legend VERMONT(I)S RESPUBLICA, 'The Republic of Vermont,' specified the issuing authority as a sovereign republic, alone among state coppers. Coley's earliest revs. showed the All-Seeing Eye in the Blazing Sun within a constellation of 13 stars for the Original 13 Colonies, in allusion to the then current CONSTELLATIO NOVA coppers—even to similar blunt rays; the legend STELLA QUARTA DECIMA, 'The Fourteenth Star,' referred to local pressure to join the Union as the Fourteenth State, which came true in 1791. Issues of 1786 revised the obv. legend to read VERMONTENSIUM RESPUBLICA (better Latin for the same meaning), and the rev. showed long pointed rays, after the 1785 CONSTELLATIO NOVA coppers.

For undetermined reasons, Harmon petitioned the legislature to permit a change in the design to approximate that similar to most other coppers then current (British halfpence and their local imitations, including the Connecticut coppers). The legislature accordingly amended the original act to specify the devices as "on the one side, a head with the motto AUCTORITATE VERMONTENSIUM, abridged—on the reverse, a woman, with the letters, INDE: ET LIB:—for Independence and Liberty." This copied the Connecticut coppers; the rev. inscription is not Latin but French, *Indépendance et Liberté:* There is no Latin cognate for the first word. As Harmon's franchise was to expire July 1, 1787, he petitioned for an extension, which was granted on better terms than expected: His franchise was to extend for eight years longer, the first three free of any tax, the remaining five to cost him 2½% of his gross coinage, to be paid directly into the state treasury (Act of Oct. 24, 1786).

Col. Coley first made the "Baby Head" obv., imitating one of James F. Atlee's counterfeit Connecticut coppers of 1786. A few weeks (months?) later, Abel Buell's son William, age 14, fled to Vermont to escape hostile Indians and brought along a pair of device punches made by his father for the Bust Left dies: Sipsey {1964}. These copied the 1786 Connecticut pattern, but bore a wheat sheaf on shield, unlike the latter. Only two obvs. and three revs. were made from them, and these dies broke down quickly; local steel was rare and of poor quality, local copper no better. Well-struck pieces without planchet defects are unobtainable. To avoid trouble, Harmon made most of his coppers slightly heavier than standard: about 60 or even 55 to the lb. rather than the prescribed 63. At 63 to the pound they were lighter than Birmingham coppers, which were already an annoyance because of short weight; at 60 they matched the Birmingham standard; at 55 they were a little lighter than Irish halfpence but less likely to be refused in change.

Disappointed in the receipts, Col. Coley joined his New York silversmith partner Daniel Van Voorhis (later of Machin's Mills, Newburgh) in petitioning the New York State legislature for a coinage franchise: Feb. 16, 1787; *Journal of the N.Y. Assembly,* 1787, p. 53, cited by Crosby, loc. cit. In desperate need for dies, Harmon was receptive to approaches from the newly formed Machin's Mills firm. On the following June 7, Harmon signed a contract with the latter, giving them 60% of all profits from his Vermont operations in exchange for 40% of the profits from all other Machin's Mills operations on the condition that Machin's designer-engraver James F. Atlee would furnish the Vermont mint with sufficient dies; Crosby quoted the contract in full, Newman {1958} analyzed its terms.

Coins struck under the June 7 agreement have the Atlee head (sometimes called "Standard Head" to distinguish it from Atlee's other device punch): a large bust of George III, though with the legal Vermont inscription. Revs. come with either of two seated figure punches, both showing the British shield with simplified Union Jack (no fimbriation on crosses). Most vars. are rare; in upper grade levels, all are rare, most unobtainable. Worse still, the Machin's Mills coiners began making Vermont coppers on their own, one of the commonest of these showing a Vermont obv. with a worn-out BRITANNIA rev. Others showed the standard Vermont head contradicted by the legend GEORGIVS III REX. Both endangered Harmon's franchise and bondholders: Newman {1958}. Still others showed crudities of execution such as the famous Inverted C blunder. Many were overstruck on counterfeit Irish halfpence dated 1781–82; these halfpence, allegedly from a Smithfield button maker, had briefly circulated in America: Christmas II, p. 13.

In July 1789, partly owing to Machin's Mills, partly to floods of lightweight Birmingham pieces, coppers of all kinds fell to about 25% of their former purchasing power, in most places becoming unacceptable in trade at any valuation. Harmon abandoned his franchise and left Vermont for the "New Connecitcut" (Western Reserve) area of what is now Ohio, where he gave up coining for salt making; he died there (Salt Spring tract, Weathersfield Township, Trumbull County), Oct. 29, 1806. No doubt both Harmon and his fairweather friends from Newburgh would have been incredulous at the prospect of their primitive coppers becoming rare collectibles.

Crossreferences are to RR = Richardson {1947}, which uses and extends the Ryder {1919} numbers, and to KB = Bressett {1976}.

VERMONT COPPERS
Landscape Design, 1785–86

Designer, Engraver, Col. William Coley (devices specified by legislature). Mint, Harmon & Co., Rupert. Composition, pure copper. Diameters, at first 17/16″ = 27 mm, later 16–18/16″ = 25–28 mm. Weight standard, 111 grs. = 7.2 gms. = 63 to the lb. Authorizing Acts, June 15, 1785; Oct. 27, 1785.

Grade range, POOR to UNC. GOOD: All legends and date readable. VERY GOOD: Some contours of hills clear. FINE: Some details of rays, sun face, and internal structure of plow clear. VERY FINE: Part of internal strands of hair in eyebrow of All-Seeing Eye discernible; eyes and part of facial structure of obv. sun face clear. EXTREMELY FINE: Iris and part of pupil in All-Seeing Eye clear; most rays clear. EXCEPTIONS: Buckled dies and uneven strikes; grade by surface.

Issues of Oct.–Dec. 1785

711   1785 VERMONTS. 2 vars.
Price for var. ill. (RR 2 = Bressett 1-A); the other, with ray pointing well beyond period after RES. (RR 3 = KB 2-B), is rarer. Weights vary greatly: 77.5 grs. = 5.02 gms. (Earle:1995) to 185 grs. = 11.99 gms. (Parsons:142). Were the heaviest issued before the Act of Oct. 27 authorized coinage at lower weight?

712   1785 VERMONTIS.
RR 4 = KB 3-C. Weight range 91–120 grs. = 5.9–7.78 gms. For the other VERMONTIS, with sun rising at observer's l., see **735**.

Issues of Jan.–Sept. 1786

713   1786 VERMONTENSIUM. 3 vars.
RR 6 = KB 4-D (7 trees; ray points between ES); RR 7 = KB 5-E (ill.); RR 8 = KB 6-E (point of plowshare above 7).

Last is rarest. The var. ill. is often weak in central obv. from die failure.

Issues of Oct. 1786–June 1787

Designer, Engraver, as noted below. Mint, Physical Specifications, as above. Authorizing Act, Oct. 24, 1786.

Grade range, POOR to EX. FINE (usually POOR to VG). GOOD: Part of date and all legends visible (but see EXCEPTIONS). VERY GOOD: Part of details of armor and drapery show. FINE: Some hair details clear. VERY FINE: Some wreath details clear. EXCEPTIONS: Always on defective planchets. Die breaks on some vars. also obscure details. Grade by surface.

714   1786 "Baby Head."
RR 9 = KB 7-F. 4 wheat sheaves on shield. By Coley. Usually in low grades. Punchlinked with **713**. Copied from **746**. Robison:194, VF, $3,000.

715   1786 Bust l. 2 vars. Rare.
Buell hubs, one wheat sheaf on shield. Always weak; prohibitively rare above F. RR 10 = KB 8-G (ill.; same as Crosby, Pl. V, 1); RR 11 = KB 9-H, obv. as **716**, doubled rev. die. 111.6–127.9 grs. = 7.23–8.29 gms. Sanborn Partridge discovered the wheat sheaf device: *CNL* 6/74, p. 438.

716   1787/6 Bust l. Very rare, 12–15 known.
Same hubs. RR 15 = KB 9-I. Heavy die break destroys most of date, which must have been 1787/6 because the 1786 date was in the hub, altered by Coley's hand. Always weakly struck on crude defective planchets. One is known overstruck on a specimen of **712**: B&R RCR 39 (7/81), $6,995.

Issues of July 1787–88

Designer, Engraver, James F. Atlee. Mint, Rupert. Physical Specifications, Authorizing Acts, as above.

Grade range, POOR TO UNC. GOOD: All legends and date legible if on flan and not destroyed by die breaks, die failure, or planchet defects. VERY GOOD: Part of details of armor and drapery show; wreath outlines partly visible. FINE: Most details of armor, part of hair above wreath, over half drapery, and most shield stripes clear. VERY FINE: Over half wreath details show; usually, part of hair on female head clear. EXTREMELY FINE: Only few tiny spots of wear on isolated high points; grade by surface.

717 1787 Standard head, obv. pellet stops. 2 vars.
RR 34 = KB 10-J = Crosby, Pl. V, 2 (ill., Ex. rare). Price for the other var., RR 14 = KB 10-K: same obv., rev. as **718**. Often overstruck on CONSTELLATIO NOVA coppers, especially **1114**.

718 1787 Same, no obv. stops. 2 vars.
Price for var. ill., RR 12 = KB 11-K. The other var., RR 32 = KB 12-K, is Ex. rare; it has very wide legend, I touching armor, break through UCT. Both vars. usually overstruck on CONSTELLATIO NOVA coppers as preceding.

719 1788 Standard head, pellet stops, single exergue line. 4 vars.
RR 19, 20, 38, 21 = respectively, KB 13-L, 10-L, 10-N, 10-R (last ill.). Short seated figure as above. All rare; the rarest, RR 38 (3 or 4 known, discovered by Richard Picker), has date crowded far to r., final 8 almost under curl of shield.

720 1788 Same but double exergue line. 2 vars. Very rare.
RR 37, 23 = KB 10-M, 10-O; price for latter (ill.). On RR 37 (2 or 3 known, discovered by A. D. Hoch, 1960), E T L I B is extremely wide, B nearly in line with exergue.

721 1788 Similar, tall seated figure. 2 vars. Very rare.
RR 36, 22 = KB 10-P, 10-Q, latter ill. RR 36 (7 not lower than 1 88) was discovered by Bressett, *NUM* 2/55, p. 162; cf. 1975 EAC:418.

722 1788 No obv. pellets; short seated figure. Rare.
RR 17 = KB 14-S. Not to be confused with next!

723 1788 Faint centered period midway N . A
RR 16 = KB 15-S. Period gradually fades out. Unlike preceding, all letters away from device.

724 1788 Cross stops both sides. 2 vars.
RR 25, 26 = KB 16-T, 16-U. Price for former (ill.); latter (Ex. rare) has branch hand opposite E, and a long break joining both E's: 1975 EAC:426.

Later RR 25's, struck at Machin's Mills after Harmon abandoned his mint, come overstruck on counterfeit Irish halfpence (dated 1781 or 1782, weighing about 97 grs., for 72 to the lb.?), or still later (with heavier obv. breaks) on small crude planchets at about 108–116 grs. (for 60 to the lb.); both issues are very rare. For the var. with cross stops only on obv., see **727**.

Issues of 1788–89

MACHIN'S MILLS, Newburgh, N.Y.

Designer, Engraver, James F. Atlee. Mint, Machin's Mills. Physical Specifications, as above, except often lighter weight.

Grade range as above. Specimens overstruck on other coppers will show a jumble of letters; sometimes those of the undertype (normally 1781–82 counterfeit Irish halfpence) will obscure the Vermont legends.

GROUP I: "BASTARD HEADS"

725 1787 BRITANNIA rev.
RR 13 = KB 17-V. Grade by obv. only; rev. always weak, date not legible, possibly ground off die after it had been used with 4 different Tory copper obvs.: See **995.** 111.8–116.8 grs. = 7.24–7.57 gms.

726 1788 Round head, one obv. star.
RR 27 = KB 18-W. Crosby, Pl. V, 3. Obv. device punch of some 1788 Connecticuts. 116–126 grs. = 7.56–8.16 gms. Sometimes apparently struck in brass.

GROUP II. STANDARD HEADS

727 1788 Cross stops obv. only.
RR 24 = KB 16-S. Heavily broken obv. of **724.**

728 1788 Two obv. stars; rev. crosses. Very rare.
RR 28 = KB 21-U. Reused rev. of **724.** Always overstruck on counterfeit Irish halfpence of 1781–82. Always in low grades. Cf. 1975 EAC:435, G–VG, $2,300.

729 1788 Same obv.; 3 rev. stars. Ex. rare.
RR 33 = KB 21-Y. Legend apparently * INDE* *ETLIB with B touching shield. Always overstruck on counterfeit Irish halfpence. No specimen shows complete legends. Discovered by Howard H. Kurth, *NSM* 10/42.

730 1788 Four obv. stars. Very rare.
RR 29 = KB 22-U. Rev., crosses, as **724, 728.** Sometimes overstruck on counterfeit Irish halfpence of 1781–82. Sometimes in brass. Late strikings are on small crude planchets.

731 1788 ET LIB INDE 2 vars. Very rare.
Price for RR 18 = KB 19-X (V E R M O N wide); the other var., RR 35 = KB 20-X (VERMON close, discovered by Damon G. Douglas), is much rarer. Both always overstruck on counterfeit Irish halfpence of 1781–82; legends usually incomplete.

732 1788 Inverted C. 15–18 known.
RR 30 = KB 23-S. Discovered by Dr. Edward Maris, 1875; Crosby, p. 372; ANS {1914}, Pl. 8. Always on small crude flans, usually much of the C off flan. Obv. severely buckled. Usually in low grades. 1975 EAC:437, VF, $6,000; Roper:331, 138 grs. = 8.942 gms., VF (complete C), $13,200.

733 1788 GEORGIVS. III. REX. Rare.
RR 31 = KB 24-U. Reused rev. of **730** always weak, date seldom visible; rev. reappears on **855.** Usually on defective flans, often rough; later strikings come also on small crude

flans like next. Compare **999**. In SI is one with obv. **999**, rev. L of **719**.

734 1785 (i.e., 1789) IMMUNE COLUMBIA. Very rare. RR 1 = KB 26-Z. Always on small crude flans, about 60 to the pound, usually severely defective; almost never shows full date or legends; usually in low grades. Struck after the Machin's Mills people retrieved the 1785 die among Walter Mould's effects from the Morristown (N.J.) mint. Garrett:551, VG, $3,400, Roper:316, $1,540. For the similar IMMUNE with Tory obv., see **1000**.

UNIDENTIFIED PRIVATE MINT
(BUNGTOWN MINT?)

735 1785 VERMONTIS. Sun rises at observer's l. Ex. rare. RR 5. Date entirely within circle formed by legend. Discovered by Dr. Augustine Shurtleff before 1859; ill. Dickeson {1860}; first auctioned, Bache I:2572. Crosby, p. 181. Specimens come cast or struck; always in low grades.

iv. CONNECTICUT COPPERS
(1785–89)

Two members of the State Assembly, Joseph Hopkins and Samuel Bishop (both signers of Oct. 1777 fractional notes), joined with John Goodrich and James Hillhouse to petition the legislature for a coining franchise. Their fellow legislators authorized them on Oct. 20, 1785, to coin 2.4 million coppers, "of the standard of British halfpence," to weigh 150 grs. each. (The actual British standard was 46 to the lb. avoirdupois = 152.17 grs. each; Barnsley, *CNL* 2, (1/61), p. 9, says the intended weight was 144 grs.) The state treasury was to collect 5% of the gross amount coined, after inspection to verify weight and purity. Despite the authorized weight equating them to halfpence, the coins passed not at 24 to the shilling but at 18, and in New York at 14. Before the "Company for Coining Coppers" (the legal mint, Water St., New Haven) dissolved, June 1, 1787, the partners managed to issue 1,407,000 that passed inspection: Crosby, pp. 222–23; *CNL* 1973, p. 412; Breen {1976B}.

Statutory legends AUCTORI:CONNEC: 'By authority of Connecticut,' and INDE:ET LIB: = *Indépendance et Liberté* = 'Independence and Liberty,' were imitated on the Vermont coppers. Dies for both legal and illegal Connecticut coppers were made by Abel Buell of Killingworth—mechanical genius (convicted 20 years earlier of altering 1762 Connecticut 1s and 2s6d notes to 30s: Wroth {1958}; Newman {1976A}, p. 74)—using hubbing methods later to be adopted at the Philadelphia Mint. Except for **741**, all Connecticut coppers of 1785 came from the Company for Coining Coppers.

Those with mailed bust l. were first coined in 1786; Buell adopted this new design to distinguish them from 1786-dated counterfeits then being made in quantity by James F. Atlee. Atlee's imitations occasioned complaints in the State Assembly, May 1786: Crosby, p. 220. The rare 1785s with bust l. were made after vars. with the same obv. dies and 1786-dated revs.; using up old dies was cheaper than making new ones.

Study of die linkages, punch linkages, and planchet stocks established the mints of issue of practically all later coppers purporting to be official Connecticut issues; these results were first published in 1975 EAC and Breen {1976B}, but the present classification supersedes both. The draped-bust coins dated 1786 originate in the legal mint, as do the earliest of 1787 and the "Hercules Heads." By this time James Jarvis was a minority stockholder in the legal mint, and the design changes in some part reflect both the successive reorganizations and Buell's quality-control methods.

As of June 1, 1787, Jarvis became majority stockholder in the Company for Coining Coppers. He dissolved the firm and reorganized it as a legal mint for making FUGIO cents (then known as "Congress Coppers" or "Mind Your Business Coppers"). Though a token shipment of FUGIOs did go to the federal Board of Treasury in May 1788, the principal business of Jarvis & Co. was the illegal manufacture of 1787-dated, draped-bust Connecticut coppers. Jarvis had gone to Europe to obtain copper and use of a factory to make dies and stamp some 32,149,468 FUGIOs, but other mints would not deal with him without payments in silver or gold (paper Treasury notes were not acceptable). In his absence, his father-in-law Samuel Broome managed the New Haven mint, embezzling over 30 tons of federally owned copper earmarked for FUGIO coinage to make the Connecticuts, which passed at a higher rate though of lower weight. Jarvis had obtained the copper from Col. William Duer (head of the Board of Treasury, who had gotten Jarvis the coinage contract in exchange for a $10,000 bribe), but never paid for it. Congress voided the Jarvis & Co. franchise in Sept. 1788 and sued the firm. Abel Buell deeded his share in the enterprise to his son Benjamin, and fled to Europe until the heat was off (he had reason to fear the law, having a cropped ear and a brand mark on his forehead as souvenirs of an earlier encounter). The coins of Jarvis & Co. comprised the 1787-dated draped busts with small letters; these are punchlinked with the FUGIOs and struck on blanks of identical texture. For more on this firm see Chap. 15.

Later, representatives of Machin's Mills bought out the Jarvis & Co. equipment, and made other draped-bust coins dated 1787 and 1788, in addition to all the mailed-bust-right coins of both years and all the mailed-bust-left coins dated 1788, among others. After Benjamin Buell received the deed to his father's share in the coining business, he began making Connecticuts on his own (April 1789); these have mailed bust l. with triple leaves and paired berries in wreath, and Ms. Liberty holds a wheat ear. Design excellence contrasts with amateurish letter spacing and blunders (e.g., INDL for INDE); all are backdated 1787, in one die 1787/88! Young Buell sold his equipment to a representative of Machin's Mills within a few weeks, as we later find these same device punches used with Atlee's distinctive letter punches.

Some of the more famous type coins have still other sources. The "Horned Bust" and "Laughing Head" coins of 1787 originate with Walter Mould of the Morristown Mint, a legal coining facility for the State of New Jersey; they have the same letter punches as his New Jersey coppers. But as Mould had no franchise from the legislature to make his Connecticuts, the latter are technically circulating counterfeits (though not penalized by any law then or now). Mould also sold his equipment to representatives of Machin's Mills about July 1788, enabling him to flee to Ohio to avoid debtor's prison. The 1787 "Muttonhead," notable for a topless Ms. Liberty, is another counterfeit of the day. Still others, dated 1786, are ascribed to the "Bungtown" counterfeiters in and near the Rehoboth/North Swansea, Mass. area: Newman {1976B}, Breen {1976B}. One of these copies the 1785 "African" head (itself a local imitation); another has a BRITANNIA rev.

Some of the famous spelling errors on Connecticut coppers are the result less of illiteracy than of broken punches (AUCTOPI, ET LIR); others are from wrong choice of punches (AUCTOBI, CONNFC). The FNDE reflects force of habit: A workman fresh from lettering FUGIO dies received a Connecticut die blank and punched FU before noticing (or being reminded) that INDE was wanted instead. The two overdates are both Benjamin Buell's work; the 1787/8 earlier mentioned may represent deliberate backdating, but the 1787/1877 is a corrected blunder.

In all, over 340 vars. are known from six different mints and at least two isolated individual sources. The field is by far the most complex in all colonial coinages, and in some ways the most rewarding: Not only is there an extreme diversity of types, there is always the continuing possibility of new discoveries. Partly because the Miller book is hard to find, partly because it is hard to use without 1975 EAC, partly because the latter catalog is itself no longer easily found, fewer than half the Connecticut coppers seen in coin show bourses are attributed. This explains how even in the last couple of years alert collectors have managed to cherrypick extreme rarities and unlisted vars.

CONNECTICUT COPPERS

Designer, Abel Buell. Engravers, Mints, various. Composition, copper. Diameter, $18/16'' = 28.6$ mm (varies). Weight standard, 150 grs. $= 9.72$ gms.; observed range 37–241.4 grs. $=$ 2.4–15.64 gms. Authorizing Act, Oct. 20, 1785.

Grade range, POOR to UNC. GOOD: Devices outlined; all legends and date readable. VERY GOOD: Partial details of wreath, armor, and drapery. FINE: Some details of hair above wreath clear; over half details of armor or drapery. VERY FINE: Over half wreath details; nearly full details of armor or drapery. EXTREMELY FINE: Few isolated rubbed spots on highest points; grade by surface. EXCEPTIONS: Many vars. are struck from worn, buckled, heavily broken, or severely clashed dies, showing local weaknesses; others are on flans with severe defects developed before striking; for details see 1975 EAC.

Issues of Oct. 1785–Early 1786

All with Grapevines on Shield

I. COMPANY FOR COINING COPPERS,
Water St., New Haven

736   1785 Mailed bust r., small face, short ribbons.
20 vars. Ribbons entirely within circle of legends; colons in legends (but compare **738, 741**). The so-called ETLIR var.

has base of B open, from a broken punch; not rare. Many vars. struck at 52 to the lb. or lighter.

737   1785 Bust r., large face, long ribbons.
3 vars. Ribbons divide mail and A; colons in legends (but compare next and **741**). Crosby, Pl. V, 6. Many struck at 52 to the lb.

738   1785 Similar, periods in legends. Very rare.
Miller 1-E, allegedly a mint alteration of 6.3-G.1. ANS's weighs 130 grs. = 8.428 gms.

739   1785 Mailed bust l., no obv. colons. Rare.
2 obv. vars. (Miller 7.1-D, 7.2-D). Struck after **755** and other 1786s with that obv. 1975 EAC:27–28. Always weak in centers; always in low grades.

740   1785 Mailed bust l., colons in obv. legend. About 10 known.
Miller 8-D, rev. as last. Same comments. That ill. is one of the finest: Craige, 1975 EAC:29.

II. UNIDENTIFIED PRIVATE MINT

741 1785 "African" head. 2 vars.
Miller 4.1-F.4 (ill.), 4.2-F.6 (same letter punches, similar head, hair brushed back; 2 known? *CNL* 1/73, p. 386). 133–140 grs. = 8.61–9.07 gms., for 52 to the lb. Possibly among coins made for Maj. Eli Leavenworth? Vermont RR 3 (**711**) comes overstruck on former. *CNL* 10/79, p. 701.

Issues of 1786

I. BY JAMES F. ATLEE. Busts to r.

Designer, Engraver, James F. Atlee. Mints, New York City and possibly Rahway Mills (N.J.). Composition, copper. Diameters, 17.5–19.5/16″ = 28–30 mm. Weights, variable, as noted. Grade range and standards, as preceding.

742 1786 Large head, ETLIB INDE Rare.
Miller 1-A. Grapevines on shield, unlike most to follow. 84–124 grs. = 5.4–8.04 gms., for 60 to the lb.? Almost always shows "double chin" die crumbling; die reground, bridge of nose gone. *CNL* 1/73, p. 384. Usually in low grades. See next.

743 1786 Medium head, ETLIB INDE Very scarce.
Miller 2.1-A. ANS {1914}, Pl. 12. About 90–102 grs. = 5.8–6.61 gms., for 72 to the lb.? Usually weak in centers. Discovered by Dickeson {1859}.

744 1786 Broad shoulders, INDE. ET LIB. 6 or 7 known.
Low periods in obv. legend. Miller 2.2-D.2. Discovered by Dr. Edward Maris, 1875; Crosby, p. 372; Crosby:975. Small flans, date usually not visible; 84–96 grs. = 5.4–6.2 gms., for 80 to the lb.? Always in low grades.

745 1786 Narrow shoulders, centered obv. periods. 4–6 known.
Miller 2.1-D.3. Weight range as **743**. Usually in low grades.

746 1786 Tallest head, colons in obv. legends. Very rare.
Miller 3-D.1 (ill.), 3-D.4 (similar, B close to exergue, much rarer). 106–173 grs. = 6.87–11.2 gms., heaviest and lightest being 3-D.1's. Usually in low grades.

II. COMPANY FOR COINING COPPERS, Water St., New Haven

Mailed Busts Left

Designer, Engraver, Abel Buell. Mint, Water St., New Haven. Physical Specifications, Authorizing Act, as above.

Grade range and criteria as for 1785. In some dies, drapery details (rev.) are weak even at EXTREMELY FINE; grade by surface. Dies are completely hubbed (mechanically identical) except for punctuation, borders, some ornaments, berries in wreath, leaves in branch.

747 1786 Coarse serrated borders both sides. No obv. colons.
M. 4.1-G.
748 1786 Same, with obv. colons. 2 vars.
M. 5.1-H.1, 5.4-G (ill.; Crosby, Pl. V. 8).

749 1786 Coarse serrated obv. border, fine rev. dentils. 2 vars.
M. 5.4-N, 5.4-O.1. Price for latter; former (rev. of **756**) is very rare.
750 1786 Obv. dentils fine, rev. coarse; cross after INDE. Rare.
M. 5.8-F.

751 1786 Same, no cross after INDE. 2 vars. Rare.
   M. 5.2-H.1, 5.7-H.1.
752 1786 Fine dentils both sides. 10 vars.
   Many struck at 52 or even 60 to the lb.
753 1786 Same, no rev. colons.
   M. 5.9-B.1, 5.5-M, 5.6-M.

754 1786 Similar. Sword var., obv. colons. Very rare.
   M. 5.14-S. Sword hilt and shell guard above shield; no
   knuckle guard, ferrule, or quillon; pellet pommel. Hilt points
   at T. Always in low grades. 1975 EAC:61; LM 10/73,
   Roper:234, 138.5 grs. = 8.97 gms.

755 1786 Sword var., no obv. colons. 2 or 3 known.
   M. 4.2-S. Obv. pictured at **739**; rev. as preceding. Discovered
   by Norman Bryant. *CNL* 3/64, p. 28; 1975 EAC:39.
756 1786 "Hercules" head. Rev., fine dentils.
   M. 5.3-N. Rev. usually weak from extreme clashing. Obv.
   from usual hub but drastically altered and deepened by hand.

757 1786 "Hercules." Rev., coarse serrations. 4 or 5 known.
   M. 5.3-G; Crosby, Pl. V, 9. Rev. ill. at **748**. Cf. 1975 EAC:63.
758 1786 "Hercules." No rev. colons. 3 known.
   M. 5.3-B.2. 1) Ellsworth, Garrett:1345, EF, $3,700. 2)
   Miller:1838, Boyd estate. 3) Craige, Bowers, 1975
   EAC:62, F.

Draped Bust Left
Blank shields

759 1786 No blunt stars in obv. legend. Very rare.
   M. 6-K. Usually, 86 weak. Garrett:1349 weighed 166.7
   grs. = 10.8 gms.

760 1786 Blunt stars in obv. legend. Ex. rare.
   M. 7-K. Obv. of **801**; rev. as last, 86 weak. Crosby, Pl. V, 10.
   Roper:235, 138.5 grs. = 8.97 gms., VF, $495.

III. BUNGTOWN MINTS (North Swansea, Mass.?)

761 1786 Imitation "African" head. Ex. rare.
   M. 2.3-T. First described in Betts {1886}. 1) Ill. *CNL* 3/64.

762 1786 BRITA NNIA Ex. rare.
   M. 2.4-U. Rev. of **975**. 1) Barnsley. Discovered by A. D.
   Hoch.

Issues of 1787

I. UNLOCATED PRIVATE MINT (New York City?)

763 1787 First Muttonhead; INDE ET.LIB Ex. rare.
   M. 1.2-mm. Discovered by R. A. Vlack, *CNL* 2,2 (4/61). 1)
   Vlack, Groves:352, VG, $700 (1974). 2) N.J. pvt. coll. 3)

Mass. pvt. coll. 4) MHS II:44, "VF," $1,150 (1973). 5) Pvt. coll.

764 1787 Second Muttonhead, early issue; INDE.ET LIB. Rare.
M. 1.2-C, before regrinding. 133.7–150 grs. = 8.67–9.72 gms.

765 1787 Second Muttonhead, late issue.
Same dies, after drastic regrinding. Note topless Ms. Liberty. Lettering and date almost never legible. Believed an intentional alteration to simulate old worn coppers long accepted in circulation, and to conceal its origin: Betts {1886}; cf. Garrett:2226. 123–151 grs. = 7.97–9.78 gms. Also alias "Bradford Head," Dickeson's "Bull Head."

II. MORRISTOWN (N.J.) MINT, 1787–88

Designer, Engraver, Walter Mould and Benjamin Dudley. Mint, Morristown. Mintmark, star in base of cuirass. Physical Specifications, as before, mostly struck at 60 to the lb.
Grade range and standards, as above.

766 1787 Mailed bust r., "horseshoe" U's. Ex. rare.
M. 1.3-L. Discovered by Dr. Edward Maris. Crosby, p. 215. Same punches as Mould's coarser dies for New Jersey coppers, **937–40.** Rev. fails at E. and IN. 102.6 grs. = 6.648 gms., possibly for 68 or 70 to the lb.

767 1787 Mailed bust l. Scarce.
"Hornless Horned Bust." M. 4-L (but compare next); rev. as last, earlier state. 136.6–138 grs. = 8.85–8.94 gms., probably for 52 to the lb.

768 1787 Horned Bust.
Later states of same dies; that ill. is one of the latest. Some are on small thin flans, 105–115.5 grs. = 6.8–7.48 gms.

769 1787 Same dies, broad Jersey flan. Rare.
29–31 mm, 139–160 grs. = 9.01–10.37 gms., as on **936–45.**
770 1787 First "Laughing Head."
M. 6.1-M. Same punches as **766.** Small thin flans, 60 to the lb. Garrett:1353, UNC., $8,000. This and **771** discovered by Dickeson {1859}.

Ex J. W. Garrett: 1353. Courtesy Bowers & Ruddy Galleries, Inc.

771 1787 Second "Laughing Head."
M. 6.2-M. Same punches. 101–118 grs. = 6.55–7.65 gms.

Ex J. W. Garrett: 1354. Courtesy Bowers & Ruddy Galleries, Inc.

III. BENJAMIN BUELL, April 1789
(Backdated Issues)

Wheat Ear Revs.; Grapevines on Shields
1. Hand-Cut Prototype Obv.

772 1787 Rev. crosslets. Rare.
M. 9-D. Rev. reappears on **789.**

773 1787 Same obv. rev., blunt star ornaments. Rare.
M. 9-E. Rev. reappears on **777.** 113.5–184 grs. = 7.354–11.92 gms., probably representing batches at 60 and 40 to the lb.

774 1787/88 (!) Same obv.; IND ET LIB. Rare.
M. 9-R. Crosslets in legends. Wheat ear altered to bouquet, crosslets for flowers. Rev. of **782.** Believed intentional backdating; see introductory text.

2. Triplet Head; Large Letters, Small Dates

775 1787 Blunt stars in legends. 3 vars.
M. 11.1-E, 11.2-K, 11.3-K. Device punch has triple leaves and paired berries in wreath; worn specimens may not show berries. First obv. reappears in **866–68;** second var. is Crosby, Pl. V, 14; third is exceedingly rare, and always shows a break at (C)O.

776 1787 No punctuation or ornaments.
M. 2-B. Rev. reappears in **790.**

3. Triplet Head, Wheat Ear; Medium Letters, Small Dates

777 1787 Crosslets. Rev., blunt stars. Very rare.
M. 10-E. Rev. of **773.** 133 grs. = 8.62 gms.

778 1787 Pheons.
M. 14-H. Pheons are heraldic arrowheads. Crosby, Pl. V, 15. Only the rare earliest state shows extra pheon following T of ET. 102–116 grs. = 6.61–7.52 gms.

779 1787 Branch hand divides IN DE. Rare.
M. 5-P. Discovered by Dr. Edward Maris. Crosby, p. 216. No cinquefoils; compare next. Crosby, Garrett:1352, 127 grs. = 8.229 gms. Usually in low grades. Anthony Terranova discovered one, EF (ill.), overstruck on a counterfeit 1781 Irish halfpenny.

4. Triplet Head, Wheat Ear; Small Letters, Cinquefoils

780 1787/1877 Branch hand divides IN DE. Very scarce.
M. 12-Q. CONNEC corrected from CONNC. Obv. reused in **869.** Usually in low grades. Garrett:1356, "AU," $2,400, 127.3 grs. = 8.249 gms.

Ex J. W. Garrett: 1356. Courtesy Bowers & Ruddy Galleries, Inc.

781 1787 CONNECT Rev., INDE ET LIB
M. 15-F. Rev. reappears in **791–92.** Crosby, Pl. V, 20; Dickeson {1859}.

782 1787/1788 (!) CONNECT Rev., IND ET LIB Ex. rare.
M. 15-R. Crosby, Pl. VI, 1. Rev. of **774:** wheat ear altered to
bouquet, crosslets for flowers. Usually in low grades. Appleton, MHS, Robison:130, "About EF," $1,800; Roper:244,
109.9 grs. = 7.121 gms., VF, $825.

783 1787 CONNECT Rev., INDL ET LIB Very rare.
M. 15-S. Crosby, Pl. VI, 2. Cinquefoils at date. Always with
heavy break destroying IB.

IV. MACHIN'S MILLS, Newburgh, N.Y.
July 1787–July 1789?

See also Issues of 1788 for additional mulings.
Shields blank except as noted.

1. Mailed Busts R.

784 1787 Figure seated r., ETLIB INDE 2 known.
M. 1.4-WW. Discovered by Lyman Low ca. 1884. Ill. Betts
{1886}, fig. 1. 1) Low, Col. Walter Cutting (1886), Low 5/
23–24/1898:141, $16, S. H. & H. Chapman, Dr. Hall, Brand,
B. G. Johnson, Eric P. Newman. 2) Mrs. R. Henry Norweb.

785 1787 Small head, ETLIB INDE
M. 1.1-A; Crosby, Pl. V, 11. Always on small crude
planchets, about 104–116 grs. = 6.74–7.52 gms., like **732,**
734, and next, possibly for 64 or 66 to the lb. Like **734,** struck
between July 1788 and July 1789. Often in low grades.

786 1787 Small head, INDE ETLIB Very rare.
M. 1.1-VV. Small crude flans as last, often rough. Obv. reused with a 1788 Vermont rev. to make **855.** Always in low
grades. Discovered by Dr. Thomas Hall, Jan. 1897.

787 1787 Round head, pellet after CONNEC. 2 vars. Ex. rare.
M. 52-G.2 (2 known, ill., discovered by Ted Craige); M. 52-
G.1 (rev. of next, under 10 known). Rev. device punch of
1788, grapevines on shield. The discovery coin (ill.) is ex
Wayte Raymond, Maj. Alfred Walter, NN 60:364, Craige.

2. Mailed Bust L.; Atlee Rev. Device Punch

788 1787 Broad shoulders. Ex. rare.
M. 3-G.1; Crosby, Pl. V, 12. Grapevines on shield.

3. Mailed Bust L., Wheat Ear

789 1787 Sharp 6-pointed stars; crosslets in rev. legend.
M. 13-D. Rev. of **772.** The 8 is made from 2 small zeros;
lettering as in Atlee's 1788 mailed-bust-left coins. Made after
takeover of Benjamin Buell's equipment, April 1789. Obv. is
apparently Atlee's attempt to copy the Triplet Head. 133.7–
139.5 grs. = 8.66–9.04 gms., for 50 or 52 to the lb. Crosby,
Garrett:1351, AU, $2,700.

4. Draped Bust L.; Wheat Ear

790 1787 Four fleurons; wheat ear, no rev. punctuation. 4 or 5 known.
M. 37.6-B. Rev. of **776.** Most are in low grades. 1975 EAC:171.

791 1787 Cinquefoils and periods; wheat ear, cinquefoils. 9–12 known.
M. 32.4-F. Obv. earlier used in **874,** rev. **781.** Discovered by Dr. Thomas Hall. 1975 EAC:81 traces 8 survivors, most in low grades.

792 1787 Similar, CONNLC., large letters; same rev. About 12–15 known.
M. 50-F. Obv. shattered, earlier used in **876–77.** 1975 EAC:82; Roper:256, 124.8 grs. = 8.087 gms., VF, $396.

V. COMPANY FOR COINING COPPERS,
New Haven
Jan.–June 1, 1787

Blank Shields

1. Mailed Bust L.

793 1787 "Hercules." Very rare.
M. 7-I; Crosby, Pl. V, 13. Obv. of **754–56.** Roper:240, 129.6 grs. = 8.398 gms., VF, $1,100.

794 1787 Largest head; blunt rev. stars.
M. 8-N, 8-O. Hand-engraved obv.

795 1787 Largest head; rev. crosses. Unique?
M. 8-a.1. 1) Barnsley, *CNL* 3/64.

2. Draped Bust; Large Letters

796 1787 AUCTORI/ET LIB Blunt stars only.
At least 13 vars.
797 1787 AUCTOPI:/ETIIB. Blunt stars. 3 vars.
M. 40-kk.1, 41-ii, 42-kk.2, last Crosby, Pl. V, 23. First (rare) lacks obv. colons.

798 1787 AUCTOPI/ETLIB 2 vars. Ex. rare.
M. 40-N, 42-o. Former lacks obv. colons.
799 1787 AUCTORI/ET LIB Crosses; rev., blunt stars. Very rare.
M. 25-m.
800 1787 Same but ETIIB Rare.
M. 26-kk.1. About 145–163.1 grs. = 9.4–10.57 gms.
801 1787 Blunt stars/Crosses. Ex. rare.
M. 29.1-a.2. Obv. of **760;** larger date, T lacks l. base. 1975 EAC:120.
802 1787 Crosses both sides. 7 vars. Very scarce.
133.3–150.2 grs. = 8.638–9.733 gms.

VI. JARVIS & Co., New Haven
June 1, 1787–Sept. 1788

1. Smaller Letters; Crosses in Rev. Legend

803 1787 Crosses in obv. legend, AUCTORI: 9 vars.

804 1787 Same but AUCIORI:
M. 38-GG. For the other AUCIORI see **806.**
805 1787 Fleurons in obv. legend. 2 vars. Rare.
M. 48-g.5 (ill., Ex. rare); 53-FF.

2. Composite Ornament After INDE:

806 1787 Obv. crosses, AUCIORI:
M. 38-l.2. Compare **804.**

807 1787 No obv. ornaments. Very rare.
M. 16.3-l.2.
808 1787 Large obv. fleurons; ET-LIR: Very scarce.
M. 34-ff.1.

809 1787 Same obv.; ETLIB. 3 or 4 known.
M. 34-k.3. 1) ANS. 2) Ex Dr. Hall. 3) 1975 EAC:143.
810 1787 Small obv. fleurons/2 crosses. 4 vars.
M. 37.5-e, 37.9-e, 37.7-h.2, 37.15-h.3.

811 1787 Similar, AUCTOBI: Very rare.
M. 39.1-h.1. Compare **820–21.** Almost always in low grades.
Roper:252.

812 1787 Small obv. fleurons/Cross and scroll.
M. 37.3-i. The scroll is behind female head.

813 1787 Four small fleurons/2 scrolls. 5 vars.
Weakly struck pieces may show only 3 obv. fleurons. Not to
be confused with **814–15.**
814 1787 Similar/2 scrolls, ETLIR 3 vars.
Same comment. Not to be confused with last or next.
815 1787 Three small fleurons/2 scrolls, ETLIB Ex. rare.
M. 36-k.3. Not to be confused with weak strikings of **813–14.**
816 1787 Four obv. fleurons/Paired fleurons, ET-LIB: 2 vars.
Weak strikings are not to be confused with **817–19.**

817 1787 Same but ETLIR 3 vars.
Not to be confused with **816** or **818–19.**
818 1787 Three obv. fleurons/Paired fleurons, ETLIB Very
scarce.
M. 36-l.1. Not to be confused with weak strikings of **816–17.**
819 1787 Three obv. fleurons/Paired fleurons, ETLIR Ex.
rare.
M. 36-ff.2. Not to be confused with **816–18.**
820 1787 Four small fleurons, AUCTOBI/ETLIR Ex. rare.
M. 39.1-ff.2; Crosby, Pl. V, 22. Obv. of **811.**
821 1787 Similar, AUCTOBI/ETLIR Rare.
M. 39.2-ee.

3. "Transitional" Punctuation (Machin's Mills?)

822 1787 Four small fleurons/Blunt stars, large date. 2 vars.
Rare.
M. 37.8-LL, 37.12-LL.
823 1787 Four small fleurons/2 cinquefoils after INDE: 2 or 3
known.
M. 37.12-TT. Cinquefoils after INDE: altered from crosses,
as on **826.** 1) ANS. 2) 1975 EAC:170.
824 1787 Four cinquefoils/Composite ornament, ETLIB:
Very rare.
M. 33.16-l.2; 33.21-k.4 (ill.).

825 1787 Same but ETLIR 3 or 4 known.
M. 33.13-ff.1. Rev. of **808.** 1975 EAC:167.

FOUR OBV. CINQUEFOILS HENCEFORTH
(Unless Otherwise Noted)

4. Two Cinquefoils After INDE:

826 1787 Three rev. cinquefoils altered from crosses. Ex. rare.
M. 33.21-EE, 33.30-EE, 33.30-SS, 33.36-SS, 33.47-TT. Some

of these (ill.) also have 2 obv. cinquefoils altered from crosses. 1975 EAC:174–78. Both features are hard to see in the usual low grades.

827   1787 Hyphen between ET-LIB: 2 vars.
   M. 33-9-s.2; 33.39-s.1. Normal cinquefoils henceforth unless noted.

828   1787 No hyphen in ETLIB: 5 vars.

829   1787 No hyphen in ETLIR: 5 vars.
830   1787 No cinquefoil after ETLIB: 6 vars.

831   1787 No cinquefoil after AUCTORI: or ETLIB: 2 vars.
832   1787 No cinquefoil after AUCTORI: or ETLIR:
   M. 31.1-gg.1.

5. Three Cinquefoils After INDE:

"Standard type" = colons after AUCTORI: CONNEC: INDE: ETLIB: with cinquefoils before and after all words. **833–40** deviate only in the named features, **841–47** only in blundered or corrected letters.

833   1787 First obv. cinquefoil missing; ETLIR:
   M. 30-hh.1. Obv. of **848**.
834   1787 Second obv. cinquefoil missing. Ex. rare.
   M. 44-Z.10.
835   1787 Second obv. and last rev. cinquefoils missing. 2 vars.
   M. 44-W.4, 44-W.5.

836   1787 Only last rev. cinquefoil missing. Very scarce. 9 vars.

837   1787 First rev. cinquefoil missing. 3 vars. Very rare.
   M. 33.19-q, 33.43-q, 33.4-q. INDE: corrected from INDN.

838   1787 Cinquefoil before ETLIB: missing.
   M. 33.6-KK. Doubled obv. die: 3 ribbon ends.
839   1787 AUCTORI/O: No colon after INDE Unique?
   M. 33.22-II. Description from Miller; F. C. C. Boyd estate.
840   1787 Extra cinquefoil before CONNEC: Ex. rare.
   M. 49-Z.1. Rev. of **843**, INDE: corrected from INDN: 1) Barnsley.   2) Buckley (ill.).   3) Reported. Discovered by Frederick Canfield. A new var., "M.49.2-Z.26," has cinquefoils higher above head; normal E. Discovered by Steve Tannenbaum, April 1986.

841   1787 CONNFC: with colons. Very scarce.
   M. 33.37-Z.9. Compare **843**.

842   1787 ETLIR: 3 vars. Rare.
843   1787 INDE:/INDN: 4 obv. vars.
   Rev. of **840**. Late obv. states of 33.19-Z.1 (not rare) make this resemble CONNFC:; not to be confused with **841**.
844   1787 INDE:/IDDE: 3 vars. Ex. rare.
   M. 33.12-Z.21, 33.2-Z.21, 33.2-Z.22.
845   1787 ETLIB:/ETLIR: 15 vars.
   Compare next.

846 1787 "B = R + L." Very rare.
  M. 33.28-Z.23. The B was made by punching an L and an R.

847 1787 Standard type. At least 29 vars.

6. Transitional Punctuations

848 1787 Colons; rev. periods. Rare.
  M. 30-X.1. Obv. of **833**, first cinquefoil missing.
849 1787 Periods; rev. colons. 2 vars. Ex. rare.
  M. 32.4-Z.3, 32.4-Z.20. Obv. of **791, 874**. Survivors are in too low grade to determine from die state if struck at Machin's Mills.

7. Periods in Legends

850 1787 CONNFC. Dashes in rev. legend.
  M. 43.1-Y. Crosby, Pl. V, 18.

Ex J. W. Garrett: 1368. Courtesy Bowers & Ruddy Galleries, Inc.

851 1787 CONNFC. No dashes. Very rare.
  M. 43.2-X.4. Late reground state of a CONNEC. die. Discovered by Canfield, 1920. Cf. 1975 EAC:276.

852 1787 CONNEC. 8 vars.
853 1787 Small obv. letters, FNDE.
  M. 32.5-aa. IN of INDE corrected from FU; the letterer was evidently fresh from doing FUGIO obvs. Compare next.

854 1787 Large obv. letters, FNDE. Very rare.
  M. 32.8-aa. Same rev.; obv. earlier used on **875**. Always in low grades, unevenly struck; that ill. is possibly finest known.

Issues Dated 1788

I. MACHIN'S MILLS, Newburgh, N.Y.

1. Mailed Bust R.; Vermont Rev.

855 1788 Small head/Crosses, British shield. 16–20 known.
  M. 1-I; KB (VT.) 25-U; Crosby, Pl. V, 24. Obv. of **785–86**, advanced die failure between TOR and neck; rev. of **724, 728, 730, 733**. Always on small crude flans, 80.9–107.6 grs. = 5.24–6.972 gms. Usually in low grades. Struck after July 1788, probably June–July 1789. Craige, 1975 EAC:287, F, $2,200.

2. Mailed Bust R.; Jarvis & Co. Rev.

856 1788 "Boxer" head/Cinquefoils. 16–20 known.
  M. 6-H. Obv., 6-pointed stars. B made from R and L punches. Usually in low grades. Struck after takeover of Jarvis & Co. equipment, Sept. 1788. Cf. 1975 EAC:294. See introductory text.

3. Mailed Bust R.; Atlee Rev., Grapevines on Shield

857 1788 5-pointed obv. stars.
  M. 2-D. Rev. of **871, 999**. Often on defective planchets. Obv. often shows heavy breaks.

858 1788 Round head, quatrefoils before A and after B. 2 vars. Very rare.
M. 3-B.1, 3-B.2. Almost always overstruck on CONSTEL-LATIO NOVA coppers, **1114.**

859 1788 Round head, quatrefoils after legends. 3 vars. Very rare.
M. 5-B.2, 4.1-B.1 (Crosby, Pl. V, 25), 4.1-B.2. Same comment. 109.6–114.1 grs. = 7.1–7.39 gms., for 60 to the lb. Undertype usually **1114.**

860 1788 Round head, quatrefoil after C only; regular branch. Very rare.
M. 4.1-K. Compare next. Sometimes overstruck on **1114** as last 2.

4. Mailed Bust R.; Wheat Ear
Nos. **861–70** Struck April–July 1789

861 1788 Quatrefoil after C; wheat ear. 6–8 known.
M. 4.2-R. Always overstruck on CONSTELLATIO NOVA coppers, most often **1114.** Always in low grades. 1975 EAC:293. See introductory text.

5. Mailed Bust L., Triplet Head; Jarvis Rev.

862 1788 Large letters, CONNLC. Very rare.
M. 13-A.1. Benjamin Buell head; blank shield. In date 8's

made from S's, from a font for Tory halfpence letters. Struck at 60 to the lb.

6. Mailed Bust L., Triplet Head; Wheat Ear

863 1788 Three obv. stars. 2 vars.
M. 11-G (ill.), 10-C (very rare: no star before A). Sharp 6-pointed stars. Latter usually overstruck on CONSTELLATIO NOVA coppers **(1114).**

864 1788 Four obv. stars; no quatrefoil. 2 vars.
M. 12.2-C (ill.), 12.1-F.1. Same stars. Former usually overstruck on **1114** as preceding. Both struck at 60 to the lb.

865 1788 Four obv. stars; quatrefoil after B. 2 vars.
M. 12.2-E, 12.1-E.

866 1788 Large letters, blunt stars; quatrefoil after B. Very rare.
M. 7-E. Obv. is a die of **775.** Struck at 60 to the lb.

867 1788 Same obv.; ET before face, star after B. 15–20 known.
M. 7-F.2. Struck at 60 to the lb. Almost always in low grades. Garrett:1376, "AU," $2,100. Discovered by Dr. Thomas Hall, 1895.

Ex J. W. Garrett: 1376. Courtesy Bowers & Ruddy Galleries, Inc.

7. Mailed Bust L., Triplet Head; Atlee Rev.

868 1788 Same obv. ETLIB behind head. Ex. rare.
M. 7-K. Obv. of **866,** rev. of next. Always in low grades. 1975 EAC:306.
869 1788 Cinquefoils; ET * LIB * behind head. Ex. rare.
M. 8-K. Obv. of **780.** Always in low grades. 1975 EAC:307.

8. Mailed Bust L., Atlee Obv.; Wheat Ear

870 1788 One obv. star; quatrefoil after B. Very rare.
M. 9-E. Rev. of **865–66.**

9. Draped Bust L.; Atlee Rev.

Struck After Sept. 1788

871 1788 Cinquefoils; sharp 6-pointed stars.
M. 16.1-D; ANS {1914}, Pl. 12. Usually with heavy breaks at foot. Struck at 60 to the lb. Rev. of **857, 999.**

II. JARVIS & CO., New Haven (?)

1. Draped Bust; ET L. of Face

872 1788 No obv. periods. 3 vars. Rare.
M. 14.1-L.2, 14.1-S, 14.2-A.2.

873 1788 Period only after C. 2 vars. Rare.
M. 15.1-L.1 (ill.), 15.2-P. See note to next.

874 1788 Two obv. periods; correct legends. 3 vars. Very rare.
M. 16.4-A.2, 16.4-L.2, 16.7-P. First 2 from obv. of **791, 849.** Weakly struck specimens may be mistaken for **873.**
875 1788 Same but INDL. Very rare.
M. 16.2-O; Crosby, Pl. V, 27. Obv. later used for **854.** 1975 EAC:314–15; Roper:264, 135.7 grs. = 8.793 gms., VF, $418.

876 1788 CONNLC./INDL. Very rare.
M. 17-O. Same rev. Obv. later reused for **792.** Discovered by W. W. Hays.
877 1788 CONNLC./INDE. Ex. rare.
M. 17-Q. Same obv. 1975 EAC:323; Roper:266, 150 grs. = 9.72 gms.

2. Draped Bust; ETLIB. Behind Head

878 1788 IN DE., 178 8.

M. 16.3-N. Berry punches mark lips. See next.

879 1788 Same, reground dies, overstruck on Massachusetts cent. 6–8 known.

All seen to date are on **968,** early recognized as counterfeit and bought up cheaply.

880 1788 INDE. 3 vars.

M.16.1-H, 16.5-H, 16.6-H. Rev. of **856.** Struck at Machin's Mills. Sometimes very thin: ANS has one weighing only 37 grs. = 2.4 gms.

v. NEW JERSEY COPPERS
(1786–89)

The prime promoter of this coinage was the young Revolutionary War hero, Gen. Matthias Ogden, then a member of the State Assembly. When the three English émigrés, Thomas Goadsby, Albion Cox, and Walter Mould, turned up early in 1786 with proposals to manufacture copper coins for the State of New Jersey, Ogden succumbed to the common delusion that coining coppers could make coin manufacturers rich. Not only did Ogden exert his political influence in the Assembly to insure passage of a bill awarding the would-be coiners a contract, he also—in a stupendous gamble—gave his own profitable franchise (carrying mail between New York and Philadelphia) to his fellow Assemblyman Daniel Marsh in exchange for Marsh's vote for the coinage bill, he arranged that the coiners should lease Marsh's gristmill for their mint site, and he even became their bondholder and their guarantor of payment to Marsh in the event of default.

Accordingly, on June 1, 1786, the "Act for Establishing a Coinage of Copper in This State" became law. It authorized the three coiners to make 3 million coppers to pass current at 15 to the New Jersey shilling. The coins had to weigh 150 grs. each (that being the legislature's idea of the proper weight of Tower Mint halfpence), and the coiners had to complete the project no later than June 1, 1788. For this privilege they had to pay 10% of their output in quarterly installments to State Treasurer James Mott: 300,000 coppers or the equivalent in current New Jersey paper currency. Each coiner had to deposit a bond with at least two sureties, binding them to faithful performance of their duties.

Their mint site, known as Rahway Mills, was on the east bank of the Rahway River, at what is now St. George's Ave. at School St., next to present-day Koos Bros. Department Store, in what is now Rahway but was then still part of Elizabeth Town. They executed the lease (at £130 per year) on June 22, 1786. The mint site is marked by a plaque, replacing the original one (ill. *NUM* 11/54, p. 1179) which had been unveiled April 20, 1954, by Mrs. Sophia Meyner, mother of the then Gov. Robert B. Meyner.

As the authorizing act specified such "marks and inscriptions" as the State Supreme Court should direct, Walter Mould,

a pupil of the Wyons at Birmingham, brought over sample impressions from various dies (some Wyon's, some his own) for the Justices to select. That chosen is heraldically described as "nag's head sinister on torse, plough below, legend NOVA CAESAREA, date in exergue; reverse, arms, argent, six pales gules, a chief azure, motto E PLURIBUS UNUM." Though the obv. clearly refers to New Jersey, deriving from the crest on the state arms found on paper currency of 1781, 1784, and 1786, the rev. does not: It commemorates the union of the Original 13, and was originally intended for Mould's proposal to make coppers for the Confederation (rejected Aug. 18, 1785).

Before coinage could begin, Goadsby and Cox quarreled with Mould, alleging that he had been uncooperative in obtaining or constructing machinery, and that he had failed to find sureties for his bond. They then petitioned the state legislature Nov. 17, 1786, to permit them to coin their 2 million coppers independently of Mould's million; this was granted Nov. 22. Coinage thereafter began at Rahway Mills, at first using the services of Benjamin Dudley as diesinker (who may have traveled a circuit performing such work), later those of James F. Atlee, until about June 1, 1787. They sent off their first quarterly tithe to Treasurer Mott on March 16, 1787.

In the meantime, Mould filed his surety bond on Jan. 18, 1787 (only three days before the deadline), and moved to Morris County on or before April 1. He leased the John Cleve Symmes house "Solitude," later known as Holloway House, as mint site, at least partly because the property contained a copper mine. The site is about two miles west of Morristown, on the Sussex Turnpike; it has been for some years jointly occupied by the Sisters of the Good Shepherd and the Rabbinical College of New Jersey. During part of the time, Mould also used Dudley's diesinking services. All the coins unearthed in the garden and from behind the fireplace are of varieties Douglas had independently attributed to this mint: Sipsey {1964}; Douglas {1951}.

Both Rahway Mills and Mould's mint were plagued by lawsuits, among others that of Benjamin Dudley, alleging nonpayment of agreed-on sums for services rendered (most likely diemaking). Cox went to debtor's prison, from which he managed to escape and board ship for England; only with the utmost difficulty could Thomas Pinckney (U.S. minister to Great Britain) persuade him in 1792 to return as Assayer of the Philadelphia Mint. (This accounts for the lack of tithes from Rahway Mills between April 6 and Oct. 4, 1787.) Goadsby seized the Rahway mint equipment and began coining elsewhere on his own (the Horse Head Left coppers), so that Matthias Ogden had to pay the entire rent of the empty Rahway Mills. Ogden obtained a court order recovering the copper ingots, blanks, rollers, dies, punches, coin press, etc., and resumed operations, at first alone, later with the aid of Gilbert Rindell, in an attempt to recover his rent payments. Ogden paid his tithes to Treasurer Mott in the name of "Goadsby & Cox" except for the final one, which Rindell delivered July 3, 1788: Mott {1783–99}. Goadsby, in the meantime, fled to Vermont.

After the Rahway Mills franchise expired in June 1788, Ogden moved his equipment to his family home (the Old Armstrong House, on the then Water St. in Elizabeth Town), at what is now 941–959 Elizabeth Ave., and began making overstrikes on any old coppers which had passed at lower rates than 15 to the shilling. Some of these overstrikes used old leftover 1786 or 1787 dies from the Rahway Mills operation; others (the Plaited Manes group) used newly made dies, all backdated 1787. The crudity of these coins came to the attention of the legislature, but they could neither stop the operation nor outlaw the coins.

In the meantime, Mould realized that he could remain solvent only by devising a sideline which would yield profit without need of paying any tithes to the State Treasurer. This sideline was the manufacture of imitation Connecticut coppers: the two "Laughing Heads," the Horned Bust, and a bust-right coin with the same rev. **(766–71).** When Dudley sued Mould, the latter sold a part interest in his franchise to John Bailey, of New York City; Bailey, between Jan. and April 15, 1788, struck the "Running Horse" Jersey coppers. These are punchlinked to the Brasher Doubloons, NOVA EBORACS, and EXCELSIORs. Mould prepared to leave the state to avoid following Cox into debtor's prison. When Dudley's lawsuit and Mould's insolvency came to Ogden's attention, Ogden (as their bondholder) went to the Court of Chancery and petitioned for a writ of *ne exeat statum*—which order, forbidding Mould to leave the state, was granted July 19, 1788. Before process servers could reach Mould, he contacted representatives of Machin's Mills, sold them his equipment, and fled to Ohio, where he died in 1789. This explains how the Machin's Mills people came to use Mould's old IMMUNE COLUMBIA die in mulings with Vermont and Tory Copper obvs. **(734, 1000).** Mould's bondholders shipped his final tithe to Treasurer Mott on Jan. 29, 1789, indicating that he had coined his full million coppers; the actual number was probably larger.

The "Serpent Head" **(914),** a thin brassy imitation of one of the regular Rahway Mills Curved Beam vars. **(909),** is thought to be the var. which flooded the New York City area around the beginning of March 1787: Crosby, p. 291. It has been dubiously attributed to one Hatfield, operating out of either his Staten Island hideaway or a barn near Elizabeth Town. The ruder counterfeits **956–58** may have been by several makers, but some of them probably came from the "Bungtown Mints" in and near North Swansea, Mass.

After taking over the equipment of Jarvis & Co., about Sept. 1788, the Machin's Mills people began issuing Jersey coppers. These are the familiar and plentiful Camel Heads. All are overstrikes on other coins. The three obv. dies have some of the same larger letter punches as the last Draped Bust Connecticuts dated 1788, many of which are known to have been made in Machin's Mills. Collectors have in recent decades begun paying attention to the undertypes of these coins; rare undertypes have commanded enormous premiums. We illustrate a famous one (a GEORGE CLINTON) from the F. C. C. Boyd estate. Collectors are urged to attempt to decipher undertypes both on the Camel Heads and on the Plaited Manes; possibilities always exist of new discoveries.

NEW JERSEY COPPERS

Designer, Wyon. Engravers, Mints, various. Composition, copper. Weight standard, 150 grs. = 9.75 gms. Diameter, 18/16″ = about 29 mm (varies). Authorizing Act, June 1, 1786.

Grade range, POOR to UNC. GOOD: Outlines of devices complete, all letters and date legible. VERY GOOD: Partial internal details of stripes. FINE: At least half details of stripes and mane. VERY FINE: Over half details of azure; usually, number of twists in torse (below head) countable, some inner mane details present. Above VF, grade by surface. EXCEPTIONS: On overstrikes, undertype details often interfere with legibility; Plaited Manes are often multiple-struck. Many other vars. are unevenly struck from buckled or broken dies, unequally weakening details.

I. PROTOTYPES (Spring 1786):
Wyon's Mint, Birmingham

881 1786 Date below beam; stop after A. Ex. rare.
Maris 8-F. 1) Bushnell, Parmelee, Ten Eyck, Newcomer, Ellsworth, Garrett:1393, EF, $52,000, 116.4 grs. = 7.543 gms. 2) English museum, Roper:299, 125.8 grs. = 8.152

gms., VF+, $41,800, enl. photo. 3) James Goudge, 127.5 grs. = 8.262 gms.

882 1786 Date below beam; no stop after A 2 vars. Ex. rare.
Crosby, Pl. VI, 17; Maris 7-E (ill.), 4 or 5 known; 7-C (unique), rev. as next. Struck at 60 to the lb. Parmelee, Newcomer, Green, Picker:181, EF. $57,750.

883 1786 Coulterless, "micro" date; extra wide legend. 3 known.
"Maris 8½-C." 1) Garrett:1394, 146.1 grs. = 9.467 gms., F, rough, $1,700. 2) Pvt. coll., ex Dorothy Kraisman. 3) Pvt. coll., ex Picker. Rev. reused by Mould at Morristown: See **936.**

II. RAHWAY MILLS
(Nov. 1786–late 1787):
Goadsby & Cox

Issues of 1786 [all kinds 109,890+]

1. 1786 Coulterless

884 1786 Wide shield. 4 vars. Rare.
Maris 9-G, 11½-G, 11-G (Crosby, Pl. VI, 18; MHS I:92, unique, ill.), and 12-G (obv. ill. at **886**); price for 12-G, others Ex. rare. 135.2–148.7 grs. = 8.76–9.64 gms.

885 1786 Wide shield, stop after A. 10–12 known.
Maris 10-G. Discovery coin, Maris, Garrett:1395, VF–EF, $6,000. 133.7–148.9 grs. = 8.664–9.649 gms.

886 1786 Narrow shield. 3 vars. Very rare.
Maris 11-H, 11-hh, 12-I (ill.). 151–167.3 grs. = 9.784–10.84 gms.

887 1786 Narrow shield, stop after A. 3 vars. Ex. rare.
Maris 10-gg (ill.), 10-h, 22-P. 126 grs. = 8.16 gms.

2. 1786 with Coulter; Curved Beam

888 1786 Small date. Narrow shield. 7 vars.
141–173.7 grs. = 9.14–11.26 gms.

889 1786 Small date, stop after A., narrow shield. Ex. rare.
"Maris 21½-R." 1) Ryder, Boyd estate, discovered in 1903, ill. ANS {1914}, Pl. 9. 2) Picker coll., ill., 152.4 grs., $5,280.

890 1786 Small date, widest shield. 3 vars.
Maris 24-M, 19-M (ill.), 20-N (chief point to S). 141.4–158.5 grs. = 9.16–10.27 gms. Price for second or third; first Ex. rare: *CNL* 12/69, p. 42.

891 1786 "Bridle," widest shield. 2 vars.
Maris 18-M (ill.), 18-N. Price for former. Early impressions without the "bridle" will price as **890.** 135.8–156 grs. = 8.8–10.11 gms.

892 1786 "Bridle," medium shield. Very rare. 2 vars.
Maris 18-J (ill.), 18-L (Ex. rare, rev. of **899**). Price for 18-J. 133.3–150 grs. = 8.638–9.72 gms.

893 1786 Large date, widest shield. 2 vars.
Maris 21-N, 21-O (ill.). Price for 21-N (chief point to l. side of S). 136–170.2 grs. = 8.81–11.03 gms.

894 1786 Large date, narrow shield. 2 vars. Scarce.
Maris 21-R (ill., rare); 21-P (Crosby, fig. 41; ANS {1914}, Pl. 9). Price for latter. 141–148.5 grs. = 9.14–9.62 gms.

3. 1786 Straight Beam

895 1786 Small date and shield, no sprigs. Very rare.
Maris 17-K. Price for specimens without any trace of over-striking or die failure. For ill. (later state) see **923;** for this obv. with other revs., **924–25.**

896 1786 Large date and shield. 10 vars.
137.4–163.2 grs. = 8.903–10.58 gms.

897 1786 Large date, borderless shield. Very scarce.
Maris 16-S (unique), 25-S (ill.), 26-S. 136.8–162.3 grs. =
8.864–10.52 gms. Price for 25-S.

Issues of 1787 [all kinds 1,351,130+]

4. 1787 Straight Beam

For Broad flans and/or "Horseshoe" U's, see MORRIS-
TOWN MINT.
For Overstrikes, see ELIZABETH TOWN MINT.

898 1787 Knobless handles. 2 vars.
M. 52-i, 33-U. 137–155.2 grs. = 8.88–10.06 gms. See next.

899 1787 Square grips; medium shield.
M. 28-L. Grips at handle ends are often weak. 133.2 grs. =
8.631 gms. See next.

900 1787 Square grips; borderless shield.
M. 28-S; Crosby, Pl. VI, 21. Rev. of **897**. 145.7 grs. = 9.44
gms.
901 1787 Round knobs, blundered A; sprigs. Ex. rare.
"Maris 27-j." CAESAREA over CAESRREA. Obv. of **902**;
rev. of **908**. Discovered by Lorin G. Parmelee in the 1880s.
902 1787 Round knobs, blundered A; borderless shield. Very
scarce.
Maris 27-S. 160.1 grs. = 10.37 gms.

903 1787 Round knobs; second U over S. Very scarce.
Maris 55-m. Discovered in 1875: Crosby, p. 372. 143.8–158.4
grs. = 9.318–10.26 gms.

904 1787 Round knobs; PLURIRUS Very rare.
Maris 55-l. B open at base (broken punch). 146.8–148.1
grs. = 9.512–9.597 gms. Usually in low grades. Roper:308,
VG, $264.

905 1787 Round knobs; normal legends. 3 vars.
Maris 29-L, 30-L, 32-T (ill.). 146.5–156.6 grs. = 9.493–10.14
gms. Price for var. ill.

906 1787 Knobless, straight beam bent up at end; 13 stripes.
M. 31-L, 45-d, 45-e, 44-d, 43-d, 43-Y. 143.1–162.4 grs. =
9.273–10.52 gms.

907 1787 Knobless, straight beam bent up at end; 14 stripes.
Ex. rare.
M. 44-c. Rev. of **911–13**. Discovered by M. W. Dickeson
before 1859. Usually in low grades. 7 vertically shaded stripes
(normally 6).

5. 1787 Curved Beam

For overstrikes, see ELIZABETH TOWN and MACHIN'S
MILLS.
For broad flans and/or Horseshoe U's, see MORRISTOWN
MINT.
For the "Serpent Head," see **914**.

For Chief Point Low, see **917–22.**
For straight beam bent up at end, see **906–7.**

908 1787 Small date, stop after A.; sprigs below shield.
Maris 53-j. Dies by Benjamin Dudley; punchlinked with Morristown issues **941–44.** This var. occasioned Dudley's lawsuit against Goadsby & Cox.

909 1787 Widest obv. legend.
Maris 46-e. Imitated by **914.** Massive obv. die failures usually weaken details. Rare without clash marks from shield. 151.6 grs. = 9.824 gms.

910 1787 Close legend; 13 stripes. 7 vars.
Includes coins with smallest head. 138.2–176.5 grs. = 8.96–11.44 gms. One (M.68-w) seen weighing 203 grs. = 13.2 gms.

911 1787 Large head; 14 stripes. Very rare.
Maris 41-c. 7 vertically shaded stripes (normally 6): rev. of **907.** Usually in low grades. 150–155.2 grs. = 9.72–10.06 gms. See next.

912 1787/77 Large head; 14 stripes. Very rare.
Maris 42-c. Same rev. Corrected blunder. MHS I:99, vg, $550 (1970), is probably finest; 152.1 grs. = 9.856 gms.

913 1787 Smallest head; 14 stripes.
Maris 38-c. 152.9 grs. = 9.908 gms.

III. UNCERTAIN PRIVATE MINT
(Hatfield's, Staten Island?)

914 1787 "Serpent head."
Maris 54-k; Crosby, Pl. VI, 23. Imitation of **909,** believed the var. flooding the New York City area in Feb.–March 1787. Most are on thin flans, 110–119.7 grs. = 7.12–7.756 gms.; few heavier, 126.1–146 grs. = 8.171–9.46 gms. 2 worn examples seen in brass.

IV. GOADSBY ISSUE (Jan.–Feb. 1788)

915 1788 Head 1.; small shield, close legend. 2 vars. Very scarce.
Maris 49-f (larger head, rarer); 50-f (ill.). Plough design after that on 1781 and 1785 Pennsylvania notes: Newman {1976A}, pp. 310, 314. Usually in low grades; defective flans, weak dates often off flan. Finest known, Ellsworth, Garrett: 1448, unc., $26,000. 138.2–152.2 grs. = 8.995–9.86 gms.

916 1788 Head 1.; large shield, wide legend. Rare.
Maris 51-g; Crosby, Pl. VI, 27. Obv. S corrected from C. 147.3–166.1 grs. = 9.55–10.77 gms. Finest is probably Newcomer, Garrett:1449, ef, $2,100. Usually in low grades.

V. MATTHIAS OGDEN ISSUES (Feb.–June 1788)

All backdated 1787. [538,980+]

917 1787 Chief point low, large shield.
Maris 48-g, Rev. of **916** but struck later; often with break across shield. Many struck at 52 to the lb., others heavier: about 130–160.1 grs. = 8.4–10.38 gms. Forms majority of Ogden's output. Often in VF–EF.

918 1787 Same obv. Chief point low, small shield. Scarce.
Maris 48-f. Rev. of **915** but struck later; central rev. failure. 142.5–152.3 grs. = 9.24–9.869 gms.

919 1787 "Goiter"; chief point low, small shield. Rare.
Maris 37-f. The "goiter" is a die defect. 165.85 grs. = 10.75 gms.

920 1787 "Goiter"; old Rahway shield. 2 vars. Rare.
Maris 37-J (ill.), 37-Y. 138.6–167.5 grs. = 8.981–10.86 gms.

921 1787 "Goiter"; crude shield, pales of 3. Three or 4 known.
Maris 37-X. Blunt base and chief points. Die failure weakens rev. 156.7 grs. = 10.16 gms. Rev. copied from **944**. Maris, Garrett, Picker:211, $1,760.

922 1787 No goiter; crude shield, pales of 3. Two known.
Maris 48-X. Obv. of **917**. Discovered by Jacob N. Spiro about 1950.

VI. ELIZABETH TOWN MINT (July 1788–1789): Ogden & Rindell

1. Overstrikes, Backdated 1786 or 1787

Weights are those of undertypes, usually 60 to the lb.

923 1786 Small date, straight beam; small shield without sprigs.
Maris 17-K. Dies of **895**.

924 1786 Small date, straight beam; large shield.
Maris 17-J. Rev. of **892**.

925 1786 Small date, straight beam; small shield with sprigs.
Maris 17-b. The 5-pointed stars on rev. recur in Plaited Mane vars. Often with advanced die failures.

926 1787 Smallest head; small shield with sprigs. Ex. rare.
Maris 38-b. Same rev. Obv. of **913**. Always in low grades.

927 1787 Huge conical ears, solid torse. 6 known.
Maris 36-J. Rev. of **892**. Obv. punchlinked with **988**. Severe die rust below CAESAREA. Finest known, Garrett:1432, "EF," $9,000.

2. "1787" Plaited Manes

928   1787 Deer head; large shield.
Maris 34-J.

929   1787 Deer head; small shield, sprigs, 5-pointed stars. Very rare.
Maris 34-V, 40-b (ill.). Latter discovered by M. W. Dickeson.

930   1787/1887 Similar; large shield. Very rare.
Maris 35-J. Always in low grades. Upper loop of 8 clearly visible below crossbar of first 7.

931   1787/1887 Sprigs, 6-pointed stars. Ex. rare.
Maris 35-W.   1) Crosby, Parmelee, Mills, Canfield, NJHS, ill.   2) Brand estate.

932   1787 Quatrefoil before N. 6–8 known.
Maris 70-x. Heavy break obliterates *E * P. Crudely struck. Always in low grades. Discovery coin, Maris, Garrett:1475, "VG," $4,300.

933   1787 Quatrefoil after A. Ex. rare.
Maris 71-y. Heavy die failure at CAESARE affecting one ear and part of head. No specimen shows entire legends. Crudely struck. Always in low grades. Discovery coin, Maris, Garrett:1476, "VG," $3,000.

934   1787 Two 5-pointed obv. stars. Rare.
Maris 72-z; Crosby, Pl. VI, 24. Less crude than last 2.

935   1787 Obv. star only after A. Rare.
Maris 73-aa. Die failure destroys NOVA. Always crudely struck. Many different undertypes including foreign coins.

VII. MORRISTOWN MINT (April 1787–July 1788): Walter Mould

All but the last 1788's are on broad flans, 30–31 mm.
1787 [All kinds 830,000+]

1. 1787 Curved Beams, Coarse Dies by Mould

936   1787 Hybrid; extra wide legend. Very scarce.
Maris 6-C; Crosby, Pl. VII, 19. Obv. of **937** by Mould; rev. of **883** by Wyon. Usually in low grades. 132.4–147 grs. = 8.579–9.98 gms.

937   1787 PLURIBUS, "horseshoe" U's.
Maris 6-D; Crosby, Pl. VII, 20. Rev. is Mould's crude copy of **936;** always with some stage of die break, often severely

rusted. 149.8–158.8 grs. = 9.707–10.29 gms. Sometimes on smaller flans.

938 1787 PLURIBS* 2 vars.
Maris 60-p (ill.), 61-p (Crosby, Pl. VI, 22; lump on mane). Price for former. 145.6–164.8 grs. = 9.435–10.68 gms.

2. 1787 Straight Beam, Coarse Dies by Mould

939 1787 Tall narrow shield. Rare.
Maris 59-o. Planchets normally defective in centers. 144.2–148.5 grs. = 9.344–9.623 gms.

940 1787 Wide shield. 2 vars.
Maris 64-t (ill.), 64-u (rare, rev. of **946**). Planchets normally defective. The 64-t sometimes comes on narrow flans (29 mm). 149.6–171 grs. = 9.7–11.08 gms.

3. 1787 Curved Beams, Fine Dies by Dudley

Sprigs below shield are Dudley's "signature."

941 1787 Stop after A.; medium shield.
Maris 62-q. 147.1–148.9 grs. = 9.532–9.649 gms.

942 1787 Stop after A.; very tall shield. Unique?
"Maris 62-r." Obv. of **941**, rev. of **944**. Discovered by Richard August in 1974.

943 1787 No stop after A; medium shield. 2 vars.
Maris 63-q, 63-s (ill.). 144.4–149.6 grs. = 9.357–9.694 gms.

944 1787 No stop after A; very tall shield. Rare.
Maris 63-r. Often weak on stripes. 138.6–158.8 grs. = 8.981–10.29 gms.

1788 [All kinds 170,000+]

4. 1788 Coarse Wide Dies

945 1788 Hybrid; stop after A. 2 known.
"Maris 64½-r." Obv. by Mould, rev. of **944**. Discovered by Lyman Haines Low in the 1920s. 1) Low, W. W. C. Wilson, Newcomer, Ellsworth, Garrett:1468, "EF," $11,000 (clipped planchet). 2) Canfield, N.J. Historical Society.

5. 1788 Coarse Narrow Dies by Mould

946 1788 No obv. stars; wide shield.
Maris 65-u. Planchets normally defective. 150.1 grs. = 9.726 gms.

947 1788 Braided mane; wide shield. Ex. rare.
Maris 66-u. Obv. as **948**, rev. as **946**. 1) Maris, Garrett, Picker:241, $1,980 (worn), 136.5 grs. = 8.85 gms. 2) Newcomer, Garrett:1470, "VF," $3,400. 3) Ross, Ryder, Boyd estate. 4) Reported. Obv. copied from **944**.

948 1788 Braided mane; sprigs. Ex. rare.
Maris 66-v; ANS {1914}, Pl. 9. 107.7–155.5 grs. = 6.979–10.08 gms. Usually in low grades. S (6/75), Robison, Roper:312, F, $715.

949 1788 Stars, brushed mane; sprigs.
Maris 67-v. Rev. sharper than obv. 139.6–151.9 grs. = 9.046–9.843 gms.

VIII. BAILEY'S MINT, New York City
(Jan.–April 15, 1788): John Bailey

Mintmark: Running Horse in Rev. Legend

950 1788 Star and quatrefoil; horse follows M. Ex. rare.
Maris 76-cc. 1) Maris, Garrett:1482, 128.6 grs. = 8.34 gms., "VF," $15,000. 2) Jacob N. Spiro, pvt. coll. 3) Ex Anthony Terranova. 4) Dr. Hall, Brand, Boyd estate (ill.).

951 1788 Similar; horse begins legend. Very rare.
Maris 74-bb. Usually weak, coulter and swingletree not visible. Finest is probably Maris, Garrett:1480, VF (scratched), $1,200, Terranova, pvt. coll., 142.4 grs. = 9.23 gms. Kosoff estate:4116, VF, $1,760.

952 1788 Three obv. quatrefoils; horse begins legend.
Maris 75-bb; Crosby, Pl. VI, 25. 142.6–146.1 grs. = 9.24–9.467 gms.

953 1788 Similar; horse after first quatrefoil.
Maris 77-dd, 78-dd (3 stages of heavy obv. die failure, latest ill.; Crosby, Pl. VI, 26). 140.5–162.3 grs. = 9.104–10.52 gms. This and 950–52 all punchlinked with NOVA EBORAC and EXCELSIOR coppers and with the Brasher doubloons, qq.v.

IX. MACHIN'S MILLS, Newburgh, N.Y.
(1787–89): Thomas Machin & Co.

954 n.d. (1789?) NOVA * CESEREA 2 known.
Maris 69-w. Massive die failure obliterates most of plough and horse head. Both survivors are on small crude planchets. Discovered by Dr. Edward Maris in NYC between 1875 and 1881. 1) Maris, Garrett:1474, "G–VG," $2,700, 131.7 grs. = 8.54 gms. (ill.) 2) Boyd estate.

955 1787 Camel heads. 3 obv. vars.
Maris 56-n, 58-n (ears between A C, rare), 57-n (one ear about touches A: Ex. rare). Always overstruck on other coins. Rare undertypes, such as the GEORGE CLINTON from the Boyd estate (ill.), command high premiums.

X. BUNGTOWN MINTS, North Swansea, Mass.? (1786–89?)

956 1786 As ill. Unique?
Maris 80. 1) Maris, Garrett, Picker:247, $13,750, 128.3 grs. = 8.32 gms.

957 1787 As ill. Ex. rare.
Maris 81, "83-ii" (ill., 3 known), "84." Some are overstruck on counterfeit British halfpence. The "83-ii" was discovered by Maris about 1885; Garrett:1487, $7,750, 105 grs. = 6.81 gms.

958 1788 Unique?
Maris 79-ee. Clark, Boyd estate.

vi. MASSACHUSETTS CENTS AND HALF CENTS (1787–89)

After several petitions reached the Massachusetts state legislature in 1786 seeking exclusive franchises to coin copper and silver, similar to the copper coinages already authorized by Connecticut, New Jersey, and Vermont, the General Court decided instead to establish a state mint. Possibly they realized that the risks in private franchised coinage were greater than they wished to run. Accordingly, on Oct. 17, 1786, the state passed an act authorizing construction of a mint to coin gold, silver, and copper, and specifically directing issue of copper cents and half cents, to bear such devices as the Governor should approve, receivable for all taxes and other payments. No more was heard about gold or silver coins (presumably for lack of bullion), but the authorities appointed the Boston goldsmith Capt. Joshua Wetherle as mintmaster to make copper cents and half cents.

On June 27, 1787, the Council notified Wetherle of the chosen devices. Obvs. of both denominations were to show a stand-ing Indian, holding bow and arrow, with one star above; this device recurs on militia buttons, but we have not yet been able to date their first use: Albert {1974}, MS 17, 19. Revs. were to feature an eagle displayed, with state name and date. Uniformity with the federal standard was intended, but the authorizing act (quoted in Crosby) does not specify the coins' weight, nor has other documentation surfaced. Observed weights average very close to those of genuine Tower Mint British halfpence and farthings. The weight range for cents is 146–165 grs. = 9.46–10.7 gms., compared to the Tower standard of 46 to the lb. = 152.17 grs. = 9.861 gms. The range for half cents is 75–83 grs. = 4.8–5.4 gms.; those dated 1788 are uniformly about 76 grs. = 4.9 gms. These standards are a little heavier than those for the "Congress Coppers" or FUGIOs (44⁴⁄₉ to the lb. = 157.5 grs. = 10.21 gms.).

Dies for the 1787 and earlier 1788 coins were made by Paul Revere's pupil Joseph Callender (1751–1821), of Half-Square Court, State St. (near the present Congress Square), Boston; these have open S's. Because the General Court thought Callender's fees too high (24 shillings per die), Wetherle hired Jacob Perkins of Newburyport (1766–1849) to make the remaining 1788 dies (both denominations). Perkins's dies have closed S's shaped like 8's. Perkins was to receive 1% of the coins struck from his dies instead of any other fee.

Bullion used for the earliest coins consisted of some 3,500 lbs. of rough copper (sprues, mortars, brass cannons, etc.) then in custody of Hugh Orr but belonging to the state. This required costly and troublesome refining; even so, many planchets showed splitting and occasional cavitation.

As the expense of operating the mint exceeded the revenue the coins brought in by some $3,990.93, the legislators thought of closing the mint and awarding a private coining franchise to one John May. But they abandoned this attempt after attorneys reminded the General Court that the United States Constitution, ratified by Massachusetts and already in effect, forbade any state to coin money. Wetherle's authority to make copper coins ended Jan. 23, 1789; the total was £1,048 2s 7d = $3,490.43, of which £3 18s 10d = $12.80 constituted Perkins's 1%: a paltry sum for making 13 dies! This implies that $1,280 (both denominations together) were coined from Perkins's dies as against $2,210.43 from Callender's, all between Aug. 30, 1788, and Jan. 21, 1789; but no extant records enable us to break down these figures into amounts coined of cents or half cents. For some years afterward, the state continued to accept the coins in tax payments at the rate of 108 cents = 6 shillings.

Callender's prototype (**959**) usually comes overweight. On eagle's breast shield, CENT is in relief; this detail wore away faster than anything else, doubtless explaining the change to incuse CENT on all later dies. This suggests that a device punch was in use for the eagle; if so, either it was incomplete (lacking arrows and branch?) or peripheral details had to be added by hand. The prototype Indian die was heavily reworked and used with the "Horned Eagle" rev. (the horn is a die defect atop eagle's head) to make the first regular var. (**960**). Counterfeiters promptly imitated the latter, producing **968,** the only hornless 1787 cent with four leaves on branch. After these were identified and rejected, late Connecticut coiners (Jarvis & Co.? Machin's Mills?) bought them up to use as planchets for the 1788 draped-bust var. **879.** All subsequent Massachusetts cents, including some very rare later counterfeits with very large dates, have five leaves on branch.

Massachusetts copper coins comprise several important historical "firsts": They are the only state issues to conform to the 1786 Acts of Congress proposing a federal decimal coinage; the Cents are the only ones to bear their denominations; the Half Cents are the only ones ever issued by a state. Despite their historical interest, they have suffered unjustly from neglect by collectors. This neglect can be traced to unsatisfactory var. descriptions in Ryder {1919A}, which in turn copied Crosby {1875}. Philip Greco's photographic plates (1960), showing and renumbering most of them, are rare and difficult of access, even in fuzzy third-generation copies, and the lack of accompanying descriptions or of information about rarity has limited their usefulness. Vlack's plates (1978) are almost equally elusive. Lack of a monograph comparable to Kessler {1976} remains one of the widest gaps in Early American numismatics.

MASSACHUSETTS CENTS AND HALF CENTS

Designer, Joseph Callender, after specifications by Governor and Council. Engravers, Joseph Callender and Jacob Perkins. Mint, Joshua Wetherle's, 910 Washington St., Boston. Composition, copper. Diameters: Cents, 18.5–19/16″ = 29–30 mm; Half Cents, 15/16″ = 24 mm. Weight standards, uncertain: See introductory text. Authorizing Act, Oct. 17, 1786.

Grade range, POOR to UNC. GOOD: Devices outlined; all letters and numerals legible except (HALF) CENT. VERY GOOD: Partial details on tunic and feathers. FINE: About half tunic details; partial vertical stripes; C T legible on shield. VERY FINE: CENT clear, EN weak; all major feather contours clear except at tops and edges of wings. EXTREMELY FINE: Isolated tiny spots of wear only; grade by surface. EXCEPTIONS: On **959**, CENT is in relief and not fully legible even in VF; some Half Cents are weak and vague on tunic even in mint state.

1. ISSUES DATED 1787: WETHERLE'S MINT

959 1787 Prototype Cent. "Transposed Arrows." Ex. rare.
Ryder 2a-F; Crosby, Pl. VI, 5. CENT in relief. Discovered by Joseph J. Mickley before 1867. 1) Appleton, MHS, Laird Park, Robison:103, "F," $3,500, 165.45 grs. = 10.72 gms. 2) Parsons, Garrett:582, "F," $5,500, 185 grs. = 11.99 gms. 3) Essex Inst., $17,000, Roper:220, 168.9 grs. = 10.94 gms., VF, $7,700. 4) Bushnell:778, DeWitt Smith, Brand II: 960, "VG–F." 5) Parmelee, Mills, Jackman, pvt. coll., ill. in Crosby. 6), 7) Rumored.

960 1787 Cent. 4 leaves. "Horned Eagle."
Ryder 2b-A; ANS {1914}, Pl. 4. 157.9–159 grs. = 10.23–10.31 gms. For hornless Four Leaves coins, see **968.**

961 1787 Cent. 5 leaves, period before .COMMON
Ryder 3-G; Crosby, Pl. VI, 6. 158 grs. = 10.24 gms. The period has been called a rust pit, but it is round and in much higher relief than unquestioned rust pits.

962 1787 Cent. 5 leaves, no period, single exergue line. 3 vars.
Ryder 6-G, 2b-G, 8-G. Small date; same rev. Exergue line below tail thin, unlike **969,** with which this could possibly be confused.

963 1787 Cent. Similar, double exergue line. 6 vars.
142–166.3 grs. = 9.21–10.78 gms. Use a glass: The 2 lines are often too close together to show in photographs.

964 1787 Half Cent. Thin rev. letters. Very rare.
Ryder 1-D, 6-D; Crosby, Plate VI, 12, 11. Thin numerals, footless 1 in date. Former 88.5 grs. = 5.73 gms. A third var., "Ryder 4-D," was first reported in 1962 by Philip Greco, but remains unverified.

965 1787 Half Cent. Same. "White metal" (tin?) trial piece. Unique.
"Ryder 7-D." Discovered by Richard August.

966 1787 Half Cent. Heavy letters, wide date spaced 17 87.
Ryder 2-A, 3-A, 5-A, 6-A. Second and third, Crosby, Plate VI, 9, 10. 73–78.5 grs. = 4.73–5.09 gms.

967 1787 Half Cent. Heavy letters, close date.
Ryder 4-B (AS nearly touch, rare), 4-C (arrow piercing period, ill.); former, Crosby, Pl. VI, 13, 14; latter, ANS {1914}, Pl. 4. 69.3–81.4 grs. = 4.49–5.27 gms.

2. UNIDENTIFIED PRIVATE MINTS

968 1787 Cent. 4 leaves, no horn. Ex. rare.
Ryder 1-B. See introductory text. 146–149.9 grs. = 9.46–9.712 gms., heaviest in ANS.

969 1787 Cent. 5 leaves, large date. Ex. rare.
Ryder 5-I (Bushnell:775), 7-H (ill.; Crosby, Pl. VI, 7). Heavy single exergue line. Both are by the same maker, imitating **962.** No specimen of 5-I available for examination; 7-H's weigh 155.8–158.9 grs. = 10.1–10.29 gms. 1) Mills, Earle:2006, Picker:140, UNC., $6,875, 156.1 grs. = 10.115 gms. 2) NN 43:845.

3. ISSUES DATED 1788.
WETHERLE'S MINT
DIES BY CALLENDER. OPEN S'S

970 1788 Cent. Period after S. 12 vars.

971 1788 Cent. No period after S 2 obv. vars.
Ryder 6-N, 13-N, latter first ill. ANS {1914}, Pl. 4. 160.8 grs. = 10.42 gms.

4. DIES BY PERKINS.
CLOSED S'S LIKE 8'S

972 1788 Cent. 9 vars.
Specimens (usually red UNC.) with small E next to star are copies struck after WW II by the Springfield, Mass., coin dealer Henry Evans.

973 1788 Half Cent. 2 vars.
Ryder 1-B (ill.; Crosby, Pl. VI, 15), second 8 high; Ryder 1-A (Crosby, Pl. VI, 16), with even 88, is very rare. Same comment as to **972.**

vii. THE BUNGTOWN MINTS

The Swansea Township area (North Swansea and Rehoboth, Mass.), formerly Barneyville, was unofficially known for over a century as "Bungtown," even among natives, though at least three other communities (notably Westerly, R.I.) shared this insulting nickname. Newman {1976B} brilliantly elucidated *Bungtown* as meaning 'Buttsville,' after *bung,* 'anus' (a locution documented as early as Urquhart's 17th-century translation of Rabelais). *Bungtown* itself was 18th-century and later East Coast (primarily New England) slang for any filthy backwoods town; in the 1780s it also designated lightweight copper coins coming from any such place (Newport *Mercury,* Aug. 13, 1787). Of the four communities known locally as "Bungtown," one (Swansea Township) had been notorious as a hotbed of counterfeiting activity at least since 1716, and in the 1780s specifically as a source of counterfeit coppers.

Considerations of style and punch linkage indicate that several "Tory Coppers" and imitation state coppers, of known American origin but unrelated to the Machin's Mills output, may share a common source. We do not claim that all these originated from the one firm, nor yet that only one group of makers of counterfeit coppers operated out of "Bungtown," but we can be absolutely certain that these coppers are American, that they are of the 1784–89 period, and that in their own day any New Englander would have called them Bungtowns or Bungtown Coppers.

The Bungtown imitations of state coppers were described and pictured earlier: The Connecticuts are nos. **761–62,** the New Jerseys **956–58.** The unique CONSTELLATIO NOVA with only 12 stars **(1115)** appears to have the same source, as do the "Tory Coppers" described immediately below. These are not to be confused with the "Tory Coppers" by Machin's Mills **(992–97)** or by Walter Mould **(1002–9).** However, all such coppers of American origin share a peculiarity which at one time induced erroneous attribution of them all to Machin's Mills: Crosses on the Union Jack are unfimbriated, whereas normally on even the crudest British counterfeit halfpence the crosses are fimbriated (shown on the coins as narrow extra outlines to all eight arms).

Anonymous imitations of other state coppers are of different styles and may have different local origins. This remark applies to New Hampshire **707** and **709–10,** Vermont **735,** Connecticut **741, 763–65,** Massachusetts **968–69,** and to the 1786 CONSTELLATIO NOVA, **1116.**

974   1784 Copper. Very rare.
Vlack 14-84A. Grand Central:76A; Roper:289, 93.1 grs. = 6.03 gms.

975   1786 Copper. Unique?
Vlack 16-86A; ill. Betts {1886}, p. 8, and on Vlack plate. Rev. of **762.**   1) C. Wyllys Betts, Ted Craige, Dr. Arthur Kahn, Brown Library I:850. 2 similar vars. dated 1781 and 1785, dubiously ascribed to the Bungtown mints, are now claimed by Eric P. Newman to be of British origin.

CHAPTER 7

PROPOSED, SPECULATIVE, AND UNDERGROUND NEW YORK ISSUES

i. ATLEE'S *NON VI VIRTUTE VICI* (1786)

On March 29, 1786, John Mycall's Newburyport newspaper *The Essex Journal and Merimack Packet: or, the Massachusetts and New-Hampshire General Advertiser* printed this news item:

> New York, Connecticut and Vermont have authorized a person in each of those states to coin coppers; numbers of them are now in circulation; they are in general well made, and of good copper, those of New York in particular. Was a person authorized in this State for the same purpose, it would undoubtingly prevent the manufacture of those made of base metal.

Mycall, or whoever wrote his copy, was evidently unaware that no New York law franchised manufacture of coppers. But something in the devices and inscriptions of those then current convinced him that the coins were an official issue. Though he did not describe the coppers, the only possible candidates are those with a rude Washington portrait and the inscriptions NON VI VIRTUTE VICI, 'Not by violence but by excellence have I conquered,' and NEO-EBORACENSIS, 'At New York.' No other coppers dated 1786 or earlier referred in device or inscriptions to New York.

Two vars. exist: the first (**976**, with large head) evidently a pattern, the second (**977**, small head) apparently passed out as samples to VIPs and afterward circulated generally. All were struck at the regular Birmingham standard of 60 to the pound, like the Virginia halfpennies and unofficial coppers of many kinds then in circulation, but slightly heavier than the Vermont coppers familiar to Mycall. With the dubious exceptions of the GEORGIUS TRIUMPHO and 1784 "Ugly Head," they bear the earliest domestic attempts at coin portraiture of Washington.

Their legends ostensibly allude to Washington's military victories (though the redcoats did not evacuate New York until Nov. 26, 1783, long after Cornwallis's surrender). However, they are equally interpretable as alluding to the coins themselves: "Not by force [= legal mandate], but by excellence [= weight and quality of copper] have I overcome [sc. public resistance] in New York, 1786."

Date and letter punches link these coins with the 1786 bust-right imitation Connecticuts and the 1786 Rahway Mint New Jersey coppers, therefore to James F. Atlee before his association with Machin's Mills. The time element proves that the NON VI VIRTUTE VICI coppers antedated by over eight months Atlee's association with the Rahway Mint (Nov. 1786), so that their most likely place of mintage was Atlee's private

mint in New York City. They are almost certainly contemporary with his counterfeit Connecticuts **742–46**. Their seated-figure device with scales probably alludes to that on the 1785 IMMUNE COLUMBIA **1117–22**. If Mycall knew of these latter, this circumstance possibly explained his belief that the coppers had some kind of official status. Official or otherwise, in New York they passed at 14 to the shilling, along with all other types of coppers (state coins, foreign issues, and bungtowns), pursuant to agreement among New York merchants, Dec. 24, 1753. NY *Gazette* 12/24/1753 and 12/31/53, cited in *CNL* 4/73, p. 401.

NON VI VIRTUTE VICI COPPERS

Designer, Engraver, James F. Atlee. Mint, Atlee's, NYC. Composition, copper. Diameter, $^{18}/_{16}''$ = about 29 mm. Weight standard, 60 to the lb. = 116.67 grs. = 7.56 gms.

Grade range, FAIR to UNC. No grading standards established.
976 1786 Large head pattern. 2 known.
  Baker 13a. Stop after VICI. Rev., flag on liberty pole. 1) Boyd estate. 2) Ex Fuld coll. Obv. recurs on **1134**.

977 1786 Small head. Very rare.
  Baker 13; Crosby, Pl. VIII, 4. No stop, no flag. Occasionally on heavier blanks, e.g., Parmelee, Smith, Bement, Ellsworth, Garrett:594, EF, $12,000, 134.1 grs. = 8.691 gms., for 52 to the lb. I have not seen the die-struck counterfeit mentioned in 1979–83 Yeoman Guide Books.

ii. THE BAILEY AND BRASHER PATTERNS (1787)

Though many petitions to the New York State legislature sought franchises for manufacturing copper coins, political pressure was applied by interests which strongly opposed them all. In the first place, any such authorization would give one firm a monopoly and end the profitable game of importing lightweight Birmingham coppers. Crosby quotes an early 1787 estimate that the profits to coiners of Birmingham coppers, or therefore to any others of the same weight standard (60 to the pound), were in the neighborhood of 96% (pp. 290–92). In the second place, some members of the state legislature adopted a high moral tone, objecting to copper coinage in general and to lightweight Birmingham imports in particular, characterizing them all as a serious loss to the citizenry, but without recommending any alternative. This led to the hostile Report of March 3, 1787, and that in turn to the "Act to regulate the Circulation of Copper Coin, passed April 20, 1787" (Crosby, pp. 294–95), which attempted to prohibit the circulation of any coppers weighing under 1/3 oz. avoirdupois (145.833 grs. = 9.45 gms.), and pegging even these at 20 to the shilling effective Aug. 1, 1787, down 30% from the then (1753–89) current 14 to the shilling. This law was unenforceable and appears to have been a dead letter from the day of its passage. Nevertheless, it had its covertly intended effect: It ended any further petitions for legitimate coinage franchises, without preventing the profitable import of lightweight coppers from the Birmingham "Hard Ware Manufactories."

Among the petitions which the new law estopped were those of John Bailey and Ephraim Brasher, submitted Feb. 11, 1787. Bushnell's reference to these (Crosby, p. 290) does not allow us to deduce whether they were separate or together; but as John Bailey's "running horse" Jersey coppers of 1788 (**950–53**) are punchlinked with the Brasher Doubloons, the two makers (neighbors at 22 and 77 Queens St.) were closely associated: Sipsey {1964}. Accordingly, the Bailey and Brasher patterns are identified as all those coins whose devices and inscriptions proclaim an intended New York circulation and which share letter punches with Bailey's Jersey coppers: Breen {1958C}. There are two classes: the EXCELSIOR coppers and the Brasher Doubloons. (Their NOVA EBORAC coppers are not patterns: They were issued in quantity. See next section.)

The EXCELSIOR design follows the New York arms as found on that state's paper currency issue of April 18, 1786, as engraved by Peter Maverick. Their heraldic blazoning: "Sun rising over three mountains, sea in foreground, all proper; crest, eagle surmounts demi-globe on torse; dexter supporter, Liberty, with cap and pole; sinister supporter, Justice, with scales." EXCELSIOR, 'More excellent, more noble,' is the state motto: Newman {1976A}, p. 244.

Following these are Ephraim Brasher's famous Doubloons, the only gold coins whose inscriptions allude to any of the Original 13. There are two designs; that better known (and probably first) has for obv. the New York arms with NOVA EBORACA COLUMBIA EXCELSIOR, with rev. United States arms and usual motto rearranged UNUM E PLURIBUS. The signature BRASHER is for the New York goldsmith and silversmith Ephraim Brasher (1744–97: rhymes with glazier), a neighbor and friend of George Washington. Various specialists have theorized, without evidence, that Brasher originally intended these dies for a proposed coinage of coppers. However, there are no copper strikings, and the gold impressions—hallmarked by Brasher with his EB in oval, as a guarantee of metallic content —approximate the then current Spanish weight standard, so that they would pass at par with Spanish and Latin American doubloons, equated to 16 Spanish dollars apiece. Most likely their unfamiliar design met with resistance, so that Brasher sub-

stituted another design, imitating the then common Philip V Lima doubloons; he hallmarked these similarly. His EB in oval also occurs on many foreign gold coins of the period, guaranteeing their weight and metallic content (e.g., Garrett:2342–46), reflecting assays ordered in 1792 by Alexander Hamilton, Secretary of Treasury, but not paid for until 1796 ("Estimated Expenditures for the Year 1796," in *ASPF*-I; *AJN* 7/1892, p. 20; Decatur {1938}). Extended discussions are at Garrett:607 and 2340.

The following survivors have EB hallmark on wing:

1. Adam Eckfeldt, Mint Cabinet, SI. 406.8 grs. = 26.36 gms. Worn. Clain-Stefanelli {1970}, fig. 15.
2. E. Cogan, J. F. McCoy, J. N. T. Levick, Woodward 10/1864:1540, Colin Lightbody, G. F. Seavey, L. G. Parmelee, A. C. Zabriskie, V. Brand, B. G. Johnson, F. C. C. Boyd, Rev. William H. Owen, Yale Univ., unidentified thieves (May 1965, recovered 1967), Stack's, offered Jan. 1981 at $650,000. 29.8 mm. 407.5 grs. = 26.41 gms. Crosby, Pl. IX, 24. This piece's history oddly recalls that in Raymond Chandler's *The High Window* (1942), filmed as *The Brasher Doubloon* (1947), though the coin in the film was a fake.
3. J. T. Raymond, H. P. Newlin, R. C. Davis, J. G. Mills, James Ten Eyck, V. Brand, R. Friedberg estate, RARCOA, Auction 79:1433, $430,000, W. Perschke. 407.405 grs. = 26.399 gms. Ill.
4. M. A. Stickney, J. W. Ellsworth, Wayte Raymond, J. W. Garrett, JHU, Garrett:607, UNC., $725,000. 407.945 grs. = 26.434 gms. ANS {1914}, Pl. 10
5. Philadelphia sewer (1897), unidentified laborers, S. H. & H. Chapman, A. W. Jackman, Waldo Newcomer, Col. E. H. R. Green, William Randolph Hearst, B. G. Johnson, F. C. C. Boyd estate, New Netherlands, Mrs. R. Henry Norweb, ANS (1969). 411 grs. = 26.63 gms.
6. B. Max Mehl (July 1933), Lammot duPont, Willis H. duPont; stolen at gunpoint Oct. 1967, retrieved July 1968. 408.3 grs. = 26.45 gms.

Brasher's unique half doubloon remained long controversial because Edgar Adams inexplicably believed it merely a clipped doubloon; however, it is much thinner than the doubloons, and its edge is normal. Proskey, Newcomer, and B. G. Johnson recognized its authenticity (1928); for other details see Winter {1983}.

The Boston diesinker Merriam made a pair of copy dies in 1861 for Alfred S. Robinson, and struck prooflike impressions in copper and brass [25 each]. These have letters and date much larger than the genuine and in more modern style; the EB on wing "hallmark" is in the die. They are rare and not deceptive: Crosby, Pl. IX, 27.

Mint Cabinet Curator DuBois, sometime in the 1860s, made gilt electrotype copies of the Mint Cabinet specimen. These show edge seams and will not ring (see Ring Test in Glossary).

THE EXCELSIOR COPPERS

Designer, Engraver, John Bailey (after Maverick). Mint, Bailey's, NYC. Composition, copper. Diameter, 18/16″ = 28.6 mm. Weight standards, variable, as noted.

Grade range, FAIR to AU. No grading standards established.

978 1787 Transposed Arrows. 3 or 4 known.
Crosby, Pl. VII, 24. Blundered die? Arrows in dexter claw.

Eagle *on globe* sinister (faces observer's r.). 1) Parsons, Ellsworth, Garrett:600, 165.5 grs. = 10.72 gms., "VF," $26,000. 2) Eric P. Newman. 3) Dr. Hall, Brand, NN 35:177, battered. Crosby gives weight of one of these as 123 grs. = 7.97 gms., for 55 or 56 to the lb.

979 1787 Eagle *on globe* sinister. 10–12 known.
Crosby, Pl. VII, 23. Usually in low grades. Garrett:598, 153.3 grs. = 9.94 gms.; Roper:272, EF, $4,125, 148.4 grs. = 9.616 gms., for 46 to the lb.

980 1787 Eagle *on globe* dexter. 15–20 known.
Crosby, Pl. VII, 22. Usually in low grades. Weight range 134.4–148.9 grs. = 8.709–9.649 gms., for 50 to the lb. Garrett:599, "AU," $17,500.

BRASHER'S DOUBLOONS

Designer, Engraver, Ephraim Brasher and John Bailey. Mint, Bailey's or Brasher's, NYC. Composition, gold, probably $11/12$ = 917 Fine. Diameter, about $18/16''$ = 28.6 mm. Weight standard, probably 411.429 grs. = 26.66 gms., for 14 to the troy lb., as a guess at Spanish standard. Edge, plain.

Grade range, FINE to UNC. No grading standard established.

981 1787 New York Doubloon. EB hallmark on wing. Ex. rare.
Rulau-E NY 82B. See introductory text for discussion and roster.

982 1787 New York Doubloon. EB hallmark on breast. Unique.
Rulau-E NY 82A. Same dies. 1) Bushnell, Garrett:2340, VF, $625,000. 411.5 grs. = 26.66 gms.

983 1787 New York Half Doubloon. Same dies. Unique.
Said to weigh 204 grs. = 13.2 gms. 1) Noncollector accumulation, unidentified lady (1928), David Proskey, Boyd, Col. Green, Frank Smith, Maj. Ball, Josiah K. Lilly, SI.

984 1742 (i.e., 1787?) Lima Style Doubloon. 2 known.
Rulau-E NY 82C. Note signature BRASHER N.Y. Discovered by J. W. Scott, 1894. 1) Scott, "Paris":813, Ten Eyck, Garrett, Bernstein, Kagin, 408 grs. = 26.4 gms. Discovery coin, discussed in Kagin {1957}; narrow thick flan. 2) Newcomer, Garrett:2341, 407.3 grs. = 26.39 gms. (ill.)

iii. THE *NOVA EBORAC* COPPERS

When the New York State legislature adopted Assemblyman Brooks's moralistic hostility to private coinage proposals, John Bailey (possibly with Brasher's help) struck large quantities of coppers vaguely like others already in circulation. Probably these appeared before Aug. 1, 1787 (when the Act of April 20 took effect); possibly Bailey continued making them thereafter as well. Bailey's coppers show an anonymous male head facing r. with domed hair (copied from one of Abel Buell's 1785 Connecticut obvs.) and legend NOVA EBORAC; revs. have the usual seated figure, here with motto VIRT. ET LIB. for VIRTUS ET LIBERTAS, 'Strength and freedom.' Their letter and quatrefoil punches match those on 1787 EXCELSIOR patterns and the Brasher Doubloons, as well as on Bailey's 1788 Jersey coppers **950–53,** which establishes their origin: Breen {1958C}. Possibly the first var. (**985,** Large Head) was a pattern; it is even conceivable that this one represented Bailey's Feb. 11, 1787, petition, while the EXCELSIOR patterns represented Brasher's petition of the same date—or vice versa: Which one cannot be plausibly guessed.

This first variety's spacing and layout problems betray an inexperienced hand. Its obv. die promptly collapsed owing to improper hardening; survivors are very rare. The wide weight range suggests that the earliest ones, intended for presentation to legislators reviewing the petition, were specially struck on heavy blanks, while later ones, intended for circulation, were on thinner planchets.

Two less rare vars. followed; that with figure seated r. also shows evidence of inexperience, as the device was cut very deeply into the die, ideally for higher relief, but in practice instead resulting in weak striking. The other is always unevenly struck. These were issued in quantity; they circulated at least until the July 20, 1789, copper panic, and most survivors are well worn.

The small-head coin is of entirely different style. It shares letter punches with Gilbert Rindell's clandestine Jersey coppers **927–35,** which circumstance establishes its origin in Elizabeth Town, N.J., most likely after July 1788 at Matthias Ogden's secret mint. (Rindell stayed lifelong in Elizabeth Town; his coinmaking activities coincided with his association with Gen. Ogden, who brought home the coining press and other equipment from the defunct Rahway Mills.) Almost all survivors are in low grades. No specimen yet examined shows an undertype, unlike the Ogden & Rindell Jersey coppers; this may have to do with poor preservation, or with deliberate avoidance of overstriking. It may even mean that these NOVA EBORAC coins were the first issue from the Elizabeth Town Mint, before the rolling mill and blank cutter failed and the partners had to resort to stamping New Jersey dies on any available discredited coppers.

NOVA EBORAC COPPERS

Designer, John Bailey. Engravers, Bailey, Gilbert Rindell. Mints, Bailey's, NYC; Ogden & Rindell, Elizabeth Town, N.J. Composition, copper. Diameters, variable, as noted. Weight standard, mostly 60 to the lb.; others as noted.

Grade range, FAIR to UNC. GOOD: All inscriptions legible if on flan. VERY GOOD: Some details of armor and drapery show. FINE: Some leaves separated, partial hair details above them. VERY FINE: Over half hair details; part of New York arms clear. Higher grades—grade by surface. EXCEPTIONS: **985** will normally be weak between face and EBORAC; **986** will normally be weak on either date or female head or both; **987** will normally be weak in central rev. and on legs; **988** is often weak at profile from die buckling in field.

985   1787 Large head. Figure seated l. 15–18 known.
Crosby, Pl. VIII, 9. Discovered by Lorenzo H. Abbey before

1861: Attinelli {1876}, p. 30. Obv. die buckled early, affecting area between face and EBORAC, often weakening profile. Usually in low grades. 120–156.9 grs. = 7.78–10.17 gms., probably representing batches at 60 and 46 to the lb. Broad flans, about 18/16″ = 29 mm. Garrett:595, AU, $8,750.

986   1787 Medium head, figure seated l.
Crosby, Pl. VIII, 11. 17/16″ = about 27 mm (varies). Usually 60 to the lb.; Garrett:596, EF, $1,150, 133.1 grs. = 8.62 gms., for 52 to the lb. Tops of some letters often off flan; see also EXCEPTIONS above. Anthony Terranova reports one overstruck on a counterfeit Irish halfpenny, probably of 1781 or 1782.

987   1787 Figure seated r.
Crosby, Pl. VIII, 10. 17/16″ as last. Usually 60 to the lb. Often with heavy die break at foot; cinquefoil after B weakens. See EXCEPTIONS above. Crosby, Garrett:597, EF, $2,400.; Roper:268, UNC., $5,500.

988   1787 Small head. 8–10 known.
Crosby, Pl. VIII, 12. By Gilbert Rindell, Elizabeth Town, N.J. Approximately 16–17/16″ = 25–27 mm. 120–142 grs. = 7.78–9.21 gms., for 52 to the lb.? See introductory text. Almost always in low grades. Roper:270, "VF," rough, $3,300. Enl. photos.

iv. ATLEE'S PATTERNS FOR THOMAS MACHIN, MARCH 1787

According to the *Journal of the Assembly of the State of New York,* the petition of Thomas Machin for a franchise to coin coppers in and for the state was referred to committee on March 3, 1787. The committee's chairman was the same Mr. Brooks who was responsible for the wording of the March 5 report disapproving all such petitions on moralistic grounds (Crosby, pp. 290–92).

By what probably transcends coincidence, on April 18, 1787, the very day that the New York Senate passed the bill intended to outlaw all coppers weighing under 1/3 oz. each, Capt. Machin formed a partnership with the die engraver James F. Atlee and four others to make "Hard Ware" (then current euphemism for copper coins). Atlee was no newcomer to diesinking: He had already made the NON VI VIRTUTE VICI coppers and many imitation Connecticuts; he was then principal engraver at Rahway Mills (Nov. 1786–June 1787), the legal coining facility for the State of New Jersey.

Atlee was thus the logical candidate to make the necessary sample coppers to accompany Machin's March 1787 petition; and when the Rahway Mills enterprise failed three months later, Atlee joined Capt. Machin at Newburgh for the clandestine Machin's Mills enterprise: See next section.

The coppers in this section are deduced to be those Atlee made to accompany Machin's original March 1787 petition. Their lettering positively identifies them as his work; their devices and inscriptions establish their intent. Use of Gov. Clinton's portrait was most likely Capt. Machin's deliberate bow to his longtime friend and host (see following section). We need not assume that Atlee copied the EXCELSIOR rev. from Bailey's coppers (979–80); more likely both Atlee and Bailey were copying Peter Maverick's engraving of the state arms on the then current New York paper currency (April 18, 1786, pictured in Newman {1976A}, p. 244). Note that in Atlee's version, the demi-globe rests directly on shield (rather than on a torse), and the supporters are transposed.

The GEORGE CLINTON was discovered by an East Poultney, Vt., grocer about 1859; W. C. Prime was first to publish news of its discovery in *Harper's,* March 1860. The first three examples found were all overstruck on specimens of **1137.** Bolen's struck copies (1869) are deceptive, but readily identifiable by the date, in which 1 is shaped like I and the tops of 787 are in a straight line: Crosby, Pl. VIII, 27. On originals, the 1 is shaped like J, and the top of the 8 is above the tops of 7's. (Compare Ford {1950}, Kenney {1952}, which references use a much less convenient method for distinguishing them.) Bolen's copies are nearly as rare as originals: silver [2], copper [40], brass [5], together with the copper mules: Clinton with standing Indian [5], Clinton with eagle on demi-globe [5], New York arms with eagle on demi-globe [5]. Unlike the genuine, his eagle die lacks the hyphen between NEO and EBORACUS; A's are normal, whereas Atlee's original A punch is broken at upper l.

Atlee kept his original standing-Indian die after moving to Machin's Mills, and sometime in 1789 muled it with a "Tory Copper" obv. (1001); the coiners must have abandoned quality control, picking up any dies still even briefly usable no matter how crude their workmanship or how ludicrous their combined inscriptions.

Bolen's copy of the standing-Indian pattern has nine feathers in headdress, tops of ND even, and A's normally formed, whereas Atlee's original die has seven feathers in headdress, top of D above top of N, and both A's are broken at upper l. In 1869 Bolen combined this copy die with the state arms rev. described above for the Clinton: silver [2], copper [40], brass [5]. He also muled this obv. with the eagle on demi-globe, in the same metals and quantities: Crosby, Pl. VIII, 27–29.

Other struck copies of the Clinton pattern have inaccurate modern letters and numerals. Casts and electrotypes of the genuine are identifiable by the ring test (see Glossary), edge seams, and bubble marks.

ATLEE'S PATTERNS FOR THOMAS MACHIN, MARCH 1787

Designer, Engraver, James F. Atlee. Mint, NYC or Rahway Mills. Composition, copper. Diameter, $17/16''$–$18.5/16''$ = 27–30 mm. Weight standards, mostly 46 to the lb. (vary).

Grade range, POOR to EX. FINE. No grading standards established.

989 1787 GEORGE CLINTON, 8–10 known.
Crosby, Pl. VIII, 5. 145.3–166.5 grs. = 9.41–10.79 gms., for 46 to the lb. Beware struck copies, casts, and electrotypes; see introductory text. Finest known, Appleton, MHS II:31, UNC., $34,000 (1973). At least 3 are overstruck on early impressions of **1137:** 1) Ten Eyck, Garrett:603, VF, $29,000. 2) Jenks, Groves:335, $21,000, Park, Robison:154, $14,000.

990 1787 Standing Indian/State arms. About 12 known.
Crosby, Pl. VIII, 6. 127–166 grs. = 8.25–10.76 gms., probably for 55 and 46 to the lb. (Enl. photos.) Beware struck copies, casts, and electrotypes; see introductory text. Garrett:601, EF, $21,000. J. D. Parsons describes one with die rust in shield: B&R RCR 45, p. 5 (Aug. 1982).

991 1787 Standing Indian/Eagle on demi-globe. 6–8 known.
Crosby, Pl. VIII, 7. 121.8–153 grs. = 7.9–9.92 gms., probably for 60 and 46 to the lb. (Enl. photos.) Beware struck copies, casts, and electrotypes; see introductory text. Garrett:602, "AU," $37,000; Roper:276, "EF," $10,450; Parmelee,

Ten Eyck, Wurtzbach, Brand II: 958, UNC. For the muling with the "Tory Copper" obv. see **1001**.

v. THE COINAGES OF MACHIN'S MILLS, NEWBURGH, N.Y.

Capt. Thomas Machin was born March 20, 1744/5 (O.S.), four miles from William Wood's hometown of Wolverhampton, Staffordshire, England. He became a "practical engineer" under James Brindley, building canals for the Duke of Bridgewater, but emigrated to New York in 1772 to investigate New Jersey copper mines. He moved to Boston and quickly joined the rebellious colonists at the Boston Tea Party (1773), taking an arm wound at Bunker Hill, and being commissioned a lieutenant in Col. Henry Knox's Regiment of Artillery, Jan. 18, 1776. Through April and May 1776 he took part in erecting "fortifications for the defence of the Town and Harbor of Boston." On July 21, 1776, Washington sent him to Fort Montgomery on the Hudson, under Gen. (later Gov.) George Clinton, under orders to complete necessary works of military engineering. On Jan. 1, 1777, Machin became brevet Captain, U.S. Artillery. Clinton later assigned him to aid in constructing the 1,700-foot, 186-ton "Great Chain" across the Hudson to obstruct British ships. This went into use April 20, 1778. In the meantime, Machin had become a friend and frequent houseguest of Gen. Clinton (see preceding section). After Machin took a chest wound on Oct. 6, 1777, at the battle of Fort Montgomery and Fort Clinton (which he had helped fortify), he recuperated at Clinton's home. During the rest of the war he fortified West Point and various other locales, including Yorktown (1781). Clinton gave him a commission as Captain, March 1783, retroactive to Aug. 21, 1781.

After the war Machin settled in New Grange (now Newburgh), buying land fronting on Orange Lake (later known as Machin's Lake or Machin's Pond). In 1784 he built a house 1/8 mile east of the lake, later known as the Mint House. On March 3, 1787, Machin submitted a petition to the State Assembly, praying for a franchise to coin coppers in and for the state (see preceding section); this went to a committee headed by the moralistic Mr. Brooks, which predictably rejected it (and all its rivals) two days later. On April 18, the State Senate passed a bill intended to outlaw all copper coins weighing under 1/3 oz. each. On the same day, Machin formed a partnership to manufacture "Hard Ware" (copper coins) and to secure coinage contracts with the United States or individual states. His partners included Samuel Atlee, brewer of porter (a malt liquor originally blending ale with stout) and owner of certain equipment (mills? presses?); James F. Atlee, engraver with the New Jersey mint at Rahway Mills; James Giles, attorney and bookkeeper, of 58 Maiden Lane, in New York City; James Grier and David Brooks, presumably press operators.

During the next couple of months, James Atlee's employers at Rahway Mills awaited a decision on their bid to make copper coins for the federal government, unaware of their rival James Jarvis's decisive $10,000 bribe to Col. William Duer (head of the Board of Treasury): See Chap. 15. Finding themselves cheated out of a contract they alone among local minters could have fulfilled, weakened by internal dissension, and plagued by lawsuits, the Rahway Mills people were not receptive to any proposed contract with Machin & Co. James Atlee, sensing that Rahway Mills's remaining days were few, abandoned New Jersey for Newburgh, not to return.

Machin's Mills expanded when the partners signed an agreement with the coiners at the Rupert, Vt., mint (Reuben Harmon, Col. William Coley, and associates) binding Atlee to furnish dies thereafter for the Vermont coinages on condition that 60% of the Vermont profits go to Machin's Mills in exchange for 40% of the profits of the Newburgh mint. (Charles Bushnell furnished a copy of the contract, reprinted in Crosby and explained in Newman {1958}.) Thereafter, the Vermont coppers bore the "Standard Head" and a seated figure with the same simplified British shield as did Atlee's later "Tory Coppers" made at Machin's Mills; later, some regular-design Vermont coins **(725–34)** were actually made in Newburgh.

In July 1787, Capt. Machin began secret operations at the Mint House. To this period are assigned, by evidence of punch linkage, the "Tory Coppers": imitation George III halfpence with that same simplified cross in the British shield, dates as pictured below. (Those dated 1747 and 1771–76 large date are the work of Walter Mould: See **1002–9**. Those dated 1784 and 1786 are attributed in Newman {1976B} to the "Bungtown" Mints: **974–75**.) One of the 1787 revs., with large date, comes later with a Vermont obv. **(725)**; two "Tory Copper" obvs. come with Vermont and Connecticut revs. **(733, 998–99).**

Machin's son Thomas provided the interesting details that neighbors suspected the Mint House operations to be illegal because much work went on at night, with workmen wearing hideous masks to frighten off any children not already repelled by the noise of the rolling mills, blank cutters, and coining press: *CNL* 3/83, p. 806. But no law forbade private copper coinage.

In July 1788, representatives of Machin's Mills bought out Walter Mould's equipment from the Morristown (N.J.) mint, enabling Mould to flee the state for Ohio just ahead of a court order which would have sent him to debtor's prison. Thereafter, the Newburgh mint produced pieces using some of Mould's old punches and dies, notably the Vermont and George III mulings with his 1785 IMMUNE COLUMBIA die **(734, 1000).**

After Congress voided Jarvis & Co.'s FUGIO franchise, Sept. 1788, representatives of Machin's Mills went to New Haven and bought out the Connecticut minting equipment. Thereafter, the Newburgh output included the "Club Rays" FUGIO coppers and various imitation Connecticuts using Abel Buell's device punches: **856, 871,** and others sharing these dies, many with the same large letters used for the "Camel Head" New Jersey coppers **(955).**

After April 1789 they also bought out Benjamin Buell's equipment. Machin's Mills then diversified to make imitation Connecticuts with the Triple Leaves mailed-bust and/or Wheat Ear revs., many with letter and numeral punches matching those on Atlee's own earlier dies: **790–92, 861–70.** During this final period, quality controls broke down; many crude strikings, blundered dies, and incongruous combinations date to April–July 1789.

Simms {1845} claimed that under 1,000 pounds of coppers were "manufactured" in 1789, "previous to which little seems to have been done." This would still mean over 60,000 coppers, exclusive of larger quantities of overstrikes (Vermonts on Irish halfpence, Connecticuts on CONSTELLATIO NOVA coppers, New Jerseys on anything and everything); nor does it count the output of 1787–88. A more reasonable estimate might be between 100,000 and 200,000 coppers in all. However, more reliable information awaits rediscovery of the Machin family papers, which may survive in possession of his descendants (where Simms had seen them?), or in one of the local historical societies. Whatever the amount, Machin's enterprise was struck down by the New York "copper panic" of July 20, 1789, after which, through 1790, coppers passed at about 1/4 their former value or less. Further details are in Trudgen {1983}.

Machin, a longtime rebel and a prime exponent of free enterprise, met no legal disapproval for his coining operations. A Masonic officer and a member of the Society of the Cincinnati, Machin died, greatly honored, on the evening of April 3, 1816. Nothing has been learned of the later fate of James Atlee or the other partners; but their products include some of the rarest and most interesting—if among the ugliest—copper coins ever intended to circulate within the continental United States.

MACHIN'S MILLS ISSUES

Designer, Engraver, James F. Atlee (except on dies obtained from other mints). Mint, Machin's Mills, near Newburgh, N.Y. Composition, copper. Diameters, variable, about $^{17-18/16}{''}$ = 27–29 mm. Weights, variable, about 83–117 grs. = 5.4–7.56 gms., for 60 to 84 to the lb.

Grade range, POOR to UNC. No grading standard established. Many are weak, uneven strikings on crude, defective planchets.

1. "TORY COPPERS."

992 1776 CEORCIVS III REX/Very small date. Ex. rare.
Vlack 9-76B. C not corrected to G. Obv. reused on **1001.** 1) Stepney hoard (ca. 1790), Eric P. Newman: ill. here and

Newman {1958}. 2) Newman. 3), 4), 5) R. August. 6) Lepczyk 5/4–5/84: 512, VG, $1,540. For similar coins with large 1776 date, see **1008;** 1777, see **1009;** 1747–75, **1002–7.** (Enl. photos.)

993 1778 Small date. 2 vars. Very scarce.
Vlack 12-78B, 13-78B. Note the small 8. Rev. device punch reappears on **726.**

994 1778 Large date. Scarce.
Vlack 11-78A. Note the large 8. For similar coins dated 1784, 1786, see **974–75.**

995 1787 Large date. 5 obv. vars.
Vlack 18-87C, 19-87C, 20-87C, 21-87C, 23-87C. Rev. reappears on **725,** badly worn, nearly illegible, and broken.

996 1787 Small date. 4 vars.
Vlack 17-87A, 17-87B, 17-87E, 21-87D. The rarest of these

(17-87E) has closely spaced date and a big break joining TA to thigh.

997 1788 Scarce.
Vlack 23-88A.

2. MULES

998 1787 Round head, GEORGIVS III REX/INDE ET LIB
3 known.
Vlack 13-87CT. Obv. as next; rev. ill. at **787.** 1) R. August. 2), 3) Pvt. colls. Discovered by Dickeson: {1860}, Pl. XX, 9. Barnsley, *CNL* 4/75.

999 1788 Similar. Rare.
Vlack 13-88CT. Rev. of **857, 871.** In SI is one with rev. L of **719,** ex Mendel L. Peterson; 113.9 grs. = 7.383 gms. Discovered by Ron Guth, 5/9/86. For the similar piece with Vermont standard head and crosses in INDE + ET. LIB +, see **733.**

1000 1785 CEORCIVS III. REX./IMMUNE COLUMBIA.
Very rare.
Crosby, Pl. VII, 32; Vlack 15-85NY. C not corrected to G. Small crude flans, date rarely visible, dies buckled. Associated in time with **732, 734, 785–86, 855, 954,** and latest strikings of **730** and **733,** probably May to July 1789.

Ex J. W. Garrett: 1336. Courtesy Bowers & Ruddy Galleries, Inc.

1001 n.d. (1789) CEORCIVS III REX/Standing Indian. 3 known.
Vlack 9-87NY. Obv. of **992.** C not corrected to G. Always on small crude flans as last; always weak at upper obv., lower rev. 1) Mickley, Bushnell, Parmelee, pvt. coll. Ill. Newman

{1958} and Guide Book. 2) Mills, Bascom, Newcomer, Garrett:606, $20,000, 118.1 grs. = 7.65 gms; ill. 3) "Devonshire," Roper:277, $5,775, 80.7 grs. = 5.23 gms.

3. IMITATIONS OF STATE AND FEDERAL COPPERS

VERMONT. See **725–34.**
CONNECTICUT. See **784–92, 855–71.**
NEW JERSEY. See **954–55.**
FUGIO. See **1317–20.**

vi. THE MOULD-ATLEE "TORY COPPERS"

These pieces have long been confused with similar coins made by James F. Atlee at Machin's Mills (above). However, as they are punchlinked with some of Walter Mould's pattern dies and ultimately with the 1783–85 CONSTELLATIO NOVA coppers, they obviously have a different origin.

Walter Mould, Wyon's pupil, emigrated from Birmingham to the USA in 1785. Before the official rejection of Mould's petition for a franchise for federal copper coinage (Aug. 18, 1785: Taxay {1966}, p. 28), and possibly through part of 1786, Mould appears to have made a living of sorts by coining imitation British halfpence ("Bungtown coppers," more recently "Tory coppers"), circulating them in the New York area, eastern New Jersey, and possibly Connecticut and Pennsylvania. These are not, of course, the "base halfpence" current in Pennsylvania and banned in public payments by the Supreme Executive Council's proclamation of July 14, 1781: The time element rules that out. Crosby, pp. 169, 172, attempted to identify the latter with the British coppers bearing evasive legends such as GEORGE RULES/BRITONS ISLES. However, there is evidence that the "evasion coppers" were made about 1789–1805, and that most vars. never circulated in the USA (Thompson {1949}); S. K. Harzfeld began popularizing them in American collecting circles about 1878: Newman {1976B}, p. 151. Most likely, the lightweight coppers annoying Pennsylvania authorities were counterfeit British halfpence of George III, dated 1770–75.

As the coins here under consideration share letter punches with Wyon's CONSTELLATIO NOVA coppers, they might reasonably have been attributed to Wyon's mint in Birmingham (see Chap. 11). However, there are good arguments against such attribution. 1) The devices are too crude to have been Wyon's work. 2) After Wyon landed the contract to make CONSTELLATIO NOVA coppers for Gouverneur Morris and others, this coiner was too much in the public eye to risk trouble by counterfeiting obsolete regal halfpence. 3) Specimens have turned up in noncollector accumulations in New York and New Jersey, but to date not in any groups of coppers from Britain. 4) Wyon would not have made the careless error of leaving the British Union Jack on the shield unfimbriated. British-made counterfeit halfpence, like the genuine, normally show the fimbriations as extra outlines to the eight cross arms on the shield. Neither the present coins nor the similar ones later made in Machin's Mills **(992–97)** ever show fimbriated crosses. The only hypothesis that reasonably fits the observations is that Mould brought his tools over here from Birmingham and made his "Bungtown coppers" before he found any other source of income. Though no legal penalties existed for making them, most likely Mould kept his enterprise secret. After all, he was in the persona of an honest entrepreneur with diemaking and coining skills, petitioning for a contract to make copper coins for the states and the Confederation. This petition may have been his occasion for selling punches to Atlee, who took them first to Rahway, then to Machin's Mills.

THE MOULD-ATLEE "TORY COPPERS"

Designer, Walter Mould (after Richard Yeo). Engravers, Mould and J. F. Atlee. Mint, Mould's, 23 Williams St., NYC and/or Atlee's, NYC. Composition, copper. Diameters, about $^{17-18/16}''$ = 27–28.6 mm. Weight standard, mostly 60 to the lb. = 116.67 grs. = 7.56 gms.

Grade range, POOR to UNC. No grading standard established; grade by surface. Many are weak, uneven strikings.

1002 1747 GEORGIVS. II. REX. Large obv. pellets. Rare.
Vlack 1-47A. Usually in low grades. Any offered from different dies must show identical letter punches.

1003 1771 GEORGIVS. III. REX. Scarce.
Vlack 2-71A, 3-71B, 4-71C. All have same letter punches as var. ill. The 2-71A has some punches later used by Atlee on **742–46, 992;** its obv. device reappears on **992:** a condition discovered by Gary A. Trudgen.

1004 1772 Similar. Very rare.
Vlack 5-72A, 6-72B, 7-72B, 24–72C. Same comment.

1005 1774 Similar. GEORGIVS. Rare.
Vlack 3-74A, 8-74A, and unlisted. Same comment.

1006 1774 Same but GEORGIUS Ex. rare.
Vlack 7-74A. Same rev. as **1005.** Herstal:826; Roper:283.

1007 1775 Similar. GEORGIVS.
Vlack 4-75A. Same letter punches as preceding coins. Any offered from different dies must show identical letter punches.

1008 1776 Large date. 2 vars.
Vlack 6-76A (ill.) and unlisted. Same comments; but for the 1776 small-date coin see **992.** One has been seen overstruck on a Spanish 8 maravedis.

1009 1777 Double exergue line. Ex. rare.
Vlack 10-77A. Provenance uncertain, though conceded to be American. For later dates of "Tory coppers" see **974–75, 992–97.**

CHAPTER 8

POSTREVOLUTIONARY PRIVATE ISSUES

i. MARYLAND SILVERSMITHS
(1783–90)

After the Boston Mint closed in 1682, nobody attempted to make silver coins for local American circulation for a century. Where Spanish and Mexican dollars and fractions were readily accepted by weight, there was no acute need to melt them down for conversion into shillings or fractions in local designs and exchange rates. Where not enough silver bullion was available, there was little reason for making dies to coin it.

But almost exactly 100 years after the death of Boston mintmaster John Hull, another silversmith attempted to follow in his footsteps, both in creating a silver circulating medium and in attempting to obtain some kind of local recognition. This was Capt. John Chalmers (1750–1817), Continental Army recruiting officer, sometime Methodist preacher, later Sheriff of Baltimore: Perlitz {1948}; Schab {1984}.

To judge from its devices, Chalmers's first coinage was intended for a proposal to the Continental Congress, which met in Annapolis Nov. 1783–Aug. 1784. This is the "Rings" Shilling pattern, with its script lettering "Equal to ONE Shi" above clasped hands. Its rev. device obviously alludes to the United States in Confederation: a chain of 12 linked rings with a thirteenth within, interlinked with the three lowest; 13 stars, 11 within rings, the other two flanking a liberty cap on pole arising from within the thirteenth ring. Above the cap is the All-Seeing Eye. The iconographic message is clearly "These 13 equal states are united in liberty under God." Chalmers's choice of device was apparently influenced by the Third Maryland Regiment's flag, carried at the Battle of Cowpens, Jan. 17, 1781: 13 red and white stripes, with a blue canton containing 12 stars in a circle around a thirteenth in the center. However, no details of the Chalmers proposal have survived.

Though no state or national coinage franchise followed, Chalmers realized that no law prevented him from making local silver coins of honest weight and fineness. Accordingly, he issued shillings of a new design in quantity. Obv. shows two clasped hands in wreath. Rev. bears a peculiar symbolic device which may be read as a lesson to local citizens: Within a circular field, a hedge separates a serpent from a pair of doves squabbling over a worm. Crosby was unable to read this iconographic message because he thought the worm was a branch. However, it is clearly "While you states go on squabbling over trivialities [boundary disputes?], you don't notice what is coming over to devour you!" This was a warning that a strong centralized government, then being recommended in many quarters, might well destroy the hard-won status of individual states as independent sovereign entities under the Confederation—which in fact did happen when the Constitution was adopted. The Confedera-

tion, of course, had long been on the verge of collapse owing to money problems created by the Revolution. Chalmers may even have adopted this extreme states' rights or antifederalist position because the Confederation had rejected his coinage proposal.

With the Sixpence we discover the designer's identity. In the crescents that end the arms of the crosses flanking the clasped hands, on all vars., are letters T and S, evidently for Chalmers's friend Thomas Sparrow. Sparrow was a local silversmith who had become famous for his elaborate border cuts on Maryland notes of 1767–74, many signed T S, and during the Revolution for his inflammatory antiroyalist woodcuts on the Maryland July 26, 1775 notes, also signed T S (Wroth {1958}, p. 40; Newman {1976A}, pp. 131–34). The clasped hands occur on Sparrow's Maryland state seals: Schab {1984}.

Aside from a single tin trial piece, all the Chalmers coins are in silver, probably Spanish standard (65/72), but possibly French (11/12) or sterling (925) fineness. All have edges reeded by file, probably to reduce weights to within intended limits. Observed weights cluster closely around 56 grs. for Shillings, 28 for Sixpences, and 14 for Threepences, suggesting that Chalmers adhered to a recognized standard. The only logical one in Annapolis during the 1780s was the 1781 Maryland exchange rate, equating the Spanish dollar to 7 shillings 6 pence. Given the Spanish standard as 417.75 grs. = 27.07 gms., this works out to 55.7 grs. = 3.609 gms. per Shilling: a close enough fit that we may take this as what Chalmers intended.

Brogdon {1938} quotes early silversmith sources to the effect that Chalmers's bullion source was cut money: eighths and quarters cut from Spanish and Mexican dollars, many lightweight. This implies that his coins of honest weight could yield little or no profit. Most likely his coins advertised his family business.

In the present section we also include the tiny issue of commemorative Threepence pieces by Col. Standish Barry (Nov. 4, 1763–1844), silversmith on Market St., Baltimore (1784–85), thereafter in partnership with Joseph Rice as Rice & Barry (1785–87), later alone on Baltimore St., and still later as a merchant on North Gay St., 1796–1808. Barry was prominent in public affairs; he was a colonel in the First Rifle Regiment. The exact occasion for manufacture of his Threepence coins is unknown, most probably the opening of his new store on Baltimore St. (Brogdon). All known specimens show some degree of die failure; planchets are crude and mostly too narrow to accommodate the entire design. Their weight standard is apparently identical to that of Chalmers's. Most survivors are in low grades.

JOHN CHALMERS'S ISSUES

Designer, Engraver, Thomas Sparrow. Mint, Chalmers's, Fleet and Cornhill Sts., Annapolis. Composition, silver. Diameters, Shilling, $^{14}/_{16}''$ = 22 mm; Sixpence, $^{11}/_{16}''$ = 17.5 mm; Threepence, $^{1}/_{2}''$ = 13 mm (all vary slightly). Weight standard, Shilling, 55.7 grs. = 3.609 gms.; Sixpence, 27.85 grs. = 1.805 gms.; Threepence, 13.92 grs. = 0.902 gms. Edges reeded by file to adjust weights to standard.

Grade range, POOR to EX. FINE. No grading standards established.

1010 1783 "Rings" Pattern Shilling. 5 known.
Crosby, fig. 68. Discovered by Joseph J. Mickley before 1867. Always weak at script letters, less so at cap: Chalmers had not yet learned how to harden a die properly. 1) Mickley, Bushnell, Parmelee, Brock, Univ. of Pa., Ward, Forman, Ford, the discovery coin. 2) Newman. 3) Norweb, SI. 4) Jenks, Garrett:1313, 54.2 grs. = 3.51 gms., double-struck, $75,000, Roper:175, $24,200. 5) Lauder:177, POOR, plugged, $2,000.

1011 1783 "Birds" Shilling. Short worm. Scarce.
Crosby, Pl. IX, 5. Hedge extends between N's. Ornament after G conceals an erroneous S (a condition discovered by Richard Picker). 54–59 grs. = 3.5–3.8 gms. Lightweight counterfeits exist, usually with plain edges.

1012 1783 "Birds" Shilling. Long worm. Rare.
Crosby, Pl. IX, 6 and fig. 69. Hedge extends from N to I. Obv. always weak in center (die failure). Rarer than preceding in all grades. 44–56 grs. = 2.9–3.6 gms.

1013 1783 Sixpence. Large date 17.83 Ex. rare.
Crosby, Pl. IX, 8. The "period" dividing date is the end of one of the ornaments. 1) Robison:74, "EF," $3,000. 2) Roper:179, VF, $1,870, 27.3 grs. = 1.77 gms. 3) 1976 ANA:26, worn, $1,500.

1014 1783 Sixpence. Period after large date 1783. Ex. rare.
Crosby, Pl. IX, 7. 25.8–28 grs. = 1.67–1.8 gms. Garrett:1310, VF, $5,750.

1015 1783 Sixpence. Small date, 8-pointed star after SIX. Very rare.
Narrow numerals, unlike preceding. Large fleurons in cross. Robison:73, others.

1016 1783 Sixpence. Same dies. Tin trial piece. Unique?
NN 48:767. Genuineness doubted.

1017 1783 Sixpence. Small date, 6-pointed star after SIX. Ex. rare.
Small fleurons in cross. 1) ANS.

1018 1783 Threepence. Very rare.
Crosby, Pl. IX, 9. 10.7–14 grs. = 0.69–0.91 gms. Borders usually incomplete. Garrett:1308, AU, $7,500; Roper:180, UNC., $5,500.

STANDISH BARRY THREEPENCE

Designer, Engraver, Standish Barry. Mint, Barry's, Baltimore. Composition, silver. Diameter, about $^{1}/_{2}''$ = 13 mm (varies). Weight standard 13.92 grs. = 0.902 gms.

Grade range, GOOD to AU. No grading standard established.

1019 1790 Threepence. Ex. rare.
Crosby, Pl. X, 23 and fig. 72. 12.1–14 grs. = 0.79–0.91 gms. Always on small flans, tops of some letters usually off. Obv. die often buckled, obscuring hair details. 1976 ANA:27, "AU," $10,500. Enl. photos.

Ex J. W. Garrett: 1517. Courtesy Bowers & Ruddy Galleries, Inc.

ii. MOTT'S TOKENS (1789)

Generally believed the first American merchant's advertising tokens or store cards (in parallel with those then being made in Britain for circulation and for collectors), Mott's coppers bear a design which was to become identified with U.S. gold for a century. The firm of William and John Mott, of 240 Water St., New York City, as late as 1822 imported watches, jewelry, and silverware; their tokens display on one side a grandfather clock called a "regulator," on the other an eagle which is the nestmate of the Reich eagle found on federal gold coins 1807–1908, and may have been its actual prototype: Bushnell {1864}.

They come on thick and thin flans, the thin almost four times rarer. Some thin-flan specimens show peculiar edge ornamentation consisting of tiny raised and incuse square areas alternating like the black squares on adjacent rows of a chessboard. Despite claims that the thick-flan specimens may have been made as late as 1794–95 (to pass at par with federal cents), die-break evidence indicates that thick- and thin-flan specimens alternated, and we still do not know which came first.

Adams {1920} claims a British lettered edge: This is unconfirmed, but if it exists and is not an overstrike on a British token, it would indicate a Birmingham origin for these pieces. To date no punch linkage has been demonstrated between the Mott tokens and anything else.

They probably circulated at first as regular Birmingham coppers (14–18 per shilling), at least until the July 1789 copper panic. After 1793 the thick-flan coins doubtless passed as cents. Most come well worn; true mint-state survivors are exceedingly rare. Even EF examples seldom show full inscriptions, as the dies wore down, broke down, and rusted, obscuring many letters on either side. A well-struck specimen with fully legible clock face and completely clear inscriptions is a rarity.

MOTT'S TOKENS

Designer, Engraver, Mint, uncertain (Mott's, NYC?). Composition, copper. Diameter, thick flan, $18/16'' = 28.6$ mm; thin flan, $17.5/16'' = 27.8$ mm (both vary). Weights, variable, as noted.

Grade range, VG to UNC. No grading standard established; grade by surface. On coins with broken and rusted dies, inscriptions are normally partly obscured, clock face partly illegible, even near mint state. The perfect-die coin ill. is exceptionally clear and must not be taken as typical!

1020 1789 Copper. Plain edge, thick flan.
Crosby, Pl. IX, 17; Adams {1920} NY 610. 163.6–171 grs. = 10.6–11.08 gms., for 40 to the lb. Early and late states; but compare **1022**.

1021 1789 Same. Plain edge, thin flan. Very scarce.
Adams NY 611; Wright {1972} 728. 108–122 grs. = 7–7.91 gms., for 60 to the lb. Early and late states; but compare **1025**.
1022 1789 Same. Plain edge, cent weight. Very rare.
Apparent standard, 208 grs. = 13.48 gms. Mostly late state. 1) Garrett:1516, EF, $1,300, 202.5 grs. = 13.13 gms. 2) Roper:337, EF, $550, 233.4 grs. = 15.12 gms.; others.
1023 1789 Same. Jumbo piedfort. Unique?
Extra broad borders distinguish this from last. 1) C. E. Bullowa, 1980.
1024 1789 Same. Ornamented edge, thick flan. Ex. rare.
1) Dr. Spence:755, "AU," $850 (1975).
1025 1789 Same. Ornamented edge, thin flan. Very rare.
Adams NY 612. 103–110 grs. = 6.66–7.14 gms., possibly for 64 to the lb. Usually in low grades. Robison:209, "EF," $625; Roper:338, UNC., $1,265.

1026 1789 Same dies. Lettered edge. Untraced.
Adams NY 613, which gives edge as PAYABLE AT LIVERPOOL LONDON OR BRISTOL. See introductory text.
1027 1789 Same dies. Pewter trial piece. Ex. rare.
Adams NY 613A. 1) Heifetz:343, Ford.

iii. *TALBOT, ALLUM & LEE* CENTS (1794–95)

During 1794–95, despite fairly large-scale operations by the Philadelphia Mint, copper coinage of acceptable weight and purity remained in short supply. At this juncture, probably inspired alike by the success of Mott's tokens and the profitable import business in British "Hard Ware," the New York firm of Talbot, Allum & Lee, of 241 Water St., importers of goods from India, contracted with Peter Kempson & Co., Birmingham, England, for at least two tons of tokens of the usual halfpenny size. However, these were to be cents rather than halfpence, as their inscriptions (1794) and edge lettering (1795) spell out. They went into circulation and stayed there, despite being lighter than federal cents, possibly because over half were of the familiar and trusted Tower Mint weight standard, and the rest were only a little under it (50 rather than 46 to the lb.), all reassuringly heavier than the thin, sleazy coppers which had become discredited in July 1789.

The first var. erroneously omitted NEW YORK; its stock rev. broke at once, and its ship die was discarded because of the blunder. Later vars. dated 1794 are mostly common and usually come in circulated condition. Their edge device, PAYABLE AT THE STORE OF, appears also on a few tokens made for British collectors: D&H Hamps. (Emsworth) 11c, (Gosport) 41b; Warwickshire (Birmingham) 50f, all of great rarity.

Those dated 1795 were formerly considered rare, but a hoard found in Britain after WW II yielded many UNC. examples, mostly brown to light olive, fewer original red. Their edge device (unusable on circulating British tokens because of the cent denomination) nevertheless appears on some very rare vars. aimed at collectors: D&H Essex (Braintree) 4b; Suffolk (Blything) 19b, (Ipswich) 35g; Sussex (Chichester) 17b; Warwickshire (Birmingham) 60c.

On April 5, 1795, the Philadelphia Mint bought some 1,076 lbs. (about 52,000 tokens) from William Talbot, and cut them down to make half-cent planchets. Many of the tokens were of the 1795 issue; the half cents are 1795's without pole, though struck in spring 1796. At least two large cents dated 1795 are overstruck on these tokens, one a Sheldon 75 in SI, the other a new var. (Sheldon NC-2) in private hands; edge letterings remained intact.

Mr. Lee retired in 1796, and the firm dissolved in 1798 (Bushnell {1858}, {1864}; Crosby, p. 336); no more tokens were ordered, but the older ones continued to circulate. In the meantime, Elias Boudinot, Philadelphia Mint Director, bought the remaining undistributed stock from William Talbot, Dec. 12, 1796, and ordered them cut down into half-cent planchets. Almost all these tokens were dated 1795; the half cents included two vars. dated 1797, the "1 over 1" and Centered Head coins.

The Talbot, Allum & Lee tokens are by far the largest merchant token issue for American circulation, effectively bridging the gap between Birmingham "Hard Ware" of the 1780s and Philadelphia Mint cents. They have remained popular for over a century. Their small number of designs led their coiners to make other vars. for collectors, some with unfamiliar edges, others with alien revs. Though the latter did not circulate, they have been brought back to the USA by coin collectors ever since the 1850s. The list below is the most comprehensive yet attempted; other vars. possibly still exist in British collections.

TALBOT, ALLUM & LEE CENTS

Designer, Engraver, Thomas Wyon. Mint, Kempson's, Birmingham. Composition, copper. Diameter, $^{18}/_{16}'' = 28.6$ mm. Weight standards, variable, as noted. Edges, PAYABLE AT THE STORE OF (1794); WE PROMISE TO PAY THE BEARER ONE CENT (1795), except as noted.

Grade range, GOOD to UNC. GOOD: Devices outlined, all inscriptions and date legible. VERY GOOD: Partial drapery details. FINE: Over half drapery details, partial waves; rope on bale almost complete. VERY FINE: Over half hull details. EXTREMELY FINE: Isolated tiny wear spots on a few high points. Higher levels: grade by surface. EXCEPTIONS: **1028** and most mules are unevenly struck.

1028 1794 Cent. Without NEW YORK. Ex. rare.
Adams {1920} NY 880; Fuld {1956} 1. Struck at 46 to the lb. Usually in low grades, G to F, often rough. Garrett:1536, "VF," $2,100, 144.8 grs. = 9.39 gms.; Roper:347, 147.7 grs. = 9.571 gms., EF, $990.

1029 1794 Cent. With NEW YORK; rev., large &. Thick flan.
Crosby, Pl. IX, 19; Adams NY 878A; Fuld 2. 46 to the lb. = 152.17 grs. = 9.86 gms. average.

1030 1794 Cent. Same dies. Thin flan. Rare.
50 to the lb. = 140 grs. = 9.072 gms.; observed, 140.5 grs. = 9.1 gms.
1031 1794 Cent. Same dies. Plain edge. 3 or 4 known.
Adams NY 878. Merkin 10/66:43. 153.75 grs. = 9.96 gms., for 46 to the lb.
1032 1794 Cent. Small &'s. Usual edge. 2 vars.
Adams NY 879. Price for the var. ill., Crosby, Pl. IX, 18 = Fuld 4. The other var., Fuld 3, has N of NEW entirely beyond A, and is very rare. Both vars. seen at 46 to the lb., as **1029.**

1033 1794 Cent. Similar. Plain edge. 2 or 3 known.
Same dies as both vars. of **1032**: "Fuld 3A," discovered by Robert Bashlow; Fuld 4A, Boyd estate. Former 151.5 grs. = 9.81 gms., for 46 to the lb.
1034 1794 Cent. Similar. Silver OMS. Usual edge. 3 known.
Dies of Fuld 4 (see **1032**). 1) BM, 178.4 grs. = 11.56 gms. 2) Murdoch:934, Chapman, Ryder, Boyd estate. 3) Europe (1984), Ivy/Heritage 5/30/85:511, Terranova, 179.5 grs. = 11.63 gms.
1035 1795 Cent. Thick flan. Usual edge.
Crosby, Pl. IX, 20; Adams NY 881; Fuld 1. 151–156.5 grs. = 9.78–10.04 gms., for 46 to the lb. The ill. is of a proof, Morton:604.

1036 1795 Cent. Thinner flan.
Struck at 50 to the lb., 140 grs. = 9.07 gms.
1037 1795 Cent. Same dies. Edge, CURRENT EVERY WHERE. Unique?
Adams NY 881A; Fuld 1A. Parmelee, Jenks, Ryder, Boyd estate. This edge recurs on at least 15 vars. of British tokens, mostly from Kempson's mint; most often on tokens of R. Campin, Haberdasher, Norwich (D&H Norfolk 20–21), whose 1793 stock rev. reappears on Kempson's Emsworth coppers.
1038 1795 Cent. Same dies. Edge, twin olive leaves. Unique?
Adams NY 881B; Fuld 1B. Ex C. E. Clapp, Clarke, NN 48:787.
1039 1795 Cent. Same dies. Plain edge. 2 known.
Adams NY 882; Fuld 1C. 149 grs. = 9.66 gms., for 46 to the lb.

Mules with British Token Dies: 1794

1040 1794 Rev., BIRMINGHAM HALFPENNY 1793 London edge. Rare.
Bushnell {1858} 3; Birchall 38, p. 11; Atkins 34; Adams NY 883; D&H Warwickshire (Birmingham) 54; Fuld Mule 1. Small & as in **1032**. Edge, PAYABLE IN LONDON and ornaments.

1041 1794 Same dies. Plain edge. Ex. rare.
Fuld Mule 1A. Bushnell, Ryder, Boyd estate.
1042 1794 Same dies. Brass. Ex. rare.
Adams NY 883A. Ex Cohen:2317 (1875), Haines coll.
1043 1794 Same obv. Rev., stork. Warehouse edge. Scarce.
Bushnell 4; Birchall 25, p. 48; Atkins 31; Adams NY 885; D&H Hamps. (Petersfield) 52; Fuld Mule 2. Struck at 46 to the lb. Edge, PAYABLE AT THE WAREHOUSE LIVERPOOL x x x, intended for Kempson's imitation Liverpool

halfpence, D&H Lancs. (Liverpool) 89; it recurs on other Wyon/Kempson issues aimed at collectors: D&H Cambridgeshire 14a, Middlesex 1035b, Sussex 17d.

1044 1794 Same dies. London edge. Ex. rare.
Adams NY 884; D&H Hamps. (Petersfield) 52a; Fuld Mule 2A. Edge as **1040.** NN 60:424; Bolt, Laird Park:71.
1045 1794 Same dies. Plain edge. Ex. rare.
D&H Hamps. (Petersfield) 52b; Fuld Mule 2B.
1046 1794 Same dies. Brass. Untraced.
Adams NY 885A. Ex Cohen:2316 (1875).
1047 1794 Same obv. Rev., bust, EARL HOWE etc. London edge. Scarce.
Bushnell 2; Atkins 28; Adams NY 887; D&H Hamps. (Emsworth) 25; Fuld Mule 3. Always unevenly struck and with break joining HOWE & T, as ill. The Howe die is from one of the tokens made for the Emsworth grocer and tea dealer John Stride. Edge as **1040.** Richard, Earl Howe (1726–99), was the Admiral Howe of the 1779 Rhode Island ship tokens; the legend alludes to his triumphal return after a victory over the French at Ushant, June 1, 1794.

1048 1794 Similar, point of cap to E. Tin. Plain edge. Unique.
Adams NY 887A; Fuld Mule 4. Rev. of D&H Hamps (Emsworth) 23. Boyd estate.

1049 1794 Same obv. Rev., bust, IOHN HOWARD etc. London edge. Scarce.
Bushnell 1; Atkins 25; Adams NY 886; D&H Hamps. (Portsmouth) 56; Fuld Mule 5; Bell {1968} 14, p. 25. Always unevenly struck, as ill.; varying amounts of rev. die rust. Edge as **1040.** John Howard (1726–90), sheriff of Bedford, was a prison reformer. His testimony before Parliament led to pas-

sage of laws (1794) greatly improving inmates' living conditions. Vlack's specimen counterstamped with head of John the Baptizer on platter was for circulation in Malta, 1814, *CNL* 4/68, p. 15.
1050 1794 Same. Plain edge. Ex. rare.
NN 60:428. Intermediate state of die rust.

Mules with British Token Dies: 1795

1051 1795 Regular obv. Rev., BLOFIELD CAVALRY. Vine edge. Ex. rare.
Bushnell 5; Atkins 11; Adams NY 888; D&H Norfolk (Blofield) 10; Fuld Mule 6. Edge, sinuous line with dots for leaves. Other edges may exist. Bolt, Laird Park: 74; Dr. Spence:762.

1052 1795 Same obv. Rev., cathedral. Fear God edge. Ex. rare.
Atkins 60; Adams NY 888A; D&H Yorkshire (York) 65; Fuld Mule 7. Edge, FEAR GOD AND HONOUR THE KING. x x Bolt, Laird Park:75. This edge, from 1 Peter 2:17, recurs on another very rare Wyon/Kempson concoction, D&H Hamps (Petersfield) 47a.

1053 1795 Same. Demand edge. Unique?
Rulau-E NY 888C. Edge, PAYABLE ON DEMAND. 1) Baldwin, Ford, Fleischer:578. Discovery (1960) announced by R. A. Vlack, *CNL* 10/61, p. 2.
1054 1795 Same. Plain edge. Ex. rare, untraced.
Bushnell 6; Adams NY 888B; D&H Yorkshire (York) 65a; Fuld Mule 7A. Other edges may exist.

iv. JACOBS'S *THEATRE AT NEW YORK* PENNY (1796)

During the 1790s, the largest theater in New York City was the Park Theatre, on Park Row about 200 feet north of Ann St.; its stage entrance was at the end of an alley still known as Theatre Alley (joining Beekman and Ann St.). The theater seated about 2,372. Designed by the architect Brunel, this building externally never looked much like his conception (the Penny copies Brunel's rendering: Hemstreet {1901}). Its cornerstone was laid May 5, 1795; construction began the following June 1. The proprietors petitioned city authorities for permission to erect a portico above the sidewalk, but for unknown reasons the bureaucrats refused, and from then until the theater burned down its exterior remained "barbarous . . . a miserable barrack" (as one observer described it about 1809). After many delays and some difficulties in financing the project, the Park Theatre opened on Jan. 29, 1798, with *As You Like It*. During its first decade, actors often played to half-empty houses; during 1809–10 the Park was the only theater in operation in the city, but during the next decade it was the most famous one. It burned to the ground after a performance, May 25, 1820; its proprietors, John Jacob Astor and John K. Beekman, promptly rebuilt it, but fire again attacked the site on July 4, 1821, and reopening was delayed until the following Sept. 1. It hosted the American premiere of Beethoven's *Fidelio,* Sept. 3, 1839. This jinxed theater again fell victim to fire on the night of Dec. 16, 1848, when a pile of playbills hanging at the prompter's entrance was blown or brushed against a gas jet (John and Damia Francis, personal communication).

The Penny is uniform with the remainder of the series of notable buildings depicted on penny tokens by the engraver Jacobs for Skidmore, the coin dealer and ironmonger of High Holborn St., London. Some have claimed that these Pennies were used as admission tickets; for this there is no evidence, and against it is the proof state of all known survivors, even as with Jacobs's other penny tokens of this series.

Nothing is known of the origin or purpose of the ANTIENT SCOTTISH WASHING mule, though its fabric proves it a fanciful production aimed at some coin collector.

JACOBS'S THEATRE AT NEW YORK PENNY

Designer, Engraver, B. Jacobs (except as noted). Mint, Skidmore's, High Holborn St., London. Composition, copper (except as noted). Diameter, $21.5/16'' = 34$ mm. Weight standard, apparently $17\frac{1}{2}$ to the lb. $= 400$ grs. $= 25.92$ gms. Proofs only.

1055 n.d. (1796?) Penny. Proof. Promise edge. 10–12 known?
Adams {1920} NY 892; D&H Middx. (London misc.) 167; Wright {1972} 1130. Edge, WE PROMISE TO PAY ON DEMAND THE BEARER ONE PENNY x as on other Jacobs penny tokens. The rumor of 2 minor vars. remains unconfirmed. 402.8–409.8 grs. $= 26.1$–26.55 gms. Garrett:1529, $8,000; Roper:355, $4,400.

1056 n.d. Same dies. Plain edge. Unverified.
Adams NY 893. Beware of cast or electrotype copies.
1057 n.d. Mule penny. Obv. as 1055. Tin. Unique?
Wright 1130A; Rulau-E NY 894. Rev. of Wyon's 1797 Loch Leven penny, D&H Kinrosshire 1 (p. 413), depicting a woman with her feet in a tub, explaining the archaic (supposedly comic) inscription. Exposure of her legs in the process

doubtless recalled the incident leading to creation of the Order of the Garter, hence the Order's motto appears too: HONI SOIT QUI MAL Y PENSE, 'Shame on whoever thinks ill of it.' Discovered in the 1890s by Dr. Benjamin P. Wright.   1) Wright, Boyd, Ford coll.

v. THE *CASTORLAND* DEMI ÉCUS (1796)

Among the less known American side effects of the French Revolution was the flight to upper New York State (even before the Reign of Terror) by many families who justly feared the Revolutionary Tribunal (1792). Among the sites selected by a group of these exiles was a tract of 630,000 acres occupying much of the present Lewis and Jefferson Counties on the Beaver River. Representing the entire group, Pierre Chassanis bought this tract from William Constable on Aug. 31, 1792, for 52,000 "louis sterling" (Pounds?). Chassanis issued a prospectus in Oct. 1792, subdividing the tract into 100-acre lots offered at the equivalent of $152.88 apiece. The 41 leading subscribers (who had bought a total of 818 of these lots) met on June 28, 1793, at Chassanis's Paris home, 28 rue de Jussienne, and adopted a constitution as the "Compagnie de New-York." The Company seal bore for device a beaver (in French, *castor*) nibbling at a maple tree, with CASTORLAND in exergue. Trustees of the Company and others took ship for America, arriving on Sept. 7, 1793; they got short shrift from local authorities, who did not welcome any influx of French-speaking aliens. The colonists set about to farm the land, tap maple trees for sugar, and hunt and trap furbearing animals. They built a mill, a forge, and a canal, and they founded two villages, Castorville (now known as Castorland) and Carthage—this latter an ominous name, as the colony perished as abjectly as its original namesake.

In 1796, Chassanis—who had been unable to emigrate to his lands during the Terror—and the new trustee Rudolph Tillier (successor to M. Desjardins, one of the original trustees) managed to persuade the Paris Mint to strike silver half écus as a proposed currency for the colony, with distinctive designs by one of the DuViviers (probably Benjamin). Tillier brought the coins to the settlement, where they went into circulation; most survivors are well worn.

Some of their peculiar design features require explanation. The obv. shows a head ambiguously interpretable as France or the Colony, laureate for divine favor, veiled for respectability, and coroneted with what looks like the crenelated tower of a brick fort, probably one built in the colony. Legend FRANCO-AMERICANA COLONIA, 'French-American Colony,' identifies the settlement; CASTORLAND in exergue alludes to the company seal. Rev. depicts the Goddess Ceres, patroness of agriculture, looking at a freshly tapped maple tree, whose sap flows into an open vessel. In her right hand is a cornucopia for agricultural abundance, in her left a drill for tapping maple trees; at her right foot a wheat sheaf and small sickle, in exergue a beaver (for *Castorville,* 'Beaver Town,' on the Beaver River). SALVE MAGNA PARENS FRUGUM, 'Hail, great mother of crops,' is from Virgil, *Georgics* 2:173; the original line continued *Saturnia tellus, magna virum,* making the meaning 'Hail, great Saturnian land, mighty mother of crops and men.'

Epidemics decimated the colony and killed off most of the cattle during the excessively severe winters of 1794–95 and 1795–96, and one trustee, Pharoux, drowned with all his surveying instruments; misfortune mounted and most of the colony's funds were stolen in spring 1796. The honesty of Tillier, Chassanis's main representative, came into grave doubt. As a result of these adversities more and more of the surviving colonists abandoned their holdings and departed, some for

France, others for Louisiana and elsewhere. Gouverneur Morris filed suit on behalf of Chassanis (who never did settle on his lands), attempting to recover everything from Tillier, who promptly fled to Louisiana. Chassanis died in Paris, Nov. 28, 1803. Various New Yorkers bought parcels and plots of land. Amid increasing scandal, the Company finally dissolved July 1, 1814, and its Swiss creditors took over everything; today nothing remains but the local names and the few surviving coins: Morin {1938}.

Some have claimed that the original coins were merely souvenirs or "honorariums for attending meetings." Both the weight standard and the survivors' circulated state argue against any such conclusion. Being good silver, the coins were readily acceptable in trade; their weight standard indicates that they would have been locally valued at 1/2 écu = 1/2 French crown = 5/9 Dollar in New York currency, or higher elsewhere. Each piece was heavier than either a federal half dollar or a pair of 2-real pieces.

Gadoury {1978} gives 14.744 gms. (= 227.53 grs.) as standard for French half écus 1774–92; if this is meant for 16⅔ to the marc, it should be 228.9 grs. = 14.83 gms. Observed weight range of silver originals matches or exceeds this standard, while even the earliest restrikes are lighter. Copper originals vary more widely but appear to have been struck to the same weight standard as the silver coins, suggesting a denomination of 15 deniers.

Original dies have oldstyle lettering; on obv., A is below M, 1 of date embedded in a border bead. On rev., S is far below AL, M below AG, UG touch, remainder irregularly spaced. All originals seen to date have traces of rust near vessel handle but no bulge at PARENS and no break at final S; restrikes from these dies show both failures in various states. I first described the sequence in NN *Numisma* 11–12/56, p. 65.

Later lightweight restrikes are from a copy rev.; subsequent ones from several pairs of copy obv. and rev. dies. The period during which any given restrike was made can be ascertained by inspecting the mint director's symbol beside the metal designation (OR, 'gold,' ARGENT, 'silver,' CUIVRE, 'copper' or BRONZE) on edge. Before 1821 this was a rooster; 1822–42, an anchor; 1843–45, a ship's prow; 1846–60, a hand; 1860–79, a bee; 1880–present day, a cornucopia *(SCWC,* p. 605). Some coins made 1897–1920 may have no symbol. Earlier restrikes (before about 1900) are brilliant proofs; later ones have matte finish. No information is available on quantities issued or relative scarcity of any of the later restrikes.

THE **CASTORLAND** DEMI ÉCUS

Designer, Engraver, DuVivier. Mint, Paris. Composition, silver, 11/12 Fine, except as noted. Weight standard, 227.53 grs. = 14.74 gms. (?), except as noted. Diameter, 20–21/16″ = 32–33 mm.

Grade range (originals), VG to AU, all mint-state examples seen being Proofs. FINE: About half details of hair, leaves, and drapery. VERY FINE: About 3/4 details of hair, leaves, and drapery. EXTREMELY FINE: Isolated tiny spots of wear on cheek, hair, knees, breasts, etc.

1058   1796 Demi Écu. Original. Silver. Reeded edge. Very rare.
223–238.5 grs. = 14.45–15.45 gms. See introductory text. Garrett:1519, Proof, $4,250.

1059   1796 15 Deniers? Original. Copper. Reeded edge. 6–8 known?
195.7–249.2 grs. = 12.68–16.15 gms. Garrett:1520, Proof, $2,100. Kosoff Estate: 4134, AU, $2,035.
1060   1796 Brass OMS. Original. Reeded edge. Unique?
Mills, Garrett:1522, 220.7 grs. = 14.31 gms.
1061   1796 Gold OMS. Original or earliest restrike? Reeded edge. Untraced.
Gschwend:96. If meant for 3 louis d'or = 72 livres, this would weigh about 354.13 grs. = 22.947 gms. Not to be confused with **1069,** which is from different dies.
1062   1796 First restrike. Same dies. Silver. Reeded edge. Very rare.
Without ARGENT on edge. Buckling at PARENS (at first very faint); later, break through final S into field. Earliest impressions are almost indistinguishable from originals except by weight. 178–196.7 grs. = 11.53–12.75 gms., possibly for 21 to the marc = 179.87 grs. = 11.65 gms.
1063   1796 Same. Copper. Reeded edge. Very rare.
Earle:2066. Same comments. ANS's weighs 126 grs. = 8.17 gms., for 30 to the marc?
1064   1796 Second restrike. Same dies, broken, bulged. Silver. Rare.
ARGENT on edge. 178 grs. = 11.53 gms. May exist with reeding over ARGENT.
1065   1796 Same. Copper. Rare.
CUIVRE on edge. May exist with reeding over CUIVRE.
1066   1796 Third restrike. Same obv., copy rev. Silver.
Vertical serifs to rev. letters. ARGENT on edge, with or without reeding.
1067   1796 Third restrike. Same. Copper. CUIVRE on edge.
Comes with or without reeding over CUIVRE.
1068   1796 Third restrike. Same. Copper. Plain edge.
Without CUIVRE. ANS, others.
1069   1796 Later restrike. Copy dies. Gold. Rare.
OR on edge. See introductory text. Garrett:1524, 302.5 grs. = 19.6 gms., for 12½ to the marc?
1070   1796 Later restrike. Copy dies. Silver.
ARGENT on edge. See introductory text.
1071   1796 Later restrike. Copy dies. Copper.
CUIVRE on edge. See introductory text.
1072   1796 Later restrike. Copy dies. Bronze.
BRONZE on edge. See introductory text.

vi. *MYDDELTON'S* KENTUCKY PATTERNS (1796)

Philip Parry Price Myddelton (his born name lacked the "Myddelton") managed to come into possession of an enormous land tract in Kentucky. During 1795–96, he persuaded hundreds of English farmers and laborers to emigrate to his Kentucky lands, promising them steady employment.

During his preparations for full-scale operation, anticipating that his people would need some kind of small change, Myddelton went to the Boulton & Watt Soho Mint in Birmingham and ordered sample halfpence made from specially designed dies by Conrad H. Küchler. Their devices are remarkable for their beauty as well as their iconography. On obv., Hope (with anchor) presents two children to Liberty, who holds a liberty pole. Behind Ms. Liberty is a cornucopia, in allusion to Kentucky's fertility; between her and the children is a wreathed seedling, symbolic of Myddelton's project. On rev. is Britannia, dejected, her spear inverted (a clear reference to the defeat at Yorktown), with the scales of Justice and the fasces on the ground. She looks at a liberty cap which has sprung up from the ground like some kind of mushroom. This rev. device must have been considered seditious, if not treasonable. In Aug. 1796, authorities flung Myddelton into Newgate prison, charging him with "brain drain," literally "enticing artificers to emigrate to the United States," ending his ambitious project (*CNL* 12/63, p. 12).

At least one of the dozen or so silver proofs retains its original, snugly fitting cylindrical metal case; this is only slightly larger than the coin. The silver strikings' weight indicates Myddelton intended a florin (2 shillings) denomination, over 50 years before the Tower Mint made any. Tower Mint shillings weighed 66 to the troy lb. = 87.28 grs. = 5.655 gms., 1763–1919; Myddelton's silver proofs weigh double that. His copper pieces were coined at 40 to the lb., too heavy for Tower halfpence (which had not been struck since 1775), and heavier still than Birmingham "Hard Ware."

Mintage figures were found by Richard Margolis in a manuscript volume, "Rough Medal Ledger," in Soho Mint Archives, Central Reference Library, Birmingham. Myddelton returned 46 of the original 50 silver pieces; more may have been made later.

The mules with the COPPER COMPANY OF UPPER CANADA rev. were made by coiners at the Soho Mint a few years later (Willey says 1802–3), as samples. They have no more direct American relevance than the Talbot, Allum & Lee mules, but are collected as associated items; they are shown below along with Noël-Alexandre Ponthon's Canadian pattern halfpenny, to which the rev. belonged. (This latter was made for Gov. Simcoe of Canada, but his recall in 1796 broke off negotiations with Boulton.) About 1894, one J. Rochelle Thomas struck copies for sale to collectors: gold [3?], silver [12], bronze [50], tin [12?], lead [3?], and a few uniface trials. Their lettering is modern, with tails of R's on rev. curling upward, entirely unlike the originals: Ford {1951B}. Ponthon's halfpenny is not actually relevant to American prefederal coinages, but has been consistently collected as such for many generations, partly because of its rev. die's association with **1076**. As Thomas's copies have deceived many, illustration of originals is necessary.

THE 1796 **MYDDELTON** PATTERNS

Designer, Engraver, Conrad Heinrich Küchler (except **1077**). Mint, Boulton & Watt, Birmingham. Composition, silver, 925 Fine; copper. Diameter, $^{18.5}/16'' = 29.4$ mm. Weight standard, silver, 33 to the troy lb. = 174.546 grs. = 11.310 gms.; copper, 40 to the lb. = 175 grs. = 11.34 gms. Plain edges.

Proofs only.

1073 1796 Pattern Florin. Silver. [50+] 15–20 known.
Crosby, Pl. IX, 22; Rulau-E Ky. 2. 173.7–180 grs. = 11.26–11.67 gms.; only one reported above 177 grs. (Crosby). Enl. photos. Aulick, Garrett:1527, $6,750; Roper:349, $5,500. Boulton sold these at 2s6d each, without mention of denomination; he delivered the initial batch to Myddelton on March 8, 1796.

1074 1796 Pattern Halfpenny. Same dies. Copper. [7+] 8–10 known.
Rulau-E Ky. 1. 161.4–177 grs. = 10.63–11.47 gms. Ellsworth, Garrett:1526, $9,500, Auction 82:1010, $5,000; Roper:350, $5,720. Boulton sold these at 6d each, as "bronzed"; the first mention is dated March 19, 1796.

1075 1796 Uniface trial of unfinished rev. of preceding. Tin. Unique?
Without inscription. 1) British collection of Soho Mint strikings, James D. King.

1076 1796 (i.e., 1802–3) Copper Mule Halfpenny. Ex. rare.
Crosby, Pl. IX, 23; Breton 722; Haxby-Willey 261. 138.2–166 grs. = 8.955–10.8 gms. Robison:223, $3,000; Roper:351, $3,960.

1077 1794 Pattern Halfpenny. Same rev. Copper. Ex. rare.
Breton 721; Haxby-Willey 259; Willey A2. By Ponthon. Legend = 'We spread around fertility and wealth.' Mills, Garrett:1528, $3,600, Auction 82:1013, $1,700. As the Murdoch coll. (1903) pictured neither the tin OMS nor the uniface die trials, we are not sure these are originals instead of J. Rochelle Thomas's struck copies: See introductory text.

vii. ISSUES FOR SPANISH FLORIDA

Owing to the original Line of Demarcation (the notorious Pope Alexander VI's decision of May 5, 1493) which divided the Western Hemisphere between Spanish and Portuguese claimants, Florida remained a Spanish possession until Feb. 10,

1763, when the British took it over from the *Capitanía de la Florida.* In 1783 the Spaniards regained the territory, only to find in 1803 that the United States claimed part of it as among the lands transferred in the Louisiana Purchase. Unlike Gaul, Florida was divided only into two parts, of which *Florida Occidental* (West Florida) included also the southern sections of what are now Mississippi, Alabama, and Louisiana; its capital was Pensacola. On Oct. 27, 1810, Pres. Madison signed a proclamation taking possession of this area as far east as the River Perdido. *Florida Oriental* (East Florida) comprised the huge peninsula, the majority of Spanish Florida; its capital was San Agustín, now St. Augustine. In 1819, the United States bought the whole tract from the Spanish government for $5 million.

During the entire time Spain possessed Florida, the monetary needs of the wealthier colonists appear to have been met by circulation of Mexican silver dollars; there were almost no local issues, and the pieces described below are the only ones ever claimed for the Capitanía de la Florida. About the first there has been some doubt; skeptics have claimed that the individual named on rev. (Juan Estevan de Peña) in affixing the name "Florida" was using a matronymic rather than identifying the locale. However, its fabric suggests a proclamation 4 Reales (half Mexican dollar), like its 1789 counterpart; this would be confirmed were Peña identifiable as a local high official: See below. In support of the belief that it is a coin rather than a medal is Dickeson's report {1859} that Mickley's discovery example turned up in circulation as a half dollar, presumably before 1857 while foreign silver coins were legal tender in the USA. About the 1789 piece there has never been any controversy.

Proclamation pieces were a kind of commemorative issue struck by order of territorial or district governors, city mayors, bishops, or colleges on the coronation of each new Spanish king. Most bear portraits of the new king (often, in the New World, imaginary effigies), with the coronation year; revs. vary, legends may be Spanish, Latin, or macaronic combinations. Those judged to be coins have weights fitting into the Spanish coinage system. That makes the proclamation 4 Reales pieces the direct unacknowledged ancestors of our modern commemorative half dollars!

Designers, engravers, and mints are unknown but certainly local. Physical specifications below. The coins are so rare that grade is irrelevant.

1078 1760 Proclamation 4 Reales. Silver. Ex. rare.
Dickeson {1859} Pl. VIII, 1; Herrera 56 (Pl. 29); Betts {1894} 454; Medina 63; Grove K-21; Rulau-E Fla. 1. 21/16" = 33 mm. Die-struck or cast. Rose = *Florida*, 'flowery'? 1) Ex Mickley, pierced. 2) Woodward 18:394, "VF" (Feb. 23–26, 1874). Others in private colls.

1079 1789 Proclamation 4 Reales. Silver. Ex. rare.
Herrera 133 (Pl. 55); Betts {1897} 10; Medina 148; Grove C-58. Discovered by Adolfo Herrera, 1882. 21/16" = 33 mm. 213 grs. = 13.8 gms. Die-struck or cast. 1) Clarke III:3644, L.I. specialist. Macaronic legend would read as LA FLORIDA ORIENTAL PER ZESPEDES PROCLAMATUR 1789 if written in full = 'East Florida, 1789 (Coronation) proclaimed by (Gov. Don Vicente Manuel de) Zespedes.' The

jasmine between lion and castle = Florida among Spanish domains (the lion and castle meaning the kingdoms of Leon and Castile united as Spain).

1080 1789 Same. Bronze. Ex. rare.
Die vars. exist. ANS, pvt. colls.

viii. THE TEXAS JOLAS (1817–18)

Owing to a chronic shortage of low-denomination copper coins of any size (locally called *jolas),* in 1817 Gov. Martínez of the Presidio (Fort) of San Fernando de Bexar (later San Antonio), Tex., authorized one Manuel Barrera, merchant and jeweler, to coin 8,000 jolas, to pass current at 1/2 Real apiece. No specimen of this issue has survived. We may conjecture that they were copper, 15–20 mm, with initials MB, date 1817, and value 1/2. Apparently because Barrera could not redeem his coinage, it was withdrawn Dec. 6, 1818, when Martínez granted a similar coining monopoly to the local postmaster, José Antonio de la Garza, again authorizing 8,000 specimens. These also remained untraced until 1959, when about 60 were unearthed on the banks of the San Antonio River, the first by visitors James J. Zotz (Sr. and Jr.) and Richard Zotz, the rest by local laborers. Dr. G. W. Vogt published the historical details in *CW* 4/23/80. Their incuse five-pointed star on blank backs is believed to represent the earliest use of the Texas "Lone Star" symbol.

Weight range, 23.3–26.9 grs. = 1.51–1.74 gms. The coins are rare enough, and crudely enough made, that grading is all but impossible and hardly relevant.

1081 1818 1/2 Real or Jola. [All kinds 8,000] Numerator near J. Rare.
J.A.G. = José Antonio de la Garza. 18–20 mm. 35–40 known. Morton:607.

1082 1818 1/2 Real or Jola. Numerator near G. Very rare.
15–17 mm. 20–25 known. Morton:608.

ix. THE OREGON BEAVER
TOKENS (1820)

Only a single issue qualifies as a colonial circulating medium for the Pacific Northwest. This is the 1820 NORTH WEST COMPANY token, made in Birmingham by John Walker & Co. for Canadian promoters of a beaver-trapping enterprise which in 1812 bought out John Jacob Astor's interest, attempting to break the Hudson's Bay Company monopoly. Its stock die with TOKEN 1820 apparently portrays the Regent, later King George IV. With a single exception, survivors are pierced; they were dug up in the Columbia and Umpqua River Valleys (Oregon) areas. They are believed to have represented one beaver pelt apiece.

Earlier students assigned them to Canada because this Oregon area was under Canadian influence, though not officially a British territory. Their Colonial American relevance is established because the Oregon/Northwest Territory area, then an unexplored wilderness, later became part of the continental USA, and because the tokens were actually used in trade between Umpqua trappers and the Company's buyers, presumably at Company stores, just as in present-day Alaska other tokens are used in trade between Inuit natives and storekeepers.

Willey says that the rivalry between the Hudson's Bay Company and the "Nor'westers" degenerated into open war, weakening the latter until in 1821 the survivors had to merge with the Hudson's Bay Company to avert bankruptcy: *CNJ* 28,2, pp. 66–67 (2/83). This may explain the lack of subsequent token issues.

OREGON BEAVER TOKENS

Designer, Engraver, unknown. Mint, John Walker & Co., Birmingham. Composition, brass, copper. Diameter, about

$18/16'' = 28.6$ mm. Weight standards, brass, apparently 50 to the lb. = 140 grs. = 9.072 gms.; copper, 40 to the lb. = 175 grs. = 11.34 gms.

Grade range, FAIR TO VERY FINE; almost always pierced. No grading standards established.

1083 1820 Beaver Token. Brass. Pierced. [all kinds 5,000] Rare.
Breton 925; Curto 15; Haxby-Willey 297A; Willey C29; Rulau-E Ore. 1. ANS's weighs 137.38 grs. = 8.902 gms. Almost always in low grades, including the couple of dozen in the Umpqua River Valley hoard, found about 1976.

Ex J. W. Garrett: 1530. Courtesy Bowers & Ruddy Galleries, Inc.

1084 1820 Beaver Token. Same dies. Copper. Pierced. Ex. rare.
Haxby-Willey 297; Willey C29; Rulau-E Ore. 2. Security edge. 1) ANS, 169.04 grs. = 10.954 gms. 2) Ford. 3) Ferguson, Banque du Canada. 4) Theis, 1979 F.U.N.:125. 5) L.I. specialist. 6) Garrett:1530, "EF," 166.1 grs. = 10.76 gms., $1,600. 7) Roper:356, 157.9 grs. = 10.23 gms., "F," $660.

CHAPTER 9

CONTINENTAL CONGRESS PATTERNS (1776)

In anticipation of Congress managing to obtain a loan of silver bullion from France, unidentified intermediaries sought out the Freehold, N.J., engraver Elisha Gallaudet with a proposal he could hardly refuse (Newman {1959B}). Gallaudet was then best known for his ornamental cuts on the 1774–76 NEW-YORK WATER WORKS notes, and for the sundial and links devices on the Feb. 17, 1776 Continental Currency fractional notes (ill. in Newman {1976A}, pp. 36, 236). Under cover of secrecy, the agents commissioned Gallaudet to prepare dies for a mintage of coins of various denominations. These would serve a dual function: on the one hand, demonstrating to the world the United Colonies' national sovereignty the same way other nations showed theirs; on the other, propping up the paper Continental notes, showing all concerned that these were exactly what they purported to be, promissory notes redeemable in coin.

Accordingly, the agents transmitted orders to the United Colonies' official note printers, Hall & Sellers, to omit the $1 denomination from the July 22, 1776 and later plates of Continental Currency notes; and a similar hint dropped to the New York State authorities and their note printer Samuel Loudon induced them to drop the $1 denomination from the Aug. 13, 1776 State note issue. Evidently all assumed that enough bullion would arrive to make the coins an effective circulating medium, and that they would replace some of the paper issues.

For devices they chose the same ones Gallaudet had placed on the fractional Continental notes, after sketches by Benjamin Franklin. The obv. consisted of a sundial with CONTINENTAL CURRENCY around; the rev. AMERICAN CONGRESS on a label enclosing WE ARE ONE and surrounded by a glory of rays; around, 13 conjoined links, each bearing the name of one of the United Colonies: the same as would appear on Abel Buell's prototype dies for James Jarvis's FUGIO coppers. This sundial rebus deserves further comment, as most people today have forgotten their childhood games with rebuses. Above the sundial is a blazing sun with a face and the word FUGIO, 'I [Time and/or the Sun] am fleeing.' Any 1770s child old enough to read could have grasped the meaning: "Usable time (daylight hours, business hours) flies away; therefore mind your business." This warning was aimed alike at farmers and merchants and at the patriots in their struggle against British redcoats. Though this rebus is credited to Franklin, it is made up of older elements. Barton {1813} describes an eight-day clock David Rittenhouse had constructed in 1756 for his brother-in-law, bearing the mottoes TEMPUS FUGIT and GO ABOUT YOUR BUSINESS. Rittenhouse, an inventor, artist, scientist, then America's foremost astronomer (later Mint Director, like Newton a century earlier in Britain), had designed border elements for 1776 New Jersey notes; he and his friend Francis Hopkinson may have worked on the layout sketch for Gallaudet, as Hopkinson did with some of the Continental Currency plates: Newman {1976A}, pp. 34, 213–14. The Soleil or Sun with Face, personifying Time and/or God, was familiar in the Masonic Lodges to which Franklin and many of the other Founding Fathers belonged; it dates back at least to the medieval Tarot decks. Newman {1983} demonstrated Franklin's role in designing the linked rings device.

Unfortunately, the French bullion did not arrive, and the paper depreciated, and all that remained of the dream were these sample coins. They first reached print in Watson {1789}, pp. 135–37; Bishop Watson gave their weight as 10 dwt = 240 grs. (a little too high), and wrongly estimated their composition as 12/13 tin, 1/13 lead. Because Crosby (p. 306) quoted Watson, these coins have traditionally been called pewter. They are actually tin with less than 5% trace elements (largely natural antimony alloy) but no lead, whereas pewter normally contains predetermined proportions of tin and lead. Nondestructive analyses done on several genuine specimens in 1963–64 proved that they uniformly contain 95+% tin, no lead; specific gravity range 7.15–7.45. Peck {1964}, Appendix 13, gives sp. gr. of pewter "95:5" (95% tin, 5% lead), as 7.46; pewter "98:2," as 7.35; pure tin as 7.29; "coinage tin," as 7.22 to 7.33 depending on the trace elements (natural alloys).

The signature EG FECIT on **1094–95** means 'E(lisha) G(allaudet) made it.' Unlike his earlier dies, the rev. of this one has N of AMERICAN full size, and N. HAMP'S is to l. of MASSACHS. The misspelling CURENCY represents a spacing problem. On the other hand, the singular error CURRENCEY occurs on all three plate vars. of Feb. 17, 1776 $1⁄6 notes, which according to Newman {1959B} were Gallaudet's work.

The traditional name "dollars" for all these coins has lately come under attack. Its sole rationales were size, the existence of a few silver strikings, and Bishop Watson's guesswork. Whatever the tin pieces might have represented, the copper and brass strikings most likely were pattern pence. On Sept. 2, 1776, the Continental Congress valued its paper dollars at par with the Spanish, equating the British shilling of 12 pence to 2/9 dollar: Solomon, p. 40. This works out to 54 pence or 108 halfpence to the dollar. As the copper and brass impressions are much heavier than Tower Mint halfpence, their makers and recipients would have thought of them as pennies; nobody had yet proposed to divide the Spanish dollar of 8 Reales into 100 units, let alone named such hypothetical unit a "cent."

Dr. Montroville Wilson Dickeson had some unidentified engraver make dies copying the CURRENCY var. (without EG FECIT), apparently for the 1876 Centennial celebration. They are of modern workmanship, with small modern letters (upright serifs and marked contrast between thick and thin elements), and come on perfectly round blanks with proof surface and plain edges. Before WW I, the New York coin dealer Thomas L. Elder acquired the dies and made restrikes; in 1961–62 Q. David Bowers did likewise. Bowers's restrikes were supposedly only in pewter; we have no reliable data about Elder's, though a specimen overstruck on an 1876 double eagle has lately come to light. Robert Bashlow had transfer dies made from the Dickeson dies (lest the latter break), and about 1962 he made restrikes in silver [2,000], goldine (brassy), and bronze. A few months later, the Boy Scouts of America rented the hubs and made many aluminum impressions, relettered and with a new rev. commemorating their annual Jamboree. Dickeson's original impressions (which come muled with various other dies) show full shading at sundial; the Elder, Bowers, and Bashlow restrikes show far less, finally none. During the 1976 Bicentennial celebrations there was a brief flurry of collector demand for many of these vars.

More deceptive are old casts made from genuine 1776 coins. They are porous, sometimes also showing raised bubbles or blebs around letters. Edge leaves are crude or absent. Unlike the genuine, they often have a high lead content, sometimes enough to leave a trace on paper—"You can write your name with them," as one young collector put it. Authentication of low-grade specimens is necessary.

CONTINENTAL CURRENCY PATTERNS

Designers, Benjamin Franklin, David Rittenhouse, and possibly Francis Hopkinson. Engraver, Elisha Gallaudet. Mint, Gallaudet's, Freehold, N.J.? Composition, 95+% tin, remainder antimony and trace elements, except as noted. Diameter, $25/16'' = 40$ mm (varies). Weights, tin, 232–285.59 grs. = 15.03–18.51 gms.; copper, brass, about 222–234 grs. = 14.4–15.17 gms., both possibly for 30 to the lb., matching Birmingham standard (60 halfpence = 30 pence to the lb., i.e., 233.33 grs. = 15.12 gms.). Edge, twin olive leaves, except as noted.

Grade range, VERY GOOD to UNC. No grading standards established.

1085 1776 Prototype Penny? Beaded links. Brass. 2 known.
Crosby, p. 305; Newman 1-A.   1) Newman, 250 grs. = 16.2 gms.   2) Spink (11/10), Brand II:955, $26,400.

1086 1776 Second Prototype. Partly beaded links. Tin. 2 known.
Newman 1-B. Altered dies of **1085.** Discovered in England

ca. 1970. Not to be confused with **1089;** note pronounced glory of rev. rays. 1) Spink, Merkin, Picker:117, $7,700. 2) Pvt. coll.

1087 1776 Penny. Same dies. Brass. 5 or 6 known.
Newman 1-B. Discovered by J. Carson Brevoort. 1) Jay, Laird Park:109, $9,500. 2) Robison:82, 222.15 grs. = 14.395 gms. (worn), $4,600. 3) Roper:198, 244.8 grs. = 15.86 gms., EF, $8,250. 4) Kern, Carter:204, 223 grs. = 14.45 grs., EF, $11,000.

1088 1776 Penny. Same dies. Copper. Unique?
Newman 1-B. 1) Lermann, Garrett:1489, 222.9 grs. = 14.44 gms, "EF," $11,000.

1089 1776 "Dollar." Unbeaded links. Tin.
Crosby, Pl. VIII, 15; Newman 1-C. Altered dies of **1085–86.** Glory of rays attenuated, especially at RESS M R; border beads incomplete.

1090 1776 "Dollar." Same dies, jumbo flan, plain edge. Unique.
1) Pressman, Pine Tree Auctions, Joseph P. O'Hara.

1091 1776 Dollar. Same dies. Silver. Unique?
Newman 1-C. Edge has chevrons spaced farther apart than the normal twin olive leaves. 1) Dr. Clay, Seavey, Parmelee, Mills, Garrett:1491, worn, $95,000, J. J. Ford, 375 grs. = 24.3 gms., for 90% of Spanish standard? Said to be overstruck on a cut-down 8 Reales.

1092 1776 "Dollar." CURRENCY. Tin.
Crosby, Pl. VIII, 16; Newman 2-C. UNC. specimens are mostly dull, unlike **1089** or **1095.** Ellsworth, Garrett:1492, $16,500, brilliant.

1093 1776 Penny. Same dies. Copper. Small flan. Unique?

1094 1776 Penny. EG FECIT. Brass. Unique?

1095 1776 "Dollar." Same dies. Tin.

Crosby, Pl. VIII, 17; Newman 3-D. Full size N in AMERI-CAN. Dies usually cracked through links. UNC. survivors are often prooflike.

1096 1776 Dollar. Same dies. Silver. 2 known.

Newman 3-D. 1) Earle:2132, $2,200, Brand, Boyd, Ford? 2) British sale 12/1886, Chapman Bros., Mc-Coye:238, Chapman, $3,000, Granberg, Woodin, Newcomer, Green, Newman. Ill. *NUM* 6/09, p. 177; ANS {1914}, Pl. 13. 363.5 grs. = 23.55 gms., for 7/8 of Spanish standard? In T. Grand:10 was one supposedly ex Granberg, Col. Green; not verified, same as 1)? Both said to be overstruck on cut-down 8 Reales coins.

1097 1776 "Dollar." CURRENCEY. Tin. Plain edge. Ex. rare.

Newman 4-D. 1) Newcomer, Green, Eric P. Newman, 285.5 grs. = 18.5 gms. 2) British coll., NN/Seaby 11/

70:429, Roper:202, $6,050, 277.3 grs. = 17.97 gms. 3) British coll., Anthony Terranova, 257.7 grs. = 16.7 gms.; sp. gr. 7.27 ± 0.01. 4) Pvt. coll.

1098 1776 "Dollar." Square ornament after CURRENCY. Tin. Unique?

Newman 5-D. Reworked obv. of **1097**; Y corrected from E, ornament conceals original Y. One of the few rare instances of a die altered after actual use. 1) Brand, Norweb.

CHAPTER 10

MORRIS'S CONFEDERATION PATTERNS
(1783)

In 1782, Gouverneur Morris (1752–1816), Assistant Superintendent of Finance for the Confederation, proposed what was at once the most ingenious and the most cumbersome coinage system ever devised in Western Civilization. Its unit of account (or Unit for short) was ¼ grain (actually 0.01742 gms.) silver, equated to ¹/1,440 Spanish dollar. Its coins were to be of 10,000 Units in gold, 1,000 and 100 Units in silver, with possible intermediate denominations. Its purpose was to reconcile various conflicting moneys of account then in use in 12 of the Original 13 Colonies. (South Carolina's system, which contained the factor 13, could not be reconciled with the rest.) Its timing was meant to tell the world that the United States of North America under the Articles of Confederation was a sovereign nation exercising its supreme prerogative by coining precious metals.

To implement this coinage system, Robert Morris, Superintendent of Finance (no relation to Gouverneur), hired Benjamin Dudley, a British die engraver then living in Boston (and later known for his work with the New Jersey coppers), to supervise establishment of a mint, and to make dies and coins. Dudley brought along three workmen, whose families remained with the Philadelphia Mint for generations: John Jacob Eckfeldt (father of later Chief Coiner Adam Eckfeldt), John Swanwick, and A. Dubois. Though neither a suitable mint building nor a source of silver bullion became available, Robert Morris offered Francis Hopkinson the directorship of the Mint, and hired Samuel Wheeler to make rolling mills after Dudley's models. Dudley also designed screw presses, but it is not known if he constructed any or used Gallaudet's. Morris paid Dudley $72 on May 5, 1783, for "sinking, casehardening, &c., four Pair of Dies for the Public Mint" (Letter of Francis Hopkinson to Thomas Jefferson, May 12, 1784; Robert Morris's Diaries, cited in *Historical Magazine,* Second Series, I, pp. 30–32 [Jan. 1867]; Crosby, p. 310, from "Expenses for Contingencies, Jan.–July 1783"). These were for **1099, 1101, 1103,** and **1105.**

On April 2, 1783, Benjamin Dudley delivered the first sample coin, No. **1099,** to Robert Morris; **1101** and probably at least three specimens of **1103** followed on April 22. Lack of silver bullion made the mint project a dead letter; the Confederation could neither tax nor force the states to tax citizens, and after the 1778–80 debacle of Continental notes, its credit rating was effectively zero. From the surviving coins, we can learn much of what was originally intended. Their devices are uniform: the All-Seeing Eye in glory with 13 stars and CONSTELLATIO NOVA, 'The New Constellation'; and within a closed wreath U.S and numerical value, LIBERTAS . JUSTITIA . 1783 around. Fineness was supposed to be 926 (25 grains silver + 2 grains copper for the 100 Units piece, and proportionately); in actuality, at least the 1,000 Unit coin was struck in pure silver,

sp. grs. 10.5, according to nondestructive tests made at Johns Hopkins Univ. in 1959.

Their legend CONSTELLATIO NOVA refers to the 13 original United Colonies, represented by the 13 stars. This device ultimately derives from a Resolution of the Second Continental Congress, June 14, 1777 (published Sept. 2): "That the flag of the United States be thirteen stripes, alternate red and white; that the union be thirteen stars, white in a blue field, representing a *new constellation.*" (Emphasis added.) This flag differed from its predecessor (the 1776 Continental or Grand Union flag) in replacing the Union Jack canton with the starry circle. The new flags only became available in 1783, but remained in use until May 1, 1795, when the stars and stripes were increased to 15 (World Almanac). This starry circle concept was echoed on the coppers Morris ordered struck in Birmingham in 1785 (see following chapters). In combination as given on the coins, the legends make a rude Latin hexameter verse:

Lī-bēr-/tās Jūs-/tĭ-tĭ-ă//cōn-stēl-/lā-tĭ-ŏ/nō-vă
'Liberty and Justice: Newly Spelled in Stars.'

Use of hexameters this way (prolonging the syllables whose vowels are marked with ⁻'s) made the slogan the equivalent of an advertising jingle, to remind all who might read it of what this country was organized to further.

Only in 1979 was the complex history of these coins finally unraveled with the discovery of the long missing 5 Unit copper coin, mentioned in Samuel Curwen's Diary (May 15, 1784, cited in Crosby, p. 312). This piece turned up in Paris in 1977, and made the front-page headline in *Coin World,* Jan. 9, 1980. There are still gaps; in particular, other 100 Unit coins must have been made, and probably other 5 Unit coins as well, quite aside from the mystery posed by the lightweight Second Quint **(1102),** which uses an obv. die differing from any of the eight original dies cited above. We know about the extra 100 Unit coins because Thomas Jefferson's Account Book contains an entry dated May 11, 1784, recording that he had "left with C[harles] Thomson [Secretary of the Continental Congress] as specimens of coins 1.8 D," evidently the Mark, or 1,000 Units, the first Quint, or 500 Units, and three Bits of 100 Units each = 1,800 Units, for a total 1.8 Spanish dollars. Joseph J. Mickley, around the Civil War, borrowed the two largest from one of Charles Thomson's descendants (probably his nephew John Thomson, of Newark, Del., who had found them in a secret compartment of his uncle's desk) to make soft-metal cast copies; the latter still occasionally show up from old collections, being for the decades before coin photography the only clue to the appearance of the originals **(1099, 1101).** After Capt. John W. Haseltine (Philadelphia coin dealer) somehow learned of Mickley's source, he wrote to all Charles Thomson's locatable descendants, claiming to have heard that one of them had a coin collection for possible sale. Rathmell Wilson, of Wilmington, Del., finally sold Haseltine the two original proofs in May 1872, and their later history is well known (see below). However, the smaller coins did not turn up among Thomson's descendants. One 100 Units with leaved edge (1103) appeared in a London pawnshop (T. F. Cloud's, 207 High Holborn St.), between 1882 and 1884; L. E. Shorthouse bought it for 2s3d and consigned it to the Roxbury (Mass.) coin dealer William Elliot Woodward for his 73rd auction (April 2, 1885), where it was reserved at $550 and failed to sell. The plain-edge 100 Unit (1104) also showed up in England; it went from the J. G. Murdoch collection (1903) successively to Robert Garrett and John Work Garrett, who resold it as a duplicate after obtaining the Shorthouse coin.

In Oct. 1870, William P. Brown, coin dealer, of 28 John St., New York City, published a description of a second type 500 Unit piece (1102) owned by a young man of that city who had it of his grandfather as an heirloom (*The Curiosity Cabinet*, v1n2, 10/1870; *Mason's Monthly Coin & Stamp Collectors' Magazine*, 11/1870). The coin shortly sold to Sylvester Sage Crosby, who authenticated it because its rev. die is identical to 1101. However, the piece is underweight, does not ring, does not match the standard description of the others, and has a date "2 Dec." pin-scratched in field in 18th-century script: possibly either the date of manufacture or that of receipt by an early owner. These deviations strongly suggest a later and unrecorded abortive attempt to revive the Morris-Dudley project. The latter also makes more understandable both the plain-edged 100 Unit coin (1104) and the hitherto unpublished piece next to be described.

In 1959, a West Coast collector sent me for authentication a holed 1,000 Unit coin with plain edge (1100), which on nondestructive testing at Johns Hopkins Univ. proved to be of lower-grade silver than 1099. It is apparently not a cast but a struck piece, and its centering differs from that of the original Mark (1099). I was unable to account for its inconsistencies with the latter, and returned it without certificate, in extreme puzzlement. No photographs were taken, but the late Robert Bashlow (then 20 years old) made two (unholed) casts in gold, about a dozen in silver, and less than a dozen in copper, in the tradition of Joseph J. Mickley, as a permanent record of this mysterious piece. It is herein listed as "genuineness unconfirmed" because in 1959 I did not know any way to account for a plain-edged piece; I had not yet learned that one 100 Unit has a plain edge, nor that the second Quint is of lower fineness. Appropriate tests of genuineness are now possible; they include diffractometry, to compare proportions of trace elements with those in the second Quint. Should 1100 prove genuine, it will probably also rate front-page coverage by the numismatic press. In the meantime, further search continues among the papers of Jefferson, the Morrises, and other involved officials.

ROBERT MORRIS'S PATTERNS FOR THE CONFEDERATION

Designer, Engraver, Benjamin Dudley. Mint, Dudley's, Philadelphia. Composition, silver $25/27$ = 926 Fine (varies). Diameters, as noted. Weight standard, Mark, 270 grs. = 17.42 gms.; Quint, 135 grs. = 8.71 gms.; Bit, 27 grs. = 1.74 gms.; 5 Unit (copper), apparently 92 to the lb. = 76.09 grs. = 4.93 gms. Edges, leaved, except as noted.

Proofs only.

1099   1783 Mark = 1,000 Units. Leaved edge. [1+] Unique. Crosby, Pl. VIII, 1. Pure silver; 1.3" = 33 mm. 269.8 grs. = 17.417 gms. Enl. photos. Ex Benjamin Dudley, April 2, 1783; Robert Morris; William Hemsley Committee of Continental

Congress; Robert Morris; Thomas Jefferson; Charles Thomson; John Thomson (nephew); Samuel E. Thomson (son of John); Rathmell Wilson (before May 28, 1872); Capt. John W. Haseltine (Dec. 18, 1872); Henry S. Adams; S. S. Crosby; Lorin G. Parmelee; Harlan P. Smith (Parmelee's agent protecting the coin?); S. H. & H. Chapman; George H. Earle; Col. James W. Ellsworth; M. Knoedler Galleries; Wayte Raymond; John Work Garrett; Johns Hopkins Univ. (1942–79); Garrett:622, $190,000; John Jay Ford, Jr. Ill. in Parmelee; ANS {1914}, Pl. 10; *Papers of Thomas Jefferson* (vol. VII); and all the standard guidebooks. Cast copies exist in soft metal; see introductory text.

1100   1783 Second Mark. Same dies. Plain edge. Unique? Genuineness not yet confirmed. Pierced. Low-grade silver. See introductory text for original and casts in gold, silver, or copper.

1101   1783 First Quint = 500 Units. Leaved edge. [1+] Unique. Crosby, Pl. VIII, 2. Almost $17/16$" = 27 mm. 133.98 grs. = 8.682 gms. Enl. photos. Made by Benjamin Dudley, April 22, 1783; remainder of pedigree as 1099, except Garrett:620,

$165,000, Ford. Ill. in same places as **1099.** Same comment about Mickley's soft-metal casts.

1103 1783 Bit = 100 Units. Leaved edge. [3+] Unique? ANS {1914}, Pl. 10. ⁷/₁₀″ = 18 mm. 27.75 grs. = 1.798 gms. Enl. photos. Presumably made by Benjamin Dudley about April 22, 1783, then Robert Morris, the William Hemsley Committee, Robert Morris, Thomas Jefferson, Charles Thomson, unidentified pvt. colls., T. F. Cloud (London pawnbroker), L. E. Shorthouse, Lorin G. Parmelee, S. H. & H. Chapman, Col. J. W. Ellsworth, M. Knoedler Galleries, Wayte Raymond, John Work Garrett, Johns Hopkins Univ. (1942–79), Garrett:619, $97,500, Ford. See introductory text.

1102 1783 Second Quint. Weakly leaved edge. Unique. Crosby, Pl. VIII, 3. ¹⁵/₁₆″ = 24 mm. 109.72 grs. = 7.11 gms. Enl. photos. Unidentified young NYC collector (1870), W. P. Brown, S. S. Crosby, Lorin G. Parmelee, S. H. & H. Chapman, J. W. Ellsworth, Knoedler Galleries, Wayte Raymond, J. W. Garrett, Johns Hopkins Univ. (1942–79), Garrett:621, $55,000, Walter Perschke. Does not ring (dumb or cracked flan?); date "2 Dec." is faintly pin-scratched in field. Ill. in same places as **1099.** See introductory text.

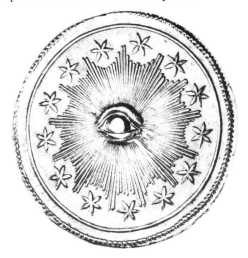

1104 1783 Second Bit. Plain edge. Unique?
Diameter about as **1103;** 26 grs. = 1.68 gms. J. G. Murdoch (before 1903), Robert Garrett, John Work Garrett, Wayte Raymond, Guttag Bros. (52 Wall St., NYC, May 2, 1923, circular), Col. E. H. R. Green (?), B. G. Johnson, Eric P. Newman.

1105 1783 5 Units. Copper. Plain edge. [1+] Unique?
$^{23}/_{24}$″ = 24.35 mm; 75.15 grs. = 4.87 gms. Benjamin Dudley, Robert Morris, William Hemsley Congressional Committee (?), Josiah Bartlett, M.D., Judge Samuel Curwen (May 15, 1784), British pvt. colls., an English coin dealer in Paris

(1977), Fred S. Werner, Dec. 11, 1977, Ford, Feb. 14, 1978. Ill. *Coin World,* 1/9/80, p. 1; Breen {1984}, pp. 27–28.

CHAPTER 11

PROPOSED CONFEDERATION CONTRACT ISSUES

i. WYON'S *CONSTELLATIO NOVA* COPPERS (1783–86)

After silver bullion for Gouverneur Morris's proposed federal coinage proved elusive (see preceding chapter), Morris traveled to England, and in 1785 apparently ordered coppers from Wyon's mint in Birmingham. These were similar to Dudley's 5 Unit piece (**1105**), except for lacking any mark of denomination. Because of Morris's position as Assistant Superintendent of Finance for the Confederation, and because the coppers explicitly alluded to the new American flag device, many London newspapers believed the coins were official issues ordered by the Continental Congress:

> The American Congress have lately made a copper coinage which is now in general circulation: one side of the halfpenny bears this circular inscription, *Libertas et Justitia;* round a central cypher U.S. On the reverse is a sun rising amidst Thirteen Stars, circularly inscribed *Constellatio Nova.*

That paragraph, or one similarly worded, appeared between March 11 and 14, 1786, in the London *Morning Herald,* the *Public Advertiser,* the *London Chronicle,* and the *Morning Chronicle and London Advertiser.* It was invariably among general news, unsigned, and without cited source. The last-named paper issued a correction (March 16, 1786, p. 3):

> A correspondent observes, that the paragraph which lately appeared in several papers, respecting a copper coinage in America, is not true. The piece spoken of, bearing the inscription, "Libertas et Justitia, etc." was not made in America, nor by the direction of Congress. It was coined at Birmingham, by the order of a merchant in New York. Many tons were struck from this dye, and many from another; and they are now in circulation in America as counterfeit halfpence are in England.

All the above were quoted by Eric Newman in *CNL* 10/73, p. 422.

Crosby, p. 331, quotes (via Bushnell) a claim in *Massachusetts Centinel,* May 10, 1786, that "over forty tons were issued from one die alone, and many more from another" *(CNL* 4/73, p. 402). At the regular Birmingham standard of 60 to the lb. (at which many of these were struck), assuming long tons as usual, this would have meant some 5,376,000 coppers. If the *Centinel* meant the total issue, that averages 672,000 coins per rev. for the eight revs.: far too high for the period (200,000 would have been ample). I conjectured long ago that "forty" was a mishearing of "fourteen," which gives a corresponding figure of 1,881,600 pieces = 313,600 coins per rev.: still too high. How-

ever, as the earliest ones were struck at 50 at the lb., possibly the actual number made is still smaller, and we may take 1.4 million to 1.6 million (say 12 long tons) as a reasonable upper limit.

At least a half dozen batches were made, only the first (Morris's?) at 50 to the lb., later ones at 55, 60, 64, and 72 to the lb., with the vast majority at the regular Birmingham standard. After Morris resold the first few dozen (?) casks to New York merchants, others more profit-minded got into the act; there was, after all, no legal monopoly on the design. Its "Up the Union!" message was good public relations, and the Vermont coiners promptly put it to use on their 1785–86 plough-type or landscape-type coppers (**711–13**) as propaganda for their Republic's campaign to join the Union.

All answer to the same general description: All-Seeing Eye in glory of rays, punctuated by 13 stars, CONSTELLATIO NOVA around; circular wreath enclosing U.S, LIBERTAS ET JUSTITIA around. On the 1783's, the word ET is omitted, and the U.S is roman, copying **1105**; on the 1785's, the US monogram is in script, deriving from Continental Army buttons: Albert {1974} GI 5. The 1783 date is commemorative; all the coins were struck in 1785–86.

All vars. come in low grades, VG to VF; all are prohibitively rare in mint state, indicating that they were promptly accepted in trade. As they preceded the state coppers by some months, they were for a while the major small change in the Eastern Seaboard area, though they had plenty of competition in Birmingham counterfeit halfpence. By 1787–88 their value had fallen, and the Vermont and Machin's Mills coiners bought them up cheaply in quantity to overstrike with Vermont and Connecticut dies: See **717–18, 858–61, 863–64.** I have seen one proof of the 1783 with blunt rays, struck twice from polished dies on an imperfectly polished blank, and have heard of another. Three of the ray dies were combined with the Wyon/ Mould IMMUNE COLUMBIA to make the patterns **1117, 1119,** and **1122.**

Eric Newman's unique coin dated 1785 with only 12 stars (**1115**) is probably from one of the Bungtown mints. On the other hand, the var. dated 1786 is an American imitation, too good in quality for the Bungtown mints, but not yet traced to any other source: Its letters and numerals are of unfamiliar style.

These coppers were all formerly called NOVA CONSTELLATIO pieces, but if you hold one so that the eyebrow is above the eye, clearly CONSTELLATIO comes first; in addition, the hexameter jingle cited in the preceding chapter preserves its rhythm only if CONSTELLATIO comes first—a situation forgotten or ignored by Benjamin Dudley when he cut the dies for the silver coins. All the 1786 London newspaper accounts read the coppers as CONSTELLATIO NOVA, which is better Latin.

The engraver was George Wyon, III (1744–97), probably with his teenaged twin assistants, Thomas Wyon and Peter George Wyon (b. 1767). Wyon's pupil Walter Mould lettered some dies; these letter punches recur in the Mould-Atlee Tory Coppers (Chap. 7, Sect. vi). More detailed records may be impossible to locate unless some were saved from the fire which destroyed Wyon's mint before 1790. The Wyons, partly because of these coppers, later became very famous; three generations of this family served as die engravers and medalists for the Tower and private mints.

WYON'S CONSTELLATIO NOVA COPPERS

Designer, George Wyon, III, after Benjamin Dudley. Engravers, George Wyon, III, and assistants Thomas and Peter George Wyon. Mint, Wyon's, Birmingham, England. Composition, copper. Diameters, 16–$17/16'' = 25$–27 mm. Weight standards, variable (see introductory text).

Grade range, GOOD to UNC. GOOD: All letters legible; date may be weak. VERY GOOD: All leaves clear (see EXCEPTIONS). FINE: Some internal details in leaves; some eye details; almost all rays clear except at innermost ends. VERY FINE: Some eyebrow details clear; iris distinct (except 1106). EXTREMELY FINE: Tiny isolated wear spots only on highest points of some leaves, inner and outer ends of some rays, iris and pupil, part of eyebrow; part of pupil will be clear. EXCEPTIONS: On 1106 and 1116, leaves are always weak (die failure); on 1110–11 with rusted dies, rays and stars will be blurry even in mint state. Grade by surface.

1106   1783 Large U.S Usually weak.
Crosby 1-A; Pl. VII, 25. Earliest strikings at 50 to the pound (140 grs. = 9.07 gms.; observed, 138–140 grs. = 8.94–9.07 gms.); later ones at 55 to the lb. (127 grs. = 8.24 gms.); still later at 60 to the lb. (116.7 grs. = 7.56 gms.). These price the same. Dies always show injuries in rays, later clashing, breakage, and rust; borders now weak.

1107   1783 Small U.S Pointed rays.
Crosby 2-B; Pl. VII, 27. Small flans, border dentils off. Many struck at 60 or 55 to the lb. as above, others at 72 to the lb. (97.2 grs. = 6.3 gms., observed 95–110 grs. = 6.16–7.13 gms.). These price the same. Mills, Garrett, Roper:203, 123.4 grs. = 7.996 gms., UNC., $1,980.

1108   1783 Same. Silver OMS. Unique?
   1) Richard Picker (1973), Groves, 6.87 grs. = 4.451 gms.
1109   1783 Blunt rays, CONSTELATIO
Crosby 3-C; Pl. VII, 26. Small flans like 1107; some at 60 to the lb., others at 52 (134.6 grs. = 8.72 gms.). Garrett:610 is

heavy at 153.3 grs. = 9.934 gms. The solitary proof has full border dentils (very unusual) and needle-sharp details of eye, stars, and leaves.

1110   1785 Blunt rays, CONSTELATIO
Crosby 1-B; Pl. VII, 23. Struck between early and late impressions of next. Always with break in leaves and some rust on rays side. Some struck at 60 to the lb., others at 55 (compare 1106–7). Parsons:333, "UNC.," was described as on broad flan, $19/16'' = 30$ mm.

1111   1785 Pointed rays, narrow 5, pellets at date, coarse dentils.
Crosby 3-B; Pl. VII, 29. Rusted dies; varying states of break in leaves. Some struck before 1110, others after; some at 60 to the lb., others at 64 (109.4 grs. = 7.09 gms.; observed, 107–112 grs. = 6.93–7.26 gms.). These price the same.

1112   1785 Similar, closest date, no pellets. Rare.
Crosby 2-A. Same comments. Usually weak in centers. Struck at 60 to the lb. Robison:95, "EF," $600.

1113   1785 Wide 5, pellets flank date, fine dentils. Scarce.
Crosby, 4-C (ill., rare), 4-D; price for 4-D. The 4-D has 2 overlapping leaves above script U. Mostly struck at 60 to the lb.; some 4-D's are light at 106 grs. = 6.87 gms., for 64 to the

lb., others heavier at 123.6–132.8 grs. = 8.01–8.61 gms., probably for 55 to the lb. These price the same.

1114 1785 Scanty wreath, widest date. Rare.
Crosby 5-E. Often shows die rust. Struck at 60 to the lb., though Garrett:613 was heavy at 131.9 grs. = 8.547 gms. Used in quantity as undertypes for Vermonts **717–18** and Machin's Mills coins of Connecticut type **858–61, 863–64.**

BUNGTOWN MINT (North Swansea, Mass.?)

1115 1785 Only 12 stars. Unique?
1) B. M. Douglas, Eric P. Newman.

UNCERTAIN AMERICAN MINT

1116 1786 Ex. rare.
Crosby, Pl. VII, 33. Note roman U.S as in 1783. Almost always in low grades; Garrett:617, "F," $6,500. Struck at 60 to the lb.; observed, 98.8–123 grs. = 6.4–7.97 gms.

ii. WYON'S *IMMUNE COLUMBIA* PATTERNS (1785)

Little is known of Wyon's mint in Birmingham because its records reportedly perished by fire before 1790. However, of this much we can be sure: This institution enjoyed special favor with high American officials, among others Gouverneur Morris; and it produced several family engravers who later received Crown appointments to the Tower Mint in London. In addition, one of its pupils was Walter Mould, who in 1785 emigrated to America, becoming one of the legal coiners for the State of New Jersey, and bringing along several dies and other ironmongery, including the 1785 IMMUNE COLUMBIA obv.

When the Morris-Dudley 1783 project for a mint in Philadelphia proved abortive, and all further plans were suspended after Robert Morris resigned as Superintendent of Finance (1784), the next step was Gouverneur Morris's order for the CONSTELLATIO NOVA coppers from the Wyon mint. As the Con-

federation officials were still interested in creating some kind of national coinage, the Wyons designed patterns for a possible contract coinage. Ideally, inscriptions and devices would link these to Gouverneur Morris's coppers and thence to the original 1783 silver project (see preceding two chapters). Designs would be adaptable to coinage in gold or silver (should bullion become available) as well as copper.

Wyon's first pattern obv. depicts an allegorical female figure seated on a crate (for international commerce), offering the scales of Justice, and holding a pole with flag and liberty cap. When Walter Mould lettered this die, somehow he managed to commit a grammatical blunder, replacing the needed adjective IMMUNIS by the adverb IMMUNE. The construction IMMUNE COLUMBIA would have merited a beating in any British elementary school. Under the circumstances, perhaps we need seek no further reason why Mould emigrated to the USA. When he fled New Jersey in July 1788 to avoid debtor's prison, this blundered die went with his other ironmongery to Machin's Mills, Newburgh, N.Y., where James F. Atlee used it to make the crude strikings **734** and **1000.**

The original intention in the phrase "Immunis Columbia" was to enable the coins' legends to make another rude hexameter verse or jingle:

Īm-mū-/nīs Cō-/lūm-bǐ-ă//cōn-stēl-/lā-tǐ-ŏ/nō-vă.

'The sky's New Constellation: Columbus's taxfree land.'
Immunis connotes "not subject to penalties, imposts, liens, etc." A brave sentiment, but clearly only propaganda or wishful thinking, as the new nation was even then floundering in unpaid debts.

WYON'S IMMUNE COLUMBIA PATTERNS

Designer, Engraver, George Wyon III (lettering by Mould). Mint, Wyon's, Birmingham. Composition, Weight Standards, as below. Diameter, 17/16″ = 27 mm.

Grade range, VERY GOOD to UNC. No grading standards established.

1117 1785 Pattern copper. Pellet and cinquefoil in legend. About 12 known.
Crosby, Pl. VII, 30 and fig. 54. Rev. of **1107.** Struck at 46 to the lb. = 152.17 grs. = 9.861 gms. Bispham, Parsons, Ellsworth, Garrett:1334, "EF," $15,000.

1118 1785 Pattern guinea. Same dies. Gold. Unique?
Overstruck on a guinea. 1) Beebee & Parshall, N.Y. (May 8, 1843), Matthew A. Stickney (May 9, 1843), Mint Cabinet in trade for an 1804 dollar, SI.
1119 1785 Pattern copper. Pointed rays, no punctuation. 5 or 6 known.
Crosby, Pl. VII, 31 and fig. 53. Rev. of **1111** before it rusted. Some struck at 60 to the lb. Garrett:1332, "EF," $18,500, 121.1 grs. = 7.85 gms.

1120 1785 Pattern Shilling (?) Same dies. Silver. Ex. rare. Edge diagonally reeded. 75.1–92 grs. = 4.87–5.96 gms., possibly for Tower shilling standard. Garrett:1333, "VF," $25,000, is heavy at 133.7 grs. = 8.67 gms. Compare next.

1121 1785 Pattern Shilling (?) Same dies. Silver. Plain edge. 2 known.
1) Roper:210, 86.4 grs. = 5.6 gms., F–VF, $4,400. 2) Lauder:191, plugged, withdrawn. Mid-19th-century forgeries exist from copy dies (letters differ), made for Dr. Francis S. Edwards (d. 1866); Crosby, Pl. X, 26; Ex. rare.

1122 1785 Pattern copper. Blunt rays, CONSTELATIO. 2 known.
Rev. of **1109.** 1) Dr. B. B. Miles:932, $100, "Hawkins," Heman Ely:1010, Parmelee:593, Mrs. Norweb. 2) Maris, Garrett:1335, "VG," $17,000, Roper:212, $11,000, 109.1 grs. = 7.07 gms.

Ex J. W. Garrett: 1335. Courtesy Bowers & Ruddy Galleries, Inc.

iii. WYON'S PATTERNS
CONFEDERATIO DECADS (1785–86)

Thomas Jefferson's "Propositions Respecting the Coinage of Gold, Silver, and Copper," May 13, 1785 (written while he was in Paris), recommended the device of an Indian trampling on a crown, with MANUS INIMICA TYRANNIS, 'This hand is hostile to tyrants' *(Papers of Thomas Jefferson,* VII, p. 202). A deleted paragraph of the Report of the Grand Committee of Continental Congress suggested the name "Decad" for the larger copper coin, valued at 1/100 Spanish dollar, and for its device a sketch of the union of 13 stars in a circle with a serrated border representing rays, surrounded by CONFEDERATIO 1785 *(JCC,* XXVIII, pp. 354–58; *Papers of Continental Congress,* no. 26, pp. 537–42, Record Group 11, National Archives.) [ill.]

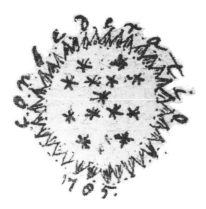

That paragraph was deleted from the printed report, either by acting chairman Hugh Williamson, or by vote of the Committee. However, Jefferson knew of the Committee's inner workings, and he would surely have known of the proposed designs (if indeed he was not their instigator), as well as of Wyon's facilities. He was, therefore, the most logical go-between for transmitting the recommended designs and inscriptions to Wyon, even for patterns for a possible contract coinage should mint equipment no longer be locally obtainable.

Wyon promptly made dies for pattern Decads, to the following general description—here given in detail because the illustrations may not convey all the iconographic subtleties:

Obv., the Goddess Diana (patroness of hunters), at altar, trampling a crown, and holding her usual attributes (bow, arrow, and quiver). On the altar is a helmet deliberately resembling a liberty cap. INIMICA TYRANNIS AMERICA(NA), 'America, hostile to tyrants.' Any reference to hunting was then taken as symbolic of freedom: Only a free man can hunt his dinner.

Rev., cantoned cross of 13 stars within a glory of rays, long and short. CONFEDERATIO, 'Union,' 1785. Large or small stars; the large-star die more closely resembles the original sketch in *Papers of Continental Congress.*

When Walter Mould arrived in the USA in 1785, he brought along some impressions from these two pairs of dies, and probably also several associated dies. We have no details of Wyon's proposal for contract coinage, but this may have been associated with, or even confused with, Mould's own petition for a coinage contract franchise, Aug. 18, 1785: Taxay {1966}, p. 28; see following section. The dies' origin in Wyon's mint is proved by their punch linkage with the CONSTELLATIO NOVA coppers; however, some later come muled with dies evidently made by other hands, suggesting that the dies traveled with Mould.

Because of the complexity of the group of mulings, we list all the dies before enumerating their combinations. This enables some comparisons and attributions less conveniently made in the main text.

Obv. 1 was the IMMUNE COLUMBIA die previously described.

Revs. A, B, and C were the three CONSTELLATIO NOVA dies found with obv. 1. Numbering hereinafter is continuous with these.

Obv. 2. Diana at altar, as above. INIMICA TYRANNIS AMERICA. Crosby {1875}, rev. A. By Wyon.

Obv. 3. Diana at altar; AMERICANA. Crosby, rev. B. By Wyon.

Obv. 4. Uniformed bust r., GEN. WASHINGTON. Crosby, rev. D; Maris {1881}, obv. 4. Shares some punches with rev. A. Workmanship would be fairly crude for Wyon but is unusually good for Mould.

Obv. 5. Script US (S coils around the body of U) monogrammed within wreath of 30 pairs of leaves, LIBERTAS ET JUSTITIA 1785. Crosby, rev. C; an unused die of the CONSTELLATIO NOVA coppers.

Obv. 6. Allegorical figure vaguely like obv. 1, but female seated on globe rather than crate. IMMUNIS COLUMBIA 1786. By Wyon; shares punches with obv. 1 and the CONSTELLATIO NOVA coins. Crosby, rev. F = Maris, obv. 3. Possibly made in 1785 for use in 1786, and brought over here by Mould.

Rev. D. Within circle of short rays, 13 large stars arranged 1 + 3 + 5 + 3 + 1, CONFEDERATIO 1785. Crosby, obv. 1.

Rev. E. Similar, but small stars within long rays. Crosby, obv. 2. Brought to the USA by Mould.

Rev. F. Arms, argent, six pales gules, a chief azure; * E * PLURIBUS * UNUM * with very wide legend nearly encircling device. Crosby, rev. G = Maris, rev. C. Prototype die of the New Jersey coppers used with one of Wyon's 1786 "Date

Below Plowbeam" obvs. (882) and with the prototype of the accepted design (883); later taken to the Morristown Mint by Walter Mould and muled with one of his coarsest obvs. to make 936 (Crosby, Pl. VII, 19).

The above number-letter designations in combination are used in all listings to follow through 1133. Combinations 2-D and 3-E (1123–24), the "regular" CONFEDERATIO pattern coppers, are among the most prized of all American Colonial issues, and were so even before C. Lynn Glaser {1962}, then 18 years old, published the tie-in with the Continental Congress's deliberations. These two are now cherished still more, especially 1123, as this is nearest to the description and sketch in *Papers of Continental Congress.*

Their legend again forms a rude hexameter verse (false quantities and all), even though for reasons of layout it would have to be read rev. first:

Cōn-fĕ-dĕ-/rā-tĭ-ŏ//Ā-mē-/rī-ca = in-ĭ-/mī-că tў-/rān-nīs.
'American Union, Tyranny's Foe!'

Why then the other reading with AMERICANA, which destroys any possible scansion? Probably because Wyon thought it worthwhile to give alternative versions to whoever might be in a position to order contract coinage on behalf of the Confederation, even as Obadiah Westwood was to do a few years later (via Thomas Ketland & Sons) with the Washington Cents of 1791.

The combination 3-D (AMERICANA with large stars) was reported to Crosby, most likely by Charles Ira Bushnell, but its existence remains unconfirmed. Crosby's illustrations (Pl. VII, 11 and fig. 56) were made from other coins. Most likely his informant had a Bolen copy which he believed genuine (see below).

Combinations of the above dies not found in this section will be found in Sect. iv; but check the list of Bolen copies below first!

In 1863, John Adams Bolen, of Springfield, Mass., made copy dies of the AMERICANA and both large- and small-stars revs. Bolen's copy of obv. 3 is readily identifiable: a) Dot in Y of TYRANNIS, Bolen's secret mark. b) Open S (on original, S is closed: lower serif extends up to meet middle stroke). c) Tops of ME apart (on original they join). His copy of the large-stars die D has stars closer to rays than the original, and no extra serif on first E. His copy of the small-stars die E has no extra spines from long rays at RAT, nor does the long ray extend up far above bases of those letters, which features are visible on all originals sharp enough to show them. Bolen struck each design in silver [2], copper [40], and brass [1]; there are no silver or brass originals. Bolen's copper copies weigh 145.8–156.6 grs. = 9.45–9.5 gms., nearer the originals than most forgeries. There is also a unique brass muling of Bolen's two CONFEDERATIO revs.

WYON'S CONFEDERATIO PATTERN DECADS AND MULES

Designer, Engraver, Thomas Wyon. Mint, Wyon's, Birmingham. Composition, copper. Diameter, about 18/16″ = 28.6 mm. Weight standards, variable, as below.

Grade range, POOR to UNC. No grading standards established.

1123   1785 Pattern Decad. 2-D: AMERICA ./Large stars. 7 or 8 known.
Crosby, Pl. VII, 13. Some struck at 46 to the lb., others at 60: Garrett:1329, VG, $9,500, 112.4 grs. = 7.283 gms.;

Roper:214, "F," $18,700, 112.2 grs. = 7.27 gms. Rev. progressively bulges in center. Enl. photos.

1124   1785 Pattern Decad. 3-E: AMERICANA ./Small stars. 8–10 known.
Crosby, Pl. VII, 12 and fig. 57. Struck at 46 to the lb. Ham, Breisland, Laird Park:126, "VF," $47,000, Roper:215, $17,600, 142.7 grs. = 9.247 gms. Bolen's copies have dot in Y: See introductory text. Enl. photos.

1125 1785 Pattern Decad. 4-D: Washington/Large stars. 7 or 8 known.
Crosby, Pl. VII, 14; Baker 9. Some coined at 52 to the lb. = 134.6 grs. = 8.72 gms. Roper:216, 129 grs. = 8.359 gms., VF, rim dents, $8,800. Garrett:1331 is on a thin flan, 87 grs. = 5.6 gms., "FINE, rough," $6,500. If Mould completed the obv., this and next may belong in the following section.

1126 n.d. (1785) Pattern Decad. 4-F: Washington/Arms. 3 known.
Crosby, p. 352; Baker 11; Maris {1881} 4-C. Long miscalled "New Jersey Washington" because of the rev. 1) Crosby, Parmelee, H. P. Smith, James Ten Eyck, Newcomer, Garrett:1390, "VF," $50,000, 128.6 grs. = 8.34 gms., for 55 to the lb. (ill.) 2) Parsons, Brand, Fuld, Roper:298, VF–EF, $11,550, pierced, 130.8 grs. = 8.476 gms. Ill. ANS {1914}, Pl. 39, Baker {1965}, Yeoman Guide Book. 3) Boyd estate.

1127 1785 Mule Decad. 5-D: Wreath/Large stars. Unique?
Crosby, Pl. VII, 10. Dated on both sides. Shurtleff, Crosby, Parmelee, Ryder, Boyd estate, 103 grs. = 6.67 gms. (worn), possibly for 60 to the lb.
1128 1786 Mule Decad. 6-D: IMMUNIS COLUMBIA./ Large stars. Unique?
Crosby, Pl. VII, 16; fig. 55. Different dates on both sides. Morris, Brock, Univ. of Pa., Ward, Newman, 160 grs. = 10.37 gms., for 46 to the lb.?

1129 1786 Pattern Decad. 6-F: IMMUNIS COLUMBIA./ Arms. 7 or 8 known.
Crosby, Pl. VII, 17; fig. 58; Maris 3-C. Miscalled "New Jersey IMMUNIS" from the rev. Some struck at 52 or 55 to the lb.; Roper:297, EF, $7,150, 128.4 grs. = 8.32 gms. Gar-

rett:1389, EF, $17,000, is heavy at 153.4 grs. = 9.94 gms., for 46 to the lb. Finest is probably 1976 ANA:61, UNC., $22,000.

iv. MOULD'S AND BAILEY'S PATTERNS (1786–87)

One of Walter Mould's earliest acts on arriving in the USA was to submit a petition to the Continental Congress for a coinage franchise. This petition was referred to the Board of Treasury, Aug. 18, 1785, but got no further.

However, Mould apparently submitted sample coins, from dies he had brought over from Wyon's mint in Birmingham, muled with others of his own manufacture. He retained the old IMMUNE COLUMBIA die as a closet skeleton, avoiding use of it either because it was so completely identified with the Wyon proposal or because he did not wish further attention to its glaring error; later he sold it to James F. Atlee, who used it at Machin's Mills, 1789.

The coins attributed to Mould are in turn mixed up with those ascribed to John Bailey. We have already seen that Bailey made Jersey coppers early in 1788 **(948–51).** Bailey testified under oath, Aug. 1, 1789, that he had made none since April 15, 1788, and that "what he so made previous to the said fifteenth of April was in conformity to, and by authority derived from, an Act of the State of New Jersey, entitled, 'An Act for the establishment of a Coinage of Copper in that State, passed June the first, 1786' " (Crosby, p. 283). The only way Bailey could have obtained such authority was by buying into the Mould enterprise. Most likely Mould sold him not only part of the action but a variety of old dies and other ironmongery. Bailey's motive was obvious: He expected to profit by circulating Jersey coppers without paying tithes to the state. Mould's motive was more obvious: He needed cash to stay out of debtor's prison; as it was, in July 1788 he managed to evade it only by abandoning his mint, selling his equipment to Machin's Mills, and fleeing the state. The evidence that Mould sold dies to Bailey is **1133,** which combines one of the Wyon CONFEDERATIO dies (evidently brought to the USA by Mould) with a crude eagle die dated 1787 that shares punches with Bailey's Jersey coppers and the NOVA EBORACs.

Such mulings of dies made 3,000 miles apart introduce confusion. For the moment, the only coins herein attributed to Bailey are those bearing at least one die sharing punches with his Jersey coppers; it is possible, however, that some of the other coins attributed to Mould may have come from dies Mould sold to Bailey, in particular those listed above with the Washington obv. We earlier encountered a similar situation with the Brasher Doubloons.

Because this series is continuous with the CONFEDERATIO patterns above, the letter designations of revs. continue from those.

Rev. G. 1786 Eagle. By Walter Mould.

Rev. H. 1787 Eagle. By John Bailey. From the EXCELSIOR series.

WALTER MOULD'S PATTERN COPPERS

Designers, Engravers, Wyon and Mould. Mint, private, NYC? Composition, copper. Diameters, 17–18/16″ = 27–29 mm. Weight standards, variable, as below.

Grade range, FAIR to UNC. No grading standards established.

1130 1786 Pattern copper. 4-G. Washington/Eagle. 2 known.
Crosby, p. 318; Baker 10. Struck at 60 to the lb. 1) Few-

smith, Appleton, MHS. 2) Robert R. Prann (ca. 1947), Kagin.

1131 1786 Mule copper. D-G. Large stars/Eagle. Ex. rare.
Crosby, Pl. VII, 15. Revs. of **1123** and **1130:** both sides differently dated. 1) Mills, C. E. Clapp, ANS, 150.2 grs. = 9.734 gms., for 46 to the lb. 2) Benjamin Haines (1863), Lightbody, Bache, Seavey, Parmelee, Appleton, MHS, George J. Bauer, 134 grs. = 8.72 gms. = 52 to the lb.

1132 1786 Mule copper. F-G. Arms/Eagle. Unique?
Crosby, Pl. VII, 18. Revs. of **1126** and **1130.** 1) Stickney, Ellsworth, Garrett:1391, UNC., $37,500, 133.3 grs. = 8.63 gms., for 52 to the lb. A second rumored.

JOHN BAILEY'S PATTERN COPPERS

1133 1787 Mule copper. E-H. Small circle of stars/Eagle. Ex. rare.
Crosby, Pl. VII, 21. Rev. of **1124:** both sides differently dated. 1) Lilliendahl, Seavey, Parmelee, Brand, Norweb, 114 grs. = 7.39 gms., for 60 to the lb. 2) Reported.

v. ATLEE'S PATTERNS FOR THE CONFEDERATION (1787)

Before James F. Atlee became a full-time partner at Machin's Mills, he worked at first as a freelance die engraver (making the 1786 NON VI VIRTUTE VICI coppers and the 1786-dated counterfeit Connecticuts with bust facing r.). Later, from the end of Nov. 1786 until the end of May 1787, Atlee made dies for Rahway Mills, the legal New Jersey mint of Goadsby & Cox, under supervision of Gen. Matthias Ogden. All these coins share letter punches with coppers that Atlee made for the Vermont mint in 1787 pursuant to the contract between Machin's Mills and the legal Vermont coiners. The terminus of June 1, 1787, coincides not only with Atlee's departure for Newburgh but also (more than coincidentally?) with Benjamin Dudley's lawsuit which flung Albion Cox into debtor's prison and broke

up the Rahway Mills operation. In the meantime, Atlee had bigger projects in mind: contract coinage for the Confederation, either in conjunction with Rahway Mills or on his own.

To this purpose, in both 1786 and 1787 Atlee made pattern coins for a Confederation contract coinage. As the blanks for both are entirely unlike those found on most Machin's Mills coppers, the question arises of where and under what auspices he made them. This question can now be answered.

On March 23, 1787, Gen. Ogden, bondholder for Rahway Mills, submitted a petition to the Continental Congress praying for a franchise to make coppers for a national coinage. This was routinely referred to the Board of Treasury. Unfortunately for Ogden, the Board's nefarious chief, Col. William Duer, had already decided to give the contract instead to James Jarvis, in consideration of a $10,000 bribe. However, as Ogden had offered better terms (including 15% of the gross to be paid into the Treasury), the award of the FUGIO contract had to await Jarvis's offer to match those terms. Ogden could have fulfilled his contract, having the Rahway facilities and local copper mines; Jarvis could not, defaulted, and stayed in Europe to avoid a $10,842 court judgment against him. (Other details are found under Connecticut Draped Busts and FUGIO coppers, Chaps. 6 and 15.)

In the meantime, while Ogden was awaiting the bad news, he struck sample coins for submission to Congress from dies made by Atlee at Rahway Mills. These were almost certainly the earliest of the 1787 IMMUNIS COLUMBIA coppers. (Over a century ago these were recognized as patterns for the Confederation: Vattemare {1861}, p. 40; but later collectors who could not read the coins' Latin inscriptions could neither remember nor reconstruct the insight.) Those dated 1786 were presumably Atlee's earliest (unsuccessful) effort to make this design for Gen. Ogden. Those dated 1787 were obviously a much more careful effort. Blanks used for the common later state match in fabric those found on many of the later Rahway Mint Jersey coppers (**908–14**). Those overstruck on other coppers were probably trial impressions: Breen {1979}.

That over 100 survive today in all grades points to a sizable issue—certainly thousands, possibly tens of thousands. Most likely after Ogden's petition failed, before the Rahway Mills operation broke up, he ordered quantities struck for circulation; there was no local law against it, and the New York act regulating copper-coin circulation would not take effect until Aug. 1. In the meantime, these passed side by side with other coppers in New York at 14 to the shilling, and in other states at local rates wherever merchants would accept coppers at all.

ATLEE'S PATTERNS FOR THE CONFEDERATION

Designer, Engraver, James F. Atlee. Mints, NYC and Rahway Mills. Composition, copper. Diameters, Weight Standards, variable, as noted.

Grade range, **1134–35,** as shown; **1136–37,** G to UNC. No grading standards established.

1. For Atlee's Own Proposal

1134 n.d. (1786) NON VI VIRTUTE VICI. Large head/ Arms. Unique?
Baker 12. Obv. of **976,** rev. unused elsewhere. 1) Parmelee,

H. P. Smith, Clarence S. Bement, Col. James W. Ellsworth, John Work Garrett, Johns Hopkins Univ. (1942–79), Garrett:1388, FAIR, $16,500, 112.6 grs. = 7.296 gms.

1135 1786 IMMUNIS COLUMBIA/Eagle, transposed arrows. 2 known.

AJN 10/1885, p. 40; *AJN* 7/01, Pl. facing p. 20. Discovered by Dr. Edward Maris. Possibly struck at Rahway Mills. 1) Benjamin Titus, Maris:501, H. P. Smith, Dr. Thomas Hall, Virgil Brand estate, pvt. coll. 2) Roper:213, EF, $23,100, 143.3 grs. = 9.286 gms.

2. For Gen. Matthias Ogden's Proposal

1136 1787 IMMUNIS COLUMBIA Broad flan, full date. Very rare.

Crosby, Pl. VIII, 8. Diameter, 18–19/16″ = 28–30 mm. Some struck at 46 to the lb.; observed, 142.7–154 grs. = 9.247–10 gms. Some are overstruck on Jersey coppers: Garrett:605, UNC., $21,000.

1137 1787 Same dies. Narrow flan.

Diameter 16–17/16 = 25–27 mm. Date partly or wholly off flan. Usually shows few or no border dentils. Struck at 52 to the lb.; about 129–136 grs. = 8.4–8.82 gms. Garrett:604, 144.8 grs. = 9.39 gms., F–VF, $2,400, has ornamented edge (raised dots in rows and columns), added (experimentally?) after striking, possibly at Rahway Mills.

CHAPTER 12

MISCELLANEOUS NONLOCAL IMPORTS

i. RHODE ISLAND SHIP TOKENS (1779)

There are three vars. of this mysterious issue. The first shows the word *vlugtende,* in error for Dutch *vluchtende,* "fleeing," below Adm. Howe's flagship (**1138**); makers scraped this word off most of them after striking, producing **1139**. Later, they reannealed the die and engraved an ornament to conceal the word (**1140**). All three come in brass, generally on cast blanks with file marks on edges. Their garbled Dutch legends have been variously misinterpreted, largely because nobody bothered to look up the events in the Revolution to which the tokens alluded.

Adm. Richard Howe (1726–99), Earl Howe, the pro-American member of the Peace Commission, portrayed on **1047–48**, was ousted from the commission without stated cause. His brother, Gen. William Howe, sent a detachment under Gen. Henry Clinton to occupy Newport, R.I., Dec. 8, 1777. (These are the same Gens. Howe and Clinton who only a little earlier had been distributing counterfeit Continental notes from H.M.S. *Phoenix* in New York Harbor.) During the summer of 1778, about 10,000 American militia, under Maj. Gen. John Sullivan, tried to retake Newport with the help of about 4,000 French troops under Adm. Comte d'Estaing. As the French began to disembark on Aug. 9, 1778, at Conanicut Island (in Narragansett Bay west of Newport), Adm. Howe arrived. Admiral d'Estaing hastily reembarked and went out to confront Howe; but as they jockeyed for battle positions a sudden storm dispersed both fleets. On Aug. 20, d'Estaing limped back to Newport for repairs; on Aug. 30, the Americans, learning of Howe's approach, abandoned the tiny island (the 1778 event alluded to on the obv. of the Ship Tokens). But 15 months later, on Oct. 25, 1779, Howe himself had to abandon not Conanicut but Rhode Island itself: the event mentioned on the tokens' ship side, accounting for the word *vlugtende* originally present below the ship.

These satirical pieces, long obscure and mysterious, may now be read as "The Americans had to run away in 1778; now there goes Adm. Howe the same way in 1779." This fails to explain why the sails are furled: Howe's ship would be going nowhere fast. Possibly the engraver meant this detail to emphasize the satirical content. Why the word *vlugtende* was removed, first from the coins, then from the die, is still obscure. Most likely the makers feared British reprisals.

Judging by their preservation, these tokens circulated with other coppers, side by side with the CONSTELLATIO NOVA and various base Birmingham "Hard Ware," at a time when anything of suitable size and weight would serve as small change. They come in all grades (rarely mint state), unlike medals, which were not spent. Their legends do not suggest local

Rhode Island circulation, which is why the tokens are listed here rather than in Chap. 8.

The Providence, R.I., coin dealer Horace M. Grant issued a struck copy of **1141** in 1936; this is instantly identifiable by initials HMG in the waves. The Grant copies are rare and not deceptive.

RHODE ISLAND SHIP TOKENS

Designer, Engraver, Mint, unknown. Composition, brass, except as noted. Diameter, about $^{20}/_{16}'' = 32$ mm. Weight standard, variable, as noted.

Grade range, VERY GOOD to UNC., mostly FINE to EXTREMELY FINE. No grading standards established.

1138 1779 *vlugtende* below ship. Brass. Unique?
Betts 561. Jencks-Paine (1866), Ellsworth, Garrett:1325, EF, $16,000, Roper:170, $9,900, 151.1 grs. = 9.8 gms., for 46 to the lb.

Ex J. W. Garrett: 1325. Courtesy Bowers & Ruddy Galleries, Inc.

1139 1779 *vlugtende* scraped off coin. Brass.
Betts 562. 132–137.6 grs. = 8.56–8.916 gms., for 52 to the lb. Roper:171 is heavy at 159.2 grs. = 10.32 gms., for 46 to the lb.? First publication, Shoen Shujin, *Seiyo Sempu* (Illustrated Catalog of European Coins), Kyoto, ca. 1785, cited in *CNL* 47, v15n3, p. 570 (10/76).

1140 1779 Same. Pewter trial piece. Ex. rare.
1) NN 51:182. 2) Merkin 3/68:2, Roper:173, AU, $3,520, 169.1 grs. = 10.96 gms. One of these may be ex Earle:2025. Others reported.

1141 1779 Ornament below ship. Brass.
Betts 563. Occasionally silvered. Many struck at 46 to the lb., e.g., Garrett:1327, 151.5 grs. = 9.82 gms.

1142 1779 Same. Pewter trial piece. About 6 known?
1) Parsons, Ellsworth, Garrett:1328, $5,000, 129 grs. = 8.36 gms. 2) NN 48:792, from England. 3) NN 51:183, from England. 4) Burnheimer:502. 5) NERCG, "Commonwealth" sale; this and 4) possibly represent reappearances of 2) and 3). One of these is probably Roper:174, VF (tin pests), $687.50, 134.1 grs. = 8.69 gms.; the other possibly Kagin 332:1006 (Long Beach sale, 2/2–4/83), 135.03 grs. = 8.75 gms.

ii. THE BACKDATED "1781"
NORTH AMERICAN TOKEN

Ever since Crosby's day, a century ago, collectors have suspected that this mysterious token was of later date than 1781. One of the reasons is that its obv. device first occurs on Irish tokens reading CAMAC, KYAN & CAMAC, made in Dublin, 1792, by William S. Mossop, Sr., for the Hibernian Mine Company at Ballymurtagh (near Arklow seaport, County Wicklow), later imitated by many other firms in hundreds of vars. Another is P. Napoléon Breton's testimony {1894}, at his number 1013, to the effect that the "North American" had been in circulation "up to recent times," which probably means 1858, when decimal coinage for Canada began displacing the lightweight coppers serving until then as small change. A third is that similar devices are found on Canadian coppers dated 1820 and 1833. Nevertheless, fanciers of Early American Colonial coppers, ever since Dickeson {1859}, have considered the NORTH AMERICAN TOKEN collectible. Among other reasons, these tokens have shown up in noncollector accumulations with other nonlocal pieces, notably the "1783" backdated Washingtons: a clue to their period of origin. They generally come well worn, and close examination of the few really choice ones explains the fact: The dies were cut in low relief then deliberately scratched and banged up so that the coins struck from them would simulate much older coppers long accepted in circulation, rather than anything new and likely to arouse suspicion.

Douglas Winter, then (1977) aged 18, investigated punch linkages between the NORTH AMERICAN TOKEN and others of similar design, and discovered that this "1781" piece shares letter punches with two tokens by William Mossop, Jr. (1788–1827), datable to the 1810–20 period. These are the backdated "1804" Pawnbrokers Office halfpenny, Davis {1904} (Dublin) 57, and the 1813 Neville & Co. halfpenny, Davis (Dublin) 59, both known to be by the younger Mossop. Mossop's name was first speculatively linked to the NORTH AMERICAN TOKEN by J.(ohn) F. J.(ones), *NUM* 6/37, but proof was lacking until Winter demonstrated the punch linkage. Both the Mossop tokens with this punch linkage have similar devices, but the "1781" has even closer look-alikes in a Canadian nonlocal copper, Breton 894 = Charlton 148 (reading ONE HALFPENNY TOKEN 1820/TRADE AND NAVI-

GATION), and an Irish piece reading HIBERNICUS 1820 (NN 54:513); Seaby {1961} Dublin 68, p. 229. Similar considerations of style induced Winter to assign the 1817–19 period as the most probable time of issue.

This circumstance enables us to account for its importation. During the War of 1812, an embargo prevented the Philadelphia Mint from importing cent planchets from Boulton & Watt in Birmingham. The coiners made cents in limited quantities through 1814, exhausting the prewar supply of blanks, without filling the need for local small change. To make matters worse, when the British invaded our shores, banks suspended specie payments, and all coins were hoarded. The Treasury stopped silver and gold coinage, and issued notes in various low denominations, but because these notes were fundable in 7% bonds, speculators bought them up at once. Still worse, in Jan. 1816 a fire destroyed one of the Mint's outbuildings containing the mills for rolling gold and silver ingots into strip, therefore preventing manufacture of planchets for any coinage whatever until repairs could be completed. As a result, the Mint made no more cents until the end of 1816 (when Boulton & Watt shipped several tons of planchets); no silver until 1817, no gold until 1818. During this period, New York and Philadelphia merchants, in need of small coins to make change, ordered a variety of tokens from Birmingham and Dublin mints. Among these may now be named not only the backdated "1783" Washingtons (Chap. 14), but also the "1781" NORTH AMERICAN TOKEN.

Why was it backdated 1781? Winter {1978} has suggested that this date commemorates Cornwallis's surrender.

THE "1781" NORTH AMERICAN TOKEN

Designer, Engraver, William Mossop, Jr. Mint, Mossop's, Dublin. Composition, brass, copper. Diameter, about $^{17.5}/_{16}$" = about 27.5 mm. Weight standard, 60 to the lb.

Grade range, FAIR TO UNC. GOOD: Date and legends readable, devices outlined. VERY GOOD: Partial drapery details. FINE: Partial waves; over half drapery. VERY FINE: Over half waves; partial hull details. Higher levels—grade by surfaces. EXCEPTION: Uneven weak strikes are the rule. Choice survivors show numerous die scratches in field. No specimen is completely sharp; apparently the dies were softened and banged up (see introductory text).

1143 1781 Token. Brass.
Crosby, Pl. IX, 21; Breton 1013; Haxby-Willey 15a. 112–117 grs. = 7.26–7.58 gms.

1144 1781 Token. Same dies. Copper.
Haxby-Willey 15. 109.2 grs. = 7.076 gms.

iii. THE BAR COPPER (1785)

The New Jersey *Gazette,* Nov. 12, 1785, described a recent arrival among circulating coppers from Birmingham "Hard Ware" makers:

A new and curious kind of coppers have lately made their appearance in New York. The novelty and bright gloss of which keeps them in circulation. These coppers are in fact similar to Continental buttons without eyes; on the one side are thirteen stripes and on the other U.S.A. as was usual on the soldiers buttons. If Congress does not take the establishment of a Mint into consideration and carry it into effect it is probable that the next coin which may come into circulation, as we have a variety of them, will be the soldiers old pewter buttons, for they are nearly as variable as the coppers above described and hardly so plenty.

The Continental buttons mentioned are scarce collectibles (Albert {1974} GI 2); several vars. exist. According to the minutes of the revolutionary Supreme Executive Council, these buttons were made of pewter comprising 75% lead, 25% tin, which would hardly have served for coins: Stewart {1924}, p. 116.

Note that the Great Seal of the United States (1782) represents the Original 13 Colonies as stripes, though easing the count by alternating red and white; this precedent accounts for the stripe or bar device on the coppers' rev. They were struck at considerably lighter weight than the normal Birmingham standard of 60 to the lb.; until the New York copper panic (July 1789), they surely passed with the rest at 14 to the shilling. This circumstance makes the old name "Bar Cent" a misnomer not worth preserving.

We may conjecture that whichever New York merchant ordered them furnished their Birmingham maker with a uniform button as a prototype. At the apparent weight standard of 84 to the lb., a cask containing one cwt (112 lbs.) would have comprised some 9,408 coppers. Crosby, p. 333, quotes Charles Ira Bushnell as attributing these to Wyon's mint in Birmingham; at the time there was no other operation whose name has been preserved, certainly no other with any pretense to legitimacy.

Survivors mostly come F to VF, seldom better or much worse; in mint state they are prohibitively rare. Normally they come on thin narrow blanks with incomplete border dentils. They antedate the period when Birmingham mints were coining coppers with lettered or ornamented edges. No other coins have shown up overstruck on Bar Coppers.

There are more forgeries of the Bar Copper than of any other coins of the period. All genuine examples have a tiny spine protruding from near end of second bar, pointing at third; usually there is also a tiny die crack joining two bars almost at center of the coin. These marks are absent from any of the die-struck forgeries, though they may show on cast or electrotype copies of originals. Crosby, p. 333, mentions two vars., "that on the plate the rarest," but the other var. has never shown up; it was probably a Bolen copy.

About the earliest of the forgeries reliable historical information exists. In 1862, the Springfield (Mass.) medalist John Adams Bolen made accurate copy dies (without the spine or central crack) and struck impressions in copper [65], later selling the dies to the Roxbury coin dealer William Elliot Woodward. Woodward turned the dies over to one of the three Lovetts in New York, ordering silver impressions [12]. Charles Ira Bushnell somehow learned that Lovett had the dies, and privately ordered other strikings; in his estate (1882) were later strikings in nickel, brass, and tin. Bolen's coppers are minutely lighter than some originals: 81–81.8 grs. = 5.25–5.3 gms. (as against Bolen's 80.8–87.2 grs. = 5.24–5.65 gms.). They normally come in mint state, though a few have been rubbed to simulate originals.

Less is known of the five or six later issues of forgeries; these are mostly struck from cruder dies than the originals, sometimes on cast blanks. Crosby, fig. 79, shows an undersized piece, brazenly called the "Bar Half Cent," in which the letters USA are not monogrammed; this apparently dates to the 1858–73 period. At the other extreme is a deceptive (and not impossibly contemporaneous) coin which showed up at the 1982 ANA

Convention in Boston. This is overstruck on a Bengali (Prinsep) 1/2 Anna, A.H. 1195 = A.D. 1780, KM126, Craig 704; broad irregular flan, about $^{19-20}/16'' = 30$–32 mm, 197.5 grs. = 12.8 gms.

THE BAR COPPER

Designer, Engraver, George Wyon, III. Mint, Wyon's, Birmingham. Composition, copper. Diameter, varies, as below. Weight standard, apparently 84 to the lb. = 83.3 grs. = 5.4 gms.

Grade range, FINE to UNC. No grading standards established; grade by surface only.

1145 n.d. (1785) Copper. Spur from second bar.
Crosby, Pl. IX, 25. Round flan, about $^{15.5}/16''$ (varies). 80.8–87.2 grs. = 5.24–5.65 gms. Note spur from second bar, partial crack from sixth to seventh bars, recutting above end of sixth bar; forgeries lack these (see introductory text). Border often incomplete. Breisland, Roper:334, UNC., $2,530.

1146 n.d. (1785) Same dies. Broad oval flan. 2 known.
$16.5 \times {}^{17.5}/16'' = 26.2 \times 27.8$ mm. Weight not recorded. The crack is plain; shadow on ill. obscures the spur from second bar, though both examples show it. Thought to be some kind of special presentation or souvenir striking. 1) English pvt. coll., Metropolitan Coin Co. FPL, n.d. (ca. 1962). 2) England, Lester Merkin (ill.).

iv. THE *AUCTORI PLEBIS* COPPERS

The design most often seen with this legend closely copies **847**, the Jarvis & Co. draped-bust Connecticut issue. Collectors have therefore long cherished the AUCTORI PLEBIS as a kind of nonlocal adjunct to the Connecticut series. Its devices suggest that the maker intended American circulation. Most likely whichever New York or Philadelphia merchant ordered them furnished a Connecticut copper for prototype. Moreover, in Britain, AUCTORI PLEBIS, 'By authority of the commoners,' had an antiroyalist flavor, as did INDEP. ET LIBER, 'Independence and Liberty,' quite aside from its being copied from the Connecticut rev. legend.

There are two probable periods of issue: between early 1788 and July 1789 (before the New York copper panic interrupted the profitable business of importing lightweight Birmingham coins); and (less likely) 1794–95. We know that they were already around in 1795, because Prattent pictures one on p. 54, and his book (illustrating then current British token halfpence) was published on Jan. 14, 1796. Prattent's index (reproduced by photo offset in *CNL* 43, p. 477 (v14n1), 4/75) lists the design as follows:

American o. A Head, s: Auctori Plebis R. Britannia, & c. 54

The listing "American" induced Crosby (p. 342) to say "probably struck for use in America." However, Crosby confused matters by comparing the rev. device to Wyon's Emsworth halfpenny tokens of 1793–94, D&H Hamps. (Emsworth) 9–11e, and Wyon's Norwich tokens, D&H Norfolk (Norwich) 20–21d. The Emsworth tokens show a sailing ship and EMS-WORTH; the 1793 also comes with an obv. showing dove and cornucopia with PEACE AND PLENTY, while the Norwich token obvs. advertise R. Campin's haberdashery. All these come from Kempson's mint in Birmingham; the Emsworth items were made on behalf of the local grocer and tea dealer John Stride, whose dies were also favored for making some of the TALBOT, ALLUM & LEE mules (**1047–48**). However, it is unwise to assume that Wyon had anything to do with the AUCTORI PLEBIS; there is no similarity of style, and none of the punches match.

Nor is it even certain that the maker of the 1787 AUCTORI PLEBIS made any of the rarer vars. with bust to r. The latter usually have revs. reading HISPANIOLA ('Haiti') and the fictitious date 1736, or NORTH WALES or BRITAINS ISLES and the equally fictitious date 1756. These peculiar legends link them to the series of "evasion" halfpence common in England, like the Washington NORTH WALES coins **1294–99** and hundreds of types of sleazy coppers whose devices copy regal halfpence, but whose inscriptions are meant to deceive the illiterate, such as GEORGE RULES for GEORGIVS III REX, or BRITAINS ISLES for BRITANNIA, or HISPANIOLA or NORTH WALES for HIBERNIA. R. C. Bell calls them "album weeds": {1968}, p. xv. "Evasion" halfpence mostly come from the period 1789–1805: Thompson {1949}. Both the Washington NORTH WALES and the AUCTORI PLEBIS coppers are included herein because of their obv. inscriptions. The IC who signed **1149** is unidentified; possibly he intended to be taken for the (also unidentified) IC who signed several medals (1788–89) celebrating the "recovery" (actually temporary remission) of King George III.

Crosby claimed that some of the coins with bust r. have revs. "effaced by attrition." Examples examined to date do not confirm this, but indicate that the pieces (**1152–53**) were in fact struck uniface. Their obv. inscriptions justify their inclusion.

A tentative assignment to William Lutwyche's mint in Birmingham follows from the fabric of "evasion" coppers, but to date no student has found any punch-linkage evidence connecting the 1787's to the backdated pieces with bust r., nor any of the latter to the Washington NORTH WALES.

THE **AUCTORI PLEBIS** COPPERS

Designer, Engraver, —— Arnold, William Mainwaring, and/or Roger Dixon, others? Mints, Lutwyche's (and others?), Birmingham. Composition, copper. Diameter, $^{17}/_{16}"$ = 27 mm (varies). Weight standard, 60 to the lb. = 116.67 grs. = 7.56 gms.

Grade range, FAIR to EX. FINE, always weak. No grading standard established; grade by surface only.

1147   1787 Copper. Bust l.
Crosby, Pl. IX, 15; Atkins {1889}, "Imitations of Regal

Coinage," p. 385, no. 7; *CNL* 1 (see introductory text). The recent forgery has large hollow cinquefoil before AUCTORI and may not show date: ill. *NUM* 11/64, pp. 1492–93.

1148   1736 Bust r./Harp, HISPANIOLA Blundered date 17336. Ex. rare.
Atkins 8; *CNL* 3; NN 56:62, no. 5.

1149   1736 Head r., signed IC. Rev. similar, normal date. Ex. rare.
CNL 4; NN 56:62, no. 1.

1150   1756 Same obv. Rev., harp, NORTH WALES 1756. Ex. rare.
NN 56:62, no. 2.

1151   1756 Same obv. Rev., seated figure, BRITAINS ISLES 1756. Ex. rare.
NN 56:62, no. 3.

1152   n.d. Bust r., ornaments in legend, uniface. Ex. rare.
CNL 2; NN 56:62, nos. 6, 7 (early and late states). Cf. NN 51:207. 105–112.8 grs. = 6.81–7.31 gms., possibly for 64 to the lb.

1153   n.d. Bust r., no ornaments in legend, uniface. Ex. rare.
Kurth {1943}, Pl. IX, lower l.; *CNL* 5; NN 56:62, no. 4. Other vars. may exist.

v. THE STARRY PYRAMID HALFPENCE (1792–94)

Masonic symbolism gave these tokens their device and their name; an intended nationwide circulation dictated their inscriptions. The Pyramid consists of 15 blazing suns or stars, each stamped with the initial of one of the states, echoing the CONSTELLATIO NOVA motif. The Original 13 form the Masonic Unfinished Pyramid configuration, originally appearing on some Continental Currency issues, later on the rev. of the Great Seal of the United States (1782), reproduced on the backs of today's $1 notes. On the Continental bills and the Great Seal, the Unfinished Pyramid is surmounted by the All-Seeing Eye in

glory, with the motto ANNUIT COEPTIS, 'He [God] hath smiled on our efforts.' But on the token, the Pyramid is instead completed by suns marked V for Vermont (admitted to the Union in 1791) and K for Kentucky (admitted in 1792); the makers must have assumed that Kentucky would close the roster of states. (Had they believed other states were still to be admitted to the Union, nothing would have been simpler than to arrange the stars in rows of 4, 5, and 6, and again surmount the group with the Eye.) As there are only 15 states, the period of issue is certainly between 1792 and June 1796, with 1792 as the most probable year. (Tennessee's admission, June 1, 1796, provided a terminus for manufacture of the dies, though the coins may well have circulated afterward.) The earliest mention in print: Birchall {1796}, p. 96, called them United States coins.

Their obv. legend, UNANIMITY IS THE STRENGTH OF SOCIETY, is a pep talk for the new nation, while the Great Seal's motto E PLURIBUS UNUM, 'Out of many, one,' refers to the stable configuration of states into one union. Both inscriptions suggest that the makers intended a nationwide circulation, not a local Kentucky destination; outside Lexington, the new state was a wilderness where coins would have been about as useful as at the North Pole.

On the scroll (a petition?) is OUR CAUSE IS JUST, which is more problematical. If this refers to the former British colonies in America, it is strangely late; if it refers to Kentucky, the words allude to settlers' struggles ever since 1783 to secede from Virginia and join the Union as a separate state—again pointing to a date early in 1792, when the federal congress was considering admission of Kentucky as the fifteenth state.

Workmanship on these tokens suggests one of the very finest diemakers. There are only two likely possibilities: John Gregory Hancock and George Wyon, III. Wayte Raymond claimed that the tokens were made in Lancaster, England, following Crosby, p. 343; this attribution is impossible, being based solely on the edge lettering PAYABLE AT LANCASTER LONDON OR BRISTOL, common on Lancaster token halfpence. The latter, however, at least through 1792, were made for Thomas Worswick, Sons & Co., bankers, of New Street, Lancaster, by John Gregory Hancock at Westwood's mint in Birmingham; no Lancaster private mint is known. The minute lettering found on many of the Lancaster tokens is a Hancock mannerism, similar to that found on the Starry Pyramid pieces, though no punch linkage has yet been found between them. Wyon, working at Kempson's mint (also in Birmingham), could have imitated Hancock's style; however, the planchets on which some of the Starry Pyramid coins come are from firms whose tokens originated with Westwood's mint, making the attribution to Hancock more plausible. Nor is it coincidence that the same remark holds for some of the 1791 Washington cents known to have originated with Hancock: See Chapt. 14.

We do not know which New York or Philadelphia merchants ordered the shipments from the Westwood mint, but the Starry Pyramid coins circulated widely along the Eastern Seaboard, while the floundering Philadelphia Mint's cents remained unfamiliar curiosities. The plain-edge coins continued to circulate for some years, as they come in all grades down to GOOD, rarely mint state. Weight data indicate that there were several batches, probably made at different times for different merchants: one on extra-heavy Macclesfield blanks at 35 5/7 to the lb. = 4,000 to the cwt, another and much larger shipment on Tower standard blanks at 46 to the lb.

On the other hand, those with lettered edges rarely show signs of circulation (more often they come cleaned by ignorant owners), and they have the look of pieces intended for sale to British collectors; over 95% are in prooflike mint state, which remark also holds for the other and rarer edges.

These coins have long been popular among collectors, partly because of the Kentucky connection (especially with those who

wished to include them as tied in with individual states), partly because of their attractive design and the obvious American relevance of their inscriptions. They should become still more popular now that their symbolism has been elucidated.

THE STARRY PYRAMID HALFPENCE

Designer, Engraver, John Gregory Hancock. Mint, Westwood's, Birmingham. Composition, copper. Diameters, variable, as below. Weight standards, various, as noted.

Grade range, GOOD to UNC. GOOD: Inscriptions legible except on scroll. VERY GOOD: Part of JUST shows; most state initials clear. FINE: Partial hand details; OUR . . . IS JUST is legible. VERY FINE: Part of CAUSE legible. EXTREMELY FINE: Full scroll motto (CAU may be slightly weak); isolated tiny wear spots on hand and scroll. For higher levels, grade by surface.

1154 n.d. Halfpenny. Plain edge. Macclesfield standard. Rare. Crosby, Pl. IX, 26. Atkins 33c; D&H Lancs. (Lancaster) 59c. 192–198 grs. = 12.44–12.83 gms. 1.16–1.185" (about 18.5–19/16") = 29.3–30 mm. Border dentils usually incomplete.

1155 n.d. Same. Plain edge. Tower standard.
Birchall {1796} 1, p. 96. 150.8–154.9 grs. = 9.77–10.04 gms. 1.122–1.15" (about 18/16") = 28.5–29.2 mm. Border dentils usually incomplete. Often with die cracking near scroll. Garrett:1531, UNC., $1,400; usually F to EF.

1156 n.d. Same. Large Lancaster edge. Heavy London standard.
Edge, PAYABLE IN LANCASTER LONDON OR BRISTOL. Birchall {1796} 2, p. 96. 174–187.5 grs. = 11.28–12.15 gms. Broader flans, border dentils usually complete though narrow. Sometimes with die cracking near scroll. Crosby, Garrett:1533, AU, $1,000; others.

1157 n.d. Same. Large Lancaster edge. Tower standard. Rare. Atkins 33; D&H Lancs. (Lancaster) 59; Bell {1968} A5, pp. 240–41. 149–153 grs. = 9.66–9.91 gms. Rarely with edge blunders (slippage): LANCASTERNDON (Parsons:306); LANCASTER OR BRISTOL (Gregory:2213).

1158 n.d. Same. Small Lancaster edge. Irish standard. Ex. rare.
Same edge words, smaller letters. 132–137 grs. = 8.56–8.88 gms. 1) 1973 GENA:60. 2) Pvt. coll.

1159 n.d. Same. Bedworth edge. Ex. rare.
Edge, PAYABLE AT BEDWORTH NUNEATON OR HINKLEY. Discovered by Dr. Charles Clay, of Manchester, England, before 1871. 1) Mrs. Norweb. 2) Reported. This edge belongs to D&H Warwickshire (Coventry) 242a, one of the regular Lady Godiva halfpence. No data on weight or diameter.

1160 n.d. Same. Asylum edge. Unique? Untraced.
Atkins 33a; D&H Lancs. (Lancaster) 59a. Edge, AN ASYLUM FOR THE OPPRESS'D OF ALL NATIONS. Listed on the authority of Atkins {1889}.

1161 n.d. Same. Fieldings edge. Unique?
Edge, PAYABLE AT I. FIELDINGS MANCHESTER * 176.5 grs. = 11.44 gms., for Heavy London standard (40 to the lb.). 1.197" (about 19/16") = 30.4 mm. Early die state. Discovered by Richard Picker. CNL 6, p. 2 (v3n1), 1–3/62.

This edge belongs to tokens of John Fieldings, D&H Lancs. (Manchester) 127, 135.   1) Picker:279, UNC., $1,595.

1162 n.d. Same dies. Diagonally reeded edge. Very rare.

Atkins 33b; D&H Lancs. (Lancaster) 59b. 142.4–148.8 grs. = 9.227–9.642 gms., most likely for Tower standard. $1.187 \pm 0.01'' = {}^{19}/_{16}'' = 30.15 \pm 0.25$ mm. Full dentilation. The diagonal reeding is widely spaced, unlike that on the Washington Grate halfpence, SUCCESS tokens, or 1792 Federal patterns. It could be simulated by hand alteration, but the diameter and weight combination rule out deception; plain-edge coins at this weight are almost never so broad. Discovered by Dr. Charles Clay before 1871. Aulick, Garrett:1532, UNC., $2,300; Roper:344, UNC., $770.

1163 n.d. Same dies. "Vine edge." Unique.

1) Newman coll. No data on weight or diameter. Edge is probably like that on **1051**: sinuous line and dots.

1164 n.d. Same dies. Silver OMS. Unique? Unverified.

vi. THE *FRANKLIN PRESS* COPPERS (1794)

These tokens' device is apparently intended for the press at Watts's Printing Works, Wyld St., Lincoln's Inn Fields, London, where Benjamin Franklin worked between Jan. and July 1726. Franklin revisited the press in 1768, while living about 20 minutes' walk away (at Mrs. Stevenson's boarding house on Craven St.). The press became famous because of Franklin's association with it; later owners affixed a plaque detailing its history. After Watts died in 1763, the firm of Cox & Bayliss (later Cox & Son) bought the entire establishment. In 1842, John Boyles Murray brought the press to Washington, D.C., where it was exhibited in the Patent Office Building, later at the 1876 Centennial; today the press is in the Smithsonian Institution.

Nothing is known of the occasion for which the tokens were made, though their fabric suggests that coin collectors, not storekeepers, were their intended buyers. These coppers have turned up in unattributed groups of token halfpence from Britain, but to date in no American noncollector accumulations. Their learned Latin legend would have discouraged ordinary circulation; it means "Thus [by the power of the press] learning is disseminated and liberty shall spring forth," a sentiment singularly appropriate to Franklin, but strangely recondite for William Lutwyche, to whom Raymond H. Williamson {1958} attributes the tokens. D&H quoted an anonymous claim in "Bazaar Notes" {1882} that these coppers were made for Cox & Bayliss.

Pye ({1795}, {1801}) assigned no diesinker, maker, nor proprietor. From internal evidence in both editions, he never got close enough to Lutwyche to assemble usable data: He did not even learn Arnold's given name. This manufacturer had ample reason for secrecy: Much of his output comprised sleazy "evasion" coppers and counterfeits of other firms' tokens.

The ASYLUM edge, properly referring to America, occurs irrelevantly on D&H Lancs. (Lancaster) 40, (Liverpool) 120a; Middx. (London, Lackington's) 351a, 369; Wales (Anglesey)

430a; Ireland (Wicklow, Cronebane) 40, all of which are attributed on other grounds to Lutwyche; the Lancaster, Welsh, and Irish tokens are Lutwyche's counterfeits of the time.

Most survivors show a die break within the press; unbroken die coins are scarce though not rare. The tiny defect at RT is always present and does not increase in size. Only the one pair of dies is accepted as genuine; the "new variety" which appeared about 1961–62, with different lettering, is believed a modern forgery: Vlack {1965}, p. 95.

THE **FRANKLIN PRESS** COPPERS

Designer, Engraver, —— Arnold, William Mainwaring, or Roger Dixon? Mint, Lutwyche's, Birmingham. Composition, copper. Diameter, ${}^{17-17.5}/_{16}'' = 27$–27.8 mm. Weight standard, 60 to the lb. = 116.67 grs. = 7.56 gms.

Grade range, FINE TO UNC. EXTREMELY FINE: Few isolated tiny spots of wear on lintel, toggle joint, handle, etc. Lower and higher levels—grade by surface.

1165 1794 Plain edge.

Crosby, Pl. IX, 16; Atkins 222a; D&H Middx. 307a; Bell {1968} 25, p. 20. Perfect-die examples (ill.) are scarcer than those showing break within press. Border dentils usually incomplete. The alleged proof offered in Burdette G. Johnson's FPL#31 (n.d., after 1926) remains unlocated.

1166 1794 Same dies, lettered edge. Unique?

Atkins 222; D&H Middx. 307. Edge, AN ASYLUM FOR THE OPPRESS'D OF ALL NATIONS.   1) British pvt. coll.

1167 1794 Same dies, diagonally reeded edge. Unique?

1) Baldwin, Ford.

1168 1794 Same obv.; East India rev. Unique?

Rev. device is bale mark of British East India Company: VEIC in rudely quartered heart, 4 above. This device occurs on several of Lutwyche's Manchester tokens. Struck on penny-token blank, 230.16 grs. = 14.913 gms., for 30 to the lb. 1) Woodward 69:408 (10/13/1884), Twining:1102, ANS.

CHAPTER 13

CHURCH AND COMMUNION TOKENS

Normally this field would be outside the scope of Colonial coinages, but as the Albany Church Penny (1790) has been accepted as within the field, inevitably a few others herein listed will prove to have a comparable claim, incidentally forcing a redefinition of the term "token," and conceivably stimulating a search through junk boxes for similar items.

Coppers or other tokens used solely within churches perpetuate an idea going back at least to the Reformation. The 1635 Liturgy of the Scottish Presbyterian Church spells out that each Saturday night all members of the congregation intending to partake of communion (bread and wine) the next morning were to gather at the meeting house or church, and on recognition by the pastor, each would receive a token of such membership. On Sunday morning, as each one came to the communion service, (s)he would return the token for subsequent use. Tokens therefore constituted a kind of proof of membership whose purpose was to prevent hostile outsiders (royal spies, etc.) from attending services and betraying members during the decades when all such unorthodox religious observances were illegal. This 1635 account indicates that the custom was to continue in the same manner in which it had been conducted since the earliest days of the Reformation. Tokens remained in use until well into the 1880s; in some Presbyterian churches of the more ancient observance, they continued into the present century.

They come in many styles, and they formerly showed up in dealers' junk trays. They occur round, square, rectangular, octagonal, or oval; lead is the most frequent metal. They are sometimes die-stamped, more often incused with initials alluding to the location of the church and sometimes its pastor's name. Not often are the American tokens dated, and sometimes the initials are cryptic, befitting their original outlaw purpose. Unless a token matches a description in a contemporaneous source, there is no automatic way to tell if such a piece is from the 18th or 19th century, let alone its city or state of origin. Very little research has been done on American church tokens, either those strictly for Presbyterian communion usage or those accepted in collection plates. These two classes are often confused and sometimes overlap (as when the parishioner is expected to give an offering to pick up his church token on Saturday night). The ultimate source of the listings below is Warner {1888}, though oddly he omitted the Albany Church Pennies.

By their very nature, any given issue of pre-1800 American church tokens must be rare, restricted to the few dozen (at most, few hundred) members of any one congregation simultaneously in attendance. (This remark does not apply to Scottish tokens, as their congregations grew very large.)

We list only those definitely datable to 1800 or earlier. All are very rare; makers are unknown, grading irrelevant. *In all following descriptions, assume that the metal is lead and the shape round unless otherwise specified.*

1169 NEW YORK. n.d. (1790) Albany. Copper. [1,000] About 6 known?
First Presbyterian Church, Jan. 4, 1790. Counterstamped on worn-out coppers, about 18/16″ = 28.6 mm. Woodworth {1853, 1860}; Rulau-E NY 1. 1) Woodward 4/1863:2079, Appleton, MHS I:178, Roper:340, $2,530. 2) Jenks:5507, Garrett:1518, holed. 3) Clapp, Schulman 4/59:1173.

1170 n.d. (1790?) Albany. Copper. Equally rare.
Adams {1920} N.Y., Albany 1; Rulau-E NY 1A. Same comments. The D may represent a pastor's initial. 1) Woodward 4/1863:2080, Appleton, MHS, 1976 ANA:78, $7,000. 2) Pvt. coll., ill. 3) Robison, Roper:341, $2,200.

1171 1785 Cambridge. Lead, like all to follow. Ex. rare.
Obv., in 2 lines, A.C/C.E (= Associated Church, CambridgE). Rev., in 2 lines, T.B./1785 (= Pastor Thomas Beveridge). Square, 15/16″ = about 24 mm on a side. The town, in Washington County, N.Y., was later called Coila.

1172 1799 New York City. Associated Church/N.York 1799. Very rare.
Inscriptions all in script. Rulau-E NY 622. Oval, about 11/16″ × 15/16″ = 17 × 23+ mm. 1) ANS. 2) Groves:348. 3) Altman-Haffner:686. Others reported.

1173 1793 South Argyle. Ex. rare.
Obv., in 2 lines, A.E/C.N (= ArgylE CongregatioN). Rev., in 2 lines, T.B/1793 (= Pastor Thomas Beveridge). Square, 13/16″ = about 21 mm on a side. The church was in South Argyle, Washington County, N.Y.

1174 PENNSYLVANIA. n.d. (1784). Bethel. Ex. rare.

Obv., B.C incuse (= Brush Creek Congregation). Oval, 11/16 × 12/16″ = about 17.5 × 19 mm. Bethel was in Westmoreland County.

1175 n.d. (1778). Buffalo. Ex. rare.

Obv., script B in sunken square, raised border around. Square, 11/16″ = 17.5 mm on a side. Issued by Pastor Matthew Henderson, Buffalo Congregation, Washington County, Pa.

1176 n.d. (1795) Deer Creek. Ex. rare.

Obv., within large multipointed star, D. Square, 10/16″ = 15.9 mm on a side. Deer Creek was in Lawrence County, Pa.

1177 n.d. (1792) Mill Creek, Pa. Ex. rare.

Obv., M incuse (= Mill Creek). Rev., A incuse (= Pastor Anderson). Square, 10/16″ on a side, as last. Mill Creek was in Beaver County.

1178 1799. Philadelphia. Ex. rare.

Identical to **1170** except Philada in script instead of N.York. Oval, 13/16″ × 16/16″ = about 20.6 × 25 mm. Apparently by the same maker as the New York Associated Church token.

1179 n.d. (1752) Stony Ridge, Pa. Ex. rare.

LS incuse on square flan, various sizes. Brought from Scotland by the evangelist Rev. John Cuthbertson; remained in use in the Stony Ridge (Cumberland County) congregation for decades after the original revival meeting of Aug. 23, 1752.

1180 1748 Welsh Run, Pa. Ex. rare.

Obv., CC. Rev., 1748. Square, 14/16″ or about 22.2 mm on a side.

1181 SOUTH CAROLINA. 1800 Charleston. Ex. rare.

Obv., communion table, cloth, cup, and plate, THIS DO IN REMEMBRANCE OF ME. Rev., burning bush, NON TAMEN CONSUMEBATUR, 'Yet it was not consumed.' Edge, PRESBYTERIAN CHURCH, CHARLESTON S.C. 1800. Silver. Engraved. Rulau-E SC 8. [150] + [150 second batch] (different work?). Plundered by Union soldiers during the Civil War; few recovered. The similar pieces struck in pewter, Rulau-E SC 10, were made about 1836–37 for black parishioners [about 400] from dies by Robert Lovett, and these tokens suffered the same fate as the silver.

1182 VERMONT. 1791 Barnet. Ex. rare.

In 3 lines, R-C/D-G/B-T 1791 = Reformed Church, (Pastor) David Goodwillie, BarneT. Square, 14/16″ or about 22.2 mm on a side.

1183 n.d. (1790) Ryegate. Ex. rare.

In 2 lines, A C R/VT. Square, 10/16″ or 15.9 mm on a side. A C R = Associated Church, Ryegate.

CHAPTER 14

WASHINGTON COINS, TOKENS, AND CIRCULATING MEDALETS

i. THE *GEORGIVS TRIUMPHO* COPPER (1783)

Long popular among collectors who knew little about it, this has become still more popular now that detailed study has yielded some of the surprising truth about it. It was long believed ambiguous, muling a rude head of George III (copied from the 1775–76 and 1781–82 Irish halfpence, Seaby {1961} H236–40) with one of the usual Birmingham counterfeit British halfpenny dies. Its legends seemed evasively readable whatever the outcome of the war: in praise of King George if the redcoats won, in praise of Washington if the colonists won, but with familiar devices insuring circulation either way: Folksong buffs would see it as a kind of "Vicar of Bray" among coppers.

Closer attention shows, however, that by 1783 King George had no possible triumph coming; and had his redcoats counterattacked after both Yorktown and the British evacuation of New York, the legend VOCE POPOLI (Italianate spelling of VOCE POPULI, 'By the voice of the people') would have been colossal irony. In the actual context of Washington's heroically wresting victory from an army of redcoats vastly outnumbering the colonists, both the triumph and the voice of the people had definite relevance. The coin's rev. device, in this context, reveals its meaning: The weaving frame before Ms. Liberty's (?) legs contains 13 vertical stripes representing the United Colonies (as on the Great Seal of the United States, 1782); at its corners, completing the design and holding it upright, are four fleurs de lys, obviously alluding to French aid in obtaining victory for Washington. This means that the obv. device attempted to represent Washington when no engraved portraits were accessible to copy.

Discovery of several "Plaited Mane" Jersey coppers (935), made in 1788–89, overstruck on specimens of the GEORGIVS TRIUMPHO, proves that this Washington piece, unlike any others dated 1783, was actually struck in the 1780s. All other Washingtons bearing date 1783 originated in Birmingham about 1817–20 (See Sect. iii, below).

Robert A. Vlack claimed in *CNL,* v17n2, p. 651 (7/78), that the GEORGIVS TRIUMPHO circulated first in Georgia, then in Virginia (despite Jefferson's well-known claim that coppers were never in use in that state), many later being "destroyed or mutilated" allegedly because the bust was taken for George III; still later (according to Vlack) others went to Jamaica and Florida. Confirmation from noncollector accumulations from these areas would be welcome but is so far unavailable.

THE GEORGIVS TRIUMPHO COPPER

Designer, Engraver, Mint, unknown. Composition, copper. Diameter, about $^{17.5}/_{16}'' = 27.5$ mm. Weight standard, 60 to the lb. = 116.7 grs. = 7.56 gms.

Grade range, FAIR to EXTREMELY FINE. GOOD: All legends legible, though rev. may be weak, date blurred. VERY GOOD: Partial details on tapestry and hair. FINE: Some wreath details on back of head. VERY FINE: All major wreath outlines clear. EXTREMELY FINE: See ill. EXCEPTION: Coins from broken dies (some in much later state than ill.) show marked weakness around the breaks. Grade by surface.

1184 1783 Copper.
Crosby, Pl. IX, 14; Baker 7; Bell {1968} A4, p. 240; Vlack 30-Z. Garrett:1699 is heavy at 135.5 grs. = 8.78 gms. This may mean another batch at 52 to the lb. = Irish halfpenny standard; not enough have been weighed for confirmation.

ii. THE "UGLY HEAD" COPPER (1784)

What little is known about this legendary rarity has had to be pieced together by comparing the traceable specimens: four coppers and two "white metal" trial pieces. Obv. is a caricature (of Tory persuasion?), with legend WASHINGTON THE GREAT D:G: Rev. shows date 17 84 in two lines within a circle of links bearing initials of states, after the style of the 1776 Continental Currency patterns and fractional notes, with which its maker must have been familiar, though the order of the states differs from that on the Continentals by having C (Connecticut) between R.I. and N.Y. instead of just right of M.B. (Massachusetts Bay).

All specimens were discovered in this country decades ago; the only British association with any of them is the Royal Navy's Arrow and Cross countermark found on one, and its significance is unknown. Mint, engraver, and weight standards are unknown. The issue is so rare that grade is irrelevant.

1185 1784 "Ugly Head" copper. 4 known.
Snowden 74; Crosby, Pl. X, 3; Baker 8. $^{17/16''} = 27$ mm. 1) Dr. Gibbs, Mint Cabinet (before 1860), SI. 2) Cogan 4/ 1863, Appleton, MHS; countermarked Arrow and Cross, 102 grs. = 6.61 gms. 3) Roper:369, $14,850, 93 grs. = 6.03 gms. 4) K.L. Stockdale. 98.243 grs. = 6.366 gms. (pierced). Found by a teenage boy under a porch in Ijamsville, MD., late 1930's.

1186 1784 Same dies. White-metal trial piece. Ex. rare.
1) Dr. Valentine:227 (Elder 12/8–10/27), Cy Hunter, Arthur Conn, Maurice Gould estate, L.I. specialist, 158.21 grs. = 10.252 gms. According to Ford, 56% silver, 20% tin, 19% lead, 4% antimony, traces of copper and iron. Several electrotypes exist. 2) I. F. Wood, Nicholas Petry, Col. James W. Ellsworth, Garrett:1700, $3,600, 125.5 grs. = 8.14 gms. Alloy untested.

iii. THE BACKDATED "1783" BIRMINGHAM TOKEN CENTS

These coins remained a mystery for a century. They circulated extensively along the Eastern Seaboard, apparently as cents; specimens come in all grades down to FAIR. They have shown up in noncollector accumulations, generally associated with cents as late as the 1820s, and sometimes with the 1781 NORTH AMERICAN TOKEN. Specialists in Colonials and Washington pieces have collected them since the late 1850s, when restrikes began showing up from London. Allusions to the restrikes in the first major American bestsellers for coin collectors—Dickeson {1859} and Snowden {1860}—increased interest in the originals. Most collectors took for granted that these were products of the 1780s; even Crosby included them among "those struck in the eighteenth century" (p. 349).

That view could not survive after skeptics pointed out that the UNITY STATES cent plagiarizes in all details of rev. (except the Y) the federal Draped Bust cents of 1796–1807, evidently intending to attract little attention to itself by its difference in obv. device. Its legend UNITY STATES OF AMERICA recalls the "evasion" halfpence of 1789–1805 mentioned in Chap. 12, Sect. iv, under the AUCTORI PLEBIS coppers; their legends, like this one, were meant to deceive the illiterate—suggesting an attempt to evade anticounterfeiting laws (though that of 1806, to be sure, applied only to gold and silver). This theory is strengthened by the makers' use of rough planchets with some kind of impressed gridwork near borders, obscuring the word UNITY.

But when the Fulds {1964} deduced the identity of the T.W.I. whose initials appear on several vars. of both Military

Bust and Draped Bust token cents, the riddle was read. Much evidence already connected these coppers to Boulton & Watt's Soho Mint, near Birmingham, England: 1) working dies were made from complete hubs to accommodate an enormous standardized issue (a Boulton technique then well beyond the capacity of other private mints: Even the Philadelphia Mint did not successfully achieve it until 1836!); 2) the peculiar edge ornamentation of some of the small Military Busts first occurs on British coins and tokens in and after 1799, many from the Soho Mint; 3) rev. on all is a seated figure with liberty cap, loosely copying those engraved by Conrad H. Küchler in 1797 at the Soho Mint for Boulton's "Cartwheel" pence; 4) W. J. Taylor made his restrikes using hubs obtained with the ironmongery he had bought from the Soho Mint's effects: See details below. But evidence for the original 1815–20 striking period did not appear until the Fulds deciphered the undertype on a unique (?) Draped Bust coin (Winsor, Mills, Brand, Fuld, MHS II:99, $350); this proved to be a rare colliery token of I (= John) WALKER, FLIMBY PARK, Davis-Waters 70. The Walker firm owned collieries (coal retail outlets) from 1800–74; Davis and Waters {1922}, p. 288. A search for the initials T.W.I., found in exergue on some revs., yielded the name Thomas Wells Ingram, engraver with the Soho Mint in and after 1820, possibly for some years earlier. I had earlier noticed the capital I on truncation of original Draped Bust token cents, between toga folds above 3; this fell into place as another Ingram signature.

Clearly, Boulton intended no fraud by using the 1783 date: It obviously commemorated both the Treaty of Paris ending the Revolution, and Washington's disbanding the Continental Armies. Since 1797, Boulton & Watt had been making current coins for Britain and cent planchets for the Philadelphia Mint; their Soho Mint, though not above making occasional fancy items for collectors, was too much in the public eye to attempt anything fraudulent. Most likely, New York and Philadelphia merchants openly imported these "1783" Washingtons by the dozens or even the hundreds of kegs, at a fraction of a cent apiece; no law forbade import or circulation of private tokens. At 60 to the lb. = 6,720 to the cwt = 134,400 per long ton, these were not only profitable, they were a familiar way of dealing with shortages of small change, easier than waiting for more expensive federal cents, which (lacking legal-tender quality) had no advantage over tokens. The obvious occasion for such large orders in the 1815–20 period was the coin shortage of 1815–17, mentioned above concerning the "1781" NORTH AMERICAN TOKEN. Most likely the merchant who ordered the Draped Bust coins sent along a UNITY STATES as prototype; the one who ordered the Military Busts may have furnished a Large or Small Eagle cent or a sketch.

Were further evidence of their late date needed, the Draped and Military Bust Washingtons were still circulating as late as 1853: Thompson {1848}; Lord {1853}, p. 24. Many have noticed that the portrait on the Military Busts more nearly resembles Wellington than Washington.

In 1848, the coin dealer W. J. Taylor, of 33 Little Queen St., Holborn, London (later of 70 Red Lion St.), purchased a quantity of scrap metal from the rubbish of the just-closed Soho Mint, among which were numerous hubs, device punches, and working dies: Peck {1964}. These included the hubs for the Draped Bust Washingtons. Taylor sank working dies from them and struck many impressions during the 1850s, some possibly as early as 1851 (as **1197** suggests) for the Industrial Exposition at the London Crystal Palace, others possibly as late as 1860 (earlier students have repeatedly specified 1858). Fuld, in his marginal addenda to Baker {1965}, suggests 1850 for restrikes with plain edges, 1860 for those with ornamented edges. Whatever their date of striking, all have remained in demand among collectors ever since the 1860s.

THE BACKDATED "1783" BIRMINGHAM TOKEN CENTS

1. Unity States

Designer, Engraver, unknown. Mint, uncertain, Birmingham. Composition, brassy copper. Diameter, 18/16″ = 28.6 mm. Weight standard, 60 to the lb. = 116.7 grs. = 7.56 gms.

Grade range, FAIR to UNC. GOOD: Date and legends legible, though tops of letters and bases of date will be weak or obscured by grid. VERY GOOD: Partial drapery and hair details. FINE: Some leaves on head distinct; partial internal details in leaves, both sides. VERY FINE: Over 3/4 details of drapery and leaves on head, their outlines clear. EXTREMELY FINE: Few tiny isolated rubbed spots on drapery and leaves (both sides). EXCEPTION: Artificial roughening in grid pattern near borders on **1188**.

1187 1783 UNITY STATES. Triple leaf at F. Unique?

Vlack 27-X. Layout of wreath exactly as on 1797–1807 federal cents: 16 leaves l., 19 r., triple leaf at F. No border grid roughening. Possibly discouraged as infringing on the federal design. Discovered by James D. King. 1) HR 12/72:128, King, 28.2 mm, 111.1 grs. = 7.2 gms. Enl. photos.

1188 1783 UNITY STATES. Berry below F.

Vlack 27-W. Same obv. die; leaves differently arranged. Note that the portrait resembles Napoleon Bonaparte. Usually found F to AU, rarely higher, never brilliant. Their American distributor was supposedly one James Kean, of Philadelphia: CCJ 2/1884, p. 26, earlier source not cited.

2. Draped Bust Cents, No Toga Button

Designer, Engraver, Thomas Wells Ingram. Mint, originals, Soho, Birmingham; restrikes, W. J. Taylor's, London. Composition, originals, copper; restrikes, as below. Diameter, 18/16″ = 28.6 mm. Weight standard, originals, 60 to the lb. = 116.7 grs. = 7.56 gms.; restrikes, apparently 48 to the lb. = 145.8 grs. = 9.45 gms.

Grade range, originals, FINE to UNC. VERY FINE: 3/4 drapery and wreath details; berries clear on both sides. EXTREMELY FINE: Few isolated tiny rubbed spots; no drapery or leaf details blurred. Unknown in mint state. Restrikes: proofs only, some copper strikings bronzed (artificially patinated matte in mint).

1189 1783 Cent. Original, small date. Plain edge. 2 minor vars.

Crosby, Pl. X, 2; Baker 2; Vlack 13-J, 15-K. Signed I = Ingram, between toga folds above 3; borders narrower than on restrikes.

1190 1783 Cent. Same, thin flan. Rare.

103–108 grs. = 6.67–7 gms., probably for 66 to the lb.; apparently represents a later order by a different merchant.

1191 1783 Soho restrike, small date. Brass. Plain edge. 2 known.

A) Heavily clashed and rusted original dies. In INDEPENDENCE, bases of I and second D, serifs of second N broken, as are tops to most E's. Rev. clash marks are from drapery, profile, and back hair. 133 grs. = 8.62 gms. 1) Clarke III:3612, Jonathan Kern, Daniel Presburger coll. Ill. B) Second var.: crack through bases of 83. Vlack 15-J. 127.47 grs. = 8.26 gms. 1) Ezra Cole:1297 (B&M 1/23–25/86), Mike Ringo.

1192 1783 Taylor restrike, large date. Copper. Plain edge. Very rare.

Baker 3; Vlack 14-J, 16-K. Sometimes bronzed. Price for 14-J, with base of 7 repunched. Robison:233, $500; Roper:359, 150.7 grs. = 9.765 gms. Dangerous counterfeits exist; these have matte surfaces and beveled edges, unlike the genuine.

1193 1783 Taylor restrike. Similar. Copper. Center-grained edge.

Baker 3; Vlack 14-J, 17-L. Sometimes bronzed. Price for 14-J. Diagonal reeding along middle of edge (cylindrical surface).

1194 1783 Taylor restrike. Similar. Silver. Plain edge. Ex. rare.

Baker 3; Vlack 14-J. Repunched base of 7. 1) Reported.

1195 1783 Taylor restrike. Silver. Center-grained edge. Very scarce.

Baker 3; Vlack 17-L. Edge as **1193**. Robison:232, $875; Roper:362, 134.8 grs. = 8.734 gms.

1196 1783 Taylor restrike. Gold. Ex. rare.

Mentioned in Fuld's marginal note to Baker 3 {1965}; allegedly from same dies as last. 1) H. Chapman 1909, Brand, pvt. coll. 2) Reported.

1197 1851 Mule restrike. Copper. Rare.

Vlack MEL-K. The kangaroo die was for tokens Taylor sold at the Crystal Palace exhibition (see introductory text). The seated figure rev., or one like it, survived into the 1960s, and may still exist. Roper:360, 103.1 grs. = 6.68 gms., $550.

3. Draped Bust Cents with Toga Button

Designer, Engraver, uncertain (local imitation of preceding). Mint, uncertain, Birmingham. Composition, copper. Diameter, 17.5/16″ = 27.8 mm. Weight standard, 60 to the lb. = 116.7 grs. = 7.56 gms.

Grade range, FAIR TO FINE. GOOD: Outlined devices, legible date and letters. VERY GOOD: Partial drapery details, few leaves separated. FINE: Over half drapery details. EXCEPTION: Centers always weak. That ill. at **1198** approaches VF and is one of the sharpest extant.

1198 1783 Cent. No period after final S; rev., dot within D. Very scarce.

Baker 5. On this and next, Liberty sits on crate (unlike **1189–97**); in exergue, T.W.I. and E.S, imitating **1201-3**. Always in low grades.

1199 1783 Cent. Period after final S.; no dot in D. Very rare. 3 minor vars. Always in low grades.

1200 1783 Cent. Similar but blunder INDEPEDENCE. Unique?

Vlack 24-T. Imitation by another Birmingham mint, probably William Lutwyche's. 1) British pvt. coll., NN 60:488, T. L. Craige estate.

4. Military Bust Cents

Designer, Engraver, Thomas Wells Ingram, after Edward Savage. Mint, Soho, Birmingham. Composition, copper. Diameter, 17.5/16 = 27.8 mm. Weight standard, 60 to the lb. as foregoing.

Grade range, GOOD to ABOUT UNC. VERY GOOD: Partial details on collar, wreath, and drapery. FINE: Most wreath leaves distinct. VERY FINE. All buttons clear, over half drapery distinct. EXTREMELY FINE: Star on epaulet clear, fringes without blurring; few tiny isolated rubbed spots.

1201 1783 Cent. Small bust, center-grained edge. Rare.

Baker 4 footnote; Vlack 1-A. Very fine border beads; W far from bust. Edge like **1193** but less deeply impressed. Sometimes with obv. cracked as next. In exergue, T.W.I. = Thomas Wells Ingram; E.S. = Edward Savage, portraitist. Roper:365, EF, 118.8 grs. = 7.698 gms.

1202 1783 Cent. Small bust, plain edge. Scarce.

Same dies, often cracked, sometimes shattered. A second var., NN 60:473, has severe rust and different breaks; no duplicate seen to date.

1203 1783 Cent. Large bust. At least 10 minor vars.

Crosby, Pl. X, 1; Baker 4. Coarse border beads. Dies differ mostly in minute details of hand strengthening on some letters and/or location of cracks.

5. The Double Head Cent

Designer, Engraver, unknown. Mint, uncertain, Birmingham. Composition, copper. Diameter, 17.5/16″ = 27.8 mm. Weight standard, apparently 56 to the lb. = 125 grs. = 8.2 gms.

Grade range, VERY GOOD to ABOUT UNC. FINE: Most leaves on both wreaths distinct. VERY FINE: All buttons clear on both sides; fringes clear, all leaves distinct. EXTREMELY FINE: Few tiny isolated rubbed spots only; grade by surface. EXCEPTIONS: The concentric lathe marks in fields (raised on coin) are in the die.

1204 n.d. (1815–20?) Cent. Plain edge.
Baker 6; Vlack 28-Y. 124–129 grs. = 8.04–8.36 gms. Placed here because the portraits resemble those with the Large Military Busts; specimens have shown up in noncollector accumulations with the latter.

1205 n.d. Cent. Same dies. Center-grained edge. Ex. rare.
Similar edge to **1201**; diagonal reeding slants up to r. 124 grs. = 8.04 gms.   1) NYPL:2105, "EF," $1,127.

iv. HANCOCK'S WASHINGTON CENTS (1791–93)

John Gregory Hancock, Sr. (1775–1815), was a juvenile engraving prodigy, becoming one of the finest artists in the history of 18th-century British diemaking (Peck {1964}, p. 239, note 1). While working for the Birmingham token manufacturer Obadiah Westwood, Hancock received the honorific assignment for making dies for two types of cents portraying George Washington, as samples for a proposed federal contract coinage, ordered by W. and Alex. Walker, Birmingham. These are the famous Large Eagle and Small Eagle cents. Hancock's portrait punch derived from an engraved copy of Pierre Eugène DuSimitière's drawing. The Small Eagle device shows eight stars, probably for the eight states where these coppers would be circulating; this design recurs on U.S. army buttons of 1792: Albert {1974} GI 24, pewter, 23 mm.

Walker shipped a cask (conjecturally one cwt = 112 lbs., about 4,000 cents, estimated as about 2,500 Large Eagle and 1,500 Small Eagle) to the firm's Philadelphia associates, Thomas Ketland & Sons, for distribution to cabinet officials, senators, representatives, and other VIPs (Thomas Digges's letter to Thomas Jefferson, March 10, 1793: quoted by Julian {1962B} and Taxay {1966}, p. 53). Between Dec. 21, 1791, and the end of March 1792, Congress was debating the Morris coinage bill, which sought to establish a national mint and a federal coinage system. Sect. 10 of the bill proposed that the coins portray Pres. Washington. Some of Ketland's people, or their friends in the administration, showed some of the sample cents to Washington, who rejected the proposal as "monarchical," and reportedly objected on principle to any private contract coinage. The relevant section of the Morris bill had to be rewritten; its final version, which became law on April 2, 1792, called instead for "an impression emblematic of liberty," taken to mean a personification. (Presidential portraits were not again

seriously considered until 1866, and reached coinage for circulation only in Aug. 1909.) However, in 1791 sample cents went into circulation and stayed there, so that their usual grade is VF. Strictly uncirculated specimens (especially of the Small Eagle) are rare, those with original mint red more so. Birchall ({1796}, p. 96) listed the Small Eagle cent as no. 3 of "United States coins," made by Birmingham coiners; for his nos. 1 and 2, see **1155–56**.

Those with other edge inscriptions, or with different revs., were made up later, probably 1793–94, mostly for sale to British collectors. Many of the 1793/2 Ship Halfpennies were evidently imported to circulate, as they also came worn, almost never with mint surface: Pye {1801} said, "These were sold in small quantities to any person who would purchase them."

HANCOCK'S WASHINGTON CENTS

Designer, Engraver, John Gregory Hancock, Sr. Mint, Westwood's, Charles St., Birmingham. Composition, copper (except as noted). Diameter, 19/16″ = 30 mm (except as noted). Weight standards, regularly Macclesfield = 355/7 per lb. = 4,000 per cwt = 196 grs. = 12.7 gms.; exceptions noted.

Grade range (on **1206, 1217, 1223, 1226** types): VERY GOOD to UNC. FINE: Partial epaulet details; main roll of wig (above ear) clear, some hair details above and below. VERY FINE: Over half hair and feather details; most of epaulet clear. EXTREMELY FINE: Few tiny isolated rubbed spots. Grade by surface. EXCEPTIONS: The 1793/2 Ship Halfpenny, especially in later clashed die states, is weak on head and epaulet, and die failure obliterates parts of rigging; grade by surface only.

1206 1791 Cent. Large eagle. Macclesfield standard. [About 2,500+]
Crosby, Plate X, 5; Baker 15; Atkins Non Local 173; D&H Middx. 1049. Edge, UNITED STATES OF AMERICA . x . (reads either way). One blank planchet seen with this edge: 192 grs. = 12.4 gms. N.B.: Similar pieces dated 1789 (Baker 14, D&H Middx. 242, Kenney 7) are G. H. Lovett's fantasies for Alfred S. Robinson (1863); ill. at Garrett:1743. Silver (Byron White coll.); copper [100]. 32 mm.

1207 1791 Cent. Same dies. Small thin flans. Ex. rare.
166.8–170.45 grs. = 10.81–11.02 gms., possibly for 41⅔ to the lb. = 7 dwt = 168 grs. 1) Noreweb. 2) NN 60:490. 3) NN/Seaby I:432. Cf. Elder 2/5/24:1722, 3/19/24:2688, 10/9/24:726, 6/28/26:2302 (Noreweb's coin?). Obv. die rusted and cracked, though less so than on **1223**.

1208 1791 Cent. Same dies. Plain edge. Untraced.
1) W. A. Lilliendahl, H. A. Smith, J. N. T. Levick, Jencks-Paine:1787 (1866). Beware electrotypes and cast copies.

1209 1791 Cent. Same dies. Gold. Unverified.
Edgar H. Adams, *Elder Monthly* 2,2, 12 (4/07). Beware gilt copper specimens.

1210 1791 Same, from unfinished dies; without ONE CENT. Copper. Unique?
Edge, BERSHAM BRADLEY WILLEY SNEDSHILL (on blank for Hancock's John Wilkinson Iron Master tokens, D&H Warwickshire 332–445). 1) W. C. Prime, Gilbody, Breen, Fuld, 1983 ANA:105, $1,265, ANS, 182.7 grs. = 11.84 gms., possibly for 38 to the lb.

1211 n.d. (1791) Uniface obv. device-punch trial, Macclesfield edge. Unique?

Crosby, Pl. X, 4, and p. 352. Edge, PAYABLE AT MAC-CLESFIELD LIVERPOOL OR CONGLETON . x . This edge represents blanks for Roe & Co. Macclesfield halfpence, D&H Cheshire 8–60 (also by Hancock). 1) Hancock's widow, Dr. Charles Clay, S. S. Crosby, G. M. Klein, Mills, Ryder. Ill. ANS {1914}, 194 grs. = 12.57 gms., for Macclesfield standard.

1212 1791 Uniface trial of completed obv. Unique?

Macclesfield edge, as last. 1) Baldwin.

1213 n.d. (1791) Uniface rev. device-punch trial. Unique.

No branch, no arrows; motto letters incised retrograde for layout. Plain edge. 1) Ellsworth, Raymond, Garrett:1703, $1,650, 161.6 grs. = 10.47 gms.

1214 n.d. (1791) Uniface incomplete rev. trial. Unique?

No heavy outline around shield. BERSHAM edge as **1210**. 41474 and other numbers scratched on blank back, significance unknown. 189.7 grs. = 12.29 gms. 1) Hancock's widow, Capt. Davenport, Seavey, Colburn, Bushnell, Woodward (1884), T. Harrison Garrett, John Work Garrett, Johns Hopkins Univ. (1942–79), Garrett:1701, $1,550.

1215 n.d. (1791) Uniface trial of completed rev. 2 known.

Heavy outline around shield. Edge, PAYABLE AT SHREWSBURY, representing blanks for Salop Woollen Manufactory halfpence, D&H Shropshire (Shrewsbury) 19–21, by Hancock. 1) Woodward (1884), Garrett:1702, $1,900, 167.6 grs. = 10.86 gms. 2) Hepner, Tralins, Kagin.

1216 n.d. (1791?) Mule. Draped bust l. of George III. Unique?

Crosby, pp. 354–55. Edge, twisted scrollwork. $19.5/16'' = 31$ mm. 215.4 grs. = 13.96 gms. Obv. of Peck 924, whose rev. imitates the 1770–75 Tower halfpence but is dated 1796. 1) Dr. Charles Clay, James E. Root, Isaac F. Wood, James Ten Eyck, Waldo Newcomer, Col. E. H. R. Green, B. G. Johnson, F. C. C. Boyd, NN 60:491, L.I. specialist.

1217 1791 Cent. Small eagle. Regular edge. [1,500+]

Crosby, Pl. X, 7; Atkins Non Local 174; Baker 16; D&H Middx. 1050. Weight and edge as **1206**. Die failure at WA. Proof in original case, Bache I:3273 (3/1865), untraced.

1218 1791 Cent. Same. Macclesfield edge. Ex. rare.

Edge as **1211**, probably same weight standard. 1) Bushnell, Parmelee, Mills, Ryder, Boyd estate. 2) Appleton, MHS. 3) Krugjohann:65, James D. King. 4) Hatie:175, possibly same as one of foregoing.

1219 1791 Cent. Same. Worswick edge. Unique? Untraced.

Atkins Non Local 174a; D&H Middx. 1050a. Edge, PAYABLE AT THE WAREHOUSE OF THOS. WORSWICK &

SONS . x . representing blanks for Lancaster halfpence, D&H Lancs. (Lancaster) 9–28.

1220 1791 Cent. Same dies. Brass. Regular edge. 2 known.

1) Capt. Davenport, Bache, Colburn, Seavey, Lightbody, Levick, Bushnell, Ellsworth, Garrett:1706, $1,600, 187.9 grs. = 12.18 gms. 2) Fuld, Roper:373, EF, $2,200, 188 grs. = 12.18 gms. Beware gilt copper examples.

1221 n.d. (1791) Uniface trial of incomplete obv. Copper. Unique?

No coat buttons. Edge, PAYABLE AT THE WAREHOUSE OF THOMAS & ALEXR. HUTCHISON, representing blanks for Hutchison's 1790–91 Edinburgh halfpence, by Hancock, D&H Lothian (Edinburgh) 22–37. 192.4 grs. = 12.47 gms., for Macclesfield standard. 1) Hancock's widow, Davenport, Colburn, Seavey, Bushnell, Parmelee, Woodward (1884), Garrett:1707, $2,900.

1222 1791 LIVERPOOL HALFPENNY. Laurel wreath. Pewter. Unique?

Rev. of D&H Lancs. (Liverpool) 1791.88–89 = 1792.100–2. $18.5/16'' = 29.4$ mm. 1) B. G. Johnson estate, Schulman 4/51:1077, NN 35:557, Futter, Mehl, Norweb, 156.5 grs. = 10.14 gms. Cf. Fuld's marginal note to Baker 17 {1965}.

1223 1791 LIVERPOOL HALFPENNY. Oak wreath. Copper. Very rare.

Crosby, Pl. X, 6; Baker 17; Atkins Non Local 64; D&H Lancs. 116. Edge, PAYABLE IN ANGLESEY LONDON OR LIVERPOOL. About $18/16'' = 28+$ mm. Struck at 50 to the lb. = 140 grs. = 9.07 gms.; observed, 134.8–140 grs. = 8.73–9.07 gms. Rev. of D&H Lancs. (Liverpool) 1793.107 = 1794.115, 117. About 20 known. Obv. die always cracked and rusted; rev. always broken atop mainmast. Edge represents blanks for Kempson's imitations of Westwood's Parys Mines tokens, D&H Anglesey 271–297, etc. Planchets always a little too narrow, tops of letters and base of date usually off flan. Grade range VF–UNC., usually EF; not over 5 UNC. Reported with blundered edges (in D&H); this may mean the piece ex Dr. Clay, Isaac F. Wood colls., with half of edge device inverted.

1224 1791 Same dies. Plain edge. Unique?

1) Baldwin. Beware electrotype copies, casts.

1225 1793/2 Ship halfpenny. Copper. Anglesey edge.

Crosby, Pl. X, 14; Baker 18; Atkins Non Local 175; D&H Middx. 1051; Bell {1968} A3, p. 238. Edge as **1223**. 163–172.8 grs. = 10.56–11.2 gms., possibly for 41 2/3 to the lb. = 168 grs. = 7 dwt = federal cent standard. Early strikings (ill.) command a premium; usual late strikings are from severely clashed and buckled dies, overdate gone along with much of rigging; rust on collar, hair details vague. Still later strikings develop breaks at AS, GT, and bust. May exist on lightweight flans at 50 to the lb.

1226 1793/2 Same dies. Copper. Plain edge. 3 known.
D&H Middx. 1051a; Fuld marginal note to Baker 18 {1965}. 1) Unlocated British coll., source of D&H listing. 2) Fuld, Roper:376, 159.5 grs. = 10.34 gms., VF, $770. 3) N.J. specialist, 1975 EAC:491, 160 grs. = 10.37 gms. Beware electrotype copies.
1227 1793/2 Same dies. Brass. Anglesey edge. Unique?
Baker 18 footnote. 1) Mickley, Bushnell, Ellsworth, Garrett:1710, $3,300, Roper:377, VF, $990, 158.3 grs. = 10.26 gms. Late die state.

v. HANCOCK'S MULTI-DENOMINATIONAL PATTERNS (1792)

Little is known of these, though much is conjectured. Letter punches they share with earlier issues prove their origin with engraver Hancock at Westwood's mint. Crosby believed them medals; however, they evidently circulated as cents. They were almost certainly made between submission of the 1791 cents and receipt of word that Washington had rejected the whole idea of contract coinage. Lack of any mark of denomination, at least on the 1792-dated pieces with eagle rev., definitely suggests that the silver strikings may have been meant for samples of the half-dollar denomination, the solitary gold piece for the $10 (before choice of any specific weight standard, though Eric Newman believes that his unique specimen of the last was a special presentation piece). Low weights on gold and silver strikings compared to those demanded by the Morris bill cannot be adduced as a contrary argument; like any other silver or gold coins of the period, these would have been valued only by weight. Westwood did not know the terms of the Morris bill or he would have approximated them; he did not follow Hamilton's 1786 or 1791 recommendations, because they would have eliminated most of his possible profit.

This leaves the pieces with inscriptions on rev. and/or the BORN VIRGINIA obv. as medals; but as they were not fancy enough to please British token collectors, they were dumped into a keg and shipped to the USA (probably mixed with other coins—Ship halfpennies?) as one more cask of "Hard Ware" to circulate as cents. At 40 to the lb., a one-cwt cask would have contained 4,480 pieces, only a fraction of which bore these designs. In the 1790s, federal cents were seldom seen, but the size of these Washingtons surely means the two passed side by side. As federal cents were not legal tender, they had no advantage over lightweight imports; heavier ones would be hoarded, lighter ones spent as quickly as possible.

Whatever their original purpose, Hancock's 1792 coppers stayed in circulation, as the rare survivors are almost all in low grades. The least rare **(1239)** must have been made in some quantity (the majority of the single keg?); its rev. die caved in, producing many survivors with central bulges. Its obv. was preserved (as the last of its kind?), brought over to Massachusetts

by Jacob Perkins on one of his ocean crossings, and in 1959 Albert Collis struck many uniface impressions **(1242–46)** from a transfer die made from it before presenting the original die to the ANA in 1960.

HANCOCK'S MULTIDENOMINATIONAL PATTERNS

Designer, Engraver, Hancock. Mint, Westwood's, Birmingham. Composition, copper, silver, gold (fineness undetermined). Diameters, $19-20/16'' = 30.2-31.8$ mm. Weight standards, copper, 40 to the lb. = 175 grs. = 11.34 gms.; silver, gold, as noted.

Grade range, FAIR to UNC. No grading standards established.

1228 1792 Eagle Cent. Rejected obv., final T below shoulder. Unique?
Edge, UNITED STATES OF AMERICA . x . 1) Newman. Cf. Fuld's marginal note to Baker 21 {1965}.

1229 1792 Eagle Cent. Regular obv. Copper. Lettered edge. 4–6 known.
Crosby, Pl. X, 10 and p. 356; Baker 21. Edge as **1228**. Ellsworth, Garrett:1712, $8,000, Roper:380, $2,860 (worn). 179–180 grs. = 11.61–11.66 gms.

1230 1792 Eagle Cent. Copper. Plain edge. 6 or 7 known?
Baker 21. Similar pieces dated 1789 (Baker 14) are fantasies from G. H. Lovett's dies, struck for A. S. Robinson (1863); see specifications at **1206**.
1231 1792 Half Dollar. Same dies. Silver. Lettered edge. 5 or 6 known?
Crosby, p. 356; Baker 20. Edge as **1228**. $20/16'' = 31.8$ mm. 182.95–187 grs. = 11.86–12.12 gms., possibly for 30 to the troy lb. = 192 grs. = 12.44 gms. Robison:245, EF, $44,000, Roper:379, $35,200.
1232 1792 Half Dollar. Same dies. Silver. Plain edge. 4 or 5 known?
Baker 20.
1233 1792 Ten Dollars (?). Same dies. Gold. Lettered edge. Unique?
Baker 20A. Edge as **1228**. Out of round, 31×32 mm, for $20/16''$. 251.5 grs. = 16.3 gms. (worn), possibly for $22\frac{1}{2}$ to the troy lb. = 256 grs. = 16.59 gms. 1) Gustavus Adolphus Myers, Col. Mendes I. Cohen, Parmelee, H. P. Smith, Wayte Raymond, Col. Green, B. G. Johnson, Eric Newman. Edward Cogan conjectured (following Col. Cohen?) that this was Washington's pocket piece; cf. *CW* 1/29/75 and ANS {1976}, pp. 206–7.

1234 1792 Same obv.; inscription, first die. Copper, plain edge. Very rare.
Crosby, Pl. X, 11; Baker 59; ANS {1914}, Pl. 6. 30–31 mm, for $^{19}/_{16}"$. 176–179 grs. = 11.4–11.6 gms. Usually in low grades.

1235 1792 Same. Copper, lettered edge. 4 known?
1) Mickley, Col. Cohen, Appleton, MHS. 2) Stickney, Ellsworth, Garrett:1733, 179 grs. = 11.6 gms., $6,000. 3) Roper:400, $880 (worn, B M scratched in obv. field). 179.3 grs. = 11.62 gms. 4) Brevoort, Parmelee (1876), I. F. Wood, pvt. coll.
1236 n.d. (1792) BORN VIRGINIA/Eagle. Copper. Plain edge. 3 known?
Crosby, Pl. X, 12; Baker 22. $^{19}/_{16}" = 30$ mm. 1) Mickley, Cohen, Holland, Appleton, MHS, 173 grs. = 11.21 gms. 2) Newcomer, Brand, Norweb. 3) Unnamed German coll., Brand, B. G. Johnson, Schulman (1951), pvt. coll.

1237 n.d. (1792) Same obv., uniface. Original. Copper. Unique?
1) MHS. Not to be confused with the Collis Restrike **1245**.
1238 n.d. (1792) BORN VIRGINIA/Inscription, first die. Copper. 3 known.
Crosby, Pl. X, 13; Baker 60/59 {1965}. Date 1775 below CAN A; G L of GENERAL very close to border. 1) Appleton, MHS. 2) Parmelee, Norweb. 3) Fuld, Groves:433. Compare next.

1239 n.d. (1792) BORN VIRGINIA/Inscription, second die. Copper. Rare.

Baker 60. $^{19.5}/_{16}" = 31$ mm. 169.2–186.4 grs. = 10.96–12.08 gms. Plain edge. Date 1775 below ICAN; G L of GENERAL far from border. Rev. normally bulged in center. Usually in low grades. Deceptive counterfeits exist; authentication is necessary.
1240 n.d. (1792) Half dollar? Same dies. Silver, plain edge. 4 or 5 known?
Most are holed and plugged. 1) Winsor, Ellsworth, Garrett:1734, $9,000, 160.8 grs. = 10.42 gms., possibly for 36 to the troy lb. = 160 grs. = 10.37 gms. 2) Laird Park:196, $15,000, Robison:263, $5,500. 3) Roper:402, EF, $16,500, 172.6 grs. = 11.18 gms.
1241 n.d. (1792) Half dollar? Same dies. Silver, lettered edge. 2 known?
1) Bushnell:1244. 2) Fuld, Picker, plugged.
1242 n.d. Same obv. uniface. Collis Restrike. Platinum. Unique.
Ill. of **1245**. See introductory text.

1243 n.d. Same. Gold. [7] Ex. rare.
1244 n.d. Same. Silver. [22] Very rare.
1245 n.d. Same. Copper. [5,019]
Broad flan, $^{21}/_{16}" = 33.3$ mm. 274.3 grs. = 17.77 gms. (probably varies). Normally bright red UNC. Not to be confused with **1237**.
1246 n.d. Same. Lead. Unique.

vi. "HANCOCK'S REVENGE": THE "ROMAN HEAD" CENTS (1792)

When news of Washington's rejection reached Birmingham, John Gregory Hancock (doubtless with Westwood's gleeful consent, possibly even at his instigation) undertook an extraordinary piece of revenge. As Washington's spokesmen had compared the idea of presidential portraits on coins to the practices of Nero, Caligula, and Cromwell, so Hancock's (and/or Westwood's) idea was to portray Washington on a coin as a degenerate, effeminate Roman emperor. Hancock's satirical masterpieces, the "Roman Head" cents, manage to convey this impression—with a subtle resemblance. Their eagle attempts to "cock a snook" with his nearer wing; the Small Eagle die's eight stars have shrunk to six. The dozen or so survivors were privately distributed among Hancock's and Westwood's friends in Birmingham; their existence was kept secret for over 40 years lest it become an "international incident"! Beginning as tokens of incredible spite, these cents have become among the most highly coveted of Washington items: Breen {1971A}.

1247 n.d. (1792) First Roman head. Pewter. Uniface. Unique?
Note blunder PRESEDENT: lettered by Hancock's apprentice John Jordan? $^{18.5}/_{16}" = 29.4$ mm. 88.6 grs. = 5.74 gms. 1) Lincoln, Glendining 3/21/35:188, Elder 9/20/35:1672, B. G. Johnson, Schulman 4/51, NN, Fuld, Picker,

unidentified thieves, Aug. 1971. Cf. Fuld's marginal note to Baker 19 {1965}.

1248 n.d. (1792) Second Roman head. Copper. Uniface. Unique?
I.G.HANCOCK. F. below head. Edge, PAYABLE AT MACCLESFIELD LIVERPOOL OR CONGLETON . x . ¹⁹⁄₁₆″ = 30 mm. 197.4 grs. = 12.79 gms., for Macclesfield standard. 1) Spink, Merkin, Picker, unidentified thieves, Aug. 1971.

1249 Third or "regular" Roman head. Copper. Very rare. Crosby, Pl. X, 9; Baker 19. Edge, UNITED STATES OF AMERICA . x . x . x . (different from the 1791 cents). ¹⁹⁄₁₆″ = 30 mm. 196–198.5 grs. = 12.7–12.85 gms., for Macclesfield standard. About 12–15 known, all proofs (several impaired, one worn—apparently a pocket piece); at least 5 are impounded in museums.

vii. THE BACKDATED "1794" WASHINGTON DOLLARS

Unidentified parties fabricated these between 1859 and 1864 to deceive prominent collectors; their initial target may have been Mint Director James Ross Snowden, who had bought the "1793" Washington half cent from its maker Edwin Bishop during the same period, and who showed himself willing to trade rarities for unfamiliar Washington items for the Mint Cabinet Collection. As Snowden either refused the piece or left office before he could buy it, other customers had to be found. Woodward, in the McCoy sale (May 1864), gave a frustratingly ambiguous account, from which we learn that apparently only the one silver and two copper pieces showed up, obv. die breakage preventing manufacture of any others. They appear herein because conceivably mistakable for a British speculative issue of the 1790s.

1250 "1794 Dollar." Silver. Unique?
Baker 28. 1) Unlocated. Ill. of **1251.**

1251 Same. Copper. 2 known.
Baker 28. 1) Holden, Mrs. Norweb. 2) Pvt. coll.

viii. KEMPSON'S PENCE AND HALFPENCE (1795–1800)

Despite Washington's rejection of the Obadiah Westwood proposal for a contract coinage with presidential portraits, hope still lurked in the hearts of the Birmingham token makers, who after all could not depend for their entire income on the whims of London and provincial coin collectors, nor compete effectively with Matthew Boulton for Caribbean contract coinages.

And so, when rumors leaked back to England in 1795 that the infant federal mint in Philadelphia was in trouble and likely to be abolished, Kempson & Sons began making pence and halfpence which might conceivably keep their names before the American authorities as possible recipients of a national coinage franchise—over and above what they could earn by selling mules and odd edge letterings to wealthy collectors.

Whether or not they ever managed to interest any legislators or Cabinet members in this proposal, Kempson & Sons did export considerable quantities of their sample coins for circulation. Survivors come in a wide range of conditions; the really choice ones have mostly come out of British collections and dealers' stocks.

The undated penny, **1254,** was first mentioned in print by Samuel Birchall, {1796}, p. 4, no. 24. It must have been known in 1795, as Lutwyche's imitations bear that date.

The Kempson firm was also responsible for two types of tradesmen's tokens made for Clark & Harris, dealers in grates, stoves, etc., in Wormwood St., Bishopsgate, London; these are the Grate Halfpennies. They also circulated over here, probably as cents; the rare Small Buttons coins seldom come anywhere near mint state, though many red uncirculated Large Buttons coins have shown up from British numismatic sources.

About the REPUB. AMERI. pennies very little is known. They circulated little, as few of the 1796 and to date none of the Funeral type (1800) show signs of wear. Wyon inaccurately copied the Collyer and Chapman engraving of Joseph Wright's portrait etching (1790), but was proud enough of the result to sign it.

KEMPSON'S PENCE AND HALFPENCE

1. THE *LIBERTY AND SECURITY* SERIES

Designer, Engraver, pence, Thomas Wyon; halfpence, Arnold, Dixon, and/or Mainwaring. Mint, pence, Kempson's; halfpence, William Lutwyche's, both Birmingham. Composition, copper, except as noted. Diameters, variable, as noted. Weight standards, pence, 23 to the lb. = Tower standard = 304.3 grs. = 19.72 gms.; halfpence, various, as noted.

Grade range, undated penny, FINE to UNC.; dated penny, FAIR to UNC.; halfpence, FINE to UNC. GOOD: Date and legend readable. VERY GOOD: Partial wig details. FINE: Half details of wig and uniform; on undated penny, partial epaulet details. VERY FINE: Over 3/4 wig and epaulet details; most wing feathers show. EXTREMELY FINE: Few tiny isolated rubbed spots; nearly full breast feathers. EXCEPTIONS: Halfpennies normally come weak on upper part of head, lower part of shoulder, eagle's breast, and central shield, even when fields are covered with mint luster.

1252 n.d. (1795?) Pattern penny. Pewter. 2 known.
Note rev. engine-turned rim, like next. 1) Norweb. 2) NN 36:548, Fuld (ill.). Cf. Fuld's marginal note to Baker 30 {1965}.

1253 n.d. (1795) Penny. Engine-turned rims. Copper. 8–10 known.
Edge, AN ASYLUM FOR THE OPPRESS'D OF ALL NATIONS :: 21–21.5/16″ = 33.3–34 mm. 300–314 grs. = 19.44–20.34 gms. Discovered by Dr. Charles Clay before 1871. Compare following. Enl. photos.

1254 n.d. (1795) Penny. Same dies, plain rims. Asylum edge. Copper.
D&H Middx. (Political & Social) 243; Baker 30; Atkins 42; Rulau-E Non Local 1. Edge, diameter, and weight range as last. Often prooflike. Rarely gilt.

1255 n.d. (1795) Penny. As last, plain edge. Copper. 2 known? 1) Hillyer Ryder (before 1930), Wayte Raymond, W. L. Breisland, Laird Park:188, "AU," $1,150. Discovery coin. 2) 1960 MANA, Fuld, *CNL* v2n2 (4/61). Beware electrotype copies (seam on edge).

1256 n.d. (1795) Penny. Same dies. Brass. Unique?
Baker 30 footnote (cites Woodward sale, 4/28/1863). 1) Heifetz:368. Probably has same edge as **1253**. Must not be confused with gilt copper.

1257 n.d. (1795?) Mule Penny. Pewter. Unique?
Rev. of **1253** (engine-turned rim) muled with slave token obv., showing slave in chains, legend AM I NOT A MAN AND A BROTHER, from D&H Middx. (Pol. & Social) 235 bis 1, made for the Society for the Suppression of the Slave Trade. Plain edge. 1) Norweb, ANS, probably ex Heifetz:369. 204.9 grs. = 13.277 gms.

1258 1795 Penny. Bust r. ASYLUM edge. Copper. 10–12 known.
Crosby, Pl. X, 17; Baker 32; Atkins 43; D&H Middx. (Pol. & Social) 244. 20.5/16″ = 32.5 mm. 291.6–310 grs. = 18.9–20.09 gms. Edge as **1253**. Rulau-E Non Local 2. Believed made by Lutwyche's mint as circulating imitation of **1254**. Mostly in low grades, one gilt (ex Dr. Clay, Cauffman, Kirk, Fuld), one with counterstamped initials (ex G. M. Klein, 1888). Roper:395, AU, $6,600.

1259 1795 Penny. Same dies. Plain edge. Unique?
Rulau-E Non Local 2A. 1) Aston coll.

1260 1795 Halfpenny. Similar. London edge.
Baker 31; Atkins 176a; D&H Middx. 1052a; Bell {1968} A2, pp. 236–37. Edge, PAYABLE AT LONDON LIVERPOOL OR BRISTOL. 18.5/16″ = 29.4 mm.; 146–153 grs. = 9.46–9.92 gms., for 46 to the lb. Others weigh 136–140 grs. = 8.81–9.07 gms., for 50 to the lb.; these price the same.

1261 1795 Halfpenny. Same. Birmingham edge. Rare.
Baker 31 footnote; Atkins 176; D&H Middx. 1052. Edge, BIRMINGHAM REDRUTH AND SWANSEA, followed by symbols for Sun, Mercury, Saturn, Moon, Venus, Jupiter, and Mars in that order. Small thin flans, about 116 grs. = 7.56 gms., for 60 to the lb. Edge represents blanks for Birmingham Mining & Copper Co., D&H Warwickshire 77–101, 108–110, 117a, many of these being Lutwyche's imitations. Roper:391, AU, $577.50, 128.3 grs. = 8.31 gms.

1262 1795 Halfpenny. Same. Plain edge. Very rare.
Baker 31 footnote; Atkins 176c; D&H Middx. 1052c. Small thin flans, borders incomplete. 102.8–114.7 grs. = 6.67–7.43 gms., possibly for 65 to the lb., though Fuld conjectured that

these flans originally had lettered edges, possibly at 60 to the lb., removed before striking.

1263 1795 Halfpenny. Same. Asylum edge. Very rare.
Baker 31 footnote; Atkins 176b; D&H Middx. 1052b. Edge as **1253** but smaller letters. Only 12 traceable as of 1968 (NN 60:504). Ellsworth, Garrett:1727, "VF," 151.3 grs. = 9.81 gms., for 46 to the lb.; Robison:256, "AU," $950; Roper:392, AU, $660, 148.1 grs. = 9.6 gms.

1264 1795 Halfpenny. Same. Edge, LIVERPOOL OR LONDON Unique? Untraced.
Parmelee:632.

1265 1795 Halfpenny. Same. Edge, LONDON . LIVERPOOL Unique? Untraced.
Mills:1510.

1266 1795 "Irish" Mule Halfpenny. London edge. Copper. Very scarce.
Atkins 8; D&H Dublin 9. Edge as **1260**. Irish standard = 52 to the lb. = 134.6 grs. = 8.72 gms. Dated both sides. Usually weakly enough struck to look worn. Roper:394, 137.3 grs. = 8.897 gms.

1267 1795 Mule Halfpenny. Same. Plain edge. Ex. rare.
1268 1795 Mule Halfpenny. Same. Pewter OMS. Ex. rare.
1269 1795 "Fame" Mule Halfpenny. Copper. Unique? Unlocated.
Atkins 12; D&H Cork 13; Rulau-E Non Local 7. Fame l., blowing trumpet; FOR THE CONVENIENCE OF THE PUBLIC. Rev., arms die of **1260–63**. Diameter, weight, edge not described, probably same as **1266**. Device as on tokens of J.E. Co., Cork, D&H 1 and its imitation D&H 2 (latter probably by Lutwyche). Listed only on Atkins's {1889} authority.

2. GRATE HALFPENCE, FOR CLARK & HARRIS

Designer, Engraver, Thomas Wyon. Mint, Kempson's, Birmingham (D&H says Good's). Composition, copper. Diameter, 18/16″ = 28.6 mm. Weight standard, 50 to the lb. = 140 grs. = 9.07 gms.

Grade range, VERY GOOD to UNC. FINE: Roll of hair over ear complete; partial epaulet details. VERY FINE: Over half details of hair and epaulet. EXTREMELY FINE: Few tiny isolated rubbed spots only. EXCEPTIONS: Most Small Buttons coins are weakly struck; grade by surface. Almost never shows more than traces of rev. border dentils, with either obv. or any edge.

1270 1795 Halfpenny. Small coat buttons. Scarce.
Crosby, Pl. X, 15; Baker 29 footnote; Atkins 202; D&H Middx. 284. Edge diagonally reeded, down to r. 139–144 grs. = 9–9.33 gms.

1271 1795 Halfpenny. Large coat buttons; same edge.
Crosby, Pl. X, 16; Baker 29; Atkins 201a; D&H Middx. 283a. 137.2–145.5 grs. = 8.89–9.43 gms.

1272 1795 Halfpenny. Same dies. Edge reeding slopes up to r. Ex. rare, untraced.
Atkins 201b; D&H Middx. 283b.

1273 1795 Halfpenny. Same dies. Brass. Unique?
Baker 29 footnote; D&H Middx. 284. Edge as **1270.** 1) Bushnell, Ellsworth, Garrett:1721, $2,600, Roper:386, EF, $880, 147.7 grs. = 9.58 gms.

1274 1795 Halfpenny. Same dies. London edge. Copper. 4 or 5 known.
Baker 29 footnote; Atkins 201; D&H Middx. 283. Edge as **1260.** 1) Robison:251, UNC., $950. 2) Roper:387, UNC., $632.50, 144.4 grs. = 9.357 gms. First published, Birchall {1796} 126, p. 68; rediscovered, *AJN* 7/1877, p. 23.

THE **REPUB. AMERI.** PENNIES

Designer, Engraver, Thomas Wyon. Mint, Kempson's, Birmingham. Composition, as noted. Diameters, about 33 mm as previous pence. Weight standard, uncertain, possibly same as previous pence.

Grade range, VF to AU; mint-state specimens seen to date are Proofs. EXTREMELY FINE: Isolated tiny wear spots on main roll of wig, part of collar and ruff, truncation, scroll, fasces, and cannon butt. Otherwise grade by surface.

1275 1796 Penny. Copper. Plain edge. Rare.
Baker 68; D&H Middx. (Pol. & Social) 245; Rulau-E Non Local 22. Usually in proof state. Robison:264, $420.

1276 1796 Penny. Copper. Lettered edge. Unique? Unlocated.
1) Parsons:607, F. Edge, [ON DEMAND?] IN LONDON LIVERPOOL & ANGLESEY (slippage blunder, bracketed words omitted), representing a blank for Anglesey (Parys Mines) pence, either D&H 90 or 256a (latter AND ANGLESEY). Fuld, in marginal note to Baker 68 {1965}, conjectured the missing word as PAYABLE, but this wording is not confirmed on any token in D&H.

1277 1796 Penny. Tin. Plain edge. Ex. rare, untraced.
Baker 68.

1278 n.d. (1800) Funeral Penny. Copper. Plain edge. Ex. rare.
Baker 69. D&H Middx. (Pol. & Social) 245 bis (p. 542). Birth
and death dates below bust; birth date FEB.11. is O.S., 1732
corrected from 1752. Death date is erroneously given as
DC.21. instead of DEC.14. 1) Fleischer:611. 2) Gar-
rett:1759, $450. 3) 1981 ANA:2632.

1279 n.d. (1800) Funeral Penny. Copper. Jumbo piedfort. Ex.
rare.
Reported in Garrett:1759 as overstruck on a 1797 Soho Mint
"Cartwheel" penny; 1.4″ = 35.8 mm, 3 mm thick, standard
437.5 gr. = 28.35 gm. = 16 to the lb.
1280 n.d. (1800) Funeral Penny. Copper. Lettered edge. Untraced.
Reported in 1981 ANA:2632.
1281 n.d. (1800) Funeral Penny. Tin. Rare.
Baker 69; D&H Middx. (Pol. & Social) 245 bis (p. 542).

ix. THE *SUCCESS* TOKENS

Though both Baker and the late J. Doyle DeWitt believed
that these pieces were made to celebrate Washington's Second
Inaugural (March 1793), and that their inscription refers to his
Second Inaugural Address, there is no documentation. DeWitt
may have accepted William Elliot Woodward's theory (in Mat-
thews:1894) that Jacob Perkins of Newburyport, Mass., made
them, to be "worn" at the Inauguration. In absence of original
holders, this suggests that Woodward may have confused these
coins with Perkins's medals worn at Washington's funeral.

The only evidence the tokens provide about their period of
issue is the rev. device, which shows the All-Seeing Eye (usually
too weak to make out) in glory, with 15 stars for the 15 states in
the Union: an obvious allusion to the old CONSTELLATIO
NOVA device of 1783–85, and evidence of manufacture during
1792–95, as Tennessee became the sixteenth state June 1, 1796.
This is consistent with the Baker-DeWitt theory.

Baker believed these were made in the USA; however, no
contemporary advertisements or descriptions have been located,
nor are the SUCCESS pieces punchlinked to any other domestic coins or tokens. As specimens have been recovered from
both British and American collections, the question is still
moot.

The two sizes led some older collectors to call them, unwisely, "halfpence" and "farthings." Specimens of the larger
size come in a wide range of conditions, indicating that they
were either carried as pocket pieces or (more likely) spent, possibly as half cents.

DeWitt mentions copper restrikes, but all impressions seen to
date in any metal are originals. There are three obv. vars. of the
larger size, all with the same letter punches and a single rev. die,
which does not show notable deterioration with any of them.
Only one pair of dies is known for the smaller size; the latter
more often comes choice, suggesting that specimens were saved
as souvenirs, not spent: No copper coin then circulating in the
USA was of that size.

THE SUCCESS TOKENS

Designer, Engraver, Mint, unknown. Composition, as noted.
Diameter, large, 1″ = 25.4 mm; small, ³/₄″ = 19.4 mm. (both
vary slightly). Weight, variable, as noted.

Grade range: Large, GOOD to UNC.; small, VERY FINE to
UNC. VERY GOOD: Partial hair details. FINE: All of principal
roll of hair and curls visible; partial epaulet, partial hair details.
VERY FINE: Most of epaulet shows. EXTREMELY FINE: Isolated
tiny rubbed spots on highest points only. EXCEPTIONS: Broken die examples will be weaker in immediate vicinity of the
break on one side of it. Most survivors in both sizes are weak at
All-Seeing Eye.

1282 n.d. (1792–95) Large. "Roman" nose. Brass. Reeded
edge. Rare.
Snowden 93; Baker 266; DeWitt GW 1792-2. G E apart
(both times); l. foot of R weak or missing; feet of T weak.
59.4–68.1 grs. = 3.85–4.41 gms. Garrett:1738, VF, $325.

1283 n.d. Same dies. Brass. Plain edge. Very rare.
1) NN 60:510.   2) Roper:406, 63 grs. = 4.08 gms.
1284 n.d. Same dies. Copper. Ex. rare.
DeWitt 1792-2. 1) Discovery piece, Jenks:1654 (1880).
65.5–80.5 grs. = 4.28–5.22 gms. Beware electrotypes.
1285 n.d. Same dies (?). Silver OMS. Unique? Untraced.
1286 n.d. (1792–95) Large. "Bob Hope" nose. Brass. Reeded
edge. Very rare.
Baker 265; DeWitt GW 1792-1. GE and GT close. Note direction of die break. Sometimes silvered. 57.9–67.7 grs. =
3.75–4.39 gms. Perfect dies, Garrett:1739–40, $2,900, $3,800,
latter gilt; broken die, Garrett:1736; cf. Laird Park:197, UNC.
$1,500.

1287 n.d. Same dies. Brass. Plain edge. Very rare.
Garrett:1737; NN 60:509; Roper:403, 72.2 grs. = 4.678 gms.
1288 n.d. (1792–95) Large. Straight nose. Brass. Plain edge.
Ex. rare.
Baker 265A. G E and G T apart. Note direction of die break.
Cf. Laird Park:198, UNC., $1,000. May exist with reeded
edge.

1289 n.d. (1792–95) Small. Brass. Reeded edge. Rare.

Snowden 94; Baker 267; DeWitt GW 1792-3. 12–12.5/16″ = 19.4–20 mm. 27.4–30.6 grs. = 1.78–1.92 gms. Without or with original silvering: Laird Park: 199–200; NN 60:511; Garrett:1741, $2,400; Robison:266.

1290 n.d. Same dies. Brass. Plain edge. Very rare.

NN 60:512; Robison:267; Roper:407, 34.9 grs. = 2.26 gms.

1291 n.d. Same dies. Copper. Plain edge. Ex. rare.

DeWitt GW 1792-4, called a restrike. 1) Garrett:1742, original, 27.9 grs. = 1.81 gms. (worn).

1292 n.d. Same dies. Silver OMS. Unique?

1) Brand, NN, Fuld, Roper:409, EF, scalloped edge, $1,045.

1293 n.d. Same dies. Pewter trial. Reeded edge. Unique?

THE WASHINGTON *NORTH WALES* COPPERS

These are among the most mysterious of all Washington coppers. They first reached print in Snowden {1861}. All we know about them is deduction from resemblances to British "evasion" halfpence, which series in turn (after over 60 years of misunderstanding) was first correctly analyzed in Thompson {1949}: See Chap. 12, Sect. iv, AUCTORI PLEBIS.

We can be reasonably sure that these coins came from Birmingham sometime in the 1790s—during Washington's presidency. Their obv. die's error GEORGEIVS testifies less to fraudulent intent or incompetence than to carelessness. Their irregularities of surface (typical of many of the "evasion" coppers) suggest that the dies were banged up before final hardening to suggest that any coins struck from them were old halfpence long accepted in circulation. All their revs. are of types commonly found on evasion halfpence, traced by collector-oriented mulings to the Birmingham token maker William Lutwyche. The obv. die broke early after severe clashing, probably explaining why it does not come muled with anything else.

Intent to circulate in America is proved both by the Washington portrait and the fabric. Actual circulation is proved by the worn condition of most survivors, even aside from the appearance of wear imparted by weak, uneven striking from deliberately weakened dies. No mint-state specimen is even rumored.

THE WASHINGTON NORTH WALES COPPERS

Designer, Engraver, uncertain (Arnold, Mainwaring, or Dixon?). Mint, apparently Lutwyche's, Birmingham. Composition, brass, copper. Diameter, 17/16″ = 27 mm. Weight, variable.

Grade range. FAIR to EX. FINE. No grading standards established; grade by surface.

1294 n.d. First "Evasion." Brass. Medium flan.

Baker 34. Star atop crown; harp divides 2 sixfoils. 97.5–111 grs. = 6.32–7.2 gms. (for 66 to the lb.?). That ill. is one of the finest known, very nearly EF.

1295 n.d. Same dies. Brass. Small thin flan.

91–96.1 grs. = 5.9–6.23 gms., for 72 to the lb.? Garrett:1731. It is not known whether this or **1294** is rarer.

1296 n.d. Same dies. Copper. Lettered edge with LONDON. 8–10 known.

Baker 34 footnote; D&H Middx. 1052 bis. Edge, PAYABLE IN LANCASTER LONDON OR BRISTOL. 139–154 grs. = 9.01–9.98 gms., for 50 to the lb. Blundered edges exist, e.g., Robison:260 (LANCASTER overlaps LONDON), F, $775. Discovered by Dr. Charles Clay of Manchester, before 1871; discovery coin, Dr. Clay, Crosby, Breisland:875, $1,600, Gil Steinberg; Roper:397, F, $990.

1297 n.d. Same dies. Copper. Lettered edge without LONDON. Unique?

Edge, PAYABLE IN LANCASTER OR BRISTOL, in tall narrow letters spaced apart. Later die state than **1294–96.** 1) Discovered in London, 1974; later Forman-Taxay Associates 12/74:112A.

1298 n.d. Second "Evasion." Brass. Plain edge. 7 or 8 known.

Baker 35. Same obv., clashed, broken; rev. fleur de lys atop crown, harp divides 4 cinquefoils. Always in low grades. Discovery coin, Crosby, Parmelee, Brand, NN, Breisland:876, $1,800, Gil Steinberg; Roper:398, VG, $1,155, 108.3 grs. = 7.018 gms.

1299 n.d. Third "Evasion." Copper? Bust r. Unique? Untraced.

Snowden 101; Baker 36. 1) Described by Snowden {1861}: Only TON of obv. legend shows; rev., crowned harp, "star at each side of crown"—legend probably is * NORTH * (crown) * WALES * as in D&H Warwickshire 330, 468. Said to be 17/16″ = 27 mm.

CHAPTER 15

JAMES JARVIS'S "FUGIO" FEDERAL CONTRACT CENTS

On April 21, 1787, Congress passed a resolution authorizing a contract coinage of cents. A further resolution of July 6 specified the devices of a sundial with FUGIO, date, and Benjamin Franklin's motto MIND YOUR BUSINESS, and on rev., 13 linked rings, with WE ARE ONE in central field. These devices were copied from those adopted for the Feb. 1776 Continental Currency fractional notes and tin patterns. The major contender for the contract had been Gen. Matthias Ogden, of Rahway Mills (Chap. 6, Sect. v), whose samples were the 1787 IMMUNIS COLUMBIA coppers (Chap. 11, Sect. v). However, in the meantime, his rival James Jarvis had given Col. William Duer, head of the Board of Treasury, a $10,000 bribe. Duer manipulated matters so that Jarvis got the contract instead, even giving him almost 32 long tons (71,174.5 lbs.) of federally owned copper at a nominal 11¼ pence sterling per pound for the coinage. Jarvis was required to coin a total of 345 tons (some 32,149,468 pieces in all) at the rate of 44 4/9 coppers per lb., repaying the government for the copper in coins made from it.

Jarvis's plan for fulfilling his contract was to buy a controlling interest in the New Haven mint, originally operated by the Company for Coining Coppers (Chap. 6, Sect. iv), which firm possessed the legal franchise for making Connecticut coppers. By June 1, 1787, Jarvis owned 56¼% of the total stock, on which date he ended coinage of Connecticut coppers, and directed Abel Buell to prepare device punches and working dies for the FUGIO cents. In the meantime, the federal copper had reached the mint site on Water St., New Haven. Jarvis set up the operation with his father-in-law Samuel Broome as superintendent, then left for Europe to attempt to obtain more copper (preferably as ready-made rolled blanks, which would have saved him 99% of the trouble facing any mintmaster at the time) and facilities for multiplying dies on an unprecedented scale. He first approached Matthew Boulton at the Albion Works (later renamed the Soho Mint) near Birmingham, England, largest and most prestigious of all private mints. However, Boulton would not even discuss the project unless on cash terms: good Spanish or Mexican silver, not depreciated paper, not even drafts on the Continental treasury.

During Jarvis's prolonged absences, Samuel Broome continued to operate the New Haven mint, embezzling the federal copper to strike over 3 million draped-bust Connecticut coppers. Most of these were dated 1787; they have the same letter and numeral punches as the FUGIO cents, and the copper is of the same texture. To minimize suspicion, on May 21, 1788, the Jarvis mint shipped 8,968 lbs. of FUGIOs from about 24 pairs of dies (398,577 pieces in all) to the Treasurer of the United States, supposedly representing 15% of the initial coinage (i.e., [2,657,180]). Many of these cents averaged slightly under legal weight (155 instead of 157.5 grs. each, for 45 to the lb.); others averaged about 143 grs. (for 49 to the lb.). Most were of the regular STATES UNITED vars., a minority with UNITED STATES. They circulated but little; the "Congress Coppers" (as they were then known) were of unfamiliar enough design that many shopkeepers preferentially circulated older coppers of the everyday bust and seated-figure pattern common to Birmingham "Hard Ware" and state issues. A smaller quantity of FUGIOs went to Massachusetts; we take the reference in Eckfeldt & DuBois {1842}, p. 141, claiming that the FUGIOs were made in Massachusetts to mean they circulated there. Much the same significance can be attached to early auction references to "Massachusetts Cents 'Mind Your Business 1787,' " e.g., lot 200, Leavitt, Delisser & Co., N.Y., May 17, 1856 (cited by Douglas, in CNL 3/77, p. 582).

Unsurprisingly, Jarvis & Co. did not make any other large quantity of FUGIOs, at least ostensibly pending Jarvis's return; they preferred instead to make Connecticuts at 50 or even 55 to the lb. (instead of the heavier federal standard of 44 4/9) for larger profits. Nor did the firm pay the Treasury a cent for the 30-odd tons of copper. On Sept. 16, 1788, Congress voided the Jarvis contract for default, leaving the Jarvis mint no further legal reason for existence.

Thereafter, representatives of Machin's Mills bought up the Jarvis equipment (enabling Broome to flee the country), and continued to strike Connecticut coppers on their own, light-weight, many dated 1788, some of them muling Jarvis & Co. dies with Atlee's (790–92, 856, 862, 871, etc.). They struck the Musket Butt Rays and Club Rays FUGIOs; the copper on these matches in texture that on many Machin's Mills issues, but differs from that used on the regular FUGIOs. The G punch differs from Buell's, and was probably intended for GEORGIVS in "Tory" coppers. James C. Spilman has shown that the vars. 1314–18 used the original Jarvis hubs, but that the sundial device punch was severely injured or defaced so that each working die had to be extensively hand-tooled to produce the "clubs," contrary to normal practice. Issues were on heavy blanks, probably in little demand, certainly yielding scant profit, and quickly abandoned.

Abel Buell, fearing possible indictment as a coconspirator with Jarvis and Broome in the massive embezzlement, and remembering his own earlier brush with the law (which in 1762 had cost him part of one ear and earned him a brand mark on his forehead), deeded his house to Jarvis, Jan. 21, 1789, his share in the original Connecticut franchise to his son Benjamin, and fled to Europe. Young Buell began coining Connecticuts in 1789, only to sell out to Machin's Mills; his father stayed overseas for two years. In the meantime Jarvis and Broome sailed to Paris, where they vainly tried to set up a subsidiary of Boulton's mint. Congress obtained a judgment of $10,842.24 against Jarvis, but never managed to collect a cent.

On July 7, 1789, Congress managed to find a buyer for what was left of the 8,968 lbs. of FUGIOs in Treasury vaults. This was Broadway merchant Royal Flint, a Duer crony. Flint repaid $1,323.33 (⅓ the purchase price), but on July 20 the New York copper panic collapsed the purchasing power of all kinds of copper coins to about 25% of its former level. Sheriffs hauled Flint off to debtor's prison; Col. Duer followed him there in 1792: *CNL* 12/69, p. 47.

Most remaining uncirculated survivors are from a keg deposited in 1788 at the Bank of New York, 48 Wall St., which keg remained unopened until 1856. Thereafter, bank officers began distributing samples from it to VIPs and favored depositors: Prime {1861}, Chap. VI. Even a century later, dignitaries and occasional friends of bank officers still received individual specimens with accompanying leaflets (printed about 1957); text by Polly Beaton, after information supplied by Damon G. Douglas, reprinted in *CNL* 20, p. 54, v6n6 (7–9/67). The number of FUGIOs originally in the keg is not precisely known, but if the keg contained one cwt (a common and practical size at the time), there would have been just under 5,000. About 1948, the last remnant (some 1,641) became the subject of Damon G. Douglas's monograph (ms. at ANS, partly published in *CNL*). The ANS museum retains a large selection of vars. donated by the bank. All known survivors of the rare UNITED Above STATES var. came from this keg (a dozen were still there in 1948), as did all known mint-state examples of several other vars. Douglas's study established that the same mint struck all these on two batches of blanks (143 and 155 grs. average) during a very short period of time, which is reasonable enough. The keg contained neither prototypes nor coins using a prototype die, nor any of the Musket Butt or Club Rays vars.

We now come to the so-called "New Haven restrikes," which (on the guinea-pig principle) appear to be so named because they are neither restrikes nor made in New Haven. For obvious commercial reasons, their issuers published as little as possible, and what they did publish was deliberate obscurantism. There are three conflicting but overlapping accounts: 1) *AJN* 1/1873, ascribing the "discovery" of the dies to Maj. Horatio N. Rust; 2) *AJN* 7/1887, p. 22, the obituary of Charles Wyllys Betts (1844–87), which identified Betts, then (1858) age 14, as the finder; 3) undated (1879–86) newspaper clippings, reproduced in *CNL* 5/76, p. 549. This last is our major source, as it is Rust's own account of the "discovery."

Supposedly, when Rust, living in New York, heard (1860) that the FUGIO coinage had been made in New Haven, he decided to spend a day there to learn everything he could about the issue and "if possible find the dies." (How would he have gotten the idea that any were still extant?) He first visited local newspaper offices, passing most of the day "in a vain search for information," then in the evening he found himself in the eastern part of the city with a coin collector who told him, "I had never thought of this before, but Broom[e] and Platt, general jobbers in hardware, had a contract for a part of that coinage and the strong box and other effects belonging to that house are in a hardware store on Chappel [sic] street." Rust's unnamed informant also provided the interesting but unverified item that "while Broom[e] and Platt were doing the coinage that, they being insolvent, they were liable to arrest if they passed off their hands [lands?]." Rust immediately visited the store (conveniently open after hours?) "and found a pair of the dies used as paperweights on the cashier's desk," later amended to two pairs and one odd die, and learned on inquiry that "the other die had

been loaned to a man in Bridgeport and never returned." Rust then purchased the dies, "took them to Waterbury, Conn., and struck several hundred for cabinet specimens. I had one struck in gold and several in silver and for many years used them as exchanges in collecting coins. I printed an account of finding the dies on a slip, which I gave with each restrike, that all might know what they were. After coming to California I sold the dies to a coin collector in Philadelphia. Recently I noticed in an eastern paper that a Ring cent in gold had been found. Probably it is the one I struck in 1860."

In Parsons:1762, Henry Chapman printed the text of one of Rust's "slips" (the only verification of their existence): "First United States Cent, known as the Ring or Franklin Cent. July 6, 1787, the United States Government ordered the minting of its first coin. Messrs. Groome [sic] & Platt, New Haven, Conn., did some part of the coinage. About the year 1860 the undersigned found (and still retains) the original dies among their effects in New Haven. The dies were taken to Waterbury, Conn., and a few coins struck for cabinet specimens, the enclosed being one of the restrikes. Horatio N. Rust, Chicago, 1875." This auction also contained a steel FUGIO obv. die. Rust must have been reasonably famous about 1860, when the New York City dealer Augustus B. Sage portrayed him on a token, no. 8 of "Sage's Numismatic Gallery" series.

Unfortunately for Rust's credibility, there are at least two gold impressions; the "collector in Philadelphia" must have sold the dies at once to a New York City dealer (Sage?), though the Philadelphia collector-dealer J. Colvin Randall had some of the dies after about 1878. Most of all, Rust's story must be condemned as false because the dies were made by a technique which had not been perfected in the 1780s, and there are more dies than he admitted to "finding." There is also no direct evidence that Betts was in any way connected with FUGIO dies. Betts became famous during his teens for a remarkable series of fantasy coins purporting to be of colonial relevance, from dies he engraved by hand onto worn-out coppers and hammered onto lead or copper blanks. When Betts went to Yale he ended such pranks; W. Elliot Woodward auctioned Betts's collection of dies and impressions as an addenda to the McCoy sale (May 1864). Many of these are now in the ANS museum; none are deceptive.

If any of the FUGIO dies actually came from any New Haven hardware store, they must have been planted there to give them a spurious Broome & Platt pedigree to support a concocted story of their origin. The five surviving "New Haven restrike" dies are short cylinders, unfit for coinage, rusted, one (Newman 105) broken from striking a few silver specimens. Except in rust patterns, all are indistinguishable, even to identically placed (hubbed) date numerals, letters, and dentils: far beyond 1787 technology, though ironically fulfilling what Abel Buell had been attempting in 1786! Two revs. are in the ANS museum, one obv. each in ANS, Yale, and Mattatuck Historical Society; see ills. in Taxay {1968}. Spilman (*CNL* 24, pp. 39–44, v7n4, 12/68) believed that all these dies were made at Scovill's mint, in Waterbury, by a transfer process already known in the 1850s, from a Club Rays prototype coin (**1315**). Scovill's was the only known mint then operating in Waterbury.

According to George W. Cogan (Bangs & Co., 12/29/1883:27) and Lyman Haines Low (12/18/14:6), three of Rust's dies had been sold to "a New York City dealer" (Sage?), who tried in vain (via one of the Lovetts?) to make impressions, and who later sold them (broken?) to J. Colvin Randall about 1878. Like much of Randall's material, they later turned up in Haseltine's possession. Haseltine, significantly, never admitted to making any, probably recognizing that they were unfit for coinage. Some few silver impressions appear to be from the obv. die, Newman 105 in ANS, broken at sundial; these may represent the abortive Sage/Lovett attempt. Certainly the copper and brass impressions are not from any of the surviving dies, nor could they have been made from them. Possibly the five surviving dies may have been intended only as salable impressions from the copy hubs used for sinking two pairs of normal steel working dies; only plaster impressions are known from the rest.

From these same hubs (narrow pointed chin to sun face, thin links) came still other dies, with numerous impressions (**1333–45**), made for Charles Ira Bushnell. Crosby noncommittally listed Bushnell's impressions (pp. 300-1) as though all were authentic original pattern strikings of the 1780s, though surely, among all students of Early American coinages then active, Crosby would have noticed the identity of the thin links on one of these revs. with the "New Havens." Either Bushnell did not allow Crosby enough time to study the coins (his usual practice with other series), or else Crosby found it politic to keep his suspicions to himself. We may take their origin at Scovill's mint as certainty because of the workmanship. Most likely this institution concocted these fantasy pieces for Bushnell during the 1860s, at about the same time it was fabricating many rare vars. of Washington medals and Hard Times Tokens for him.

JAMES JARVIS'S FEDERAL **FUGIO** CONTRACT CENTS

Designer, Engraver, Abel Buell. Mints, Jarvis & Co., New Haven; Machin's Mills, Newburgh, N.Y. Composition, copper. Diameter, 18/16″ = 28.6 mm. Weight standard, 157.5 grs. = 10.21 gms. = 44⅘ to the lb.; most are underweight. Authorizing Acts, Resolutions of Congress, April 21, 1787; July 6, 1787.

Grade range, POOR to UNC. GOOD: Date, FUGIO, and MIND YOUR BUSINESS legible, with enough of UNITED STATES (any position) to enable identification as to type. VERY GOOD: Part of Roman numerals on sundial visible. FINE: More than half Roman numerals legible. VERY FINE: All Roman numerals show (unless destroyed by die breakage); both cinquefoils at UNITED STATES clear. EXTREMELY FINE: Few tiny isolated rubbed spots; rays should not show more than minimal blurring even near sun face; all features of sun face should show. Visual grading is in Kessler {1976}. EXCEPTIONS: Below VF, **1313** will show only one 8-pointed star; **1314** is weak at FUGIO.

I. JARVIS & CO., New Haven

1. Prototypes

1300   1787 Cent. Cross after date/AMERICAN CONGRESS Ex. rare.
Crosby, Pl. VII, 3; Newman 1-CC. Note 8's for S's in CONGRESS. 1) Bushnell, Garrett:1495, EF, $17,500, 144.6 grs. = 9.37 gms. 2), 3) Reported, unverified. Beware electrotype copies.

1301   1787 Cent. Cross after date/Rimmed label. Ex. rare.
Newman 1-Z. Label has raised rims; WE ARE ONE engraved in larger letters than on any other die. Both dies were

later used on production coins (group 2). Miller, Garrett:1496, VF, $1,200, 150.2 grs. = 9.733 gms.

2. Regular Issues from Prototype Dies

1302   1787 Cent. Cross after date/UNITED STATES Rare.
Newman 1-B. ARE corrected from ONE, outline of O clear around A. Usually in low grades. Roper:410, VF, $462, 141.4 grs. = 9.163 gms.

1303   1787 Cent. Cross after date/STATES UNITED Very rare.
Newman 1-L. Usually in low grades. Roper:411, VF, $550, 163.9 grs. = 10.62 gms.
1304   1787 Cent. Widest date/Rimmed label. Rare.
Newman 19-Z. Rev. of **1301**. Usually in low grades. Miller, Garrett:1505, VF, $1,750, 170.3 grs. = 11.04 gms.; Roper:421, EF, $1,430, 122.1 grs. = 7.91 gms.

1305   1787 Cent. Close date/Rimmed label. Very rare.
Newman 12-Z. Same rev. Usually in low grades.

3. Regular Issues, UNITED Above STATES

1306   1787 Cent. Very rare.
Crosby, Pl. VII, 4; Newman 11-A. Rev. broke at once. All survivors are in or near mint state, from the Bank of N.Y. keg. Laird Park:115, UNC., $5,250 (1976); Garrett:1501, EF, $4,200, 130.6 grs. = 8.463 gms. (worst known?); Roper:417, UNC., $3,190, 145.3 grs. = 9.415 gms.; Lauder:220, UNC., $3,700.

4. Regular Issues, UNITED STATES

1307 1787 Cent. ARE corrected from ONE. 2 vars.
Newman 8-B, 11-B. Rev. of **1302.**

1308 1787 Cent. Normal ARE. 6 vars.
Compare next.
1309 1787 Cent. 1 over lazy 1. Ex. rare.
ANS {1914}, Pl. 4; Newman 10-G. Always in low grades.
Obv. ill. at **1312.**

5. Regular Issues, STATES UNITED

1310 1787 Cent. Close date. At least 28 vars.
Many in mint state from the Bank of N.Y. keg.

1311 1787 Cent. Widest date. 2 vars. Rare.
Newman 19-M, 19-SS. Obv. of **1304.** Always in low grades.
1312 1787 Cent. 1 over lazy 1. Rare.
Newman 10-T. Obv. of **1309.** Usually in low grades.
Roper:416, VF, $484, 158.6 grs. = 10.28 gms.

1313 1787 Cent. Rev. 8-pointed stars on label. Scarce.
Crosby, Pl. VII, 5; Newman 15-Y. Always with break from
dial to lower r. base. In lower grades only one 8-pointed star
will show. 122.9–160.8 grs. = 7.97–10.42 gms.

II. MACHIN'S MILLS, Newburgh, N.Y.

All Struck Between Sept. 1788 and Early July 1789

1. Musket Butt Rays ("Club Rays, Concave Ends")

1314 1787 Cent. FUCIO. 2 vars. Ex. rare.
Newman 2-C (ill.), 23-ZZ (discovered by T. L. Craige, 1963).
Usually in low grades, weak at FUCIO. C not corrected to G.
Roper:412, VF, $4,290 (2-C). Price for var. ill.

1315 1787 Cent. Similar, FUGIO/UNITED STATES. Ex.
rare.
Newman 5-F (ill.), 5-HH (discovered by Richard Picker,
1965). Crosshatched shading, not stippling, around wreath
and gnomon of sundial, unlike the Jarvis mint obvs. This obv.
was the prototype copied on the "New Haven restrikes," but
rev. links are thick, unlike the latter. Usually in low grades.
Lauder:219, F, $2,400.

1316 1787 Cent. Similar, FUGIO/STATES UNITED.
Unique?
Newman 24-MM. Discovered by Anthony Terranova, early
1979.

2. Club Rays, Round Ends

1317 1787 Cent. 15 club rays. Rare.
Crosby, Pl. VII, 6; Newman 3-D. One club ray overlaps dial.
Usually in low grades. Miller, Garrett:1497, EF, $1,100, 150.2
grs. = 9.74 gms.

1318 1787 Cent. 10 club rays. Scarce.
  Newman 4-E. Partly filled 8. Usually in low grades.
  Roper:413, VF, $742.50, 162.1 grs. = 10.5 gms.

III. SCOVILL'S MINT, Waterbury, Conn., 1860–77

Designer, Engraver, unknown, after Buell. Mint, Scovill's.
Composition, Diameters, Weights, variable, as noted.

Found in mint state only (varying tone) except for pieces
mishandled by collectors or dealers. EXCEPTION: **1324–25**
are overstrikes on other coins and grading is impossible.

1. "New Haven Restrikes"

Pointed Chin, Thin Links, End of Final 7 Broken

1319 1787 (i.e., 1860–77) Copper restrike. 2 vars.
  Newman 104-FF, 105-JJ, latter Ex. rare; price for former. On
  104, right-hand large fleuron below gnomon is high; in 105, it
  is low, and there is a heavy break r. of sun face. Revs. differ in
  rust patterns. Discovery specimen of 105-JJ, Parsons:1762,
  with Rust's original printed ticket (see introductory text).
  Copper is sometimes yellowish rather than reddish; these
  strikings are not to be confused with brass. 139–144 grs. =
  9–9.33 gms., for 50 to the lb. But compare **1321–22**.

1320 1787 Similar. Silver. Ex. rare. 2 vars.
  Newman 104-FF, 105-JJ. 177–180 grs. = 11.47–11.66 gms.,
  for 32 to the troy lb.; not connected with 1853–73 federal
  silver coin standard. First auction record, Finotti:1513
  (1862), suspected even then of being a restrike. Bryant, Robi-
  son:292 (104-FF), $650; Roper:422, $577.50.
1321 1787 Similar. Brass. Buckled dies. Rare.
  Newman 104-FF. Buckling most obvious in central obv. 139–
  162.7 grs. = 9–10.54 gms. First auction record, Woodward
  4/1863:2051. May exist from 105-JJ dies: Roper:423, 162.7
  grs. = 10.54 gms.
1322 1787 Last strikings, red copper.
  Newman 104-FF. Obv. buckled and shattered, rev. severely
  rusted; obvious edge shear marks, unlike the 1860–77 impressions.
1323 1787 Same dies? Gold. Ex. rare.
  Newman 104-FF? 203 grs. = 13.16 gms., possibly for 28 to
  the troy lb.; not connected with 1837–1933 federal gold coin
  standard. 1) Ex Yale. 2) Norweb. 3) Ex James Kelly,
  1946. Discovery specimen, Pratt:1467 (1879); cf. Smith:1170
  (1885). As Maj. Rust admitted to making only one, either he
  was lying, or a later owner of the dies struck extras, or both.

1324 n.d. Uniface rev., narrow links. Copper, on cent. Unique?
  Overstruck on a 1798 cent.   1) Edwin Blow (1961), Picker,
  pvt. coll., "Promised Lands":344, 1977 ANA:62, Spilman.
1325 n.d. Same (?) rev., uniface, on copper 2 Sols. Unique?
  Overstruck on 1792 French 2 Sols, Monneron issue, KM
  T25. Pierced.   1) Spilman.

2. Restrikes, "Patterns," Fantasy Pieces, Etc.

1326 n.d. Rays extend into links. Copper. Unique?
  Crosby, 4-A (fig. 47); Newman-Taxay 102-GG.   1) Dickeson, Bushnell, Parsons. Possibly restruck from experimental
  prototype dies; round sun face, unlike **1333–45**.

1327 n.d. Same dies? Gold. Unique.
  1) Norweb. Dies said to be still more rusty.
1328 n.d. Obv. as last, uniface. Lead. Unique?

1329 Same obv.?/Fantasy inscription. Gold. Unique?
  Rev., U.S. CENT BY J.JARVIS 1787.   1) Boyd estate.
1330 Rev. as **1326**/Fantasy inscription as last. Gold. Unique?
  1) Boyd estate.
1331 Hub impression, type of **1326**. White metal. Unique?
  AJN 1/02, pp. 76–80.   1) Dr. Hall, Brand, Kagin.

1332 Rev. hub impression. White metal. Unique?
  Newman DD.   1) Dr. Hall, Brand, NN 36:533, Newman.
  Other vars. reported.

1333 n.d. Fantasy piece. Copper. Ex. rare.
Crosby, Pl. VII, 2; fig. 46. Newman 101-AA. 1) Bushnell,
Bache II:1823, Appleton, MHS. 2) Hoffman, Chambers,
Brevoort, Parmelee:663, Dr. Hall, Brand, pvt. coll.

1334 n.d. Same. Silver. Unique?
Newman 101-AA. 1) Hoffman, Maris, pvt. coll.
1335 n.d. Same. Gold. Unique? Unverified.
Newman 101-AA.
1336 n.d. Same. White metal. Unique.
Newman 101-AA. 1) Newman.
1337 n.d. Fantasy piece, eye in center. Copper. Ex. rare.
Crosby, fig. 45; Newman 101-BB. 1) Bushnell, Whit-
man:339, Dr. Sloss, 137 grs. = 8.88 gms. 2) Reported.

1338 n.d. Same. Brass. Unique?
Newman 101-BB. 1) Whitman:340, Brock, Univ. of Pa.,
Ward, Dochkus, Ford, Sloss, Dr. Spence:743, $3,100, 128.5
grs. = 8.33 gms.
1339 n.d. Same. Silver. 2 known.
Newman 101-BB. 1) Bushnell, Maris, Ellsworth, Gar-
rett:1508, 152.8 grs. = 9.9 gms. 2) Bushnell, Whitman:338,
Brock, Univ. of Pa., Ward, Dochkus, Ford, Sloss, Spence:744,
$4,200, 154.8 grs. = 10.03 gms.
1340 n.d. Stars in links, strong impression. Copper. Ex. rare.
Newman 101-EE. 1) Bushnell, Whitman:342, 141.5 grs. =
9.169 gms. 2) Pvt. coll., weight unavailable.

1341 n.d. Same. Silver. Ex. rare.
ANS {1914}, Pl. 11; Newman 101-EE. 1) Bushnell, Whit-
man:341, Brock, Univ. of Pa., Ward, Dochkus, Ford, Sloss,
Spence:745, $3,100, 150.5 grs. = 9.75 gms. 2) Granberg,
Woodin, Newcomer, Wayte Raymond, Garrett:1509, 151.1
grs. = 9.79 gms.
1342 1787 Same rev. Brass. Unique?
Newman 103-EE, strong rev. impression. 1) Bushnell,
Whitman:344, 125 grs. = 8.12 gms.

1343 1787 Same. Copper. Reported. Untraced.
Dies of Newman 103-EE.
1344 1787 Same. Silver. Ex. rare.
Newman 103-EE. 1) Strong impression (Crosby 1-B),
Bushnell, Whitman:343, 133 grs. = 8.62 gms. 2) Strong impression, Lauder:230, $1,600. 3) Weak impression (Crosby
5-B and Pl. VII, 1), Bushnell, Bache II:1822, Hoffman, Brevoort, Parmelee:662, Dr. Hall, Brand, B. G. Johnson, Eric P.
Newman.
1345 1787 Same. Gold. Unique?
Newman 103-EE. Weak impression. 1) Parmelee:661, Frossard, Brand, pvt. coll. Obv. said to be severely broken and
bulged in center.

CHAPTER 16

THE U.S. PROVISIONAL AND PATTERN ISSUES OF 1792

These are most easily understandable in the context of rival coinage proposals simultaneously being made in 1791 for consideration by the Second Congress: Julian {1962A}. After Alexander Hamilton's report of Jan. 28, 1791, recommended a national coinage in the denominations of $10 and $1 gold, $1 and 10¢ silver, cent (264 grs.) and half-cent copper, the lame-duck First Congress, on its final session day (March 3), resolved that a national mint should be established. But as yet there were neither laws to implement this resolution, nor technicians to staff any such mint, nor bullion to coin therein; which left the field wide open for both British and American contenders.

On the one hand there were proposals to have our national coinage made by Boulton & Watt at their Soho Mint near Birmingham, then the most prestigious and technically advanced private mint in the world. Not only were negotiations going on directly with Boulton, there was a would-be agent of Boulton, one John Hinkley Mitchell, who seems to have had in mind establishment of a subsidiary or agency of Boulton in the USA: Taxay {1966}, pp. 39–51.

Then there were Thomas Jefferson's attempts to hire Jean Pierre Droz (the Swiss engraver, who had lately quarreled with Boulton and was in process of leaving his employ) as Engraver and possibly Director of the federal mint.

On a third hand, Messrs. W. and Alex. Walker, Birmingham merchants, ordered sample cents of two designs to be struck by Obadiah Westwood's private mint in that city, from dies by the then 16-year-old John Gregory Hancock, Sr. (probably the foremost artist in that line aside from Droz), for submission to Congress via Walker's American agents Thomas Ketland & Sons, Philadelphia. These were the familiar Washington Large and Small Eagle cents, **1206** and **1217**: Julian {1962B}.

But because of arguments presented by Thomas Paine, Jefferson came to oppose any private contract coinage whatever, particularly foreign and/or copper; for which reason further negotiations with Boulton were dropped, though Jefferson continued to try to induce Droz to come to Philadelphia. Jefferson went so far as to have Paine's arguments published *(National Gazette,* 10/17/1791; *American Museum* magazine, 10/1791), where they would quickly become familiar to Congress and all others concerned. Evidently Jefferson also convinced Washington on this score, for on Oct. 25, 1791, the day after the Second Congress began, Washington reminded the legislators that it was now up to them to enact laws implementing their earlier resolution to found a federal mint. Washington's words—"strongly recommend the carrying into immediate effect"—sounded to Congress enough like an ultimatum that on Oct. 31 the Senate formed a committee under Robert Morris to devise such a bill. Morris had been Superintendent of Finance, and he was remembered both for the silver CONSTELLATIO NOVA patterns **1099–1105** and the Birmingham coppers with the same inscription. Here Morris found himself in the paradoxical position of having to introduce a bill not only excluding contract coinage but establishing a coinage system similar to one he had opposed in 1783; but introduce it he did, on Dec. 21. In the meantime, Morris hired people to make sample coins conformable to his bill. These included Peter Getz (1768–1804), of Lancaster, Pa., a self-taught diesinker, goldsmith, and silversmith, as Engraver. Unfortunately, Getz used Hancock's Large and Small Eagle cents as prototypes. John Harper, the Trenton saw maker and mechanical expert, an associate of Albion Cox at Rahway Mills (above, Chap. 6, Sect. v), forged and hardened Getz's dies. The Getz coins were apparently struck in Harper's coach house on Sixth St., near Chestnut St., Philadelphia, a few blocks from the future federal mint.

Most likely the coinage (which shows evidence of haste) was completed before Dec. 21, 1791, despite the 1792 date, so that Morris could pass out samples to senators and representatives at introduction of his bill. The first of these is believed to have been **1346,** the unique Large Eagle half dollar, struck after the rev. die had been defaced with a chisel mark. This piece has a pedigree stretching continuously back to 1831, and a probable further source back to 1792. It was stolen before its scheduled appearance in the Garrett auction, and the coin later recovered at a convention aboard H.M.S. *Queen Mary* (as an "electrotype") has generated doubts.

However, what the legislators saw were copper and silver strikings of the Small Eagle type **(1347–51, 1352–53)**, showing a heraldic eagle based on the 1782 Great Seal design. The silver specimens–possibly 35–40 in all–are thought to have been distributed Dec. 21 to the senators (numbering 26, plus John Adams, Washington's Vice President, presiding), with a few going to other VIPs. Though they lack any mark of value, their intent to represent half dollars is conclusively proved by their conformity to the Morris bill in designs, inscriptions, and (sometimes) weights.

Of the copper strikings, some went to the 66 representatives in attendance at this session, others probably also to the senators, still others to other VIPs, total probably 100–150 specimens. They deviate from the Morris bill's terms by showing an eagle, most likely for want of time to make a third rev. die. Weights of different batches vary, but at least some early-state coins cluster around 264 grs., the figure Hamilton and Morris had agreed on for cents, which satisfactorily establishes their intended denomination.

These, then, were the "original Washington cents of 1791" struck under Adam Eckfeldt's supervision. The unfortunate similarity of devices between these and the Hancock cents caused the latter to be mistaken for the former for generations.

Adam Eckfeldt (*Historical Magazine,* 9/1861, pp. 277–78) told how he had supervised the coining, but mention of the date 1791—which was not the date on the coins—abetted the confusion. However, it was probably the Hancock cents (rather than Getz's) which gave rise to Washington's adamant objections to presidential portraits on coins as "monarchical." One of Thomas Ketland's people attempted to put samples of the Hancock cents into Washington's hands, according to Thomas Digges's letter to Thomas Jefferson, March 10, 1793: Julian {1962B}; Taxay {1966}, p. 53.

Washington's views quickly became known in Congress, and on March 24, 1792, a representative proposed striking out the words in Sect. 10 of the Morris bill calling for presidential portraits on coins, and replacing them with "a device emblematic of liberty." In support of that motion, Rep. John Page (Democratic-Republican, Va., who had served under Washington during the French and Indian Wars) not only echoed the presidential objection, but prophetically pointed out that however pleased they might be with the incumbent, there was no reason to believe that their descendants would be pleased with some of his successors! On March 26, the amended bill passed the House, and went to the Senate, where it was rejected and returned to the House. In the ensuing debate, Rep. John Francis Mercer (Democratic-Republican, Va.) insisted that it was no real compliment to Washington to portray him on coins, since he would share that honor with Caligula, Nero, and Heliogabalus (see **1247–49**), and Rep. Page amplified that notion with enough passion to silence further objections. The amended act passed at once, the Senate concurred the next day, and Washington signed it into law on April 2, 1792. This act is the ultimate legal basis for all subsequent American coinage laws; it has traditionally been known as "Statute One."

However, with the abandonment of the original Morris plan with Washington's portrait, Peter Getz's chance for the mint engravership vanished. Evidently he retained his dies and made occasional later strikings from them. These are identifiable by a growing die defect on A of STATES together with rust marks among the stars. The specimen overstruck on a British silver coin may have belonged to this group; certainly that overstruck on a large cent (1794 or 1795, from the style of edge lettering) belongs there. Getz's small eagle design recurs on U.S. army buttons: Albert {1974} 25A, 25B, 25C. The 1796 dollar, from the same rev. die in still worse condition, probably dates from when there was great pressure in Congress to abolish the Mint. Most likely it was intended to give some idea of what Getz could produce in that denomination (without making new dies unless the project were to approach reality).

On July 9, 1792, Rittenhouse wrote to Washington, asking (and receiving) permission to strike cents and small silver: Julian {1967}. On July 13, Adam Eckfeldt and other workmen hired for the Mint struck 1,500 half dismes from Birch's dies. Letter punches were almost certainly by Jacob Bay, the Germantown, Pa., maker of printing types who continued to make letters and numerals at the federal Mint until his death in one of the yellow fever epidemics. These half dismes conformed in composition, weight, and designs to the Mint Act of April 2, 1792, and were official issues of the United States, though struck before the nation acquired the site on which the First Mint would be built. The actual striking took place on a press stored in John Harper's cellar, at Sixth and Cherry Sts., a few blocks from the Mint site.

Eckfeldt turned over the half dismes to Thomas Jefferson, Secretary of State, for use in presentation to domestic and foreign VIPs. Choice of this denomination represented both commitment to the decimal system and the most economical use possible of $75 worth of silver bullion, some of which reportedly came from melting down Washington's old tableware (surviving presidential tableware at Mount Vernon is Sheffield

plate). The coins were legal tender, and some went into circulation (they come in all grades of preservation); for which reason Washington referred to them in his Annual Address, Nov. 1792, as "a small beginning" in coinage. His hearers—and the foreign readers of the printed text of his speech—understood the enormous political significance of this action. Coinage of silver, for centuries a royal prerogative, was understood everywhere to be an expression of national sovereignty. Coinage issued by a national mint pursuant to statute law conveyed this intention far more effectively than coppers ordered from any Birmingham token factory. Their historic context has for over 120 years made these half dismes among the most prized among American silver coins.

After authorities bought the site at Seventh St. and Sugar Alley and converted the old Shubert distillery building into the First Mint, sometime between Sept. and Dec. 1792, Henry Voigt as Chief Coiner struck a few silver dismes, from an obv. die by Adam Eckfeldt (matching that of the 1793 half cents, possibly after a drawing by Mint Director David Rittenhouse) and a rev. by Birch. Their denomination, like the half disme, emphasized the Administration's commitment to the decimal system.

The name *disme,* 'tenth,' later (about 1836) anglicized to *dime,* is a neologism of the polymath Simon Stevin van Brugghe, alias Simon Stevinus (1548–1620). Stevin invented the decimal system as a convenient alternative to fractions, and published it in a pamphlet, *De Thiende* {1585}. His printer, Christoffel Plantijn, simultaneously issued a French version, *La Disme,* whose full title translates as 'The Decimal System: easy instructions for simplifying all arithmetical calculations found in business, by using whole numbers without fractions.' Robert Norton's English translation, *Disme: the art of tenths, or, Decimall arithmeticke* (Stevin {1608}), had much effect on financial calculations, but little on coinage so long as Continental monetary systems remained obdurately nondecimal: The everyday British division of the pound into 20 shillings = 240 pence, the Spanish dollar = 8 Reales, and the French livre tournois = 20 Sols = 240 to 300 deniers, let alone the more complex Dutch and Germanic systems, could not be ignored in favor of any alternative. But after the French Encyclopedists rediscovered Stevin's work through Albert Girard's revision (Stevin {1634}) and publicized the decimal system as a scientific necessity, their American devotees Franklin, Hamilton, Jefferson, and Rittenhouse favored a decimal coinage as a clean break with the past. Merely by being decimal—by including the dollar and its tenth part or disme—this coinage system declared its independence of all others then known. The French revolutionists were to follow suit in 1794.

To the same period doubtless belongs the pattern quarter dollar by the portraitist Joseph Wright (b. July 16, 1756): Chamberlain {1954}. Its rev. shows an eagle on a segment of a globe, surrounded by 87 minute stars; this die broke on the second copper striking. Wright's workmanship on this pattern was of high enough quality to earn him the Mint engravership during the summer of 1793; however, he died on Sept. 12 or 13 of that year during one of the annual yellow fever epidemics, having completed only one project (the device punch for the 1793 Liberty Cap cents) and possibly one earlier working die (the 1793 "Periods" cent obv.): Death notice, *National Gazette,* Saturday, 9/14/1793, cited in Brady {1977}; cf. also Groce and Wallace {1957}, p. 105.

For the pattern cents of 1792, we can do no better than to quote Thomas Jefferson's historic letter to Washington, Dec. 18, 1792:

"Th:Jefferson has the honor to send the President two cents made on Voigt's plan by putting a silver plug worth ¾ of a cent into a copper worth ¼ cent. Mr. Rittenhouse is about to make a few by mixing the same plug by fusion with the same quantity of copper. He will then make of copper alone of the same size, & lastly he will make the real cent as ordered by Congress, 4 times as big. Specimens of these several ways of making the cent may now be delivered to the Committee of Congress now having the subject before them" (Record Group 104, Treasury Section, National Archives).

The historic "Silver Center" cents comprise possibly a dozen authentic specimens and a larger number of dangerous counterfeits. Cost of making the blanks doubtless revealed the project's impractical side. Voigt's billion cents ("mixed by fusion") were equally impractical: They could be imitated by copper without any silver content, and only chemical analysis could tell them apart. The idea of small copper cents weighing not much more than half a Birmingham copper pleased nobody. That left only the large coppers, "the real cent as ordered by Congress."

We can make educated guesses why the first var., known only from the unique tin striking, **1372**, was rejected: Its frizzy hair (a probable prototype for the half disme) doubtless suggested a slave woman, no suitable "impression emblematic of liberty"; the reverse's G.W.PT (= George Washington President) conveyed some of the same monarchical flavor as the rejected version of the Morris bill. However, there are still many unanswered questions about the copper strikings, not the least of which is the engraver's identity: Even his given name has long been disputed.

Carlson {1982} argues that the British engraver, cameo carver, and miniaturist William Russell Birch made these dies, probably in March 1792. Some weeks or months after passage of the Mint Act of April 2, Birch altered both dies, making Ms. Liberty's lips thinner and hair smoother (to suggest a more Anglo-Saxon type?), signing his name on the truncation, reworking the wreath and replacing G.W.PT by enlarged ribbons and 1/100. Sprays of berries on the revised rev. were the prototype for those on the 1793 wreath cents and half cents. These may be the cent dies mentioned in Rittenhouse's July 9 letter to Washington: Julian {1967}. Carlson's reconstruction has these revised dies finished by September, and suggests that Chief Coiner Voigt's Sept. 11 purchase of six lbs. of old copper may have been for initial strikings of the revised design, most probably with plain edges. This weight of copper would have made fewer than 200 specimens even at the lightest recorded weight; the actual number was more likely well under 100, especially if struck to the 264-grs. standard called for by the Mint Act.

Those struck Dec. 18–31, 1792, pursuant to Jefferson's letter, are more likely those with either of two variant edge letterings. They are lighter in weight, possibly anticipating authorization of cent coinage at lower weight (Act of Jan. 14, 1793). Mint Director Rittenhouse's own coin (Garrett: 2349) has lettered edge and weighs 220.5 grs., suggesting an intended standard of 224 grs. = 9.33 dwt = 31¼ to the lb. = 3,500 to the cwt: arithmetically more convenient than the figure Congress authorized. Not enough specimens have been weighed to verify or dismiss a conjecture that the different edge devices all represent different weight standards.

Based on Jefferson's words, the large Birch Cents have an excellent claim to be counted as the first regular United States cents, and include the only ones struck to the original weight standard called for by the Mint Act of 1792 rather than its 1793 amendment. All of the 1792 issues are among the most historic and the most highly prized of United States coins.

THE U.S. PROVISIONAL AND PATTERN ISSUES OF 1792

I. PETER GETZ'S COINAGES, Dec. 1791

Designer, Engraver, Peter Getz, after Hancock and the Great Seal. Mint, Harper's coach house, Sixth St., Philadelphia. Composition, silver, copper. Diameters, variable. Weight standard, silver, 208 grs. = 13.48 gms.; copper, 264 grs. = 17.11 gms. (both vary).

Grade range, FAIR to UNC. No grading standards established.

1346 1792 Prototype Half Dollar. Large Eagle. Unique.
Baker 23. Die canceled before striking. About $21.5/16'' = 35$ mm. 194.7 grs. = 12.62 gms. 1) Getz, Morris (?), Sen. Rufus King (?), his son Charles King (1831), Bossuet the cobbler, W. J. Howard (1858), G. N. Dana, Rev. Joseph Finotti (1862), Charles Ira Bushnell, Lorin G. Parmelee, S. H. & H. Chapman, Allison W. Jackman, Waldo Newcomer, John Work Garrett, Johns Hopkins Univ. (1942–79), Garrett:1713, $16,500. Howard cut his initial H within the U on rev. See introductory text.

1347 1792 Half Dollar. Small eagle. Silver. Plain edge. Narrow flan. Ex. rare.
Appleton XXIII; Baker 24. $20/16'' = 32$ mm; 192.9–234 grs. = 12.5–15.16 gms. Beware casts, electrotypes. Note rounded high relief of shield; see next. Ill. of **1353**.

1348 1792 Half Dollar. Same. Silver. Plain edge. Wide flan. Ex. rare.
Appleton XXIV; Baker 24. $22/16'' = 35$ mm; 204–214.1 grs. = 13.2–13.88 gms. Usually in low grades. Garrett:1714, VF, $24,500; Roper:381, EF, $17,050. Idler's struck copy (Crosby, Pl. X, 25) has modern letters, flat shield (originally with COPY in relief below stem—often effaced), narrow flat borders, 34 mm; dies by John S. Warner, Philadelphia, ca. 1860. Later mulings exist of either die with Idler's advertisement die. A second die-struck forgery is Baker 26, Garrett:1718, ex Fonrobert:6103, Anthon V:407. This has a caricature portrait, the blunder PRESIDENTI, and only 11 arrows; 213 grs. = 13.8 gms.

1349 1792 Half Dollar. Same. Silver. Overstruck on other coins. Ex. rare.
1) On Charles II half crown, 1679. 218.4 grs. = 14.15 gms. Bogert, W. C. Prime, Ford.

1350 1792 Half Dollar. Same. Silver. Edge, circles and rectangles. 5 known?

1351 1792 Half Dollar. Same. Silver. Leaved edge. 2 known.
Edge, twin olive leaves, after the style of the 1776 CONTI-

NENTAL CURRENCY and 1783 CONSTELLATIO NOVA patterns. 1) Zabriskie, Brand, NN, Wayte Raymond, Boyd estate. 2) Ford, 248.78 grs. = 16.121 gms. (plugged).

1352 1792 Cent. Same dies. Copper. Plain edge, narrow flan. Rare.

Baker 25. 20/16″ = 32 mm; 219.9–273 grs. = 14.25–17.7 gms.; Garrett:1715, UNC., $32,000. 265.8 grs. = 17.23 gms. Dies usually aligned opposite to current coins. Compare **1356–58**. Beware casts and electrotype copies. See next.

1353 1792 Cent. Same dies. Copper. Plain edge, broad thin flan. Very rare.

22/16″ = 35 mm. Same weight range. Dies usually aligned as on current coins. Hall, Brand, Breisland, Laird Park:182, "EF," $7,500. Compare **1354–58.** Beware casts and electrotype copies. Idler's copy (see **1348**) is 34 mm, 210.7 grs. = 13.65 gms.

II. UNOFFICIAL GETZ STRIKINGS, 1792–96?

Rev. Rusted at Stars and A of STATES

1354 1792 Cent. Same dies. Copper. Normal flan. Very rare. If without extensive rust at stars and A, this qualifies as **1352.** May exist in silver. Beware casts and electrotype copies.

1355 1792 Cent. Same. Copper. Federal-cent size. Plain edge. Unique?

19/16″ = about 30 mm. 1) Harte:2041. Weight not recorded: If overstruck on a plain-edge cent, standard is 168 grs. = 10.89 gms.

1356 1792 Cent. Same. Copper. Federal cent edge. Unique? Edge, ONE HUNDRED FOR A DOLLAR; overstruck on a cent of 1794 or 1795. Standard weight 208 grs. = 13.48 gms. 1) Kagin, *CNL* 4/61, p. 2. 30.5 mm. 202.3 grs. = 13.2 gms.

1357 1792 Cent. Same. Copper. Ornamented edge. Very rare. Edge, circles and rectangles. 22/16″ = 35 mm. Most were holed and plugged: Were they worn as funeral medals? Anthon, Garrett:1716, $34,000, Roper:383, UNC., $24,200, 190.2 grs. = 12.32 gms.

1358 1792 Cent. Same. Copper. Jumbo piedfort. Ex. rare. 22/16″ = 35 mm. Die alignment as modern coins. 1) C. Jay, 328 grs. = 21.31 gms. 2) Leidman, Bowers, Essex, Herdman, Terranova. 330 grs. = 21.39 gms.

1359 1796 Dollar (?). Same dies, date altered in die. Silver. Unique.

Snowden {1861}, Pl. XI, 43; Baker 33. 24/16″ = 38 mm; 361 grs. = 23.39 gms. Borders added to both sides by hand. Edge ornamented with rectangles. Overstruck on a cut-down Spanish or Mexican 8 Reales. 1) H. Drumheller coll., unknown intermediates, Louis R. Karp (summer 1960), 1962

ANA:1976, pvt. coll. *CNL* v2n2 (4/61); *NSM* 11/61, pp. 2882–85.

III. COINS STRUCK AT HARPER'S CELLAR BY MINT PERSONNEL

Designer, Engraver, William Russell Birch? Mint, Harper's cellar, Sixth and Cherry Sts., Philadelphia. Composition, silver 892.4 + Fine, copper. Diameter, 11/16″ = 17.5 mm. Weight standard, 20.8 grs. = 1.35 gms. Authorizing Act, April 2, 1792.

Grade range, FAIR to UNC. GOOD: Devices outlined, date and all legends legible. VERY GOOD: Partial hair and feature details. FINE: Most ringlet curls outlined; partial hair above ear. VERY FINE: Over half hair details; microscopic details of some ringlets; most feathers outlined except on breast. EXTREMELY FINE: Isolated tiny rubbed spots only. EXCEPTIONS: Even UNC. will not show full breast or leg feathers; one curl immediately above ear, another immediately below will be partly flat (see ill.). Adjustment marks (see Glossary) are common and do not constitute injury.

1360 1792 Half Disme. Silver. [1,500] Very scarce.

Crosby, Pl. X, 19; Judd 7. Diagonally reeded edge. 20.37–21.14 grs. = 1.32–1.37 gms.; sp. gr. 10.3 ± 0.01. Possibly 200–250 survive in all grades, including perhaps 20 UNC.; Dr. Judd, Auction 80:592, UNC., $20,000. Many are holed and plugged. Beware solid silver casts; these have vertically reeded edges, and run a little heavy: 21.8 grs. = 1.412 gms. Enl. photos.

1361 1792 Same dies. Copper trial piece. Plain edge. Unique? Judd 8. 1) Mickley estate (1878), Lohr, Hinman, "Century":51, Roper:428, $20,900.

IV. COINS STRUCK AT FEDERAL MINT, Sept.–Dec. 1792

Designers, Engravers, various, as noted. Mint, Seventh St. and Sugar Alley, Philadelphia ("First Mint"). Composition, silver 892.4 + Fine; copper. Diameters, Weight Standards, various, as noted. Authorizing Act, April 2, 1792.

Grade range, FAIR to UNC. No grading standards established.

1362 1792 Disme. Copper. Diagonally reeded edge. Very rare. Crosby, Pl. X, 18; Judd 10. 14.5/16″ = 23 mm. Garrett:2352, 58.6 grs. = 3.8 gms., AU, $54,000, Marvin Brauder. Obv. by Adam Eckfeldt, after Rittenhouse?; rev. by Birch. About 14 known. Enl. photos.

1363 1792 Disme. Copper. Plain edge. 2 known.
Judd 11. 1) Mint, Maris:147, Garrett:2353, 61.1 grs. = 3.96 gms. 2) Lohr, Hinman, "Century," Roper:429, $19,800. Beware casts, electrotype copies.
1364 1792 Disme. Silver. Diagonally reeded edge. 2 or 3 known.
Judd 9. Weight standard, 41.6 grs. = 2.696 gms. 1) Norweb. Date effaced, 57 grs. 2) Dr. Judd, L.I. specialist. 3) Reported.
1365 1792 Pattern quarter dollar. Copper. Reeded edge. 2 known.
Crosby, Pl. X, 21; Judd 12. 18/16″ = 28.6 mm. Designer, En-

graver, Joseph Wright. See introductory text. 1) Rittenhouse, Eckfeldt, Mint Cabinet, SI. Clain-Stefanelli {1970}, fig. 18. 175.5 grs. = 11.37 gms. 2) Rittenhouse, Cogan 4/1863:1074, Bushnell, Parmelee, Brand, NN, Dr. Judd, pvt. coll., 179.5 grs. = 11.63 gms., broken rev. die. Enl. photos. Beware electrotype copies of the SI coin, with plain edges.
1366 1792 Same. White-metal trial piece. 2 known.
Judd 13. 1) Lohr, CMB, *ANS,* jumbo piedfort. 2) Norweb.
1367 1792 Same obv. uniface. White metal. Unique.
Bushnell, Garrett:2354, B&R RCR 39, p. 10 (7/81), 480.8 grs. = 31.16 gms.
1368 n.d. (1792) Rev. of **1365,** uniface. White metal. Unique. Same provenance as **1367.** 432.9 grs. = 28.06 gms.
1369 1792 Silver Center Cent. Reeded edge. About 12 known. Crosby, fig. 109; Judd 1. Designer, Engraver, Henry Voigt. 15/16″ = 24 mm.; weight standard 69.12 grs. = 4.48 gms.: See introductory text. Dangerous counterfeits exist; authentication is mandatory. Survivors:
1. Ellsworth, Wayte Raymond, Garrett:2347, UNC., $95,000, 70.5 grs. = 4.57 gms.

2. Gschwend, Brock, Univ. of Pa., Ward, Ford, Norweb, UNC.

3. Davis, Jenks, Newcomer, Boyd, Lohr, "River Oaks," Hughes, pvt. coll., SI, AU.

4. Morris, Sloss, Mitkoff, 1974 GENA:1272a, $105,000, N.J. pvt. coll., EF–AU. Enl. photos. Ill. *CW* 5/8/74.

5. Stearns:280, $4,000, EF, L.I. specialist. Copied by the forgers.

6. Cogan 4/1863, Bushnell, Parmelee, Smith, Earle, Wurtzbach, Brand, Roach, Neil, NN 52:104, Romano, EF, scratched.

7. Mickley, Cohen, Dohrmann, Woodward 93:816 (2/1/1887), Smith, Wurtzbach, Brand, KS 3/18/64:1106, Gibson, Roper:425, $19,800, VF.

8. Boyd, Newman. EF or better.

9. Warner, Winsor, Lauder:233, $44,000, Weinberg, EF–AU.

10. Seavey, Woodside, Elder 10/07, Judd, Leidman, pvt. coll. Forgers copied this one too.

11. Brand, Morgenthau 311:78, G. All ill. in Rubin {1985}.

Two perforated blanks in Congress Hall, Philadelphia, were found by Frank Stewart in excavations (1909) at First Mint site.

1370 1792 Cent. Same dies. Billon. No silver plug. Reeded edge. 2 known?

Same diameter, weight standard. 2 supposedly authenticated by chemical test: 1) N.J. pvt. coll., ex HR 11/69. 2) Hinman, "Century," *Bowers Review,* pp. 18–20 (1973–74), Douglas Robins (*CW* 12/4/74:24), 1975 Sub. Wash.:59, ANA coll. 78.2 grs. = 4.549 gms. See next.

1371 1792 Cent. Same dies. Copper, no silver plug. Reeded edge. Ex. rare.

Crosby, Pl. X, 22; Judd 2. Same diameter, weight standard. 1) SI. Clain-Stefanelli {1970}, fig. 16. 2) Appleton, MHS. 3) Seavey, Maris, Garrett:2348, 63.1 grs. = 4.09 gms. Dangerous forgeries exist; authentication mandatory. The plain-edge specimens are casts, often showing small central circle on rev., proving that their prototype was a Silver Center cent.

1372 1792 Large Cent. Rejected dies. White metal. Unique.

Judd 6. 20/16″ = 31.8 mm; 104.5 grs. = 6.78 gms. Obv. prototype for the Half Disme. See introductory text. Ex Sotheby 3/7/1888:423, Verity, Bascom, Ellsworth, Garrett:2350, $90,000. Enl. photos.

1373 1792 "Birch" Cent. Copper. Plain edge. Ex. rare.

Crosby, Pl. X, 20. Judd 3. 20/16″ = 31.8 mm. 1) Jay, Laird Park:201, UNC., $42,000, 226 grs. = 14.65 gms. Beware casts and electrotype copies. Crosby's weight range, 209–286 grs. = 13.54–18.53 gms., including this and next 2; heavier range may signal compliance with the 1792 Mint Act standard = 264 grs. = 17.11 gms. Enl. photos. See introductory text.

1374 1792 "Birch" Cent. Same dies. Copper. 2 stars on edge. Ex. rare.

Judd 4. Edge, TO BE ESTEEMED * BE USEFUL * Compare next.

1. Rittenhouse, Ellsworth, Garrett:2349, UNC., $200,000. 220.5 grs.

2. Bushnell, Parmelee, Jenks, Green, KS 4/3/59:1166, EF.

3. 1955 ANA:1421, "VF."

4. HR 11/69:3739, "VF," $6,500.

5. S 12/69:604, B&R RCR 27–32 (1976–77), Harte:2070, Hellwig:1539, very worn, 201 grs. = 13.03 gms.

6. Dr. Judd, Roper:426, S 12/84:611, F/VG, 200 grs. = 13 gms.

Others reported. 1981 ANA:2730, "VF," 193 grs. = 12.5 gms., was withdrawn; Kagin 301:1371, "EF, $52,000," is probably one of 2), 3) or 4) above.

1375 1792 "Birch" Cent. Same dies. Copper. One star on edge. Ex. rare.

Judd 5. Edge, TO BE ESTEEMED BE USEFUL * Leaves flank star. 1) Kagin 166:228 (10/31/53), 202:713 (3/20/56), 221:1392 (10/18/58), Lauder:235, $3,520 (very worn).

V. APOCRYPHA

We owe the impressions pictured below to Dr. Montroville Wilson Dickeson, traveler, journalist, artist, numismatist, archaeologist. Dickeson, sometime in the late 1850s, managed to get his hands on at least two (possibly as many as four) of Adam Eckfeldt's rejected dies for embossing revenue stamp paper (ca. 1797–1817), probably among Mint ironmongery sold as junk (1816 or 1833), but for reasons unknown, he thought they might have belonged to the group of 1792 federal provisional issues, and he had some local engraver make a rev. stating such a claim. Impressions were probably made at different times, as the amount of rust on both dies (and breakage on **1376**) varies greatly. Mules exist between these dies and rusted half-eagle and quarter-dollar restrike dies dated 1804–5; are all extremely rare, probably made in the 1859–78 period. Dickeson's die with the inscription was offered for sale in the 1950s, but it has since vanished; no recent impression is reported: Adams, *NUM* 5/12, p. 186; Breen {1951B}.

1376 Eagle on shield. Copper. Rare.

1377 Same. White metal. Ex. rare.

1378 Eagle on half shield. Copper. Rare.
Kosoff Estate: 1163–64, $385 and $302.50. 161.9–162.7 grs. = 10.49–10.54 gms.

1379 Same. White metal. Ex. rare.
Kosoff Estate: 1165. $187. 128.3 grs. = 8.31 gms.

1380 Similar, eagle on rock. Copper. Untraced.
Ill. in Dickeson {1859}; confused with **1378?**

1381 Similar, eagle on half globe. Copper. Untraced.
Ill. in Dickeson {1859}; confused with **1376?**

1382–1500 Reserved for possible later discoveries in all Colonial or Prefederal series.

Part Two

FEDERAL
MINOR COINAGES

CHAPTER 17

HALF CENTS

i. THE RITTENHOUSE-ECKFELDT DESIGN (1793)

These are the first federal coins to depict a liberty cap, antedating the cents by four months. They are also the only ones to have the head with cap and pole turned to l., explicitly acknowledging the design's ultimate prototype as Augustin Dupré's (1782) LIBERTAS AMERICANA medal (Betts {1894} 615; Loubat 4), then familiar from specimens presented to congressmen and VIPs. They are the smallest and thickest of all half cents for circulation (aside from occasional rare pieces struck on cut-down large cents), and the only ones before 1831 with borders of round beads. They are also the only half cents with two leaves following DOLLAR on edge—a circumstance connecting them in time with one batch of 1793 wreath cents sharing this feature **(1645).**

The first blanks were 7/8″ in diameter; these coins may fail the Ring Test (see Glossary). Later planchets were cut out at 15/16″. Different striking force spreads flans to different extents so that the two batches are not always easily distinguishable.

The two obv. dies match in style the 1792 Disme. Their attribution to Adam Eckfeldt rests on his own testimony: On Nov. 4, 1803, he deposed under oath that before becoming Assistant Coiner (Jan. 1796) he had been working "in the Engraver's Department," and in Colburn:2021 (1863) an uncirculated specimen on broad flan was described as Eckfeldt's present to its former owner as "a sample of his work." Edgar Adams *(NUM* 2/11) quoted another claim to the same effect.

Beaded borders afforded little protection for coins as high in relief as these, for which reason subsequent dates instead show serrated borders (see 1794).

Their three revs. match those of the wreath cents of summer 1793, deriving ultimately from the large Birch Cent of 1792, much the same kind of laurel (?) leaves being used on all, with similar sprays of berries unlike olive or laurel. Most probably Eckfeldt worked from sketches furnished by David Rittenhouse.

Letter punches are by the Germantown typefounder Jacob Bay, who had been working full-time for the Mint as a punch cutter since Dec. 24, 1792 (Stewart {1924}, p. 76). After making several alphabets for the various denominations and several graded sets of numeral punches, which remained in use for the next few years, Bay died in one of the annual yellow fever epidemics.

All 35,334 were minted between July 20 and Sept. 18, on copper blanks cut from strip rolled from a variety of sheet and scrap copper. Over 20 survive in mint state (evidently as souvenirs, first of their kind), and at least 20 more in AU. Most others are well worn, and their population has been estimated at 500–550, or slightly over 1.5% of the original mintage. See discussion in Breen {1984}, pp. 30, 67–83.

Half cents did not become legal tender until passage of the Coinage Act of July 23, 1965, PL 89-81.

THE RITTENHOUSE-ECKFELDT DESIGN

Designer, Engraver, Adam Eckfeldt, after sketches by David Rittenhouse. Mint, Philadelphia. Composition, copper. Diameters, 7/8″ and 15/16″ = 21.4–24.6 mm (vary). Weight standard, 104 grs. = 6.74 gms. Authorizing Acts, April 2, 1792; Jan. 14, 1793.

Grade range, POOR to UNC. GOOD: All legends and date legible (exception below); part of eye shows. VERY GOOD: Eye fully clear; some detail at hair ends. FINE: Half hair detail; partial cap detail; edges of leaves and some berry sprays show. VERY FINE: Partial hair ribbon; partial inner leaf details; partly clear berry sprays. EXTREMELY FINE: Isolated tiny rubbed spots; hair ribbon mostly clear; all locks separate; nearly full leaf veins. ABOUT UNCIRCULATED: Tiny rubs on brow, shoulder, veins of leaves above H. EXCEPTIONS: On **1501,** HALF CENT may be only partly legible even in FINE grade, from central die failure. Enl. photos, all by Jack Collins.

1501 1793 Periods after AMERICA. and CENT. [7,000]
Breen 1; CMM 1. HALF CENT usually weak; obv. sometimes with die striations before face, rev. sometimes with heavy break at upper r. rim. Coined July 20. Ex. rare in UNC. Enl. photos.

1502 1793 No periods; short ribbons and stems. [28,334]
Breen 2, 3; CMM 2, 3. Obv. as ill. or as **1501.** This and next coined July 26–Sept. 18. Sometimes on broad flans (15/16″).

1503   1793 No periods; long ribbons and stems.
Breen 4; CMM 4. The majority var. Obv. die often rusty.
Many in or near UNC. Sometimes on broad flans (15/16").

The piece with a Washington obv. (Baker 27) is a concoction by Edwin Bishop ca. 1859, made to sell to Mint Director J. R. Snowden.   1) SI. Ill. Breen {1984}, p. 80.   2) MHS.

ii. SCOT'S LIBERTY CAPS (1794)

This date is notable for the Philadelphia Mint's first attempt to emulate Abel Buell's 1786 Connecticut experiment by creating completely hubbed dies. Device punches were no novelty (Joseph Wright had created one for the Liberty Cap cents in summer 1793), but a complete hub (including wreath, all lettering, and border dentils) was then a new experiment. After only three half-cent revs. were sunk from it, the attempt was abandoned, not to be revived for this denomination until 1840. (It was tried on cents between late 1798 and late 1800; then again on cents late in 1834, silver in Nov. 1836, gold in 1838.) The reason is clear enough: insufficient striking force in the presses used for sinking hubs into working dies, so that many details had to be redone by hand (letters repunched, leaves and berries strengthened), with too little saving in time or cost to warrant continuation. To make matters worse, these "Heavy Wreath" revs. have borders too weak to provide adequate protection, and the coins wore down quickly.

The other two revs. are called "Cent Type"; wreaths copy those on cents of this year, in style and engraving technique.

There are three types of head, all crudely copied from Wright's 1793 Liberty Cap cent design, rather than from the previous half cents. The first has head much too high in field; the device punch used for the second unaccountably made only three working obvs.; and the last ("High Relief Head") has head so deeply incised into the die that a normal blow would not bring out full details, even newly struck coins looking weak: Compare **756–58**.

Borders are serrated, unlike 1793. That on the High Relief Head die is correspondingly deep, intended to afford protection against wear and to enable the coins to stack.

Neither of the two types of edge lettering for this date matches that of 1793 or that of 1795. The one designated Large Edge Letters has tall, wide, shallow letters spaced close together, O larger than D in DOLLAR. The other, Small Edge Letters, has narrow letters spaced well apart and more deeply impressed, and D is high and about the same size as O. Dr. Edward Maris {1869} first described these, but because Gilbert {1916} chose to ignore the variation, collectors forgot about them, and specialists are still cherrypicking rare edge letterings.

SCOT'S LIBERTY CAPS

Designer, Engraver, Robert Scot. Mint, Composition, as preceding. Diameter, 15/16" = 23.8 mm (varies). Weight, Authorizing Act, as preceding.

Grade range, POOR TO UNC. GOOD: Part of eye shows; date and legend weak but legible. VERY GOOD: Hair ends show detail; eye clear. FINE: Partly separated locks; some cap details.

VERY FINE: Partial leaf veins; at least half hair details. EXTREMELY FINE: Only narrow rubbed areas from forelock to ear and along high ridge of shoulder. EXCEPTIONS: High Relief Heads may not show all rev. letters in G, and they will appear flat above and below ear even in VF; Heavy Wreaths (**1504–7, 1511**) will appear flat on leaves even in F. Enl. photos, all by Jack Collins.

1504   1794 [all kinds 81,600] Pointed 9, large edge letters.
Breen 1a; CMM 1a. In date 79 first punched too low, then corrected. Usually dark. Only 3 or 4 real UNCs. Enl. photos.

1505   1794 Same, small edge letters. Very rare.
Breen 1b; CMM 1b. Discovered by Dr. Edward Maris. Always in low grades, unobtainable above F.

1506   1794 Knobbed 9, normal relief head, large edge letters. Very rare.
Breen 2a, 3a; CMM 2b, 5b. Same dies as next; almost always in low grades. Ill. of **1507**. Both first reported by Comdr. W. C. Eaton, 1921.

1507   1794 Same, small edge letters.
Breen 2b, 3b; CMM 2a, 5a. Second var. (very scarce) has date spaced 1 79 4. On both, hair looks soft even in EF. Ill. at **1506**.

1508   1794 Similar head, cent type wreath, large edge letters. Ex. rare.
Breen 4a, 5a, 6a; CMM 6b, 3b, 4b. Same dies as next; always in low grades, evidently struck on leftover blanks. Ill. of **1509**.

1509   1794 Same, small edge letters.
Breen 4b, 5b, 6b; CMM 6a, 3a, 4a. Price for third var. (ill. at **1508**), which sometimes shows drastically clashed dies. The

others have date spaced 1 79 4; first (rev. of **1510,** T of CENT rests atop leaf tips) very rare.

1510 1794 High relief head, cent type wreath. Very rare.
Breen 7; CMM 7. Usually in low grades. Small edge letters from now on.

1511 1794 High relief head, heavy wreath.
Breen 8, 9. Price for latter (ill.): T of CENT leans l., common in all grades below mint state. Former is rare; T leans r.

iii. GARDNER'S LIBERTY CAPS
(1795–97)

These were the Mint's darkest days. Adverse criticisms poured in from all sides; congressional opponents mounted a massive investigation explicitly aimed at finding cause to repeal the Mint Act of April 2, 1792 and revert to profitable contract coinage from Birmingham token factories. Few coins were made, and gold and larger amounts of silver spent most of their time in bank vaults rather than in public circulation. Even in Philadelphia, if you were very lucky, your pay envelope would most likely have contained worn and/or cut-up Spanish and Mexican silver coins, together with British and Irish coppers which were better spent without close examination in the hope that the storekeepers would do likewise. If you were not so lucky, your wages would have consisted mostly of a horrid little pile of irredeemable scrip issued by this turnpike company, that general store, or Jedediah Jukes's Bank in Lower Jackrabbit Crossing.

To make matters worse, annual yellow fever epidemics since 1793 had killed off half a dozen of the Mint's most valuable personnel. Bullion was scarce; foreign coins remained legal tender, so that there was little incentive to go to the expense of having them recoined. Tool steel was locally unavailable; the Mint ordered it from England, and the quality was very uneven, many dies quickly chipping and splitting. Copper gears (for the Mint's primitive rolling mills) wore down quickly; breakdowns were frequent, and these mills were the weakest and most unreliable part of minting operations, forcing numerous interruptions and delays.

No wonder, then, that the half cents show evidence of being emergency issues. Mint Director Boudinot's correspondence deals largely with the desperate search for good copper, preferably ready-made blanks fit for press, which would bypass the rolling mills and cutting presses. In April 1795, he bought 1,076 lbs. [= about 52,000] TALBOT, ALLUM & LEE token cents from their New York importers; most were cut down into half-cent planchets early in 1796 and stamped from 1795 No Pole **(1517)** dies, without being rolled to proper thickness: "token stock." Smaller quantities [about 1,963] were struck during the same period on blanks cut down from "spoiled cents" (mostly pieces struck far off center or otherwise mismade); these come without and with visible cent undertypes. The latter are in greater demand, especially if attributable. Most "cent stock" 1795's were not rolled down to proper half-cent thickness. This was to save the Mint's primitive rolling mills for gold and silver blanks, where weight tolerances were far narrower and deviations legally more dangerous. Cent-stock coins thus often weigh more than the 1793–94 issues, though made after adoption of the reduced weight standard. Dies were used long after they would normally have been discarded for breakage. In 1799, some 12,167 were coined from dies dated 1797; and in spring 1800, 20,978 more were overstruck on cents (the Low Head coins). Some of these last show cent undertypes dated 1797–98 or even 1800. Unlike the 1795's, the 1797-dated cent-stock coins were rolled down, but they vary greatly in weight.

On Dec. 12, 1796, Boudinot bought 1,914 lbs. of TALBOT, ALLUM & LEE tokens from William Talbot. If all were at 46 to the lb., there were 88,044; if at 50 to the lb., they totaled 95,700. Cohen estimates 90,527, which is probably within 1% of the correct figure. They were rolled down for use with 1797 "1 above 1" and "Centered Head" dies.

Mint-state survivors of 1795–97 are rarer than those of 1793; some vars. are unknown choice. No Low Head coin is known in mint state. Some vars. on cent stock come only in low grades. On the other hand, over ¼ of the surviving 1796's with pole are in AU or UNC., suggesting origin in a tiny hoard.

Lettered-edge coins, struck between Oct. 1 and Dec. 1, 1795, are at the old 1793–94 standard, 104 grs. = 6.74 gms. Mint Director Boudinot halted coinage owing to a rise in copper prices and petitioned Secretary of State Thomas Jefferson to obtain authority to lower the weight to 84 grs. = 5.44 gms. Pres. Washington complied by issuing a proclamation dated Jan. 26, 1796, retroactive to Dec. 27, 1795. During the next five months coinage continued using 1795-dated dies. Mintage figures herein are based not on published Annual Reports but on daily coinage records in the National Archives. A fuller discussion is in Breen {1984}.

The occasional plain-edge 1795's at 1″ diameter rather than the normal 15/16″ are on blanks thought to have been cut out with the half-eagle blank cutter rather than the normal half-cent cutter. This variation is too recent a discovery to enable accurate estimates of rarity.

All these coins are from an obv. device punch by John Smith Gardner, matching in style his cent "Head of 1795" punch. Gardner was Assistant Engraver from Nov. 1794 through March 31, 1796; he was responsible for these device punches and presumably also for the wreath revs. accompanying them, which makes the 1797 revs. leftover dies from early 1796. As Scot was extremely jealous of his engravership (despite progressively failing eyesight), we need seek no further for the reason that his assistants (Gardner, Eckstein, John Reich) received pittances, no raises, and doubtless much adverse criticism, inducing them to quit and leave Scot without further rivals.

The dates and vars. of the Gardner Liberty Cap design include some of the greatest rarities in the series, as well as some of the most interesting impressions—including the token-stock and cent-stock overstrikes. Mint error strikings (off centers, brockages, double and multiple strikes, etc.) are more often seen of coins dated 1795 and 1797 than for all other dates 1793–1857 inclusive, and the possibility of new discoveries remains wide open. Many collectors include in this category the cent-stock coins and those struck on cut-down copper impressions of half-dollar dies, but strictly speaking these testify less to quality-control failure than to official economy efforts; see the discussions in Breen {1984} under dates 1795 "Issues of 1796," 1797 "Backdated Issues of Spring 1800," and the chapter "Oops!" All such strikings give the Gardner half cents an individuality not possessed by any others in the series.

GARDNER'S LIBERTY CAPS

Designer, Engraver, John Smith Gardner, after Scot. Mint, Composition, as before. Diameter, 15/16″ and rarely 1″ = 23.8 and 25.4 mm (varies). Weight standards: lettered edge (Oct. through Dec. 1795), 104 grs. = 6.74 gms.; plain edge (Jan. 1796 on), 84 grs. = 5.44 gms. Authorizing acts: lettered edge, Jan. 14, 1793; plain edge, Washington's proclamation, Jan. 26, 1796, retroactive to Dec. 27, 1795. See introductory text.

Grade range, POOR to UNC.; grade standards, as for 1794. EXCEPTIONS: Most cent-stock coins are on grossly defective planchets; token-stock coins often have some details obscured by traces of ship's rigging or hull. Specimens of **1514** with break slanting down above HALF may be too weak in that area for HALF CENT to be legible even in VF. The 1796 no pole is always weak at hair behind ear, from the break. Many 1797 Low Heads are porous. Enl. photos, all by Jack Collins.

I. LETTERED EDGE

1512   1795 Date I795. [14,800]
Breen 1; CMM 1. Letter I for 1 in date. Delivered Oct. 27, 1795. Possibly 10 UNCS. One seen on thin flan, 77.1 grs. = 5 gms.

1513   1795 Date 1,795. [10,800]
Breen 2a; CMM 2a. "Punctuated Date," from a die break; normal 1. Die fails at AME. Delivered Dec. 1, 1795. Possibly 6 UNCS. One seen at 104.2 grs. with plain edge (lettering omitted in error); but compare next.

II. PLAIN EDGE

1514   1795 Date 1,795. [30,000]
Breen 2b, 3, 4; CMM 2b, 3, 4. Price for third var., with rev. break slanting down above HALF. First var. (dies pictured

above **1513**) is very rare; second var. (leaf point between UN) is rare and usually in low grades. All delivered Jan. 22, 1796.

1515   1795 No pole, date I795, rolled stock. [30,127]
Breen 5a, 6a; CMM 5a, 6a. Reground obv. of **1512**. Price for second var. (ill. of **1517**); the other rev. (double leaf at IT, not triple) is scarcer. Not to be confused with next 2. Struck after Feb. 28, 1796.

1516   1795 Same, cent stock. [1,963]
Breen 5b, 6b; Cohen 5b, 6b. Thick crude flans, 100.5–124 grs. = 6.51–8.04 gms.; heavier examples may exist. Rarer still if cent undertype is attributable; usually on 1795 Sheldon 76b (ONE CENT high) and 78 (CENT central). One is reported on a 1796 Liberty Cap cent. See introductory text. Delivered March 12, 1796.

1517   1795 Same, token stock. [Approx. 52,000]
Breen 6c; incl. in CMM 6a. Undertypes are more often 1795 than 1794 TALBOT, ALLUM & LEE tokens; that ill. at **1515** is on a 1794. Specimens with attributable undertypes are in demand; those with plain token dates are rare. See introductory text. Struck between March 18 and June 8, 1796.

1518   1796 No pole to cap. [Incl. in 1,390] About 24 known. Breen 1; CMM 1. Almost always with horizontal obv. break; always with hair weak behind ear, as ill. Beware worn specimens of **1515–17** offered as "1796 with weak date." On the genuine, 6 is from the 9 punch rotated; rev., triple leaves both at IT and r. of LF, outer berry below first T of STATES. Beware electrotypes and cast copies. Finest known: 1) Winsor, Earle, Ellsworth, Atwater, Eliasberg, UNC. 2) Murdoch, Newcomb, Pierce, Showers, Willis duPont, Ketterman, pvt. coll., UNC. 3) Riley, Brand, "Dupont," D.N., TAD, S 3/15/75:823, UNC., $34,000, Tettenhorst, McGuigan. The next 3 grade F, the rest lower. Delivered Oct. 24, 1796. Enl. photos.

1519   1796 With pole. [Incl. in 1,390] Rolled stock. Rare. Breen 2a; CMM 2. Only the one var.; rev. as last. Beware electrotypes, cast copies, 1795's with weak or altered dates. Usually in low grades, though there are 7 UNCS. and 4 AU's. 12 "Edwards Die" coins were made for Dr. Frank Smith Edwards (ca. 1865) in NYC; they have much larger letters than the genuine, and normally come UNC. See ill. in Breen {1984}, p. 166.

1520 1796 With pole, cent stock. Ex. rare.
Breen 2a. Thick flan, 105 grs. = 6.8 gms. (worn).
1521 1797 1 above 1 in date, rolled stock. [27,525+]
Breen la; CMM 1. Mintage incl. **1524**. Date first begun far too high, crowded into bust, then corrected. See next 2. Shattered die coins are thought to be among the [12,167] of 1799. Ill. of **1523**.

1522 1797 Same dies, cent stock. [1,164] Ex. rare.
Breen 1b. Mintage incl. **1525**. Discovered by M. H. Bolender, 1934. See introductory text. Always in low grades.
1523 1797 Same dies, token stock. [Est. 90,527]
Breen lc; incl. in CMM 1. Mintage figure incl. **1526**; see introductory text. Usually from unbroken dies. Ill. at **1521**.
1524 1797 Centered head, knobbed 9. Rolled stock.
Breen 2a; CMM 2. Incl. in **1521** mintage.

1525 1797 Same dies, cent stock. Ex. rare.
Breen 2b. Discovered by Dr. Charles Ruby. Incl. in **1522** mintage. See introductory text. Always in low grades; usually sold as mint errors. Weights vary, as low as 75 grs. = 4.86 gms.
1526 1797 Same dies, token stock. Very rare.
Breen 2c, incl. in CMM 2. Discovered by Dr. Charles Ruby. First published in 1954 ANA:86. Mintage incl. in **1523**.
1527 1797 Low head, pointed 9. Lettered edge. [Incl. in 20,978 overstruck in 1800]
Breen 3a; CMM 3b. Always on cent stock, struck April 29– June 5. Diameter, 7/8″ = 21.2–22.5 mm. Different batches

weigh 73.3–78.4 grs. = 4.75–5.08 gms. and 93–97 grs. = 6.03–6.29 gms.; heavier examples may exist. Edge lettering differs from any foregoing, parts of tops and bases of letters usually off. Usually in low grades, often porous; sometimes with crack from chin to rim. Ill. of **1529**.

1528 1797 Low head, gripped edge. Very rare.
Breen 3b; CMM 3c. The gripping consists of transverse marks, some in relief. Mintage included in preceding. Always on cent stock. Always in low grades; unknown F. Independently discovered by Matthew Stickney and Sigismond K. Harzfeld before 1890. Varying states of obv. crack: See next.
1529 1797 Low head, plain edge. Very scarce.
Breen 3c; CMM 3a. Mintage included in **1527**. Always on cent stock. Usually in low grades, often porous. Varying states of obv. crack, sometimes very heavy. Ill. at **1527**.

iv. SCOT'S DRAPED BUSTS (1800–8)

Only in 1800 did Scot get around to adapting Gilbert Stuart's draped-bust design of summer 1795 to the half cents, and here only in a version more drastically oversimplified even than on the cents of 1796. Even then, the rev. used through early Aug. 1802 was a leftover Gardner die of the 1795–97 type, the last appearance of this design (single leaves at top) on American coinage.

The first coins of 1800, and all of 1802, were struck on cent stock: blanks rolled and cut down from misstruck cents. Only rarely are traces of undertype visible, especially on 1800's.

Arrival of several tons of Welsh copper blanks from Boulton & Watt, July 8, 1800, signaled a new beginning. Dies were evidently of tougher steel, as they lasted longer than any earlier ones; the single Stemless Wreath rev. (the commonest die of the denomination, 1793–1857) forms the majority of survivors dated 1805–6 and nearly half those dated 1804. Its blunder has the same explanation as that on the stemless cents: The wreath device punch lacked stem ends, which had to be added by hand, and Scot carelessly omitted them.

Very rarely, coins dated 1804 come on cent stock; the dates 1803–8 may also exist on blanks made from cut-down spoiled cents. This reflects not error but economy; the coiner had to account for every Boulton & Watt planchet, and do everything to minimize spoilage because Congress would appropriate funds for more planchets only on the basis of how many coins were actually issued. Unsurprisingly, mint errors in this period are plentiful: Quality control had to yield to quantity.

Again for reasons of economy, many dies were used into later years: The mintage figures for 1804–5 included many coins dated 1803, those for 1805–6 included many dated 1804, that for 1807 included many dated 1806. Coins dated 1807 are readily found worn but seldom in mint state, the best ones being weak strikings from worn dies. Those dated 1808 represent the final appearance of this design; the normal date obv. was evidently made in 1806 with final digit omitted, the 8 punch breaking in the meantime, as its final 8 is made up of two zeroes.

Uncirculated survivors dated 1800 are mostly from two

hoards found in New England: brown UNCs. from a group found before the turn of the century, red ones (usually spotty) from one found in Boston in the 1930s. Mint red 1806's with large 6, also usually spotty, are from a hoard of at least 200 found by Henry Chapman about 1906; these are always weak at upper wreath.

SCOT'S DRAPED BUSTS

Designer, Engraver, Scot, after Gilbert Stuart. Mint, Philadelphia. Composition, pure copper. Diameter, $^{15}/_{16}'' = 23.8$ mm. Weight standard, 84 grs. = 5.44 gms. Authorizing acts, as before.

Grade range, POOR to UNC. GOOD: Partial eye; date and letters readable. VERY GOOD: Partial hair details, part of main drapery fold shows, eye clear. FINE: At least two drapery folds; part of curl before ear; partial separation of ribbon folds behind head, partial hair details. VERY FINE: All drapery folds show, though rubbed; clear complete line demarcating hair from skin; partial internal details to leaves. EXTREMELY FINE: Isolated rubbed spots on leaves; isolated rubbed areas on hair from forehead to l. of ear, just above shoulder, and back of head. EXCEPTIONS: Vars. from buckled dies may not show HALF CENT clearly even in F; 1802, 1805 small 5 stems, 1807 are often weak on hair. Enl. photos, all by Jack Collins.

1530   1800 Cent stock. [Incl. in 20,978] Very rare.
Breen 1a; incl. in CMM 1. Border dentils strong; die scratch from corner of F to above adjacent L. Weight varies. Specimens with attributable undertype are Ex. rare. Struck April 29–June 5. Mintage figure includes **1527–29**. Discovered by W. H. Cottier (1882).

1531   1800 Boulton stock. [190,552+]
Breen 1b; incl. in CMM 1. Border dentils weak, die scratch at LF gone. Always with die flaws from E of UNITED to C of CENT and others parallel to these. Struck Sept. 17–Dec. 12. Average weight 82.5 grs. = 5.346 gms. Many UNCs. from hoards: See introductory text.

1532   1802/0 Rev. of 1800. Very rare.
Breen 1; CMM 1. Cent stock only. Always in low grades (unknown in VF), rev. always weak. That ill. (enl. photos) is one of the finest.

1533   1802/0 [all kinds 14,366+] New rev.
Breen 2; CMM 2. Cent stock only. Usually in low grades, HALF CENT weak. Struck Aug. 1802. Rusted-die coins are believed to be among the 5,900 on cent stock delivered Aug. 8, 1803.

1534   1803 Five berries on left branch, wide fraction. 2 vars.
Breen 1, 2; CMM 1, 2. Price for B-1 (line from fraction bar to r. ribbon, ill.); the other var. (no line from bar; berry below E of UNITED joins leaf) is rarer, usually in low grades, and often with rim break above STAT. Average 86 grs. = 5.5 gms. Mintage report [97,900]; probable figure [381,900], many struck in 1804.

1535   1803 Close fraction.
Breen 3; CMM 3. Struck in 1804 or 1805 after all 1804-dated coins with this rev. die. Almost always with bulge at 18; often, shattered dies.

1536   1803 Six berries on left branch. Very scarce.
Breen 4; CMM 4. Paired berries below first T of STATES. Struck in 1805.

1537 1804 Crosslet 4, stems, close date and fraction.
Breen 1 (ill.), 9, 3; CMM 1, 10, 2. Price for second var., with break from rim to top of R in AMERICA; others are rarer, especially last, with low 4 as on one die of **1539**. Average weight for 1804 = 86 grs. = 5.5 gms. Mint report [1,055,312] includes many dated 1803; probable figure, [771,312+].

these by die state. The "spiked chin" and "protruding tongue" (enl.) are from die injuries: Obv. struck a bolt.

1538 1804 Crosslet 4, stems, wide date, close fraction.
Breen 8; CMM 9. Always with some stage of break from rim to R of AMERICA. Very rare in UNC.

1541 1804 "Spiked chin," close fraction.
Breen 7; CMM 8. Break from R to border; early rev. of **1538**.

1539 1804 Crosslet 4, stems, close date, wide fraction. Very rare.
Breen 2, 4; CMM 4, 3. Price for former, with low 4 (well below base arc line of 180); other is Ex. rare. Both usually in low grades. Not to be confused with **1537** or next.

1542 1804 Crosslet 4, stemless wreath.
Breen 11; CMM 12. UNC. survivors are usually dull. Most, possibly all, were struck in 1805.

1540 1804 "Spiked chin," wide fraction.
Breen 4a, 5, 6; CMM 5, 7, 6. Price for last (ill.). All 3 revs. often show bizarre extensive rim breaks; specialists collect

1543 1804 Plain 4, stemless wreath.
Breen 10; CMM 13. Many struck in 1805–6. Usually with weak borders and long, light vertical crack in l. obv. field. Many UNCs. survive.

1544   1804 Plain 4, stems to wreath.
  Breen 12; CMM 11. Usually in low grades; die failure weakens HALF CENT. Struck in 1805.

1545   1805 Medium 5, stemless.
  Breen 1; CMM 1. Top of 5 normally doubled. Rev. of **1542–43.** Probable mintage [694,464] includes many stemless 1804's.

1546   1805 Small 5, stems. Rare.
  Breen 2, 3; CMM 2, 3. Usually in low grades. Not to be confused with next; note shape of 5, smaller than 0, away from drapery. Price for B-3, with bulge in r. obv. field.

1547   1805 Large 5, stems.
  Breen 4; CMM 4. Mint report [814,464] includes **1545–46** and many dated 1804. Often confused with preceding; note long top stroke to 5 touching drapery. Prohibitively rare UNC., though at least 6 AU's exist.

1548   1806 Small low 6, stems. Very scarce.
  Breen 1; CMM 2. Usually in low grades; note shape of 6. Not to be confused with next or **1551;** 6 on same base arc line as 180.

1549   1806 Small high 6, stems. Very rare.
  Breen 2; CMM 3. Obv. as next, 6 nearly touches bust; rev. of preceding, develops severe rim break lower r. Always in low grades, unknown above F.

1550   1806 Small high 6, stemless.
  Breen 3; CMM 1. Obv. as preceding. UNCs. are usually dull. Mint report [356,000]; probable figure, **1548–50,** [555,000+].

1551   1806 Large 6, stems.
  Breen 4; CMM 4. Probably struck in 1807. Sometimes confused with **1548–49,** but 6 embedded in drapery. Common in spotty red UNC. from the Chapman hoard; these are always weak at top of wreath. Probable mintage [239,000+].

1552 1807

Breen 1; CMM 1. Mint report [476,000] mostly includes coins dated 1806; probable figure [38,000+]. Price for usual late state with weak border dentils. Early states with strong dentils are rare and unknown choice; mint-state survivors are dull with weak dentils.

1553 1808/7 2 rev. vars. Scarce.

Breen 1, 2; CMM 1, 2. Price for latter (ill.); only one UNC. known, and rare late states have heavy obv. rim breaks at top. B-1 (leaf almost touching D) is Ex. rare and almost always in low grades.

1554 1808 Normal date.

Breen 3; CMM 3. Only the one var., though late strikings show 9 or even only 7 berries (originally 10) from die wear; in these states dentils are weak. Mint report [400,000] may include some dated 1807.

v. REICH'S "CLASSIC HEADS" (1809–29)

Once Robert Scot had managed to land the lifetime post of Mint Engraver, Nov. 1793, he became an instance of the Peter Principle ("Employees tend to be promoted to a level above their competence"). Scot had been a competent engraver of bank-note plates in the 1780s, but as a diesinker or maker of device punches 20 years later he was still barely marginal. Probably because he knew he was out of his depth and feared displacement by a competitor, Scot was reluctant to tolerate the continued presence of an assistant (despite having become wealthy through his bank-note work). And so John Smith

Gardner had to go, after only 16 months, in late March 1796. As early as May 1801, Thomas Jefferson wrote to Mint Director Boudinot, recommending appointment of John Reich (1768–1833) as Scot's assistant. Chief Coiner Henry Voigt rescued Reich from indentured servitude (into which the engraver had sold himself to escape from the Napoleonic Wars and obtain passage to the USA), and put him to work in a variety of capacities, but—presumably from Scot's opposition—never allowed him to design coins. To judge by medals signed by Reich, he was by far the best diesinker then working in the area. We may thus attribute to Scot's intransigence the Mint's failure to name Reich Assistant Engraver.

Matters came to a head in March 1807 when the new Director, Robert Patterson, wrote to Pres. Jefferson that Scot's "advancing age" (62) made his "good health" (for which read competence to perform his duties) doubtful; and Reich, his only possible successor, was on the point of returning to Europe, war or no war. On April 1, with Jefferson's approval, Reich was named Assistant Engraver at the pittance of $600 per year, with the specific assignment of improving all our coin designs, i.e., replacing Scot's conceptions. He began at once with the half eagles and half dollars, the cents and quarter eagles following in 1808, the dimes and half cents in 1809.

On the copper coins he placed a curious conception of Liberty, misnamed "Turban Head" by the coin dealer Édouard Frossard (who probably had never seen a real turban), but more appropriately called "Classic Head." This latter name is from Ebenezer Locke Mason, Jr. (*Mason's Coin and Stamp Collector's Magazine* 2/1868, p. 9). Vattemare {1861}, p. 29, quoted an old rumor that it portrayed Dolley Madison. Whoever may have been the live model, if any, this is the strangest device "emblematic of liberty" before the presidential heads. A profile similar to that common to numerous Greek statues of boy athletes is adorned only by a fillet or narrow ribbon inscribed LIBERTY. Its nearest possible prototype is apparently Polykleitos's *Diadoumenos*, or 'Athlete Tying the Fillet,' which shows this ornament identically placed. But the fillet was never worn by women, only by boy athletes; it was a prize for winning town games, and is ancestral to today's blue ribbons awarded to show dogs, cacti, or coin displays. Rev. is a wreath of the Christmas kind enclosing HALF CENT. Head and wreath are from device punches, but not stars, dates, surrounding legends, nor borders.

The Mint exhausted its last prewar shipment of planchets from Boulton & Watt in 1811; no more could be ordered afterward because of the embargo on trade with Britain during the War of 1812.

Reich's design was replaced on cents in 1816 by Scot's "Matron Head" caricature: Possibly some critic with pretensions to classical education had noticed its masculine character. On March 31, 1817, Reich resigned in disgust: He had received no pay increase in 10 years, and Scot had replaced most of his best designs with dismal copies. Scot hung on, with neither assistance nor competition, until he died in Nov. 1823, aged 79. For unknown reasons, instead of rehiring Reich, the Mint called in another bank-note-plate man, William Kneass.

In late 1825, orders by Jonathan Elliott & Co., Baltimore, occasioned resumption of half-cent coinage. Instead of following Scot's example and creating a new and inferior design, Kneass made dies using Reich's old device punches. The anticipated larger demand for this denomination never materialized; coinage was again stopped in 1829, and at least 234,000 were melted in 1830–31 for alloying gold and silver: Julian {1972B, 1984}. Mint-red survivors of all these dates are very rare except for 1828 13 Stars, which often comes in spotted mint red from the Collins hoard, discovered by Benjamin H. Collins in 1894. This hoard contained a single 1811, and apparently originally numbered 1,000; as late as 1955, a remnant containing several hundred pieces was in the holdings of F. C. C. Boyd.

The 1811 "restrike" was struck outside the Mint about 1859 from genuine dies (the regular Close Date obv. with the 1802 rev.), which the teen-aged Joseph J. Mickley had retrieved in 1816 among rusted and broken dies sold by Mint personnel as scrap metal. For many years the coin dealer Capt. John W. Haseltine used to claim that only six were struck; the correct number appears to be 12, of which 11 are traced: Breen {1984}, pp. 315–17.

REICH'S "CLASSIC HEADS"

Designer, Engraver, John Reich. Composition, Mint, Diameter, Weight, Authorizing Acts, as before.

Grade range, FAIR to UNC. GOOD: Partial LIBERTY; all stars, date, and letters show; wreath outlined. Tops of letters and outer points of stars may be worn into rim. VERY GOOD: Clear eye, full LIBERTY, distinct rims. FINE: Partial hair details, partial leaf details. VERY FINE: Over half hair and leaf details; hair ribbon clear. EXTREMELY FINE: Isolated rubbed spots above and below LIBER and on back curls; isolated worn spots on leaves, though most will show many internal details. EXCEPTIONS: 1809 straight date, 1811, and 1828 12 Stars normally come weak on some curls; 1810 is flat on l. stars even in mint state. Enl. photos, all by Jack Collins.

1555 1809 [all kinds 1,154,572+] "Inner Circle," 0 in date over smaller 0.
Breen 1; CMM 4. Rarely found choice; stem end and lower r. leaves weak even in mint state. Average weight, 1809–11, 84.47 grs. = 5.474 gms.

1556 1809 Straight date, normal 0. Scarce.
Breen 2, 3; CMM 1, 2. Price for latter (ill.); rarely found above VF. Former (berry below tail of R) is very rare.

1557 1809 Curved date. 2 vars.
Breen 4, 6; CMM 3, 6. But compare next.

1558 1809/6
Breen 5; CMM 5. Date spaced 180 9, the 9 first cut inverted, then corrected.

1559 1810 [215,000−]
Only the one var. Most of the reported mintage was dated 1809. L. stars flat; parts of wreath often weak.

1560 1811 [all kinds 63,140] Wide date.
Breen 1; CMM 1. About 7 mint-state survivors; that ill. is a prooflike presentation piece, in SI: Compare Breen {1977}, p. 37. With rim break over 1 or 2 stars, Ex. rare; with this break extended over 4 stars, only very scarce.

1561 1811 Close date.
Breen 2; CMM 2. Same rev. Less scarce in ordinary grades, prohibitively rare choice.

1562 "1811 Restrike." [12?]

Breen {1977}, p. 255; {1984} pp. 315–17; Cohen, p. 124. Same obv.; rev. of 1802, both dies rusted, strengthened. See introductory text.

1563 1825 [63,000+]

Breen 1 (ill.), 2; Cohen 1, 2. The vars. differ mainly in spacing of date. 2 proofs known, both with only obv. die polished ("one-sided proofs"). Letter and numeral punches hereafter are by Christian Gobrecht.

1564 1826 Normal date. [234,000–]

Breen 1, 2, die states II–V {1984}; Cohen 1, 2. Respectively with or without crisscross die file marks r. of date. Some of the reported mintage doubtless bore date 1825. B-2 is very rare with heavy rim break touching 2 stars (state V).

1565 1826 over horizontal 6. Very rare.

Breen 2, state I; dies of CMM 2, in earliest state. Discovered by Jack Beymer. Later strikings, with only a fragment of extra 6 at base, will price as preceding.

1566 1828 [all kinds 606,000–] 13 stars.

Breen 1, 2; CMM 1, 3. Probably some of reported mintage bore date 1826; others were delivered in 1829. Two minor positional vars. Common in spotty red UNC. from the Collins hoard: See introductory text. 3 proofs reported.

1567 1828 12 stars.

Breen 3; CMM 2. Usually soft on curls. Very rarely with any trace of mint red.

1568 1829 [487,000–]

Only one var.; UNCS. are normally brown, rarely red. 4 proofs reported. Part of the reported mintage bore date 1828.

vi. KNEASS'S MODIFIED "CLASSIC HEADS" (1831–36)

Mint authorities had thought themselves finished with half cents, but in 1831 an enormous order from the merchant Washington Cilley specified 400,000 of this denomination. Engraver William Kneass made sharpened-up copies of the old Reich hubs, somewhat after the fashion of his copies of the old Scot hubs for half eagles and quarter eagles (1829). Letter and numeral punches are by Christian Gobrecht.

The first date of this design, 1831, is the only one with large stars. For long believed to exist only in proof state, this mintage of 2,200 is now known to have consisted of business strikes, of which possibly 1% survive: See enumeration in Breen {1984}, pp. 341–42. Original proofs of 1831 are from the same dies as the business strikes, some experimentally bronzed to prevent discoloration. However, the majority of proofs offered as 1831 "originals" or "large berries" are in fact restrikes made 1858–59 from the original obv. die and the repolished 1836 original rev., which cracked during striking of one of the later batches: Breen {1977}, pp. 256–57; {1984}, pp. 344–45. Most collectors until recent years have made little distinction among these, content to have either var. so as to show large berries. The Small Berries coins are restrikes made later in 1859 or 1860 (possibly 1868) from a rev. originally made for restrikes dated 1840–48. This concoction first came to collectors' attention about 1879, when Capt. John W. Haseltine claimed that only 12 had been struck (Frossard {1879}; Haseltine auctions, June, July, and Oct. 1879).

Later dates of this series are notable for the discovery of hoards of spotted mint-red survivors, numbering in the thousands for both 1833 and 1835. Guttag Bros. discovered the 1833 hoard, Elmer Sears the 1835, both during the Great Depression; the coins at first sold at 25¢ each, and in the mid-1950s, when quantities were released in New York, they brought a few dollars apiece. On the other hand, the date 1832 seldom comes with mint red, and the 1834 is not easily found so, there being no hoards to swell their numbers.

The date 1836 is found only on proofs, though quantities of coins dated 1834 and 1835 were delivered during that calendar year. As with 1831, several batches of restrikes were made in 1858–59, with similar properties, and using the original rev. and the anachronistic 1840–48 replacement die. This last was first published by Haseltine (7/27/1879:101) as "the only one I ever saw" (from William Idler); two more were in the estate of former Mint Director Henry R. Linderman in 1888.

Julian {1984} has shown that mintage figures are too confused to mean anything; the total for circulation 1831–35 is [693,000], but this cannot be effectively portioned by dates on coins.

KNEASS'S MODIFIED "CLASSIC HEADS"

Designer, Engraver, William Kneass, after Reich. Composition, Mint, Physical Specifications, Authorizing Acts, as before, but Diameter 14.5/16″ = 23 mm.

Grade range, VERY GOOD to UNC. FINE: About half hair details; some internal leaf details. VERY FINE: Nearly full hair details with some flatness at forelock, near ear, near top of head, shoulder, etc.; all leaves show some internal details. EXTREMELY FINE: Few tiny isolated rubbed spots only. EXCEPTIONS: Original proofs have rounded borders; restrikes have "squared" borders. For details see Breen {1977}, {1984}. Enl. photos, all by Jack Collins.

1569   1831 Original. [2,200 + ?P] Very rare.
Breen 1; CMM 1. Rev. of 1832, point of high leaf under r. side of S (compare next). Small date, large stars; alterations from later dates have small stars. Most of the couple of dozen business strikes are VG to VF. See roster of survivors in Breen {1984}, pp. 341–42.

1570   1831 First restrike. [?P] Rare.
Breen 2; Cohen PR2, 2a, 2b. Rev. of 1836, point of high leaf under l. side of S, but struck after the 1836 restrikes. About 30 proofs known. Most are from uncracked dies, average weight 81.8 grs. = 5.3 gms.; fewer show various states of rev. cracks (ill.), average 76.7 grs. = 4.97 gms. See roster of survivors in Breen {1984}, p. 345.

1571   1831 Second restrike, small berries. [?P] 4 known.
Breen 3; Cohen SR 15. Rev. from 1840–57 hub, die file marks above RICA. Usually flat in centers.   1) Steigerwalt, Clapp. Eliasberg estate.   2) Byron Reed, OCL.   3) King Farouk, R. E. Naftzger.   4) Brobston, Miles, pvt. coll., 76.6 grs. = 4.96 gms.

1572   1832 [? + ?P]
Breen 1, 2, 3; CMM 1, 2, 3. Small stars from now on. UNC. are usually dull, seldom red. Proofs are known from all 3 revs.

1573   1833 [? + ?P]
Breen 1; CMM 1. Possibly as many as 30 proofs (ill.), thought to be in celebration of opening of the new Mint building. Prooflike business strikes are normally from cracked and clashed dies, unlike the proofs. Mint red UNC. are common from the Guttag hoard (see introductory text).

1574   1834 [? + ?P]
Breen 1; CMM 1. Delivered in 1835. Julian {1972B}. The 1834 is scarcer in all grades than 1833, and much rarer in mint state. Possibly 18–20 proofs survive.

1575   1835 Small date. [? + ?P]
Breen 1, 2; CMM 1, 2. Delivered in 1836, retained and released in driblets through 1848. Mint red UNCs. are plentiful from the Sears hoard (see introductory text). Proofs exist from both revs., rarer than 1834: Breen {1977}, p. 61.

1576   1836 Original. [?P] Very rare.
Breen 1a; Cohen EO 12. Rounded borders; 84 grs. = 5.44 gms. About 30 proofs reported, 3 in museums, 4 others worn. See roster in Breen {1984}, pp. 366–68.

1577   1836 First restrike, from original dies. [?P] Very rare.
Breen 1b; Cohen PR1, PR1a. About 12 proofs; others probably exist, represented as originals. Sharp inner rim immediately outside beads, broad borders with knife-rims outside; see ill. in Breen {1977}, p. 257. Rev. of **1570** but struck before the latter. Weight range, 77.8–82.4 grs. = 5.04–5.34 gms. See roster in Breen {1984}, p. 369.

1578   1836 Second restrike, small berries. [?P] 5 known.
Breen 2; Cohen SR16. Struck on the same occasion as **1571**; see introductory text.   1) Byron Reed, OCL.   2) Lyman, Ryder, Raymond, Kortjohn, 77.3 grs. = 5.01 gms.   3)

Woodin, Jackson, Newcomer, Green, Johnson, Eric Newman, 77.6 grs. = 5.03 gms.   4) G. H. Hall, Brobston, Showers, 78.1 grs. = 5.06 gms.   5) "Dupont," TAD, Tettenhorst, 79.5 grs. = 5.15 gms. All are proofs with flat centers.

vii. GOBRECHT'S CORONET HEADS
(1840-57)

After 1835, when the Mint found its vaults clogged with half cents which found no customers, Mint Director Robert Maskell Patterson resolved to strike no more for circulation until those had been distributed. Paradoxically, in 1840, Patterson decided to include this denomination in the dozen or so proof sets made up each year for presentation to visiting dignitaries; accordingly, he ordered the new Engraver, Christian Gobrecht, to make complete hubs from which working dies could be sunk and dates quickly added. These would serve also for eventual completion of working dies for business strikes, should demand ever resume for this denomination: which it did in Nov. 1849.

Gobrecht's hubs copied those on his 1839-43 cents, "Head of 1840." Through 1848, all original half cents came from a single proof die, on which hand retouching had disproportionately enlarged 10 of the 11 berries: the "Large Berries" type. This die was retired to the Coiner's Vault in late 1848 or 1849, as later proofs (except for the 1849 small date and one 1852 var. and a few restrikes of other dates) showed normal small-berry revs. like the dies for business strikes.

The obv. hub suffered a dent before the 1841 working die was sunk from it; this shows below ear on all later dates except 1854. On the single obv. of that year, Longacre noticed it and added fine hair detail by hand to correct it, but he had forgotten about it by 1842.

Of the 1840-48 (and 1849 small date) group of proof-only coins, the 1841 original and one var. of 1848 restrike occur more often than all the rest (a couple of dozen or more of each), despite the 1841 obv. die cracking at the very beginning of use. When pristine, originals of 1840-41 are more brilliant than any others, and lighter in color; these planchets were experimentally reeded on edge before insertion into the plain-edge collar (reason unknown): a condition discovered by Richard Picker. Of the remaining proof-only dates in the forties, mostly a dozen or fewer apiece are known; some restrikes are rarer than originals, others less rare. A few off-weight restrikes were made in 1859 using the old large-berry rev. die, including at least five dated 1852: a combination not found on originals: Breen {1977}, pp. 71-93, 259-62; {1984}.

The business strikes, 1849-57, are a most frustrating group. The 1849 large date and 1853 are excessively difficult to find in red mint state, though brown ones (and cyanided pieces attempting to simulate pristine coins) are always available for a price. Small hoards of spotty red coins turned up for 1851, 1854, 1855, and 1857. The 1854's comprised a bag of 1,000 specimens, discovered in the early 1930s by A. C. Gies, the Pittsburgh hoarder; the 1855's may have numbered as many as 500. There were apparently only 100-300 each of the rest. All have long since been dispersed.

Why none were coined for circulation between 1836 and late 1849 is explained by an entry in Box 41, General Correspondence File, Records of the Bureau of the Mint (National Archives): Inventory of Coins on Hand, June 30, 1848, including the line "Half Cents in Vault, 5 kegs, $410.00." These 82,000 comprised the undistributed remainder of the 539,000 half cents of 1834-35 13 years after their original coinage and storage. Evidently the Mint could not then dispose of more than about 16,000 half cents per year; nevertheless, when coinage resumed, it was in larger amounts.

The same cause explains why none were coined for circulation in 1852: The few orders that came in were filled by 1851's still on hand. However, at least three different vars. of restrikes of this date were made on at least eight different occasions, 1858-60. The most coveted of these has the old large-berry rev. of 1840-49; of the commonest (that with the 1856-57 rev.) over 50 are known. Original proofs are not positively identified to date; they should weigh 84 grs. = 5.44 gms. apiece, and not have one of the known restrike revs. Restrikes weighed to date are lighter or heavier.

The restrikes were made 1858-60 on various nights by various Mint personnel with access to the Coiner's Vault collection of old dies, with the connivance of Theodore Eckfeldt, the Mint's night watchman, who had been earlier fired for theft but rehired to avoid disgracing his family (which had included Mint officials since 1792). Eckfeldt had peddled plain-edge 1804 dollars and restrike patterns in 1858-59 until Mint Director Snowden found the dies and sealed them in a carton (July 8, 1859). Eckfeldt acted as distributor for the half cents and other restrikes, operating out of Dr. M. W. Dickeson's store on Buttonwood St., later through the coin dealer William Idler. Because the Mint no longer ordered half-cent planchets, Eckfeldt and his friends had to use a 15/16" blank cutter to make them from any available copper stock; only limited quantities could be made each night, and at least seven batches or "series" are distinguishable by weight and texture, three each from First and Second Restrike revs., one from the old large-berry die which was rediscovered later. Restrikes were made up in date sets in each series: The rev. was left in press while 1840-48 obvs. were used for a few impressions each, to avoid danger of die breakage. As the First Restrike rev. buckled (it had been earlier used on coins dated 1856, 1857, 1852 and 1840-49 small date, in that order), Eckfeldt's accomplices made up the Second Restrike die from the original hub, and on one occasion (Series VI) used it with the old 1831 and 1836 obvs. (see previous section). Snowden discovered this operation too and sealed up all these dies July 30, 1860. These and the other carton were reopened by the later Director Henry R. Linderman, May 18, 1867; some few extra strikings followed in 1868, after which the dies were destroyed: Breen {1984} pp. 383-85, 463-65; Newman-Bressett {1962}, pp. 85-88.

Planchets for business strikes 1849-57 came from Crocker Bros. & Co., Taunton, Mass., which firm landed the federal contract partly because (unlike some of its competitors) it was willing to accept payment in copper coins. The Mint was under pressure to find a domestic supplier after the Boulton & Watt mint closed; and even into recent years the Mint Bureau has relied on private industry to supply base-metal planchets, following a precedent established by Elias Boudinot in 1796.

Later dates for circulation needed only one obv. die per year. Relative scarcity conforms well to reported mintages except for the uncirculated specimens from the hoards. However, 1857 in worn state is scarcer than it should be, because Mint Director James Ross Snowden ordered the Mint's remaining stocks melted after the denomination was abolished in Feb. 1857. Unfortunately, no record has turned up showing the amount melted.

Snowden ordered 50 copper-nickel half-cent proofs struck July 1856 to show congressmen and others what the proposed new alloy would look like before the 1856 Flying Eagle cent dies were ready. Restrikes of this issue are rarer than originals and mostly better struck. The occasional worn specimens were probably congressional pocket pieces.

Many sets of electrotype copies were made from the Mint Cabinet collection's set of half cents: 1831, 1836, 1840–48 large berries, 1852 First Restrike. Electrotypes may retain proof surface, but they will fail the Ring Test (see Glossary), their weight is far too high, and they have either seams on edges or scrapes to conceal them.

GOBRECHT'S CORONET HEADS

Designer, Engraver, Christian Gobrecht. Mint, Philadelphia. Composition, copper. Diameter, as before. Weight, 84 ± 3.5 grs. = 5.443 ± 0.227 gms. (Act of Jan. 18, 1837); observed tolerances narrower. EXCEPTION: Restrikes weigh 68.2–83 grs. = 4.42–5.4 gms.; thick-flan restrikes 96–98 grs. = 6.2–6.4 gms. (other exceptions as noted in main text). Authorizing Acts, as before.

Grade range, VERY GOOD to UNC., 1849–57; proofs sometimes also come circulated and grade similarly. FINE: Beads on bun sharp; most hair strands intact except above ear, at forelock, on bun, and a few other small spots. VERY FINE: Strands separated except on lovelock (below ear). EXTREMELY FINE: Few tiny isolated rubbed spots only.

Original, Large Berries, 1840–49
Note modifications at ribbon, leaf below (CENT) T

"First Restrike," Small Berries
Reverse of 1856–57: broken wreath, local doublings

"Second Restrike," Small Berries
Die file marks between border and RICA

1579 1840 Large berries. About 18 known.
   Breen 1; Cohen PO 1. Originals have squashed edge reeding (see introductory text). At least 2 restrikes from these dies, normal plain edge, 81.3–81.8 grs. = 5.27–5.3 gms.
1580 1840 Small berries, First Restrike. 6 known.
   Breen 2; Cohen SR 2.
1581 1840 Small berries, Second Restrike. 12–15 known.
   Breen 3, Series IV, VI; Cohen SR 17. See introductory text.
1582 1840 Same. Thick flan. 3 or 4 known.
   Breen 3, Series V.
1583 1841 Large berries. About 24 known.
   Breen 1; Cohen PO 2. Originals have squashed edge reeding like 1840 (see introductory text). Obv. die almost always cracked.
1584 1841 Small berries, First Restrike. 4 known.
   Breen 2; Cohen SR 3. The crack is heavier than on originals.
1585 1841 Small berries, Second Restrike. About 9 known.
   Breen 3, Series IV, VI; Cohen SR 18. Same comment.
1586 1841 Same. Thick flan. 3 known.
   Breen 3, Series V.
1587 1842 Large berries. About 13 known.
   Breen 1; Cohen PO 3. Second star repunched.
1588 1842 Small berries, First Restrike. About 13 known.
   Breen 2; Cohen SR 4.

1589 1842 Small berries, Second Restrike. About 10 known.
Breen 3, Series IV, VI; Cohen SR 19.
1590 1842 Same. Thick flan. About 4 known.
Breen 3, Series V.
1591 1843 Large berries. About 21 known.
Breen 1; Cohen PO 4. Repunched 8. About 5 of these are off weight (78.8–87.9 grs = 5.11–5.7 gms.) with pronounced knife-rims, believed restrikes made at the same occasion as the 1852.
1592 1843 Small berries, First Restrike. 25–30 known.
Breen 2; Cohen SR 5.
1593 1843 Small berries, Second Restrike. About 6 known.
Breen 3, Series IV, VI; Cohen SR 20.
1594 1843 Same. Thick flan. 2 known.
Breen 3, Series V. 1) Eliasberg. 2) Pvt. coll.
1595 1844 Large berries. About 16 known.
Breen 1; Cohen PO 5.
1596 1844 Small berries, First Restrike. 5 known.
Breen 2; Cohen SR 6.
1597 1844 Small berries, Second Restrike. About 10 known.
Breen 3, Series IV, VI; Cohen SR 21.
1598 1844 Same. Thick flan. Only one reported.
Breen 3, Series V. 1) Bryant, Ryder, pvt. coll., 96.2 grs. = 6.23 gms.
1599 1845 Large berries. About 14 known.
Breen 1; Cohen PO 6. One restrike from these dies, ex Brobston, weighs 79.5 grs. = 5.15 gms.
1600 1845 Small berries, First Restrike. About 7 known.
Breen 2; Cohen SR 7.
1601 1845 Small berries, Second Restrike. About 10 known.
Breen 3, Series IV, VI; Cohen SR 22.
1602 1845 Same. Thick flan. 5 known.
Breen 3, Series V.
1603 1846 Large berries. About 18 known.
Breen 1; Cohen PO 7. Date engraved, not punched. Several show incuse mark in central rev. from foreign matter adhering to die.
1604 1846 Small berries, First Restrike. 4 known.
Breen 2; Cohen SR 8.
1605 1846 Small berries, Second Restrike. About 12 known.
Breen 3, Series IV, VI; Cohen SR 23.
1606 1846 Same. Thick flan. 5 known.
Breen 3, Series V.
1607 1847 Large berries. About 20 known.
Breen 1; Cohen PO 8. At least 2 are restrikes with high knife-rims, 80.9 grs. = 5.24 gms. and 86 grs. = 5.57 gms.
1608 1847 Small berries, First Restrike. 3 known.
Breen 2; Cohen SR 9. Discovered by Q. David Bowers about 1955.
1609 1847 Small berries, Second Restrike. About 18 known.
Breen 3, Series IV, VI; Cohen SR 24.
1610 1847 Same. Thick flan. 6 known.
Breen 3, Series V.
1611 1848 Large berries. About 14 known.
Breen 1; Cohen PO 9. Date too large; sixth star repunched. Same comment as to **1607** except that the lightweight restrike weighs 79.3 grs. = 5.14 gms., and the thick one (ex Farouk) may exceed 87 grs.
1612 1848 Small berries, First Restrike. Over 25 known.
Breen 2; Cohen SR 10. Beware alterations from 1849 large date: These will have the wrong reverse.
1613 1848 Small berries, Second Restrike. 2 known.
Breen 3, Series VI; Cohen SR 25.
1614 1848 Same. Thick flan. 2 known.
Breen 3, Series V. 1) Eliasberg. 2) Norweb.
1615 1849 Small date, large berries. About 14 known. Proofs only.
Breen 1; Cohen PO 10. Numerals from quarter-eagle logo-

type. Time of issue disputed. Discovered by Edward Cogan (10/18/1860:639). At least 2, possibly more, are restrikes, weighing as little as 81.3 grs. = 5.27 gms.

1616 1849 Small date, small berries, First Restrike. About 15 known.
Breen 2; Cohen SR 11. No Second Restrike yet reported.
1617 1849 Large date. [39,864 + ?P]
Breen 4; Cohen 1. Prohibitively rare with full original mint red, though brown UNCs. are available for a price.

1618 1850 [39,812 + ?P]
Breen 1; Cohen 1. About 12 proofs known. Most half cents hereafter went to post offices.
1619 1851 [147,672 + ?P]
Breen 1; Cohen 1. Part of a third 1 (base and lower upright) weakly visible at r. of date. A second obv. was made but not used. About 8 proofs known. The [46,794] of Jan. 20 were from a Crocker shipment, average 83.99 grs. = 5.44 gms.; the [100,878] of July 14 were from another Crocker shipment, avg. 83 grs. = 5.38 gms. UNCs. from the hoard are spotty mint red and often not sharply struck.
1620 1852 Original. Small berries. Proofs only. Untraced.
Breen 1. 84 grs. = 5.44 gms. Rev. different from any to follow. Most recently reported from the Winsor proof set (1895).
1621 1852 Small berries, First Restrike. Proofs only. Over 50 known.
Breen 2; Cohen SR 12. Rev. of 1856–57 proofs; 77.8–82 grs. = 5.04–5.31 gms.; 2 known at 87 grs. = 5.64 gms. Alterations from 1853 are not deceptive; they have the wrong rev. die.
1622 1852 Small berries, Second Restrike. Thick flan. About 8 known.
Breen 3; Cohen SR 26. Rev. of 1840–48 Second Restrikes, ill. above. 96.2–97.2 grs. = 6.23–6.3 gms.
1623 1852 Large berries. Restrike only. 5 known.
Breen 4; Cohen SR 1. Usually called "original" by dealers who stupidly fear that the label "restrike" might lower the price. 1) Mills, Clapp, Eliasberg estate. 2) Rice, Dunham, Brobston, Lauder: 316, $27,500, 83 grs. = 5.38 gms. 3) Brock, Univ. of Pa., Ward, Dochkus, Forman, Miles, pvt. coll. 4) Alvord, Boyd (fire damage). 5) James Aloysius Stack estate. See extended discussion in Breen {1984}, pp. 444–46.
1624 1853 [129,694]
One pair of dies. Ex. rare in pristine mint red, though plentiful in brown UNC. The blanks cost the Mint 42¢/lb., repre-

senting a net loss of almost 1¢/lb. in face value independent
of labor and equipment costs. No proofs reported.

1625   1854 [55,358 + ?P]
2 minute vars. of rev.: without or with rust pit near top of
upright of I(TED). Common in spotty red UNC. from the
Gies hoard (see introductory text). About 30 proofs. A single
copper-nickel proof (Judd 155), ex Farouk coll., remains unlocated.

1626   1855 [56,500 + ?P]
One var. only., struck April 28; avg. 83.28 grs. = 5.396 gms.
Possibly 40 proofs.

1627   1856 [40,230 + 200+P]
2 minute vars. of rev., without or with rust pit on I (die of
1854), delivered Dec. 18, 1856. Rarer in pristine red UNC.
than 1854–55. Borders are normally weak on business
strikes, even prooflike gems, but not on real proofs. Proofs
with either of these revs. are Ex. rare. The 200 proofs of July
25 (Cohen SR 13), 84 grs. = 5.44 gms., are from the die later
used for 1857 proofs and still later for First Restrikes; in
addition there are possibly a dozen restrikes averaging 81.8
grs. = 5.3 gms. each.

1628   1856 Prototype copper-nickel, 90:10. Ex. rare. Proofs
only.
Adams-Woodin 216. Pale lemon color, often toned or faded.
69.4–70.68 grs. = 4.497–4.58 gms., possibly for 100 to the lb.
avoir. or 82½ to the lb. troy. Weak strikings only. Compare
next.

1629   1856 On copper-nickel cent blank, 88:12. [50+P]
Adams-Woodin 217; Judd 177. Pale warm gray, often toned
or faded; originals (July 1856) weakly struck (ill.), rarer
restrikes less so. Standard, 72 grs. = 4.67 gms. (observed
70.98–73 grs. = 4.599–4.73 gms.)

1630   1857 [35,180− + 266+P]
Business strikes (Jan. 14) have tiny lump on r. side of first A
in AMERICA; many melted later. Proofs from this die are
Ex. rare. Most proofs (Cohen SR 14) are from the 1856 rev.,
including possibly a dozen restrikes at 81.8 grs. = 5.3 gms.,
8–10 more at 87–91.5 grs. = 5.64–5.93 gms.

viii. HULSEMAN'S HALF CENT
TOKEN (1837)

While the Philadelphia Mint was unable to circulate its own
product during the "Hard Times" depression, private manufacturers made and circulated large quantities of copper and brass
tokens, now generally called Hard Times tokens. Some were
anonymous propaganda items aimed largely at Andrew Jackson's disastrous fiscal policies (which had led to the depression)
or at Martin Van Buren's financial floundering. Others (a minority) were advertising pieces ostensibly redeemable in cash at
the issuers' stores; many others aimed at general circulation,
avoiding any possible demands on makers for redemption: John
J. Ford's euphemism for these is "neutral money substitutes."
The piece pictured below is one of these last. The dies were by
Edward Hulseman, of 80 Nassau St., New York City; we have
not yet been able to ascertain if striking was at the Scovill Mint
(Waterbury, Conn.) or at H. M. and E. I. Richards' mint in
Attleboro, Mass., as others Hulseman dies appear on tokens
struck in both places. Collectors of half cents have long been
interested in this token, as the only one of its denomination; we
owe its original popularity to Wayte Raymond, who made space
for it in his "National Album" pages (1930s–40s, ancestral to
the Meghrig coin holders and Whitman albums). Issue was
large, certainly at least in the tens of thousands. Survivors are
plentiful in all grades except red mint state, but most often they
come in F to VF; grade by surface. No weight standard known;
the only one weighed was 77.8 grs. (for 90 to the lb.?). F. C. C.
Boyd had a hoard of over 100 specimens as an adjunct to his
holdings of Hard Times tokens; most of these were in or near
VF grade.

1631   1837 Token.
Low 49; Breen {1984}, p. 487; Cohen, p. 124. The coin ill. is
sharper at claws, arrow butts, legs, head, and tops of wings
than normal.

CHAPTER 18

LARGE CENTS

i. VOIGT'S CHAIN DESIGN
(March 1793)

Aside from the "real cent as ordered by Congress" (the Birch Cents of 1792, above, Chap. 16), the first regular coins minted by the federal government on its own machinery and within its own premises were the 36,103 Chain cents struck at the infant Philadelphia Mint, March 1–12, 1793, from four obv. and two rev. dies by Henry Voigt. Coinage halted because the Mint ran out of blanks.

Voigt was Chief Coiner, and considered the ablest man available here or overseas for the post, but the blacksmith's and mechanic's skills appropriate to a coiner are very different from those needed for hand-cutting steel dies. Accordingly, his designs were kept simple, like their brethren the Silver Center Cents of 1792. Once the layout drawings had been assembled, imparted to the die blank by transfer wax, and incised by hand, an apprentice could safely enter lettering and numerals. While Birch was unavailable, and before Joseph Wright sought the position, the Mint had no Chief Engraver: Nobody had yet been found with the specialized skill needed for making device punches, a necessity for mass production of dies for millions of substantially identical coins. If the head of Ms. Liberty was to have any appreciable relief (it could not be much, given the small hand presses then in use), then the revs. must be of simple open layout with plenty of blank space in central areas. The chain device was an obvious reference to those on Continental fractional currency of Feb. 1776, Continental tin patterns of 1776, and 1787 FUGIO cents (above, Chap. 15), though now with the issuing authority spelled out as UNITED STATES OF AMERICA. Use of the decimal fraction 1/100 both reaffirmed the government's commitment to the decimal system and attempted to reach the then large class of people who could recognize numerals but not read words. Jacob Bay (the Germantown type founder) had been making letter punches full-time for the Mint since Dec. 1792, and either he or Voigt could easily have cut a link punch to assemble the chain design.

However, the choice of a chain device appears to have been ill-timed: Many remembered the FUGIO debacle, others deplored any attempt to associate liberty with the chains of slavery. Dr. Sheldon quoted some unnamed critic as alluding to "Liberty in chains" (probably from the numerous specimens of **1635** from clashed dies showing traces of a chain before Ms. Liberty's neck and face).

Not that the obv. was above criticism, either: Despite extremely fine lines, the hair looks disheveled, then connoting failure of respectability and either madness or savagery, explaining Carlile Pollock's oft-quoted comment (1/25/1796), "A plough and a sheaf of wheat would be better than an idiot's head with flowing hair which was meant to denote Liberty, but which the world will suppose was intended to designate the head of an Indian squaw" (Letter to Gen. Williams, quoted in *CCJ* 2/1877, p. 28). Sheldon {1949} also cited an anonymous gibe at the "wild squaw with the *heebie jeebies,*" supposedly antedating by over a century Billy DeBeck's coinage of the phrase in *Barney Google*. (Unfortunately, the Good Doctor had "misplaced" his source when I asked him about it in 1958; nor did he ever locate the "wild squaw" again.)

Unlike later cents prior to 1909, the border consists of a plain raised lip without beading. Because this plain border either did not strike up too well, or wore down too fast, or both, beads had to be added to the Wreath cent dies (following section), even as to the half cents. Without it, the coins most likely would not stack: a frequent complaint at any change of design even in recent years.

Die steel was of poor quality: The toughest rev. (AMERICA spelled out) lasted under 29,000 impressions, the toughest obv. **(1635)** less than 15,000, and other dies far less.

The edge device, popularly "vine and bars," consists of alternating panels of sinuous line with trefoils and of vertical reeding; this remained in use through **1644.** Occasional examples with plain edge are mint errors. Beware electrotype copies (see Glossary); these normally show edge seams where the two halves are joined. Authentication of plain edge specimens is mandatory.

Of the 36,103 coined, probably about 5% (1,500–2,000) survive today in all grades (mostly low because of the inadequate borders): perhaps ten in UNC., a dozen in AU, and 35 in EF, saved as first of their kind.

Less than a week after the coins first appeared, *The Mail, or Claypoole's Daily Advertiser* (Philadelphia, March 18) ran this story, promptly copied in other papers up and down the East Coast:

> The American cents . . . do not answer our expectations. The chain on the reverse is but a bad omen for liberty, and Liberty herself appears to be in a fright. May she not justly cry out in the words of the Apostle, "Alexander the coppersmith hath done me much evil: the Lord reward him according to his works!"

Everyone new that this barb (2 Timothy 4:14) was aimed at Alexander Hamilton, the illegitimate mixed-race statesman commonly misbelieved to be in charge of the Mint. This was Director Rittenhouse's cue to order a change in design for the next cents to be struck. And so, for the first time (but not the last), bad newspaper publicity forced the Mint to abandon an adopted design, unintentionally creating rarities in the process.

Large cents were not legal tender until 1965 (PL 89-81).

VOIGT'S CHAIN DESIGN

Designer, Engraver, Henry Voigt. Mint, Philadelphia. Composition, copper. Diameter, $17/16'' = 27$ mm (varies: 25–28 mm). Weight standard, 208 grs. = 13.48 gms. Edge, vine and bars. Authorizing Acts, April 2, 1792; Jan. 14, 1793.

Grade range, POOR to UNC. GOOD: Outlines of head and chain complete, all letters and date legible though weak. VERY GOOD: Eye fully clear; some detail at and near ends of hair. FINE: About half hair details. VERY FINE: Ear clear, most hair details intact except at demarcation between hair and skin. EXTREMELY FINE: Isolated rubbed spots only. Surface may require raising or lowering of grade; at the UNC. level, color is important in judging quality. Specialists use criteria agreed on in the Early American Coppers Society. EXCEPTION: Obv. of **1632** is always weak.

1632   1793 [Chain, all kinds 36,103] Widest date; AMERI.
Sheldon 1. "Chain, AMERI." Loring estimates about 7,000 coined with this rev. Obv. always weak. Sometimes with crack through TAT, rarely with heavy break at these letters. Enl. photos.

1633   1793 Widest date; AMERICA
Sheldon 2. Usually better struck than last. Loring estimates about 5,000 coined. Enl. photos.

1634   1793 Widest L I B E R T Y 2 known
Sheldon NC-1. 1) Stornay, Chapman, Steigerwalt, W. F. Johnson, Dr. Hall, Wurtzbach, Brand, Clapp, ANS. (ill.) 2) Exman, Loring, Shalowitz, Adams, Robinson S. Brown, Jr., much worn.

1635   1793 Close date, no periods.
Sheldon 3. "Leaning R" obv.; note prominent sternocleido-

mastoid muscle (from behind jaw down to bust point). Often with clash marks from chain before neck and face: "Liberty in chains." Loring estimates about 15,000 coined.

1636 1793 Periods after date and LIBERTY.

Sheldon 4. That ill. ("The Coin!") is a prooflike presentation piece on exceptionally broad flan, possibly given the extra blows (to bring up design) which make a proof: Breen {1977}, p. 30; Mickley, Crosby, Dr. Hall, Virgil Brand, Hines, Dr. Sheldon, R. E. Naftzger coll. Obv. possibly by Joseph Wright? Hair style and periods suggest his 1792 pattern quarter dollar. Loring estimates about 9,000 coined. Enl. photos.

ii. THE RITTENHOUSE-ECKFELDT WREATH DESIGN
(April–July 1793)

Between April 9 and July 17, 1793, the Coiner's Department delivered 63,353 cents, from seven pairs of dies made by Adam Eckfeldt and assistants, after sketches most likely furnished by David Rittenhouse. These are the famous and coveted Wreath Cents, created in an attempt to improve the Mint's public image after newspaper attacks ridiculing the Chain design (previous section). Unlike any other American coins, these show a leafy sprig between head and date; unlike any other coins except the Voigt and Birch cents of 1792 and the half cents of 1793, their berries occur in linear sprays.

Which plant the wreaths depicted has been controversial for over a century. The best evidence suggests that Rittenhouse had in mind a composite wreath, including for symbolic reasons both cotton leaves (the trefoils) and laurel, probably bay laurel (Laurus nobilis, 'Laurel of Apollo'), native to the Greek islands and Italy, but brought to the Atlantic coast colonies in the 1600s. In folklore, this plant was associated with victory and peace; in superstition, it was a charm against lightning striking any place where it grew or was hung or strewn. It was also used for wreaths crowning victors in town games. It was smoked by priestesses at Delphi to induce the altered state of consciousness enabling divination and prophecy, though Rittenhouse may not have known this last. (R. Graves, *The Greek Myths,* § 20.2.) Had he intended the leaves to represent olive, most likely the wreath would have shown its oily fruits rather than the still unidentified linear berry sprays.

Only the first obv. die has large date and letters, like the Chain cents. On its inception, April 4, the Coiner made up a few (five or six?) prooflike "specimen strikings" on brilliantly polished planchets (Breen {1977}, p. 30), followed by a few thousand normal impressions, during which time the obv. chipped and crumbled at rim. Later obv. dies have smaller date and LIBERTY, to produce a less crowded effect; all differ in shape of sprig. The next to last of these has the same trefoils in sprig as all revs. of this design; this was discovered by Richard Winsor before 1869 and misnamed "Clover Leaf," later "Strawberry Leaf," though as early as 1896 Crosby gave reasons for identifying the leaves as cotton. The final die-pair (narrow leaves all leaning r.) usually comes on blanks whose edges were lettered ONE HUNDRED FOR A DOLLAR rather than ornamented with vine and bars as formerly; these are thought to have been included among the 12,001 struck July 6–17.

Possibly between 6% and 7% survive of the original 63,353 mintage: 4,000 to 4,500 in all grades, of which over 30 qualify as mint state and many more in EF to AU grades, thanks largely to British collectors who saved them as colonial issues, and partly to local citizens who squirreled them away as novelties. This survival proportion is higher for 1793 Wreaths than for any other pre-1800 cents for which it can be even approximately ascertained. No hoards have been discovered, but then (unlike many following issues) no abnormal selective destructive forces have operated to lower the number of survivors.

In the meantime, Rittenhouse hired as acting engraver the famous portraitist Joseph Wright, whose cameos convinced authorities that he could probably create suitable device punches. Wright's first task was to make one for the cents, effectively signaling the end of the Wreath type. Shortly after creating the Liberty Cap device punch, Wright perished of yellow fever, Sept. 12 or 13, 1793 (see Chap. 16 above); his design went into use posthumously, being preferred to the Wreath type (despite the primitive vigor of the latter) if only because the device punch enabled multiplication of obv. dies.

The Wreath cents are the first American coin design created in direct response to public opinion; they remain today one of the most popular of all.

THE RITTENHOUSE-ECKFELDT WREATH DESIGN

Designer, Adam Eckfeldt, after Rittenhouse. Engravers, Eckfeldt and assistants; letters by Jacob Bay. Mint, Philadelphia. Composition, copper. Diameter, $^{17}/_{16}'' = 27$ mm; range 26–29 mm. Weight, as preceding. Edges, as preceding through **1643; 1644–45,** lettered ONE HUNDRED FOR A DOLLAR. Authorizing Acts, as preceding.

Grade range, POOR TO UNC. GOOD: Device outlines complete, date and all letters legible. VERY GOOD: Eye clear; some hair details. FINE: About half hair details. VERY FINE: Ear clear, most hair details intact (worn on parts of locks nearest ear, neck, and temple). EXTREMELY FINE: Tiny rubbed spots only on few highest points. At higher-grade levels surface may require raising or lowering grade; at the UNC. level, color is important in judging quality. Specialists use criteria agreed on in the Early American Coppers Society.

1637 1793 [Wreath, all kinds 63,353] Large date and LIBERTY.
Sheldon 5. That ill. ("The Atwater Coin") is a prooflike presentation striking: Breen {1977}, p. 30. Later strikings show crumbling at beads over LI; date sometimes weak. Enl. photos.

1638 1793 Small date and LIBERTY henceforth; broad leaves.
Sheldon 6 (ill.), 7; price for var. ill., which usually shows bulges in obv. field. Sheldon 7 (very rare) often has weak date.

1639 1793 Narrow leaves, no horizontal twig, no periods. Unique?
Sheldon NC-5. 1) LeGras, Frossard, Parmelee, Hall, Brand, Clapp. ANS. Discovered by Édouard Frossard, 1881. Compare next.

1640 1793 Same obv.; period after AMERICA. Very scarce.
Sheldon 10. Discovered by George F. Seavey before 1869.

1641 1793 Narrow leaves, horizontal twig.
Sheldon 8 (ill.), 9 (commoner; bow large and heart-shaped).

1642 1793 Same obv.; period after AMERICA. 4 known.
Sheldon NC-4. Rev. of **1640.** Always in low grades. Discovered by Édouard Frossard, 1897.   1) Ruby, Portman, Robinson S. Brown, Jr. 2) Davidson, Paschal, Sheldon, Naftzger. 3) Gilbert, Brand, Williams, Starr, Jack H. Robinson.   4) Bowman, Hall, Brand, Clapp, ANS.

1643 1793 Trefoil sprig. 4 or 5 known.
Sheldon NC-2, NC-3. Also called "cotton leaf," formerly "strawberry leaf." Always in low grades. The 2 vars. differ slightly in rev.   1) NC-2 (unique): Winsor:823, Crosby, Hall, Brand, Williams:6, Starr:6, $50,600, Naftzger, 26.5 mm.   2) NC-3: Sampson, Parmelee:671, Steigerwalt, Hall, Brand, pvt. coll., VG.   3) Merritt, Haines, Frossard, Saltus, ANS (ill.),

ABOUT GOOD, 28mm.   4) Rabin, *NUM* 9/41, p. 736, Kelly, 1949 CSNS, Starr:7, $51,700, Tatnall Starr. ABOUT GOOD, very rough, 27 mm, 206.1 grs. = 13.36 gms.   5) Reported.

1644   1793 Narrow leaves all lean r. Vine and bars edge. Rare.
Sheldon 11a. Planchets often defective. Discovered by Edward Groh before 1869.

1645   1793 Same dies. Edge, 2 leaves after DOLLAR. Very scarce.
Sheldon 11b. Planchets often defective. Discovered by L. Bayard Smith before 1869.

1646   1793 Same dies. Edge, one leaf after DOLLAR.
Sheldon 11c. Planchets often defective. Often weak in central obv. and showing clash marks from AMERICA before face.

iii. WRIGHT'S LIBERTY CAP DESIGN (Sept. 1793–Jan. 1794)

During Joseph Wright's last few weeks of life, before he succumbed to yellow fever, he designed a device punch for the cent, deriving his design at some distance from Dupré's LIBERTAS AMERICANA medal (ill.), but with head fac-

ing r. Wright's Liberty Cap head is more delicate in detail than any later device in American coinage, though the preservation of survivors does not usually allow this to be noticed. For the rev., Wright drew a simple two-branch olive wreath, with fraction 1/100 below. Working revs. could be easily made thereafter by using individual punches (13 for letters, one for leaves, one for beads and berries, two for numerals 1 and 0), adding bows, ribbon ends, stems, and any other necessary details by hand.

This famous Liberty Cap design was to be copied successively by Robert Scot, John Smith Gardner, and various apprentices.

Four obv. and two rev. working dies were completed between late July and early Sept. 1793, the heads from the single device punch (containing head and cap but no pole); letters, numerals, and beaded borders were entered by hand. Dimensions of the obv. device punch required the circle of border beads to be broader than formerly; accordingly, planchets were cut to measure 1/16″ broader. As weight remained unchanged, the blanks had to be minutely thinner; the struck coins therefore ring better than their predecessors (see Ring Test in Glossary).

Wright died five or six days before the single delivery, 11,056 pieces (Sept. 18, 1793), so that he most likely never saw any of the coins made from his dies (unless indeed the presentation specimen preceded all the rest). The regular strikings used the four obvs. and two revs. in six combinations; their true sequence is controversial, though the first obv. used was apparently the one with vertical bisecting break.

Both revs. gave way in the center, weakening ONE CENT, so that most 1793 Caps look more worn than they actually are, quite aside from the role of dishonesty and greed in exaggerating the grade of most offered at private sale and many at public auction. The rev. buckling was largely because Adam Eckfeldt had not yet invented a technique for hardening dies to prevent it. At that period, dies were hardened by being heated red and dipped into cold water; this meant that too often their interiors remained less hard than the surfaces, and they quickly buckled. Eckfeldt experimentally hardened some dies by spraying them with cold water under pressure, which largely solved the problem; the technique thereafter became common: See discussion in Breen {1984}, p. 20.

Only a little over 2% of the original mintage survives, possibly under 250 pieces in all, mostly in low grades; possibly as many as six grade AU to UNC., eight EF. That ill. at **1647** is by far the sharpest striking known, though cleaning has slightly obscured its original surfaces; it is believed to have originated as a prooflike presentation striking. It was successively owned by the Chapman brothers, Thomas Cleneay, Peter Mougey, Clarence S. Bement, Col. James W. Ellsworth (one of the executives of the World's Columbian Exposition), Wayte Raymond, William Cutler Atwater, and Louis Eliasberg. Two are known with finer surfaces but neither has so much sharpness of hair detail. The Liberty Caps are the most famous of the 1793 cents and possibly the most prized of all large cents.

When the Mint hired the bank-note-plate engraver Robert Scot on Nov. 23, 1793—one of its worst blunders ever—the Director failed to learn beforehand that Scot knew no more about making a device punch than he did of the Aztec language. Accordingly, pending his learning his trade, Scot used the Wright punch for his first three cent obvs. for 1794, producing the famous "Heads of 1793," though abandoning border beads in favor of heavy serrations so that the coins could stack. Of the 11,000 delivered, Jan. 13, 1794, under 5% survive, mostly well worn.

The vast majority of alleged 1794 "Heads of 1793" offered, except among specialists, are misattributed. To end this abuse, all three obvs. are pictured below with both revs. If a 1794 described as "Head of 1793" does not match one of these obvs., it belongs with the Scot or Gardner groups (in following sections).

WRIGHT'S LIBERTY CAP DESIGN

Designer, Joseph Wright. Engravers, Wright and Scot. Composition, copper. Diameter, 18/16″ = 28.6 mm (varies, 27.5–30 mm). Weight standard, as before. Edge, ONE HUNDRED FOR A DOLLAR. "First edge" = leaf after DOLLAR points down, as before; "Second Edge" = leaf after DOLLAR points up, as through Dec. 1794. Authorizing Acts, as before.

Grade range, POOR to UNC. GOOD: Device outlines complete, part of eye shows, date and all letters legible. VERY GOOD: Eye clear; some hair details. FINE: About half hair details; some internal leaf details. VERY FINE: Hair details clear except l. of ear, immediately bordering neck, and at temple; on 1793's, ear may not be clear. EXTREMELY FINE: Few tiny rubbed spots only (forelock, eyebrow, hair r. of cap, hair l. of ear, l. part of truncation); few other hair details may be soft: Coin ill. at **1648** grades at this level. At higher levels, surface may require raising or lowering grade; near mint state, color affects quality. Specialists use criteria agreed on in the Early American Coppers Society. EXCEPTIONS: Planchets often show streaks, laminations, and cracks; these do not affect grade but should be mentioned. Both 1793 revs. fail in center, weakening or obliterating ONE CENT.

1647   1793 [11,056] 6 vars.
Price for var. ill. (Sheldon 13); others are all rarer, especially those from the other rev. (single leaf at F, pointed r. ribbon, ONE CENT weak). Usually in low grades. That ill. is a presentation striking (see introductory text).

1648   1794 Head of 1793. [All kinds 11,000] First var., first edge. Rare.
Sheldon 17a. Wide straight date; blundered N of CENT, first rotated 180° then corrected (note serif at lower r. corner). Discovered by Dr. Edward Maris before 1869. See next. Enl. photos. Nos. **1648–55** all coined Jan. 10–13, 1794.

1649   1794 Same dies, second edge. Unique?
Sheldon NC-4. Leaf after DOLLAR points up.   1) Borcky, Garrabrant, Shab, Smith, Sheldon, Naftzger, much worn. First identified by C. Douglas Smith, 1950.
1650   1794 Head of 1793. "Double chin," blundered N, first edge. Ex. rare.
Sheldon 18a. Usually in low grades. Enl. photos. (of **1651).**

Note repunched 1. Discovered by Édouard Frossard before 1879.

1651 1794 Same dies, second edge.
Sheldon 18b. Leaf after DOLLAR points up. At least 10 grade AU or better.
1652 1794 Head of 1793. "Double Chin," longest stems, first edge. Very rare.
Sheldon 19a. Same obv.; extra-long stems lying close to nearly straight ribbons, oversize border serrations nearly touch many letters. Usually in low grades. Rev. reappears on **1656.** Discovered by Harlan P. Smith before 1906.

1653 1794 Same dies, second edge. Rare.
Sheldon 19b. Leaf after DOLLAR points up. Usually in low grades. Discovered by Dr. Maris before 1869.
1654 1794 Head of 1793. Close straight date; same rev. First edge. Unique?
Sheldon NC-7. Leaf after DOLLAR points down. The discovery example shows both edge devices, from being mistakenly run twice through the edge-lettering machine. 1) Bashlow, Naftzger. Discovered by Robert Bashlow, 1961.
1655 1794 Same dies, second edge. Very scarce.
Sheldon 20. Leaf after DOLLAR points up. Usually in low grades. Discovered by Dr. Maris before 1869.

iv. SCOT'S LIBERTY CAPS
(Feb.–Nov. 1794)

Until recently, students of cents assumed that Robert Scot engraved all 39 obvs. of this year by hand. Only in the 1950s were five Gardner obvs. identified as from a single device punch (see following section); only in the 1960s, were the first three proved to be from Wright's 1793 hub. Many specialists, ever since the original Dr. Maris publication {1869}, have commented on the remarkable degeneration of style throughout 1794, though they did not realize that this was partly from mistakenly assuming that all were Scot's work. In June 1984, I discovered that Scot's obvs. came from two device punches, the first for Sheldon 21-40, the second for Sheldon 41–66. As with the half-cent obvs., Scot reengraved the hair on each, adding date, LIBERTY, and border by individual punches. A few dies in this section, unusually crude for this period of Scot's career, are ascribed to other assistants of shorter tenure, notably Frederick Riche. Among the 27 obv. dies attributed to Scot, there is a definite trend to simplification and lower relief. This was partly for saving time in completing dies. But more importantly, it reflected Scot's learning the practical necessity of keeping relief low, both to save wear and tear on dies and to enable details to be brought up more clearly on available presses.

Many vars. of this year acquired sobriquets ranging from obvious ("Starred Reverse") to fanciful ("Patagonian," "Venus Marina," "Egeria," "Amatory Face," "Coquette"), most of the latter awarded by Dr. Maris {1869}. Maris originally intended these as mnemonics, but without adequate photographs they failed of their purpose. The most notable naked-eye vars. are all illustrated below; for the rest, readers are referred to Sheldon {1958}.

The "Starred Reverse" (1663) is possibly the most famous of the 1794's, and certainly the most coveted; its rev. die, which has smaller letters than normal, was reworked from that of **1665,** adding a circle of 94 tiny five-pointed stars—apparently from the punch Wright had used on the rev. of his 1792 pattern quarter dollar—possibly as an anticounterfeiting device. The regular border serrations were enlarged, in some instances partly overlapping the stars. According to Lyman Low, this var. was allegedly first commented on before 1850 by A. J. Gilbert, elder brother of the Ebenezer Gilbert who wrote monographs on cents and half cents; it first came to collector attention in 1877. Most survivors are much worn, and the few high-grade ones have accordingly brought very high prices. The solitary EF coin (ill.) realized $15,000 in a 1972 auction, at which many collectors expressed willingness to go as high as $10,000. In B&M 4/10/86:446, it brought $45,100. One of the other famous ones, "Missing Fraction Bar," unintentionally repeats the blunder found on Voigt's 1792 Silver Center Cents.

The first 15 obvs. of this group have smaller date numerals than the later ones, but the difference is not pronounced enough to attract much attention. Most noticeable here is that on the later dies, 7 is appreciably taller than 1, and the crosslet and foot of 4 are closer together than on former dies.

Some revs. have wreaths cut by hand; on the rest, at least three, possibly four, device punches were used for wreaths. Berries and sometimes extra leaves were individually punched, stems lengthed by hand. Why wreath punches lasted so briefly compared to head punches is unknown.

SCOT'S LIBERTY CAPS

Designer, Engraver, Robert Scot and assistants. Mint, Physical Specifications, Authorizing Acts, as preceding, except that diameters vary: $^{17-18}/_{16}'' = 27-29$ mm. Edge, as "Second Edge" of preceding.

Grade range, POOR to UNC. Grade criteria as preceding except that in VERY FINE expect fully clear ear. EXCEPTIONS: Buckled dies will weaken some letters. Specialists use grading criteria agreed on in the Early American Coppers Society.

1656   1794 [all kinds 807,500] Flat pole.
Sheldon 21. Rev. of **1652–55.**

1657   1794 Tall numerator. 2 vars.
Sheldon 24 (ill.) and 23. Latter (rare) with date much farther from bust, usually shattered obv.

1658   1794 Divided Date 17 94. Three rev. vars.
Sheldon 26 (ill.), with die chip from O(F), 25, and NC-8 (last Ex. rare, with 4 berries below R). Note dots at bases of LI.

1659   1794 Single leaf at I(CA). 2 obv. vars.
Sheldon 28 (ill.), with ends of 5 locks in vertical line, and 27; latter has buckled obv. and is very rare.

1660   1794 "Tailed rev." 2 obv. vars.
Sheldon 29, 30. Long tails to R and r. ribbon.

1661   1794 "Wheel Spokes." Ex. rare.
Sheldon 33. Always in low grades, rev. buckled, ONE CENT often not legible. Most show all 6 breaks. Discovered by W. W. Hays.

1662   1794 Single berry l. of bow. Very rare. 6 vars.
Sheldon 34–38 and NC-1. The least rare (S-35) has exceptionally delicate lowest lock; price for this var. or for S-38 (large die chip in field behind hair).

1663 1794 Starred Reverse. Rare.
 Sheldon 48. Usually in low grades, often on defective flans. See introductory text. Enl. photos.

1665 1794 "Fallen 4."
 Sheldon 63. Small letters, tailed R(ICA). Obv. attributed to Frederick Riche. Rev. was reworked to make **1663.** Enl. photos.

Jack Collins

Jack Collins

1664 1794 "Office Boy Reverse." Scarce.
 Sheldon 56. N of ONE first rotated 180°, then corrected; note serif at lower r. Rev. attributed to Frederick Riche. Enl. photos.

1666 1794 Missing Fraction Bar. Rare.
 Sheldon 64. Small letters. That ill. is prooflike, possibly a presentation piece.

1667 1794 Widest date, "Split Pole." Very rare.
 Sheldon 66. Die crack at pole on all but 3 survivors. Usually

in low grades. The only other var. with date this wide is still rarer (Sheldon 37, above, incl. in **1662**).

1668   1794 Normal. 30 vars.

Compare **1648–67**; see next section.

v. GARDNER'S LIBERTY CAPS
(Dec. 1794–April 1796)

In Nov. 1794, Director Rittenhouse hired John Smith Gardner as Acting Assistant Engraver. Gardner was later well known as inventor of the "Stenographic Telegraphic," a possible ancestor of the later stenotype machines; but in his Mint days, his assignments were to make letter punches (since Jacob Bay had died), then to enter legends and borders, finally to raise device punches from matrixes, at first Scot's (for silver and gold denominations, 1794–95), later also his own (cent "Head of 1795," half-cent head 1795–97, small-head 1795 half dollars). These are simplified versions of Scot's designs, in lower relief, with locks clipped shorter. He was originally paid $2.25 per day, but on Aug. 11, 1795, he successfully petitioned Mint Director DeSaussure for a raise to $3 per day, making his annual salary $936. His final payment record, dated March 31, 1796, specifies "78 days' work as Assistant Engraver @ 3.00." He evidently left the Mint shortly afterward; based on Scot's later tactics, we may surmise that jealousy was at work: Scot had a sinecure and feared competition or especially replacement.

Because of the need for numerous dies for dollars and half dollars early in 1795, cent coinage was interrupted until the following October. The next cent delivery was 37,000 lettered-edge 1795's, Dec. 1, from three pairs of dies, their obvs. from Gardner's device punch. The new Mint Director, Elias Boudinot, at once interrupted coinage: Every 100 cents cost the Mint $1.22 to make, owing to a sudden rise in copper prices to 36¢/ lb. following the temporary failure of the Anglesey (Wales) Mines. Boudinot then petitioned Pres. Washington to authorize reduction of official cent weight, preferably at 7 dwt = 168 grs. rather than the previous 8 dwt 16 grs. = 208 grs. Washington granted this verbally, Dec. 27, 1795, but his only public announcement about it was a proclamation, Jan. 26, 1796, retroactive to "the said twenty-seventh day of December," possibly to permit Boudinot to issue cents at the new weight in quantity before newspaper attacks on lightweight copper coins could force unfavorable congressional attention. Between Dec. 28 and 31, 1795, the third pair of dies (Sheldon 76) went back to press, producing 45,000 cents at the new weight, delivered Jan. 1, 1796. From then through March 12 there were 456,500 more, making 501,500 in all. Many show evidence of great haste and carelessness; more factory rejects (freaks or mint errors) went into circulation bearing date 1795 than any other in the series (1797 is a close second), still others were retained in the Mint and cut down to make half cents. All these thin-flan coins have plain edges.

In the meantime, the Coiner's Department had experimentally struck a few 1795 cents on Talbot, Allum & Lee tokens (the best of these is the Sheldon 75 in the Smithsonian Institution), and a few others with reeded edges (Sheldon 79). The former were thin enough to risk rejection by a public long since dissatisfied with lightweight British coppers; the latter proved a needless frill. Copper, at the new weight standard, was unlikely to attract specialists in clipping and shaving, whereas they made protective edges necessary for gold and silver coins until the Mint stopped using those metals.

GARDNER'S LIBERTY CAPS

Designer, Engraver, John Smith Gardner (after Scot). Mint, Physical Specifications, Authorizing Acts, as preceding. Grade range and criteria as preceding.

LETTERED EDGE, THICK PLANCHET
208 grs. = 13.48 gms.

1669   1794 First Gardner head. 6 vars. [80,000]
Sheldon 67–71. Maris's "Roman Plicae." Delivered Dec. 16–24, 1794. The rarest var., Sheldon NC-3, has 1 in date almost touching hair, and rev. of **1670**; the second rarest (Sheldon 68) has bisecting obv. break. Others are always available for a price.

Jack Collins

1670   1794 Head of 1795. [20,021]
Sheldon 72. Device punch continues through **1677**; note shape of lowest curl, which differs from all preceding. Delivered Dec. 31, 1794.

Jack Collins

1671 1795 [Thick, all kinds 37,000] Double leaf atop r. wreath.

Sheldon 75. One in SI has British edge lettering, from the Talbot, Allum & Lee token on which overstruck.

1672 1795 Single top leaves, ONE CENT centered.

Sheldon 74 (obv. as last) and 73 ("hyphen" die defect joins RT; rare).

1673 1795 Similar, ONE CENT high. Rare.

Sheldon 76a. Coinage halted, Dec. 1, 1795. One known (experimental?) on thinner planchet with lettered edge; weight not ascertained.

PLAIN EDGE, THIN PLANCHET
168 grs. = 10.89 gms.

Specifications as before except weight and edge. Authorizing Act, Presidential Proclamation, Jan. 26, 1796, retroactive to Dec. 27, 1795.

1674 1795 [Thin, all kinds 501,500] ONE CENT high.

Sheldon 76b, dies of **1673.** One other obv. die known (Sheldon NC-2, unique?), with date spaced 1 79 5, top of 5 buried in bust; the lone worn survivor is overstruck on a 1794 Talbot, Allum & Lee token, though no edge lettering shows. 1) Merkin 3/69:649, Naftzger.

1675 1795 Rev. type of 1796, very fine details. Very scarce.

Sheldon 77. Rev. often weak.

1676 1795 ONE CENT centered.

Sheldon 78. N(ITED) normally weak. Planchets often peppered with tiny defects. Jack Beymer discovered a second var., NC-3 (still unique): obv. **1673**, rev., (CEN)T rests on 2 leaf points.

EXPERIMENTAL REEDED EDGE

1677 1795 Rev. of 1796. 6 known.

Sheldon 79. Edge reeding vertical as on silver and gold coins. Rev., "Type of 1794," later used on **1684.** Always in low grades.

1) Woodward 108:866 (4/16–18/1890), Steigerwalt, Lewis, McGirk, Clapp. ANS. 2) Millard, Book, Clapp, Newcomb, Kelly, Peterson, Kagin, Sheldon, Naftzger. 3) Downing, Austin, Brotman, FCI, Loring, Robinson S. Brown, Jr. 4) Proskey, Buskirk, Newcomb, Hines, Sheldon, Paschal, Shalowitz, Brotman, Korsing, pvt. coll. 5) House of Davis McKinney (1963–68), unverified. 6) Sheldon, Downing, Ruby, Brotman, pvt. coll. Holed brockage of obv.

vi. HARPER'S "JEFFERSON" CENTS (1795)

Attacks on the Mint as an extravagance, costing more to run than the face value of the coins it produced, continued and redoubled. During 1795, a congressional committee began hearings investigating the possible advantages of abolishing it and signing coinage contracts with private firms either locally or in Birmingham: the same profitable expedient Jefferson had been opposing for years. John Harper, who had been briefly associated with Albion Cox at Rahway Mills (above, Chap. 6, Sect. v), and who had provided room and equipment for striking some of the 1792 federal provisional coinages (above, Chap. 16), as well as continuing to furnish equipment for the infant Philadelphia Mint, testified and struck sample coins at these hearings, Feb. 1795. These coins illustrated his proposals to make cents, should the mint actually be abolished.

For many years this episode was known only from Stewart {1924}; the coins were not identified. In 1952 I drew the connection in timing between Harper's proposal and the mysterious "Jefferson" cents dated 1795, which are obviously not productions of the federal Mint, but which are too heavy to have been a practical exercise in counterfeiting. Paraphrasing Mint Director Boudinot's report of Feb. 8, 1796, Stewart recorded that Harper made the dies and struck the coins at his own expense,

and that the congressional committee members paid him from
their own pockets for the cost of the copper (which gave them a
semi-official status). Stewart added also that Harper later declined an appointment as Assistant Coiner (presumably under
Adam Eckfeldt), and that after Mint Director Boudinot learned
that Harper still had his dies, he confiscated them, promising
reimbursement. Boudinot allegedly managed to induce Congress to appropriate $100 for the purpose. Whatever the truth
of this last (and it is possible that the $100 was covered by some
such noncommittal label as "contingent expenses"), clearly
Harper got special treatment, extraordinary for a possible competitor: Julian {1964}.

We owe the name "Jefferson cents" or "Jefferson heads" to
Ebenezer Locke Mason, Jr., who popularized the issue by making large quantities of electrotype copies of the Fewsmith specimen (see ill. of **1679**) for sale at 50¢ each. The name doubtless
comes from a (possibly unintentional) resemblance of the profile
to that of Jefferson: Mason's *Coin Collector's Magazine,* 1869, p.
73. These electrotypes are lead with copper coating; they fail
the Ring Test (see Glossary) and show edge seams. Later dealers have attempted to sell them as authentic. They are not to be
confused with the early casts, which circulated and which are
thought to have been made by Harper after Boudinot confiscated his dies. There was no legal penalty for doing so; federal
cents were not legal tender, anticounterfeiting laws affected
only gold and silver.

JOHN HARPER'S "JEFFERSON" CENTS

Designer, Engraver, John Harper. Mint, Harper's, Philadelphia? Composition, copper. Diameters, variable. Weight standard, not certain, possibly 37½ to the lb. = 186.67 grs.

Grade range, POOR to EXTREMELY FINE (see ill. of **1678**). No
grading standard established.

1678   1795 "Jefferson." Lettered edge. 3 known.
Sheldon NC-1. Border dentils complete; longer fraction bar
than next. Edge lettering differs in style from federal issue. 1) Newlin, Maris, Newcomer, Hines, Downing, Sheldon, Naftzger, ill. 2) HR, W. R. T. Smith. 3) Clayton L.
Wallace, B. K. Thurlow, Mayflower 12/8/67:126, Naftzger,
Loring, Shalowitz, Adams, Robinson S. Brown, Jr.

1679   1795 "Jefferson." Plain edge. Very rare.
Sheldon 80. Border dentils generally incomplete; shorter fraction bar. See introductory text. That ill. is ex William Fewsmith, J. Colvin Randall, George H. Clapp, now ANS, 186
grs. = 12.1 gms. One is overstruck on a 1794 Federal cent:
Downing, 52 ANA:1716, Bareford, Halperin, Loring. Beware
electrotype copies. Compare next.

1680   1795 Same. Early cast, for circulation. Very rare.
Solid copper, but porous with briefer ring than preceding. See
introductory text.

vii. SCOT'S FINAL LIBERTY
CAPS (May–June 1796)

Almost immediately after John Smith Gardner left the Mint,
Robert Scot replaced his cent device punch with a new one
copying it. This punch was too high in relief so that the six obv.
dies sunk from it often produce weak impressions. Most 1796
Liberty Cap cents are weaker on rev. than on obv. because the
heads take up too much of the available metal. The six obvs.
were muled with seven revs. to produce 11 combinations for a
total of 109,825 coins, April 18–May 10, 1796, the last use of
the various copies of Wright's design on cents.

Obverse device is in high relief; revs. are usually weak in
centers. Most survivors are therefore in low grades, and possibly 2½% of the original mintage remains, compared with
about 3% of 1794 and possibly 4% to 5% of 1795 plain edge.
The set of 11 die vars. is very difficult to complete in acceptable
condition, even though no single var. is of extreme rarity.

SCOT'S FINAL LIBERTY CAPS

Designer, Engraver, Scot. Mint, Philadelphia. Physical Specifications, Authorizing Acts, as for 1795 plain edge.

Grade range, POOR to UNC. Grading standards, as for 1795
plain edge. EXCEPTIONS: Rev. usually weaker than obv. so
that ONE CENT is seldom clear even in FINE; "split grades"
are the rule, e.g., obv. FINE or VF, rev. GOOD or VG. Many are
on rough, dark planchets; evenly struck specimens and those on
high-quality planchets command a premium.

1681   1796 [Liberty caps. All kinds 109,825+] Straight date. 4
rev. vars.
Sheldon 84–87. Price for var. ill. (S-84, leaf touches F), or 87
(double leaf l. of ONE); the other 2 are much rarer. Die
failure weakens 96.

1682   1796 Wide curved date. 5 vars.
Sheldon 83, 88–91.

1683 1796 Close date. 2 rev. vars.
Sheldon 81, 82. Price for former (ill., double leaf at UN); 82 is very scarce.

viii. SCOT'S DRAPED BUSTS
(July 1796–Dec. 1807)

Adam Eckfeldt said that the changeover from Caps to Draped Busts occurred in July 1796, a few months after he had become Assistant Coiner. (Mason's *Coin and Stamp Collector's Magazine,* Dec. 1867.) After the May 10 delivery of Liberty Caps, cent coinage was again interrupted. With Eckfeldt's help, Scot made a new matrix, or original die, rudely copying the Gilbert Stuart drawing previously used for designing silver coins, and Eckfeldt raised a device punch to make 19 working obvs. to bear this date. The next cent deliveries were completed between Oct. 13 and Dec. 23, 1796: [363,375]. From this same device punch other dies were made, dated 179_ with final digit omitted, for possible use in 1797 or 1798 or even 1799 as needed; its final appearance is on an obv. redated 1800/1798. It is generally called "Head of 1797" or "Style I Hair" to distinguish it from the next device punch, the Head of 1799.

Vattemare {1861}, p. 25, repeats the preposterous old rumor that the obv. portrayed Pocahontas!

Sometime in 1798, the device punch chipped at top, the point and parts of waves of topmost curl (below BERT) breaking away; and it began to give way at center. This made a replacement necessary: the Head of 1799. The new device punch was used on the last 14 obv. dies to be dated 1798, but most coins from them were actually struck in 1799. This device punch also appears on both obvs. dated 1799, and (with the single exception above) on all later cent obvs. through 1807. It is possible that at some time between 1799 and 1807 new obv. device punches were raised from the same matrix; these would not be distinguishable except in minute details of hand finishing.

During 1796–99 and again in 1803, Mint operations had to be suspended in August or September through late fall while all personnel fled the city to escape the yearly yellow fever epidemic. Each winter, the old dies (or all that could still be even briefly used) were retrieved from the vaults, degreased, and hastily combined in any convenient pairings to make many small batches of cents. These "emergency" coinages include many of the most famous type coins in the series, notably all the 1798's with Reverse of 1796 (single leaves atop wreath) and many 1796's with rusted or severely broken dies.

Planchets come from a variety of sources. The best ones represented the initial shipment (418,000, Aug. 1797, at 0.645¢ each) from Boulton & Watt. Many uncirculated survivors from this group came from the "Nichols find," a bag of 1,000 pieces brought by Sen. Benjamin Goodhue to his daughters in Dec. 1797 or early 1798, and preserved by them and their descendants in the Salem, Mass., area. They reached numismatic channels about 1863 when David Nichols, of Gallows Hill (near Salem), began selling them to coin dealers. Representative examples of the coins from this group (dated 1796 and 1797, but all struck in late 1797) are illustrated. These planchets were mostly used for the vars. 1796 Sheldon 119, 1797 Sheldon 123 and 135, with sprinklings of others vars.: 1796 S-104 rusted dies and 118; 1797 S-122, 136, 137; 1798 S-154: See Sheldon {1958}. However, many of the poor rough planchets and dark lenticular blanks found on earlier 1796's recur on these later dates as well. The 1799's and most 1800's are on dark rough flans referred to in Mint records as "black copper," which was evidently not as durable as other kinds, subject instead to rapid deterioration so that many survivors are illegible or nearly so. These inferior planchets (388,333 in all) came from Coltman Bros. (Governor & Company of Copper Miners), and cost more (0.695¢ each) than Boulton's, aside from having to be scoured to make them even marginally acceptable for coinage. For this reason, Mint Director Boudinot gave Boulton his planchet orders as nearly exclusively as possible, despite local objections to favoring a British firm over its American competitors. For further details see Julian {1975}.

There are three different types of revs. on 1796 cents. The first, called "Type of 1794" (Sheldon's revs. S, U, V), has broad serrations for border, with 14 leaves l., 17 or 18 r., arranged exactly as on 1794 cents; one of the three revs. first appeared on the 1795 reeded-edge cents, **1677.** Next comes the "Type of 1795," copying **1675:** single leaves at top of each branch. Eight working dies were of this type, in addition to the seven found with the 1796 Liberty Caps; four were reused with obvs. dated 1797 and 1798. Finally there is the "Type of 1797," with 16 leaves l., 19 r., in a layout which continued unchanged through 1807. The first five dies made of this type (Sheldon revs. I, K, O, and R of 1796; 1797 rev. K) have small fraction, like previous types; later ones all have larger fraction. This Type of 1797 wreath is from a device punch comprising only wreath stem, leaves, and ribbons; stem ends, berries, and berry stems had to be added by hand, and were sometimes forgotten (Stemless Wreaths, Three Errors, Nine Berry vars.).

Later still, Scot and Eckfeldt attempted a complete rev. hub, and managed to sink 44 working dies from it: the last ones of 1798, the 1799 rev., all of 1800, Sheldon revs. A, B, and E of 1801, and 1802 rev. I. The experiment was then abandoned as a failure, not to be revived until Oct. 1834. This was because the Mint's hubbing press (presumably the one normally used for dollars and medals, the largest of the five in the Coiner's Department) was too weak to produce more than a vague sketchy impression, so that all 44 of these dies required extensive hand finishing. When Scot had to resume making working dies with only the wreath impressed by a device punch, he began making increasing numbers of blunders. His Stemless, 1/000, Corrected Fraction, and similar evidences of failing sight and/or attention have long been popular among collectors, though mostly not rare. In 1801, not less than four different working revs. bore the same preposterous error 1/000! One of these was put aside after brief usage, but was resurrected, annealed, corrected to 1/100, and rehardened in 1803 when the Mint's supply of die steel began to run short. Most likely Scot had apprentices enter the lettering thereafter.

Most of the really interesting vars. of this design—and most of the rarest—come from the Mint's troubled years, 1796–1801, during most of which time its personnel lived in daily anxiety over possible abolition. Afterward, for reasons not completely understood, die steel was of better quality so that dies lasted longer, and the coins themselves are more durable so that more choice survivors are known. The final var. of 1807 (Common Large Fraction) is possibly the most plentiful die combination of the design.

Collectors of this series are recommended to use Sheldon {1958}, pending appearance of the new Breen-Bland text. Scarce and even rare vars. are still being cherrypicked (discovered unattributed), and the possibility represents more an investment than a gamble. At worst, you will be exposed to some of the best writing and research in American numismatics; and you might even become interested enough to join the Early American Coppers Society, whose publication *Penny Wise* records ongoing research in an often delightfully readable manner. (For membership information: John D. Wright, 1468 Timberlane Dr., St. Joseph, Mich. 49085.)

SCOT'S DRAPED BUSTS

Designer, Engraver, Robert Scot, after Gilbert Stuart. Mint, Composition, Physical Specifications, Authorizing Acts, as before.

Grade range, POOR to UNC. GOOD: Date and all lettering legible. VERY GOOD: Partial eye, partial hair detail, major drapery fold shows. FINE: Clear eye, about 2/3 hair detail, most drapery folds clear; partial veins to leaves. On Type of 1795 revs., hollows in leaves, sharp demarcations between neighboring leaves in pairs or triplets. VERY FINE: More than half of all hair lines distinct; ear and adjacent curl clear. EXTREMELY FINE: Isolated tiny rubbed spots above brow, behind eye, on shoulder; almost full leaf veins. At higher-grade levels, surface may require raising or lowering of grade; near mint state, color affects quality. Specialists use grading criteria agreed on by the Early American Coppers Society.

I. 1796 REV. TYPE OF 1794

Leaves 14 l., 17 or 18 r.; Coarse Serrations; double r.
Terminal Leaf; Only One Leaf Below C(ENT); Small Berries,
6 or 7 l., 7 r.

1684   1796 [all kinds 363,375+] Wide curved date. Scarce. Sheldon 106–108. Usually in low grades. Price for 108, with coarse obv. dentils.

1685   1796 Close curved date. Sheldon 101, 102, 109. Usually in low grades. Obv. rims usually weak: Coltman blanks.

1686   1796 Same, "LIHERTY." Sheldon 103. B first rotated 180°, then corrected. Enl. photo of this detail at **1698.** Discovered by W. Earle Hidden, 1903.

1687   1796 Close straight date. Sheldon 110–112 and NC-5. All have 96 close. Price for S-110, with LI repunched.

II. 1796 REV. TYPE OF 1795

Single Terminal Leaves (Top of Each Branch),
Leaf and Berry Distribution Variable

1688   1796 Close straight date. Sheldon 92, 98, 99 (price for 92). Usually in low grades. All have 96 close.

1689   1796 Close curved date. Rare. Sheldon 116, NC-4. Usually weak at rims (Coltman blanks). Always in low grades.

1690   1796 Wide curved date. Sheldon 93, 95, 96, 97, and NC-2. Price for 93 (ill.) or 97.

III. 1796 REV. TYPE OF 1797

Leaves 16 l., 19 r., Layout as 1797–1807;
Berries 5 or 6 l. + 4 to 6 r.: 9 = 5 + 4,
10 = 5 + 5, 11 = 6 + 5, 12 = 6 + 6

a. SMALL FRACTION

1691 1796 Close straight date, 9 berries. 9 known.
Sheldon NC-1. Always in low grades.

1692 1796 Close curved date, 10 berries. Very rare.
Sheldon 100. Almost always in low grades; rim weak
(Coltman blanks).

1693 1796 Wide curved date, 10 berries. Very rare.
Sheldon 94. Same comment as to preceding; flans often
rough.

1694 1796 Wide curved date, 11 berries. 9 known.
Sheldon NC-3. Same comments. Discovered by C. E. Clapp,
1933.

1695 1796 Wide straight date. Rare.
Sheldon 117. Same comment as to **1693**. This and next 4
struck after Nov. 6, 1797, many on Boulton blanks.

1696 1796 Wide curved date. Very rare.
Sheldon 113. Almost always with die crack at 179. Struck
just before **1708.**

1697 1796 Close curved date. Very scarce.
Sheldon 105, 114, 115, NC-6. Usually in low grades, rev.
unevenly struck. Compare next 2.

1698 1796 Same, "LIHERTY."
Sheldon 104. Obv. of **1686**. Late strikings (Dec. 1798?) show
heavily rusted dies (ill.).

1699 1796 Close curved date, 12 berries.
Sheldon 118 (ill.), 119 (same obv., rev. of **1709**). Former (very rare) has berry below D; usually in low grades. S-119, the Nichols find var. (see introductory text) usually comes VF to UNC., weak in central obv. and peppered with minute central defects. Struck just before **1709**.

I. 1797 REV. TYPE OF 1795

Single Terminal Leaves

1700 1797 Wide date, plain edge.
Sheldon 120a. Rev. weaker than obv. Mint record [897,510] includes some dated 1796.

1701 1797 Same dies, gripped edge.
Sheldon 120b. Same comment. Some "grip marks" are incuse, some embossed, irregularly spaced.
1702 1797 Close date, same rev., gripped edge.
Sheldon 121b. Central obv. weak, rev. weaker still.

1703 1797 Close date, same rev., plain edge. Ex. rare.
Sheldon 121a, NC-1. Usually in low grades.

II. 1797 REV. TYPE OF 1797

a. SMALL FRACTION

1704 1797 Triangular chip in r. obv. field. Rare.
Sheldon 134.

b. LARGE FRACTION, Straight Tails to R's

Stems to Wreath Unless Noted, Berries Distributed as in 1796

1705 1797 Wide date, 97 close, 9 berries.
Sheldon 136. Usually with vague flat leaves; later, rusty dies. Compare **1707**.

1706 1797 Same obv., 11 berries.
Sheldon 137.

1707 1797 Close date, 9 berries. 2 known.
Sheldon NC-6. Date evenly spaced, rev. of **1705**. Discovered by Raymond Chatham, 1958.

1708 1797 Close date, 11 berries. Very rare.
Sheldon NC-5. Discovered by A. C. Gies. Struck between **1696** and **1697**.

1709 1797 Close date, 12 berries.
Sheldon 123 (ill., closest date) and 135 (obv. of **1707**). "Nichols find" vars.: See introductory text.

1710   1797 Close date, 10 berries, M corrected from E.
Sheldon 128 (ill.), 129. Price for former, with 1 and tops of both 7's touching device; 129 (date free of drapery) is very rare.

1711   1797 Close date, 10 berries, normal. 14 vars.
Those with closest date (Sheldon 122, NC-2, NC-3), obv. ill. at **1709**, are all rare and usually in low grades.
1712   1797 Stemless wreath. 4 vars.
Price for Sheldon 131 (ill.) with break behind hair ribbon; the others are much rarer.

c. LARGE FRACTION, Curly Tail to Obv. R

1713   1797 Stems to wreath. Rare.
Sheldon 142. Usually on granular planchets.
1714   1797 Same obv.; stemless wreath. Rare.
Sheldon 143. Same comment. The new style lettering continues through 1807 (except for a few old revs. reused, and for the first few 1798 obvs., made earlier with final digit omitted).

I. 1798 HEAD OF 1797 ("Style I Hair")

a. Straight Tail to Obv. R; Large 8

1715   1798 Closest date; straight tail to rev. R.
Sheldon 145 (ill.), 144 (very rare); price for former, with fraction bar joined to r. ribbon. Flat strikings, often in low grades. Mint record for 1798 [979,700] includes many dated 1797, some dated 1796.

1716   1798 Curly tail to rev. R.
Sheldon 146–149. Price for 148 (ill.), with spur on back of 9; the others are all rare and usually in low grades.

b. Curly Tail to Obv. R; Large 8

1717   1798/7 Three vars.
Sheldon 150–152. Price for 152 (ill.) with high leaf point r. of S; others are scarcer and always weak on obv. device.

1718   1798 Straight tail to rev. R.
Sheldon 154. Central obv. weak. The best ones are on Boulton planchets, like the Nichols find coins (see introductory text). Discovered by Dr. C. E. McGirk.

1719   1798 Curly tail to rev. R.
Sheldon 153.

c. Small 8, Rev. Type of 1795

1720   1798 Widest date.
Sheldon 155.

1721   1798 Close date. Ex. rare.
Sheldon 156. Almost always in low grades, centers weak. Discovered by Dr. C. E. McGirk.

d. Small 8, Rev. Type of 1797

1722   1798 Wide date. 2 rev. vars.
Sheldon 161 (ill., lump on r. side of O(NE)); 160 (rarer, lines to rim from tops of ER). Price for 161.

1723   1798 Close date. 6 vars.
Sheldon 157, 159, 162–4, NC-1; and compare 2 following. Not to be confused with Head of 1799 vars. S-162–63 show chipped, worn device punch (see introductory text).

1724   1798 Same, widest L I B E R T Y, A M E R I C A. 6 known.
Sheldon NC-2. Always in low grades. Discovered by Henry C. Hines.

1725   1798 Same, close LIBERTY, widest A M E R I C A.
Sheldon 158.

II. 1798 HEAD OF 1799 ("Style II Hair")

a. Large 8, Rev. Type of 1797

1726   1798 Normal legend.
Sheldon 166, 167. Usually with badly cracked rev. dies.

1727   1798 Blundered legend. Very scarce.
Sheldon 165. Second T of STATES inverted (rotated 180°), then corrected.

b. Small 8, Rev. Type of 1795

1728   1798 Rusted obv. Ex. rare.
Sheldon 178. Always in low grades, usually rough. Discovered by J. A. Walker before 1914.

c. Small 8, Rev. Type of 1797

1729   1798 Rev., straight tail to R.
Sheldon 177, 182–4. Price for 184: low 9, defect from upper l. corner of 7, die cut from r. ribbon across final A. Others all much rarer.

1730   1798 Large over small fraction. Scarce.
Sheldon 181. Shattered obv. die.

1731   1798 High 98, small fraction, blundered E.
Sheldon 179. E of AMERICA first entered "reversed" (ro-

tated 180°) then corrected; note extra serifs at l., part of up-right at r.

1732 1798 Small fraction, normal dies. 13 vars.
Most are from rev. hub of 1799 (see introductory text); many were struck during 1799, after next 2. At least one shows part of edge lettering of a 1788 Anglesey Mines token: ANS, S-176.

1733 1799/8 Two rev. vars.
Sheldon 188 (enl. photos) and NC-1. Price for former; latter (4 known) has outer leaves opposite (CEN)T free of wreath stem. Beware altered dates; the genuine has curl point between BE, unlike any 1798's with equally wide dates. A few S-188's have heavy breaks at upper r. obv. Mint report [904, 585] comprises mostly coins dated 1798.

both strong. Rim break in dentils above F A preceded the die chip between (ON)E and (CEN)T. Beware altered dates and electrotype copies. Enl. photos.

1735 1800/1798 Head of 1797 ("Style I hair"). 4 rev. vars.
Price for Sheldon 191; others all rarer. Usually dark. All revs. from hub of 1799 (see introductory text). Mint report [2,822,175] may include some dated 1798 and 1799.

1736 1800/179 Head of 1799 ("Style II hair"). 7 vars.
Usually dark. Same comment about revs.

1737 1800 Normal date. 18 vars.
Same comments. Vars. with bizarre or extremely extensive die breaks are mostly rare and of great interest both to cent specialists and mint-error fanciers.

1738 1801 Pointed first 1; normal fraction. 6 vars.
Mint record, [all kinds 1,362,837]. Price for Sheldon 213 (ill., wavy parallel cracks before face); others are all rarer.

1734 1799 Normal date.
Sheldon 189. Usually on dark rough flans. Most have weak date, strong LIBERTY; a minority vice versa; very few have

1739 1801 Pointed first 1; Three Errors rev.
Sheldon 219. Only one stem to wreath, 1/000, and "IIN-ITED" (U first inverted, then corrected). Often unevenly struck. Rev. of **1742,** often cracked.

1740 1801 Pointed first 1; 1/000.
Sheldon 220. Same obv., reground. Both dies later shattered.

1741 1801 Blunt 1's; normal fraction. 4 vars.
Sheldon 216, 217, 222, 224. Price for any except 217 (very rare: LIBERTY far r., curl point below I, obv. of next).

1742 1801 Blunt 1's; Three Errors. Very rare.
Sheldon 218. LIBERTY far r.; uncracked rev. of **1739.**

1743 1801 Blunt 1's; corrected fraction.
Sheldon 221. Denominator has 000 changed to 100.

1744 1801 Blunt 1's; 1/000.
Sheldon 223 (ill.), NC-3. Price for former, with l. stem extended into a long point; NC-3 has normal stem, and berry is opposite center of (ON)E.

1745 1802 Error rev., 1/000.
Sheldon 228, rev. ill. at **1744.** Mint report [3,435,100] includes many dated 1801.

1746 1802 Stemless wreath. 2 vars.
Sheldon 231, 241; latter (ill.) has double fraction bar and part of extra S below final S. Price for either.

1747 1802 T over Y. 2 rev. vars.
Sheldon 232 (ill.), 233. Price for former (long fraction bar almost touches both ribbons); latter is scarcer.

1748 1802 Nine berries, none opposite (ON)E. Rare.
Sheldon 238. Obv. die injured, rev. shattered, weak at l. Discovered by Dr. C. E. McGirk.

1749 1802 Nine berries, none opposite (CEN)T. 5 vars. Sheldon 234–6, 239, 240.

1750 1802 Ten berries, normal type. 9 vars.
1751 1803 Stemless wreath.
 Sheldon 243. Rev. of 241 **(1746).** Mint report [2,471,353] includes many dated 1802.

1752 1803 Corrected fraction.
 Sheldon 249. Always with "mumps" (die chipped below jaw).

1753 1803 Small date and fraction, 11 berries.
 Sheldon 263. Six berries on l. branch.

1754 1803 Small date and fraction, 10 berries. Close fraction. 14 vars.

1755 1803 Same. Extra wide fraction. 2 vars.
 Sheldon 245 (ill.) and NC-1. Price for former; latter (very rare) has top r. leaf point between E S.

1756 1803 Small date, large fraction, 11 berries.
 Sheldon 257. Six berries on l. branch.

1757 1803 Small date, large fraction, 10 berries.
 Sheldon 258–261. Many were struck in 1804. High-grade forgeries exist of S-260: See ANACS {1983}, p. 37.

1758 1803 Large date and fraction. Pointed 1 in date.
 Sheldon 265. Often rough.

1759 1803 Large date, small fraction. Pointed 1 in date. Rare.
 Sheldon 264. Obv. of **1758,** rev. of **1753,** but struck later; shattered dies. Almost always in low grades. Often misat-

tributed; see enls. of details. Discovered by J. A. Walker before 1914.

1760 1804 Only the one var. Scarce.
Sheldon 266. Mint report [756,838] comprises coins dated 1803. Most high-grade examples have been recolored or otherwise tampered with. Beware casts, electrotypes, and altered dates. On the genuine, 0 in date aligns with O in OF. 3 die states are often collected as though separate vars. State I (perfect dies) is slightly scarcer than III; State II (obv. rim break at RTY only) is scarcest; State III (rim breaks at RTY and MERIC) is least scarce. See next.

1761 "1804 Restrike." Copper.
Struck about 1858 by parties unknown (Mickley? Dickeson?) from rusted dies retrieved from scrap metal sold by the Mint in 1833. Obv. altered from 1803 Sheldon 261; rev. of 1820. Both dies hand-strengthened. Normally comes tan to brown UNC., not red.

1762 "1804 Restrike." White metal. 2 known.
Discovery coin, Fewsmith:2434 (1870). One of the 2 was Shinkle:1.
1763 "1804 Restrike." Uniface obv., white metal. Unique?
Pvt. coll., ex Parsons:344, Shinkle:2.
1764 "1804 Restrike." Uniface rev., white metal. 2 known.
1) Parsons:348, Shinkle:3, pvt. coll.   2) Chapman, Hines, Blaisdell, 1971 ANA:253. This rev. also comes with an 1810 obv., below.
1765 1805 Blunt 1.
Sheldon 267 (ill.), 268 (scarcer, rev. of next). Mint report [941,116] includes coins dated 1803, and possibly 1804 and 1805. High-grade forgeries exist of S-267.

1766 1805 Pointed 1.
Sheldon 269. Rev. of next.

1767 1806
Sheldon 270. Mint report [348,000] includes some dated 1805. Cent press broke down for several months, interrupting coinage.
1768 1807/6 Large 7, pointed 1.
Sheldon 273. Mint report [727,221] probably includes some dated 1806. Borders often weak.

1769 1807/6 Small 7, blunt 1. Rare.
Sheldon 272. Usually in low grades, often porous. Discovered by Dr. C. E. McGirk.

1770 1807 "Comet."
  Sheldon 271. Distinctive die flaw, visible even in low grades. Central obv. often weak.

Jack Collins

1771 1807 Small fraction.
  Sheldon 274; "Eclipsed Comet" (271 without comet flaw, rare).

1772 1807 Large fraction. 2 obv. vars.
  Sheldon 275 (scarce), 276. Often porous or with weak borders. S-276 comes with rev. at any angle desired to obv., all

the way around the clock; positional sets are often collected. Many believed struck in 1808.

ix. REICH'S "CLASSIC HEADS" (1808-14)

John Reich's first assignment as Assistant Engraver, 1807, was to improve the designs of all current denominations—i.e., to replace the unsatisfactory Scot designs. His contribution to the cents was the "Classic Head" device punch, copied a year later on the half cents; the latter would be revived in 1825 for half cents and copied by Kneass on gold coins (1834–38) in various modifications. In the introductory text on half cents, 1809–29, we already saw how the name "Classic Head" was originally proposed in 1868 by Ebenezer Locke Mason, Jr., forgotten in favor of Frossard's misnomer, and lately revived; we have also seen the probable reason for its early abandonment on cents: The fillet was worn not by women but as a prize by boy athletes who had won town games. Most likely some classically educated critic pointed this out to Mint officials, who had already had a bellyful of bad publicity about the Chain cents and Flowing Hair dollars—not to mention claims that Reich had portrayed his "fat mistress" on the 1807 half dollars and half eagles.

The relatively few dies of this type were apparently tougher than any earlier or most later ones for many decades, averaging a then unprecedented 300,000+ impressions apiece. Apparently Boulton's latest shipment of tool steel surpassed any previous consignments. A by-product is that the Classic Head coins are, in worn state, commoner than any earlier or many later types, though in strictly mint state they are difficult to find, despite several tiny hoards. Boulton's planchets for this period, however, were not up to the quality of some earlier shipments; dates 1808-9, 1811, 1813 are often dark and porous even in high grades.

For the absence of mint-red survivors of 1814, however, the explanation testifies to prolonged official ineptitude. During the War of 1812, an embargo prevented the Mint from obtaining any more copper planchets from its normal supplier (Boulton & Watt, Birmingham, England), and all cent coinages through 1813 were made from backlogged blanks on hand. In 1814, for reasons never made clear, the Treasury ordered the Mint Director to make no more cents until further notice. No half cents had been coined since 1811, no half dismes since 1805, no eagles or silver dollars since 1804 (the dollars struck that year being dated 1802 and 1803 large 3), and the few banks lucky enough to have half eagles and half dollars on hand hoarded them. What people had to spend was bank notes and irredeemable scrip: Current foreign silver and gold (legal tender until 1857) vanished into hoards. The coin shortage became acute, and the Mint received complaints, but the Director's letters requesting authority to resume coinage were in vain. For even more mysterious reasons, the Treasury refused, all year long, to issue warrants authorizing the Mint Director to pay his workmen. After 11 months of futile correspondence, Mint Director Patterson in Dec. 1814 overrode Treasury policy and ordered Chief Coiner Adam Eckfeldt to coin all the remaining copper blanks into cents. These promptly went into workmen's pay envelopes for back salaries, and were spent at once.

The coin shortage continued. No cents were coined in 1815 because no planchets were on hand, and the Mint had no domestic suppliers. Patterson was not about to go back to buying clippings and scrap copper on the open market for rolling and cutting into cent blanks; the marginally functional rolling mills had to be saved for gold and silver. As soon as the embargo was lifted, Patterson ordered more cent planchets from Boulton & Watt, but none arrived until the end of 1816. Individuals unaware of this history have fraudulently made many "1815" cents since the Civil War, deceiving more than their share of collectors; these fakes are usually altered from genuine cents of 1813, more rarely from 1845 (!) or 1816.

During the shortage, East Coast merchants acted as their fathers had done in previous decades: They imported coppers from overseas. To date, the coppers circulating in the USA from this occasion have been identified as including, among others, the "1783" Washingtons (from Boulton & Watt and William Lutwyche), and the "1781" NORTH AMERICAN TOKEN (from William Mossop, Jr., Dublin). These circulated freely long after the Mint resumed cent coinage; there was then no law against the practice, and federal cents were neither legal tender nor had any other advantage over the private tokens. Meanwhile, private entrepreneurs (said to have been working out of Mexico) coined immense quantities of white-metal half dollars, mostly Flowing Hair design, with a variety of dates from 1787 (!) and 187 (!!) to 1814; one of the more grotesque of these is pictured in Taxay {1963}, others by Ford in *CCJ* 11/50.

Mint Director Patterson, pending arrival of a planchet shipment from Boulton, began negotiating with other metal fabricators, notably Revere Copper & Brass Co. However, he found that they could mostly meet neither Boulton's prices nor the Mint's specifications. Boulton continued to get the majority of the Mint's orders until the 1830s, despite much adverse criticism from the American firms who wanted the contract instead.

Meanwhile, Robert Scot made a new device punch for the cent obvs., which was the opposite of an improvement, and must have struck Reich as a public insult (doubtless leading to his resignation the following March). It had exactly one advantage: It silenced any possible further criticism of the Mint for making coins showing a Greek boy athlete as Lady Liberty. Anything, even Scot's ugly new Matron Head design, would have seemed better than enduring more newspaper attacks.

REICH'S "CLASSIC HEADS"

Designer, Engraver, John Reich. Mint, Philadelphia. Composition, Physical Specifications, Authorizing Acts, as before.

Grade range, POOR to UNC. GOOD: Outlined devices; LIBERTY, date and letters legible. VERY GOOD: Partial hair detail; eye and ear clear. FINE: About 2/3 hair details; partial internal details to leaves. VERY FINE: Most hair details intact except above eye and around ear; half or more internal leaf details. EXTREMELY FINE: Isolated tiny rubbed spots only. At higher levels, surface may require raising or lowering of grade. Near mint state, color affects quality. Specialists use grading criteria agreed on by the Early American Coppers Society.

1773 1808 [all kinds 1,109,000] Twelve Stars.
Sheldon 277. First star weak owing to failure of rev. die; rarely do all 13 stars show plainly. Often dark. Reported mintage probably includes at least 102,000 dated 1807.

1774 1808 Thirteen Stars.
Sheldon 278–79. Often dark and unevenly struck, borders weak or incomplete.

1775 1809 Over smaller 9. [222,867]
Sheldon 280. Often dark. Rev. always stronger than obv.; softness on hair is common even in EF. Reported mintage probably includes 47,367 coins dated 1808.

1776 1810/09 [all kinds 1,458,500] Coarse obv. dentils.
Sheldon 281. Same comment as to **1774.**

1777 1810 Normal date, coarse obv. dentils.
Sheldon 285. Obv. die usually cracked. Unevenly struck. Lower-grade coins are usually dark; the few mint-state survivors are mostly red and slightly prooflike, from a tiny hoard discovered in the 1930s.

1778 1810 Fine dentils. 3 vars.
Sheldon 282–84. Often dark and unevenly struck.

1779 "1810 Restrike." White metal. 2 known.
Judd 41. Obv. apparently **1777**, much rusted; rev. of **1761–64**. 1) Lyman Wilder, Howard D. Gibbs, 1952 ANA:1990, Dr. Sloss, pvt. coll. (ill.) 2) Stack's, *NumRev* v1n2, p. 24 and Pl. *V* (9/43).

1780 "1810 Restrike." Uniface obv. White metal. Unique?
Judd Appendix A. For the uniface rev., see **1764.**

1781 1811 [all kinds 218,025] Normal date
Sheldon 287. Stars flat at l. Usually dark. Mint report probably includes many dated 1810.

1782 1811/0
Sheldon 286. Usually dark and on rough or defective flans. The "dash" below (ON)E is a chip out of die. See next.

1783 1812 [all kinds 1,075,500] Small date, center stroke of 8 thin.
Sheldon 291 (rev. of **1782**, ill.), 290. Price for latter; there was a small hoard, AU–UNC., mostly brown. S-291 usually worn, dark, obv. die cracked.

1784 1812 Large date, center stroke of 8 thick.
Sheldon 288 (ill.), 289 (point of high leaf ends almost midway between S O). Price for latter; many were in the same hoard as **1783**, brown AU to UNC. S-288 is very rare in mint state.

1785 1813/12 [all kinds 418,000] Rare early state of next.
Sheldon 293. Price only if curve of 2 is plain behind 3, mid-stroke of 2 partly visible near and above knob of 3. Later states price as next.

1786 1813 Wide date, close star.
Sheldon 293, later states. Often weak at upper l. stars.

1787 1813 Close date, distant star.
Sheldon 292. Last star more than its width away from 3.

1788 1814 [all kinds 357,830] Crosslet 4.
Sheldon 294. Not found in full mint red; see introductory text.

1789 1814 Plain 4.
Sheldon 295. Same comment. Often comes with double profile, or with die crumbling below chin, or with long obv. die crack.

x. SCOT'S "MATRON HEADS" (1816–35)

When cent coinage resumed at the end of 1816 (after its 1815 hiatus while the Mint was out of copper planchets), the new issues bore a spectacularly ugly head of Ms. Liberty by Robert Scot, the Christmas wreath of 1808 being continued without appreciable change. (See introductory text, Sect. ix.) This head has not had a permanent and universally accepted name. Back around 1950, Dr. Sheldon said that it "resembled the head of an obese ward boss instead of a lady," from which remark I unofficially christened these coins "Tammany Cents," after the notorious New York City home of generations of obese political ward bosses. As Tammany was originally the name of a Native American chief, the use of that name for these cents was criticized in many quarters. Some of the Early American Coppers Society people thereafter began calling this particular caricature "Matron Head," which may have to do until someone finds a name more descriptive of this characterless slattern. Vattemare {1861}, p. 26, quotes an ancient and scurrilous rumor that she was the wife of Mint Director Robert Patterson.

Various minor modifications followed, most obviously a new head punch (differing mostly in the hair) in 1818, but the basic concept remained the same until Christian Gobrecht's two new portraits (1839). Dies were reasonably tough, averaging over 100,000 impressions apiece, some of them far more, though none in a class with Reich's (previous section). All dates are readily obtainable in F, though 1823 will cost more than others. However, you may have to wait several years for choice mint-state survivors of some dates (1823, 1829–30 small letters in particular); UNCs. of 1824 have mostly been hoarded by one specialist.

Beyond doubt the most spectacular var. in the series is the 1817 with 15 stars. In worn condition this is common; in AU there are possibly 15–20 survivors, with possibly a dozen more in mint state, only two of which are full or nearly full mint red: unusually low for the date. Though some collectors have claimed symbolism as a reason for this var., there is no documentation; it looks instead like an error in spacing the stars. Scot (whose eyesight must have been failing long since) punched in the first six stars too close together, and had to add the other nine in nearly equal spacing to avoid an embarrassing gap between the last one and the device. Better to issue blundered coins than to waste die steel.

The dates 1816–20 are common in mint red from the Randall hoard. About 1868, a Georgia merchant found a buried keg of cents and gave them to a wholesaler in payment of a debt. The wholesaler sold them to Wm. H. Chapman & Co., "Buyers & Sellers of Everything Cheap," a Norwich, N.Y. department store, at 90¢ per 100. The store passed them out in change as a publicity stunt; but their customers mostly refused them as "Chapman's counterfeits." John Swan Randall, a Norwich (N.Y.) collector, bought the remainder from the Chapmans at the same price, and for years thereafter slowly dispersed them among coin collectors. Some believed the coins were restrikes, but Edward Cogan, "Father of the Coin Trade," published Randall's own account of the hoard, and the rumors died. Randall died Jan. 1, 1878; Cogan's 60th Sale, May 6–9, 1878, offered the remainder of the hoard as part of Randall's estate: 85 1817's, 1,464 1818's, 67 1819's, and 500 of "various dates." Some 1819's brought $1.28 each, most of the others 5¢ to 7¢ each. The vars. are 1817 Newcomb 14, 1818 N-10, 1819 N-8, 1820 N-13 (these two called "Connected Stars" from die breaks), 1820 N-15, and 1825 N-9. The 1816 N-2 and 1819 N-9 apparently came from other hoards, though traditionally believed part of the Randall find. Most Randall cents are spotty red or partly red mint state with many bag marks; the 1820 N-13 is by far the best struck, 1818 N-10 the commonest, outnumbering all other vars.—1816–39 inclusive—in that condition. Beyond doubt, Randall—not to mention the Georgia merchant—would have been struck dumb to learn that a century later their coins would be selling for over $100 apiece! Cohen {1985}.

Letter and numeral punches 1816–24 are by Henry Starr. Thereafter, Christian Gobrecht (1785–1844), inventor and bank-note-plate engraver, began furnishing letter and numeral punches to the Mint. He also made dies for medals, which have become very popular among collectors, but whose excel-

lence then helped him in his years-long campaign to become Engraver of the Mint.

During part of 1829–31 the cent press repeatedly malfunctioned, producing weak strikings; the worst ones are Small Letters coins.

Mint reports omit the date 1823; apparently all business-strike cents of this date were made in 1824 or later (proofs were not mentioned in the Director's Annual Reports). The 1823 was long believed scarce enough in upper grades that when Joseph J. Mickley found the broken original obv. die among batches of scrap metal sold by the Mint (1833), he and his friends eventually decided to make restrikes, using an 1813 rev. from a similar source. These dies suffered still more extensive breakage, but continued to be used at intervals for decades, at least until a later owner defaced them. I heard in 1951 from the late Homer K. Downing that they were privately offered for sale, no longer fit for use, but have no further details. Their then owners understandably must have feared federal seizure.

In Oct. or early Nov. 1834, William Kneass (1780–1840), Engraver of the Mint since Scot's death, completed the first working die from a new complete rev. hub, including all letters and border elements. Previous hubs had included only the wreath, dash, center dot, and ONE CENT, all other lettering being entered by hand into each die; and ONE CENT normally was weakly enough impressed by the hub to require hand strengthening on each working rev. The new complete hub (the first of its kind since 1798–1801) served to make revs. for more than half the cents of 1835 (see following section) and all of 1836; Christian Gobrecht replaced it in 1837 with one that had smaller letters. Nevertheless, for reasons of economy, the coiners continued to use up earlier revs. at least through mid-1835.

Kneass's last cent dies for 1834 bore a unique feature: For the first time since the 1793 Liberty Caps, borders consisted of round beads. These dies were first used for proofs, Nov. 1834, on behalf of the State Department. Special Agent Edmund Roberts was assigned the task of establishing diplomatic relations with the King of Siam (Ph'ra Nang Klao), the Imam of Muscat (Sayid Sayid bin Sultan), the Mikado of Japan, and the Emperor of Cochin-China. Part of his mission included delivering official gifts from the American government to these monarchs; part of these diplomatic presents were cased proof sets of U.S. coins. The above-mentioned cent dies, originally made for this purpose, later served for business strikes (in 1835?); in the meantime their obv. had been used with a different rev. from the new complete hub of 1835. However, for unknown reasons, Kneass at once abandoned the beaded borders; his last dies of 1835 with hand-cut borders reverted to radial lines, as ever since 1795.

In 1834, the mint shipped 100,000 cents to Venezuela for small change. What local denomination they corresponded to is uncertain: either 1 real or—later—1 centavo? (Julian {1972B}).

SCOT'S "MATRON HEADS"

Designer, Engraver, Robert Scot (rev. by Reich; later copy device punches by Kneass after Scot; letters after about 1824 by Gobrecht). Mint, Philadelphia. Composition, Physical Specifications, Authorizing Acts, as previously.

Grade range, POOR to UNC. GOOD: Date and all lettering legible, devices outlined, part of eye, part of ear show, part (most often nearly all) LIBERTY visible. This grade is collectible only for extreme rarities. VERY GOOD: Eye and ear clear, full LIBERTY, about half their detail. FINE: Over half hair details, partial internal leaf details. VERY FINE: At least ¾ hair details, over half internal leaf details. EXTREMELY FINE: Few isolated rubbed spots: Hair below LIBER, curls bound by cord, curls before ear and near shoulder, high points of leaves. At higher levels, surface may require raising or lowering of grade; near mint state, color affects quality. Specialists use grading

criteria agreed on by the Early American Coppers Society. EX-
CEPTIONS: 1829–31 Small Letters will show localized weaknesses even when there is mint luster in fields.

1790   1816 [all kinds 2,820,982] Close date.
8 vars. Price in AU and UNC. is for Newcomb 2 (ill.), the
hoard var., identifiable by date spacing 181 6 with rim breaks
at r., and leaf points almost under r. edges of final S, F, C(A):
See introductory text. This obv. also comes, rarely, with 2
other revs. (N-1, 3, latter ill. at **1791**). Other vars. are common in low grades but rare in mint state.

1791   1816 Widest date.
Newcomb 9. Usually in low grades.

1792   1817 [all kinds 3,948,400 + ?P] 15 stars.
Newcomb 16. Usually blunt on forelock and a couple of
other spots in hair, even UNC.; r. border often weak so that
the rim break above AM does not show.

1793   1817 Thirteen stars, as all to follow. Wide date.
Newcomb 8, 10, 11, 12.

1794   1817 Divided date, 18 17.
Newcomb 9.

1795   1817 Close date. Randall hoard var.
Newcomb 14. Note position of 1 before bust. See introduc-
tory text. This obv. comes, less often, with a different rev.
(N-15); this will price as next.

1796   1817 Close date, other vars.
Newcomb 1–7, 13, 17. The ill. is of a proof.

1797   1818 [all kinds 3,167,000 + ?P] Close date, head of
1817.
Newcomb 1–5. The rare one, N-4, has date crowded between
stars, and obv. bulged or buckled.

1798   1818 Wide date, head of 1817.
Newcomb 8, 9, 10. Price in UNC. is for N-10 (ill.), Randall
hoard var., alias "Connected Stars": See introductory text.
The piece with 14 stars (Maris coll., 1886) is not Mint work;
unique, unlocated.

1799   1818 Head of 1819.
Newcomb 6, 7. Proofs reported but unlocated. Compared to
previous head, this has simplified hair contours below LIB-
ERTY.

1800   1819/8 [all kinds 2,671,000 + ?P] Center stroke of 8 thick.
Newcomb 1. Obvious overdate, 1 away from bust; compare next. At least 2 proofs reported.

1801   1819/8 Center stroke of 8 thin.
Newcomb 2. In date 1 almost touches bust. Overdate often unclear; often sold as "Large Date." Note that this 8 is punched over one of the other style; see detail enlargement.

1802   1819 Small close date, oldstyle letters.
Newcomb 3, 5, 6. Wide dull triangular serifs on C's and S's, as in 1816–18. Compare no. **1804.**

1803   1819 Small wide date, oldstyle letters.
Newcomb 9, 10. UNC. N-9's from the hoard often show blurred borders on both sides. See introductory text. The proofs Newcomb {1944} reported remain unlocated.

1804   1819 Small close date, modern letters.
Newcomb 4. Sharp vertical serifs on C's and S's, unlike no. **1802.** Rev. always rusted. Usually in low grades.

1805   1819 Small wide date, modern letters.
Newcomb 7, 8. Price for latter (ill.); former (rare) has rev. of no. **1804** and usually comes in low grades. N-8's from the hoard (see introductory text), usually spotted red UNC., often show blurred borders. Modern letters continue through following years. Proofs reported are unconfirmed.

1806   1820/181 [all kinds 4,407,550 + ?P] Large date.
Newcomb 1. Large 1820 over smaller 181; Head of 1819. The die was an 1818 product; when it was made, minus final digit, the question was whether it would be needed for late 1818 or 1819. One proof seen.

1807   1820 Large normal date, curled 2.
Newcomb 9.

1808   1820 Widest large date, plain 2. "Connected Stars."
Newcomb 13. Randall hoard var. (see introductory text). Most are EF to spotty red UNC. The ill. is of a proof, believed unique, ex Winsor, Smith, Morgan, Clarke.

1809   1820 Large date, plain 2, other vars.
Newcomb 10, 11, 12, 14. N-11 has longest peak to 1; N-10, 14 have date spaced 18 20, former with 3 fused dentils near U, latter (very rare) with I below R-CA, high leaf ending about below center of final S. 2 proofs of N-10.

1810   1820/1819 Small date.
Newcomb 2. Date spaced 1 82 0; part of 9 visible at lower l. of 0.

1811   1820/181 Small date.
Newcomb 3. Date spaced 1 820; nothing within 0.

1812   1820 Small date. Obv., curled tail to R.
Newcomb 4, 5, 6, 8, 15; price for last (many UNCs. from

Randall hoard). At least one proof known, ex Mougey, Sleicher, Ryder colls.

Ex J. W. Garrett: 140. Courtesy Bowers & Ruddy Galleries, Inc.

1813   1820 Small date. Obv., straight tail to R. Scarce.
Newcomb 7.
1814   1821 [389,000 + ?P]
Newcomb 1, 2, respectively with final 1 low or 8 low. Over a dozen proofs of former (ill.).

1815   1822 [all kinds 2,072,339 + ?P] Wide date.
10 vars. Over a dozen proofs.

Ex J. W. Garrett: 145. Courtesy Bowers & Ruddy Galleries, Inc.

1816   1822 "Divided" date, spaced 1 8 22.
Newcomb 3.
1817   1822 Close date.
Newcomb 1, 2. Former scarcer, usually in low grades; latter has leaf point at r. side of C(A). One proof of each var.
1818   1823/22
Newcomb 1. Omitted in Mint reports (see introductory text); many believed delivered in 1824/25. Usually in low grades. That ill. is one of 4 known proofs. Newcomb, Starr:161, $16,500.

1819   1823 Normal date.
Newcomb 2. Obv. die comes more often broken than intact. Usually in low grades. The unique proof, Finotti, Brock, Ward, Starr:162, brought $29,700. See next.

1820   1823 Restrike. Issue of 1862. [49] Very rare.
Obv. of preceding, with rim breaks, but without bisecting obv. crack. Struck for Joseph J. Mickley (see introductory text). Usually dark and most often simulated by later coins with the crack tooled off. Ill. of **1823.**

1821   1823 Restrike. Issue of 1863–79.
Same dies, obv. cracked across, rev. uncracked.
1822   1823 Restrike. Silver. Issue of 1879. [12+]
Same dies. Struck for John W. Haseltine, possibly later also for Stephen K. Nagy. Rev. cracked in an arc. Auction 80:1383, $5,000.
1823   1823 Restrike. Issues of 1879–1900+. Copper.
Same dies, more heavily cracked. See introductory text. Ill. above **1820.**
1824   1824/22 [All kinds 1,262,000]
Newcomb 1, 5. Latter (rare) has rev. of no. **1819.** Both usually in low grades.

1825   1824 Close date.
Newcomb 2.

Ex J. W. Garrett: 148. Courtesy Bowers & Ruddy Galleries, Inc.

1826 1824 Divided date, 18 24.
Newcomb 3.

Ex J. W. Garrett: 149. Courtesy Bowers & Ruddy Galleries, Inc.

1827 1824 Wide date.
Newcomb 4.

Ex J. W. Garrett: 150. Courtesy Bowers & Ruddy Galleries, Inc.

1828 1825 [all kinds 1,461,100 + ?P] Small A's.
Newcomb 3, 6, 8. All have short top to F as in 1824. Proofs unconfirmed.

Ex J. W. Garrett: 151. Courtesy Bowers & Ruddy Galleries, Inc.

1829 1825 Large A's. Short top to F. Closest date. Scarce.
Newcomb 1. Usually in low grades, dark and porous.
1830 1825 Large A's. Short top to F. Normal date.
Newcomb 7, 9. At least 5 proofs of latter; a few UNCs. (some prooflike) were in the Randall hoard (see introductory text).

1831 1825 Large A's. Long top to F. Widest date. Scarce.
Newcomb 10. Very rare UNC.
1832 1825 Same, normal date.
Newcomb 2, 4.

1833 1826/5 [All kinds 1,517,425]
Newcomb 8. Date spaced 1 8 26; top of 5 within 6. Rare UNC.

Ex J. W. Garrett: 155. Courtesy Bowers & Ruddy Galleries, Inc.

1834 1826 Widest date.
Newcomb 9.
1835 1826 Close date, traces of star at 6.
Newcomb 1. Two (later only one) star points just r. of 6; star originally misplaced, then effaced.
1836 1826 Close date, normal.
5 vars.
1837 1827 [2,357,732 + ?P]
12 vars. At least 15 proofs known.
1838 1828 [all kinds 2,260,624 + ?P] Normal large date.
9 vars. Center of 8 thin; see detail ill. of next. At least 3 proofs.
1839 1828/88 Blundered large date.
Newcomb 6, 7. Part of 8 shows between 82; various states of die rust.

1840 1828 Small date.
Newcomb 10. Center stroke of 8 thick. This size of numerals remained standard through 1833.

1841 1829 [all kinds 1,414,500 + ?P] Large letters, tall 1.
Newcomb 1, 2, 4, 6. On all large-letter vars., bases of TAT nearly touch. At least 6 proofs of N-6 (high, wide date).

1842 1829 Large letters, short 1.
Newcomb 7, 8. Price for latter (ill., first star close to end of bust); former rare, usually weak, with first star far from bust, sixth star well to r. of coronet point.

1843 1829 Small letters, tall 1.
Newcomb 3, 5. Small-letter coins 1829–33 have bases of T A T far apart, narrow A's. Always unevenly struck; usually in low grades. N-3 (closer date) is scarcer.

1844 1829 Small letters, short 1.
Newcomb 9. Wide date, 1 leans r. Always unevenly struck; usually in low grades.

1845 1830 [all kinds 1,711,500 + ?P] Large letters.
10 vars. Letters as in 1828. At least 5 proofs known.

1846 1830 Small letters.
Newcomb 6. Letters as in nos. **1843–44.** Rev. of 1831 N-11. Always unevenly struck (usually weak on hair and parts of leaves); usually in low grades, unobtainable UNC.

1847 1831 [all kinds 3,359,260 + ?P] Small letters.
Newcomb 11, 4, 5 (struck in 1835), 3, 2 (struck in 1833, last with blunt 1's: repolished obv.). Price for N-11 (rev. of no. **1846**) or N-3 (ill.). The ill. is one of the dozen or so proofs, made before the business strikes.

1848 1831 Large letters. Obv., curled tail to R.
7 vars. 5 proofs, all "one-sided" (rev. fields not mirrorlike).

1849 1831 Large letters. Obv., straight tail to R.
Newcomb 9. A single "one-sided" proof, ex Miller, Ryder.

1850 1832 [all kinds 2,362,000 + ?P] Small letters.
Newcomb 1, 2. Mint report apparently includes many dated 1831. Three proofs known.

Ex J. W. Garrett: 165. Courtesy Bowers & Ruddy Galleries, Inc.

1851 1832 Large letters, wide date.
Newcomb 3.

1852 1833/2 [All kinds 2,739,000 + ?P]
Newcomb 4, earliest state. One proof known. Later die states, with 2 faded out, price as next. Mint report includes many dated 1831.

1853 1833 Normal date.
6 vars. Small letters only.

1854 1834 [all kinds 1,855,100 + ?P] Large date and stars, small letters.
Newcomb 5. Rev. of 1831 and 1835. Usually dark and in low grades. Mint report probably includes many dated 1831–33.

1855 1834 Large date, stars, and letters.
Newcomb 6, 7. Latter Ex. rare and usually comes in proof state.

1856 1834 Small date, letters, large stars.
Newcomb 1 (close date) and 2 (wider date, ill.), equally common.

1857 1834 Beaded borders; large date, small stars, letters.
Newcomb 3. C of AMERICA leans backward; N of

UNITED first punched rotated 180°, then corrected: Note extra serif lower r. The dozen or so proofs were made in Nov. 1834 (see introductory text); some business strikes followed in 1835, after next.

1858 1834 Same but serrated rev. borders.
Newcomb 4. Rev. from complete hub of 1835 (Type of 1836). Struck after the proofs of no. **1857** but before the business strikes.

1859 1835 [all kinds 3,878,400 + ?P] Head of 1834, large date.
Newcomb 1, 9. Latter (very rare) has high leaf ending under r. edge of final S; price for former.

1860 1835 Head of 1834, small date, hand-punched rev. letters.
9 vars. Mostly in low grades except for Newcomb 5, of which there was a tiny hoard of UNCs. 3 proofs known. Must not be confused with any to follow.

1861 1835 Same; rev. from hub of 1836.
Newcomb 6. Not to be confused with preceding or next.

xi. THE KNEASS-GOBRECHT TRANSITIONAL HEADS (1835–39)

We shall probably never know for certain whether the "Head of 1836" design, found on the last four cent obvs. of 1835, all of 1836, and the first seven of 1837, was made by Kneass just before his paralytic stroke, or by Christian Gobrecht, who took over the engravership during Kneass's disability. It is a copy of the old Scot "Matron Head" concept, simplified and with sharper point to coronet. All coins struck from dies made from this new hub have the completely hubbed revs. introduced about the end of 1834, except for the single 1837 Plain Hair Cord, Small Letters var., which uses a new rev. hub by Gobrecht. This latter remained in use through early 1839. Gobrecht modified the head slightly for the final 1836 obv., but in this period he (like his counterpart William Wyon at the Tower Mint) was notable for making minute improvements by hand on many working dies, a practice later abandoned.

Two obvs. of 1837 (round end to bust) show a still different device punch, by Gobrecht, abandoned for unknown reasons in favor of the "Head of 1838," which uses a beaded hair cord.

Working dies of all cents of 1838 are from a single pair of hubs, but these dies all required hand strengthening, accounting for the distinct vars. They divide into two groups, made before and after an injury to the hub knocked off the upper serif from E of LIBERTY.

The year 1839 was marked by no less than four different transitional heads before the Mint Director finally approved a fifth to continue into later years:

1. *Head of 1836.* Plain hair cords. The lone 1839 die to show this is an overdate, 1839/6; its date punches are those used in 1837. As this obv. die split across early, survivors are very scarce, uncirculated specimens prohibitively rare. The overdate was long disputed, but high-resolution macrophotographs have settled the question. Some believe the 9 was an inverted 6; this is undecidable.

2. *Head of 1838.* Beaded hair cords. Two obv. dies.

3. *"Silly Head."* A modification of preceding; hair is more piled up on top, the profile altered—no improvement. Both obvs. from this device punch come with the same rev. as the 1839/6.

4. *"Booby Head."* Readily identifiable by Ms. Liberty's sharply angular truncation line (between back of neck and shoulder) at lower r., defining a triangular area behind *and below* which are parts of one and the same lock of hair. Revs. are from a new hub lacking the line below CENT; most working dies from this hub were drastically reground, for unknown reasons, so that many berries and some leaves are stemless.

The names "Silly" and "Booby," as here used, date back to June 1868, when Ebenezer Locke Mason, Jr., tried to standardize them in his *Coin and Stamp Collector's Magazine.* Earlier, they had been inconsistently applied; both Dickeson {1859} and Snowden {1860} transposed them.

All these types are in progressively lower relief in an attempt to increase die life. Probably more than half the total mintage of 1839 cents consisted of "Booby Head" coins.

Whatever Kneass's other merits as an artist may have been, they certainly did not extend to designing coins. Much the same must be said for Gobrecht, though the latter was luckier in choice of models to translate into metallic form. Doubtless Scot's early jealousy, which dictated Mint policy for generations (aversion to use of outsiders' designs: the "Not Invented Here" principle), ultimately accounts for the wretched artistic quality of United States cents.

THE KNEASS-GOBRECHT TRANSITIONAL HEADS

Designers, Engravers, William Kneass and Christian Gobrecht, after Scot. Mint, Composition, Physical Specifications, Authorizing Acts, as previously, except that the Act of Jan. 18, 1837 set weight at 168 ± 7 grs. $= 10.89 \pm 0.45$ gms.

Grade range, POOR to UNC. Grading standards, as before.

1862 1835 Type of 1836. 5 vars.
Newcomb 7, 8, 14, 15, 16. Coins attributed as "N-17" are from severely rusted dies of N-7. The unique N-7 proof is ex Reed, Holland, Merkin.

1863 1836 [2,111,000 + ?P]
7 minor vars. Possibly 8 proofs.

1864 1837 [all kinds 5,558,300 + ?P] Type of 1836.
Plain hair cord, narrow end of bust, large letters. Not to be confused with either of next 2. About 5 proofs (ill.).

1865 1837 Plain hair cord, small letters.
Newcomb 5. Obv. head of preceding, rev. as **1867**. UNC. survivors seldom show mint red, and are often blunt strikings.

1866 1837 Wide, round end to bust, large letters.
Newcomb 6, 7. ("Newcomb 8" is an earlier die state of N-7.) 3 proofs known, including Starr:335, 339.

1867 1837 Type of 1838.
Newcomb 9, 10, 11. Beaded hair cord, small letters. 4 proofs of N-10 (ill.). Compare next.

1868 1837 Same, "Accessory E." Rare.

Newcomb 12. Extra E imbedded within leaves below E(RICA), a condition discovered by Jules Reiver. Coronet point aims at middle of sixth star, unlike other obvs. of this period. Usually in low grades.

1869 1838 [6,370,200 + ?P]

16 vars. Those with perfectly formed E of LIBERTY are slightly scarcer than those with upper l. serif of E weak or missing. About 12 proofs of N-11.

1870 1839/6 [all kinds 3,128,661] Head of 1836.

Newcomb 1. Plain hair cord. Usually in low grades; very rare above VF. Rarely shows obv. die horizontally split across.

1871 1839 Head of 1838.

Newcomb 2, 3.

1872 1839 "Silly" head.

Newcomb 4, 9. Latter (shattered obv. die) scarcer. Both vars. have rev. of no. **1870**.

1873 1839 "Booby" head; no line below CENT.

10 vars. See introductory text.

xii. GOBRECHT'S BRAIDED HAIR CORONETS (1839–57)

Sometime during 1839 one of the Philadelphia art galleries exhibited Benjamin West's painting *Omnia Vincit Amor,* 'Love Conquers All,' before a collector bought it. Gobrecht, though secure for life as Mint Engraver, evidently believed he needed a new profile of Ms. Liberty for the cents (and half cents, should any more ever be coined). Preferably, this should be one whose intrinsic quality would abort any hostile criticism (had some already been aimed at the "Booby" heads?). And so he sketched the head of Venus from the Benjamin West painting (compare the ill. in Vermeule {1971}) as a model for his final working hub for cents. Vattemare ({1861}, p. 26), nevertheless, dismissed it as "a female head resembling everybody and nobody." A single working obv. dated 1839 from the new hub **(1874)** went into use that year. The "Head of 1840" continued into 1843. Revs. were also from a new complete hub; smaller letters than before, while the only elements needing to be entered into obvs. were dates.

Evidently several other working dies had been made for 1839 use, at least with dates 18 , 183 , or 1839. These remained unused until 1840, when they were ground down and redated; usually only fragments of the 1839 dates show. The weirdest of these shows small 1840 date over larger 18; this die was used on a minority of business strikes and on all the proof cents of 1840 —a most extraordinary piece of carelessness!

Types continued unchanged through the first half of 1843. The first two cent obvs. of 1842 had small dates as previously, while later dies in this denomination (like the quarters, half dollars, and eagles) bore larger dates.

Gobrecht created new obv. and rev. hubs later in 1843: "Type of 1844." Obvs. show head repositioned; revs. have larger lettering. As the obv. hub went into use after the rev., a small minority of transitional cents ("Obv. of 1842, rev. of 1844") appeared in the meantime; these have become popular.

As the newest steam presses proved powerful enough to impart these designs to working dies without hand modification (other than punching in dates from two- to four-digit logotypes), vars. thereafter became mostly very slight, consisting principally of minute shifts in date position, with occasional accidents: minute doublings, die file marks, die chips, rust pits, cracks, crumbling. The main exceptions: three different date logotypes for 1846, two of them (Medium and Tall) being also used on eagles and half dollars.

An overdate is known for 1849, and others are claimed for 1844 and 1851. In the last two, a date logotype was first entered into the working die rotated 180°, then corrected, producing 1844/81 and 1851/81. These, like the obviously repunched dates on many obvs. 1844–48, testify to the new Engraver's timidity and incompetence at this blacksmith's chore. James Barton Longacre (1794–1869) was hired as Engraver on Gobrecht's death in 1844. Like Gobrecht, he had begun as a portrait engraver on bank-note plates. Unlike him, Longacre had no previous experience in die sinking, his appointment coming as a political plum plucked from the pie by Secretary of State John C. Calhoun. While on one hand the medal business was firmly in Franklin Peale's hands, on the other the Kneass-Gobrecht mechanization processes had left the Mint without need of an Engraver except when new designs or new denominations were necessary. Longacre had nothing to do for his first four years in the Mint except punch in date logotypes. Meanwhile, the Mint establishment under Director Robert Maskell Patterson repeatedly attempted to oust him. Their opposition to him was largely political: partly from Longacre's connection with Calhoun (earlier and later senator from slave-holding South Carolina), partly because Longacre was an outsider, not related to the interlocked Pennsylvania families who had been running the Mint for generations. "Not Invented Here," in short.

The mysterious 1848 Small Date was evidently a product of private enterprise, possibly made in New York: Newcomb {1944}, pp. 203–4; Julian {1972A}. It is included less for tradition than because inexperienced collectors may otherwise be deceived about it. The seven survivors:

1. J. N. T. Levick (May 29, 1865), Cogan (Nov. 1871), Brevoort, Parmelee, Ropes, Mougey, Elder, Proskey, Hines, Sheldon, Downing, 1952 ANA:2207. The discovery coin (ill. in main text).
2. G. M. Klein, J. A. Thurston (1888), "G," untraced, possibly same as one of next few.
3. W. B. Hale, B. Max Mehl, G. Discovered spring 1939.
4. Dr. W. E. Chapman, J. G. MacAllister, G. H. Clapp, ANS, VG.
5. Mehl, Newcomb, Starr estate, VG.
6. Essex Inst.:225, overstruck on an 1840 Large Date cent.
7. Denis W. Loring, triple-struck.

During the 1850s, the most outstanding vars. include different date logotypes: upright and slanting 5's for 1855 and 1856, large and small dates for 1857. Of an entirely different kind is the 1855 "Twelve Stars": Here, foreign matter adhered to the obv. die, preventing the sixth star from showing fully on the coins.

Large-cent coinage continued only through Jan. 1857. Anticipating passage of the new Mint Act (signed into law Feb. 21, 1857), Mint Director Snowden stopped coinage, and reassigned workmen in various departments to prepare tens of millions of copper-nickel cent planchets, hundreds of dies to stamp them, and the presses necessary for this operation. Snowden {1860} said that most of the 1857 copper cents were melted; however, the number or weight of the destroyed coins has not been ascertainable. The general public hoarded 1857's, so that in all grades short of full mint red the date is available at a price.

Other dates in this period are plentiful in red uncirculated state from old hoards: 1850 Newcomb 7, 1851 Newcomb 2, 1852 Newcomb 3, 1853 Newcomb 25, 1855 Newcomb 4, 1856 Newcomb 14, and possibly other vars. Some of these hoards

appear to have come from banks' cash reserves during the 1933 Bank Holiday, when examinations of vault assets yielded quantities of obsolete coins. There may have been a full keg or more of 1853's, which would mean at least a ballpark figure of 3 cwt = 336 lbs. = 14,000 specimens.

Planchets for most cents of this period came from Crocker Bros. & Co., Taunton, Mass., which firm enjoyed a virtual monopoly partly because its output met Mint standards, partly because (unlike many of its competitors) it would accept payment in copper coins.

GOBRECHT'S BRAIDED HAIR CORONETS

Designer, Engraver, Christian Gobrecht. Mint, Composition, Physical Specifications, Authorizing Acts, as previously.

Grade range and specifications, as previously, except that (aside from a few extreme rarities) these are not usually collected below VF. Attribution to Newcomb {1944} or G&R {1986} is seldom possible below that grade level, and very difficult below UNC.

1874 1839 Type of 1840.
2 minute rev. vars.

1875 1840 Large date, like 1839. [1,534,093]
6 obv. dies. Some show traces of 1840/39 overdate, never distinct. Mint report comprises Jan. 31–June 30.
1876 1840 Small date. [928,597 + ?P]
5 obv. dies. Compare next.
1877 1840 Small date over large 18.
Newcomb 2. Proofs (about 15 known, ill.) and business strikes.

1878 1841 [1,597,367 + ?P]
6 vars. of business strikes, a seventh (Newcomb 1) for the approximately 25 proofs.
1879 1842 Small date. [214,945 + ?P]
Date as last 3. Two pairs of dies for business strikes, one of these obvs. (Newcomb 1) also used for the 6 proofs. Mintage figure includes deliveries through Jan. 31.

1880 1842 Large date. [2,168,445 + ?P]
　　6 obv. dies known; 3 or 4 proofs.

1881 1843 [all kinds 2,425,342 + ?P] Type of 1842.
　　Over 12 vars., some with minor repunching on dates. About
　　15 proofs (Newcomb 14, ill., and 2 other vars.).

1882 1843 Obv. of 1842, rev. of 1844.
　　Newcomb 4, 13. Larger letters. Usually in VF or lower
　　grades.

1887 1845 [3,894,804 + ?P]
　　About 22 minor vars., a few with minute repunching on date.
　　About 10 proofs known.
1888 1846 [all kinds 4,120,800 + ?P] Small date, open 6.
　　Newcomb 9, 10 with various revs. Round knob of 6 well
　　away from loop. At least 3 proofs of N-10. Compare next.
1889 1846 Small date, closed 6.
　　Wedge-shaped knob of 6 almost or quite touches loop; see ill.
　　of next. Over 20 minor vars., several with minute repunching
　　on 1, 18, 4, or 46. At least 18 proofs.
1890 1846 Doubled small date.
　　Newcomb 4. Date first punched well to l., then corrected.
　　One proof known, ex Hines, Blaisdell.

1883 1843 Type of 1844. 4 vars.
　　Newcomb 5, 6, and unlisteds. G&R 13–16. Repositioned
　　head, as all to follow.
1884 1844 [2,398,752 + ?P]
　　At least 7 vars.
1885 1844/81 Blundered obv.
　　Newcomb 2. See introductory text.

1891 1846 Medium date.
　　Newcomb 11. Same logotype as on most half dollars of this
　　date.
1892 1846 Tall date.
　　Newcomb 12, 13, 14, 16; Breen 22 (4 proofs known); unlisted
　　vars. Same logotype as on a minority of half dollars of this
　　date.
1893 1847 [6,183,669 + ?P]
　　Over 40 minor vars.; at least 12 proofs. 3-digit logotypes were
　　in use, so that some few vars. have 47 close, others 47 farther
　　apart. At least 6 vars. show traces of repunching on 1, 18, or
　　84. See next 3.
1894 1847 over small 7. Scarce.
　　Newcomb 2, 31. Usually in low grades; very rare in UNC.

1886 1844 Part of 18 in bust. Proofs only. About 18 known.
　　Breen 8. Serif of 1 protrudes from above end of bust; upper
　　curve of 8 shows just below neck.

1895 1847 Double date, horizontal.

Date first punched to l., then mostly effaced and corrected. Newcomb 3 shows traces of original date at upper l. of digits; Newcomb 1 (with several revs.) shows similar traces at l. bases of all digits.

1896 1847 Double date, vertical.

Newcomb 18, early state. Logotype (containing 184) first entered too high, then corrected. Later die states with this repunching faint command less of a premium.

1897 1847 Thin weak date. Very rare.

Newcomb 17, 36, and unlisteds.

1898 1848 [all kinds 6,415,799 + ?P] Open 4.

Crosslet of 4 distant from base. At least 20 vars., some with traces of repunching on 48 (Newcomb 20); see next.

Ex J. W. Garrett: 194. Courtesy Bowers & Ruddy Galleries, Inc.

1899 1848 Open 4, double date, horizontal.

Date first punched to l., then mostly effaced and corrected. Newcomb 3, 4. Former (much scarcer) has first 8 touching bust.

1900 1848 Closed 4.

Crosslet of 4 long and almost touches base. At least 22 vars., several with traces of repunching on 184, 18, 84 or 4. Possibly 18 proofs.

1901 1848 Small date. 7 known.

Not Mint work; included less for reasons of tradition than to avoid confusing inexperienced collectors. See introductory text. All are in low grades, G to F. 151–159.4 grs. = 9.78–10.33 gms.

1902 1849 [4,178,500 + ?P]

Over 27 vars. Possibly 16–20 proofs.

1903 1849/8 Scarce.

Newcomb 8, early state only. Later states with most traces of 8 gone will price as preceding.

1904 1850 [all kinds 4,426,844 + ?P] Closed 5.

Cusp of 5 touches knob. At least 18 vars.; 8–10 proofs known.

1905 1850 Open 5.

Cusp of 5 well away from knob. At least 7 vars.

Ex J. W. Garrett: 196. Courtesy Bowers & Ruddy Galleries, Inc.

1906 1851 [9,889,707]

Over 50 minor vars. from 43 obv. and 47 rev. dies.

1907 1851/81 Blundered date.

Newcomb 3, early state: See introductory text. Later states, with most of the blunder effaced, command less of a premium. Dangerous forgeries exist; authentication recommended.

1908 1852 [5,063,094 + ?P]

Over 25 minor vars. from 19 obv. and 21 rev. dies; possibly 12 proofs. A few vars. have faint traces of repunching on 52, 18, or 1. See next.

1909 1852 Double date. Rare.

Newcomb 7, earliest state. Date logotype first entered low and to l. of final position, then corrected. Later states, with most of the extra outlines gone, will price as preceding.

1910 1853 [6,641,131]

Over 40 vars. from 37 obv. and 43 rev. dies, several with traces of repunching on one or more digits (Newcomb 4, 9, 19, 22). See next 2.

1911 1853 Double date.

Newcomb 20. Logotype first entered slanting more sharply down to r., then corrected. Another var., Newcomb 10, shows fainter traces of repunching below tops of all digits; this commands less premium.

1912   1853 Obviously repunched 1.
Newcomb 13, 28.

1913   1854 [all kinds 4,236,156 + ?P] 5 4 separated.
Over 28 vars.; 54 closer or more distant.

1914   1854 54 touch each other.
.Newcomb 12. Proofs (possibly 50?) and business strikes.

1915   1855 [all kinds 1,574,829 + ?P] Upright 5's.
12 pairs of dies plus intermulings: 9 pairs with upright 5's, 3 with slanting. See next 3.

1916a   1855 Slanting 5's, 13 stars, normal ear.
Newcomb 9 early state, 10 early state, 11 (proofs only). Over 100 proofs of N-10 (minute die chip on front edge of coronet); business strikes of N-9, 10.

1916b   1855 Slanting 5's, knob on ear.
Newcomb 9 late state. The knob (chip out of die) varies greatly in extent. Date slants far up to r., 5 exceptionally close to star.

1917   1855 Slanting 5's, Twelve stars.
Newcomb 10 late state. See introductory text. Usually proof-like mint state, red or partly red; saved as curiosities?

1918   1856 [all kinds 2,690,463 + ?P] Upright 5.
Mint records say 19 pairs of dies for business strikes (including 8 obvs. with upright 5), a twentieth for proofs.

1919   1856 Italic 5.
12 obv. dies incl. in above; proofs only (over 100 known) of Newcomb 5 (ill.).

Ex J. W. Garrett: 204. Courtesy Bowers & Ruddy Galleries, Inc.

1920   1857 [all kinds 333,456− + 238+P] Large date.
Newcomb 1, business strikes only. From the logotype for half dollars and eagles. Only the earliest state shows tops of extra 18 in dentils below 8: ANACS 1983, p. 40. See introductory text.

1921   1857 Small date.
Business strikes Newcomb 2, 4; proofs Newcomb 3, 5.

1922   1868 Exact type of 1844–57. Copper. Proofs only. 6–8 known.
Judd 610. 1981 ANA:14, $5,300. *Pièce de caprice,* probably made for Mint Director Henry R. Linderman.

1923   1868 Same. Nickel. Proofs only. 4 or 5 known.
Judd 611.

CHAPTER 19

SMALL CENTS

i. LONGACRE'S FLYING EAGLES
(1856–58)

As early as the 1840s, the Mint found that the large copper cents were increasingly unpopular. The coins stimulated adverse criticisms: ugly, too heavy, too often filthy. Many banks and stores refused them (the coins were not legal tender then, though oddly they now are!); others would accept them only at a discount compared to silver or gold, quoting the same merchandise at different prices according to the kind of money tendered for payment. By 1851–53, the 1795 situation had returned: Every 100 cents cost the Mint $1.06+ to coin. Something had to be done, quickly.

As early as 1837, the eccentric New York City dentist Dr. Lewis Feuchtwanger had begun proposing his own alloy as a coinage metal preferable to copper. This was "argentan," alias "American Silver" or German silver, containing copper, nickel, zinc, tin, antimony, and various trace metals, but varying in proportions too much to suit the Mint. We may fairly deduce Feuchtwanger's motives from his repeated offers to sell unlimited quantities to the Mint. During the 1837–44 Hard Times, Feuchtwanger's own small cents circulated freely beside other private tokens, along with irredeemable bank notes and scrip, while the Mint's own coins were hoarded. Understandably, his proposal was remembered in 1850–51 when the issue of replacing the large copper cent became an acute problem.

In 1850, Rep. Samuel Vinton (Whig, Ohio), Chairman of the House Ways and Means Committee, notified the Mint of a proposal to issue ring-shaped cents of billon (10% silver, 90% copper). Four successive Mint Directors (Robert Maskell Patterson, G. N. Eckert, William Pettit, and James Ross Snowden) protested this and later similar proposals on the perfectly reasonable grounds that the cost of manufacturing planchets and ejecting newly struck coins would make such cents an impossible proposition. Racism was also a factor: Annular coins suggested to many the cast brass Chinese cash with their square holes and their minuscule purchasing power.

Meanwhile, Joseph Wharton (then holder of a monopoly on nickel mines in the Western Hemisphere) began writing pamphlets advocating his metal for coinage: It then had no commercial use and was unpopular among metallurgists because it was excessively difficult to work. As Wharton was closely connected with the Mint's ruling families, and moreover had immense political influence, Mint and Treasury authorities paid close attention to all his proposals for the next 30 years.

By late 1853, when the Mint was losing money on every cent it made, and copper blanks threatened to become unobtainable at any price, James C. Booth (then Melter and Refiner, and one of the foremost chemists of his day) proposed two simplified versions of Feuchtwanger's metal, which would also earn

money for Wharton. The lighter-colored of these consisted of 40% nickel, 40% copper, 20% zinc; the darker 30% nickel, 60% copper, 10% zinc. Booth still later attempted a third alloy, 40% nickel, 60% copper. None of these was practical: The two ternary alloys, when bright and new, were easily confused with silver; when dulled, they respectively resembled tin and lead—raising the fear of counterfeits in those metals. Booth's 40-60 cupro-nickel alloy proved impossibly difficult to melt, roll, cut into blanks, and strike; the planchets were hard enough to damage steel dies! Nevertheless, partly because the Mint establishment and Congress were thickly seeded with Wharton's friends, experiments with nickel continued. Protests quickly followed that the metal was justifying its old name *Kupfer-Nickel,* 'devil's copper,' requiring the very fires of hell even to melt!

Finally, in early 1856, Mint Director Snowden (one of Wharton's longtime friends and neighbors from the Delaware Water Gap area of Pennsylvania) decided on an alloy of 88% copper, 12% nickel, at a weight of 72 grs. (4.666 gms. = 80 to the troy pound), for the new cents. In July 1856 he sent the Treasury a batch of 50 half cents struck on blanks of this new alloy, and his congressional friends accordingly pushed through a bill to authorize the new coinage. This became law Feb. 21, 1857.

Snowden approved for these coins a modification of the old Gobrecht flying-eagle motif, which had been appearing on many pattern cents of 1854–55. The rev. device was Longacre's wreath, originally used in 1854 for the $3 and large-size $1 gold coins. During the remainder of the year many hundreds of 1856 Flying Eagle cents were made. We have not been able to learn exactly how many, but Archives records show that at least 634 were passed out in that year to Treasury officials, senators, representatives, and other VIPs; hundreds more were certainly made, and probably over a thousand restrikes in 1858–59 from dies dated 1856. Not all restrikes can be distinguished from originals.

The 1856 Flying Eagle cents successively became prized souvenirs, collectibles, and objects of hoarding. George W. Rice (onetime ANA Secretary) owned 756 specimens. Many of these doubtless found their way into Col. John A. Beck's hoard (accumulated in the 1920s and held until 1974 in the Mellon National Bank of Pittsburgh). Many of Beck's had evidently come from circulation, as the part of the hoard I examined in Nov. 1974 consisted largely of low-grade survivors. A more comprehensive history and review of this issue is in Breen {1977}, Chap. XV.

On May 25, 1857, when the new Flying Eagle cents were ready for initial quantity distribution, Mint Director Snowden ordered two booths to be set up in the Mint yard, with signs reading, respectively, CENTS FOR CENTS and CENTS FOR SILVER, and that the Mint's gates be opened to the public. Newspapers carried press releases about the new cents (thereafter popularly called "nickels" or "nicks" for short), which were to be exchanged at these booths for old copper cents and worn-out or cut-up foreign silver coins. People queued up in lines blocks long to make the exchanges. Thousands of the new cents were saved as souvenirs; uncirculated survivors are plentiful even today at a price.

Snowden believed he was ridding the country of the twin nuisances of filthy old cents and of fractional foreign silver of dubious value (much of it counterfeit, even the genuine often worn far below bullion value). As with many of this stubborn bureaucrat's other projects, this was a gross error: Snowden was merely trading a tolerable nuisance for a worse one. The foreign silver coins had been legal tender, receivable for all kinds of payments including postage stamps and some taxes; the nickel cents were not. They quickly filled shopkeepers' cashboxes to the exclusion of almost everything else; they began to be legally refused in trade. Cartloads of complaints reached the Mint, but nothing was done, either to make the new cents legal tender (they did not become so until PL 89-81, the Coinage Act of 1965!), or about stopping the exchanges. This, even before the scandal about the "1804" dollars (see Chap. 29, Sect. iv), represented the beginning of the Mint's decades-long foul repute. Taxay {1966}, pp. 232–241.

As with the large cents since late 1839, dies were completely hubbed except for dates. Vars. are mostly minor except for the change in letter size and the two rev. hubs.

Proofs of 1857–58 are finally achieving recognition as rarities. For many generations they were undervalued in comparison to the 1856, partly because they came up too seldom to be touted as rare, partly because of the enormous collector demand for the 1856 in any grade as a date.

Sharp UNC. business strikings of 1857–58, with full feather and leaf details, are seldom offered. The usual weaker strikings eventually stimulated Snowden to authorize a design change late in 1858, to the first "Indian" head type: See following section.

LONGACRE'S FLYING EAGLES

Designer, Engraver, James Barton Longacre, obv. after Gobrecht, after Titian Peale. Mint, Philadelphia. Composition, copper 88%, nickel 12%. Diameter, 3/4" = 19 mm. Weight standard, 72 ± 4 grs. = 4.666 ± 0.259 gms. Authorizing act, Feb. 21, 1857.

Grade range, POOR to UNC. GOOD: Devices outlined; date and all letters legible, though tending to blur into rims. VERY GOOD: Eye clear; few feather and leaf details. FINE: Feather ends in tail and wing at r. all distinct. VERY FINE: Over half wing-feather and wreath details, complete tail-feather details. EXTREMELY FINE: Few tiny isolated rubbed spots only. EXCEPTIONS: Many unworn 1856 coins are undecidable if made as proofs or business strikes. Business strikes of 1857–58 are often weak at parts of tail and wingtip and some leaves, but surfaces will fit higher grade. However, even the weakest uncirculated ones will usually have full breast feathers.

1924   1856 [all kinds 634+] High leaf at C, low leaf at T.
Judd 180. Breen 1-B, 2-B have thin date and open 6 (enl. photos); Breen 5-D has heavier date, closed 6, knob touching

loop. Rarely with minute center dot above N. (Breen {1977}, Chap. XV.) Compare next 2.

1925   1856 Similar. Both leaves low; wide open E's. Rare.
Judd 180. Thin shallow date, open 6. Breen 2-C. Enl. photos.

1926   1856 Similar. Both leaves high.
Judd 180. Center dot just below serif of N. Breen 3-D, 4-D, 5-D. Over half the survivors of this date are Breen 5-D's. Beware alterations from 1858: Shape of 5 on all genuine 1856's is as in enl. ills. above; 5's on 1857 and 1858 coins are as in ills. below. ANACS {1983}, p. 43.

Omitted vars. are known only from copper strikings, or only in noncirculating pattern combinations, including the dateless coins and those with garnished shield rev., all believed 1858–59 products, all very rare. Enl. photos.

1927   1857 [all kinds 17,450,000 + ?P] Closed E in ONE.
Relief veins in maple leaves; high leaves at C T; see ill. at **1930.** Proofs have die file marks above NI; under 12 traced. Counterfeits from spark erosion dies have short raised vertical line between 57 and minute raised lumps on ONE CENT.
1928   1857 Wide open E's in ONE CENT.
Incised veins in maple leaves; low leaves at C T; see ill. at **1933.** Minor doubled obv. dies are known. ANACS {1983}, p. 42; Wexler {1984}.
1929   1857 Double date. Very rare.
Several positional vars. CW 5/13/70:61. Not examined recently enough to tell which rev.

Courtesy ANACS

1930 1858 [all kinds 24,600,000 + ?P] Large letters, nearly closed E in ONE.
Rev. as **1927.** Under 20 proofs traced (enl. photos).

1931 1858/7 Same type rev. Rare.
Always with broken wingtip and tiny triangular chip in field midway between date and abdomen. Early states (most of top of 7 present) are much rarer than later states (only top r. corner of 7 showing); latter are weak at date and letters and usually in low grades.

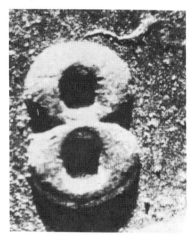

1932 1858 Large letters; rev. wide open E's. Rare.
NN 60:534.
1933 1858 Small letters; rev. wide open E's. Very rare.
A M apart, unlike any preceding. Business strikes and proofs, some of the latter from prototype rev. of **1925.** Enl. photos.

1934 1858 Small letters; rev. closed E's.
Business strikes and proofs [80+?]. Minor doubled obv. dies are known: Wexler {1984}.
1935 1858 First Transitional Type. Leaves in clusters of 5. [60+ P?]
Judd 191A. Regular obv., small letters. Prototype rev. of 1859 design. U normal or lacking inner r. serif. Included in

regular sets of 12 pattern flying-eagle cents: See introductory text of following section. Compare next 2.

1936 1858 Similar, leaves in clusters of 6. Proofs only.
Judd 191B. Adopted rev. of 1859.
1937 1858 Large letters; leaves in clusters of 5. Proofs only. Ex. rare.
Judd 196. May also exist with leaves in clusters of 6.

ii. LONGACRE'S COPPER-NICKEL "INDIANS," NO SHIELD (1858–59)

Probably owing to the characteristic weakness of striking of the Flying Eagle cents (at eagle's head, tail, and wingtips, the areas of wreath directly opposite these, and sometimes elsewhere), Mint Director Snowden directed Longacre to prepare other cent designs, one of which would replace the Flying Eagle as of Jan. 1, 1859.

The result was some 60–100 12-piece sets of pattern cents. These comprised three obvs. (flying eagle with small letters, smaller eagle, and "Indian" head), each combined with four revs. (adopted "cereals" type of 1857; oak wreath without shield; oak wreath with rococo ornamental or "garnished" shield; and adopted "laurel" [olive?] wreath of 1859). One of the 12 in each set was thus identical to the regular issues of 1858; three others qualified as transitional types (combinations of designs adopted and to be adopted), one of the latter becoming Snowden's eventual choice. A very few sets were made up with another flying-eagle die having large letters.

These sets were sold to collectors; few remain intact because customers broke them up almost at once, inserting brilliant proof cents of regular or transitional designs into date sets, leaving the rest with their groups of patterns.

Several hundred extras were made of the transitional designs, most of all of the type finally adopted. Of this last there were at least three obv. dies, differing primarily in date position; they come in proof state and as business strikes. Many of the latter occur in F to EF grades, evidently spent by Treasury or VIP recipients; others were sold or traded to collectors, particularly for Washington medals—the Director's hobbyhorse (he was then working on his magnum opus: Snowden {1861}) and official excuse for all such sales of offbeat "cabinet coins." Snowden apparently chose the "Indian"/laurel wreath combination because it was in lowest relief of all the candidates, striking up better than some others.

The myth of Longacre's "Indian" cent model has been retold for generations. Obviously no Native American profile, this was evidently a white female, and early legend had it that she was the Engraver's little daughter Sarah (later Mrs. Sarah Longacre Keen), supposedly sketched while playing with a toy warbonnet. Mrs. Keen herself came to believe the story. Unfortunately for legends and illusions and childhood memories, this identical profile recurs—with many different headdresses—in Longacre's sketchbooks from 10 years earlier, always with the same adult proportions, always with the same long "Greek" nose forming an approximately straight line from tip to forelock. Longacre himself referred to this profile in letters and official memoranda (in the National Archives) as that of the *Venus Accroupie,* 'Crouching Venus,' apparently one of the Greco-Roman statues of Venus then housed in a Philadelphia museum. He first placed it on the 1849 gold dollar, then on the 1849 double eagle, later on the 1854 three-dollar piece and the second and third gold dollar designs (1854, 1856), before modifying the headdress for the cent to give it "a more national character."

The 1859 cents are remarkably uniform except for one very rare corrected blunder (the Double Date); they normally come softly struck, with feather and curl details not as sharp as on later issues. This may account for Snowden's decision to change the design again late in the same year: See following section. With the adoption of the oak wreath and shield of 1860, the laurel wreath vanished from American coin designs as a major design, not to return except on the nickel 3¢ pieces of 1865–89.

These copper-nickel "Indians" did not become legal tender until 1965 (PL 89–81).

LONGACRE'S COPPER-NICKEL "INDIANS," NO SHIELD

Designer, Engraver, James Barton Longacre. Mint, Philadelphia. Composition, Physical Specifications, Authorizing Acts, as preceding.

Grade range, FAIR to UNC. GOOD: Date and all letters legible except LIBERTY; devices outlined. VERY GOOD: At least LI Y or L TY or parts of LI TY show. FINE: Full LIBERTY. VERY FINE: About half hair details, over half feather details. EXTREMELY FINE: Few tiny isolated rubbed spots only. EXCEPTIONS: Even mint-state survivors sometimes show soft feather details; weak areas should show mint luster.

1938   1858 Second Transitional. Low date; rev. wide open E's. Proofs only.
Judd 213. Rev. of **1925**. Base of 1 much nearer border than top of 1 is to bust.

1939   1858 Similar. Centered date; rev. wide open E's. Proofs only.
May also exist with closed E rev. of **1927**.
1940   1858 Prototype. Centered date; leaves in clusters of 5. Proofs only.
Judd 208. Base of 1 about as far from border as top of 1 is from bust. 2 obv. dies. Enl. photos.

1941   1858 Centered date; leaves in clusters of 6.
Found in all grades. The 2 types of wreath (this and preceding) first publicized in Hetherington:529–30, but forgotten until this writer described them in the 1971 ANA offering of the Blaisdell pattern cents. See ill. at **1943**.
1942   1858 Low date; leaves in clusters of 5. Rare.
Auction 82:834, "UNC.," $750; also comes in proof state.
1943   1858 Low date; leaves in clusters of 6. Rare.
Found in all grades and in proof state. Enl. photos.

1944   1859 Leaves in clusters of 6. [36,400,000 + 800+P]
180 pairs of dies, averaging over 200,000 impressions per pair. Many minute positional vars. Often weakly struck. Proofs are rarer than the mintage figure suggests; probably many were melted or spent. Proofs may exist with leaves in clusters of 5.

1945   1859 Obvious double date. 4–6 known.
Discovered by this writer (1953); first ill., *Coins* 11/76, p. 49. The coin here ill. is 1977 ANA:474. Other less obvious repunched dates bring less.

iii. LONGACRE'S COPPER-NICKEL "INDIANS" WITH SHIELD (1859–64)

Late in 1859, apparently to remedy imperfect striking quality of the existing cent devices, Mint Director Snowden again ordered Longacre to submit alternative rev. designs, one of which would be adopted Jan. 1, 1860. Snowden's choice proved to be a new device: ONE CENT within oak wreath, small shield above, evidently in preference to Longacre's 1856–59 rococo "garnished" shield pattern.

Many hundreds were struck from the prototype dies, almost all in business strike form; I have seen only two proofs. Their VIP recipients spent them, so that many survivors are in F to EF grades. At coin shows in the 1950s I used to cherrypick transitional 1859's from groups of regular cents; nobody then cared enough to turn them over! More recently, these have become recognized as an interesting adjunct to the regular series, like the 1882 nickels without CENTS.

Two obv. hubs are known for 1860, the earlier and far rarer one (sharp pointed bust) the same one used for 1858–59 "Indians," the later one (rounded tip to bust) continuing into 1864. No information is available about the time of change or the quantities struck.

By late 1860 banks and merchants were learning that Snowden's exchanges had flung more cents into circulation than could be conveniently absorbed. After the New York banks suspended specie payments, Dec. 28, 1860, silver and gold coins vanished from circulation. Storekeepers were faced with the dismal prospect of accepting bags of cents or piles of irredeemable "shinplasters" (scrip and wildcat bank notes). It did not help at all that cents (not legal tender until 1965) were legally refusable; neither merchants nor the general public had anything else. For a few months, supplies of silver 3¢ coins and gold dollars helped slightly, but then they too vanished.

Congress, believing that Snowden's withdrawal of legal-tender foreign silver coins from circulation might have worsened this situation, repealed the clause in the Act of Feb. 21, 1857 which had authorized the practice. Nevertheless, Snowden went on buying dwindling supplies of foreign silver coins with nickel cents for another year, until Lincoln replaced him in office with nickel's bitter opponent James Pollock.

However, by Dec. 1862, even the nickel cents had disappeared from circulation. By 1863, what the average working citizen was likely to find in his pocket or pay envelope was a variety of "shinplasters", tattered federal fractional currency, and privately made cent-sized "copperhead" tokens (now called Civil War tokens), many without issuer's name or address. No law then existed against circulation of even irredeemable tokens or paper notes.

In the meantime, Joseph Wharton, the nickel promoter, had gone to Canada to open up new nickel mines, but at first even these failed to provide enough ore to fill mint orders, and the price went up so high that cents once again cost more than face value to produce: 1795 and 1853 again, only worse. Even more excruciatingly from the government's side, nickel ore had to be paid for in full, in advance, and in gold: and the Treasury had little to spare of that beyond what had to go to munitions makers for the Union Army.

The result (as again in 1942) was a variety of further experiments: thinner nickel, aluminum, aluminum-bronze, oroide (a brassy costume jewelry alloy, named after its alleged resemblance to gold), pure copper in various weights. Finally, Mint Director Pollock, inspired by seeing thousands of vars. of "copperheads" freely circulating while legal nickel cents vanished,

decided "when you can't lick 'em, join 'em," and recommended that Congress authorize issue of cents in "French bronze" at 48 grs. apiece: close to the average weight of the "copperheads." "French bronze" was legally defined as a mixture of 95% copper, 5% tin and zinc (proportions to be determined by the Director). Cents would henceforth have limited legal-tender quality, and private tokens would no longer be legal to issue. This became law April 22, 1864. However, a few copper-nickel blanks remained in the hoppers, and a few cents of 1864 L and 1865 are known on them, e.g., Dr. J. H. Litman's double-struck 1865 (*Mint Error Collector Bulletin* v2n1, 1/58). The 1863 L coins are thought to have been made later as *pièces de caprice*.

Owing to hoarding activities during the Civil War, uncirculated nickel cents of 1860–64 are still plentiful; occasional bags of 100 or 500 were still encountered during the 1950s, but they have been long since dispersed. The extra premiums on 1861 and 1864 derive more from comparative mintage figures than from actual scarcity.

LONGACRE'S COPPER-NICKEL "INDIANS" WITH SHIELD

Designer, Engraver, Mint, Physical Specifications, Authorizing Acts, as previously.

Grade Range, Grading Standards, as previously. EXCEPTION: Mint-state specimens often show weakness on feather tips; specimens sharply enough struck to show all four diamonds on ribbon will command higher premiums.

I. HUB of 1858: Pointed Tip to Bust, No L on Ribbon

1946 1859 Prototype. Very scarce. [100+ + ?P]
Judd 228. Usually UNC., sometimes worn; only 2 proofs seen.

1947 1860 Pointed bust. Very rare.
Same hub as 1858–59; tip of bust has *sharp* point. Proofs and business strikes. Not to be confused with next.

Courtesy Don Slouffman, Paramount Coin Corp.

II. HUB of 1860–64: Rounded Tip to Bust, No L on Ribbon

1948 1860 [all kinds 20,566,000 + 542+P]

Proofs and business strikes. Actual number of proofs made was in excess of the 1,000 included in silver sets (cent to dollar). Some 514 were sold with the sets, 28+ individually, others melted. Enl. photos.

1949 1861 [10,100,000 + 400+P]

Same comment as to preceding, except that of the original 1,000+ proofs, over 600 were melted with unsold sets. 92 obv. dies, 85 revs.

1950 1862 [28,075,000 + 550+P]

Usually with light date, less often with heavy 2 or heavy date. 197 obvs., 396 revs.

1951 1863 [49,840,000 + 460+P]

Minor positional vars. only; probably over 250 pairs of dies.

1952 1863 Reeded edge. 4 proofs known.

Judd 300. Kosoff Estate: 1051–52, $1,045, $715. Business strikes also exist, but their reeded edges differ and were probably applied outside the mint.

1953 1863 L Pointed bust. Proofs only. 4 or 5 known.

Judd 302. Hub of 1864; possibly struck in 1864–65. L = Longacre. For the bronze specimens see following section. Enl. photos.

1954 1864 No L. Rounded tip to bust. [13,740,000 + 370+P]

Often weak. The proof mintage figure represents the number of silver sets issued (including cents) before bronze cents were authorized.

1955 1864 Similar, partly repunched date. Rare.

NN 57:53; 1983 Midwinter ANA:133, repunched 86. Other vars. probably exist, perhaps from dies also used for bronze strikings.

1956 1864 L Pointed bust. Ex. rare.

Judd 358. See ill. at **1961** for a bronze proof from the same dies as the copper-nickel proofs. 1977 ANA:2168A. Circulated specimens are thought to have been struck on leftover nickel blanks after April 1864.

1957 1865 Ex. rare.

Judd 404. Same comments as to last. None examined recently enough to say if from Plain 5 or Fancy 5 date logotype. Judd mentions 3 vars. and thin flan proofs (46.6 grs. = 3.02 gms.).

iv. LONGACRE'S BRONZE "INDIANS" (1864–1909)

Mint Director Pollock's objections to nickel as a coinage metal were based on many reasons: It was difficult to melt and more difficult to work, it was hard enough that the planchets damaged dies, and perhaps worst of all, it had become so expensive that nickel cents cost more than face value to make. This was independent of his political opposition to Joseph Wharton, nickel's monopolist and promoter. Accordingly, Pollock pushed his friends in the Senate and House to hasten passage of a bill to authorize cent and 2¢ coinage in "French bronze" (see preceding section), which became the Act of April 22, 1864. These pieces were to have a limited legal-tender quality, unlike any of their predecessors: a provision of dubious constitutionality.

Earlier cents coined under this new act are from the same hub seen on 1860–64 nickel cents, with rounded tip to bust, and no engraver's initial. Later ones (at least 18 obv. dies, probably more) show a narrower, sharper bust point and Longacre's initial L on ribbon: the famous 1864 L cents. These are common in ordinary grades (mostly too worn for the L to show), but scarcer in EF to UNC. Many evidently went to England during and after the Civil War, as during 1950–70 thousands of specimens were retrieved there in all grades. The L continued on all cents of this design through 1909.

On Jan. 18, 1873, Chief Coiner Archibald Loudon Snowden formally complained about the "closed" 3's on date logotypes, correctly alleging that on small denominations the 3 could be mistaken for an 8. The Director at once ordered the Engraving Department to prepare new "open 3" logotypes for all denominations.

Minor coinage was interrupted from Feb. 16, 1885, until late in 1886, explaining limited quantities minted for both dates.

A new obv. hub was introduced in 1886, producing two vars. of that year, generally referred to as "Type II." This hub, by Charles E. Barber, is a slavish copy of the Longacre design in minutely lower relief. A roll of uncirculated 1886 Type II's (50 pieces) brought $30,000 in Auction 81:593.

Most planchets 1864–1907 had come from Scovill's mint in Waterbury. Beginning sometime in 1908, the Philadelphia Mint resumed manufacture of its own blanks. These cannot readily be distinguished. *NUM* 3/08, p. 92.

The first San Francisco cents appeared in Nov. 1908.

The whole series of bronze "Indians" remained for some years under a cloud, owing to numerous counterfeits of 1877 and 1909 S, and a smaller number of genuine 1909 cents with false S mintmarks cemented on. The fake 1877's differ in position of 7's from the genuine. Though these were readily identified, more dangerous forgeries have since appeared, particularly of 1864 L, 1866–78, 1908 S, 1909 S. Authentication is recommended. See also ANACS {1983}, pp. 44–47.

Until recent decades, few collectors studied this series more than superficially; this is why neither the overdates nor the 1873 Double LIBERTY were discovered until the 1950s and later. As it was to the Mint's advantage to maximize stereotypy, so it is to the collector's advantage to find out where the Mint had failed to do so. That way there is more fun to the game.

LONGACRE'S BRONZE "INDIANS"

Designer, James Barton Longacre. Engravers, Longacre and assistants; Hub of 1886 by Charles E. Barber. Mints, Philadelphia (no mintmark), San Francisco (mintmark S on lower rev.). Composition, "French bronze" = 95% copper, 5% tin and zinc. Diameter, 3/4″ = 19 mm. Weight standard, 48 ± 4 grs. = 3.11 ± 0.26 gms. through 3/31/1873; later, 48 ± 2 grs. = 3.11 ± 0.13 gms.

Grade range, POOR to UNC. Grading standards, Exceptions, as previously.

I. HUB of 1860–64: Rounded Tip to Bust

1958 1863 No L. Prototype. [100+P]
Judd 299. 48–49.8 grs. = 3.11–3.23 gms. Dies generally aligned 180° from normal. Possibly over 200 proofs exist; some circulated survivors, no business strikes. Thick-flan specimens, said to be pure copper, 65–74.6 grs. = 4.21–4.83 gms., are frankly experimental and very rare.

1959 1864 [all kinds 39,233,714 + 100+P] No L.
Mint report includes 1864 L. Various minor repunchings on dates. At least 100 proofs were with the sets issued in July 1864.

II. HUB of 1864–86: Pointed Bust, L on Ribbon

1960 1863 L. [?P] 4 or 5 proofs known.
Judd 301. Same dies as **1953.**

1961 1864 L. [Incl. in **1959** mintage]
At least 18 obv. dies differing in date positions and minor repunchings. Enl. photo is of a proof; note long spine on neck below ear (not found on business strikes). About 10 proofs known.

Note location of L, almost in straight line between O(F) and 4, or between final S and final A. Specimens too worn to show L (G or VG) are identifiable by shape of bust point, but will price as **1959.**

1962 1864 L. Obvious double date. Very scarce.

1963 1865 [all kinds 35,429,286 + 500+P] Fancy 5.
Rounded knob to 6. Business strikes only. Various minor repunchings at date. Distinctly scarcer than Plain 5. Proof mintage (plain 5) based on number of silver sets issued.

1964 1865/4 Fancy 5. Ex. rare.
Earliest die states show corner of 4 between 65 and part of crossbar. 2 vars.

1965 1865 Plain 5.
Flat knob to 6, ending in a point. Business strikes and proofs, latter usually dull. The tiny lump on 8 is in the date logotype and shows on all Plain 5 coins, both cents, and 2¢. Minor date repunchings exist; but see next.

1966 1865/4 Plain 5. As ill. Ex. rare.
ANACS 10-5-77-H(5A).

Courtesy ANACS

1967 1865 Plain 5. Obvious multiple-punched date. 2 vars. Very rare.

1968 1866 [9,826,500 + 725+P]
Proof mintage represents number of silver sets.

1969 1866 Final 6 plainly repunched.
Top of extra 6 high. Sometimes called "1866/6."

1970 1866 Repunched 66. Rare.
Date first entered to r. of final position, then corrected.

1971 1866 Doubled obv. die. Very rare.
Doubling plainest at LIBERTY. "Charmont":1327.

1972 1867 [9,821,000 + 625+P]
Normal or with various minor date repunchings. Authentication recommended. ANACS {1983}, pp. 44–45. Proof mintage represents number of silver sets.

1973 1867 Strongly repunched 1. Very scarce.
Ivy Cambridge:118.

1974   1867 over "small" 67. Scarce.

Top of the original or smaller 7 differs slightly in shape from the final 7. Discovered by Q. David Bowers, early 1959: *Empire Topics* 5 (Feb.–March 1959).

1975   1868 [10,266,500 + 600+P]

Various minor repunchings on dates. Proofs sometimes have dies aligned 180° from normal. Proof mintage represents number of silver sets. Authentication recommended; see ANACS {1983}, pp. 44–45.

1976   1869 [6,420,000 + 600+P]

Proof mintage represents number of silver sets. Authentication recommended.

1977   1869/69 Scarce.

Business strikes only. Discovered by this writer about 1953. Rare earliest states show part of 8 within 9 ("1869/9/8"); later states do not. Not to be confused with next. Authentication recommended.

Courtesy ANACS

1978   1869/8 Ex. rare.

2 die vars., both with part of extra loop of 8 but not extra knob to 9. Long controversial. Business strikes only; usually in low grades. Discovered by this writer about 1954. Cf. 1982 ANA:117 (UNC., $900); Ivy Cambridge:124. Authentication recommended.

1979   1870 [5,275,000 + 1,000+P]

Minor positional vars. of business strikes, one with repunching atop 1, which fades. Proof mintage represents number of silver sets.

1980   1871 [all kinds 3,929,500 + 960+P] 71 about touch.

Date logotype as on 2¢. Proofs and business strikes. Proof mintage represents number of silver sets. Authentication recommended.

1981   1871 7 1 apart.

Date logotype as on later 2¢. Proofs and business strikes. Enl. photo. Authentication recommended.

1982   1872 [all kinds 4,042,000 + 950+P] Heavy date, 18 touch.

Proofs and business strikes. Proof mintage represents number of silver sets.

1983   1872 Thinner numerals, 1 8 apart.

Business strikes only to date. Dates in straight line 1872–1880.

1984   1872 Heavily repunched 2 ("1872/2"). Very rare.

1983 Midwinter ANA:145. Later states with only fainter traces of extra 2 price as preceding.

1985   1873 Closed 3. [1,002,000 + 1,100+P] Normal.

Business strikes and proofs. Proof mintage represents number of silver sets. For explanation of Closed and Open 3's see introductory text. Enl. photo.

1986   1873 Closed 3. Double LIBERTY. Very scarce.

Double entry from obv. hub; doubling also on eye, feathers, etc. Later, die cracked through base of date. Wexler {1984}. Discovered by this writer about 1957. Business strikes only; usually in low grades. Possible finest known, Hinman, "Century," Harte III:6, nearly UNC., cleaned. A second obv. has minor doubling only on ERTY and some feathers; this is rare but less obvious and has commanded less of a premium.

1987 1873 Open 3. [10,674,500]
Business strikes only. Minor date repunchings. Enl. photo. Permitted weight deviation hereafter ± 2 grs. = ± 0.13 gms.

1988 1874 [14,187,500 + 700+P]
Proof mintage represents number of silver sets. 69 obvs., 93 revs.
1989 1874 Obviously doubled 4. Proofs only. Very rare.
The 4 was first punched too low. Found on a tiny minority of proofs.
1990 1875 [13,528,000 + 700+P]
Proof mintage represents number of silver sets. Normal or with traces of partial date repunching. 68 obvs., 99 revs.
1991 1875 Obvious repunching at bases of 18. Rare.
Later states, with most traces faint or gone, price as preceding.
1992 1875 Plainly doubled 5. Proofs only. Rare.
Top of extra 5 above 5. Forms a small minority of proofs.
1993 1876 [7,944,000 + 1,150+P] Small knob to 6.
Proof mintage represents number of silver sets. 39 obvs., 53 revs. Also reported with large knob to 6 (one of the dime date logotypes); these are hard to distinguish and price the same.
1994 1877 [852,500 + 510+P]
Proof mintage represents number of silver sets. 3 obvs., 2 revs. + 4 revs. left over from 1876 (were these all used?). Authentication recommended; see ANACS {1983}, pp. 46–47.
1995 1878 [5,797,500 + 2,350P]
Proofs occasionally show double base to 1.
1996 1879 [16,228,000 + 3,200P]
Same comment; "Charmont":1369.
1997 1879 Double date, plainest on 8 9. Proofs only. Rare.
Forms only a small minority of proofs.
1998 1880 [38,961,000 + 3,955P]
Proofs sometimes show traces of repunching on second 8. A minor doubled obv. die is known: Wexler {1984}.
1999 1881 [39,208,000 + 3,575P]
Numerals always irregularly placed, the 81 out of line with 18, in an attempt to make a curved date out of a straight logotype.
2000 1881 Bases of 1's plainly repunched. Proofs only. Rare. 1982 ANA:1632, others.
2001 1881 Final 1 obviously repunched. Rare.
2 or 3 vars., business strikes and proofs. Other less obvious date repunchings are less rare and command lower premiums.
2002 1882 [38,578,000 + 3,100P]
2003 1883 [45,591,500 + 6,609P]
Proofs of this and following dates through 1886 are often iridescently toned, from holdings by the late Wayte Raymond.
2004 1883 Plainly repunched 3. Proofs only. Rare.
Forms only a small minority of proofs.

2005 1883, second 8 over 7. Ex. rare.
Discovered by Bill Fivaz. Probably was 1883/79.

2006 1884 [23,257,800 + 3,942P]
2007 1885 [11,761,594 + 3,790P]
Some proofs show traces of repunching on 5. Ivy Cambridge:161.
2008 1886 [all kinds 17,650,000 + 4,290P] "Type I."
Feathers placed as before, lowest points to C; final A close to curl. Proofs and business strikes.

III. HUB of 1887–1909: Lowest Feather to A

2009 1886 "Type II."
Lowest feather to A; final A distant from curl. Proofs and business strikes. First publicized by James Reynolds, Flint, Mich., *NSM* 8/54, p. 920. See introductory text.
2010 1887 [45,223,523 + 2,960P]
A minor doubled obv. die is known. Wexler {1984}.
2011 1888 [37,489,832 + 4,592P]
2012 1888/7 Very rare.
Business strikes only. Almost always with break in dentils above TE(D). Discovered by James F. Ruddy about 1970. Usually in low grades.

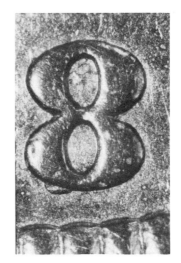

Courtesy Ted Clark

2013 1888 Last two 8's obviously repunched. Very rare.
Discovered by Delma K. Romines, 1979.
2014 1889 [48,866,025 + 3,336P]

2015 1889 Obviously repunched 9. Very rare.
Discovered by Bill Fivaz.

2016 1889 Obvious double date. Ex. rare.
Discovered by Bill Fivaz. *ETCM* 4/77, p. 27.
2017 1890 [57,180,114 + 2,740P]
2018 1891 [47,070,000 + 2,350P]
2019 1891 Double-punched 91. Very rare.

2020 1891 Double date. Very rare.
2021 1892 [37,647,087 + 2,745P]
Several vars. of partly repunched dates, none obvious. Some proofs show traces of repunching on base of 1: 1983 Midwinter ANA:1979.
2022 1893 [46,640,000 + 2,195P]
2023 1894 [16,749,500 + 2,632P]
2024 1894 Obvious double date. Very scarce.

2025 1895 [38,341,474 + 2,062P]
2026 1895 Partly repunched date. Proofs only.
The var. with repunching on 1 9 ("Charmont":1419) may be an earlier state of that with repunched 9 (LM 11/65:173). Compare next.
2027 1895 Plainly repunched 895. Very scarce.
Price for vars. ill., a) with traces of third 5 far too high, or b) date first entered well to r. Another, less obvious, occurs on proofs (NN 51:749); almost equally rare.

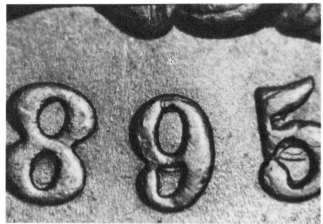

2028 1896 [39,055,431 + 1,862P]
Normal or with minor partial date repunching.
2029 1897 [50,464,392 + 1,938P]
Proofs sometimes show traces of repunching on base of 1.
2030 1897 Base of extra 1 protrudes from throat. Very rare.
Discovered by Jack Beymer.
2031 1898 [49,821,284 + 1,795P]
2032 1899 [53,598,000 + 2,031P]
2033 1899/7 (?) Very rare.
Discovered by Bill Fivaz. Compare next.

Courtesy Alan Herbert

2034 1899 Obviously repunched final 9. Rare.
2035 1899 Obvious double date. Ex. rare.
Entire date first entered well to r., then corrected. 1983 Midwinter ANA:196.

2036   1900 [66,831,502 + 2,262P]
Proofs occasionally show minor repunching at bases of 19. 1983 Midwinter ANA:205.
2037   1901 [79,609,158 + 1,985P]
Occasional minor traces of repunching on dates 1901–7.
2038   1902 [87,374,704 + 2,018P]
Proofs 1902–9 of this design have devices semibrilliant, not frosted; fields remain mirrorlike as before.
2039   1903 [85,092,703 + 1,790P]
2040   1903 Obviously repunched 3. Very rare.
Discovered by Bill Fivaz. At least 2 vars.

2041   1904 [61,326,198 + 1,817P]
2042   1905 [80,717,011 + 2,152P]
2043   1906 [96,020,530 + 1,725P] Closed 6.
Knob of 6 heavy and touches loop. Proofs and business strikes.
2044   1906 Open 6.
Knob of 6 smaller, away from loop. It is uncertain if this represents a different logotype, a repolished die, or a weaker impression.
2045   1907 [108,137,143 + 1,475P]
2046   1907 Triple 7. Rare.

2047   1907 "Large over small date." Very rare.
Original date apparently wider spaced. Publicized by Alan Herbert. Other partial or minor repunchings of dates have attracted less collector attention.

2048   1908 [32,326,317 + 1,620P]
2049   1908 S [1,115,000]
Minor positional vars., 2 with traces of repunching on S. Beware of specimens made by cementing an S to genuine Philadelphia coins. Authentication recommended.
2050   1909 [14,368,470 + 2,175P]
2051   1909 S [309,000]
Mintmark is from same punch as on 1908 S. Beware of cast counterfeits, fakes struck from false dies, and genuine Philadelphia coins with false S mintmarks cemented on. Authentication is urgently recommended. Pristine mint-state specimens are ordinarily pale golden yellow, often weak but with mint frost on the weak areas.

v. BRENNER'S "WHEAT EAR" LINCOLNS (1909–58)

We owe the Lincoln design to a coincidence. The Lithuanian immigrant sculptor Victor David Brenner developed an obsession with the martyred President, and during the years just before Lincoln's birth centennial he modeled portrait medals and plaques. These came to the attention of Pres. Theodore Roosevelt, and probably played a part in Brenner's winning a commission to portray him on the Panama Canal service medal. During the sittings, Brenner became a close friend of Roosevelt. The President confided in Brenner about his "pet crime" (improving all our coin designs, favoring domestic artists above Mint Engraver Barber's mediocrity), and invited him to submit cent models.

Brenner's original cent rev. copied the then current French 2-franc piece. The moment that Mint Director Leach found this out, he used the fact as an excuse to reject the new design. Undaunted, Brenner brought the Mint Bureau a new rev. on Feb. 17, 1909; this featured two stylized ears of durum wheat (the kind used today in making spaghetti). Brenner had signed his full name on the obv. model, but on Leach's orders he removed his signature, substituting V.D.B. at bottom rev. Owing largely to pressure from the White House, this version was approved, and the new cents appeared on Aug. 2, 1909. Newspaper attacks on the use of the initials promptly followed, and people hoarded the new coins as souvenirs, correctly expecting that later cents would drop the initials. An alternative proposal to substitute a modest B on truncation of shoulder was so strongly objected to by Barber, on grounds then obscure, that Brenner's signature in any form was dropped instead. (After all, Barber had been using an initial B on the truncation of his silver coins since 1892, and it would not do for anyone to mistake his designs for Brenner's or vice versa.) Brenner's initials were not restored until Jan. 1918, a convenient few months after Barber's death; they remain there today, on lower edge of truncation, about 7 o'clock. Taxay {1966}, pp. 330–38.

Barber modified the portrait in 1916: Lincoln's coat and cheeks are less wrinkled; the vigor of the design is attenuated.

In this period the best known rarities are some of the matte proofs: ultrasharp medallic impressions, struck twice or more from the dies and given special finishes for collectors, notably 1909 V.D.B., 1915–16, and the clandestine 1917. These normally come stained from the sulfite-containing paper in which the Mint shipped proof sets; the inevitable result has been cleaning, sometimes so drastic as to render their proof status forever undecidable. See Breen {1977}, pp. 211–19; Albright {1983}. Authentication is urgently recommended.

The 1909 S V.D.B. has been extensively counterfeited, earlier by casting and by inserting spurious S mintmarks onto genuine cents, more recently by dangerously deceptive false dies. ANACS {1983}, pp. 48–51. Uncirculated specimens with dash-shaped rim nick above I(N) and acute accent-shaped rim nick above (W)E are among these last: CW 2/9/83, p. 1. Authentication of this date is mandatory.

Many mintmarked issues through the 1920s are comparatively weak on hair details, even in mint state; sharp strikings of some of these can almost be called rare, and they bring premiums several times as high as ordinary uncirculated impressions even of the same color and surface.

A rarity of another kind is the 1922 "Plain," a genuine emergency issue caused by a collision between Denver Mint necessity and Philadelphia Mint policy. When the Denver institution had to fill its orders (amounting to 7,160,000 cents in all) even after learning that the Engraving Department in Philadelphia would ship no more dies (the rest of the year had to be devoted to Peace dollars), the last half million cents were made Feb. 26–March 3 from an obv. die already worn out and further weakened by regrinding to efface clash marks. In its later states, this obv. die (No. 30) wore down so far that the mintmark eventually vanished. Many worn examples survive, but few in or near mint state. Forgeries exist, made by scraping the D off normal 1922 D cents, but comparison with the enlarged ill. will immediately enable detection. Further details are in Craig {1964} and ANACS {1983}, pp. 62–63.

A different type of rarity is overmintmarks. The first of these, 1944 D/S, was discovered as recently as 1962. In the same general class can be mentioned the 1909 with S over lazy S, produced by the same kind of blunder and correction that gave us the 1877 S over lazy S quarter dollar; evidently inspection procedures in the Engraving Department were no more perfect even after 30 additional years of experience. Discovery of other modern rarities of this same kind may be attributed to intensified study of coins recovered from circulation or from rolls or bag lots. Nor is the end in sight.

Rarities of a still different kind are the world famous 1943 bronze and 1944 steel cents. Because copper had become a scarce strategic metal during WW II, efforts to find a substitute (including, among other things, plastics, ceramics, and noncuprous alloys) eventually resulted in adoption of the wretched expedient of low-carbon steel with an 0.0005″ coating of zinc. Because the two metals are well apart in the electropositive series, they form a "couple" in moist atmospheres, and quickly corrode. Cents of this dross ("steelies") were coined in 1943 in enormous quantities, but they immediately proved a failure. When new they were often mistaken for dimes (numerous accidental strikings on dime planchets made matters worse!), and when corroded they looked like slugs, even to being nicknamed "lead pennies." Fortunately for some few collectors, but unfortunately for the peace of mind of Mint bureaucrats, at the end of 1942 some bronze blanks were left over in a hopper attached to one of the cent presses, and at least 40 were struck by accident early in 1943, being mixed with a normal production run of steel cents, and managed to leave the Mint undetected. Considering the enormous coinage orders that had to be filled, inspection had to be cursory.

For many years after the war, rumors persisted that the Ford Motor Company would give a new car as a prize to anyone turning in a genuine 1943 bronze cent (usually called "43 copper cent"). As one might expect, fraud artists promptly copperplated ordinary "steelies" and began attempting to sell their wares. (A magnet will instantly detect one of these; real bronze coins are nonmagnetic.) The car company vainly issued indignant denials of the rumors. Spokesmen for the Mint repeatedly denied that any such coins had been made, but the rumors refused to die—with good reason.

In early 1947, a Dr. Conrad Ottelin reported discovering a bronze 1943 cent (NUM 6/47, p. 434); this coin either has not become available for authentication, or else has not been connected with Ottelin's name. However, a few weeks earlier, Don Lutes, Jr., then aged 16, found one in change at his high school cafeteria (Pittsfield, Mass.), and I had the pleasure of authenticating the piece when it came to my attention in 1959. It was one of the first two (both found by youths) to achieve nationwide publicity, the other being Marvin Beyer's, also recovered from circulation (about 1958). Rumors of four- and five-figure prices followed, but the first public auction of a 1943 bronze cent did not actually result in the coin's changing hands until 1974. (Beyer's coin went into the 1958 ANA Convention auction—only to be withdrawn by the boy's father at the last moment, resulting in widespread protests as the auctioneer's book reportedly contained bids well into five figures.) In the meantime, over a dozen others have been authenticated, but there are tens of thousands of forgeries.

In the early 1960s a New York coin firm played a mean practical joke: Some member copperplated a bag lot of 5,000 "steelies" (most likely too spotted, stained, and corroded to be worth retailing), and dropped the coins singly in strategic locations where the general public would be sure to notice. For the next six months, coin dealers throughout the New York City area (including, one hopes, the perpetrator) were plagued by phone calls from finders. Counterfeit 1943 bronze cents from false dies began showing up about 1961; some were stamped on genuine cent blanks bought from coin dealers, others on homemade blanks, still others on genuine cents of other dates, notably and stupidly 1944 and later years! By 1965, the Mint Bureau was issuing press releases ignorantly denying the genuineness of any 1943 bronze cents (including, if they had only known, the one owned by Mint Engraver John R. Sinnock!), such releases in one instance including the infamous line "The Mint makes no mistakes," which has gone down in history beside "Rum, Romanism, and Rebellion" (Coins 11/67, p. 33; NNW 11/28/81, p. 16; CW 11/18/81).

Authentication of purported examples is mandatory. However, over 99% of specimens offered will fail one of the following tests, whereas the genuine will pass them all:

1. Nonmagnetic.
2. Weight standard 48 grs. = 3.11 gms.
3. Same long-tailed 3 as on steel cents.
4. Exceptionally sharp strikings (note especially clear V.D.B. on truncation), with borders built up almost as on matte proofs. (This is because the dies were set to come apart only to the lesser thickness of steel blanks, so that they compressed bronze blanks much more.)

At least with the 1944 steel cents (which are rarer than the 1943 bronze), publicity has been less in quantity, fantasy, and stupidity. Richard Fenton found the first one in change, about 1945 (*NSM* 10/60, p. 2855), but Harold Berk first reached print with one (*Mint Error Collector Bulletin* v1n2, 12/56). The explanation is much the same: Leftover steel blanks remained in a hopper and were stamped early in 1944 mixed with regular shell-case bronze cent blanks, managing to escape inspection the same way as the 1943's. No forgeries are known. Several survivors are corroded, and in at least one instance the zinc coating had to be stripped away to enable legibility—a practice long common with the "steelies." Steel cents of either date are already rare in pristine spotless mint state, and will eventually become unobtainable, so unstable is the zinc coating. No protective holder, spray, or chemical treatment is yet known that will indefinitely retard deterioration of the zinc layer. No chemical treatment will reverse the process. Even stripping and replating with zinc produces surfaces entirely different from the pristine original one.

Steel blanks ordered by the Mint for 1943 cent coinage were also used in Philadelphia for executing foreign coinages (Belgian 1944 2 francs); there is no way to distinguish these from leftover 1943 cent blanks. Quality control was lax enough that the two weight standards (41.5 and 42.5 grs. = 2.69 and 2.75 gms.) cannot be distinguished; the coins' weights fall in a wide range.

Cents dated 1944–45 are in "shell case bronze" (95% copper, 5% zinc), because official orders required salvage of all empty shell cases. Salvaged cases were originally intended to be recycled in several ways, as the armed forces' supply of copper (their principal ingredient) was running low. Formerly, fighting ships' "hot shellmen" jettisoned the burning hot empty cases; but under recycling orders they instead passed them on to ungloved mates, who had to find a place to stack them in darkness, while the ship pitched, tossed, and yawed, and other men fell over them. Infantrymen often risked their lives retrieving them on battlegrounds. For various bureaucratic reasons, these spent shell cases did not go back to munitions makers for reconversion into other shells; they went instead to the three mints to make cents: Moser {1982}.

When proof coinage was resumed 1936–42 and again in 1950, authorities intended to revive the pre-World War I brilliant finish. However, Mint personnel had long forgotten precisely how earlier dies and planchets were proofed, and so the earliest 1936 proofs (and, for similar reasons, the earliest 1950's) come with a satiny finish, the later ones extra brilliant with some mirrorlike surface even on devices. Beware of polished or plated pieces simulating proofs! Look always for extra sharpness of relief details (compared to uncirculated business strikes of the same dates), broad borders with no rounding on either inner or outer rims. If in doubt, have the piece authenticated.

Minor repunching is found in mintmarks in most years; such coins command slight to moderate premiums above the values of normal specimens of the same date and mintmark. We list herein only the more spectacular instances, which are also the most valuable. The same remark holds for doubled obv. or rev. dies, which result from misaligned blows from the hub at manufacture of working dies.

Coins dated 1937 with reeded edges (usually found with 5¢ pieces similarly treated) were made in Philadelphia for the 1941 ANA convention, reportedly either 100 or 104 pairs. Despite old rumors (some originating with F. C. C. Boyd) that the Mint clandestinely issued them so, for the Philadelphia dealer Ira S. Reed, more likely private parties reeded ordinary cents. Obviously more could be made the same way anytime.

In 1955, a mismade obv. die managed to slip past inspectors long enough to make a few tens of thousands of impressions, even as similar though less obvious ones had done in 1917 and 1936. Sydney C. Engel, of the coining room, decided to release the batch of 10 million cents containing about 20,000 to 24,000 from the doubled obv., rather than ordering the whole lot destroyed: Engel {1970B}. The 1955's turned up in quantity (often as change in cigarette vending machines) in the Boston area, various cities in western Massachusetts, and parts of upper New York State. *NSM*, 1/56, p. 5, published the first reports, from Ameil Druila (Greenfield, Mass.) and W. S. Meadows (Newton Highlands, Mass.). Pristine survivors have proved very scarce; the majority turned up in circulation, and most "UNCIRCULATED" specimens offered to date have been cleaned or even recolored, or qualify only as "sliders" (borderline cases). After prices soared on these, forgers made many cast copies and later many more from false dies. On casts, details are notably inferior to the genuine; on the die-struck pieces, numerals are differently positioned (see ills. in 1966 ANA Convention catalog and ANACS {1983}, pp. 64–66). Authentication is recommended.

Information about numbers of dies used for particular date-mintmark combinations is fragmentary. Wallace {1954} gives figures which indicate that from 1912–1920 the Philadelphia Mint's average number of cents coined per obv. die went from 345,146 to 403,246, Denver's 381,075 to 403,262, San Francisco's from 211,152 to 476,256; by 1948 this last had improved to 560,000 (590,000 per rev.). All these figures indicate that the number of obvs. per year ranged from a few dozen to a few hundred. For more recent figures, see Glossary at **proof dies.**

Rumors of specimens dated 1959 but bearing the old wheat ear rev. have not yet been confirmed by examination of a genuine example. The Mint Bureau has naturally denied the issue of anything of the kind.

BRENNER'S WHEAT EAR LINCOLNS

Designer, Engraver, Victor D. Brenner. Mints, Philadelphia (no mintmark), San Francisco, Denver (respectively, S or D below date). Composition, 1909–42, 1946–58, French bronze, as formerly; 1943, low-carbon steel with 0.0005" zinc coating; 1944–45, bronze from recycled shell cases, 95% copper, 5% zinc. Diameter 3/4" = 19 mm. Weight, 1909–42, 1944–58, 48 ± 2 grs. = 3.11 ± 0.13 gms.; 1943 steel, 41.5 and 42.5 grs. = 2.689 and 2.754 gms. (variable, overlapping, not distinguishable), with the same permitted deviation. Authorizing Acts, as previously.

Grade range, POOR to UNC.; not collected in low grades except for certain "key" (low mintage) dates. GOOD: Devices outlined; all numerals and letters legible (except V.D.B. on truncation, 1918–); lettering distinct from rims. VERY GOOD: Half of lines (awns) show in upper wheat ears. FINE: All awns in wheat ears distinct. VERY FINE: All kernels completely separate. Cheek and jaw bones will show wear but will be distinctly separated. EXTREMELY FINE: Few tiny isolated rubbed spots only; grade by surface. EXCEPTIONS: All steel cents must be graded by surface; spotless coins command a premium (see introductory text). 1944 steel (not 1943) is always weak on rims and high points. 1955 doubled obv. and some S and D coins 1918–35 will be vague on beard, hair, and coat details, but mint-state specimens show luster on the weak areas. 1922 "Plain" always shows weaknesses as in enlarged ill.; one of its two revs. is also weak, the other normal.

2052   1909 V.D.B. [27,995,000 + 420P]
Released Aug. 2. Pristine business strikes are often pale and streaky, from the original William Pukall, A. C. Gies, and Wayte Raymond holdings. On many business strikes, one or more periods after V.D.B. will be weak or absent (filled die). Proofs come in 2 styles: satin finish or matte (see Breen {1977}, pp. 211–17; Albright {1983}); authentication mandatory.

2053   1909 V.D.B. Doubled obv. die. Presently very rare.
3 vars. Wexler {1984}. Doubling is plainest on date and LIBERTY. Discovered by Everett Zuidmeer. *NNW* 6/3/78.

2054   1909 S V.D.B. [484,000]
At least 6 obv. dies. Generally all 3 periods in V.D.B. sharp. Beware of forgeries; see introductory text. Authentication mandatory; see ANACS {1983}, pp. 49–52, 78–79. The late John Zug bought 25,000 from the San Francisco Mint at issue and resold them at 1¾¢ apiece, ca. 1918. Cited by George Fuld in Van Cleave:5012 (Kagin 2/1/86).
2055   1909 "Plain" (no V.D.B.). [72,700,000 + 2,198P]
For proofs see refs. at **2052**. A few revs. show V.D.B. was filed off dies. Wexler {1984} lists a minor doubled rev. die.
2056   1909 Doubled obv. die. Presently very rare.
Not in Wexler {1984}.
2057   1909 S "Plain" (no V.D.B.). [1,825,000]
At least 7 obv. dies, some the same as with V.D.B. revs. A few revs. show that V.D.B. was filed off dies. Mintmarks vary in position. Specimens with ridges on shoulder and numerals, and tiny "pimple" above l. stem end, are counterfeits: *NUM* 12/82, p. 2959. Authentication recommended. See ANACS {1983}, pp. 53–55.

2058   1909 S over lazy S. Scarce.
RPM 2; *CW* 5/10/78, p. 34. Later states showing less of original S bring lower premiums.

2059   1910 [146,798,813 + 2,405P]
Proofs are usually satin finish, though ANS has one with matte finish. See refs. cited at **2052**. The claim that specimens were made from worn or reground 1909 V.D.B. revs. remains unverified.
2060   1910 S [6,045,000]
Mintmarks vary in position; this remark holds for all subsequent S- and D-Mint cents. Same comment as to preceding about V.D.B. revs.
2061   1910 S Double S. Presently very rare.
RPM 1, 2. S first entered respectively far too low or too high.
2062   1911 [101,176,054 + 1,733P]
Proofs are usually satin finish, like 1910; less often matte, like 1912. See refs. cited at **2052**.
2063   1911 S [4,026,000]
2064   1911 D [12,672,000]
First released in May. *NUM* 11/11, p. 396.
2065   1912 [68,150,915 + 2,145P]
Proofs are matte, more granular than 1909 V.D.B. See refs. cited at **2052**.
2066   1912 S [4,431,000]
2067   1912 D [10,411,000]
2068   1913 [76,529,504 + 2,848P]
Proofs are matte, similar to 1913. See refs. cited at **2052**.
2069   1913 S [6,101,000]
Pristine specimens vary from rose to tangerine color.
2070   1913 D [15,804,000]
2071   1914 [75,237,067 + 1,365P]
Proofs are matte, similar to 1911–13. The oldstyle brilliant proofs alleged to have come from the maker of the 1913 Liberty nickels proved to be counterfeits.
2072   1914 S [4,137,000]
Pristine specimens are darker than previous S mints.
2073   1914 D [1,193,000]
6 obvs., 7 revs. Often mistakenly called rare, though a hoard of at least 700 UNCIRCULATED specimens existed until the early 1950s. Many types of forgeries exist: struck counterfeits, cast counterfeits, mintmarks added to genuine 1914

Philadelphia cents, and alterations from 1944 D; ANACS {1983}, pp. 56–61. Authentication is mandatory. Enl. photos.

2074   1915 [29,090,970 + 1,150P]
Proofs are matte, differing minutely in texture from 1914. See refs. cited at **2052**. As well-struck UNCs. are sometimes deceptively similar, authentication of alleged proofs is mandatory.

2075   1915 S [4,833,000]
2076   1915 D [22,050,000]
2077   1916 Modified portrait. [131,832,627 + 1,050P]
Proofs (ill.) have finer matte finish, most like 1915. See refs. cited at **2052**. Authentication mandatory. The modified portrait continues through 1917.

2078   1916 S Modified portrait. [22,510,000]
2079   1916 D Modified portrait. [35,956,000]
2080   1917 [196,429,785 + ?P]
Proofs (clandestinely made) have the same finish as 1916. See refs. cited at **2052**. Authentication mandatory.

2081   1917 Doubled obv. die. Presently very rare.
Discovered by Andrew Frandsen. *NNW* 9/3/77. Usually in low grades. 2 vars.

2082   1917 S [32,620,000]
2083   1917 D [55,120,000]
2084   1918 [288,104,634]
V.D.B. restored to truncation henceforth on cents from all mints.

2085   1918 S [34,680,000]
Often weakly struck.

2086   1918 D [47,830,000]
2087   1919 [392,021,000]
2088   1919 S [139,760,000]
2089   1919 D [57,154,000]
2090   1920 [310,165,000]
Wexler {1984} shows a minor doubled obv. die.

2091   1920 S [46,220,000]
2092   1920 D [49,280,000]
2093   1921 [39,157,000]
2094   1921 S [15,274,000]
Often weakly struck.

2095   1922 D [7,160,000]
Coined Jan.–Feb., from 20 obvs., 27 revs. Mintage figures include next.

2096   1922 "Plain."
Struck about Feb. 26–28, from final obv. (No. 30); [507,000] in all. Price only for obv. die state ill. (last few thousand made); rev. die worn (blurred wheat ears) or normal. Usually low grades, very rare UNC. Auction 86:512, UNC., $4,620. Earlier states show weak or fragmented D and bring less premium. Fakes (usually genuine 1922 D's with removed D) lack the incomplete coat or lettering peculiarities of the genuine. See introductory text. Enl. photo.

2097   1923 [74,723,000]
2098   1923 S [8,700,000]
UNCs. when brilliant are often weak on hair; sharper UNCs. (from different rolls) are usually darker.

2099   1924 [75,178,000]
2100   1924 S [11,696,000]
UNCs. from the Gies, Pukall, and Raymond holdings are often weak. Sharp specimens are unusual and command higher premiums.

2101   1924 D [2,520,000]
9 obvs., 11 revs.

2102   1925 [139,949,000]
2103   1925 S [26,380,000]
UNCs. are often weak. Several vars. of repunched mintmarks: RPM 1–3.

2104   1925 D [22,580,000]
Same comment.

2105   1926 [157,088,000]
A minor obv. doubled die discovered by Richard Simone. *CW* 5/27/70, p. 61.

2106   1926 S [4,550,000]
Often weak.

2107   1926 D [28,020,000]
2108   1927 [144,440,000]
Delma K. Romines discovered a doubled obv. die, plainest on 27 and LIB; presently very scarce. Ill. Wexler {1984}.

2109   1927 S [14,276,000]
Often weak.

2110   1927 D [27,170,000]

2111   1928 [134,116,000]

2112   1928 S [all kinds 17,266,000] Small s.
Mintmark as in previous years. Often weak.

2113   1928 S Large S. Presently scarce.
Taller, sharper serifs on mintmark. Often weak. At least 3 vars. of repunched mintmarks: RPM 1, 2, 3.

2114   1928 D [31,170,000]

2115   1929 [185,262,000]
A minor obv. doubled die discovered by Norman O. Mink. *CW* 5/27/70, p. 61. Wexler {1984} ill. a minor rev. doubled die.

2116   1929 S [50,148,000]
Often weak.

2117   1929 D [41,730,000]

2118   1930 [157,415,000]

2119   1930 S [24,286,000]
Often weak. Wexler {1984} ill. a minor doubled obv. die; similar ones exist in many later dates and mintmarks.

2120   1930 D [40,100,000]

2121   1930 D Filled zero. Scarce.
Chipping of this working die removed center of zero; entire digit is a solid blob.

2122   1931 [19,396,000]

2123   1931 S [866,000]
More often seen UNC. than in lower grades. The Scharlack hoard contained over 200,000 red UNCIRCULATED specimens, many weak. Numerous counterfeits exist; authentication recommended. Specimens with disproportionately long tail to 3 (nearly touching 9) and scattered raised granules in upper l. rev. field are fakes: ANACS {1983}, p. 59.

2124   1931 D [4,480,000]

2125   1932 [9,062,000]

2126   1932 D [10,500,000]

2127   1933 [14,360,000]
Pristine specimens are often tangerine color.

2128   1933 D [6,200,000]

2129   1934 [219,080,000]
Long tail to 3 as in 1943, 1953. Wexler {1984} ill. a doubled obv. die, most noticeable by extra thickness in date and LIBERTY.

2130   1934 D [28,446,000]
Same comments. Often weak.

2131   1935 [245,388,000]

2132   1935 S [38,702,000]
Often weak.

2133   1935 D [47,000,000]

2134   1936 [309,632,000 + 5,569P]
Proofs come with satin finish ("Type I") or extra brilliant ("Type II"); because of dangerous forgeries, authentication is mandatory. Business strikes often have leg of R(TY) weak or missing.

2135   1936 Doubled obv. die. Presently very rare.
Doubling is plainest on date, ear, and letters. 5 vars.; price for

that ill., less obvious ones bring lower premiums. Usually in low grades. Independently discovered by Roger Martin, Herman A. Klouser, and John E. Bayides; *CW* 5/27/70, p. 61. One of the 5 vars. (Wexler {1984} 2-O-V) shows impressions from 2 hubs, one with l. upright of R(TY) broken, the other normal. Compare ills. *NUM* 3/86, p. 447.

2136   1936 S [29,130,000]

2137   1936 D [40,620,000]

2138   1937 [309,170,000 + 9,320P]
Proofs are extra brilliant. Forgeries may have been made by buffing or plating business strikes; they will not have the extra sharp relief details of the genuine. Authentication recommended.

2139   1937 S [34,500,000]

2140   1937 D [50,430,000]

2141   1938 [156,682,000 + 14,734P]

2142   1938 S [15,180,000]

2143   1938 D [20,010,000]

2144   1939 [316,466,000 + 13,520P]
Doubled obv. dies exist, one plainest at motto (very scarce), the other plainest on 19, ear, eyelid, and BERTY (rare).

2145   1939 Unequal 9's. Proofs only.
Second 9 smaller, unusually thin—evidently from excessive lapping of this obv. die. Forms a minority of proofs of this date.

2146   1939 S [52,070,000]

2147   1939 D [15,160,000]

2148   1940 [586,810,000 + 15,872P]

2149   1940 S [all kinds 112,940,000] Small s, plain 4.
Mintmark as in previous years; lower serif slants.

2150   1940 S Small s, "crosslet" 4.
Plain serifs on crossbar and base of 4, representing a different master die.

2151   1940 S Large S, "crosslet" 4.
Long, sharp vertical serifs to S as in later years. See ills. in RPM.

2152   1940 S Large S over small s, "crosslet" 4.
RPM 4. Compare last. Discovered by Delma K. Romines. *CW* 1/27/82, p. 80.

2153   1940 D "Crosslet" 4. [81,390,000]
As **2151**; may exist with plain 4.

2154   1941 Plain 4. [887,018,000 + 21,100P]

2155   1941 Doubled obv. die. Presently rare.
Doubling plainest on LIBERTY and TRUST. 5 vars. Usually in low grades. 1977 ANA:4618–9, unc., $200, $160.

2156   1941 S [all kinds 92,360,000] Small s.
Mintmark punch as in 1939 and earlier years. Many minor vars., some with repunched s.

2157 1941 S Large S.
Mintmark punch as in 1942–44.

2158 1941 D [128,700,000]
2159 1942 [657,796,000 + 32,600P]
2160 1942 S [85,590,000]
2161 1942 S Doubled obv. die. Presently rare.
2 vars. RPM 1. Discovered by Delma K. Romines, 1979. Doubling plainest on motto and 9.
2162 1942 D [206,698,000]
2163 1943 Bronze. Very rare.
See introductory text. The estimate of about 40 known is from ANACS. Finest, J. R. Sinnock, 1981 ANA:414, $10,000. Authentication mandatory.
2164 1943 S Bronze. About 6 known.
See introductory text. Authentication mandatory.
2165 1943 D Bronze. About 24 known.
Same comment.

ZINC COATED STEEL, 1943

2166 1943 Steel. [684,628,670]
Mintage began Feb. 27. See introductory text. Often with weak 4. Seldom pristine. Beware specimens stripped and replated. Millions were recalled and dumped into the ocean, probably killing many fish by zinc poisoning.
2167 1943 S Steel. [191,550,000]
Same comments, except date of inception not recorded.
2168 1943 D Steel. [217,660,000]
Same comments as to preceding.
2169 1943 D Steel. Obvious double D. Presently rare.
RPM 1. D first punched over half its own diameter southwest of final position. *CW* 5/10/78, p. 34.
2170 1944 Steel. Very rare.
Always weakly struck; see introductory text. Finest, J. R. Sinnock, 1981 ANA:415, $3,500.
2171 1944 S Steel. Very rare.
Same comments. Harte III:787, 41.5 grs. None examined recently enough to tell which style S (see 1944 S Bronze).
2172 1944 D Steel. Very rare.
Same comments. Harte III:786, 42.3 grs.

SHELL CASE BRONZE, 1944–45

2173 1944 [1,435,400,000]
See introductory text.
2174 1944 S [all kinds 282,760,000] Sharp vertical serifs to S. Mintmark as in 1941–43. Discovered by Delma K. Romines. *Coins* 1/83, p. 68. Compare next. A minor doubled obv. die

exists, discovered by Edward Ordjuowicz, *CW* 5/13/70, p. 61.
2175 1944 S Blunt serifs to S. Mintmark as in 1945 and later. Discovered by Delma K. Romines. *Coins* 1/83, p. 68.
2176 1944 D [430,578,000]
2177 1944 D over S.
OMM 1, 2. Discovered by Delma K. Romines, 1962. Price for OMM 2 (S shows within and l. of D). OMM 1 (S partly above D, ill.) is rarer; 1978 ANA:220, $400.

2178 1945 [1,040,515,000]
2179 1945 S [181,770,000]
2180 1945 D [226,268,000]

FRENCH BRONZE RESUMED, 1946–62

2181 1946 [991,655,000]
Shell-case bronze specimens of this or next 3 may exist; they could be identified only by spectroscopic tests proving the absence of tin.
2182 1946 S [all kinds 198,100,000] Blunt serifs to S.
This and next discovered by Delma K. Romines. Forms a small minority of total.
2183 1946 S Sharp serifs to S.
2184 1946 D [315,690,000]
2185 1947 [190,555,000]
2186 1947 S [all kinds 99,000,000] Blunt serifs to S.
This and next discovered by Delma K. Romines. Same comment as to **2182.**
2187 1947 S Sharp serifs to S.
2188 1947 D [194,750,000]
2189 1948 [317,570,000]
2190 1948 S [all kinds 81,735,000] Blunt serifs to S. Presently very rare.
This and next discovered by Delma K. Romines.
2191 1948 S Sharp serifs to S.
2192 1948 D [172,637,500]
2193 1949 [217,775,000]
2194 1949 S [64,290,000]
2195 1949 D [153,132,500]
2196 1950 [272,635,000 + 51,386P]
Early proofs are satiny; later ones very brilliant as in 1951–64.
2197 1950 S [118,505,000]
2198 1950 D [334,950,000]
2199 1951 [284,576,000 + 57,500P]
Wexler {1984} ill. a proof with doubled obv. die; presently rare.
2200 1951 S [136,010,000]
2201 1951 D [625,355,000]

2202 1951 D over S. Scarce.
  OMM 1. Traces of S within D.
2203 1952 [186,775,000 + 81,980P]
2204 1952 S [137,800,004]
2205 1952 D [746,130,000]
2206 1952 D over S. Scarce.
  At least 2 vars. OMM 1 and new; neither obvious.
2207 1953 [256,755,000 + 128,800P]
  Long-tailed 3 (all 3 mints) as in 1934, 1943.
2208 1953 S [181,835,000]
2209 1953 D [700,515,000]
2210 1954 [71,640,050 + 233,300P]
2211 1954 S [96,190,000]
  The "SJ" var. has a defect at S looking like part of curve of a
  D. Alan Herbert says this is a die break, but no earlier or
  later states are reported.
2212 1954 D [251,552,500]
2213 1955 [330,580,000 + 378,200P]
2214 1955 Doubled obv. die. [20,000+]
  Mintage included in preceding. Usually F to AU, rarely pristine; "UNCs." are usually cleaned or even recolored. Price
  only for var. ill. Because of counterfeits, authentication is
  mandatory. See introductory text. Scarcer but less spectacular doubled obv. dies show extra outlines plainest at motto or
  LIBERTY; these bring lower premiums, as do the minor
  doubled rev. dies: Wexler {1984}.

Courtesy ANACS

2215 1955 S [44,610,000]
  The San Francisco Mint closed during this year, reverting to
  "Assay Office" title. Robert Friedberg's hoard numbered
  some 7 million UNC. specimens; these have been long since
  dispersed.
2216 1955 D [563,257,000]
2217 1956 [420,745,000 + 669,384P]
2218 1956 D [1,098,210,100]
2219 1956 DD. Presently very rare.
  RPM 8. Mintmark first punched far too low, then corrected;
  lower D mostly effaced and faint, but complete and separate
  from upper D.
2220 1957 [282,540,000 + 1,247,952P]
2221 1957 D [1,051,342,000]

2222 1958 [All kinds 252,525,000 + 875,652P]
  A doubled obv. die has just been identified (plainest on LIB-
  ERTY and motto); presently Ex. rare. Discovered by Charles
  Ludovico.
2223 1958/7
  Several vars., all with only faint traces of 7; at least as much
  of 7 must show as on the ill. to command a premium. A 1957
  working hub (the 7 only imperfectly effaced) was used for
  creating a 1958 master die; working hubs and working dies
  derived from the latter showed various traces of 7, or most
  often none. First reported by Alan Herbert, *NNW* 7/15/78,
  p. 12.

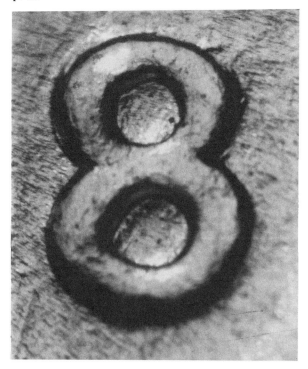

Courtesy Krause Publications

2224 1958 D [All kinds 800,953,000]
  Reported with repunched mintmarks, including one with
  faint traces of horizontal D in field l. of normal mintmark;
  discovered by Harry Ellis: *Errorscope/Errorgram* 11/83, p.
  40.
2225 1958/7 D
  Several vars.; explanation as for **2223**. At least as much of 7
  must show as on the ill. to command a premium. Discovered
  by Robert Wilharm, *NNW* 4/22/78, p. 1.

vi. GASPARRO'S MEMORIAL REVERSE LINCOLNS (1959–   )

The current Lincoln Memorial cent rev. was Frank Gasparro's first accepted design for a circulating coin; Gasparro was
then Assistant Engraver of the Mint. It has proved technically
adequate, if recognizability after long wear is the test; Gasparro's initials FG, above r. end of ground, are clear even on worn
specimens. But as usual with the Mint, artistic considerations
have had to be subordinated to the necessity of minimal relief—
some would say sacrificed. Don Taxay has made the caustic
comment that the result "looks at a glance more like a trolley
car." {1966}, p. 339. It is an oversimplified copy of the Lincoln
Memorial building as depicted on the $5 bill, minus the foliage.

On normal strikings, rarely can Daniel Chester French's heroic statue of Lincoln (here strangely dwarfed) be seen at all; never on 1959–60 coins. The whole concept is continuing testimony to the truism that buildings make poor coin designs (compare the Jefferson nickel). The blame for this artistic disaster presumably rests on the then Director of the Mint, or whichever other bureaucrat prescribed the device, rather than on Gasparro. This design was intended to commemorate the 150th anniversary of Lincoln's birth, even as the original Brenner head had been intended for the 100th; but here, as there, we have been left to guess the intent solely by knowing the dates. Pres. Eisenhower, apparently without the artistic discrimination of a Theodore Roosevelt, approved the design on Dec. 20, 1958; mintage began on the following Jan. 2.

In 1960 a change in the matrices resulted in small and large dates. Mint Director W. H. Brett vainly denied this (NSM 5/60, p. 1565), but it has since been confirmed. For a few days or weeks, working hubs of both types were simultaneously in use sinking working dies, and the same kind of blunder occurred as the one which had produced the 1942/41 dimes, here yielding small over large dates and vice versa. Any single working die requires several blows from a working hub to sink the design in enough detail for use. However, to eliminate stress-hardening and brittleness, the working die must be annealed between successive blows ("entries") from the hub. If a partly completed working die is returned to the wrong hubbing press, the result is just what did occur.

On the other hand, the so-called large and small date vars. of 1970 are misnomers; the real difference here is in the position of 7 in date, which on one working hub was level at top with 9-0, and on another was lower. Again, some coins show evidence that both hubs were used to make a single obv. die.

The alleged 1969 cents with doubled obv. die have been condemned as forgeries made by Mort Goodman. All were supposedly recovered by the Secret Service during preparation of the Justice Department's successful prosecution: CW 8/12/70, p. 1; 8/19/70, p. 3. On the other hand, the 1969 S doubled obv. die coins are genuine, produced by an accident in diemaking of the same kind which yielded the more famous 1955.

The next var. to stimulate public enthusiasm was the 1972 doubled obv. die; this managed to reach Time Magazine. Only "Variety I" (ill.) has continued to command high premiums—and attract counterfeiters' attention. The 7 other obvs. with visible doubling are nowhere nearly so spectacular, requiring a strong glass, and they have generated less interest.

Quantities issued of the Lincoln Memorial design have far surpassed those of any other coin of any denomination or type since coinage began: in excess of 170 billion to date! Maximal stereotypy has induced collectors to look more and more closely to find any deviations interesting enough to collect as vars. We are under no illusion that we have seen them all.

Beginning in Sept. 1962, owing to the scarcity of tin, cents began to be made in brass, the composition fixed through 1981 at 95% copper, 5% zinc. Only spectroscopy readily distinguishes them. They differ little in color or durability from the former French bronze. Until about 1981, collectors still indifferently called both bronze, but Mint reports properly refer to tinless cents as brass.

Beginning in Nov. 1974, the Bureau began coining cents at the West Point Depository. Under the flimsy excuse that this is only a subsidiary of the Philadelphia Mint, coins made at West Point have remained without mintmark, and official reports of quantities struck have been lumped with those from Philadelphia. Omission of mintmarks on these is beyond doubt another episode in the century-old feud between the Mint and coin collectors. Authorities have been heard to express fear that if mintmarks are added, more coins will be "withheld from circulation" by collectors, dealers, and speculators: three classes very distinct to everyone except the Mint Bureau, which has stupidly and paranoidly assumed that all were one and the same, and which has grossly exaggerated the effects of hoarding on circulation. This same defective reasoning underlay the omission of mintmarks on all U.S. coins 1965–67 and more recent proposals to abolish them altogether; it was even spelled out in Bureau press releases lamely excusing delaying distribution of uncirculated Susan B. Anthony mini-dollars until authorities could accumulate a stockpile of 500 million (most of which never left Treasury vaults).

Yet another instance of official paranoia occurred during the singular episode of the aluminum cents. During the fall of 1973, owing to a sudden rise in copper prices and the prospect of cents once again costing more than their face value to manufacture, the Mint Bureau sought alternative coinage metals. In line with one of these proposals, the Philadelphia Mint made over 1.5 million aluminum cents, of regular design, dated 1974. When the vending machine industry condemned this proposal as requiring expensive replacement of their counterfeit-detection devices, Mint Bureau authorities—in their usual panic lest collectors obtain specimens—recalled the entire mintage, and counted the whole million-plus quantity individually before melting the lot. Alas for such plans, several congressmen and other official recipients of the experimental coins either refused to return them, or claimed that they had been lost or misplaced, so that 12 remain in private hands and one in the Smithsonian Institution. Their legal status is dubious; at the moment, public offering of one of these coins would probably result in confiscation, though its hapless owner could always take his case to court, but in the meantime the coin would have been destroyed, rendering the question moot: a likely course of events that would exactly parallel similar disputes over the legality of mint-error cents struck on dime blanks or foreign planchets during the 1950s. In its ill-considered efforts to prevent coin collectors from obtaining curiosities cheaply, the Mint Bureau has unintentionally created a rarity already quoted above $10,000.

Over the years since 1909, Lincoln's portrait has been repeatedly modified, even aside from Morgan's restoring Brenner's initials V.D.B. in 1918. Most of the minute changes have been in the direction of oversimplifying and blurring details in the interest of lower relief, especially since WW II, whereas from 1909–17 one could usually make out Lincoln's many small distinct ringlets. During the 1970s the President has been made to look as though his hair and beard were overenthusiastically pomaded.

Because the Mint Bureau remained concerned about rises in the price of copper, authorities let it be known that they would welcome alternative proposals. Exotic metals (repeatedly proposed in the past) would not do, if only because of the vast quantities needed. Jerry T. McDowell, president of the metal and chemical division of the Ball Corp. (Greeneville, Tenn.), successfully approached Dr. Alan Goldman of the Mint Bureau with a proposal to replace copper with zinc. Treasury plans to implement this idea received a setback in mid-1980 by a lawsuit from the Copper & Brass Fabricators Council (subsequently dismissed). Predictably, the Treasury in July 1981 announced its decision to change the cent from brass to copper-coated zinc. Equally predictably, the successful bidder for the contract to produce the new planchets was the Ball Corp., July 22, 1981; its metal division has done the actual fabrication.

In Sept. 1982, the Mint redesigned the cent obv. as described in the main text below. Skip Nashawaty first reported specimens in circulation. This design modification was intended to reduce relief and increase die life from about 700,000 to 1.5 million impressions per die. Zinc does not harden further at striking, so that the new ("Type II") coins can now be struck at only 31 tons per square inch rather than the initial 41 (up from 40 for bronze), still at 130 per minute. Collars are now 0.749" (formerly 0.747″); they enlarge minutely in service but are not discarded at Denver or San Francisco until they reach 0.753″.

The copper-coated zinc composition has proved nearly as unsatisfactory as the 1943 zinc-coated steel, and for similar reasons: The two metals form a "couple" in moist atmospheres. To date, no storage technique, not even the Mint's own plastic holders for proof sets, will prevent cents from discoloring. Some cynics have speculated that the Mint Bureau may even prefer this situation as discouraging collectors from "withholding from circulation" even the proofs. However, annealing has minimized the quantities of cents showing surface blisters.

In recent years Mint Bureau production statistics have become notable for delays and inconsistencies. Mintage figures quoted below are subject to revision.

Mintmarks are hammered into each working die by hand, except on proofs 1985– ; on the latter the S is in the master die and therefore identical on working hubs and dies.

GASPARRO'S MEMORIAL REVERSE LINCOLNS

Designer, Engraver, Frank Gasparro, obv. after Brenner. Mints, Philadelphia and West Point (no mintmark), San Francisco (mintmark S), Denver (D): mintmarks below date. Composition, French bronze 1959–62, brass 1962–81, zinc (copper coated) 1982– . Physical Specifications, as before, but the zincs weigh 38.58 ± 1.54 grs. = 2.5 ± 0.1 gms.; core is 99.2% Zn, 0.8% Cu, plated with pure copper, total content 97.6% Zn, 2.4% Cu. Authorizing Acts, as before, but brass composition pursuant to Act of Sept. 5, 1962, Title 31, US Code, Sect. 5112, gives weight of brass cent as 3.11 gms., diameter as 0.750″, but leaves specifications for zinc cents to be decided by the Secretary of Treasury.

Grade range, VERY GOOD to UNC. Grading standards, as before, but generally collected only UNC. or Proof.

2226 1959 [609,715,000 + 1,149,291P]
Production began Jan. 2; first release, Feb. 12, 1959.

2227 1959 D [1,279,760,000]
Many vars. of repunched D's this year and all to follow; only the most spectacular are listed.

2228 1960 [all kinds 586,405,000 + 1,691,602P] Small date.
Top of 1 minutely above top of 9. Probably under 200,000 proofs, possibly under 100,000. Edward Zigata (NSM 11/60, p. 3454) reported large-date proofs in sets around the second week in Feb. 1960, so that the change may date to before Jan. 31.

2229 1960 Large over small date. Proofs only? Presently scarce.
Possibly 3 vars.; sometimes uncertain which hub was impressed first. Discovered by Edward Zigata (same ref. as **2228**). See ill. in ANACS {1983}, p. 67. Compare discussion by Donald L. Keys in "Collector's Clearinghouse," CW Feb.–March 1966. Wexler {1984}.

2230 1960 Large date. [Included in **2228**]
Top of 1 below top of 9. First reported by Philip Montagna and Benson C. Balderdash, NSM 5/60, p. 1284.

2231 1960 D [all kinds 1,580,884,000] Small date.
Top of 1 minutely above top of 9.

2232 1960 D Small over large date; double D. Scarce.
RPM 1 (p. 78). Entirety of second D (weak) rests atop main D. Discovered by Donald L. Keys, NSM 10/62, p. 2776. Kramer 60N12.

2233 1960 D Large date.
Top of 1 below top of 9. Many repunched mintmark vars.

2234 1960 D Same, D over lazy D. Presently rare.
RPM 9.

2235 1961 [753,345,000 + 3,028,244P]
2236 1961 D [1,753,266,700]
2237 1961 D over lazy D.
RPM 1. Discovered by John Kolyska, NSM 10/61, p. 2837.

2238 1962 [All kinds 606,045,000 + 3,218,019P]
Total includes both French bronze and brass (see introductory text). At least 6 minor doubled obv. dies and 7 doubled rev. dies exist. Wexler {1984}.

2239 1962 D [1,793,148,400]

2240 1963 [754,110,000 + 3,075,645P]

2241 1963 D [1,774,020,400]
A doubled obv. die exists: cusp of extra 3 in lower part of 3. *EVN* 1/81; *CW* 6/18/86, p. 62.

2242 1964 [2,648,575,000 + 3,075,762P]
The much publicized multiple strikes of this date proved to have been made by impressing homemade dies into genuine coins; the perpetrators went to prison. Diameters of genuine pieces would be correct at 0.745″–0.75″ = 18.9–19.1 mm. The fakes were too large. At least 6 minor doubled rev. dies exist. Wexler {1984}. Many struck in 1965 from 1964 dies, pursuant to Act of 9/3/64.

2243 1964 D [3,799,071,500]

2244 1965 [1,497,224,900 + 2,360,000 SMS]
SMS = Special Mint Sets, prooflike, produced at San Francisco without mintmark. Business strikes from Philadelphia and Denver (no mintmark) reported together. See introductory text.

2245 1966 [2,188,147,783 + 2,261,583 SMS]
Same comment.

2246 1967 [3,048,667,100 + 1,863,344 SMS]
Same comment.

2247 1968 [1,707,880,970]

2248 1968 S [258,270,004 + 3,041,506P]
Proofs henceforth issued only from San Francisco.

2249 1968 D [2,886,269,600]

2250 1969 Modified portrait. [1,136,910,000]
Head smaller from now on, from all mints. The alleged doubled obv. die coins are counterfeits made by Mort Goodman, which led to his conviction and imprisonment. Ill. Wexler {1984}.

2251 1969 S Modified portrait. [544,375,000 + 2,934,631P]

2252 1969 S Doubled obv. die. Presently very rare.
Doubling is obvious on motto and date. Independently discovered by Cecil Moorhouse and Bill Hudson. *CW* 7/8/70, p. 1. Moorhouse's coin came 6/16/70 in a lot of 5 rolls from the San Francisco Federal Reserve Bank via the Belmont branch of Bank of America. Secret Service agents seized it in the mistaken belief that it was one of the Goodman counterfeits, but later returned it as genuine. *EVN* v4n2, p. 4, Feb. 28, 1981. About 15 are traced, only one UNC. Wexler {1984}. Ill. *NUM* 10/85, p. 2001.

2253 1969 D Modified portrait. [4,002,832,000]

2254 1970 Low 7. [1,898,315,000]
Top of 7 below 9-0.

2255 1970 S [all kinds 690,560,004 + 2,632,810P] Low 7.
As preceding. Most business strikes and proofs are of this type. A doubled obv. die exists, plainest at date, motto, and LIBERTY. Steiner & Zimpfer {1974}, p. 69; *CW* 7/18/76; Wexler {1984}. Presently very rare.

2256 1970 S Level 7. Presently scarce.
Numerals aligned at top; E(RTY) weak, horizontal strokes shorter than usual. Business strikes (possibly 2 obvs.) and proofs (1 obv.). Engel {1970A}. Publicized by Alan Herbert, *Coins* 10/78 and often since.

2257 1970/70 S Presently very scarce.
2 vars.; dies received blows from each hub (low and level 7). Publicized by Alan Herbert. Doubled die of class C (see Glossary).

2258 1970 D Low 7. [2,891,438,900]
May exist with level 7. Reported with low 7 over level 7, similar to **2257.**

2259 1971 [1,919,490,000]

2260 1971 Doubled obv. die. Scarce.
Doubling plainest at LIBERTY. Other less obvious doublings are known; these command smaller premiums. Wexler {1984}.

2261 1971 S [525,100,054 + 3,224,138P]

2262 1971 S Doubled obv. die. Proof. Presently very rare.
Discovered by Harry Forman, *CW* 4/16/75. Wexler, *EVN* 4/30/82, p. 8; Wexler {1984}. 2 minor vars.

2263 1971 D [2,911,045,600]

2264 1972 [2,933,255,000]

2265 1972 Doubled obv. die, "Variety I."
Price only for the obv. ill.; 7 other obvs. show minute traces of doubling, and command smaller premiums. Released Aug. 2–9, 1972. Discovered by Michael Bauer. First publicized by Harry Forman. Wexler {1984} estimates about 75,000 released. Counterfeits exist (ANACS {1983}, pp. 69–71, and another var. with spine from head up into field below space after WE); authentication recommended.

2266 1972 S [376,932,437 + 3,267,667P]
Minutely doubled obv. dies exist; they command little premium over normal proofs, though very rare.

2267 1972 D [2,665,071,400]
Same comment; the same remark applies to most subsequent dates.

2268 1972 D No V.D.B. Presently rare.
Discovered in 1973. Explanation uncertain—improper grinding of a working die? The Mint unconvincingly attributes it to foreign matter in die.

2269 1973 Modified dies. [3,728,245,000]
Initials FG enlarged, other minor changes.

2270 1973 S Modified dies. [317,167,010 + 2,769,624P]
Same comment.
2271 1973 D Modified dies. [3,549,576,588]
Same comment.
2272 1974 Modified rev. [4,232,140,523 + 128,957,523 WP]
WP = West Point issue, Nov.–Dec. No mintmark. *CW* 1/
26/83, p. 7. Modified revs. on coins from all mints; initials
FG again smaller.
2273 1974 Aluminum. [Net 13] Ex. rare.
See introductory text.
2274 1974 S Modified rev. [409,421,878 + 2,617,350P]
Same comment as to Philadelphia coins.
2275 1974 D Modified rev. [4,235,098,000]
2276 1975 [5,451,476,142 + 1,577,294,142 WP]
WP = West Point, 1975– ; no mintmark.
2277 1975 S [2,845,450P] Proofs only.
2278 1975 D [4,505,275,300]
2279 1976 [4,674,292,426 + 1,540,695,000 WP]
2280 1976 S [4,149,730P] Proofs only.
2281 1976 D [4,221,592,455]
2282 1977 [4,469,930,000 + 1,395,355,000 WP]
The "1977/6" cents are fakes by Stephen Von Zimmer. *CW*
7/13/77, 8/3/77.
2283 1977 S [3,251,152P] Proofs only.
2284 1977 D [4,194,062,300]
2285 1978 [5,266,905,000 + 1,531,250,000 WP]
2286 1978 S [3,127,781P] Proofs only.
2287 1978 D [4,280,233,400]
2288 1979 [6,018,515,000 + 1,705,850,000 WP]
2289 1979 S "Type I." [2,848,155P] Proofs only.
Mintmark from old punch, filled, blurred, or blobby. See
next.
2290 1979 S "Type II." [829,000P] Proofs only.
Mintmark from new punch, clear with rounded serifs.
Mintage figure from Alan Herbert, "Give Us an S!", *NNW* 7/
23/83, pp. 12, 16.
2291 1979 D [4,139,357,254]
One reported without initials FG. *CW* 5/14/86, p. 82. Others
probably exist, from an overpolished die.
2292 1980 [6,230,115,000 + 1,576,200,000 WP]
Dwight Stuckey discovered a doubled obv., plainest at date
(irregular openings in 80); to date 28 found. Wexler {1984},
Appendix.
2293 1980 S [3,554,806P] Proofs only.
S as 1979 "Type II."
2294 1980 D [5,140,098,660]
2295 1980 D over S. Presently very scarce.
OMM 1–6. Price for OMM 1 or 2, S far to northwest or
directly above D.
2296 1981 [6,611,305,000 + 1,882,400,000+ WP]
See **2300.**
2297 1981 S "Type I" [3,464,083P]
"Type I" = worn mintmark punch of 1979: Round serifs join
middle, forming an 8. Reportedly, 880,445,000 without mintmark; these cannot be told from **2296** and may be included in
the latter. Compare next.
2298 1981 S "Type II." [599,000P] Proofs only.
"Type II" = new mintmark punch: wide S, serifs free of middle. Publicized by Alan Herbert: *NNW* 8/21/82, *CW* 11/10/
82, p. 70.
2299 1981 D [5,573,235,677]
Several vars. of D over S, only microscopic traces of S. OMM
1–4.
2300 1982 "Type I," large date. Brass. [all kinds
9,125,280,000 + 1,990,005,000 WP]
Officially "High Relief"; 2 close to rim. 48 grs. = 3.11 gms.
Mintage figure includes both metals. WP (no mintmark) figure includes some dated 1981; other sources say

1,904,400,000 WP, which may exclude the backdated 1981's.
Corrected figures are anticipated. A doubled obv. die exists.

2301 1982 "Type I," large date. Zinc.
Issue began Jan. 6, 1982 at West Point. *CW* 1/6/82, p. 1.
Often discolored; see introductory text.
2302 1982 "Type II," small date. Brass.
Officially "Low Relief"; 2 its own width away from rim. First
trial strikings Sept. 3; first reported in circulation by Bill Olsen, Oct. 9; *CW* 10/27/82, p. 3.

2303 1982 "Type II," small date. Zinc.
Issue began Dec. 1982. Often discolored; see introductory
text.
2304 1982 S "Type I," brass. [3,857,479P] Proofs only.
New S punch, lower serif wedge-shaped with lower vertical

point. Issue began Jan. 18, 1982. Reportedly 1,587,245,000 business strikes were made without mintmark; these cannot be told from **2300.** *NNW* 2/26/83.

2305 1982 S "Type II," brass. Untraced.
Proof samples made, reportedly all destroyed at the Mint.

2306 1982 D [all kinds 6,012,979,368] "Type I," brass.
Issue ended Oct. 21, 1982.

2307 1982 D "Type I," zinc. [About 100,000,000]
Issue began Oct. 27, 1982. Often discolored.

2308 1982 D "Type II," zinc. [Incl. in preceding]
Same comments. Mint Bureau denies any of Type II were made in brass.

2309 1983 Zinc. [7,571,590,000 + 2,004,400 WP]
Often discolored. At least 3 minor doubled obv. dies exist. Rev. often weak. A drastically overpolished rev. die yielded specimens reading CFNT. *CW* 6/15/83, p. 72; *CW* 5/14/86, p. 82.

2310 1983 Doubled rev. die. Zinc.
Discovered by John Barkanic, Aug. 1983. *NNW* 11/12/83, p. 1; *CW* 4/11/84, p. 70. Doubling obvious on ONE CENT, less on UNITED AMERICA; note separated double dots in Latin motto. A few thousand have shown up to date, mostly around Lewistown, Pa. Ill. *USA Today* 5/31/84, p. 1.

2311 1983 S Zinc. [3,228,648P]
Often discolored. Reportedly, 180,765,000 without mintmark; these cannot be told from **2309** and may be included in the latter.

2312 1983 D Zinc. [6,476,199,428]
Often discolored.

2313 1984 [8,151,079,000]
Some lack initials FG (overpolished rev. die).

2314 1984 Doubled obv. die.
Doubling plainest at ear and beard. According to Robert N. Brock, about 2,000 have shown up. Other vars. exist.

2315 1984 S Proofs only. [3,198,999P]

2316 1984 D [5,569,238,906]

2317 1985 [4,951,904,887 + 696,585,000 WP]
Coinage at West Point suspended because of Gramm-Rudman Act cutbacks: *CW* 2/5/86, p. 3.

2318 1985 S Proofs only. [3,348,814P]

2319 1985 D [5,287,399,926]

2320 1986

2321 1986 S

2322 1986 D

2323–2369 Reserved for future issues.

CHAPTER 20

LONGACRE'S TWO-CENT PIECES (1863–73)

In 1806, and again in 1836, proposals were made in Congress to authorize coinage of 2¢ pieces in billon (copper with some small proportion of silver). The former project died quickly after Mint Director Robert Patterson sent the bill's prime mover, Rep. Uri Tracy (D.-N.Y.), two planchets of the intended alloy, together with a common brass button, to show how easily counterfeiters could imitate billon's general appearance without using any silver. However, the 1836 proposition was another story, and for some months Christian Gobrecht and Franklin Peale experimented with sample coins (10% silver, 90% copper, at 60 grs. = 3.888 gms. each) to investigate physical properties, resistance to wear, and ease of imitation by counterfeiters. After pickling some pieces, abrading others, silverplating still others, and so on, they came to the same conclusion as their predecessors of 30 years earlier. Legislators dropped this denomination from the then pending Mint Bill, not to revive it in any form for another generation.

But the third time, the proposal originated not in Congress but in the Mint itself. On Dec. 8, 1863, Director James Pollock wrote to Salmon P. Chase (Lincoln's Secretary of Treasury), recommending a 2¢ piece in French bronze (the alloy earlier chosen for the new cents). Pollock submitted for Chase's approval samples of two designs, one with a Washington head, the other with shield and arrows in saltire (similar to that adopted), preferring the latter—probably because it was in lower relief. Secretary Chase concurred, but stipulated that the motto GOD OUR TRUST be changed to IN GOD WE TRUST. This wording was evidently influenced by the motto of Chase's alma mater, Brown University, IN DEO SPERAMUS, 'In God we hope.' Pollock's proposal was written into the pending Mint Bill, which became law April 22, 1864.

A few of the earliest proofs, and a few thousand business strikes, came from the prototype die with small letters in motto, April 1864. Other working dies 1864–70 are from a new hub with large motto letters. Illustrations in the main text exhibit the differences more clearly than any verbal description. This prototype die with small motto also comes with the 1863 pattern rev. showing CENTS much curved, in copper, bronze, and aluminum proofs; these are extremely rare. Carl W. A. Carlson discovered a restrike of the 1864 large-motto proof; this has the new hub of 1871 (see below).

On the other hand, the 1863 large-motto coin claimed as a prototype may be a product of sometime between late 1864 and 1870, as its rev. die was made after the hub was injured (missing top serif to D of UNITED), as in many coins dated 1865–70, but unlike most 1864's.

In 1865 there are two different styles of date, from the same logotypes used for the cents. Proofs show plain 5; business strikes, including the 1865/4, have plain or fancy 5. Rarity of the other overdate, 1869/8, is explained by immediate die failure: All show some stage of a break through bases of 18 left-ward to border, becoming heavy enough to require prompt discard of this obv.

William Barber (who succeeded to the Mint engravership after Longacre's death, Jan. 1, 1869) made a new hub for the 1871–73 coins; berries are smaller and more distinct from stems. All working dies sunk from it show minor doubling on some letters of motto.

The year 1871 also comes with the same two different date logotypes as the cents: 71 about touching or well apart. This same distinction occurs on several other denominations. In all instances, the logotype with 71 about touching comes on dies furnished to branch mints before the end of 1870, that with 7 1 apart occurs on later vars. We therefore list the former first also for this denomination.

Business strikes of 1872 mostly occur in low grades, and they are far rarer than the proofs. Several uncirculated survivors are reported; to date all but four have turned out to be dull proofs. Dangerous counterfeits exist from spark-erosion dies; they have roughness on wreath and large 2. Working dies of the authentic ones are described in the main text. Many examples of this date (proofs and business strikes alike) were among the obsolete issues melted on July 10, 1873, after this denomination was abolished.

Two-cent pieces circulated at first because of the Civil War coin shortage; but after the war, fewer banks called for this denomination, and mintages dwindled, coinciding with increased coinage of nickel 5¢ pieces. This was believed—rightly or wrongly—to reflect lack of public acceptance of the denomination. Accordingly, the Act of March 3, 1871 authorized the Mint to redeem and melt these coins. Large mintages of cents, 1873–76, in fact came from bullion obtained from wholesale meltings of half cents, large cents, and 2¢ coins. Nor was any protest heard when the congressional committee working on the 1873 Mint Bill (later the Act of Feb. 12, 1873) decided to omit the denomination: Carothers {1930}, pp. 200–13. By its effective date, the only 1873 2¢ pieces coined were proofs with closed 3, some of them very dull like the 1864–65 issue; they have the rev. of 1870–72 proofs. Open 3 coins were made at some later time, probably clandestinely; they are much rarer, and have a rev. not seen earlier.

Two-cent coins had limited legal-tender status by the 1864 act; they achieved full legal-tender status by the Coinage Act of 1965 (PL 89-81).

The series has long been undervalued. We suspect that with recent publicity over some of its more dramatic vars., collectors' interest may be rekindled.

LONGACRE'S TWO-CENT PIECES

Designer, Engraver, James Barton Longacre; hub of 1871 by William Barber, after Longacre. Mint, Philadelphia. Composition, French bronze, 95% copper, 5% tin and zinc. Weight, 96 ± 4 grs. = 6.221 ± 0.259 gms. Diameter, $^9/_{10}'' = 23$ mm. Plain edge. Authorizing act, April 22, 1864.

Grade range, POOR to UNC. GOOD: Devices outlined; date, all rev. letters, and at least IN GOD legible. VERY GOOD: WE in motto weakly legible. FINE: Motto complete, WE weak, partial leaf details. VERY FINE: Over half leaf details both sides; WE clear. EXTREMELY FINE: WE bold; isolated tiny rubbed spots only. Surface and color affect higher grade levels.

2370 1863 Prototype? Large motto. Proofs only. Ex. rare.
Judd 316. Top serif of D missing as in coins of late 1864–70. Enl. photo.

2371 1864 Prototype. Small motto.
Note letter shapes. O D far apart; little distinction between thick and thin elements in those letters; first T(RUST) almost or quite touches ribbon fold, leaf below it has plain stem. Business strikes usually show plain rev. cracks through bases of legend. Proofs (12–15 known?) have repunched ER in AMERICA. Enl. photo. Dangerous forgeries exist; authentication recommended.

2372 1864 [all kinds 19,847,500 + 100+P] Large motto; Normal date and D.
OD almost touch; boldface motto letters (heavy thick vertical elements, thin horizontal ones); first T(RUST) away from ribbon fold; stem to leaf below fold is much less distinct because of other leaves above and below. Business strikes (over 20 vars.) sometimes have dies aligned 180° away from nor-

mal. Proofs are normally dull; they were included with the 100 sets issued July 1864, though others were doubtless made for sale separately from the sets. For the proof restrike see **2379.**

2373 1864 Similar. Repunched 18. Normal D.
Several vars.
2374 1864 Similar. Repunched 64. Normal D.
Several vars.
2375 1864 Similar. Double date. Normal D. Rare.
Several vars.
2376 1864 Similar. Partly triple date. Normal D. Very rare.
2 vars.: a) Newport:134; b) 1977 FUN:193.
2377 1864 Double motto. Normal D. Scarce.
Kliman 30. Doubled obv. die.

2378 1864 D of UNITED lacks upper serif.
Thought to be the last var. of the year; see introductory text. Rev. like **2370.**
2379 1864 Restrike. Hub of 1871. Proofs only. Ex. rare.
Elongated berry below l. end of ribbon; remodeled ornament below WE. Repunched 1. Discovered by Carl W. A. Carlson, 1983. "NY Coll.":1075.
2380 1865 [all kinds 13,640,000 + 500+P] Fancy 5; normal D.
Leftover 1864 rev. Fancy 5 comes only on business strikes. In all, 92 obvs., 108 revs. Proof mintage comprises the silver sets (plain 5).
2381 1865 Fancy 5. Normal date. Top serif of D missing.
Many vars. D of UNITED lacks top serif henceforth; see introductory text.
2382 1865 Fancy 5. Partly repunched dates.
Several vars. 1982 ANA:1692–94, others.
2383 1865 Fancy 5. Double date. Rare.
Date first entered slanting down to r., then corrected. Other vars. possible. Discovered by Mike Kliman, June 1978. Cf. *ETCM* 8/78, p. 27.
2384 1865 Fancy 5. Blundered date. Rare.
Date first punched far too low, then corrected. Note top

stroke of 5 protruding to l. from upright. Later die states (showing only traces of extra 86 and only a fragment of the extra 5) are less rare.

2385   1865 Fancy 5. Triple date. Very rare.

Discovered by this writer about 1953. Later die states show only doubling; these price as **2383.**

2386   1865/4 Fancy 5. Very rare.

Note corner of 4 between 65. Not to be confused with previous vars. "Durham," 1980 ANA:1181, "UNC.," $1,250.

2387   1865 Plain 5.

Business strikes and proofs. Many positional vars. Several vars. of partly repunched dates. Date elements as in **1965–67.**

2388   1865 Plain 5. Double date. Scarce.

Kliman 20.

2389   1866 [3,177,000 + 725+P]

Various minor partly repunched dates exist. Proof mintage comprises those with silver sets.

2390   1867 [2,938,750 + 625+P]

Proof mintage comprises those with silver sets.

2391   1867 Double date. Very rare.

2392   1867 Double motto. Scarce.

Kliman 8. Doubled obv. die. Discovered by this writer, 1953. Auction 82:519, "UNC.," $1,550. Usually in low grades.

2393   1868 [2,803,750 + 600+P]

Proofs have serif of D restored by hand to working rev.; ornament below WE weak.

2394   1868 Repunched 1.

On the proofs, the repunching is plainest at base of 1; on business strikes, at top of 1. 1982 ANA:1698.

2395   1868 Partly repunched date.

Kliman, 1, 2, 8, others. Either 18 or 68 will show extra outlines.

2396   1869 [1,546,500 + 600+P]

2397   1869 Repunched 1. Very rare.

1975 Sub. Wash.:87.

2398   1869 Repunched 18. Rare.

Repunching plainest at tops. 1982 ANA:1699, "UNC.," $900.

2399   1869/8 Very rare.

Kliman 10. Usually in low grades; see introductory text. Always with some stage of the die crack. Note traces of extra 186, evidence of use of 2 date logotypes. Discovered by this writer, Oct. 9, 1954, at the New England Numismatic Association convention, Hartford, Conn.

2400   1870 [861,250 + 1,000+P] Normal date.

Proofs have weak stripes at center and a horizontal die scratch l. of 2.

2401   1870 Double date. Rare.

Kliman 3. Business strikes and proofs; latter, 1983 Midwinter ANA:274.

2402   1871 New hubs. [All kinds 721,250 + 960+P] 71 about touch.

All coins 1871–73 are from William Barber's new hub: smaller berries more clearly distinct from stems; elongated berry below l. end of ribbon; redesigned ornament below WE; repositioned motto letters. Proofs have the 1870 rev. Several vars. of business strikes.

2403 1871 Same. Repunched 71. Scarce.
Kliman 1.
2404 1871 Same. Double date. Rare.
Repunching plainest at final 1. 1982 ANA:1704.
2405 1871 Double motto. Rare.
Doubled obv. die, like the 1867 but less spectacular.

2406 1871 7 1 well apart. Rare.
Business strikes only. Date logotype as on later cents. 1982 ANA:1703.
2407 1872 Straight date. [65,000− + 950−P]
Proofs often dull; some (not all) have rev. of 1870. Dull proofs are apt to be mistaken for rare UNC. business strikes. Usually in low grades; the few UNCs. have date slanting down (2 nearer border than 1), obv. rim break at 8:30, rev. cracks at UNIT and from ribbon to final A. Dangerous counterfeits are described in introductory text. Authentication recommended for any alleged UNCs. without these breaks. 1975 Sub. Wash.:89; Harte III:264. Many melted, July 10, 1873. A doubled obv. die is reported.

2408 1873 Closed 3. Original. [600−P]
Knobs of 3 nearly touch; 2 revs., one of them that of 1870. Often dull, occasionally sold in error or cupidity as "unlisted business strikes." Many melted, July 10, 1873. Enl. photos.

2409 1873 Open 3. Restrike? Rare.
Knobs of 3 over a knob's width apart. Usually weak in central azure and upper third to sixth red stripes. Sometimes carelessly made. Possibly 10 times as rare as preceding. Discovered by S. W. Freeman before 1957; first publicized in Boosel {1960}. Enl. photo.

CHAPTER 21

LONGACRE'S NICKEL THREE-CENT PIECES (1865–89)

By March 1864, the Philadelphia Mint was running out of nickel for cent planchets, and its requirements were so immense that even Joseph Wharton's newly opened Canadian mines could not supply the want. During 1863, cent coinage had required over 32 tons of nickel for the 12% alloy specified by law: a huge output for what was then a chemical curiosity costly and difficult to extract from its ores.

Mint Director James Pollock, a bitter opponent of the use of nickel for coinage, seized this opportunity to urge passage of a bill to abolish nickel cents and authorize issue of minor coins (1¢, 2¢, 3¢) in French bronze. This bill became law April 22, 1864, over powerful opposition from Wharton's friends in Congress—minus the reference to 3¢ pieces. (The latter would have been the same size as the old large cents, but weighing 144 grs. = 9.33 gms. each; surviving patterns show them with the 1844–57 cent head. Most likely, had they been authorized, obsolete large cents would have been spent as 3¢ coins, especially victimizing the blind and the illiterate.) Yet Pollock appears to have agreed with other Treasury people that the 3¢ coin was a worthwhile denomination.

Why 3¢? Not, as one might suppose, to replace the now vanished silver 3¢ coins, alias fish scales or trimes (Chap. 23 below); nor yet merely to lower the quantities of cents needed for nationwide circulation; but mostly to retire the unpopular 3¢ fractional notes, which had been authorized by the Act of March 3, 1863. Like the trimes, these fractional notes (ill.) found their major use in post offices. One would send a letter on its way; a pack of 100 would buy a sheet of stamps. They were the smallest in size and value of any fractional notes; they quickly became foul things of rags and tatters; they were easily

lost. More than any higher denomination, perhaps, they continued to be known by the derisive term "shinplasters." While the public complained about these notes, they willingly received and spent millions of cent-size "copperheads" (today known as Civil War tokens: over 10,000 varieties!), despite occasional newspaper stories about how makers had refused to redeem them. Here, as in Canada a generation earlier, the motto "Pure Copper Preferable to Paper" held true; the public in the 1860s, like their ancestors in the 1780s and 1830s, remained readier to use even anonymous irredeemable tokens than paper notes. Some of the tokens even read SUBSTITUTE FOR SHIN PLASTERS.

This was the opportunity Wharton's supporters had been awaiting. Until March 1865 they put unceasing pressure on Rep. John Adam Kasson (R.-Ia.), their chief opponent, finally convincing him that anything, even Wharton's latest proposal for coins of 25% nickel, would be better than further proliferation of shinplasters. At which moment, they presented him with a draft of a bill which would authorize coinage of nickel 3¢ pieces at 30 grs. each, to be legal tender to 60¢ (while cents and 2¢ pieces would thereafter be legal tender only to 4¢: petty spite!). These were to be paid out in exchange for 3¢ notes, which would thereafter be canceled. Implication: The coins would replace a like number of shinplasters, and eventually replace the entirety of that issue less lost notes, souvenirs, and rags too filthy to identify as genuine. Kasson introduced the bill; it passed both houses without debate (such was congressional hatred of shinplasters!) and became law the same day, March 3, 1865.

Longacre resurrected a Liberty head with coronet and rib-

bon, first used on experimental cents and quarter eagles (1857, 1860)—though the profile is suspiciously similar (minus the coronet) to the *Venus Accroupie* used on his other designs since 1849. For rev., he placed the Roman III from the trimes within the laurel wreath of the 1859 cents. These designs remained unaltered through the end of the denomination (1889).

Most coined 1865–76 were actually used in retiring over 17 million 3¢ notes, the remainder primarily for stamps; this pattern is reflected in diminishing quantities coined in later years, as fewer 3¢ notes were brought in for redemption. After 1876 (except for 1881), most coined were proofs for the regular minor proof sets; the dates 1879–80, 1882–87 are rarer as UNC. business strikes than in proof state. This has led to the unscrupulous offering dull proofs as rarer business strikes—even in the proof-only dates 1877–78, 1886, 1887/6.

Minor coinage was interrupted from Feb. 16, 1885, until late in 1886, explaining low mintage of business strikes and presence of a leftover die to make into the 1887/6.

We list first a prototype collected as a pattern (the Heavy Ribbons coin) because specimens have been retrieved from proof sets of 1865. Its obv. die was later used with a normal Thin Ribbons rev. die found on 90% of the regular (double date) proofs of that year.

The oversized proofs dated 1868 (³⁄₄″ = 19 mm) are patterns, made for sets with 1¢ and 5¢ coins of similar design, to illustrate still another of Joseph Wharton's proposals to increase the Mint's use of nickel.

Overdates (except for 1887/6) are discoveries of recent years. The 1866, **2416,** is a still unsolved problem: What is the 6 punched over? Many 1869 double-date coins have been mistakenly offered as overdates. Rumors of 1873/2 and some others remain unverified. The 1877/6 was controversial until Douglas Winter found a die state early enough to show that the traces of extra digit l. of final 7 is in fact part of a 6. The 1878/7 is actually the very earliest state of the normal 1878; repolishing of this obv. effaced all traces of the extra 7. The 1882 filled 2 has been occasionally offered as "2 over 1," but this appears to be wishful thinking. On the other hand, the 1883/2 is the real thing, as the curve of 2 within top of 3 matches part of the 2 in 1882 but not the 3.

We owe the change from closed to open 3 in 1873 to a complaint by the Chief Coiner, Jan. 18, 1873, that the 3's in the date logotypes furnished by the Engraving Dept. could be readily mistaken for 8's. Even in the 1950s and early 1960s, occasional 1873 proofs (especially toned or tarnished or dull) showed up mislabeled "1878." In the 1878, the two 8's are identical—unlike the 8 and final digit in 1873 closed 3.

Many of 1888–89 were melted (for recoinage into 5¢ pieces) when the denomination was abolished (Act of Sept. 25, 1890), following a change in postal rates. Millions of earlier 3¢ nickels went back from banks to the Philadelphia Mint, accounting for large coinages of Liberty head nickels from 1890–93. PL 89-81 made them legal tender (7/23/65).

Stereotypy of design probably contributed to collector neglect of this series; little attention was paid even to rare vars. Possibly this situation is about to change.

LONGACRE'S NICKEL THREE-CENT PIECES

Designer, Engraver, James Barton Longacre. Mint, Philadelphia. Composition, 25% nickel, 75% copper. Diameter, ⁷⁄₁₀″ = 17.9 mm. Weight standard, 30 ± 4 grs. = 1.94 ± 0.26 gms. = 192 to the troy lb. Plain edge. Authorizing Act, March 3, 1865.

Grade range, FAIR to UNC.; not usually collected below VERY

FINE. GOOD: Devices outlined; date and letters legible. VERY GOOD: About half of ribbing on III shows; rims distinct. FINE: Curls well defined; partial leaf and hair details. VERY FINE: Over half leaf and hair details. EXTREMELY FINE: Isolated tiny rubbed spots only. EXCEPTIONS: Many dates come weakly struck; mint-state examples will show luster on the weak areas.

2410 1865 Prototype. Heavy ribbons. Proofs only. 10–12 known?
  Judd 410. Breen 1-A. Ribbons run into dentilated border. See introductory text. Enl. photos.

2411 1865 Extra high date, thin ribbons. Proofs only. Very rare.
  Breen 1-B. Same obv.; rev. as next. Not to be confused with any to follow.

2412 1865 [all kinds 11,382,000 + 400+P] Double date west. Proofs, Breen 2-B (over 90% of proofs of this date are from these dies). Parts of extra digits at upper l. Enl. photos. A similar configuration on business strikes, presently rarer than the proofs, was discovered by Bill Fivaz; obv. badly cracked from bust through 18 to rim below 6. *CW* 12/8/82, p. 70. Proof mintage is that of silver sets issued after this denomination was authorized.

2413   1865 Double date, vertical. Rare.
  Date first punched too low, then corrected. Discovered by this writer about 1953. Cf. 1977 FUN:2001; *CW* 4/26/78 p. 44; *CW* 12/8/82, p. 70.

2414   1865 Normal date.
  136 obvs., 228 revs. Sometimes with minor traces of repunching on date. Weak strikings and defective planchets are common. A recent discovery by Tom Miller shows part of top of extra 5 above border below 65: probably very rare.

2415   1866 [4,801,000 + 725+P]
  Various minor vars. with traces of repunching on dates. See next. Proof mintage is that of silver sets.

2416   1866 "Overdate." Rare.
  Identity of digit within final 6 uncertain. Has been called "6 over 5" and "6 over small 6." Possibly the lines within loop of 6 represent knob and loop of another 6 originally entered far too low.

2417   1867 [3,915,000 + 625+P]
  Same comments as to 1866.

2418   1868 [3,252,000 + 600+P] Normal thin numerals.
  Same comments as to 1866. For oversize proofs, see introductory text.

2419   1868 Extra heavy date. Proofs only.
  Forms a minority of proofs. Under a strong glass, not only do numerals touch, they show traces of repunching.

2420   1869 [1,604,000 + 600+P]
  Same comments as to 1866. Wider numerals than formerly; same logotype as on shield nickels.

2421   1869 Double date. Scarce.
  Date first punched too low, then corrected. Hirt:58; others. Discovered by this writer, 1955. Sometimes mistakenly offered as an overdate.

2422   1870 [1,335,000 + 1,000+P]
  Same comments as to 1866.

2423   1870 Double date, plainest on 0. Proofs only.
  Forms a minority of proofs.

2424   1870 Obvious double date. Rare.
  So-called "large over small date." Actually the first entry from the date logotype was too low, well to left, lighter and/or weakened by repolishing before correction.

2425   1871 [604,000 + 960+P] 71 about touch.
  Same comments as to 1866. Only the one date logotype. Has been hoarded.

2426   1871 Double date. Scarce.
  Business strikes only.

2427   1872 [862,000 + 950+P]
  Same comments as to 1866.

2428   1872/72 Obvious doubling on 72. Proofs only.
  Forms a minority of proofs.

2429   1872 Obvious double date west. Very rare.
  Business strikes only. Date first entered to l. of final position.

2430   1873 Closed 3. [390,000 + 1,100+P]
  Knobs of 3 almost touch; see introductory text. All proofs of this date and denomination have closed 3.

2431 1873 Open 3. [783,000]
Knobs of 3 farther apart and smaller. Business strikes only. Hereafter, permitted weight deviation is ± 2 grs. = ± 0.13 gms.

2432 1874 [790,000 + 700+P]
Same comments as to 1866.

2433 1874 Obviously repunched date.
Business strikes only.

2434 1875 [228,000 + 700+P]
Same comments as to 1866. Apply a magnet to any specimen of this or next, UNC. or proof; 2 of each were made in pure nickel for Joseph Wharton: Julian {1969}. Pure nickel is magnetic, cupro-nickel is not.

2435 1876 [162,000 + 1,150+P]
7 obvs., 11 revs.; 3 revs. were held over for 1877 use. Same comments as to 1875.

2436 1876 Plainly repunched date.
Business strikes only.

2437 1877/6 [all kinds 510+P] Proofs only.
Earliest state only: repunched base of 1; traces of 6 l. of final 7. Discovered by Douglas Winter: Ivy Phoenix:323; Ralston:501; Rhodes:485. Comprises a small minority of 1877's. Dull specimens are sometimes sold as "unlisted business strikes." See next.

2438 1877 Normal date.
Fragmented leaves (lapped die). Comprises the vast majority of 1877's. Said to come with high and low dates. 1982 ANA:251–52, :1750. Proof mintage represents the number of silver sets; actual number is probably nearer to 800 or 900. One pair of dies for business strikes remained unused; its rev. and the 3 leftover 1876 revs. were most likely held over for 1878–79 use. Often dull, sometimes sold as "unlisted business strikes."

2439 1878/7 Very rare. Proofs only.
Actually the very earliest die state of next. Obvious remnants of crossbar of 7 in upper loop of final 8, shaft of 7 in lower loop. Discovered by Jack Collins, Aug. 1977. See next.

2440 1878 [2350P] Proofs only.
Both 8's identical in size and shape, unlike 1873 Closed 3 (which is sometimes mistaken for this date). Second 8 microscopically repunched at base (1982 ANA:1751), filled; later, only partly filled; still later, clear, from successive repolishings of dies. Dull specimens have been offered as "unlisted business strikes."

2441 1879 [38,000 + 3,200P]
More often offered in proof state than in business strike form.

2442 1880 [21,000 + 3,955P]
Many proofs and several dozen UNC. business strikes came from a hoard once owned by Virgil Brand, the Chicago beer tycoon.

2443 1881 [1,077,000 + 3,575P]
Date normal or with traces of repunching in 88 (several vars.). Proofs and business strikes. Compare next.

2444 1881 Obvious double date. Proofs only. Scarce.
Comprises a minority of proofs. Later, this obv. die was repolished, effacing all extra digits except traces of extra 8's within 88; in this state it prices as preceding. Discovered by Lester Merkin about 1965.

2445 1882 [22,200 + 3,100P]
Filled 2 (not an overdate) or clear 2. Many proofs are dull; some have been offered as "rare business strikes." The 1882/1 remains unconfirmed.

2446 1883 [4,000 + 6,609P]
Dull proofs are often sold as "rare business strikes."

2447 1883/2 Ex. rare. Proofs only.
Curve of 2 within top of 3, not matching inner outline of top of 3; die file marks within 883, apparently to efface other traces of overdate. Discovery coin, 1973 GENA:602.

2448 1884 [1,700 + 3,942P]
Business strikes are very rare, often simulated by dull proofs.

2449 1885 [1,000 + 3,790P] Normal date.
Same comment as to 1884. 1982 ANA:1771, UNC., $650. See next.

2450 1885 Partly repunched date. Proofs only.
Repunching clearest on 18 and 5. 1982 ANA:266.

2451 1886 [4,290P] Proofs only.
Often dull or granular, sometimes sold as "unlisted business strikes." 3 die states. I: Repunching at base of 6. II: Normal closed 6, knob touches loop. III: Normal open 6, knob free (repolished die).

2452 1887 [all kinds 5,000 + 2,960P] Normal date.
UNCS. and proofs (same comment as to 1884) have 7 much farther from curl than either overdate die (see next). Normal date proofs are more than twice as scarce as the overdates; they were in the earliest proof sets of the year, preceding the overdates. The rare earliest state of one proof obv. shows repunching at bases of 18. Business strikes (mostly UNC.) are scarcer than proofs.

2453 1887/886
Forms the vast majority of proofs. Only the earliest (rare) show as much of the 6 as the ill.; later strikings show only traces of outer l. part of 6 (price for latter). Business strikes (rare) show part of extra base of 1 between 18. Discovered by Andrew Madsen Smith (the Mint's publicity agent) before 1935, in his hoard of proof sets.

2454 1888 [36,500− + 4,582−P]
Some proofs show traces of repunching on second 8. Business strikes (mostly UNC.) are scarcer than proofs; early states sometimes show repunching on last two 8's. Many were melted in 1890 when the denomination was abolished.

2455 1889 [18,125− + 3,436−P] Normal date
Same comments as to 1888. See next 2.

2456 1889 Obviously repunched 1. Proofs only.
Comprises a minority of proofs.

2457 1889 Obviously repunched 89. Very rare.
1982 ANA:1781.

CHAPTER 22

FIVE-CENT PIECES

i. LONGACRE'S SHIELD DESIGN, WITH RAYS (1865–67)

When silver coins began disappearing from circulation during the Civil War, the four denominations most affected (half dimes, dimes, quarters, and half dollars) were replaced first by postage stamps. These proved entirely unsuitable, becoming first impossibly filthy sticky messes, then too short in supply to serve as a circulating medium. The shortage of stamps killed John Gault's invention of encased postage; pay envelopes thereafter were crammed with "copperheads" (see Chap. 19, Sect. iv, introductory text) and low-denomination private scrip, alias "shinplasters," often filthy and tattered. Gen. F. E. Spinner's invention of Postage Currency (federal paper fractional notes exchangeable for stamps) came next, then Fractional Currency proper. The latter, of the same denominations as the vanished coins (plus the 3¢ after 1863), though neither legal tender nor redeemable in silver, could still be exchanged in quantity by banks and merchants for greenbacks (Demand Notes and Legal Tender Notes), which in turn could be used for buying interest-bearing Treasury bonds: their main advantage over the private tokens and scrip. Despite these assurances of value, the federal fractional notes (the 5¢ more than higher denominations) quickly became as much a nuisance as the 3¢, and shared the name of "shinplasters."

After the war, these notes went on circulating, despite mounting public protests. Something had to be done; not enough gold or silver was available to retire federal fractional notes at face value, even if Congress would authorize such action. However, the Act of March 3, 1865 had provided a precedent in authorizing coinage of nickel 3¢ pieces to retire the 3¢ notes (see Chap. 21, introductory text). A similar plan therefore seemed feasible for disposing of 5¢ notes.

When Congress discovered that the new Third Issue 5¢ (ill.) portrayed not the explorer William Clark (of the Lewis and Clark "Corps of Discovery" expedition), as they had expected, but instead Spencer M. Clark, of the Currency Bureau, their immediate infuriated response was to pass a bill retiring the 5¢ denomination, and another to forbid portrayal of any living person on federal coins or currency, April 7, 1866. (This was knowingly violated for generations afterward, being invoked only against Clark and Gens. Grant and Sherman.) Clark kept his job only because Treasury Secretary Salmon P. Chase intervened on his behalf. *CWA,* p. 300.

Now that the 5¢ notes had to go, something had to be found for a substitute. The logical choice was a nickel 5¢ piece uniform with the 3¢, proportionally weighing 50 grs. to the 3¢'s 30 grs. Mint Director James Pollock, though opposed as always to nickel coinage, prepared a bill authorizing such issues at 60 grs. apiece—an obvious sop to the congressional friends of Joseph Wharton, the nickel-mine monopolist. The House committee under Rep. Kasson (see preceding chapter) raised this to 77.16 grs., ostensibly to express the weight as an exact 5 gms., but in reality to increase the size of Mint orders for nickel bullion from Wharton. This bill was reported out of committee and passed both houses without debate the same day, becoming the Act of May 16, 1866. Either Wharton's name carried an influence in Congress equal to that of Almighty God, or the congressmen were in such haste to be rid of shinplasters that they would accept any halfway reasonable substitute, or they were still infuriated at the chutzpah of Spencer M. Clark in

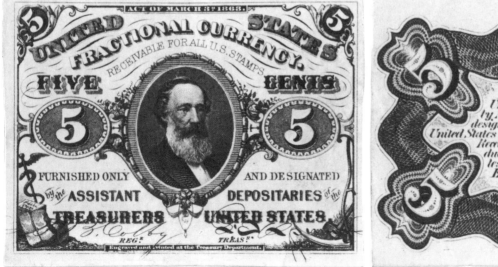

portraying himself on the 5¢ notes—possibly all three. Taxay {1966}, pp. 243–45.

Nickel 5¢ pieces were legal tender up to $1 (in violation of the Constitution, like the greenbacks themselves); they were to be paid out for 5¢ Postage Currency or 5¢ fractional notes of all series, which paper must be canceled immediately, in parallel with the 3¢ act (preceding chapter). The coins were immediately accepted and have remained part of our pocket change ever since.

Not that even this measure was successful in ridding the country of 5¢ notes. Over 44.8 million had been issued of this denomination in Postage Currency, almost 56 million of the Second Issue 5¢ (bronze ovals), and over 13 million Third Issue fractional 5¢ with Clark's portrait: in all almost 114 million, more than the entire mintage of half dimes since 1794. By 1884, only 76.7 million 5¢ notes had been canceled, leaving over 37.2 million still in public hands—mostly in such wretched condition that banks and public officials since then have refused to redeem them on the grounds that they could not tell if the notes were genuine or counterfeit!

During late 1865 and early 1866, while the 5¢ coinage bill was still being talked about in Congress, Longacre prepared a var. of pattern dies for the new nickel 5¢ piece. Mint Director Pollock rejected the Lincoln head outright, alleging intense Southern opposition (how had he heard of it?). He gave no reason for failure to adopt any of the Washington head types. Pollock appears not to have liked any of Longacre's submissions, but he finally expressed a mild preference for the shield design, possibly partly because of its correspondence to the 2¢, partly because it was in lowest relief and might strike up better on nickel blanks than the other designs, with a little less wear and tear on dies. (Even so, weak imperfect strikings are common; and nickel blanks, for generations, caused more die breakage than all other denominations put together! Shield nickels are commoner from cracked dies than from intact ones.) As designs were discretionary with Treasury Secretary Hugh McCulloch, needing no congressional approval, Pollock's choice—unopposed in Washington—became law. The shield design was promptly ridiculed as "the ugliest of all known coins," while even Joseph Wharton called its obv. "a tombstone surmounted by a cross overhung by weeping willows." These scurrilities were typical of many appearing in early newspapers and coin trade magazines commenting on the new issue. (Carl Allenbaugh quoted others in *NNW* 5/13/78, p. 1.) Similarly, the rays between stars came in for attack, often as "stars and bars," from believers in the delusion that treasonous elements in the Mint had chosen to honor the Southern rebels. (They might have cited Longacre's use of his longterm friendship with John C. Calhoun to obtain the engravership of the Mint; but bigots rarely knew enough history then or now.)

At least this much was true: Rays between stars impaired the coins' striking quality. Chief Coiner A. Loudon Snowden in Jan. 1867 refused to make any proofs of this type for sets (R. W. Julian, personal communication). Official complaints reached Treasury Secretary McCulloch, who on Jan. 21, 1867, ordered that subsequent nickels omit the rays. Proofs with rays, evidently clandestine, have become major rarities (12–15 known); they come from a single pair of dies, before and after repolishing. As prooflike early business strikes from other dies are far less rare, diagnostic criteria for the real proofs are necessary. State I: Roughness at base of all white stripes except that farthest l.; outer leaf below RU detached but not hollow; rev. ray below T(ES) hollow, dentils 3:00–5:00 attenuated. State II: Same dies repolished; leaf below RU hollow; ray below T(ES) incomplete; dentils at 2:30–5:00 still thinner, weaker. This supersedes the account in Breen {1977}, p. 132; State I (at least 5 known) was discovered by Ed Hipps in 1979.

LONGACRE'S SHIELD DESIGN WITH RAYS

Designer, Engraver, James Barton Longacre. Mint, Philadelphia. Composition, nickel 25%, copper 75%. Diameter, 13/16" = 20.6 mm. Weight standard, 77.16 ± 2 grs. = 5 ± 0.13 gms. Plain edge. Authorizing Act, May 16, 1866.

Grade range, POOR to UNC. GOOD: Date and all lettering legible including motto. VERY GOOD: Partial shield lines. FINE: Half leaf details. VERY FINE: Nearly full shield lines. EXTREMELY FINE: Few tiny isolated rubbed spots, mostly on leaf tips. EXCEPTIONS: Business strikes even in full UNC. are apt to show isolated weaknesses on some parts of shield lines and rays; mint luster on weak areas. Grade by surface; dull gray suggests grades below mint state.

2458   1865 Prototype. Proofs only. Very rare.
Judd 416. Center dot on rev., same die as next. I have not seen the business strike from severely clashed dies (date 1865 clashed between rim and TES) in "N.Y. Coll.":1182.

2459   1866 Center dots both sides. [125+P] Proofs only.
Same rev. as last. Mintage began about June 10, 1866. Proof mintage figure represents number of silver sets delivered thereafter.

2460   1866 No center dots. [14,742,500]
Business strikes only. Many vars. have partial repunchings on dates; compare next 2.

2461   1866 Double date. Rare.
At least 4 vars. Compare next.

2462 "18666" Very rare.
Date first entered far to r. Almost entire 6 visible r. of final 6. Usually in low grades. Discovered by Barney Bloom, *NUM* 9/49, p. 559. Another var. shows about 2/3 of extra 6; price for former.

2463 1867 [2,019,000 + ?P] Normal date.
Enl. photos are of one of the clandestine proofs (State II): See introductory text. Several vars. of business strikes show minor partial repunchings on date.

2464 1867 Double date.
Several vars.; original numerals may appear l. or r. or above or below final position. Compare next. See also ill. *NUM* 3/86, p. 445.

2465 1867 Triple date. Very rare.
On one var., one of the extra dates is below final position, the other a little to r.; on another, parts of extra 1 and 7 show to l. and r.

ii. LONGACRE'S SHIELD DESIGN, WITHOUT RAYS (1866–83)

It might be equally appropriate to credit this version of the basic Longacre design either to Treasury Secretary Hugh McCulloch (who on Jan. 21, 1867, ordered omission of rays from the 5¢ revs.) or to Chief Coiner Archibald Loudon Snowden,

who had made the original complaints about how the rays impaired the coins' striking quality.

Two new rev. hubs went into use in 1868 and 1869, differing primarily in positions of some stars. The later 1869 hub ("Rev. of 1870") continued until the design was discontinued. I announced these changes in *Numisma* 11–12/55:3483–86.

Alleged prototypes exist dated 1865 and 1866; because of their use of dies from 1868–69 hubs, most vars. are suspected of being clandestine products of late 1868, made for Mint Director Henry R. Linderman.

Overdates are all discoveries of recent decades. In 1869 there are two very different date logotypes (narrow and wide numerals); the narrow-numerals coins match the style of 1868, and all genuine 1869/8's are of this type. Wide-numerals coins offered as overdates invariably prove to be repunched dates. The rare 1873/2's are all from the Open 3 logotype (see below); the 1878/7 is an early state of the regular die; and there are at least five 1883/2 obvs., a situation not matched since the 1820s when the superannuated Engraver Robert Scot's eyesight must have been failing. Aside from these, major vars. are mostly doubled or tripled dies (slightly misaligned successive entries from hub onto working dies) or repunched date logotypes. Here, as with the nickels with rays, coins from cracked dies are seen more often than those without cracks.

On Jan. 18, 1873, the Chief Coiner formally complained to the Director that the date logotypes furnished by the Engraving Department ("Closed 3") were too easily mistaken for 1878; a new set of logotypes ("Open 3") quickly followed. I have seen 1873 Closed 3 coins offered as 1878's; genuine 1878's have both 8's identical in size and shape, and the date (of the 1876–82 style) is larger, wider, and heavier than that of 1873.

Counterfeits dated 1870 through 1876 are plentiful; most are dated 1871, 1874, or 1875. These circulated in the 1870s, principally in New York and New Jersey, and they still sometimes show up unrecognized in collections. They are immediately identifiable by having shield and letters differing from the vars. here illustrated; these genuine device elements do not change over the years because the same hubs mechanically transferred them to all working dies.

The dates 1877 and 1878 were issued only in proof state, though many are dull with rounded borders. Predictably, some dealers have offered such coins as "rare unlisted business strikes." Other proofs were carelessly made and distinction between them and prooflike business strikes is sometimes very difficult; authentication is recommended.

Over half the 1882's show a filled 2; these are occasionally offered as "1882/1" (possible though not confirmed), or as "1883/2." The real 1883/2 coins have date very widely spaced, like the normal 1883 but entirely unlike the 1882: Check the enlarged illustrations.

A rare proof pattern dated 1882 matches the regular issue except for lacking the ball above date. This may be found in sets of nickels, not distinguished from a regular 1882; its original purpose remains unknown.

Another and still rarer 1882 was struck from regular proof dies in a special grooved collar producing five equally spaced raised bars on edge: the "blind man's nickel," first described by Capt. John W. Haseltine in his auction of March 1, 1883. Though only four or five have been reported to date, others probably exist; have you checked yours?

LONGACRE'S SHIELD DESIGN, WITHOUT RAYS

Designer, Engraver, Mint, Physical Specifications, Authorizing Acts, as preceding, except that after April 1873 weight is 77.16 ± 3 grs. = 5 ± 0.194 gms. Grade range, standards, and comments as preceding.

2466 1865 "Prototype." (Restrike?) Proofs only. Ex. rare.
Judd 418. Obv. of **2458;** rev. hub of 1869. Kosoff Estate:
1059, $2,640.

2467 1866 Transitional. Original. Ex. rare.
Judd 507. Obv. of **2459,** with center dot; rev. prototype die, 2
center dots. 1976 ANA, Kennedy, S 12/11/80:453, $2,400;
Kosoff Estate:1064, $1,650.

2468 1866 Transitional. Restrike. Ex. rare.
Judd 507. Same obv.; rev. of 1868, no center dots.

2469 1867 [28,890,500 + 625+P] Normal date.
Rev. from hub continuing through part of 1868: stars point to
l. foot of A(TES), r. foot of E(S), between AM, and l. foot of
R. Many minor positional vars. of date, several with partial
repunchings. Proof mintage represents number of silver sets.

2470 1867 Double date. Several vars.
All 4 extra digits partly visible; none so spectacular as vars.
ill. for 1866. One obv. shows part of extra 7 emerging from r.
side of ball above date.

2471 1867 Triple date. Very rare.
Similar to **2465.**

2472 1868 [28,817,000 + 600+P] Rev. of 1867, normal date.
Many positional vars., some with minor partial repunchings
on dates (but see next 7). Proof mintage represents number of
silver sets.

2473 1868 Rev. of 1867. Date crowded into ball.
Outline of ball incomplete, overlapped by 8 or 6 or both.

2474 1868 Rev. of 1867. Date slants crazily down to r.
Final 8 much nearer border than 1.

2475 1868 Rev. of 1867. Double date.
Several vars. One, found only on proofs, has loop of extra 8 at
middle of final 8.

2476 1868 Rev. of 1868.
New hub, found only in this year: Stars point to center of
A(T), l. foot of E(S), to M, and center of R. Business strikes
only?

2477 1868 Doubled obv. die. Very rare.
Not seen recently enough to check rev. type. Similar to **2492.**
See ill., *NNW* 7/15/86, p. 6.

2478 1868 Obvious double 68. Rev. as **2476.** Rare.
Date first entered slanting down to r., then corrected slanting
up to r. (1977 MANA:1668, others). Less spectacular
repunched dates bring smaller premiums.

2479 1868 Rev. of 1870. Reported.
Same hub as **2483.**

2480 1869/8 Narrow numerals, rev. of 1867. Ex. rare.
Business strikes only; usually in low grades. Discovered by
this writer, 1960. Not to be confused with next or **2484.** Die

breaks at date probably explain early discard of this obv. and
consequent rarity.

2481 1869 Narrow numerals, rev. of 1867. Rare.
Discovered by this writer, 1959. *Numisma* 26:742.

2482 1869 [all kinds 16,395,000 + 600+P] Wide numerals.
Rev. of 1867.
Business strikes and proofs; many positional vars. Compare
next. Proof mintage figure represents number of silver sets.

2483 1869 Wide numerals. Rev. of 1870.
New hub. Stars point to l. foot of A(TES), r. foot of E(S) (as
in 1867), to M (unlike 1867), and r. side of upright of R.
Often with incomplete D, (E)S, C(ENT)S: see "Clearinghouse," *CW* 9/12/73, 5/14/80.

2484 1869 Wide numerals. Double date. Scarce.
Several vars., that ill. the rarest; others have both dates free
of ball and are sometimes mistaken for the real 1869/8
(above). Rev. as **2483;** may exist with rev. as **2469.**

2485 1870 [4,806,000 + 1,000+P]

Proof mintage represents number of silver sets. May exist with rev. of 1867 or 1868. One seen with doubled rev. die.

2486 1870 Double date. Rare.

Date first punched l. of final position; parts of all 4 extra digits visible. "Gilhousen":73. Vars. with only traces of repunching command lower premiums.

2487 1870 Doubled obv. die. Very rare.

CW 10/6/82.

2488 1871 [561,000 + 960+P]

Proof mintage represents number of silver sets. In date 71 about touch; date without or with several vars. of partial repunchings. Usually in low grades; often hoarded. Beware of early circulating counterfeits; see introductory text.

2489 1871 Obvious double date. Very rare.

1975 Sub. Wash.:97.

2490 1872 [6,036,000 + 950+P] Normal shield and date.

Many minor vars.: 2 clear or partly filled or completely filled; or with traces of repunching on date.

2491 1872 Double date. 3 vars. Rare.

Parts of all 4 extra digits clear.

2492 1872 Doubled obv. die. 2 vars. Very scarce.

Note crisscrossing shield lines (azure and gules) and double annulet below cross. *CW* 5/12/82. Rarer on business strikes than on proofs.

2493 1873 Closed 3. [436,050 + 1,100+P]

Knobs of 3 almost or quite touch, 3 smaller than 8; see introductory text. Proof mintage represents number of silver sets. All proof nickels of this date have Closed 3; the earliest ones

sometimes show traces of repunching on 1. Several vars. of business strikes. First publicized by Harry X Boosel.

2494 1873 Closed 3. Doubled obv. die. Ex. rare.

Similar to **2492**. Grand Central:1104.

2495 1873 Open 3. Normal. [4,113,950]

Knobs of 3 well apart. Several minor vars. including partly repunched dates, one with much of extra 3 between 73. Compare next 2.

2496 1873/1872 Open 3. Ex. rare.

Discovered by this writer about 1957. All digits show double punching at bases; the 1872 logotype was first entered low and slanting up to r., then the 1873 Open 3 logotype was repeatedly and heavily entered, to obscure traces of over-

date. 1) Breen, Kagin (1957), ill. 2) Kagin, Eliasberg estate. 3) Reported. Compare next.

2497 1873 Second overdate. Ex. rare.

Doubled obv. die, upper details similar to ill. of **2492** but double annulets closer together, slightly fewer crisscross lines in central shield. It is not certain if the original date was 1872 or 1873. Discovered by Bill Fivaz. Cf. MacFarland I:288, UNC., $400.

2498 1874 [3,538,000 + 700+P]

Date weak or strong, varying in position, occasionally with traces of repunching, most often with repunched 4 (proofs and business strikes). Proof mintage represents number of silver sets.

2499 1874 Double date. Very scarce.

Parts of all 4 extra digits clear. Usually business strikes; a proof was listed in Ivy Cambridge:453, later Rhodes:608.

2500 1875 [2,097,000 + 700+P] Normal.

Positional vars., some with traces of repunching on date. Proof mintage represents number of silver sets. Business strikes often weakly struck, often hoarded. Beware old circulating counterfeits (see introductory text).

2501 1875 Double date. Rare.

Parts of all 4 digits plain. Rhodes:610, others.

2502 1875 Plainly doubled 18. Rare.

Ivy Cambridge:455. Possibly late state of foregoing?

2503 1875/874 (?) Very rare.

The 875 are punched over other digits; only the 4 is uncertain (it is not another 5). 1977 FUN:205.

2504 1875 Doubled obv. die. Very rare.

Similar to **2492.** Discovered by Bill Fivaz. Business strikes.

2505 1876 [2,530,000 + 1,150+P]

Proof mintage represents number of silver sets. Many minor positional vars., some with partial repunchings on dates. In all, 119 obvs., 68 revs., averaging a little over 21,200 coins per obv. die–about 1/10 the corresponding figure for other denominations. Beware early struck counterfeits; see introductory text.

2506 1876 Double-punched date.

Proofs and business strikes.

2507 1876 Tripled obv. die. Ex. rare.

Triple annulet below cross; overlapping shield stripes; extra outlines on leaves and ornamental border of shield. Discovered by Bill Fivaz; *CW* 5/12/82. The reported doubled obv. die may be a later state of this.

2508 1877 [510+P]

Proofs only; mintage figure represents number of silver sets. One obv. die, 4 revs. left over from 1876. Often dull, sometimes sold as "rare unlisted business strikes."

2509 1878/7 [Incl. in 2,350P] Rare.

Earliest die state of next; clear shaft of 7 in lower loop of 8. Discovery coin, "Gilhousen":81. See enl. photo in B&R RCR 38, p. 18 (7/81).

2510 1878 Normal date. [2,350P]

Later obv. die states of preceding, traces of final 7 repolished off die. Often dull, sometimes sold as "unlisted business strikes."

2511 1879 [25,900 + 3,200P]

Normal or with partly repunched dates (several vars.), most notably in proofs. Compare next 3.

2512 1879 Triple date. Rare. Proofs only.

See enl. ill. in B&R RCR 39 (7/81), p. 18; Steig:295, $825. Later repolished die states command lower premiums and will be cataloged as preceding or next, depending on how much of extra digits show.

2513 1879 Double date.

At least 2 vars. of proofs. Later die states will price as **2511.**

2514 1879/8 Very scarce.

At least 2 vars. Forms a small minority of proofs. Hellwig, S 12/11/80:490, $1,250. Only 2 business strikes reported to date: 1) 1983 Midwinter ANA:403. 2) Ted Clark.

Courtesy ANACS

2515 1880 [16,000 + 3,955P] Normal date.

Dull proofs are apt to be miscataloged as rare business strikes. See next.

2516 1880 "Dropped 8." Proofs only.

Second 8 first entered very low, then corrected. Thought to have begun life as a double date, but no specimen shows traces of other extra digits. Forms a large minority of proofs; same comment as to preceding.

2517 1881 [68,000 + 3,575P]

Same comment as to **2515.**

2518 1882 [11,472,900 + 3,100P] Filled 2.

Business strikes and proofs; many minor vars., some with partial or complete date repunchings. Alleged overdates ("1882/1") remain unverified; see introductory text.

2519 1882 Clear 2.

Comprises a minority of business strikes and proofs. See next 2.

2520 1882 Clear 2, "blind man's nickel." Proofs only. 4 or 5 known.

Judd 1697. Five raised bars on edge (see introductory text). 1) J. C. Mitchelson, CSL. 2) Woodin, Newcomer, Boyd, Curtis, 1958 ANA, Neumoyer, Kagin, pvt. coll. 3) Woodin, Newcomer, Judd, HR 11/69, Kagin 11/73, 1977 ANA:2158, 1983 ANA:3013. 4), 5) Reported. Others may exist masquerading as **2519**.

2521 1882 Clear 2. No ball above date. Proofs only. Very rare.

Judd 1693. At least 2 have been retrieved from sets of proof nickels into which they had been sold as regular issues (early 1950s). Kosoff Estate:1120, $1,430.

2522 1883 Shield. [1,451,500 + 5,419P]

Date normal or with partial or minute repunching; many minor vars. Business strikes and proofs. Compare next 5.

2523 1883 Double date.

At least 2 vars. of proofs; others of business strikes. Rarest has date first entered far too low (ill.); late states may be mistaken for next.

2524 1883/1882 2 partly left of 3. Rare.

At least 3 vars.; over 90% show only part of middle curve of 2 between knobs of 3. Earlier states with clear 2 (ill.) command a far higher premium; 1980 ANA:1550, UNC., $3,800. Occasionally an 1882 Filled 2 is offered as 1883/2; the 1882 has close date, the 1883 very wide date.

2525 1883/2 2 within 3. Scarce.

At least 2 vars., one found on proofs; upper curve and part of knob of 2 within upper half of 3. *Numisma* 27 (11/60), pp. 6–7, for this and next.

2526 1883/2 "18823." Ex. rare.

Fewer than 5 reported of the earliest die state with almost the entire 2 in space between 83 (discovered about 1954). Later

reground die states (rare) show top and base outlines of 2 between 83 with traces of middle curve l. of space between knobs. Last state (ill.) no longer shows top of 2; Hirt:62, others. The die break is at first very faint, later heavy; earlier states lack it.

2527 1883/2 2 partly to r. of 3. Ex. rare.

Date 1882 first entered far to r.; parts of 2 peep out from r. edge of 3. Discovered by this writer about 1954; 3 or 4 known.

iii. BARBER'S LIBERTY HEADS, WITHOUT CENTS (1882–83)

In 1881, Mint Director A. Loudon Snowden ordered Charles E. Barber, Engraver of the Mint, to prepare pattern dies for cent, 3¢, and 5¢ coins to illustrate another of Wharton's coinage proposals. This was for a uniform nickel coinage, all three denominations alike save for size and weight. Obv. featured a profile of Liberty, copied from a Greco-Roman marble head, onto which Barber (imitating Morgan's dollar design) had affixed several wheat ears, cotton bolls, etc., above and behind the coronet. Revs. displayed value in Roman numerals within a rococo wreath of wheat, corn, and cotton. No action was taken on the proposal in 1881; but as it was still pending in 1882, Barber made more dies for various similar 5¢ pieces during that year. In line with one of Wharton's earlier recommendations (1877), the new coins were to be broader than shield nickels had been, so that they would ring better, making counterfeiters' task more difficult.

No action followed in 1882, either. Under official orders, Barber continued making pattern dies well into 1883. Some of these came with revs. which announced their experimental alloys: PURE NICKEL, 75 N 25 C, 50 N 50 C, 33 N 67 C: alloys which had been rejected over 20 years earlier as impossibly difficult to work into homogeneous strip free of splits or bubbles, or else hard enough to damage dies. It developed that Congress was not about to vote any more nickel cents into law, but Treasury Secretary Charles Folger approved of the idea of improving the 5¢ design. The version he chose had stars (rather than lettering) around head, and motto below wreath without CENTS: a stupid blunder. Specimens of this adopted design, dated 1882, went to Folger and various other officials, who spent them, kept them for pocket pieces, or possibly used them for barroom betting; whatever the reason, most survivors are circulated. Ever since the 1957 Central States convention in St. Louis, when Bernie Marshfield won a prize for exhibiting one of these 1882 No CENTS nickels in solitary splendor, this prototype has been in extreme demand, like the 1865 Rays and 1866 No Rays nickels, the 1856 Flying Eagle cents, and the 1865 silver coins with motto.

Accordingly, Barber made working hubs and dies, from which came almost 5.5 million 1883 No CENTS coins. At which point, as Herman Melville put it, "the whole powder-train went up." People noticed that the coins had no mention of CENTS, and began saving these "mistake" nickels on the correct assumption that the design would be changed to incorporate the necessary word. (Unsurprisingly, they are still plentiful in high grades, mostly VF to AU.) But worse was to follow.

Unscrupulous persons reeded the edges of many of these coins, goldplated them, and palmed them off on the unwary as new $5 gold pieces. At least one famous court case reportedly involved a deaf-mute, Josh Tatum, who did the actual "shoving" so that his victims could never testify under oath that he had *called* the coins anything whatever. Thousands of the original "Racketeer" nickels, with partly rubbed-off gold wash, survive today; many with reeded edges, some with plain. Other parties, aiming at coin collectors, have within the last 30 years gilt ordinary centless nickels and sold them as "Racketeer" coins, thereby exposing themselves to this epithet, but doubtless crying all the way to the bank.

Protests multiplied. Mint Director Snowden at once ordered Barber to modify the rev. Barber's first and better idea was to place the word CENTS on a scroll across V; this was inexplicably rejected in favor of the more crowded arrangement with CENTS below and the Latin motto in minute letters above. However, the centless nickels were not withdrawn, many reportedly going to the Mississippi Valley and the West Coast, where minor coinage was always in short supply: Gibbs {1983}. Only the proliferation of the new type with CENTS finally ended the gilding racket.

BARBER'S LIBERTY HEADS, WITHOUT CENTS

Designer, Engraver, Charles E. Barber. Mint, Philadelphia. Composition, Physical Characteristics, Authorizing Act, as before, except Diameter $\frac{5}{6}'' = 21.2$ mm.

Grade range, POOR TO UNC. GOOD: Devices outlined, date and letters legible except LIBERTY. VERY GOOD: LI Y or L TY or parts of four letters of LIBERTY legible. FINE: LIBERTY completely legible. VERY FINE: Over half hair and leaf details; I of LIBERTY bold. EXTREMELY FINE: Isolated tiny rubbed spots only. EXCEPTIONS: Weak and even mediocre strikings will not show all corn grains even in mint state; look for mint luster on weak points. However, there are tens of thousands of "sliders," borderline cases, apt to be offered as mint state; look for traces of rubbing on cheek and hair, with grayed fields having less mint luster than full mint-state nickels of any date.

2528　1882 Prototype. Exact type of 1883. Very rare.
　　　Judd 1690. Over ¾ the known survivors are in VF or EF grade, though they originated as proofs. Perfect proofs are Ex. rare: Auction 82:63, $4,300.

2529　1883 [all kinds 5,474,000 + 5,219P] Normal date.
　　　Many minor vars., some with traces of repunching on one or more digits. Usually found VF to AU; probably over half the mintage was saved as curiosities. See introductory text. Rarely, proofs will have the prototype rev., with BU repunched.

2530　1883 Obviously repunched 1. Rare.
　　　Plain double serif at upper l.
2531　1883 Double date. Rare.
　　　Parts of all 4 extra digits visible.
2532　1883 Obvious doubling at 18. Proofs only. Very rare.
　　　LM 11/65:202; 1983 Midwinter ANA:419.
2533　1883 Base of extra 1 crosses middle of 1. Rare.
　　　Discovered by Elliot Landau before 1958.

2534　1883 Doubled obv. die. Ex. rare.
　　　Doubling is plainest at LIBERTY.

iv. BARBER'S LIBERTY HEADS, WITH CENTS (1883–1913)

After the new rev. with CENTS replaced the centless type, no further official changes followed until the design was abandoned in Dec. 1912.

Vars. are few and confined entirely to dates, though doubled dies may exist. Many dates in the 1880s come with repunched second 8, reason unknown; others have repunched final digits.

The only var. of this kind to have kindled public imagination to date is 1899/8. I found one of these, much worn, in 1953, and suspected it to be an overdate, as second 9 is extra wide and solid (upper and lower parts are completely filled and featureless); proof remained impossible for two decades, as all specimens that turned up were in similar condition, revealing nothing, even under a microscope. But since 1971 a few high-grade examples have appeared, showing plain traces of 8 at final 9. As this 8 is from the regular 1898 logotype, the combination is wider than final 9, accounting for the peculiar contours. However, these are possibly from a different obv. die, as none shows the 8 solidly filling final 9.

Proofs are more readily available than business strikes for a few dates, notably 1885–86. (Minor coinage was interrupted from Feb. 16, 1885, through the end of 1886, explaining limited mintages of both dates.) In 1888–89 most proofs were carelessly made on a batch of planchets that did not polish well; they are dull and apt to be taken for business strikes. These may have come from the 10 tons of blanks ordered from Benedict & Burnham. Really brilliant proofs of either date, with full mirror fields and frosty devices, are rare. Some later proofs, notably 1903–4, are found more often cleaned than not; many dates of proofs come stained or spotty. The explanation is apparently the chemically active (sulfite-containing) paper in which the Mint shipped proofs.

Uncirculated survivors, especially 1884–96, come from rolls saved by A. C. Gies, William Pukall, and Wayte Raymond during the 1930s and 1940s; these have long since been dispersed. Raymond published catalogs and marketed various types of coin albums in order to create and develop a market for single coins at retail; to him this was the only imaginable justification for hoarding rolls. But for many issues those rolls are our primary original source for high-grade specimens.

In 1912, for the first time in the history of this denomination, working dies for 5¢ pieces were shipped to the Denver and San Francisco branch mints. Many uncirculated specimens were saved of both, mostly from Denver. The mint-state San Francisco survivors invariably show weakness on forelock and some other parts of hair; apparently all came from the same handful of rolls. Numismatic counterfeits have been made by altering 1912 D coins, and more often by adding S mintmarks to genuine Philadelphia coins. Authentication is recommended.

Mintage at Philadelphia ended Dec. 13, 1912. A letter of that date from Mint Director George H. Roberts in Washington to Philadelphia Mint Superintendent John H. Landis said, "Do nothing about 5¢ coinage for 1913 until the new designs are ready for use." Nevertheless, one Samuel W. Brown of North Tonawanda, N.Y., later mayor of the town, formerly Assistant Curator of the Mint Cabinet Collections, and in 1912–13 Clerk or Storekeeper of the Mint, advertised in the Dec. 1919 *Numismatist* to pay $500 apiece for any 1913 Liberty Head nickels offered. In the Jan. 1920 issue he raised his offer to $600 each, "In Proof if possible." He exhibited five in all at the following ANA convention (Aug. 1920). In Jan. 1924, the Philadelphia coin dealer August Wagner placed a tiny advertisement in *The Numismatist* offering the set for sale. They went to Stephen K. Nagy, later to Wayte Raymond, thence to Col. E. H. R. Green (son of the notorious Hetty Green, the stingy millionaire "Witch of Wall Street"), thereafter (1942) to Burdette G. Johnson of the St. Louis Stamp & Coin Co., who dispersed them. Presumably, dishonest employees in the Coiner's Dept. clandestinely struck them for Brown, who waited until certain people had either died or retired from the Mint Bureau to pretend to buy his five through appropriate advertising. Their later history follows.

1. F. C. C. Boyd, A. Kosoff, King Farouk, Nasser's government, "Palace Collections of Egypt":1695A, withdrawn, privately sold via A. Kosoff and S. Kaplan to Mrs. R. Henry Norweb; by her donated to the Smithsonian Institution (1977). Proof.

2. Eric P. Newman, A. Kosoff, Louis Eliasberg estate. Proof.

3. James Kelly, Fred Olsen, Olsen:1551, King Farouk, Mehl, Neil:2798, Edwin Hydeman:280, Kosoff, $100,000 (10/3/72), WWCI (i.e., John B. Hamrick and Warren E. Tucker), Q. David Bowers, A-Mark, R. L. Hughes, Superior Galleries, Jerry Buss:366, $385,000, Reed Hawn. Dull, scratched UNC. Cf. *CW* 7/26/78, p. 1; *Sports Illustrated* 6/18/79. This was the piece featured on the TV program *Hawaii Five-0* in 1974; Kosoff's sale to WWCI got into the *Guinness Book of World Records.* Ill. at **2583.**

4. James Kelly, Numismatic Fine Arts 2:1058 (5/21/46), $2,450, Dr. Conway A. Bolt, R. J. Reynolds, Reynolds family. UNC., nicked. This piece was last seen with George O. Walton and has not shown up since he was killed en route to a coin show, Wilson, NC.

5. James Kelly, J. V. McDermott, 1967 ANA:2241, "UNC., partly rough," $46,000, Aubrey E. Bebee. The coin I saw is EF, nicked, scratched, cleaned; exhibited at hundreds of conventions, reportedly used by McDermott for barroom betting. Cf. *NSM* 3/58, 7/68, and 12/71.

During the Great Depression, the Fort Worth, Tex., dealer B. Max Mehl carried on a years-long newspaper advertising campaign (which he later admitted had cost him over a million 1930s dollars!), offering to buy for $50 apiece any 1913 Liberty head nickels offered. This offer was not bona fide, being merely a come-on to promote sales of his *Star Rare Coin Encyclopedia,* which went through over 30 editions despite being of no numismatic value. The major effect of Mehl's publicity was threefold: It made Mehl very wealthy through peddling his worthless book; it made the 1913 Liberty head nickel one of the most famous of American coins; and it stimulated the ungodly to make thousands of altered dates (mostly from 1903, 1910 or 1912) pretending to be 1913's.

BARBER'S LIBERTY HEADS WITH CENTS

Designer, Engraver, Charles E. Barber. Mints, Philadelphia (no mintmark), San Francisco 1912 (mintmark S), Denver 1912 (D), both below dot l. of CENTS. Physical Specifications, Authorizing Acts, as previously.

Grade range and standards, as previously.

2535   1883 [all kinds 16,026,000 + 6,783P]
Minor positional vars. of date; few very minor partial repunchings.

2536   1883 Triple-punched 1. Ex. rare.
Discovered by Delma K. Romines, 1979.

2537   1884 [11,270,000 + 3,942P]
Same comments. Sometimes with second 8 repunched; not rare.

2538   1884 Obviously repunched 4. Rare.

2539   1884 Double date. Proofs only. Rare.
Later states show only the obviously repunched 1 (NN 51:462); still later ones show only traces of the extra 1. These will price as **2537.**

2540   1885 [1,473,300 + 3,790P]
More readily obtained in proof state than as choice business strikes. For why mintage was limited see introductory text. Enl. photos. Beware casts and fraudulently altered dates. Proofs rarely show repunched first 8. 1982 ANA:331.

2541   1886 [3,326,000 + 4,290P]
Normal, or with repunching on second 8, or minutely within 6. See next.

2542   1886 Obviously repunched 86. Proofs only. Very scarce.
Comprises a minority of proofs. 1982 ANA:334, $850.

2543   1887 [15,260,692 + 2,960P]
Normal or with traces of repunching: base of 1, second 8, or tops of 1 and of second 8.

2544   1888 [10,715,901 + 4,582P]
Proofs are normally dull: See introductory text. Business strikes come without or with minor repunchings; but see next 2.

2545   1888 Double date. Proofs only. Rare.
Comprises only a small minority of proofs. All 4 digits double.

2546   1888 Obviously repunched 1. Proofs only. Very scarce.
Not the same die as last. Comprises a minority of proofs. Not to be confused with business strikes showing traces of repunching on base of 1.

2547 1889 [15,878,025 + 3,336P]
Same comments as to **2544.** See introductory text.
2548 1890 [16,256,532 + 2,740P]
2549 1891 [16,832,000 + 2,350P]
2550 1892 [11,696,897 + 2,745P]
2551 1892 Repunched 1 2. Proofs only. Rare.
Repunching clear below upper serif of 1 and below 2. Comprises only a small minority of proofs.
2552 1892 Plainly repunched 18. Rare.
Business strikes only. 1982 ANA:1874.
2553 1893 [13,368,000 + 2,195P]
Minor positional vars. for both proofs and business strikes.
2554 1893 Obviously repunched 1. Proofs only. Very rare.
Comprises only a tiny minority of proofs.
2555 1894 [5,410,500 + 2,632P]
2556 1894 Obviously repunched 4. Rare.
Comprises a minority of proofs. The 4 was first punched too low and too far l.
2557 1895 [9,977,822 + 2,062P]
Some proofs show traces of repunching in 5.
2558 1896 [8,841,048 + 1,862P]
2559 1897 [20,426,797 + 1,938P]
2560 1898 [12,530,292 + 1,795P]
Occasionally with partial repunchings on date, proofs and UNCS.
2561 1898 Double date. Proofs only. Very rare.
NN 51:479; Ivy Cambridge:484.
2562 1898 Overdate. Ex. rare.
Final 8 extremely heavy; impossible to tell if over 7 or 6 even under a microscope. Hirt:1120, proof; compare Rhodes:678, UNC.
2563 1899 [26,027,000 + 2,031P]
2564 1899/8 Very rare.
Usually in low grades, where final 9 is solid and broader than its neighbor. The UNCs. are apparently from a different die (ill.). Discovered by this writer, 1953. See introductory text.

2565 1900 [27,253,733 + 2,262P]
2566 1901 [26,478,228 + 1,985P]
Various minor vars. with traces of repunching on dates, UNC. and proofs.
2567 1902 [31,487,581 + 2,018P]
Sometimes shows angle of 2 filled by die crumbling; not an overdate. Others have traces of repunching on base of 1.
2568 1903 [28,004,930 + 1,790P]
Normal or with traces of repunching on base of 1.
2569 1904 [21,403,167 + 1,817P]
Minor vars. exist with partial date repunchings.
2570 1905 [29,825,124 + 2,152P]
2571 1906 [38,612,000 + 1,725P]
2572 1907 [39,213,325 + 1,475P]
Same comment as to **2569.**

2573 1908 [22,684,557 + 1,620P]
2574 1908 Double date. Very rare.
Date first entered too low, then corrected; plainest at 19 8.
2575 1908 Heavily repunched 1. Presently very rare.
1 first entered too high and to r. 1983 Midwinter ANA:457.
2576 1908 Overdate. As ill. Ex. rare.
The 0 appears to be over a 9, the 8 over an unidentifiable digit. Discovered by this writer, July 1978, in a coll. consigned to Pine Tree Auctions.

2577 1909 [11,583,763 + 4,763P]
2578 1910 [30,166,948 + 2,405P]
2579 1911 [39,557,639 + 1,733P]
2580 1912 [26,234,569 + 2,145P]
Mintage officially ended Dec. 13.
2581 1912 S [238,000]
See introductory text. Uncleaned mint-state specimens are apt to have a bluish tint; many are from the H. E. McIntosh hoard of 60, discovered about 1953. Beware fraudulent alterations from next, or inserted mintmarks. Mintage began Dec. 24.

2582 1912 D [8,474,000]
2583 1913 Clandestine issue. 5 known.
See introductory text. Beware fraudulent alterations from 1903, 1910, or 1912. Enl. photos.

v. FRASER'S INDIAN AND BISON, RAISED GROUND (1913)

The Act of Sept. 25, 1890 (Mint Director J. P. Kimball's brainchild), which abolished the 3¢ nickel, gold dollar, and $3 piece, also forbade any changes in coin design oftener than every 25 years—ostensibly to discourage counterfeits of new types, but actually to discourage coin collectors. Treasury Secretary Franklin MacVeagh was informed by his son Eames on May 4, 1911, that during his term of office only one coin denomination could be improved in design without special legislation: the nickel 5¢. The Treasury Department communicated with James Earle Fraser, who produced a pair of original models in June 1911 suitable for the reducing lathe; MacVeagh promptly approved these. (Fraser's galvanos, dated 1912, are still on a wall in the Philadelphia Mint; smaller versions called "electrotrials" have appeared in various recent auctions.)

For obv., Fraser made a composite portrait of three aged chiefs: Iron Tail (Custer's opponent at Little Big Horn), Two Moons, and John Big Tree. The result is immediately identifiable as Native American, but cannot be attributed to any one tribe. It is nevertheless only the second realistic depiction of an Indian on American coinage (the first is on the 1908–29 gold $2½ and $5 coins), and it is apparently also the last.

Fraser chose to depict on rev. not a European buffalo but an American bison, old Black Diamond, then living in Central Park Zoo in New York City. Nevertheless, the coin's public nickname has always been "buffalo nickel," partly because of A. A. Milne's lines about the "biffalo-buffalo-bison," partly because the distinction was and still is unclear to most people other than zoologists. After Black Diamond was slaughtered, the firm of A. Silz sold the meat as "Black Diamond Steaks" for $2 per lb. Silz had the head mounted; Diamond Jim Brady vainly tried to buy it on a "name your price" basis. After Silz retired, 1927, the head went to his employee Benjamin H. Mayer, whose daughter Marjory Mayer Curnen exhibited it at the 1985 ANA Convention. *NUM* 3/86, pp. 429–30.

Perhaps more than coincidentally, Native American and bison motifs were being featured on American currency and stamps at the same time. On the then current (Series of 1899) $5 silver certificates was G. F. C. Smillie's splendid portrait of Chief Running Antelope; and the Series of 1901 $10 Legals featured Marcus Baldwin's magnificent bison, modeled from Pablo (1895–1914), then in the Washington, D.C. zoo (Lynn Glaser, *NSM* 7/59, p. 1636). A few years earlier, the 1898 Trans-Mississippi Exposition stamps included an orange 4¢ depicting a mounted brave pursuing a bison.

Between Treasury approval of the design and the manufacture of master dies, a vending machine company executive claimed that the new coins would not pass his counterfeit-detection device, and demanded numerous minor changes. After the Mint acceded to these, he made still further demands. In the end, Secretary MacVeagh told the Mint authorities to proceed with Fraser's design as originally approved, and let the vending machine companies change their apparatus instead.

During the monstrous fuss made by the vending machine executive, the Engraving Department made two different types of experimental pieces, both similar to the design adopted but without Fraser's initial F below date. Of the first, with normal flat top to 3 (diameter 0.839″ = 21.3 mm), 11 survive from an original mintage of 17, Jan. 13, 1913; of the second, with round top to 3 (0.869″ = 22.1 mm), 4 were struck Feb. 13, but only one is in private hands. Possibly some of the former survive in collections, mistaken for normal 1913's; have you checked yours? Taxay {1966}, pp. 340–46.

Many uncirculated examples of the regular 1913 "Type I" or Raised Ground were saved as first of their kind. Occasional rare matte proofs used to be unwittingly displayed in bourses as choice ordinary business strikes; now the problem is to find matte proofs that are not business strikes mislabeled! Real matte proofs are much sharper in central detail than are business strikes, and their borders are noticeably broader than normal, with pronounced sharp inner and outer rims. Many were mistakenly spent.

There are no marked vars. of this type within its single year. Some specimens will show minute to microscopic die doubling (same principle as the 1955 doubled die cents), or minute repunching on a mintmark, but so far collectors have paid little attention to these. Others, more often met with, are from clashed dies, showing parts of the Latin motto below chin, and occasionally other details from either die impressed retrograde on the other.

As early as April 1913 it became apparent that the denomination FIVE CENTS would wear down rapidly. This discovery led to modification of the design: See following section.

FRASER'S INDIAN AND BISON, RAISED GROUND

Designer, Engraver, James Earle Fraser. Mints, Philadelphia (no mintmark), San Francisco (mintmark S), Denver (D). Mintmarks below space between FIVE CENTS. Composition, Physical Specifications, Authorizing Acts, as before.

Grade range, FAIR to UNC. GOOD: Date and inscription legible. VERY GOOD: Half horn visible. FINE: Full obv. rim; 2/3 of horn shows. VERY FINE: Full horn (outlined, not rounded relief); cheekbone distinct though with a worn line. EXTREMELY FINE: Isolated rubbed spots only, notably on hair ribbon and above and behind temple. NOTE: Usually collected by beginners in G–VG, by others only in UNC.

2584 1913 Prototype. No F below date; flat top to 3. [17, net 11]
Diameter 0.839″ = 21.3 mm. Struck Jan. 13, 1913. 1), 2) SI; others in private colls. See introductory text.

2585 1913 Second Prototype. No F; round top to 3. [4, net 3]
Diameter 0.869″ = 22.1 mm. Struck Feb. 13. 1), 2) SI; 3) Pvt. coll. The fourth was destroyed. See introductory text.

2586 1913 With F below date. [30,992,000 + 1,520P]
The F is Fraser's initial. Mintage began Feb. 17: *NUM* 3/13, p. 130. Ill. is of a proof; note borders and device details, especially Indian's skin, hair, feathers, and rugosity of bison's hide. Enl. photos.

2587 1913 S [2,105,000]
Mintmark varies in position: midway between E C, nearer to E, nearer to C, high or low, rarely touching E or C. Occa-

sionally with minute double punching. Often with clash marks (see introductory text).

2588 1913 D [5,337,000]

Same comments as to last.

vi. THE FRASER-BARBER INDIAN AND BISONS, STRAIGHT GROUND (1913–38)

As soon as the discovery was made (April 1913) that the mound bearing FIVE CENTS would have to be modified so that the words would not wear away at once, the necessary procedure was obvious: place FIVE CENTS within a recess. That should have been enough.

Unfortunately, professional jealousy reared its stupid head, and Mint Engraver Charles E. Barber could not bear to leave well enough alone after executing the one necessary minor change. Henceforth, not only does the bison stand on a straight platform whose base defines the recess for FIVE CENTS, but the portrait and bison are notably modified. Gone is much of the rugosity of Black Diamond's hide, gone too are many details of the Indian's hair, wrinkles, and feathers. Fields are smoothed out. These multiple minor changes greatly diluted the vigor of Fraser's original design. Nor did they improve either striking quality or resistance to wear; many coins of the 1913 II–1915 issue are weak in centers, unlike 1913 "Type I" from any mint. Dates wear down more rapidly than those on the 1913 "Type I" coins; Barber could have placed date in a recess, but for unknown reasons he did not.

Barber again modified the design in 1916. Coins of 1916–38 should be known as "Type III": LIBERTY is henceforth much sharper, Indian's nose longer, and many other details have again been changed. Not that this helped; striking quality and resistance to wear are still worse, dates becoming quickly illegible. Some mintmarked nickels 1918–35 are virtually unknown well struck. Uncirculated survivors from the original Gies, Pukall, and Wayte Raymond rolls show flatness on hump and horn—but enough mint luster so that nobody could downgrade the coins.

Proofs of 1913 "Type II" through 1917 show more detail than any business strikes, but they are not in a class with the 1913 Raised Ground proofs. Many were mistakenly spent. Surfaces resemble the Lincoln cent proofs of the period, being uniformly minutely granular with a satiny effect. Borders are slightly broader than normal, with sharp inner rims. Many deceptive business strikes have been understandably sold as matte proofs. Those of 1917 were not publicly distributed; the first one turned up about 1976 in a broken set sold by the Philadelphia dealer Ira S. Reed (ca. 1930) to Robert E. Lee.

Proofs of 1936–37 are again different: Mint personnel had forgotten the former proofing techniques in the ensuing two decades. The first ones of 1936 (like the proof cents of that year) are of satin finish and unusual sharpness, though over half the survivors are impaired, probably from being spent. Later or second-style 1936's are very brilliant, like the 1937's, even on devices; beware buffed or plated coins, which will not have the extra sharpness.

Because all dies of this design were completely hubbed except for mintmarks, vars. come from hubbing accidents or mintmark repunching or overpunching (with one outstanding exception). Hubbing accidents produced such extraordinary anomalies as the 1916 doubled die (from the same process that produced the more famous 1955 doubled die cents). Minor doublings, often at profile or date, exist for many dates; they have mostly remained unnoticed and without the popularity of the cents.

A similar cause explains the 1918/7 D coins. During the fall of 1917, when (under emergency wartime conditions) working dies were simultaneously being prepared in unusual haste for both 1917 and 1918, one working obv. was returned to the wrong hubbing press after being softened (annealed) between blows from the hub, thus receiving entries from hubs of both years. Dangerous counterfeits exist; only the one genuine die is known. Study the enlarged photo, and particularly check the 7 and 8 in date, as forgers have added either a 7 to genuine 1918 D or an 8 to genuine 1917 D coins. Rumors of 1918/7 coins from Philadelphia and S mints are based on worn examples with atypical loops to 8's; explanation still awaits discovery of choice ones from these same dies.

The repunching that produced the 1938 D over S coins is not from accident nor blundering but from economy. Once the authorities decided not to ship any buffalo nickel dies to San Francisco for 1938 coinage, the revs. already earmarked for the San Francisco Mint were overpunched with D's for Denver. *ETCM* 4/77, p. 4. (On the other hand, the similar 1937 D/S is a blunder.)

A different blunder created the famous 1937 D Three Legs var.: excessive regrinding of a die to remove clash marks. Die clashing is a common accident in any mint: A tiny metal fragment or the like comes into the hopper among blank planchets, thence to the feeder—where it jams the mechanism and delays or prevents a planchet from reaching the dies. At which point, the dies, having no blanks to stamp, strike each other instead, often repeatedly, each leaving traces of their designs on the other. Routine procedure then is to stop the press, condemn and discard the dies which have become defaced by clashing, clear out the feeder, replace the dies with new ones, and resume normal operations. At the time of the 1937 accident, the pressman (a Mr. Young), then a newcomer, was under pressure to complete a quota, so instead of replacing a pair of clashed dies he took an emery stick and ground off the clash marks, in the process removing the bison's foreleg and weakening many other details. These coins escaped into sealed sacks among normal ones, in quantity, before inspectors condemned the dies and many impressions. From mint sacks the Three Legs coins reached the Federal Reserve branch banks and the general public. Strictly mint-state coins (full mint luster on the weak areas) are very rare, though specimens in VF to AU are always available for a price. During about 1957–64 forgers simulated many by grinding off the foreleg from normal coins; these are readily identified by lacking the peculiarities of the genuine, as only a single pair of dies suffered at Mr. Young's hands. Study the enlarged ill.; cf. Craig {1964}, ANACS {1983}, p. 75.

On the other hand, the 1935 and 1936 Two Legs coins have lately been proved counterfeit, the 1936 unmintmarked and "S" coins having the same obv. die. All are overweight despite apparent extreme wear; the blebs or raised lumps on surfaces of both dates, and the distortions of lettering, are inconsistent with Mint technology of the period.

More dangerous fakes of D- and S-Mint coins have turned up since 1983. These are genuine Philadelphia coins with mintmarks embossed: The forger drilled a hole into edge below space between FIVE CENTS, then used a tool somewhat like needle-nosed pliers with hard plastic or leather on lower jaw, and a reversed incuse mintmark on the other. Inserting the lower jaw into the hole, the forger squeezed the handles, raising the mintmark. The hole was then filled with solder and the edge filed down to remove evidence. Authentication recommended: ANACS {1983}, pp. 78–79.

Coins dated 1937 with reeded edges were made in Philadelphia and first offered for sale at the 1941 ANA Convention. They normally come with reeded edge cents of the same date; supposedly only 100 (others say 104) sets were made. Despite reports at the time that the Mint had issued them with reeded edges, they were apparently made by private parties. But even if someone at the Mint had clandestinely made them, there is no way such pieces could be distinguished from others privately made later.

THE FRASER-BARBER INDIAN AND BISONS, STRAIGHT GROUND

Designer, Engraver, Charles E. Barber, after Fraser. Mints, Physical Specifications, Authorizing Acts, as before.

Grade range and standards, as before. EXCEPTIONS: Weakly struck branch-mint coins through 1935 must be graded by surface; even the most brilliant will sometimes fail to show rounded relief detail to horn, or fringe on tail.

2589   1913 "Type II." [29,856,186 + 1,514P]
Enl. photos are of a matte proof. A doubled obv. die is reported.

2590   1913 S "Type II." [1,209,000]
Often with clash marks. Weak strikings are frequent. Mintmark positions vary as in **2587**; minor repunchings occur. The same remarks hold for later S and D mint coins.
2591   1913 D "Type II." [4,156,000]
2592   1914 [20,665,463 + 1,275P]
2593   1914 S [3,470,000]
UNCS. often are partly prooflike.
2594   1914 D [3,912,000]
Sharp strikings are commoner than on other D mints in the decade 1915–25.
2595   1915 [20,986,220 + 1,050P]
Proofs usually show arc crack on bison's shoulder and chest.
2596   1915 S [1,505,000]
Same comment as to **2593**.
2597   1915 D [7,569,500]
2598   1916 "Type III." [63,497,466 + 600P]
Note profile details, sharper LIBERTY, on all to follow. Enl. photos. Proofs (ill.) are very rare. Rarely, business strikes from drastically repolished dies (to remove clash marks) will have F weak or absent.

2599   1916 Doubled obv. die. Ex. rare.
Usually in low grades.

2600   1916 S [11,860,000]
Same comment as to **2593**.
2601   1916 D [13,333,000]
The doubled obv. die reported has not been authenticated.
2602   1917 [51,424,029 + ?P]
Proofs have similar finish and striking quality to 1916; only 7 have been authenticated to date. All show traces of double striking; several have die cracked through L(IB). Auction 86:1039, Proof, $6,600.
2603   1917 S [4,193,000]
2604   1917 D [9,190,800]
2605   1918 [32,086,314]
2606   1918 S [4,882,000]
Often weak.
2607   1918 D [8,362,000]
Often weak.
2608   1918/17 D Scarce.
Only the one die (ill.); usually in low grades. Later strikings show crack slanting down to r. from hair just above top of knot into jaw. See introductory text. Authentication recommended. Discovery first announced in Bluestone 1:62 (10/24/31). Possibly 6 genuine UNCS. survive. Fred Logan, Joe Flynn, $12,000 (1975), Ohio pvt. coll., $25,000 (5/86), Jack Hertzberg, pvt. coll.; $45,000 (1979), pvt. coll.; S 1/15/85:121, $23,500. *CW* 6/4/86, p. 70.

Courtesy ANACS

2609   1919 [60,868,000]
2610   1919 S [7,521,000]
Usually weak; sharp strikes command a high premium.
2611   1919 D [8,006,000]
Same comment.

2612 1920 [62,093,000]
2613 1920 S [9,689,000]
Often weak.
2614 1920 D [9,418,000]
Same comment as to **2610**.
2615 1921 [10,663,000]
Broadfaced 1's in date with top serifs, this year only. Better struck than 1916–20 Philadelphia coins.
2616 1921 S [1,557,000]
Same comments as to last (about date numerals) and as to **2610**.
2617 1923 [35,715,000]
Same comment as to **2615**.
2618 1923 S [6,142,000]
Same comments as to **2610**. Buffalo Bob discovered an S/D; only 2 reported.
2619 1924 [21,620,000]
2620 1924 S [1,437,000]
Same comments as to **2610**, though there are a few more bold strikes. An obviously repunched S has recently been discovered by Jack Beymer.
2621 1924 D [5,258,000]
As preceding.
2622 1925 [35,565,100]
2623 1925 S [6,256,000]
Same comments as to **2620**.
2624 1925 D [4,450,000]
Same comments as to **2610**. Bold strikes are Ex. rare. Minor doubled obv. dies exist for this and some other dates in the period.
2625 1926 [44,693,000]
2626 1926 S [970,000]
Same comments as to **2620**.
2627 1926 D [5,638,000]
Same comments as to **2610**.
2628 1927 [37,981,000]
2629 1927 S [3,430,000]
Same comments as to **2620**.
2630 1927 S Doubled obv. die. Ex. rare.
Doubling plainest at date. Discovered by Bill Fivaz.
2631 1927 D [5,730,000]
2632 1928 [23,411,000]
2633 1928 S Small s. [6,966,000]
May exist with large S, like the cent. Often weak.
2634 1928 D [6,436,000]
Same comment as to **2610**.
2635 1929 [36,446,000]
2636 1929 S [7,754,000]
Same comments as to **2610**.
2637 1929 D [8,370,000]
Same comment as to **2610**.
2638 1930 [22,849,000]
2639 1930 Tripled obv. die, plainest at date. Ex. rare.
Discovered by Delma K. Romines before 1971. *CW* 5/26/82.
2640 1930 S [5,345,000]
Same comments as to **2610**.
2641 1931 S [1,200,000]
Same comment as to **2610**.
2642 1934 [20,213,003]
2643 1934 D [7,480,000]
Often weak.
2644 1935 [58,264,000]
For the "Two Legs" coins see introductory text. A doubled rev. die has been recently discovered; usually in low grades. Doubling plainest on FIVE CENTS. Steiner & Zimpfer [1974], p. 66.
2645 1935 S [10,300,000]
Often weak.

2646 1935 D [12,092,000]
Often weak.
2647 1936 [118,997,000 + 4,420P]
2 styles of proofs; authentication recommended: See introductory text. For the "Two Legs" coins see introductory text. A reground die produced "Three Legs" coins, like **2654** but without raised dots and with more of foreleg intact. *CW* 5/14/86, p. 82.
2648 1936 S [14,930,000]
A markedly repunched S has been discovered.
2649 1936 D [24,814,000]
2650 1937 [79,480,000 + 5,769P]
Proofs are very brilliant; see introductory text.
2651 1937 S [5,635,000]
2652 1937 D [17,826,000]
A minor doubled obv. die is known. See next 2.
2653 1937 D over S? Presently very rare.
OMM 1. Discovered by Mike O'Reilly; *NNW* 9/16/78, 9/30/78. The discovery coin (one of only 8 traced to date) is Sieck-Harte:753.
2654 1937 D Three legs.
See introductory text. Only the one var.; compare all offered to illustration. Look for the stream of raised minute dots from below middle of belly to ground (this inspired derisive epithets); note details at hoof and fur adjacent to missing leg. Usually VF to AU, very rarely UNC. (That here ill. falls minutely short of the grade.)

2655 1938 D [7,020,000]
Several vars. of repunched mintmarks, some popularized as "D over D." None is rare.
2656 1938 D over S.
3 rev. dies. The most obvious (ill.) is OMM 1: triple D repunched over S; OMM 2, 3 are harder to identify and bring less. Discovered, March 1962, by C. G. Langworthy and Robert Kerr. *CW* 9/14/62, p. 1. See introductory text.

vii. SCHLAG'S JEFFERSON DESIGN (1938–   )

As soon as the Act of Sept. 25, 1890 permitted, Treasury officials announced a competition for a new design to replace the buffalo nickel. Evidently authorities already wished to rid us of personified liberty in any form as quickly as possible, substituting a series of presidential portraits to go along with the set on the then current stamps. Competing sculptors had to submit two plaster models, one of obv. portraying Thomas Jefferson, the other of rev. depicting his home "Monticello." Judges were to be Nellie Tayloe ("Ma") Ross, then Director of the Mint, and three sculptors; prize, $1,000; deadline, April 15, 1938.

On April 24, the judges announced the winner among some 390 entrants as Felix Schlag. However, the federal Fine Arts Commission rejected Schlag's side view of the building, and a Treasury directive demanded that it be changed to a front view (minus the graceful tree). All lettering had to be made much narrower, of 19th-century style, and squeezed closer, to leave room for the building's name—probably on behalf of those who would not recognize it, so different was the final conception from the original even as seen on $2 bills. Schlag complied—refusal would have meant forfeiture of the prize—and production of the coins began during the second week of Sept. 1938. Taxay {1966}, pp. 367–70.

Schlag issued 150 numbered, autographed, and notarized plaques, each containing a brilliant proof nickel with a photograph of his original rev. and explanatory text (2659). Almost none of these were sold then; a few were given away and the rest were retrieved decades later in a coin dealer's estate. They still occasionally come on the numismatic market. Dennis Brown has #1.

There have been many minor changes in the portraiture since 1938, mostly in details of Jefferson's peruque and its ribbon, though the appalling rev. needed improvement far more; even today it is unusual to find a nonproof nickel on which even six steps are complete and clear, all windows better than vaguely outlined. (Some "full steps" nickels command enormous premiums.) The blame here rests on whichever Mint Bureau officials insisted on a building (seldom if ever an effective coin device)—and a front view at that. Bureaucrats, not being artists, apparently could not realize that they were mandating impossible layout restrictions. Even mechanically this design proved to have serious flaws, most of all an area of high relief (steps and front portico) opposite another area of higher relief (hair near ear), to the detriment of both: A single blow from the dies at normal striking force simply cannot adequately bring up the design. Art was sacrificed this time not even to economics but to sheer stupidity.

During 1942, nickel became a strategic metal, having many uses in munitions making (appropriately for a metal whose original name meant Devil's Copper). There was too much industrial demand for nickel for existing sources to supply both the War Department and the Mint Bureau. During high-level discussions aimed at discovering a possible substitute for the standard 25% nickel alloy, authorities learned at once that most nickel-free alloys would prove useless. There were two fatal obstacles: coin phones and vending machines, alias "legal receptacles," where 5¢ pieces found much of their use. Counterfeit-detecting devices in most of these checked not only weight but electrical resistance, and the proposed alloys could not be tailored to match the manufacturers' specifications. Unlike 1913, this time it was unthinkable to demand that proprietary firms

close down millions of phone booths and vending machines long enough to retune their slug rejectors to accommodate both the old nickels and a possibly ephemeral new alloy. It would be simpler in every way—and far less costly—to choose a nickel-free alloy with the same electrical resistance as the former cupro-nickel, keeping blanks at the same weight as before.

After much experimentation, the Mint Bureau's metallurgists found that a ternary alloy of 35% silver, 56% copper, and 9% manganese satisfied the coin phones' and vending machines' electrical resistance specifications. The Act of March 27, 1942 accordingly authorized minting of 5¢ pieces in this alloy (promptly dubbed "wartime silver"), and the new issue began Oct. 8, 1942, continuing through Dec. 1945. To distinguish them at once from regular nickels, the new coins bore large mintmarks above the dome; those from Philadelphia are the only domestic coins prior to 1979 to bear a P mintmark. First test runs, May 13, 1942, occasioned many fire alarms: *NUM* 6/42, p. 461.

Many wartime silver 5¢ pieces come with minor splits ("lamination defects") owing to difficulties in making the new alloy homogeneous. They also tarnished irregularly, in streaks, for the same reason; the copper, silver, and manganese oxidize at different rates and to different colors. However, when new, cupro-nickel and wartime silver look similar, though the latter is whiter. This meant that the two alloys could be confused in the Mint; and in fact this happened, producing the 1942 P and 1943 P "nickel nickels" and 1946 "wartime silver nickels," on obsolete blanks. Several of these turned up in circulation or in ordinary roll or bag lots. Like the 1943 bronze and 1944 steel cents, these were struck on leftover blanks which happened to remain in the hopper at completion of earlier press runs. The easiest test for these is the ring test (see Glossary): All nickel 5¢ pieces of the same type produce the same note, whereas all wartime silver specimens will produce a note of another pitch.

On the other hand, the nickel alloy 1944 coins without mintmark are circulating counterfeits made by Francis Leroy Henning, of Erial, N.J.; these appeared in the Camden, N.J., area, Oct. 1954–June 1955. Coin collectors publicized them, aiding in apprehension and conviction of the forger.

In 1966, Felix Schlag's initials FS were added below bust, thanks to a campaign started by *Coin World*. Two proofs were made for a ceremony honoring Schlag as the unsung designer: *Coinage* 8/73, p. 8.

Because the Mint Bureau unrealistically blamed coin collectors' alleged hoarding activities for a coin shortage (1964), mintmarks were omitted 1965–67. But beginning in 1968, mintmarks (larger than those used 1938–42, 1946–64) were placed on obv. just past date, producing a somewhat crowded effect. Thenceforth, all proofs bear the S mintmark, except for a few tiny batches from which the S was omitted by error. Philadelphia coins 1980– bear mintmark P. Mintmarks are hammered into each working die by hand, except on proofs 1985– ; on the latter S is in the master die and therefore identical on working hubs and dies.

Aside from those made on obsolete blanks and the unmintmarked proofs, the most coveted of Jefferson nickels are overmintmarks: 1949 D/S, 1954 S/D, 1955 D/S. The last of these is probably from Mint economy measures, as the San Francisco Mint's closure in 1955 meant that dies earmarked for that branch could be put to use in Denver instead. Doubled-die coins of 1939 and 1945 have not yet been publicized enough to create a demand reflecting their actual rarity; the 1939 is almost unobtainable in mint state. The overdate 1943/2 P reached the front page of *Coin World* at Christmas 1978: eloquent proof that we have not yet reached the end of discoveries even in this stereotyped series.

However, the rarest of all Jefferson nickels have remained among the least known. These include the 1942 S with rev. of

1941 (found in circulation about 1961 and still unique), and two proof 1966's in Schlag's possession.

Nickels today are struck at 55 tons force, 120 per minute; average die life has been boosted to above 300,000 impressions.

In recent years Mint Bureau statistics have become notable for delays and inconsistencies. Mintage figures quoted below are subject to revision.

Collectors interested in a more specialized approach to this denomination may find it worthwhile to write to the PAK Club (Adolf Weiss, president), Box 1205, Montclair, N.J. 07042. This group is notable for sponsoring essay contests for young collectors. Possibly as the vars. herein described and pictured become better known, the Jefferson nickel series will outlive its earlier dull repute.

SCHLAG'S JEFFERSON DESIGN

Designer, Engraver, Felix Schlag. Mints, Philadelphia (mintmark P as noted), San Francisco (mintmark S as noted), Denver (mintmark D as noted). Composition, 25% nickel, 75% copper, 1938–42, 1946– ; wartime silver, 35% silver, 56% copper, 9% manganese, Oct. 1942–Dec. 1945. Diameter, Weight, Edge, Authorizing Acts, as before, except wartime silver alloy authorized by Act of March 27, 1942; Title 31, U.S. Code. §5112, gives diameter as 0.835".

Grade range, GOOD to UNC. GOOD: Devices outlined, date and all letters legible. VERY GOOD: Second porch pillar from r. nearly gone, other three weakly visible. FINE: All four pillars visible, though second from r. will be weak especially at base; partial eyebrow and hair lines. VERY FINE: Most hair detail intact; all pillars plain including base of second from right. EXTREMELY FINE: Isolated tiny rubbed spots only. Base of pediment (above pillars) visible but weak. NOTE: Except for certain "key" dates and rare vars., seldom collected below UNC. Sharp specimens with six steps clear and complete ("full steps") command higher premiums.

1. CUPRO-NICKEL. Small mintmark r.
of building

2657   1938 [19,496,000 + 19,365P]
Star before date smaller than on later years, but normally formed. Proofs and business strikes. Enl. photos.

2658   1938 Irregular dot before date. Proofs only.
Extremely thin shallow letters, star attenuated enough to form an irregular dot, much smaller than normal and not immediately recognizable as a star. From a drastically overpolished die. Comprises a minority of proofs.
2659   1938 Proof in original numbered autographed plaque. [150P] (See illustration next column.)
See introductory text. Included in above proof mintage.

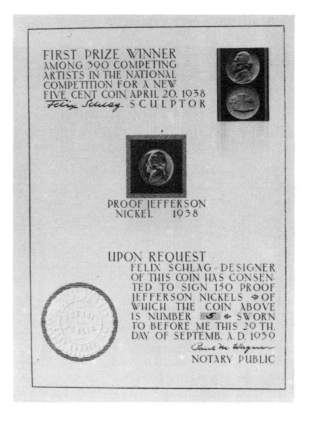

2660   1938 "Large over small date." Presently very rare.
Bases of differently shaped 938 above lowest strokes. Explanation uncertain, possibly an initial blow to the die blank from a hub which was discarded at once. Adolf Weiss coll.
2661   1938 S [4,105,000]
Repunched mintmarks exist for this and most to follow.
2662   1938 D [5,376,000]
2663   1939 [all kinds 120,615,000 + 12,535P] Rev. of 1938.
Larger star henceforth. Top step thin. Comprises over 99% of proofs and under 20% of business strikes. Compare next.

2664   1939 Rev. of 1940.
Top step heavy—much thicker than lower steps, unlike preceding. Comprises over 80% of business strikes. Proofs (discovered by Tom Miller) are presently very rare. This distinc-

tion first published by Bernard Nagengast. New hub introduced Feb. 21, 1939.

2665   1939 Doubled rev. die.
2 vars., both with Rev. of 1940. Price for "Variety I" (ill.); the other var. is rarer but less obvious, letters in UNITED STATES and FIVE CENTS thickened by doubling. Discovered about July 1939 by Malcolm O. E. Chell-Frost, who had confused them with **2664** because of Acting Superintendent Dowd's letter of 9/18/39. *NUM* 2/43, p. 104. Usually in low grades; very rare UNC.

2666   1939 S [all kinds 6,630,000] Rev. of 1938.
Top step thin, as **2663.** Comprises about 2/3 of survivors. Usually in low grades.
2667   1939 S Rev. of 1940.
Top step heavy, as **2664.** Comprises about 1/3 of survivors. Usually in low grades.
2668   1939 D [all kinds 3,514,000] Rev. of 1938.
Top step thin, as **2663.** Comprises possibly 60% of survivors. Usually in low grades; pumped into circulation early, not saved in bag lots. Beware alterations from 1959 D; on the genuine, the 3 is like that on other 1939's, entirely unlike the 5 of 1959.
2669   1939 D Rev. of 1940.
Top step heavy, as **2664.** Comprises possibly 40% of survivors. Same comments.
2670   1940 [all kinds 176,485,000 + 14,158P] Rev. of 1938. Presently very rare.
Top step thin, as **2663.** Proofs only, to date. Discovered by Bill Fivaz.

2671   1940 Rev. of 1940.
Top step heavy, as **2664.** Proofs and business strikes. Comprises over 99% of proofs.
2672   1940 S [39,690,000]
Rev. of 1940 only; may exist with Rev. of 1938.
2673   1940 D [43,540,000]
Same comment.
2674   1941 [203,265,000 + 18,720P]
2675   1941 S [all kinds 43,445,000] Small s.
Mintmark from punch used 1938–40; roundish serifs. Compare next.
2676   1941 S Large S.
Large sharp serifs to S, as on cents of later years. Only one rev. die seen to date. Comprises a tiny minority of the mintage.

2677   1941 D [53,432,000]
2678   1941 D over lazy D. Presently very rare.
Not in RPM. D first entered horizontal, curve down, then corrected, like **2681.** Discovered by Bob Salwasser, *CW* 5/11/83, p. 82.
2679   1942 [49,789,000 + 29,600P]
Business strikes are often granular.
2680   1942 D [13,938,000]
Usually in low grades (no bag lots saved). Mintage interrupted to prepare for the new coinage.
2681   1942 D over lazy D. Presently very rare.
RPM 1. Discovered by Joseph L. Diodato, 1962. *CW* 9/14/62, p. 1.

2. WARTIME SILVER. Large mintmark above dome unless noted

2682 1942 P [57,873,000 + 27,600P]

The proofs were hoarded; many were added to proof sets purchased earlier in the year, creating what are regularly sold as 6-piece sets. No more proofs were coined until 1950. On this and all to follow through **2701**, numerous vars. of repunched mintmarks exist; most require a strong glass to discern. Ill. of **2685**.

2683 1942 P On obsolete cupro-nickel blank. Ex. rare.
See introductory text.

2684 1942 S Rev. of 1941 S. Unique?

Discovered in circulation by Ken Frith about 1961; later Herstal:89, 1975 Sub. Wash.:104, Robert Bashlow estate. Mintmark from the same punch as **2676**; presumably a 1941 S rev. remained in press with the 1942 obv. in anticipation of orders for nickel coins, but nothing was made until after the wartime silver alloy went into use.

2685 1942 S Mintmark above dome. [32,900,000]
Ill. at **2682**.

2686 1943 P [271,165,000]
Oddly shaped star on all vars. of this date from all 3 mints.

2687 1943/1942 P

Horizontal base of 2 visible within 3, even on worn examples. Usually in low grades; difficult to find in mint state. 1982 ANA:372, "unc.," $650. Discovered by Delma K. Romines, 1948, but not confirmed as an overdate until late 1977, when Bernard Nagengast discovered a mint-state specimen (ill.); *CW* 12/25/78, p. 1. Pieces with spurlike crack from lower loop of 3 are not overdates.

2688 1943 P Two Eyes.
Lettering and date also show multiple impressions. Discovered by Bill Fivaz. *ETCM* 6/78, p. 27.

2689 1943 P On obsolete cupro-nickel blank. Ex. rare.
Discovered about 1964. See introductory text.

2690 1943 S [104,060,000]

2691 1943 D [15,294,000]
Often hoarded.

2692 1944 P [119,150,000]
Star redesigned. Those without mintmark are counterfeits; see introductory text.

2693 1944 P On obsolete cupro-nickel blank. Ex. rare.
See introductory text.

2694 1944 S [21,640,000]

2695 1944 D [32,309,000]

2696 1945 P [119,408,100]
Over 40 vars. of repunched P. John Wexler's P over D is unverified.

2697 1945 P Doubled rev. die. Scarce.
Discovered by this writer about 1952, and independently by many others. Most seen are UNC. Price for the var. ill.; a second rev., less obvious, with lightly repunched P, commands lower premiums.

2698 1945 S [58,939,000]
Often weakly and unevenly struck.

2699 1945 S Triple S. Presently very rare.

2700 1945 D [37,158,000]

2701 1945 D Widely doubled D. Very rare.
RPM 14. Also called "1945 DD." The 2 D's overlap half a D's width l. and r., one being faint. Other repunched D's (26+ vars.) bring lower premiums. Discovered by Bill Fivaz; *ETCM* 8/78, p. 28.

3. CUPRO-NICKEL RESUMED. Small mintmark r. of building

2702 1946 [161,116,000]
Sometimes granular. See next.
2703 1946 On obsolete wartime silver blank. Ex. rare.
See introductory text. At least 4 authenticated to date. Ring test (see Glossary) will match that of any 1942–45 wartime silver 5¢. May exist from S or D mints.
2704 1946 S [all kinds 13,560,000] Sharp vertical serifs to S. Distinction discovered by Delma K. Romines. Forms about 90% of this date.
2705 1946 S Knob-tailed S.
Same comment. Forms about 10% of this date.
2706 1946 S Doubled obv. die. Ex. rare.
Discovered by John Wexler, July 1979.
2707 1946 D [45,292,000]
2708 1946 D over lazy D. Very scarce.
Cf. RPM 2. As ill., like **2678, 2681.** Discovered by Adolf Weiss, 1978.

2709 1947 [95,000,000]
Sometimes granular.
2710 1947 S [all kinds 24,720,000] Sharp vertical serifs to S.
Same comments as to **2704.**
2711 1947 S Knob-tailed S.
Same comments as to **2705.**
2712 1947 D [37,822,000]
2713 1948 [89,348,000]
Often granular.

2714 1948 S [all kinds 11,300,000] Sharp vertical serifs to S. Same comments as to **2704,** except that this forms about 85% of this date.
2715 1948 S Knob-tailed S.
Forms about 15% of this date.
2716 1948 D [44,734,000]
2717 1949 [60,652,000]
Often granular.
2718 1949 S [9,716,000]
Often weakly and unevenly struck.
2719 1949 D [36,498,000]
2720 1949 D over S. Scarce.
OMM 1. Discovered by Andrew Jacubowski ca. 1972. Other vars. exist. *CW* 3/1/78, p. 48.

2721 1950 [9,796,000 + 51,386P]
Sometimes granular. Earlier proofs are satin finish; later ones much more brilliant, like 1951 and later years.
2722 1950 D [2,630,030]
Rarely found circulated. Most of the mintage went in rolls and bags to speculators, contributing to the evil repute in which the Mint Bureau has held all collectors. One Milwaukee dealer had 8,000 rolls = 160,000 pieces, all UNC. Beware alterations from 1959 D and possibly other dates.
2723 1951 [28,552,000 + 57,500P]
Often dark.
2724 1951 S [7,776,000]
2725 1951 D [20,460,000]
2726 1952 [63,988,000 + 81,980P]
Often dark.
2727 1952 S [20,572,000]
2728 1952 D [30,638,000]
2729 1953 [46,644,000 + 128,800P]
Business strikes usually dark, often weak uneven impressions.
2730 1953 S [19,210,000]
Usually weak uneven strikes.
2731 1953 D [59,878,000]
2732 1954 [47,684,050 + 233,300P]
Same comments as to **2729.**
2733 1954 S [29,384,000]
Usually weak uneven strikes.
2734 1954 S over D. Scarce.
OMM 1. Always weak uneven strikes. Later die states with D weak command lower premiums. Steiner & Zimpfer [1974], p. 65.

2735   1954 D [117,183,060]
2736   1954 D over S. Presently Ex. rare.
Discovered by Philip Scott Rubin, 1978. Middle stroke of S plain within D.
2737   1955 [7,888,000 + 378,200P]
Usually dark. One proof has tripled rev. die, plainest at letters; very rare.
2738   1955 D [74,464,000]
Often granular.
2739   1955 D over S.
At least 10 revs. "Variety I" (ill.) is scarcest. Other vars. with S less clear command less premium. Discovered by Arthur Lehmann, Jr., 1962. *CW* 9/14/62, p. 1; 3/1/78, p. 48; 5/10/78, p. 34.

2740   1956 [35,216,000 + 669,384P]
2741   1956 D [67,222,940]
2742   1957 [38,408,000 + 1,247,952P]
Larger star than formerly. Usually dark: peculiarity of alloy?
2743   1957 D [136,828,900]
Larger star, as above.
2744   1958 [17,088,000 + 875,652P]
Same comment as to **2742.**
2745   1958 D [168,249,120]
Same comment as to **2743.**
2746   1959 [27,248,000 + 1,149,291P]
Smaller star (as 1939–56) henceforth. Often dark, like 1957–58.
2747   1959 D [160,738,240]
Smaller star.
2748   1960 [55,416,000 + 1,691,602P]
2749   1960 D [192,582,180]
Usually weak uneven strikes, as are subsequent D mints through 1970.
2750   1961 [73,640,100 + 3,028,144P]
2751   1961 D [229,342,760]
2752   1962 [97,384,000 + 3,218,019P]
2753   1962 D [280,195,720]
2754   1963 [175,784,000 + 3,075,645P]
2755   1963 D [226,829,460]
2756   1964 [1,024,672,000 + 3,950,762P]
Many struck in 1965 from 1964-dated dies, pursuant to Act of 9/3/64.
2757   1964 D [1,787,297,160]
Same comment.
2758   1964 D PLURIDUS. Very scarce.
R I far apart, r. uprights of U's thin. From a die heavily

reground ("stoned") to remove clash marks. The erroneous D is from regrinding obliterating center of B. Discovered 1973; described by Robert Leonard, *NNW* 12/11/82, p. 6.
2759   1965 [136,131,380 + 2,360,000 SMS]
SMS = prooflike coins in sets, 1¢ to 50¢, produced at San Francisco without mintmarks, while no proofs were struck.

4. DESIGNER'S INITIALS ADDED; MINTMARK OBV.

2760   1966 [156,208,283 + 2P + 2,261,583 SMS]
Initials FS (= Felix Schlag) added below truncation henceforth. For the 2 proofs, see introductory text. For SMS see above.

2761   1967 Modified rev. [107,325,800 + 1,863,344 SMS]
Door, window lines, and porch strengthened. For SMS see **2759.**

2762   1968 S [100,396,004 + 3,041,506P]
Mintmark follows date henceforth. Proofs from San Francisco only hereafter.
2763   1968 D [91,227,880]
2764   1969 S [120,066,000 + 2,934,631P]

2765   1969 D [202,807,500]
2766   1970 S [232,852,004 + 2,632,810P]
About 10,000 were released with dies aligned 180° from normal.
2767   1970 D [515,485,380]
2768   1971 Modified rev. [106,884,000]
French windows between outer and inner pillars have slanting tops; balconies, pillars, lintel, and window lines all strengthened; top step thinner. Probably exists with 1967–70 rev. For proofs without mintmark, see **2770.**

2769   1971 S Modified rev. [3,220,733P] Proofs only.
See next.
2770   1971 [S] No mintmark. Proof. [1,655] Very rare.
Mintage included in preceding; mintmark omitted from one die by error. Authentication recommended. Discovered in a proof set Dec. 29, 1971; the Mint Bureau confirmed it and provided the mintage figure.
2771   1971 D Modified rev. [316,144,000]
May exist with 1967–70 rev.
2772   1972 [all kinds 202,036,000] Type of 1970.
Not to be confused with any to follow.
2773   1972 Obv. of 1970, rev. of 1971.
Same comment. This and last minted Jan.–Aug.
2774   1972 New obv.; rev. of 1970.
Note prominent ‹-shaped Adam's apple. Queue retouched.
2775   1972 New obv.; rev. of 1971.
This and last minted Sept.–Dec. Cf. *NNW* 10/31/72; *CW* 10/11/72, p. 1; *CW* 10/18/72, p. 3; 11/1/72, p. 1.
2776   1972 S [3,260,996P] Proofs only.
Obv. type of 1970, rev. type of 1971. Other types may exist.
2777   1972 D [all kinds 351,694,000]
Obv. type of 1970, rev. type of 1971. Minted Jan.–Aug. Probably exists with rev. type of 1970.
2778   1972 D New obv.; rev. of 1971.
Minted Sept.–Dec.
2779   1973 [384,396,000]
2780   1973 S [2,760,339P] Proofs only.
2781   1973 D [261,405,400]
2782   1974 [601,752,000]
2783   1974 S [2,612,568P] Proofs only.
2784   1974 D [277,373,000]
2785   1975 [181,772,000]
2786   1975 S [2,845,450P] Proofs only.
2787   1975 D [401,875,300]
2788   1976 [367,124,000]
2789   1976 S [4,149,730P] Proofs only.
2790   1976 D [563,964,147]

2791   1977 Modified dies. [585,376,000]
Hair details, windows, and doors strengthened.

2792   1977 S Modified dies. [3,251,152P] Proofs only.

2793   1977 D Modified dies. [297,313,422]
2794   1978 [391,308,000]
2795   1978 S [3,127,781P] Proofs only.
2796   1978 D [313,092,780]
2797   1979 [463,188,000]
2798   1979 S "Type I." [3,009,175P] Proofs only.
Mintmark as before, filled, blurred, or blobby.
2799   1979 S "Type II." [668,000P] Proofs only.
Mintmark clear, with rounded knobs. Figure from Alan Herbert.
2800   1979 D [325,867,672]
2801   1980 P [593,004,000]
Mintmark P on Philadelphia coins henceforth.
2802   1980 S [3,554,806P] Proofs only.
Mintmark as 1979 S "Type II."
2803   1980 D [502,323,448]
2804   1981 P [657,504,000]

2805 1981 S "Type I." [3,565,083P] Proofs only.
Mintmark as 1979 S "Type II," now filled or like an 8. See ills. in *CW* 11/10/82, p. 70.

2806 1981 S "Type II." [498,000P] Proofs only.
Mintmark open, round knobs away from middle stroke. See ills. in *CW* 11/10/82, p. 70.

2807 1981 D [364,801,843]

2808 1982 P [all kinds 292,355,000] Type of 1981. Presently scarce.
Always weak in centers. Dwight Stuckey *(CW* 12/1/82, 2/2/83) found fewer than 20 among 20,000 examined.

2809 1982 P Obv. of '81, rev. of '82. Presently very scarce.
Rev., legend farther from rim; internal details of building sharper, most notably front door, lintel, arches, and dome supports. Stuckey (ibid.) found fewer than 10 among 20,000 examined.

2810 1982 P Obv. of '82, rev. of '81. Presently very scarce.
Obv., letters and numerals thinner, sharper (including initials FS); sharper points to star; more pronounced serifs to 1 2; sharper folds in ribbon. Stuckey (ibid.) found fewer than 10.

2811 1982 P Type of '82.
Obv. as **2810,** rev. as **2809.** The majority var.

2812 1982 S [all kinds 3,857,479P] Type of '81. Proofs only.
Estimated about [1,500,000P], Jan.–May 1982.

2813 1982 S "Type II." [Incl. above] Proofs only.
Estimated about [2,350,000P], in and after June 1982.

2814 1982 D [all kinds 373,726,544] Type of 1981.
As **2808.** Weak centers. No information on relative scarcity.

2815 1982 D Obv. of '81, rev. of '82.
As **2809.** Weak obv. Same comment.

2816 1982 D Obv. of '82, rev. of '81.
As **2810.** Weak rev. Same comment.

2817 1982 D Type of 1982.
As **2811.** Same comment.

2818 1983 P [561,615,000]

2819 1983 S [3,228,648P] Proofs only.

2820 1983 D [536,726,276]
A minor doubled rev. die exists. *CW* 7/13/83, p. 66.

2821 1984 P [746,769,000]

2822 1984 S Proofs only. [3,198,999P]

2823 1984 D [517,675,146]

2824 1985 P [647,114,962]

2825 1985 S Proofs only. [3,348,814P]

2826 1985 D [459,747,446]

2827 1986 P

2828 1986 S

2829 1986 D

2830–2899 reserved for future issues.

Part Three

FEDERAL SILVER
AND
SANDWICH-METAL
COINAGES

CHAPTER 23

LONGACRE'S TRIMES

i. BILLON, "Type I" (1851–53)

While a committee under Sen. Daniel Stevens Dickinson (D.-N.Y.) was preparing a bill changing postal rates, the question of how stamps could be bought loomed large. "Shinplasters" (private or state bank notes and merchants' scrip of all kinds) were not acceptable. Spanish and Mexican silver coins were, like many other types of foreign silver, but most had already vanished into hoards. Almost any piece offered would have to be weighed and tested to make sure it was genuine and not too lightweight—an inconvenient procedure, and not calculated to maintain goodwill. American silver coins were virtually unobtainable. Copper cents and half cents were extremely unpopular; any merchant who offered 95 large cents in change with a 5¢ cigar paid for with a Mexican dollar (let alone with a gold dollar) would be risking a fight! Federal copper coins were not legal tender and thus could be refused by anyone demanding payment in silver; they had no notable advantage over shinplasters, becoming equally filthy in a few months after issue, and even more inconvenient to carry around.

Why was silver coinage unobtainable? Immense discoveries of gold in California had forced down the world market price of gold in terms of silver, which shift was experienced as a rise in the price of silver reckoned in gold dollars. Little silver was brought to the Mint. The tiny amounts of silver dollars coined mostly did not reach the public; bullion dealers were buying up half dollars in quantity for resale in the Caribbean islands or Europe, where they were worth over face value and melted in quantity. Quarters were going the same way; smaller silver was hoarded. Something had to be done, quickly.

Since postal rates were to be lowered from 5¢ to 3¢ prepaid, the obvious answer was a 3¢ coin of some kind of base metal. Senators apparently remembered a couple of earlier minor coinage proposals that had failed because the low grade billon (10% silver, 90% copper) could be too easily counterfeited. Sen. Dickinson therefore wrote into his bill a clause authorizing issue of a 3¢ coin in high-grade billon, 75% silver, 25% copper. This bill passed and became the Act of March 3, 1851, effective June 30.

As the act left designs up to the Treasury, Secretary Thomas Corwin requested sample coins from Mint Director Robert Maskell Patterson. These were of two radically different designs. The first (Judd 125) was Franklin Peale's 1850 Liberty Cap (copied from Gobrecht's 1836 gold dollar patterns); the second, Longacre's, featured a shield within a six-pointed star. Patterson actually preferred the former, but reluctantly recommended the latter, because it was in lower relief, therefore easier

to strike and conducive to longer die life. Corwin's approval followed promptly. Taxay {1966}, pp. 219–20.

The new 3¢ coins were minted in large quantities, went immediately into circulation, and stayed there, which is why most survivors are in low grades. They substituted for the vanished Mexican cuartillas (1/4 real = 3 1/8¢) and—in larger numbers—for reals and medios (1/2 reals); they were welcome where copper cents were not; they bought immense quantities of stamps, and for two years they were the only readily available American coin of lower denomination than the gold dollar. This was because they were worth less than their face value as bullion, and promised no profit to would-be exporters or melters. They nevertheless became unpopular, being easily lost and having a tendency to become discolored and filthy. They quickly acquired the nickname of "fish scales." (Nobody called them "trimes": This later neologism, invented by Mint Director James Ross Snowden, hardly got into use outside coin-collecting circles, if there.) Breen {1974}.

Coinage was interrupted March 31, 1853, in anticipation of a new act of Congress which would change weight and fineness to conform to the standard for silver coins with arrows.

Vars. of this first type are mostly minor. Dies were totally hubbed except for dates and mintmarks (latter 1851 O only), which details had to be entered by hand. Other vars. probably remain to be described; collectors did not examine these coins in detail until recent years, and the numbers of working dies are so large that repunchings, overdates, blunders, or doublings are likely.

Though the denomination was abolished in 1873, trimes are again legal tender by a clause in the Coinage Act of 1965 (PL 89-81).

LONGACRE'S TRIMES, "Type I"

Designer, Engraver, James Barton Longacre. Mints, Philadelphia (no mintmark), New Orleans (1851; mintmark O r. of opening of large C). Composition, billon, 75% silver, 25% copper. Weight, 12.375 ± 0.5 grs. = 0.802 ± 0.032 gms. Diameter, 9/16″ = 14.3 mm. Plain edge. Authorizing Act, March 3, 1851.

Grade range, POOR to UNC. GOOD: Devices outlined, tops of letters and outer points of stars blurred, everything legible. VERY GOOD: Rim almost complete, over 2/3 shield lines. FINE: Almost complete horizontal and vertical shield lines, over half shield borders. VERY FINE: Almost complete outer and inner borders to shield. EXTREMELY FINE: Isolated tiny rubbed spots on ribs of star, few high points of shield border, parts of large C, and star points. In higher levels, surface is critical for grading.

2900 1851 [5,446,400 + ?P] Heavy numerals.
40 obvs., 36 revs. Only 4 proofs known (enl. photos), apparently made to celebrate inception, June 30, 1851.

Ex J. W. Garrett: 1549. Courtesy Bowers & Ruddy Galleries, Inc.

2901 1851 Thin numerals.
Serifs hair-thin.
2902 1851 Double date. Very rare.
Heavy numerals.

2903 1851 First 1 repunched.
2904 1851 O [all kinds 720,000] Thin O.
7 pairs of dies. One proof reported, 1976 ANA:482, $7,500.

2905 1851 O Heavy O.
Minor positional vars.
2906 1851 O Double-punched O. Very rare.
2907 1851 O Dash follows date. Very rare.
The dash may be part of a third 1. Merkin 4/72:197.
2908 1852 [18,663,500 + ?P] Heavy date.
109 obvs., 44 revs. Minor positional vars. The unique proof is in the ANS museum.
2909 1852 Thin shallow date.
Hair-thin serifs.
2910 1852 Repunched 1.
2911 1852 Double date. Very rare.
Date first punched to r., then corrected. Ill. is of a later state; earlier states (still rarer) have plain double outlines at r. of all 4 digits.

2912 1852 Incomplete star. Very rare.
Large hollow areas within star, from drastically repolished dies. 6 pairs of dies went to the New Orleans branch, but no 1852 O coinage followed.
2913 1853 [11,400,000] Heavy date.
Over 60 pairs of dies. Coinage completed between Jan. 12 and March 31.
2914 1853 Thin date.
Hair-thin serifs to 1.
2915 1853 Partly repunched date.
6 obv. dies dated 1853 were shipped to the New Orleans branch; the 12 old revs. remained on hand. No 1853 O coinage followed.

ii. LONGACRE'S SILVER TRIMES, "Type II" (1854–58)

By Feb. 1853, silver coins (other than "Type I" trimes, popularly "fish scales") could not be had in the USA. As soon as the tiny batches of half dimes, dimes, and quarters without arrows had left the Mint, bullion speculators bought up all they could from local banks and melted them down for export as silver bars, at considerable profit. On Feb. 21, Congress finally passed an act reducing the standard weights of silver coins (except, oddly, silver dollars and "fish scales") to figures which would make melting unprofitable. Silver dollars were ignored for sentiment (so that the tiny coinages continued to vanish); trimes were disregarded, presumably because they were still worth under face value as bullion.

On March 3, Congress passed a supplemental "Deficiency Act" aimed at plugging loopholes left open by the Feb. 21 law. Among various other provisions, 3¢ coins were brought into line with other subsidiary silver; henceforth they would be struck in standard (900 Fine) silver at lower weight. Again, the new design was discretionary with the Treasury. Longacre suggested the simplest modification recognizable from a distance; Mint Director Eckert approved. This consisted of raising the rim of the star and adding two extra outer rims, making three in all. On rev., Longacre added a bunch of arrows and an olive branch above and below III. In the Mickley collection (1867) was a prototype proof of the new design, dated 1853; this is unlocated, though it reportedly showed up at the 1952 ANA Convention in New York. The first 1854's were released on May 22, 70,000 pieces. Taxay {1966}, p. 223; Breen {1974}.

For uncertain reasons, "Type II" trimes are usually weaker than earlier or later designs, and in mint state they are much rarer. Quantities struck were surprisingly limited, possibly because plenty of "Type I" coins were still in circulation—especially going into and out of post offices. Weak uneven strikings are the rule; many specimens have fine parallel field striations, apparently because these were not polished off the dies.

LONGACRE'S SILVER TRIMES, "Type II"

Designer, Engraver, Longacre. Mint, Philadelphia. Composition, silver 90%, copper 10%. Weight, 11.52 ± 0.5 grs. = 0.746 ± 0.032 gms. Diameter, Edge, as before. Authorizing Act, March 3, 1853.

Grade range and standards, as before. Weak uneven strikes are the rule; above EF, surface is critical.

2916 1853 Prototype. Proof. Unlocated, ex J. J. Mickley (1867).

2917 1854 [671,000 + ?P] Knob of extra 5.

Part of 5 between bases of 85. This obv. was used on over 80% of business strikes and on many of the surviving proofs. Enl. photos.

2918 1854 Normal date, heavy. Scarce.

No trace of extra 5 between 85. One obv. has star almost touching 5, another with date still heavier and lower (business strikes). A few proofs are known with die file marks above TED (enl. photos); this obv. may exist on business strikes.

Ex J. W. Garrett: 1551. Courtesy Bowers & Ruddy Galleries, Inc.

2919 1854 Normal date, thin and shallow. Rare.

No trace of extra 5 between 85; hair-thin serifs, crossbar, and crosslet.

2920 1855 Double date. [139,000 + ?P]

Proofs show most of the extra 855; business strikes usually show only corners of extra 5's within open loops of 55.

2921 1855 Normal date, quadruple outlines to star. Very rare.

Comprises under 5% of business strikes (entire mintage delivered June 21). Discovered by this writer, 1956; *Numisma* 7–8/56:4209. Three pairs of dies for this date; the third has not been identified.

2922 1856 [1,458,000 + ?P]

25 pairs of dies. Often weak at date.

2923 1857 [1,042,000 + ?P] Heavy date.

Business strikes and proofs.

2924 1857 Thin shallow date.

Business strikes only.

2925 1858 [1,604,000 + ?P] Heavy date, normal.

Business strikes and proofs.

2926 1858 Heavy date, repunched 8's. Rare.

Business strikes only. 1976 EAC:1242.

2927 1858 Thin shallow date.

Business strikes only.

with cents and larger silver and gold coins. With the assistance of Anthony C. Paquet (whose influence is seen in the narrow lettering), Longacre prepared new matrices and hubs, which were used to sink working dies complete except for dates.

Among the most notable features of the new "Type III" design are the narrow letters spaced well apart, two thin, closely spaced, raised outlines to star, and some of the smallest numerals ever used for coin dates. (In 1860–63 we find the smallest dates of all, on this denomination and on the gold dollars; later dates are a little larger, probably to save strain on official eyes.)

Mintages were smaller than in "Type II," yet the coins of 1859–62 are far more often seen in all grades than those of 1854–58. This can be credited to a combination of better striking quality, better resistance to wear, and hoarding. On Dec. 28, 1861, East Coast banks (beginning with the largest ones in New York) suspended specie payments for the duration of the Civil War. This meant that they would no longer give any kind of coins in exchange for any paper currency, even for federal greenbacks. Beginning that same day, silver coins began vanishing from banks and stores into hoards, many of them in Central America. Greenbacks (the term then meant the new Demand Notes of 1861), being without backing in gold or silver, were spent in haste lest they depreciate in purchasing power, and the process intensified further after the Legal Tender notes began showing up in mid-1862. Simultaneously, less and less silver went to the mints for coinage, and what small quantities were struck (mostly from uncurrent or worn-out coins melted for the purpose) disappeared at once into hoards. Accordingly, later dates of trimes, 1863–73, are represented in collectors' hands almost entirely by proofs.

Vast quantities of counterfeits appeared during the war, dated 1859–62 inclusive; most are 1861's. Dates are always larger than on the genuine issue; letters are apt to be irregularly spaced and wider than the genuine. They are struck in some pale gray metal resembling German silver.

Forgeries of **2946** (the 1864 restrike) appeared in summer 1984, allegedly from England. Date is high and thin, especially base and crossbar of 4; all seen to date have a dent on lower left corner of obv. star.

The Mint Act of Feb. 12, 1873 abolished the denomination. On the following July 10, the Philadelphia Mint held some 74,000 trimes in its stock of uncurrent silver issues, together with 2,258 old proof silver dollars and larger quantities of unsold proofs, mostly 1871–73 silver coins without arrows. These were all melted (Boosel {1960}, p. 19). The 74,000 trimes represent proofs of 1872–73, nearly the entire production run of 1863–72, and many of 1862 and earlier years. We need seek no further for reasons why these later dates have remained so elusive. As uncirculated business strikes of several denominations found their way into dozens of proof sets in the 1860s, possibly those are the main source for surviving uncirculated gem trimes of 1863–68.

This series is notable for overdates, mostly discoveries of recent decades. The 1862/1 is attributable to economy at the Mint, not error; the 1863/2 proofs are all restrikes, possibly representing an unused original obv. of the year; but no ready explanation arises for the 1866 or 1869. See Breen {1974}.

iii. LONGACRE'S SILVER TRIMES, "Type III" (1859–73)

Though Archives documentation has not yet surfaced, most likely Mint Director James Ross Snowden ordered Longacre to revise the "Type II" design for improved striking quality, as

LONGACRE'S SILVER TRIMES, "Type III"

Designer, Engraver, Longacre. Mint, Philadelphia. Physical Specifications, Authorizing Acts, as before.

Grade range, VERY GOOD to UNC.; standards as previously.

2928 1859 [365,000 + 800−P] Normal date.

Minor positional vars. Many of the unsold proofs were melted, others distributed as business strikes. Enl. photos.

2929 1859 Repunched 18. Rare.

"Charmont":1628; others.

2930 1860 [286,000 + 538+P] Heavy date.

Originally 1,000 proofs were delivered March 8 with the sets; the named figure represents those sold in the ensuing year, the remainder being melted or spent. Positional vars. exist.

2931 1860 Thin date. Rare.

Hair-thin serifs of 1, bases and tops of 860.

2932 1860 Partly repunched date. Rare.

2933 1861 [497,000 + 400−P] Heavy date.

Originally 1,000 proofs were delivered April 15 with the sets, but over 600 were melted as unsold. Business strikes sometimes come with dies aligned 180° from normal (*Numisma* 24:80–83, 11/58). 15 obvs., 16 revs. Large-date coins are counterfeits.

2934 1861 Thin numerals. Rare.

Similar to **2931**.

2935 1861 Obvious double date. Very rare.

Numisma 24:73, 11/58.

2936 1861 Partly repunched date.

One var. shows repunching plainest on 6, another on final 1. 1982 ANA:1725–26.

2937 1862 [343,000 + 430+P] Thin numerals.

Some 550 proofs were delivered Jan. 27 with the sets; 430 were sold through Feb. 1863, possibly a few more later, the rest melted in 1873. Positional vars. exist. 10 obvs., 12 revs.

2938 1862 Heavy numerals.

Large-date specimens are counterfeits; see introductory text.

2939 1862 Double date. Very rare.

Numisma 24:95–96, 11/58.

2940 1862/1 Very scarce.

Usually with some stage of die crack from rim through first 1 toward star. Discovered by John Cobb, 1963.

2941 1863 Thin date, normal 3, closed top to D. [460P] Proofs only.

2942 1863 Thin numerals, lightly repunched 3. [21,000−] Very rare.

Unknown to exist as business strikes before the mid-1950s. NN 54:173. Often with clashed dies, later bulged at upper r. obv. Usually found UNC. Business strikes mostly melted in July 1873. Top of D almost closed.

2943 1863 Normal date, open top to D. Restrike. Proofs only. Ex. rare.

Grand Central:928. Copper and aluminum strikings from the same dies are listed as Judd 321–22. The open top to D is from an injury to the hub, found regularly 1866–73. Rev. reused for following.

2944 1863/1862 Restrike. Proofs only. Very rare.

Heavy 1863 punched over lighter 1862. Open top to D as last. Rev. of 1864; struck after the proofs of early July 1864 but before the business strikes of late Aug. 1864, which show this same rev. cracked. Discovered by Don Taxay, 1962. *NSM* 10/62, p. 2787; NN 57:336; Breen {1974}; Robison: 689, $2,500.

2945 1864 Base of 4 repunched. [12,000− + 470P]

Top of D almost closed. Some dies for proofs (with the sets) and for later business strikes, delivered Aug. 30. The latter often show rev. crack at 4:00 (Robison:691, $3,400); rarely obv. crack through 18 (1982 ANA:1731). Business strikes mostly melted in July 1873. Auction 86:1560, UNC., $2,310.

2946 1864 Normal 4, open top to D. Restrike. Proofs only. Ex. rare.

3 seen in silver: 1) Starr estate. 2) Gibbons II:2443. 3) Pvt. coll. Dangerous forgeries exist; authentication is mandatory: See introductory text. Copper and aluminum strikings from these dies are listed as Judd 375–76.

2947 1865 Repunched 1 65 [8,000− + 500P] Very rare.

Unknown to exist in business strike form until discovered in 1956 (NN 48:852); most were melted in July 1873. Proofs from these dies more often show only traces of repunching on 65, which fade. In all, 4 obvs., 2 revs. for business strikes, probably not all used.

2948 1865 Repunched 1 5. Proofs only.

Extra outlines at r. sides of these digits; die repolishing effaces them, so that later states price as next.

2949 1865 Normal date. Proofs only.

2 vars., first a later state of preceding, other with tops of 65 filled, tops of TE(S) joined. Former developed crack from rim into field l. of date.

2950 1866 [22,000− + 725P] Top of final 6 double. Proofs only?

Top of D open from now on, unless corrected by hand on an individual working die.

2951 1866 Lightly repunched 66. Rare.
Extra outlines within tops of 66; spine from star point between 86, on proofs and earlier business strikes; later UNCS. show heavy die clash marks and finally a rim break above F. Hirt:315. Auction 86:1561–62, $2,970 each.

2952 1866 Overdate. Very rare.
Identity of digit within final 6 uncertain. Discovered in 1958. NN 51:349; Landau:335. Most business strikes melted, July 1873.

2953 1867 [4,000– + 625P] Normal date.
Most are late states of following. Most business strikes melted, July 1873.

2954 1867 Double date. Rare.
Several vars., proofs and business strikes. Later states show extra outlines on 1 67 or only on 67; still later ones, with these outlines attenuated, will price as preceding.

2955 1868 [3,500– + 600P] Normal date.
Business strikes (very rare) were mostly melted in July 1873.

2956 1868 Repunched 1 6. Proofs only. Rare.

2957 1869 [4,500– + 600P] Normal date.
Same comment as to **2955.**

2958 1869 Obvious double date. Proofs only. Very rare.

2959 1869 Repunched 69. Business strikes. Very rare.
1982 ANA:1737, few others.

2960 1869/8 Ex. rare.
The 6 is over a differently shaped 6; base of 8 plain within lower part of 9, the curves not matching. Overall configuration resembles **2480.** Proofs discovered by Don Taxay about 1962; cf. 1977 ANA:711. John Dannreuther reports a business strike with cracked rev. die.

2961 1870 [3,000– + 1,000–P]
Same comment as to **2955**, though less rare. Normal or partly repunched dates (3 vars.).

2962 1871 [3,300– + 960–P]
Always with 71 about touching. Same comment as to **2955**, though less rare. At least 3 minor positional vars. of proofs. A small hoard of proofs (under 100) turned up in the John Zug estate (Bowie, Md.) before 1964; long since dispersed.

2963 1872 [1,000– + 950–P]
Top of D restored by hand. Same dies for proofs and business strikes (latter Ex. rare, mostly melted July 1873). Some of the worn survivors may have begun life as proofs.

2964 1873 Closed 3. [600–P]
Earliest impressions (rare) show repunched 1; this fades out. 1982 ANA:238, 240. Later impressions show rusty dies: restrikes? The Mint's publicity agent, Andrew Madsen Smith, had a hoard of at least 300. Others were melted in July 1873.

CHAPTER 24

HALF DIMES

i. SCOT'S FLOWING HAIR DESIGN (1794–95)

For uncertain reasons, the Birch design used on the 1792 half disme (Chap. 16) was abandoned in favor of the flowing hair design found on the dollar, half dollar, and copper coins of 1794. Scot's first concept is represented by a unique copper pattern in the Smithsonian Institution (Judd 14), similar to that adopted but without stars and with HALF DISME below eagle: Clain-Stefanelli {1970}, fig. 19. We do not know when this piece was made, but it may well have been in fall 1794, contemporaneously with the half dollars and with the copper dollar without stars (Judd 18). As the larger circulating coins bore no mark of denomination (being acceptable only by weight), the accepted half-disme design omitted these words. (Nevertheless, Mint records until about 1835–36 often spelled this denomination the same way as in 1792–94; only in 1837 did the coins begin to call themselves HALF DIME. *Disme* must originally have rhymed with "steam"; there is no record of when people began to rhyme it with "time.")

Little is known of the accepted design's origins. Scot apparently copied it from the cents, omitting the liberty cap; but it is reminiscent of Wright's original 1793 cent design only in the same way that the Lincoln Memorial on the present-day cent is reminiscent of the actual building. These heads were mostly engraved until well into 1795 as Scot did not at the outset know how to make a device punch, and one that he finally did make for half dismes broke at the tip of the bust.

His attempt to make these half-disme designs match the larger silver coins reflects a Mint policy which became obsessive for over a century: All gold coins should share a common design, all silver another, all copper a third (preferably like the silver but minus the eagle). Mint Director David Rittenhouse derived this policy from British and French coins of the period.

On the other hand, if the letter quoted below is in any way typical of public opinion, we need seek no further reason for abandonment of the Flowing Hair silver designs: "Nothing can be more wretched: an unmeaning fool's head on one side, and something that resembles a turkey cock on the other. Oh, shame, shame, shame! The Eagle of America mantling the arms of the United States, as we see it on the City Hall, would have been a dignified impression, and on the other side, if the President's head should be too *aristocratic,* a plough and a sheaf of wheat would be better than an Idiot's head with flowing hair, which was meant to denote Liberty, but which the world will suppose was intended to designate the head of an Indian squaw." (Carlile Pollock, Letter to General Williams, of Salem, N.Y., Jan. 25, 1796, quoted in *CCJ* II, 2, p. 28, Feb. 1877. Italics in original.)

The four 1794-dated vars. were all struck in 1795; the last

and least rare (close date, F rests on leaf) followed the first two dated 1795, which share the same rev. die before it cracked with the 1794 obv. Mint records show no half-disme deliveries until March 30, 1795 [7,756]; most of these were dated 1794, along with a smaller part of the later 1795 deliveries [78,660]. This implies that about 10 times as many 1795's were coined as 1794's, and POOR to AU survivors actually do occur in this ratio. In mint state the ratio is affected by about 15 pristine 1794's, saved as first of their kind, and by the Wadsworth-Rea hoard of about 100 UNC. 1795's found about 1880 and dispersed by the garrulous Roxbury coin dealer William Elliot Woodward. Most of this hoard consists of the last three vars. of 1795 (see below).

All 1794–1805 half dismes have vertically reeded edges imparted by the Castaing machine (see Glossary and Newman-Bressett {1962}) before devices were stamped; close collars for reeding edges did not come into use until 1828–29.

It will be convenient to list the 14 vars. of this type. In the following, B = Breen, H = Hilt (from Hilt {1980}), V = Valentine (from Valentine {1975}), R = Rarity (Sheldon scale: see Glossary), P means "Prooflike presentation coins are known": Breen {1977}, pp. 31–32. Rarity ratings mostly agree with those in Reiver {1984}.

1794: B.1-A. **(2965)** Wide date; r. branch ends in double leaf. H-2B; V-1; low R-7; P. Possibly 3 UNCs. Randall, Garrett:226, AU+, $7,500.

B.2-A. **(2966)** Close crowded date; same rev. H-1B; V-2; R-5; P. Ill.

B.2-B. **(2966)** Close crowded date; berry almost touches (UN)I. H-1A; V-3; low R-6.

B.3-C. **(2966)** Close date far from bust; F rests on leaf. H-3C; V-4; R-4; P. Rev. of next two, cracked.

1795: B.1-A. **(2967)** Head of 1794. First star between second and third curls; F rests on leaf, uncracked. H-4C; V-1; high R-6; P.

B.2-A. **(2967)** Same head, date far from bust, star far from L; same rev., early. H-5C; V-10; high R-7. Discovered by Charles Steigerwalt about 1900; best is Holmes:2576, UNC., most others low grades.

B.3-B. **(2967)** Same head, broken bust point, straight date, high 1; berry below l. foot of A(M). H-6D; V-2; R-7. Robison, Auction 82:65, UNC., $6,000.

B.4-B. **(2968)** Only 6 curls, sixth and seventh stars far apart; same rev. H-7D; V-3; high R-7. 1) Valentine Plate, Holmes:2566, UNC.   2) Garrett:227, AU, $9,000. Few others in lower grades.

B.5-B. **(2968)** Only 6 curls, sixth and seventh stars close, widest date; same rev. H-8D; V-9; R-7. About 6 known. "Autumn":10, UNC., $3,200.

B.5-C **(2968)** Only 6 curls, same obv.; no berries below wings. H-8E; V-7; R-8. 1) T. L. Smith estate:185, UNC.   2) Valentine Plate, Holmes:2572, VF. Ill.

B.6-C. (2967) E almost touches hair; same rev. H-9E; V-8; R-7. About 5 known; P. 1) Eliasberg. 2) Maris, Garrett:228, $4,500.

B.7-C. (2967) L low, I B apart; same rev. H-10E; V-5; low R-3. Many UNCs. from the hoard. Often, crack from Y to nose.

B.7-D. (2967) Same obv.; berry almost touches S(T). H-10F; V-6; R-4. Fewer UNCs. from the hoard.

B.8-E. (2967) B E apart, TY low, last star touches bust point; outer berry between UN. H-11G; V-4; R-3; P. Ill. Many UNCs. from the hoard. Often, rim break at TY and adjacent stars. Counterfeits (seemingly AU grade) have granular surfaces and filled triangle of first A in AMERICA.

The Milton Holmes coll. (1960) contained the first complete set ever assembled.

SCOT'S FLOWING HAIR DESIGN

Designer, Engraver, Robert Scot. Mint, Philadelphia. Composition, silver 892.43 (1,485/1,664), remainder copper. Diameter, about 2/3″ = 16.5 mm. Weight 20.8 grs. = 1.348 gms. Reeded edge. Authorizing Act, April 2, 1792.

Grade range, POOR TO UNC. GOOD: Devices outlined, no internal detail; date and all legends legible. VERY GOOD: Eye visible; traces of hair and feather details. FINE: Some hair details l. of brow and near curl ends; some wing-feather details. VERY FINE: Over half hair and wing-feather details, partial inner-leaf details. EXTREMELY FINE: Isolated tiny rubbed spots. EXCEPTIONS: Some vars. normally come weak in centers or with weak curl tips; mint-state specimens have mint luster on the weak areas. Adjustment marks (file marks on planchets before striking to reduce weight to legal standard) are common and do not constitute damage; grade as though without them, then mention their location and extent.

2965 1794 [all kinds 7,756—] Wide date. Very rare.
Breen 1-A. Right branch ends in double leaf. Delivered March 1795; see introductory text. Possibly 3 UNCs. Enl. photos.

2966 1794 Close date. Very scarce.
Price for Breen 3-C (majority var.: See introductory text). Other vars. (Breen 2-A, 2-B) are nearly as rare as last and will bring about as much. Delivered March 1795. Enl. photos.

2967 1795 [all kinds 78,660+] 7 curls.
Price for Breen 7-C, 7-D, 8-E (see introductory text). Many

UNCs. from the hoard are available for a price. Other vars. (Breen 1-A, 2-A, 3-B, 6-C) are all very rare. Enl. photos.

2968 1795 Six curls. Very rare.
Breen 4-B, 5-B, 5-C. Price for 5-B (see introductory text). Usually in low grades. Hilt attributes this device punch to John Smith Gardner. Enl. photos.

ii. THE SCOT-ECKSTEIN DRAPED BUST/SMALL EAGLE (1796–97)

More nonsense has been written about the half dismes of this design than about all others put together. We are now able to substitute truth for folklore and dealers' fantasies.

We owe the creation of this design to the ambitions of the new Mint Director, Henry William DeSaussure, who defined his twin goals as the manufacture of gold coins and the improvement of all silver coin designs. DeSaussure induced the illustrious portraitist Gilbert Stuart to furnish a sketch of Ms. Liberty; this drawing (completed about Aug. 1795, in Newport, R.I., but now lost) was modeled after Mrs. William Bingham, née Ann Willing (Snowden {1861}, p. 177). Alas for grandiose plans: Scot's deficiencies as Engraver required hiring of John Eckstein to create "models" (for translation into device punches?), and Eckstein's merits were not enough to recommend him for any further Mint work. Eckstein may also have been responsible for the eagle with its too, too solid clouds. Whatever subtlety Stuart's buxom drawing ever had was lost in conversion to device punches. Worse still, some fault in them, or in the press used for sinking their designs into working dies, or both, produced central weakness on nearly all vars. of this design in all denominations—perhaps worst of all on these half dismes.

There are only two obvs. dated 1796 for this denomination, both of which have been called overdates; the less scarce one (not an overdate) has also been touted as a purported blundered die, "LIKERTY," making three alleged types in all. If your 1796 has berry below E(D), it is the overdate; if the berry is below D, it is the other var. The "LIKERTY" is a later die state of the latter, with top and base of B weakened. Some of the 10,230 minted may have borne date 1795.

Despite generations of contrary cataloging, the order of types in 1797 is chronologically 15 stars, then 16, finally 13. This is only logical; the 15-star dies were left over from fall 1795, with final digit omitted, as was then common practice. The 16-star die, like its counterparts in all other silver and gold denominations, was made in 1796 alluding to Tennessee's admission to the Union as the sixteenth state (June 1), but if any presentation strikings were made of the half dismes, they have not shown up. And the permanent shift to 13 stars followed Mint Director Elias Boudinot's realizing that the Mint could not go on indefinitely adding new stars as new states entered the Union.

Date punches on the 15-star die (like those on the 1796's) are those used on the last vars. of 1795. This is the least rare var. of 1797, and the die continued in use long after breakage and clashing marred it. A single prooflike presentation piece survives, sent by Mint Director Boudinot to Matthew Boulton in England, as a sample of the best the Mint could then produce; this specimen went from the Boulton estate to Waldo Newcomer and Harold Bareford, but it did not appear in the auction of Bareford's coins.

On the 16-star die we find two different 7's, indicating that when the die was made in 1796 its final digit was omitted. The 179 are from the same punches as on the last vars. of 1795 and both of 1796; the 7 punch must have cracked, chipped, or been mislaid in the meantime. One of the two rev. dies of 1797 16 stars has outer berry below D (Valentine 3); the other, less rare (Valentine 4), has outer berry between NI instead: the shattered resurrected die of 15-star coins. Obv. in this last combination is usually marred by heavy clash marks. This var. may have been minted at the end of some later year following one of the annual yellow fever epidemics, when the Mint reopened in haste and made emergency coinages from any old dies that would hold up, however briefly.

On the 13-star die, both 7's are large, unlike any preceding; rev. is again different, a leaf touching r. base of final S. Most survivors are in low grades.

These emergency coins represent the Mint's darkest hours; they constitute a tremendous challenge to today's collectors.

THE SCOT-ECKSTEIN DRAPED BUST/SMALL EAGLE

Designer, Robert Scot after Gilbert Stuart. Engravers, Scot and John Eckstein. Mint, Physical Specifications, Authorizing Acts, as before.

Grade range, POOR to UNC. GOOD: Devices outlined, date and letters legible. VERY GOOD: Over half rims intact; traces of hair details, mostly lower l. FINE: About half wing feathers; partial drapery folds. VERY FINE: Over half hair details (generally 3/4 or more except in centers); most wing feathers visible, claws partly visible, internal detail in most leaves. EXTREMELY FINE: Isolated tiny worn spots only. At higher levels, surface is critical. EXCEPTION: Most 1797's are weak in centers even in. UNC., claw at l. and eagle's eye indefinite.

2969 1796 [all kinds 10,230—] Double-punched 6. Very scarce.
Valentine 1; Hilt 13H. Berry below D. The "LIKERTY" is a late, lapped die state; top and base of B gradually weaken, finally vanish. See introductory text. Enl. photos. Bareford:29, UNC., $28,000.

2970 1796/5 Rare.
Valentine 2; Hilt 12I. Berry below E(D), not D. Note that 5 touches bust while 6 is free. At least 6 UNCs., incl. Maris, Garrett:229, $60,000.

2971 1797 Fifteen stars. [18,144]
Valentine 2; Hilt 14J. Usually weak in centers; the piece ill. is much sharper than normal. Enl. photos.

2972 1797 Sixteen stars. [16,620+]
Valentine 3, 4 (ill.); Hilt 15K, 15J. Usually weak in centers; often from heavily clashed dies, as ill. Usually in low grades. See introductory text. Enl. photos.

2973 1797 Thirteen stars. [9,763—] Very rare.
Valentine 1; Hilt 16L. Usually in low grades; possibly 7 EF's, 3 or 4 AU's, no UNCs. known. Neil, Bareford:30, AU, $7,250. See introductory text. Enl. photos.

iii. SCOT'S HERALDIC EAGLE DESIGN (1800–5)

As always, the smallest denominations were among the last to receive the dubious benefit of Scot's design changes. Scot copied the heraldic eagle device from the Great Seal of the United States (1782), though on all six device punches of this design he committed the heraldic blunder (or piece of saber-rattling bravado?) of placing the warlike arrows in the eagle's dexter claw (its own right, observer's left), outranking the olive branch of peace in the sinister claw. On the actual Great Seal (as copied on the backs of current dollar bills) this blunder does not occur. No Archives documentation explains the change; we may never know if it was Mint Director Boudinot's militant hyperpatriotism, or merely a Scot error blindly repeated from one device punch to its bigger or smaller look-alikes. Circumstances favor the latter guess. Patterson and Dougall cite evidence that Scot engraved the Great Seal. They even quote the engraver Alexander Lawson (1773–1846): "He [Scot] had no knowledge of animals or figures," and add that this "harshly critical commentary . . . is consistent with the scrawny, odd-shaped eagle of the Great Seal die of 1782." {1978}, pp. 115–19.

This design appeared first on 1796 quarter eagles, perhaps originally intended for presentation pieces celebrating Tennessee's admission to the Union as the sixteenth state: All three dies have 16 stars above eagle. Next it showed up on half eagles and eagles in 1797, and on dollars and dismes in 1798, reaching the half dismes only in 1800, half dollars in 1801, quarter dollars in 1804. On all the smaller gold and silver denominations, especially the half dismes, through miscalculation it presents a much more crowded appearance than on the dollars, eagles, or half dollars.

The only date of this type which can be had in mint state, well struck, without many years' waiting, is 1800. Of 1802 no UNCS. is traced, of 1801 only one, and of 1803–5 only a few.

For 1800, three obvs. are known. That with a tall perfectly formed 8 is still unique; after this punch broke, for unknown reasons it was never replaced, and subsequent dies through 1805 either have an 8 made out of overlapping circles (the other two 1800 obvs., 1802, and 1803 large date) or engraved, crude and narrow, like a schoolboy's effort (1801, 1803 small date, 1805).

The so-called LIBEKTY die was made with a broken or otherwise defective R punch; this was promptly replaced, but the die remained in use through part of 1801.

Specimens dated 1801, and most of those dated 1803 and 1805, are among the most poorly struck coins ever issued by the Philadelphia Mint. All are weak on parts of drapery and the rev. areas exactly opposite (clouds and most stars above eagle's head); and this weakness caused many to look worn after only a few days or weeks in circulation.

The most famous date in the half-disme series is 1802. When the first specimen was recorded in 1863, only three could be traced (all much worn), respectively, in the W. A. Lilliendahl, John F. McCoy, and Joseph J. Mickley colls. Twenty years later, when the early variety specialist Harold P. Newlin sent his monograph (1883) to press, only 16 1802's were known. In 1935, James G. MacAllister (coin dealer and cataloger associated with the illustrious Wayte Raymond) debunked the "16 known" figure, claiming that he could trace 35, mostly in the POOR to VG range. Nobody has attempted a more recent comprehensive head count, but the probable number is somewhere between 35 and 45. Of these, none rate UNC., only two approach AU, five more are EF or thereabouts, four others VF, and the

other two to three dozen are in low grades. One of the two top examples (Betts, Haines, Burton, Newlin:85, Garrett:234, EF–AU) brought $45,000; the other (the Valentine Plate coin) remains unlocated.

As deceptive counterfeits exist of this rarity, detailed description is necessary. The genuine has large 8 (made of overlapping circles), large 2; 1 is free of curl, bases TY below R below E. Its rev. is the same as 1801: Leaf touches C (not A); first S nearer to T than to wing. Later strikings show a crack through TED and sometimes also lumpy rim breaks above TED and below tail. The counterfeits have small crude 8 as in 1801, with oddly shaped 2; they are apparently electrotype shells of solid silver (from molds made from a genuine 1801, the negative altered in the date), cemented together without lead filling. They ring more briefly than the genuine; they may show false edge reeding; weights will vary.

Nearly as coveted as the 1802, though with less reason, is the 1805. This usually comes VG to VF; only one UNC. survivor is traced (Merkin, Reed Hawn:560, $4,500 [1973]), a second being reported, followed by possibly seven EF's including Randall, Garrett:236 at $10,000. Parmelee's was AU but has been repeatedly cleaned.

Mintage was interrupted, and no more were coined until July 1829. No reason has been recorded for the discontinuance. Possibly banks preferred the more readily available Mexican medios (1/2 real = 1/16 dollar coins), which were legal tender side by side with the federal coinages.

SCOT'S HERALDIC EAGLE DESIGN

Designer, Engraver, Robert Scot, obv. after Stuart, rev. after the Great Seal. Mint, Physical Specifications, Authorizing Act, as before.

Grade range, POOR to UNC. GOOD: Devices outlined, date and letters (except motto) legible. VERY GOOD: Over half rims intact; traces of hair details, mostly at lower l.; few motto letters. FINE: Partial drapery folds; about half wing feathers and motto letters. VERY FINE: Over half hair details (3/4 or more except in centers); partial internal details to most wing feathers. EXTREMELY FINE: Isolated tiny worn spots only; grade by surface. EXCEPTIONS: Coins of 1801, 1803, 1805 always show local weaknesses; see introductory text.

2974 1800 Normal LIBERTY [24,000]; 8 made of overlapping circles.
Valentine 1. Some 14,000 went on March 25 to the Bank of Philadelphia; the other 10,000 the next day to William Cooper. About 20 survive in UNC., evidently saved as first of their kind. Enl. photos.

2975 1800 Similar; tall perfectly formed 8. Unique?
Breen 3. First star very far from curl. Ex Philip Straus estate, NN 53:438.
2976 1800 LIBEKTY. [16,000]
Valentine 2. Broken top to R suggesting a K. Delivered in early 1801. Rev. as last 2, now with heavy injury (clash mark?) at BUS. At least a dozen survive in mint state.

2977   1801 [27,760]
   2 minor vars., differing principally in location of die failures.
Mintage includes 9,950 reported at the beginning of 1802.
Usually in low grades. Note location of weak areas on drapery, on wing, in and below clouds; usually these are more
extensive (that ill. is exceptionally well struck for this date:
enl. photos). Allenburger, Bareford:35 ($8,000), Auction
82:69 ($7,000), UNC., is apparently unequaled.

2978   1802 [3,060] Rare.
   Note location of weak areas. Usually in low grades. Dangerous fakes exist. See introductory text. Enl. photos.

2979   1803 [all kinds 37,850] Small date. Very rare.
   Valentine 3. Small narrow 8; rev. of 1801–2, leaf touches C.
Usually in low grades. Neil, Bareford:36, "UNC.," $7,500.

2980   1803 Large date. Very scarce.
   Large 8 from overlapping circles, like 1800. Usually in low
grades. One var. (V-1, ill.) has rev. of preceding, the other
(V-2) has rev. of 1805: Leaf touches A, not C. Enl. photos.

2981   1805 [15,600]
   Small misshapen 8. Later, break below and r. of date. Usually
in low grades. See introductory text. Enl. photos.

iv. THE KNEASS-REICH CAPPED BUST HALF DIMES (1829–37)

Coinage of this denomination resumed July 4, 1829, from
new dies by William Kneass (Scot's successor as Engraver),
vaguely after John Reich's half-dollar design of 1807. Like the
dimes of 1828, these half dimes have a plain raised rim encircling a border of round beads. Because they were struck in a
grooved "close collar," which imparted the reeded edge, their
diameters were thereafter uniform. Earlier dates had been given
reeded edges before striking by passing the blanks through a
Castaing machine. This consisted of spring-loaded parallel bars,
one fixed, the other actuated by gear train and long lever. These
were set apart to the intended coin diameter (minutely less than
that of the blanks) and were grooved to impart edge reeding.
(For larger denominations, the bars were lettered or ornamented.) Coins so made varied in diameters because planchets
expanded on being stamped. New coins, struck in close collars,
could no longer have lettered edges; but in compensation, as the
collars prevented planchets from spreading on impact, the
metal flowed instead into crevices, simultaneously producing
reeded edges, raised protective rims, and sharper impressions
on lettering, stars, and borders. Mint correspondence of the
period mentioned the close collar as a major technological improvement.
   Half dimes of 1829 show two different rev. device punches,
each consisting of eagle, arrows, olive branch, and inscribed
scroll, but no other lettering. The first punch, "Triple Stripes,"
shows three lines in each pale gules (nearly vertical shield
stripe, shaded to represent heraldic red); the second, "Double
Stripes," shows only two. The former appears only on three
working dies of 1829; the latter on all the rest, through 1837
when the design was changed.
   Coins dated 1829–32 sometimes come with cracked revs.
originally used with obvs. of later date, indicating that old obv.
dies were carried to the new Second Mint building in 1833–35
and indiscriminately used as long as they would remain fit for
service to save time of making new dies. The 1832 "No Berries"
var. is part of this group; its rev. die is almost worn out.
   Letter and numeral punches in this period were by Christian
Gobrecht, who later succeeded the paralyzed and dying William Kneass as Engraver of the Mint. As a new set of numeral
punches went into use in 1835, we find large and small dates,
large and small 5 C. in all possible combinations. In ordinary
grades the large date with large 5 C. is slightly more often
found than the others; in mint state, the small date with small 5
C. has become commonest owing to a hoard of at least 100
specimens found in a Boston bank in 1969 and dispersed by Q.
David Bowers.
   Mintage of this design was stopped in June 1837, in anticipation of a change to the Liberty Seated design (see following

section). Some part of the limited mintage [871,000] probably bore date 1836. Only four vars. of Capped Busts bear date 1837: three with large 5 C. (one Ex. rare), a fourth (rare) with small 5 C. All these revs. are apparently left over from 1835; the last had actually been used in that year.

Most of the vars. described below have been known only to specialists. Values are largely conjectural, based on approximate relative scarcity or rarity of the various die combinations. We are only beginning to learn about this neglected series; new die vars. are still being discovered (at the rate of one about every two years), and it is by no means certain that we have seen all the important ones. For easy attribution, with rarity ratings, see Reiver {1984}.

The change of spelling from *disme* to *dime,* earlier occasional, became official on the coins only with the new design of 1837. Originally the word must have rhymed with "steam"; the new pronunciation, rhyming with "time," is thought to date to this period, perhaps concurrently with the new anglicized spelling.

THE KNEASS-REICH CAPPED BUST HALF DIMES

Designer, William Kneass, after John Reich. Engraver, Kneass. Mint, Physical Specifications, Authorizing Act, as before, except Diameter ⅝″ = 15.9 mm.

Grade range, GOOD to UNC. GOOD: Designs outlined, date and all letters legible except parts of LIBERTY and of motto. VERY GOOD: LIBERTY fully legible; few wing feathers clear. FINE: Full motto; parts of ear, clasp, and half of wing feathers show. VERY FINE: Some leg and neck feathers; ear and clasp completely clear. EXTREMELY FINE: Isolated tiny rubbed spots only; grade by surface. NOTE: Usually not collected in low grades, except by beginners.

2982 1829 [all kinds 1,230,000+ + ?P] Triple rev. stripes.
3 rev. dies; Valentine 3, 7, 2. Possibly 20 proofs. First made for the cornerstone of the Second Mint, Chestnut and Juniper Sts. Enl. photos.

2983 1829 Double rev. stripes.
13 vars. Possibly 9 proofs. Many business strikes were actually coined in 1831–35 (economy, not skulduggery): See introductory text. Minor repunchings of date or 5 C. or both. For enl. photo of Double Stripes rev., see below.

2984 1830 [1,240,000+ + ?P] Normal.
13 vars. Same comments. Under 12 proofs.

2985 1830 C over horizontal C in AMERICA.
Valentine 1. Price only for earliest die state, the blunder plain. NN 57:360. Later states with it weak (traces of curve between serif and tail, no extra thick stroke at base) will price as **2984.**

2986 1831 [1,242,000− + ?P] Normal eye.
4 vars. Many of the reported mintage bore dates 1829, 1830. At least 20 proofs.

2987 1831 No pupil to eye.
V-6, 7, 2.

2988 1832 [965,000+ + ?P] Normal.
In all 14 vars. Many of this date were delivered in 1833. About 7 proofs, incl. 1982 ANA:291, $5,200.

2989 1832 No berries. Very scarce.
V-3 (ill.); Breen 10 (diff. obv.). From worn-out die of 1829. Not to be confused with V-1, 5B, 6, or 7, in which berries are small and weak but clear. Usually in low grades. Enl. photos.

2990 1832 C over horizontal C.
V-1. Rev. of **2985,** the blunder less plain.

2991 1832 O over much larger O. Very rare.
V-4; Breen 12. Latter (rarer) with 1 in date too high (LM 9/70:241); price for former.

2992 1833 [1,370,000− + ?P] Wide even date.
V-4, 6. Both with sixth star repunched; latter repolished state with lowest curl forming large hollow loop. Reported mintage includes at least 4 vars. dated 1832 and others of earlier dates.

2993 1833 Wide even date; O over much larger O. Very scarce.
V-3. Rev. of **2991** but struck earlier. Enl. photos.

2994   1833 Extremely heavy obv. rim.
V-5, 1, 2. Tops of 83 nearly touch. Possibly 3 proofs.

2995   1833 Irregular date. Scarce.
V-7; Witham 8, Reiver 9. Date spaced 1 8 33, final 3 high. Price for first (ill.); the others are Ex. rare.

2996   1834 [1,480,000— + ?P] Normal.
4 vars. At least 20 proofs, including one in the King of Siam's cased proof set (Breen {1977}, pp. 57–59). Most of the reported mintage consisted of coins dated 1833, 1832, and possibly earlier. See next.

2997   1834 3 over reversed 3.
V-5, early states. The 3 was first rotated 180° from normal, then corrected; extra knobs plain within 3. Publicized by Q. David Bowers. Price for early states; later ones (traces of extra 3 faint or almost indistinguishable) will price as preceding. The lump in 8 is from chipping of the die; it is not found on the earliest states.

2998   1835 [all kinds 2,760,000+ + ?P] Large date and 5 C.
V-3, 8, 2, 4; Breen 11. Reported mintage includes many of earlier dates; but other 1835's were delivered in 1836–37. Possibly 5 proofs, including Bareford:44, $2,600. Enl. photos.

2999   1835 Large date, small 5 C.
V-9, 10. Enl. photos.

3000   1835 Small date, large 5 C.
V-5, 6 Enl. photos. At least 2 proofs.

3001   1835 Small date and 5 C.
V-1, 7. Many mint-state V-7's survive, from the Boston hoard (see introductory text): close date, tops of S's filled. At least 2 proofs. Enl. photos.

3002 1836 [all kinds 1,900,000+ + ?P] Large 5 C.
V-3, 5; Breen 7; V-4 late state only. Small dates henceforth (same punches as **3000–1**); 5 C. as in **2998**. Fine border dentils henceforth. At least 6 proofs. Reported mintage included many dated 1835. See next.

3003 1836 Large 5 C., 3 over reversed 3.
V-4 early state only; same type of blunder as **2997**. Discovered by Kamal Ahwash. 1977 ANA:745.

3004 1836 Small 5 C.
V-6, 2, 1.

3005 1837 [all kinds 871,000– + ?P] Large 5 C.
V-1, 3, and 2 others. Normal or repunched 7. At least 6 proofs. Mintage included many dated 1836, possibly some dated 1835. Enl. photos.

3006 1837 Small 5 C. Scarce.
V-2; rev. of 1835. Often in low grades. 1980 ANA:1375, UNC., $3,500. Enl. photos.

v. THE SULLY-GOBRECHT LIBERTY SEATED DESIGN, NO STARS (1837–38)

Uniformity of design through all denominations of the same metal remained a fetish with successive Mint Directors ever since David Rittenhouse's day (1792–95). We have already seen how Robert Scot used similar "Flowing Hair" heads on dollar, half dollar, and half disme, probably adapted from the cent (1794–96); how Gilbert Stuart's portrait of Mrs. Bingham as Ms. Liberty appeared on dollars (Oct. 1795), extending to all other silver and copper by 1800; how Scot's heraldic eagle did likewise, 1796–1804. We have also seen how John Reich's capped-bust design of 1807 made a slower progress of contagion from half dollars through all other silver by 1815, finally reaching the half dimes in 1829. Accordingly, when Christian Gobrecht's new Liberty Seated device (after Thomas Sully) was adopted on the silver dollar, Dec. 1836, Mint Director Robert Maskell Patterson at once ordered that the same starless design be translated into working dies for all other silver denominations as quickly as practicable. For the dimes and half dimes, the rev. was to consist of a simple laurel wreath enclosing denomination, instead of the revised Reich eagle which continued on the larger coins. Of course, all this redesigning had to be shoehorned into a schedule already demanding dozens of dies for cents and half dollars in designs continued or modified from earlier years. This is why the new conception did not reach quarter dollars until 1838, or half dollars until 1839.

After the final deliveries of Capped Bust half dimes in June 1837, the Director stopped coinage to await completion of working dies of the new design. On July 25, regular coinage began, with some 20 proofs struck to celebrate the new occasion. Adam Eckfeldt kept one of these for what was to become the Mint Cabinet Collection (now in the Smithsonian Institution); others went to Treasury Secretary Levi Woodbury and various VIPs. At least 12 are traceable today, many evidently kept as pocket pieces or curiosity cabinet items long enough to acquire nicks and scratches. As usual with new designs, the public saved many as novelties. Uncirculated survivors are always available for a price, though pressure from collectors of type coins has launched that price into orbit.

During the remainder of 1837, a total of 1,405,000 half dimes followed, from possibly four pairs of dies of the new design. The first of these (used on proofs and business strikes) has date in a curved line, with tall vertical peak to 1 and thick center to 8, as in 1836–37 Capped Busts: "Large Date." The other three obvs. have straight date, with flat top to 1 and thinner center to 8, as in 1838: "Small Date." Size differences are microscopic, and the old sobriquets (mentioned above for identification) should be dropped.

Two pairs of dies were made that fall or winter, dated 1838, mintmarked O, and shipped to the New Orleans Mint on April 10, 1838, arriving May 3. After many delays, the newly established branch finally managed to issue somewhat over 70,000 half dimes from these dies, which coins promptly went into circulation and stayed there. They passed locally at par with Mexican medios, alias picayunes (from Créole *picaillons,* 'tiny ones'), better known as half reals or half bits = 1/16 Dollar = 6¼¢ each. For this reason, most 1838 O survivors are in low grades; uncirculated specimens are very rare, evidently because the locals did not save them as curiosities. New Orleans mintage figures herein and in later sections follow reconstructions in Julian {1977}.

Later dies for both mints had stars added near border, again copying the silver dollar. Never again were our coins to be so free of clutter as they had been on this ephemeral 1837–38 design.

THE SULLY-GOBRECHT LIBERTY SEATED DESIGN

Designer, Thomas Sully (obv.), Christian Gobrecht (rev.). Engraver, Gobrecht. Mints, Philadelphia (1837), New Orleans (1838, mintmark O below IM). Composition, silver 90%, copper 10%. Weight, 20.625 ± 0.5 grs. = 1.336 ± 0.032 gms. Edge, Diameter, as before. Authorizing Act, Jan. 18, 1837.

Grade range, POOR to UNC. GOOD: Devices outlined, date and all letters legible except LIBERTY. VERY GOOD: Traces of drapery and shield details; LI Y or L TY legible on shield. FINE: All of LIBERTY legible though weak; partial drapery and shield details, about half leaf details. VERY FINE: LIBERTY bold, scroll complete though its raised rim may be blurred; partial hair details. EXTREMELY FINE: Isolated tiny rubbed spots only; complete raised rims to scroll. EXCEPTION: Rusted die state of second var. of 1838 O.

3007 1837 [all kinds 1,405,000 + 20 + P] Tall peak to 1.
At least 3 rev. dies. Proofs and earliest business strikes show triple punching on 8, partial repunching on other digits; later strikings, from repolished obv. die, no longer show partial extra digits. See introductory text. Enl. photos.

3008 1837 Flat top to 1.
At least 4 vars. Much rarer choice than foregoing. See introductory text. Enl. photos.

3009 1838 O [70,000+]
2 pairs of dies, both ill. (enl.) because of grading problems. What we take to be the first var. (V-1) has date level and centered; earliest strikings show repunching on base of first 8, later ones have several cracks from rim to device: "Gilhousen":169. In most die states weak flat strikings are common (as ill.). Prohibitively rare UNC. Robison:834, $4,500; private sale record $10,000 (1983). The second var. (V-2) has date low, slanting up to r.; later strikings (enl. ill.) show obv. die extensively rusted, drapery and date weak, numerals distorted, eventually hardly legible—probably explaining the 2 Augustus Heaton {1893} thought might have been dated 1837. In these late die states (made in 1839?), grading is done by surface and rev. details only. No mint-

state specimens survive; possibly 3 qualify as AU or better: 1) Ahwash (ill.). 2) Newlin, Garrett:252. 3) Rhodes:540.

3010 1838 [2,255,000+ + ?P] Normal stars.
At least 15 vars. About 5 proofs. Many were delivered in 1839 from 1838 dies. Enl. photos.

vi. GOBRECHT'S LIBERTY SEATED DESIGN, WITH STARS (1838–40)

From Jan. 1838 through Nov. 1840, half-dime working dies came from the old starless hub of 1837, but with 13 stars hand-punched into each die (about 18 obvs. in all for Philadelphia, 10 for New Orleans). Stars therefore vary notably in spacing, never completely even; they also vary slightly in size according to how heavily they were entered into each die, or how much the working dies were later repolished. Double punching on stars is the rule, not the exception.

However, the real 1838 Small Stars vars., first described in Valentine {1931} and then forgotten for a generation, are from three obvs. which had severely rusted and were vigorously reground to remove the rust. We are fortunate enough to show "before" and "after" states of a single die, the former qualifying as Large Stars, the latter as Small Stars.

In all, some 4,218,150 (plus an unknown number of proofs) of this design came from Philadelphia, with an additional 1.8 million from New Orleans. The old hubs were then abandoned in favor of the new Hughes design, allegedly an improvement, in actuality the exact opposite: See next section.

Like their dime counterparts, the so-called "partial drapery" coins of 1838 are any half dimes showing a heavy die clash mark from (DIM)E between forearm and knee: NN 57:376.

Most of the coins reported in 1839 actually bore date 1838.

On the New Orleans dies, three different mintmark punches occur: large, medium, and small O, the first from the 1838 punch.

The very rare Large Letters 1840 O is sometimes called a "transitional" coin because it combines an adopted obv. of earlier type with a rev. from the new Hughes type. We do not know for certain when this coin was struck, nor even when its rev. die arrived. The var. is obvious to the naked eye, which makes all the more remarkable its remaining unknown until 1976.

New Orleans mintage figures are from Julian {1977}. Archives records from this branch's earlier years are incomplete and confusing, complicated by official incompetence and dishonesty; the true figures may never be known, but these are as near as we are likely to approach them.

3011 1838 Small stars.
Reground obv. dies; at least 3 vars. That ill. is from same obv. die as preceding. Cf. 1982 ANA:1795, UNC., $775. Enl. photos.

GOBRECHT'S LIBERTY SEATED DESIGN, WITH STARS

Designer, Engraver, Mints, Physical Specifications, Authorizing Acts, as before.

Grade range and standards, as before.

3012   1839 [1,069,150− + ?P] Normal date.
V-1. Many of the reported mintage bore date 1838.
3013   1839 Repunched 39.
V-2. Business strikes and about 4 proofs. Later strikings with only 9 showing repunching bring less premium.
3014   1839 O [1,104,039+] Large O. Very rare.
V-1. Note mintmark shape (1838 O punch). Usually in low grades. Enl. photos. At least one var. has rev. of **3009**.

3015   1839 O Medium oval O.
V-4, 5.
3016   1839 O Small round o.
V-2, 3, 6. In all 6 pairs of dies. Sometimes shows repunching on 1 9 (enl. photos).

3017   1840 [1,034,000 + ?P]
At least 9 vars., coined April–Sept. 1840 only. At least 5 proofs; Allenburger, Bareford:59, Proof, $10,000. A tiny hoard of prooflike UNCs. turned up in Berkeley, Calif., about 1961; these have weak dentils.

3018   1840 O [all kinds 695,000] Small letters; large round O. Rare.
V-1. Usually in low grades.
3019   1840 O Small letters; medium oval O. Very scarce.
V-2. Usually in low grades.
3020   1840 O Small letters; small round o.
Several vars. In all, 6 obvs., 7 revs., with other dies left over from 1839. All dies shipped between Jan. 15 and Aug. 24; coinage completed in November. All are very rare UNC.
3021   1840 O Large Letters, "Transitional." Ex. rare.
Rev. of Hughes type (see next section). Besides the larger letters, note split berries ("open buds"); only 13 leaves on each branch instead of the former 14. Discovered by Kamal Ahwash. Cf. *Gobrecht Journal* v2n6 (7/76), pp. 28–29, and "Prudential":252. Possibly part of the Dec. 1840 coinage (see next section), from a leftover obv. Usually in low grades. Enl. photos.

vii. THE HUGHES-GOBRECHT DESIGN, EXTRA DRAPERY (1840–53)

Allegedly as a design improvement, but actually for more unworthy reasons, Mint Director Robert Maskell Patterson hired the Anglo-American miniaturist Robert Ball Hughes (1806–68) during fall 1840 to prepare a modified Liberty Seated design. Hughes's totally redrawn conception of Ms. Liberty (popularly known as "With Drapery") fattened her arms, enlarged her head, flattened her bosom, replaced her décolleté by a high collar, chipped away much of her rock, moved her shield to an upright position, and replaced her thin Greek chiton by a much heavier fabric (of at least army-blanket thickness), with a peculiar bulla or heavy pendant (on half dimes and dimes only) on its lower edge, lest the garment ride up far enough to reveal her ankles. Over her elbow, in what must have been an extremely uncomfortable position for Hughes's model, if any, hangs a bulky cloak or himation, irregularly folded: "extra drapery from elbow." (Chamberlain {1958}.)

As usual, this design appeared first on the larger denominations: dollars, quarters, dimes, finally half dimes in 1840. (It never did get to the half dollars, which is just as well.) The story was given out that these changes were intended to improve striking quality and design, but either the Mint's officials were incompetent to judge either one, or they were perpetrating another of their numerous official lies of the period, or even both. From 1840 through 1858, weak uneven strikings in all denominations (though least on the half dollar) are the rule, not the exception. "Full head" coins (showing full facial and hair details) are rare and for some dates unknown except in proof state. No business strikes of this new design ever come as well struck as the best ones of 1837–40.

The real reason for this design change appears to have been that century-long bugaboo, from which we are not yet completely freed, known as Respectability. After Queen Victoria made the mistake of marrying the petty German prince known later as "Albert the Good," everybody who claimed to be anybody on either side of the Big Pond began aping the royal style; nor was the Philadelphia Mint an exception. (Note that the Queen's profile appears on some 1875 20¢ patterns and all 1876 silver-dollar patterns.) Unfortunately, Prince Albert's Biedermeier governesses and tutors had inculcated in him an insanely unreal standard of modesty; the then extremist Wesleyan and Calvinist churches abetted such prudery (though Jesus had never said anything that would serve to encourage them). And so the day was not far off when signers on paper currency had to be of the same gender; when books by male and female authors could not stand side by side on respectable bookshelves unless the authors were married to each other; when a bull could be mentioned only as a "gentleman cow," and even then only with a blush; when legs of pianos (modestly called "limbs") were draped, and no other kind could ever be named; and when petticoats had to be multiplied ninefold lest someone have the obscene experience of seeing an undraped knee. By 1840, "respectability" was already well on the way to these extremes; beyond doubt it motivated Hughes and probably also Patterson in attempting to ensure that our coinage would offend nobody: (Breen {1972B}.)

To make counterfeiters' tasks harder, the new hubs included stars as well as letters, so that thereafter the only elements needing to be hammered by hand into working dies were dates and mintmarks. At this blacksmith's chore (specified in his job definition), the new Mint Engraver, James Barton Longacre, was timid and inefficient, but Chief Coiner Franklin Peale's workmen were no better, and some of the resulting blundered dies have become famous. Among the half dimes possibly the most notable are various triple dates, the 1848/7/6, the 1849/8/6, the 1848 large date (in which a dime logotype was used by mistake), and the 1858 over inverted date. Longacre had used his friendship with Sen. John C. Calhoun (then Secretary of State) to obtain the Mint engravership on Gobrecht's death (1844). As Calhoun was from a slaveholding state, and as Longacre was not connected with any of the Mint's ruling families (Patterson, Eckfeldt, Peale, Dubois), this circumstance made the new Engraver anathema to the Mint Establishment, which used every possible excuse and subterfuge in attempts to oust him—in vain. Julian has gone so far as to suggest that some of the notorious die blunders were not Longacre's work at all, but rejects made by workmen in the Coiner's Department and used anyway: possibly ammunition for the Patterson-Peale campaign to dispose of Longacre?

On the other hand, the regular 1849/6 overdates (not the 1849/8/6) are from an entirely different cause, and they are the only overdates known to have been mentioned in Mint correspondence. In 1846 the New Orleans Mint had five half-dime obvs. but used none; the Superintendent later returned them to George Eckfeldt at the Philadelphia Mint "to be fitted for service of 1849."

During the earlier 1840s, half dimes circulated, especially in the South, at par with Mexican medios = 6¼¢ apiece (see introductory text to previous section), explaining the low grade of many O-Mint survivors. But after the California gold rush began, the lowering in the price of gold reckoned in silver dollars was experienced in the East as a rise in the price of silver reckoned in gold dollars. This went far enough that it became profitable either to hoard silver coins or to melt them: They were then worth more than face value as bullion. Silver coins vanished from circulation, and little silver came into the Mint. Coins of 1849–53 without arrows are notable for low mintages and for lower survival ratios; all are much scarcer than one could expect even from their mintage figures.

The only way small silver coins could continue to circulate was official weight reduction to a point where melting would no longer be profitable. This took place in 1853 (see next section). In Jan. 1856, the current 1840–52 type resumed, minus arrows, but at the lower weights authorized in 1853. Type collectors wishing completeness ideally would have to have specimens of both the pre-1853 issues and the lighter 1856–58; in practice, many are content with only one, as the design was resumed unaltered.

THE HUGHES-GOBRECHT DESIGN, EXTRA DRAPERY

Designer, Robert Ball Hughes, after Gobrecht. Engraver, Gobrecht. Mints, Philadelphia (no mintmark), New Orleans (mintmark O below IM). Physical Specifications, Authorizing Act, as before.

Grade range and standards, as before. EXCEPTION: Hair details and some central drapery details may not be clear even in mint state; look for mint luster on the weak parts. See introductory text.

3022 1840 "With drapery." [310,085 + ?P]
3 vars., coined Nov.–Dec. 1840. Rev. from large-letters hub

logotype has high 5, and 845 touching (less apparent on weakly impressed dies or weak strikings). Possibly 8 proofs. Robison:848, $3,200.

3039 1845 Double date. Scarce.

V-5. Often sold as "1845/3," but the extra fragments at 5 do not match the 3 of 1843. The extra curve at r. of 5 shown on the Valentine Plate has not been found on any survivor from these dies: possibly foreign matter on the plate coin?

seen first on **3021;** this continues through 1859. At least 2 proofs known; Auction 81:68, $4,200. Enl. photos (of **3023**).

3023 1840 O "With drapery." [240,000−]

V-5. Small round o. Coined Dec. 1840, from a single pair of dies sent Dec. 2. Obv. die split across, from rim above cap through R to rim left of date. Usually in low grades; prohibitively rare in or near mint state. That ill. (above **3022**) falls short of mint state but is one of the finest known. Reported mintage may include **3021** and possibly earlier vars.

3024 1841 [1,150,000 + ?P]

At least 8 minor positional vars.; possibly 8 proofs.

3025 1841 O [all kinds 815,000] Small round o.

3 positional vars. In all, 6 obvs., 5 revs., with others left over from 1840. Very rare UNC.

3026 1841 O Medium oval O. Scarce.

V-3, 4. Very rare UNC.

3027 1841 O Large wide O. Ex. rare.

Neil 4 (1927), Neil:1711. Discovered by A. G. Heaton before 1893.

3028 1842 [815,000 + ?P]

Possibly 8 proofs.

3029 1842 O [all kinds 350,000+] Small round o.

5 pairs of dies. Ex. rare UNC.

3030 1842 O "No drapery." Ex. rare.

Merkin 9/68:157. Drastically lapped die, drapery grossly incomplete at elbow and breast. Heavy clash mark at (I)M.

3031 1843 [1,165,000 + ?P]

Larger dates through 1848. Several vars. with partly repunched dates. Possibly 5 proofs (V-1A, normal dates).

3032 1843 Double date. Scarce.

Several vars. Part of all 4 extra digits show. Business strikes and possibly 8 proofs. *Gobrecht Journal* 11/77, p. 6.

3033 1844 [430,000 + ?P] Normal date.

V-1, 2. Business strikes and at least 9 proofs (both vars.).

3034 1844 Partly repunched date.

V-3. Business strikes and at least 2 proofs.

3035 1844 Triple date. Very scarce.

Breen 4. Business strikes and at least 4 proofs. *Gobrecht Journal* 11/77, p. 7.

3036 1844 O [all kinds 220,000−] Small round o.

V-2. Usually in low grades, rev. aligned 180° from normal. Mintage probably included some dated 1842. Three pairs of dies sent; only one var. seen of each mintmark size.

3037 1844 O Large O. Rare.

V-1. Almost always in low grades. Farouk, Bareford:71, UNC., $6,250. Five pairs of dies shipped for 1845 O coinage remained unused.

3038 1845 [1,564,000 + ?P]

At least 11 vars., normal or partly repunched dates. Date

3040 1846 [27,000 + ?P]

Business strikes (V-1, shield point above r. upright of 1) are usually in low grades, prohibitively rare UNC.: Garrett (1976):105, $7,000. Proofs (Breen 2) have shield point above l. upright of 1; possibly 14–18 survive: Bareford:73, $7,750. Die difference first described by W. W. Neil.

3041 1847 Normal date. [1,274,000 + ?P]

4 vars. Usually in low grades. Possibly 10 proofs survive.

3042 1847 Obviously repunched 18. Rare.

V-1. Date crowded into base. Always in low grades.

3043 1848 [all kinds 668,000 + ?P] Large date. Very scarce.

V-1 (2 rev. vars., without and with die file marks through CA). Date from dime logotype, top of 1 nearly touching shield. Usually in low grades. 1976 ANA:617, UNC., $1,200.

3044 1848/7/6 Medium date. Ex. rare.

Serif of 7 at upper l. of 8; traces of 6 at lower l. Triple-

punched 4. Always with heavy die file mark in field r. of date, joining rim to rocky base. Later states show less of underdigits. Usually in low grades. Discovered by Jack Collins, 1976. Harte III:926, AU, is possibly finest.

3045 1848 Medium normal date.
At least 8 vars. Business strikes and possibly 12 proofs.

3046 1848 Double date. Very scarce.
Breen 8. Doubling plainest on 48; die later repolished, traces of doubling remain on final 8 (commands less premium).

3047 1848 O [all kinds 600,000] Large O.
At least 3 vars. Usually in low grades. 1982 ANA:1800, "UNC.," $1,400.

3048 1848 O Medium oval O.
At least 3 vars. NN 57:392; 61:257. In all, 6 pairs of dies.

3049 1848 O Small round o. Ex. rare.
Breen 6. Discovered by W. W. Neil before 1927; NN 54:1271. So rare that its existence was long controversial. Rev. possibly left over from 1844, and/or reused in 1850.

3050 1849 [all kinds 1,309,000 + ?P] Partly repunched date.
Several vars., plainest Breen 10 (ill.); those with less obvious repunching command less premium. No completely "normal" date (without repunching) is reported. Possibly 5 proofs, incl. Garrett (1976):107, $3,500; on some proofs with repunched 9, rev. is rotated 180° from normal alignment. Not to be confused with any to follow.

3051 1849/48 (?)
Several vars. Business strikes and possibly 6 proofs. Bill Fivaz believes some of these (ill.) are 1849/horizontal 9; this is uncertain.

3052 1849/8/6 Very rare.
Upper parts of 6 within 9; lower half of 8 above knob and in field below and to r. of 9: not to be confused with next. Later impressions (less rare) show less of the extra 8 at lower r.; these command less premium.

3053 1849/6
Several vars., from 5 1846 O obv. dies returned to Philadelphia (see introductory text). The others differ minutely in position; all show either top of (lower) loop of 6 at middle r. of 9, or upper l. curve of 6 within loop of 9, or both.

3054 1849 O [140,000−] Rare.
2 minor vars. In all, 12 obvs. and 2 revs. shipped, most remaining unused. Part of the reported mintage may have been dated 1848. Almost always in low grades. Bareford:80, UNC., $1,800.

3055 1850 [955,000 + ?P]
At least 12 minor vars.; possibly 10 proofs. Garrett (1976):109, $2,600.

3056 1850 O [all kinds 690,000] Large wide O.
V-1, 2. In all, 6 obv. dies (not all used?), 11 old leftover revs.

3057 1850 O Medium oval O. Scarce.
V-3. Unknown in mint state.

3058 1850 O Small round thin o. Rare.
V-4. Severely rusted rev., possibly left over from 1848 or even 1844. Unknown choice.

3059 1851 [681,000− + ?P]
In all, 7 obvs., 5 revs., possibly not all used; possibly 5 proofs. Many melted of this and next few; see introductory text.

3060 1851 O [860,000−]
3 vars. 12 obvs., 6 revs., mostly unused. Many melted; see introductory text. Usually in low grades; best ones generally prooflike. Auction 80:1120, UNC., $3,800.

3061 1852 [1,000,500− + ?P]
4 obvs., 6 revs. Possibly 10 proofs; Garrett (1976):111, $2,000. Many melted.

3062 1852 O [260,000−]
2 vars. 6 obvs. shipped, mostly unused; leftover revs. from 1850–51. Many melted. Usually in low grades; very rare choice.

3063   1853 No arrows. [135,000 –]

Probably most melted in the Mint. Only one var., struck in 2 batches: [50,000] Feb. 19, [85,000] Feb. 22; coinage then stopped, pending effective date of the new Mint Act of Feb. 21. UNCS. are from a small hoard discovered by Harold P. Newlin. Survivors show varying states of clash marks. Beware altered dates from 1858 (the ill. will detect these); beware coins with arrows removed (these will be underweight). Enl. photos.

3064   1853 O No arrows. [160,000 –]

Only one var.; leftover rev., repunched mintmark. The other 5 obv. dies remained unused. Date always weak. Beware altered dates from 1858 (the ill. will detect these); beware coins with arrows removed. At least 3, possibly 5 UNCS. (ill.), all prooflike; about 5 others EF–AU, but most are in low grades. Weak strikings are usual; grade by surface. Enl. photos.

viii. ARROWS AT DATE (1853–55)

The discovery of immense quantities of gold in California, 1848–56, had the consequence of lowering gold's price reckoned in (Spanish or Mexican) silver dollars; in practice, this was experienced on both coasts as a rise in the price of silver (bullion or coins) reckoned in gold dollars, eventually above face value. By 1851 silver coins vanished from circulation. Some were hoarded; many others were melted down for shipment in ingot form to Caribbean countries and Europe, exactly as happened in the mid-1960s. This situation rapidly produced hardship. The only coins in circulation, 1851–early 1853, were gold dollars, "fish scales" (3¢ silver: Chap. 23, introductory texts to Sects. i, ii), large cents, occasional half cents, junk foreign coins, and merchants' tokens. Federal copper coins were not legal tender and could be legally refused by storekeepers; they had no real advantage over merchants' tokens. Into this gap came an inundation of irredeemable "shinplasters": private scrip, paper currency promising (often falsely) redemption on demand in other bank notes or occasionally in coin, *if* one could ever find the backwoods banks of issue, or *if* one could catch the issuers before they left the state.

Nothing quite like this had happened before in American history, and nobody knew what to do about it. Eventually Mint Director George N. Eckert (in office 1851–53) decided to reduce official silver coin weights (oddly excluding the silver dollar) down to where melting would no longer be profitable. He managed to persuade an uncomprehending Congress that this would work, and accordingly an equally uncomprehending Pres. Millard Fillmore signed into law the Act of Feb. 21, 1853 proportioning weights of half dimes, dimes, quarters, and half dollars to a theoretical dollar of 384 grs. (down from 412.5).

There was no time to make samples of new designs for Treasury approval, yet it was absolutely essential to distinguish between heavier old-tenor and lighter new-tenor silver coins as they came from the mints, and as they would later be brought in for redemption and melting. Eckert devised the idea of some kind of distinctive mark to be added to existing designs, eventually ordering Longacre to add arrows beside dates. All half dimes to be struck after April 1, 1853 (like their larger siblings), would bear this marking.

Eckert resigned; Thomas M. Pettit briefly succeeded him. Longacre prepared some 78 new obv. dies for 1853 Philadelphia half dimes, 18 for New Orleans, and 2 for San Francisco, all with arrows at date. (The two pairs of 1853 S half-dime dies went to Augustus Humbert's provisional mint in San Francisco, alias the "U.S. Assay Office," just in case that institution could solve the problem of obtaining parting acids and issue regular coins at legal fineness: Chap. 40. The 1853-dated dies remained unused; San Francisco would issue no half dimes for another 10 years.)

During the remainder of 1853, the Philadelphia Mint made over 13 million half dimes with arrows (the largest mintage of the series!), the New Orleans branch 2.2 million. These coins went into circulation and stayed there, for which reason they are not often seen in perfect mint state. Until recent decades coin dealers would not stock them in any grade because they were so common in G to VF, and in higher grades they were neglected because nobody thought them worth keeping. This led in recent years to an intense demand among type collectors for gem survivors, and a corresponding tendency to exaggerate the grade of the common EF's and AU's.

Use of arrows continued through Dec. 1855; the new Mint Director, James Ross Snowden, thereafter countermanded it. Many of the larger mintages of 1853–54 came from bullion obtained by melting old-tenor coins (see previous section). Uncirculated survivors of 1854–55 are a little easier to obtain than those of 1853, as by then there were plenty available for circulation, and some of the newer coins began to accumulate in vaults and bank sacks. The 1855's are often weak at dentils, sometimes also at dates.

ARROWS AT DATE

Designer, Engraver, Mints, Physical Specifications, as before, except Weight 19.2 ± 0.5 grs. = 1.244 ± 0.032 gms. Authorizing Act, Feb. 21, 1853.

Grade range and standards, as before.

3065   1853 Arrows. [13,210,020 + 5P]
In all, 78 obvs., 80 revs., which figure may include **3063.** Proofs were issued in sets with dimes, quarters, and halves, March 3, 1853; 1976 ANA:631, $3,200. Regular coinage began April 26. Many "sliders" or borderline cases masquerade as mint state (see introductory text). Arrow and date positions vary. Enl. photos.

3066   1853 O Arrows. [2,200,000]
18 obvs. shipped; at least 8 revs. on hand. The 6 surviving No Arrows obvs. were defaced before June 9, 1853. Arrow and date positions vary. V-5 (Merkin 9/68:183) shows the severest clash marks yet seen on a U.S. coin of the period. The mythical "1853/1" publicized by Heaton {1893} proved to have vertical die break through 3: V-2 (rare).

3067   1853 O Arrows. Obviously repunched 3. Rare.
Discovered by W. W. Neil; Neil:1727. Break develops from 1 to border.

3068   1854 [5,740,000 + ?P]
Many minted from silver obtained by melting some $1 million in old-tenor coins returned in fall 1853 from New Orleans. Arrow and date positions vary; 5 4 free but vars. may exist with 54 touching. Proofs are very rare; those on broad flans with plain edge are experiments struck in argentan (a kind of German silver) to show how this base alloy could be mistaken for silver.

3069   1854 Date overlaps base. Rare.
V-1; Neil 3. Discovered by W. W. Neil before 1927. Later, dies severely clashed.

3070   1854 Heavily repunched 1. Scarce.
NN 50:355.

3071   1854 O [1,560,000]
8 obvs., 4 revs. Date and arrow positions vary; 5 4 free, but vars. may exist with 54 touching. Rare in mint state, though "sliders" abound as in 1853.

3072   1854 O Mintmark extremely thin, incomplete. Very rare.
Merkin 9/68:185, others. Heavily clashed dies.

3073   1855 [1,750,000 + ?P]
17 obvs., 18 revs. Arrows normally high, barbs slightly overlapping rocky base; date positions vary slightly. Dentils often weak, especially on obv. Proofs are very rare: Bareford:93, $8,000.

3074   1855 O [600,000]
6 obvs., 4 revs. Arrow positions as last; date positions vary slightly. Sometimes from heavily rusted or clashed dies. Very rare in mint state: Hawn, Fraser, Auction 80:1122, $2,300. One proof known.

ix. ARROWS OMITTED (1856–59)

Mint Director Snowden's order to omit arrows on the coins of 1856 made Longacre's task easier. Coinage continued at the new weight standard, in somewhat lower quantities.

Half dimes and other small coins of 1856–58 normally show weak border dentils except in proof state. In an attempt to correct this and some other weaknesses, Longacre sent the old obv. hub to be reannealed (softened), retouched it, and ordered it rehardened. Coins dated 1857–58 from both Philadelphia and New Orleans, and 1859 O, were mostly made from dies sunk from the retouched hub. These show more drapery detail near pole, and a dent on innermost point of third star (counting clockwise from lower l.). Rocky baseline near foot wavy (formerly straight). Dentils remain weak except on proofs. This was at best a temporary stopgap; in 1859 a new hub was made for Philadelphia half dimes (see next section).

Coins of 1856–58 are often collected by type collectors as representing the Hughes-Gobrecht design since 1840, as the major change was in the weight, not the dies. This is a matter of individual taste.

In this period the most spectacular vars. are double dates and the 1858 over inverted date. There is also a report of an "1856 over 54" proof, said to have date entirely repunched and larger than usual (Neil:1648, ex S. Hudson Chapman coll., 1929, possibly ex Eavenson:102). This has led to examination of several earlier states of the regular V-2 proofs, but so far none has exactly matched the description of the Neil coin, nor has the latter shown up. Regular V-2 proofs do not show totally repunched dates, nor are dates larger than normal; the var. remains a numismatic ghost which has refused to be exorcised.

ARROWS OMITTED

Designer, Engraver, Mints, Physical Specifications, Authorizing Acts, as before.

Grade range and standards, as before. EXCEPTION: Border dentils weak except on proofs.

3075　1856 [all kinds 4,880,000 + ?P] Upright 5, curved top; open 6.
31 pairs of dies. Knob of 6 away from loop. Business strikes only. V-4, 5, 6, 7, others. Enl. photos.

3076　1856 Upright 5, curved top; closed 6.
Knob of 6 touches loop; see ill. at **3078.**
3077　1856 Same, obvious double date. Very rare.
Merkin 10/66:230.
3078　1856 Upright 5, straight top; closed 6. Proofs only. Very rare.
V-2. Strong dentils. See introductory text.

3079　1856 O [all kinds 1,100,000] Open 6; large O.
6 obvs., many leftover revs. Usually, closed 5 (knob touches upright).
3080　1856 O Closed 6; large O.
Same comment.
3081　1856 O Same, double date. Rare.
3082　1856 O Similar, small o. Ex. rare, untraced.
V-5. Two pairs of dies for San Francisco remained unused.
3083　1857 [all kinds 7,280,000 + ?P] Unretouched hub. Rare.
V-1 and unlisted (latter with very thin shallow date, NN 61:276). Compare following; see introductory text.
3084　1857 Retouched hub. Closed 5.
Dent on inner point of third star (see introductory text).

Knob of 5 touches upright. Business strikes have weak dentils; the coin ill. (enl.) is a very rare proof (V-3).

3085　1857 Retouched hub. Open 5.
Knob of 5 well away from upright. Business strikes only. V-2, 5, 6, others. A hoard of about 75 (which vars.?) turned up at 1976 ANA Convention.
3086　1857 O [all kinds 1,380,000] Unretouched hub.
4 vars. See introductory text.
3087　1857 O Retouched hub. Large O.
Many vars. See introductory text. Newcomb (ANS {1914}) claimed one with medium oval O; difference from large O, if any, unverified. A hoard of at least 9 UNCs. turned up in 1982.
3088　1858 [3,500,000 + ?P]
Retouched hub only. Possibly 80+ proofs. Business strikes are usually weak in centers. UNCs. are plentiful from a hoard.
3089　1858 Short pole. Very rare.
V-5; Ivy Cambridge:423. Drastically lapped obv.: pole ends below hand, cap suspended above fingertip, elbow drapery fragmented.
3090　1858 Double date. Very rare.
Breen 10. Date first entered far too high, top of 1 touching

rocky base, then corrected half its height lower. Merkin 9/70:262; *Gobrecht Journal* 3/76. At least 10 times as rare as next.

3091   1858 over inverted date. Rare.
Breen 9. Tops of inverted digits show a little above middle of date. Discovered by Jesse Patrick, mid-July 1963. Cf. Q. David Bowers in *CW* 2/2/66, and *Gobrecht Journal* 11/79, p. 30; Auction 81:73, UNC., $3,000. Not to be confused with preceding.

3092   1858 O [1,660,000]
Minor positional vars. A hoard of about 20 UNCS. surfaced in late 1982; some were in "N.Y. Coll.":1155–65.
3093   1859 O [560,000]
10 obvs. shipped Dec. 1858, for 1859 use; probably not over 2 were used, with leftover revs.

x. PAQUET'S MODIFIED DESIGN
(1859–60)

In early 1859, for Philadelphia Mint half dimes only, Longacre's new assistant Anthony C. Paquet (1814–82) prepared a new obv. hub; this was not copied on other denominations. It is most notable for hollow stars, slimmer arms, smaller cap, larger head. Coiffure, profile, and drapery folds are all altered. The treatment is not in any way a real improvement. The new hub occurs on both the 1859 Philadelphia obvs., and reappears on the 1859 and 1860 fantasy coins without UNITED STATES (3096–97).
   The latter were struck by order of Mint Director James Ross Snowden to provide collectors with something special, ostensibly for trades to benefit the Mint Cabinet collection of Washington coins and medals, and to make Snowden's new book {1861} more comprehensive. Supposedly only 100 of this 1860 concoction were minted—business strikes only, though never circulated. Proofs are reported (Allenburger, 1952 ANA:516), though I have not seen this coin. All others shown me as such have proved to be the regular strikings with weakness at rock and upper l. wreath, and field striations from imperfect die pol-

ishing. Compare "Dupont":1409 and Lohr:277, also called proofs.
   On the other hand, the similar 1859 (commonly miscalled "transitional") comes only in proof state, possibly 12–15 survivors being traceable. As neither obv. nor rev. die has been identified on any other coins to date, we are unable to guess when or under what circumstances they were minted, but they are certainly *pièces de caprice,* and may even be afterthoughts inspired by Snowden's little eccentricity of 1860.
   Before the end of 1859, Longacre made entirely new hubs for the 1860 dime and half dime. Many have suspected that Paquet's limitations as a coin designer induced Longacre to ease him out; all his efforts are notable for a stiffness well beyond even that associated with our most Victorian Mint Engravers, William and Charles E. Barber. Paquet nevertheless continued to make occasional dies for Mint medals as late as 1875.

PAQUET'S MODIFIED DESIGN

Designer, Engraver, Anthony C. Paquet, after Hughes, after Gobrecht, after Sully. Mint, Philadelphia. Physical Specifications, Authorizing Acts, as before.
   Grade range and standards, as before; rarely collected in low grades.

3094   1859 [340,000 + 800 − P] Repunched 18, low date.
V-2. See introductory text. This var. comprises the majority of proofs (many later melted). Later business strikes show little double punching on 18, eventually none. Enl. photos.

3095 1859 Repunched 1 59.

V-1. In all, 6 obvs., 8 revs., mostly unused. Proofs (a minority) and business strikes. Die later repolished, thereafter showing only bases of 1 9 repunched, and even these fade.

3096 1859 Rev. type of 1860. Proofs only. Possibly 12–15 known.

Judd 232. Right ribbon end clear of wreath. 1976 ANA, Robison:883, $6,000.

3097 1860 Similar. [100]

Judd 267. Both ribbon ends touch wreath. Obv. usually

shows field striations, and always shows some trace of long die scratch from l. end of rocky base to border. Usually weak at rock and upper l. wreath; ill. (enl.) is one of the sharpest strikings known. Proofs are unverified; see introductory text.

xi. LONGACRE'S "CEREAL WREATH" DESIGN (1860–73)

From Longacre's abortive group of pattern half dollars of 1859, only one design actually managed to win official approval. This was "Newlin's Wreath of Cereals," one of Longacre's more fanciful productions, including sprigs of corn, wheat, oak, and maple. We have not managed to find out precisely what was Newlin's connection with it (did he provide a sketch?), nor whether this was the Mint hanger-on Harold P. Newlin (who gave the Mint Cabinet some important coins, and in 1883 wrote the first monograph on half dimes), or someone else with this family name. Whatever its actual origin, the name dates back at least to the 1880s. Half dimes issued from Jan. 1860 through the end of the series (March 1873) bore this wreath, uniformly with the dimes from 1860 through 1916. Longacre again modified Ms. Liberty's effigy in lower relief; the statutory legend now surrounds her in place of the stars, because to place it on rev. would have required reducing wreath and HALF DIME to impossibly small proportions.

Coins of this new design were issued from the Philadelphia Mint in all years 1860–73, though most business strikes 1863–68 which left the Mint at all went to Latin American melting pots. For long no uncirculated (nonproof) 1864's were known to exist, and the date was believed proof-only; other dates 1863–67 were very rare in all grades. But about 1956–57 a few uncirculated 1864's, '66's, and '67's began showing up, several of them extracted from original proof sets of these years, still in Mint wrappers. (This apparently testifies less to skulduggery than to carelessness at the Mint: In the 1860s there was too little profit in proof sets to make any difference.) Today these dates are still rare though far less so. A small hoard of 1864's, business strikes and proofs, was broken up in 1974; I saw 14 proofs from it. Other tiny hoards have more recently shown up, but the market has not sagged; date collectors are normally ready to accept either proofs (regularly saved) or the rarer business strikings, and the latter have begun to command enormous premiums.

The New Orleans Mint issued a quantity in 1860 only. Two pairs of dies were shipped for 1861 use; no coinage followed under the Union, but it is unknown if the Confederacy struck any after the rebels seized the Mint that spring.

At San Francisco, half-dime coinage began in 1863 and continued each year through 1873, though the unique 1870 S coin was not known until 1978 (see below). Over half the known survivors of 1863–69 had been made into cuff links, tie tacks, buttons, pins, etc., going along with a coin-jewelry fad which peaked in the 1870–83 period. This treatment left solder marks in central obv. or rev., or plain scraping and retooling to remove traces; such coins are numismatically beyond redemption. The fad affected other small coins: dimes, gold dollars, quarter eagles, and California fractionals, both the circulating issues of 1852–56 (Chap. 43, Sect. iii) and the jewelers' issues of 1859–82 (Breen {1983}). Until 1968 no uncirculated specimen was known of many of the San Francisco dates, but two tiny hoards showed up in New York: 10 to 20 each of 1863 S, 1864 S, and 1866 S. About a dozen 1871 S's appeared in England in 1977; about 100 1872 S's at the 1964 ANA Convention, and about 150 more in 1974. Most of these 1872 S's have mintmark below wreath.

During early 1978, a specimen dated 1870 S was found in a junk tray. This coin came into the possession of RARCOA (Rare Coin Company of America, a Chicago coin firm), was authenticated, went on display at the 1978 ANA Convention in Houston, was publicized in *NNW* 9/9/78, p. 1, and later sold to John Abbott for $425,000. In "Four Memorable Colls.":174, it sold at $176,000 to Martin Paul; Auction 86:1053, $253,000. Its S mintmark is within wreath, like the 1871 and early 1872 revs.; it has prooflike surfaces. We suspect, but cannot prove, that it is a duplicate of one in the cornerstone of the second San Francisco Mint building (the "Granite Lady" on Fifth St. near Mission), which was laid in 1870, and which is known to contain other 1870 S mintages including the three-dollar piece (Chap. 34 below). In later 1872, the Engraving Department reverted to placing mintmark below wreath; the reason for the brief change has never been revealed.

Overdates are, for unknown reasons, far less frequent in this design than in its predecessors, and a couple of those reported have either remained controversial or failed to pass inspection. Perhaps the most famous of these numismatic ghosts is the 1865/3 S, publicized in a Frossard sale in 1894, and rediscovered in a New Netherlands auction, Dec. 1963. Kamal Ahwash insisted that this was only an earlier die state of a known var., and that whatever is in the 5 does not match curves of either a 2 or a 3. At present the question is moot, though the coin does show something at the 5 for which no ready explanation occurs. Similarly, the 1862/1, reported in 1977, has not passed examination—or at least no convincing specimen has shown up. On the other hand, there are at least three vars. of 1861/0. Ted Clark, the overdate specialist, claimed to have discovered one at the 1975 ANA Convention, but the first publicity occurred when Kamal Ahwash cataloged one for 1977 ANA:801. All three vars. are illustrated in *Gobrecht Journal* 11/82, pp. 5–7. The 1860 logotype was mostly effaced, but various traces of 0 show at lower l. of final 1.

Restrikes were made, about 1870–71, of regular proofs dated 1863 and 1864 and possibly other dates. Their rev. die is the same one found on some proofs of 1870; obv. dies are from a worn or injured state of the hub, with open top to D of UNITED, as found on almost all working dies of 1871–73 inclusive. These proof restrikes dated 1863–64 come in copper and aluminum; silver strikings are Ex. rare, only one seen of 1863, three of 1864. Dr. Daniel W. Valentine, who first pointed out the open D on the copper proofs {1931}, did not draw the obvious conclusion that these were restrikes, possibly because the technique of comparing proof rev. dies had not yet been perfected.

Growing use of shield nickels (Chap. 22, Sects. i, ii) made half dimes less and less necessary, except on the West Coast and in the Southwest, where the bulk of survivors turned up.

As a result, when the framers of the Mint Act of 1873 were deciding which denominations to abolish as superfluous, they chose to retain the nickel 3¢ and 5¢ coins instead of trimes and half dimes. (This was at least partly a sop to Joseph Wharton, who had been for two decades continuously promoting the use of nickel for coinage—from the mines of which he was the monopolistic owner.) Accordingly, issuing of half dimes ceased, ending a denomination which had been struck off and on for nearly 80 years. But it was a serious mistake, as none of the branch mints struck cents or other minor coins; and a by-product was one of the worst blunders in the history of coinage: the 20¢ piece (Chap. 26). Not until 1908 were cents struck at any branch mint, nor any nickels until 1912; and not until then did the United States begin to supply adequate small change to its inhabitants west of the Mississippi.

LONGACRE'S "CEREAL WREATH" DESIGN

Designer, Engraver, James Barton Longacre, after Hughes, after Gobrecht, after Sully. Mints, Philadelphia (no mintmark), New Orleans (1860, mintmark O below wreath), San Francisco (1863–73, mintmark S below wreath except 1870–early 1872 in which it is within wreath). Physical Specifications, Authorizing Acts, as before.

Grade range and standards, as previously. NOTE: Not usually collected in low grades. Beware S-mint coins with traces of solder in central obv. or rev.: see introductory text.

3098 1860 [799,000 + 535 + P]
Originally 1,000 proofs struck with the sets, March 8; only 535 sets sold, with a few individual extra half dimes, the rest melted. Date varies from thin to fairly heavy (enl. photos).

3099 1860 Plainly repunched 1 0. Rare.
Date logotype entered twice, first slanting up to r., then corrected level. Doubling plain at 1 0. Valentine 4; Neil 3, Neil:1667. Discovered by W. W. Neil before 1927. *Numisma* 5/57:279; Rhodes:556. Later states with repunching faded off 1 price as preceding.

3100 1860 O [1,060,000 + ?P]
Mintmark normally thin and delicate, less often heavier. Possibly 4 proofs known.

3101 1861 [3,361,000 + 400−P]
Originally 1,000 proofs in sets, April 15; under 400 sold, the rest mostly melted. 42 obv. and 43 rev. dies. Many minor positional vars.

3102 1861/0 Very rare.
3 vars. See introductory text. "Capitol City":204, UNC., $2,200.

3103 1862 [1,492,000 + 550−P]
21 pairs of dies. Some 430 proofs sold with the sets, most others melted; Julian discovered that a few remained on hand as late as 1877.

3104 1862 Double date. Rare.
Discovered by W. W. Neil between 1927 and 1945. Neil:1673. Ill. *Gobrecht Journal* 11/82, p. 7; cf. "Charmont":2342.

3105 1862 Date slants grotesquely up to r. Ex. rare.
V-4; Neil 4. Extreme clash marks forced immediate discard of this obv.; Merkin 10/66:237, and cf. Rhodes:564. Enl. photos. 2 proofs reported. 3 pairs of 1862 S dies to San Francisco; no coinage followed.

3106 1863 Original. [18,000 + 460P]
Closed top to D of UNITED; heavily repunched 18. Rare business strikes were all delivered May 26, after the proofs from the same dies.

3107 1863 Restrike. Proofs only. Ex. rare.
Open top to D of UNITED; recutting at r. side of 1; rev. of 1870, clash mark at M. See introductory text. One silver impression seen (others probably exist); 2 or 3 in copper.

3108 1863 S [100,000]
3 pairs of dies (Nov. 1862). Usually in low grades; UNCs. are from the tiny hoard (see introductory text), many cleaned.

3109 1864 Original. [48,000 + 470P] Very scarce.
Closed top to D in UNITED. 4 vars. Date usually low with heavy 4 (V-1), rarely central. Business strikes often show heavy clash marks; a few have the old 1863 rev. with crack from rim to wreath at r. Clifford:1482, UNC., $2,100. The rarest of the proofs have crack from rim to top of head; these also come with the 1863 rev. The mintage figure, from Julian, may include some coins dated 1863. Capt. Roy Ash attempted a census of this date, and found fewer than 56 business strikes, of which about 20 are UNCs. from the hoard (many cleaned) with a few from original proof sets (see introductory text), the rest mostly badly worn pieces, some of which may have begun life as proofs: *Gobrecht Journal* 11/77. We suspect that the true total is 80–100 survivors in all grades.

3110 1864 Restrike. Open top to D. Ex. rare.
Date high, slanting up to r.; rev. of 1870 proofs, clash mark below M. Enl. photos. Also found in copper and aluminum. Probably made about the same time as the 1863 restrike, **3107.** Enl. photos.

3111 1864 S [90,000]
2 pairs of dies shipped Oct. 1863. Usually in low grades. The hoard contained 14 when I saw it (1971), some UNC., others cleaned enough to fall slightly short of mint state; these were the first top-grade coins known. See introductory text. Earliest states show repunched 1.

3112 1865 [13,000 + 500P]
2 pairs of dies made for business strikes (only one used?); 2 obvs. also for proofs. Usually with parts of 865 filled in. The tiny lump on r. side of 8 is in the logotype and occurs on other denominations, notably cents and 2¢ pieces. Auction 86:1573, UNC., $2,090.

3113 1865 Double base to 1. Proofs only. Rare.
Discovered by W. W. Neil before 1927.

3114 1865 S Heavily repunched date. [120,000]
V-1 and Breen 3. Usually in low grades, Ex. rare choice; not represented in the hoard.

3115 1865 S "Overdate." Ex. rare.
Discovered by W. M. Friesner before 1894; see introductory text. Earliest state of foregoing?

3116 1865 S Normal date, no repunching.
V-2. Two obv. dies shipped Nov. 1864.

3117 1866 [10,000 + 725P]
2 minor vars. of proofs, 2 of business strikes. The rare earliest state of one proof die shows triple outlines on final 6.

3118 1866 Repunched date, plainest at 18. Proofs only. Very rare.

Later states with repunching faded price as preceding.

3119 1866 S [120,000]

6 obv. dies shipped; the only one noticed has what looks like part of 8 just l. of skirt pendant. Usually in low grades; only 8 were in the hoard (1968) when it was shown to me. Auction 86:1574, UNC., $4,400.

3120 1867 [8,000 + 625P]

4 minor vars. of proofs (Breen {1977}, p. 133), one of business strikes, the latter usually with die clash marks. 1980 ANA:1427, UNC., $5,000.

3121 1867 S [120,000]

Usually in low grades, very rare choice. Auction 81:655, UNC., $2,500.

3122 1868 [88,600 + 600P]

One var. of business strikes (rare), 2 of proofs.

3123 1868 S [280,000]

One pair of dies, used until they wore down and shattered. Not as rare in mint state as previous S mints.

3124 1869 Normal date. [208,000 + 600P]

At least 5 minor vars.

3125 1869 Double date. Very rare.

V-2, earliest die state only; later states, with doubling mostly gone, will price as preceding.

3126 1869 S [230,000]

6 obv. dies sent Oct. 1868. Normal or with light repunching on 18.

3127 1870 [353,600 + 1,000P]

At least 7 minor vars.

3128 1870 S Mintmark within wreath. Unique?

6 pairs of dies shipped Dec. 1869; no record of coinage. Discovered early spring 1978; see introductory text. Filled S, die reused for **3130.** 19.599 grs. = 1.27 gms.; sp. gr. 10.316; 107 edge reeds. Enl. photos.

3129 1871 [1,873,000 + 960−P]

Obv. Top of D open from now on (hub injury) except where corrected by hand on an occasional working die. Bases of 18 touching or, on weaker impressions, barely free. Proofs often show rust on seated figure. The minus sign alludes to extensive melting of 1871–73 proofs July 10, 1873.

3130 1871 S Mintmark within wreath. [160,000]

4 pairs of dies received Dec. 16, 1870. Obv., top of D repaired; rev. of **3128.** Only the earliest die state shows repunching on 1. Formerly believed rare, but 2 hoards have turned up since WW II, and UNCS. (mostly cleaned) have been available for a price; see also introductory text.

3131 1872 [2,947,000 + 950−P]

Top of D open. Same comments as to **3129** except for rusty dies. See next.

3132 1872 Doubled obv. die. Ex. rare, 4 known.

Discovered by Chuck and Marian Leber. Note triple stripes to shield, and base of extra N joining diagonal. 1983 Midwinter ANA:883. Enl. photo.

3133 1872 Double date. Proofs only. Rare.

V-2, earliest state.

3134 1872 S Mintmark in wreath. [475,000]

4 obvs. shipped Nov. 1871; leftover revs. Coined Jan.–June 1872.

3135 1872 S Mintmark below wreath. [362,000]

4 revs. shipped Nov. 1871; coined Sept.–Dec. 1872. See next. 2 hoards, mostly of this type, have turned up since 1964; see introductory text.

3136 1872 S Blundered obv. Ex. rare, 4 known.
Discovered by Kamal Ahwash. Date triple-punched in final position; traces of a fourth date show above, and next to bulla (skirt pendant) are traces of tops of a fifth 1 and 8!

3137 1873 Closed 3. [712,000— + 600—P]
4 minor vars. Many proofs melted July 10, 1873; some business strikes melted then, others later used for recoinage into other denominations.

3138 1873 S Closed 3; S below wreath. [324,000]
4 obv. dies shipped Nov. 1872; leftover revs. Occasional lapped dies show knobs of 3 a little farther apart, but not enough to call it a different var.

CHAPTER 25

DIMES

---

i. THE SCOT-ECKSTEIN DRAPED BUST/SMALL EAGLE DISMES (1796–97)

This one denomination was the crucial test of whether the federal coinage system would be fully decimalized as Congress intended. Congress in 1786 had adopted a coinage system calling for a silver dollar equated to the Spanish, with a smaller denomination of 1/10 its value, called a disme. (For the name's origin, see Chap. 16, introductory text.) Alexander Hamilton's system, adopted in 1791, required two gold coins of $10 and $1, two silver coins of $1 and 10¢ (latter called a "tenth"), and two coppers (cent and half cent). Modified to eliminate the gold dollar, and to include five intermediate denominations (the half disme, quarter and half dollar, and quarter and half eagle), this system became law with the Mint Act of April 2, 1792, the ultimate basis of later coinage acts to the present day. Its fully decimal character depended on simultaneous use of coins of $10, $1, 10¢ (called dismes) and 1¢, eventually supplanting the Spanish division of the dollar into eighths or bits.

However, actual coinage of dollars and dismes did not follow for some years. Silver coinage could not be legally made until late in 1794, because neither Assayer Albion Cox nor Chief Coiner Henry Voigt could post $10,000 surety bonds. The first coinage of dismes for general circulation consisted of 22,135 pieces delivered between Jan. 18 and May 27, 1796, from five obv. and four rev. dies in six combinations. These dies were by Robert Scot and John Eckstein, loosely following Gilbert Stuart's portrayal of Mrs. William Bingham (née Ann Willing) as Ms. Liberty (Chap. 24, Sect. ii, introductory text). Several dozen were saved in mint state as souvenirs, the first of their kind. Col. E. H. R. Green (son of Hetty Green, the "Witch of Wall Street") accumulated many 1796 dimes, including most of the really choice survivors, but following his death, dealers dispersed the hoard to date collectors.

It will be convenient to list the six vars. Equivalents are to Hilt {1980} and Davis {1984}.

Davis 1. LI nearly touch, L low, almost always with lumpy break joining first star to rim; five berries, leaf point almost touches O. Hilt 1A. Over 250 known; dozens UNC. The Cass, "Empire," Jimmy Hayes coin without the break is a prooflike presentation piece. In Hayes:16 (Stack's 10/22/85) it brought $44,000.

Davis 2. Low date, 6 equidistant between drapery and border, fifteenth star touches drapery; five berries, one (inner) between l. bow and lowest leaves. Hilt 2B. Rare, very few UNC.

Davis 3. Closest date, first star away from curl; four berries, leaf joins U, outer berry just r. of D. Hilt 3C. Rare, possibly three UNC.

Davis 4. Same obv.; four berries, triple leaf at ST. Hilt 3D. Very scarce, but at least six UNC.

Davis 5. Notched stars, first touching second curl; same rev. Hilt 4D. Rare, more so than Davis 2. No UNC. known.

Davis 6. Dot before L, widest L I B E R T Y; four berries, outer berry below T(A). Hilt 5E. Over 200 known; possibly 12 UNC.

The coins of 1797 are far rarer than those of 1796. Their reported mintage of 25,261 may possibly include as many as 3,864 dated 1796 (delivered Feb. 28, 1797); the 6,380 of March 21, if not further 1796's, were probably 16-star coins, like the 9,099 of May 26. The 3,958 of June 20 were most probably 1797 13-star coins, like the 1,000 of June 30 and the final 960 of Aug. 20, 1797. On Aug. 28 the Mint closed down because of a yellow fever epidemic, reopening in November. However, no more dismes were coined until July 1798, by which time the Heraldic Eagle dies were ready (see next section). All subsequent disme obvs. bore only 13 stars because Mint Director Boudinot realized in 1797 that the Mint could not go on indefinitely adding new stars as new states joined the Union. A very few 13-star coins come from severely rusted dies; these may be the 960 of Aug. 20, or possibly products of a later winter after an epidemic. In low grades, the 13 Stars var. is only slightly rarer than the 16 Stars; in mint state, both are Ex. rare, the 13 Stars prohibitively rare.

THE SCOT-ECKSTEIN DRAPED BUST SMALL EAGLE

Designers, Engravers, Robert Scot and John Eckstein, after Gilbert Stuart. Mint, Philadelphia. Composition, silver 892.43+ Fine (1,485/1,664). Diameter, 12.5/16″ = 19.8 mm (varies). Weight, 41.6 grs. = 2.696 gms. Reeded edge as on all to follow. Authorizing Act, April 2, 1792.

Grade range, POOR to UNC. GOOD: Devices outlined, no internal details; date and all legends barely visible (tops of some letters may be blurred). VERY GOOD: Traces of hair and feather details. FINE: Some hair details l. of brow and near ends of curls; partial drapery folds; about half wing feathers. VERY FINE: Over half hair details—generally 3/4 or more except near centers; most wing-feather details, claws partly visible, some internal detail in most leaves. EXTREMELY FINE: Isolated tiny worn spots only; grade by surface. EXCEPTIONS: Even prooflike 1796's may not show breast feathers nor full leg feathers; eagle's head may be weak. Die break weakens date in 1797 16 Stars even in FINE. NOTE: Most UNC. 1796's are prooflike or satiny, not frosty.

3139 1796 Four berries. [22,135+]
4 vars.; see introductory text. Price for Davis 6; other vars. are rarer. Total mintage may be as high as 32,379 (incl. 10,244 of Feb.–March 1797). Enl. photos.

3140 1796 Five berries.
2 vars.; see introductory text. Price for Davis 1 (ill.); Davis 2 is rarer. Enl. photos.

3141 1797 Sixteen stars, pointed 9. [9,099?]
Davis 1; Hilt 6F. See introductory text. Always with die break from rim to rim crossing top of date; this break becomes heavy, weakening date. Usually in low grades; probably fewer than 5 UNC. Enl. photos.

3142 1797 Thirteen stars, knobbed 9. [5,918?]
Davis 2; Hilt 7F. See introductory text. Usually in low grades. Not over 3 known UNC.

ii. SCOT'S HERALDIC EAGLE DISMES (1798–1807)

Robert Scot's scaled-down copy of the heraldic eagle from the Great Seal of the United States first appeared in 1796 on quarter eagles. Though disme and quarter-eagle dies were of identical size and were occasionally interchanged, for unknown reasons no dismes were issued with the new rev. until July 1798. Either as a heraldic blunder or as an ill-timed piece of bravado, Scot placed the arrows in the eagle's dexter claw, relegating the olive branch for peace to the less honorable sinister claw (Chap. 24, Sect. iii, introductory text). Scot's earliest dies of this type bore 16 stars above eagle (1796 quarter eagles, 1797 half eagles), but during 1797 Mint Director Boudinot decided that the Mint could not go on indefinitely adding new stars to coin dies with every new state joining the Union. This is why 1798 disme obvs. show only 13 stars. But the first rev. shows 16 stars because it is actually the 1797 quarter-eagle rev. reused. This is also the only disme rev. from the Long Neck device punch; the other three revs. from it were used on 1796 quarter eagles.

The earliest 1798 disme obv. is also distinctive in having a tiny 8 punched over a much larger 7, with no attempt to conceal or efface the latter: an unusual way of making overdates, not found later in any denomination. Overdates normally indicated Mint economy, not mere blunders; dated dies were too costly to discard merely because their year of date had elapsed. This unsightly overdate is part of the reason why Scot habitually omitted the final digit from dates if there was any chance the die would be held over for a later year.

Beginning in 1797 we find, in various denominations, two rev. star arrangements, "arc" and "cross." On the former, the stars are in a row of six nearest clouds, a row of five in a parallel arc below, with twelfth below beak and thirteen behind head. On the latter, stars are in straight lines obliquely crossing, forming diamond-shaped patterns: a peculiarity pointing to a single (still unidentified) apprentice in the Engraving Department. The cross arrangement occurs on dismes of 1798 and 1804–5, the latter suspected of being leftovers; on dollars of 1798–99; quarter eagles of 1804 (14 stars, reused on dismes, also believed leftovers); half eagles of 1798–99; and two eagle dies of 1797. The arc arrangement occurs 1797–1807 on all denominations.

Mint delivery warrants specify 27,550 dismes, July 23, 1798. Some specialists believe that many (possibly all) the dismes delivered in 1800 bore date 1798: March 25, 1800, [16,760] to the Bank of Philadelphia; March 26, [5,000] to William Cooper. This explains why 1798 is much easier to find than 1800. Similarly, Davis and collaborators interpret later deliveries as follows:

March 16, 1801:	9,260 dated 1800?
Sept. 30, 1801:	8,120 dated 1800 or 1801?
Dec. 1, 1801:	14,190 dated 1801?
Dec. 26, 1801:	3,070 dated 1801?
July 22, 1802:	10,975 dated 1802?
March 1803:	31,380 dated 1802 and 1803.
Sept. 1803:	1,660 dated 1803.
June 1804:	8,265 dated 1803 or 1804?
Sept. 1805:	67,540 dated 1804 and 1805.
Dec. 1805:	53,240 dated 1805.
March 1807:	80,000 dated 1805 and 1807.
June 1807:	95,000 dated 1807. More detailed break-

downs are speculative.

The best reason for thinking that the revs. of 1804–5 with cross arrangement are leftovers from 1798 is that (like the 1798 dies) they have narrow A's. A wider A punch went into use

1801–7, beginning with the second rev. of 1800 (almost certainly made in 1801).

Cast counterfeits have recently appeared of 1800 Wide A's. These are lightweight and show a short horizontal raised mark extending to l. of crossbar of A in STATES.

The date 1801 is the least rare of the 1800–4 group in worn condition, but both vars. are Ex. rare in VF or higher grades, and in mint state so rare that their existence was long controversial.

Three quarter-eagle revs. of 1802 also were used to make dismes in the same year. This date also usually comes worn, not over six mint-state survivors being recorded. The four vars. are as follows:

Davis 1. Star almost touches L; top l. rev. star obviously repunched. Rev. of quarter eagle ($2.50) B-4; crack, wing tip to r. rim. Only one seen: Copeland:469, Munoz IV:58. Rev. reappears on 1803 Davis 1.

Davis 2. Same obv.; arrow tips extend only to l. tip of l. foot of N. Usually, shattered rev. Rare.

Davis 3. Same obv.; arrow tips extend nearly to center of N. Rev. of $2.50 B-1, reappearing on 1803 Davis 2. Very rare.

Davis 4. Star far from L; "Needle Beak," lower prong piercing twelfth star. Rev. of $2.50 B-2, reappearing on 1804 $2.50 (13 stars) and 1804 Davis 1. Very scarce.

Two of the four vars. of 1803 are Ex. rare; all are weak in central obv., most also in central rev., no more than 10 EF's known:

Davis 1. Close 03, 3 tilts l.; top l. rev. star obviously repunched, die of 1802 Davis 1. Ex. rare, possibly four known.

Davis 2. Same obv.; arrow tips extend nearly to center of N, die of 1802 Davis 3. Crack, CA to rim. Very rare.

Davis 3. Same obv.; narrow A's. Very scarce.

Davis 4. Wide 0 3, 3 tilts r., top parallel drapery; arrow tips extend only to l. tip of l. foot of N, die of 1802 Davis 2. Rare.

The 1804 was formerly believed rarest of all because of its low reported mintage. Of its two vars., Davis 1 (13 rev. stars) has the repolished 1802 Needle Beak rev.; Davis 2 (14 rev. stars) has the repolished 1804 quarter-eagle rev., with narrow A's. Both vars. are rare, and in mint state apparently unknown.

The 1805 obv. comes first with an arc-arrangement rev. with wide A's and five berries (Davis 1), and more often with a cross-arrangement rev. with narrow A's and four berries (Davis 2). There are many UNCs. of the latter; many are thought to have been delivered in 1807. These vars. were formerly distinguished in catalogs only by numbers of berries; star arrangement and A's can be identified on specimens too worn to count berries, explaining the method of listing herein.

The single 1807 var. has a rev. first used on 1805–7 quarter eagles. During production runs of dismes, the dies clashed at least nine times; late impressions are therefore weak on letters, stars, and part of date, earlier (unclashed) die states are far harder to find.

SCOT'S HERALDIC EAGLE DISMES

Designer, Engraver, Robert Scot. Mint, Physical Specifications, Authorizing Acts, as before.

Grade range, POOR to UNC. GOOD: Devices completely outlined, no internal details except (sometimes) partial shield stripes; tops of some letters may be blurred; only a few motto letters visible. VERY GOOD: Traces of internal hair and feather details; partial motto. FINE: Some hair details l. of brow and near ends of curls; half wing feathers; generally, over half motto. VERY FINE: About 3/4 hair details—usually, nearly full except above and l. of brow and behind ear; nearly full wing feathers (tips and tail may be weak); motto weak but complete. EXTREMELY FINE: Isolated tiny rubbed spots; grade by surface. EXCEPTIONS: Dates 1801–3 are apt to be weak in centers;

1798–1805 are usually weak at stars above and r. of eagle's head. Over 4/5 of 1807 are weak at stars and letters from multiple clash marks.

3143 1798/7 [all kinds 27,550+] Rev., 16 stars.
Davis 1; Hilt 8D. Small 8 over larger 7. Rev. of 1797 quarter eagle. See introductory text. Usually weak in centers. Enl. photos.

3144 1798/7 Rev., 13 stars. Very rare.
Davis 2; Hilt 8E. Cross arrangement: See introductory text. Possibly 3 UNCs. Always weak in centers; usually in low grades. Enl. photos.

3145 1798 Small 8. Rare.
Davis 3; Hilt 9G. Usually in low grades. Enl. photos.

3146 1798 Medium 8.
Davis 4; Hilt 10G. Rev. arc arrangement, die of 1798 quarter eagle; reused in next. Usually weak in central rev. and l. obv. Probably many made in 1800.

3147   1800 Narrow A's. [Mint report 21,760] Very scarce.
Davis 1. See introductory text. Probably not over 5 UNCS.
Enl. photos.

3148   1800 Wide A's. Rare.
Davis 2. Rusted obv.; rev. of 1801, probably delivered in
1801. Probably not over 5 UNCS. Beware counterfeits; see
introductory text. Enl. photos.

3149   1801 [Mint report 34,640]
2 vars., commoner (ill.) with rev. of preceding, scarcer with
rusty rev. die ("7 berries": rust pits simulate extra berries),
leaf overlaps base of I. Usually in low grades. Possibly 5
UNCS. Enl. photos.

3150   1802 Normal. [Mint report 10,975] Rare.
3 vars.; price for Davis 2: See introductory text. Usually in
low grades; no mint-state specimens seen.
3151   1802 Needle Beak. Very scarce.
Davis 4; see introductory text. Possibly 3 UNCS. known.

3152   1803 Close 03; wide A's. [Mint report, 33,040] Very rare.
Davis 1, 2. See introductory text.

3153   1803 Close 03; narrow A's. Very scarce.
Davis 3. See introductory text. Prohibitively rare UNC.

3154   1803 Wide 0 3. Rare.
Davis 4. Usually in low grades.
3155   1804 Rev., 13 stars. [Mint report, 8,265] Very rare.
Davis 1. Repolished "Needle Beak" die of **3151.** See introductory text. Usually in low grades.

3156   1804 Rev., 14 stars. Very rare.
Davis 2. Repolished quarter-eagle rev. of **6119.** See introductory text. Usually in low grades.

3157   1805 Rev., wide A's, arc arrangement, 5 berries.
Davis 1. See introductory text.
3158   1805 Rev., narrow A's, cross arrangement, 4 berries.
Davis 2. See introductory text.

3159   1807 [165,000]
Only one var.; see introductory text. Early-state specimens
with full border dentils on both sides are rare.

iii. REICH'S CAPPED BUSTS
(1809–27)

The new Reich designs, first used on half dollars in Sept.
1807, represented a distinct mechanical advantage over all previous types of design found on U.S. silver coins, whatever their
aesthetic demerits. Heretofore, hubs or device punches imparted only the head or bust and eagle to working dies. Some
24–27 elements had to be added by hand to each Scot obv., 34–
37 to each rev. (date, stars, and letters): aside from arrows,
berries, sometimes also leaves and shield stripes, and occasionally other details. Many details had to be strengthened by hand
repunching or other retooling. These operations required that
the die be annealed, then each individual element hammered
into the die blank enough times to make a deep enough indent.
Each working die took many hours to complete. With the Reich

designs, the number of elements needing to be entered by hand dropped to 17 per obv., 24 per rev., with far fewer elements requiring hand strengthening. This entailed a saving in time per working die, and an improvement in die life. Its ultimate object was not only economy but increasing ease in detection of counterfeits and allowance for possible great expansion in quantities of coinage.

This expansion eventually became a daily reality for half dollars, but not for dismes. Local banks seldom ordered the smaller denominations coined from the bullion they deposited; merchants habitually preferred to use the old familiar Spanish and Mexican fractional silver coins, which were as much legal tender as federal silver. The small quantities of dismes that did reach circulation stayed there; strictly uncirculated specimens are rare.

All 1811 dismes have date 1811 over 1809, from an unused 1809 die; on late impressions from shattered dies, the numerals 09 within 11 are hard to see. This same font of numerals— much smaller than any later used prior to 1837—makes its last appearance on the scarce 1814 Small Date obv.

The final var. of 1814 shows a peculiar blunder: STATESOFAMERICA as one word. Remaining in good condition after the final delivery, this die stayed in Scot's vault for six years (a closet skeleton?), being exhumed for the first var. of 1820. This rev. went back into the vault, and in 1833 it was among old dies sold as scrap metal to private parties (Mickley? Dickeson?). It eventually went to Robert Bashlow, the promoter of the Confederate cent centennial restrikes. About 1962, Bashlow had some 536 impressions struck in various sizes and thicknesses from this badly rusted die in Edinburgh, Scotland— in platinum, gold, silver, bronze, and lead. Some were uniface; others bore a fantasy obv. reading GOD PRESERVE PHILADELPHIA AND THE LORDS PROPRIETERS (sic) 1869 M (in honor of Joseph J. Mickley, who had made similar restrikes a century earlier from other dies discarded by the Mint). The spelling PROPRIETERS is in obvious allusion to no. **191** above. In no case could any of these restrikes be mistaken for any current coin. Nevertheless, on Bashlow's return from Edinburgh, the Secret Service seized the die and all impressions (aside from any remaining in Scotland). The late Curator of the Smithsonian Institution's Division of Numismatics, Dr. Vladimir Clain-Stefanelli, made vain efforts to have the die and impressions placed in the National Collections, but Secret Service agents reportedly destroyed everything. Their ostensible (but irrational) reason was that they believed the die a counterfeit and a danger to the current coinage of the nation! This policy testified to official stupidity, lack of humor, lack of comprehension of numismatics, and most of all to a disposition to continue a vendetta which had been going on between the Mint Bureau and coin people since 1858: Breen {1962B}.

Dismes of 1820 are listed herein differently from all previous catalogs. Traditionally they have been collected only as having large and small 0 in date, but this distinction is very difficult to see without having both types at hand for physical comparison (ordinary halftone ills. in actual size do not enable certainty), and the coins are often mislabeled, quite aside from reflecting little difference in rarity. A division at once more rational and more easily recognizable by the naked eye is into two styles of lettering. "Oldstyle" letters (as in 1809–14 coins) have wedge-shaped serifs, with little distinction between thick and thin elements. "Modern" letters (as in 1821–37) have sharp, narrow vertical serifs with marked distinction between thick and thin elements. A glance at 10 C. affords instant identification; the wedge-shaped and sharp vertical serifs in the C. can be distinguished from about as far away as the letters can be read. These punches are by Henry Starr; dates and replacement letters after 1824 are by Christian Gobrecht.

Reported mintage figures are unreliable as a clue to scarcity.

Mintage reported for 1822 must have consisted mostly of coins dated 1821; all 1824's were included in the 1825 delivery. Also, at least 90,000 of the reported mintage for 1828 evidently bore date 1827.

REICH'S CAPPED BUSTS

Designer, Engraver, John Reich; dies later mechanically completed by Robert Scot and apprentices. Mint, Physical Specifications, Authorizing Acts, as previously, except Diameter, $3/4'' = 19 \pm 0.2$ mm.

Grade range, FAIR to UNC. GOOD: Devices outlined, no internal details except white shield stripes; tops of some letters may be blurred. VERY GOOD: LI Y or L TY will be clear; traces of eye, ear, and clasp; partial motto, few wing feathers. FINE: About half hair, drapery, and wing-feather details; motto clear but weak; full LIBERTY. VERY FINE: Ear, clasp, and over 3/4 hair and feather details clear; do not expect detail at eyebrow. EXTREMELY FINE: Isolated tiny rubbed spots only, mostly at hair above eye and ear; clasp sharp. Grade by surface. EXCEPTIONS: Weak uneven strikings mentioned at individual dates.

3160   1809 [51,065]
Mintage includes 6,355 delivered in 1810. Normally weak at l. stars and UNITED. Ex. rare in mint state.

3161   1811/09 [65,180]
Later impressions have shattered dies. L. obv. dentils often weak. Possibly 12 UNCs.

3162   1814 [all kinds 421,500] Small date.
Davis 1. Small narrow 8 as in 1809–11. Possibly comprised initial delivery [34,500]. Usually in low grades; no more than 6 UNCs. traced. Usually weak at upper obv. Enl. photos.

3163   1814 Large date, no period after C
Davis 3, 4. Broad 8, taller than 1. Both vars. are common.

3164 1814 Large date, period after C., normal legend. Scarce. Davis 2. Enl. photos.

3165 1814 Same but STATESOFAMERICA one word. Scarce.
Davis 5. Fewer than 10 UNCS. Enl. photos.

3166 1820 [all kinds 942,587+] STATESOFAMERICA one word. Scarce.
Davis 1. Rev. of last; see introductory text.

3167 1820 Oldstyle letters, normal spacing.
Davis 8. Tall 0 in date, taller than 1. One proof known. See introductory text. Enl. photos.

3168 1820 Modern letters, smaller c in 10 c.
Davis 10, 11. See introductory text. Enl. photos.

3169 1820 Modern letters, large C in 10 C. Blundered rev.
Davis 2. "Office boy" rev.: part of another letter between D S; ME join at tops and feet; many letters repunched and irregularly spaced.

3170 1820 Modern letters, large C in 10 C., normal.
Davis 3, 4, 5, 6, 7, 12. In date 0 no taller than 1. Most were struck in 1821.

3171 1820 Same, tall 0 in date.
Davis 9, 13. At least one proof known. Most were struck in 1821. In date 0 taller than 1.

3172 1821 [all kinds 1,186,512—] Large date.
7 vars. Curved base to 2. Mintage includes many dated 1820. At least one proof known. Enl. photos.

3173 1821 Small date.
Davis 8, 9, 10. Flat base to 2; quarter-eagle punches. 3 or 4 proofs known. Enl. photos.

Ex J. W. Garrett: 1585. Courtesy Bowers & Ruddy Galleries, Inc.

3174 1822 [100,000—] Very scarce.
Usually in low grades. Specimens offered as "UNC." should show as much detail as that ill. 2 proofs seen, a third reported. Mintage consisted mostly of 1821's. Enl. photos.

3175 1823/22 [400,000] Small E's.
Davis 1. E's as in 1809–22, less tall than T-D or T-S; rev. of 1821. Enl. photos.

3176 1823/22 Large E's.

Davis 2, 3. E's as in 1824–27, taller than adjacent letters. One proof reported. Enl. photos.

3177 1824/3/2 [100,000–]

Davis 1, 2. Mintage included in initial delivery, Aug. 1825. Earliest state with both 3 and 2 visible around 4 (possibly 3 proofs, few business strikes) very rare. Enl. photos. Price for later state with 3 not visible; last ones show only blurry traces of 2 around 4. The second rev. var. (Davis 2, rev. of 1825, ERI joined) is Ex. rare.

3178 1825 [410,000]

5 vars. At least 9 proofs known.

3179 1827 [Mint report 1,305,000]

13 vars. Part of reported mintage may have been dated 1825; but at least 90,000 delivered Jan. 1828 bore date 1827. At least 12 proofs.

3180 1827 Obviously repunched 7.

Davis 1. The very earliest die state appears to be 1827/5; traces of 5 fade (die wear or repolishing).

iv. KNEASS'S CAPPED BUSTS
(1828–37)

William Kneass succeeded to the Mint engravership after Robert Scot died in 1823. His primary assignments were to devise methods for rapidly multiplying working dies, and if possible to improve designs. In addition, following Matthew Boulton's recommendations of years before, he was expected to find methods for standardizing design elements and sizes, so that any deviation could be rejected as counterfeit.

Among the mechanical improvements Kneass introduced was what Mint people called a close collar (Eric Newman uses the term "collar die"). This is a heavy steel slug into which a hole is bored in the exact diameter of a finished coin. If intended for gold or silver coinage (or modern clad coins), its cylindrical wall is grooved to impart a reeded edge at the exact moment of striking; otherwise plain. A close collar fits just above the rev. die, forming the coining chamber confining each blank as it is stamped. After striking, one and the same continuous motion of the flywheel causes the upper die to retract, the lower die to rise through the collar (ejecting the newly minted coin), and feeder fingers to push the coin into a receiving bin. Then the lower die sinks again below the collar, the upper die begins to descend, another blank is released from the hopper and guided by the feeder fingers into the coining chamber, resting atop the lower die, whereupon the sequence repeats. This process enormously speeds up coinage, saving the time of separately reeding edges of blanks before striking (previously done by the Castaing machine: See Glossary and Newman-Bressett {1962}), and imparting "a mathematical equality to diameters" (to quote Mint Director Samuel Moore, 1829); it is the basic method still in use. Earlier issues had been struck in an open collar, which

positioned the blanks on the rev. die but did not confine them, as this would have flattened edge reeding or lettering.

However, even this increase in mechanization did not yet render identical a whole year's output of a denomination, though this was the ideal toward which Mint practice strove. Dies still required hand entry of dates, stars, and letters (see introductory text to previous section). This is why we find two sizes of dates in 1828, and four different styles of 10 C. in 1829. Nor were diameters as nearly equal as hoped: Not all collars were of the same size.

The 1828's involve mysteries, not the least of which is when they were struck. The 70,000 delivered on Jan. 11 and the 20,000 of Jan. 19 were surely dated 1827; the 15,000 of Feb. 1828 and the 20,000 of the final delivery may have comprised 1828 Small Date. However, the 1828 Large Dates were mostly (perhaps all?) struck in 1829, after the 1829 Davis 1, by evidence of die breakage.

As with the half dismes, the first rev. device punch showed "triple stripes": three lines in each pale gules (nearly vertical stripe) in shield. The change to "double stripes" (two lines in each pale gules) occurred in 1831. This means that the 1829's with double stripes must have been made in 1831 or later, parallel with similar backdated half dismes of the period.

Again as with the half dismes, borders of round beads appear for the first time since 1793. Kneass did not revert to the older types of radial dentilated borders until 1835, though border beads in the meantime tended more and more to be crowded against one another and against the raised rims so that they differed less in general appearance from the earlier dentilated borders.

Coinage was halted in late June 1837 to permit introduction of the new Gobrecht design: See next section.

About 1836–37 Mint records began consistently using the spelling "dime" rather than the former "disme." By 1837 it was standardized enough to be spelled out on the new design; presumably by then people were pronouncing it to rhyme with "time" rather than the former "steam."

The Mint Act of Jan. 18, 1837 lowered official weight to 41.25 ± 0.5 grs. $= 2.673 \pm 0.032$ gms. This should have affected all 1837 Capped Busts; we suspect leftover blanks were used up first, undetectably because they were within Mint tolerances for the new issue.

KNEASS'S CAPPED BUSTS

Designer, John Reich. Engraver, William Kneass. Mint, Physical Characteristics, Authorizing Acts, as before, except Diameter varies: 0.72–0.74″ = 18.3–18.8 mm. (Collars vary; narrowest 1832–35.) Weight (1837 only), 41.25 grs. = 2.67 gms.; Authorizing Act, Jan. 18, 1837.

Grade range and standards, as before.

3181 1828 [Mint report 125,000] Small date, flat base to 2.

Davis 1. Coarse rev. border beads. Possibly [35,000 + ?P]. At least 5 proofs; at least 6 business strikes with claims to mint state, plus many sliders. Enl. photos.

3182   1828 Large date, curved base to 2.
Davis 2. Fine rev. border beads. Ex. rare in mint state. Struck after next. Enl. photos.

Ex J. W. Garrett: 1593. Courtesy Bowers & Ruddy Galleries, Inc.

3183   1829 [all kinds 770,000+ + ?P] Extra large 10 C. Very scarce.
Davis 1. Curved neck 2. Same rev., earlier die state only. Usually in low grades. Discovered by this writer, 1955. Reported mintage for 1829 includes many dated 1828. Lohr:391 (unseen) was described as obv. proof, rev. UNC.; similar "one-sided proofs" exist for many other issues in the 1817–37 period. Enl. photos.

3184   1829 Large 10 C., coarse rev. border beads.
Davis 2. Same obv.; rev. similar to **3181**. The best UNCs. are from a tiny hoard released by one of Paul Revere's descendants about 1956.

3185   1829 Small 10 C., curved-neck flat-base 2.
Davis 3, 4, 5, 6. Small 10 C. vars. have round o in 10 C. At least 8 proofs reported.

3186   1829 Same, straight-neck flat-base 2.
Davis 7, 8. At least 3 proofs reported.

3187   1829 Same, small over large 10 C. Very scarce.
Davis 9. Usually in low grades; prohibitively rare UNC. Discovered by Q. David Bowers, 1965.

3188   1829 Small 10 C.; curved-base 2. Ex. rare.
Davis 10. Always in low grades. Discovered in Dayton, Ohio, 1973. Rev. reused in 1830. Enl. photo.

3189   1829 Medium 10 C., triple stripes. Very scarce.
Davis 11. Narrow oval 0 in 10 C. Usually in low grades; prohibitively rare UNC. Discovered by Don Frederick, 1976. Rev. reused in 1830. See introductory text.

3190   1829 Medium 10 C., double stripes. Scarce.
Davis 12. Narrow oval 0 in 10 C. Rev. of 1831. Enl. photos.

3191   1830 [510,000− + ?P] Small 10 C., round o.
Davis 1, 2. Revs. of 1829. Reported mintage includes many dated 1829.

3192   1830 Period after medium 10 C.
Davis 3, 5 (late), 6 (early), 7, 8. Period often weak. At least 4 proofs.

3193   1830 No period after medium 10 C Rare.
Davis 6, late die state (drastically repolished die).

3194   1830/29 Period after medium 10 C.
Davis 4, 5, early states. Discovered by Kenneth W. Lee, 1959; the discovery coin first publicized in NN 54:1911, later Gene Edwards, 1982 ANA:1928. Early states show traces of 29 within 30 and serif of 2 at lower r. of 3. Later states (less rare) show progressively less of overdate. At least one proof reported.

3195 1831 [771,350+ + ?P] Triple stripes.
Davis 1, 2, 5. Reported mintage includes coins dated 1829 and possibly 1830. See introductory text. Enl. photos. Proofs reported.

3196 1831 Double stripes.
Davis 3, 4, 6. See introductory text. Enl. photos. Proofs reported.

3197 1832 [522,500− + ?P] Level 2.
Davis 1, 2, 5. Reported mintage includes many dated 1831.
3198 1832 High 2.
Davis 3, 4, 6, 7. Obv. possibly made in 1830 or 1831, final digit omitted; configuration as in **3201**. One proof reported.
3199 1833 [485,000 + ?P] High 1.
7 vars. Reported mintage includes many dated 1832 (Davis 6, 7). At least 4 proofs.
3200 1833 Even date. Rare.
Davis 2. Oversized dentil below 1 in date.
3201 1833 Final 3 high.
Davis 5, 7.

3202 1834 [635,000 + ?P] Large perfect 4; normal D.
Davis 1, 3. Price for former; latter (very rare) has RI touching with traces of top of another I between them. At least 3 proofs of former.
3203 1834 Large perfect 4, extra large D. Rare.
Davis 2. D from a font intended for half dollars. Discovered by this writer in 1975 ANA:224. Enl. photos.

3204 1834 Large imperfect 4, doubled leaves. Rare.
Davis 4. Crossbar of 4 partly broken off. Leaves touch dentils in 3 places. Enl. photos.

3205 1834 Large imperfect 4, arrow shaft through middle talon.
Davis 5, 6. Latter with crossbar completely broken off. At least 3 proofs.
3206 1834 Small 4.
Davis 7. Usually in low grades. At least 2 proofs. Enl. photos.

3207 1835 [1,410,000+ + ?P] Center of 8 thick, widest date.
Davis 1, 2, 3, 9. "Horned" 8 (partly repunched). At least 6 proofs.
3208 1835 Same; all shield rims equally thick. Scarce.
Davis 4. Possibly 3 or 4 proofs. Enl. photos.

3209 1835 Center of 8 thin; curved top to 5.
Davis 6, 7, 8. Many were struck in 1836.
3210 1835 Center of 8 thin; small straight top to 5.
Davis 5. Enl. photos.

3211 1836 [1,190,000 − + ?P] Short obv. dentils.
Davis 2. Center of 8 thick, repunched over another 8 with center thin. Most of the reported mintage was dated 1835. At least 3 proofs. Enl. photos.

3212 1836 Long obv. dentils; center of 8 thick.
Davis 1. Many 1835's followed this var.

3213 1836 Long obv. dentils; center of 8 thin.
Davis 3.

3214 1837 [359,500 + ?P] Center of 8 thick.
Davis 1, 4. Weights unchecked; see introductory text.

3215 1837 Center of 8 thin.
Davis 2, 3. Same comment. Proof: Paramount 2/77, Auction 82:666, $4,200. Mintage interrupted, June 1837, to allow introduction of the new Gobrecht design: See next section.

v. THE SULLY-GOBRECHT LIBERTY SEATED DESIGN, NO STARS (1837–38)

In triumph, Mint Director Robert Maskell Patterson on June 30, 1837, ordered the newly completed Gobrecht dies to be placed into the dime press, and some 30 brilliant proofs struck for presentation to Treasury officials and other VIPs. About 20

of these proofs survive today, mostly cleaned, some scratched; one is in the Smithsonian Institution, from the Mint Cabinet collection where Chief Coiner Adam Eckfeldt had placed it.

The rejoicing was not only for the new design, but for several technological breakthroughs. Obv. shows Gobrecht's rendering of the Thomas Sully design, showing Ms. Liberty seated on a rock and holding a scroll inscribed with her name, closely following the device on the dollars coined Dec. 1836–March 1837, without stars. The only details requiring hand entry into each working die were dates. On this small scale, a four-digit logotype could impart the entire date with a single blow—reducing the needed hand entries from 17 per obv. die to one, saving time, cost, wear and tear on punches, and doubtless lengthening die life. And for the first time in the Mint's history, working revs. were successfully sunk from a complete hub, reducing needed hand entries from 24 per rev. to none (or one for those with mintmarks). From 1798–1801 the Mint had attempted to create cent revs. this way, but the 40-odd working dies so made all needed so much hand strengthening that Adam Eckfeldt abandoned the experiment, even as with several half-cent revs. in 1794. Eckfeldt tried again on cents 1835–37, but again the letters, berries, and some other details needed hand strengthening. For the time being, only the dime and half-dime revs. were completely hubbed, but even this deserved celebration as a major advance over anything hitherto possible, and as a small-scale fulfillment of Matthew Boulton's dream (1797) of total mass-production coinage, not to be completely implemented at Philadelphia until Dec. 1921.

Another and more important reason for attempting such total stereotypy of coin designs was security against counterfeiting. Hereafter, any coin of the new design which did not match the genuine in every detail of devices (date and mintmark positions aside) would be automatically rejected as counterfeit: precisely the view held to the present day in the Bureau of Engraving and Printing, which has rendered United States currency probably safer from counterfeiting than any other in the civilized world.

Large date 1837's were saved as first of their kind, and they are always available in mint state for a price. Not so the small dates, which comprised probably under ⅓ of the total mintage, and which were not saved in quantity.

Mint Director Patterson ordered stars added to all 1838 and subsequent dies. (Alleged 1838's without stars or mintmark have been repeatedly reported, but to date all seen have proved to be counterfeits.) However, before this order went into effect, two pairs of dime dies had been made up and mintmarked for the newly opened New Orleans Branch Mint. They were shipped April 9, 1838, and these and the corresponding half dimes are the only mintmarked coins of this design without stars.

Owing to incredible mismanagement, illness of key personnel, turnover of workmen, defalcations, etc., coinage at New Orleans was delayed, and its true amount not known for almost 140 years. The first 30 dimes struck, May 7, 1838, were for presentation purposes (though oddly not proofs); 10 went into the cornerstone of the New American Theatre in New Orleans, the other 20 to local VIPs. Some 367,434 more followed in June and July, and an additional batch in early 1839 from 1838-dated dies: quantity uncertain, known to be at least 32,600 and possibly as high as 121,600: Julian {1977}. These at once went into circulation and stayed there, almost none being saved as souvenirs. As the Superintendent of the New Orleans Mint explained in later correspondence with Patterson, these coins were in demand, passing readily as bits or one-real coins = ⅛ Mexican Dollar = 12½¢ each. Given a choice, merchants preferred to spend these lightweight coins (41.25 grs.) and hoard the 25% heavier one-real coins (standard 52 grs.). Survivors are well worn, mint-state specimens exceedingly rare. As with the half dimes, die deterioration (rust and chipping) rendered the obv. of one 1838 O var. abnormally weak and rough, so that after only brief circulation the coins look wretched; these Rusted Die coins are thought to be the batch delivered in early 1839.

As mentioned under the corresponding half dimes, never again was our coinage to be so free of clutter; and for many generations no more dimes were to be so well struck.

THE SULLY-GOBRECHT LIBERTY SEATED DESIGN, NO STARS

Designer, Thomas Sully (obv.), Christian Gobrecht (rev.). Engraver, Gobrecht. Mints, Philadelphia, 1837, New Orleans, 1838 (mintmark O above bows). Composition, silver 0.900, copper 0.100. Diameter, 7/10″ = 17.9 mm. Weight, 41.25 ± 0.5 grs. = 2.673 ± 0.032 gms. Authorizing Act, Jan. 18, 1837.

Grade range, POOR to UNC. GOOD: Date and all letters legible except LIBERTY. VERY GOOD: L TY or LI Y legible on scroll. FINE: Full LIBERTY; partial drapery and leaf details. VERY FINE: LIBERTY fully strong and even; nearly full drapery and leaf details. EXTREMELY FINE: Edges of scroll distinct above and below LIBERTY; isolated tiny rubbed spots only, mostly on thighs, breasts, parts of rock, and leaf tips.

3216 1837 [all kinds 682,500 + 30+P] Large date.
Flat top to 3. Proofs have sharply defined spur above T(A), faint die scratch through ES O. This same rev. reappears on early business strikes, with the die scratch gone, the spur increasingly blurry. Many UNCs. were saved as first of their kind. See introductory text. Enl. photos.

3217 1837 Small date.
Round top to 3, as in 1838. Usually in low grades; much rarer in mint state than preceding. Auction 81:1533, "UNC.," $3,500. 2 minor vars. Enl. photos.

3218 1838 O [406,034+]
2 pairs of dies, received May 3, 1838, not defaced until June

21, 1839. The first var. is apparently that ill., with rim break at r.; the rare later impressions of 1839 are thought to be those from severely rusted obv. die, mintmark without plain repunching. Usually in low grades, the first var. Ex. rare UNC., the rusted-die coins unknown choice. See introductory text. Enl. photos.

vi. GOBRECHT'S LIBERTY SEATED DESIGN, WITH STARS (1838–40)

All dimes from 1838 through Sept. 1840 (Philadelphia) and 1839 through Dec. 1840 (New Orleans) came from working dies sunk from the No Stars hubs of 1837. However, each working obv. had 13 stars individually entered by hand, often irregular in spacing.

What is apparently the first of these obvs. has unusually small stars, from use of the punch intended for half dimes. This scarce var., long unrecognized and often cherrypicked, most likely formed at least part of the initial delivery of 30,000 pieces, March 31, 1838; obv. promptly cracked through first five stars. A larger star punch was used for all remaining dies of this type, increasing the cluttered effect.

On the other hand, the "partial drapery" var. of 1838 is not a result of hand alteration, nor yet of a different hub; as the enlarged illustrations show, it is the remains of severe clash marks from ONE DIME, after the rest were effaced from obv. field by regrinding and repolishing. For decades, collectors have accepted it as a legitimate var., possibly by analogy with the "no drapery" and "drapery" half dollars of 1839.

Some dies of 1839 give the superficial appearance of an overdate, though we have as yet seen none with unequivocal evidence of 8 within 9. Unseen early die states may yet qualify.

Three different mintmark punches were in use: Large Round O (1.2 mm), the punch of 1838; Tall Narrow O (1.1 mm); Small Round o (0.8 mm), intended for quarter eagles. Uniformity in mintmarks was not yet among the Mint's fetishes.

In all, 4,026,115 dimes of this type were coined at Philadelphia (plus an unknown number of proofs), compared to 2,501,600 in New Orleans; after which Mint Director Robert Maskell Patterson insisted on a design change, intended and erroneously billed as an improvement: the Hughes design, called "With Drapery," or more properly "Drapery from Elbow": See next section.

GOBRECHT'S LIBERTY SEATED DESIGN, WITH STARS

Designer, Engraver, Mints, as before, except New Orleans mintmark O (1839–40) above bows. Physical Specifications, Authorizing Acts, as before.

Grade range, POOR to UNC. Grade standards, as before.

3219 1838 Small stars. [30,000] Scarce.
Ahwash 1. Half-dime star punches. Discovered by Howard Newcomb before 1914. Rev., repunched D(IME). See introductory text. Enl. photos.

3220   1838 Large stars. [1,962,500+ + ?P]
At least 8 vars. aside from that to follow. Stars always unevenly spaced; usually several show repunching. The largest-star punch remained in use through 1840. At least 3 proofs known. Enl. photos.

3221   1838 "Partial drapery." Scarce.
Ahwash 6. Clash mark from E: See introductory text. Discovered by F. C. C. Boyd, before 1943.

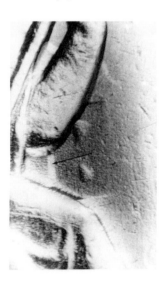

3222   1839 [all kinds 1,053,115 + ?P] Normal date.
At least 5 vars. Possibly 3 proofs, incl. Auction 82:1609, $6,750. Reported mintage includes many dated 1838.
3223   1839 Repunched 39. Scarce.
Ahwash 2. See introductory text.
3224   1839 Repunched 9. Scarce.
Ahwash 4. See introductory text.
3225   1839 O [all kinds 1,326,600+] Large round O. Ex. rare.
Ahwash 7. Rev. of 1838. Mintmark 1.2 mm. Enl. photos.

3226   1839 O Tall narrow O.
4 pairs of dies. Mintmark 1.1 mm, narrow. Enl. photos.

3227   1839 O Small round o.
Ahwash 1, 2. Two pairs of dies (6 pairs shipped in all). Mintmark 0.8 mm. Enl. photos.

3228   1840 "No drapery." [981,000 + ?P]
Hub of 1838–39. At least 8 vars. struck April–Sept. only. At least 5 proofs. Compare next.
3229   1840 Same, "Extra hair."
Ahwash 6. Die file marks l. of throat, from lip to shoulder, give the appearance of additional hair.

3230   1840 O "No drapery." [1,175,000] Small round o.
Hub of 1838–39. 6 obvs., 7 revs. Mintmark 0.8–0.9 mm.
3231   1840 O Same; tall narrow O. Very rare.
Mintmark as in **3226**; apparently from the single leftover 1839 rev. One reported with rev. of **3225**.

vii. THE HUGHES-GOBRECHT DESIGN, "EXTRA DRAPERY" (1840–60)

Late in 1840, Mint Director Robert Maskell Patterson ordered that the dimes and half dimes follow the silver dollars in adopting the new Robert Ball Hughes modified effigy. Like its smaller and larger counterparts, this new portrait has fatter arms, larger head, no décolleté, flatter contours concealed by bulkier drapery for "respectability," smaller rock, shield upright with enlarged scroll, and the useless cloak or himation over her elbow, making her pose extremely uncomfortable. Like the half dime, but none of the larger denominations, the dime obv. also shows a heavy pendant or bulla pulling drapery down to nearer the ground, lest someone catch sight of a feminine ankle: See Chap. 24, Sect. vii, introductory text. As on all other denominations from then on until the design was abandoned, stars are in the hub, their positions standardized to make counterfeits easier to detect.

Less familiar are the changes on rev., first publicized by Dr. John R. McCloskey and Kamal Ahwash of the Liberty Seated Collectors' Club. Hereafter, letters are larger, wreath has open buds. A single exception exists (3236), from a leftover rev. of 1839–40; this is an extremely rare discovery of recent years. On the other hand, the 1841 "No Drapery" is not a reversion to the old 1838–40 design, but the result of drastic regrinding and repolishing of a die used on a few proofs of this year; it is one of the rarest of all Liberty Seated coins.

As an abject submission to the new goddess of Respectability, alias Mrs. Grundy, the new design doubtless pleased the clergy; as an aesthetic enhancement, it was a failure; as a technological advance, it was a disaster. Though ostensibly meant to improve striking quality of the coins, the new design usually comes worse struck than its predecessors, often flat on heads and parts of drapery even in pristine mint state.

Aside from the arrows of 1853–55 (see next section), the only major variations in this design are in dates and mintmarks, which still had to be entered by hand. Dates were normally added to working dies by logotypes or gang-punches comprising three or sometimes four digits. At this blacksmith's chore, the new Mint Engraver, James Barton Longacre (appointed after Gobrecht's death, 1844), was timid and tentative, making many blunders. (Robert W. Julian says that some of these should be blamed on workmen in the Coiner's Department under Franklin Peale, though Longacre admitted that entering dates had been his chief task between 1844 and early 1849, the period most notable for such blundered dates. It has been cynically suggested that some few of these were deliberately allowed to reach circulation, as part of Patterson's and Peale's campaign to oust Longacre.) Many doubled dates are known through 1856, though there are no major blunders among the dimes.

On the other hand, the three mintmark sizes for New Orleans (similar to those in the previous section) are not errors; mintmark sizes were not yet standardized.

In an early instance of what is now called "media hype," the late Frank C. Ross, hack writer from the Kansas City area, hoarded 1844 dimes and for years publicized how rare this date was, going so far as to award it the sobriquet "Little Orphan Annie." He gave no reason for this nickname; my conjecture is that Ms. Annie's sententious gems of reactionary wisdom dated from about 1844. Dimes of this year are rare only in mint state; in all grades, 1846 is much harder to find, but for decades it brought less than the 1844 owing to Ross's publicity for the date he possessed.

Early O mint coins are very difficult to find in mint state, some dates being all but unknown in that grade. The reason is the same as for 1838–40 O mints (previous section): Dimes continued to pass in the New Orleans area at par with one-real coins (12½¢ each), circulating preferentially to the latter because of Gresham's law: Merchants would hoard the heavier Mexican coins.

Dates 1849–53 are scarcer than mintages suggest: Many were melted in 1853 as worth over face value (see next section).

THE HUGHES-GOBRECHT DESIGN, "EXTRA DRAPERY"

Designer, Robert Ball Hughes, after Gobrecht, after Sully. Engraver, Gobrecht. Mints, Philadelphia, New Orleans

(mintmark O above bows). Physical Specifications, Authorizing Acts, as before.

Grade range, POOR to UNC. Grade standards, as before. EXCEPTIONS: Many coins with full LIBERTY will otherwise grade VERY GOOD; flatness of striking is usual, most of all on hair, central drapery, and often stars.

3232 1840 [377,500]
New rev. hub, open buds. Delivered Dec. 1840. Difficult to find choice. Enl. photos.

3233 1841 [1,622,500 + ?P]
One proof seen (N.Y. State specialist set). Business strikes come with and without very minor repunching on first 1 (latter Ahwash 1).

3234 1841 Double date. Very rare.
Not in Ahwash. Plain repunching at 184, or at bases of 841. NN 47:1072, others.

3235 1841 "No drapery." Ex. rare.
Ahwash 2. Excessively lapped die. Discovered by F. C. C. Boyd. 1) Col. E. H. R. Green's proof set, pvt. coll. *Num. Review* 3, p. 29 (1943). 2) ABOUT EF, cleaned, naturally retoned, formerly proof. F. C. C. Boyd, WGC:519, NN 57:466, Kagin, 1973 MANA:1107, $52,000. Enl. photo.

3236 1841 O [all kinds 2,007,500] Small letters, rev. of 1839–40. Ex. rare.
Ahwash 1. Large round O, 1.2 mm, like 1838 O. Always in low grades. See introductory text. Another, very worn, has a small o rev. of **3230.**

3237 1841 O New rev., large letters, medium O.
At least 2 vars. Oval O, 1 mm. Usually in low grades.

3238 1841 O Similar, small round o.
At least 2 vars. Mintmark 0.8 mm. In all, 10 obvs. and 9 revs. shipped. Usually in low grades.

3239 1842 [1,887,500 + ?P]
Many minor positional vars.; some dates heavier (logotype impressed more vigorously). Possibly 4 proofs known.

3240 1842 O [all kinds 2,020,000] Medium O.
Possibly 4 vars. Mintmark 1 mm. Usually in low grades.

3241 1842 O Small round o. Rare.
Mintmark about 0.8 mm. 7 pairs of dies shipped. Usually in low grades.

3242 1843 [all kinds 1,370,000 + ?P]
Dates larger, 1843–48. Many minor positional vars.; about 8 proofs. Ahwash 3 and 5 have minor repunching within 3; not to be confused with next.

3243 1843 Double date. Very rare.
　　2 vars., Ahwash 2 and unlisted.
3244 1843 Very thin shallow date. Very rare.
　　Not in Ahwash. Hair-thin serifs.
3245 1843 O [150,000]
　　Usually in low grades; prohibitively rare choice. 4 obv. dies
　　shipped; revs. (medium O, about 1 mm) left over from 1842.
　　Always weak on head, foot, and parts of leaves.
3246 1844 [72,500 + ?P]
　　Usually in low grades. Much hoarded; see introductory text.
　　Possibly 8 proofs. 3 pairs of dies shipped for 1844 O coinage;
　　they remained unused, obvs. later defaced.
3247 1845 [all kinds 1,755,000 + ?P]
　　Many minor vars.; 845 touch except on the weakest impres-
　　sions.
3248 1845 Repunched 45. Proofs only. Ex. rare.
　　About 7 known. Not to be confused with next.
3249 1845 Double date.
　　Ahwash 2, possibly other vars.

3250 1845 O [230,000]
　　Large O, 1.3 mm, as in later years. 4 obvs., 2 revs. shipped; 6
　　old revs. on hand. Only one var. seen. Usually in low grades;
　　weak on head, foot, and parts of leaves. Prohibitively rare
　　UNC. 5 pairs of dies were shipped for 1846 O coinage; obvs.
　　were returned unused. For 1847 O, 2 obvs. were shipped be-
　　fore Nov. 12, 1846; for 1848 O, 6 pairs. All remained unused.
3251 1846 [all kinds 31,300 + ?P] Scarce.
　　Possibly 10 proofs survive; these have date slanting down
　　to r.
3252 1847 [all kinds 245,000 + ?P] Normal date.
　　Possibly 8 proofs. Compare next.
3253 1847 Date overlaps base. Rare.
　　Top of 1 nearly touches shield. Not to be confused with vars.
　　in which date just touches base; these price as preceding.

3254 1848 [481,000 + ?P]
　　Possibly 8 proofs.
3255 1849 [all kinds 839,000 + ?P] Normal date.
　　Possibly 4 proofs.
3256 1849/8 Obvious overdate. Proofs only. Ex. rare.
　　Not in Ahwash. Most of final 8 clear around 9. Starr estate.
3257 1849/8 Concealed overdate. Very rare.
　　Ahwash 3. Parts of 8 clear in 9. Not to be confused with any
　　to follow.

3258 1849 Repunched 49. Rare.
　　Not in Ahwash.
3259 1849 Repunched 9. Rare.
　　Not in Ahwash. Not to be confused with either of preceding.
3260 1849 Extra thin date. Rare.
　　Serifs of 1 and 4, tops and bases of 8 and 9 hair-thin.
3261 1849 O [all kinds 500,000] Large O.
　　Ahwash 1, 2. Mintmark 1.3 mm. Always in low grades;
　　rarely with rev. rotated at various angles to obv. 12 obv. dies
　　shipped; leftover revs.
3262 1849 O Small round o. Rare.
　　At least 3 vars. Mintmark 0.8 mm. Date sometimes shows
　　traces of repunching. Almost always in low grades. Discov-
　　ered by Howard Newcomb before 1914. Rarely with rotated
　　rev. as preceding.
3263 1850 Closed 5. [1,931,500 + ?P]
　　Knob of 5 touches cusp except on weakest impressions.
　　Many minor positional vars.; dates vary from light to heavy.
　　Possibly 4 proofs. UNCs. are mostly from a hoard (about 30
　　pieces) discovered about 1977.
3264 1850 O [all kinds 510,000] Large O.
　　At least 2 vars. Mintmark 1.3 mm.
3265 1850 O Medium round O. Very rare.
　　Ahwash 3. Mintmark 1.1 mm.
3266 1850 O Small round o. Rare.
　　Mintmark 0.8 mm. In all, 6 obvs.; revs. selected from 14
　　leftover dies.
3267 1851 [1,026,500 + ?P] Closed 5; normal date.
　　Knob touches cusp. In all, 9 obvs., 7 revs.; positional vars.
　　exist. One proof reported, not located.
3268 1851 Closed 5; final 1 repunched.
　　Ahwash 4.
3269 1851 Closed 5; repunched 51. Rare.
　　Ahwash 5. Cf. NN 46:249 and "Gilhousen":358.
3270 1851 Open 5. Rare.
　　Knob well away from cusp. Ahwash 3.
3271 1851 O [all kinds 400,000] Open 5; large O.
　　Mintmark 1.3 mm. Usually in low grades. In all, 12 obvs. and
　　6 leftover revs., not all used.
3272 1851 O Small round o. Ex. rare.
　　Mintmark 0.8 mm. Not in Ahwash. Last specimen seen 1957.
3273 1852 [1,535,000 + ?P]
　　In all, 15 obvs., 19 revs.; possibly 8 proofs. Various positional
　　vars.: date higher, lower, or slanting. Earle, Ryder,
　　Bareford:211, Proof, $8,000.

3274 1852 Double date. Very rare.
Ahwash 4.
3275 1852 O [all kinds 430,000] Large O. Rare.
6 obvs. shipped, not all used; leftover revs. Only one rev. var. seen; mintmark 1.3 mm, thin. Usually in low grades. A second minor var. may exist. 12 1853 obvs. without arrows were shipped to New Orleans but were defaced unused; 14 leftover revs. remained on hand.
3276 1853 No arrows. [95,000]
High and low dates, respectively Ahwash 1 and 2; these probably correspond to the 2 deliveries, respectively [55,000] Feb. 17, [40,000] Feb. 19. Mint-state survivors mostly come from a batch (small hoard?) rescued by Harold P. Newlin before 1883.

viii. ARROWS AT DATE (1853–55)

When news reached the East of immense discoveries of gold in California, nobody thought to speculate on what the new supply would do to price scales; certainly nobody expected that it would drive up the price of silver until coins began disappearing from circulation. Yet precisely that happened. The larger supply of gold—uncompensated by any comparable discoveries of silver—meant that its price fell in terms of silver dollars: Banks, merchants, and bullion dealers experienced the change as a sharp rise in the price of silver reckoned in gold dollars: The silver in two half dollars (or four quarters, or 10 dimes) became worth about $1.06 in gold, at which point it became profitable to melt down silver coins in quantity, sell the ingots for gold, trade the gold for silver coins at face value, and repeat the process in what Carothers {1930} called an "endless chain." This quickly exhausted local supplies of silver coins up and down the Eastern Seaboard, leaving a gap between cents and gold dollars filled only by worn billon "fish scales" (3¢ coins or trimes), worn-out and often counterfeit Spanish and Mexican fractional silver, wildcat bank notes, and irredeemable paper scrip, alias "shinplasters."

After much dithering, Mint Director George N. Eckert finally hit on the idea of reducing official weights of silver coins to a point at which the "endless chain" would no longer be profitable. He managed to persuade an uncomprehending Congress to go along with his scheme, and the Mint Act of Feb. 21, 1853 accordingly reduced the weight of the dime from 41.25 grs. (2.673 gms.) to 38.4 grs. (2.48 gms.), proportionally with other coins through the half dollar.

As with the other denominations, there was no time to prepare new designs for Treasury approval, yet it was absolutely essential to distinguish old-tenor (pre-1853 heavier standard) from new-tenor (lighter standard) coins. Eckert decided that some kind of obvious distinguishing mark was the answer, and he ordered addition of arrows flanking dates on all new-tenor coins above the 3¢. This practice continued through 1855.

Anticipating a large mintage, Longacre prepared about 50 pairs of dime dies for Philadelphia Mint use, a dozen pairs for New Orleans, and two pairs for Humbert's Provisional Mint at San Francisco (alias "U.S. Assay Office of Gold") in case this institution managed to obtain enough parting acids to make standard gold and silver coins. On March 3, 1853, five proof sets were struck using the new dies with arrows: half dime through half dollar only. Survivors are of the highest rarity. Regular coinage with arrows began a month later: over 12 million dimes in Philadelphia, 1.1 million in New Orleans. These coins went into circulation and stayed there, so that worn survivors are common, while mint-state ones are scarce. Few saved them for souvenirs; dealers did not bother to stock them. I myself saw badly worn specimens in circulation as late as 1943, while dealers' buying lists in the 1920s and '30s refused to offer

any premium above face value for them in any grade. Small wonder that type-collector pressure has priced gems into orbit.

During the next couple of years, much of the silver coinage came from bullion obtained by melting down old-tenor coins. Uncirculated specimens of 1854–55 are proportionally scarcer than 1853's, as mintages dwindled. More dimes were minted 1853–55 with arrows than in the entire period 1796–1840. Today they represent interesting mementos of a monetary emergency created by the operation of economic laws nobody understood.

ARROWS AT DATE

Designer, Engraver, Mints, Physical Specifications, as before, except Weight, 38.4 ± 0.5 grs. = 2.48 ± 0.032 gms. Authorizing Act, Feb. 21, 1853.
Grade range and standards as before.

3277 1853 [all kinds 12,173,000 + 5P] Open 5.
Proofs minted March 3; business strikes began April 26. Knob of 5 away from cusp. Arrows vary in position. Occasional minor repunchings on numerals or arrows. Enl. photos.

3278 1853 Similar. Arrow shaft merges with 1.
Ahwash 4. Shaft actually covers serif of 1.
3279 1853 Similar. Heavy date, closed 5.
Ahwash 6. Knob of 5 joins cusp. Date high, touching base; other positional vars. probably exist.
3280 1853 O [1,100,000] Closed 5.
Large O (1.3 mm) only; 12 obvs., 14 revs.
3281 1853 O Thin numerals, open 5. Rare.
Hair-thin serifs of 1, tops and bases of 853.
3282 1854 [4,470,000 + ?P] Heavy date, 54 touch. Rare.
Not in Ahwash; "Gilhousen":367. On all vars. from both mints, arrows normally touch border, l. arrow almost or quite touches rocky base.
3283 1854 Thin numerals, 5 4 apart.
Ahwash 1; "Gilhousen":368. Minor positional vars. of date; otherwise same comment as to preceding.
3284 1854 Double-punched date. Very rare.
Not in Ahwash. 1982 ANA:382.
3285 1854 O [1,770,000] 5 4 free.
Large O (1.3 mm) only; 10 pairs of dies. Long considered rare in mint state, but a small hoard (18 pieces) turned up in Dec. 1981. Compare 1982 ANA:383–395.
3286 1854 O Similar, incomplete mintmark.
Not in Ahwash. Upper half of O missing (obliquely punched into die). Discovered by F. C. C. Boyd. Ill. *Gobrecht Journal* 11/77, p. 22.
3287 1854 O 54 about touch. Rare.
Not in Ahwash.
3288 1854 O 54 about touch; doubled obv. die. Very rare.
Not in Ahwash. "Gilhousen":369. Doubling plainest at stars at r. 2 pairs of dies were shipped to San Francisco, but remained unused.
3289 1855 [2,075,000 + ?P]
13 obvs., 10 revs. Very minor positional vars.

3290 1855 Obvious double date. Proofs only. Very rare.
The 8 pairs of dies for 1855 O and the 3 pairs for 1855 S remained unused.

ix. ARROWS OMITTED (1856–60)

At the end of 1855, the new Mint Director, James Ross Snowden, ended use of arrows at dates, easing Longacre's task. Coinage from melted old-tenor silver continued in dwindling amounts.

The first Philadelphia dimes of 1856 bore a large date, from the logotype used on half cents and three-dollar pieces. These are believed to comprise most of or possibly all the first delivery [150,000], March 3, 1856. Possibly because this date was crowded in the exergual space, Longacre used a small-date logotype (same as on quarter eagles) thereafter for both proofs and business strikes from all three mints.

Business strikes began to issue from the new San Francisco Branch Mint (which had become an official mint in 1854) beginning in 1856. As there were few coin collectors in that area, few mint-state specimens were saved; survivors are mostly in low grades. Exorbitant local price scales insured that any silver coins (mostly foreign) circulated there about as cents did on the East Coast: Even silver dollars were small change (one would buy a bowl of soup).

Sometime around Nov. 1859, at Mint Director Snowden's request, Longacre prepared new original dies, hubs, and working dies, with legend on obv. (see next section). However, the 1860 S coins are of the old design; they were made from four obvs. shipped Nov. 2, 1859, with leftover revs. from 1858. On the other hand, sometime thereafter, possibly with Snowden's approval, the Coiner's Department made possibly a dozen proofs combining an 1859 obv. of regular type with the new wreath of 1860, producing a combination lacking any mention of UNITED STATES OF AMERICA. These doubtless went to the same collectors who bought the similar half dimes (Chap. 24, Sect. x).

ARROWS OMITTED

Designer, Engraver, as before. Mints, as before but San Francisco added (mintmark S above bow). Physical Specifications, Authorizing Acts, as before.

Grade range and standards, as before.

3291 1856 Large date, upright 5. [150,000−]
4 minor vars.: Kenneth R. Hill, *Gobrecht Journal* 7/78, p. 15. See introductory text. Usually in low grades, rare in mint state. Enl. photo.

3292 1856 Small date, slanting 5. [5,630,000+ + ?P] Closed 6.
In all, 28 pairs of dies. Closed 6 = knob touches loop. Many minor positional vars.

3293 1856 Same, double date. Very rare.
Ahwash 4. Double punching plainest at 18. Later states with most doubling gone price as preceding.

3294 1856 Open 6, thin numerals. Scarce.
Ahwash 5. Open 6 = knob well away from loop.

3295 1856 Doubled obv. die. Proofs only. Very rare.
Doubling plainest at skirt; line joins loop of R to border. Apparently all 1856 proof dimes are from these dies.

3296 1856 O [all kinds 1,180,000] Large O.
Mintmark 1.3 mm. In all, 16 obvs., 8 revs., plus others left over from 1853–55. Some vars. have very minor date repunching; compare next.

3297 1856 O Large O; double date. Scarce.
Ahwash 2, 3. Former with date first punched level, then "corrected" slanting far up to r.; latter vice versa.

3298 1856 O Medium round O. Rare.
Ahwash 5. Mintmark 1.1 mm. Usually in low grades. Usually weak at head, foot, and parts of leaves.

3299 1856 O Small round o. Ex. rare.
1954 ANA:618; not since located. Mintmark would be about 0.8 mm.

3300 1856 S [70,000] Normal S.
Large S, 1.3 mm, as on 3-dollar coins and half dollars. In all, 6 obvs., 2 revs. Usually in low grades; Ex. rare choice.

3301 1856 S Double-punched S. Ex. rare.
Earliest die state of preceding. "Dupont":1592; 1978 FUN:348. Later states with only faint traces of doubling price as preceding.

3302 1857 [5,580,000 + ?P] Heavy date, closed 5.
Closed 5 = knob touches cusp. Minor positional vars. Proofs have peak of 1 repunched and rev. of 1856 proofs.

3303 1857 Same, obviously repunched 1. Scarce.

3304 1857 Thin numerals, open 5.
Ahwash 3. Open 5 = knob away from cusp.

3305 1857 O [1,540,000] Large O, heavy date, closed 5.
Mintmark 1.3 mm. Ahwash 1, 2, 3; first (with minutely repunched date) is very rare.

3306 1857 O Medium O, thin date, open 5. Rare.
Mintmark 1.1 mm. Ahwash 4, 5. Discovered by Howard Newcomb, before 1914. A small o coin (round o, mintmark 0.8 mm) was offered in G. H. Hall:691 but remains unverified.

3307 1858 [1,540,000 + ?P] Heavy date, closed 5.
Closed 5 = knob touches cusp. Many minute positional vars.; dates usually slant down to r. The proofs (possibly about 80 made) have blank lapped area between elbow of pole arm and body; die file mark from A(M) to border.

3308 1858 Thin numerals, open 5. Rare.
Not in Ahwash. Open 5 = knob away from cusp. Thin serifs, bases, and tops of numerals.

3309 1858 O [200,000] Large thin O only.
Usually in low grades; very rare UNC.

3310 1858 S Medium S. [60,000] Rare.
Mintmark 1.1 mm. 4 pairs of dies shipped. Usually in low grades; very rare UNC. Auction 81:1154, UNC., $6,600.

3311 1859 [430,000 + 800−P]
At least 3 positional vars. of date. Many of the proofs were melted as unsold, or spent.

3312 1859 O [480,000] Large heavy O. Rare.
Mintmark 1.3 mm, top and bottom thick.

3313 1859 O Large thin O.
Ahwash 1. Same mintmark punch, top hair-thin.

3314 1859 O Medium O.
Ahwash 2. Mintmark 1.1 mm, top and bottom fairly heavy. Usually in low grades. A small o coin was claimed in the G. H. Hall coll. (1945) but remains unverified.

3315 1859 S Medium S. [60,000]
6 obvs. shipped Nov. 1858; leftover revs. Usually in low grades; Ex. rare UNC.

3316 1860 S [140,000]
4 obvs. shipped Nov. 2, 1859; leftover revs. 2 minor posi-

tional vars. On one, top stroke of S is heavy: mintmark rotated 180°? *Gobrecht Journal* 36, p. 39 (7/86). Compare **6068.** Usually in low grades; Ex. rare UNC. Auction 86:562, UNC., $8,250. The large S mentioned in Granberg:505 (1913) remains unverified.

PIÈCE DE CAPRICE: WITHOUT STATUTORY LEGEND

3317 1859 Proofs only. Very rare.
Judd 233. Ahwash traced only 6 but estimated 12 survive. *Gobrecht Journal* 11/77, p. 21. Robison:1082, $8,500. Enl. photos.

x. LONGACRE'S "CEREAL WREATH" DESIGN (1860–91)

"As Maine goes, so goes—New Hampshire," and similarly every design change in the half dime exactly paralleled a change in the dime. That for 1860, the final one for the half dime, was one in a long series for the dime—supposedly (like that of 1840) to improve striking quality. On orders of Mint Director Snowden, Longacre made new original dies, with statutory inscription on obv. instead of stars. Rev. was a reduction of one of his 1859 pattern half dollars, with what was then called "Newlin's Wreath of Cereals" enclosing value. Striking quality, which had for two decades varied from mediocre to impossibly weak, improved little or not at all.

Why Newlin's name was associated with this wreath of corn, wheat, maple, and oak leaves has not yet been ascertained; it appears in many auction catalogs of the 1870s and '80s. Conjecturally, either Newlin (the Mint hanger-on Harold P. Newlin?) furnished a sketch or more likely suggested this combination of important crops to (in Longacre's words) "give the reverse a more national character," this being then deemed an important issue. In several successive modifications by William Barber (1876) and Charles E. Barber (1892), this design remained on dime revs. 1860–1916: Longacre's most durable creation save for his double-eagle devices (1849–1907), easily outdistancing his "Indian" cent (1859–1909).

Late in 1860, to improve striking quality, Longacre made a modified obv. hub differing in details around upper shield and hand. The earlier dies, called "Type I" or "Five Lines" shield, showed five vertical lines (tops of two pales gules and part of a third) between scroll and azure; the later ones, "Type II" or "Six Lines" shield, show six instead, and the hand differs.

Coins of this new design were issued from Philadelphia in all years (except 1874, in which all dimes bore arrows at date: See next section); from New Orleans only in 1860 and 1891, the former very rare; from San Francisco in every year except 1860,

1873–74 (arrows only), and 1878–83; and from Carson City every year 1871–78 except 1874 (arrows only). Philadelphia issues 1863–67, 1879–81 were issued for circulation only in small amounts, and survivors therefore are mostly proofs, which were, after all, meant to be saved. Tiny hoards of all these dates have shown up in recent years. S-Mint coins through 1872 are very rare in mint state, some years apparently unknown choice. Early Carson City coins are all very rare, the 1873 CC without arrows represented by a unique mint-state example in the Eliasberg estate that has been traced back to Philadelphia Mint Superintendent Archibald Loudon Snowden; this coin was probably retrieved from the 1874 Assay Commission meeting. Official orders deliberately limited the Carson Mint's output for political reasons, and this limitation in turn was intended to provide an official excuse for abolition! By the time the official limitation was removed (1875), bullion depositors had already formed the habit of shipping their metal to San Francisco instead, enriching Wells Fargo and other shipping companies, though at risk of losing shipments to robbers and hostile Indians.

LONGACRE'S "CEREAL WREATH" DESIGN

Designer, James Barton Longacre, obv. after Hughes, after Gobrecht, after Sully. Engravers, Longacre; William Barber for "Type II" rev. 1876–91. Mints, Philadelphia 1860–91 (no mintmark), New Orleans 1860, 1891 (mintmark O below wreath), San Francisco 1861–77, 1884–91 (S below wreath except in part of 1875), Carson City 1871–78 (CC below wreath except in part of 1875). Physical Specifications, Authorizing Acts, as before.

Grade range, FAIR to UNC.; Grade Standards, as before.

3318 1860 [all kinds 606,000 + 527+P] "Type I" shield.
Also called "Five Lines" shield: Note detail above E and shape of hand. Originally 1,000 proofs minted in sets; at least 527 sold, rest mostly melted or spent. On this and all subsequent dates, ribbon ends occur free of leaves above, or almost touching, or occasionally touching; dates vary from lighter to heavier. Enl. photos (of **3320**).

3319 1850 "Type II" shield. Proofs only. Ex. rare.
Also called "Six Lines" shield: Note detail above E and shape of hand. Discovered by Douglas Winter. 1982 ANA:1951, $1,100. Enl. photo.

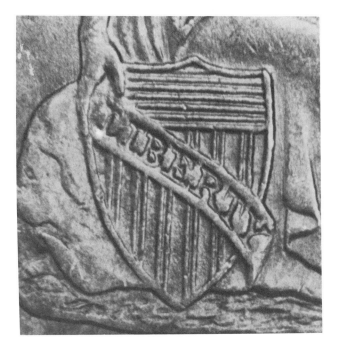

3320 1860 O "Type I" shield. [40,000] Rare.
Very small thin mintmark (0.7 mm); only one var. known. Ill. above **3318.** Usually in low grades; planchets often porous or rough. 2 pairs of dies shipped for 1861 O coinage remained unused by the Union; it is doubtful if the CSA issued any after taking over the Mint.

3321 1861 [all kinds 1,883,000 + 400−P] "Type I" shield. Very rare.
Business strikes only. In all, 47 obvs., 46 revs.; numbers of Types I and II not known.

3322 1861 "Type II" shield.
Business strikes and proofs. Of 1,000 proofs originally minted with sets, over 600 were melted or spent as unsold.

3323 1861 S "Type I" shield. [172,500]
Very small s (0.8 mm) as in later years. 4 pairs of dies shipped; to date 2 minute rev. vars. are reported. Usually flat on head, toe, and part of central drapery. Most survivors are in low grades; prohibitively rare in mint state.

3324 1862 [847,000 + 550−P] Thin numerals.
"Type II" shield henceforth. 17 pairs of dies. Business strikes ("Gilhousen":395) and proofs come with thin numerals (hair-thin serifs and tops and bottoms of digits). Some proofs were melted in 1863 as unsold. One rare rev. has a heavy die cut joining NE (Montfort Johnsen, *Gobrecht Journal* 11/79, pp. 8–15).

3325 1862 Heavy numerals.
Business strikes and proofs ("Gilhousen":394) come with heavy numerals (thick serifs and tops and bottoms of digits). Positional vars. exist.

3326 1862 Double-punched 1. Very rare.
"Gilhousen":396.

3327 1862 S [180,750]
In all, 10 obvs., 2 revs., with others left over from 1861. Usually weak on head, toe, and mintmark. Usually in low grades; prohibitively rare in EF.

3328 1863 [14,000 + 460P]
Only one var. reported; business strikes (coined in March) are much rarer than proofs (coined in 3 batches, March 5–May 26).

3329 1863 S [157,500]
7 obvs. shipped; leftover revs. Usually weak on head, part of rock, toe, bow knot, and mintmark. Usually in low grades.

3330 1864 [11,000 + 470P] 64 apparently touch.
Business strikes (coined in August) are rarer than proofs.

3331 1864 6 4 apart.
Business strikes (rare) and proofs, latter with the 1863 rev.

3332 1864 S [230,000] 64 almost touching.
4 pairs of dies shipped Oct. 1863. Heavy date. Usually flat on head, foot, part of wreath, bow knot, and mintmark. Usually in low grades; Ex. rare UNC.

3333 1865 [10,000 + 500P]
2 pairs of dies; 2 very minor positional vars. Business strikes (all coined in April) are much rarer than proofs; some business strikes have rev. 180° from usual alignment (Ahwash 2b). Auction 86:1594, UNC., $3,740. Only the very earliest proofs (1982 ANA:1954) show traces of repunching on 865.

3334 1865 S [175,000] Thin weak mintmark. Rare.
Ahwash 1. Four obv. dies shipped Nov. 1864. Usually flat on head, foot, lower wreath, and mintmark. Usually in low grades; prohibitively rare UNC. Auction 86:565, UNC., $5,060.

3335 1865 S Heavy bold mintmark. Ex. rare.
Not in Ahwash; "Gilhousen":403. Prohibitively rare choice.

3336 1866 [8,000 + 725P]
2 minor vars. of proofs; 2 of much rarer business strikes (from proof dies; struck in January). Some original proof sets, still in the mint wrappers, contained UNC. business strikes; these are thought to be the source of most gem survivors.

3337 1866 S [135,000] Thin weak mintmark. Rare.
Ahwash 1, 2, respectively date high (slanting down to r.) and lower. 6 obvs. shipped. Usually weak on same areas as **3334.** Usually in low grades, prohibitively rare UNC.

3338 1866 S Heavy bold mintmark. Ex. rare.
Not in Ahwash; "Gilhousen":406. Same comments as to last.

3339 1867 [6,000 + 625P] Normal date.
Ahwash 1, 2. Proofs and rarer business strikes, latter coined Jan. 29. 2 minor vars. of proofs.

3340 1867 Repunched date. Proofs only? Rare.
2 vars., doubling plainest on 18 or 1 7. Comprises a minority of proofs. I have not seen the business strike mentioned in 1982 ANA:1961.

3341 1867 S [140,000]
2 minor positional vars. Usually weak in same areas as previous S mints; usually in low grades, prohibitively rare UNC.

3342 1868 [464,000 + 600P] Normal date, heavy.
Ahwash 1. In date 18 almost touch; thick serifs to 1. Business strikes only. Henceforth, many dates show broken tops to first S and O(F), from damage to obv. hub.

3343 1868 Normal date, thin numerals.
Ahwash 2, 4. In date 1 8 well apart; hair-thin serifs to 1. On both obvs., dates slant down to r.; A-4 apparently only for proofs.

3344 1868 Double date. Rare.
Ahwash 3. Doubling plainest above bases of 18; date first punched slanting down to r., then corrected.

3345 1868 Blundered die. Proofs only. Ex. rare.
Base of extra 1 just r. of base point of shield; base of a third 1

just below second. Discovered by this writer, Nov. 1965; discovery coin went in Merkin 4/66:185. All show die rust in central drapery.

3346 1868 S [260,000] Normal rev.

2 minor rev. vars. Usually weak in same areas as previous S mints but less so. Usually in low grades; Ex. rare UNC.

3347 1868 S Doubled rev. die. Very rare.

"Gilhousen":410. Doubling obvious on ribbons and parts of wreath; mintmark far to r.

3348 1869 [256,000 + 600P]

Minor positional vars. in proofs and business strikes; latter rare in EF and very rare above.

3349 1869 S [450,000]

6 obvs. shipped Oct. 1868. At least 2 positional vars. of mintmark. S is heavier than before and apt to be blurry; probably heavier impressions from same (worn) S punch, 0.8 mm. "Gilhousen":412–13. Usually weak in same areas as previous S mints; usually in low grades but a little less rare UNC. than earlier S mints.

3350 1870 [470,500 + 1,000P]

Several minor positional vars. of business strikes and proofs. One obv. of business strikes has part of upper serif of 1 repunched (Ahwash 4); this becomes blurry. Most business strikes are weak on head, base of shield, lower part of rock, and foot and parts of drapery.

3351 1870 Double 0 in date. Rare.

Ahwash 3. Extra outline plainest above base. Also called 1870/0.

3352 1870 S [50,000] Rare.

6 pairs of dies shipped Dec. 1869; only one var. seen, coined in November. Mintmark lighter as in 1861–68. Usually weak in centers (notably at value), head, bow knot, ribbons, and mintmark. Usually in low grades, often rough. Formerly prohibitively rare UNC., but in 1977 a hoard of about 15 turned up in England.

3353 1871 [752,650 + 960–P] Normal date.

Several minor positional vars. of business strikes and proofs, all with 71 about touching (only the one logotype for this denomination). Usually weak in same areas mentioned for 1870. Some proofs melted as unsold, July 1873.

3354 1871 Double-punched 18. Proofs only. Very rare.

Not in Ahwash; discovered in Garrett set (1976). Comprises a tiny minority of proofs. Later, repunching fades out or is repolished off die; these will sell as preceding.

3355 1871 S [320,000] Normal date.

4 pairs of dies received Dec. 16, 1870. Ahwash 2, 3; former with rev. of 1870 S. Usually weak in same areas as 1870 S; usually in low grades, Ex. rare UNC. Auction 86:1598, UNC., $1,650.

3356 1871 S Double date. Ex. rare.

Ahwash 1. Doubling plain on all digits; later states show it clearly only on 18.

3357 1871 CC [20,100] Very rare.

Mintage began in Feb. [6,400]. 3 minor vars., all with wider-spaced edge reeding (only 89) than other mints. Usually in low grades; prohibitively rare above VF. Holmes:2782, "UNC.," is possibly finest.

3358 1872 [2,395,500 + 950–P]

Several minor positional vars.; Ahwash 1 shows minor repunching on 2. On dies with heavier dates, 18 about touch. Some proofs melted as unsold, July 1873.

3359 1872 Double date. Very rare.

Not in Ahwash.

3360 1872 S [190,000]

4 pairs of dies shipped Nov. 1871; June and Dec. deliveries (respectively [130,000] and [60,000]) cannot be distinguished. S (0.8 mm) narrower than formerly. Usually flat on head, foot, and lower wreath. Usually in low grades; Ex. rare UNC.

3361 1872 CC [35,480]

2 obvs. shipped (were both used?); 2 minor rev. vars., the second die (crack through CC and r. ribbon) continuing through 1874. Mintage figure after Julian; var. data from McCloskey, *Gobrecht Journal* 11/79, p. 27. Edge reeding as in 1871 CC. Always weakly and unevenly struck. Usually in low grades, prohibitively rare EF.

3362 1873 No arrows. Closed 3. [1,508,000 + 600–P]

Positional vars. of UNCs. and proofs. All delivered Jan. 15–Feb. 28; some proofs melted July 10, 1873. Enl. photo.

3363 1873 Same, double date first punched to l. Very rare.

Not in Ahwash; discovered by Kenneth R. Hill, *Gobrecht Journal* 3/79, p. 7. Business strikes only. Extra bases of digits plain to l. of final position.

3364 1873 No arrows. Open 3. [60,000] Very rare.

Ahwash 3, 4. Business strikes only. Almost always weak on head and foot; prohibitively rare in mint state. 4 obvs. shipped for 1873 S No Arrows coinage remained unused. Enl. photo.

3365 1873 CC Closed 3. No arrows. [12,400] Unique?

Only the one obv.; rev. of second 1872 CC var. Delivered Feb. 5, 1873; most believed melted after July 1873. The unique survivor is traced to a parcel of assay coins shipped to Philadelphia, early 1874, thence to A. Loudon Snowden, John W. Haseltine, Stephen K. Nagy, H. O. Granberg, William H. Woodin (later Secretary of Treasury), U.S. Coin Co. sale of Granberg coll., Rudolph Kohler (dealer), pvt. coll., Adolphe Menjou, James Kelly, Louis Eliasberg, Sr.; it remains in the Eliasberg estate. This coin first came to the attention of the numismatic world in Granberg's display at ANS {1914}. Counterfeits exist; date positions differ from the genuine. Authentication mandatory. Tied with 1894 S as most famous of all dimes; tied with the 1876 CC Twenty Cents as most famous of all Carson City coins. Enl. photos.

xi. LEGEND AND ARROWS AT DATE (1873–74)

Among the provisions of the omnibus Mint Act of Feb. 12, 1873 was one attempting to introduce metric weights for our national coinage. The nickel 5¢ coins were already supposed to weigh 5 gms. apiece (though in practice they varied enough to be useless as weight standards); henceforth the dime, quarter dollar, and half dollar were to weigh, respectively, 2.5, 6.25, and 12.5 gms. each. This provision hardly merits praise. Mint tolerances were broad enough on all denominations that the coins could not be safely used as weights (let alone legally), even if there was any reason at the time to use metric weights outside a laboratory. The new weights differed little enough from the old that beyond doubt planchets made before the new standard could have been used and many doubtless were: 38.58 ± 1.5 grs. completely overlaps 38.4 ± 0.5. There is no foolproof way to distinguish new and old planchets, and no way to identify coins struck on obsolete blanks. Over 100 years after this act of Congress, the USA still lags behind the rest of the civilized world in introducing metric weights and measures; and though our silver coins had metric weights 1873–1964, this feature had no discernible effect on public awareness of the metric system.

For reasons unknown, the new coins were given a distinguishing mark: a reappearance of arrows at dates. Older issues were theoretically to remain current, though the incomplete records indicate that many pieces without arrows were melted down beginning July 10, 1873. These included silver from both San Francisco and Carson City; and the Philadelphia Mint also melted proofs of 1871–73 without arrows in all denominations, as well as unsold 2¢, silver 3¢ and half dimes, proofs and business strikes. These mass meltings possibly account for the rarity of earlier Carson City coins.

Dimes with arrows at date have long been prized as type coins, and some dealers long since began promoting them as alleged rarities, which fact is evidence less of scarcity than of cupidity. Quantities made were ample in Philadelphia, moderately small in San Francisco, and really small only in Carson City: this last from official orders restricting coinage to amounts well below capacity (see introductory text of previous section). Enough survive from the 5,327,700 Philadelphia business strikes and 1,500 proofs that the coins are always available for a price. The 695,000 S mints pose no severe problems except in mint state, in which condition both dates are very scarce. On the other hand, the Carson City issues (1873 Arrows [18,791] and 1874 [10,817]) are both rare, only a tiny fraction of 1% surviving in all grades; mint-state specimens are prohibitively rare, and the 1874 CC is of extreme rarity in any condition: Newcomb (NUM 6/12, p. 198) said all six known were "from circulation."

Some 500 proof sets of silver coins with arrows were struck in 1873, with the trade dollar included; there were extras of some denominations including possibly 300 more dimes. Collectors routinely broke up these sets in order to add the dimes to their date runs of that denomination, and similarly with the other denominations. This accounts for the rarity of original sets. However, most collectors interested in pre-1936 proof sets have been content with assembled sets. These can usually be identified by different kinds of cleaning on individual specimens: See Breen {1977}, pp. 144–47.

Arrow positions vary on both 1873 and 1874. However, whether higher or lower, arrow points on 1873 are level, whereas they point up on 1874. Claims of large and small arrows for either date remain unverified.

The new metric weights continued for almost a century, but their importance to the Mint has consisted solely in a multiplicity of decimal points in the operations of strip rolling, planchet cutting, and planchet weighing. They have remained as another instance of government tokenism.

LEGEND AND ARROWS AT DATE

Designer, Engraver, Mints, Physical Specifications, as before, except that William Barber modeled the arrows, and Weight is 38.58 ± 1.5 grs. = 2.5 ± 0.097 gms. Authorizing Act, Feb. 12, 1873.

Grade range and standards, as before.

3366   1873 Arrows. [all kinds 2,377,700 + 800P] Heavy date, 18 about touch.
Open 3 only. Positional vars. exist. Enl. photos (of **3371**).

3367   1873 Arrows. Thin numerals, 1 8 apart.
Minor vars. Proofs and business strikes.
3368   1873 Arrows. Doubled obv. die. Ex. rare.
Ahwash 7 (discovered by Kamal Ahwash after publication). Doubling is plainest at shield; die lapped and repolished to efface other evidence.

3369   1873 S [all kinds 455,000] Small thin s.
Ahwash 1. Mintmark 0.7 mm, clear, unlike the 1871–72 dies.
3370   1873 S Taller narrower S. Very rare.
Not in Ahwash. Mintmark 0.8 mm, but of different style from anything earlier. Discovery coin, "Gilhousen":426. Cf. Menjou, Herdman, 1982 ANA:402; Rhodes:836.
3371   1873 CC Arrows. [18,791] Very rare.
Only one var. seen; ill. above **3366**. Rev. of second 1872 CC var. and of **3365**. Often on porous or rough planchets. Usually in low grades; prohibitively rare above VF, apparently only one UNC. verified (ex Boyd, WGC, Boosel, 1975 ANA:269, $13,000).
3372   1874 [2,940,000 + 700P] Normal.
Arrowheads slant up, unlike 1873. Minor positional vars.

3373 1874 Double-punched 4. Rare.

Not in Ahwash. NN 53:359. An earlier state shows faint repunching on base of 7.

3374 1874 S [240,000] Small thin s. Very rare.

Not in Ahwash. Rev. of **3369.** "Gilhousen":429. Usually in low grades.

3375 1874 S Minute s. Rare.

Ahwash 1. Mintmark square in outline, filled, 0.63 mm. "Gilhousen":430. Usually in low grades; Ex. rare in mint state. Kern, Bareford:245, UNC., $4,000. Both vars. ill. by McCloskey, *Gobrecht Journal* 36, pp. 20–21 (7/86).

3376 1874 CC [10,817] Ex. rare, possibly 6–8 known.

Rev. of **3365, 3371.** Usually in low grades, porous or rough. Finest is possibly Miles:725. Numerous forgeries have been made in the Harrisburg, Pa., area by adding CC mintmarks to genuine Philadelphia dimes; they do not show the diagnostic crack through mintmark.

xii. ARROWS OMITTED (1875–91)

We have not yet ascertained whether it was the Mint Bureau Director in Washington or the Superintendent at Philadelphia who gave Mint Engraver William Barber orders to omit arrows from dates of dimes beginning in Jan. 1875. The effect was a resumption of the previous design, though at the new metric weight.

Large mintages of 1875–77 were intended to retire 10¢ fractional notes, once Congress had passed a Specie Resumption Act. The Engraving Department's quota of working dies more than tripled. Possibly as an attempt to solve the problem of weak imperfect strikings (common on business-strike dimes for many years), William Barber created a new working rev. hub, commonly "Type II." The old "Type I" revs. (1860–77) had E of ONE about touching wreath; the new "Type II" revs. (1876–91) had this E far from wreath, with various other minor modifications. These improved neither the overall concept nor striking quality, but appear primarily to have satisfied Barber's need to feel he was doing something about the problem. (Much the same comment can be made about the changes he made in quarter and half-dollar revs. in this period.) These changes, and the mintmark vars. (S or CC within wreath during part of 1875 only; several different types of S punches), constitute minor relief from major stereotypy.

On the other hand, low mintages of 1878–81 are attributed to Rep. Richard P. "Silver Dick" Bland, whose unremitting pressure induced Congress to pass the Act of Feb. 28, 1878 (over a veto) mandating coinage of silver dollars in such enormous quantities that time and machinery available for production of lower denominations had to be drastically curtailed. A coin shortage ensued at once. The Treasury finally ruled that Morgan dollar coinage thereafter must be limited to the legal minimum. Bullion from retired obsolete coins was thereafter earmarked for making dimes, most of all in 1887 and 1891, while quarters and halves remained in short supply. Reasons for low San Francisco dime coinage, 1884–86, remain unknown.

ARROWS OMITTED

Designer, Engraver, William Barber, after Longacre. Mints, Philadelphia, New Orleans (1891 only, mintmark below wreath), San Francisco (mintmark S below wreath except part of 1875), Carson City (mintmark CC below wreath except part of 1875). Physical Specifications, Authorizing Acts, as before.

Grade range and standards, as before.

3377 1875 [10,350,000 + 700P]

At least 50 minor positional vars.

3378 1875 S [all kinds 9,070,000] Mintmark within wreath.

Large S, 1 mm. Minor positional vars.

3379 1875 S Minute s below wreath.

Ahwash 5, 6, other positional vars. Mintmark 0.63 mm or less than ribbon thickness.

3380 1875 S Small s below wreath.

Ahwash 4; many positional vars. Mintmark 0.7–0.8 mm, about ribbon thickness, from punch used in 1861–74.

3381 1875 S Tall narrow S below wreath. Rare.

Not in Ahwash; discovered by Howard Newcomb before 1914. Mintmark almost 1 mm—well in excess of ribbon thickness.

3382 1875 CC [all kinds 4,645,000] Wide C C in wreath.

9 obvs., 8 revs. requisitioned Feb. 12, 1875, by William Sty Doane, Coiner. Distance between C C nearly the width of either C; compare following. Several minute positional vars. Fine edge reeding as in 1876, or coarser reeds (89) as in 1871–74.

3383 1875 CC Close CC in wreath. Very rare.

Not in Ahwash. The C's are about half as far apart as on last.

3384 1875 CC Close CC below wreath. Scarce.

Ahwash 3, 4; other positional vars. Fine edge reeding as in 1876.

3385 1876 [all kinds 11,460,000 + 1,250P] "Type I." Large knob to 6.

Ahwash 1. Business strikes and a majority of proofs; many minor positional vars. Rev. hub as on 1860–75: E of ONE nearly touches wreath (see introductory text). In all, 79 obvs., 69 revs., of which 11 were held over for 1877 use.

3386 1876 "Type I." Small knob to 6.

Ahwash 2, 3, others. Business strikes and a minority of proofs. One die shows repunching on 1 6.

3387 1876 "Type II." Large knob to 6. Rare.

Ahwash 8, 9, others. E of ONE far from wreath, as 1878–91; see introductory text. Business strikes only.

3388 1876 "Type II." Small knob to 6. Rare.

Ahwash 4, 5, 7, others. Business strikes only.

3389 1876 "Type II." Small knob to 6; repunched 1. Rare.

Ahwash 6. Business strikes only.

3390 1876 S [all kinds 10,420,000] "Type I." Small knob to 6; small s.

Ahwash 1. E in ONE nearly touches wreath, as 1861–75; see introductory text. Mintmark 0.8 mm as 1861–74. Minor positional vars.

3391 1876 S "Type I." Large knob to 6; small s.

Ahwash 2, others (e.g., 1982 ANA:1913).

3392 1876 S "Type I." Same; repunched 1 6. Rare.

Ahwash 3.

3393 1876 S "Type I." Taller narrow S. Very rare.

Not in Ahwash. Mintmark 0.9 mm—well over ribbon thickness. See next.

3394 1876 S "Type II." Large knob to 6; taller narrow S. Very rare.

Ahwash 4. E in ONE far from wreath, as 1884–91; see introductory text. Mintmark as preceding.

3395 1876 S "Type II." Large knob to 6; small s. Very rare. Ahwash 5. The only var. noticed to date has strongly repunched 6; others may exist. Mintmark 0.8 mm as 1861–74. Head, foot, and lower shield flat.

3396 1876 CC [all kinds 8,270,000] "Type I." Small knob to 6.

Ahwash 3, 4, others. E in ONE nearly touches wreath, as 1871–75; see introductory text. CC varies in position. One var. has partly repunched date.

3397 1876 CC "Type I." Small knob to 6. Doubled rev. die. Rare.

Not in Ahwash. Doubling plainest at E's; rusted obv. and rev.

3398 1876 CC "Type I." Large knob to 6.

Ahwash 1, 2.

3399 1876 CC "Type I." Same, doubled obv. die. Very scarce.

Ahwash 5, 6. CC vary in spacing. 1982 ANA:1974. Usually in low grades. Deceptive cast counterfeits exist; authentication recommended.

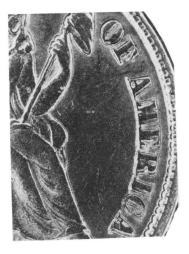

3400 1876 CC "Type II." Small knob to 6. Ex. rare.

Ahwash 7. E of ONE far from wreath. Auction 82:696.

3401 1877 [all kinds 7,310,000 + 490P] "Type I." Very rare.

Ahwash 1. E of ONE nearly touches wreath; see introductory text. Business strikes only; made from any of the 11 leftover 1876 revs., and from several of the 44 obvs. for this year.

3402 1877 "Type II."

E of ONE far from wreath; see introductory text. Many minor positional vars. Proofs and business strikes. 37 rev. dies made.

3403 1877 S [all kinds 2,340,000] "Type I." Ex. rare, reported, untraced.

E in ONE nearly touches wreath, as 1861–75; see introductory text.

3404 1877 S "Type II." Tall S. Very rare.

Not in Ahwash. E in ONE far from wreath; see introductory text. Mintmark 0.9+ mm, narrower than on next, most like **3393–94.**

3405 1877 S "Type II." Small s.

Many minor positional vars. Mintmark 0.8 mm as 1861–75.

3406 1877 CC [all kinds 7,700,000] "Type I." Normal date. Rare.

Ahwash 1, others. E in ONE nearly touches wreath, as 1871–75. From old leftover revs.

3407 1877 CC "Type I." Repunched 1 and final 7. Very rare.

Ahwash 2.

3408 1877 CC "Type I." Repunched 18. Very rare.

Ahwash 3.

3409 1877 CC "Type II." Normal date.

Ahwash 4–7, others. E in ONE far from wreath. CC vary in position and spacing.

3410 1877 CC "Type II." Repunched 1. Very scarce.

Ahwash 8. Price for early state with repunching plain; those with it faded will price as preceding.

3411 1878 [all kinds 1,678,000 + 800P] "Type I." Very rare.

Ahwash 1. E in ONE nearly touches wreath. Business strikes only; discovered about 1975.

3412 1878 "Type II."

E in ONE far from wreath. Business strikes and proofs. Minor positional vars. Only 677 proofs sold; the other 123 were released into circulation in 1879. Julian [1986].

3413 1878 CC [all kinds 200,000] "Type I." Very rare.

Ahwash 1. E in ONE nearly touches wreath. Bareford:256, UNC., $1,500.

3414 1878 CC "Type II."

Ahwash 2, 3. E in ONE far from wreath. Those with incomplete wreath are from a drastically repolished rev. (Ahwash 3); most survivors are UNC. and prooflike, e.g., "Gilhousen":444; Auction 81:1157, $2,300.

3415 1879 [14,000 + 700P] Repunched 18. Very rare.

Business strikes. 1982 ANA:412–13.

3416 1879 Repunched 1. Rare.

Ahwash 3. Business strikes. Later states with traces of extra 1 faded will price as **3418.**

3417 1879 Repunched 9.

Business strikes (very rare) and proofs.

3418 1879 Normal date.

Ahwash 1. Proofs usually show incomplete drapery near shield.

3419 1880 [36,000 + 1,355P]

Ahwash 1. Same comment as to preceding. Business strikes are rarer than proofs.

3420 1881 [24,000 + 975P]

Proofs have 2 minor positional vars. of date. Business strikes are rarer than proofs.

3421 1882 [3,910,000 + 1,100−P] Normal date.

Minor positional vars. Many proofs have incomplete drapery near shield. Some proofs were melted early in 1883 as unsold.

3422 1882 Plainly repunched 2.

Ahwash 1. Proofs and a few business strikes.

3423 1882 Repunched 1. Rare.

Ahwash 2. Business strikes only.

3424 1883 [7,674,673 + 1,039−P]

Minor positional vars. Some proofs were melted in 1884 as unsold.

3425 1884 [3,365,505 + 875P]

3426 1884 S [all kinds 564,969] Small s.

Mintmark about 0.8 mm, about thickness of adjacent ribbon. Usually in low grades.

3427 1884 S Large boldface S. Very rare.

Ahwash 1. Mintmark 1 mm, about 1½ times thickness of ribbon. Usually in low grades.

3428 1885 [2,532,497 + 930P] Normal.

Business strikes and proofs. Minor positional vars.

3429 1885 Repunched 1.

Ahwash 1. Business strikes only.

3430 1885 S [43,690] Large boldface S.

Mintmark as on **3427.** Usually in low grades, planchets often rough; Ex. rare UNC.

3431 1886 [6,376,684 + 886P] Normal date, small knob to 6.

Business strikes and proofs. Minor positional vars.

3432 1886 Repunched 6, large knob to 6.

Ahwash 2. Business strikes only.

3433 1886 Repunched 88. Very rare.

Not in Ahwash. Business strikes only. 1982 ANA:2003.

3434 1886 S [206,524]

Mintmark as on **3427.** As scarce as 1884 S but not so highly publicized.

3435 1887 [11,283,229 + 710P] Normal date.

Business strikes and proofs. A minority of proofs have incomplete drapery near shield.

3436 1887 Repunched 1.

Ahwash 1. Business strikes only. Repunching plainest at top.

3437 1887 S [all kinds 4,454,450] Large boldface S.

Several minor vars. S as in **3427, 3430, 3434,** often partly filled. Ahwash 3 shows a die file mark within S; not to be confused with next.

3438 1887 S Large over small S. Very rare.

Ahwash 4. Rev. die probably left over from 1884.

3439 1888 [5,495,655 + 800P] Normal date.

Minor positional vars. in business strikes and proofs. Incomplete drapery near shield on a minority of proofs (Ahwash 2).

3440 1888 Heavy date, final 8 obviously repunched. Rare.

Date slants down to r., thick serifs; final 8 first punched still lower, then corrected. The earliest state may show doubling on more digits.

3441 1888 S [1,720,000] Normal.

3442 1888 S Doubled rev. die. Very rare.

Ahwash 2.

3443 1889 [7,380,000 + 711P] Heavy date, closed 9.

Knob of 9 touches loop. Business strikes and proofs. Many minor positional vars., one with traces of repunching on 18 (1982 ANA:2015).

3444 1889 Thin numerals, open 9.

Knob of 9 away from loop. Comprises a large minority of proofs; may exist in business strike form.

3445 1889 S [all kinds 972,678] Large S.

Mintmark as on 1885–88 S coins. Minor positional vars.; sometimes with traces of repunching on 1 or S. Enl. photos.

3446 1889 S Small s. Closed 9. Rare.

Ahwash 4, 5. Mintmark 0.7 mm (less than thickness of ribbon). Discovered in 1959. Without or with minute repunching on S. "Gilhousen":464; 1982 ANA:2018. Compare next.

3447 1889 S Small s. Open 9. Rare.

Same mintmark; knob of 9 away from loop. Enl. photos.

3448 1890 [9,910,951 + 590P] Closed 9.

Knob of 9 touches loop. Minor positional vars.

3449 1890 Open 9.

Knob of 9 well away from loop. Business strikes and proofs (latter usually with date slanting down to r.).

3450 1890 S [all kinds 1,423,076] Large S.

Mintmark 0.9 mm but wider than formerly. Minor positional vars., some with traces of repunching on S.

3451 1890 S Large S over small. Very rare.

RPM 1; Ahwash 3.

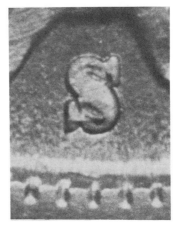

3452 1890 S Small s. Rare.

Ahwash 2. Mintmark 0.8 mm, about thickness of ribbon, and more compact than other types.

3453 1891 [15,310,000 + 600P] Closed 9.

Knob of 9 touches loop. Business strikes and proofs. Minor positional vars., some with dates slanting down to r., some with minute traces of repunching.

3454 1891 Open 9.

Ahwash 2, 3, others. Knob of 9 well away from loop. Same comments as to preceding.

3455 1891 Open 9. Double date. Very rare.

Ahwash 6. Date first entered to l., then repunched to r.

3456 1891 "Two Tails." Rare.

Not in Ahwash. Knob and tail of extra 9 within lower part of

9. Discovered by J. R. McCloskey. *Gobrecht Journal* 11/77, p. 11.

3457 1891 O [all kinds 4,540,000] Open 9.
   Ahwash 2. Knob of 9 well away from loop. Mintmark 1 mm. Compare all to follow.

3458 1891 O Open 9. Double-punched mintmark.
   Ahwash 5.

3459 1891 O Double date and mintmark. Rare.
   Ahwash 4. Date first entered high, then corrected lower. Die crack through mintmark; not to be confused with 1891 O/S. 1982 ANA:2028.

3460 1891 O Closed 9. Normal.
   Ahwash 1, 3, others. Knob of 9 touches loop.

3461 1891 O Closed 9. Double-punched mintmark.
   Ahwash 6.

3462 1891 O over horizontal O. Ex. rare.
   RPM 2; Ahwash 7. Closed 9.

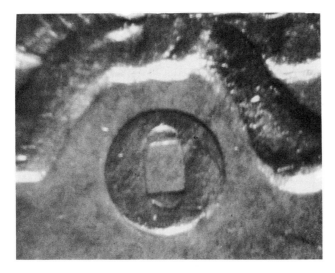

3463 1891 O over S. Normal date. Very rare.
   Ahwash 8. Discovered by this writer about 1962.

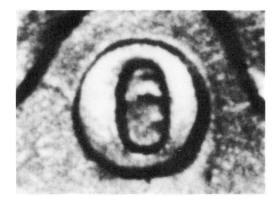

3464 1891 O over S. Double date. Very rare.
   Not in Ahwash. Repunching plainest on 189. Robison:1149. Later states with repunching indistinct will price as preceding.

3465 1891 S [all kinds 3,196,116] Open 9, broad S.
   Ahwash 1. Mintmark as in **3450**. Minor positional vars.

3466 1891 S Open 9. Large over small s. Very rare.
   RPM 1; Ahwash 5. Bareford:270.

3467 1891 S Closed 9, broad S.
   Ahwash 2. Mintmark as in **3450**. Minor positional vars.

3468 1891 S Closed 9, small s. Rare.
   Ahwash 4. Mintmark 0.8 mm, like **3452**. Discovered by Howard Newcomb before 1914.

3469 1891 S Same. Obviously repunched first 1. Very rare.
   Ahwash 3. Repunching distorts l. base of 1.

xiii. BARBER'S DESIGN (1892–1916)

Mint Director James Putnam Kimball was always prone to misunderstand wordings of Acts of Congress, attaching meanings the legislators never originally intended. Kimball is perhaps best known for redefining the term "pattern" in his 1887 Annual Report in order to distort a couple of clauses in the 1873 and 1874 Mint Acts to justify escalating a witchhunt against coin collectors. (Because he had vainly tried in 1886 to obtain an aluminum proof set of 1885, he decided that nobody else could ever again have anything of the kind; and he promulgated ex post facto regulations outlawing private ownership of unadopted designs, including coins openly sold by his predecessors in the Directorship. For him, but nobody else, "pattern" meant only the first year of an adopted design. No statute law confirms his view.) Almost equally irrationally, by assuming that the word "authorized" in another clause of the 1874 Mint Act referred only to Congress, Kimball got the idea that no improvement of coin designs could be undertaken without further legislation: He even went so far as to condemn as "illegal" the 1878 Morgan dollar and 1883 Liberty Head nickel designs! Using this manifestly absurd reasoning, Kimball induced his friend Sen. Justin Morrill (R.-Vt.) to introduce a bill which would authorize the Treasury to change coin designs only after current designs had been in use for 25 years. This became the Act of Sept. 26, 1890.

Implementing Kimball's eccentric idea, the Treasury shortly afterward announced a competition among 10 of the best-known American artists for new coin designs—only to find that they jointly rejected the terms, proposing far more favorable ones. The artists complained that the prize money was too small to make the competition worthwhile (the amount has not been learned), especially given the stringent legal limitations; the time limit was too short; and the nine unsuccessful contestants would have been expending enormous labor without compensation. The Treasury's riposte was to throw the competition open to the public. Judges were to be Augustus St. Gaudens, Henry Mitchell (a then well-known Boston engraver of gems and seals), and—most stupidly—Mint Engraver Charles E. Barber. Barber's record, since his accession in 1879, was notable for only two things: dullness and adamant opposition to outsiders' designs. His presence among the judges was the kiss of death. Unsurprisingly, most of the best artists in the USA boycotted the contest on the same grounds as before. The Treasury circular of April 4, 1891, giving details of the competition, elicited about 300 entries. Of these 300, only two were thought worth even an honorable mention; Barber made certain that no prize would be awarded. The new Mint Director, Edward O. Leech, called the contest "too wretched a failure" ever to be tried again, and ordered Barber to prepare the designs himself—which is exactly what Barber had wanted all along. Taxay {1966}, pp. 286–88.

However, Barber must have been feeling unusually lazy. He left the rev. design as it had been since 1860, with minor simplifications. His obv. was a mirror image of the Morgan dollar head, with much of Miss Anna Willess Williams's back hair cropped off, the rest concealed (most likely for Respectability: 1 Cor. 11:6. See Chap. 24, Sect. vii, introductory text) within a disproportionately large cap. A plain laurel (?) wreath replaced the assorted vegetation on the dollar. Barber's initial B appears at the truncation of neck.

The series is most notable for stereotypy, though recent researches have turned up several overdates, most notably the 1893/2 (on both proofs and business strikes). The 1905 O with "microscopic" o (from a punch intended for mintmarking quarter dollars) has proved to be a rarity in upper-grade levels, only one mint-state specimen being reported.

However, the most famous of all Barber dimes is beyond doubt the 1894 S. Of only 24 minted (all as proofs), reported June 30, 1894, only a dozen are traced. These were special strikings made by Mint Superintendent J. Daggett for a group of banker friends. Each of eight persons received three; Daggett gave his three to his daughter Hallie, telling her to put them away until she was as old as he was, at which time she would be able to sell them for a good price. On the way home, the child supposedly spent one for a dish of ice cream, but kept the other two until 1954, when she sold them to the coin dealer Earl Parker. As Parker had three, someone's memory is evidently at fault. The story has been written up several times, notably in *CW* 9/13/72 and 6/27/73, and differently in Breen {1977}. The roster of genuine survivors there constructed is amended and updated as follows:

1. Waldo Newcomer, F. C. C. Boyd, WGC:756, Neil:1433, Mehl, Hydeman:387, Empire Coin Co., A. Buol Hinman, "Century":724, Paramount, Leo A. Young, Auction 80:1578, $145,000, Ron Gillio, 1986 NCNA, $93,100, pvt. coll.

2. John H. Clapp, Eliasberg estate.

3. John H. Clapp, Louis Eliasberg, Sr., "H. R. Lee":348, N.Y. pvt. coll. This and preceding published in New York *Herald Tribune* 2/7/42 and *NUM* 3/42, p. 237.

4. James Aloysius Stack estate.

5. Mintmaster J. Daggett, Hallie Daggett, Earl Parker (1954), Dan Brown, Chicago pvt. coll.

6. Mintmaster J. Daggett, Hallie Daggett, Earl Parker (1954), W. R. Johnson, Abner Kreisberg, World-Wide Investments; later offered by Q. David Bowers, $97,500. (Ill.)

7. Mintmaster J. Daggett, "a relative," Earl Parker, James Kelly, Malcolm Chell-Frost, F. S. Guggenheimer:772, Kagin, 1973 MANA:1114, $52,000, Superior Galleries, Jerry Buss:617, $50,600, Michelle Johnson. Impaired proof, scratched near border and mintmark.

8. Charles A. Cass, "Empire":881, Bowers, Mrs. Norweb. Maple leaf below D weak, flat.

9. J. C. Mitchelson, CSL. Unverified.

10. Rappaport, Kagin, Reuter, Kreisberg, Bowers, "eastern pvt. coll." Not seen.

11. Retrieved from circulation (1957: the ice cream specimen?), Friedberg, Kagin, NN 51:581, Kagin, HR 11/69, J. G. Johnson, pvt. coll., 1980 ANA:1804, $31,000, 1981 ANA:2921, $25,500. GOOD.

12? Romito, Montesano, consigned to Stack's, 1942, withdrawn "for personal reasons"; worn, circular obv. cut. Unverified.

Dangerous forgeries exist. Some are made from genuine 1894 dimes to which S mintmarks have been fraudulently affixed; others altered from 1894 O; still others have been brought back in quantity from the Philippines, 1975–78 *(CW* 1/4/78, p. 50). These last show suspicious marks around date, and their S mintmark is of the wide open type common to 1899–1916 coins, altogether unlike those of 1892–98. Genuine specimens have minute rectangular defects on base and top of E of DIME, just beyond upright but a little l. of center of horizontal strokes.

Though dealers have called many other Barber dimes "rare," no individual date or mintmark qualifies as such. A. C. Gies, William Pukall, and Wayte Raymond obtained rolls of all of them prior to 1934, Raymond's in conjunction with his far-sighted promotion of coin albums. Wayte Raymond intended that his rolls become a source of individual specimens for collectors buying his albums, never a means of manipulating markets. Most of these rolls were broken up in the 1940s and 1950s, though in the 1978 ANA Convention auction an original roll of 1912's brought $14,000, and a similar roll of 1911 D's $14,500.

BARBER'S DESIGN

Designer, Engraver, Charles E. Barber, after Morgan (obv.) and Longacre (rev.). Mints, Philadelphia (no mintmark), New Orleans (mintmark O below wreath), San Francisco (mintmark S below wreath), Denver (mintmark D below wreath). Physical Specifications, Authorizing Acts, as before.

Grade range, POOR to UNC. GOOD: Date and all letters legible except LIBERTY. VERY GOOD: LI Y or L TY show. FINE: Full LIBERTY, though some letters will be weak. VERY FINE: All letters in LIBERTY evenly clear; many internal details in leaves. EXTREMELY FINE: Few tiny isolated rubbed spots only; edges of headband clear. EXCEPTIONS: Occasional weakly struck examples may be weak on LIBERTY even with mint luster; grade by surface. NOTE: Usually collected by beginners in GOOD to VG, by advanced collectors in UNC. and Proof.

3470 1892 [12,120,000 + 1,245P] Normal date.
Minor positional vars. Right ribbon end touching or free of wreath on proofs and business strikes of this and later dates (lapped dies). Rarely, chip out of die joins 2 to truncation. Rev. thin r. ribbon through 1900. Enl. photos (of **3488).**

3471 1892 Repunched 2. Very scarce.
Ruby, "Gilhousen":474.
3472 1892 Double date. Very rare.
Proofs and business strikes; former Hirt:72, latter (ill.) Bill Fivaz.

3473 1892 O Large O only. [3,841,700]
3474 1892 S Large S only. [990,710]
S as on silver dollars, vertical serifs nearly or quite touching middle stroke. This style S continues through 1898; see ill. of 1894 S, above **3470.**

3475 1892 S Double-punched S. Thin date. Rare.
"Gilhousen":477. Thin serifs to 1, thin tops and bases to other numerals.

3476 1892 S Double-punched S. Heavy date. Rare.
"Gilhousen":478. The double S discovered by Howard Newcomb before 1914.

3477 1893 Normal date. [3,340,000 + 792P]
Minor positional vars.

3478 1893 Repunched 3.
Several positional vars.

3479 1893/2 Very rare.
At least 4 vars.; business strikes and proofs (only a tiny minority of proofs). Discovered by this writer, Feb. 1961; *CW* 3/16/61, p. 1. 1982 ANA:2036, "UNC.," $800. Proofs are far rarer than business strikes.

3480 1893 O [1,760,000]

3481 1893 S [all kinds 2,491,401] Normal date and S.

3482 1893 S "Ugly 3." Rare.
Extra curve at outer r. of 3, between loops; named after the similar 1823 half dollar. Claimed as possible overdate; unconfirmed.

3483 1893 S Double-punched S.
Several vars., extra outlines at r. or l. Compare next.

3484 1893 S Triple S. Very scarce.
Mintmark first punched far to r., then to l. of final position.

3485 1893/2 S Ex. rare.
1977 ANA:4624, VF, $250.

3486 1894 [1,330,000 + 972P]
Several positional vars.: 4 touching truncation, barely free, or more distant. A hoard of nearly 100 proofs was dispersed in New York about 1967–68.

3487 1894 O [720,000]

3488 1894 S [24] Proofs only. Ex. rare.
See introductory text. Enl. photos above **3470.**

3489 1895 [all kinds 690,000 + 880P] Normal date.
Proofs come with 5 touching or free of truncation. Business strikes (several minute positional vars. of date) come with

normal ribbons or, rarely, with upper ribbon behind head fragmented (lapped die).

3490 1895 Double date. Rare.

3491 1895 O [all kinds 440,000] Heavy mintmark.

3492 1895 O Very thin mintmark.
Top and bottom hair-thin.

3493 1895 S [all kinds 1,120,000] Normal date and mintmark.

3494 1895 S Normal date, double S. Scarce.

3495 1895 S Double 95 and S. Rare.
Date first punched slanting upward to r., 5 touching bust, then corrected more nearly level. "Gilhousen":487.

3496 1896 [2,000,000 + 762P] Normal date.
Minor positional vars. Business strikes and proofs.

3497 1896 Partly repunched date. Scarce.
Business strikes only.

3498 1896 O [610,000] Normal date.

3499 1896 O Extra heavy date. Scarce.
Discovered by Dr. Charles L. Ruby. Date repeatedly repunched but extra outlines blurred. Serifs thick, 96 closed —knobs join loops.

3500 1896 S [575,056]

3501 1897 [10,868,533 + 731P]
Proofs and business strikes come with 7 touching truncation or free. One var. with incomplete wreath (7 free) is from drastically repolished dies: Landau:490.

3502 1897 O [666,000] Normal date.

3503 1897 O Base of 1 obviously repunched. Scarce.

3504 1897 O Bar joins 97. Ex. rare.
It is uncertain if the heavy extension from crossbar of 7 to upper part of 9 is part of another 7 or a cut or break in the die. *Numisma* 5/57:491.

3505 1897 S [1,342,844] Normal S.

3506 1897 S Double S. Scarce.
S first punched to r. of final position (1983 Midwinter ANA:591) or to l. (Rhodes:905).

3507 1898 [16,320,000 + 735P] Normal date.
Business strikes and proofs.

3508 1898 "Overdate." Very rare.
Curved line within loop of final 8, not matching any curve of another 8; most like part of middle stroke of a 2. "Gilhousen":494.

3509 1898 O [2,130,000] Normal date.

3510 1898 O Extra heavy date. Rare.
Similar to **3499.**

3511 1898 S [1,702,507] Normal date.

3512 1898 S Very thin numerals. Rare.
Serifs of 1 and tops and bases of 898 hair-thin.

3513 1898 S "Overdate." Ex. rare.
Part of extra 9 within 9; traces of another digit (loop of 6?) within final 8—curve not matching any part of 8. Die crumbling above final 8. Only 3 seen to date.

3514 1899 [19,580,000 + 846P] Normal date.

3515 1899 Double date. Rare.

3516 1899 O [2,650,000]

3517 1899 S [1,867,493] Normal S.
Mintmark broader, serifs slanting and well away from middle stroke.

3518 1899 S Repunched 9 and S. Very scarce.
Numisma 12/59:438. Later, repunching on 9 fades out: "Gilhousen":500.

3519 1900 [17,600,000 + 912P] Normal date.
Business strikes and proofs. Positional vars. exist.

3520 1900 Final 0 double. Rare.
Business strikes only.

3521 1900 O [2,010,000]
Mintmark varies greatly in position. *Numisma* 12/59:440 has O far to l.; "Gilhousen":502 has O leaning crazily to l. Scarcity levels not yet known.

3522 1900 S [5,168,270] Normal date.

3523 1900 S Final 0 double. Rare.
Similar to **3520**.

3524 1901 [18,859,665 + 813P] Normal date.
New hubs (1901–16); N away from ribbon; all top leaves longer, sharper; leaf below final S especially longer, nearly touching S. Rev. Thicker r. ribbon end, extra fold on underside. Old hub revs. continue intermittently through 1905. J. R. McCloskey, *CW* 7/2/80, p. 76.

3525 1901 Double 19. Rare.

3526 1901 Double 01. Proofs only. Rare.
"Gilhousen":505; 1982 ANA:2048. Comprises about 5% of proofs of this date.

3527 1901 O [5,620,000] Normal mintmark. Both rev. hubs.

3528 1901 O Double O. Very rare.
Mintmark first punched well to r. Discovered about 1978. 1983 Midwinter ANA:597.

3529 1901 O over horizontal O. Very rare.
RPM 1. Discovered by Tom Miller, 1976.

3530 1901 S [593,022] Old rev. hub.

3531 1902 [21,380,000 + 777P]
Proofs 1902–15 have devices semibrilliant rather than frosty as heretofore.

3532 1902 O [4,500,000]
Rarely with lower half of 2 filled by die chip: "Gilhousen":510.

3533 1902 S [2,070,000]

3534 1903 [19,500,000 + 755P]

3535 1903 O [8,180,000] Normal date.

3536 1903 O Repunched 3. Rare.
3 first entered to l. of final position.

3537 1903 O "Double knobs." Very rare.
3 first entered to r. of final position; both sets of knobs to 3 are plain. "Gilhousen":513.

3538 1903 S [613,500] Normal date. Old rev. hubs.

3539 1903 S Repunched 3. Rare.
"Gilhousen":514.

3540 1904 [14,600,357 + 670P]

3541 1904 S [800,000] New rev. hub.

3542 1905 [14,551,623 + 727P] Normal date.
The irregularities within 5 on all dimes of this year from all 3 mints are in the logotype, not evidence of overdate. But see next.

3543 1905 Repunched 5. Proofs only. Very scarce.
Comprises a minority of proofs.

3544 1905 O [all kinds 3,400,000] Large O.
See note to **3542**.

3545 1905 O "Microscopic" o. Rare.
Mintmark about half normal size, from the punch used for mintmarking quarter dollars. Almost always in low grades; prohibitively rare above VF, only one reported UNC. Discovered by Howard Newcomb: *NUM* 6/12, p. 198. See note to **3542**.

3546 1905 S [6,855,199]
Both rev. hubs. See note to **3542**.

3547 1906 [19,957,731 + 675P] Normal date.

3548 1906 Double 6. Scarce.
Business strikes only. NN 54:1259.

3549 1906 O [2,610,000] Normal date.

3550 1906 O Repunched 6.
Discovered by Dr. Charles L. Ruby.

3551 1906 S [3,136,640] Normal date.

3552 1906 S Repunched 6. Very scarce.
"Gilhousen":524. Under high magnification, the 6 is triple-punched.

3553 1906 S over "inverted" S. Very rare.
"Charmont":2995. S first cut rotated 180°, then corrected.

3554 1906 D [4,060,000] Normal date.

3555 1906 D Double 6. Very scarce.

3556 1907 [22,220,000 + 575P]

3557 1907 O [5,058,000]

3558 1907 S [3,178,470]
Sometimes with traces of repunching on S.

3559 1907 D [4,080,000]
A repunched date exists.

3560 1908 [10,600,000 + 545P] Normal date.

3561 1908 Triple 8. Rare.
"Gilhousen":530. One of the 3 punchings of 8 is at an odd angle to the other 2. Not to be confused with following.

3562 1908 Overdate. Proofs only. Very rare.
Hirt:1181. Uncertain digit within 8, possibly a 6.

3563 1908 O [1,789,000] Normal date.

3564 1908 O Double-punched 8. Very scarce.
Outline of extra 8 within upper loop.

3565 1908 S [3,220,000]

3566 1908 D [7,490,000] Normal date.

3567 1908 D Double date. Rare.
NN 57:540. On one var. (ill.) date first entered far too high; on another, too low and to r.

3568 1908 D Triple 8. Rare.

3569 1909 [10,240,000 + 650P]

3570 1909 O [2,287,000]
Hoarded because final year from this Mint.

3571   1909 O over reversed D. Presently very rare.
First entered with D rotated 180°, then corrected with O; upright and traces of serifs of erroneous D visible at r. Discovered by Michael Pollack, 1974. ANACS 7294.

3572   1909 S [1,000,000] Normal date.

3573   1909 S Final 9 double. Rare.
NN 54:1254.

3574   1909 D [954,000]

3575   1910 [11,520,000 + 551P]

3576   1910 S [1,240,000]

3577   1910 D [3,490,000]

3578   1911 [18,870,000 + 543P]

3579   1911 S [3,520,000]
Sometimes with traces of repunching on S. 1982 ANA:2061.

3580   1911 D [11,209,000]

3581   1912 [19,350,000 + 700P]

3582   1912 S [3,420,000]
Rarely with traces of repunching on S. Rhodes:947.

3583   1912 D [11,760,000]

3584   1912 D Double D. Very rare.
Not in RPM. Mintmark first entered too low, then corrected.

3585   1913 [19,760,000 + 622P]

3586   1913 S [510,000]
Much hoarded.

3587   1914 [17,360,250 + 425P]

3588   1914 S [2,100,000]

3589   1914 D [11,908,000]

3590   1914 D Blundered D. Presently Ex. rare.
RPM 1. Mintmark first entered far too high and r., overlapping stem, then corrected. *CW* 5/7/86, p. 86.

3591   1915 [5,620,000 + 450P]
Numerals for this year and following, for both mints, cruder than on any previous dates since 1844–46; reason unknown.

3592   1915 S [960,000]
Rarely with traces of repunching on S. RPM 1; 1984 Midwinter ANA:882.

3593   1916 [18,490,000]
No proofs reported of this design. Proof sets officially consisted only of cent and 5¢.

3594   1916 S [5,820,000]

xiv. WEINMAN'S WINGED CAPS (1916–45)

By late 1915, everyone from the Secretary of Treasury down to the general public had become tired of the Barber silver coin designs—with the possible exception of Barber himself. The Act of Sept. 26, 1890 (see introductory text to previous section) required that 25 years elapse from adoption of a coin design to its replacement. Accordingly, with a "fiscal 1917" (July 1, 1916) target date, the Treasury announced another competition for dime, quarter, and half-dollar designs. The prize was sufficiently larger than its 1891 counterpart to attract attention from some of America's better sculptors, and on March 3, 1916, Mint Director Robert W. Woolley announced that Adolph Alexander Weinman's dime and half-dollar designs would receive the prizes in their categories, while the quarter-dollar design prize went to Hermon A. MacNeil (see Chaps. 27, Sect. xiv, and 28, Sect. xv, introductory texts). Woolley accordingly wrote to Mint Engraver Charles E. Barber, thanking him for his own rejected submissions, and asking him to cooperate when the Weinman and MacNeil relief models would arrive at the Philadelphia Mint (not later than May 1, 1916). Barber became sullen and totally uncooperative. In subsequent work with George T. Morgan (the nearly forgotten Assistant Engraver, who had designed the silver dollar in use 1878–1921), Weinman found

satisfactory cooperation, but Morgan's illness delayed completion of the galvanos. Nevertheless, the new coins were ready by June 1916, though distribution began Oct. 28. Taxay {1966}, pp. 347–49.

Weinman's new design depicted Elsie Stevens (Mrs. Wallace Stevens) as Ms. Liberty in a close-fitting winged cap. Ignorant people at once mistook this for a head of Hermes or Mercury in the winged hat *(petasos)*, evidently through unfamiliarity with the original Greek vase paintings and statues. Hermes's petasos is flat and broad-brimmed, in general outline more like one of the commoner types of flying saucers, whereas Ms. Liberty's brimless winged cap more nearly resembles 1920s cloche hats worn by flappers. Coin dealers, who of all people should have known better, perpetuated the solecism "Mercury dime" for generations. "Weinman design" or "Winged Cap dime" is preferable. Ted Schwarz identified Weinman's model as the wife of the poet in *NNW* 1/20/79, p. 16; but compare *CW* 1/10/73.

Beyond doubt, the rev. device had something to do with the USA's impending entry into WW I: the Roman *fasces,* before its infamous association with Mussolini's Blackshirts. This consists of the executioner's axe bound within a group of rods. Commonly interpreted as "the power of life or death," in practice it means the power to kill or to make one's victim wish (s)he were dead; in ancient Roman law it connoted the power to kill mercifully by the blade or mercilessly by the rods. Weinman's symbolic message in this design (surrounded by greenery, like the iron fist in the velvet glove) was clearly an updated "Don't tread on me": something like "The USA can instantly punish with any penalty up to and including death, therefore beware, enemies of liberty!" One wonders how many young collectors even thought of these connotations, especially after the war.

Nevertheless, this gruesome device has acquired a kind of mystique among collectors. In recent years, many have noticed that mint-state Weinman dimes are often more or less blurry in centers, most often on the horizontal thongs or "bands" holding the rods. Increasingly often, pieces with clearly defined thongs ("split bands") bring high premiums, most of all for "100% split bands." The diagram below illustrates how the percentages are used; but remember that exaggeration is common and occasional separations have been fraudulently enhanced by handtooling. Mint-state prices herein are for normal coins with 75% or less bands; premiums for 90% to 100% split-bands coins are sometimes double to quadruple normal prices.

This was the first dime design to be completely imparted to working dies by hubs including dates. Therefore, aside from the 1916 prototypes, the only vars. in any given date will be those created by changes in mintmark size (1917, 1928, 1934, 1941,

GUIDE TO "SPLIT BANDS" TERMINOLOGY

The bands are at center of reverse

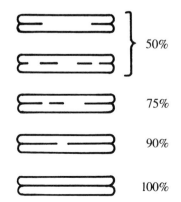

1942, 1945), mintmark position (minor only), mintmark repunching (many dates, mostly minor), or hubbing errors. These last are of two kinds: doubled dies and overdates. A working die must receive at least two blows from a hub to show the design in enough detail to impart it to the coins. But between blows in the hubbing press it becomes stress-hardened and brittle, requiring annealing. Replacement of a partly completed working die in the hubbing press at a minute angle to initial position, or minutely displaced in any direction, produces a "doubled" die, showing extra outlines to devices. An accident of this kind in fall 1941, when dies were simultaneously being prepared for 1941 and 1942 dimes, had two working obvs. going by error to two different presses, producing the famous 1942/1 and 1942/1 D overdates. Similar pieces dated 1918 have been repeatedly reported (from very worn pieces culled from circulation) but remain unconfirmed.

Aside from the 1916 prototypes and matte proofs, there are no extreme rarities; and if we count only normal date-mintmark combinations, there are no real rarities at all. The same three individuals who hoarded almost all 1892–1947 issues in roll lots (A. C. Gies, William Pukall, and Wayte Raymond) favored this design; uncirculated survivors of many dates of Weinman dimes mostly come from their holdings.

WEINMAN'S WINGED CAPS

Designer, Adolph Alexander Weinman. Engraver, Weinman, assisted by Morgan. Mints, Philadelphia (no mintmark), San Francisco (mintmark S), Denver (D), both r. of (ON)E. Physical Specifications, Authorizing Acts, as before.

Grade range, POOR to UNC. GOOD: All letters and date legible; generally, rods in fasces all blurred. VERY GOOD: Half the rods distinguishable. FINE: All seven rods plus the half rod adjacent to blade clear; diagonal thongs worn nearly flat. VERY FINE: Both diagonal thongs clear. EXTREMELY FINE: Braids and hair before ear clear; tiny isolated rubbed spots only, even on diagonal thongs. EXCEPTIONS: UNCs. of certain dates come weakly struck; these show mint frost on weak areas. NOTE: Beginners collect these in GOOD or VG; advanced collectors prefer UNC. Intermediate grades tend to be neglected save for the "key" dates 1916 D, 1921, 1921 D, and overdates. For "split bands" see introductory text.

3595   1916 First prototype, no AW. Ex. rare.
At least 4 vars.; see enl. ills. in *CW* 8/19/70, p. 34. Enl. photos. Kosoff Estate:1129–30, AU $4,400, VF $880 (scratched).

3596   1916 Second prototype, with AW. Ex. rare.
AW is Weinman's monogram, as on all subsequent dimes of this design. Truncation line straight at lower l., forming angle with shoulder curve, ending close to 6; two berries above (ON)E; stems and ribbon ends longer than in next; obv. and rev. rims narrow and shallow. Newcomer, Raymond, 1958 ANA:74, Bareford:318, Proof, $7,000. Compare next.

3597   1916 [22,180,080 + ?P]
Released Oct. 28. Satin-finish proofs (not publicly distributed, 4 or 5 known) are sharply enough struck to make even the best "full split bands" business strikes look weak; authentication recommended. Warning: Many choice business strikes have deceptive broad borders simulating proofs. Ill. of **3599.**

3598   1916 S [10,450,000]
3599   1916 D [264,000]
Released in November. Coinage stopped so that personnel could devote full time to making quarter dollars. Wagner {1973}. 4 pairs of dies, ill. ANACS {1983}, pp. 80–81. Enl. photos above **3597.** Forgeries are plentiful, most often fabricated by affixing mintmarks to genuine Philadelphia coins, or by altering S to D on genuine 1916 S coins. The Busby gang made thousands in Los Angeles (1958); others made tens of thousands more in Milwaukee ca. 1968–73, and elsewhere in later years, in all grades. Cast counterfeits also exist. Authentication is mandatory!

3600   1917 [55,230,000]
May exist in matte or satin-finish proof, like all other denominations of this date.
3601   1917 S [27,330,000]
3602   1917 D [9,402,000]
Mintmark larger than on 1916 D; may exist with same mintmark as latter.
3603   1918 [26,680,000]
The "overdates" reported from badly worn examples remain unconfirmed.
3604   1918 S [19,300,000]
Same comment. UNCs. are often weak.
3605   1918 D [22,674,800]
Same comments.
3606   1918 D Excessively thin motto letters. Rare.
Die drastically overpolished; neckline indistinct near (US)T.
3607   1919 [35,740,000]
3608   1919 S [8,850,000]
UNCs. are often weak.
3609   1919 D [9,939,000]
One var. has "broken nose": die lapped to remove clash marks, effacing top of bridge of nose. This feature has been reported for many later dates and may exist for all.
3610   1920 [59,030,000]
3611   1920 S [13,820,000]
UNCs. are often weak.
3612   1920 D [19,171,000]
3613   1921 [1,230,000]
Usually in low grades. UNCs. (often weak) are in short supply because the hoarders could find only a few rolls. Genuine specimens have thick 1's with concave sides and very slight serifs, with open loop to 9; falsely altered dates have straight 1's with pronounced serifs, closed loop to 9.
3614   1921 D [1,080,000]
11 obvs., 8 revs. Same comments.

3615   1923 [50,130,000]
Note: Dimes dated 1923 D are circulating counterfeits made before 1950, possibly by the makers of the "1930 D" (below).

3616   1923 S [6,440,000]
UNCS. are often weak.

3617   1924 [24,010,000]

3618   1924 S [7,120,000]
UNCS. are often weak.

3619   1924 D [6,810,000]

3620   1925 [25,610,000]

3621   1925 S [5,850,000]
UNCS. are often weak.

3622   1925 D [5,117,000]
UNCS. are often weak.

3623   1926 [32,160,000]

3624   1926 S [1,520,000]
UNCS. are often weak.

3625   1926 D [6,828,000]
Same comment.

3626   1927 [28,080,000]

3627   1927 S [4,770,000]
UNCS. are often weak.

3628   1927 D [4,812,000]
Same comment.

3629   1928 [19,480,000]

3630   1928 S [all kinds 7,400,000] Small s.
Mintmark as 1916–27. UNCS. are often weak.

3631   1928 S Large S. Scarce.
Broader mintmark with pronounced sharp serifs. UNCS. are often weak.

3632   1928 D [4,161,000]

3633   1929 [25,970,000]

3634   1929 S [4,730,000]

3635   1929 D [5,034,000]

3636   1930 [6,770,000]
Note: Dimes dated 1930 D are circulating counterfeits made before 1950, possibly by the maker of the similar "1923 D."

3637   1930 S [1,843,000]
UNCS. are often weak.

3638   1931 [3,150,000]

3639   1931 S [1,800,000]
UNCS. are often weak.

3640   1931 D [1,260,000]

3641   1931 D Doubled obv. die. Very scarce.
Discovered by Tom Miller, 1978. Usually in low grades.

3642   1934 [24,080,000]
UNCS. are often weak.

3643   1934 D [all kinds 6,772,000] Small D.
Mintmark as on silver dollars. Rarely, with brilliant prooflike fields from repolishing dies to efface clash marks.

3644   1934 D Large D.
Mintmark as on quarter dollars and later dimes. Compare next.

3645   1934 D Large over small D. Presently very rare.
RPM 1. Discovered by Bill Fivaz. *ETCM* 4/77, p. 28.

3646   1935 [58,830,000]

3647   1935 Doubled obv. die. Presently very rare.
Plainest on date and motto. Discovered by Delma K. Romines, May 1979.

3648   1935 S [15,840,000]

3649   1935 D [10,477,000]

3650   1936 [87,500,000 + 4,139P]
2 finishes on proofs: "Type I," satin finish, only about 8 seen to date; "Type II," extra brilliant, like 1937. Buffed or plated pieces are sometimes offered as proofs; authentication recommended.

3651   1936 S [9,210,000]

3652   1936 D [12,132,000]

3653   1937 [56,860,000 + 5,756P]
Proofs are extra brilliant; same comment as to 1936.

3654   1937 S [9,740,000]

3655   1937 D [14,146,000]

3656   1938 [22,190,000 + 8,728P]

3657   1938 S [8,090,000]

3658   1938 D [5,537,000]

3659   1939 [67,740,000 + 9,321P]
Normally with double ribbon end l. of D(IME). Compare next.

3660   1939 Single ribbon end. Proofs only. Presently very rare.
1973 GENA:620–21. "Broken nose" as mentioned at **3609**. This and single ribbon end come from excessive repolishing of dies to efface clash marks.

3661   1939 S [10,540,000]
UNCS. are often weak.

3662   1939 D [24,394,000]

3663   1940 [65,350,000 + 11,872P]
Some proofs have "broken nose": cf. **3609, 3660.**

3664   1940 S [21,560,000]
Repunched mintmarks exist for this and many later years.

3665   1940 S Doubled obv. die. Presently scarce.
Discovered by Delma K. Romines, 1979.

3666   1940 D [21,198,000]

3667   1941 [175,090,000 + 16,557P]

3668   1941 S [all kinds 43,090,000] Small s.
Mintmark as in 1935–40.

3669   1941 S Large S.
Mintmark as in 1942–44. Constitutes a slight majority of the year.

3670   1941 S Large S over small s. Presently Ex. rare, 3 or 4 seen.
Not in RPM. Small s partly above the large and leans l. Discovered by Don Taxay before 1971.

3671   1941 D [45,634,000]
Rarely with minutely doubled obv. die (plainest at motto): Note irregular elongated dots between words, and notches on top strokes of TR-T, tops of 1's, and crossbar of 4. Similar doubled dies exist for many later dates and mintmarks.

3672   1942 [205,410,000 + 22,329P]

3673   1942/41 Only one var.
Discovered by Arnold Cohn, *NSM* 3/43, p. 154. Usually in low grades. UNCS. are from 4 rolls discovered in 1954. Many found in circulation, Phoenix, Ariz., 1943. Many types of forgeries exist; authentication recommended.

Courtesy Alan Herbert

3674 1942 S [all kinds 49,300,000] Small s.
Same punch as in 1935–40. Comprises about 10% of specimens checked.
3675 1942 S Large S.
Same punch as in 1943–44. Comprises about 90% of specimens checked.
3676 1942 D [60,740,000]
3677 1942 D Double D. Presently rare.
Publicized by Alan Herbert.

3678 1942/1941 D
Only one var.; repunched D. Usually in low grades; Ex. rare UNC.: 1981 ANA:538, "UNC.," $12,000. Discovered by Delma K. Romines, 1962. This obv. has double motto visible only under high magnification.

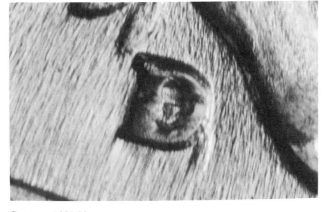

Courtesy ANACS

3679 1943 [191,710,000]
3680 1943 S [60,400,000]
3681 1943 D [71,949,000]
3682 1944 [231,410,000]
UNCs. are often weak.
3683 1944 S [49,490,000]
3684 1944 D [62,224,000]
3685 1944 D Obvious double D. Presently very rare.

Courtesy ANACS

3686 1945 [159,130,000]
UNCs. are often weak; "full split bands" very unusual.
3687 1945 S [all kinds 41,920,000] Large S, normal.
3688 1945 S Small s.
Also called "micro" s. See ill. in RPM, p. 170. Discovered by Bernard J. Maier, *NUM* 3/47, p. 244.
3689 1945 S Large over small s. Reported, unseen.
This may prove to be a grotesquely repunched mintmark.
3690 1945 S over horizontal S. Reported, unseen.
RPM 3. Unknown if large or small s.
3691 1945 D [40,245,000]

xv. SINNOCK'S ROOSEVELT DESIGN, SILVER (1946–65)

Pres. Franklin D. Roosevelt's sudden death (1945) induced Treasury officials to propose that his portrait be immediately placed on a coin of regular issue, without awaiting his birth centenary as had been done for Lincoln. (Of the other presidents who died in office, Lincoln, W. H. Harrison, Garfield, and McKinley were all portrayed on federal paper currency; McKinley's face showed up on two different commemorative gold dollars; Kennedy's still appears on the half dollar at this writing; but nobody bothered to propose such honors for Warren G. Harding.)

The only denominations then available without special legislation were the Lincoln cent, the Weinman or Winged Cap dime, and the Walking Liberty half dollar. For unknown reasons, officialdom chose the dime. Mint Engraver John R. Sinnock created models featuring a large head in low relief, which he submitted to the federal Fine Arts Commission via Acting Mint Director Leland Howard, Oct. 12, 1945. The Commission disliked them, and gave reasons in a conference. Sinnock thereafter submitted modified models, with IN GOD WE TRUST reduced in size and moved from below neck to before it; date moved below neck; LIBERTY moved from overhead to before face; and a little more detail added to jaw and cheekbones. Presumably the Commission approved these, though the new design was not much improvement on the old, and no improvement whatever on Weinman's except for eliminating the fasces in favor of a torch and making the vegetation more recognizably an olive branch for peace.

The new coins were rushed into production to coincide with the 1946 "March of Dimes" birth defects fund-raising campaign. Taxay {1966}, pp. 371–75.

The illustrious black sculptor Selma Burke claimed that Sinnock adapted his design from her bas-relief of Pres. Roosevelt: *CW* 2/2/83, p. 34. Considering that Sinnock had also copied and signed John Frederick Lewis's design for the 1926 Sesquicentennial half dollar, Ms. Burke's claim is probably valid.

As with the Weinman design, working dies have been completely hubbed, dates and all, so that the only sources of variation have been changes of hub (1946, 1964), doubled dies, and mintmark vagaries. The hub changes deserve further attention.

On 1946 "Type I," Y is farther from forelock than on any later years, and Sinnock's initials JS are small, weak, and often misshapen. The 1946 S and D "Type I" were discovered only in recent years. On 1946 "Type II," Y is nearer forelock, as in subsequent years, and initials JS are larger, plain, and well shaped.

Similarly, the first few working obvs. of 1964 Philadelphia and the first few dozen for 1964 D have pointed tail to 9 and plain upper serif to 1 in date; the rest have blunt (sawed-off, almost rectangular) tail to 9 and no serif to 1, representing a new obv. hub.

Sinnock's initials JS proved a source of political controversy from the beginning of issue, like engraver's initials on so many other U.S. coins. Reactionary superpatriots, supporters of the unlamented Sen. Joseph R. McCarthy, believing (against all evidence) in Roosevelt's Communist "leanings," began spreading stupid, unfounded, and malicious rumors that the JS instead stood for Joseph Stalin. These rumors eventually reached Congress, at which point the Treasury demanded that they be squelched. Accordingly, the Mint issued press releases properly identifying JS as Sinnock, and the extremists adopted other tactics: See Chap. 28, Sect. xvii, introductory text. Taxay {1966}, p. 375.

All dates and mintmarks were coined in enormous quantities. Despite everything Leland Howard could do to discourage the practice, bag lots went to dealers, investors, and speculators, though never in amounts large enough to cause shortages of circulating change. Howard nevertheless blamed collectors for the coin shortage of 1964–65, whereas its real cause was blocked flowback: Vending machine and telephone company employees did not collect receipts from machines often enough to return them to circulation. See next section.

SINNOCK'S ROOSEVELT DESIGN, SILVER

Designer, John R. Sinnock, after Selma Burke. Engraver, Sinnock. Mints, Philadelphia 1946–65 (no mintmark), San Francisco 1946–55 (mintmark S), Denver 1946–64 (D). Mintmarks l. of torch base. Physical Specifications, Authorizing Acts, as before.

Grade range, GOOD to UNC.; generally collected only UNC. FINE: Flame worn smooth; all vertical lines on torch show, but no horizontals. VERY FINE: Only slight wear on hair above ear; partial horizontal lines on torch, vertical lines plain. EXTREMELY FINE: Isolated tiny rubbed spots only, otherwise full details of torch, flame, leaves, hair. EXCEPTIONS: Many UNCS. are weakly struck; look for mint luster on weak areas, especially base of torch, adjacent horizontal lines, and those immediately below torch.

3692 1946 [all kinds 255,250,000] "Type I."
Y far from forelock; small weak misshapen JS (see introductory text). Coinage began Jan. 30, 1946. Enl. photos.

3693 1946 "Type II."
Y nearer forelock as on all later years; JS large, bold, clear.

3694 1946 S [all kinds 27,900,000] "Type I." Presently very scarce.
Same hub as **3692**.

3695 1946 S "Type II." Trumpet-tailed S.
Same hub as **3693**. Tail of mintmark flared like "bell" of a trumpet. This mintmark punch continued through 1955 concurrently with next.

3696 1946 S Similar. Knob-tailed S.
Tail of mintmark ends in oval knob. See ills. in RPM, pp. 172–73.

3697 1946 S Doubled rev. die. Very scarce.
RPM 1, 2. Discovered by Tom Miller, 1977. 2 vars.: double- or quadruple-punched S. Both have knob-tailed S.

3698 1946 S Triple S. Very scarce.
RPM 4. Knob-tailed S.

3699 1946 D [all kinds 61,043,500] "Type I." Presently very scarce.
Same hub as **3692**.

3700 1946 D "Type II."
Same hub as **3693**.

3701 1947 [121,520,000]

3702 1947 S [34,840,000] Trumpet-tailed S.
See **3695**.

3703 1947 S Knob-tailed S.
See **3696**.

3704 1947 S Sans-serif S. Scarce.
Mintmark (this year only) possibly intended for coins made for foreign governments.

3705 1947 S over D. Presently very rare.
Discovered by Lewis Lawton before 1963; rediscovered by Hugh Campbell (1978) and publicized in *CW* 10/12/83, p. 70. Cf. RPM 1, called S over horizontal S; knob-tailed S.

3706 1947 D [46,835,000]
3707 1948 [74,950,000]
3708 1948 S [35,520,000] Trumpet-tailed S.
Mintmark as in **3695**.
3709 1948 S Knob-tailed S.
Mintmark as in **3696**.
3710 1948 D [52,841,000]
3711 1949 [30,940,000]
3712 1949 S [13,510,000] Trumpet-tailed S.
3713 1949 S Knob-tailed S.
3714 1949 D [26,034,000]
3715 1950 [50,130,114 + 51,386P]
The first proofs are satiny; later ones more brilliant as in later years.
3716 1950 S [20,440,000] Trumpet-tailed S.
3717 1950 S Knob-tailed S.
3718 1950 D [46,803,000]
3719 1950 D Doubled rev. die. Scarce.
First published in *EVN* 3/31/82, p. 11.

3720 1951 [103,920,102 + 57,500P]
3721 1951 S [31,630,000] Trumpet-tailed S.
3722 1951 S Knob-tailed S.
3723 1951 D [56,529,000]
3724 1952 [99,040,093 + 81,980P]
3725 1952 S [44,419,500] Trumpet-tailed S.
3726 1952 S Knob-tailed S.
3727 1952 D [122,100,000]
3728 1953 [53,490,120 + 128,800P]
3729 1953 S [39,180,000] Trumpet-tailed S.
3730 1953 S Knob-tailed S.
3731 1953 D [136,433,000]
3732 1953 D over horizontal D. Presently very rare.
RPM 3.
3733 1954 [114,010,203 + 233,300P]
3734 1954 S [22,860,000] Trumpet-tailed S.
3735 1954 S Knob-tailed S.
3736 1954 S Without JS. Presently very scarce.
Discovered by Mark Bauer, Sept. 1983. Motto weak (overpolished die).
3737 1954 D [106,397,000]
3738 1955 [12,450,181 + 378,200P]
3739 1955 S [18,510,000] Trumpet-tailed S.
3740 1955 D [13,959,000]
3741 1956 [108,640,000 + 669,384P]
3742 1956 D [108,015,100]
3743 1957 [160,160,000 + 1,247,952P]
3744 1957 D [113,354,330]
3745 1958 [31,910,000 + 875,652P]
3746 1958 D [136,465,000]
3747 1959 [85,780,000 + 1,149,291P]

3748 1959 D [164,919,790]
3749 1960 [70,390,000 + 1,691,602P]
No clear-cut division between "pointed" and "blunt" 9's; some coins are difficult to assign to either class. A doubled obv. die exists on proofs; Ex. rare.
3750 1960 D [200,160,400]
Same comment.
3751 1961 [93,730,000 + 3,028,244P]
3752 1961 D [209,146,500]
3753 1962 [72,450,000 + 3,218,019P]
3754 1962 D [334,948,380]
3755 1963 [123,650,000 + 3,075,645P]
3756 1963 D [421,476,530]
3757 1964 [all kinds 929,360,000 + 3,950,762P] Pointed 9.
Plain upper serif to 1. *NSM* 3/65, p. 732. Business strikes (estimated under 2 million) and proofs. See introductory text.

3758 1964 Blunt 9.
No serif to 1. *NSM* 3/65, p. 732. Business strikes (estimated over 927,000,000) and proofs. See introductory text. For clad strikings see following section. Many coined in 1965 from 1964-dated dies, pursuant to Act of 9/3/64.

3759   1964 D [all kinds 1,357,517,180] Pointed 9.
      As **3757**. Estimated under 40 million.
3760   1964 D Blunt 9.
      As **3758**. Estimated above 1,317,000,000.
3761   1965 On obsolete silver blank. Ex. rare.
      Weight 38.58 grs. = 2.5 gms. Milton G. Cohen coll. For explanation see following section.

xvi. CLAD ISSUES (1965–   )

While the so-called "coin shortage" of 1963–65 was going on, the Mint Bureau found that the price of silver bullion was going up and the supply was going down. As this was also the period when the Treasury was releasing its hoard of silver dollars to the general public, some officials blamed coin collectors' and hoarders' greed for silver. For this, as for the "coin shortage" itself, the Bureau first hunted scapegoats, only then solutions. Leland Howard was one among many Mint officials who ignorantly and maliciously attempted to blame coin collectors for both problems, unwittingly (?) continuing the Mint's century-old feud: Breen {1962B}.

I was one of several columnists to point out then that coin hoarders' activities (grossly overestimated by the Mint Bureau then as now) contributed almost nothing to the "coin shortage" compared to its main source, inhibited flowback. The missing coins, far from inhabiting bank vaults and coin shops, were spending 28–30 days out of every month in vending machines, parking meters, and telephone booths; personnel did not collect nearly often enough from these "legal receptacles." Once they did, the "coin shortage" ended, but the Mint Bureau's official policy of exaggerating hoarders' activities did not: See Chap. 31.

As the price of silver began climbing, the Mint Bureau found supplies shorter. As in 1942 with cents and nickels, the solution most attractive to officialdom was a change of metal, but any substitute for silver would have to pass vending machines' counterfeit-rejection devices. (The vending machine industry estimated that conversion of these devices in their millions of machines would take a minimum of five years and astronomical costs.) The Bureau consulted the Battelle Institute, which eventually recommended adoption of clad metal, commonly known as "sandwich metal," consisting of thin cupro-nickel layers bonded to copper cores. The Coinage Act of July 23, 1965 made this recommendation law.

In adopting this concoction, the Mint Bureau abandoned counterfeit-detection methods thousands of years old, perhaps cynically recognizing that the purchasing power of dimes and quarters had already become low enough that these coins would no longer attract counterfeiters' attention. "Sandwich metal" dimes are lightweight by almost 10%, like counterfeits (2.27 gms. instead of the former 2.5); slick to the touch, like cast counterfeits; and show less design detail than did former silver coins, easing forgers' tasks. They are struck at 35–40 tons, 130 per minute; die life is 250,000–400,000 impressions.

During 1965–67, the Mint Bureau omitted mintmarks, in a deliberate attempt to discourage coin collectors from retaining new dimes found in circulation. Proofs were not coined; the only things the Bureau offered to its former proof-set customers were "Special Mint Sets," made in San Francisco, vaguely prooflike at best but with neither the sharpness nor the eye appeal of previous proofs. As these ersatz proofs sold only half as well as the genuine, the Mint Bureau resumed manufacture of proof sets in 1968, moving all mintmarks to obv. (producing a crowded effect on dimes) and—in an unprecedented shift— designated the San Francisco Mint under its 1851–53 title of "U.S. Assay Office" to do all subsequent proof strikings.

Nevertheless, occasional proofs since then have shown up without S mintmark. These (aside from the Aug. 1974 proto-type Bicentennial coins) are not Philadelphia issues but regular San Francisco proofs from dies with S mintmark omitted in error. These "S-less" proofs are all very rare, the 1968 (**3768**) and 1975 (**3793**) arguably the rarest of all 20th-century dimes. Partly to avoid similar omissions, beginning in 1985 each year's master die for proofs contains the S mintmark.

The 1964 on clad metal was made in 1965 while both silver and clad-metal dimes were being struck (the former to complete earlier quotas). A few blanks of each type reached the wrong press.

Beginning in 1980, Mint Bureau directives required a P mintmark on all Philadelphia coins above the cent. A furor predictably began in Dec. 1982 when several collectors discovered new dimes without P. The independent discoverers were Walter Placzawkis, Andrew Macdonald, and Lane Durkee: *NNW* 1/29/83, p. 1; *CW* 1/26/83, p. 70. As the coins mostly turned up in rolls of 1982 P dimes in the Sandusky, Ohio, area, ultimately from Mint bags obtained from the Cleveland Federal Reserve branch, the logical presumption is that they were in fact from Philadelphia rather than Denver; San Francisco coined only proof dimes that year. During ensuing months, a total of 8,000–10,000 showed up, traceable to a shipment sent to a Sandusky amusement park. These are all sharp strikes. A Toledo dealer presently holds over 1,700 of them.

In late Aug. 1983, more 1982 no-P dimes turned up in Pittsburgh, to date possibly 5,000. These, unlike the Sandusky group, are mostly weak strikes, largely at lower r. obv. rim, into which the 2 of date blurs. Though they are fewer, they bring only about half the premium of the Sandusky coins. Both kinds are illustrated in *NNW* 10/22/83, p. 3. Because a mintmark could be easily removed, authentication is recommended. The same remark holds about the 1983 without mintmark.

Like the "S-less" proofs, the 1982 dimes without mintmark resulted from an Engraving Department error: Someone forgot to add the P mintmark to a single working die, and nobody caught the error until after some coins had been released.

In recent years Mint Bureau production statistics have become notable for delays and inconsistencies. Mintage figures quoted below are subject to revision.

CLAD ISSUES

Designer, Engraver, as preceding. Mints, Philadelphia (1965–79, no mintmark; 1980–   , mintmark P above date), San Francisco (1968–   , mintmark S above date, proofs only), Denver (1968–   , mintmark D above date). Diameter, 0.705″ = 17.907 mm. Composition, "sandwich metal," pure copper core bonded to outer layers of cupro-nickel (75% copper, 25% nickel). Weight, 35 ± 1.4 grs. = 2.268 ± 0.09 gms. Authorizing Acts, July 23, 1965; Title 31, U.S. Code, §5112.

Grade range, F to UNC.; standards, as before. To date, collected only in UNC. or Proof.

3762   1964 Struck by error. Ex. rare.
      See introductory text. For the converse error (1965 silver) see **3761**.
3763   1965 [1,652,140,570 + 2,360,000 SMS]
      Released beginning 3/8/66. *CWA*, p. 176. SMS = Special Mint Sets, prooflike, struck at San Francisco: See introductory text.
3764   1966 [1,382,734,540 + 2,261,583 SMS]
      Those dated 1966 were struck after 8/1/66.
3765   1967 [2,244,007,320 + 1,863,344 SMS]
      A doubled obv. die exists, plainest on motto and date; Ex. rare.
3766   1968 [424,470,400]
3767   1968 S [3,041,506P] Proofs only.
      See next.

3768 1968 [S] No mintmark. Proof. About 6 known.
Found in proof sets in the Mint Bureau's sealed plastic containers: *CW* 6/26/68. The discovery example reappeared in 1982 ANA:1210, $6,000. Minute spine within loop of 6.
3769 1968 D [480,748,280]
3770 1969 [145,790,000]
3771 1969 S [2,934,631P] Proofs only.
3772 1969 D [563,323,870]
3773 1970 [345,570,000]
3774 1970 Doubled rev. die. Presently rare.
3775 1970 S [2,632,810P] Proofs only.
See next.
3776 1970 [S] No mintmark. Proof. [2,200] Very rare.
Mintage figure included in preceding. Specimens were found in proof sets in the Mint Bureau's sealed plastic containers, Jan. 6, 1971; the Bureau on March 3 confirmed that a single die had produced 2,200 "S-less" coins.
3777 1970 D [754,942,100]
3778 1970 D Doubled rev. die.
2 vars. Discovered by Ed Raser, Dec. 1978.
3779 1971 [162,690,000]
3780 1971 S [3,220,733P] Proofs only.
3781 1971 D [377,914,240]
3782 1972 [431,540,000]
3783 1972 S [3,260,996P] Proofs only.
3784 1972 D [330,290,000]
3785 1973 [315,670,000]
3786 1973 S [2,760,339P] Proofs only.
3787 1973 D [455,032,426]
3788 1974 [470,248,000]
3789 1974 S [2,612,568P] Proofs only.
3790 1974 D [571,083,000]
3791 1975 [585,673,900]
3792 1975 S [2,845,450P] Proofs only.
See next.
3793 1975 [S] No mintmark. Proof. Ex. rare, 2 known.
Discovered in a proof set in the Mint's sealed container. *CW* 2/22/78, p. 1; *NNW* 3/11/78, p. 3. The second example was described in *CW* 7/5/78.
3794 1975 D [313,705,300]
3795 1976 [568,760,000]
3796 1976 S [4,149,730P] Proofs only.
3797 1976 D [695,222,774]
3798 1977 [796,930,000]
3799 1977 S [3,251,152P] Proofs only.
3800 1977 D [376,607,228]
3801 1978 [663,980,000]
3802 1978 S [3,127,781P] Proofs only.
3803 1978 D [282,847,540]
3804 1979 [315,440,000]
3805 1979 S "Type I" S. [2,940,175P] Proofs only.
Filled, blurry, or blobby S.
3806 1979 S "Type II" S. [737,000P] Proofs only.
Clear S. For ills. of both S's see Chap. 31.
3807 1979 D [390,921,184]
3808 1980 P [735,170,000]
See introductory text.
3809 1980 S "Type II" S. [3,554,806P] Proofs only.
May exist with "Type I" S as **3805.**
3810 1980 D [719,354,321]

3811 1981 P New hubs. [676,650,000]
JS smaller, less distinct; rev. higher relief, flame about touches S, its internal divisions gone; larger dots nearer to Latin motto.
3812 1981 S New hubs. "Type I" S. [3,440,083P] Proofs only.
As **3811.** Mintmark as **3805,** worn, shaped like 8. See next.
3813 1981 S New hubs. "Type II" S. [623,000P] Proofs only.
As **3806.** Open S, round serifs free of middle stroke.
3814 1981 D New hubs. [712,284,143]
3815 1982 P [519,475,000]
3816 1982 [P] No mintmark.
See introductory text. Price for sharp strikes (Sandusky group, estimated at 8,000–10,000); flat strikes, with 2 blurring into rim (Pittsburgh group, about 5,000 discovered late Aug. 1983) bring about half as much. See ills. in *NNW* 10/22/83, p. 3. Authentication recommended.

3817 1982 S [3,857,479P] Proofs only.
New S mintmark, with vertical serifs. May exist with "Type II" S as **3813.**
3818 1982 D [542,713,584]
3819 1983 P [647,025,000]
3820 1983 S [3,228,648P] Proofs only.
3821 1983 [S] No mintmark. Proofs only. Presently scarce.
Discovered by Robert J. Lewis, about May 1983. *CW* 7/6/83, p. 1. Found in about 100 proof sets identified to date.
3822 1983 D [730,129,224]
3823 1984 P [856,669,000]
3824 1984 S [3,198,999P] Proofs only.
3825 1984 D [704,803,976]
3826 1985 P [705,200,962]
3827 1985 S Proofs only. [3,348,814P]
3828 1985 D [587,979,970]
3829 1986 P Modified design.
IN WE farther from border, AM CA not touching; sharper device details. Described by Herbert Hicks, *NUM* 2/86.
3830 1986 S Modified design.
Same comments.
3831 1986 D Modified design.
Same comments.
3832–3870 Reserved for future issues.

CHAPTER 26

WILLIAM BARBER'S TWENTY-CENT PIECES (1875–78)

A coin of the denomination of 20 cents, called a "double disme," had been proposed at least as early as 1791, and then reproposed in 1806, actually reaching Congress; but the legislators correctly realized then—as their successors 70 years later did not—that simultaneously issuing coins of such nearly identical value as 20¢ and 25¢ could lead only to confusion. The proposal did not recur until Feb. 1874, when Sen. John Percival Jones (R.-Nev.) introduced a bill to authorize coinage of silver 20¢ pieces.

Charity would call Jones's motives confused; cynicism something else. Minor coins were not then being struck at any branch mint, and only small quantities of dimes and quarters at Carson City. Half dimes (the bulk of small change in the Wild West during the late 1860s and early '70s) began vanishing from circulation after the framers of the 1873 Mint Act abolished the denomination; and many survivors were ending up as jewelry. Storekeepers priced many items at 10¢ to 15¢ apiece; owing to the lack of half dimes or minor coins, people paying with quarter dollars had to accept being shortchanged, receiving a "short bit" (i.e., a dime). Sen. Jones believed, or claimed to believe, that mintage of 20¢ pieces would solve this problem; whereas the obvious, necessary, and sufficient solution was issue of cents and nickels at San Francisco—not to be started until 1908 and 1912, respectively. One suspects that Jones's hidden agenda was to help enrich the owners of western silver mines, who were furiously seeking reparations after the 1873 Mint Act had lowered Mint orders for their output by abolishing trimes, half dimes, and silver dollars. But whatever the Senator's real motives, Mint Director Henry R. Linderman supported the bill, and other legislators went along with it, largely as a favor to Sen. Jones. Pres. Grant signed the bill into law March 3, 1875.

In the meantime, Linderman ordered Philadelphia Mint Superintendent James Pollock to begin obtaining designs and submitting for approval pattern coins of the new denomination. (This could have been done without the metallic samples, but Linderman was a coin collector, and patterns were among his specialties.)

The first of these bore an extravagantly elaborate seated Liberty design by the French-born sculptor Joseph Alexis Bailly; its rev. (large 20 CENTS in wreath) was probably concocted by William Barber. (Barber had succeeded to the Mint engravership on the death of Longacre, Jan. 1, 1869.) Pollock sent Linderman samples on Aug. 7, 1874, commenting that it too closely resembled the quarter dollar, in effect ordering Barber to prepare alternative designs. One of these, a bust long known as the "sailor head," Judd 1392, actually portrayed the young Queen Victoria as Ms. Liberty!

However, Treasury policy as always (prior to 1916) favored uniformity of design within the series of coins of a single metal, so that the design Linderman finally approved, April 12, 1875, proved to be the most confusingly similar to the quarter dollar among all the candidates.

As approved, the prototype (**3871**) copied Barber's eagle from the trade dollar, and his low-relief copy of the old Sully-Gobrecht-Hughes design then common to current silver coins. As a favor to the illiterate, the coin had a plain edge. On April 15, Pollock proposed to "improve" the design by enlarging the word LIBERTY and placing it in relief on the shield scroll, rather than incuse as on all other silver coins. This change made these letters the area of the coin destined to wear most quickly to illegibility. Nothing has been learned about the modification of leaves on rev. of **3872**. Taxay {1966}, pp. 262–63.

Twelve proofs were made of 1875 S, about June 1, 1875. These are from a single pair of dies: horizontal die file marks in shield below BER, spine l. from pole just below little finger; l. pendant of T(S) broken away, as is lower serif of adjacent S; die file mark from leaf point above that T to adjacent S. These dies were later used (retaining initial polish) on business strikes, still later cracking. About six proofs are traced, almost all cleaned or impaired or both; they have unusually broad borders, needle-sharp central drapery and feathers. Authentication of purported proofs is mandatory.

Twenty-cent pieces were coined for circulation in 1875–76 only, and for proof sets 1875–78 inclusive. Public confusion between them and quarter dollars was immediate and universal, and the coins were extremely unpopular. They had no effect whatever on the "short bit" problem; overcharging continued without hindrance as always. A bill to repeal the Mint's authority to manufacture these coins was introduced in July 1876, finally becoming law May 2, 1878. Coins on hand in all mints had to be melted down, by order of Mint Director Linderman, May 1, 1878, for recoinage into other denominations.

Actually, Linderman had authorized melting of the CC stock of 12,359 coins (amount on hand March 1, 1877) effective March 19, 1877. This created a rarity: Possibly 18 survive of 1876 CC, some of them impounded in estates. All genuine 1876 CC's show doubling on LIBERTY, which is not true of the forgeries created by adding mintmarks to 1876 Philadelphia coins, or by joining split halves (obv. 1876 Philadelphia, rev. 1875 CC). The earliest auction records were Davis:1506 (1890) and Frossard 168:324 (Dec. 10, 1900). Pedigree history of the survivors follows; all are UNCIRCULATED unless otherwise noted.

    1. F. C. C. Boyd, WGC:487, Kern:1642, Hydeman:405, Joe Flynn, Armand Champa, Winget, Tebo, 1975 ANA:349, $45,000, QS 11/76:349, $63,500, Arnold/Romisa:2211, $44,000, Reed Hawn, Auction 85:1653, $52,500 to the book. Rim nick below end of rock. Ill. **3878.**

    2. Knapp:145, Neil:1194, Pelletreau:661, Wolfson:771, Miles:874, C. W. Henderson:439, $39,500, Jack Spivack and Jules Karp, Auction 80:110, $85,000, Auction 83:625, $66,000, AU, nick on lower upright of I(CA).

    3. John H. Clapp, Eliasberg estate.

    4. Atwater:884. Nick below r. wing.

    5. Col. E. H. R. Green, J. V. McDermott, James Kelly, Guggenheimer:779.

    6. Menjou:662. Possibly same as no. 4?

    7. Stoddard, Col. Green, Shuford:813, $6,350. Harshly cleaned.

    8. G. H. Hall:802, "VF." Possibly later C. H. Deetz:1512 (1946).

    9. B. Frank:622, E. A. Carson, Willing:72, Auction 82:707, $25,000, VF, banged up. Not the same as no. 8.

    10. George H. Smoots, Mehl 2/23/32:548, VG. Not seen; supposedly cherrypicked in Nevada.

    11. Kreisberg/Schulman 5/20/66:1166, $12,750. Possibly same as one of nos. 4, 5, 6 above, or as next.

    12. Maryland estate, Bowers, C. A. Cass, "Empire":995, A. Buol Hinman, "Century":831.

    13. Maryland estate, Bowers, 1977 ANA:1143 in set.

    14. Maryland estate, Bowers, 1959 ANA:2026.

    15. Maryland estate, Bowers, CSNA 10/27–30/60:927. Rub above eagle's head and neck.

    16. Frossard 168:324 (12/10/1900), $28, S. Benton Emery, Emery & Nichols:492, $66,000.

At least two others reported. The Maryland estate (1957) reportedly contained 10 in all, of which I examined four; if so, this source may account for no. 11, and there may be four or five others. That in 1983 ANA:2229 came with an incorrect pedigree identifying it as no. 2; it is not positively identified, nor is one reportedly ex R. L. Hughes, "Pacific":659, $35,500, nor is the Gene Henry, Ken Goldman coin in B&R FPLs 1976–77. Part of the difficulty is that many of the UNCs. look so much alike that auction catalog illustrations will not distinguish them.

Of the total production for circulation [1,351,540], some 390,220 were officially melted 1895–1954, most of all in 1933.

WILLIAM BARBER'S TWENTY-CENT PIECES

Designer, Engraver, William Barber, obv. after Hughes, after Gobrecht, after Sully. Mints, Philadelphia (no mintmark), San Francisco (1875, S below eagle), Carson City (1875–76, CC below eagle). Diameter, 7/8″ = 22 mm. Plain edge. Weight standard, 77.16 ± 1.5 grs. = 5 ± 0.097 gms. Composition, silver 0.900, copper 0.100.

Grade range, POOR to UNC. GOOD: Date and all letters legible except LIBERTY. VERY GOOD: Shield outline plain, few drapery lines, L Y visible. FINE: Partial drapery and feather details, three or parts of four letters in LIBERTY legible. VERY FINE: Full LIBERTY (some letters not as strong as rest), over half

drapery and feather details. EXTREMELY FINE: Few tiny isolated rubbed spots; LIBERTY completely bold.

3871 1875 Prototype. Small date. Proofs only. Very rare.
    Judd 1411. LIBERTY incuse; leaves about NT overlap. Design approved April 12, 1875. Specimens have been retrieved from original proof sets of the year. May exist with rev. of next. Enl. photos.

3872 1875 Regular issue, large date. [38,500 + 2,790P]
    Leaves above NT do not overlap. Design modification approved April 15. Mintage began May 19: San Francisco *Examiner,* 5/20/1875, p. 2. Proofs may exist with rev. of preceding. Enl. photos.

3873 1875 S [1,155,000 + 12P] Filled S.
    Mintage began between June 1 and 17. For proofs, see introductory text.

3874 1875 S Clear S. Scarce.

3875 1875 S "$ variety." Very scarce.
    Obvious extra serifs at top and bottom of S simulating ends of vertical line in $. Mintmark first entered leaning crazily to l., then corrected. NN 57:583.

3876 1875 CC [133,290 −]
    Mintage began June 1, 1875: San Francisco *Evening Bulletin,* 6/4/1875, p. 3. Minor positional vars. of date and CC, one with traces of repunching on 5; 1982 ANA:2119. Often flat in centers and/or on upper wings. The 12,359 ordered melted March 19, 1877, contained some 1875 CC's as well as most of the 1876 CC mintage.

3877 1876 [14,750 + 1,260P]
    2 pairs of dies for business strikes, others for proofs. One of the 2 production revs. has hollows in wings, defect joining wingtip to (T)S, and minor doubling on STAT; the other lacks these. No information yet as to which is scarcer.

3878   1876 CC [10,000 —] Very rare, 16–18 known.
Double LIBERTY; only the one pair of dies used among 6
obvs. and 4 revs. shipped (destroyed 1/20/77). See introductory text.

3879   1877 [510 —] Proofs only.
2 pairs of dies, only one used, second rev. held for 1878.
Many melted.

3880   1878 [600 —] Proofs only.
Of 760 struck, only 600 sold, rest melted. Many survivors are
impaired.

CHAPTER 27

QUARTER DOLLARS

i. THE SCOT-ECKSTEIN DRAPED BUST/SMALL EAGLE (1796)

The story behind this ephemeral design goes back to summer 1795. The new Mint Director, Henry William DeSaussure (David Rittenhouse's successor for a few months) defined his two principal ambitions on taking office: first, placing gold into circulation; second, improving all current coin designs (a slap at Scot's flowing-hair concept as seen on all federal silver and copper then circulating). To implement the second of these, DeSaussure persuaded the illustrious portraitist Gilbert Stuart to prepare a portrait of Ms. Liberty. Stuart chose as his model Mrs. William Bingham, née Ann Willing, of Newport, R:I., and his sketch went to the Mint about Aug. 1795: Snowden {1861}, p. 177. During the last couple of weeks in October, silver dollars were issued bearing the new design, which must have lost a great deal in translation; that fall, device punches were completed for all the smaller silver denominations. Stuart must have been gravely disappointed with the coins; their unsatisfactory aesthetic quality surely accounted for suppression of the story of his connection with the Mint. Aside from Snowden's footnote, we hear no more of it until April 1887 (*AJN* 21, p. 95). Stuart's dissatisfaction can be blamed partly on Robert Scot, the bank-note-plate artist who obtained the Mint engravership without knowing how to sink a die or make a device punch, and partly on his temporary assistant, John Eckstein, who was hired to make "models" (device punches?) for the new Draped Bust designs.

Eckstein is credited (if that is the proper word) with the design of the small eagle on its cloud-shaped cushions, within that oversized wreath of olive and palm branches. In 1795, this wreath was understood as a compliment to DeSaussure's southern homeland; by 1796, when his successor Elias Boudinot ordered manufacture of quarter dollars of this design, it was already an anachronism.

As both obv. dies contained only 15 stars, they must have been completed before anyone realized that Tennessee would most likely join the Union as the sixteenth state; but many of the impressions struck from them followed Tennessee's admission, June 1, 1796.

In all, only 6,146 were coined, in four batches, from two obv. dies and a single rev.:

April 9, 1796	1,800
May 27	2,530
June 14	1,564
Feb. 28, 1797	252

Many of these were saved as first of their kind. When Col. E. H. R. Green inherited his mother's millions, he became a collector of (among other things) railroad cars, pornographic films, and coins; and among his immense numismatic holdings was a hoard of over 200 uncirculated 1796 quarter dollars, of which at least 100 were more or less prooflike—their fields more mirrorlike than on the others. A. Kosoff and Andre DeCoppet dispersed many of these to date and type collectors during the 1940s. Decades of publicity about the alleged rarity of this single-year type coin managed to push prices into the five-figure level.

Over 90% of specimens from the Col. Green hoard are High 6 coins, weak at eagle's head. This weakness has been dubiously attributed to die wear, but a simpler explanation is that a design flaw placed the part of Ms. Liberty's shoulder in highest relief directly opposite eagle's head and top of palm branch, leaving insufficient metal to fill all these details at a single blow from the dies. One obv. die broke, but the rev. remained intact, so that there is still a certain amount of doubt which of the two vars. came first, and therefore whether the very rare Low 6 coins belong among the initial 1,800 or the 252 of Feb. 1797—or whether the latter are the still rarer broken-die examples of the High 6.

Presentation strikings exist from both obvs. in earliest states, suggesting several occasions some months apart. Low 6: 1) Eliasberg estate; 2) Ex Allenburger coll. High 6: 1) Ten Eyck, Holmes, Cornell-Oglethorpe:824, $27,000; 2) Newcomer, Green, MacAllister, Clarke, NN 47:1557 (Breen {1977}, p. 34). Eagles' heads on presentation strikings of both vars. are stronger than usual; all fields are unusually prooflike, without adjustment marks (file marks on planchets before striking, to reduce weights to legal limits).

Dangerous cast counterfeits exist of the Low 6, first identified at the 1982 ANA Convention. These are all (to date) from a worn example, identifiable at long range by sharing the identical field scratches before face, nick just l. of twelfth star (counting clockwise from lower l.), rev. nick above ER and on final A (ANACS {1983}, pp. 88–89).

Browning numbers, used for all quarter-dollar vars. from 1796 through 1838 Capped Bust, derive from Browning {1925}, originally in an edition of only 50 copies, with eight photographic plates (contact prints). About 1950, John J. Ford, Jr., retrieved the original negatives and issued a second limited printing, using unissued copies of the original printed text with new contact prints; these plates are on far heavier, stiffer paper than the originals, and of higher photographic quality. Various later photo-offset reprints are of lower quality. I summarized ensuing researches in Breen {1954A}, but these notations are obsolete. Duphorne's recent pamphlet lists the original Browning vars. in serial order, unaccountably relegating the half dozen new discoveries to an appendix rather than integrating them with the text. George Frederick Kolbe plans to issue a revised version of Browning, with additional notes by me and other specialists. Listings in sections to follow have been reconciled with the manuscript of this last.

THE SCOT-ECKSTEIN DRAPED BUST/ SMALL EAGLE

Designers, Robert Scot, John Eckstein, after Gilbert Stuart. Engravers, Scot, John Smith Gardner. Mint, Philadelphia. Diameter, approx. $1^{1}/12'' = 27.5$ mm. Reeded edge. Composition, silver $0.89243+ = 1,485/1,664$, remainder copper. Weight standard, 104 grs. = 6.74 gms. Authorizing Act, April 2, 1792.

Grade range, POOR to UNC. GOOD: Date and all letters legible. VERY GOOD: Deepest drapery folds show; partial details of curls, hair, and feathers. FINE: All drapery folds show. VERY FINE: Over half hair and feather details except at eagle's breast and knees; only l. side of drapery is indistinct. EXTREMELY FINE: Few tiny isolated rubbed spots only. EXCEPTION: Eagle's breast, leg feathers, and, usually, also his head will be flat even on uncirculated specimens. Compare ills.; see introductory text. NOTE: Many show adjustment marks, generally in fields running into borders (file marks on blanks before striking, to reduce weight to legal limits).

3881   1796 [6,146] Low 6. Very rare.
Browning 1; Hilt 2A. Curl point under center of B. Sometimes with eagle's head clear. Possibly 22–25 known, of which 2 are presentation strikings, about 6 UNCs., 8 EF. Cast counterfeits exist: See introductory text. Enl. photos (presentation striking).

3882   1796 High 6. Scarce.
Browning 2; Hilt 1A. Curl point under curve of B. Eagle's head flat except on presentation pieces. Mint-state survivors often have prooflike surfaces, from the Col. Green hoard. Many are on planchets showing splits or chips at edges. The coins with shattered obv. die (the 252 of Feb. 1797?) are Ex. rare, possibly 4 or 5 known; discovery coin (ill.) was in a Glendining & Co. sale, March 1935.

ii. SCOT'S HERALDIC DESIGN (1804–7)

In 1796 Scot concocted a new rev. for the quarter eagles, possibly for presentation pieces in connection with Tennessee's admission to the Union. This new device punch copied the Great Seal of the United States, though with the heraldic solecism (or tasteless saber rattling) of placing the warlike arrows in the eagle's dexter claw, relegating the olive branch of peace to the sinister or less honorable side. Compare Chap. 24, Sect. iii, introductory text. In line with standard Mint practice of the day (probably a policy established by the first Director, David Rittenhouse), each new design had to be extended to all other denominations in the same metal. By 1804, Scot finally made a rev. device punch of this type for the quarter dollars, and it remained in use through 1807. Letters, numerals, extra arrowheads, stars, and berries had to be added by hand to each of the 14 working obvs. and 12 revs. Most of the 19 die combinations are rare; in choice mint state, any var. of this design is less often offered than the 1796.

Two vars. exist of 1804, from two obvs. combined with a single rev. The less rare (Browning 1, Hilt 3B) has low 4 in date, with die cut between eighth and ninth stars, visible even on FAIR specimens; only seven UNCs. survive, and prices on the best ones have far surpassed those of 1796. The other var. (Browning 2, Hilt 4B) has date spaced 18 04 with 4 almost touching bust, but no die cut between stars; bases of BE are much closer together. About nine or 10 survive of this one, mostly in low grades.

Of the five 1805 vars., one is common, one scarce, the other three of great rarity. It will be convenient to list them:

Browning 1. 5 leans l., first star less than its own diameter from curl; rev. of 1804, wings touching D and almost touching F. Possibly 15 survive.

Breen 5. Same obv.; long stem nearly touches C, which joins tail; wing touches D, other wing farther from F. Two traced, a third reported: Bergen:9; Harte III:1062.

Browning 2. 5 leans l., much too close to 0, R weak; rev., wide space between dentils above E(S). Scarce. Obv. die discarded by the Mint as junk (1816 or 1833), retrieved by Joseph J. Mickley, and in the 1850s or later (rusted and broken at rims) it was muled with a rusted revenue stamp die **(1376)** showing eagle on shield. Of this concoction two copper strikings are known, probably made for Dr. Montroville Wilson Dickeson, who owned the revenue stamp die.

Browning 3. 5 leans r., I has r. foot broken away; rev. of Browning 2. Common.

Browning 4. Low 1; four berries on branch. Possibly eight to 12 known, mostly in low grades. Its rev. was reused in 1806–7; its obv. was softened at year's end by annealing, and overdated to 1806/5. This was contrary to usual Mint practice, and represents the same emergency as the similar 1806/5 half dollars and quarter eagles from previously used 1805 dies: The Engraving Dept. was running out of die steel.

A similar roster of the 10 1806-dated vars. follows.

Browning 1. 1806/5. Feet broken off I T. Rev. as 1805 Browning 4. Common. **(3886)**

Browning 2. Normal date henceforth. Feet broken off I T, 0 6 apart; C of 25 C. touches final A. Very scarce. **(3887)**

Browning 3. Same obv.; 5 free of tail and arrows, long spine from lowest r. leaf to tail of R. Common. **(3887)**

Browning 4. Normal I T; same rev. Scarce. **(3888)**

Browning 5. First star nearly twice its own diameter from curl; die scratch from rim to second feather on l. wing. Very rare. **(3888)** Its obv. die was also resold as junk by the Mint; a single copper striking mules it with an unlisted 1807 (?) large fraction cent rev. David Henderson, ex Empire Topics 3, MBS 11/26/58:83.

Browning 6. Bases of RT nearly touch, T lower; same rev. Rare. **(3888)**

Breen 10. Same obv.; arrows extend nearly to r. side of N (instead of center as on last two), no die scratch to l. wing. Die buckles at branch. Possibly five or six known. **(3888)** Discovery coin (unrecognized), Stickney coll.

Browning 7. Same obv.; branch touches center of top of C. Rare. Usually in low grades. **(3888)**

Browning 8. Same obv.; C crowds feathers to l., its r. top touches branch, its lower l. curve showing part of an erroneous A. Very rare. Usually in low grades. **(3889)**

Browning 9. Stars exceptionally far from L Y, branch far from C. Common. Usually, obv. die reground, removing parts of lowest curls. Comprises a large part of the 1807 deliveries. **(3888)**

The two 1807 vars. represent a change of type. Browning 1 has small date and stars with the old 1805 Four Berries rev.; Browning 2 has large date and stars with a five-berry rev., and is much rarer. Probably over half the reported mintage was dated 1806. No more would be coined until 1815.

SCOT'S HERALDIC DESIGN

Designer, Engraver, Robert Scot, obv. after Stuart, rev. after the Great Seal. Mint, Philadelphia. Physical Specifications, Authorizing Acts, as before.

Grade range and standards, as before, except that remarks about eagle's head and knees do not apply. EXCEPTIONS: Usually weak at clouds below ES and at adjacent stars, even in mint state.

3883   1804 [6,738]
2 obv. vars. Price for Browning 1 (ill.); the other is very rare: See introductory text. That ill. falls slightly short of mint state.

3884   1805 Five berries. [121,394]
4 vars.; see introductory text. Price for Browning 2 (ill.) or 3, with gap between dentils above E(S); other vars. are very rare.

3885   1805 Four berries. Very rare.
Browning 4. Usually in low grades. Dies altered at Mint to make next. See introductory text.

3886   1806/5 [All kinds 286,424+]
Browning 1. Same dies as last. Many coins of this date were delivered in 1807.

3887   1806 Normal date, defective I T obv.
Browning 2, 3. Price for latter (5 free of tail). Same broken I and T punches on obv. as **3886**. See introductory text.

3888   1806 Normal I T; normal C.
6 vars. Price for Browning 4, 7, or 9 (see introductory text); others are all rarer.

3889   1806 C of 25 C. corrected from A. Very rare.
Browning 8. Always in low grades. See introductory text.
3890   1807 [140,343−] Large date and stars, 5 berries. Scarce.
Browning 2. Tall 1 missing l. base.

3891 1807 Small date and stars, 4 berries.

Browning 1. Short 1 with normal base. Edge reeding sometimes weak. Enl. photos.

iii. REICH'S CAPPED BUSTS, WITH MOTTO (1815–28)

John Reich was a German engraver who sold himself into
indentured service to reach the USA during the Napoleonic
wars. As early as 1801 he sought a post in the Philadelphia
Mint, but Chief Engraver Robert Scot was unwilling to tolerate
any outsiders, presumably fearing replacement. However, by
1807 Scot's age and health (probably eyesight) were already a
source of enough official concern that the Mint authorities began looking for assistant engravers. On April 1, 1807, they
hired Reich, at $600 per year (even then a pittance for so de-
manding a job). Reich's first assignment was indeed a slap at
Scot: He was to redesign all denominations.

Reich's new conception for the silver coins was an uncom-
monly buxom effigy of Ms. Liberty, wearing a mobcap inscribed
with her name. (This was for generations misnamed a turban by
people who never saw a real one; and even from the beginning it
was taken to represent the *pilleus* or Phrygian liberty cap,
whereas Reich actually intended it as a fashionable headdress,
somewhat like that on some portraits of Martha Washington.)
Contemporaneous newspaper scurrility attacked the device as
portraying "the artist's fat mistress." Reich placed it first on
half dollars and half eagles, fall 1807; then quarter eagles
(1808), dismes (1809), and finally quarter dollars, the next time
banks ordered them (1815). Sporadic mintages of this denomination reflect public preference for Spanish and Mexican 2-real
coins, which were legal tender at par though lighter in weight;
heavier federal quarters tended to be hoarded, finally many being melted in 1853.

Mintage figure for this date includes 20,003 delivered Jan. 10,
1816, from the 1815-dated dies. The small quantity is from bullion scarcity during the War of 1812. Less than 12 hours after
this 1816 delivery, a fire broke out in one of the Mint's outbuildings, ruining the rolling mills and blank cutters so that no
more gold or silver could be coined until extensive repairs were
complete (late 1817). Most of the 1815-dated coins went to
Bailly Blanchard, Cashier, Planters' Bank of New Orleans.

Many specimens dated 1815, and a far smaller number dated
1825 (but, oddly, no intervening dates), show a small counterstamped E above head; about 1/10 that number show instead an
L. Either counterstamp is always in the same spot and from the
same punch. Survivors of both dates with E or L are usually in
EF to UNC. (Similar specimens with an R have been reported,
many years ago, but I have not located one for study.) Ever
since these were first noticed, in the 1870s, collectors suspected
them to have official origin, reflecting some kind of experiment;
but no Archives records mention anything so interpretable.
Some have speculated that the E and L mean respectively Excess and Light; but countermarked specimens of both dates
have proved to be of normal weight. I conjectured in 1982 that
these coins were school prizes, E = English, L = Latin, which

would account for the high grade of survivors: They were kept
with other prizes, not spent.

Letter punches before 1824 were by Henry Starr; later ones
by Christian Gobrecht.

One of the 1818 obvs., Browning 2 (crack in field above cap
through three upper r. stars), was among dies sold as scrap
metal in 1833. In 1862, someone combined it with an 1818 cent
rev. (Newcomb 10), making a unique overstrike on an 1860
quarter dollar; this is listed as Judd 45. It was successively in
the John K. Wiggin, Parmelee, Woodin, Brenner, Clarke, and
Welch collections. It sold privately at $4,400 (1981).

Both 1819's with small 9 have colon after 25 C: instead of
period. That with uneven date (spaced 1 819) is very rare, because the obv. broke at date and probably lasted only a few
hours in press.

The 1822 was blundered rev. (25 over 50) is very rare, not
because of die failure, but because this die was laid aside in
horror as soon as impressions were examined. It was briefly
resurrected in 1828, when the new Mint Engraver William
Kneass could blame it on his late predecessor, and excuse its
exhumation on grounds of economy.

Coinage reported for 1823 appears to have consisted largely
of 1822's and possibly earlier dates. The 1823/22 obv. die
cracked at once. Beware altered dates; all genuine 1823/22
quarters have incomplete arrows as illustrated.

The following survivors are traced:

1. J. N. T. Levick, William Fewsmith, pvt. colls., B. G.
Johnson, Elmer Sears, Waldo Newcomer, Morgenthau 305:109
(1933), A. J. Allen, Morgenthau 418:599 (1940), G. H. Hall,
Clinton Hester, Jerome Kern:1407, F. S. Guggenheimer:334,
R. L. Miles:893, Speir estate sale:16, $44,000, Reed Hawn:272,
$32,000, Auction 80:1176, $87,500, Auction 86:127, $46,200,
Proof.

2. B. G. Johnson, Virgil Brand, C. David Pierce, 1947
ANA:914, Edgar Levy:16. AU, scratch joins second and third
stars.

3. "Dupont":1798. EF, obv. field dig.

4. B. G. Johnson, F. C. C. Boyd, WGC:72, Louis Eliasberg
estate. ABOUT EF.

5. Atwater:674, Grant Pierce:608, B&R FPL 8/65, $4,750,
1976 ANA:956, $16,000, Pullen & Hanks sale, Long Beach 2/
82:380. VF+, prooflike. Faint die crack, rim to hair r. of 3.

6. Parmelee:947, H. O. Granberg, W. H. Woodin, Col.
E. H. R. Green, Charles M. Williams, Menjou:690,
Baldenhofer:400. VF. Ill. ANS {1914}; Browning {1925}, Pl.
IV.

7. J. Colvin Randall, Garrett:637, $13,500, Pullen & Hanks
2/5–6/82:380, $14,000. F.

8. Neil:892. F. Heavy die crack, rim to hair r. of 3, to near
center dot.

9. Allenburger:800, Jerome Kern:1408, J. A. Stack:22.
VG–F.

10. French's 2/58, NN 54:1407, Bergen:52, $6,000, VG.

11. Frossard 4/26/1900, NN 49:1147, R. Picker, pvt. coll.
ABOUT VG.

12. Atwater:675, B. Frank:640, B&R RCR's 11–16 (1971–
72), 1978 ANA:719. ABOUT VG, deep nick r. of first star.

13. J. H. Clapp, Eliasberg, "H. R. Lee":386, NN 49:1148,
1970 ANA:665. G–VG, rim nick at second arrowhead.

Six others are known in still lower grades.

Rarity of quarters dated 1827 remains unexplained. Possibly
12 survive from the original dies, all proofs or former proofs;
the reported mintage of 4,000 business strikes is likely to have
consisted mostly or wholly of coins dated 1825. Joseph J.
Mickley (1799–1878), "Father of American Coin Collecting,"
obtained four proofs from the Philadelphia Mint in late 1827 as

change for a dollar (probably Spanish or Mexican); for decades these were the only ones known. In 1858–59 workmen in collusion with Theodore Eckfeldt (the Mint's night watchman and fence) retrieved the 1827 obv. from the Coiner's vault and surreptitiously made about a dozen silver restrikes and possibly five copper ones, using a rusted and cracked 1819 rev. with flat base to 2. At least three early silver restrikes are overstruck on other old quarters (one dated 1806); others, with dies more rusty, show no trace of undertype, representing a second batch. No specimen of this latter group has been made available for weighing to ascertain if it was on a current quarter-dollar planchet (96 grs. = 6.22 gms.) rather than on a broader blank specially cut; nor is it known how many survive of each: Photographic ills. are no help. Mint Director James Ross Snowden ended these operations July 30, 1860, seizing all the old dies and sealing them in a carton in his own vault.

The roster of surviving 1827 original quarters is corrected and extended from Breen {1977}.

1. Adam Eckfeldt, Coiner, Mint Cabinet, SI. Cleaned.

2. Mint, J. J. Mickley, Rev. Joseph Finotti, George F. Seavey (1873):41, Lorin G. Parmelee:975, Col. E. H. R. Green, Burdette G. Johnson, James Aloysius Stack estate:29, $50,000, San Diego specialist. Ill. Browning {1925}, Pl. V.

3. Mint, J. J. Mickley, J. F. McCoy:508, Jeremiah Colburn, Heman Ely:244, T. Harrison Garrett, John Work Garrett:641, $190,000.

4. Mint, J. J. Mickley, G. F. Seavey (1863):226, J. N. T. Levick, Woodward 10/1864:437, F. S. Edwards:1202 (1866), Lewis White:177 (1876), R. Coulton Davis:1425, Charles M. Williams, Adolphe Menjou, King Farouk, N.Y. State pvt. coll. Discolored, probably cleaned, like many of Farouk's coins.

5. Mint, J. J. Mickley, Mickley:1706, Reichardt family, J. P. Reakirt, Mrs. R. Henry Norweb (ill.).

6. G. W. Massamore, Thomas Cleneay:1339, John G. Mills:999, W. B. Wetmore:396, Waldo Newcomer, A. J. Allen, George H. Hall, Clinton Hester, Jerome Kern:1412, Wayte Raymond, NN 49:1149, D.N., TAD, 1976 ANA, Auction 80:1177, $70,000, Marcus Johnson Brown:2981 (misidentified as 3 above), $64,900, pvt. coll.

7. H. O. Granberg, William H. Woodin, Rev. Wm. H. Owen, Yale Univ., unidentified thieves.

8. F. C. C. Boyd, WGC:89, W. W. Neil:897, F. S. Guggenheimer:539, R. L. Miles:898, Speir sale:20, $40,000, R. Hughes, 1977 ANA:1175, Auction 79:581, $45,000.

9. Alvárez, QS 9/73:670, $28,000, Reed Hawn:275, $27,000, Robison:1284, $26,000. Rim nick upper obv.

10. Found in circulation in Hudson, Mich., 1893; Nicholas Petry sale, John H. Clapp, Eliasberg estate. VF.

The 1827 restrikes are more difficult to distinguish by ills. in coin auctions.

The following roster includes all traceable survivors; all are proofs or prooflike.

1. F. C. C. Boyd. WGC:90. Vertical field scratch r. of second star.

2. Ten Eyck:521, Newcomer, Col. E. H. R. Green, A. Buol Hinman, "Century":855, B&R RCR's 19–25 (1974–77). Ill. Browning {1925}, Pl. VIII.

3. Menjou:697, Edgar Levy:20.

4. "Dupont":1803, Baldenhofer:403, Gene Sanders, Rob Kolesar, Mal Varner, John Dannreuther, Auction 85:677, $20,900. Discoloration before nose. Border nick over final A. 101 grs. = 6.6 gms.

5. Atwater:679, Grant Pierce:612, KS 4/67:1321, Jay:180, Delp:56, Reed Hawn:274, Robison:1285.

6. Charles A. Cass, "Empire":1026.

7. B. Frank:643, Wolfson:789.

8. Miles:899, S 9/75:182, $13,000, 1978 ANA:722, $10,250. Cleaned, most proof surface gone.

9. Neil:898, J. A. Stack:30, San Diego specialist. Early state, overstruck on an early quarter.

10. J. H. Clapp, Eliasberg estate. Early state, overstruck on an 1806 quarter.

11. Bowers Review 2 (3/61), Empire Review 19 (4/64). Broad border at l. rev.

12. Kensington:1213, $18,000.

Allenburger:834 is untraceable (ill. is erroneously repeated from Atwater:679) but is probably one of nos. 4, 6, 7, 8, or 11. Atwater:680 (not ill.) is thought to be another of those five.

The date 1828 is marked by reuse of the old 1822 blundered rev.; it represents the last appearance of the motto E PLURIBUS UNUM on this denomination prior to 1892.

The Mint's new close collar was not to be used on this denomination until 1831: See next section.

REICH'S CAPPED BUSTS, WITH MOTTO

Designer, John Reich. Engravers, Scot and Reich. Mint, Philadelphia. Composition, Physical Specifications, Authorizing Acts, as before, except Diameter 17/16" = 27 mm.

Grade range, POOR to UNC. GOOD: Date, letters all legible except for LIBERTY and E PLURIBUS UNUM. VERY GOOD: Full LIBERTY, partial motto; some hair, drapery, and feather details; rim well defined. FINE: Shoulder clasp distinct. VERY FINE: Ear details sharp. EXTREMELY FINE: Complete hair and feather details, isolated tiny rubbed spots only. NOTE: To qualify as UNCIRCULATED, specimens must not show any trace of rubbing on hair just above eye or ear, or just below Y.

3892 1815 [89,235]
Mintage figure includes [20,003] of Jan. 10, 1816, from 1815 dies; these may be the coins with heavy clash marks. Many offered as "UNC." fall short of the grade because of rubbing on hair above eye. For those with E or L counterstamp above cap, see introductory text.

Ex J. W. Garrett: 628. Courtesy Bowers & Ruddy Galleries, Inc.

3893 1818/5 [361,174+] Overdate; large 5, broad dentils. Browning 1. Mintage figure includes also normal-date coins; others were included in 1819 deliveries. Top stroke of 5 plain within upper loop of 8. Rev. dentils broader than on any to follow. Compare next.

3894 1818/5 Rev. Small 5, narrow dentils. Ex. rare. Top stroke of 5 plain within upper loop of 8, as last; revs. of Browning 3 and 6. See next.

3895   1818 Normal date, broad obv. dentils, narrow rev. dentils.
Browning 3, 8 (ill.), 9, 10. First from the overdate die relapped so that 5 no longer shows within 8. Others have 3 dentils squeezed below date. The ill. is of the unique proof.

3896   1818 Narrow dentils both sides.
Browning 2, 4, 5, 6, 7. Price for first, with long crack in field above cap extending through 3 upper r. stars; others are rarer.

3897   1819 [144,000−] Small 9, colon after 25 C:
Browning 3. Mintage report includes many dated 1818.

3898   1819 Same, irregular date. Very rare.
Browning 4. Date spaced 1 819. Two cracks through date rapidly worsen. Dies generally misaligned (rotated about 45°). Usually in low grades.

3899   1819 Large 9, period after 25 C. Scarce.
Browning 1, 2. Modern 5, unlike preceding. Usually in low grades.

3900   1820 [127,444] Large date, large 0, normal 1.
Browning 3. Base of 2 in date heavy. Normally cracked through date and l. stars.

3901   1820 Large 0, long peak to 1.
Browning 1, 2. This long serif is also found on some cents of the year. Possibly 6 proofs survive from both revs. Usually in low grades.

3902   1820 Small date, small o.
Price for Browning 4 (ill.), rust pits between leaf and 2. At least one "one-sided" proof known (obv. mirror field, rev. frosty field). The other var. (not in Browning) has the same obv. with another rev., leaf l. of 2 joined to border; discovered by this writer in 1951, this remains very rare. Both vars. were struck in 1821.

3903   1821 [216,851+ + ?P]
5 minor vars.; possibly 16 proofs. Mintage includes many dated 1820.

3904   1822 [64,080+ + ?P] Normal 25 C.
Browning 1. Possibly 6–8 proofs.

3905   1822 Blundered rev., 25 over 50. Very rare.
Browning 2. Usually in low grades. Possibly 6 proofs (ill.), of which 4 were in the Brand estate.

3906   1823/2 [17,800− + ?P] Very rare, 18–20 known.
Most of the reported mintage must have been dated 1822, possibly some 1821. Usually in low grades. Only the one var.; note incomplete arrows. Fraudulently altered dates will not have this feature. For the roster of survivors see introductory text.

3907   1824/2 [24,000? + ?P]
Only one var.; 2 within and around 4 fades out. Usually in low grades; Ex. rare UNC. The unique proof is from the J. W. Haseltine, R. Coulton Davis colls. Auction 86:128, $11,000. Mintage figure is the initial delivery, Dec. 1825.

3908 1825/2 [144,000— + ?P] Very rare.

Browning 1. Wide date, unlike next; rev. of last (elongated barb on lowest arrow). Usually in low grades. Mint report [168,000] is thought to include the 1824's, as above.

3909 1825/3 Close date; rev. small 5.

Browning 2. Date originally 1825/4/3; both 4 and 3 show only on earliest strikings. With this rev., the 3 is usually plainer. 6–8 proofs known. Found with the same E and L counterstamps as 1815: See introductory text.

3910 1825/4 Same obv.; rev. large 5.

Browning 3. Obv. (date originally 1825/4/3) reground, revealing traces of 4 and weaker traces of 3. First publicized as "1825/4" by W. Elliot Woodward, July 1884 ("European" coll.). Found, rarely, with the same E and L counterstamps as preceding: See introductory text.

3911 1827/3 Original. [4,000? + ?P] Proofs only traced. Ex. rare.

Browning 1. Curved base to rev. 2, rev. of 1828: Compare next. For roster of survivors see introductory text.

3912 1827/3 Restrike. Proofs only. About 12 known.

Browning 2. Flat base to 2, rev. of 1819. Early strikings with minimal obv. die rust are overstruck on older quarters; later impressions show no traces of undertypes. For roster of survivors see introductory text.

3913 1828 [102,000 + ?P] Normal.

Browning 1, 2, 4. At least a dozen proofs. Auction 86:1090, Proof, $14,300.

3914 1828 Rev. 25 over 50. Rare.

Browning 3. Rev. of **3905**. Usually in low grades.

iv. KNEASS'S CAPPED BUSTS, NO MOTTO (1831–38)

Mint Director Samuel Moore triumphantly laid the cornerstone of the new Mint building ("Second Mint," Juniper and Chestnut Sts.) on July 4, 1829, though not all machinery was to be installed for another 3½ years. On the same day, Moore notified Treasury Secretary Levi Woodbury that coinage of half dismes had begun, embodying several mechanical improvements which he proposed to extend to all other denominations as soon as possible. Notable among these were wide, raised protective rims around a beaded border, and a "close collar" (called by Eric Newman and others a "collar die"), which confined planchets at striking, simultaneously reeding edges of gold and silver pieces, and imparting what Moore called "a mathematical equality" to their diameters. This improvement was extended at once to dismes, quarter eagles, and half eagles, but it was not to reach other denominations for some years; on quarter dollars the next opportunity was in 1831.

For the new issues, Moore ordered Scot's successor in the engravership, William Kneass, to improve the designs, omitting the motto E PLURIBUS UNUM, 'One made up of many,' as redundant, expressing nothing more than the phrase UNITED STATES. The Treasury Department attempted to force its restoration, but Moore traveled to Washington, D.C., to justify his action, and the new coins remained without the motto until 1892, when it was restored as part of Barber's copy of the Great Seal on the new design.

Kneass kept the basic Reich composition, but imparted an unaccustomed slickness to the devices, aside from omitting the motto. His first rev. die of the new type (Browning 1) shows two berries on branch, added by hand in imitation of those on the dismes and half dismes of 1829, but omitted on all later dies. The last vars. dated 1831 have large date (tall 1's punched over short 1's), and were almost certainly struck in 1832.

A new rev. device punch occurs in 1833, but was promptly abandoned. Many survivors from both vars. of this date show rusted dies, suggesting that they were coined in some later year.

One var. each of 1833, 1834, and 1835 lack period after 25 C; though none is really rare, the 1834 and 1835 without period comprise less than a quarter of the total of each date, explaining a higher speculative price.

The large mintage of 1835 apparently satisfied circulation needs for a while; mintages of 1836–38 were considerably smaller, part of the quantities reported for each year including coins of earlier date.

Mintage of 1837 legally had to be of the new lower weight mandated by the Act of Jan. 18, 1837. However, old blanks could have been used and probably were, as the legal "remedy" (deviation in weight) overlapped the former standard.

Coinage of this design was halted in midyear to allow preparation of dies for the new Liberty Seated design.

KNEASS'S CAPPED BUSTS, NO MOTTO

Designer, Engraver, William Kneass, after John Reich. Mint, Philadelphia. Composition, 1831–36, as before; 1837–38, silver 0.900, copper 0.100. Diameter, $^{19}/_{20}'' = 24.3$ mm. Reeded edge. Weight standard, 1831–36, 104 grs. = 6.74 gms. 1837–38, 103.125 ± 1 grs. = 6.68 ± 0.065 gms. Authorizing Act, 1831–36, April 2, 1792; 1837–38, Jan. 18, 1837.

Grade range, FAIR to UNC. GOOD: Date and all letters legible except LIBERTY. VERY GOOD: Partial drapery, hair and feather details; full LIBERTY. FINE: Shoulder clasp distinct. VERY FINE: Shoulder clasp sharp, ear details clear. EXTREMELY FINE: Complete hair, drapery, and feather details with isolated tiny rubbed spots only. NOTE: Beware specimens offered as "UNCIRCULATED" which show rubbing on hair above eye or behind ear.

3915 1831 [398,000+ + ?P] Small date and letters, with berries.
Browning 1. Curve-based 2. One of the berries is in field between 2 lowest pairs of leaves; the other touches leg feather above stem. One proof is in ANS; 2 others reported.

3916 1831 Small date and letters, no berries, short, broad arrowheads.
Browning 2. Flat-based 2. Possibly 7 or 8 proofs.

3917 1831 Similar, long, narrow arrowheads.
Browning 3, 4 (latter ill.). Price for var. ill., eighth star about its own width away from cap; Browning 3 (rare) has eighth star close to cap.

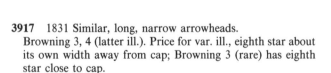

3918 1831 Small date, large letters. Rare.
Browning 6. Curve-based 2. Long arrowheads almost touch border. Very rare in mint state. This and next 2 probably coined in 1832.

3919 1831 Large date and letters, long arrowheads.
Browning 5. Tall 1's corrected from short 1's in date; same rev. Possibly a dozen proofs known.

3920 1831 Large date and letters, short arrowheads. Unique? Not in Browning; Breen 7. Rev. of **3922,** arrowheads far from border. Discovered by this writer in ANS, where it had lain unrecognized for generations. Ill. *NSM* 2/54, p. 144.

3921 1832 [320,000− + ?P] Long arrowheads.
Browning 1. Rev. of **3918–19.** One proof reported. Many of the reported mintage bore date 1831.

3922 1832 Short arrowheads.
Browning 2. Rev. of **3920.** At least 3 proofs known. Rare in mint state.

3923 1833 [156,000− + ?P] Period after 25 C.
Browning 1. Possibly 2 or 3 proofs. Auction 86:1091, Proof, $11,000. The majority of business strikes are from rusted dies (struck 1834–35?).

3924 1833 No period after 25 C; different eagle.
Browning 2. Rusty obv.; O(F) corrected from an F. At least 2 proofs reported.

3925 1834 [286,000 + ?P] No period after 25 C
Browning 1. Rev. of last. 2 proofs seen, others reported.

3926 1834 Period after 25 C.
Browning 2, 3, 4, 5. All vars. of this date have crosslet 4. At least 6 proofs.
3927 1835 [1,952,000+ + ?P] Coarse dentils both sides.
Browning 1, 2. High 3 in date. At least 2 proofs known.

3928 1835 Coarse obv. dentils, fine rev. dentils. Very scarce.
Browning 3. Same obv. (high 3), more advanced cracks. Very rare in UNC.

3929 1835 Fine obv. and rev. dentils; period after 25 C. Scarce.
Browning 4, 5, 6, 8.

3930 1835 Similar, no period after 25 C
Browning 7. Coarse rev. dentils. Rare UNC. At least 3 proofs known. Enl. photos.

Ex J. W. Garrett: 649. Courtesy Bowers & Ruddy Galleries, Inc.

3931 1836 [471,000 + ?P]
4 vars. Browning 3 has a larger 6 but the difference is slight and difficult; not rare. Probably 5 proofs known. Many of reported mintage bore date 1835.
3932 1837 [252,400 + ?P] Coarse obv. dentils. Rare.
Browning 1. Obv. die left over from 1835, final digit not added until 1837. Usually in low grades. New weight standard. Part of the reported mintage probably bore date 1836.

3933 1837 Fine dentils.
4 vars. At least 4 proofs known. Price for Browning 2 (rev. of next).
3934 1838 [366,000– + ?P]
Browning 1. Rarer choice than some earlier dates. The unique proof is from the Straus and Gardner colls. Part of the reported mintage probably bore date 1837.

v. THE SULLY-GOBRECHT LIBERTY SEATED DESIGN (1838–40)

During summer 1838, the new Engraver, Christian Gobrecht, completed device punches for the new quarter dollars. These copied neither the dollars of 1836 nor the half dollars of 1837–38, but combined the dollars' Liberty Seated motif by Thomas Sully with a version of the old Reich-Kneass eagle; the denomination was for the first time expressed as QUAR. DOL.

In Sept. 1838, Mint Director Robert Maskell Patterson sent 20 "specimens" of the new design to Treasury Secretary Levi Woodbury. The term "specimens" was Patterson's; we do not know if any were proofs, but in any event only one proof has surfaced to date.

Regular production coinage began Sept. 29, 1838. Only 466,000 were struck, a figure oddly close to the annual totals for 1839 and 1840 O of this design. That made this type, in the original Sully-Gobrecht conception, one of the shortest-lived of all: 1,274,346 total, a figure exceeded by the last four dates of Capped Busts and the first three of the Hughes modified design, which replaced it in late 1840.

Understandably, these "No Drapery" coins have lately become recognized as scarce in all grades and very rare in mint state. They are called "No Drapery" only in contrast to the Hughes design (see next section), which has extra bulky drapery at elbow.

THE SULLY-GOBRECHT LIBERTY SEATED, "NO DRAPERY"

Designer, Christian Gobrecht, obv. after Thomas Sully, rev. after John Reich and William Kneass. Engraver, Gobrecht. Mints, Philadelphia (no mintmark), New Orleans (mintmark O below eagle). Physical Specifications, Authorizing Acts, as in 1837–38 (see preceding section).

Grade range, FAIR to UNC. GOOD: Date and all letters legible except LIBERTY. VERY GOOD: Partial drapery and feather details, LI Y or L TY legible. FINE: Full LIBERTY. VERY FINE: Over half drapery and feather details; LIBERTY uniformly strong. EXTREMELY FINE: Edges of scroll and drapery clasp completely clear; complete drapery and feather details, isolated tiny rubbed spots. EXCEPTION: Many specimens of 1840 O are weakly struck in centers with flat heads.

3935 1838 [466,000 + ?P]
Mintage began Sept. 13. Only one proof reported. Enl. photos.

3936 1839 [491,146 + ?P] "Type I": straight claws. Presently very rare.
Rev. of 1838. Discovered by Dr. John R. McCloskey, 1974. *Gobrecht Journal* 11/77, pp. 16–17.

3937 1839 "Type II": curved claws.
Tongue to eagle, as preceding, but unlike next. The unique (?) proof, WGC:147, has not been examined recently enough to determine type.

3938 1840 O "No drapery." [382,200] Mintmark far to l.
Different rev. hub: no tongue to eagle. Narrow dentils far from stars and legends. 3 pairs of dies, of which 2 belong to this var. Bodine 2. Coined April–Nov. 1840. Usually weak at dentils, stars, and parts of devices. At least 13 were in the New Orleans hoard (see next section).

3939 1840 O Similar; mintmark to r. Rare.
Discovered by Howard Rounds Newcomb before 1914. WGC:319, where called Ex. rare. Bodine 1. Usually in low grades, weak flat strikings like that ill. Only 2 were in the New Orleans hoard.

vi. THE HUGHES-GOBRECHT DESIGN, EXTRA DRAPERY (1840–53)

Mint Director Robert Maskell Patterson, never one to let a good thing alone, decided that the Gobrecht designs needed improvement. He hired the Anglo-American miniaturist Robert Ball Hughes to rework the effigy of Ms. Liberty. Besides fattening her arms, chipping away much of her rock, and enlarging the scroll with her name, Hughes's major contribution consisted in covering up much of her exposed skin in the interests of "Respectability," and in particular burdening her with an impossibly bulky cloak over the crook of her elbow, which uncomfortable position doubtless explains her grimace: Chamberlain {1958}; cf. introductory texts to Chap. 24, Sect. vii, and Chap. 25, Sect. vii. (Unlike the smaller denominations, the Hughes device punch here did not show the lead weight from base of skirt.) The new revs. are also attributed to Hughes.

As an "improvement" in either aesthetic quality or striking characteristics, these changes add up to a net loss. During this entire period, on coins from both Philadelphia and New Orleans, flat striking is the rule, not the exception—unlike 1838–39.

In this period there is one major rarity: the 1842 with small date, as in 1840–41. This is known only in proof state, not over six impressions being confirmed to exist. The roster of survivors is amended from Breen {1977}:

1. Mint Cabinet, SI, from a proof set.
2. R. C. W. Brock, J. Pierpont Morgan, ANS, from a proof set.
3. Oscar G. Schilke estate, from a proof set.
4. James Aloysius Stack estate:55, $41,000, 1978 ANA:731, $32,500, Stack's, $42,500, Reed Hawn.
5. A. Buol Hinman, "Century," R. L. Miles, Steckler:39, $50,000, Bowers, Robison:1304, $22,000, Auction 86:597, $23,100.
6. Jerome Kern, Vermont pvt. coll.

The date 1849 O is also rare in all grades; its mintage is not known with certainty, but is thought to have been included in the initial 1850 delivery [16,000]. Survivors are mostly in low grades; only one is reported with any claim to mint state (ex J. A. Stack, Reed Hawn, Robison:1317, $5,500), followed by possibly four others above EF.

Actually, all dates except for 1841 are rare in mint state; the 1841's have become obtainable for a price because of a small hoard (under 50), discovered sometime before 1970. Striking quality of most dates from either Philadelphia or New Orleans made survivors look worn after a day or two in public hands, and the amount of circulation that would reduce an earlier coin to VF made these look like candidates for the melting pot.

On the other hand, the dates 1840 O and 1841 O have become readily obtainable in upper grades short of mint state owing to a hoard discovered in the French Quarter of New Orleans, Oct. 29, 1982, during excavations at the foundation site of the new Meridien Hotel. The coins (over 1,000) were largely Mexican, Peruvian, and Bolivian silver 8 Reales and 2 Reales, ca. 1821–40, but included a single 1798 federal dollar, various federal half dollars 1811–37, federal quarter dollars dated 1805–38, 1840 O no drapery (see previous section), 1840 O with drapery (at least seven, mintmark low or high), 1841, 1841 O (at least 40), 1842 (O?) (one): James Cohen, *CW* 11/24/

82, p. 1. Passersby waded into the mud to retrieve specimens washed up by heavy rains. Many survivors show chalky discoloration and matte surfaces, or have been cleaned to minimize evidence of flood damage, but otherwise show little or no evidence of wear. This hoard also yielded the discovery specimen of the 1841 with doubled rev. die.

After quantities of gold discovered in California 1848–49 began reaching world markets, price levels of gold (reckoned in silver dollars) sank, or what is the same thing, silver bullion prices rose sharply in terms of gold dollars: enough to stimulate mass meltings of silver coins as worth more than face value. The ensuing coin shortage led to reduction in official coin weights in 1853 (see following section) and wholesale melting of old-tenor silver, so that many dates 1848–53 No Arrows have become very scarce.

THE HUGHES-GOBRECHT DESIGN, EXTRA DRAPERY

Designer, Robert Ball Hughes, after Gobrecht, after Sully. Engraver, Gobrecht. Mints, Philadelphia (no mintmark), New Orleans (mintmark O below eagle). Physical Specifications, Authorizing Acts, as before.

Grade range and standards, as before. EXCEPTION: Heads, central drapery, and eagle's leg at l. are often flat even in mint state. NOTE: Beware coins offered as "UNC." that show rubbing on knees and thighs.

3940 1840 [188,127 + ?P]
New rev. hub; longer dentils. 2 vars. Ill. of **3943**.

3941 1840 O [43,000+] Large O. Very rare.
Rev. most like **3938**, but border dentils reworked, closer to legend, and mostly doubled. Always weak in feathers below shield and on part of wing at r. Bodine 5. WGC:320. Usually in low grades. See McCloskey's comments in *Gobrecht Journal* 36, pp. 10–12 (7/86).
3942 1840 O Medium O.
At least 2 positional vars. of mintmark. Several came from the New Orleans hoard: See introductory text.
3943 1840 O Small o.
Without or with rust on dies, e.g., WGC:322–23. Only a single pair of dies shipped Dec. 2, 1840; mintage includes others delivered in 1841. Ill. above **3940**. Bodine 3, 4.
3944 1841 [120,000 + ?P]
4 proofs known. Mint-state specimens are from a small hoard; see introductory text.
3945 1841 Doubled rev. die. Very rare.
Doubling is plain to naked eye at ED STATES OF. Discovery coin was in the New Orleans hoard.
3946 1841 O [452,000−]
Mintage includes many dated 1840; 5 obvs., 4 revs. shipped, some of the revs. also used with the 1840 obv. One die shows minor doubling, plainest on shield, LIBERTY, and first 3 stars. At least 3 positional vars. Many came from the New Orleans hoard: See introductory text.

3947 1842 Small date. Ex. rare, 6 known. Proofs only.
Date as in 1840–41. For roster of survivors see introductory text.

3948 1842 Large date. [88,000 + ?P]
Usually in low grades. One proof is in a N.Y. State specialist coll., ex WGC:151; not over 2 others reported.

3949 1842 O Small date. [157,000]
All coined from a single pair of dies shipped Dec. 18, 1841. Reported mintage may include coins dated 1841. Usually in low grades; virtually unobtainable EF. Rev. often weak at azure from foreign matter adhering to die.
3950 1842 O Large date. [612,000]
From 3 obvs., 7 revs. Positional vars. exist. Very rare choice.
3951 1843 [645,600 + ?P]
Minor positional vars. of date. Possibly as many as 8 proofs.
3952 1843 O [968,000] Small o.
Mintmark as in 1842. In all, 5 obvs., 7 revs. Minor positional vars. Usually in low grades.

3953 1843 O Large O. Very rare.

Rusted dies; possibly struck in 1844. Always in low grades; unobtainable choice. "Gilhousen":626.

3954 1844 [421,200 + ?P]

Minor positional vars., some with minute traces of repunching on 4's, or on 18. Five proofs traced.

3955 1844 Double date. Very rare.

Repunching obvious on all 4 digits. "Gilhousen":627, Auction 82:1126. Compare WGC:155–56, perfect or shattered rev. die.

3956 1844 O [740,000] Heavy claws.

Centered date. Medium O henceforth unless otherwise noted. Ex. rare UNC.

3957 1844 O Thin claws.

High date. Either this rev. was given one blow too few from the hub, or it was heavily repolished attenuating details: Preservation of available specimens has not enabled certainty.

3958 1844 O First 4 obviously repunched.

WGC:332; Edwards, 1982 ANA:2134, UNC., $4,400. In all, 5 pairs of dies. 4 more pairs shipped for 1845, 4 more for 1846, but all remained unused. The 4 1846-dated obvs. were returned to the Philadelphia Mint. Unlike the similar situation in half dimes, we have seen no unequivocal evidence of their reuse as overdates; but see **3973–74.**

3959 1845 [922,000 + ?P] Thin numerals.

Narrow sharp serifs to 1 and 4.

3960 1845 Heavy numerals.

Thick blunt serifs to 1 and 4.

3961 1845 over smaller 5. Scarce.

Usually cracked through date to 1.

3962 1845 Partly repunched date.

At least 2 vars.; price for that with 45 repunched (WGC:161) —sometimes mislabeled "1845/43." Compare preceding and next.

3963 1845 Repunched 845. Proofs only. Ex. rare, 6 known.

Outlines show l. of final position.

3964 1845 Entire date doubled. Rare.

3965 1846 [510,000 + ?P] Normal date.

Date placed high, central, or low; some vars. show traces of repunching. Possibly 12 proofs known.

3966 1846 "Dropped 6." Very rare.

In date 6 first punched far too low, then corrected; extra knob between knob and loop.

3967 1846 Repunched 46. Rare.

Not impossibly some are later states of next. Repunching differs from **3966** in position.

3968 1846 Entire date doubled. Very rare.

WGC:164–65.

3969 1847 [734,000 + ?P] Normal date and rev.

Positional vars. exist. Possibly 10 proofs.

3970 1847 Normal date; doubled rev. die. Rare.

Doubling plainest on QUAR.DOL.

3971 1847 Repunched 47; doubled rev. die. Very rare.

Same rev. as preceding.

3972 1847 O [368,000]

Usually in low grades; unknown choice. 2 rev. vars. 4 pairs of dies shipped before Nov. 12, 1846. Six more pairs for 1848 O, shipped before Dec. 31, 1847, remained unused.

3973 1848 [146,000 + ?P] Partly repunched date.

Several vars.; parts of extra 48 (?) or extra final 8 (?) visible. Some of the more obscure ones of this and next may have begun as 1848/6, from the 4 1846 obvs. returned from New Orleans (see note to **3958**); compare next. Possibly 10 proofs.

3974 1848 Double date. Rare.

Several vars., e.g., "Gilhousen":633 and Garrett (1976):159; another on a proof ex Howard Newcomb. Same comment as to last. One rev. has a tiny round hole (center punch in hub?) atop farthest l. gules (red, relief) stripe in shield; this peculiarity recurs on other revs. as late as 1858. The "dashed" date _1848 (traces of extra 1848 below date) belongs here.

3975 1848 Triple date. Very rare.

Ill. ANACS {1983}, p. 90. Later states qualify as preceding.

3976 1849 [340,000 + ?P]

One rev. as described under **3974**. Three proofs known.

3977 1849 O [16,000 − ?] Very rare.

6 obv. dies (not canceled until April 10, 1850); only one var., its rev. also found with an 1850 obv. Mintage believed included in initial 1850 delivery. See introductory text. Prohibitively rare UNC.

3978 1850 [1,908,000 −] Thin date, open 5.

Knob of 5 well away from cusp. Minor positional vars. 2 proofs known.

3979 1850 Same, part of extra 1 in border. Ex. rare.

Park Forest:2366. Die heavily repolished in fields to efface remaining traces of misplaced date. See ANACS {1983}, p. 90.

3980 1850 Heavy date, closed 5. Rare.

Knob of 5 touches cusp.

3981 1850 O [396,000 −] Thin date, open 5.

Knob of 5 free of cusp. The minus sign in this and following mintages alludes to mass meltings through 1855: See introductory text.

3982 1850 O Heavy date, closed 5. Rare.

Knob of 5 touches cusp. Minor positional vars. Sometimes from heavily rusted dies: 1982 ANA:2135. In all, 6 obvs., 15 leftover revs. from 1844 and later years.

3983 1851 [160,000 − + ?P]

In all, 4 obvs., 6 revs. Only one proof reported, untraced.

3984 1851 O [88,000 −]

Usually in low grades; Ex. rare UNC. In all, 7 obvs., 3 revs.

3985 1852 [177,060 − + ?P]

In all, 5 pairs of dies. 2 proofs known.

3986 1852 Double date. Very rare.

Apparently unobtainable UNC.

3987 1852 O [96,000 −]

Almost unobtainable UNC. In all, 6 obvs. made, only 4 shipped. For 1853 O no arrows, 10 obvs. and 6 revs. were shipped in addition to a dozen revs. on hand; all remained unused, and 4 obvs., 12 revs. were defaced before June 9, 1853.

3988 1853 No arrows. [44,200 −]

Always with doubling on 3 and usually on 5; formerly called "1853/2" in error. 2 indistinguishable batches, [20,800] Feb.

Ex J. W. Garrett: 658. Courtesy Bowers & Ruddy Galleries, Inc.

7, [23,400] Feb. 19. Mint-state survivors, as with the dimes and half dimes, originated with Harold P. Newlin (before 1883). Forgeries, made by altering genuine 1858's, are readily detectable: All genuine 1853's have identical date elements; 1858's are lightweight at 96 grs. = 6.22 gms. compared to 1853 No Arrows at 103+ grs. = 6.68 gms.

vii. ARROWS AND RAYS (1853)

During 1851–53, authorities realized that no matter how much silver could be located for coinage, no silver coins were going to remain in circulation. Immense discoveries of gold in California had lowered the market price of gold in terms of silver. In the East, this situation was experienced as sharp rises in the price of silver reckoned in gold dollars, eventually to a point where bullion dealers found they could make "endless chain" profits by melting down silver coins bought for face value and reselling the bullion. All the mints' output of silver vanished into hoarders' hands, and most of it went to bullion dealers; less and less silver reached the Mint for coinage, reflected in the diminishing mintages of 1850–52 (see previous section). This "endless chain" could not be allowed to continue, as with the disappearance of silver coins there was no effective legal medium of exchange of lower value than gold dollars. Cents could be refused by storekeepers (and often were), as they were not legal tender; and the vanished silver coins were replaced by an inundation of irredeemable scrip, which could be refused by the same storekeepers who passed it out, and which could not be used for buying stamps or paying taxes.

Mint Director George N. Eckert devised the plan of reducing the weight of silver coins to a figure which would eliminate bullion dealers' profits and thus discourage further melting. Somehow he managed to persuade a puzzled Congress that this tactic would work, and his plan became law by the Act of Feb. 21, 1853, which authorized coinage of quarters at 96 grs. compared with the former 103⅛.

The new coins had to have an identifying mark to distinguish them from earlier heavier issues. Eckert chose arrows flanking date, with rays behind eagle. James Barton Longacre (Gobrecht's successor in the Mint engravership) added rays by hand to a working rev., and had this die hardened to raise working hubs from which 120 working rev. dies were sunk. Variations in length or thickness of rays, or presence or absence of a pseudo-border around them, have to do with the number and depth of impressions of the hub into each working die, and the amount of subsequent relapping. The 1853 date logotype was sunk into a wider steel bar and arrows added; this was hardened and used to raise the new logotype for dating some 119 working obvs.

On March 3, 1853, five proof sets were struck, consisting of half dimes, dimes, quarters, and half dollars with arrows, the two larger denominations with rays in rev. field. These sets have been long since broken up; individual survivors are of the highest rarity.

The first business-strike quarters [780,000] followed on April 26. During the rest of the year a total of 15,254,200 quarters emanated from the Philadelphia Mint: the largest annual coinage and the largest number of dies made and used for a single denomination for any year until then. This total exceeded all quarter-dollar issues 1838–53 put together. There were also 1,332,000 issued at New Orleans from four pairs of dies—the largest single issue of this denomination from a branch mint until then. These coins all went into circulation and stayed there; no melting followed. This explains both the commonness of worn 1853 Arrows quarters and the rarity of strictly mint-state specimens: Nobody bothered to save them. For decades until the 1950s, coin dealers refused to stock them. Worn ones were still occasionally seen in circulation as late as 1941; I saw one in a church collection plate (Wheeling, W. Va.) in that year.

One of the strangest vars. in U.S. coinage is the 1853/1854, which I discovered in the Hirt collection (1976). This obv. must have been made during fall 1853, when dies were being prepared for both this year and 1854; an obv. die intended for 1853 was first given a blow with the 1854 logotype (whose arrows were differently placed), then several heavier blows with the 1853 logotype. Later states show only part of upright of 4 within 3; rarer earlier states show also part of the extra 85 and both sets of arrows.

On the off chance that the provisional United States branch mint at San Francisco (operating then under the nom de guerre "United States Assay Office of Gold") might manage to solve its problems with parting acids (to extract silver from raw gold ore so that the ingots would be within legal limits of 50 parts silver per thousand), the Philadelphia Mint shipped two pairs of quarter-dollar dies with arrows and rays; but no 1853 S coins followed.

For reasons never publicized, the incoming Mint Director, Col. James Ross Snowden, decided to drop rays from the later issues, while retaining arrows at dates for the time being: See following section.

ARROWS AND RAYS

Designer, Engraver, James Barton Longacre, after Hughes, Gobrecht, Sully. Mints, Philadelphia, New Orleans, as before. Diameter, Composition, as before. Weight, 96 ± 1 grs. = 6.22 ± 0.065 gms. Authorizing Act, Feb. 21, 1853.

Grade range and standards, as previously. NOTE: Beware coins with rubbing on knees and thighs (usually also cleaned), offered as "UNC."

3989   1853 [15,254,200 + 5P] Normal date.
Proofs coined March 3; Auction 80:1184, $25,000. First business strikes, April 26. Dates differ in position and heaviness. Occasional obvs. show traces of repunching on dates and arrows. Rays differ in thickness, length (slightly), and presence or absence of pseudo-border: See introductory text. In all, 119 obvs., 120 revs.

3990   1853 Double date. Rare.
All 4 digits show repunching.
3991   1853/1854. Very rare.
See introductory text. Note upright of 4 within 3, and position of extra arrow shaft above r. arrow shaft; these show even on worn specimens of the later die states, as will traces of differently shaped 5. Ill. is of one of the earlier die states; these are rarer and bring higher premiums than later states

showing less of the 1854 date. The latter show heavy rev. clash marks, suggesting that obv. regrinding effaced both clash marks and the more obvious traces of overdate. Prohibitively rare in mint state; see Rhodes:1053.

3992   1853 O [1,332,000]
In all, 4 pairs of dies; see introductory text. Very rare UNC.
3993   1853 O Solid O. Ex. rare.
A chip out of die left mintmark completely filled on coins. Compare ill. in *Gobrecht Journal* 27 (7/83).

viii. ARROWS, NO MOTTO (1854–55)

The new Mint Director, Col. James Ross Snowden, felt that continuation of arrows at dates of silver coins would remain necessary to distinguish the new issues instantly from heavier old-tenor issues, which were being melted as worth $106.60 per $100 face value. For unknown reasons, Snowden ordered that rev. dies be made from the old hub without rays.

The number of dies made for Philadelphia quarters is unknown, but likely to have been 80–100 pairs, sufficient for a mintage of over 12 million, much of it from melted old-tenor silver. Twelve pairs of dies went to the New Orleans branch, correctly anticipating a larger issue than that of 1853. And on the off chance that the new San Francisco branch might obtain enough parting acids to make coins of legal fineness, two pairs of 1854 S dies went there, but remained unused.

The most distinctive var. of this issue is beyond doubt the 1854 O Huge O. This mintmark differs from all others in the series, being both larger (1.75 × 1.65 mm) and grossly thicker throughout, and fairly crude in shape; adjacent device details are attenuated. Most likely this die was received at New Orleans without mintmark, and the O added by hand. See discussion by Harry E. Smith in *Gobrecht Journal* 36 (7/86), pp. 3–5.

Both branch-mint issues of 1855 are Ex. rare in mint state, reason unknown. The first 1855 S struck was a brilliant proof; it went from Robert Aiken Birdsall (the new Superintendent) to the W. W. Long Museum, Dr. Edward Maris (1886), and various private collections, believed to be the same piece reappearing in the Grant Pierce collection (1955), thereafter Groves:440 at $6,500 (1974), MTB, $14,750 (1978) to Joseph L. Ellison, MTB 12/78:2527, Auction 86:1615, $24,200.

Snowden decided in 1855 that thereafter too few old-tenor silver coins would be brought in to require continuation of the distinguishing mark. As of Jan. 1, 1856, arrows would no longer appear at dates, though the coins would continue at the new weight.

ARROWS, NO MOTTO

Designer, Engraver, as before. Mints, Philadelphia (no mintmark), New Orleans (mintmark O below eagle), San Francisco (S below eagle). Physical Specifications, Authorizing Acts, as in 1853.

Grade range and standards, as before.

3994 1854 [12,380,000 + ?P] Normal date, 5 4 free.
Possibly 10 proofs survive. Dates vary slightly in position and heaviness; some show very minor traces of repunching. On one var., left arrow is shorter than r., and has straight barbs, evidently from an overpolished die: apparently rare.

3995 1854 Repunched 1. Rare.
1974 GENA:1353.
3996 1854 Heavy date, 54 touch. Rare.
The distinction is similar to that on the cents of this year.
3997 1854 O [1,484,000] 5 4 free; medium O.
In all, 12 pairs of dies.
3998 1854 O Very thin weak O. Very rare.
Hair-thin top and base of mintmark. Harte III:432, others.
3999 1854 O Repunched mintmark. Rare.
1982 ANA:2138, others.
4000 1854 O Partly repunched date. Scarce.
4001 1854 O Very small round o. Ex. rare.
From the punch used for mintmarking gold dollars.
4002 1854 O Huge O. Very rare.
See introductory text. Discovered by this writer in 1954. Usually in low grades; prohibitively rare above EF.

4003 1855 [2,857,000 + ?P]
Arrows smaller than in 1853–54. In all, 26 obvs., 20 revs., probably not all used. Possibly 20 proofs known.
4004 1855 O [176,000]
In all, 12 pairs of dies shipped, not all used. Usually in low grades.

4005 1855 S [396,400 + 1+P]
Large S only (1.7 mm); 4 pairs of dies, 3 positional vars. known. Usually in low grades. For the unique proof see introductory text.

ix. ARROWS OMITTED (1856–66)

Beginning in Jan. 1856, quarter dollars were issued without arrows at date, though continuing at the new weight standard mandated by the Act of Feb. 21, 1853. Silver coinage in California was by now a reality, limited by the amounts of parting acids available. Continuing high prices in the San Francisco area meant that dimes and quarters were locally treated much as were cents and trimes back east; silver dollars were explicitly referred to in San Francisco branch-mint correspondence as "small change." This is why the S Mint smaller silver coins 1856–65 are all rare in decent preservation and Ex. rare or even unknown in mint state; there were few coin collectors in the West, if any, and nobody else thought them worth saving.

On the other hand, Philadelphia coins of the war years 1863–65 are also rare as business strikes. Mintages were limited because New York banks had suspended specie payments in Dec. 1861; silver was hoarded, and little reached the Mint for coinage. These dates are principally represented by proofs, which were meant to be saved. Discovery of uncirculated specimens in original proof sets traced directly to the Mint has given rise to the suspicion that most mint-state business strikes of those years have this origin. Proof sets were largely broken up, quarters being added to date runs of quarters (and similarly for all other denominations); few collectors bothered to distinguish between business strikes and proofs of a given year for their date runs, just as before Heaton {1893} few bothered to distinguish between Philadelphia and branch-mint coins. These fundamental distinctions began to receive collector attention only in recent decades, since Wayte Raymond began publishing his Standard Catalogues in 1934.

In 1859, Longacre modified the quarter-dollar design with the help of Anthony C. Paquet. The old or "Type I" obvs. (1840–59) have single hair ribbon, fingers of pole hand are nearly straight. The new or "Type II" obvs. (1859–65) have double hair ribbon, fingers of pole hand more curved, index finger elongated. The old or "Type I" revs. (Philadelphia 1840–61) have eagle's eye hollow, claws closed, heavy arrowheads nearly touching one another; the new or "Type II" revs. (Philadelphia 1859–65) have eagle's eye solid and convex, claws shorter and open, arrowheads smaller and a little farther apart. All New Orleans quarters through 1860 O have only "Type I" revs.; those from San Francisco through 1865 likewise, largely because these were all leftover dies from 1855–58. During 1859–61 "Type I" and "Type II" obvs. were indiscriminately paired with I and II revs. on Philadelphia business strikes. Information on these changes is as yet too recent to be certain of rarity levels, and other vars. may exist. In particular, 1859 may exist with obv. "Type II," rev. "Type I." Any of the possible combinations may also occur on proofs or business strikes.

The unique 1866 coin without motto is a fantasy piece, struck in a set with the half dollar and silver dollar, long after authorization to adopt the new design with motto (Act of March 3, 1865: See next section). This set was made up for the Mint's favorite druggist, Robert Coulton Davis. Because Davis had told the Mint people where to go to seize the plain-edged 1804 dollars during the 1858 scandal, and reputedly because he provided Mint personnel with their usual ration of laudanum (Brown's Mixture, a tincture of opium, then legal and not even attacked by the prohibitionist Temperance Unions), successive Mint Directors and other high officials gave Davis almost any odd patterns and restrikes or other fantasy coins he wished, even to making up many to order. The set later went to H. O. Granberg, William H. Woodin (FDR's Secretary of Treasury), Waldo Newcomer, F. C. C. Boyd, Wayte Raymond, Col. E. H. R. Green, King Farouk, Edwin M. Hydeman, and Lammot duPont. It was among the coins stolen from the duPont family at gunpoint in Oct. 1967.

ARROWS OMITTED

Designer, Engraver, Mints, as before. Physical Specifications, Authorizing Acts, as 1853–55.
Grade range and standards, as before.

4006   1856 [7,264,000 + ?P]
Upright 5 only; 72 pairs of dies. The proofs (under 30 known?) have a vertical bulge in r. rev. field, from AM through wing to arrows.
4007   1856 Obviously repunched 6. Rare.
4008   1856 O [968,000]
12 obvs., 6 revs. Occasionally shows traces of repunching on base of mintmark.
4009   1856 S [286,000] Normal large S.
12 pairs of dies, probably not all used. Mintmark above R ("S to l.") or above space between R D ("S to r."), *Gobrecht Journal* 11/78, p. 12. Usually in low grades; prohibitively rare UNC.
4010   1856 S Large S over small s. Very rare.
RPM 1. Discovered by William Cutler Atwater before 1946, and independently by others since. NN 57:648. Always in low grades.

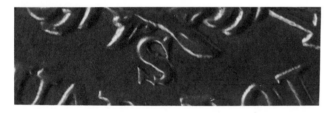

4011   1857 [9,644,000 + ?P]
Number of dies unknown but probably larger than for 1856; only minor positional vars. to date, one with traces of repunching on serif of 1. Proofs have the rev. described for 1856; under 20 known? Mint-state survivors are largely from a hoard of 40 specimens, discovered about 1974.
4012   1857 O [1,180,000]
Very rare UNC.
4013   1857 S [82,000] Large S.
S 1.7 mm. Usually in low grades; Ex. rare UNC. 2 minor vars.: S touches stem or S touches feather.
4014   1857 S Medium S. Ex. rare, reported.
S 1.3 mm.
4015   1858 [7,368,000 + 80?P]
Minor positional vars. of dates. Proofs have base of 1 faintly repunched (this repunching fades out); most proofs show multiple lint marks (incuse impressions from lint adhering to dies: Someone failed to wipe them clean before starting the press run).
4016   1858 O [520,000]
Ex. rare UNC.
4017   1858 S [121,000] Large S.
In all, 12 obvs., 2 revs., the latter shipped in March. Usually in low grades; unobtainable UNC.
4018   1859 [1,344,000 + 800−P] "Type I" obv. and rev.
Single hair ribbon; closed claws. See introductory text. "Type

I" proofs are very rare; discovery coin, Philip More:2597. Relative rarity of "Type I" business strikes not yet known. Enl. photos.

4019   1859 "Type I," obv. "Type II" rev. Very rare. Proofs only? Enl. photos.

4020   1859 "Type II," obv. "Type I" rev. Probably exists. See **4018** and next.

4021 1859 "Type II" obv. and rev.

See introductory text. Most proof quarters of this date are "Type II"; the majority were melted as unsold. Ill. of **4039**.

4022 1859 O [260,000] "Type I" obv. and rev.
Ex. rare UNC.

4023 1859 S [80,000] "Type I" obv. and rev. Large S.
S 1.7 mm. Usually in low grades; Ex. rare UNC. 6 obvs. shipped Nov. 1858.

4024 1860 [804,400 + 542P] "Type II" obv., "Type I" rev. Ex. rare.
Business strikes only. Compare **4027**.

4025 1860 "Type II" obv. and rev.
Business strikes and proofs. Of 1,000 proofs originally made, 542 were sold, the rest melted.

4026 1860 O [388,000] "Type I" rev. Normal O.
Very rare UNC.

4027 1860 O Same, thin O. Scarce.
Mintmark timidly entered; hair-thin top and base. A later state, showing only part of O, has been mistaken for **4024**.

4028 1860 S [56,000] "Type I" rev. Very rare.
Large S, 1.7 mm. 4 obvs. shipped Nov. 2, 1859; leftover revs. Usually in low grades.

4029 1861 [4,853,600 + 400−P] "Type I" rev. Presently very rare.
Discovered at 1979 ANA Convention by Jerald Hueber. *Gobrecht Journal* 11/79, p. 31. Doubtless from a leftover rev. die.

4030 1861 "Type II" rev.
75 obvs., 80 revs.; of 1,000 proofs made for sets, fewer than 400 sold, the rest melted. All proofs seen to date have "Type II" rev.

4031 1861 S [96,000] "Type I" rev.
Large S, 1.7 mm; 6 obvs., leftover revs. Usually in low grades. 4 obvs. shipped to New Orleans, but no 1861 O coins were issued before the rebels seized the branch mint in April 1861.

4032 1862 [932,000 + 430+P] "Type II" rev.
11 obvs., 12 revs.; 550 proofs struck for sets, somewhat over 430 sold, rest melted.

4033 1862 S [67,000] "Type I" rev.
Large S, 1.7 mm; 8 obvs., leftover revs. Usually in low grades; prohibitively rare UNC. 4 obvs. shipped Nov. 1862 for 1863 S coinage remained unused.

4034 1863 Normal date and legend; "Type II" rev. Proofs only. [460P]
3 minor vars.; see Breen {1977}, pp. 120–21. Compare next. For the coins with motto rev., see next section.

4035 1863 Partly doubled date and legend; "Type II" rev. [191,600]. Very rare.
Bases of extra 18 show above bases of 18; doubled rev. die. See next.

4036 1863 Normal date; doubled legend. Very scarce.
Rev. of preceding. Business strikes only.

4037 1864 "Type II" rev. [93,600 + 470P]
Business strikes are rare; they have die chip on thigh, unlike proofs. For coins with motto rev., see next section.

4038 1864 S "Type I" rev. [20,000] Very rare.
Large S, 1.7 mm. Date partly repunched. 4 obv. dies shipped Oct. 1863; leftover revs. Only the one var. seen to date. Almost always in low grades; prohibitively rare UNC. Auction 86:142, $2,310.

4039 1865 Normal date; "Type II" rev. [500P] Proofs only.
Date centered, or low and slanting up to r., latter rarer. As a slanting date also occurs on proof restrikes of the gold dollar and $3 coin, is this quarter var. also a restrike? For coins with motto, see next section.

4040 1865 Partly repunched date; "Type II" rev. [58,800] Rare.
Parts of extra digits at 1 and between 65. Business strikes only.

4041 1865 S "Type I" rev. [41,000] Rare.
Thin numerals, large S, 1.7 mm. 5 obvs. shipped Nov. 1864; only the one var. seen. Almost always in low grades; prohibitively rare UNC.

4042 1866 No motto. Unique proof.
Judd 536. See introductory text and Breen {1977}, p. 264. Hydeman sale, $24,500.

x. MOTTO ADDED (1866–73)

The Act of March 3, 1865 (another of those wartime omnibus bills) not only authorized another issue of compound interest notes, and fixed the weight and terms of issue of nickel 3¢ coins, but also mandated that henceforth all silver and gold coins of suitable size would bear the motto IN GOD WE TRUST. Almost everyone has heard the story of how Rev. M. R. Watkinson (of Ridleyville, Pa.) wrote to Treasury Secretary Salmon P. Chase, Nov. 13, 1861, proposing addition of a religious motto to our coinage; his historic letter was for many years on display at the Chase Manhattan Bank Money Museum while this was still at Rockefeller Center in New York. Watkinson's action directly led to Chase's choice of the wording IN GOD WE TRUST rather than its various proposed alternatives (GOD AND OUR COUNTRY, GOD IS OUR SHIELD, GOD OUR TRUST). Chase was doubtless influenced by the wording of the motto of his alma mater (Brown University in Providence, R.I.) which was IN DEO SPERAMUS, 'In God we hope'; this in turn derived from the motto of colonial Rhode Island.

Whatever Chase's actual rationalization, his wording became law; it first appeared in circulation on 2¢ pieces in 1864, then shield nickels, gold $5 to $20, and silver 25¢ through $1 in 1866. R. Coulton Davis (see introductory text to previous section) described, and probably originally owned, alleged prototype sets with the adopted motto, dated 1863, 1864, and 1865, in silver, copper, and aluminum; reputedly the seven 1865-

dated silver sets were for Treasury approval of the design of motto scroll. As one of the 1865 silver dollars with motto is overstruck on an 1866 dollar (both dates plain), the whole story has become dubious; evidently at least some of the 1865 coins with motto, and possibly all, must join their brethren dated 1863–64 as restrikes made about 1868, most likely for Mint Director Henry R. Linderman.

Issues of quarter dollars for circulation, 1866–73, were very limited. Little bullion came in after the war during the continuing suspension of specie payments; any silver was worth over its face value in greenbacks. Probably over 80% of specimens in collectors' hands, dated 1866–70, are proofs from broken sets, many of them cleaned or impaired. S-Mint coins are very rare in mint state through 1873; CC-Mint coins 1870–73 are of great rarity in all grades, because issues were deliberately kept limited for political reasons by official policy emanating from the Philadelphia Mint—which limitation was in turn urged as reason for abolishing the Carson City branch!

In 1873, Philadelphia coins without arrows come with "closed" or "open" 3, the former with knobs very close together. When the Chief Coiner found that the closed-3 dates (especially on smaller denominations: cent, half dime, gold dollar, quarter eagle) could be mistaken for an 8, he filed an official complaint with the Director, and the Engraving Department under William Barber had to make up a complete set of date logotypes with open 3. Later issues with arrows at date (see following section) all had open 3; mintmarked silver coins without arrows all had closed 3.

Mintage was interrupted in March 1873 to enable preparation of new dies with arrows at date, and allegedly blanks at the new weight standard, mandated by the omnibus Mint Act of Feb. 12, 1873: See next section. This had the effect of creating rarities, of which the two most famous are beyond doubt the 1873 CC dime and quarter dollar without arrows. Only four of the quarters are traced:

1. Carson City Mint (in parcel of assay coins, Feb. 1874), A. Loudon Snowden, J. W. Haseltine and Stephen K. Nagy, H. O. Granberg, Mehl 54:358 (7/16/19), William H. Woodin, Waldo Newcomer, F. C. C. Boyd, WGC:378, Eliasberg estate. UNC.

2. James Aloysius Stack estate:136, $80,000, William Grayson, 1980 NY Met.:519, $205,000, Bob Riethe and Greg Holloway. UNC. (ill.)

3. Mrs. R. Henry Norweb. Described as UNC; unseen.

4. Ex Abner Kreisberg. Described as VF; unseen.

MOTTO ADDED

Designer, Engraver, as before (motto scroll by Longacre). Mints, Philadelphia (no mintmark), San Francisco (small s below eagle), Carson City (small cc below eagle). Physical Specifications, as before. Authorizing Act, March 3, 1865.

Grade range and standards, as before. NOTE: Beware coins offered as "UNC." with rubbing on knees and thighs.

4043   1863 "Prototype" (Restrike). [5P?] Proofs only.
Judd 335. Probably struck in 1868. See introductory text. Ill. of **4047.**

4044   1864 "Prototype" (Restrike). [5P?] Proofs only.
Judd 386. Same comment.

4045   1865 "Prototype" (Restrike?) [7P?] Proofs only.
Judd 425. At least some struck in or after 1866.

4046   1866 [16,800 + 725P]
Many mint-state business strikes were retrieved from proof sets.

4047   1866 S [28,000]
Usually in low grades; prohibitively rare UNC. Without or with curve of another S within lower part of mintmark; latter ill. above **4043.** Six pairs of dies shipped: obvs. Nov. 1865, revs. March 1866.

4048   1867 [20,000 + 625P]
Same comment as to **4046.**

4049   1867 S [48,000]
Same comments as to **4047;** same rev., with part of extra S within mintmark. Auction 86:145, UNC., $3,960.

4050   1868 [29,400 + 600P]
Same comment as to 1866. The majority of proofs have plain rust pit in die below B, and base of final 8 repunched; this repunching fades out. Only the earliest die state shows repunching on 1: 1982 ANA:2148.

4051   1868 S [96,000]
Normal S (rarer) or rev. of 1867 S. 1982 ANA:2149–50; Ivy Cambridge:841. Usually in low grades; Ex. rare UNC. Only the earliest die state shows traces of repunching on 1.

4052   1869 [16,000 + 600P]
Business strikes are very rare. Those with long spine through fourth and fifth stars were made as proofs. The proof rev. with die rust below wing at l. and above U(NI) continued in use through 1871.

4053   1869 S [76,000]
Rev. of **4049.** Usually in low grades; Ex. rare in mint state. 8 obvs. shipped Oct. 1868. One die (discovered by Jack Beymer) shows traces of top of extra 9 within lower part of 9, and traces of 86 in dentils below date.

4054   1870 [86,400 + 1,000P]
Proofs have the rusted 1869 rev. Business strikes (much rarer) lack it but have die rust on seated figure.

4055   1870 CC [8,340] Very rare.
Usually in low grades; prohibitively rare UNC. Only one var.: top of C(A) straight; small round c c widely spaced, l. c lower, rev. of 1871–73 (Larry Briggs, in *Gobrecht Journal* 11/83, pp. 3–7). Beware falsely added mintmarks. Mintage began April 20 [3,540].

4056   1871 [118,200 + 960P] 71 about touch.
Long serifs to 1's. Found on a minority of proofs, and on nearly all business strikes. BER usually weak. This is the earlier date logotype, found on branch-mint obvs. shipped before the end of 1870.

4057   1871 7 1 apart.
Short serifs to 1's. Found on the majority of proofs. Business strikes are rare; LIBERTY normal.

4058   1871 S 71 about touch. [30,900]
4 obvs. received Dec. 16, 1870. Minute s, one of the revs. left over from 1866. Usually in low grades; Ex. rare in mint state, though about 6 turned up in England, 1977.

4059   1871 CC 71 about touch. [10,890] Very rare.
Only the earliest impressions show triple punching on 1's. Rev of 1870. Usually in low grades; only 2 UNCs. reported: 1) Eliasberg estate.   2) Giacomo Opezzo, J. A. Stack estate, Reed Hawn, F. Sweeney, M. B. Simons (obv. prooflike). *Gobrecht Journal* 3/79, p. 4.

4060   1872 [182,000− + 950−P]
Business strikes are rarer than mintage figure suggests; most likely many were melted after July 10, 1873, with other No Arrows coins. The proof rev. with die cut from l. border of

shield was reused in 1873 (without and with arrows) and again occasionally as late as 1880.

4061   1872 S [83,000]

Minute s as before. 4 obvs. shipped Nov. 1871. Very rare in mint state.

4062   1872 CC [22,850−]

At least 2 minor positional vars. of date; rev. of 1870–71. Many melted after April 1, 1873. Very rare above EF.

4063   1873 Closed 3. [40,000− + 600−P]

Business strikes are very rare, included in the initial delivery of the year; many melted (with some proofs) after July 10, 1873. Two obv. dies. Enl. photo.

4064   1873 Open 3. [172,000−]

Many melted after July 10, 1873. Business strikes only, though in the Boosel coll. (ex Philip Straus estate) was one with proof obv., UNC. rev. Enl. photo. The 4 obvs. shipped to San Francisco Nov. 1872 remained unused.

4065   1873 CC Closed 3. [4,000−] Ex. rare, 3 known.

Mostly melted after April 1, 1873. Rev. of 1870–72. See introductory text.

xi. ARROWS AND MOTTO (1873–74)

The Mint Act of Feb. 12, 1873, in addition to abolishing several denominations (2¢, trime, half dime, silver dollar), creating the trade dollar, and moving the Mint Directorship out of Philadelphia to a new bureau in Washington, attempted to introduce the metric system in our coinage. Quarter dollars issued after April 1 were to weigh 6.25 gms. apiece: an increase of 0.45 grs. (0.03 gms.) or less than 5% of gross weight per coin—a paper complication. As James Blish had *Star Trek's* Mr. Spock say, "A difference which *makes* no difference *is* no difference." As the new standard was less than ⅓ of the Mint's remedy (allowable deviation from standard weight of each planchet), old blanks could have been legally used and probably were. If Congress's intention was to familiarize people with the metric system, it was both irrelevant and futile; if the purpose was to make the new coins serve as weights, the remedy of ± 1.5 grs. (= almost ± 0.1 gms.), as with the 5¢ nickels, rendered any such attempt self-defeating. The new metric weights continued through 1964, but their importance to the public has been zero, and to the Mint solely a proliferation of decimal points.

For uncertain reasons, the new coins were to bear a distinguishing mark; this proved to be arrowheads at date, exactly as 20 years earlier. We conjecture that this was to enable distinction (at subsequent Assay Commission meetings?) between coins made under the previous administration and those made under supervision of the new Mint Bureau.

Older coins were theoretically to remain current. However, the admittedly incomplete surviving records of this period indicate that quantities of 1873 No Arrows coins and earlier dates were melted during the months following July 10, 1873, along with the abolished denominations, including both proofs and business strikes. Both San Francisco and Carson City branch mints received orders to melt all obsolete coins on hand—accounting for rarity of many issues of 1871–73.

Quarter dollars of 1873–74 with arrows have long been prized as type coins and promoted as "rarities" to a degree incredible among people not intimately familiar with the coin trade ca. 1960–85. Mintages were ample except at Carson City, where earlier (politically motivated) orders to limit coinage remained in effect. In mint state the 1873 S is very rare, the 1873 CC prohibitively rare, the 1874 S common, though usually advertised as rare. A hoard of 80–100 uncirculated 1874 S quarters turned up in a West Coast bank about 1949; they were dispersed one at a time, more frequently after 1974, to dealers and type collectors, so as not to depress prices.

Most of the proof sets went to date collectors, who promptly broke them up to add the new issues to their date runs of dimes, quarters, and halves. Existing proof sets of 1873–74 were mostly reassembled in recent years; this remark applies particularly to sets combining coins without and with arrows. One extraordinary exception was a cased double set (two of each, cent to dollar and trade dollar, including duplicate silver coins without and with arrows), presented Sept. 30, 1874, to Charles A. Whitney by Mint Superintendent James Pollock, and containing a document of presentation signed by eight Mint officials.

For reasons still uncertain, authorities decided to omit arrows after the end of 1874.

ARROWS AND MOTTO

Designer, as before. Engraver, William Barber (for the arrows). Mints, as before. Physical Specifications, as before, except Weight 96.45 ± 1.5 grs. = 6.25 ± 0.097 gms. Authorizing Act, Feb. 12, 1873.

Grade range and standards, as before.

4066 1873 Open 3. [1,271,200 + 540P]

Minute positional vars.; rarely traces of repunching at base of 3. Proofs have the 1872 rev. with die cut at l. border of shield. Ill. of **4071.**

4067 1873 S Open 3. [156,000] Normal S.

Minute s as before. 2 minor positional vars. Very rare UNC.

4068 1873 S Open 3. Double S. Rare.

Mintmark first punched much too low, then corrected. "Rays" (plain die file marks) above head.

4069 1873 CC Open 3. [12,462] Very rare.

Rev. of 1870–72. Usually in low grades; prohibitively rare above EF. UNC.: Granberg, Mehl 54:359 (7/16/19).

4070 1874 [471,200 + 850P]

Arrows smaller and tilt upward at points, unlike those of 1873.

4071 1874 S [392,000]

Arrows as on preceding; mintmark as on 1873 S. See introductory text.

xii. ARROWS OMITTED (1875–91)

Beginning in Jan. 1875, quarters no longer showed arrows at date, though they continued to be made at the new weight standard.

Vars. in this period remained obscure until recent years. The first to be discovered was 1877 S over lazy S, before WW I (by H. O. Granberg), forgotten until the 1950s. For many years this was believed Ex. rare; during the 1970s many low-grade specimens turned up, mostly from later die states showing little of the horizontal S. Early die states with both S's clear are still very rare.

William Barber made a new rev. hub copying Longacre's original. The old Longacre hub (1866–80) shows TATE closely spaced at bases; the new Barber hub (1875–91) has these letters farther apart. We still do not know for certain if all the mintmark vars. of 1875–76 exist with both hubs, nor yet how rare are particular ones; other combinations probably exist. The same comment holds about the different mintmark sizes found in 1875–77.

Large mintages of 1875–77 were to retire 25¢ fractional notes.

Philadelphia issues 1879–90 were very limited; most survivors are proofs with a minority of prooflike uncirculated pieces, some of them probably (as in the 1860s) retrieved from proof sets. Circulated examples are rarely seen. As with half dollars, the reason for tiny quarter-dollar mintages is primarily the fatally stupid Bland-Allison Act of Feb. 28, 1878. This mandated coinages of silver dollars so immense as to monopolize the Mint's equipment, from bullion bought at artificially inflated prices: a frank subsidy whose sole purpose was to enrich owners of Western silver mines. Dollar-coinage quotas were so large that there was no time to prepare enough dies for smaller denominations, nor could bullion be bought for the latter; nor could any dollars be melted down for recoinage into smaller denominations. While silver dollars clogged Treasury vaults and banks, stores and employers suffered from a shortage of

smaller silver coins, and vain protests flooded the Mint Bureau until 1892.

The series ends with a rarity, the 1891 O: the only issue from New Orleans of this design. This tiny mintage [68,000] is difficult to find in any grade, and in mint state it is both very rare and in demand from type collectors. Occasion for the two brilliant proofs is uncertain; most likely they memorialized resumption of quarter-dollar coinage from this branch, the first since the Civil War.

ARROWS OMITTED

Designer, Engraver, Mints, Physical Specifications, Authorizing Acts, as before, except that the "Type II" hub is by William Barber, and mints include also New Orleans (O below eagle).

Grade range and standards, as before. Philadelphia coins 1879–91 rarely occur below EF; most are proofs. The majority have been cleaned.

4072 1875 [4,292,800 + 630P] "Type I" rev. Rare.

TATE close at bases. 1982 ANA:2157. Enl. photo.

4073 1875 "Type II" rev.

T A T E spaced apart at bases. 1982 ANA:2158–59. Enl. photo.

4074 1875 over "small" 5. "Type II" rev. Rare.

Business strikes only. Probably began as a double-punched date, the obv. reground and repolished to efface extra outlines.

4075 1875 S [680,000] "Type I" rev. Minute s. Rare.

Mintmark as in 1866–74. At least 2 positional vars.

4076 1875 S "Type II" rev. Minute s.

Auction 82:1643, others.

4077 1875 S "Type II" rev. Medium S, wide. Rare.

4078 1875 S "Type II" rev. Tall narrow S. Rare.

"Gilhousen":706, others.

4079 1875 CC "Type II" rev. [140,000]

None reported with "Type I" rev. To date 2 rev. vars. seen, out of 8 obvs. and 5 revs. requisitioned by William Sty Doane, Coiner, Feb. 12, 1875.

4080 1876 [17,816,000 + 1,410P] "Type I" rev. Rare.

In all, 101 obvs., 108 revs.; "Type I" revs. are leftovers from 1875. The few proofs use the 1872 rev. with die cut at l. border of shield; business strikes are less rare.

4081 1876 "Overdate." Very rare.
Part of what may be a 5 within loop of 6; remainder of original date mostly effaced.

4082 1876 "Type II" rev. Normal.
Many vars., several with traces of repunching at 1 or 76. Business strikes and proofs. Some proofs have dash in field just down from berry above Q.

4083 1876 "Type II" rev. Repunched 876; berry in field. Rare.
Rev. die drastically lapped; upper berry broken away (stem effaced). Ivy Cambridge:846.

4084 1876 S [8,596,000] "Type I" rev.; medium S, wide. Rare.

4085 1876 S "Type II" rev.; medium S, wide.

4086 1876 S "Type II" rev.; tall, narrow S.
Hetherington:366, others.

4087 1876 CC [4,944,000] "Type I" rev. Small wide c c. Rare.
McCloskey 1; rev. of 1870–73. Fine reeding (153 reeds). "Charmont":3180. *Gobrecht Journal* 11/78, pp. 23–25.

4088 1876 CC "Type I" rev. Small close cc. Scarce.
McCloskey 2. C's 0.7 mm tall. Fine reeding as last.

4089 1876 CC "Type I" rev. Tall CC. Scarce.
McCloskey 3. C's 1 mm tall.

4090 1876 CC "Type II" rev. Small cc.
McCloskey 4–7. Some show traces of repunching on 6 or CC. Edge, 113, 122, or 153 reeds. The minutely repunched date ill. in ANACS {1983} p. 90 may belong here; no specimen examined recently enough for attribution.

4091 1876 CC "Type II" rev. Tall CC.
McCloskey 8, 9. Fine reeding (153).

4092 1877 [10,911,200 + 880P] "Type II" rev.
80 obvs., 72 revs. None reported with "Type I" rev., though proofs may exist from the 1872 rev.

4093 1877 S [8,996,000] "Type II" rev. Large S.
S 1.1 mm. May exist with "Type I" rev.

4094 1877 S "Type II" rev. Small s. Scarce.
S about 0.8 mm.

4095 1877 S "Type II" rev. Medium S over horizontal S. Rare.
RPM 1. That ill. is from one of the rare earlier states. Later states (after die was repolished) showing less of the horizontal S bring lower premiums. See introductory text. Discovery specimen, Granberg coll. ("Prominent American":711); Green {1936} claimed only 4 were known. Collectors began cherrypicking others about 1955.

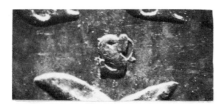

4096 1877 CC [4,192,000] "Type II" rev. Tall wide C C.
McCloskey 6. May exist with "Type I" rev.

4097 1877 CC "Type II" rev. Tall close CC.
McCloskey 4, 5.

4098 1877 CC "Type II" rev. Double date, tall wide C C.
McCloskey 2. Repunching plainest on bases of 77. See enl. ill. in *Errorgram* 12/82, p. 7.

4099 1877 CC "Type II" rev. Double date, tall close CC.
McCloskey 3. Same comments.

4100 1877 CC "Type II" rev. Small cc. Very rare.
Not in McCloskey.

4101 1878 [2,260,000 + 800 – P] "Type II" rev.
Of 1232 struck, 800 were delivered, 677 sold, 123 released into circulation. Julian {1986}. Proofs may exist with "Type I" rev. from the 1872 die.

4102 1878 S [140,000] "Type II" rev.
Much scarcer than its mintage figure suggests.

4103 1878 CC [996,000] "Type II" rev.
Several minor vars.: CC upright or leaning r.; former sometimes (about 1/3 of survivors) from "canceled" die, showing long raised line (die cut) along upper thigh. "Gilhousen":717.

4104 1879 "Type I" rev. Proofs only. Ex. rare.
Rev. of 1872, with the die cut at l. border of shield. See next.

4105 1879 [13,600 + ?P] "Type II" rev.
Proofs and business strikes. Much hoarded. Usually proofs or prooflike business strikings, rarely circulated. Internal records of the Mint insist only 250 proofs were coined, but more survive; the older figure of 1,100 proof sets for the year is likely to include interpolated business strikes and/or mixed dates. Breen {1977}, p. 163.

4106 1880 "Type I" rev. Proofs only. Ex. rare.
Rev. of 1872, as in **4104**. See next.

4107 1880 [13,600 + 1,355P] "Type II" rev.
Proofs and business strikes. Much hoarded. Usually proofs or prooflike business strikings. Breen {1977}, p. 166.

4108 1881 [12,000 + 975P]
"Type II" rev. from now on. Same comment as to preceding. Breen {1977}, p. 168.

4109 1882 [15,200 + 1,180?P]
Same comments. Breen {1977}, p. 171, for explanation of uncertainty in proof mintage figure.

4110 1883 [14,400 + 1,039?P]
Same comments. Breen {1977}, p. 174.

4111 1884 [8,000 + 875P]
Proofs have 84 in date touching; business strikes have these digits barely apart. Breen {1977}, p. 176. Almost all nonproof survivors are prooflike mint-state pieces, many formerly sold as proofs while the proofs cataloged higher; today, dull or cleaned proofs are often sold as "rare business strikes." Indiscriminately hoarded.

4112 1885 [13,600 + 940P]
Same comments as to 1881–83; Breen {1977}, p. 179.

4113 1886 Open 6, normal 1. [5,000]
Business strikes. Knob of 6 clearly free of loop; l. base of 1 vertically above center of dentil. Compare next. Much hoarded; usually found in prooflike mint state, generally cleaned. Breen {1977}, p. 181; compare comments to 1884.

4114 1886 Closed 6, base of 1 repunched. [886P] Proofs only. Knob of 6 touches or about touches loop; l. base of 1 above space between dentils. Much hoarded; many survivors come from a hoard of over 100 held by Charles E. Green (Chicago dealer who operated under the name of his wife, R.[uth] Green) and dispersed in the 1960s. Breen {1977}, p. 181.

4115 1887 [10,000 + 710P] Much hoarded. Proofs have level date, l. base of 1 vertically above a point barely r. of l. edge of a dentil; business strikes (normally prooflike mint state) have date slanting slightly down to r., l. base of 1 above space between dentils. Breen {1977}, p. 184.

4116 1888 [10,000 + 800P] For unknown reasons, less hoarded than previous dates. Breen {1977}, p. 187.

4117 1888 S [1,216,000] Usually in low grades. 3 vars. On one, LIBERTY weak or incomplete; on another, LIBERTY is normal, but claws, neck feathers, and lower rev. rim are weak.

4118 1889 [12,000 + 711P] Much hoarded. Breen {1977}, p. 189.

4119 1890 [80,000 + 590P] Breen {1977}, p. 189.

4120 1891 [3,920,000 + 600P]

4121 1891 O [68,000] Rare. Usually in low grades; see introductory text. 2 proofs known (discovery coin, "Prominent American":685); one, 1980 ANA:2024, brought $51,000.

4122 1891 S [2,216,000] Positional vars. in date and mintmark.

xiii. BARBER'S DESIGN (1892–1916)

The Mint Act of Sept. 26, 1890 (Mint Director James P. Kimball's brainchild) specified that thereafter coin designs could be changed only after they had been in use 25 years. As of 1891, dimes, quarters, and half dollars were eligible. (The Act also made nickels and dollars eligible, though they were not to be redesigned for another generation.)

Implementing Kimball's ideas, the Treasury announced a contest for new designs; details are in Chap. 25, Sect. xiii, introductory text. The presence of Mint Engraver Charles E. Barber (whose opposition to outsiders' designs was as immovable as the Pyramids) guaranteed that no entry would win a prize, let alone reach actual coinage. When Mint Director Edward O. Leech condemned the competition as a "wretched failure," he assigned the designing to Barber, which is what the Engraver had wanted all along. Taxay {1966}, p. 288.

Barber's new obv. was a mirror image of the Morgan dollar head, with most of Ms. Anna Willess Williams's hair cropped off and the rest modestly concealed within her enlarged cap. A plain laurel (?) wreath replaced the assorted vegetable matter in the brim; the religious motto was moved above, now that the Latin motto would appear on the eagle's scroll.

The Barber rev. harked back to that of 1804 (**3883**), copying Robert Scot's adaptation of the Great Seal of the United States, though this time without Scot's blunder in positioning arrows and olive branch. In the quaint but precise heraldic terminology: "an eagle, barbed and langued [= with feathers and tongue depicted], displayed, in a glory of 13 stars; on his breast the arms of the United States, argent, six pales gules, a chief azure; in his beak a scroll inscribed E PLURIBUS UNUM; in his dexter claw an olive branch of 13 leaves, in his sinister claw a sheaf of 13 arrows." The "stars" were a blunder, not being proper heraldic stars (estoiles) but molets or spur rowels, this misunderstanding apparently deriving from the appearance of these charges in George Washington's arms. There was no attempt to show heraldic shadings for colors of leaves, feathers, claws, or tongue—only on the shield, where as usual vertical lines represent gules (red) and horizontal lines azure (blue). The whole composition is Germanically stolid, prosy, crowded (especially on rev.), and without discernible merit aside from the technical one of low relief. His 1891 prototype (Judd 1761, in SI) was still worse: It included the clouds, crowding the design elements more even than Scot's.

Coins of 1892 from all mints, including proofs, come from two rev. hubs. "Type I" (1892 only) has eagle's wing covering less than half of E(D); "Type II" (1892–1916) has wing covering more than half of E including its entire crossbar, and the other wing overlaps much of R. "Type I" coins are scarcer from all mints and in all grade levels, and form a minority of proofs.

In 1901 a new obv. hub was put into use; leaves and berries are enlarged, inner ribbon ends form a rounded obtuse angle. (On the 1892–1900 dies, they form a rounded acute angle.) This modification continued through 1916. In late 1900 Barber also made a new rev. hub; wingtips extend beyond tops of E's, unlike former dies. David Lange, "Collectors' Clearinghouse," *CW* 11/12/80, p. 94.

Major vars. are very few, but in this series the kind of observation which has yielded new ones in other denominations is only beginning, and most likely new discoveries will be made, comparable to the 1893/2 dimes. Some collectors have begun paying attention to mintmark positions; the only ones likely to represent deliberate changes are here listed. "Mintmark far to left" (1892 only) is above l. part of R; "mintmark far to right" (1893–97) is above D, close to arrow butts. Usually the mintmark is in space somewhere between center of R and space between R D; this became standard.

There are no rare dates or mintmarks. William Pukall, A. C. Gies, and Wayte Raymond during the 1930s accumulated rolls of all Barber coins. (Rumor says no more than one or two rolls each of 1896 S, 1901 S, and 1913 S could be found, and perhaps three rolls of 1913 and several others.) These are the sources of most mint-state survivors of the scarcer O and S mints. Scarcity levels generally follow mintage figures. The final New Orleans issue, 1909 O, is unexpectedly scarce in mint state, apparently because few locals bothered to save them.

Proofs of all dates are available for a price; 1892 "Type I," 1913, 1914, and 1915 are the scarcest, price levels of the last three being kept higher by continuous hoarding. No proofs are reported for the final year 1916, and possibly none were made.

BARBER'S DESIGN

Designer, Engraver, Charles E. Barber. Mints, Philadelphia (no mintmark), New Orleans (mintmark O), San Francisco (S), Denver (D). Mintmark below tail. Physical Specifications, Authorizing Acts, as before.

Grade range, POOR to UNC. GOOD: Date and all letters legible except LIBERTY and motto on scroll. VERY GOOD: LI Y or L TY legible; partial motto. FINE: Full LIBERTY; most motto letters legible. VERY FINE: All of LIBERTY sharp; full motto. EXTREMELY FINE: Fully defined leaves and feathers; ribbon edges bold; isolated tiny rubbed spots only. NOTE: Beware coins offered as "UNC." which show rubbing on forelock, cheek, wingtips, and central tail feathers. True mint-state coins show no rubbing at all.

4123   1892 [all kinds 8,236,000 + 1,245P] "Type I" rev.
Wing covers less than half of E in UNITED; crossbar shows.
Comprises a minority of both business strikes and proofs. See
introductory text.

4124   1892 "Type II" rev.
Wing covers over half of E of UNITED including crossbar.
Comprises the majority of both business strikes and proofs.
See introductory text.

4125   1892 O [all kinds 2,640,000] "Type I" rev. Mintmark far
to l. Presently rare.
As **4123**. "Gilhousen":741. See introductory text. Probably
the first die mintmarked; this position does not recur.

4126   1892 O "Type I" rev. Mintmark normally placed.
Comprises a minority of this mintage.

4127   1892 O "Type II" rev.
As **4124**. Comprises the majority of this mintage. Some UNCS.
are from a roll (20) found on the West Coast about 1956.
Some show traces of repunching on mintmark.

4128   1892 S [all kinds 964,079] "Type I" rev.
As **4123**. Comprises a minority of this mintage.

4129   1892 S "Type II" rev.
As **4124**. Comprises the majority of this mintage.

4130   1893 [5,444,023 + 792P]

4131   1893 O [3,396,000]

4132   1893 O Mintmark far to r.
ANS {1914}, Newcomb display; Rhodes:1128–29.

4133   1893 O Same, over larger O. Presently very rare.
RPM 1, as triple O (small o double-punched); traces of larger
O above.

4134   1893 S [1,454,535]

4135   1893 S Mintmark far to r.
ANS {1914}, Newcomb display; "Gilhousen":745; Rhodes:
1130.

4136   1893 S Double S. Presently Ex. rare.
RPM 1. Mintmark first punched far to r., then partly effaced
and corrected in nearly central position. Discovered by Tom
Miller.

4137   1893 S Double-punched date. Presently very rare.
Discovery coin: the proof in 1975 Sub. Wash.:186.

4138   1894 [3,432,000 + 972P]

4139   1894 O [2,852,000]

4140   1894 O Mintmark far to r.
ANS {1914}, Newcomb display; "Gilhousen":747; others.

4141   1894 S [2,648,821]

4142   1894 S Mintmark far to r.
ANS {1914}, Newcomb display; 1984 Midwinter ANA:1060;
others.

4143   1895 [4,440,000 + 880P]

4144   1895 O [2,816,000]

4145   1895 O Mintmark far to r.
ANS {1914}, Newcomb display; "Gilhousen":751.

4146   1895 S [1,764,681]

4147   1895 S Mintmark far to r.
ANS {1914}, Newcomb display; "Gilhousen":752. Ill. *CW*
6/15/83, p. 72. Some have repunched S.

4148   1896 [3,874,000 + 762P]

4149   1896 O [1,484,000]

4150   1896 S [188,039]
Usually in low grades.

4151   1897 [8,140,000 + 731P]

4152   1897 O [1,414,800]

4153   1897 S [542,229]

4154   1897 S Mintmark far to r.
"Gilhousen":759; Auction 80:1207; Rhodes:1143; others.
From a leftover rev. of 1893–95?

4155   1898 [11,100,000 + 735P]
Occasionally shows traces of repunching on base of 1.

4156   1898 Obviously repunched 98. Very rare.
NN 54:340.

4157   1898 O [1,868,000]

4158   1898 S [1,020,592]

4159   1898 S over O? Ex. rare.
NN 54:1163. Not to be confused with the ordinary
repunched S, RPM 1.

4160   1899 [12,624,000 + 846P]

4161   1899 Double date. Ex. rare, reported.

4162   1899 O [2,644,000]

4163   1899 O Overdate. Ex. rare.
Final 9 over another digit, which is apparently not another 9.
1978 FUN:451.

4164   1899 S [708,000] Heavy filled S.

4165   1899 S Clear thin S. Presently very rare.
"Gilhousen":766.

4166   1900 [10,016,000 + 912P]
Reported with old and new rev. hubs. See introductory text.

4167   1900 O [3,416,000] Same comments.

4168   1900 S [1,858,585] Same comments.

4169   1901 New hubs. [8,892,000 + 813P]
May exist from the old rev. hub. See introductory text.

4170   1901 O New hubs. [1,612,000]
Same comments.

4171   1901 S [72,664] New hubs.
Same comments. Usually in low grades.

4172   1902 [12,196,967 + 777P]
Proofs 1902–15 have devices semibrilliant rather than frosty
as formerly.

4173   1902 O [4,748,000]

4174   1902 S [1,524,612]

4175   1903 [9,669,309 + 755P]

4176   1903 O [3,500,000]

4177   1903 S [1,036,000]

4178   1904 [9,588,143 + 670P]

4179   1904 Obviously repunched 19. Proofs only.
"Gilhousen":781. Comprises a tiny minority of proofs.

4180   1904 O [2,456,000]

4181   1905 [4,967,523 + 727P]

4182   1905 O [1,230,000]

4183   1905 S [1,884,000]

4184   1906 [3,655,760 + 675P]

4185   1906 O [2,056,000]

4186   1906 D [3,280,000]
Probably exists in proof state, like other denominations of
this year; occasion, inception of coinage at the new branch
mint.

4187   1907 [7,192,000 + 575P]

4188   1907 Repunched 7. Proofs only. Presently rare.
1982 ANA:2212; 1984 Midwinter ANA:1060; others.

4189 1907 O [4,560,000]

4190 1907 S [1,360,000]

4191 1907 D [2,484,000]

4192 1907 D Obviously repunched 7. Presently rare.
Date first entered to r. of final position, traces of extra 190 effaced. "Charmont":3253; Rhodes:1169.

4193 1907 D Obviously repunched 19. Presently very rare.
Date first entered too high, traces of extra 07 effaced. "Charmont":3254.

4194 1908 [4,232,000 + 545P]

4195 1908 Obviously repunched 18. Presently rare.
Business strikes only.

4196 1908 O [6,244,000]

4197 1908 S [784,000]

4198 1908 D [5,788,000]

4199 1909 [9,268,000 + 650P]

4200 1909 O [712,000]

4201 1909 O Doubled rev. die. Presently Ex. rare.
Doubling plainest on legend. "Gilhousen":800.

4202 1909 S [1,348,000]

4203 1909 D [5,114,000]

4204 1910 [2,244,000 + 551P]

4205 1910 D [1,500,000]

4206 1911 [3,720,000 + 543P]

4207 1911 S [988,000]

4208 1911 S over smaller s. Presently very rare.
RPM 1. Smaller s (for double eagles?) entirely within normal S.

4209 1911 D [933,600]

4210 1912 [4,400,000 + 700P]

4211 1912 S [708,000]

4212 1913 [484,000 + 613P]
See introductory text.

4213 1913 S [40,000]

4214 1913 D [1,450,800]

4215 1914 [6,244,250 + 380P]
See introductory text.

4216 1914 S [264,000]

4217 1914 D [3,046,000]

4218 1915 [3,480,000 + 450P]
See introductory text.

4219 1915 S [704,000]

4220 1915 D [3,694,000]

4221 1916 [1,788,000]

4222 1916 D [6,540,888] Normal D.
Occasionally shows traces of repunching on second 1. 1984 Midwinter ANA:1112. All coined Nov.–Dec. in haste. Wagner {1973}.

4223 1916 D Double D. Ex. rare.
Parallel uprights and curves of 2 D's (l. and r.) on early states: NN 54:1180. Later states (RPM 1) show uprights blurred together. Compare next.

4224 1916 D Large over small D. Ex. rare.
RPM 2. Ill. ANACS {1983}, p. 33. The small D (proper punch for the dime) was first entered low and leaning r., then the larger punch entered higher and leaning l. *NUM* 8/82, p. 2036. This was earlier thought to be D over S; what is touching tail is uncertain.

xiv. MACNEIL'S LIBERTY STANDING DESIGN, NO STARS BELOW EAGLE, "Type I" (1916–17)

By the Act of Sept. 26, 1890 any coin design could be changed only after 25 years' tenure. The Barber quarter's statutory lease was due to expire in 1917—though it could have remained in production decades longer, like the Lincoln cent. On Dec. 28, 1915, the Treasury announced another competition for new designs for the dime, quarter, and half dollar, evidently having forgotten the dismal results of its 1891 contest (Chap. 25, Sect. xiii, introductory text). On March 3, 1916, Mint Director Robert W. Woolley advised Mint Engraver Charles E. Barber that the designs submitted by Hermon Atkins MacNeil (1866–1947) had been approved for the quarter dollar as of Feb. 28, and that MacNeil would have to visit the Engraving Department to confer with Barber about mechanical requirements for relief models. Barber was, as usual, completely uncooperative with this outside input; George Morgan, the then almost forgotten Assistant Engraver (best known as the designer of the silver dollar), was much more helpful. On May 23, MacNeil's galvano models, suitable for electrotyping and reduction to coin size, were approved—minus the two dolphins which had originally flanked Ms. Liberty's feet, or the religious motto on the fold of drapery crossing her arm. One of the original plaster models is reproduced in Cline {1976}.

Jumping the gun by several weeks, the Philadelphia Mint coined some 52,000 quarters of the new design, Dec. 16–31, 1916, telling the general public nothing of the act; these were released, with the first 1917's, on Jan. 17, 1917. Ever since then, the 1916's have been in continuous demand, and touted as rarities, though they are always available for a price in any grade desired.

As early as *NUM* 5/17, MacNeil's model for Ms. Liberty was identified as Dora Doscher (Mrs. H. William Baum), later an actress in silent films under the name of Doris Doree. She was also the model for Karl Bitter's *Diana* (in the Metropolitan Museum of Art) and for the female figure in his Pulitzer Memorial Fountain in NYC. More recently, the story proved to be a deliberate coverup. Robert Curran (Newburgh, N.Y., *Evening News,* Sept. 19, 1972, cited also in *NUM* 5/78 and in Cline) quoted the Broadway actress Irene MacDowell as describing how she had posed for MacNeil. Mrs. MacDowell's name had remained a secret because her husband (one of MacNeil's tennis partners) disapproved. Photographic evidence indicates a composite portrait, but beyond doubt Irene MacDowell was the principal model.

Before Barber completed the working hubs for 1917, he modified the original master die. On 1916 quarters, leaves are broad and close together; on 1917's, they are narrower and farther apart, especially the two immediately l. of L; configuration of drapery above 19 differs; position of toes (above 7) differs; star below W is closer to line, and all stars are in higher relief. These distinctions enable identification of 1916's too worn to be read; see ANACS {1983}, p. 90.

But even these modifications were irrelevant to the most serious design flaw of all: The date is on an exposed plaque unprotected by raised rim, so that it wears down to illegibility long before anything else. That problem was not to be solved until the beginning of 1925, when the date was placed within a recess: See Sect. xvi below.

A second problem found on 1916's—and continuing on all dates through 1930, though paradoxically least of all on 1917 "Type I"—is that Ms. Liberty's head is apt to show less than half its design details. "Full head" mint-state coins show clear details of hair and leaves above ear, with full facial features; in all dates (1917 "Type I" least of all) they bring substantial premiums over ordinary uncirculated examples.

Full Head: Minimum Acceptable Detail

Cline claims that full heads are coins from new dies; more likely they are a matter of how the coins were struck. We are not prepared to ascribe the variation to die failure without more evidence from successive states of a single working die, especially because head details, shield bosses, inescutcheon, hand, breast, central drapery, knees, and toes differ greatly in definition on coins from the same dies without appreciable extension of cracks, and some coins from cracked dies have sharper head details than other coins from earlier states of the same dies.

Ornithologists claimed that the eagle had the "head of a

hawk, the wings of an eagle, the body of a dove": Schwarz {1974}.

However, still another feature of the new design, though cherished by the general public, proved the downfall of MacNeil's own conception. Followers of the unlamented Anthony Comstock, who had waged war on "immorality," noticed that Ms. Liberty's drapery exposed her right nipple, including (on the sharpest strikings) a realistic areola. Through their Society for the Suppression of Vice, the guardians of prudery at once began exerting political pressure on the Treasury Department to revoke authorization for these "immoral" coins, and to withdraw them from circulation. By the time they reached Treasury Secretary William G. McAdoo, their success was in sight: See next section, introductory text. Nevertheless, the Treasury refused to recall the coins already in circulation, and the general public saved enormous quantities of 1917 "Type I" as first of their kind. McAdoo and others falsely claimed that the "Type I" coins would not stack, as an argument for changing their design: Dolnick {1954}. But the real reason for its discontinuance was unquestionably prudery of the kind H. L. Mencken and George Bernard Shaw used to call comstockery. American official morality was no more ready in 1917 for a seminude coin than it had been in 1896–98 for a seminude Ms. Electricity on the $5 "Educational" notes. Whatever we may think today of Comstock, his enormous political clout then all too accurately reflected the abysmal state of national consciousness.

At least two prototypes are reported, matching the regular 1916 coins except without MacNeil's initial M on wall r. of date; these presumably followed the patterns Judd 1796, 1796a. Owing to unsupported claims of illegality and threats of seizure as contraband, specimens are still mostly inaccessible for study and photography. Extensive search has failed to locate any statute law supporting such claims or threats against private holders of such coins. The only source adduced even among Treasury agents (during the 1950s and 1960s at least) is the uncredited warning in Judd (4th ed., p. 219), which is obviously not evidence that will stand up in any court! Their rationale was originally a witchhunt begun by Mint Director James Putnam Kimball in 1887: See introductory text to Chap. 25, Sect. xiii. Clauses in the Mint Act of 1873, originally aimed at Mint officials, controlling the physical characteristics of coins to be placed in circulation, became twisted in Kimball's mind to justify his rigorism, which sought to outlaw any collector having anything which Kimball could not obtain—even unto cabinet coins publicly sold by his predecessors. This distorted reasoning rendered many irregular Mint productions (patterns, trial pieces, experimental coins, and off-metal error strikings) subject to seizure, especially during the McCarthyist 1950s. In 1982, the then Treasurer of the United States, Angela M. Buchanan told me in a letter that seizure of off-metal mint-error coins was no longer Treasury policy, and that the Mint Bureau did not wish to continue in an adversary relationship with collectors. However, no official decision has reversed Kimball's attempt at ex post facto legislation by fiat, nor have collectors dared risk exhibiting their prizes dated after 1907.

Aside from the prototypes, no date or mintmark is rare. Hoarders, most of all A. C. Gies, William Pukall, and Wayte Raymond, accumulated many UNC. rolls in the 1930s, especially from cash reserves of failed banks. Too many alleged mint-state survivors are cleaned "sliders"; look for rubbed knees.

MACNEIL'S LIBERTY STANDING, "Type I"

Designer, Engraver, Hermon A. MacNeil. Mints, Philadelphia (no mintmark), San Francisco (mintmark S), Denver (mintmark D). Mintmark between star and drapery above l.

end of date plaque. Physical Specifications, Authorizing Acts, as before.

Grade range, POOR to UNC. GOOD: All letters legible; date positively readable though its top will be weak; toes worn off, as are drapery lines on l. leg (at observer's r.). VERY GOOD: Date completely clear; drapery lines show above l. leg. FINE: High curve of r. leg (at observer's l.) flat from thigh to ankle, drapery lines on it visible at sides; only slight wear on l. leg. VERY FINE: Garment hem crossing r. leg visible though worn. EXTREMELY FINE: Sharp toes and garment hem across r. leg; isolated tiny rubbed spots only. NOTE: "Full head" uncirculated coins (see introductory text and enl. photo of upper half for minimum acceptable detail) command a premium varying from 150% to 400+% over price levels for ordinary UNCs. Coins with full head bring still higher prices if full details remain on knee, central drapery, and shield including bosses and inescutcheon (central smaller shield).

4225   1916 Prototype. Without M. 2 or 3 known?
Judd 1795. Enl. photos. See introductory text.

4226   1916 with M. [52,000 + ?P]
Usually in low grades. Mint-state survivors are mostly from 2 hoards of 100 and 80 specimens dispersed between 1944 and 1976. Nearly all have flat heads; I have seen no true full-head coin in over 30 years. 2 satin-finish proofs reported; these will have full heads and exceptionally sharp central details. Enl. photos.

4227   1917 "Type I." [8,740,000 + ?P]
True full heads are plentiful; tens of thousands of UNCs. survive: See introductory text. Enl. photos. Counterfeits have heavy crude lines in panels, 5 uneven, exaggerated stripes in inescutcheon. To date possibly 6 satin-finish proofs are reported. These have exceptionally sharp central details. Breen {1977}, p. 219.

4228   1917 S "Type I." [1,952,000]
Usually softly struck; full heads are scarce. Beware "sliders": See introductory text.

4229   1917 D "Type I." [1,509,200]
Cline {1976}, p. 78, claims large and small mintmark vars.; we are not convinced these are different punches rather than heavier and lighter impressions from the same punch on different working dies.

xv. THE BARBER-MACNEIL DESIGN: STARS BELOW EAGLE, "Type II" (1917–24)

On Jan. 11, 1917, Hermon A. MacNeil, designer of the new quarters, wrote to Mint Director F. J. H. von Engelken requesting permission to modify the design—despite many of the coins' having already reached circulation. At the Director's suggestion, MacNeil conferred with Treasury Secretary W. G. McAdoo, and at the latter's request, the Engraving Department admitted MacNeil to supervise the initial stages of transferring his modifications to metal. On April 16, McAdoo wrote to Rep. William Ashbrook (D.-Ohio), Chairman of the House Committee on Coinage, Weights, and Measures, enclosing a draft of an act which would permit the specific modifications requested—increasing concavity of fields, repositioning the eagle higher in field, placing three of the 13 stars below eagle, respacing the inscriptions. MacNeil alleged that the dies, as finished in the Mint, were untrue to his original conception—in which valid claim we may see the hand of Charles E. Barber at work, even as in 1913 on the "Type II" buffalo nickels, and still worse in 1907–8 on the St. Gaudens gold designs.

Ashbrook introduced McAdoo's bill on April 30, falsely alleging that the "Type I" coins then in circulation would not stack—provoking a storm of criticism of the Mint. As enacted, July 9, 1917, Public Law 27 specified that no change should be made in the devices other than those above specified: *Congressional Record*, 65th Congress, 1st Session, pp. 1568, 4223; cited also in Carothers {1930}, p. 293.

However, in the meantime, some supporters of the late Anthony Comstock had reached the Treasury Department demanding recall of the quarters on the grounds of alleged obscenity. The power of the Society for the Suppression of Vice was already too familiar: They had forced the Treasury in 1898 to recall some 35 million "Electricity" (Educational Series) $5 silver certificates for the same reason. And so, without anything being written into the *Congressional Record* (let alone the law) except that McAdoo did not like the "Type I" designs, the coins as issued from 1917 "Type II" on contained one illegal alteration: Ms. Liberty's décolleté was replaced by a coat of medieval chain mail—a grotesque anachronism, even if one naively assumed its adoption to have purely symbolic origin in the USA's involvement in the World War. Taxay {1966}, pp. 349–52.

The new type failed technically even worse than aesthetically. Whereas the 1917 "Type I" coins were generally well struck and full-head coins plentiful, the new "Type II" coins were the exact opposite. Coins with heads struck up well enough for discernment of details of hair and ear—let alone the leaves above ear—are the exception, and in some dates they are almost unobtainable. Worse yet, dates are weaker still, wearing down more rapidly than on "Type I." This defect did not come to official attention until the end of 1924 (see next section); and it is justly blamed on Charles E. Barber, whose last work at the Mint appears to have been his revisions on the quarter dollar. We therefore attribute this design jointly to him and MacNeil.

Full Head: Minimum Acceptable Detail

In this type, one major rarity exists: the 1918/7 S. During autumn 1917, immense wartime coinage quotas had to be filled in haste. The Engraving Department was simultaneously making dies for 1917 "Type II" and 1918; in particular, 1918-dated dies for the branch mints had to be ready well before the year's end, so that the Denver and San Francisco facilities could proceed at once with coinage of this denomination. One working die received a blow from a 1917 hub, routinely went to the annealing furnaces to be prepared for subsequent blows, but through error returned to the wrong press and received its other blow from a 1918 hub. (This annealing between blows is neces-

sary to prevent working dies from becoming stress-hardened and brittle enough to shatter on subsequent impressions from the hub.) Inspection failed to detect the error, and this obv. die was mintmarked for San Francisco and used—briefly—in coinage. Collectors first noticed the var. in 1937, and retrieved most survivors from circulation then and during the next few years. Its first auction appearance was in Bluestone 12/4/37:741, where a mint-state specimen (one of possibly six now known) sold for the then astronomical figure of $26.25. Dangerous counterfeits exist, made during the 1950s and 1960s to deceive gullible collectors; but as there is only one die var. of the genuine, the enlarged ills. will enable instant detection of forgeries.

A Midwest dealer has claimed 1918/7 Philadelphia and Denver coins, from very worn specimens. We have not seen these, and the vars. remain unconfirmed.

No date or mintmark is rare in mint state, owing to activities of the hoarders Gies, Pukall, and Raymond, who retrieved many original bank rolls during the 1930s, especially from cash reserves of failed banks. However, not many rolls turned up of 1921 or 1923 S.

The Barber-MacNeil Design, "Type II"

Designer, Engraver, Charles E. Barber, after Hermon A. MacNeil. Mints, Physical Specifications, as before. Authorizing Act, July 9, 1917.

Grade range and standards, as before. NOTE: Full-head mint-state coins bring 200% to 600% above ordinary UNCs. The enlarged ill., left column, shows minimum detail acceptable for full-head pricing.

4230 1917 "Type II." [13,880,000]
4231 1917 S "Type II." [5,552,000]
Full heads are very scarce.
4232 1917 D "Type II." [6,224,000]
Full heads are rare, as for next 2.
4233 1918 [14,240,000]
Same comment.
4234 1918 S [11,072,000]
Often weak. Same comment.
4235 1918/1917 S. Very scarce.
Usually in low grades; only 6 mint-state specimens are known, none with full head. See introductory text. Dangerous forgeries exist; genuine specimens match the var. here ill., enl. Note position of 7 within 8, die defect in field r. of toes, and other microscopic features here highlighted. Single or

double clash marks below TR; the later states show clashed E (from Latin motto) next to lower knee and upper calf r. of fourth star (counting up).

4236 1918 D [7,380,000]
Usually weak at top of date and breast feathers. Full heads are rare.

4237 1919 [11,324,000]

4238 1919 S [1,836,000]
Often weak. Full heads are very rare.

4239 1919 D [1,944,000]
Dates usually weak. Full heads are prohibitively rare.

4240 1920 [27,860,000]

4241 1920 S [6,380,000]
Often weak. Full heads are very rare.

4242 1920 D [3,586,400]
Dates are usually weak at top. Full heads are very scarce.

4243 1921 [1,916,000]
Usually in low grades. Usually weak at lower half of date, even on rare full-head coins. Shape of 1's differs from later issues. Beware pieces fraudulently altered from 1924; on these the 1's do not match.

4244 1923 [9,716,000]

4245 1923 S [1,360,000]
Full heads are rare. Fraudulent alterations from 1928 S are easily detected by having recessed dates (see next section).

4246 1924 [10,920,000]
Numerals thinner.

4247 1924 S [2,860,000]
Often weak. Full heads are very rare.

4248 1924 D [3,112,000]
Often weak. Full heads are prohibitively rare.

xvi. RECESSED DATES, "Type III" (1925–30)

By late 1924, Mint authorities finally realized that Barber had blundered. Coins were coming in from banks, obviously of the 1917–24 design, but with dates completely worn off, whereas many earlier quarter dollars dating back to the mid-

1870s were still circulating and legible. The only possible answer short of replacing the design (which would have required another Act of Congress) was to go ahead and modify the existing hubs at date, saying nothing about the change.

No longer is the date on a raised panel exposed to wear faster than any other detail; instead, from Jan. 1925 until the end of the series, dates are in a recess, well protected from wear. Unfortunately, nothing else was done about the relief modeling, so that striking quality remained as before; most mint-state survivors are softer strikes than their 1917–24 predecessors, drapery contours being vague even on the best full-head coins, and the latter are virtually unknown for some dates.

Full Head: Minimum Acceptable Detail

There are no major vars. and no rarities in this period, though the 1927 S has proved unexpectedly difficult to locate in mint state. Probably not more than a couple of rolls were available to the sources of the Gies, Pukall, and Raymond hoards.

RECESSED DATES, "Type III"

Designer, Engraver, George T. Morgan, after Barber and MacNeil. Mints, Physical Specifications, Authorizing Acts, as before.

Grade range and standards, as previously, except that dates are clear even in GOOD. See note to previous section about full-head coins. Enlarged ill. shows minimum acceptable detail for full-head pricing.

4249 1925 [12,280,000]
Full heads are rare.

4250 1926 [11,316,000]
Full heads are rare. Some coins from worn dies show 6 distorted like G or 6/0 (not overdate): *CW* 2/1/84, p. 70.

4251 1926 S [2,700,000]
Usually in low grades. Full heads are very rare. Beware forgeries made by cementing S mintmarks to genuine Philadelphia coins!

4252 1926 D [1,716,000]
Plentiful in mint state from bags recovered from banks in the early 1930s. Usually weak at head and drapery; full heads are prohibitively rare.

4253 1927 [11,912,000]

4254 1927 S [396,000]
Usually in low grades. Mint-state survivors are weak at head and drapery; full heads are prohibitively rare. Beware forgeries made by cementing S mintmarks to genuine Philadelphia coins!

4255 1927 D [976,000]
Plentiful in mint state for the same reason as 1926 D. Full heads are rare.

4256 1928 [6,336,000]

4257 1928 S [2,644,000] Small s. Presently scarce.
Mintmark usually distant from star; same punch as on earlier S mints, with little difference between top, middle, and bottom curves. Compare next. Often weak; full heads are rare.

4258 1928 S Large S.
Mintmark usually touches star; the S punch is tall, boldface, with heavy middle element. Often weak. Full heads are rare.

4259 1928 S Obviously repunched large S. Presently rare.
RPM 1. Auction 80:159, UNC., $3,850. S first entered to r. and leaning l., then corrected. This may be Cline's "large over small s": *NUM* 11/77, p. 2297.

4260 1928 D [1,627,600]
Plentiful in mint state for same reason as previous D mints. Often weak; full heads are very scarce.

4261 1928 D over S? Presently very rare.
Curve of S (?) within D. Crack, lowest l. star through pedestal to designer's initial M; another from drapery through ankle to rim at 4:30. Described by Douglas Winter in 1984 Midwinter ANA:1152. Another possible die is RPM 1: traces of S (?) between star and repunched D.

4262 1929 [11,140,000]

4263 1929 S [1,764,000]
Mint-state specimens are no longer scarce, owing to a hoard of 100 found in California in early 1975. Full heads are scarce.

4264 1929 D [1,358,000]
Often weak. Full heads are very rare.

4265 1930 [5,632,000]

4266 1930 S [1,556,000]
Often weak. Full heads are prohibitively rare. The 1931's alleged by Cline remain unconfirmed to exist. His own source (the late dealer James Kelly) claimed to have seen one decades ago, but Kelly's own credibility has been justly impugned.

xvii. FLANAGAN'S WASHINGTON DESIGN, SILVER (1932–65)

Following the precedent of the Lincoln cent (first issued in 1909 to commemorate the centennial of the martyred President's birth), the Treasury proposed in early 1931 that the half dollars to be issued in 1932 should honor Washington's birth bicentennial by portraying him. Accordingly, the Treasury and the Washington Bicentennial Commission cosponsored another design competition, with cooperation of the federal Commission of Fine Arts. Terms of the contest specified that the Washington portrait on obv. should be based on Houdon's bust (1785) preserved at Mount Vernon. Congress changed matters by deciding that not the half dollar but the quarter should be so honored (Act of March 4, 1931); a Washington half dollar had to wait another 50 years: See Chap. 39.

The winner of the competition was Laura Gardin Fraser, distinguished sculptor, best known among coin collectors for the Oregon Trail commemoratives. Taxay {1966}, p. 364, illustrates Mrs. Fraser's models, which would have made splendid coins.

Unfortunately, Treasury Secretary Andrew W. Mellon (one of the world's wealthiest men, and reputedly one of the stubbornest) refused to agree to the two commissions' adjudication. A second competition, judged Oct. 27, 1931, again awarded the prize to Mrs. Fraser, and again Mellon refused to consent. It has been learned that Mellon knew all along who had submitted the winning models, and his male chauvinism partly or wholly motivated his unwillingness to let a woman win. Mellon chose the John Flanagan design, which he had favored from the beginning.

Early in 1932, Ogden L. Mills succeeded Mellon, and the Commission of Fine Arts wrote to the new Secretary urging that he approve the winning entry for production coins. Mills refused to contradict Mellon's judgment, and named Flanagan as the designer of the new quarter dollar. Taxay {1966}, pp. 360–66.

How valid the Commissions' objections to the Flanagan design were can be judged by the ills. of 1932 and 1934 Light Motto: On even mint-state specimens of this first type, obv. motto IN GOD WE TRUST is always faint, often blurred; after a little wear, it is often illegible. Washington's hair and facial features often require some imagination to discern.

Accordingly, during 1934, not one but two hub changes were made, producing medium and heavy motto types; both occur on Philadelphia and Denver quarters, replacing the original light motto of 1932–34. Coins of 1935 all have the medium motto; those of 1936–64, the heavy. This last is most quickly identifiable by the middle vertex of W, which is taller than outer strokes. At least six more modifications of the design followed, none wholly satisfactory; in 1938, for instance, the profile was sharpened, and again in 1944, with changes in shape of peruque and ribbon. The 1944 version showed designer's initials JF somewhat misshapen; these were redrawn for 1945.

There are no rare dates. A. C. Gies, William Pukall, and Wayte Raymond hoarded rolls of all dates and mints from the beginning, though few of 1932 D or 1936 D were ever available. On the other hand, overmintmarks and doubled dies (discoveries of recent years) do include some real rarities. Generally, the more obvious they are, the rarer, and the higher their premiums.

Large and small mintmarks exist for 1941 S; large D's alleged for 1934 and 1936 have proved on microscopic examination to be instead heavily repunched.

Business strikes and proofs 1937–64 are from different rev. hubs. On coins for circulation ("Type A" rev.), relief is low, ES almost touch, and adjacent leaf extends only to top arrow point. On proofs ("Type B" rev.), relief is higher, E S are apart, and leaf extends above top arrow point. In 1956–64, both types of rev. occur on business strikes; possibly on earlier years, though none are yet reported.

When the clad or sandwich-metal coinage began (1965: See next section), the rev. was again modified. One var. of silver quarter, 1964 D "Type C" rev. has this modified hub; this is similar to "Type A" but shows two leaves touching tops of AR, and other leaves are elongated. Almost certainly this coin was made in 1965 during final use of silver planchets. The 1964 Philadelphia may also exist with this rev. Data on hub changes are from Herbert Hicks (personal communication).

FLANAGAN'S WASHINGTON DESIGN, SILVER

Designer, Engraver, John Flanagan, obv. after Jean Antoine Houdon. Mints, Philadelphia (no mintmark), San Francisco (mintmark S), Denver (D). Mintmarks below wreath. Physical Specifications, as before. Authorizing Act, March 4, 1931.

Grade range, FAIR to UNC. GOOD: All letters legible (see EXCEPTIONS) and flat but separated from rim; no hair lines near face. VERY GOOD: Bold even rims, tops of letters near them flat; wingtips outlined. FINE: Some hair lines show about ear; some breast feathers show, though faintly. VERY FINE: Nearly complete hair lines r. of brow and near ear; nearly complete feathers. EXTREMELY FINE: Isolated tiny rubbed spots only on two rolls of hair (before and behind ear), top of legs, center of breast; design details otherwise complete, partial mint luster.

EXCEPTIONS: On 1932 (all mints) and 1934 "Type I," obv. motto will be weak and blurry even in VF, and may be partly blurry even in EF. On mint-state specimens of these and some later dates, base of bust, eagle's breast, and both outer wing edges may be weak; look for mint frost on weak parts. NOTE: Beware "sliders" offered as "UNC." showing rubbing on rolls of hair near ear, cheek, and eagle's breast.

4267   1932 [5,404,000]
Released Aug. 1, 1932. Much hoarded. Enl. photos (of **4269**).

4268   1932 S [408,000]
Numerous "sliders" are offered as "UNC.": See NOTE above.
4269   1932 D [436,000]
Same comment as to preceding. More difficult to find pristine than 1932 S because fewer rolls were saved. Mintmark sometimes lightly repunched or almost solid. Beware forgeries made by affixing D's to genuine 1932 quarters. See enl. ills. of genuine in ANACS {1983}, p. 91; only the single D punch was used. Ill. above **4267**. Jack Beymer discovered sharp and dull cusps to 3; it is uncertain if the latter represents an overpolished die or a different hub. Research is continuing. On the former, cusp has an elongated point; on the latter, a rounded right angle.
4270   1934 [31,912,052] Light motto, "Type I."
Same hub as 1932. Estimated about 500,000 coined.

4271   1934 Medium motto, "Type II."
Same hub as 1935. Estimated about 28 million coined. Note shape of W. Dangerous forgeries exist. *NUM* 6/86, p. 1173.

4272   1934 Medium motto, doubled obv. die. Very scarce. Price for the var. ill. Later states, after obv. die was repolished, showing less obvious doubling, bring lower premiums, as do those from a second doubled obv. showing faint doublings on TRUST.

4273   1934 Heavy motto, "Type III."
Same hub as 1936–37. Estimated about 3.4 million coined. Note shape of W. First distinguished from preceding in *Numisma* 11/58:250.

4274   1934 D [3,527,200] "Type II."
As **4271**. Estimated about 1 million coined.
4275   1934 D "Type II." Obvious double-punched D.
4276   1934 D "Type III."
As **4273**. Estimated about 2.5 million coined.
4277   1935 "Type II" only. [32,484,000]
4278   1935 S "Type II" only. [5,660,000]
Often weak.
4279   1935 D "Type II" only. [5,780,000]
4280   1936 "Type III" only. [41,300,000 + 3,837P]
All proofs seen to date are of the second or extra-brilliant style. Breen {1977}, p. 226.

4281 1936 Doubled obv. die. Presently very rare.
Doubling plain at date and LIBERTY, obvious at motto. ANACS {1983}, p. 33. Discovered by Delma K. Romines, 1961.

4282 1936 S "Type III" only. [3,828,000]
4283 1936 D "Type III" only. [5,374,000]
Usually in low grades. Beware "sliders" offered as "UNC." Beware forgeries made by affixing D mintmarks to genuine Philadelphia coins.
4284 1936 D Clearly repunched D.
Several vars. including RPM 1 and *Numisma* 4/59:85. One var. shows minute triple punching under $40\times$ magnification.
4285 1936 D over horizontal D. Very rare.
Not in RPM. Mintmark first punched rotated 90° from normal, with upright at top, then corrected. Usually in low grades.
4286 1937 "Type A" rev. [19,696,000]
See introductory text. Business strikes only.
4287 1937 Doubled obv. die. Presently ex. rare.
Doubling obvious at motto and date. ANACS {1983}, p. 33; discovery reported in *NUM* 8/82, p. 2036.
4288 1937 "Type B" rev. [5,542P] Proofs only.
See introductory text.
4289 1937 S "Type A" rev. [1,652,000]
See introductory text.
4290 1937 D "Type A" rev. [7,189,600]
See introductory text.
4291 1938 "Type A" rev. [9,472,000]
Modified profile from now on. See introductory text.
4292 1938 "Type B" rev. [8,045P] Proofs only.
Same comment.
4293 1938 S "Type A" rev. [2,832,000]
Same comment. Also with repunched mintmark. *Numisma* 11/58:410.
4294 1939 "Type A" rev. [33,540,000]
See introductory text.
4295 1939 "Type B" rev. [8,795P] Proofs only.
See introductory text.
4296 1939 S "Type A" rev. [2,628,000]
See introductory text. A minor doubled obv. die exists.
4297 1939 D "Type A" rev. [7,092,000]
See introductory text. Also with repunched mintmark, RPM 1.
4298 1939 D over S. "Type A" rev. Presently very rare.
RPM 2. Discovered by Bill Fivaz.

4299 1940 "Type A" rev. [35,704,000]
See introductory text.
4300 1940 "Type B" rev. [11,246P] Proofs only.
See introductory text.
4301 1940 S "Type A" rev. [8,244,000] Small s.
See introductory text. Often weak. S as before; may exist with large S.
4302 1940 D "Type A" rev. [2,797,600]
See introductory text.
4303 1941 "Type A" rev. [79,032,000]
See introductory text.
4304 1941 Same. Doubled obv. die. Presently very rare.
Doubling plainest at motto. Discovered by Delma K. Romines, 1979. Two other vars. known.
4305 1941 "Type B" rev. [15,287P] Proofs only.
See introductory text.
4306 1941 S "Type A" rev. [16,080,000] Small s.
See introductory text. Mintmark as 1932–40: See ill., ANACS {1983}, p. 91. Often weak.
4307 1941 S Same, large S, sharp serifs.
Mintmark as 1942–44: boldface, thick midsection, sharp serifs. Often weak.
4308 1941 D "Type A" rev. [16,714,000]
See introductory text.
4309 1941 D Doubled obv. die. "Type A" rev. Presently very scarce.
Doubling plainest at motto. Discovered by Tom Miller, 1978.

4310 1942 "Type A" rev. [102,096,000]
See introductory text.
4311 1942 "Type B" rev. [21,123P] Proofs only.
See introductory text.
4312 1942 S "Type A" rev. [19,384,000] Large S, sharp serifs.
See introductory text. May exist with small s.
4313 1942 S Same. Large knob-tailed S.
4314 1942 D "Type A" rev. [17,487,200]
See introductory text.
4315 1942 D Doubled obv. die. Ex. rare.
COINS 3/76, p. 56. Doubling obvious at motto and LIBERTY. Steiner & Zimpfer [1974], p. 66.

4316 1942 D Doubled rev. die. Ex. rare.
Doubling plainest on branch and beak.

4317 1943 [99,700,000]
"Type A" rev. henceforth unless otherwise noted. A doubled obv. die exists. Steiner & Zimpfer [1974], p. 66.

4318 1943 S [21,700,000] Large S, sharp serifs.
Often weak. May exist with knob-tailed S or trumpet-tailed S.

4319 1943 S Doubled obv. die. Very rare.
Hirt:81, others. Doubling plain also at date and LIBERTY. Ill. *NUM* 3/86, p. 447. Steiner & Zimpfer [1974], p. 66.

4320 1943 D [16,095,000]

4321 1943 D over horizontal D. Ex. rare.
D first entered 90° rotated (upright at bottom), then corrected.

4322 1943 D Multiple D. Presently very rare.
RPM 6. Hook at lower l. may be part of curve of a fourth or fifth D.

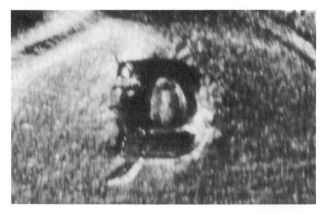

4323 1944 Sharpened queue. [104,956,000]
Designer's initials JF on truncation larger, distorted; profile slightly modified. This new hub occurs on 1944's from all mints.

4324 1944 S Sharpened queue. [12,560,000]
Same comment. Often weak.

4325 1944 S Doubled obv. die. Very scarce.

4326 1944 D Sharpened queue. [14,600,800]

4327 1945 [74,372,000]
New hub, 1945–64. JF no longer distorted.

4328 1945 Doubled obv. die. Presently very rare.
Discovered by Delma K. Romines, June 30, 1979.

4329 1945 S [17,004,001] Trumpet-tailed S.
Minute doubled dies exist: *NNW* 2/4/78, p. 30.

4330 1945 S Knob-tailed S.

4331 1945 D [12,341,600]

4332 1946 [53,436,000]

4333 1946 S [4,204,000] Trumpet-tailed S.

4334 1946 S Knob-tailed S.
Forms a small minority.

4335 1946 D [9,072,800]

4336 1946 D over S. Presently scarce.
OMM 1. Discovered by Bill Fivaz.

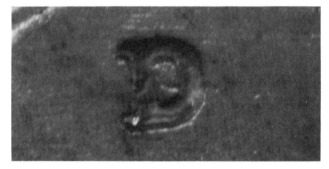

4337 1946 D Doubled rev. die. Presently ex. rare.
Discovered by Don Taxay. Doubling plainest on STATES OF.

4338 1947 [22,556,000]

4339 1947 S [5,532,000] Trumpet-tailed S.

4340 1947 S Knob-tailed S.
Same comment as to **4334.**

4341 1947 D [15,338,400]

4342 1948 [35,196,000]

4343 1948 S [15,960,000]
Knob-tailed S henceforth. May exist also with trumpet-tailed S.

4344 1948 D [16,766,800]

4345 1949 [9,312,000]

4346 1949 D [10,068,400]

4347 1950 "Type A" rev. [24,920,126]
Business strikes only. See introductory text.

4348 1950 "Type B" rev. [51,386P] Proofs only.
See introductory text. Earlier proofs are satiny, later ones very brilliant. Breen {1977}, p. 228.

4349 1950 S [10,284,004]

4350 1950 S Obvious double S. Presently rare.
RPM 1. S first punched well above its final position. Not to be confused with next.

4351 1950 S over D. Presently ex. rare.
OMM 1. Discovered by Stephen Roach ca. 1964.

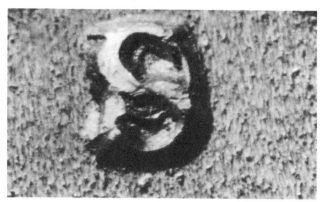

Courtesy ANACS

4352 1950 D [21,075,600]
4353 1950 D Doubled rev. die. Presently very rare.
Doubling strongest on talons. *EVN* 4/82, p. 6. Discovered by Delma K. Romines, March 1982.
4354 1950 D over S. Presently scarce.
OMM 1. Discovered by Tom Miller. Usually in low grades; rare UNC.

Courtesy ANACS

4355 1951 "Type A" rev. [43,448,102]
See introductory text.
4356 1951 "Type B" rev. [57,500P] Proofs only.
4357 1951 S [9,048,000]
4358 1951 D [35,354,800]
Jeffrey Cole discovered a D/S overmintmark. Ill. *CW* 9/10/86, p. 86.
4359 1952 "Type A" rev. [37,780,093]
4360 1952 "Type B" rev. [81,980P] Proofs only.
Herbert Hicks reports a doubled rev. die, "B/A," which received a blow from each hub. Extra outlines within AR R of QUARTER and A's of AMERICA. Presently rare.
4361 1952 S [13,707,800]
4362 1952 D [49,795,200]
4363 1953 "Type A" rev. [18,536,120]
4364 1953 "Type B" rev. [128,800P] Proofs only.
4365 1953 S [14,016,000]
4366 1953 D [56,112,400]
4367 1953 D over S. Presently ex. rare.
OMM 1. Part of S within triple-punched D.
4368 1954 "Type A" rev. [54,412,203]
4369 1954 "Type B" rev. [233,300P] Proofs only.
4370 1954 S [11,834,722]

4371 1954 D [46,305,500]
4372 1955 "Type A" rev. [18,180,151]
4373 1955 "Type B" rev. [378,200P] Proofs only.
4374 1955 D [3,182,400]
4375 1956 [all kinds 44,144,000] "Type A" rev.
See introductory text. Mintage includes business strikes of next.
4376 1956 "Type B" rev. [? + 669,384P]
Business strikes (presently rare) and proofs. See introductory text.
4377 1956 D [all kinds 32,334,500] "Type A" rev.
See introductory text.
4378 1956 D Same. D over horizontal D? Presently scarce.
RPM 1. Mintmark first entered rotated 90° (upright at top), then corrected. Discovered by Bill Fivaz.
4379 1956 D "Type B" rev.
Mintage included in **4377**; relative scarcity of the 2 types not yet known. See introductory text.
4380 1957 [all kinds 46,532,000] "Type A" rev.
See introductory text.
4381 1957 "Type B" rev. [? + 1,247,952P]
Forms about 5% of business strikes.
4382 1957 D [all kinds 77,924,160] "Type A" rev.
See introductory text.
4383 1957 D "Type B" rev.
Mintage included in preceding. Relative scarcity of the 2 types not known. See introductory text.
4384 1958 [all kinds 6,360,000] "Type A" rev.
See introductory text.
4385 1958 "Type B" rev. [? + 875,652P]
Forms a minority of business strikes.
4386 1958 D [all kinds 78,124,900] "Type A" rev.
See introductory text.
4387 1958 D "Type B" rev.
Same comments as to **4383**.
4388 1959 [all kinds 24,384,000] "Type A" rev.
See introductory text.
4389 1959 "Type B" rev. [? + 1,149,291P]
Found in all mint sets. Forms a minority of business strikes.
4390 1959 D [all kinds 62,054,232] "Type A" rev.
See introductory text.
4391 1959 D "Type B" rev.
Same comments as to **4383**.
4392 1960 [all kinds 29,160,000] "Type A" rev.
See introductory text.
4393 1960 "Type B" rev. [? + 1,691,602P]
Found in some mint sets. Forms a minority of business strikes.
4394 1960 D [all kinds 63,000,324] "Type A" rev.
See introductory text.
4395 1960 D "Type B" rev.
Same comments as to **4383**.
4396 1961 [all kinds 37,036,000] "Type A" rev.
See introductory text.
4397 1961 "Type B" rev. [? + 3,028,244P]
Same comments as to **4393**.
4398 1961 D [all kinds 83,656,928] "Type A" rev.
See introductory text.
4399 1961 D "Type B" rev.
Same comments as to **4383**.
4400 1962 [all kinds 36,556,000] "Type A" rev.
See introductory text.
4401 1962 "Type B" rev. [? + 3,218,019P]
Same comments as to **4393**.
4402 1962 D [all kinds 127,554,756] "Type A" rev.
See introductory text.
4403 1962 D "Type B" rev.
Same comments as to **4383**.

4404 1962 D over horizontal D. Presently very rare. RPM 1.

4405 1963 [all kinds 74,316,000] "Type A" rev. See introductory text.

4406 1963 "Type B" rev. [? + 3,075,645P] Same comments as to **4393**.

4407 1963 D [all kinds 135,288,184] "Type A" rev. See introductory text.

4408 1963 D Same. Doubled obv. die. Presently very rare. Discovered by Delma K. Romines, early 1979. All seen to date are from mint sets.

4409 1963 D "Type B" rev. Same comments as to **4383**.

4410 1964 [all kinds 560,390,585] "Type A" rev. See introductory text.

4411 1964 "Type B" rev. [? + 3,950,762P] Same comments as to **4393**.

4412 1964 "Type C" rev. "Transitional." Probably exists. Rev. from new hub of 1965: 2 leaves touch tops of AR. Compare **4415**; see ill. at **4418**.

4413 1964 D [all kinds 704,135,528] "Type A" rev. See introductory text.

4414 1964 D "Type B" rev. Same comments as to **4383**. Compare next.

4415 1964 D "Type C" rev. "Transitional." Presently rare. Rev. from new hub of 1965: 2 leaves touch tops of AR. See ill. at **4418**. Doubtless struck in 1965, pursuant to Act of 9/3/64, mandating continuance of 1964 dating.

4416 1965 "Type C" rev. On obsolete silver blank. Ex. rare. Milton G. Cohen coll.

xviii. WASHINGTON DESIGN, CLAD (1965–74)

During 1963–64, several phenomena combined to produce what was commonly misinterpreted as a coin shortage. On the one hand, as usual in wartime, prices rose and need increased for coins to make change; on a second, silver prices rose sharply enough to make bullion hoarding attractive to Wall Street speculators and to make far less raw silver available to the Mint Bureau for coinage; on a third, a flowback problem developed: Vending machine companies, laundromats, transit companies, tollbooth authorities, parking meter divisions of local police departments, and above all the telephone companies continued their earlier practice of collecting and depositing receipts only once or twice a month. Most coins accordingly spent over 90% of their time in locked compartments rather than moving from firms to banks to merchants to the public and back again. (I was one of several columnists to expose this problem in print.) Meanwhile, the Treasury Department was redeeming silver certificates as part of a recall program, first in silver dollars, later in other silver coins, later still in small bags of silver granules; little of this bullion ever reached the Mint Bureau.

In a triumph of stupidity, Mint Bureau spokesmen blamed coin collecting for this problem: "Withholding from circulation" was their scapegoat phrase then even as in 1979. They were either unable or unwilling to differentiate between the Boy Scout with his birthyear set for the Merit Badge, the specialist collector, the dealer in rolls and bags, and the Wall Street speculator with his vaults full of silver dollars. This was one more act in a feud dating back to 1858, when Mint officials surreptitiously made restrikes of various rare coins, peddled them to collectors and dealers with lying claims about how many had been made, and were exposed in the coin trade papers: Breen {1962B}; Newman-Bressett {1962}; Breen {1977}, pp. 249–66. Accordingly, the Mint Bureau's strategy for dealing with their

1964–65 crisis ignored the flowback aspect, and concentrated on blaming coin collectors, bullion dealers, and speculators— officially a single category. To discourage collectors, the Bureau pushed a bill through Congress to continue the date 1964 on coins until stocks were large enough to assuage their fears of hoarders (Act of 9/3/64; cf. Sect. 204, Coinage Act of July 23, 1965); they discontinued mintmarks on all denominations, 1965–67; and they stopped making proof sets (costing the Bureau some $10 million in gross annual receipts from this source: Talk about cutting off one's nose to spite one's face!): an overall policy of pinpricks. Even if they had managed to outlaw collecting of rolls or bags of coins (which was in fact advocated), this would not have ended the problem of dwindling bullion stocks.

As in 1942, when nickel and copper had become strategic minerals, the solution most attractive to the Mint Bureau was a change of metal. However, any substitute for silver would have to pass vending machine counterfeit-rejection systems, otherwise it would require that over one million machines stay simultaneously out of service pending retooling, which would take an estimated $100 million and five years to complete. The Mint consulted the Battelle Institute, which recommended adoption of clad metal, alias "sandwich metal." This consisted of thin cupro-nickel layers (75% copper, 25% nickel) bonded to pure copper cores. Pres. Johnson signed the proposal into law as the Coinage Act of July 23, 1965; his pen stroke abolished anticounterfeit tests millennia old. "Sandwich metal" quarters are lightweight by nearly 10% (5.67 gms. compared with the former 6.25); they are slick to the touch, like cast counterfeits; they show less design detail, again like most counterfeits; and in recent years they have been extensively counterfeited despite beliefs that their purchasing power had become too low to attract the ungodly.

Beginning in 1968, mintmarks were restored; henceforth they are located behind ribbon tying Washington's peruque. In an unprecedented change, the San Francisco Mint (closed in 1955) was reopened under its 1851–53 title of "United States Assay Office," and ever since 1968, this facility has made, packed, and distributed proof sets, all with the S mintmark.

Revs. are of two types, corresponding to Types B and C in previous section. "Type B" comes on all proofs and some business strikes through 1972; this has eagle in relatively high relief, E S apart, leaf extends above top arrow point, and only one leaf above R. "Type C" occurs on the vast majority of business strikes; this has lower relief, most leaves elongated, two leaves touching tops of (L)AR. Today, clad quarters are struck at 80 tons force, 130 per minute; die life averages somewhere between 250,000 and 500,000 pieces. (Proofs instead require two blows each, and dies last only a few thousand impressions: See **Proof Dies** in Glossary.) Data on hub changes are from Herbert Hicks (personal communication).

Though it hardly belongs here as a regular listing, the 1970 S proof quarter in standard silver, overstruck on a 1900 quarter, deserves mention. This is pictured in Breen {1977}, p. 231; it brought $3,000 in Winthrop:1020, reappearing in Cambridge:1440. It is almost certainly a piece of skulduggery which failed of its intended object; instead of being retrieved by the pressman who had fed the silver quarter into the proof press among regular proof blanks, it managed to leave San Francisco as part of a regular proof set.

In recent years Mint Bureau production statistics have become notable for delays and inconsistencies. Mintage figures quoted below are subject to revision.

WASHINGTON DESIGN, CLAD

Designer, John Flanagan. Engraver, Gilroy Roberts. Mints, Philadelphia (no mintmark), San Francisco (proofs only, mintmark S), Denver (D). Mintmarks behind obv. ribbon. Edge, reeded as before. Diameter, 0.955″ = 24.257 mm. Composition, outer layers 75% copper, 25% nickel, bonded to pure copper core. Weight, 87.5 ± 3.5 grs. = 5.67 ± 0.227 gms. Authorizing Acts, July 23, 1965; Title 31, U.S. Code, § 5112.

Grade range, F to UNC. Grade standards, as before. NOTE: Collected only in mint state.

4417 1964 "Transitional." Ex. rare.
Struck in 1965 during completion of the final silver quotas, but on one of the new blanks. Not examined recently enough to know if its rev. is "Type B" or "C." See introductory text.

4418 1965 "Type C" rev. [1,819,717,540 + 2,360,000 SMS]
First struck Aug. 23, at Philadelphia. These were the first coins to bear the 1965 date. Released beginning Nov. 1, 1965. This mintage figure includes coins from Denver without mintmark. SMS = Special Mint Sets, prooflike, from San Francisco, without mintmark.

4419 1966 "Type C" rev. [821,101,500 + 2,261,583 SMS]
Same comments. Those dated 1966 were all made after 8/1/66.

4420 1967 "Type C" rev. [1,524,031,848 + 1,863,344 SMS]
Same comments.

4421 1968 "Type C" rev. [220,731,500]

4422 1968 S "Type B" rev. [3,041,506P] Proofs only.
See introductory text.

4423 1968 D "Type C" rev. [101,534,000]

4424 1969 "Type C" rev. [176,212,000]

4425 1969 S "Type B" rev. [2,934,631P] Proofs only.
See introductory text.

4426 1969 D [all kinds 114,372,000] "Type C" rev.
See introductory text.

4427 1969 D "Type B" rev.
Included in above mintage. Forms under 1% of this date.

4428 1970 "Type C" rev. [136,420,000]
A doubled rev. die exists.

4429 1970 S "Type B" rev. [2,632,810P] Proofs only.
See introductory text.

4430 1970 D [all kinds 417,341,364] "Type C" rev.
See introductory text. Many doubled rev. dies.

4431 1970 D "Type B" rev.
Included in above mintage. Forms about 0.1% of this date.

4432 1971 "Type C" rev. [109,284,000]
May exist with "Type B" rev.

4433 1971 S "Type B" rev. [3,220,733P] Proofs only.
See introductory text.

4434 1971 D [all kinds 258,634,428] "Type C" rev.

4435 1971 D "Type B" rev. Presently very rare.
Included in above mintage.

4436 1972 "Type C" rev. [215,048,000]
May exist with "Type B" rev.

4437 1972 S "Type B" rev. [3,260,996P] Proofs only.
See introductory text.

4438 1972 D [all kinds 311,067,732] "Type C" rev.

4439 1972 D "Type B" rev. Presently very rare.
Included in above mintage.

4440 1973 [346,924,000]
"Type C" rev. from now on.

4441 1973 S [2,760,339P] Proofs only.

4442 1973 D [232,977,400]

4443 1974 [801,456,000]
Many were coined through 1975 retaining the 1974 date, pursuant to Public Law 93-541, Dec. 26, 1974.

4444 1974 S [2,612,658P] Proofs only.

4445 1974 S Obvious double S. Proof. Presently very rare.
Discovered by Delma K. Romines, 1979.

4446 1974 D [353,160,300]
Same comments as to **4443**.

xix. AHR'S BICENTENNIAL DESIGN (1975–76)

The story behind this mintage begins 10 years earlier, July 4, 1966, with Senate Joint Resolution 162 (80 Stat. 259), establishing the American Revolution Bicentennial Commission. This group was to consist of various congressmen, members of the executive branch, and 17 members from the general public. Its purpose was to prepare an overall program of celebrations, reporting to the President its recommendations such as commemorative coins, medals, stamps, etc. On Feb. 25, 1970, it created a Coins and Medals Advisory Panel (George Lang, chairman). Both Dr. Elvira Clain-Stefanelli, of the Smithsonian Institution, and Clifford Mishler, of Krause Publications, recommended an open competition for Bicentennial designs (Advisory Panel Report No. 3, July 29, 1970). The panel's fifth report, Dec. 24, 1970, called for changes in all denominations, with the alternative of a single Bicentennial Commemorative coin, "unique in design and composition." The ARBC endorsed this report Jan. 20, 1971, but the Treasury predictably opposed any coinage changes.

On April 19, 1971, Sen. Frank Church (D.-Id.) introduced a bill, S.1565, to authorize at least 225 million sets of two or more commemorative coins, proof or uncirculated, of special designs to be chosen in consultation with the Joint Commission of the Coinage (CW 5/5/71, p. 1). Other Bicentennial coinage bills followed, sponsored by Rep. James A. McClure (R.-Id.), and Sen. Peter H. Dominick (R.-Colo). Mint Director Mary Brooks (in an interview with David Ganz, May 8, 1972), characterized the notion of changing all six coin denominations as "a disaster" and recommended either a half cent or a gold coin, but opposed any commemorative coin of other denomination (Ganz, "Under the Glass," NNW 6/13/72, p. 8). At the second Advisory Panel meeting, Jan. 18, 1972, she had recommended double-dating all coins 1776–1976 but opposed any other change. However, she gradually retreated from her opposition, and late in 1972 she actually persuaded Treasury Secretary George Shultz to sponsor a Bicentennial coinage proposal. On Jan. 18, 1973, Sen. Mark Hatfield (R.-Ore.) introduced S.422, calling for not over 60 million Bicentennial gold coins, and Rep. White introduced HR 2190 to authorize commemorative halves or dollars. On March 3, 1973, a draft bill (drawn up by Treasury Department legal counsel) went to Congress with Shultz's covering letter; this bill called for double-dating regular coin obvs., and using special rev. designs on dollars and half dollars minted beginning July 4, 1975, "and until such time as the Secretary of Treasury may determine" (CW 3/21/73, p. 1). Mrs. Brooks proposed mintage of both proof sets and circulating coins of the new types in clad metal, recommending that buyers of either proof or UNC. silver-clad Eisenhower dollars be entitled also to buy silver-clad Bicentennial half dollars. This became HR 5244 (3/6/73, sponsored by Reps. Patman, Sullivan, and Widnall) and S.1141 (3/8/73, by Sens. Sparkman and Tower). At a hearing of the House Subcommittee on Consumer Affairs, May 2–3, 1973, ARBC's Acting Director Hugh Hall abruptly withdrew the original Advisory Panel recommendations, and favored HR 5244, only to meet opposition from

Margo Russell (*Coin World* editor), Chester Krause (*NNW* publisher), and others. At a June 6 hearing before a Senate Ad Hoc Coinage Subcommittee (Sen. William Hathaway, chairman), Mrs. Brooks recommended making Bicentennial quarters, provided that some coins could be struck at West Point: 60–100 million dollars, 125–175 million halves, 300–400 million quarters. On June 21, 1973, the Committee reworded S.1141 to permit coinage at West Point, authorize (but not mandate) a gold coin, and require 60 million Bicentennial coins to be struck by July 4, 1975; this report went to the Senate on June 25, reaching the floor July 11, when Sen. Hatfield forced an amendment to require minting gold coins.

On July 24, 1973, the House Committee on Banking and Currency issued HR Report 93-391, reprinted in the *Congressional Record* Sept. 12, recommending a new bill, HR 8789, which would authorize Bicentennial quarters, halves, and dollars, of designs to be chosen by open competition supervised by the National Sculpture Society. The House and Senate reached a compromise version of this bill on Oct. 9, which Pres. Nixon signed into law on Oct. 18, 1973, as PL 93-127 (87 Stat. 455). As passed, this act gave the Mint a deadline of July 4, 1975, to produce 45 million silver-clad Bicentennial coins.

On Oct. 23, the Treasury announced the design competition. The prize was to be $5,000 for each of the three rev. designs accepted. Each contestant was to submit one design (lettered QUARTER DOLLAR, though nobody knew for which denomination any entry would be considered); entries were to consist of a 10″ drawing or photograph of a plaster model, deadline Dec. 14, 1973. The 12 finalists would receive $750 each on completion of their plaster models. There were about 15,000 inquiries, and over 900 entries. On March 1, 1974, the six finalists were chosen; on March 6, Jack L. Ahr was named winner for the quarter dollar. Award ceremonies took place April 23–24, during National Coin Week, in Washington and Philadelphia; the three winners watched their designs transferred from galvano to master dies. On Aug. 12, at 11 A.M., the winners watched the first prototype coins struck.

A more detailed account of all of the above events is in Ganz {1976}; he was an eyewitness to many of the proceedings.

Controversy followed claims that Ahr had copied William A. Smith's "Drummer Boy" stamp, issued Sept. 28, 1973. Both obviously derive from Archibald Willard's painting *Spirit of '76* (*CW* 6/26, 7/21, and 8/28/74).

At the 1974 ANA Convention (Bal Harbour, Fla.), the Mint Bureau exhibited—under armed guard—a three-piece set of prototype Bicentennial coins, brilliant proofs, without mintmark, from the group struck Aug. 12. One of the sets went to Pres. Ford, Nov. 13, 1974, another to his appointment secretary; supposedly all the rest were melted, none even reserved for the National Collection in the Smithsonian Institution, so great is the Mint Bureau's fear that coin collectors might get their cherrypicking hands on any such rarities! One of the sets is pictured in the 1976 Yeoman Guide Book; others in *NNW* 8/27/74, p. 1 and Ganz {1976}.

Specimens were regularly issued 1975–76 for circulation from Philadelphia, West Point, and Denver; as all bear the 1776–1976 date, issues of the two years cannot be distinguished. The San Francisco Assay Office struck proof sets in both nickel-clad and silver-clad, and larger quantities of nonproof silver-clad coins, all for sale, not circulation. Silver-clad specimens were still being released as recently as 1982; only silver price rises ended distribution.

Silver-clad coins are difficult to distinguish from regular nickel-clad pieces. Legal weights are so close together that weight tests are unreliable; however, spot checks on nickel-clad quarters indicate that they tend to run a grain or two below standard, so that any piece weighing above 87.5 grs. (5.67 gms.) is worth further test. Color of the core on nickel-clad coins is

the normal reddish; that on silver-clad is much lighter though sometimes pinkish. Under a microscope, texture of cupro-nickel outer layers differs markedly from that of silver. Failing this, the ring test (see Glossary) will serve; the note varies greatly with the alloy but is the same for two quarters of the same alloy.

AHR'S BICENTENNIAL DESIGN

Designer, Engraver, obv., Frank Gasparro, after Flanagan; rev., Jack L. Ahr, after Willard. Mints, Philadelphia, West Point (no mintmarks), San Francisco (S), Denver (D). Mintmarks behind ribbon. Diameters, Edges, as before. Composition: Silver-clad issue, outer layers 80% silver, 20% copper, bonded to core of 21% silver, 79% copper; nickel-clad, as before. Weights: Silver-clad, 88.74 ± 3.09 grs. $= 5.75 \pm 0.2$ gms.; nickel-clad, 87.5 ± 3.5 grs. $= 5.67 \pm 0.227$ gms. Authorizing Act, Oct. 18, 1973.

Grade range, VF to UNC.; collected only in mint state.

4447 1776–1976 No mintmark. Proof. [3+P]
Probably silver-clad. Issue of Aug. 12, 1974. See introductory text. Not to be confused with next. Ill. *NNW* 8/27/74.

4448 1776–1976 Nickel-clad. [809,784,016 + 376,000 WP]
Coinage began April 23, 1975. Released July 8, 1975. WP = West Point issue of late 1976, indistinguishable from the others.

4449 1776–1976 S Nickel-clad. [7,059,099P] Proofs only.
The [2,909,369] issued in 6-piece sets (cent to dollar) in 1975 cannot be distinguished from the [4,149,730] issued in 6-piece sets in 1976.

4450 1776–1976 S Silver-clad. [4,294,081 + 3,262,970P]
Last coined June 22, 1976 [about 11,000,000 + 4,000,000P]; above figures represent quantities released through 1982, in 3-piece sets (quarter to dollar). Release stopped because silver bullion value rose above face value.

4451 1776–1976 D Nickel-clad. [860,118,939]

4452 1776–1976 D Doubled obv. die. Presently very rare.
Doubling strongest on LIBERTY. Discovered by Steve Magusin, 1976. *NNW* 8/14/76, p. 1.

xx. EAGLE REVERSE RESUMED
(1977–   )

After the Bicentennial celebrations were at an end, the Mint Bureau resumed coinage of the regular Flanagan design. Hubs were in lower relief with various minute modifications, most noticeable at TRUST (letters very slightly differently shaped, thinner, and spaced slightly farther apart) and leaves. Further modifications occurred in later years, mostly microscopic; the 1983 coins have LIBERTY, motto, and date farther from border than 1979–82. Research into these changes is continuing, most of all by the specialist Herbert Hicks, who has provided similar data on other denominations.

The West Point facility coined numerous quarters without mintmark; these cannot be distinguished from Philadelphia issues. Many coin collectors have urged that a mintmark W be affixed.

The single great rarity in this period is the 1977 D silver-clad; this piece (discovered by Bernie Steinbock before 1981) is on an obsolete Bicentennial blank which remained in the hopper at resumption of regular nickel-clad coinage, in exact parallel to the 1943 bronze cents and 1946 wartime silver 5¢ coins. How it got to Denver is uncertain. For a possible explanation see Chap. 29, Sect. x.

In 1979, the old S mintmark punch, "Type I" S (worn enough to produce filled, blurred blobs) was replaced; the new "Type II" S appears on a minority of 1979 proofs and on all of 1980. By 1981, this punch was worn (producing S's shaped like 8's) and was in turn replaced with a more open S having round serifs free of the middle stroke. Mintage figures are from Alan Herbert; *NNW* 8/21/82, *CW* 11/10/82, p. 70. Beginning in 1985, each year's master die for proofs contains the S mintmark.

Philadelphia coins struck in and after 1980 bear mintmark P.

EAGLE REVERSE RESUMED

Designer, Engraver, Frank Gasparro, after Flanagan. Mints, Philadelphia (mintmark P, 1980 and later only), San Francisco (S), Denver (D). Mintmarks behind obv. ribbon. Physical Specifications, Authorizing Acts, as 1965–74.

Grade range, FINE to UNC.; collected only in mint state.

4453 1977 [468,556,000 + 7,352,000 WP]
WP = West Point; no mintmark.
4454 1977 S Normal motto. [3,251,152P] Proofs only.
May exist on obsolete silver-clad blank (from **4450**).

4455 1977 S Very thin motto. Presently very rare.
Die overpolished. Forms a tiny fraction of proofs.

4456 1977 D [256,524,978]
4457 1977 D Obsolete silver-clad blank. Ex. rare.
Discovered by Bernie Steinbock. 89.7 grs. = 5.81 gms. See introductory text.
4458 1978 [521,452,000 + 20,800,000 WP]
WP = West Point.
4459 1978 S [3,127,781P] Proofs only.
4460 1978 D [287,373,152]
4461 1979 [515,708,000 + 22,672,000 WP]
WP = West Point.
4462 1979 S "Type I" S. [3,053,175P] Proofs only.
See introductory text. S filled, blurry. Ill. in Chap. 31.
4463 1979 S "Type II" S. [624,000P]
Clear S. Ill. in Chap. 31. Mintage figure from Alan Herbert.
4464 1979 D [489,789,780]
4465 1980 P [635,832,000]
4466 1980 S "Type II" S. [3,554,806P] Proofs only.
May exist with "Type I" S.
4467 1980 D [518,327,487]
4468 1981 P [601,716,000]
4469 1981 S Old S. [3,141,083P] Proofs only.
Mintmark as 1979 "Type II," now worn, closed, like 8.
4470 1981 S New S. [922,000P]
Clear S, round serifs free of middle stroke.
4471 1981 D [575,722,833]
4472 1982 P [500,931,000]
4473 1982 S [3,857,479P] Proofs only.
4474 1982 D [480,042,788]
4475 1983 P [673,525,000]
Modified obv.; see introductory text.
4476 1983 S [3,228,648P] Proofs only.
Same comment.
4477 1983 D [617,806,446]
Same comment.
4478 1984 P [676,545,000]
4479 1984 S [3,198,999P] Proofs only.
4480 1984 D [546,483,064]
4481 1985 P [775,818,962]
4482 1985 S [3,348,814P] Proofs only.
4483 1985 D [519,962,888]
4484 1986 P
4485 1986 S
4486 1986 D
4487–4549 Reserved for future issues.

CHAPTER 28

HALF DOLLARS

i. SCOT'S FLOWING HAIR DESIGN
(1794–95)

As the Chief Coiner, Henry Voigt, and the Assayer, Albion Cox, could not post the $10,000 surety bonds required for taking office (or rather for handling gold and silver bullion), only copper coins were made during 1793. On Dec. 10, 1793, Thomas Jefferson wrote to Pres. Washington recommending that bonds be reduced to a figure these officers could manage. Washington persuaded Congress to comply (Act of March 3, 1794), and at once local banks began depositing silver. Before this could be coined, the new Mint Engraver, Robert Scot, had to complete device punches and working dies. With Adam Eckfeldt's help, Scot produced an oversimplified copy of the cent head for the half dollars, and a stylized eagle punch for their revs. Individual numeral, letter, star, and leaf punches (with some hand finishing) served to complete the designs.

On Oct. 15, 1794, Voigt delivered 5,300 half dollars, followed by 18,164 more on Feb. 4, 1795, from 1794-dated dies: five pairs in 10 combinations, one of them a new discovery (**4551**), only one (ill. at **4552**) not rare. Survivors are mostly well worn; collectors were very few, and the general public remained slow to squirrel away choice ones.

During the remainder of spring and summer 1795, half-dollar coinage continued from 1795-dated dies [299,680], from 19 obv. and 22 or 23 rev. dies, the first rev. left over from 1794. Several slightly differing head- and eagle-device punches were used during the year, the final ones attributed to John Smith Gardner, briefly Assistant Engraver: the famous and rare Small Heads. These are associated with four Heavy Wreath revs. showing a small dot in lower field between ribbons; this is thought to be Gardner's "signature," to tell his dies from Scot's. The Double Date and Three Leaves coins belong with this group, evidently at the end of the mintage, summer 1795.

Coinage was interrupted to allow personnel to devote time to making silver dollars and gold coins, on orders of the new Mint Director, Henry William DeSaussure.

The vars. in this series (without or with die blunders) are nearly as individualized and distinctive as their cherished counterparts in the cents, but they have long remained neglected owing to lack of a reference work in a class with Sheldon {1958} on cents. Even Overton {1970} is unsatisfactory: It lacks ills. of three obv. and five rev. dies, lacks a rational descriptive system, lacks an emission sequence, and (perhaps worst) its illustrations obscure many distinctive features. Research is continuing on this series, and we may eventually expect a definitive text from the Bust Half Nut Club (BHNC), which has already published a supplement illustrating new discoveries.

What look like file marks on many specimens, even in mint state, are adjustment marks. Adjusters (including the first women hired by the Mint) wore leather aprons and sat with metal files. As the Weighers checked each newly cut blank, the lightweight ones were returned to the Melter and Refiner, those within legal tolerances went to the Chief Coiner, and heavier ones went to the Adjusters, who gave them a stroke or two (more if necessary after reweighing), to reduce weights to legal limits. Periodically, the contents of their leather aprons went to the Melter and Refiner. Adjustment marks, accordingly, are not counted as impairments, as they preceded stamping designs into the planchets. Note ills. of **4550, 4556.**

Irregularities at rims (as on ills. of **4553, 4556**) are from the machine used for lettering edges; these also are not counted as impairments, but they must be carefully distinguished from rim dents.

SCOT'S FLOWING HAIR DESIGN

Designer, Robert Scot. Engravers, Scot and John Smith Gardner. Mint, Philadelphia. Diameter, approx. 20.5/16″ = 32.5 mm. Edge, FIFTY CENTS OR HALF A DOLLAR (varying ornamentation between words: circles, rectangles, stars). Weight standard, 208 grs. = 13.48 gms. Composition, 892.43+ Fine silver, 107.56+ Fine copper (1,485/1,664). Authorizing Act, April 2, 1792.

Grade range, POOR to UNC. GOOD: Date and all letters legible; devices outlined. VERY GOOD: Few hair and feather details. FINE: Details at ends of curls distinguishable; some hair details clear behind ribbon; partial feather and leaf details. VERY FINE: Some detail in central hair; demarcation between hair and neck and cheek (but not temple) visible; most wing feathers intact, breast feathers partly flat. EXTREMELY FINE: Almost all hair details; isolated tiny rubbed spots only.

4550 1794 Lowest curl at second star. [5,300] Very rare.
Delivered Oct. 15, 1794. Overton 105, 106, 108 = Hilt 3C, 3D, 5D. Usually in low grades.

4551 1794 Same, looped shoulder truncation. Unique?
BHNC 109 = Hilt 2C. Loop is as in 1795 Small Heads, whence Hilt attributes this obv. to Gardner. Discovered by Robert Hilt, 11/8/76.

4552   1794 Lowest curl at first star. [18,164]
Delivered Feb. 4, 1795. Ov. 107, 101–4, BHNC 110 = Hilt 4D, 6D, 6E, 1A, 1B, new var. Price for Ov. 101 (ill.), with crack from rim to wreath between D S; others are all very rare, BHNC 110 unique (long crack, from rim through D, wing, and head to rim between F A).

4553   1795 [all kinds 299,680] Head of 1794; slender wreath. First star pierces curl, as preceding; 2 leaves on wing at TE (unlike the Heavy Wreaths, which have 3). 8 vars. Compare all following.

4554   1795 Same, Y punched over a star. Rare.
Ov. 121 = Hilt 11E. Rev. of 1794, CA repunched. The ultrasharp coin from LM 9/68:25 is thought to be a presentation piece; ill. Breen {1977}, p. 32.
4555   1795 Similar, AMEIRICA. Very scarce.
Ov. 119 = Hilt 8F. The extra I is thin, touching wingtip and serif of R.
4556   1795 Leaf divides I C. Ex. rare.
Ov. 123 = Hilt 12I. That ill. is finest known.

4557   1795 STATES over STATED. Very scarce.
Ov. 129 = Hilt 13J.

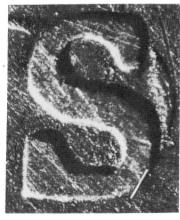

4558   1795 O over horizontal O. Very rare.
Ov. 130 = Hilt 13K. Obv. of preceding. Finest known, ex Col. Green, Clarke, Bareford:337, UNC., brought $13,000.
4559   1795 STATES over STETES. Very scarce.
Ov. 113 = Hilt 15Q. Always with field lump r. of 5.

4560   1795 Similar, first star entirely below curl; slender wreath.
9 vars. Star presents crotch, not point, to first curl; curl free of star or barely touches. But see all following.
4561   1795 Same but Heavy Wreath. Scarce.
Ov. 108, 109, 110 = Hilt 21V, 21W, 22Z. Three leaves on wing at TE, unlike any foregoing; field dot below knot (see introductory text). Hilt attributes these dies to Gardner. Compare all following.

4562   1795 As last but double date. Rare.
Ov. 112 = Hilt 16Z. Almost always with die crack between ER to hair.

4563 1795 Double date, 3 leaves below wings. Very rare.
Ov. 111 = Hilt 16Y. Always with the rev. die break. Usually
in low grades, prohibitively rare in VF; that ill. (ex Woodin
II:73, Col. Green) is finest known. Enl. photos.

4564 1795 Small head. Very rare.
Ov. 128, 126–27 = Hilt 23X, 24Z, 25Z. Note shape of lowest
curl, looped shoulder truncation, flat truncation arch, end of
bust. Usually in low grades; prohibitively rare in VF. Hilt
attributes these to Gardner.

ii. THE SCOT-ECKSTEIN DRAPED BUST/SMALL EAGLE (1796–97)

These are among the most mysterious of U.S. coin types, as
well as among the most elusive. Two obvs. dated 1796, respectively with 15 and 16 stars, were muled with a single rev., which
was carried over to make the first of the two vars. dated 1797—
again with 15 stars, not 16: Why? The mystery deepens when
we consider delivery dates: 1796, none; 1797, [60] Feb. 28, [874]
March 21 (both to the Bank of the United States in Philadelphia), and finally [2,984] May 26. By internal evidence, both 15-
star obvs. must have been made before June 1796, as the shift to
16 stars commemorated the admission of Tennessee to the
Union on June 1. Then the 16-star die must have been completed either anticipating or following the celebrations of that
time.

My tentative solution—presented only as conjecture, as no
other Archives data survive about these mintages—is that early
in 1796, a few prooflike presentation coins were struck, but as
usual not recorded as regular coinage. A second 15-star obv.
was made but (as in many other instances) omitting final digit,
for possible use later that year or in 1797 or some subsequent
year. Then, for the Tennessee celebrations, the 16-star die was
made and used only for a few prooflike presentation strikings.
No more half dollars were coined from either die until Feb.
1797. Those coined in February were 1796's with 15 stars; those
in March included some with 15 and others with 16 stars, both
obvs. cracking. Their shared rev. began to crack with the 16-
star obv. At this point the incomplete 15-star die was given a
final 7 and hardened for use, and a second rev. made ready. The
mintage of May 26 consisted mostly of coins dated 1797 from
both revs., but may have included the last of the 1796's with 16
stars.

Many high-grade survivors show vaguely prooflike surfaces,
from a tiny group once owned by Col. E. H. R. Green (peg-
legged collector of railroad cars, coins, pornographic films, etc.;
son of Hetty Green, the "Witch of Wall Street"). Real presentation strikings, from the very earliest states of both 1796 obvs.,
are much rarer: Breen {1977}, p. 35.

The portrait of Ms. Liberty is after a drawing by Gilbert
Stuart, modeled by Mrs. William Bingham (née Ann Willing),
Philadelphia socialite reputed to be one of the most beautiful
women of her day—not that either this or the Gilbert Stuart
connection could be proved by Scot's device punch. John Eckstein is credited with the eagle; the palm branches were originally a compliment to Mint Director DeSaussure's South Carolina homeland, but by the time these half dollars were made, the
device was an anachronism, as DeSaussure had long since resigned. For further details, see introductory texts to Chap. 24,
Sect. ii, and Chap. 27, Sect. i.

THE SCOT-ECKSTEIN DRAPED BUST/ SMALL EAGLE

Designers, Robert Scot and John Eckstein, obv. after Gilbert
Stuart. Mint, Physical Specifications, Authorizing Act, as before.

Grade range, POOR to UNC. GOOD: Date and all letters legible; devices outlined. VERY GOOD: Few hair and wing-feather
details; deepest drapery fold shows. FINE: All drapery folds visible; partial hair, leaf, and feather details. VERY FINE: Only
slight wear on r. drapery folds; l. side (to curls) smooth. Over
half hair details; internal details of over half of leaves and of
wing feathers. EXTREMELY FINE: All drapery lines complete to
junction with curls; few isolated tiny rubbed spots only. EX-

CEPTION: Even in mint state, breast feathers and most leg and neck feathers may not be clear, except on presentation strikings.

4565 1796 [all kinds 934+?] 15 stars. Very rare.
Hilt 2A. Usually in low grades. See introductory text.

4566 1796 16 stars. Ex. rare.
Hilt 3A. Usually in low grades. See introductory text. Robison, Auction 85:1700, VF, $22,000.

4567 1797 [2,984−] Very rare.
Hilt 1A, 1B. That without defect at numerator (ill.) is much rarer than the var. with the 1796 rev. See introductory text. Usually in low grades; rarer choice than **4565**. Auction 81:132, "UNC.," $54,000; Hawn:8, $13,750, Auction 85:750, AU, $46,750.

iii. SCOT'S HERALDIC DESIGN (1801–7)

Following the lead of the dollars (1798) and the dismes and half dismes (1800), the first half dollars minted after 1797 bore the new Heraldic Eagle design, Scot's copy of the Great Seal of the United States (1782). This device punch lacked stars, berries, and also the end of stem; it also, either from blunder or bravado, placed the warlike arrows in the eagle's dexter claw (observer's l.), the peaceful olive branch in the less honorable sinister claw. Compare Chap. 24, Sect. iii, introductory text.

For many years collectors believed in the existence of half dollars dated 1804, especially because mint reports listed a large mintage [156,519]. Early auction catalogs filled the gap by listing "1804 under 5" (the vars. now known as 1805/4); but to date the only 1804-dated halves seen are fraudulent alterations from other dates, either by removing the 5 from an 1805/4 or by fabricating a 4 from some other digit. Most likely the pieces delivered in 1804 came from 1803-dated dies, as with the silver dollars.

On the other hand, the so-called 1806/9 (formerly, in error, "1806/00") is a corrected blunder, whereas the 1805/4 obvs. reflect Mint economy in use of dated dies as long as possible. The "9" is a 6 punch first entered rotated 180° from normal. And the 1806/5 dies (one of them an actual die used in 1805, reannealed for redating, then rehardened) reflect an emergency: The Engraving Department was running out of die steel.

For many of the Mint's earliest years, its principal business was making cents, half dollars, and half eagles, which mostly found their way into bank sacks rather than public circulation. Large mintages of these denominations resulted in a proliferation of vars., mostly positional (because letters, stars, numerals, and berries had to be entered into each working die by hand), but in many instances also major (reflecting changes in punches, additions or omissions, or corrections of blunders). The complexity of listings in the 1805–6 period reflects all these factors. No really satisfactory reference work yet exists (see Sect. i, introductory text). Nevertheless, the sequence herein, though not pretending to be completely chronological, makes more sense than any previously published. (Absolute chronological sequence would place the 1805/4 vars. in the middle of the year, the small 5 coin, **4576** = Ov. 107, at the beginning.)

Mintage of this design was interrupted in summer 1807 so that the new Reich dies could be introduced: See next section. All 1807's seen to date have a new edge device without any ornaments between words, a style continued for some decades. The mintage figure [301,076], from Snowden {1860}, almost certainly includes many dated 1806.

SCOT'S HERALDIC DESIGN

Designer, Engraver, Robert Scot, obv. after Stuart, rev. after the Great Seal. Mint, Physical Specifications, Authorizing Acts, as before.

Grade range, POOR to UNC. GOOD: Date and all letters legible except for motto; devices outlined. VERY GOOD: Some few internal details of bust, hair, and wing feathers; deepest drapery fold shows; some motto letters. FINE: All drapery folds show; partial hair, leaf, feather, and stripe details; most motto letters. VERY FINE: Only slight wear on r. drapery folds, l. side (to curls) smooth; over half hair, feather, and leaf details; full motto. EXTREMELY FINE: All drapery lines complete to junction with curls; few isolated tiny rubbed spots only; generally, over half mint luster. EXCEPTIONS: Coins from buckled dies may not show full motto even in mint state; breast feathers may be weak even in mint state (look for mint luster on weak areas).

4568 1801 [30,289]
Hilt 4C (ill.), 4D; latter, with rev. of 1802 (no lumps at ED, arrows, etc.) is rarer. Usually in low grades; prohibitively rare in mint state, therefore several "sliders" have been offered as "UNC."

4569   1802 [29,890]

Rev. of second var. of 1801. Prohibitively rare in mint state.

4570   1803 [all kinds 188,234] Large 3. Rev., small stars.

Ov. 101–2. Probably the [31,715] delivered in 1803 comprised these 2, the [156,519] in 1804 the next 2.

4571   1803 Large 3. Rev., large stars.

Ov. 103. Large 3 has vertical serif at r. angle to top stroke and extending above the latter: Compare next. Large rev. stars continued through 1807. Doubtless this and next include most or all the [156,519] struck in 1804; comprises the majority of survivors of this date.

4572   1803 Small 3. Rev., large stars.

Ov. 104. Struck in 1804. Note slanting serif to 3. Rev. of **4577.**

4573   1805/4 [all kinds 211,722] Close date, 5 berries.

Ov. 101. Enlarged detail shows why this was called "1804 under 5." Normal A's (compare next). As one berry is half embedded in leaf, this rev. has also been called "4½ berries."

4574   1805/4 Close date, 4 berries.

Ov. 102. Same obv.; inner r. serif of A's broken off. Rev. reused in **4576** second var., **4582.**

4575   1805/4 Wide date. Very rare.

Ov. 103. Almost complete 4 within 5. 5 berries; often, heavy triangular break joins first 2 stars to curl. Usually in low grades. Ill. Newman-Bressett {1962}, p. 40. Enl. photos.

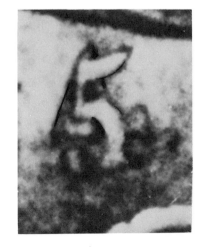

4576 1805 Small 5.
Ov. 107; BHNC 114. Quarter-dollar punch used in error. Price for 107 (normal F, A's); BHNC 114 (broken A's, Ex. rare) has rev. of **4574, 4582.**

4577 1805 Large 5; 5 berries, normal F and A's.
Ov. 112. Rev. of **4572.**

4578 1805 Same but broken serifs to A's.
Ov. 111, 113; price for 111 (2 tiny die chips above longest arrow); the other var. is very rare.

4579 1805 Similar, 4 berries, broken serifs to A's.
Ov. 110, 108.

4580 1805 As last, footless F, close date. Scarce.
Ov. 109. Lower r. serif of F broken off. This and the broken A's continue through 1806.

4581 1805 Same, widest date.
Ov. 104, 105, 106; first (ill.) is rarest. Obv. of 105–6 (die scratch down from L) was softened and overdated to 1806/5 to make **4582;** see introductory text.

4582 1806/5 [all kinds 839,576+] Knobbed 6, 4 berries.
Ov. 104. Obv. of last, altered at Mint (see introductory text); rev. of **4574.**

4583 1806/05 0 over horizontal 0 in date; 5 berries.
Ov. 101, 103.

4584 1806/5 0 over horizontal 0 in date; 6 berries.
Ov. 102. The sixth berry is in lower relief, between claw and lowest inner leaf.

4585 1806 Knobbed 6, large stars; 6 berries.
Ov. 105. Same rev. Stars almost touch border. Usually cracked through bases of 180.

4586 1806 Knobbed 6, small stars; 6 berries. Very rare.
Ov. 106. Same rev. L low; 8 repunched; stars distant from border.

4587 1806 Knobbed 6, small stars; 5 berries. Very rare.
Ov. 107. Same obv. Normal F.

4588 1806 Knobbed 6, stem not through claw. Ex. rare.
Ov. 108.   1) Discovered by this writer in the Philip Straus coll., 1951; later, NN 61:369, pvt. coll.   2) Overton coll., break through tops of UNITED.

4589 1806 Pointed 6, stem not through claw.
Ov. 109. Many struck from rusty dies (ill.).

4590 1806/9 Stem through claw. Very rare.
Ov. 110 (rim breaks at UN, ED); 111 (no breaks, rarer).

4591 1806 Pointed 6, stem through claw; normal legends.
14 vars. Usually, TY double-punched.

4592 1806 Similar, STATES over STATAS. Ex. rare.
Ov. 124. Base and r. leg of A plain within and r. of E.

4593 1807 Bust r. [301,076−] Normal F.
9 vars. Mintage includes many dated 1806. Edge device
henceforth lacks ornaments between words. All have A's
with broken serifs as in 1806.

4594 1807 Footless F. Very rare.
Ov. 108. F lacks r. base; rev. of 1806.

iv. REICH'S CAPPED BUSTS, LETTERED EDGE (1807–36)

John Reich sold himself into indentured service to escape to
the USA from the Napoleonic Wars. As early as 1801, his name
came to official attention as one of the finest engravers in the
country. Opposition from Robert Scot (who must have regarded him as a threat to his own job) prevented the Mint from
hiring him except for occasional odd temporary assignments.
But in 1807, Scot's health (for which read failing eyesight) was
a source of serious concern to officialdom; accordingly, the
Mint hired Reich as Assistant Engraver at a pittance of $600
per year.

Reich's first assignment was to create new designs for gold
and silver denominations: an insult to Scot. The first ones to
benefit from Reich's attentions were the denominations most in
demand at banks: half dollars and half eagles. Mint Director
James Ross Snowden {1860}, using Mint documents not now
located, said that the changeover occurred in Sept. 1807:
[750,500], from four obv. and three rev. Reich dies. Critics at
once attacked the design for portraying "the artist's fat mistress" (which may even have been true, though there is no evidence), and for having Ms. Liberty not only extravagantly
buxom but wearing the *pilleus,* or liberty cap, on her head. For
this the answer was immediate, as quoted by Thomas Jefferson
in 1825: The cap was meant not for the *pilleus* but for a fashionable head covering of the time—specifically a mobcap, like the
one found on portraits of Martha Washington but less elaborate
and minus the veil. Compare Chap. 36, Sect. iii, introductory
text.

Reich's eagle was copied on United States infantry officers'
buttons (dubiously attributed to Moritz Fürst): Albert {1974}
GI 50A, 50B, 51A, and later vars.

Half dollars were struck in every year and of every date except 1816. The mintage dated 1815 was delivered Jan. 10, 1816,
only hours before a fire in one of the Mint's outbuildings ruined
the rolling mills, making conversion of gold or silver bullion
into standard planchets impossible until repairs were complete
(late 1817). Most of the 1817's went to Bailly Blanchard, Cashier, Planters' Bank of New Orleans.

Reich left the Mint March 31, 1817, after 10 years of adverse
criticism and no pay increases; he remains one of the more
unappreciated figures in American coinage history: Chamber-

lain {1955}. Only in recent years was it discovered that he
signed his coinage obvs.: The "signature" consists of a notch on
one point of lowest r. star. Its last appearance is on one of the
1818/7 dies, evidently completed in 1817 before his departure.
Dies of the same type completed by Scot no longer show the
notched star. Witham {1967}.

Scot died in 1823, aged 79; his replacement was William
Kneass, who had the same assignment as Reich: Improve existing designs in all denominations (Scot had replaced the Reich
device punches with inferior copies of his own). Kneass, however, did not get around to the half dollars for over a decade.
He did complete several device punches, beginning in 1824, but
they differed only minutely from those already in use. (On the
other hand, during Scot's last six years, the half dollars featured
about a dozen overdate dies, whereas during Kneass's first six
years, the denomination showed only five overdates, which the
Mint must have seen as an improvement.)

Numeral and letter punches during this period were furnished by Henry Starr; after about 1824, by Christian
Gobrecht, the inventor, mechanical genius, medallist, and
bank-note-plate engraver who was eventually to replace Kneass
after the latter had a stroke (1835).

Edge devices differ minutely from one year to the next; sometimes several were in use during the same year; these are cur-
rently under study by Dr. Ivan B. Leaman. To date the only
ones that have received publicity are two of 1809 (the so-called
experimental edges with "XXXX"—really irregular ornaments
—and "IIII" between words) and four of 1830–31: plain between words, plaques between words bearing diagonals slanting
up to r., similar plaques with diagonals slanting down to r., and
vertical reeding between words. Complete listing of over 100
slightly differing edge devices, with the die vars. found with
each, would more than double the length of this section; we
await Dr. Leaman's book. The Overton reference on this series
needs total reworking; a true chronological sequence (possible
by combining die-state evidence, assembled by this writer and
independently by the Bust Half Nut Club, with Dr. Leaman's
researches), with accurate rarity ratings, will be necessary to
make a new text worthwhile.

Tens or hundreds of thousands of specimens 1809–36 went
directly to banks, which retained them as part of their cash
reserves, long after new laws mandated smaller sizes and lower
weights. These coins came to public attention about 1933–34,
when Pres. Roosevelt's bank holiday resulted in exhaustive
searches of many cashiers' vaults. Others showed up during the
same period owing to bank failures; still others from hoarders'
estates. Before then, the biggest single source was probably the
Economite hoard (buried by the New Harmony Society, Economy, Pa., and discovered in 1878). This contained 111,356 bust
half dollars, many close to mint state but scrubbed—including
100 1815's. For this reason, many vars. of this design come
mostly in VF to AU, "sliders" (slightly rubbed coins being mas-
queraded as "UNCIRCULATED") being common. However, truly
mint-state specimens of any date before 1836 are difficult to
find, far more so if sharp strikings.

Specimens dated 1837 and 1838 with lettered edges and 50 C.
rev. are circulating counterfeits of the period.

REICH'S CAPPED BUSTS, LETTERED EDGE

Designer, John Reich. Engravers, Reich (1807–17), Scot
(April 1817–23), Kneass (1824–35), Gobrecht (1835–36). Mint,
Physical Specifications, Authorizing Acts, as before. Edge,
FIFTY CENTS OR HALF A DOLLAR * (some vars. with
ornamentation after DOLLAR or between words).

Grade range, FAIR to UNC. GOOD: Date and all letters legible
except LIBERTY and motto; devices outlined, no internal de-

tail. VERY GOOD: LIBERTY weakly visible; shoulder clasp visible, curl above it faint, partial internal details of hair and drapery. FINE: Shoulder clasp and adjacent curl plainly outlined. VERY FINE: Clasp clear with internal detail; adjacent curl rubbed only at highest point; hair below LI distinguishable; most individual feathers show. EXTREMELY FINE: Few tiny isolated rubbed spots only; other details complete, generally over half mint luster. EXCEPTIONS: Weak strikings, especially from buckled dies, may not show certain details even in mint state; on these, parts of PLURIBUS are much weaker than rest of motto. NOTE: Tens of thousands of pieces overgraded "UNC." show rubbing on eyebrow, hair above it, hair above ear, ribbon end, and parts of drapery. These "sliders" should not command the premium of mint-state specimens.

LARGEST HEAD AND EAGLE, 1807–8

4595   1807 [750,500] Rev., 50 over 20.
Overton 111, 112. Rarely with "beard" break from jaw to upper bust. The "2" may be a 5 rotated 180°. Ex. rare UNC.

4596   1807 Small stars, widest 50 C.
Ov. 113. Stars far from border. None seen UNC.

4597   1807 Large stars.
Ov. 114. Die lumps below 7.

4598   1808/7 [All kinds 1,368,600]
Ov. 101. Part of crossbar of 7 plain within upper loop of 8.

4599   1808 Normal date.
9 vars.

SMALLER HEAD AND EAGLE, 1809–11

4600   1809 [1,405,810]
15 vars. The 2 "experimental" edges (see introductory text) command a slight premium in all grades, 10%–20% extra premium in mint state.

4601   1810 [1,276,276]
10 vars.
4602   1811 [all kinds 1,203,644] Small 8, normal.
9 vars.

4603 1811/0 Small date. "Punctuated" date 18.1'1
Ov. 101, 102. Rarely with clear 0 within and around final 1;
on late impressions (ill.), the 0 fades out. Price for earlier
impressions with 0 clear; later states price as preceding.

4604 1811 Large 8.
Ov. 103, 104. This size 8 continues through early 1817 and
makes its final appearance on one of the 1818/7 dies.

COARSE HIGH RELIEF CURLS, 1812–15

4605 1812/11 [all kinds 1,628,059] Small 8.
Ov. 102. Rev., N corrected from erroneous I.

4606 1812/11 Large 8. Rare.
Ov. 101. Same rev. Usually in low grades. Discovered by this
writer, fall 1969; discovery coin, NN MBS 12/11/69:817.
4607 1812 Normal date, large 8.
8 vars. There was a tiny hoard of sharp UNC. specimens.
4608 1813 [all kinds 1,241,903] Normal.
9 vars. At least 2 different punches for 3 in date, but the
differences are hard to describe.
4609 1813 Blundered rev., 50 C. over UNI. Scarce.
Ov. 101. Rev. later reground, effacing most of the blunder.
Price for early states (at least as much of UNI visible behind
50 C. as in ill.); later states command less premium. Mike
Danish made a census of this var. and located over 50 specimens, effectively refuting former claims of its extreme rarity.
First correctly described in *Numisma* 3–4/55:2585.

4610 1814/3 [All kinds 1,039,075]
Ov. 101. On later states, less of 3 shows, but corners of top
stroke always show.

4611 1814 "Single leaf." Very rare.
Ov. 105a. Rev. drastically lapped, eliminating uppermost leaf
below wing.

4612 1814 Extra thin date. Very scarce.
Ov. 106. Drastically lapped dies. Always with local weaknesses; the coin ill. is actually mint state!

4613 1814 STATES over STATAS.
Ov. 108.
4614 1814 Widest date.
Ov. 109. Rev., 2 center dots; extra serif at top of F. None seen
UNC.

4615 1814 Normal.
Ov. 102–5, 107.

4616 1815/2 [47,150]

Only one var., delivered Jan. 10, 1816: See introductory text. Many EF's and AU's masquerade as "UNC." Really mint-state pieces should show at least as much hair detail as that ill. Overton ill. this with rev. of **4613** in error.

4617 1817/3 [all kinds 1,215,567 + ?P] Large 8.

Ov. 101. One "one-sided" proof known, ex Newcomer, Green, Wayte Raymond. Breen {1977}, p. 40.

4618 1817/4. Ex. rare, 8 or 9 known.

Ov. 102. Discovered by E. T. Wallis, *NUM* 10/30. Large 8; I of AMERICA lacks its l. foot. Usually in low grades.

SCOT'S NEW HEADS:
Fine Curls, Low Relief

4619 1817 Small 8. "Punctuated" date 181.7

Ov. 103. The raised dot fades out; in that late die state the var. will price as **4622.**

4620 1817 Small 8. "Single leaf." Rare.

Ov. 106a. As **4611,** but different dies.

4621 1817 Small 8. Close date.

Ov. 110, 111.

4622 1817 Small 8. Wide date.

7 vars. One proof reported, ex Newcomb, Kelly 11/29–30/ 47:613.

4623 1818/7 [all kinds 1,960,322 + ?P] Small 8's.

Ov. 102. One cleaned proof reported, ex Clarke, Cox, Bauman:32.

HEAD OF 1812–15 RESUMED

4624 1818/7 Large first 8.

Ov. 101, 103. Entire top of 7 shows above final (small) 8. Die completed by Reich before his departure, March 1817: See introductory text. One proof known, ex "Alto," Patten, E. Y. Clarke:215.

HEAD OF 1818–24: Fine Curls Below LI

4625 1818 Pincer 8's.

Ov. 108. 8's open at tops. Ex. Rare UNC.

4626 1818 Close date.

7 vars.

4627 1818 Wide date.

Ov. 104–6, 115. At least 4 proofs known.

4628 1819/8 [all kinds 2,208,000 + ?P] Small 9. Italic *5.*
Ov. 101. Note the unusually narrow 9. Ex. Rare UNC.

4629 1819/8 Large 9. Italic *5.*
Ov. 102, 103. Broad boldface **9.**

4630 1819/8 Large 9. Upright 5.
Ov. 104–6. Broad boldface **9.**
4631 1819 Close date.
Ov. 107, 110, 111.
4632 1819 Wide date.
Ov. 108–9, 112–15. A one-sided proof (rev. not mirrorlike), 1979 ANA:936.
4633 1820/19 [all kinds 751,122 + ?P] Small flat-based 2.
Ov. 101. Sometimes miscalled "1820/18." Ex. Rare UNC.

4634 1820/19 Small curve-based 2.
Ov. 102.

4635 1820 Small curve-based 2.
Ov. 103. One proof reported, ex Winsor:498.

4636 1820 Widest large date.
Ov. 104, 105. Flat-based knobbed 2. One proof reported, ex Winsor:499.

4637 1820 Close large date.
Ov. 106–8. Flat-based fancy 2, no knob, as in 1821–22. Possibly 3 proofs; Breen {1977}, pp. 41–42.

4638 1821 [1,305,797 + ?P]
7 vars. Same date punches as last. Some of the reported mintage may have been dated 1820. 4 or 5 proofs reported.
4639 1822/1 [All kinds 1,559,573 + ?P]
Ov. 101–2, 106. All 3 vars. first identified as overdates in *Numisma* 3/55:2604–7. Overdate is never much plainer than

on ill.; note second 2 heavier, vertical line at its center, tiny lump within angle.

4640 1822 Button on cap.
Ov. 107. Button is on folded-down limp peak of cap, directly r. of seventh star, above BE. Ex. rare UNC.

4641 1822 Large E's. Scarce.
Ov. 114. Broken A's. Usually with rev. shattered through legend. Ex. rare UNC.

4642 1822 Small E's, normal.
9 vars. C in 50 C. varies slightly in size; no difference in scarcity. Possibly 5 proofs known; Breen {1977}, p. 44.

4643 1823 [all kinds 1,694,200 + ?P] Fancy 2, large C in 50 C.
Ov. 101. Broken 3 leans r. Later die states (less scarce) show a lump between outer curves of 3 ("patched" 3). The fancy 2 is as in 1822.

4644 1823 Fancy 2, small c in 50 c. Very scarce.
Ov. 102. "Patched" 3 leans r.

4645 Plain 2 henceforth. Broken 3.
Ov. 110, unlisted early state. Minute gap between halves of 3.

4646 1823 "Ugly" 3. Very scarce.
Ov. 110a. Middle cusp of 3 broken off; die crumbling behind 3. Not to be confused with next.

4647 1823 "Patched" 3.
Ov. 106a, 108a. Die crumbling between curves behind 3, but intact cusps, unlike preceding.

4648 1823 Normal 3. Short 1; large C in 50 C.
Ov. 103, 110–12.

4649 1823 Same. Small c in 50 c.
Ov. 104, 108, 109. Price for 104 (broken A's); others are rarer.

4650 1823 Extra tall 1; large C in 50 C.
Ov. 105, 106.

4651 1823 Extra tall 1; small c in 50 c.
Ov. 107. Fragment of extra shaft between 2 upper talons; 5 leans far r. Ex. rare UNC.

Ex J. W. Garrett: 310. Courtesy Bowers & Ruddy Galleries, Inc.

4652 1824/2/0 [All kinds 3,504,954 + ?P]
Ov. 103. Also called "1824 over various dates." The ill. shows 2 and 0 plainly; traces remain of other digits, possibly 3 and 1, but these do not always show. Punches for 182

match those of 1820–21. This hopelessly bungled die was one of Scot's closet skeletons, posthumously retrieved from his vault after Kneass succeeded him in the engravership.

4653 1824/1
   Ov. 101, 102. Same punches for 1, 8, 2 as in **4652.** Not to be confused with next or **4657.**

4654 1824/4 Tall 1; fancy 2.
   Ov. 109. The 4 was first entered well to l. of final position.

4655 1824 Tall 1, fancy 2; normal close date.
   Ov. 106, 113–14. Price for 113: 24 extra close, AT join, usually with field lump above dexter chief of shield; others are rare.

4656 1824 Tall 1, plain 2.
   5 vars.

4657 1824/4 Tall 1, plain 2; OF over CF.
   Ov. 110.

4658 1824 Short 1, plain 2.
   4 vars.

4659 1825 [all kinds 2,943,166 + ?P] Fancy 2.
   6 vars. The ill. is of a proof (Ov. 116). Fancy and plain 2's of 1825–26 first identified in *Numisma* 3/55:2621–34. Henceforth at least one new head punch each year, sometimes 2; these differ only minutely unless otherwise noted.

4660 1825 Plain 2. UNITEDSTATES as one word.
   Ov. 101. Ex. rare UNC.

4661 1825 Plain 2. Normal legend.
   9 vars. Proofs exist of several vars.

4662 1825 Plain 2. Extra large A's. Rare.
   Ov. 109. Bases of TAT almost touch. Getty:852, EF cleaned, $320.

4663 1826 [all kinds 4,004,180 + ?P] Plain 2. High 6.
   Ov. 102 (ill. is one of 4 or 5 proofs), 103. Price for former; latter, with repunching on 5, is rare.

4664 1826 Plain 2, wide date. Rare.
   Ov. 101. One proof reported. Ex. rare UNC.

4665 1826 Plain 2, close date, normal.
   Ov. 104–5, 109.

4666 1826 Plain 2, close date, OFAMERICA one word.
   Ov. 112. Crumbling fills upper half of first S and part of N.

4667 1826 Fancy 2, wide date.
   Ov. 113, 119, 120.

4668 1826 Fancy 2, close date.
   10 vars.

4669 1827/6 [All kinds 5,493,400 + ?P]
   Ov. 101, 102, 103.

4670 1827 Fancy 2, flat base. Large C in 50 C.
   39 vars. The ill. is of a proof (Ov. 107); 5 or 6 proofs known, possibly from other dies.

4671 1827 Same, extra large A's. Very rare.
   Ov. 137. Rev. of **4662.**

4672 1827 Fancy 2, flat base; normal A's, small c in 50 c. Rare.
Ov. 122, 138. The same C punch was used for C in AMER-ICA. Die file marks below beak.

4673 1827 Plain 2. Very scarce.
Ov. 109–11, 140.

4674 1827 Curve-based 2.
Ov. 146–47. Very rare in mint state.

4675 1828 [all kinds 3,075,200 + ?P] Curve-based 2, no knob.
Ov. 101–5. One proof reported (Ov. 105).

4676 1828 Curved-based 2 with knob.
Ov. 106–7. Discovery coins of both: *Numisma* 3/55:2652–53.

4677 1828 Large 8's as above, flat-based 2.
Ov. 108–9. Repunched 8's.

4678 1828 Small 8's, flat-based 2, normal large letters.
12 vars. 6–8 proofs reported.

4679 1828 Same, UNITEDSTATES one word. Scarce.
Ov. 118. One proof reported. Rev. reappears in **4686**. Ex. rare UNC.

4680 1828 Small 8's, flat-based 2, small letters. Scarce.
Ov. 119. A's in AMERICA filled. STA repunched. Discovered by this writer, 1955. Ex. rare UNC.

4681 1829/7 [all kinds 3,712,156 + ?P] Largest 5.
Ov. 101. Curve-based 2 punched over flat-based. Early states show most of top of 7, late states (less premium) little or none, though shaft of 7 remains. Ex. rare UNC.

4682 1829/7 Normal 5.
Ov. 102. Little of top of 7 shows; shaft plain. Ex. rare UNC.

4683 1829 Largest 5.
Ov. 104–5, 112. Proofs known of last 2.

4684 1829 Normal 5 henceforth. Wide open C in 50 C.
Ov. 103, 113.

4685 1829 Large C nearly closed.
10 vars. Several vars. of proofs.

4686 1829 Extra large letters, UNITEDSTATES one word.
Ov. 110. Repunched 9. Rev. of **4679**.

4687   1829 Extra large letters, normal spacing.
Ov. 116. Right bases of all T's weak, thin. None seen UNC.

4688   1830 [all kinds 4,764,800 + ?P] Small 0 in date.
16 vars. Several vars. of proofs. Compare all following.

4689   1830 Small 0; largest 5.
Ov. 106. Only one seen UNC. Getty:968, $875 (1977).

4690   1830 Small 0; extra tall 0 in 50 C.
Ov. 104. The 0 is much taller than 5. Ex. rare UNC.

4691   1830 Small 0; large letters. Very rare.
Ov. 114. Rev. of 1828. UNITEDSTATES one word.

4692   1830 Tall 0.
Ov. 120–23. Overton 119, called "medium 0," is actually a triple-punched small 0; not rare.

4693   1831 [all kinds 5,873,660 + ?P] Perfect 1's, normal.
7 vars. Compare all following. Possibly 2 or 3 proofs (Ov. 103). Top serifs plain. Coins from lapped or worn dies (Ov. 106–7) may show only very minute serifs, simulating **4695;** not rare.

4694   1831 Perfect 1's, double LIBERTY.
Ov. 106–7. First 1 too high. Die file marks l. of drapery and above cap. Doubled obv. die, doubling plainest at LIBERTY.

4695   1831 Blunt 1's.
10 vars.

4696   1832 [all kinds 4,797,000 + ?P] Large letters.
Ov. 101. Always with some state of the break at wing. Difficult to find in mint state, though always available for a price in EF or AU.

4697   1832 Small letters henceforth. Malformed arrows.
Ov. 102, 104, 113, 116–17.

4698   1832 Normal arrows. Short top to 5.
Ov. 106, 111, 118, 121. At least one proof of first.

4699   1832 Same, "dashed" date-1832.
Ov. 112 (ill.), BHNC 123. At least 3 proofs of latter.

4700   1832 Normal arrows. Long top to 5.
11 vars.

4701   1833 [All kinds 5,206,000]
11 vars. Proofs reported remain unverified except for **4703.**

4702 1833 Extra large 50 C.
  Ov. 103–4, 114. Long, heavy curved top to 5.

4703 1833 Restrike. Small 50 C. Proofs only. Ex. rare.
  Beaded borders, raised rims around them; fancy 5 as in 1836.
  Rev. of **4709, 4718.** Squashed edge lettering. Discovered by
  H. O. Granberg; "Coll. of a Prominent American":798.

4704 1834 [all kinds 6,412,000 + ?P] Head of 1833, large date
  and letters.
  Ov. 101–3. Last of these has wide open 3, cusp far from
  knobs; at least 4 proofs exist.

4705 1834 Large date, small letters. Normal 4.
  Ov. 104–5, 107–8.

4706 1834 Large date, small letters, large over small 4.
  Ov. 106. Erroneous small 4 punch probably was for half
  cents.

4707 1834 Small date and letters, small c in 50 c.
  Ov. 110, 113–14, 116. This head is not to be confused with
  any to follow.

4708 1834 Small date and letters, large C in 50 C.
  Ov. 109. Same comment.

4709 1834 Restrike. Proofs only. Ex. rare.
  Beaded borders, raised rims around them. Small 50 c., fancy
  5 as in 1836. Rev. of **4703.** Squashed edge letters. 1983
  ANA:2477; cf. J. D. Parsons, B&R RCR 4/82.

4710 1834 Head of 1835. Large C in 50 C.
  6 vars. Note contour of bust and drapery compared to previous device punches.

4711 1834 Similar. Small c in 50 c. Scarce.
  Ov. 119.

4712 1834 Similar. 0 in 50 C. over larger 0.
  Ov. 115.

4713 1834 Similar. Double date; "office boy rev." Very scarce.
  Ov. 118. R corrected from erroneous I; parts of other letters
  between ATES; crude shield stripes. Ex. rare UNC.

4714 1835/4 [All kinds 5,352,006 + ?P]
  Ov. 105. End of crossbar of 4 shows at r. of 5. Small c in 50 c.
  Ex. rare UNC.

4715 1835 Straight tops to both 5's; small c in 50 c.
  Ov. 103. Ex. rare UNC.

4716 1835 Rev., curved top to 5, large C in 50 C.
  Ov. 101–2, 104, 107, and new var.

4717 1835 Rev., straight top to 5, large C in 50 C.
  Ov. 106, 108–10. Several proofs reported.

4718 1835 Restrike. Proofs only. Ex. rare.
  Raised rims around beaded borders. Rev. of **4703, 4709:**
  fancy 5; large C in 50 C. Squashed edge letters.

4719 1836 [all kinds 6,545,000 + ?P] Straight top to 5, small
  c in 50 c.
  Ov. 104, 109 (incl. proofs), and a new var. Many UNCs. are
  from a hoard of 1,500 obtained at issue by a young man in
  Sag Harbor, N.Y., and dispersed to collectors in mid-1880.
  These probably include some of following vars.

4720 1836 Curved top to 5, small c.
  Ov. 105, 114, 123.

4721 1836 Extra heavy date; similar rev.
  Ov. 115, 119.

4722 1836/4 Similar rev.
  Ov. 118, 120–21. Date punches of 1834. Later states with
  traces of 4 faded will price as **4720.**

4723 1836 Straight top to 5, large C in 50 C.
  Ov. 103, 110.

4724 1836/4 As preceding.
  Ov. 101, 102. Later states with traces of 4 faded will price as
  4720. Several proofs exist of Ov. 102.

4725 1836 Curved top to 5, large C.
  5 vars. Several proofs exist. Compare all following.

4726 1836/4 As preceding.
   Ov. 112. Later states with traces of 4 faded will price as **4725**.
4727 1836 50/00 C. Scarce.
   Ov. 116. Note spacing of date: high distant 1, low 8. At least
   6 proofs (ill.). Later impressions with blunder fainter command lower premiums. Discovered by this writer in 1951.
   Getty:1081, UNC., $625 (1977).

4728 1836/1336; ST over IT. Scarce.
   Ov. 108. Knobs of 3 plain within loops of 8. Double dentil at
   first star. Rev. blunder fades. Later states with traces of erroneous 3 faded out will price as **4725**. Several proofs exist;
   1976 ANA:1160.

4729 1836 Straight date; ST over IT. Very scarce.
   Ov. 107. Same rev. Later states with blunder gone will price
   as **4725**. Only one UNC. seen.
4730 1836 Straight date; fancy 5.
   Ov. 106. Same obv.; rev. similar to 1833–35 restrikes, but
   normal borders. Spine from stem end; T below S-A. Several
   proofs known. Note: Coins dated 1837 or 1838 with 50 C. on
   rev. are early circulating counterfeits.

v. GOBRECHT'S CAPPED BUSTS, 50 CENTS (1836–37)

During autumn 1836, Christian Gobrecht (appointed Second
Engraver in 1835 when Kneass had his eventually fatal stroke)
completed working dies for half dollars, of a new design, intended for steam coinage at the new weight standard, to be
mandated by a bill then under consideration by Congress. As
this bill did not become law until Jan. 18, 1837, the coins dated
1836 were for long believed patterns. Robert W. Julian has
found evidence that the 1836 coinages of the new design were in
fact legal issues for circulation—at the old weight standard.
However, Mint tolerances for blanks at the old standard meant
that many were coined at 206.5 to 207 grs., which largely overlaps the legal limits of the new standard (206.25 ± 1.5 grs.).
Therefore, new standard blanks could have been used and probably were. All specimens I have weighed are within legal tolerances for either standard.

These half dollars of the new issue, dated 1836, were the first
coins made for circulation on the Mint's new steam press.
Steam coinage had been a goal of successive Mint Directors
ever since 1797, when Matthew Boulton originally demonstrated its value by coining over 34 million pennies for the government of George III, more nearly identical (and more frustrating to counterfeiters) than any similar quantity of coins had
ever been. However, for a variety of reasons, no foundry in the
USA could build a steam coinage press until 1836. The Mint's
first one was due to begin service on Feb. 22, 1836, and
Gobrecht cut dies for medalets; however, the demonstration
was aborted, and the date on the FIRST STEAM COINAGE
medalet die was altered to March 23. (These medalets became
very popular; the Mint Bureau still sells imitations.) No steam
coinage for circulation followed until Nov. 8, 1836. On this
latter date, Mint Director Robert Maskell Patterson sent 10
"specimens" (were these proofs?) of the new half-dollar design
to Treasury Secretary Levi Woodbury as "the first specimens,
executed this afternoon."

Patterson's letter continues: "The old [half dollar] coins were
struck in what we term an *open collar;* this is struck in a close
collar [see Glossary], which makes the edges of pieces thicker,
and gives a mathematical equality to their diameters." Introduction of the close collar meant that lettered edges had to be
abandoned, as the close collar compressed planchets at striking
enough to squash any lettering or ornamentation imparted to
blanks before striking—as on the 1833–35 restrike halves **4703,
4709, 4718**. Lettered edges could be imparted by collar only if
the latter were segmented and assembled in such a way as to
come apart as the lower die rose to push the finished coin out of
the coining chamber after striking. Jean Pierre Droz had experimented with this technique during his brief and unhappy time
at Boulton's mint, for which reason Thomas Jefferson vainly
sought to bring Droz to the infant Philadelphia Mint (1792–93).
However, it was beyond even Boulton's enormous technological
capacity, and the Philadelphia Mint was not to adopt it until
1907, for the new St. Gaudens eagles and double eagles. Nevertheless, close collars were perfectly adaptable to striking coins
with reeded edges, and the Mint used them for smaller silver
and gold coins beginning in 1829. Four different collars were in
use for 1837 half dollars, one of them (30.5 mm, fine reeding)
the same as 1836. The others are 29.5 mm, 30.8 mm with coarse
reeding (nearest to that of 1838 but not identical), and 31.6 mm.
This last made coins with a wider rim around border beads on
both sides, and is rare. We are not pricing them separately (except for the broadest) as nothing is known of their degrees of
scarcity, many collectors do not have micrometer calipers, and
most have neither the patience nor the eyesight to count reeds.

Instead of creating an original design, Gobrecht merely did
what Kneass would have, had the latter escaped his crippling
stroke: redrew the old Reich devices. Dropping the motto extended the practice with the then current quarter dollars and
gold coins. The wording 50 CENTS would be changed in 1838
to HALF DOL. for uniformity with the quarter dollars and
silver dollars.

GOBRECHT'S CAPPED BUSTS, 50 CENTS

Designer, Christian Gobrecht, after John Reich. Engraver, Gobrecht. Mint, Philadelphia. Composition, 1836, as before; 1837, silver 90%, copper 10%. Diameters, 1⅙ to 1⅕″ = 29.5 to 31.6 mm (see introductory text). Weight standards, 1836, as before, 208 grs. = 13.48 gms; 1837, 206.25 ± 1.5 grs. = 13.36 ± 0.1 gms. Edge, reeded. Authorizing Acts, 1836, April 2, 1792; 1837, Jan. 18, 1837 (see introductory text).

Grade range, POOR to UNC. GOOD: All legends and date legible; generally, only one or two letters of LIBERTY will show; devices outlined. VERY GOOD: At least three letters of LIBERTY legible; partial drapery, hair, and feather details. FINE: Full LIBERTY. VERY FINE: Shoulder clasp clear; over half hair details, most feathers separated. EXTREMELY FINE: All hair strands and feathers separated; only few tiny isolated rubbed spots.

4731   1836 [1,200? + ?P]
Coined Nov. 8, 1836. Doubling on bases of 50 CENTS; various states of a crack from rim down into field r. of final S. At least 12 proofs known; Garrett:329, Auction 80:741, $29,000. Enl. photos. In 1983 Grand Central:2649 and :1853, C. W. A. Carlson cataloged 2 specimens as of old and new weight standards, respectively, at 207.1 grs. = 13.42 gms. and 205.9 grs. = 13.34 gms., deducing that some were coined in early 1837 from 1836-dated dies; but see introductory text.

4732   1837 [3,629,820 + ?P]
4 different edges; see introductory text. Many slight spacing vars. in date. 4 proofs seen; Auction 82:757, $5,250.
4733   1837 "Inverted G." Very scarce.
Engraver's tool slip. Usually weak in this area, probably from attempts to efface the blunder. Willing, Auction 80:744, UNC., $1,900.

vi. GOBRECHT'S CAPPED BUSTS, HALF DOL. (1838–39)

The mid- and later 1830s were times of many brief design experiments for most U.S. coin denominations. Between 1835 and 1839, no less than seven heads were introduced on cents,

three types each on half dimes and dimes, four types on quarters, six on half dollars, five on quarter eagles, and at least five on half eagles. Little or no explanation reached the Mint files in the National Archives; obscure technical reasons doubtless explained some of these changes, equally obscure aesthetic considerations presumably dictated the rest. In particular, there is no immediate answer to why the eagle was redrawn for the 1838–39 half-dollar revs. The shift from 50 CENTS to HALF DOL. was presumably for uniformity with the quarter dollar and silver dollar.

This design is notable for the first branch-mint half dollars: 20 proofs dated 1838 with mintmark O above date, struck in Jan. 1839 ostensibly to test a press, followed by at least 178,976 similar halves dated 1839, with at least five more proofs. The 1838 O is one of the most famous of American rarities; for long the quantity minted was controversial. Beistle {1929} claimed that only three were struck; this is manifestly absurd, as his backer Col. E. H. R. Green owned seven, though either he was unwilling to let Beistle see more than three, or he bought them after 1929. The true story behind this mintage was first published in *NUM* 4/1894, p. 198, but it did not come to modern collectors' attention until the 1950s. Friesner:583 (1894) was a proof 1838 O, with an old piece of paper inscribed "The enclosed specimen coin of the U.S. branch mint at New Orleans is presented to Pres. Bache by Rufus Tyler the Coiner. It may be proper to state that not more than 20 pieces were struck with the half-dollar dies of 1838." In the National Archives (1951) I found reference to "a few" halves struck "to test a press," and Rufus Tyler's name appeared repeatedly in New Orleans records as Coiner. As all 20 evidently began life as proofs, no further explanation is needed for their absence from quarterly reports of coinage for circulation. This Tyler-Bache-Friesner coin went to Augustus G. Heaton; it is not now identified, and the Tyler document has not shown up.

The following roster is up to date as of March 1987. All are proofs unless otherwise noted.

1. Superintendent, New Orleans Mint, Mint Director Robert Maskell Patterson, Mint Cabinet Coll., SI. Clain-Stefanelli {1970}, fig. 32.
2. John H. Clapp, Louis Eliasberg estate.
3. Col. E. H. R. Green, Burdette G. Johnson, Wayte Raymond, J. G. MacAllister, Adolphe Menjou, R. E. Cox, Empire Coin Co., A. Buol Hinman, "Century":1151, Robison:1605, $70,000, Marvin Brauder.
4. J. N. T. Levick, W. Elliot Woodward 10/84, R. Coulton Davis, James B. Wilson, Waldo Newcomer, Henry Chapman, Col. E. H. R. Green, Maurice Ryan, W. W. Neil, James Aloysius Stack estate, $50,000, 1982 ANA:2320, Anthony Terranova, Kevin Lipton, G. W. Vogt, Auction 84:1666, $55,000, Florida pvt. coll.
5. Col. E. H. R. Green, William Cutler Atwater, Reed Hawn:122, $41,000, Auction 79:1569, $62,000. Field nicks midway between nose and fifth star, and hair and ninth star.
6. Col. E. H. R. Green, W. G. Baldenhofer, R. Pelletreau, Jerry Cohen, Lester Merkin, Q. David Bowers, Charles Jay, Dr. E. Yale Clarke:253, $43,000, Julian Leidman, Auction 82:1689, $47,500. Impaired. Ill. in Breen {1977} and above **4734.**
7. Col. E. H. R. Green, Wayte Raymond, F. C. C. Boyd, WGC:410, 1971 ANA:805, Oviedo:830, $40,700. EF, formerly proof.
8. Col. E. H. R. Green, "Anderson Dupont," Gotschal, 1957 ANA, TAD, Julian Leidman, Steve Ivy, Manfra Tordella & Brookes, 1983 ANA:2494, Robertson, MARCA 5/24/85:392, $35,750, 1986 ANA:4657A. Impaired.
9. New Orleans pvt. coll., Ferguson Haines, Col. E. H. R. Green, Charles A. Cass, "Empire":1344, New Netherlands, Jerry Cohen, KS 4/67:1065, Kreisberg MBS 6/29/70:1044. EF.

10. Guggenheimer:830. EF. Claimed in the catalog to be ex WGC, but ill. does not match no. 7.

In 1951, Wayte Raymond traced 11, apparently including all the above.

Attention must be drawn to the two types of rev. on the 1839 Philadelphia coins. "Type I" has large heavy letters close to border, and the eagle is that of 1838: spread talons, large shield about touching arrow feathers, three arrow butts, large area of arrow feather below stem, only one berry above H (the other is far to l. between two top pairs of leaves). This was for long the only rev. known with any Capped Bust obv.

"Type II" has medium-size narrower letters far from border, and the eagle is nearest to that regularly found with Liberty Seated obvs. later in the year: closed talons, small shield distant from arrow feathers, only two arrow butts, only a tiny remnant of arrow feather below stem, paired berries above H. Beistle {1929} may have seen it (his 1-B seems to match the description in part), but Maurice Rosen first identified it as a new design about Sept. 1972. I discovered that its rev. die was the same, or at least from the same complete hub, as the pattern Judd 95. However, with a regular obv. die, "Type II" is represented by three circulated business strikes, whereas the pattern obv. made only proofs. The roster of survivors:

1. FCI, 1973 GENA, Julian Leidman. EF. Discovery coin.
2. Julian Leidman, Stanley Scott:387, Harte:2650, 1981 GENA:1133, Kagin 333:1686 (1984 Met. NY, 3/30–31/84). VF, rim dent above (I)T; 204.8 grs. = 13.27 gms.
3. Delaware pvt. coll. EF, 205.78 grs. = 13.334 gms. Possibly same as 1.

GOBRECHT'S CAPPED BUSTS, HALF DOL.

Designer, Engraver, as before. Mints, Philadelphia (no mintmark), New Orleans (O above date). Physical Specifications, Authorizing Acts, as preceding.

Grade range and standards, as before.

4734 1838 [3,546,000 + ?P]
Minor vars. in spacing of date. 4 proofs known, one impaired. Ill. of **4736.**

4735 1838 Final 8 heavily repunched. Very rare.
1974 GENA:1513.
4736 1838 O [20P] Proofs only. Very rare.
See introductory text for history and roster. The Philadelphia Mint shipped 2 pairs of dies for this mintage, April 11, 1838; they arrived May 3. One pair was used in Jan. 1839 "to test a press"; both obvs. were defaced June 21, 1839, revs. held over for 1839 O coinage. Dangerous forgeries exist, made by affixing O mintmarks to genuine Philadelphia coins; authentication of any nonpedigreed specimen is recommended.

4737 1839 Bust. [all kinds 1,392,976 + ?P] "Type I," large letters.
See introductory text. Minor vars. exist. Enl. photos.

4738 1839 Bust. "Type II," smaller letters. Ex. rare, 3 known.
See introductory text for roster and origin of rev. type. Enl. photo.

4739 1839 O [178,976 + ?P]

Mintmark above date as in 1838 O; see introductory text. 3 pairs of dies shipped; these and the 2 leftover revs. were defaced Feb. 21, 1840. The least scarce var. has mintmark repunched at base (Beistle 2-A); the rarest, thin mintmark (Beistle 3-B): LM 3/67:354, NN 57:900. Extensively hoarded; see introductory text. The 5 known proofs have dies aligned 180° from normal, so that date is nearest to HALF DOL.; Robison:1607, $13,500. (This condition may occur on business strikes.)

vii. THE SULLY-GOBRECHT LIBERTY SEATED DESIGN, NO MOTTO (1839–53)

Following the early Mint tradition of uniformity of design of all silver coins, the Gobrecht Liberty Seated design (after Thomas Sully), adopted for silver dollars in Dec. 1836, was extended to half dollars in 1839. Rev. is similar to previous types, but inscription is at first in small letters similar to those of 1836–37.

The first obv. dies show no extra drapery at crook of elbow; later dies through 1891 have a small extra patch below it. This is nothing like the bulky cloak on the Robert Ball Hughes version found on dollars and smaller silver 1840–91. Only on half dollars does the original Sully-Gobrecht design continue (albeit with redrawn Reich eagles rather than the Peale-Gobrecht flying eagle of the 1836–39 dollars). Nor is it coincidence that the half dollars are the only denomination thereafter to come sharply struck. Coins from the 1839 "no drapery" dies went into circulation early and stayed there; mint-state survivors were until recent years so rare that their existence was controversial, but today perhaps five qualify at that level plus three proofs. Those from the three "with drapery" obvs. are nearly as rare in mint state.

Small Letter revs. continue through 1841; two of the 1841 O dies remained unused and went to press with 1842 Small Date obvs. at New Orleans. These are thought to have formed part of the initial [203,000]; they are almost unobtainable above FINE.

No reason has been found for the change to large letters in 1842; this letter size remained standard through 1891. This new rev. type has been attributed to Robert Ball Hughes.

Issues remained fairly large until 1850. The Mint's principal output in this period continued to consist of cents, half dollars, and half eagles. However, discovery of gold in California sent world market prices down in terms of silver, which trend was experienced in the East as a sharp rise in silver bullion prices reckoned in gold dollars. Eventually (1851–53) bullion dealers bought up most of the Mint's output of larger silver coins for shipment to the West Indies and Latin America, partly as coins, largely as ingots made by melting the coins: They had become worth more than face value as bulk silver. Less silver went to the mints for coinage; survivors remain very scarce, especially near mint state.

Gobrecht died in July 1844. The Mint authorities wanted nobody at all to succeed him; they then preferred to work with friendly outsiders like Charles Cushing Wright, who posed no threat to the lucrative medal business being operated by the brilliant but unscrupulous Chief Coiner, Franklin Peale (Adam Eckfeldt's successor). Unfortunately for them, James Barton Longacre (1794–1869), renowned bank-note-plate engraver and portraitist, exerted political pressure through Sen. (later Vice Pres.) John C. Calhoun, and obtained the Mint engravership as a sinecure. Owing to mechanical improvements by Kneass, Gobrecht, and Peale, manufacture of working dies was totally mechanized, and an Engraver would be needed only if new denominations were ordered. Longacre's duties, 1844–49, consisted largely of punching dates and mintmarks into otherwise completed working dies. At this donkey work his hand faltered, producing double dates, triple dates, overdates, and blunders such as the 1846 over lazy 6. These blunders—some of which may also have come from workmen in the Coiner's Department, as Julian suggests—became excuses to oust Longacre; but the real reason for official opposition to him was politics. Not only was Longacre outside the Mint's Imperial Divan (the Eckfeldts, Pattersons, Peales, and DuBois families and their cronies), but worse still, he had achieved the engravership by aid of a notorious politician from slaveholding South Carolina. On Christmas Day, 1849, Mint Director Robert Maskell Patterson privately offered Charles Cushing Wright the Mint engravership, effective as soon as the establishment could dispose of Longacre; Wright accepted. However, Longacre somehow got wind of the offer, and went over Patterson's head to Calhoun—preserving his job at the cost of 19 years of enmity from Mint officials, most of whom Longacre managed to outlive.

The final issue of this type, before adoption of the new weight standard (see next section), was from New Orleans (1853 O No Arrows): one of the most famous of American silver rarities. No record survives about this mintage, either of manufacture or disposition, except that the Philadelphia Mint shipped six obv. dies, only one of which was apparently used. There were 19 old revs. on hand from 1851 and possibly earlier years. Records of their disposition are confused; some revs. were returned to Philadelphia, others defaced (with the obvs.?) before June 9, 1853. Absence of any record of manufacture suggests that the few survivors were made for presentation purposes, only to be spent later or kept as pocket pieces. Only three survivors are traced:

1. J. W. Haseltine (before 1881), J. Colvin Randall (1885), H. P. Newlin, T. Harrison Garrett, J. W. Garrett:339, $40,000. F. 201 grs. = 13.02 gms.
2. Colin E. King:854 (1892), Col. E. H. R. Green, "Anderson Dupont," C. A. Cass, "Empire," A. M. Kagin, R. E. Cox, E. Yale Clarke:289, $24,000, Julian Leidman, Roy Ash, Leon Goodman:1712, $16,000, Delaware pvt. coll. G. 199.6 grs. = 12.93 gms.
3. H. O. Granberg, W. H. Woodin, Waldo Newcomer, Col. E. H. R. Green, Adolphe Menjou, Louis Eliasberg estate. VG.

A fourth is rumored; authentication is essential. All three genuine specimens are from the same dies; note incomplete third rev. pale gules (nearly vertical embossed stripe). Forgeries are numerous, mostly alterations from 1858 O; these have date elements grossly different in shape from the genuine, and are necessarily lightweight, generally below 192 grs. = 12.44 gms. Others could be made by grinding off arrows and rays from genuine 1853 O coins; these—even more lightweight—would show abundant evidence of monkey business at date and in fields.

Dates 1848–52 are all rarer than their mintage figures might suggest. The immense shipments of gold from California began lowering the world market price of gold reckoned in silver coins, or effectively raising the price of silver reckoned in gold dollars, until dollars, halves, and quarters became worth enough over face to be worth melting down as bullion.

GOBRECHT'S LIBERTY SEATED, NO MOTTO, 1839–53

Designer, Engraver, Christian Gobrecht; obv. after Thomas Sully, rev. after John Reich. Mints, Philadelphia (no mint mark), New Orleans (O below eagle). Physical Specifications, Authorizing Acts, as before.

Grade range, FAIR to UNC. GOOD: Date and all letters legible except LIBERTY. VERY GOOD: At least three letters of LIBERTY legible; partial rims, partial feather and drapery details. FINE: LIBERTY fully clear; most major drapery folds and over half feather details clear (leg at l. of arrow butts may be weaker). VERY FINE: All major and most minor drapery folds clear; almost all feather details clear. EXTREMELY FINE: Scroll edges and clasp clear; isolated tiny rubbed spots only (mostly on thighs and wingtips). EXCEPTIONS: Some New Orleans issues are weak flat strikings, as noted in text. NOTE: Beware alleged "UNC." coins showing rubbing on thighs and/or signs of cleaning in fields.

NO DRAPERY BELOW CROOK OF ELBOW

4740 1838 First Transitional. Original. Proofs only. 3 known.
Judd 82. Rev. of 1837, 50 CENTS. 206.25 grs. = 13.36 gms. 1) Mint, Mickley, Cohen, Parmelee, Steigerwalt, Granberg, Woodin, Newcomer, Boyd, Farris, Witham, Auction 81:321, $8,250, Merkin, pvt. coll. 2) Brock, Univ. of Pa., Ward, Dochkus, Judd, pvt. coll. 3) Brand, Farouk, Krouner, pvt. coll.

4741 1838 Same. Restrike. Proofs only. 2 known.
Judd 82. 192 grs. = 12.44 gms. Obv. differs minutely in date position.
4742 1838 Second Transitional. Proof only. Unique?
Judd 83. Obv. as **4740**; medium letters, HALF DOL., as **4734–39**. 1) Mint, SI.
4743 1839 [all kinds 1,972,400 + ?P] "No Drapery." Heavy numerals.
Closed 9 (knob joins loop). 1974 GENA:1521, others. Prohibitively rare in UNC.; many of the better ones have been drastically cleaned. Note large rock close to first star; on "with drapery" coins this rock is smaller and more distant. Rev. shows only 2 arrow butts. 2 obv. vars., differing slightly in date position.
4744 1839 Thin numerals and claws. Rare.
Open 9 (knob away from loop). 1974 GENA:1519–20, others. Same comments. 2 proofs known (enl. photos), one of them Boyd, WGC, 1976 ANA:1172, $10,000.

EXTRA DRAPERY BELOW ELBOW; SMALL LETTERS

4745 1839 Thin numerals.
"Gilhousen":968, others. Rock l. of shield smaller, farther from first star, as on all to follow. Knob of 9 away from loop.

Ex J. W. Garrett: 334. Courtesy Bowers & Ruddy Galleries, Inc.

4746 1839 Heavy numerals.
"Gilhousen":967, others. Knob of 9 joins loop. Date differs minutely in position.
4747 1840 Medium letters, rev. of 1838. [112,000–] Rare.
Beistle 1-B, 5-Ba, respectively with date level or slanting down to r. Latter rarer, ill. *Gobrecht Journal* 24, pp. 10–11 (7/82). Always with heavily cracked rev. die. 30.0 mm (other dates 30.6). Believed included in initial delivery, May 30, 1840. Usually in low grades. We have not seen Beistle 2-B (date slanting up to r.).

4748 1840 Small letters. [1,323,008+ + ?P]
Letters as in **4745–46, 4749–58**. Minor positional vars.; see next 2.

4749 1840 Same. Repunched date. Scarce.
Beistle 2a-Aa; "Gilhousen":971; Merkin 9/70:425. All 4 digits doubled; compare next.
4750 1840 Partly repunched date. 3 vars.
Repunching on 18, or 0, or 40; this last is believed a later state of preceding.
4751 1840 O Medium O, narrow interior space. [50,000] Very rare.
Mintmark .044″ = 1.12 mm. "Gilhousen":973. Rev. broke quickly; so mentioned in letter from New Orleans Mint Superintendent to Mint Director Patterson, April 18, 1840.

4752 1840 O Small round o. [150,000] Rare.
Mintmark .038″ = 0.97 mm. All seen show repunched 18.
Usually weak flat strikings (at lower force to save die wear?);
mintage figure from same source. Usually in low grades; finest is possibly ex Wilharm, Garrett, Robison, Auction 82:212.

4753 1840 O Large O. [655,100]
Mintmark .055″ = 1.4 mm; roundish interior space. At least
6 positional vars., from 7 obvs., 10 revs. (incl. **4751–52**).

Ex J. W. Garrett: 336. Courtesy Bowers & Ruddy Galleries, Inc.

4754 1841 [310,000 + ?P] Normal.
4755 1841 Obviously repunched first 1. Scarce.
Beistle 1a-B; "Gilhousen":975. Repunching on 8 is much
harder to see. Later states with repunching faded will price as
preceding.
4756 1841 O [all kinds 401,000] Narrow interior space to O.
Mintmark .05″ = 1.37 mm. At least 2 vars. A hoard of this
and next (possibly 40 UNCs.) turned up in Clearwater, Fla.
before 1957.
4757 1841 O Roundish interior space to O.
Differs from all preceding; most like **4753**. "Gilhousen":976.
At least 6 positional vars. Compare following.
4758 1842 O Small date and letters. [203,000−] Very rare.
Included in initial delivery, Feb. 28, 1842; part of this figure
comprises coins dated 1841. One obv. shipped Dec. 18, 1841;
2 revs. of 1841: Beistle 3-G (ill.) and 3-F (mintmark very
close to feather). Former rev. recurs, cracked, with 2 obvs.
dated 1841: a condition discovered by Randall Wiley. Cf. NN
57:911–12; 1974 GENA:1553–54. Usually in low grades; prohibitively rare in EF, e.g., Robison:1615, EF, $3,500; Acree,
Glassenberg, 1975 ANA:559, AU +, $2,000. Auction 86:200,
UNC., $4,180.

MODIFIED REVERSE: LARGE LETTERS

4759 1842 Small date. [191,000 + ?P] Scarce.
Numerals as preceding, matching cent **1879,** quarter **3947.**
At least 3 vars. Very rare in mint state. Wellinger, Neil,
Bareford:392, UNC., $1,200; Boyd, Auction 80:1292, Proof,
$10,000.
4760 1842 Large date. [1,821,764] Normal.
Numerals as on cent **1880,** quarter **3948;** large dates continue
through 1891. Positional vars. exist; compare following.

Ex J. W. Garrett: 338. Courtesy Bowers & Ruddy Galleries, Inc.

4761 1842 Double-punched date. Several vars.
Beistle 2-B, 3-C, others. That in Merkin 3/68:574 has date
first entered slanting up to r., then corrected.
4762 1842 Partly repunched date. Several vars.
Beistle 4-D, others. Repunched 18: "Gilhousen":978;
repunched 8 2, Merkin 9/70:426, others.
4763 1842 Triple date. Rare.
Triple outlines plainest on 842. Possibly earliest state of Beistle 2-B or 3-C. On one die, outlines show above and below
cross stroke of 2. Ill. *Gobrecht Journal* 7/85.
4764 1842 O Large date. [754,000]
7 pairs of dies shipped. Larger O henceforth except as noted,
.054″–.055″ = 1.4 mm. Mintage figure covers deliveries from
March 31 through Dec. 31.
4765 1843 [all kinds 3,844,000 + ?P] Normal.
Some show minor traces of repunching on 4 or 43: NN
57:914, others.
4766 1843 Double date. Scarce.
Beistle 3-C.
4767 1843 O [all kinds 2,268,000] Normal.
In all, 10 obvs., 15 revs. shipped.
4768 1843 O Very thin numerals. Rare.
"Gilhousen":982. Hairlike serifs. Either this date logotype
was entered timidly, or the die was too vigorously relapped,
or both.
4769 1843 O Double date.
Date first entered too low, slanting upward to r., then corrected; doubling plainest on 18. On later states the repunching on 43 gradually fades out.
4770 1843 O Small round o. Ex. rare, unlocated.
Beistle 2-B. Compare **4774–75.**
4771 1844 [all kinds 1,766,000 + ?P] Normal.
4772 1844 Partly repunched date. Several vars.
Beistle 2-B, repunched 18 (cf. NN 57:915); Beistle 3-C,
repunched 44 (earlier states also show repunching on 8).
4773 1844 O [all kinds 2,005,000] Normal date; larger O.
Mintmark about 1.4 mm as usual in this period. Some have
traces of repunching on final 4 (Beistle 6-F). The coins with
incomplete 8 (center missing), e.g., 1974 GENA:1540, are
apparently normal-date pieces with foreign matter clogging
the die at the point where loops of 8 meet.

4774 1844 O Smaller round o. Very rare.
Beistle 4-E; compare Merkin 9/70:431, in which mintmark is possibly from the regular medium punch but very thin and weakly entered. However, in view of next, a var. may exist with small o at about 1.2 mm.

4775 1844 O Blundered double date; smaller round o. Very rare.
Mintmark about 1.2 mm. Usually in low grades; prohibitively rare UNC.

4776 1845 [589,000 + ?P]
Normal or with minute traces of repunching on date. On heavier strikings 84 touch; on lighter, and/or pieces from relapped dies, 8 4 are free (same logotype). Very rare in mint state.

4777 1845 O [all kinds 2,094,000] Normal date, larger O.
In all, 14 obvs., 12 revs. Same comment as to preceding; compare next 8. On one rev., O over horizontal O (faint, use a strong glass); presently Ex. rare. Ill. *Gobrecht Journal* 24 (7/82).

4778 1845 O "No drapery." Larger O.
Beistle 3-C, 3-G, 3-H, others. Drastically lapped obv. die, not a reversion to the 1839 hub; no drapery below crook of elbow. But compare **4784–85.**

4779 1845 O Footless 1.
Beistle 7-G, 7-H. L. base of 1 missing.

4780 1845/5 O Part of extra 5 far to r. Very rare.
Part of extra 4 between 45. This may be Haseltine's "1845/41" (1881 Type Table, no. 3). It is most likely the so-called "5 over horizontal 5" in Gies 1940.

4781 1845 O Double-punched date; larger O. Several vars.
On that most often seen, repunching is plainest on 845. Robison:1627, UNC., $1,050. But compare **4783, 4785.**

4782 1845 O Triple date. Very rare.
Beistle 2-B. Ill. *Gobrecht Journal* 23 (3/82).

4783 1845 O Small round o. Normal drapery; repunched date.
Beistle 5-E, others. Mintmark about 1.2 mm, as on next 2.

4784 1845 O Small round o. "No drapery." Rare.
Beistle 4-D and unlisted: heavier and thinner dates. *Numisma* 24:450–51 (11/58).

4785 1845 O Small round o. "No drapery," repunched date. Rare.
Beistle 1-A; 5-E (drastically repolished die). Merkin 3/68:552; "Charmont":3487. Same comment as to **4774.**

4786 1846 [all kinds 2,210,000 + ?P] Small date, normal.
Same logotype as "medium date" cent **1891.** Many minor positional vars., some with traces of repunching on numerals.

4787 1846/5 Small date. Several vars. Very rare.
Beistle 1-A, 1a-B, 1b-B, and unlisteds. Discovered by J. Colvin Randall before 1881; first published in Haseltine's "Type Table" Catalog, Nov. 1881, then by Beistle in 1929, but forgotten until several specimens showed up in 1958–59. Look for tip of 5 protruding from knob of 6, or knob of 5 within loop of 6, or part of top stroke of 5 within 6.

4788 1846 over horizontal 6. Rare.
Beistle 2-A, 2-Aa. Usually in low grades. Configuration suggests that a 3-digit logotype was used for 184, as on many vars. of 1847 cents (see **1893).**

4789 1846 Tall date.
Beistle 3-Ab, 4a-Ad, 5-C, others. Same logotype as tall date cent **1892.** Compare next.

4790 1846 Tall date, spiked 4. Rare.
Beistle 4-Ac and possibly 4-C. Forgotten until rediscovery by Kamal Ahwash, 1978. The "spike" may be part of a serif from a misplaced date, the rest effaced.

4791 1846 O [all kinds 2,304,000] Small date, normal.
9 pairs of dies shipped Dec. 10, 1845–July 28, 1846. Normal date (Beistle 7-G) or with traces of repunching on 6 (Beistle 4-D). Compare all following.

4792 1846 O Same, "no drapery."

Beistle 3-C: compare NN 57:922; "Gilhousen":990; Merkin 10/73:445, and **4794, 4796.** Explanation is as in **4778.**

4793 1846 O Small date, double-punched. Rare.

Beistle 5-F; cf. Merkin 3/68:587. Later, the repunching on 46 fades out; these "recut 18" coins will price as **4791.**

4794 1846 O Small repunched date, "no drapery." Rare.

Beistle 6-A. Auction 80:1296, UNC., $9,500.

4795 1846/5 O Small date. Very rare.

Beistle 2-B, 2-C. Same comments as to **4787.** Compare following. This may explain Hetherington:252, "recut date, looks like 1846/41."

4796 1846/5 O Small date, "no drapery." Very rare.

Beistle 2a-C, 2a-D; from drastically lapped obv. Same comments as to **4787, 4778.** Traces of overdate vanish in late states; these will price as **4794.** Robison:1632. The "1846 O over horizontal 6" in Kagin 332:2388 is unverified.

4797 1846 O Tall date. Very rare.

One obv. die (the tenth for this date) shipped Sept. 11, 1846; Randall Wiley has found 3 revs. Usually in low grades. Note the ill.; previously over 90% of coins represented as this var. were misdescribed. Glassenberg, 1975 ANA:573, $1,250, UNC.

4798 1847 [all kinds 1,156,000 + ?P] Normal date.

Several minor positional vars., some with traces of repunching on digits.

4799 1847 Thin numerals. Rare.

Hairlike serifs. Same comment as to **4768.** Randall, Garrett (1976):210, Proof, $2,300.

4800 1847 Double date. Very rare.

4801 1847 Repunched 47. Scarce.

Discovered by John H. Clapp.

4802 1847/46 Ex. rare.

Beistle 1-A, 1-Aa. Traces of overdate fade (die relapped?). One proof known ("Dupont," Cass, "Empire," Hawn:161, $7,500, E. Yale Clarke:276, $9,000, Robison:1634, $6,000), and possibly 10–12 business strikes. NN, $2,500 (1962), Glassenberg, 1975 ANA:574, borderline UNC., $5,750.

4803 1847 O [all kinds 2,584,000] Heavy date.

At least 7 positional vars., one (Beistle 3-C) with repunching on 4. In all, 12 obvs., 18 revs.

4804 1847 O Thin numerals.

Beistle 5-E. Hairlike serifs. "Gilhousen":993. Same comment as to **4768.**

4805 1847 O Double date. Very rare.

Date first entered high and slanting down to r., then corrected lower. Discovered by John H. Clapp. Ill. *Gobrecht Journal* 24 (7/82).

4806 1848 [all kinds 580,000 + ?P] Open 4.

Beistle 1-A, 3-C, 5-E. Crosslet of 4 small and distant from base, as on cent **1898.** Usually in low grades.

4807 1848 Open 4, repunched 18. Very rare.

Brown Library:277; "Charmont":3491. Date first entered too high, corrected lower. Usually in low grades.

4808 1848 Closed 4. Very rare.

Beistle 2-B, 4-D, 6-Aa; 1975 ANA:579, 1976 EAC:1025. Crosslet of 4 long and almost touches base, as in cent **1900.** Usually in low grades.

4809 1848 Closed 4, obvious double date. Very rare.

Ivy Cambridge:1042.

4810 1848 Closed 4, repunched 18. Very rare.

Possibly a later state of preceding. Usually in low grades. Glassenberg, 1975 ANA:578.

4811 1848 O [all kinds 3,180,000] Open 4. Very rare.

Probably only the first obv. made; logotype as in **4806–7.** Glassenberg, 1975 ANA:580; 1976 EAC:1026; Robison:1638, UNC., $1,050; Auction 82:1181.

4812 1848 O Closed 4. Larger O.

Many minor positional vars.; 14 pairs of dies shipped. Logotype as in **4808.** Compare next.

4813 1848 O Similar, small o. Ex. rare, untraced.

Beistle 4-D (called "proof") and 6-D. Mintmark should be about 1.2 mm.

4814 1849 [all kinds 1,252,000 − + ?P] Normal date.

Minute positional vars. Many melted as worth over face: See introductory text. Randall, Garrett (1976):214, Proof, $4,000.

4815 1849 Partly repunched date.

Normally shows repunching most plainly on either 1 or 9.

4816 1849 Double date, first entered far to l. Ex. rare.

Beistle 5-E. Fewer than 6 seen to date, all but one in low grades. Cox:1920; Hirt:92. As spectacular a blunder as **4775, 4782, 4788,** but less often seen and therefore less publicized.

4817 1849 Double date, first entered to r. Very rare.
Beistle 4-D, 4a-Da, "5-A"; Merkin 9/70:440 (doubling plainest at 18).

4818 1849 O [2,310,000]
12 pairs of dies shipped.

4819 1850 [all kinds 227,000− + ?P] Closed 5.
Line joins knob to cusp; logotype as on cent **1904**. Sometimes with traces of repunching on zero. The very rare earliest state shows repunched 850.

4820 1850 Open 5. Very rare.
Knob distant from cusp; logotype as on cent **1905**. Sometimes with traces of repunching on lower part of zero. 1975 Sub. Wash.:221, others.

4821 1850 O [all kinds 2,456,000−] Closed 5.
Logotype as in **4819**. In all, 16 pairs of dies shipped. Minor positional vars., some with traces of repunching on one or more numerals. In Ten Eyck coll. one was described as with larger mintmark; cf. "Gilhousen":999. We are not convinced this is from a different punch.

4822 1850 O Open 5. Ex. rare.
Partial drapery. Discovered by Randall Wiley, 1979. Logotype as in **4820.** See next.

4823 1850 O Open 5, "no drapery." Ex. rare.
Glassenberg, 1975 ANA:584, UNC., $725.

4824 1851 [all kinds 200,750− + ?P] Normal date.
In all, 7 obvs., 11 revs., including next 2. See introductory text.

4825 1851 Repunched 851. Rare.
Beistle 1c-A. Later, repunching less obvious on final 1; 1976 EAC:1030.

4826 1851 Top of extra 1 between 51. Rare.
1978 FUN:536; compare NN 57:925.

4827 1851 O [402,000−]
20 pairs of dies shipped, few used.

4828 1851 O "No drapery." Very rare.
Discovered by Douglas Winter. UNCs. are generally somewhat prooflike. Explanation is as in **4778.**

4829 1852 [all kinds 77,130− + ?P] Normal date. Rare.
In all, 4 obvs., 6 revs. Probably the majority melted.

4830 1852 Double date, first punched low. Very rare.
Merkin 3/68:598.

4831 1852 Partly repunched date. Rare.
2 obvs. In one die, part of a second 2 shows in angle: "Gilhousen":1003.

4832 1852 O [all kinds 144,000−] Normal date.
"Gilhousen":1004, etc. In all, 12 obvs. shipped, few used; revs. are dies of previous years. The 3 proofs are from drastically repolished dies: foot not supported, parts of rev. stripes attenuated. Auction 86:203, Proof, $8,250.

4833 1852 O Partly repunched date.
Beistle 1-A, 1-B; "Gilhousen":1003. Extra outlines clearest at l. sides of 8 2.

4834 1853 O No arrows. 3 known.
No record of mintage. Only the one var.; all are in low grades. See introductory text for history, roster, and method of detecting forgeries.

Ex J. W. Garrett: 339. Courtesy Bowers & Ruddy Galleries, Inc.

viii. ARROWS AND RAYS (1853)

Because the immense quantities of gold exported from California lowered the price of bullion reckoned in silver, in effect forcing up the price of silver reckoned in gold dollars, bullion dealers began melting silver coins as worth more than face value. Silver vanished from circulation; little reached the Mint for coinage, and there was nothing between the cent and the gold dollar in circulation (1850) aside from irredeemable private scrip. Issue of billon 3¢ coins (1851) helped only a little. Something had to be done, and quickly.

Mint Director George N. Eckert proposed to Congress that weights of silver coins (except, inexplicably, the dollar) be lowered to a point at which melting would no longer be profitable. Congress did not understand why this would work, but passed his proposal nevertheless; it became the Act of Feb. 21, 1853. Henceforth half dollars would weigh 192 grs. = 12.44 gms., compared with their former 206.25 = 13.36 gms.

A distinguishing mark on the coins appeared necessary, despite lack of time to prepare and obtain approval of new designs. Eckert therefore ordered addition of arrows flanking the date and rays surrounding the eagle on all standard silver coins below the dollar.

On March 3, 1853, five proof sets were struck comprising half dimes, dimes, quarters, and half dollars with arrows. These sets were long since broken up; individual coins from them are of the highest rarity, one of the half dollars being in the Smithsonian Institution.

Production coinage began May 21 with a delivery of 80,000 halves. A total of 3,532,708 came from Philadelphia during 1853, from 49 obv. and 55 rev. dies; the 1,328,000 from New Orleans required 26 obv. and 19 rev. dies. That is less than 1/3 the then normal die life of 200,000–250,000 impressions. Possibly the operations of adding arrows and rays somehow weakened working dies; if so, this would explain why Mint Director Snowden ordered that in 1854 and later years revs. omit rays.

On the expectation that the United States provisional branch mint at San Francisco (then operating under the name of "U.S. Assay Office of Gold") might find a way to obtain enough parting acids to make gold and silver coins of legal fineness, the Philadelphia Mint shipped two pairs of half-dollar dies, but no 1853 S coinage ensued.

For generations, coin dealers believed that the issues of 1853 with arrows were so common that there would be no profit in stocking even gem UNC. survivors. As a result, nobody bothered to notice that these coins are in fact rare in pristine state. They went into circulation and stayed there (I recall seeing a few badly worn ones in church collection plates as late as 1943!), as few people saved them for souvenirs. Their recent meteoric price rise in mint state is partly from pressure from type collectors, but largely from belated recognition that few truly mint-state specimens have survived. However, there are plenty of "sliders."

The pattern of rays is standard; variations arise from degrees of lapping given to dies afterward.

ARROWS AND RAYS

Designer, Engraver, Longacre, after Gobrecht. Mints, Physical Specifications, as before, except Weight Standard 192 ± 1.5 grs. = 12.44 ± 0.097 gms. Authorizing Act, Feb. 21, 1853.

Grade range and standards, as before. NOTE: Beware "sliders"—pieces showing rubbing on thighs (and usually signs of cleaning in fields), mislabeled "UNC."

4835   1853 [all kinds 3,532,708 + 5P] Normal date, closed 5. Knob of 5 touches cusp. Many minute positional vars., among 49 obvs., 55 revs. Sometimes with traces of repunching on some numerals. Ill. of **4842.**

4836   1853 Normal date, open 5. Rare.
Beistle 9-P, 9-S. Knob of 5 far from cusp.
4837   1853 Partly repunched date.
Several vars.; not examined recently enough to tell if any are from the Open 5 logotype.
4838   1853 Double date. Rare.
Beistle 1-M, 1-Q, 1-A, 1-N, 8-N. All 4 digits show extra outlines.
4839   1853 Doubled rev. die. Very rare.
"Gilhousen":1006.
4840   1853 O [all kinds 1,328,000] Normal date.
Many minute positional vars. among 26 obvs., 19 revs. Mintage figure does not include **4834.**
4841   1853 O Partly repunched date.
Several minor vars.

4842   1853 O Blundered 1. 2 vars. Very rare.
Part of base of extra 1 from r. top of 1 in date. 1974 GENA:1566. Ill. above **4835.** Both show repunching on date; one var. has doubled obv. die.
4843   1853 O Double date. Very rare.
"Gilhousen":1008. Compare **4838, 4842.**
4844   1853 O "No drapery." Very rare.
Beistle 1-A, 1-E, 4-D; "Gilhousen":1009. Drastically repolished obv. die.

ix. ARROWS, NO MOTTO, 1854–55

The incoming Mint Director, Col. James Ross Snowden, ordered that henceforth quarters and half dollars should be issued without rays around eagle, though continuing to show arrows at dates. His reasons are likely to have included saving additional cost and time in diesinking, and increasing die life, which had sunk to about 1/3 of its usual level on coins with rays (see previous section, introductory text).

Two pairs of half-dollar dies were shipped to the new San Francisco branch mint, but no 1854 S coinage followed. A few months later, word reached Snowden of a local source of parting acids, so that the branch mint could finally begin to issue gold and silver coins at legal fineness. Accordingly, the Engraving Department shipped six obv. and four rev. dies for half dollars. At least three 1855 S proofs were made for presentation purposes, celebrating inception of this denomination. One of these went from Superintendent Robert Aiken Birdsall to Snowden, who placed it into the Mint Cabinet Collection; it is now in the Smithsonian Institution: Clain-Stefanelli {1970}, fig. 35. The other two appeared at auction in the 1950s.

This same 1855 S issue is of interest for other reasons. Among these are the vars. with and without extra drapery at elbow (the latter again from excessive relapping of dies, probably to remove clash marks); their undue rarity in mint state; and their export in quantity to China.

Most likely the last two reasons are connected; export would certainly explain rarity. Though we have not found documentation of such shipments, there is convincing circumstantial evidence. Merkin 3/68:606 was a nearly mint-state 1855 S bearing a Chinese chopmark, which qualifies as either humor or semiofficial explanation: In the middle of this half dollar is the character *chung* (shaped nearly like Greek phi) meaning 'middle' or 'half.'

In 1855, Snowden decided that thereafter too little old-tenor silver was likely to be brought in for recoinage, so that any distinguishing marks would be superfluous. Effective Jan. 1, 1856, there would no longer be arrows at dates, though the coins would continue at the 1853 weight standard.

ARROWS, NO MOTTO

Designer, Engraver, Physical Specifications, as 1853. Mints, Philadelphia (no mintmark), New Orleans (mintmark O below eagle), San Francisco (mintmark S below eagle).

Grade range and standards, as before.

4845   1854 [all kinds 2,982,000 + ?P] Normal date, 54 touch. Date logotype as on cent **1914.** On the lightest strikes, 54 do not quite touch. Many minor positional vars. Compare next 3 and **4849.** Probably fewer than 20 proofs survive. Ill. of **4852.**

4846 1854 Partly repunched date; 54 touch.
Beistle 2a-Aa (85 plainly double); other vars. are scarcer.
4847 1854 Double date; 54 touch.
Beistle 3-Ab, others. All 4 digits show double outlines.
4848 1854 Triple date; 54 touch. Very rare.
Complete double and partial third outlines on all 4 digits.
4849 1854 Normal date, 5 4 well apart.
Beistle 1-A. Date logotype as on cent **1913.**
4850 1854 O [all kinds 5,240,000] Normal date, 54 touch.
Date logotype as **4845;** same comments (except no proofs).
4851 1854 O Partly repunched date, 54 touch.
Beistle 2-B, 2-C (85 plainly double); others.
4852 1854 O Double date, 54 touch.
Beistle 4-Ca, 7-E, 12-K, unlisteds; "Gilhousen":1012; Merkin 6/68:333 (latter with crumbled rev. die). Ill. above **4845.**
4853 1854 O Triple date, 54 touch. Rare.
Beistle 5-D. Similar to **4848.**
4854 1854 O Lighter date, 5 4 well apart. Very scarce.
Beistle 9-F, 9a-G, 11-J, 13-Ba, 13-J; 1974 GENA:1571, 1574, others. Date logotype as in **4849.** In all, 55 obvs., 33 revs.
4855 1855 [all kinds 759,500 + ?P] Thin numerals.
Beistle 4-Ab, others? Hairlike serifs, bases of 8 and 5's. In all, 10 obvs., 8 revs. Possibly 12 proofs of this number, e.g., 1978 ANA:1031, $4,500; but compare **4858.**
4856 1855 Heavy numerals.
Minor positional vars. Compare next 2.
4857 1855 Same. Repunched 55.
Beistle 2-Aa. But compare next.
4858 1855/854 Heavy numerals. Very rare.
Business strikes discovered by this writer, 1970; discovery coin, Merkin 9/70:446. Part of extra 8 within 8; double knob to first 5; crossbar of 4 within final 5. 1976 ANA:1227, UNC., $1,550. Later reground die states bring less premium. Proofs discovered by Q. David Bowers; Fraser, Robison:1651, $5,000 (cleaned).

4859 1855 O [all kinds 3,688,000] Normal date.
In all, 30 obvs., 25 revs. Date usually fairly heavy.
4860 1855 O Final 5 repunched. Rare.
Beistle 6-Ca; 1975 Sub. Wash.:229.
4861 1855 O Repunched 55. Rare.
Beistle 4-C.
4862 1855 O Double date. Rare.
Beistle 1-A, 1a-C, 2-B, 3-A.
4863 1855 O Over horizontal O. Ex. rare.
RPM 1. Thin numerals. Discovered by Tom Miller, 1978. *Gobrecht Journal* 7/78, p. 18.

4864 1855 S [all kinds 129,950 + 1+P] "No drapery."
Beistle 1-A. Large S, .065″ = 1.65 mm. 3 proofs known; Breen {1977}, p. 236. Auction 86:1646, $18,700.

4865 1855 S Normal drapery.
Beistle 2-A and unlisted rev. "Gilhousen":1015, others. Large S as last. Later die states have weaker drapery below elbow. In all, 6 obvs., 4 revs.

x. ARROWS OMITTED (1856–66)

During 1858–61, Longacre created new hubs for all silver denominations. The old half-dollar rev. ("Type I," 1842–58), like those of quarter dollars and quarter eagles, shows long closed claws and large arrowheads; upper serifs of LF nearly touch. The "Type II" rev. (possibly completed with Anthony C. Paquet's assistance) has shorter open claws, smaller arrowheads spaced apart, and the upper serif of L is shorter and distant from F. Other modifications are very minor, but the whole effect is to increase apparent lightness and delicacy of the composition. Philadelphia coins 1859–65 are mostly from the new rev. hub; leftover old hub dies may exist on coins dated 1860 and later, but any survivors would be Ex. rare. However, S-Mint half dollars as late as 1864 with large S uniformly are from the old hub, as this branch mint used leftover revs. from 1856–58. This was official policy, partly for economy, partly to minimize risk in sending working dies. Overland shipments were the easy prey of stagecoach bandits, who could readily sell them to counterfeiters; ships' cargoes via Cape Horn were vulnerable to rust from salt spray and bilge water, or to shipwreck.

Pursuant to a resolution of the Secession Convention, Dec. 1860, the Southern Confederacy sent officials to the New Orleans branch mint at the end of Feb. 1861 to "take the institution into trust" (i.e., seize it: The CSA needed its silver and gold to further its war effort). On Feb. 28, the incumbent officials were confirmed in their positions on swearing allegiance to the Confederacy; refusal to swear would have meant dismissal and probably internment or other penalties. These officials included William A. Elmore, Superintendent; A. J. Guirot, Treasurer; Howard Millspaugh, Assayer; and M. F. Bonzano, M.D., Melter and Refiner. (There was of course no Engraver, as the Philadelphia Mint had furnished all working dies.) Bonzano remained on duty as a Union spy, transmitting secret reports to the Union Treasury, and almost certainly acting on secret orders to delay, minimize, or if possible sabotage any further coinage of gold and silver for the CSA. "We assume that his oath of allegiance to the CSA was done with his fingers crossed behind his back, or else in the manner of Euripides: 'My tongue an oath took, but my heart's unsworn'" (Breen {1977}, p. 239). For further details of Bonzano's activities, see Chap. 47.

One day before the rebel takeover, the Coiner delivered 330,000 regular O-Mint half dollars for the Union, with a portion reserved for assay as in former years. In March, the New Orleans branch struck 1,240,000 more for the State of Louisiana; in April, a final batch of 962,633 for the Confederacy. All

these 2,202,633 rebel strikings were from the 12 pairs of Union dies: obvs. received at New Orleans in Dec. 1860, with leftover revs. of 1858 or earlier. (The new hub coins used revs. of 1860.) It is barely possible also that rusted dies dated 1860 may have been rescued and reused. No records survive about issue of the 1861 O proof half dollars; the most likely occasions for making these would have been inception of coinage for Louisiana and for the CSA. With one remarkable exception, it is impossible to tell apart the Union, Louisiana, and CSA strikings. (However, the chances are 7 out of 8 that any given 1861 O was made for the rebels: 2,202,633 = 87% of the total 1861 O output [2,532,633].)

The lone exception is **4906**, the "Cracked Confederate Obv." This has a Union obv., cracked from rim to bridge of nose close to seventh star. In an earlier state, April 1861, this obv. appeared on the four original CSA proofs with A. H. M. Patterson's Confederate rev. (Chap. 47); but after CSA Treasury Secretary C. G. Memminger abandoned the project, the obv. stayed in press, combined with a regular Union rev. We know that these coins followed the CSA proofs, because the obv. is in later state than those—showing additional cracks from foot to rim and through several stars. Specialists have prized it ever since Beistle published it {1929} as his number 5-D.

Anticipating difficulties in obtaining enough bullion to keep the branch mint in operation, Memminger ordered its closure as of April 30, 1861; Dr. Bonzano remained there to guard it against burglars and vandals. Uncoined gold and silver bullion was placed aboard the rebel transport *Star of the West.* Bonzano stayed there until Union forces captured New Orleans, but even his efforts could not prevent Union troops from vandalizing the premises. Operations were not to resume until 1879, and the next half dollars to bear the O mintmark were dated 1892.

Dates 1861–65 from the San Francisco branch (and to a lesser extent 1863–65 from Philadelphia) were formerly believed scarce or rare. However, about 1956 unidentified individuals discovered an immense hoard in Guatemala, reflecting mass wartime shipments of coins as bullion. The Guatemala hoard coins are readily recognizable: They are dated between 1859 and 1865 Philadelphia, and between 1860 and 1865 S, most often 1861–62 from either mint, ranging from VF to nearly mint state, all cleaned with baking soda or some other abrasive. There were many hundreds of each date, possibly a couple of thousand of 1861–62. As there were no later date coins in the part of the hoard I saw (at New Netherlands Coin Co., 1956), most likely the hoard was buried about 1865 or early 1866. Either there were no 1866 S No Motto coins, or they were fished out beforehand; but I have seen none matching the hoard coins.

This means that 1866 S No Motto remains a rarity in all grades, especially choice. The variety's existence depends on a quirk of timing. Pursuant to the Act of March 3, 1865, all silver and gold coins minted after Jan. 1, 1866, large enough to bear the motto IN GOD WE TRUST, had to carry it. Obvs. dated 1866 reached the San Francisco branch before the end of 1865; but new revs. with motto were not to follow until May 1866. In the meantime, San Francisco authorities made 60,000 halves using leftover revs. without motto. Of these at most a few hundred survive in all grades, but possibly four or five in mint state.

On the other hand, the unique proof 1866 No Motto is a *pièce de caprice,* an afterthought, probably made for Robert Coulton Davis, the Mint's friendly neighborhood druggist: for its history and pedigree see Chap. 27, Sect. ix, introductory text. It was formerly considered a transitional pattern, but available evidence is overwhelmingly against this notion. The true transitionals would be the coins with motto dated 1865—if we could be sure that any were made then rather than a few years later.

ARROWS OMITTED

Designer, Engraver, Mints, Physical Specifications, Authorizing Acts, as before.

Grade range and standards, as before.

4866   1856 [938,000 + ?P]
Upright 5 only; date logotype as in cent **1918.** In all, 20 pairs of dies, probably not all used. Possibly 20–25 proofs survive, e.g., Robison:1654, $2,700.

4867   1856 O [all kinds 2,658,000] Normal date.
In all, 24 obvs., 8 revs. plus others left over from 1854–55. Minor positional vars., some with faintly repunched 6 (Beistle 4-D, 4-F).

4868   1856 O Obviously repunched 56.
Beistle 3-C. Note extra knob to 6.

4869   1856 O Double date.
Beistle 1-A. Date first entered slanting up to r., then corrected level.

4870   1856 S [all kinds 211,000] Large S only. Normal.
Beistle 2-B and unlisted. Large S, .065″ = 1.65 mm. In all, 12 pairs of dies shipped, possibly only 3 used. Usually in low grades. Auction 80:175, UNC., $5,250.

4871   1856 S "No drapery." Very rare.
Beistle 1-A; 1974 GENA:1583. Explanation as in **4778.** Usually in low grades.

4872   1857 [all kinds 1,988,000 + ?P] Normal date.
Date from logotype of Large Date cent **1920.** 18 touching or free, latter from repolished dies. Minor positional vars. Possibly 20–25 proofs survive, e.g., Auction 82:1690, $2,300.

4873   1857 Blundered date. Ex. rare.
Bases of extra date visible in rocky base far to r. of normal; base of 5 plainest, above space between 57. Discovered by Bill Fivaz.

4874 1857 O [all kinds 818,000] Normal date.
Positional vars.; date higher or lower in field. Same comments as to **4872** except no proofs.

4875 1857 O Double date. Rare.

4876 1857 S [all kinds 158,000] Large S. Rare.
Beistle 2-B. S from same punch as in 1855–56. Four obv. dies shipped; revs. were left over from the Nov. 1855 shipment. Usually in low grades.

4877 1857 S Medium S. Very scarce.
Beistle 1-A and unlisted. The latter, at least in earliest states, shows fragmentary serifs of 1 well to l. of date; discovered by Randall E. Wiley. S .055″ = 1.4 mm, as on the $3 and later halves. From dies shipped 12/4/1856, received 1/5/1857, quantity unknown. Wolfson:1170, NN, Glassenberg, 1975 ANA:606, UNC., $2,500.

4878 1858 [all kinds 4,226,000 + ?P] "Type I" rev.; normal.
See introductory text; tops of LF nearly touch, long closed claws, large arrowheads. Minor positional vars. Possibly about 80 proofs made, many showing lint marks; see ill. and discussion in Breen {1977}, p. 110.

4879 1858 "Type I" rev.; "no drapery."
Beistle 4-C; Merkin 3/68:613, 9/70:449. Thin numerals. Explanation as in **4778**.

4880 1858 "Type I" rev.; double date. Very rare.
NN 57:938. Date first punched slanting up to r., then corrected higher and level.

4881 1858 "Type II" rev. Very rare.
Beistle 4-C, 6-F? Discovered by Randall Wiley, April 1978; cf. 1978 MWNA:636. Tops of LF far apart; shorter open claws, smaller arrowheads. See introductory text. Enl. photo (of **4929**).

4882 1858 O [all kinds 7,294,000] "Type I" rev. only. Normal date.
Minor positional vars. Compare next 3. One die shows top of extra 1 at border below r. foot of 1 in date; discovered by Randall E. Wiley.

4883 1858 O "No drapery."
Beistle 1-A. Explanation as in **4778**.

4884 1858 O First Blundered Die. Very rare.
Bases of extra 18 show at edge of rocky base vertically above 18; part of another 8 (?) between 58. Discovered at 1979 ANA Convention. Cf. *Gobrecht Journal* 9, p. 31 (1977): apparently the same die. Compare next.

4885 1858 O Second Blundered Die. Very rare.
Lower fifth of final 8 in rocky base just below skirt. Discovered by William B. Bugert; ill. *Gobrecht Journal* 28, p. 21 (11/83).

4886 1858 S [all kinds 476,000] "Type I" rev. only. Large S.
Beistle 2-B. S as in 1855–56, from 4 leftover revs. 8 obvs. shipped Oct. 20, 1857; 4 more in March 1858. Usually in low grades.

4887 1858 S Medium S. Rare.
S .055″ = 1.4 mm, as in **4877**. Two positional vars., from 2 revs. shipped March 1858. ANS {1914}, Newcomb display. One has traces of extra 8 in rock above final 8. The "small s" reported in Taxay-Scott (F207, from Beistle 1-A) remains unverified; if it exists, it is a product of 1862 or later years. Most likely it is an error for the present number.

4888 1859 [all kinds 748,000 + 800 – P] "Type I" rev.
Hub of 1842–57, as in **4878**; see introductory text. Proofs and business strikes; many proofs were melted as unsold. In all, 9 obvs., 10 revs.

4889 1859 "Type II" rev.
Hub of 1860–65, as in **4881**; see introductory text. Proofs and business strikes. Same comments as to last.

4890 1859 O [all kinds 2,834,000] "Type I" rev. only. Normal date.
In all, 17 obvs.; revs. of previous years.

4891 1859 O Blundered date. 2 vars. Very rare.
Part of upper loop of extra 9 runs into border below tail of 9. Discovered by James Fairfield, 1980. *Gobrecht Journal* 19, p. 19 (11/80); 1981 ANA: 659, UNC., $500. The other var. has part of extra 9 down from rocky base.

4892 1859 S [all kinds 566,000] "Type I" rev. only. Large S.
Beistle 1-A, 2-C. S as in 1855–56. In all, 12 obvs. (6 apiece in Nov. 1858 and May 1859, not distinguishable); leftover revs. from 1854–56. Scrubbed EF's are from the Guatemala hoard: See introductory text.

4893 1859 S Same. "No drapery." Very rare.
Reported by Douglas Winter. Explanation as in **4778**.

4894 1859 S Medium S. Rare.
Beistle 2-B. S .055″ = 1.4 mm, as in 1857–58. From one of the 2 revs. shipped March 1858. Merkin 3/68:618; "Gilhousen":1027.

4895 1860 "Type I" rev. Ex. rare.
Beistle 1b-C. Rev. as in **4878**. Mintage doubtless included in next.

4896 1860 "Type II" rev. [All kinds 302,700 + 525+P]
Rev. as **4881;** see introductory text. Originally 1,000 proofs made, the rest melted. Minor positional vars. of business strikes. Scrubbed EF's are common from the Guatemala hoard: See introductory text.

4897 1860 O [all kinds 1,290,000] "Type I" rev. Very rare.
NN 57:943. Rev. hub as **4878,** evidently left over from 1856–58.

4898 1860 O "Type II" rev. Normal drapery.
Minor positional vars.

4899 1860 O Same. "No drapery." Rare.
Merkin 9/70:454. From drastically relapped obv. die.

4900 1860 S [all kinds 472,000] "Type I" rev. only. Large S.
Beistle 1-A. S .065″ = 1.65 mm, as 1855–56; from leftover 1856 revs. Upper-grade cleaned specimens are mostly from the Guatemala hoard: See introductory text.

4901 1860 S Medium S.
Beistle 2-B. S .055 ± .001″ = 1.4 mm, as in 1857–58; from leftover dies of March 1858. In "Charmont":3503 this is said to have "Type II" rev.; if so, any such piece would be a product of 1862 or later years.

4902 1861 "Type II" rev. [2,887,000 + 400−P]
Minor positional vars.; 55 obvs., 54 revs. Of 1,000 proofs struck, fewer than 400 were sold, the rest melted. High-grade cleaned pieces are mostly from the Guatemala hoard (see introductory text). A hoard of 20 UNCs. (not scrubbed) turned up in 1975.

4903 1861 O [all kinds 2,532,633] "Type I" rev. Very rare.
"Type I" coins were probably included in Union coinages [330,000]; revs. left over from 1858 or earlier. See introductory text.

4904 1861 O "Type II" rev. Normal.
Several positional vars., from 12 obvs. shipped; revs. left over from 1860. But compare next 2. Four to 6 proofs reported; see introductory text and Breen {1977}, p. 235.

4905 1861 O "Type II" rev. "No drapery." Rare.
Beistle 1-A. Drastically repolished obv. die.

4906 1861 O "Cracked Confederate Obv." "Type II" rev. Rare.
Beistle 5-D. Crack, rim to bridge of nose close to seventh star; obv. earlier used (April 1861) to make the 4 Confederate proofs (**8000**): See introductory text and Chap. 47. Usually F to EF. 1978 ANA:1039, AU, $425.

4907 1861 S [all kinds 939,500] "Type I" rev. Large S.
Beistle 1-A and several unlisteds. S .065″ = 1.65 mm, from dies left over from 1856; reportedly one shows traces of repunching on S. Plentiful in scrubbed EF from the Guatemala hoard: See introductory text.

4908 1861 S "Type I" rev. Medium S. Scarce.
S .055″ = 1.4 mm, from 2 dies left over from March 1858. Same comment as to last about the Guatemala hoard. In all, 6 obv. dies shipped.

4909 1862 "Type II" rev. [253,000 + 550−P]
In all, 8 obvs., 6 revs. Date varies in position. Many proofs melted in 1863 as unsold. Same comment as to **4907** about the Guatemala hoard.

4910 1862 S [all kinds 1,352,000] "Type I" rev.; large S.
S as in **4907,** from dies left over from 1854–56 (at least 3); 10 obvs. Same comment as to last 3 about the Guatemala hoard.

4911 1862 S "Type I" rev.; medium S.
Beistle 1-B. S as in **4908,** from at least 2 dies left over from March 1858. Same comment as to last 4 about the Guatemala hoard.

4912 1862 S "Type II" rev.; small broad s. Very rare.
Beistle 2-C and unlisted; from 2 revs. shipped April 1862. S .042 ± .001″ = 1.1 mm, its top defective.

4913 1863 [all kinds 503,200 + 460P] "Type II" rev. Closed 6.

Knob of 6 touches loop. Business strikes and proofs (latter Beistle 1-A and unlisted). Fewer of this date were in the Guatemala hoard.

4914 1863 Same, open 6.
Knob of 6 away from loop. Business strikes and proofs.

4915 1863 S "Type II" rev. [916,000]
In all, 12 obvs., 5 revs. shipped, 3 revs. used. All seen to date have closed 6, and small broad s, 2 broken at top like **4912,** the 3rd from the same punch unbroken. The report of one with small narrow unbroken s as in 1864 remains unverified. Cleaned specimens are plentiful from the Guatemala hoard; see introductory text.

4916 1864 "Type II" rev.; 64 almost touch. [Incl. in 470P of next] Proofs only.
Beistle 1-A. Heavy numerals.

4917 1864 "Type II" rev.; 6 4 apart. [379,100 + 470P]
Beistle 2-A (rare proofs); business strikes, not in Beistle. Robison:1678, UNC., $4,400. Cleaned specimens are plentiful from the Guatemala hoard; see introductory text.

4918 1864 S [all kinds 658,000] "Type I" rev., large S.
Beistle 1-A; "Gilhousen":1040. S .061″ = 1.61 mm (same punch as 1855–62, lightly impressed); 6 4 apart. Small spike atop serif of D(OL). Cf. J. R. McCloskey, *Gobrecht Journal* 14, pp. 23–25 (3/79).

4919 1864 S "Type II" rev., small broad s.
Beistle 2-B, 6 4 apart. Mintmark broken at top on one die, unbroken on another. Robison:1680, $525. May exist with 64 about touching. Many cleaned EF's from Guatemala hoard.

4920 1864 S "Type II" rev., small narrow s; 6 4 apart. Very rare.
Discovery coin, NN 47:1321. Mintmark .039 ± .001″ = .99 mm. Robison:1679, others.

4921 1864 S As preceding, 64 about touch. Very rare.
Beistle 3-C. In all, 11 obvs., 5 revs. shipped.

4922 1865 [all kinds 511,400 + 500P] "Type II" rev. henceforth. Normal date.
Minor positional vars. Scrubbed coins exist in quantity from the Guatemala hoard; choice UNCs. are mostly from a hoard of 15 found in late 1979: cf. 1981 ANA:2280, $12,750. Compare next 3.

4923 1865 Same, "no drapery." Rare.
Beistle 3-A. One minute fragment of drapery below elbow (drastically relapped die). Business strikes only; "Gilhousen":1041; 1975 ANA:636; 1982 ANA:609.

4924 1865 Double date. Rare.
Beistle 5-Aa. On "Charmont":3507, repunching is plainest at 1 5, from date logotype being first entered slanting up to r., then corrected. Another var. ill. *Gobrecht Journal* 20 (3/81).

4925 1865 Overdate. Very rare.
Merkin 4/66:345. In date, 5 punched over an unidentifiable digit. The coin reported with 1865 over inverted date (logotype rotated 180°) remains unverified.

4926 1865 S [all kinds 675,000] Small broad s.
NN 57:963; Robison:1683; others. Only one rev. Mintmark broken at top, like **4912, 4919.** Cleaned EF–AU's are common from the Guatemala hoard, but far less so than next.

4927 1865 S Small narrow s.
NN 49:1249; NN 57:962; Robison:1682; others. Mintmark as in **4920.** All seen to date show traces of repunching on 1. In all, 12 obvs.; leftover revs., at least 6 used. Common in cleaned EF–AU from the Guatemala hoard.

4928 1866 No motto. Proof only. Unique?
Judd 538. *Pièce de caprice;* see introductory text. Hydeman sale, $15,500. *Gobrecht Journal* 25, p. 13 (11/82), ill. a forgery made by removal of S and motto from a specimen of **4935.**

4929   1866 S No motto. [60,000]

Beistle 1-A. Rev. is one die of **4927;** see introductory text. Parmelee, Brand, NN 36:239, Wayte Raymond, NN 49:1250, Glassenberg, 1975 ANA:638, UNC., $2,750. Mintage interrupted pending arrival of new revs. with motto.

xi. MOTTO ADDED (1866–73)

While banks continued to suspend specie payments in and after the Civil War, little silver came to the Philadelphia Mint, and issues of half dollars remained limited. Silver was hoarded, especially during the war years while greenbacks passed at discount; the small quantities of coined silver mostly went overseas. Half dollars 1866–91 in collectors' hands today consist largely of proofs (made at the rate of a few hundred per year, to be saved, and mostly cleaned), UNC. Philadelphia coins (many retrieved from proof sets: The Mint took little notice of the difference), and random survivors from the San Francisco and Carson City mints, mostly well short of UNC.; nothing in this period is really common. The few years of fairly large mintages reflect mostly recoinage of obsolete and worn-out silver pieces, largely issued to retire fractional currency.

The Act of March 3, 1865, which is familiar to different groups of collectors for authorizing nickel 3¢ pieces and for authorizing more compound interest notes (many used as soldiers' pay), also mandated addition of the motto IN GOD WE TRUST to all silver coins above the dime, and all gold coins above the $3 piece. At least seven short silver proof sets (quarter, half, and dollar) and two short gold proof sets (half eagle, eagle, double eagle) were issued dated 1865, in the exact designs adopted in 1866, together with a larger number of copper and aluminum proofs from the same dies (for collectors, not VIPs). For generations the silver and gold coins were accepted as true transitional issues (and traded at very high prices); but in recent years their status has been flung into doubt because of discovery of a single silver dollar dated 1865 with motto, overstruck on another dollar dated 1866, with both dates plain enough to show in an auction catalog's halftone illustration ("Fairfield":32.)! Cf. Chap. 27, Sect. x, introductory text. This event forced reexamination of other denominations from these sets. Though the half dollar's rev. die has not yet been identified, the dollar's rev. is that of the two later regular proof vars. of 1866 and the two earlier of 1867, suggesting that the whole group was made up at that time—for Mint Director Linderman and Robert Coulton Davis. The similar coins dated 1863–64 with motto are almost certainly afterthoughts and may date to the same period or to as late as 1868. Certainty on this point awaits opportunity to identify their rev. dies. Whatever their actual time and occasion of manufacture, these coins will remain prized as great rarities.

Many different dates and mintmarks in this period show "partial drapery" or "no drapery" at elbow; this feature, as in previous years since 1845, results always from too-vigorous relapping or regrinding of obv. dies, usually to remove clash

marks. "No drapery" dates include, among others, 1866–68, 1870; 1868-70 S; 1870 CC: One could assemble a set of 1870 "no drapery" coins from all three mints. "Partial drapery" occurs on almost all S mints through 1877, but such coins are not counted as separate vars.

Early issues of 1873 show the 3 almost closed—knobs nearly touch. A complaint from the Chief Coiner in Jan. 1873 correctly indicated that on small denominations a closed 3 could be mistaken for an 8; the Mint Director ordered William Barber's Engraving Department to prepare new date logotypes for all denominations (except the half dime and trime, or silver 3¢) with open 3.

The new Mint Act of 1873 (see next section) mandated addition of a "distinguishing mark" (arrows at date) to identify coins at the new metric weights; obsolete coins were to be melted, which explains the disappearance of 1873 S No Arrows [5,000] and the extreme rarity of 1873 CC No Arrows [122,500]. This may also be part of the reason why S mints before 1873 are all very rare choice. Early CC mints are rare because official orders limited quantities to be issued: See Chap. 25, Sect. x, introductory text.

MOTTO ADDED

Designer, Longacre, after Gobrecht, after Sully and Reich (motto scroll is Longacre's own). Engravers, Longacre 1866–68; William Barber 1869–73. Mints, Philadelphia (no mintmark), San Francisco (S below eagle), Carson City (CC below eagle). Physical Specifications, as before. Authorizing Acts, as before plus March 3, 1865 (requiring motto).

Grade range and standards, as before.

4930   1863 "Prototype" (Restrike). [5+P?] Proofs only.

Judd 342. Open 6, knob away from loop. Possibly struck 1866–68. See introductory text.

4931   1864 "Prototype" (Restrike). [5+P?] Proofs only.

Judd 391. 6 4 apart. 1977 ANA:2178. Same comments as to preceding.

4932   1865 "Prototype" (Restrike?). [7+P?] Proofs only.

Judd 429. 1977 ANA:2180, $5,000. Same comments as to last 2.

4933   1866 [744,900 + 725P] Normal.

Proofs come without or with traces of repunching on final 6. Business strikes have higher or lower dates (at least 2 obvs. of each). See next.

4934 1866 "No drapery." Rare.
From drastically relapped die. 1982 ANA:2328, UNC., $4,200.

4935 1866 S [994,000]
Minute s, .036″ = 0.91 mm, often weak; this mintmark punch continues to 1871. Several positional vars. 6 obvs. were on hand (one was used for **4929**); 6 pairs of dies shipped in May 1866, making 12 obvs., 6 motto revs. for the year. See introductory text to previous section. Very rare choice: Auction 80:756, UNC., $3,600.

4936 1867 [449,300 + 625P] Normal.
Proofs and business strikes. Compare next.

4937 1867 "No drapery."
From drastically relapped obvs. Proofs and business strikes.

4938 1867 S [all kinds 1,196,000] Minute s.
Mintmark as **4935**; several positional vars., usually upright, approximately parallel to upright of F or D in HALF DOL. Compare next.

4939 1867 S Mintmark leans crazily to r.
"Gilhousen":1048. S almost parallel to vertical of H in HALF!

4940 1867 S "Larger S."
NN 57:966. Mintmark from same punch but heavily repunched. Compare Hetherington:273–74.

4941 1868 [all kinds 417,600 + 600P] Normal.
Date higher or lower in exergue. Compare next 2.

4942 1868 Repunched date.
Beistle 1-A. Repunching plainest on 18. A later state may be Bortin:962, with repunched 1.

4943 1868 "No drapery." Rare.
"Gilhousen":1049, others. Business strikes. Explanation as in **4937**.

4944 1868 S Normal. [1,160,000]
Several positional vars.

4945 1868 S "No drapery." Very rare.
Explanation as in **4937**. Ivy Cambridge:1053.

4946 1869 [795,300 + 600P]
At least 4 vars. of proofs, one with GOD on scroll often weak or even illegible (weak striking): Beistle 1-A. Some business strikes show base of 1 repunched.

4947 1869 S [All kinds 656,000]
8 obvs.; at least 3 old revs. Hetherington:276 claimed smaller and larger S's, as in **4940**; apparently the usual S, punched lightly or heavily. Compare next.

4948 1869 S "No drapery." Rare.
Beistle 2-B; "Gilhousen":1052; Auction 82:1691, UNC., $3,500. Explanation as in **4937**.

4949 1870 [all kinds 633,900 + 1,000P] Normal.
Positional vars. of both business strikes and proofs; compare next 2.

4950 1870 Repunched 1.
Beistle 3-Aa.

4951 1870 "No drapery." Rare.
Glassenberg, 1975 ANA:653; Auction 80:1307, UNC., $2,100. Explanation as in **4937**.

4952 1870 S [all kinds 1,004,000] Normal.
Positional vars., some with weak thin S (NN 54:1052). 6 pairs of dies shipped Dec. 1869.

4953 1870 S "No drapery."
Beistle 3-Ba; "Gilhousen":1055; Auction 80:758, UNC., $3,000. Explanation as in **4937**.

4954 1870 CC [all kinds 54,617] Normal. Rare.
CC .042″ = 1.1 mm. Mintage began with [2,000], April 9. 5 minor positional vars. from 3 pairs of dies; r. C lower or higher than l. Usually in low grades. UNCs.: 1) Cass, "Empire," Gardner, Groves:441, $13,000. 2) "Dupont," Hawn, $13,500, Halsell:725, $18,700, James Pryor. 3) Robi-

son:1694, $21,000 (r. C lower). Compare next. Beware Philadelphia coins with CC falsely added.

4955 1870 CC "No drapery." Very rare.
Beistle 1-A; "Gilhousen":1054. Carson:81, UNC. Usually in low grades.

4956 1871 [all kinds 1,203,600 + 960P] 71 about touch.
Earlier date logotype, found also on S and CC coins; positional vars. of business strikes, at least 2 vars. of proofs. Compare next.

4957 1871 7 1 well apart. Rare.
1976 EAC:1073, others. Business strikes; proofs (2 vars.) are very rare. Later date logotype, shorter serifs to 1's.

4958 1871 S [all kinds 2,178,000] 71 about touch; minute narrow s.
Mintmark as in 1866–70, .036″ = 0.91 mm.: See **4935**, compare next 4. 8 obvs. received Dec. 16, 1870, probably others in 1871; records are incomplete.

4959 1871 S Same, "no drapery." Rare.
S sometimes very weak, its upper half missing (obliquely punched). Explanation as in **4937**. Ill. *Gobrecht Journal* 11/83, by Bill Bugert.

4960 1871 S 71 about touch; small broad s.
S .042″ = 1.1 mm., as in some vars. through 1876. "Gilhousen":1058.

4961 1871 S 7 1 apart; minute narrow s. Rare.
Date logotype as in **4957**; mintmark as in **4958**. Compare next.

4962 1871 S 7 1 apart; small broad s. Rare.
Date logotype as in **4957**; mintmark as in **4960**. NN 54:1053, Glassenberg, 1975 ANA:658, Auction 82:1192, UNC., $800; 1976 ANA:1269; others.

4963 1871 CC 71 about touch. [153,950]
Usually in low grades. At least 3 rev. dies. Mintmark as on **4954**. The only 2 choice ones have proof obvs.: 1) Bauman, Groves:442, $3,750 (1974). 2) Ex Reed Hawn, $4,000 (1973). One of these (?) reappeared in Auction 85:1725, $8,250.

4964 1872 [all kinds 880,600 + 950−P] Normal.
Several positional vars.; compare next. On heavy strikings, bases of 18 almost touch; on lighter strikings and coins from lapped dies, bases are distinctly apart. Some unsold proofs were melted after July 10, 1873; some business strikes may also have perished in the same mass melting.

4965 1872 Doubled rev. die. Rare.
Merkin 6/68:337. Quadruple stripes in shield.

4966 1872 S [all kinds 580,000] Small broad s. Rare.
Beistle 2-B; mintmark as in **4960**. Positional vars. exist, from 10 pairs of dies shipped Nov. 1871.

4967 1872 S Tall narrow S.
Beistle 1-A. S .046″ = 1.17 mm. Hetherington:279, others. 2 vars. This S punch recurs in 1874–75.

4968 1872 CC [257,000−] Rare.
At least 4 pairs of dies shipped; minor positional vars. Mintmark as on **4954**. At least one reportedly shows repunching on 2: not verified. Many melted after April 1873.

4969 1873 No arrows. Closed 3. [587,200+ + 600−P]
Knobs nearly touch; same comments about 18 in date as to
4964. See introductory text. Positional vars. exist: Beistle
2-A, 2a-A, 3-A. Compare next 2.

4970 1873 Same, heavily repunched 3. 2 vars. Very rare.
Merkin 6/70:288. One obv. has 7 also repunched, less
plainly.
4971 1873 No arrows. Open 3. [214,000−] Very rare.
Beistle 4-A. Two positional vars. Knobs small and distant, as
on coins with arrows. Mintage doubtless included many
Closed 3 coins; many were melted after July 10, 1873. Usually in low grades. The Col. Green proof (Beistle 1-A), possibly later WGC:331, remains untraced.

4972 1873 S No arrows. Closed 3. [5,000−] Untraced.
Beistle 1-A: "No arrowheads are on either side of the date.
Rev. A. Perfect. Rare." In all, 10 obvs., 4 revs. shipped Nov.
1872. A worn survivor has been rumored more than once,
but to date no specimen has been authenticated. Doubtless
most, possibly all, were melted after April 1873.
4973 1873 CC No arrows. Closed 3. [122,500−] Very rare.
Smallest roundish cc, .029″ = 0.74 mm, unlike previous
dates. Many melted after April 1873. Usually in low grades.
Garrett (1976):354, $30,000, Auction 82:1693, UNC., $8,500.

xii. ARROWS AND MOTTO (1873–74)

The omnibus Mint Act of Feb. 12, 1873 (alias "Crime of '73"
—particularly among owners of silver mines and their mis-
guided partisans) affected the half-dollar series in three

ways: 1) minute adjustment in weight; 2) arrows at
dates; 3) melting of obsolete issues. None of these actions
made sense. The second gave type collectors something to compete for a century later; the third unintentionally created rarities (compare **4968–73),** while the country was still hurting for
small change as an alternative to tattered fractional currency.

Beginning in April 1873, each half dollar was to have an
exact metric weight of 12.5 gms.: 0.9 grs. = 0.06 gms. heavier
than formerly. This was nothing but a paper complication, requiring at most a microscopic adjustment in thickness of rolled
strip from which blanks were to be cut for stamping into coins.
In practice, the officially permitted remedy (tolerance of weight
deviation per coin), ± 3 grs. = ± 0.2 gms., meant that old
blanks could be used, and doubtless were, without even a tut-tut
from the Assay Commission the following February. This law
had no effect on public resistance to the metric system; 92 years
later, when standard silver coinage ended, public awareness of
the metric system remained minimal. Even today, the mints
continue to make coins to specifications named in inches and
decimalized grains. Use of coins as weights was stupidly urged
as reason to adopt metric standards; in practice, coins' weights
varied enough to make any such attempt useless.

For unknown reasons, the new silver coins (except for the
trade dollar) were to bear a distinguishing mark. Evidently remembering his predecessor's choice, Mint Director Linderman
decided that this must consist of arrows at dates. Halves of 1873
from all mints have long arrowheads, 2.9 mm from tip to end of
shaft; a few late Philadelphia dies have short arrowheads, 2.3
mm, as do all 1874 proof obvs. On the 1873's, arrowheads are
level; on 1874's, they slant. All of the 1873 issues with arrows
have the Open 3 logotype.

Though the older coins were supposed to remain current,
authorities ordered mass meltings: at the branch mints, after
April 1873; at Philadelphia, on and after July 10. These meltings affected unsold proofs and undistributed business strikes in
all silver denominations, 1872 and 1873 No Arrows issues most
of all; they also accounted for disappearance of nearly the entire
mintage of trimes, 1863–72 (Boosel {1960}, p. 19).

Type collectors have long prized the 1873–74 coins with arrows; dealers have even irrationally touted them as rare, though
the only half dollars in this group deserving that label are 1873
Short Arrows (both triple and quadruple stripes), 1874 Long
Arrows proof, 1874 Short Arrows nonproof, and both dates of
CC coins. Philadelphia mintages were fairly large because they
were made from bullion obtained by melting down obsolete or
worn-out coins; San Francisco issues were of moderate size;
whereas the Carson City emissions were deliberately limited by
official orders for political reasons, which limited output was
thereafter adduced as justifying a campaign to abolish that
branch!

Some 500 four-piece proof sets with arrows (dimes, quarters,
halves, plus the trade dollar which never bore arrows at date)
were made in 1873, with 40 extra halves; some were added to
existing proof sets without arrows, but most went to date collectors who broke up the sets to add the halves to their date runs
of that denomination (and similarly with the dimes and quarters). Proof sets offered in recent years have mostly been reassembled piece by piece. The same comment holds for 1874.

Mint Director Linderman ordered that from Jan. 1, 1875, the
coins should no longer bear arrows at dates: an end as arbitrary
as its beginning.

ARROWS AND MOTTO

Designer, Engraver, Mints, Physical Specifications, as before,
except Weight 192.9 ± 1.5 grs. = 12.5 ± 0.09 gms. Authorizing Act, Feb. 12, 1873.

Grade range and standards, as before.

4974 1873 [all kinds 1,795,000 + 550P] Long obv. arrows. Arrows 0.115″ = 2.9 mm (see introductory text). Minute positional vars. of date; several with traces of repunching on individual digits. Ivy Cambridge:1056 shows faint traces of an extra 1 at left, evidently from date first punched too high and left, then almost entirely effaced before repunching in correct position. Compare next 2.

4975 1873 Short obv. arrows, quadruple obv. stripes. Rare. Arrows 0.091″ = 2.3 mm, as in 1874 but level. Doubled obv. die, plainest at shield, hand, and parts of drapery, producing 4 (rather than the normal 3) lines per pale gules. Usually in low grades. Discovered by Harry X Boosel, about 1958.

4976 1873 Short obv. arrows, triple obv. stripes. Very rare. Beistle 10-Ad? *Numisma* 27:899 (11/60). Arrows as preceding, normal (undoubled) obv. 3 vars. Probably included in final delivery of the year. Apt to be mistaken for **4974.** Its existence was long controversial.

4977 1873 S [all kinds 228,000] Long obv. arrows. Small broad s. Ex. rare.
Arrows as on **4974;** mintmark as on **4960.** Compare next.

4978 1873 S Long obv. arrows; minute s. Mintmark .033 ± .001″ = 0.84 mm, as on some later dates. Robison:1706, UNC., $1,200. Minute positional vars., one showing traces of repunching on mintmark: 1982 ANA:2331.

4979 1873 CC [all kinds 214,560] Long obv. arrows. Smallest roundish cc. Rare.
C's .029″ = 0.74 mm. as on **4973.** "Gilhousen":1065. Usually in low grades.

4980 1873 CC Long obv. arrows. Tall boldface CC. Rare. C's .042″ = 1.1 mm. Beistle 2-B, 3-B. Usually in low grades; rarer than preceding, especially in high grades. Carson:85, UNC.

4981 1874 [all kinds 2,359,600 + 750P] Long obv. arrows. Arrows 0.115″ = 2.9 mm as on **4974,** but slanting. Minute positional vars. The only proof reported: Glassenberg, 1975 ANA:671.

4982 1874 Short arrows.
Arrows 0.091″ = 2.3 mm as on **4975,** but slanting. Beistle 1-A. Most of the proofs have been cleaned. Fewer than 6 business strikes reported, none UNC. Discovered by Charlton Meyer, Jr. Mintage included in **4982.**

4983 1874 S [all kinds 394,000] Long obv. arrows only. Tall narrow S. Very rare.
Arrows as on **4981.** Mintmark .046″ = 1.17 mm. "Gilhousen":1069. Mintmark not repunched: Compare next. Barely possibly some 1874 S var. may exist with short arrows.

4984 1874 S Same, obviously double-punched S. Rare.
NN 54:1059, Glassenberg, 1975 ANA:673, Auction 82:1194, UNC., $1,800; others. Less rare than preceding.

4985 1874 S Small broad s.
Mintmark as on **4977.** Minute positional vars. Compare next 2.

4986 1874 S Small broad s, double-punched. Very rare.
Mintmark as preceding.

4987 1874 S Minute s. Very rare.
Mintmark as on **4978.**

4988 1874 CC [all kinds 59,000] Long obv. arrows. Rare. Mintmark as on **4979.** Die chip above base of T (Y). Rev., short parallel lines down through TE(S) and atop final S; these fade. Usually in low grades. MHS II:625, UNC., $2,000 (1973). Long rumored to exist also with tall boldface CC, as on **4980.**

xiii. ARROWS OMITTED (1875–91)

Large mintages, 1875–77, served the purpose of retiring 50¢ fractional currency notes (1862–76, alias "shinplasters"). These notes were an inadequate substitute for small change ever since the banks' suspension of specie payments (Dec. 28, 1861); they were extensively counterfeited, and the genuine ones were filthy rags and tatters—so much so that in later decades the Treasury generally refused to redeem them because officials could not be sure if they were genuine or counterfeit! Public protests accumulated after the war, but not enough silver became available until the Comstock Lode discoveries—after which there was so much that the price began to fall (see Chap. 29, Sect. ix, introductory text). Philadelphia issues of 1875–77, however, largely came not from Comstock Lode bullion, but from melted obsolete coins which had accumulated at the New York Subtreasury. The Bureau of the Mint hoped that between these issues and the San Francisco and Carson City mintages from Comstock Lode silver, the nation would have adequate small change for the first time in 20 years.

Alas for bright hopes, the silver lobby (representing a group of tax-free multimillionaire mine owners), motivated by that Five Finger Word (greed, see Glossary), pushed the Bland-Allison Act into law over a presidential veto, Feb. 28, 1878, so that from then on all the mints were required to buy huge quantities of domestic silver bullion—at a price so high as to represent frank subsidy—for coinage only into silver dollars (the new Morgan dollars). Why silver dollars rather than small change? Because each silver dollar was heavier than two halves, four quarters, or 10 dimes. Quantities mandated were so immense that to fulfill the new law all the mints had to suspend or abolish coinage of smaller denominations. This accounts for the small issues of 1878 S and 1878 CC half dollars, and for the tiny mintages and consequent scarcity of Philadelphia half dollars 1879–91 (the majority of survivors being proofs). Uncirculated specimens (which are rarer than the proofs) are generally prooflike, and many have been retrieved from original proof sets: The Mint then (unlike today's collectors) remained careless about the distinction between prooflike business strikes and true proofs, despite charging a small premium for the latter.

A new rev. hub went into use in 1876; Augustus G. Heaton {1893} first described it in print, but it remained forgotten until the 1950s. The old or "Type I" hub (1866–77) has a split berry just above H; the new or "Type II" hub (1876–91), by William Barber, has this berry pointed, with other very minor changes. Proofs occur as late as 1881 using a leftover "Type I" die of 1876: See Breen {1977}, pp. 155, 158, 163, 166, 168; they are rare. No obv. changes are identified to date which would indicate a new hub rather than mechanical reproductions of working hubs.

ARROWS OMITTED

Designer, obv. and "Type I" rev., Longacre, after Gobrecht, after Sully and Reich; "Type II" rev., William Barber, after Longacre. Mints, Physical Specifications, Authorizing Acts, as before.

Grade range and standards, as before.

4989 1875 [All kinds 6,026,800 + 650P]
Many minor positional vars. See next.
4990 1875 Double date. Rare.
Beistle 2a-Aa.
4991 1875 S [all kinds 3,200,000] Small broad s. Very rare.
Mintmark .042″ = 1.1 mm, as on **4960, 4985.**

4992 1875 S Tall narrow S. Very rare.
Mintmark .046″ = 1.17 mm, as on **4967.** Hetherington:379; NN 49:1262; "Gilhousen":1072.
4993 1875 S Very small s.
Mintmark .036 ± .001″ = 0.91 mm, as on **4958.** At least 10 revs.; see next. Also reported with minute s, .033″ = 0.84 mm, as on **4978, 4987.** On weaker strikings these would be very difficult to tell apart. Also reported with "no drapery."
4994 1875 S Blundered obv. Very rare.
Base of mispunched 1 at base of rock. 1984 Midwinter ANA:1259.
4995 1875 CC [all kinds 1,008,000] Small roundish cc.
Mintmark .035″ ± 0.01″ = 0.89 mm. Beistle 1-A, 2-B. On Feb. 12, 1875, Coiner William Sty Doane requisitioned 7 pairs of half-dollar dies.
4996 1875 CC Tall boldface CC. Ex. rare (untraced?).
Mintmark .042″ = 1.1 mm. Newcomb display, ANS {1914}; Beistle 2-C.
4997 1876 [all kinds 8,418,000 + 1,520P] "Type I" rev.
Split berry above H as 1866–75; see introductory text. Business strikes and proofs. Minor positional vars. We have not verified Beistle's claim of open and closed 6's (knob distant from loop or close to it).
4998 1876 "Type II" rev.
Pointed berry above H as 1877–91; see introductory text. Business strikes only. In all, 78 obvs., 67 revs., plus leftover "Type I" revs. from 1875. Minor positional vars. Enl. photo.

4999 1876 S [all kinds 4,528,000] "Type I" rev.; very small s. Rare.
Mintmark .036″ = 0.91 mm, as in **4993.** "Gilhousen":1075; others. At least 4 positional vars. Compare next 3.
5000 1876 S "Type I" rev.; "micro" s.
Mintmark .029″ = 0.74 mm. At least 4 vars. Compare next 2.
5001 1876 S "Type II" rev. "Micro" s as last. Reported. Taxay-Scott F269.
5002 1876 S "Type II" rev. Very small s over "micro" s. Ex. rare.
Mintmark .036 ± .001″ = 0.91 mm. Randall Wiley coll.

5003 1876 CC [all kinds 1,956,000] "Type I" rev.; tall bold CC. Rare.
Mintmark .042″ = 1.1 mm. 2 revs. of **4963.** Newcomb display, ANS {1914}; Glassenberg, 1975 ANA:684; others.

5004 1876 CC "Type I" rev.; small CC.
Mintmark .035″ = 0.89 mm. At least 6 revs. Newcomb display, ANS {1914}; Glassenberg, 1975 ANA:685; others.

5005 1876 CC "Type I" rev.; smallest roundish cc. Scarce.
Mintmark .029″ = 0.74 mm. 5 revs. Newcomb display, ANS {1914}; NN 57:977.

5006 1876 CC "Type II" rev. Reported.

5007 1877 [all kinds 8,004,000 + 580P] "Type I" rev. Ex. rare.
Proof, Merkin 3/68:662 only; business strikes form under 0.1% of specimens examined of this date. See next.

5008 1877 "Type II" rev.
Minor positional vars.; 72 obvs., 62 revs. plus leftover "Type I" revs. from 1876. We have not seen the different date logotypes claimed by Beistle: 2-Aa, 87 close; 3-Ab, 8 7 apart. Drastically lapped dies could explain the difference.

5009 1877 S [all kinds 5,356,000] "Type I" rev.; normal very small s. Scarce.
Mintmark .036 ± .001″ = 0.91 mm. Glassenberg, 1975 ANA:688; others.

5010 1877 S "Type I" rev.; small s doubled ("1877 ss"). Very rare.
One of the most bizarre repositioned mintmarks known: Nearly full width of initial S shows l. of final position. On the coin ill., flat shelflike doubling on S occurred in striking; it may show differently or not at all on other specimens.

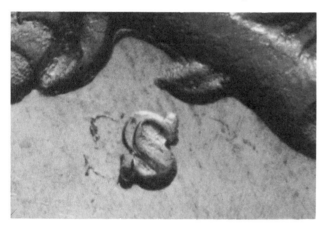

5011 1877 S "Type I" rev. Small repunched s, "no drapery." Very scarce.
1984 Midwinter ANA:1266; others. Explanation as in **4937.**

5012 1877 S "Type I" rev. "Micro" s. Scarce.
Mintmark .029″ = 0.74 mm. Minor positional vars. "Gilhousen":1078; others. See next.

5013 1877 S "Type I" rev. "Micro" s; "no drapery." Rare.
Drastically repolished obv. die.

5014 1877 S "Type II" rev. "Micro" s. Ex. rare.
Mintmark as **5012.** 1976 ANA:1280; others. See next.

5015 1877 S "Type II" rev. "Micro" s; "no drapery." Ex. rare.
"Gilhousen":1080. Explanation as in **5013.**

5016 1877 S "Type II" rev. Small narrow s.
Mintmark as **5009.** Merkin 6/68:344. Not to be confused with the small broad s of **4991.**

5017 1877 CC [all kinds 1,420,000] "Type I" rev. Smallest cc. Very rare.
Mintmark roundish, .029″ = 0.74 mm. 2 positional rev. vars. Newcomb display, ANS {1914}; Merkin 6/68:245.

5018 1877 CC "Type I" rev. Small bold cc. Very rare.
Mintmark .035″ = 0.89 mm. ANS {1914}, Society's display. "Charmont":3542 describes this as having bases of 7's repunched, widely spaced C C. But compare **5022.**

5019 1877 CC "Type II" rev. Smallest cc. Ex. rare.
Mintmark as **5017.** Newcomb display, ANS {1914}; NN 57:980; Fraser, Robison:1717, UNC., $2,000.

5020 1877 CC "Type II" rev. Small wide c c. Very scarce.
Mintmark as **5018,** about a C's width apart. Glassenberg, 1975 ANA:689.

5021 1877 CC "Type II" rev. Small close cc.
Several positional vars. Glassenberg, 1975 ANA:690; others.

5022 1877 CC Same. Obviously repunched 77.
Repunching plainest at bases. 1982 ANA:2335; others. Compare **5018.**

5023 1878 "Type II" rev. [1,377,600 + 800P]
Minor positional vars. Of 820 proofs struck, 800 were delivered, 677 sold, 123 "released into circulation." Julian [1986].

5024 1878 S "Type II" rev. [12,000] Very rare.
Only the one authentic var. Dangerous counterfeits exist; these lack the lump just below top of leftmost rev. white stripe. Genuine UNCS. are usually prooflike: Egolf, Cox, E. Y. Clarke, Lamborn, "Fairfield," Robison:1721, $16,000; Clarke, NN 47:1342; Ryan, Neil, Pelletreau:862; Brand, Miles:1391; Atwater, Hawn:289; J. A. Stack:555; Merkin 6/71:777; Walton, Glassenberg, 1975 ANA:693, Auction 80:191, $21,000, Halsell:754, $15,950. Possibly 5 others are in mint state, and perhaps 20 more in low grades. Mintage halted to put San Francisco Mint equipment into full-time use on silver dollars: See introductory text. Enl. photos.

5025 1878 CC "Type II" rev. [62,000] Rare.
Usually in low grades; Ex. rare near mint state. Auction 79, Halsell:753, UNC., $8,800. Mintage halted for same reason as at San Francisco: See preceding and introductory text.

5026 1879 "Type I" rev. [Incl. in 620P below] Proofs only.
Scarce.

Rev. of 1876, split berry above H; 2 minor obv. vars.

5027 1879 "Type II" rev. [4,800 + 620P]
Pointed berry above H. Business strikes (usually prooflike
UNC.) and proofs.

5028 1880 "Type I" rev. [Incl. in 1,355P below] Proofs only.
Scarce.
Rev. of 1876, die of **5026**.

5029 1880 "Type II" rev. [8,400 + 1,355P]
Same comment as to **5027**.

5030 1881 "Type I" rev. [Incl. in 975P below] Proofs only.
Rare.
Rev. of 1876, die of **5026**.

5031 1881 "Type II" rev. [10,000 + 975P]
Same comments as to **5027**.

5032 1882 [4,400 + 1,140P]
"Type II" rev. henceforth. Business strikes are usually prooflike UNC.

5033 1883 [8,000 + 1,039P]
Same comments.

5034 1884 [4,400 + 875P]
Business strikes and proofs both come without or with minute repunching on base of 4. Those with minute repunching
above base of 1 are proofs, but business strikes may also exist.
Same comments as to preceding.

5035 1885 [5,200 + 930P]
Same comments as to **5032**.

5036 1886 [5,000 + 886P]
To distinguish proofs from prooflike business strikes, see
Breen {1977}, p. 181.

5037 1887 [5,000 + 710P]
Same comment except p. 184.

5038 1888 [12,000 + 800P]
Business strikes are usually from clashed dies.

5039 1889 [12,000 + 711P]
Business strikes often show die cracks through sixth to ninth
stars (counting clockwise from lower l.).

5040 1890 [12,000 + 590P]

5041 1891 [200,000 + 600P]
Business strikes often show double clash marks in rev. field.

xiv. BARBER'S DESIGN (1892–1915)

Mint Director J. P. Kimball's brainchild, the Mint Act of
Sept. 26, 1890, specified that thereafter coin designs could be
changed only after they had been in use 25 years. As of 1891,
dimes, quarters, and half dollars became eligible. Implementing
Kimball's ideas, the Treasury announced the first of several
competitions for new coin designs. The first circular went only
to 10 of America's best-known sculptors, who (after conferring
among themselves) notified the Treasury that the time allotted
was too short, the prize too small (its amount has not been
ascertainable), and the cost to unsuccessful contestants in time
and effort too great unless they too were compensated for their

entries. The Treasury's response was to throw the competition
open to the public; but as one of the judges was Mint Engraver
Charles E. Barber (as notorious for opposition to outsiders' coin
designs as for dullness), none of the 300 entries won a prize, and
only two were even thought worth Honorable Mention. The
new Mint Director, Edward O. Leech, denounced the competition idea as a wretched failure, and turned over the redesigning
task to Barber, who had wanted it all along. For other details,
see introductory texts to Sect. xiii of Chaps. 25 and 27.

Barber's new obv. began as a mirror-image copy of the Morgan dollar head, though for propriety's sake he cropped off
most of Miss Anna Willess Williams's hair and concealed the
rest within her enlarged cap. Barber also removed the assorted
vegetable matter from the brim of the cap (retaining the word
LIBERTY), replacing the various stalks with a plain laurel (?)
wreath, surmounting the whole dull composition with the religious motto.

For rev., Barber aped Scot's work of 91 years earlier (**4568**)
copying the Great Seal of the United States. His earlier patterns
(dated 1891, Judd 1766, 1765, 1764, 1762) retained the clouds
above eagle; his final prototype (**5042**) sensibly dropped them,
reducing the crowded effect to tolerable levels. The adopted
Barberian design differs again from the Great Seal in scattering
the stars in field above eagle's head rather than retaining their
Star of David array as on the dollar bill. See Taxay {1966}, pp.
287–294.

No design changes occurred, though Barber made slight
modifications in 1901, 1908, and 1912. Other modifications may
exist; that of 1901 was not described in print until the 1950s,
those of 1908 and 1912 not till now.

Proofs dated 1902–15 have devices semibrilliant rather than
frosted as previously—reflecting some kind of change in manufacturing processes about which no information is available.
Most proofs in the late 1890s and early 1900s show evidence of
repeated cleaning, possibly because the original Mint wrappers
were unusually sulfurous.

There are very few major vars.; the most notable are "microscopic" mintmarks in 1892, and reportedly 1898, from mistaken use of punches intended for mintmarking quarter dollars.
Aside from these, nothing in the series can be called rare. Mint-
state survivors of all dates and mintmarks are mostly from rolls
accumulated during the 1930s by A. C. Gies, William Pukall,
and Wayte Raymond; most were dispersed before WW II. The
shortest supplies were apparently of 1901 S, 1913, 1914, 1915,
followed by 1896 S, 1897 O, 1897 S, and 1904 S. Quantities of
rolls retrieved are not proportional to mintages; 1892 O is not
nearly as rare in mint state as most later O and S coins in the
nineties, despite having the lowest mintage of these, because
more rolls were saved as first of their kind.

Most collectors were content to save proofs of 1913–15, so
that most UNC. business strikes perished; survivors are scarcer
than their mintage figures suggest. All three dates can be had as
proofs for a price, though in the late 1950s one Virginia collector hoarded many to drive the price up—reputedly over 1,000
in all!

BARBER'S DESIGN

Designer, Engraver, Charles E. Barber, remotely after Morgan, Scot, and the Great Seal of the USA. Mints, Philadelphia
(no mintmark), New Orleans (mintmark O below eagle), San
Francisco (S below eagle), Denver (D below eagle). Physical
Specifications, Authorizing Acts, as before.

Grade range, FAIR to UNC. GOOD: Date and all legends legible but not LIBERTY; tops of letters may be blurred. VERY
GOOD: LI Y or L TY show on headband. FINE: LIBERTY
completely legible but partly weak; partial wreath details, over
half of Latin motto legible. VERY FINE: LIBERTY plain; full
motto, over half wreath and feather details. EXTREMELY FINE:

Isolated tiny rubbed spots only; both edges of headband completely clear. EXCEPTIONS: Even on mint-state coins, arrow butts and adjacent claw may be weak.

5042 1891 Prototype. Exact adopted design. [2+P] Proofs only. Ex. rare.
Judd 1763. 1) Mint, SI. Others rumored.

5043 1892 [934,000 + 1,245P]
Minute positional vars. of date on this and all to follow. UNCs. of all dates are mostly from the Gies, Pukall, and Raymond rolls (see introductory text); at least one hitherto unseen roll turned up before April 1957.

5044 1892 O [all kinds 390,000] Normal medium O.

5045 1892 O "Microscopic" o. Ex. rare, 4–6 known.
Beistle 1a-B. Discovered by Howard Newcomb; in his display, ANS {1914}. Mintmark punch as on quarter dollars. Most survivors are UNC.; Auction 81:755, nicked, $4,000. Auction 86:1659, "gem," $6,600.

5046 1892 S [all kinds 1,029,028] Normal medium S.
Aside from the Gies, Pukall, and Raymond rolls (see introductory text), one original UNC. roll turned up before April 1957, another about 1974.

5047 1892 S "Microscopic" s. Reported.
Taxay-Scott F293. Mintmark punch as on quarter dollars. A specimen was described to me about 1951 but has not become available for examination.

5048 1893 [1,826,000 + 792P]

5049 1893 O [1,389,000]
Minor positional vars. of date and mintmark, as on all to follow.

5050 1893 S [740,000]

5051 1894 [1,148,000 + 972P] Normal date.

5052 1894 Repunched 4. Proofs only. Scarce.
1974 GENA:1647. Extra outlines within triangle of 4.

5053 1894 O [2,138,000]

5054 1894 S [4,048,690] Mintmark normally placed.

5055 1894 S Mintmark far to r. Very rare.
Beistle 1-C. Mintmark above O, not above D. Probably by whichever workman made the similar quarter dollars **4132, 4135,** etc.

5056 1895 [1,843,338 + 880P] Normal.

5057 1895 Obviously repunched 1. Proofs only. Rare.
1974 GENA:1648; others. Forms a small minority of proofs. Repunching clear at upper serif of 1.

5058 1895 O [1,766,000]

5059 1895 S [1,108,086]
At least one roll (not from the Gies, Pukall, and Raymond holdings) turned up before April 1957.

5060 1896 [950,000 + 762P]

5061 1896 O [924,000]

5062 1896 S [1,140,948]
Higher prices on this date have doubtless been influenced by the fame of the 1896 S quarter dollar.

5063 1897 [all kinds 2,480,000 + 731P]

5064 1897 Repunched 97. Rare.
1982 ANA:2361, UNC., $1,200.

5065 1897 O [632,000]
Difficult to find UNC. S 12/11/80:545, $7,000.

5066 1897 S [933,900]

5067 1898 [2,956,000 + 735P]

5068 1898 O [all kinds 874,000] Normal medium O.

5069 1898 O "Microscopic" o. Reported.
Beistle 2-B. Compare **5045.**

5070 1898 S [2,358,550]

5071 1899 [5,538,000 + 846P]
Some proofs show traces of repunching on base of 1. 1974 GENA:1653.

5072 1899 O [1,724,000]

5073 1899 S [all kinds 1,686,411] Normal S.

5074 1899 S Plainly double S. Rare.

5075 1900 [4,762,000 + 912P]
For possible type change see **5078.**

5076 1900 O [2,744,000]
Same comment.

5077 1900 S [2,560,322]
Same comment.

5078 1901 Modified design. [4,268,000 + 813P]
Some leaves sharper, those at R shorter; tops of W E apart; final star nearer bust; larger ear; other minor differences, compared with 1892–1900. Barely possibly, old-hub coins may exist for this year, in one or more mints, or new-hub coins may exist of 1900. Information on this change is too recent for many coins to have been rechecked, especially in lower grades.

5079 1901 O Modified design. [1,124,000]
Same comments.

5080 1901 S Modified design. [847,044]
Same comments. Part of the demand for this date has been influenced by the fame of the quarter and dime. See introductory text.

5081 1902 [4,922,000 + 777P]
Proofs henceforth have semibrilliant devices: See introductory text.

5082 1902 O [2,526,000]

5083 1902 S [1,460,670]

5084 1903 [2,278,000 + 755P]

5085 1903 O [2,100,000]

5086 1903 S [1,920,772]
Part of the demand for this date has been influenced by the fame of the dollar, quarter, and dime. See introductory text.

5087 1904 [2,992,000 + 670P]

5088 1904 O [1,117,600]

5089 1904 S [553,038]

5090 1905 [622,000 + 727P]

5091 1905 O [505,000]

5092 1905 S [2,494,000]

5093 1906 [2,638,000 + 675P]

5094 1906 O [2,446,000]

5095 1906 S [1,740,154]

5096 1906 D [4,028,000]
Proofs may exist, celebrating inception of coinage at this branch mint, as they do of the dime, eagle, and double eagle.

5097 1907 [2,598,000 + 575P]

5098 1907 O [3,946,600]

Vague soft strikes are common. The scarce "mumps var." has large swellings in cheek and throat near jawline (die failure): NN 57:1000.

5099 1907 S [1,250,000]

Positional vars., one with repunched S.

5100 1907 D [3,856,000]

5101 1908 New hub. [1,354,000 + 545P]

Differences are extremely minor; most noticeably, tops of WE again touch. The new hub appears on all 1908–11 halves seen to date; the old hub may exist on branch mints of 1908.

5102 1908 O New hub. [5,360,000]

Same comments as to **5059, 5101.**

5103 1908 S New hub. [1,644,828]

Same comments as to **5101.**

5104 1908 D New hub. [3,280,000]

Same comments as to **5101.**

5105 1909 [2,368,000 + 550P]

5106 1909 O [925,400]

5107 1909 S [1,764,000]

5108 1910 [418,000 + 551P]

5109 1910 S [1,948,000]

5110 1911 [1,406,000 + 543P]

5111 1911 S [1,272,000]

5112 1911 D [695,080]

5113 1912 Modified design. [1,550,000 + 700P]

Halves from all mints 1912–15 are from a new hub showing minute changes in leaves; tops of W E are again apart.

5114 1912 S Modified design. [1,370,000]

5115 1912 D [2,300,800]

Same comment as to **5059.**

5116 1913 [188,000 + 627P]

See introductory text. Beware forgeries made by removing S or D mintmarks.

5117 1913 S [604,000]

5118 1913 D [534,000]

Same comment as to **5059.**

5119 1914 [124,000 + 610P]

See introductory text. Beware forgeries made by removing S mintmark. Uncirculated business strikes, reputedly from 2 original bags, have long been hoarded, like the proofs.

5120 1914 S [992,000]

Specimens dated 1914 D (usually in low grades) are counterfeits made around WW II.

5121 1915 [138,000 + 450P]

Same comments as to **5119.**

5122 1915 S [1,604,000]

About 1957 a hoard of at least 5 UNC. rolls (100 pieces) turned up; this is believed not to have been part of the original Gies, Pukall, or Raymond holdings.

5123 1915 D [1,170,400]

Same comment as to **5059.**

xv. WEINMAN'S WALKING LIBERTY DESIGN (1916–47)

The same Treasury Department competition that won Adolph Alexander Weinman a prize and the commission to design the new dime for 1916 (Chap. 25, Sect. xiv, introductory text) also won him the same privilege for the half dollar, March 3, 1916. On the following May 1, Weinman's models were due to arrive at the Mint, where they met with hostility from Barber.

Weinman's design, replacing Barber's stolid Germanic conception, embodies a remarkable conceit: Ms. Liberty wears the American flag, anticipating a rebellious counterculture fad by 50 years. Striding eastward (toward wartorn Europe), she points into the sky at nothing visible (perhaps aiming a warning at German warplanes?); in the crook of her l. arm is an oversize bundle of oak and laurel branches, said to be for military and civilian honors. On her feet are Roman cross-thonged sandals; on her head is the same kind of close-fitting cap as on Weinman's dime, though here apparently wingless. On rev., the gnarled tree nearest the eagle's forward talons is said (in Mint Director Robert Woolley's Annual Report, June 1916) to be "a sapling of Mountain Pine, symbolic of America." (A singular choice, as the tree is neither exclusively American nor in any way specially remarkable save perhaps for hardihood near the timberline. This could perhaps allude to the already obsolescent American frontier culture later enshrined in Western movies, though apparently nothing Weinman said on the subject has survived.) These details are mentioned because they cannot usually be made out on even mint-state coins, so weak are most strikings.

The version of Weinman's design finally adopted was possibly the seventh revision. Silver specimens ("patterns") are known of the earlier stages, some (though regrettably not all) preserved in the Smithsonian Institution; supposedly none reached the public's hands, though worn examples exist: congressional pocket pieces? presentation coins spent during the Depression? bequests to kids whose sole interest in coins was as spending money? Those nearest to the version adopted are described below as prototypes; two others (more remote) are pictured in Judd. Some of these (unlocated) were brilliant proofs. Taxay {1966}, p. 348.

The adopted dies were in some ways inferior to their predecessors, because production coins of many dates are so weakly struck that Ms. Liberty's cap, facial details, and branch hand are blurred, as are the striations representing red stripes on the flag, many stars, and most of eagle's breast and leg feathers. Really sharp strikes occur only on the Ex. rare satin-finish proofs of 1916–17 and the old-style brilliant proofs of 1936–42. Full branch-hand coins are Ex. rare or (in many dates) unknown; oddly, 1933 S is the best struck date after 1917, and the only one in which full-hand coins are not Ex. rare. This situation is partly an artifact of hoarding activity: Most UNC. mintmarked dates between 1917 and 1929 are from rolls accumulated during the 1930s by A. C. Gies, William Pukall, and Wayte Raymond, and either these hoarders did not specially seek out sharp strikings or they could not find them. There are no truly rare dates or mintmarks, though the hoarders managed to find very few rolls of 1919, 1919 S, 1919 D, 1920 S, 1920 D, 1921, 1921 D, or especially 1921 S (reportedly only one roll of this last).

Designs are completely hubbed except for mintmarks, as on the new dimes and quarter dollars of this period. Vars. accordingly are minor: mintmark size changes (1928 S, 1934 D, 1941–42 S); mintmark position changes (obv. to rev. in 1917, and only minutely thereafter); mintmark repunching (many dates); overmintmark (1942 D/S, a discovery of recent years); incomplete flag and feathers and/or missing monogram AW (from excessive lapping of a die to remove clash marks, exactly as with the 1937 D three-legged nickel); hub doubling (from minutely misaligned second or third blows to a working die blank from the hub imparting designs to it). The 1943 "overdate" belongs in this last group, for the same reasons as the 1909/8 double eagle, 1918/7 D nickels and S quarters, and 1942/1 dimes.

However, Mint authorities knew well that the Weinman design, despite its great artistic merits, no matter how thorough Barber's original attempts to reduce relief, was technically unsatisfactory: Areas of highest relief still opposed relief areas on the other side. In a desperate effort to make the striking quality even marginally acceptable, Assistant Engraver George T. Morgan in 1918 modified the obv.; details of garment at throat are incised. This attempt was a failure. In 1937, John R. Sinnock made still another version, with only one vertical ray touching flag; in 1938, again another revision, with leaves differing in shape, and more details incised on drapery at arm below stars. This version continued until the end of the series in 1947. However, even the latest years, with presumably the best presses, seldom show even nearly full central details. This consideration may have contributed to Treasury Department decisions to replace the design in 1948: See next section.

WEINMAN'S WALKING LIBERTY DESIGN

Designer, Adolph Alexander Weinman. Engravers, Barber, Morgan, and Sinnock, after Weinman. Mints, Philadelphia (no mintmark), San Francisco (mintmark S), Denver (mintmark D). Mintmarks 1916–17 in obv. field below TR; 1917–47, near lower l. rev. border below sapling. Physical Specifications, Authorizing Act, as before.

Grade range, FAIR to UNC. GOOD: Date and all letters legible, including mintmark, if any. VERY GOOD: Partial drapery and feather details; eagle's eye visible; rims complete. FINE: At least half stripes intact; partial sandal details; at least half feather details including two upper layers below S OF AMERI. VERY FINE: Breast outlines visible; most other details present on flag and drapery except in a narrow straight line above date; gown line crossing body is partly visible; pupil of eagle's eye visible; nearly all wing feathers separate except on breast and legs. EXTREMELY FINE: Isolated small rubbed spots only; partial mint luster. UNCIRCULATED: No trace of wear; mint luster on all weak areas. NOTE: Usually collected in UNC. except by beginners. Business strikes with full head and branch hand are rare, in some dates unverified to exist; 1916–17, 1933 S least rare so. To qualify as full head, details of cap above ear must show; full-hand coins must show clear index finger and thumb (just above center of coin). Ill. of 5127 has nearly full head and hand.

5124 1916 First Prototype. Ex. rare.
Judd 1800. Note beaded borders, complete LIBERTY, smaller letters, no monogram AW. 1) Steig:1814, VG, $1,550; others.

5125 1916 Second Prototype. Ex. rare.
Judd 1799. Same but plain borders. Obv. ill. above Judd 1798.
5126 1916 Third Prototype. Ex. rare, 2 or 3 known.
Judd 1801. As next but date very small and closely spaced, not extending beyond foot; no monogram AW. Ill. NUM 1/17, p. 22. 1) Pvt. coll., worn.
5127 1916 Regular issue. [608,000 + ?P]
Possibly 5 satin-finish proofs. These have full head and hand,

broad borders and sometimes knife-rims; drapery and feather details sharp. Dangerous cast forgeries exist. Authentication recommended.
5128 1916 S [508,000]
Often weak on head and eagle's breast.
5129 1916 D [1,014,400]

5130 1916 D Double D. Presently very rare.
RPM 1. D first entered far too low and to l.

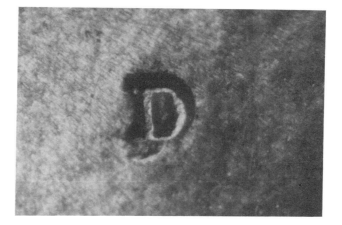

5131 1917 [12,292,000 + ?P]
Often noticeably bag-marked. At least 3 satin-finish proofs, like **5127**.
5132 1917 S Obv. mintmark. [952,000]
Often weak. "Sliders" (cleaned EF–AU) are plentiful, as are forgeries made by affixing false S to genuine Philadelphia coins.
5133 1917 S Rev. mintmark. [5,554,000]
Same comment as to **5128**.
5134 1917 D Obv. mintmark. [765,400]
"Sliders" are plentiful.
5135 1917 D Rev. mintmark. [1,940,000]
Same comment. In all, 42 obvs., 35 revs. of both types, per Alan Craig, from Denver Mint records.
5136 1918 New hub. [6,634,000]
Design details incised above bosom, 1918–36 all mints. Ill. of **5153**.

5137 1918 S New hub. [10,282,000]
Mintmark on rev. henceforth. Weak strikings, 1918–29: See introductory text.

5138 1918 D New hub. [3,853,040] Normal.
Mintmark on rev. henceforth. Often weak. See next.

5139 1918 D Without AW monogram. Presently Ex. rare, 4–6 known?
Discovered by Mrs. Genevieve Martin, *NSM* 10/60, p. 2856. All are in low grades. Cf. Jeffrey LeRose, *CW* 3/22/78, p. 38; Breen III:358. See introductory text.

5140 1919 [962,000]
"Sliders" are plentiful.

5141 1919 S [1,552,000]
Often weak. Fully UNC. survivors are seldom offered. Auction:80, $22,000.

5142 1919 D [1,165,000]
Often weak. Sharply struck UNCs. are very rare.

5143 1920 [6,372,000]

5144 1920 S [4,624,000]
Often weak; the few well-struck UNCs. are from a tiny hoard dispersed by NERCG, 1977.

5145 1920 D [1,551,000]
Often weak, especially at head.

5146 1921 [246,000]
"Sliders" are plentiful. Occasionally simulated by removing D mintmark; authentication recommended.

5147 1921 S [548,000]
Usually in low grades. Possibly all UNC. survivors are from a single roll, mostly weak strikes: 1980 ANA:2470, $24,000; one described as sharp, Ivy 3/81, $36,000.

5148 1921 D [208,000]
"Sliders" are plentiful. Denver Mint records (courtesy Alan Craig) say 2 pairs of dies, respectively yielding 165,000 and 92,672 impressions, total 257,672; probably the odd 49,672 never left the Mint.

5149 1923 S [2,178,000]
Often weak.

5150 1927 S [2,392,000]
Usually weak.

5151 1928 S [all kinds 1,940,000] Small s.
Mintmark as in cents; small rounded serifs. Often weak.

5152 1928 S Large S.
Mintmark as in some quarter dollars; larger sharper serifs. Often weak. Pieces dated 1928 D are circulating counterfeits made no later than WW II.

5153 1929 S [1,902,000] Normal.
Compare next. Ill. at **5136.**

5154 1929 S No AW monogram. Presently very rare.
From dies drastically relapped after clashing. About 15 reported to date, mostly in low grades. Discovery coin, Merkin 4/66:375. Cf. LeRose, *CW* 3/22/78, p. 38.

5155 1929 D [1,001,200]

5156 1933 S [1,786,000]
Generally better struck than previous issues.

5157 1934 [6,964,000]

5158 1934 S [3,652,000]

5159 1934 D [all kinds 2,361,400] Small D.
Mintmark as 1917–29.

5160 1934 D Large D.
Mintmark as in 1935–47.

5161 1935 [9,162,000]

5162 1935 S [3,854,000]
Often weak.

5163 1935 D [3,003,800]
Almost always weak, especially at head.

5164 1936 [all kinds 12,614,000 + 3,901P] Normal.
Proofs are extra brilliant like those of 1937; the "first style" or satin finish (found on some cents, nickels, and dimes) has not been reported. Dangerous forgeries exist, made from business strikes by buffing or plating; these can be identified by loss of detail on head and branch hand and other areas.

5165 1936 Doubled obv. die. Very rare.
Doubling obvious at letters and date. Discovered by Neil Osina, 1981; partly ill., Osina (1982). Usually circulated.

5166 1936 S [3,884,000]

5167 1936 D [4,252,000]

5168 1937 Modified obv. [9,522,000 + 5,728P]
Only one almost vertical ray touches flag; all rays thinner than before. Proofs are extra brilliant, like other denominations this year; forgeries like those described for 1936 may exist.

5169 1937 Extra-thin motto letters. Proofs only. [Incl. in 5,728P above]
Forms a minority of proofs. Obv. die excessively polished, motto letters seem farther apart. Discovery coins, 1973 GENA:617–19.

5170 1937 S Modified design. [2,090,000]

5171 1937 D Modified design. [1,676,000]

5172 1938 New hub. [4,110,000 + 8,152P]
Leaves differ in shape; more details incised on drapery at arm below stars; 2 nearly vertical rays touch flag. This new hub continued through 1947. Ill. of **5173.** Proofs: Same comment as to **5168.**

5173 1938 D New hub. [491,600]
2 positional vars. of mintmark. Much hoarded. Ill. at **5172.**

5174 1939 [6,812,000 + 8,808P]

5175 1939 S [2,552,000]

5176 1939 D [4,267,800]

5177 1939 D Obviously repunched D. Presently very rare.
RPM 1. D first punched too high, then corrected.

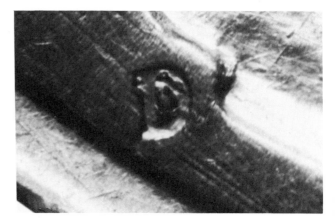

5178 1940 [9,156,000 + 11,279P] Normal.

5179 1940 Without AW monogram. Presently rare.

Both dies overpolished to remove clash marks. Survivors to date include possibly 3 proofs, one UNC. business strike, and a few in low grades. *CW* 1/10/73.

5180 1940 S [4,550,000]

Often weak.

5181 1941 [24,192,000 + 15,412P] Normal.

Proofs issued in November and December have the AW monogram, as do all business strikes seen to date.

5182 1941 Without AW monogram. Proofs only.

Proofs issued January–October are from dies excessively polished so that monogram was unintentionally removed. They probably constitute over ¾ of recorded mintage. First report: Harry C. Mathews, *NUM* 3/42, p. 207.

5183 1941 S [all kinds 8,098,000] Small s, normal.

Often weak. Mintmark as in former years. Compare next.

5184 1941 S Small s, obviously repunched. Presently very rare.

RPM 1. S first entered far too low and to l. of final position. Sometimes thought to be S over horizontal S.

5185 1941 S Large S. Presently rare.

S as in 1943–47 and on **2676**; note pronounced sharp serifs. Only one die seen to date; S leans far to r. NN 57:1035. Often weak.

5186 1941 D [all kinds 11,248,000] Normal.

5187 1941 D Obvious double D. Presently rare.

D first entered too high and to l., then corrected. 1984 Midwinter ANA:1407. Less obvious repunched mintmarks bring lower premiums.

5188 1941 D Doubled obv. die. Presently very rare.

Taxay F411. Doubling plainest on rays and motto.

5189 1942 [all kinds 47,818,000 + 21,120P] Normal.

5190 1942 Doubled rev. die.

Doubling is plainest at DOLLAR. *COINS* 3/76, p. 56. Usually circulated.

5191 1942 S [all kinds 12,708,000] Small s.

Mintmark as in 1917–41; from leftover 1941 die. Often weak.

5192 1942 S Large S. Trumpet-tailed S.

Mintmark as in 1943–47. May exist with knob tail or sharp serifs. Aram Haroutunian discovered a doubled obv. die, plainest at corner of skirt below branch.

5193 1942 S No AW monogram. Presently Ex. rare.

From rev. die excessively relapped to remove clash marks. Jeffrey LeRose, *CW* 3/22/78, p. 38.

5194 1942 D [all kinds 10,973,800] Normal.

5195 1942 D over S. Presently Ex. rare.

1) Eugene Rinn, discovery coin, 1980.   2) *CW* 10/20/82, p. 56.

5196 1943 [all kinds 53,190,000] Normal.

5197 1943 "Overdate." Presently very rare.

Possibly 1943/2, as the curvature does not match either lower or upper edge of top stroke of 3. Confirmation awaits discovery of earlier die states in unchecked rolls. Compare **5205**.

5198 1943 S [all kinds 13,450,000] Normal. Trumpet-tailed S.

May exist with overdate as preceding. Other styles may exist, as **5192**. Dave Henderson discovered one with S punched over D, the traces of D faint.

5199 1943 S Doubled obv. die. Presently very rare.

Doubling plainest at lower edge of skirt and within loop of 9.

5200 1943 S No AW monogram. Presently Ex. rare, 6 reported.

Same source and comment as to **5193**.

5201 1943 D [all kinds 11,346,000] Normal.

5202 1943 D Obviously repunched D. Rare.

RPM 1. Merkin 4/66:395.

5203 1943 D Doubled obv. die. Presently very rare.

Similar to **5199**.

5204 1943 D Doubled rev. die. Presently Ex. rare.

NN 57:1036. Doubling plainest on rays and D UST.

5205 1943 D "Overdate." Presently Ex. rare.

Similar to **5197**. Gibbons II:2959.

5206 1944 [28,206,000] Normal.

5207 1944 No AW monogram. Presently Ex. rare, only 2 reported.

Same source and comment as to **5193**.

5208 1944 S [8,904,000] Trumpet-tailed S.

Often weak. Other styles may exist.

5209 1944 D [9,769,000]

5210 1945 [31,502,000] Normal.

5211 1945 No AW monogram. Presently Ex. rare, only 4 reported.

Same source and comment as to **5193**.

5212 1945 S [10,156,000] Knob-tailed S.

Often weak. Other styles may exist.

5213 1945 D [9,966,800]

5214 1946 [all kinds 12,118,000] Normal.

5215   1946 Doubled rev. die. Presently very rare.

Doubling plainest at motto, legs, and lowest wing feathers, as ill. Usually circulated. Publicized by Bill Fivaz, *CW* 7/28/76. Other vars. reported.

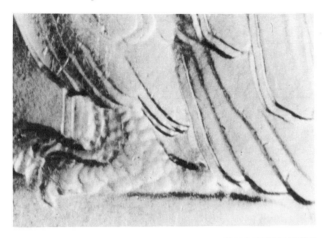

5216   1946 S [3,724,000] Knob-tailed S.

Other styles of S may exist. On some, mintmark is blurred.

5217   1946 D [2,151,000]

Much hoarded.

5218   1947 [4,094,000]

5219   1947 D [3,900,600] Normal.

5220   1947 D No AW monogram. Presently Ex. rare, only one reported.

Same source and comment as to **5193**.

xvi. SINNOCK'S FRANKLIN DESIGN (1948–63)

These were the last work of their designer, Mint Engraver John R. Sinnock. At the request of Mint Director Nellie Tayloe Ross, he completed the obv. and rev. models only a few weeks before his death (May 1947). The half-dollar design was legally changeable any time after July 1, 1941, but escalated wartime demands for coins occasioned the delay.

Acting Director Leland Howard, on Nov. 17, 1947, shipped a lead impression of an obv., with date represented by XXXX, to the federal Fine Arts Commission for its approval—but without the rev. On Dec. 1, Gilmore Clarke, Commission chairman,

wrote back to Mrs. Ross, disapproving both obv. and rev. models. (How they managed to obtain access to the latter has not been learned.) Their grounds for disapproval were the small eagle at r. of the Liberty bell (which eagle was included solely because the law had required it ever since 1792) and the plain crack in the bell, because forsooth "to show this might lead to puns and to statements derogatory to United States coinage." Taxay {1966}, pp. 376–77.

Nevertheless, the Treasury approved the design, crack and all, without setting up the competition which the Commission had urged instead (its recommendations have never had the force of law), and the coins went into production as of April 30, 1948. The evening before the first batch went to Federal Reserve Banks, about 200 of the new halves were given out to local VIPs at a dinner party, each with place cards signed by Mrs. Ross; these were normal business strikes without holders. No proofs were to follow until 1950; the earliest were satin finish, later ones brilliant as in 1951–63.

The Commission's objections to the eagle were evidently justified. On proofs of 1959–63 and some production coins of 1958–59, a new rev. hub ("Type II") went into use; this has eagle in higher relief, with only three feathers l. of perch. ("Type I" coins, since 1948, had shown eagle in low relief, with four flattened feathers l. of perch.) Not that this improvement helped much, as the eagle is seldom very clear even on proofs.

However, the derogatory remarks feared by the Commission arose not from the crack in the bell, but from Sinnock's initials JS. Ignorant paranoid superpatriots of the Sen. McCarthy persuasion, fearful of Communists under every bed, misidentified these initials (like those on the dimes in 1946) as designating Joseph Stalin, and once again these rumors required outraged official denials.

Another rumor—that the small o in oF was a mistake, and the coins with it would have to be recalled—died more quickly. However, the closet skeleton about the design took decades to be found and unwrapped. Only in the middle 1960s, when Don Taxay was working on his book on commemorative coins, did he learn and publish that Sinnock had adapted the rev. from John Frederick Lewis's original sketch for the Sesquicentennial half dollar (1926), without ever allowing Lewis's name to be used either in connection with the commemorative or the Franklin half dollar.

Because dealers saved rolls and bag lots in quantity, no officially recorded dates or mintmarks can even be called scarce. Mintmarks vary microscopically in position. Some dates with more than one rev. hub may prove to contain scarce vars., but research is still only beginning; possibilities include doubled rev. dies using both hubs, other types of doubled dies, doubled mintmarks, overmintmarks.

However, one major mystery remains, uncleared (as usual) even by official denials. Supposedly no Franklin halves were made in 1964, the Kennedy coins released on March 5 being the first coins of this denomination struck that year. Nevertheless, a New York dealer of unimpeachable repute told me on my return from a business trip that one day during my absence he had held a client in his office for several hours while vainly trying to reach me by telephone; the client had a 1964 Franklin half dollar for sale, but they did not wish to conclude the deal without my authentication. The client has never returned, nor has the coin shown up anywhere, nor has any counterfeit half dollar of this date been publicized, nor have authorities announced seizure (a probable fate in any event). There are three ways a genuine 1964 Franklin half dollar could have been made: 1) clandestine issue in 1964; 2) barely possible: In late fall 1963, when working dies were being prepared for both 1963 and 1964 use, a die could have been dated 1964, and sent to press in error; 3) experimental striking exemplifying some design modification. When orders came to hold off on issue pending change to the Kennedy design, most likely the 1964 working hub(s), dies, and impressions were destroyed. There is no way to distinguish these sources. But a provably genuine 1964 Franklin would be the half-dollar discovery of the century.

SINNOCK'S FRANKLIN DESIGN

Designer, John R. Sinnock, rev. after John Frederick Lewis; engraver, Sinnock. Mints, Philadelphia (no mintmark), San Francisco (mintmark S), Denver (D). Mintmarks above bell, just below E(S). Physical Specifications, Authorizing Acts, as before, except Weight Standard 192.9 ± 4 grs. = 12.5 ± 0.26 gms.

Grade range, GOOD to UNC. VERY GOOD: Date and all inscriptions legible except letters on bell; ear, designer's initials on truncation, and straps on beam visible. FINE: Partial hair details; partial incuse lines at bottom of bell. VERY FINE: About ¾ hair lines including some details around ear; most bell details present except for incuse lines nearest crack and parts of lettering on bell. EXTREMELY FINE: Isolated tiny worn spots only; lettering on bell intact except for few partly blurred letters at centers of top two lines. EXCEPTIONS: Many UNCS., especially S-Mint issues described as "Often weak," are vaguely struck at upper half of Franklin's head and/or parts of bell; make sure that weak areas show mint frost, not rubbing. "Full bell lines" coins show all seven incuse horizontal lines on lower quarter of bell; they bring high premiums.

5221 1948 [3,006,814]
Doubling on motto is in the master die for this date. For pieces with original presentation card [about 200], see introductory text. Ill. of **5243.**

5222 1948 D [4,028,600]
Same comment about doubling on motto.
5223 1949 [5,614,000]
5224 1949 S [3,744,000] Knob-tailed S.
Early hoarded in quantity as a "key" date. Rarely prooflike. Other styles of S may occur (sharp serifs or trumpet-tail), as in other years 1942–54.
5225 1949 D [4,120,600]
5226 1950 [7,742,123 + 51,386P]
Usually heavily bag-marked. Earlier proofs are satin finish, later ones very brilliant.
5227 1950 D [8,031,600]
A minor doubled rev. die exists, plainest at motto. Bill Fivaz, *CW* 7/28/76.
5228 1951 [16,802,102 + 57,500P]
5229 1951 S [13,696,000]
Often weak.
5230 1951 D [9,475,200]
5231 1952 [21,192,093 + 81,980P]
5232 1952 S [5,526,000]
Often weak.
5233 1952 D [25,395,600]
5234 1953 [2,668,120 + 128,800P]
Usually heavily bag-marked. This remark applies even to coins in mint sets.

5235 1953 S [4,148,000]
Often weak.
5236 1953 D [20,900,400]
5237 1954 [13,188,203 + 233,300P]
5238 1954 S [4,993,400]
Often weak.
5239 1954 D [25,445,580]
5240 1955 [2,498,181 + 378,200P]
Either die chips or clash marks created the "Bugs Bunny" var.: Franklin apparently has buck teeth. This var. is not rare but has long been popular among fanciers of Mint errors and curiosities.
5241 1956 "Type I." [4,032,000 + ?P]
As 1948–55: low relief to eagle, 4 flattened feathers l. of perch. Found on all business strikes and about 5% of proofs; compare next. Proofs formed part of [40,432P] delivered 2/56. The [2,008,000] of 2/56 cannot be told from the [2,024,000] of 12/56. Data from Myles Lambson.

5242 1956 "Type II." [Incl. in 669,384P] Proofs only.
Higher relief to eagle, only 3 feathers l. of perch. Comprises about 95% of proofs of this year. (Population estimates from Rev. Richard T. Deters, S.J.) Cf. note by W. W. Edwards, *CW* 10/5/77.

5243 1957 "Type I." [5,114,000]
As **5241.** Business strikes only. Ill. at **5221.**
5244 1957 "Type II." [1,247,952P] Proofs only.
As **5242.**
5245 1957 D "Type I." [19,966,850]

5246 1958 [all kinds 4,042,000] "Type I."
As **5241**. Business strikes only.
5247 1958 "Type II." [? + 875,652P]
As **5242**. All proofs, and about 20% of business strikes. Latter from retired proof dies.
5248 1958 D "Type I." [23,962,412]
5249 1959 [all kinds 6,200,000] "Type I."
As **5241**. About 30% of business strikes only; compare next 2.
5250 1959 "Type II." [? + 1,149,291P]
As **5242**. Proofs and about 70% of business strikes.
5251 1959 Doubled rev. die. Presently scarce.
Lower relief to eagle, only 3 feathers l. of perch. Business strikes only. This die received one blow each from Type I and Type II hubs. Note overlapping feathers, doubling on motto, clapper and hanger. *CW* 2/18/81, p. 90.

5252 1959 D "Type I." [13,053,750]
As **5241**. May exist with "Type II" rev. The same remark holds for all D mints to follow.
5253 1960 "Type I." [6,024,000]
As **5241**. Business strikes. Obv. fields flatter.
5254 1960 "Type II." [1,691,602P] Proofs only.
As **5242**. Glen Jeong found a doubled obv. die. Ill. *CW* 7/23/86, p. 71.
5255 1960 D "Type I." [18,215,812]
Same comment as to **5252**.
5256 1961 "Type I." [8,290,000]
Usually heavily bag-marked.
5257 1961 "Type II." [3,028,244P] Proofs only.
As **5242**.
5258 1961 D "Type I." [20,276,442]
Same comment as to **5252**. A doubled rev. die was recently discovered; doubling is plainest on Latin motto, HALF, and UNITED STATES.
5259 1962 "Type I." [9,714,000]
Usually heavily bag-marked.
5260 1962 "Type II." [3,218,019P] Proofs only.
As **5242**.
5261 1962 D "Type I." [35,473,281P]
Same comment as to **5252**.
5262 1962 D over horizontal D. Very rare.
RPM 3. D first entered 90° from normal (upright at top).
5263 1963 "Type I." [22,164,000]
Usually heavily bag-marked.
5264 1963 "Type II." [3,075,645P] Proofs only.
As **5242**.
5265 1963 D "Type I." [67,069,292]
5266 1964 Reported.
See introductory text.

xvii. ROBERTS'S SILVER KENNEDY DESIGN (1964–65)

About Nov. 25, 1963, Mint Director Eva Adams telephoned Chief Engraver Gilroy Roberts to notify the Engraving Department that the Treasury proposed to place a Kennedy portrait onto one of our silver coins—denomination not decided. Ms. Adams mentioned the presidential seal as a possible rev. design. On Nov. 27 she again phoned Roberts to specify the Kennedy inaugural medal as prototype for head and eagle for the new coins, which were to be half dollars. This would save much time in making original dies. (Jacqueline Kennedy had expressed a preference that her late husband's portrait not replace that of Washington on quarters; it was then doubtful if silver dollars would be coined; and nobody considered portraying Kennedy on the dime.) The Act of Sept. 25, 1890 required that any new design be authorized by Congress. However, no matter that Congress had not yet complied: Nobody expected any opposition.

The time pressure was all but unprecedented in the history of the Mint. Roberts later said that the project was barely within the bounds of possibility only because the original models for the Kennedy medals were still preserved and could be used as a basis for mechanical reductions (presumably on the Janvier portrait lathe). These reductions—first to about 5″ in diameter, thence to coin size—afforded the opportunity for reducing relief to a degree compatible with production coins, among other modifications. Medals can be made in high relief because each specimen receives multiple blows from the dies to bring design details up; production coins must be in low relief so that a single blow suffices to impart the entire design.

On Dec. 10, 1963, Pres. Johnson issued press releases recommending passage of a bill then before Congress, which would authorize this coinage. On Dec. 13, Roberts completed the first trial dies and made several impressions for delivery to Ms. Adams. On Dec. 15, she summoned Roberts to Washington to discuss the trial impressions with him, Treasury Secretary Douglas Dillon, and other officials. At the conference, all concerned approved the design, but Dillon wanted Mrs. Kennedy's opinion; two days later, they met with her and Attorney General Robert Kennedy. Aside from a tentative wish for a half-length or even full-length portrait of JFK (which Roberts rejected as impossible, there being no models usable for making the necessary galvanos, reductions, or dies, even if time permitted), Mrs. Kennedy approved of the designs, except that she preferred to de-emphasize the part in JFK's hair. This was done on the 5″ reduction, and a new trial die was made showing the recommended changes. On Dec. 27, Gilroy Roberts flew to West Palm Beach, Fla., to show newly struck impressions from this second trial to Mrs. Kennedy and Secretary Dillon, who enthusiastically approved. The next step was preparation of working hubs and production dies.

Meanwhile, back at the Capitol, Congress finally passed the authorizing act on Dec. 30, and Pres. Johnson promptly signed it into law.

Proof dies were delivered on Jan. 2, 1964, and the first press run began, eventually to comprise nearly four million proofs for the 1964 sets. On Jan. 30, production began at Denver of regular Kennedy halves for circulation, and at Philadelphia at some time during the following week. On Feb. 11, simultaneous ceremonies were held at both mints in the presence of a variety of Treasury officials, celebrating the new design; but coins were not available to the general public until March 5, when some 26 million were shipped to Federal Reserve Banks for distribution, reaching circulation about March 24. Taxay {1966}, pp. 378–80.

Almost the entire batch vanished into the hands of souvenir hunters and speculators and investors, many of these last two groups being the same cynics who had been buying and selling futures in these coins. As usual, Mint Bureau people blamed coin collectors, failing to distinguish the Boy Scout assembling type coins for his merit badge, or the scholarly specialist, from the Wall Street investor interested only in his bank balance. Coinage continued until even the hoarders were sated; not that this particularly helped, since by late 1964 silver was already rising in price enough to attract the attention of bullion hoarders, investors, and dealers, both in the USA and in Europe.

Another factor doubtless increased hoarders' attention to this issue: Paranoid superpatriots, probably some of the same people who had earlier believed former Engraver John Sinnock's initials JS on the Roosevelt dime to mean Joseph Stalin, promptly spread rumors misrepresenting Gilroy Roberts's initials GR on neck truncation of the new half dollar as the Soviet Russian hammer and sickle. These stupid rumors led to denunciations, hoarding of coins pending possible withdrawal and design change, and furious Treasury denials. In the meantime, parties in Europe were paying premiums for the new coins, and millions of them vanished into continental hands.

Because Treasury policymakers insisted on blaming coin collectors for mass hoarding, Congress passed the Act of 9/3/64 (at Treasury request) retaining the date 1964 on coins until further notice. The official rationalization labeled coin collectors as preferentially hoarding any issue with a new date; this was one of Leland Howard's fixed delusions during his tenure with the Mint Bureau, and despite all contrary evidence it still has not vanished! (See Chap. 31 on the Susan B. Anthony mini-dollars.) Because of rising silver prices, the Treasury eventually induced Congress to authorize replacement of standard silver, first by silver-clad sandwich metal (1965–70), then (1971–85) by the non-precious clad metal found on dimes and quarters: See following sections.

ROBERTS'S SILVER KENNEDY DESIGN

Designers, Engravers, obv., Gilroy Roberts (signed GR on truncation); rev. Frank Gasparro (signed FG in field r. of tail), after the presidential inaugural medal. Mints, Philadelphia (no mintmark), San Francisco (mintmark S), Denver (mintmark D); mintmarks l. of stem of olive branch. Physical Specifications, Authorizing Acts, as before, except that the design was authorized by Act of June 30, 1963.

Grade range, FINE to UNC. VERY FINE: All feathers separated except central tail feathers, and these will be at least partly separated. EXTREMELY FINE: Isolated tiny rubbed spots only; all feathers completely separated. EXCEPTION: Normally collected only in mint state; worn examples are acceptable only of the rarer vars.

5267 1964 Accented hair. [?P] Proofs only.
Estimated 100,000–120,000 proofs, from 50–60 obv. dies; in-

cluded in mintage of next. Individual hairs are more heavily incised than on coins from later dies, at and below the part. Found in proof sets with the pointed 9 dimes. *CW* 7/4/84, p. 60. Enl. photo.

5268 1964 Normal hair. [273,302,004 + 3,950,762P]
Over 40 million (Philadelphia and Denver) have long been held in European hands. Mintage figure includes many struck in 1965 from 1964-dated dies; these cannot be identified. For clad strikings see **5275**.

5269 1964 Doubled obv. die.
Other vars. are less obvious; proofs and business strikes.

5270 1964 Doubled rev. die.
Same comment except no proofs seen.
5271 1964 D [156,205,446]
Same comment as to **5268**. At least 6 vars. of repunched D. For clad strikings see **5276**.
5272 1964 D Doubled obv. die.
Several vars., none very prominent. Ill. Steiner & Zimpfer [1974], p. 70.
5273 1964 D Doubled rev. die.
Same comment.
5274 1965 On standard silver blank. Ex. rare.
Weight 192.9 grs. = 12.5 gms. Struck in early 1965 while old and new issues were simultaneously in production. See next section.

xviii. SILVER-CLAD KENNEDY ISSUES (1965–70)

During 1965 it was already apparent that domestic silver production could not indefinitely keep pace with demands from the Mint, from industry (most of all photography and electronics), and from investors. The Treasury had already allowed the latter to drain its remaining stocks of silver dollars (aside from a small reserve later earmarked for sale to collectors) in exchange for silver certificates which were then being retired from circulation; later still, authorities redeemed the latter instead with small envelopes of silver granules. No matter how immense the Mints' output of silver coins, they vanished from circulation. The Treasury chose to blame coin collectors (see previous section, introductory text); but a factor far greater than even European and Wall Street hoarding (and many orders of magnitude greater than coin collectors' activities) was the flowback problem: See Chap. 27, Sect. xviii, introductory text.

Yielding to pressure from silver mine owners for the umpteenth time, Congress saw fit to exempt the Kennedy half dollar from the nickel-clad copper ("sandwich metal") composition required in dimes and quarter dollars by a bill then pending. As finally signed into law, the Act of July 23, 1965 required the half dollar to weigh 177.47 grs. = 11.5 gms., consisting of an inner core of billon (21% silver, 79% copper), clad by outer layers of 80% silver. These coins were made in vast quantities—about 849 million for circulation, and over 5½ million proofs, 1965–70. Hoarding increased as demand for silver bullion kept pushing prices up.

The only answer to hoarding was the simple and obvious one which should have been tried at the outset: Turn deaf ears to the silver mine owners' lobbyists, and make half dollars in the same composition as the smaller denominations. If we must have sandwich metal in coinage at all, better that it be uniform in all denominations than that one issue continue to be favored by use of silver and funneled to hoarders pursuant to Gresham's law.

During 1965–67, mintmarks were omitted (to discourage coin collectors' "withholding them from circulation"), and instead of proof sets, the Mint Bureau distributed prooflike "Special Mint Sets," which were predictably a failure. Proof-set coinage resumed in 1968, thereafter from San Francisco.

SILVER-CLAD KENNEDY ISSUES

Designers, Engravers, as before. Mints, Philadelphia (no mintmark), San Francisco (mintmark S), Denver (D). Mintmarks below truncation of neck. Composition, outer layers 80% silver, 20% copper, bonded to inner core of 21% silver, 79% copper. Weight, 177.5 ± 6.17 grs. = 11.5 ± 0.4 gms. Diameter, 1.205" = 30.607 mm. Edge, as before. Authorizing Act, July 23, 1965.

Grade range and standards, as before. Normally collected only in mint state.

5275 1964 Struck by error. Ex. rare.
Coined in 1965 when both old and new issues were being simultaneously made. May exist also with D mintmark.

5276 1965 [65,879,366 + 2,360,000 SMS]
Released beginning 3/8/66. *CWA* p. 176. SMS = Special Mint Sets, prooflike, from San Francisco Assay Office, cent through half dollar, without mintmark. One of the first sets, shown by Mint Director Eva Adams to Harry Forman, is apparently indistinguishable from earlier proofs. Later SMS are of much lower striking and surface quality. Minor doubled obv. and rev. dies exist for this and almost all later dates and mintmarks.

5277 1966 [108,984,932 + 2,261,583 SMS]
SMS as defined above; ill. Minor doubled dies exist. Compare next. Those dated 1966 were all made after 8/1/66.

5278 1966 Without FG. Presently rare.
Initials of engraver Frank Gasparro, normally present between tail and eagle's leg at r., are missing owing to overpolishing of one working die to remove clash marks. Discovered by Julian Jarvis, *CW* 5/3/67; publicized by Harry Forman,

CW 11/10/82. Cf. *CW* 1/26/83, p. 70. The same accident occurs on other dates; compare **5292, 5323, 5328.**

5279 1967 [295,046,978 + 1,863,344 SMS]
Same comment as to **5277.** Business strikes are from Denver Mint but without mintmark.
5280 1968 S [3,041,506P] Proofs only.
5281 1968 D [246,951,930]
5282 1969 S [2,934,631] Proofs only.
5283 1969 D [129,881,800]
5284 1970 S [2,632,810P] Proofs only.
5285 1970 D [2,150,000]
Issued only in mint sets.

xix. NICKEL-CLAD KENNEDY ISSUES (1971-74)

Mint authorities learned that some of the same people who had been melting down standard silver coins were extending their operations to wartime silver 5¢ coins and silver-clad half dollars. Their answer was immediate: Under authority of the Act of July 23, 1965, they began issuing half dollars in the same "sandwich metal" composition as dimes and quarter dollars, and of proportionate weight.

These half dollars, like later issues in the same composition, are struck at 110 tons force, 120 pieces per minute. Die life averages somewhere between 200,000 and 500,000 business strikes.

Mint authorities viewed the coins as a triumph of technology over hoarding; others have seen them as still another example of Gresham's law in action: Compare previous section, introductory text. As there are 40 half dollars to the avoirdupois lb., it is unlikely that they will be hoarded for their copper content; considering their large mintages, it is unlikely that they are being hoarded for numismatic purposes. Yet they form only a minuscule part of circulating change today; most languish instead in banks and Treasury vaults. The reason is immediately obvious: Most "legal receptacles" (vending machines, coin phones, laundromats, fare boxes, turnstiles, parking meters, video games, etc.) accept only nickels, dimes, and quarters, alone or in combination, but refuse half dollars. Mintages, both before and after the Bicentennials (see next section), have dwindled, and rumors have abounded of possible suspension of coinage or even abolition of the denomination. Compare Chap. 31, introductory text.

NICKEL-CLAD KENNEDY ISSUES

Designers, Engravers, Mints, as before. Composition, outer layers 25% nickel, 75% copper, bonded to inner core of pure copper. Weight, 175 ± 7 grs. = 11.34 ± 0.454 gms. Diameter, Edge, Authorizing Acts, as before, plus Title 31, U.S. Code, § 5112.

Grade range and standards, as before. Normally collected only in mint state.

5286 1971 Modified design. [155,164,000]
   Minor doubled dies exist for almost all dates and mints. Release began in April. Later strikings have stronger serifs to I Y; serif of 7 weak.
5287 1971 S Modified design. [3,220,733P] Proofs only.
   May exist on leftover silver-clad blank. Same comment about later strikings.
5288 1971 D Modified design. [302,097,424]
   Same comments.
5289 1972 [153,180,000]
5290 1972 S [3,260,996P] Proofs only.
5291 1972 D [141,890,000]
5292 1972 D No initials FG. Presently very rare.
   Same comment as to **5278.** Discovered by Kip Nelson. *CW* 10/12/83, p. 70.
5293 1973 [64,964,000]
   Reported without initials FG.
5294 1973 S [2,760,339P] Proofs only.
5295 1973 D [83,171,400]
5296 1974 [201,596,000]
   Mintage includes many struck in calendar 1975 from 1974-dated dies, pursuant to PL 93-541. (Dec. 26, 1974).
5297 1974 S [2,612,568P] Proofs only.
5298 1974 D [All kinds 79,066,300]
   Same comment as to **5279.**
5299 1974 D Doubled obv. die. Presently very rare.
   Doubling plainest on motto. *EVN* 7/30/79, p. 10. Another var. has doubling plainest on TRUST, RTY, and 4; these were mostly retrieved from mint sets. At least 2 other vars., less obvious: *CW* 10/5/77, p. 54, and 11/16/77, p. 60. For Bicentennial coins, see next section; for Kennedy design dated 1977–83, see Sect. xxi below.

xx. HUNTINGTON'S BICENTENNIAL DESIGN (1975–76)

On Oct. 18, 1973, Richard Nixon signed into law an act mandating coinage with distinctive rev. designs for the United States Bicentennial. Five days later, the Treasury announced an open competition for rev. designs. The interlocking stories of the coinage act and the contest appear in detail in Chap. 27, Sect. xix, introductory text.

Despite long-term recognition that buildings generally make poor coin designs, and despite clear evidence that the view of Independence Hall echoes John R. Sinnock's 1926 Sesquicentennial quarter-eagle rev., the judges announced on March 6, 1974, that Seth G. Huntington's "Independence Hall" design was one of the three winners, and would go into production on the half dollars.

Because the authorizing act required production coinage to be ready by July 4, 1975, the Mint Bureau was suddenly under extreme time pressure, both to meet normal coinage needs and to prepare thousands of working dies of the new Bicentennial design. Mint Director Mary Brooks persuaded Congress to pass an amendment, Dec. 26, 1974 (PL 93-541), permitting continuance of the 1974 date on quarters, halves, and dollars through calendar 1975; this saved time and the cost of extra production steps in making thousands of 1975-dated working dies.

Authorities rushed the preliminary stages of the Bicentennial design (plaster model to galvano to master die, master hubs, matrices, working hubs, and working dies) to be ready for a ceremonial striking Aug. 12, 1974. On that day at least three S-less proofs of each denomination were struck. One of the three three-piece sets went to Pres. Ford, Nov. 13, 1974, one to his appointment secretary, and Mrs. Brooks brought one to the ANA Convention in Bal Harbour, Fla. (near Miami Beach), where it was exhibited under armed guard. Ill. *NNW* 8/27/74. This set was reportedly destroyed; the others were expected to be returned for destruction. We only hope that one of them will be rescued for display in the Smithsonian Institution. Failure to do so, as with several previous Mint search-and-destroy operations, testifies to official paranoia about coin collectors.

Though struck during calendar 1975 and 1976, all Bicentennial coins bear the double date 1776–1976; mintages made in the two years cannot be told apart.

Again because of time pressure, the Mint Bureau obtained another year's extension of their deadline for completing the coinage order of silver-clad Bicentennial sets. They need not have bothered: Though the coinage was in fact completed by July 22, 1976, distribution was slow. Of some 11 million three-piece silver-clad sets, less than half reached the public before soaring silver prices made the coins worth more than face value, at which point (1982) the Mint Bureau halted sales.

To date no design revisions have been found for the Bicentennial half dollars (unlike the dollars), and the only rarity is the S-less proof. Many business strikes show weak or illegible letters and stars, from foreign matter clogging the dies and/or weak striking; these command no premium above normal specimens.

The coins were seldom seen in circulation after 1977, by which time half dollars of any kind were fairly unusual in pocket change, for reasons given earlier in this chapter, Sect. xix, introductory text.

HUNTINGTON'S BICENTENNIAL DESIGN

Designers, obv., Gilroy Roberts; rev., Seth G. Huntington. Engraver, Frank Gasparro. Mints, Philadelphia (no mintmark), San Francisco (mintmark S), Denver (D). Mintmark below truncation of neck. Composition, Weight: nickel-clad, as 1971–74; silver-clad, as 1965–70, including same permitted deviation in weight. Diameter, Edge, as before. Authorizing Act, Oct. 18, 1973.

Grade range, probably VERY FINE to UNC. Normally collected only in mint state. No lower grade standards are agreed on, but by analogy with other issues, EXTREMELY FINE should show only tiny rubbed spots with partial mint luster.

5300 1776–1976 No mintmark. Proof. [3+P] Possibly survives.
   Issue of Aug. 12, 1974 (see introductory text). Probably silver-clad. Not to be confused with next. Any purported survivor must be authenticated, as specimens might be simulated by removal of S mintmark from regular proofs, or by buffing or plating normal Philadelphia coins.
5301 1776–1976 Nickel-clad [234,308,000]
   Striking started April 23, 1975. Release began July 7, 1975.
5302 1776–1976 S Nickel-clad [7,059,099P] Proofs only.
   Issued in 6-piece sets, cent to dollar.

5303 1776–1976 D Nickel-clad. [287,565,248]
5304 1776–1976 S Silver-clad. [4,294,081 + 3,262,970P]
Issue of 1976, completed July 22. Distributed in 3-piece sets, quarter to dollar. Originally some 11 million were to be struck; release continued through 1982, ended by soaring silver prices.

xxi. EAGLE REVERSE RESUMED (1977–)

After the Bicentennial celebrations ended, the Mint Bureau resumed making the regular nickel-clad Kennedy/Eagle design, as in 1971–74. Quantities were substantially lower than before, for reasons given in Sect. xix, introductory text.

In 1979, the old S-mintmark punch was worn down, producing filled, blurred blobs, "Type I" S. The Engraving Department replaced it with a clear S, "Type II" S. This new punch appeared on a minority of 1979 S and on all 1980 S dies. Enlarged illustrations of both S's are in Chap. 31. By 1981 the 1979 "Type II" S was already worn, yielding S's like 8's; the replacement punch shows an open S with round serifs free of middle stroke. Mintage figures for these issues are from Alan Herbert, using data released pursuant to the Freedom of Information Act. See also *NNW* 8/21/82 and *CW* 11/10/82, p. 70. Beginning in 1985, each year's master die for proofs contains the S mintmark.

Philadelphia coins beginning in 1980 show P mintmark.

The 1982 P coins lacking designer's initials FG (normally they show between tail and eagle's leg at r.) come from a drastically repolished die. As obv. die is also repolished enough to efface base of 1 in date, most likely the occasion was removal of clash marks, comparable to the 1937 D Three Legs nickel. Most of these 1982's without FG were released by the Cleveland Federal Reserve Bank in Ohio and parts of Indiana and Pennsylvania.

Explanation for the similar 1983 coins is much the same, though less is known about their initial distribution.

In recent years Mint Bureau production statistics have become notable for delays and inconsistencies. Mintage figures quoted below are subject to revision.

The Mint Bureau has repeatedly discussed the possibility of abolishing the denomination, but to date no action has followed. Nevertheless, for reasons given in Sect. xix, introductory text, the end of half-dollar coinage is probably only a few years away.

For the 1982 Washington commemorative issue, see Chap. 39.

EAGLE REVERSE RESUMED

Designer, Engraver, Mints, Physical Specifications, Authorizing Acts, as 1971–74.

Grade range and standards, as 1971–74. Normally collected only in mint state.

5305 1977 [43,598,000]
5306 1977 S [3,251,152P] Proofs only.
5307 1977 D [31,449,106]
5308 1978 [14,350,000]
5309 1978 S [3,127,781P] Proofs only.
5310 1978 D [13,765,799]
5311 1979 [68,312,000]
5312 1979 S "Type I" S. [3,249,175P] Proofs only.
See introductory text. Blurred, filled, or blobby S, ill. Chap. 31.

5313 1979 S "Type II" S. [428,000P] Proofs only.
See introductory text. Clear S. Mintage figure from Alan Herbert.
5314 1979 D [15,814,422]
5315 1980 P [44,134,000]
5316 1980 S [3,554,806P] Proofs only.
S as in 1979 S "Type II." May exist with "Type I" S.
5317 1980 D [33,456,449]
5318 1981 P [29,544,000]
5319 1981 S "Type I" S. [3,749,083P] Proofs only.
S as in **5316** but now worn, closed, like an 8.
5320 1981 S "Type II" S. [314,000P] Proofs only.
Clear S, round serifs away from middle stroke. Mintage figure from Alan Herbert. See introductory text, and *CW* 11/10/82, p. 70.
5321 1981 D [27,839,533]
5322 1982 P [all kinds 10,819,000] Normal.
Struck beginning Oct. 1. Compare next.
5323 1982 P Footless 1; no initials FG.
Discovered by Ron Guth. *CW* 1/26/83, p. 70. See introductory text. At least 50,000 known.

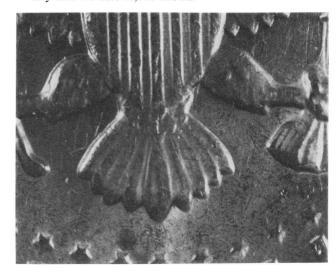

5324 1982 S [3,857,479P] Proofs only.
5325 1982 D [13,140,102]
Struck beginning Oct. 1.
5326 1982 D No initials FG. Presently rare.
Similar to **5323**, but normal 1.
5327 1983 P [all kinds 34,139,000] Modified design. Normal. All letters and date farther from rim than in 1982, in all mints.
5328 1983 P Same. No initials FG. Presently scarce.
Similar to **5326**. Discovered by James McGinn. *CW* 5/25/83, p. 82.
5329 1983 S Modified design. [3,228,648P] Proofs only.
Same comment as to **5327**.
5330 1983 D Modified design. [32,472,244]
Same comment as to **5327**.
5331 1984 P [26,029,000]
5332 1984 S [3,198,999P] Proofs only.
5333 1984 D [26,262,158]
5334 1985 P [18,706,962]
5335 1985 S Proofs only. [3,348,814P]
5336 1985 D [19,814,034]
5337–59 Reserved for future issues. For the Washington 1982 half dollars, see Chap. 39.

CHAPTER 29

SILVER AND CLAD DOLLARS

i. SCOT'S FLOWING HAIR DESIGN
(1794–95)

"Statute One," the Mint Act of April 2, 1792, authorized coinage of silver dollars at the weight of 416 grs. and the awkward fineness of 1,485/1,664 silver, 179/1,664 copper. The coins were supposed to pass at par with Spanish and Mexican dollars (the international trade coin of the day), though the primitive assaying methods available at the time prevented authorities from learning the true Spanish standard, which was 65/72 silver, 7/72 copper = 902 7/9 Fine (compared to the Philadelphia Mint's 892.43+ Fine). But because Spanish and Mexican dollars remained legal tender at par with those coined by federal authority, worn Mexican and South American "pieces of eight" circulated preferentially. Little bullion was brought in for coinage into United States dollars, and only a fraction of those reached circulation.

Albion Cox, Assayer of the Mint, complained that the prescribed fineness was too cumbersome to work with, and tried to strengthen his case by the additional (false) argument that the coins would be undesirably dark. He recommended keeping the silver content at 371.25 grs., while lowering the copper from 44.75 to 41 grs., total 412.5 grs. at 90% or 900 Fine: exactly as Congress was to authorize in 1837. But Congress in 1794 violently opposed any such change, for reasons forever obscure, whereupon Mint Director David Rittenhouse proposed instead to raise the silver content from 371.25 to 374.75 grs. out of the 416—again an increase to 900 Fine. Both Thomas Jefferson and Alexander Hamilton agreed to this notion. Expecting early Congressional approval, Rittenhouse authorized coinage of dollars at this new unauthorized standard—barely within the legal tolerance or "remedy." Congress again ignored the proposal. From the point of view of depositors of silver bullion, this meant about 3.5 grs. of extra silver had to be put into each dollar they received, representing a net loss of about 1% from what they would have received if their dollars had been struck at legal fineness. The biggest such depositor, John Vaughan, computed his total loss at some $2,260, and demanded reimbursement from Congress, which was finally approved in Feb. 1800. Julian {1978} tells the story in detail.

Silver dollars of 1794 were from a single pair of dies cut by Robert Scot, hired in Nov. 1793 as Engraver on the basis of his work on bank-note plates. The head copies that on his 1794 cents, but without the Liberty cap. Vattemare {1861}, p. 25, quotes an ancient (and necessarily false) rumor that the design covertly represented Washington as a youth. Their planchets were made from part of the Bank of Maryland's bullion deposit of July 18, 1794: 94,532 oz. of French minor coins containing 69,692.4 oz. silver; this had to be brought up to 900 Fine.

Because no press heavy enough for dollars had yet been built for the Mint, these coins were struck on the largest one at hand —that originally meant for cents and half dollars. Inspection of the copper proof with stars (Judd 19), which must have received two blows from the dies, suggested that this press would work satisfactorily for business strikes; actual minting proved otherwise. The new dollars were at once criticized for weakness of impression: "the touches of the graver are too delicate, and there is a want of that boldness of execution which is necessary to durability and currency" (New Hampshire *Gazette*, Dec. 2, 1794, cited in Taxay {1966}, p. 106). The fault, however, is less in the die than in press weakness and axial misalignment. On most survivors, obv. and rev. dies were in skew (nonparallel) planes, making the l. side of the coin weaker—especially date, stars at l., and UNITED STATES. Specimens with all these details clear are very rare, forming only a tiny minority. The peculiar mintage figure of 1,758 is believed to represent the acceptable moiety of (probably) 2,000 coined on Oct. 15, 1794, the remaining impressions (242?) being rejected as too weak, and retained in the Coiner's Vault for subsequent use as planchets: Julian {1978}, p. 51. A single example of 1795 shows plain traces of overstriking on one of these weak 1794 dollars; others probably exist.

Hilt {1980} argues that the original 1,758 dollars of Oct. 15, 1794, were only those from the earliest die state (no clash marks, no relapping, no rim breaks, with all stars and letters about equally bold), e.g., Carter:207. In support of his view is Rittenhouse's letter to Edmund Randolph, Secretary of State, Oct. 28, 1794: ". . . A large parcel of blank dollars is ready for coining, waiting for a more powerful press to be finished in order to complete them for currency." *(ASPF* I, p. 317, no. 71.) This largest press (for dollars and medals) was finished in May 1795, after which dollar coinage resumed. Hilt believes that the first dollar delivery thereafter (Warrant 8, May 6, 1795, 3,810 pieces) bore date 1794, along with possibly 1,200 of the May 16 delivery, these last being on planchets of finer texture. Against his view is that the later 1794's are all weaker strikings: the very problem which building a larger press was meant to solve! The question remains moot.

The original 1,758 pieces were turned over to David Rittenhouse for distribution to VIPs and others as souvenirs. Over 100 survivors are traceable in all grades today, including about 5 in mint state and 12–15 other borderline cases. (Survival figures are from a detailed study of pedigree records, begun by this writer about 1956, and later greatly extended, corrected, and amplified by Jack Collins.) One of a pair obtained by Sir Rowland Winn about Oct. 1795 on his visit to the Philadelphia Mint —and continuously traced from that day via the Lord St. Oswald estate to its appearance in Superior Galleries' "Gilhousen" sale (Oct. 1–4, 1973)—was bid up to $110,000, while TV cameras whirred, as a kind of apogee of the spiraling demand for these first-year dollars. The auction house later struck silver one-ounce ingots commemorating the event. (Alas for dreams of wealth: Superior Galleries later retrieved the coin from its bidder, Ralph Andrews, and sold it privately for $127,500 to Jonathan Hefferlin, who later reconsigned it to a Bowers & Ruddy auction where it realized only $75,000.)

Scot's designs continued through mid-Oct. 1795. Some 19 vars. are known from 10 pairs of dies, only three of them common. Possibly 4% of the original mintages survive in all grades.

SCOT'S FLOWING HAIR DESIGN

Designer, Engraver, Robert Scot. Letters by Frederick Geiger. Edge, HUNDRED CENTS ONE DOLLAR OR UNIT (ornaments between words). Diameter, approx. 25/16″ = 39–40 mm. Weight standard, 416 grs. = 26.96 gms. Composition, silver, officially $1,485/1,664 = 892.43+$ Fine, rest copper; actually struck at 90% silver (see introductory text). Authorizing Act, April 2, 1792.

Grade range, POOR to UNC. GOOD: Date and all letters legible (see EXCEPTIONS); devices completely outlined. VERY GOOD: Parts of eye and ear visible; partial hair and feather details. FINE: Partial hair details below ear and near tips; eye complete; partial wing, body, and tail feathers, eagle's eye clear. VERY FINE: At least half hair and feather details, some internal leaf details. EXTREMELY FINE: Isolated tiny rubbed spots only; some mint luster. EXCEPTIONS: The 1794 usually is weak at l. sides, affecting date, l. stars, and UNITED STATES (see introductory text). This weakness may make these details illegible even at the VF level.

5360 1794 [1,758+] Very scarce.
See introductory text. Over 90 of the 100+ survivors are weak as described in EXCEPTIONS. Many low-grade specimens have initials removed from fields. Possibly finest: Neil, Carter:207, UNC., prooflike, $264,000, H. Sconyers, Sup. 1/27/86:1173, $209,000. Coins with vaguely similar rev. and Washington obv. are fantasy pieces; see **1250.**

5361 1795 [all kinds 160,295−] 2 leaves below wings; 1795/ 1195.
Foot of 1 at lower r. of 7. Bolender 1, 10, 16 = Hilt 8H, 8I, 8J. Price for first: paired berries at I(CA). The other 2 vars. are Ex. rare. Mintage figure may include 3,810 dated 1794. Often weak in centers.

5362 1795 Normal wide date.
6 vars. Often weak in centers.

5363 1795 Close date. Very scarce.
Bolender 11, 3, 9, 4 = Hilt 2B, 2C, 2D, 3D. Date no wider than that ill. Usually in low grades. Carter:209, UNC., $15,400. Price for any but the first; Bolender 11 (Ex. rare) has 2 inner berries nearest tail feathers. Often on defective planchets. Watch for specimens overstruck on 1794 dollars (the only one seen to date is a Bolender 9).

Ex J. W. Garrett: 678. Courtesy Bowers & Ruddy Galleries, Inc.

5364 1795 Triple leaf below each wing; paired berries below D.
Bolender 7, "20" = Hilt 5G, 6G. Price for former (ill.); that pictured is a prooflike presentation coin: Breen {1977}, pp. 32–33. Hilt attributes these vars. and next to John Smith Gardner. Often weak in centers.

5365 1795 Same, paired berries below F.

4 vars. Price for Bolender 5 = Hilt 11-K (ill.), with long plain die cut in field l. of top curl point. Often weak in centers. Often on defective planchets.

ii. THE SCOT-ECKSTEIN DRAPED BUST/SMALL EAGLE (1795–98)

This new design represented the fulfillment of a dream for the new Mint Director, Henry William DeSaussure. On his accession, he had named his two ambitions: to place gold coinage into circulation; and to improve the design of all denominations, particularly of silver coins. To this purpose, he engaged the illustrious portraitist Gilbert Stuart, who submitted a (now lost) drawing of Mrs. William Bingham (née Ann Willing) as Ms. Liberty. John Eckstein (local artistic hack) translated this into "models" (some kind of prototypes for device punches?) for Robert Scot, losing whatever subtleties the Stuart drawing may have possessed—explaining why Stuart's family kept his role secret for decades: Snowden {1861}, p. 177; *AJN* April 1887, p. 95. Eckstein received $30 on Sept. 9, 1795, for his two "models." The second of these is likely to have been the small eagle on clouds. Use of olive and palm branches in the wreath probably represents a bow to DeSaussure's Southern origins, immediately becoming an anachronism on his resignation.

Two pairs of working dies were hastily completed, one with the obv. device punch too far to l. (crowded against stars), the other with head normally centered but with slivers from central areas (in Ms. Liberty's hair), that had probably fallen out of the die during initial hardening. Some 42,738 coins were struck from these two pairs of dies during the last two weeks of Oct. 1795. One of the two eagle dies **(5366)** cracked and was discarded; the other **(5367)** was occasionally briefly reused until it wore out with a 1798 obv. Several prooflike "specimen strikings" of 1795 survive, with many more mint-state business strikes, mostly dated 1795; these have lately become the object of intense competition among type collectors.

Hilt argues that the 23,368 of Oct. 17, 1795 (Warrant 46), were from the dies here called **5366**, the 19,370 of Oct. 24 (Warrant 49) and the 4,550 of Jan. 30, 1796, were from the dies here called **5367**, making 47,288 in all. He assumes that Scot failed to add the final 6 to the first three 1796 obvs. until later; this is fairly likely but cannot be proved. Dates on working dies normally got final digits just before hardening. Thomas Bingham was paid $48 for 96 letter punches, Oct. 19, 1795: presumably letters A B C D E F I L M N O R S T U Y, digits 1 7 8 9, in four sizes, plus replacements. In all denominations, 9 was inverted to make final 6.

The disheartened, disillusioned, and sick DeSaussure re-

signed his directorship in the face of a hostile Congress, many of whose members wanted to abolish the costly Mint in favor of the former practices: profitably passing copper coins ordered from British token factories; continuing use of foreign silver and gold coins, which were after all legal tender. Elias Boudinot succeeded him before the end of 1795.

Coinage during 1796 was larger in total amount, but was executed under increasing difficulties: die breakage; continuing anxiety over possible abolition of the Mint; and one of what proved to be a series of annual epidemics of yellow fever, forcing closure of the Mint each fall for a couple of months, and killing valuable personnel.

Previous coins showed 15 obv. stars; but on June 1, 1796, Tennessee was admitted to the Union as the sixteenth state, and subsequent dies bore 16 stars on other denominations. This change reached the silver dollars only in 1797, suggesting that the 1796-dated dies were all completed before Tennessee's admission.

Mintage in 1797 was very limited, for reasons similar to 1796. On Feb. 28, some 342 were struck, which have been tentatively identified as the Small Letters coins. These are from the worn rev. of 1795 **(5367)**, always weak so that survivors look about a full grade lower on rev. than on obv. No mint-state specimen is even rumored. Hilt's interpretation of this and later delivery figures differs (see main text).

The Large Letters coins (obv. stars 9 l., 7 r.) are conjectured to comprise the 4,941 struck in the two deliveries of May 26 and June 30, 1797. Both dies cracked, the obv. severely; the marginally usable rev. was resurrected for use with one of the 1798 obvs.

Those with stars 10 l., 6 r. are identified with the 2,493 delivered Aug. 12–28, just before the annual yellow fever epidemic. This variety's rev. rusted but failed to be cleaned up for reuse. Possibly there was too little time during preparations for closure of the Mint to regrind this die and dip it into the tub of hot grease kept for the purpose; possibly Scot or Eckfeldt thought it was too far gone.

Little is known about the two Small Eagle vars. dated 1798. It is uncertain if they represent the initial deliveries of this year or an emergency issue of winter 1798/99 following hasty reopening of the Mint after the cold weather had killed off the mosquitoes and stopped the epidemic. That with 13 stars has the cracked Large Letter rev. left over from 1797; the rarer one with 15 stars (evidently an incomplete 1796–97 die with final digit omitted) has the worn-out rev. of 1795. There is no way to know if both vars. were struck in the same month, or which came first. Evidence from the condition of rev. dies indicates only that both followed their 1796–97 usages.

This entire group of 13 vars. has probably the lowest average grade level of survivors. Some vars. are unobtainable even in EF.

THE SCOT-ECKSTEIN DRAPED BUST/ SMALL EAGLE DESIGN

Designers, Engravers, Robert Scot and John Eckstein, after Gilbert Stuart (obv.). Letters by Thomas Bingham. Mint, Philadelphia. Physical Specifications, Authorizing Act, as before.

Grade range, POOR to UNC. GOOD: Date and all letters legible, devices complete in outline. VERY GOOD: Traces of internal details of hair, drapery, and feathers; eye and ear at least partly visible. FINE: Partial hair details including curls and strands l. of ear; eye and ear completely clear; few major drapery lines clear; half wing-feather details. VERY FINE: Over half hair details; 3/4 of wing-feather details. EXTREMELY FINE: Isolated tiny rubbed spots only; inner lines in feathers and leaves clear, partial mint luster. EXCEPTIONS: Small Letters vars. dated 1797–98 all have rev. much weaker than obv.

5366 1795 [42,738+] Centered head.
  Bolender 15 = Hilt 1A. Always with slivers from die at hair. Hilt says [23,368] Oct. 17, 1795. Carter:213, UNC., $24,200.

5367 1795 Head too far l.
  Bolender 14 = Hilt 2B. Hilt says [19,370] Oct. 24, + [4,550] Jan. 30, 1796 = [23,920] total. Carter:212, UNC., $23,100. That ill. is a prooflike presentation piece: Breen {1977}, p. 33.

Ex J. W. Garrett: 680. Courtesy Bowers & Ruddy Galleries, Inc.

5368 1796 [all kinds 72,920] Small date and letters. Very scarce.
  Bolender 1, 2, 3 = Hilt 4B, 3B, 5B. Rev. of **5367**. Price for either of first 2; last (dot in field above 1, obv. of **5370**) is prohibitively rare. Usually in low grades. Hilt believes these were the 11,731 delivered March 30–May 27, 1796 (Warrants 59–63).

5369 1796 Small date, large letters, double leaf below wing. 2 known.

Bolender 6 = Hilt 3D. Outer berry below NI. The double leaf is within wreath opposite NI. Compare next. Both specimens show die broken as ill., area l. of break weak. Discovered by this writer about 1954. Hilt conjectures that these were the 390 delivered Feb. 13, 1796 (Warrant 56), and estimates 5 survivors.

5370 1796 Small date, large letters, triple leaf below wing.
  Bolender 4 = Hilt 5E. Dot above 1 in date; no outer berry at NI. The triple leaf is within wreath opposite NI. 2 die states, later and scarcer (Bolender 4A) with obv. die reground so that some outer curls are incomplete. Hilt believes these are the 21,920 struck June 14–July 29, 1796 (Warrants 65, 68, 69, 71).

5371 1796 Large date, small letters.
  Bolender 5 = Hilt 6C. The lump (die chip) above IC is always present but sometimes very small; on final impressions it is much larger than on that ill. Hilt believes these are the 34,249 coined Aug. 27–Dec. 22, 1796 (Warrants 72–78).

5372 1797 [all kinds 7,776] Stars 9 + 7, small letters. Very rare.
  Bolender 2 = Hilt 8B. Rev. of **5367**, always weak; see introductory text. That ill. qualifies as EF and probably is one of 3 finest known. In 1951 I tentatively identified these as the 342 of Warrant 81, Feb. 28, 1797. Hilt believes them the 7,776 of Feb. 28–Aug. 28 (Warrants 81–98). Carter:218, "AU," $6,600.

5373   1797 Stars 9 + 7, large letters.
Bolender 1 = Hilt 8F. Many stages of die cracks. Central obv. often weak and looks unfinished; obv. field irregularities are from repeated clash marks. In 1951 I tentatively identified these as the 4,941 of May 26–June 30, 1797. Hilt believes they were made in 1798.

5374   1797 Stars 10 + 6.
Bolender 3 = Hilt 9G. Robison:823, UNC., $10,500. In 1951 I tentatively identified these as the 2,493 of May 26–June 30, 1797 (Warrants 90, 94); Hilt believes all were made in 1798. A small minority shows heavy die rust; these were probably made after the epidemic.

5375   1798 13 stars.
Bolender 1 = Hilt 10F. Rev. of **5373,** badly cracked. Usually in low grades. See introductory text.

5376   1798 15 stars. Rare.
Bolender 2 = Hilt 7B. Rev. of **5367,** worn out, always weak.

Ex J. W. Garrett: 687. Courtesy Bowers & Ruddy Galleries, Inc.

Usually in low grades. See introductory text. "Dupont," Bareford:412, AU, is possibly finest, followed by Carter:221, $6,600.

iii. SCOT'S HERALDIC DESIGN
(1798–1803)

Robert Scot originally made his adaptation of the Great Seal of the United States in 1796, for the quarter eagles intended to be issued alluding to Tennessee's admission to the Union as the sixteenth state (they have 16 stars above eagle). Following a practice which remained traditional at the Mint as late as 1915, he made working hubs of the same designs for other denominations: half eagles and eagles in 1797, dismes and dollars in 1798, half dismes in 1800, half dollars in 1801, quarter dollars in 1804. All these contained the same heraldic blunder or tasteless military brag in showing the bunch of arrows in eagle's dexter or more honorable claw (observer's l.), the olive branch for peace in the sinister or less honorable claw (observer's r.). See Chap. 24, Sect. iii, introductory text. Working hubs for the larger denominations lacked the full bunch of arrows, berries on branch, stars above eagle's head, and protruding end of stem; these details had to be entered into each working die by hand.

The earliest dollars with this new rev. design have large 8 and knobbed 9, the latter from the 1796–97 font. They were minted early in the year, but the quantity is uncertain. All that is known is that Thomas Bingham cut a new 8 punch (small 8, for the Pointed 9 coins), and that Mint Director Elias Boudinot paid him 50¢ for it on Feb. 1, 1798; there is no record when the working obvs. bearing it went into use.

Arrangement of stars above eagle's head requires attention. On at least seven dollar dies of 1798–99, and smaller numbers of eagle, half-eagle, quarter-eagle, and disme revs., stars are in intersecting straight lines forming diamond-shaped configurations: Hilt's "cross pattern." Hilt derives this from the Great Seal (as copied on the backs of current dollar bills) and attributes all these working dies to John Smith Gardner, though the time element makes this unlikely as Gardner had long since left the Mint. More likely all come from an apprentice letterer in the Engraving Department, who either left the Mint in 1798 or was thereafter required to use the "arc pattern." (The 14-star "cross pattern" dies used on 1804 quarter eagles and 1804–5 dismes have the same letter punches as those of 1798, suggesting that they were left over from then.) The "arc pattern" (standard through 1807 on all denominations) has stars in a curved row of six, paralleling clouds, a second row of five parallel (in an arc of a smaller concentric circle), with twelfth and thirteenth stars, respectively, at beak and behind eagle's head. Earliest "arc pattern" revs. have twelfth star directly l. of beak; later ones have it below and usually touching beak.

The first four Small 8 obvs. had very widely spaced dates; that with widest L I B E R T Y (**5379**) is believed first, as it shares a "cross pattern" rev. with the Knobbed 9 group. The die was immediately reground, probably to efface clash marks, and lasted only briefly; survivors are very rare, as are Bolender 18 and 22 (incl. in **5380**) with huge arc break down through E of STATES. Later obvs. have dates spaced progressively closer; one of the last (High 8) outlived seven revs.

In 1799, some 11 obvs. and 17 revs. were combined to produce 23 vars. The earliest obv., evidently a 1798 die left over without final digit and only completed at hardening, is the famous Irregular Date: final 9 much too low, tilted crazily to r. (A common occurrence in Scot's day, doubtless explaining also both the High 8 obv. and the 1798 with 15 stars. See also Chap. 28, Sect. ii, introductory text.) The Irregular Date comes with three revs., all short-lived: **5386,** a "cross pattern" die left over from 1798; **5387,** a rusted normal die; and **5388,** with the famous 15 Stars blunder: the regular "arc pattern" began with seven stars in top row, six in second, plus the two at beak and behind head. On discovery of the blunder, Scot greatly enlarged two end clouds to conceal the two extra stars, but some points remain clear.

This rev. also comes with what is probably the second die of the year, the famous 1799/8: an obv. originally made up for the 1798 Wide Date group but mislaid or for some other reason unused. This overdate die also comes with two other revs., Bolender 1 (heavy die flaws around RI) and Bolender 2 (die flaws at ER and a bar in cloud below E of STATES—part of a misplaced E?). Aside from these, the other major vars. requiring comment are the Five Stars Facing obv., presumably a blunder rather than a deliberate experiment, and the "No Berries" rev. (Bolender 11, 12). This last is the final state of the same rev. die first seen on Bolender 16 and then with the Five Stars Facing obv., after repeated regrindings to remove clash marks.

The 16 vars. of 1800 (from 12 obvs. and 11 revs.) consist mostly of wide and close dates with variously repunched letters. The famous "AMERICAI" shows stroke of an extra letter at claw; under a glass, this appears to be the r. leg of a mostly effaced A.

Mintage reported for 1801 consisted largely of coins dated 1800; similar backdating was the rule through 1804. Aside from the proof restrikes dated 1801–3 and the fantasy coins dated 1804 (see next section), the only real rarities in this group are 1802/1 Bolender 9 (die chip in field between B and curl point), 1802 Bolender 5 (Wide Even Date), and 1803 Bolender 3 (Small Low 3, obv. field chip next to twelfth star). Only five revs. in all were made for the 1801–3 period, two of them (dollar specialists' "A" and "B" revs.) reused briefly and repeatedly. Only the two final vars. (1802 Divided Date and 1803 Large 3) are common; die-state evidence proves that these followed all the other 1803's, presumably forming the entire mintage [19,570] reported for 1804, in addition to much of the quantity reported for 1803.

The Mint Director's Report listed [321] for 1805: These were dollars of previous years, found among Spanish dollars deposited for coinage. They were not melted, merely redelivered: Stewart {1924}. This bookkeeping entry was nevertheless long mistaken for actual coinage, inspiring forgers to concoct at least one dollar with date altered to 1805.

Only in recent years have early silver dollars begun to attract collector attention as intense as the smaller denominations— despite the shortcomings of available reference books. Were some future researcher to produce a book on this series in a class with Sheldon {1958} on 1793–1814 cents, doubtless early dollars would eventually rival the cents' popularity.

SCOT'S HERALDIC DESIGN

Designer, Engraver, Robert Scot, obv. after Gilbert Stuart, rev. after the Great Seal of the United States. Mint, Physical Specifications, Authorizing Act, as before.

Grade range, POOR to UNC. GOOD: Date and all letters legible except motto on scroll; devices completely outlined. VERY GOOD: Parts of eye and ear visible; partial hair and feather details; few letters of motto show. FINE: Eye and ear completely clear; some hair details in curls and l. of ear; partial drapery lines; half wing feathers, partial motto. VERY FINE: Over half hair details, about ¾ feather details, motto completely legible. EXTREMELY FINE: All shield lines clearly separated; isolated tiny rubbed spots on highest points only; partial mint luster. EXCEPTIONS: On a few vars. with buckled or broken rev. die, motto may not be complete in VERY FINE.

5377 1798 [all kinds 327,536] Knobbed 9, cross pattern rev. Bolender 4, 5, 6, "32" (obv. B-1, rev. B-4). Price for B-6 (ill.): date high, closely spaced, 8 leans l., base of A(M) solid. Miles, Robison:1867, UNC., $8,500. Other vars. are very rare.

5378 1798 Knobbed 9, arc pattern rev. Bolender 3, 7. Price for B-3 (ill.), date wide with 79 closer; B-7 is very rare.

5379 1798 Pointed 9, widest date, cross pattern rev. Very rare. Bolender 17 (rev. of B-6, above, reground). Usually in low grades. See introductory text. Only one known in earliest state, before obv. die reground; usually, first obv. star too small, all l. stars thin, some curls incomplete.

5380 1798 Pointed 9, widest date, arc pattern rev. 8 vars. See introductory text. The Pointed 9 continues through 1799.

5381 1798 Close date, cross pattern rev.
4 vars. See introductory text. Compare following.

5382 1798 Same, but high 8.
3 rev. vars. See introductory text.

5383 1798 Close date, arc pattern rev., 5 berries.
4 vars. Compare next 2.

5384 1798 Same, but high 8.
Obv. of **5382**; 4 rev. vars.

5385 1798 Close date, arc pattern rev., 4 berries.
Bolender 8.

5386 1799 [all kinds 423,515] Irregular date, cross pattern rev.
Bolender 15. Final 9 too low, leans crazily r.; usually in low grades. See introductory text.

5387 1799 Irregular date, arc pattern rev., 13 stars. Very rare.
Bolender 13. Usually in low grades. Sieck-Harte:296, EF, may be finest.

5388 1799 Irregular date, 15 rev. stars. Rare.
Bolender 4. Same obv.; rev. as next. See introductory text.

5389 1799/8 Rev., 15 stars.
Bolender 3. The spur on lower part of loop of 9 is in the punch. Robison:1869, UNC., $5,000.

5390 1799/8 Rev., 13 stars.
Bolender 1, 2. See introductory text. Auction 81:1592, $11,000.

5391 1799 Normal date, stars 7 + 6, 5 berries.
13 vars. Compare last 5 and next 2.

5392 1799 "No berries."
Bolender 11, 12. Drastically reground rev. of next.

5393 1799 Stars 8 + 5. Rare.
Bolender 23. Seldom offered UNC.: Boyd, WGC, 1949 ANA, Bareford:415, $21,000; Auction 82:1742, $6,250; Carter:226, $9,350.

5394 1800 [all kinds 220,920+] Normal.
16 vars., some with minor repunchings on letters. Part of reported mintage was doubtless dated 1799; many more were delivered in 1801 but dated 1800.

5395 1800 "AMERICAI"
Bolender 11, 19. Part of an extra A at claw: See enlarged detail. Price for B-19, obv. die flaw near first star. B-11: Carter:228, UNC., $9,900.

5396 1801 [54,454−]
4 vars. Part of reported mintage was dated 1800. For the brilliant proof restrikes with beaded borders, see next section.

5397 1802/1 [all kinds 41,650+] Close date.
Bolender 1, 4, 9. Last (ill.) is rarest; see introductory text. Price for either of the others.

5398 1802/1 Wide date.
Bolender 2, 3. Numerals notably farther apart than in preceding.

5399 1802 Wide even date. Very rare.
Bolender 5. Obv. T perfectly formed, unlike next. For the brilliant proof restrikes with beaded borders, see next section.

5400 1802 Divided date.
Bolender 6. Date spaced 18 02; r. foot of T in LIBERTY broken off. All struck in 1804, with **5402**.

5401 1803 [all kinds 85,634−] Small 3.
4 vars. See next.

5402 1803 Large 3.
Bolender 6. Includes [19,570] struck in 1804, with **5400**. Rarely with brilliant prooflike surfaces; not to be confused with the brilliant proof restrikes with beaded borders: See next section.

iv. KNEASS'S "1804" DOLLARS AND THEIR BRETHREN

After over a century of nonsense written and talked about these legendary rarities, the truth became manifest at the 1962 ANA Convention when James C. Risk described Spink's exhibit of the King of Siam's 1834 proof set in original case, containing an "original" 1804 dollar (**5406**) and a plain 4 1804 eagle (**6848**). What follows summarizes, extends, and updates conclusions reached in Newman-Bressett {1962} and Breen {1977}.

Eckfeldt and Dubois {1842}, by illustrating an "1804" dollar without any descriptive comment, informed alert coin collectors of the day that such a piece actually existed. This had its desired effect: On May 9, 1843, Matthew Adams Stickney traveled from Boston to Philadelphia, bringing rarities, including **1118**, to trade to the curator of the Mint Cabinet Collection in exchange for an 1804. (Other collectors apparently followed his path but left no documentary evidence.)

Well before the Civil War, the 1804's were recognized as unlike all earlier dollars (except the still unreleased proof restrikes dated 1801–3). Obv. and rev. dies are from the old Scot hubs, both with hand strengthening; borders are of round beads within raised rims, like Kneass's dismes of 1828, half dismes and gold of 1829, half cents and quarters of 1831, and cents of 1834, but nothing earlier. As on many coins of 1834 but none of 1794–1824, the 4 has a flat top. Their single obv. die comes with two revs. That found on "original" or "first type" 1804's has S T widely spaced, and space between clouds below l. serif of E; eight specimens survive, of which all began as brilliant proofs, most were cleaned or impaired, and one (a pocket piece) wore down to FINE grade. The second rev. die, found on "restrike" or "second type" 1804's, has ST closely spaced, and space between clouds about below center of E; of these much more below.

On Nov. 11, 1834, the State Department ordered two cased sets of "specimens of each kind [of domestic coin] now in use, whether of gold, silver, or copper," for diplomatic presentation to the King of Siam and the Sultan [Imām] of Muscat (John Forsyth, letter to Mint Director Samuel Moore, reprinted in Breen {1977}, p. 57). As neither dollars nor eagles had been coined since 1804, either Dr. Moore or someone in the State Dept. ordered that this fictitious date appear on these denominations. Special Agent Edmund Roberts delivered the set in crimson morocco case to Sayid Sayid bin Sultan, Imām of Muscat, in 1835, as part of a crescendo of diplomatic gift exchanges which culminated in 1839 with the delivery of a full-grown lion and lioness to the Washington Zoo. The other set, in yellow morocco case, went via Roberts to King Ph'ra Nang Klao of Siam, April 5, 1836. Thereafter it passed to his successors Kings Mongkut and Chulalongkorn, by whom it was given to ancestors of a later British owner, who sold it to Spink's. In 1979 Lester Merkin sold it into a private collection for approximately $1 million.

Roberts originally also carried two similar sets for delivery to two other rulers with whom the State Dept. was specially interested in opening trade talks. Though he managed to obtain trade agreements with Siam and Muscat, Roberts died of dysentery in Macao, and the other sets (intended for the Emperor of Cochin-China and the Mikado of Japan) were returned to the Mint. Coins from the Muscat proof set eventually reached a British collector, being dispersed in Watters 1917, though the case was gone. In addition to the coins for these four proof sets, Mint authorities struck at least four others, presumably for reserve in the event that the State Dept. would make similar orders, and for trade with the few serious coin collectors who had anything outstanding for the Mint Cabinet Collections.

At some unknown date no later than 1858, unidentified parties with keys to the Coiner's Vault retrieved both original "1804" dies and the old Scot device punch, which had chipped before its 1834 use so that curl tip atop head was missing. They used this to make three new obvs., backdated 1801, 1802, and 1803. On the last two, the broken curl tip was lengthened by hand. By the time these 1801–3 restrikes were made, the rev. had developed a rust pit midway between next to lowest wing feather and top leaf of olive branch. On the original 1804 dollars this rust pit is missing; on the "1801" and "1803" it is very minute; on the "1802" it is larger, nearly half the size of a berry, suggesting that this was made months or years later. All the "1801" and "1803" restrikes, but no others, show a small depression in space between UM and shield, from a sliver of foreign matter adhering to rev. die, indicating that they were made about the same time. Blanks are atypical; weights range from 419–423 grs. = 27.15–27.41 gms., unlike either the original 1804's (struck at 416 grs. = 26.96 gms.) or the normal dollars of the 1850s (412.5 grs. = 26.73 gms.). Edges are blundered, suggesting that—like the 1804 restrikes described below—they were originally made with plain edges, then after the scandal of 1858 concealed until someone could find the original edge dies and jury-rig a Castaing machine to impart edge lettering to the finished coins.

William Idler (who had long been an agent for whichever Mint people were peddling restrikes and fantasy coins) concealed the 1801–3 restrikes until early 1876. When his son-in-law Capt. John W. Haseltine began showing them around (*CCJ* 3/1876, p. 83), local collectors rejected the coins on the theory that they had probably been fabricated within the last few months. Haseltine's protégé Samuel Hudson Chapman said in Lyman:13 (1913) that "Mint officials" had been offering them for sale in May 1876 when he entered the coin business with his brother Henry. Which Mint officials? We may never know for certain, though Patterson DuBois (long Curator of the Mint Cabinet) is the most likely candidate. DuBois, long a defender of Mint sales of pattern and experimental coins, was Chapman's source of much other inside information, and the Chapman brothers sold what seems to have been his collection as part of their "Eavenson" auction, 1903. See also Breen {1977}, p. 250.

On the other hand, we do know which Mint official peddled the restrikes of the 1804 dollar in 1858. As the original rev. had either been rusted, broken, discarded, or destroyed, or possibly seized with the 1801–3 copy obvs., the makers of the 1804 restrikes found an unused replacement die in the Coiner's Vault for combination with the original 1804 obv. They made at least 5 impressions; for the reasons above, these had plain edges. At least one of this earliest batch was overstruck on a cut-down 1857 Berne (Switzerland) Schützenfestthaler (commemorative shooting-festival thaler), Yeoman 4-S. These thalers were struck at 392 grs. = 25.4 gms.; the solitary 1804 plain-edge coin (minus the telltale Swiss edge) weighs only 381 grs. = 24.7 gms.: far too light for a legal dollar. Theodore Eckfeldt, then barely 21, had earlier been fired from the Mint for theft, but was rehired as night watchman to avoid disgracing his family, which had included Mint officials since 1792 (see Chap. 17, Sect. vii, introductory text). Eckfeldt connived with personnel in the Coiner's Department to make these and other coins, which he peddled through Dr. Montroville W. Dickeson's store on North Second St. near Buttonwood St. After Eckfeldt had sold four plain-edged 1804 restrike dollars at $75 each, a scandal broke out. Mint Director James Ross Snowden demanded that all be returned; Robert Coulton Davis (the Mint's favorite druggist) named names and locations, and after Snowden retrieved the coins, Davis got his reward: pattern and experimental coins unmatched in any other collections, even unto a unique brass gilt proof of the 1849 double eagle. Snowden placed one of the 1804 plain-edged restrikes in the Mint Cabinet Collection (it is on display today in the Smithsonian Institution), and reportedly ordered melting of the others.

Because this "Class II" restrike is more sharply struck than the original, it was for many years transposed with the latter in the Mint's display case, enabling Curators William Ewing DuBois and Patterson DuBois to claim falsely (for the benefit of later owners of "1804" restrikes) that lettered-edge impressions from this second rev. die were "originals." One of the curators made many electrotype copies; these show traces of the coin's Swiss undertype.

However, beginning apparently in 1859, and continuing into July 1860, Eckfeldt and friends struck more 1804's from the same dies, using normal dollar blanks somehow obtained from the Coiner's Department; they lettered the edges of the finished coins to avoid a replay of the 1858 scandal. Today at least six are known, proofs or impaired proofs, all with varying amounts of blundering on edge letters, some with traces of die chatter (doubling) on parts of rev., all with central weakness, and a rust spot at U which varies in size. From Eckfeldt they went to William Idler, later to Haseltine; some were shipped to respectable European auction houses to give them plausible sources. On July 30, 1860, Mint Director Snowden confiscated the 1804 die (among others) and sealed them all in a carton which remained in his office vault until May 18, 1867, when his successor Henry R. Linderman opened the carton and resealed it after making an inventory (partly quoted in Breen {1977}, p. 254), only to reopen it again in 1868, make a few impressions from some of the dies (not including the 1804: There was no usable rev.), and order all the dies to be destroyed.

The roster of 1804 "Class I" or "Original" dollars follows. All are pictured in Newman-Bressett {1962}; other ills. are mentioned below.

1. Chief Coiner Adam Eckfeldt, Mint Cabinet (1838), SI. Badly cleaned proof, nicked around ERT. Clain-Stefanelli {1970}, fig. 30.

2. Adam Eckfeldt, Mint Cabinet coll., by trade May 9, 1843, to Matthew Adams Stickney, Col. James W. Ellsworth, Wayte Raymond, William Cutler Atwater, Louis Eliasberg estate. Ill. Eckfeldt & DuBois {1842}. Cleaned, rubbed, impaired proof.

3. Adam Eckfeldt, Nov. 1834, State Dept., April 5, 1836, King Ph'ra Nang Klao of Siam (in cased proof set of 1834), King Mongkut, King Chulalongkorn, British pvt. colls., Spink's via Lester Merkin, $1 million (1979), Elvin I. Unterman Ill. Newman-Bressett and Breen {1977} as part of set. Brilliant gem proof.

4. Adam Eckfeldt, Nov. 1834, State Dept., Oct. 1, 1835, Imām Sayid Sayid of Muscat (in cased proof set of 1834), pvt. colls., C. A. Watters estate:227 (with partial proof set of 1834), Henry Chapman, Virgil Brand estate, Armin W. Brand, Charles E. Green, C. F. Childs estate (Chicago). Blue-toned choice proof.

5. Adolph Weyl 10/13/1884:159 (Berlin), S. H. & H. Chapman, James Vila Dexter, Roland G. Parvin, H. G. Brown, William Forrester Dunham, Charles M. Williams, Harold Bareford:424, $280,000, RARCOA, Leon Hendrickson and George Weingart. Ill. herein and in Breen {1977}, p. 251. Brilliant proof, dipped. Dexter (1836–99) stamped his minute initial D into cloud below O.

6. Unknown lady (ca. 1845–48), allegedly bought from the Mint; pvt. coll., E. Harrison Sanford, Lorin G. Parmelee, Byron Reed, OCL. Brilliant proof, flat stars.

7. Teller Henry C. Young (Bank of Pennsylvania, ca. 1850, supposedly retrieved from a deposit at face value), Joseph J. Mickley, William A. Lilliendahl, Edward Cogan, William Sumner Appleton, 1905, Mass. Historical Society, MHS I:625, $77,500 (1970), Chicago pvt. coll., Reed Hawn, Richard E. Raneau. EF–AU, poorly cleaned.

8. Retrieved "over the counter" at exchange office of Edward Cohen, Richmond, Va., ca. 1865, Col. Mendes I. Cohen, Henry S. Adams, Lorin G. Parmelee (pvt. sale, 1878), H. G. Sampson, Maj. William Boerum Wetmore, S. H. & H. Chapman, James L. Manning (1921), Elmer S. Sears, Lammot duPont, Willis duPont. Included in the robbery of the duPont coins, Oct. 1967.

The single "Class II" or "First Restrike" 1804 dollar is the one in SI with plain edge, overstruck on a Swiss shooting thaler, mentioned above. Clain-Stefanelli {1970}, fig. 31.

The roster of "Class III" 1804 dollars (restrikes with lettered edge) follows. All are pictured in Newman-Bressett {1962} as well as where mentioned.

1. "Koch & Co., Vienna," Capt. John W. Haseltine, O. H. Berg, Thomas Harrison Garrett, John Work Garrett, Johns Hopkins Univ., Garrett II:698, $400,000, Pullen & Hanks, Long Beach 2/5/82:1076, $190,000, Sam Colavita, Tex. pvt. coll., Einstein:1736, $187,000, Rarities Group. EF.

2. "Unnamed English source," Haseltine (exhibited 1/24/1876), Haseltine's "Centennial Sale" I:194 (3/30/1876), Phineas Adams, Henry Ahlborn, John P. Lyman, Waldo Newcomer, Col. E. H. R. Green, A. J. Allen, F. C. C. Boyd, Percy A. Smith, Amon Carter, Sr. & Jr., Carter:241, $198,000, Tex. pvt. coll. EF, cleaned. Exhibited at 1979 ANA Convention.

3. Haseltine (1883), G. M. Klein, J. Colvin Randall, Haseltine, Robert Coulton Davis, John N. Hale, R. H. Mull, Henry P. Graves, his daughter Mrs. Fullerton, Ben H. Koenig ("Fairbanks Coll."), Samuel Wolfson, Norton Simon, J. H. T. McConnell, Jr. EF, cleaned. W. E. DuBois falsely called it "original" in a letter 9/17/1878, quoted in Breen {1977}, p. 253; ill. there and herein. Exhibited at 1985 ANA Convention.

4. Mint Director H. R. Linderman, James Ten Eyck, Lammot duPont, Willis H. duPont. Brilliant proof. Involved in the Oct. 1967 armed robbery of the duPont coins; retrieved 3/31/82. On loan at the ANA Museum, Colorado Springs. At Ten Eyck:394, Mehl quotes an affidavit of July 1, 1887, in which the Director's widow Emily Linderman said the price had been so high to her late husband as to require installment payments.

5. W. Julius Driefus (Alexandria, Va.), Mint Director Oliver C. Bosbyshell, Isaac Rosenthal, Col. James W. Ellsworth, Wayte Raymond, Guttag Bros., Farran Zerbe, Chase Manhattan Bank Money Museum, ANS. VF, nicked, probably someone's pocket piece. Accompanied by a letter attesting genuineness, signed by Mint Engraver Charles E. Barber and Mint Cabinet Curator R. A. McClure, 1894.

6. William Idler, Haseltine, H. O. Granberg, William H. Woodin, William Cutler Atwater, Will W. Neil, Edwin Hydeman, A. Kosoff, reoffered with the Dr. Judd coll.:45b ("Ill. Hist.," 1962), WWCI (Tucker & Hamrick), B&R, Continental Coin Co., "Swiss pvt. coll.," Superior Galleries, 2/79, Jerry Buss:1337, $308,000, A. E. Bebee. EF, rubbed and scratched. Rust on eagle's head. Cf. CW 2/14/79, p. 1; 1/5/83, p. 57; Sports Illustrated 6/18/79.

Newman's pungent comment about the 1804 dollars remains as valid today as in 1962: "The 'King of American Coins' is an impostor, but was made for a King." Its publicity has made it possibly the most famous of American coins, though neither the rarest nor the costliest.

KNEASS'S "1804" DOLLARS AND THEIR BRETHREN

Designers, as before. Engravers, "1804," William Kneass, after Scot; "1801–3," unknown workmen. Mint, Philadelphia. Physical Specifications, as in introductory text. Authorizing Act, none. (May be legally held.)

Grade range: Irrelevant. Proofs and impaired proofs only.

5403 1801 Proof restrike. As ill. Ex. rare.
Bolender 5. Possibly 4–6 known. See introductory text. Always with obv. crack at date as ill. Note peculiar modern

numerals with vertical thick elements as in Bodoni type face. 1) Lyman, Granberg, Boyd, WGC, Newport Balboa S&L, "Autumn":303, $42,000, Ed Hipps, NERCA 1982, NYMet:1575, $46,000. Dipped. Ill. herein, *Coinage* 5/66, and in Breen {1977}, p. 250. 2) Newcomer, Green, Roe, Neil, Carter:238, $55,000, Tex. pvt. coll. Obv., additional crack, rim through B to central curl.

5404 1802 Proof restrike. As ill. Ex. rare.

Bolender 8. Possibly 6–10 known. See introductory text. In date, 2 copied from one of the "Fancy 2" half dollars in the 1820s; original 1, 8 and 0 punches retrieved from Coiner's Vault. 1) Lyman, Granberg, Boyd, WGC, "Autumn":304, $40,000, Robison:1884, $43,000, Auction 84:171, Einstein: 1734, $39,600. Ill. herein and in Breen {1977}, p. 250. 2) Newcomer, Green, Roe, Neil, Carter:239, $60,500, Tex. pvt. coll.

5405 1803 Proof restrike. Ex. rare.

Bolender 7. Possibly 6–10 known. Original numeral punches. Heavy rust marks around fourth star, lighter ones at 18. 1) Lyman, Granberg, Boyd, WGC, Golden II:3049, "Autumn":305, $40,000, Robison:1885, $39,000, Auction 84:172, Einstein:1735, $41,800. Ill. herein and in Breen {1977}, p. 250. 2) Newcomer, Green, Roe, Neil, Carter:240, $68,750, Tex. pvt. coll. 3) Auction 86:738, $55,000.

5406 1804 "Class I," or "Original." [4+P] Proofs only. 8 known.

Issue of Nov. 1834. For explanation and roster see introductory text. Authentication for any purported new specimen (not on roster) is mandatory. About 1900, John E. Kennedy, of Lowell, Mass., made many forgeries by altering genuine dollars of 1800 and possibly other dates. These have normal dentilated borders, not beaded borders. Newman-Bressett

{1962}, pp. 104–5. John Adams Bolen signed a similar piece, now in the ANS collection.

5407 1804 "Class II," or "First Restrike." Plain edge. Unique?

Issue of 1858. 1) Coiner's Dept. workmen, Theodore Eckfeldt, seized by Mint Director James Ross Snowden, Mint Cabinet Coll., SI. Ill. in Newman-Bressett {1962}. Beware electrotype copies. See introductory text.

5408 1804 "Class III," or "Second Restrike." Lettered edge. 6 known.

Issue of 1859–60. See introductory text for explanation and roster. Same comment as to **5406** about altered dates.

v. GOBRECHT'S FLYING EAGLE DESIGN (1836–39)

Christian Gobrecht (1785–1844), renowned bank-note-plate engraver and medalist, was long interested in the Mint engravership, going so far as to make two relief models which remained in the Mint for decades (they are gone or unidentified). Partly for the extra income, partly to keep his name before Mint officialdom, he furnished numerous letter and numeral punches during the 1820s. When Chief Engraver William Kneass suffered a stroke in 1835, Gobrecht succeeded him as Second Engraver, receiving an assignment from Mint Director Robert Maskell Patterson to create improved and if possible new devices for all denominations. During 1836–40, these had to be sandwiched in among brief slack periods; most of Gobrecht's time went to multiplying working dies of then current designs to accommodate a greatly increased output of coins: silver from melted old-tenor coins and new mines; gold from Africa, the Carolinas, and Georgia, and later also from French indemnity payments and the James Smithson bequest (which later was used for founding what is now the Smithsonian Institution).

Correctly perceiving the silver dollar or monetary unit as an important item in the nation's public image (even if not an important part of its circulating currency), Mint Director Patterson insisted that the designs which Gobrecht was to translate into original dies for this denomination should be of exceptional artistic merit. Influenced by a variety of seated goddesses depicted on British and other coins, Patterson chose this concept above several other possibilities, and obtained a drawing by Thomas Sully that eventually—in a much modified version—was translated into three dimensions in Gobrecht's four working obvs., 1836–39. Gobrecht's flying-eagle rev. followed Titian Peale's drawing of the Mint's pet eagle "Old Pete" (ca. 1830–36), which had suffered a broken wing and death after perching on a flywheel that began to rotate without warning.

Gobrecht signed his first working obv. die C.GOBRECHT F. in field between rocky base and date. (F = *Fecit*, 'he made it,' traditional on signed medals.) Some 18 proofs were struck in Nov. or early Dec. 1836, as samples for VIPs, with a rev. showing 26 stars in field. Criticisms of the new design denounced Gobrecht's arrogance in signing his die, though Mint Director Patterson had approved. This "name below base" obv. went back into the vault of Chief Coiner Adam Eckfeldt, from whence it was retrieved about 1858 for making restrikes (below). Originals have plain edge and die alignment I (below); restrikes have die alignment III or IV.

Somewhat more subdued criticism attacked the 26 stars, but here the explanation was easier: The authorities were reviving an original custom of the 1790s, when the number of stars on coins matched the number of states. There were 13 large stars for the Original 13 states, and 13 smaller ones for the states subsequently admitted, anticipating the admission of Michigan to the Union as the twenty-sixth.

Gobrecht's next working die for dollars showed his name on the rocky base. On Dec. 31, one warrant authorized delivery of 400 of the new dollars, with 1,034,200 halves (probably including 1,200 of the new type with reeded edge), 60,000 quarters, 250,000 dimes, and 340,000 half dimes, all at the old standard: 416 grs. = 26.96 gms., 892.43+ Fine. The same day, a second warrant authorized delivery of 600 more new dollars (at the same standard); these went to the Bank of the United States and public circulation. Survivors are found in all grades. All have plain edges and die alignment I (below).

On March 31, 1837, 600 additional dollars from the same dies left the Coiner; these also went into circulation. They are, however, from the new standards: 412.5 grs. = 26.73 gms., 900 Fine, pursuant to the Act of Jan. 18, 1837. They have plain edges and die alignment II (below). No documentation explains why this design was abandoned; possibly criticism from top officials forced Patterson's action.

On July 5, 1838, the Coiner delivered 25 proof silver dollars. These are from a new obv. similar to that of 1836 but without Gobrecht's signature; the 13 stars are restored to obv. field, as on smaller denominations. Rev. is from a die similar to that of 1836 but without stars in field. Like their predecessors, these dies went to the Coiner's Vault, to be retrieved two decades later for making restrikes. Originals have die alignment I; restrikes, III or IV (below).

On Dec. 31, 1839, the Coiner reported delivery of 300 silver dollars. These are of the same design as 1838; all are proofs, but some went into circulation. This obv. also went to the Coiner's Vault, and several vars. of restrikes followed in 1858–59. Originals have die alignment I; restrikes, III or IV (below).

During ensuing decades, dollars of these years became objects of intense demand as rarities, sometimes called patterns. Only recently (Breen {1977}, Julian {1982}) has their actual status become established. The 1,600 dated 1836 with name on base, delivered pursuant to Director's Warrants with other regular issue coins, including those sent to the Bank of the United States for release into circulation, were beyond doubt regular issues. The 300 delivered in 1839 at legal standards, and mentioned in the Director's Annual Report with other coins of regular issue, likewise qualify as regular issues, though minted as proofs. About the similar 1838's there is doubt primarily because the tiny mintage was omitted from the Director's Report; however, that negative argument loses its force when we consider that the half cents of 1836–48, quarter eagles of 1841, and other proof-only issues of regular design were also ignored in Director Patterson's reports, though clearly belonging to the regular series because included in proof sets as issued from the Mint. Other vars., with die alignments III and IV, in silver and copper, have all proved to be restrikes.

With the great collector demand came official realization that the means existed for satisfying it. Numerous collectors who wrote or visited the Mint in search of these coins offered items to the Mint Cabinet Collections in trade. Inevitably, officers and employees felt under pressure to accommodate first their friends and acquaintances (and especially VIPs), then the general public. Between 1858 and July 30, 1860, Coiner's Department personnel found all four Gobrecht obvs. and both revs., and made many kinds of proof restrikes. Some of these exactly imitated the originals except for die alignment and weight (all were at the new standard); others combined the 1836 obvs. with the 1838–39 starless rev., or the 1838–39 obvs. with the 1836 starry rev., making combinations Gobrecht never had in mind. The most comprehensive discussion is in Breen {1977}, pp. 64–69, 258–59, rendering obsolete that in Breen {1954D}, though that monograph remains a usable sourcebook for the preliminary history of this series. A more systematic tabulation is in Julian {1982}; Julian's numbers are used herein as cross-references.

The quickest way to test if a Gobrecht dollar of any date is an original or a restrike is die alignment. Four alignments are distinguishable, and no specimen is ambiguous as to which was used. To test for die alignments I and III, hold the coin (obv. up) by the edges at 9:00 and 3:00 between thumb and finger, rotate along this *horizontal* axis, and notice position of eagle. If eagle is still belly up, test for die alignments II and IV by holding the coin (obv. up) at 12:00 and 6:00 edges between thumb and forefinger, rotate along this *vertical* axis, and notice position of eagle. These procedures will yield one of the four alignments below.

Alignment I: Eagle flies "onward and upward," two pellets flanking ONE DOLLAR are level after rotation along *horizontal* axis. Originals only, 1836–39; same as most U.S. coins since 1792.

Alignment II: The exact opposite. Eagle flies "onward and upward," two pellets flanking ONE DOLLAR level after rotation along *vertical* axis. Second original issue, March 1837.

Alignment III: Eagle flies horizontally, two pellets flanking ONE DOLLAR not level (l. one low) after rotation along *horizontal* axis. Restrikes only. This alignment copies the 1856–58 Flying Eagle cents, on which eagle is intentionally horizontal.

Alignment IV: Eagle flies horizontally, two pellets flanking ONE DOLLAR not level (l. one low) after rotation along *vertical* axis. Restrikes only.

In some vars., restrikes are less rare than originals; in others, no originals exist, and the restrikes are of extreme rarity. Auction records have at last begun to reflect collector recognition of this reality rather than 19th-century moralistic objections to the skulduggery that created them. For many years, auction catalogs and fixed-price lists have minimized or omitted descriptions which would allow collectors to conclude that certain vars. are restrikes, evidently for fear that this information might discourage potential customers. Now that dealers are beginning to recognize that these fears are groundless, catalogs are more informative, and we are better able to approximate the actual populations of the rarer vars.

GOBRECHT'S FLYING EAGLE DESIGN

Designers, obv., Thomas Sully; rev., Titian Peale. Engraver, Christian Gobrecht. Mint, Philadelphia. Diameter, 25.5/16" = 39 mm. Edges, 1836 plain, 1838–39 reeded; exceptions (restrikes) as noted. Weight standards, originals of 1836 only, 416 grs. = 26.96 gms.; all others, 412.5 grs. = 26.73 gms. Composition, silver: originals of 1836 only, 892.43+ Fine; all others, 900 Fine. Authorizing Acts, originals of Dec. 31, 1836, Act of April 2, 1792; other originals, Act of Jan. 18, 1837.

Grade range, POOR to ABOUT UNC.; unworn specimens are proofs. GOOD: Date and all letters except LIBERTY legible. VERY GOOD: Traces of gown details, few feather details. At least three letters of LIBERTY legible. FINE: All letters of LIBERTY legible (some will be weak); partial details of hair, cap, upper drapery; at least half wing-feather details. VERY FINE: Over half gown and feather details; LIBERTY fully clear, scroll edges visible. EXTREMELY FINE: Isolated tiny rubbed spots only, mostly at knees, breasts, tops of wings, and eagle's breast. At least some traces of proof surface should remain. NOTE: Most surviving proofs have been cleaned; pristine (uncleaned) proofs bring a high premium over others. Beware of abrasion marks from baking soda paste or similar mechanical cleaners.

5409 1836 Name below base; starry rev. Original. [18?] Ex. rare.
Judd 58; Julian 1. 416 grs. = 26.96 gms. Die alignment I: See introductory text. Not to be confused with next. None authenticated in many years.

5410 1836 Name below base; starry rev. Restrike. Very rare.
Judd 58; Julian 6, 7, respectively die alignments III and IV: See introductory text. 1979 ANA:1037, $20,000. Possibly 25–30 survivors. Later impressions sometimes show knife-rims as on ill. of next; some show cracks through OLLA and tops of NITED STATES O. See Breen {1977}, p. 258. It is not yet known which die alignment is rarer. The copper restrikes (Ex. rare) have die alignment III.

5411 1836 Name below base; starless rev. Restrike. Ex. rare.
Judd 63; Julian 9. Die alignment III or IV. 1) Anthon, T. H. Garrett, John Work Garrett (1976):252, $19,000. 2) Woodin, Newcomer, Boyd, Farouk, Kaplan, Baldenhofer, Ostheimer, Merkin 9/68:329. 3) Maj. Lenox R. Lohr (ill.).

5412 1836 Name on base; starry rev. First Original. [1,000] Rare.
Judd 60; Julian 3. Weight, fineness as **5409**. Die alignment I: See introductory text. Issue of Dec. 31, 1836. Not to be confused with either of next 2. Usually worn, from the 600 paid out by the Bank of the United States. Pristine proofs are very rare.

5413 1836 Name on base; starry rev. Second Original. [600] Very rare.
Judd 60; Julian 4. 412.5 grs. = 26.73 gms., 900 Fine. Die alignment II: See introductory text. Usually worn; pristine proofs are Ex. rare.

5414 1836 Name on base; starry rev. Restrike. Plain edge. Scarce.
Judd 60; Julian 11, 12. Early impressions have die alignment III or more often IV; line in die slants up pointing between AT. Later impressions from repolished rev. have die alignment III; partial knife-rims, line in die slants up pointing to O(F); repunching on 83 faded out; cracks developing through OLLA and NITED STATES O. Over 2/3 of the Gobrechts offered at auction or fixed prices in the last 30 years belong to this number, including many circulated pieces (pocket pieces? spent during one of the later financial panics?).

5415 1836 Name on base; starry rev. Restrike. Reeded edge. Ex. rare.
Judd 61; Julian 14. Die alignment III or IV, unchecked. 1) DeWitt Smith, Granberg, Woodin, Newcomer, Baldenhofer:993, discovery coin, *NUM* 5/11, p. 179. 2) Farouk:1713.

5416 1836 Name on base; starless rev. Restrike. Plain edge. Ex. rare.
Judd 65; Julian 15. Die alignment III or IV, unchecked. 1) William J. Jenks, J. W. Garrett II:700. 2) Ralph J. Lathrop, Jay:173. 3) Farouk:1715.

5417 1838 Starless rev. Original. Reeded edge. [25P] Ex. rare.
Judd 84; Julian 2. Die alignment I: See introductory text. None seen in many years. Not to be confused with next 3.

5418 1838 Starless rev. Restrike. Reeded edge. Very scarce.
Judd 84; Julian 17, 18, respectively die alignments III, IV: See introductory text. Possibly 60–80 survive. Carter:244, $22,000. Later die states show knife-rims, obv. occasionally with field rust marks, rev. cracked through NITE and AMERI. Compare next. A single specimen is known overstruck on an 1859 dollar (clear date): Louis Werner (ca. 1958), A. M. Kagin. Others may exist. Kagin {1961}.

5419 1838 Starless rev. Restrike. Plain edge. 6–8 known?
Judd 85; Julian 19. Die alignment III or IV. Auction 80:801, $23,000. See partial roster in Breen {1977}, p. 259. Quality of ills. in many auction catalogs renders pedigree tracing doubtful especially after coins have been repeatedly cleaned.

5420 1838 Starry rev. Restrike. Plain edge. Ex. rare.
Judd 88; Julian 22. Die alignment III or IV. Late cracked

rev. as in **5414.** 1) Maris, Parmelee, Woodin, Newcomer, Boyd, Col. Curtis, Farouk, Randall, Baldenhofer, Ostheimer, Merkin 9/68:332 (ill. above and in Adams-Woodin {1913}). 2) Lohr, Miles, "Autumn":310, $12,000. The similar reeded-edge coin reported by Adams-Woodin (their no. 62 = Julian 25) is unverified.

5421 1839 Starless rev. Original. Reeded edge. [300P] Rare.
Judd 104; Julian 5. Die alignment I: See introductory text. Comprises under ⅓ of proof 1839's offered, but the majority of worn ones.

5422 1839 Starless rev. Restrike. Reeded edge. Scarce.
Judd 104; Julian 26. Die alignment III; may also exist with alignment IV (Julian 27): See introductory text. Later strikings show knife-rims and various states of cracks through NITED S and MERI. Over ⅔ of the proof 1839's offered belong to this number, with a smaller number of worn ones.

5423 1839 Starless rev. Restrike. Plain edge. Ex. rare.
Judd 105; Julian 28. Die alignment III; may exist with alignment IV. 1) Granberg, Woodin, Newcomer, Boyd, Menjou I:2083, Col. Curtis, Farouk, Baldenhofer, Ostheimer, Merkin 9/68:334. Lint mark below O(NE); many file marks at rounded rims (inflicted at the Mint to remove irregular sharp knife-rims: Breen {1984}, pp. 379, 398, 421, 424). 2) Jay, Miles, "Autumn":312, $12,000. Border weak below E DOLLA. 3) Allenburger, Donlon, 1975 ANA, Treglia, Pine Tree Auctions, 1978. Lint mark above space between 39. One other may survive.

5424 1839 Starry rev. Restrike. Plain edge. Ex. rare.
Judd 108; Julian 31. Die alignment III; heavily cracked rev. 1) Parmelee, DeWitt Smith, Granberg, Woodin, Brand, Boyd, Farouk, pvt. coll. 2) W. W. C. Wilson, Lenox Lohr, Miles, "Autumn":313, $15,000. *NUM* 5/11, p. 185. Rumored to exist also with reeded edge: Julian 32.

vi. HUGHES'S LIBERTY SEATED DESIGN, NO MOTTO (1840–66)

All the silver dollars of 1840–73 were made from obv. dies exemplifying the "improvements" inflicted by the Anglo-American miniaturist Robert Ball Hughes upon a hapless Ms. Liberty. Compared with the original Sully-Gobrecht conception of 1836–39, this is a sorry mess indeed: Besides chipping away much of the rock, and enlarging the scroll bearing her name, Hughes chose to fatten her arms, flatten out most of her female contours, and cover up much of her exposed skin in the interest of "Respectability," forcing her to carry a bulky cloak or himation over the crook of her elbow in what must have been a singularly uncomfortable position. (One commiserates with Hughes's unidentified model.) For no imaginable reason except possibly that some Treasury official preferred the familiar design on the Cap Bust half dollars of 1807–36, Gobrecht's magnificent flying eagle was abandoned in favor of the old John Reich "sandwich-board" eagle (as Cornelius Vermeule {1971} calls it). See Chamberlain {1958} for further details.

Mint Director Robert Maskell Patterson alleged that these changes were intended to improve striking quality; the coins prove that his claim was either wishful thinking, incompetent guesswork, or an outright lie. Dollars of 1840–65, like the quarters, dimes, and half dimes of this design, are usually flat uneven strikings, regularly weak on head, parts of drapery, eagle's neck, upper wing feathers, and claws; worst of all, perhaps, on 1854–57 survivors.

Mintages were limited. Dollars circulated very little, except in California where quantities were shipped beginning in 1854 as "small change." Shipments eastward of immense quantities of California gold forced down the world price of gold reckoned in silver dollars, raising the price of silver reckoned in gold dollars to a level which made silver dollars worth well over face value in bullion. Depositors thereafter hoarded silver, sending little to the Mint for coinage. Bullion dealers and speculators exported many coins and melted many more, especially 1850–53. Mintages of 1851–52 for circulation were very limited, and as early as 1858 Mint employees and the collectors begging for specimens recognized that these dates were already rare; for which reason proof restrikes followed quickly.

Even after the Mint adopted the new lower weight standard for smaller silver coins (Act of Feb. 21, 1853), mintage of silver dollars continued at unchanged weight, on the mistaken assumption that this was a fundamental obligation of government; these dollars circulated little and mostly went to melting pots. The dates 1854–57 are far rarer than their mintage figures suggest; no dollars were coined for circulation in 1858, and mintages 1862–65 remained low. Mint Director Snowden sold individual specimens at $1.08 each.

The Engraving Department shipped dollar dies to New Orleans for 1846–52 and 1859–61 inclusive, but the Southern branch released coins from them only in 1846, 1850, 1859, and 1860. The 1859 O and 1860 O are available in heavily bag-marked UNC., for a price, from nine bags (9,000 coins) found in Treasury vaults in 1962–63. Ten pairs of dollar dies went to the San Francisco branch in 1859, but most remained unused; two obv. dies were shipped there for 1860 coinage, two more for 1861, four more for 1862, but no more silver dollars were made there until 1870.

Many proofs of 1840–50 and 1858 are thought to be restrikes from original dies; but restrikes or no, they are very rare. The dozen proofs dated 1853 are restrikes made in late 1862 or early 1863; they first came to collector notice in the McCoy sale (1864). They have a rev. die earlier used on 1862 proofs.

In 1861–62, many earlier silver dollars which had accumulated at the New York Subtreasury were shipped to the Philadelphia Mint for melting and conversion into other denominations. This explains both the undue rarity of many dated 1848–59, and the bullion source of much Philadelphia coinage 1862–65. Most of the latter was exported to Latin American and East Indian ports.

HUGHES'S LIBERTY SEATED DESIGN, NO MOTTO

Designer, Robert Ball Hughes, obv. after Sully and Gobrecht, rev. after Reich. Engravers, Hughes and Gobrecht. Mints, Philadelphia, New Orleans (mintmark O), San Francisco 1859 (S). Mintmarks below eagle. Diameter, 1.5″ = 38.5 mm. Edge, reeded. Composition, silver 900 Fine. Weight, 412.5 ± 1.5 grs. = 26.73 ± .097 gms. Authorizing Act, Jan. 18, 1837.

Grade range, POOR to UNC. GOOD: Date and all letters legible except LIBERTY. VERY GOOD: LI TY legible; traces of gown and feather details. FINE: LIBERTY fully legible though center weak; foot and sandal clear and separate; partial feather details, most of shield border visible, claws flat but separate. VERY FINE: Over half gown details, ¾ feather details, at least half leaf details; LIBERTY and scroll completely clear. EXTREMELY FINE: Isolated tiny rubbed spots only; scroll edges raised; partial mint luster or prooflike surface. NOTE: Beware "sliders," cleaned EF-AU coins offered as "UNC." No trace of wear on UNCs. EXCEPTIONS: Weak UNCs. of 1854–57 and some other dates may be flat on head and breasts, tops of wings (most of all below ST), and talons; they will show mint surface on weak areas.

5425   1840 [61,005 + ?P]
At least 3 minor positional vars. of date on business strikes; 2 minor rev. vars. on proofs (ill.). The rev. on most original (and some restrike) proofs of 1840–49 has 2 minute points on r. slanting edge of final A: Garrett (1976):256, $5,250; Kern, Carter:246, $6,600.

Ex J. W. Garrett: 701. Courtesy Bowers & Ruddy Galleries, Inc.

5426   1841 [173,000 + ?P] Normal stars.
At least 2 minor positional vars. of date on business strikes. See next. Proofs have rev. 1840–49 described above. Kern, Carter:247, $3,960.
5427   1841 Small stars. Proofs only. Ex. rare.
Obv. drastically repolished, like the dime 3235. Probably rev. of 5425 proofs; none examined recently enough for certainty.
5428   1842 [184,618 + ?P]
At least 3 minor positional vars. of business strikes. Proofs have rev. described at 5425, and die file marks near thumb of shield hand and crook of elbow, but this obv. reappears on business strikes. "Fairfield":1045, $2,300; Carter:248, $6,875.
5429   1843 [165,100 + ?P] Heavy date.
Normal or often with traces of repunching on 4 and/or 1. At least 3 minor positional vars., often prooflike. Proofs have rev. described at 5425. Carter:249, $10,450.
5430   1843 Thin numerals.
Hairlike serifs; repunching on 4; heavy rev. die file marks in white stripes of shield. "Gilhousen":1296, others. Other vars. possible.

5431   1844 Quadruple obv. stripes. [20,000]
Doubled obv. die, plainest at shield. Rev. irreverently called "armpit" var. from many hairlike crisscross die file marks between wings and body. Usually in low grades. Compare next.

5432   1844 Triple obv. stripes. [?P] Proofs only? Very rare.
All seen are proofs or impaired proofs, with the rev. described at 5425. Enl. photos. Kern, Carter:250, $7,150. Ron

Severa (*Gobrecht Journal* 11/77, p. 31) reports seeing 2 badly worn examples; these may have begun as proofs.

5433   1845 [24,500 + ?P] Normal date.

3 vars., one with traces of repunching on 4: "Gilhousen":1298. Usually in low grades.

5434   1845 Heavily repunched 84. [?P] Proofs only. Very rare. Rev. as described at **5425.** Carter:251, $7,425.

5435   1846 Normal date. [110,600 + ?P]

At least 6 minor positional vars., without or with minute traces of repunching atop 18; often prooflike. 2 vars. of proofs, without or with traces of repunching on date; compare next.

5436   1846 Blundered date. [?P] Proofs only. Very rare.

So-called "overdate." Date first entered much too low and oblique, then largely effaced and corrected; parts of upper halves of 846 show in lower halves of final position of date (see enlargement). Rev. as described at **5425.** Carter:252, $6,875.

5437   1846 O [59,000]

3 pairs of dies: O normal, heavier, or thin and weak. 4 pairs of dies were shipped for 1847, four more for 1848, one obv. for 1849; all remained unused. UNCs. are usually bag-marked.

5438   1847 [140,750 + ?P]

At least 6 minor positional vars., often prooflike but bagmarked. Proofs have the rev. described at **5425:** Boyd, WGC, Kern, Carter:255, $6,600.

5439   1848 Normal. [15,000]

Usually in low grades.

5440   1848 "Badge var." [?P] Proofs only. Very rare.

Die chips on drapery below breast suggesting badges, decorations, or an oversized semicolon; rev. described at **5425.** Lamborn, "Fairfield," 1978 Grand Central, Auction 82:1744, $3,500; Carter:256, cleaned, $5,280.

5441   1849 [62,600 + ?P]

Earliest business strikes have "extra hair" (die file marks below chin); these fade out. Auction 82:1745, UNC., $2,000. Proofs lack this feature but have traces of rust at lower obv. border; rev. described at **5425.** Randall, Garrett (1976):266, $7,500; Carter:257, $7,425.

5442   1850 [all kinds 7,500 + ?P] Closed 5.

Knob joins cusp. Business strikes rare (many probably melted); proofs Ex. rare. 1978 ANA:1141, AU.

5443   1850 Open 5.

Knob away from cusp; repunching on base of zero, like **4820.** Business strikes and proofs. Fairfield:1063, $4,900. To date no proof shows the rev. described at **5425,** but others remain unchecked, e.g., Carter:258, $9,350. Restrike proofs have heavy crack through base of date; 2 or 3 seen. Many business strikes were melted.

5444   1850 O Closed 5. [40,000] Very scarce.

2 obvs.; revs. among 11 old dies on hand. Early impressions (rev. of 1846) show repunching on mintmark; this fades, while obv. develops cracks through stars, rev. later rusts. Usually in low grades. Rarer than mintage figure suggests (melted by bullion dealers?). 4 obvs. shipped for 1851, two for 1852, none used; all old revs. remained on hand.

5445   1851 Original, high date. [1,300 + ?P] Rare.

Rev. of 1850. Two obvs. made, 10 revs.; apparently only one pair of dies used for business strikes and original proofs, the second obv. retrieved from Coiner's Vault, 1858–59, to make proof restrikes. Fairfield, Robison:1904, UNC., $7,000; Auction 85:1265, $11,500. Original proofs are of the highest rarity; discovery coin, W. J. Jenks (1883):131. Compare Morgenthau 404:417 (7/39) and the listings in Breen {1977}, p. 93.

5446 1851 Restrike, centered date. Proofs only. Very scarce. Rev. of 1858–59. Robison:1905, $8,000; Carter:260, $9,350. The copper strikings are from the same dies.

5447 1852 Original. [1,100 + ?P] Rare.
One obv., 3 revs. made; business strikes (mostly UNC.) have only one rev. Earlier impressions show many nearly horizontal and fewer slanting die file marks within rev. white stripes of shield; later strikings (after die repolished?) show none of these, only one minute spur from r. edge of rightmost (sixth) pale gules, or "red" stripe. Original proofs (Ex. rare) have rev. white stripes filled with confused die file marks except at a small triangular sector in leftmost. Compare next.

5448 1852 Restrike. [?P] Proofs only. Very scarce.
Several rev. vars.: a) rev. of 1858–59, silver and copper strikings; b) rev. described at **5425**, silver only. Some (ill.) have pronounced knife-rims. Garrett (1976), Robison:1907, $11,000; Auction 82:1746, $14,000; Carter:261, $9,900. Other rev. vars. possible.

5449 1853 [46,110 + 12P]
2 obvs. made, one rev. The 2 deliveries, [39,000] April 21 and [7,110] Dec. 29, cannot be told apart. Proofs (12 silver, 4 copper) are all restrikes, made late 1862 or early 1863 (see introductory text); obv. die file marks from rocky base above 53: Breen {1977}, p. 262. Ely, Garrett (1976):271, $8,500; Ostheimer, LM 9/68:350, 1977 ANA:1794, $5,600, Robison:1908, $8,000, Auction 82:747, $6,500.

5450 1854 Base of 4 repunched. [33,140]
Repunching fades. Business strikes only, coined June 29. On Nov. 11, some 10,000 were shipped to California (probably to the branch mint) as "small change." Survivors 1854–57 are normally weak on head and parts of wings. One obv., 2 revs. for business strikes; 5 4 apart.

5451 1854 Spur from rocky base above 5. [?P] Proofs only.
Only the one var. of proofs; 5 4 apart. The spur looks like part of serif of an extra 4; it is visible to the naked eye. Ely, Garrett, Robison:1910, $4,750; Carter:263, $5,280.

5452 1855 [26,000 + ?P]
Business strikes (all from one pair of dies) coined June 29.

Many of these were shipped to California. A second obv. was used for proofs, with 2 revs. (one of them the 1854 proof die); possibly 60 proofs survive, some impaired. Randall, Garrett {1976}, Robison:1912, $6,500; Carter:264, $5,060.

5453 1856 [all kinds 63,500 + ?P] Normal date.
Slanting 5 only. 5 pairs of dies for business strikes. Often with "extra hair" (die file marks below chin); compare next. Most were shipped to California. Usually with flat heads: See introductory text. Proofs (only a few dozen survive) have plain die lines in field above ITE and between ES. Robison:1913, $7,000; Carter:265, $7,700.

5454 1856/4 Ex. rare.
Plain straight line (crossbar of 4) within 6. NN 47:1147–48. Later die states, with traces of overdate gone, price as preceding.

5455 1857 [94,490 + ?P]
2 pairs of dies for business strikes; often prooflike, usually weak at head, upper wings, etc. Director's Report includes the 94,000 coined June 6–30, but not the 490 of May 29. Most were shipped to California. 2 vars. of proofs, both very rare; that more often seen has the 1856 proof rev., the other a rev. found on some business strikes and reused in 1858. Robison:1914, Proof, $5,750 (which rev.?).

5456 1858 [No record; estimated 80P?] Proofs only. Rare.
2 pairs of dies made, only one obv. used; proofs have either the 1856–57 rev. described at **5453** or the 1859 rev.: Breen {1977}, p. 110. Restrikes are rumored but unconfirmed; they probably have a still different rev. The estimated mintage came to the Chapman brothers, possibly as early as 1876, from one of their Mint contacts, believed to be Patterson DuBois. Many survivors are impaired.

5457 1859 [256,500 + 800–P]
Business strikes: 3 obvs., 5 revs. made, fewer used. Proofs (microscopic repunching on base of 1) have at least 2 rev. dies, one of them that of 1858; many were melted as unsold.

5458 1859 O [all kinds 360,000] Very thin numerals.
Hairlike serifs; mintmark normal or heavy. In all, 9 obvs., 3 revs., plus other old revs. left over from 1846. Badly nicked mint-state survivors are plentiful from 3 Treasury bags (3,000 coins) released 1962–63.

5459 1859 O Normal date, heavy mintmark.
Same comments. Top and base of mintmark about as thick as corresponding parts of O in DOL.

5460 1859 O Heavy date, thin mintmark.
Same comments. Top and base of mintmark hairlike.

5461 1859 S Medium S. [20,000] Normal date.
10 pairs of dies shipped, possibly 3 used. Usually in low grades; very rare near mint state. Auction 80:809, UNC., $8,500; NN 57, Auction 81:1595, UNC., $4,000; Auction 82:789, UNC., $2,800.

5462 1859 S Obviously repunched 18. Ex. rare.
Repunching plain at bases. Ivy Cambridge:1243. On later states repunching fades out; these will price as **5461**.

5463 1860 [217,600 + 527P]
Minor positional vars. in business strikes. Originally 1,330 proofs made; 527 sold, rest melted. May exist with new rev. of **5467**.

5464 1860 O [all kinds 515,000] Heavy numerals.
Several minor rev. vars.; mintmark varies in heaviness. Common in nicked mint state from 6 Treasury bags (6,000 pieces) released 1962–63.

5465 1860 O Very thin numerals, heavy mintmark.
Hairlike serifs; rev. like **5460**. Same comment as to **5464**.

5466 1860 O Very thin date and mintmark.
Obv. as last, rev. like **5460**. Same comment as to **5464**. Rarer than last 2. Hirt:784.

5467 1861 New rev. [77,500 + 400−P]
Claws and arrowheads more delicate than formerly (ill. of **5468**); may also exist with old rev. as 1840–60. In all, 7 obvs., 8 revs. for business strikes, mostly unused. Auction 82:1752, UNC., $3,900. Of 1,000 proofs struck, at least 600 were melted as unsold.

5468 1862 [11,540 + 430+P]
One obv., 2 revs. for business strikes; rare in all grades, very rare in or near UNC. Ill. at **5467**. 1978 ANA:1154, UNC., $2,550. Of 550 proofs coined, 430 were sold in sets, most others melted in 1863 as unsold. Most business strikes were exported: See introductory text.

5469 1863 [27,200 + 460P]
Business strikes (same comment as to **5468**) have centered date; "Fairfield":1108, UNC., $2,100. Both vars. of proofs have date low in field.

5470 1864 [30,700 + 470P]
Business strikes (same comment as to **5468**) have date above center, with 6 4 free; on 3 proof obvs., date is lower or central. "Fairfield":1112, UNC., $2,900.

5471 1865 [46,500 + 500P]
Business strikes (same comment as to **5468**) have date low or central (3 pairs of dies made). Auction 81:777, UNC., $2,400.

5472 1866 No motto. Proofs only. 2 known.
Judd 540. Fantasy coin, like **4042, 4928.** 1) Robert Coulton Davis (in set), H. O. Granberg, Woodin, Newcomer, Boyd, Wayte Raymond, Col. E. H. R. Green, King Farouk, Lammot duPont, Willis duPont (ill.), stolen Oct. 1967. 2) S. H. & H. Chapman (4/22/1899), Brand, Koenig ("Fairbanks"), Wolfson:1425, $18,000, Jay:182, $15,000, Delp:91, $32,000, A-Mark, NERCG, pvt. coll.; exhibited at 1979 ANA Convention and in late 1979 at the Money Museum of the National Bank of Detroit. *CW* 9/12/79, p. 26. Compare Chap. 27, Sect. ix, and Chap. 28, Sect. x, introductory texts.

vii. LONGACRE'S LIBERTY SEATED, WITH MOTTO (1866–73)

Pursuant to the Act of March 3, 1865, the silver dollar was included among the other silver coins which had to bear the motto IN GOD WE TRUST: See Chap. 27, Sect. x, and 28,

Sect. xi, introductory texts. Mintage of motto coins began in Jan. 1866 at Philadelphia with 300 proof sets delivered Jan. 17, 23, and 29 in batches of 100 each. In March 1866, six new dollar revs. with motto were shipped to the San Francisco branch, along with six revs. apiece of quarter dollars, half dollars, and the three largest gold denominations. (Not all these dies were used during the year.)

Proofs of the same design exist dated as early as 1863. These were long believed prototypes. They originally came in three-piece sets: quarter, half, and dollar dated 1863 (Judd 335, 342, 345); 1864 (Judd 386, 391, 396); and 1865 (Judd 425, 429, 434), along with similar copper and aluminum strikings. The 1864–65 sets were first published in Parmelee:1336–38, 1347; the 1863 set in Woodside:129 as "unique," the 1864 as "5 struck," the 1865 as "7 struck." Adams-Woodin 378, 371, 367 claimed five sets struck dated 1863; this figure is from Col. A. Loudon Snowden 1909–10 when Woodin obtained quantities of pattern and experimental coins from him on donating the 1877 gold pattern $50's to the Mint Cabinet collection. As there are two gold motto sets dated 1865 (half eagle, eagle, and double eagle, Judd 445, 449, 452), long believed true transitional issues, I was prepared to accept at least the 1865 silver sets as such.

However, in 1973 I identified the 1863–5 motto-dollar revs. as those earlier used on the two latest regular proof vars. of 1866, the first two of 1867, and both of 1868 (Breen {1977}, pp. 121, 125, 128, 131, 133, 136). More revealing still, "Fairfield":27 proved to be a hitherto unseen 1865 dollar with motto, overstruck on an 1866 dollar with clear date. This opens the possibility that all were struck in 1867–68 for Mint Director Henry R. Linderman (see roster of "Class III" 1804 dollars in Sect. iv, introductory text).

Most Philadelphia dollars in collectors' hands, 1866–70, are proofs or impaired proofs. Several gem UNC. business strikes of this period have turned up in original proof sets in Mint wrappers, reflecting less venality than carelessness at the Mint. On the other hand, nicked UNCs. of 1871 and 1872 are common from original bags retrieved from Treasury holdings, 1962–63. Some dollars of 1871–72 (business strikes and proofs) were coined out of bullion from melted horns of Philadelphia's Diligent Fire Engine Co. #10: Chapman 5/27/1889:921. Many others were made from melted obsolete coins.

Doubling on G W T of motto, 1866–73, is in the hub; differences arise from the way individual working dies were hand strengthened and/or repolished.

S-Mint issues include major mysteries. Of the 1870 S there is no record of mintage. As the best survivors are prooflike, it is possible that these (like the $3 piece and possibly the half dime) were made for presentation purposes at the celebration at the cornerstone of the new Mint building (the "Granite Lady") at Fifth and Mint Sts., between Market and Mission Sts. However, most are too worn to confirm or refute this speculation.

The roster of surviving 1870 S dollars follows:

1. Cornerstone, San Francisco Mint Building, Fifth St. Proof or prooflike UNC.? Probably remains there with the second $3 piece, second half dime, and any other denominations struck.

2. Col. E. H. R. Green, Burdette G. Johnson, "Anderson Dupont":2551, Kagin, Norweb. AU+, prooflike; minute scratches at nose and O(NE).

3. James A. Stack estate (bought 1944). EF.

4. H. O. Granberg, William H. Woodin, Waldo Newcomer, W. W. Neil:202, Louis Eliasberg estate. EF, partly prooflike.

5. Compton, M. H. Bolender, A. J. Ostheimer, LM 9/68, "Gilhousen":1339, $62,500, pvt. coll., 1975 ANA:1125, $42,500, 1978 ANA:1160, $39,600, James E. Pohrer 1983 ANA:2707, $69,300. ABOUT EF, prooflike; test mark above seventh star.

6. Found in circulation before 1922 by an unidentified 18-year-old boy in Eureka, Calif.; held by him until 1978, then Donovan:1128, $32,000, Manfra, Tordella & Brookes, Auction 85:1270, $35,750. VF.

7. Matthew Adams Stickney, Col. E. H. R. Green, James Kelly, Clinton Hester, Menjou I:2181. VF, rim spots below 7, below foot, and above STA. May have been cleaned to avoid identification.

8. G. H. Hall, King Farouk, "Fairbanks," Wolfson, Miles:1612, $19,500, "Autumn":345, $39,000. VF, rim stain at TED S. Same comment as to last.

9. Norman Shultz 12/4/35:1302, 1960 ANA:1168, KS 1967:1253, $9,600. F.

10. Waldo Newcomer, Col. E. H. R. Green, Jack Roe, Jerome Kern, "Golden Jubilee":941, Carter:285, $46,750. F–VF, lower quarter of obv. pitted.

11. "Calif. Consignment," William Hesslein 12/2/26:900, F. C. C. Boyd, Hollinbeck/Kagin 95:1248 (2/23/51), Earl Skinner, NN 39:162, C. A. Cass, "Empire":1759, Kagin 250 (III):519 (1964), Kagin 274:1162 (1967) (possibly other Kagin sales). VF, initials FHI removed from obv. field.

No reason is at hand for the mintage of 9,000 specimens in 1872. And the final seated-dollar issue from San Francisco, [700], has vanished completely; apparently nobody bothered to save either of the two specimens that reached the Assay Commission in Feb. 1874, unlike the Carson City dimes. A mutilated survivor has long been rumored. Most likely the 1873 S dollars were melted along with the smaller coins without arrows, all legally defined as obsolete though still current.

The four Carson City issues pose nearly as difficult problems. Only the 1870 CC is available in top grades, and the best ones are prooflike: Were these presentation pieces? Issues of 1871–73 were still smaller, owing to politically motivated orders from the Philadelphia Mint to limit deliveries; this limitation was in turn used as a weapon in a long campaign to abolish the Carson branch mint. Claims were early made that Carson City coins were lightweight and of substandard alloy; in 1873 the Mint Bureau ordered extra sample coins to be taken at random from various deliveries and shipped to Philadelphia for test, where assays found them to be below legal limits. Instead of trying and executing the Superintendent pursuant to law, Mint authorities fired him. Publicity over these events doubtless explains why many Carson City dollars show edge test marks: Boosel {1960}. It may also explain the rarity of survivors; fewer are around than one would expect even from the low mintages, and probably as soon as they reached banks or tax collectors they went to the Mint for melting.

Because the drafters of the Mint Act of Feb. 12, 1873 abolished this denomination in favor of the trade dollar (see Chap. 30, introductory text), the silver lobby and their ignorant partisans nationwide called the bill the "Crime of '73." As if to add insult to injury, Congress in June 1874 demonetized all previous silver dollars and revoked their legal tender status: Taxay {1966}, pp. 260–61. The Act of 2/28/1878 restored it. Silver's only major commercial uses were in coinage, medals, dentistry, tableware, and jewelry; and the immense discoveries of the 1870s (of which the Comstock Lode was only the most famous among many) lowered the metal's market value reckoned in gold dollars. When the 1873 law abolished a denomination which for decades had not formed even 1% of circulating silver, the immensely wealthy owners of silver mines took this as an attack on them, and exerted every possible political effort to force the authorities to buy their output at the highest possible market price. These efforts paid off extravagantly five years later with passage (over a veto) of the new silver dollar act sponsored by "Silver Dick" Bland and John Allison: See next section.

LONGACRE'S LIBERTY SEATED, WITH MOTTO

Designers, obv. Robert Ball Hughes, as before; rev., James Barton Longacre, after Hughes, after Reich. Engravers, Longacre 1866–68; William Barber 1869–73. Mints, Philadelphia (no mintmark), San Francisco (mintmark S), Carson City (CC). Mintmarks below eagle. Physical Specifications, as before. Authorizing Acts, Jan. 18, 1837 (weight, fineness); March 3, 1865 (motto).

Grade range and standards, as before. NOTE: On GOOD coins, motto is partly legible; on VERY GOOD, over half motto letters legible; on FINE, motto is complete but IN ST will be weak; on VERY FINE, motto is bold though rubbing shows on a few letters. These criteria are *in addition to* those given for 1840–66, not instead of them.

5473 1863 "Prototype" (restrike). [5+P?] Proofs only. Judd 345. See introductory text. 1) Woodside, Woodin, Newcomer, Judd, "Ill. Hist.":295. 2) Atwater, Ewalt, Dines:790, Auction 86:473, $5,060, field rubbed. 3) Bolender, Ostheimer, LM 9/68:453. 4) Lamborn, "Fairfield":27, $2,100 (1977).

5474 1864 "Prototype" (restrike). [5+P?] Proofs only. Judd 396. See introductory text. 1) Parmelee, Woodside, Woodin, Newcomer, Judd, "Ill. Hist.":296. 2) Atwater, Ewalt:45.

5475 1865 "Prototype" (restrike). [7+P?] Proofs only. Judd 434. See introductory text. 1) Parmelee, Woodside, Woodin, Brand, Judd, "Ill. Hist.," LM 6/70:650. 2) Atwater, Ewalt:46. 3) Kern, Rumbel, 1952 ANA:2874. 4) "Anderson Dupont":2657. 5) "Old Phila. coll.," LM. 6) Lamborn, "Fairfield":32, overstruck on an 1866 dollar, $4,100. 7) Amon Carter, Sr. and Jr., Carter:278, $9,900. One of these brought $10,000 in 1976 ANA:3616; another went in 1977 ANA:2182.

5476 1866 [48,900 + 725P]

Business strikes (rare) have low date. 3 vars. of proofs: See Breen {1977}, p. 131. Two obv. and 6 rev. dies shipped to San Francisco, but no mintage followed.

5477 1867 [all kinds 46,900 + 625P] Normal date.
Business strikes are very rare. 3 vars. of proofs: See Breen {1977}, p. 133. Compare next.

5478 1867 over smaller date. [Incl. in 625P] Very rare.
Date first entered with half-dollar logotype, high and slanting down to r., then corrected with normal dollar logotype (much larger), low and level. Rev. of third proof var., but relapped; hollows in ribbon. Discovery coin, "Gilhousen":1334. Later impressions, less rare, show less of the blunder (die relapped). The "repunched 186" var. in 1983 Midwinter ANA:968 may be one of these. With 2 dubious exceptions, all seen are proofs or impaired proofs, mostly the latter.

5479 1868 [all kinds 162,100 + 600P] Normal date.
Business strikes (very rare; date very heavy on one die) and proofs.

5480 1868 Double date. [Incl. in 600P above] Proofs only. Very rare.
Doubling obvious on rare early states, less so on later states from repolished obv. die (less rare, priced as preceding). Discovery coin, "Anderson Dupont":2548. Cf. Ivy Phoenix:1028, $3,000, not one of the earliest states. See Breen {1977}, p. 136.

5481 1869 [423,700 + 600P]
Business strikes sometimes show minute repunching on base of 1; 3 minor positional vars. Auction 86:1748, "gem UNC.," $7,425. At least 3 vars. of proofs: Breen {1977}, p. 138. Four obv. dies shipped to San Francisco remained unused.

5482 1870 [all kinds 415,000 + 1,000P] Normal rev.
At least 2 positional vars. of date on business strikes. Compare next.

5483 1870 Doubled rev. die.
At least 3 vars. of business strikes, one of proofs. Doubling plainest either on feathers at l. or on lowest edges of leaves, claws, and arrows.

5484 1870 S [No record, estimated 12] Ex. rare.
No record of shipment of dies in 1869 for 1870 use. Nevertheless, Coiner J. B. Harmstead returned 2 unmintmarked revs. to the Philadelphia Mint and received 2 replacement revs., May 28, 1870. No record of shipment of obvs. until Nov. 1871: See **5492** and introductory text. Only one pair of dies: shield point midway between tip of serif and upright of 1; l. base of 1 over r. edge of dentil; date high in field (this combination unlike any found on Philadelphia or CC coins); rev. S shallow, thin, unlike 1872 S dollars or 1866–70 halves (did Coiner J. B. Harmstead cut it into this working die at San Francisco?); both dies vigorously polished, leaving upper parts of rev. white stripes mirrorlike. For roster of survivors see introductory text. Cf. **6379** and Chap. 34, introductory text.

5485 1870 CC [12,462−] CC closely spaced. Rare.
Date central or high. "Fairfield":1130, UNC., $3,400. Best ones are usually prooflike. Often with edge test marks; see introductory text. First released Feb. 10 [3,747].

5486 1870 CC Widely spaced mintmark. Scarce.
Space between C C almost full width of either C. Bareford:429, UNC., $5,000. Same comments. 3 rev. dies, one used also on **5489**, another on **5493**, a third on **5495.**

5487 1871 [all kinds 1,073,800 + 960−P] 71 about touch.
Proofs and business strikes. This logotype is the earlier one, as it appears on the 1871 CC obv. (ill.) which die was shipped west before the end of 1870. Many minor positional vars. Common in nicked UNC. from at least 2 Treasury bags (1,000 each) released 1962–63. Compare next.

5488 1871 7 1 apart. Scarce.
Proofs (rare) and business strikes (a small minority): 1982 ANA:2473.

5489 1871 CC 71 about touch. [1,376] Very rare.
Date logotype as **5487**. Wide C C as on **5486;** doubled rev. die. Usually in low grades; often with edge test marks: See introductory text. Prohibitively rare in EF: "Fairfield":1135, $2,600. Beware Philadelphia coins with added CC. Authentication recommended.

5490 1872 [all kinds 1,105,000 + 950−P] Normal.
Many minor positional vars. Heavily impressed dates have 18 touching at bases, lighter ones or repolished dies have them free (same logotype). Common in nicked UNC. from at least one Treasury bag (1,000) released 1962–63. Compare next. Some proofs melted after July 10, 1873.

5491 1872 Blundered obv. Very rare.
Part of extra 1 embedded in rock below shield, just above edge of base; parts of bases of two 2's above and just below edge of rocky base, above 2 of date. Discovery coin: 1974 GENA:1093, UNC.

5492 1872 S [9,000−]
As the 2 obvs. shipped in Nov. 1871 for 1872 use were called "extras," presumably others were shipped before, but the record has not survived. Only one var. seen to date. Usually in low grades, G to F; prohibitively rare choice. "Fairfield":1141, UNC., $2,100; Robison, Auction 82:1756, UNC., $4,500. Many probably melted after April 1873.

5493 1872 CC [3,150−] Rare.
2 obvs. shipped; only one var., top of 2 repunched. Widely

spaced C C. Many melted after April 1873. Usually in low grades, often with test marks; rev. generally sharper than obv. Bareford:430, UNC., $8,000.

5494 1873 Closed 3. [293,600− + 600−P]
Minute positional vars. Coinage ended March 29, 1873; many melted after July 10, 1873, including some 2,258 unsold proof dollars of this and previous years.

5495 1873 CC Closed 3. [2,300−] Very rare.
Widely spaced C C. Only one var. seen. Many melted after April 1873. Usually in low grades, often with test marks. 3 UNCs. turned up in a Carson City cornerstone about 1973; one of these may have been Auction 81:1598, $9,000. However, the time element precludes this source for Bareford:431, UNC., $12,000.

5496 1873 S Closed 3. [700−] Reported, unverified.
6 pairs of dies shipped Nov. 1872. Possibly the entire mintage was melted after April 1873. See introductory text.

viii. MORGAN'S DESIGN
(1878–1921)

When the Mint Act of Feb. 12, 1873 became law, the silver mine owners' lobby began to protest the discontinuance of the silver dollar and the limited legal tender of the trade dollar (see Chap. 30, introductory text). Both provisions lessened the amount of silver the mints had to buy for coinage. No matter that almost no silver dollars had circulated for decades; no matter that trade dollars were heavier (a sop to the silver lobby) or that millions were in use by importers trading in Chinese port cities. To these mine owners the only important issue was their bank balances. They convinced their powerful friends on Capitol Hill to regard any threat to silver (i.e., to their own wealth) as a threat to the nation. Persuaded by God only knows what "valuable considerations," Sen. William Boyd Allison (R.-Ia.) and Reps. Richard P. "Silver Dick" Bland (D.-Mo.), John Adam Kasson (R.-Ia.), and William Darrah Kelley (R.-Pa.) came to the same perspective.

The mine owners saw multiple threats, domestic and foreign. Domestic industries needed little silver compared to the already large requirement for coinage. The German Empire under Bismarck adopted a gold standard, and threw over 8,000 tons of silver on the market; then came enormous discoveries of silver in Nevada (the Comstock Lode being only the most famous of these). This meant that the market price of silver (reckoned in gold dollars) fell, and the Mint Bureau could buy foreign silver more cheaply. The lobby's chief legislative friends began submitting bills which would, if enacted, force the Treasury to buy enormous amounts of new domestic (not foreign, and not recycled) silver, at artificially high prices, for coinage only into silver dollars.

Mint officialdom became aware that it was only a matter of time before "Silver Dick" Bland and Sen. Allison would force some such silver dollar bill into law. Mint Director Linderman hired George T. Morgan as Assistant Engraver to prepare designs for the new coin. "Silver Dick" induced Congress to pass his silver dollar bill over Pres. Hayes's veto (one of Hayes's few sensible decisions), and it regrettably became law Feb. 28, 1878: the same day the Mint Director officially approved the Morgan design. This act mandated monthly Treasury purchases of $2 million to $4 million of new domestic silver bullion for coinage only into dollars. (Why only the one denomination? Because each silver dollar was heavier than two halves, four quarters, or 10 dimes.) The coins were commonly known as "buzzard dollars" or "Bland dollars," and after about 1892 also as "dollars

of our daddies" or "daddy dollars." The first three proofs (VAM 9) went, respectively, to Pres. Hayes, Secretary Sherman, and Mint Director Linderman, March 11, 1878, in unprecedented haste.

Morgan's design portrayed Miss Anna Willess Williams, a schoolteacher, as Ms. Liberty. Morgan, with difficulty, had persuaded her to become his model, and she sat for him five times at the home of the illustrious painter Thomas Eakins, under promise of strict secrecy. The cover story represented her head as that of "a Greek figure" at the Philadelphia Academy of Art; others noticed a resemblance to Oudine's head on French coins. Despite all precautions, some years later a newspaperman recognized her as the model, thought "Aha!" (thus exhausting his stock of bright ideas for the year), and (over protests) published the story; whereupon Miss Williams, as she had feared, did lose her job. In those days respectable ladies could not be artists' models, nor vice versa ("To Marry a Goddess," *NUM* 5/1896; Breen-Turoff {1971}).

Despite the artificially subsidized market, worldwide silver prices continued to decline, and the silver lobby continued to exert pressure on Congress to Do Something to support the market. Because the legislators did not understand the real issue any better than the average sharecropper, the bill they pushed through Congress (the Sherman Silver Purchase Act) was one of the worst blunders since the Fugitive Slave Act of 1850. This new act required the Treasury to buy 187½ tons of domestic silver every month, only for coinage into silver dollars, paying the mine owners in Treasury notes redeemable in gold. While the mine owners enriched themselves at public expense, the rest of the country was in serious trouble. By 1893 Treasury vaults bulged with silver dollars which circulated little, and bought less than gold coins (or, sometimes, less than paper!), while smaller silver coins were in short supply, and while the mine owners kept turning in the 1890 "Coin Notes" for gold, which they hoarded. As the law permitted these notes to be paid out again and again, redeemable in gold each time they returned to the Treasury, the vaults were nearly emptied of gold while the Treasury had to pay off bonds and meet international obligations payable only in gold. At the threat of Treasury default, Wall Street went into panic. Some 419 banks failed, and with them went their depositors: factories, stores, private citizens. Millions were suddenly jobless and hungry. Pres. Cleveland called Congress into special session to repeal the Sherman Act, which it did on Nov. 2, 1893—only after months of vituperous opposition from "Silver Dick" Bland.

Thereafter, dollar coinages were smaller; no more bullion was bought for the purpose. The Act of June 13, 1898 required that all remaining bullion purchased under the Sherman Act be coined into dollars. Existing stocks thus earmarked for dollars (108,800,188 in all) were exhausted by 1904, ending Morgan dollar coinage for 17 years. Most of these dollars, like their older siblings, remained in Treasury vaults until the 1960s.

The 1896 and 1900 presidential campaigns (even more than those from 1876–92) centered on the silver versus gold issue, which nobody understood, and which the silver lobby had good reason to keep obscure: The truth might cost them money; official lies might help them. "Silver Dick" Bland was the original favorite and front-runner candidate, but the egregious William Jennings Bryan captured the nomination at the 1896 convention with his "Cross of Gold" speech. The public elected William McKinley ("Boss" Hanna's candidate) instead because many feared Bryan would bring about another Sherman Act and another panic like that of 1893.

Aside from the proofs of 1878 Seven Feathers and a few individual vars., rarities in the Morgan dollar series result not from tiny mintages but from wholesale meltings after 1918, which disposed of most of the rarer branch-mint issues and apparently all 12,000 of the 1895 Philadelphia business strikes. In all, 333,022,048 silver dollars were melted 1883–1964 (VAM 1976, pp. 11–13), including probably a little under half the coinage of Morgan dollars and possibly 75% of the Peace dollars. Some 81% of this total meltage was mandated by the Pittman Act of 1918 (below), and another 52 million during WW II.

The Pittman Act (April 23, 1918) required melting of not over 350 million silver dollars. Accordingly, 259,121,554 were melted for resale to England at $1 per fine oz. (the British immediately shipped the bullion to India), and 11,111,168 for conversion into dimes, quarters, and half dollars. However, pressure from the silver lobby forced inclusion of a clause in the Pittman Act requiring purchase of enough domestic silver bullion to replace all the melted dollars. Under this authority, some 86,730,000 Morgan dollars were made in 1921 from all three mints then in operation, as the new Peace design was not yet ready: See next section.

Vars. of survivors are of many kinds, some very rare: hub changes in 1878; doubled dies (including 50 "7 over 8 tail feathers" revs. in which a new device punch was impressed to correct an earlier design); overdates in 1880–81 and 1887 (many publicized by Ted Clark); overmintmarks; repunched dates; repunched mintmarks. Only with publication of the VAM book were explanations known of many of these, though others are discoveries of more recent years, and their rarity levels are not yet certain. Even with the VAM book's extensive illustrations, classification represents a formidable problem (especially for 1878), unlisted vars. continue to turn up, and rarity levels have been affected by dispersals of major hoards, particularly Treasury holdings (below) and the Redfield hoard (407,596 pieces, of which 351,259 were graded "UNC.").

This latter may have had, in the long run, more market impact than the Treasury hoards. LaVere Redfield (d. 1974) was an eccentric Reno hard-money fanatic who hated banks and government; he once went to jail rather than pay taxes. He assembled a hoard of over 600,000 silver dollars in the 1930s and 1940s; thieves carried off many, and others were sold privately before his estate came on the market. Steve Markoff bought the hoard Jan. 27, 1976, for $7.3 million and promptly resold it to R. L. Hughes, John Love, and Paramount, which firms gradually dispersed it in a series of nationwide promotions that gave both the Redfield hoard and silver dollars generally unprecedented public interest.

One curious group of vars. of 1900 (the six (?) revs. with mintmark O punched over CC, VAM 7–12) came about because at the time the Carson City Mint was officially and permanently changed to an assay office, July 1, 1899, its three presses and all remaining coining equipment were returned in September to the Philadelphia Mint. Among the assorted pieces of ironmongery were unused working revs. for silver dollars; these were remintmarked and shipped out to New Orleans for use in 1900.

Proofs, 1881–1904, have 179 reeds on edge. Philadelphia business strikes in this period have varying numbers of edge reeds, not matching the proofs (Leroy Van Allen, personal communication).

When the 1921 dollar coinage turned out to be of the old Morgan type, the Peace Dollar's original promoter Farran Zerbe raised a monstrous fuss at the Mint Bureau. No stranger to the Treasury, Zerbe had masterminded the San Francisco Mint's exhibit at the 1915 Pan-Pacific International Exposition; his charisma had materially influenced Congress to authorize coinage of several commemorative issues (before they became scandals of the late 1930s: Chap. 39); his collection was world famous as a publicly viewed educational exhibit, later becoming the Chase Manhattan Bank Money Museum. Zerbe wielded enough political clout that the Mint Bureau could ill afford to antagonize him. And so, as a consolation prize, the Mint privately authorized coinage of limited numbers of proof 1921

Morgans from both Philadelphia and San Francisco. The Philadelphia Zerbe strikings were all carelessly made; most survivors have been badly cleaned, obscuring or rendering doubtful their proof status. Those from San Francisco are not much better: Mosher {1955}, p. 727; Breen {1977}, pp. 220, 238. When the Philadelphia coin dealer Henry Chapman heard about this, he went to Mint Engraver George Morgan, and obtained 10 proofs of much higher quality, thus creating one of the major rarities of this century with the Morgan dollars' last gasp. The original bill of sale from Morgan to Henry Chapman, dated June 11, 1921, itemizes:

"3 gold Chinese medals	$93.22
4 silver Chinese medals	4.00
10 proof silver dollars 1921	10.00
Balance due on Chinese medal dies	50.00
	157.22

Received Payment /s/ George T. Morgan."

The Chinese "medals" were strikings of the fantasy dollar, Y 332 (silver), 332a (gold), obv. Gen. Hung Hsien, rev. dragon, four characters above, four more below. Morgan had billed Chapman $100 for the dies, March 26, 1921.

Though Morgan dollars were dead, the corpse would not stay buried. From time to time during the late 1950s and early 1960s, speculators, dealers, collectors, and souvenir hunters bought bags of silver dollars from banks, subtreasuries, and the Treasury in Washington; and each November the Treasury released unchecked bags of silver dollars to the general public for Christmas purposes. Occasional windfalls were reported, such as the bags of 1894 and 1894 S dollars found in Great Falls, Mont. (1952 and 1961), but these finds received little publicity; and collectors feared to buy at higher prices because the Treasury could destroy any market at a moment's notice by releasing bags of alleged rarities.

The break came in Nov. 1962: Treasury releases included four formerly scarce dates—1898 O, 1902 O, 1903 O, 1904 O. As the 1903 O had previously been valued at up to $1,500 apiece (guidebooks even speculated that most had been melted following the Pittman Act), this event reached the front pages. Though prices dropped on these four mintmarks, public demand for the old "cartwheels" soared. Rumors named various earlier or rarer dates of Morgan or earlier silver dollars as having come out of Treasury bags: 1893, 1872, 1871, 1860 O, 1859 O, 1846 O (unconfirmed), and even 1801 (unverified). There was also a rumor that a Chicago underworld syndicate had turned up a bag of 1895's, but no coin from this alleged source has ever shown up (Breen {1977}, p. 197).

As if this were not enough, silver prices began to climb in a way that would have delighted the mine owners of 80 years before, and false reports of a coin shortage resulted in hoarding silver of all kinds. (The present writer was one of several columnists who showed that the "shortage" did not exist: It was a flowback problem; too many coins were spending over 95% of their time in vending machines and coin phones, from which they were not collected often enough to do their normal work in circulation.) Public Law 88-36, June 4, 1963, authorized the Treasury to redeem silver certificates in silver dollars or (at the Secretary's option) in silver bullion at "a monetary value equal to the face value of the certificates." No more silver certificates would be printed or issued. As the latter then formed the bulk of $1 bills in circulation, this sounded like a golden—or, more accurately, a silvery—opportunity for the general public: Nothing to lose but a little time; winnings which at worst could be spent and which just *might* contain a real jackpot. And the rush was on. From then until March 26, 1964, when the Treasury forbade release of any more silver dollars, long lines formed at the Treasury building in Washington, and rumors of valuable dates or mintmarks abounded. Some people bought and sold futures in silver dollars; others paid premiums for silver certificates. Between Jan. 1960 and Jan. 1964, the Treasury paid out over 152 million silver dollars.

However, the publicity about rare coins at face value from the Treasury revived the Mint Bureau's century-old phobia of coin collectors, and this time the officials' worst fears were confirmed. A hasty inventory showed that their shrunken holdings included 2,822,239 Carson City coins dated 1878–93 (VAM, p. 249)—many of considerable numismatic value. The Secretary of Treasury issued a ukase to the effect that after March 26, 1964, all redemption of silver certificates would take place only in silver granules. Later still, after silver prices had climbed still higher, redemption would occur only in "lawful money," defined as Federal Reserve notes or clad-metal coins: Gresham's law in action. Many who had paid premiums for silver certificates were left unable to obtain anything over face for them.

On July 26, 1967, the official government price of $1.29 per oz. for silver was rescinded. Market value of silver shortly afterward reached $2 per oz. Despite a May 1967 regulation prohibiting melting of U.S. silver coins, such meltage became common, peaking in 1980, when silver climbed to $50 per oz. (Miller {1982}, p. 3). Bowing to the inevitable, the Treasury repealed its interdict on meltings.

Recommendations from numismatic sources and the general public flooded in, suggesting that the Treasury do anything from auction its Carson City dollars to melt them down to protect the numismatic value of those already in private hands. No decision came until Dec. 31, 1970, when Pres. Nixon signed into law the Bank Holding Company Act Amendments, which (among other things) authorized the General Services Administration to sell these silver dollars in any suitable manner. The Treasury decided on mail-bid sales, and launched a massive advertising campaign. Paid for with public funds, this included several TV documentary films, at least 100,000 posters, and literally millions of brochures, given out free at post offices, banks, credit unions, and savings and loan firms (VAM, p. 247).

On Dec. 6, 1971, the Treasury turned over the remaining 2,937,695 silver dollars to GSA, which stored them in the U.S. Bullion Depository at West Point. (This figure included not only the CC's but 27,980 mixed non-CC UNCs. and 84,165 of lower grades.) Early in 1973, someone discovered that the 1880 CC dollars included many strong overdates. The Act of Dec. 31, 1970 did not permit segregation of unusual coins; however, coin people strongly urged that these be withheld pending further study. Leroy C. Van Allen and A. George Mallis went to the West Point Depository, May 4, 1973, and surveyed the group (VAM, Chap. 10).

GSA held five mail-bid sales: Oct. 1972—March 1973, June–July 1973, Oct. 1973, Feb. 1974, and April–June 1974. These disposed of almost 1.96 million CC dollars at some $55 million, bringing vociferous criticism based on a practice of requiring minimum bids that were on the high side of retail. Tactics aside, this was the biggest volume sale of numismatic material in the history of the world.

There were two final GSA mail sales: Feb. 8–April 8, 1980, and July 1980. The former offered 823,287 CC-Mint dollars (195,745 of 1883, 428,152 of 1884, and 199,390 of mixed dates 1878–93) at fixed prices: 1883 CC at $42 each, 1884 CC at $40 each, and mixed years (Treasury's choice of dates) at $20 each. The latter offered 55,847 more coins at mail-bid sale (minimum bid $180 each): 4,284 of 1880 CC, 19,996 of 1881 CC, and 31,567 of 1885 CC.

From then to the present day, every big coin convention has included dealers with quantities of dollars for sale from the Treasury/GSA holdings. Dispersal for long was slow, and one side effect has been a steep gradient in price levels from the usual run of the bag up to rare gem coins almost or quite devoid of bag marks. Heavily bag-marked specimens have even

brought less than UNC. price; valuations increase dramatically with decreasing numbers of bag marks, and the few with none at all bring very high premiums. Pristine coins (never cleaned) bring premiums above the commoner dipped ones.

The real problem is "sliders": EF's and AU's cleaned to simulate mint state. Check hair above brow, above ear, and above date, as well as wingtips and eagle's breast, to verify that weakly struck areas show mint surface, not rubbing. Some years including 1884 S and 1901 are very difficult to find in mint state, though plentiful in slider grade.

An active market has also developed for prooflike coins. No attempt is here made to price these separately; interested collectors should consult Miller {1982} for details.

MORGAN'S DESIGN

Designer, Engraver, George T. Morgan. Mints, Philadelphia (no mintmark), New Orleans (mintmark O), San Francisco (S), Carson City (CC), Denver (D). Mintmark below bow, above DO. Physical Specifications, as before. Authorizing Acts, as before plus Act of Feb. 28, 1878.

Grade range, FAIR to UNC. GOOD: Date, mintmark (if any), and all inscriptions legible; minimal internal details of hair or feathers. VERY GOOD: Partial hair and feather details; edges of some leaves partly blurred, cotton blossom on cap outlined with local blurred spots at edges; half of wing feathers show at l., 2/3 of those at r. FINE: Junction between hair and face clearly defined; two principal lines in each cotton blossom clear, lower two cotton leaves clearly distinct from cap, partial wheat grains; partial internal details to wreath leaves; over 3/4 of wing feathers on both sides. VERY FINE: Partial detail in hair above ear, elsewhere about 3/4 hair detail; internal detail intact in all cotton leaves and blossoms; partial breast, neck, and head feathers; wing feathers intact except at tips. EXTREMELY FINE: Isolated tiny rubbed spots only; partial mint luster. UNCIRCULATED: *No* trace of wear. See introductory text about "sliders," nicked coins, pristine, and prooflike coins.

Issues of 1878

I. PROTOTYPES: SEVEN TAIL FEATHERS
Morgan's Initial M on Truncation, Not Bow

5497 1878 First Prototype. Proofs only. Very scarce. [6+]
Judd 1550. Issue of Dec. 5, 1877; many (over 100?) struck later. 3 leaves in branch; long dentils both sides; small rev. stars. 2 obv. vars. Dentils nearly touch obv. legend; rev. stars show centers. The other obv. has first star much nearer bust point; ill. in Judd and VAM p. 49.

5498 1878 Second Prototype. Proofs only. Rare.
Judd 1550a. Issues of Jan.–Feb. 1878. Three leaves in branch; short obv. dentils, large flat rev. stars as on all to follow. Other die vars. may exist.

5499 1878 Third Prototype. [3P] Proofs only. Untraced.
Judd 1552. Struck Feb. 25, approved March 1 (VAM pp. 50–51). As adopted, with 9 leaves on branch; first A far from wing; *without* Morgan's initial M on bow.   1) Woodside:336, Woodin, Boyd, Farouk. Ill. *NUM* 2/12, p. 48.

II. EIGHT TAIL FEATHERS
**Morgan's Initial M on Truncation and Left Bow Henceforth
Issue of March 12–25**
[699,300+ + 500−P]

5500 1878 Thin LIBERTY, blunt beak, I(n) touches wing.
VAM type I-A1: 2 outer folds of ear equally thick. About 20 minor vars. Proofs: See Breen 1977, p. 161; Auction 81:1632, $4,200.

5501 1878 Same, but thicker LIBERTY: doubled obv. die.
VAM type II/I-A1. VAM 15–17, possibly other vars.

5502 1878 Thin LIBERTY; pointed beak, I(n) free of wing.
VAM type I-A2/A1. Doubled rev. die: Note beak, top arrowhead. VAM 23. Not to be confused with next.

5503 1878 Same but thicker LIBERTY; doubled obv. and rev. dies.

VAM type II/I-A2/A1. At least 5 vars.; doubling as last and/or parts of motto. Through March 30, 32 obvs. and 14 revs. used, including some of Group III (following). On March 18–20, Director Linderman demanded changes, including that from 8 to 7 tail feathers: See next.

III. SEVEN OVER EIGHT TAIL FEATHERS
Issue of March 26–April 4+
[544,000+]

5504 1878 Normal obv.; 3–5 extra tail feathers.

VAM type II-B/A. Obv. die not doubled. Thick LIBERTY; outermost fold of ear thinner than its neighbor, doubled rev. dies. In all, 50 revs. were altered to make Group III. VAM 32, 34, 36, 37, 39, others.

5505 1878 Same, 7 extra feathers ("14 Feathers"). Presently rare.

VAM 41. Not to be confused with any to follow.

5506 1878 Doubled obv.; 3 to 5 extra tail feathers.

VAM type II/I-B/A. VAM 33, 38, 40, 44, others. Compare next 2.

5507 1878 Doubled obv.; doubled talons. Presently very scarce.

VAM 30, 45.

5508 1878 Doubled obv.; doubled legs.

VAM 31, 43.

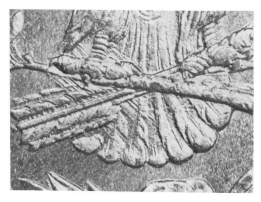

IV. SEVEN TAIL FEATHERS, PARALLEL ARROW
FEATHERS
Issue of April 4–June 28
[4,900,000− + 200−P]

5509 1878 Normal, thin LIBERTY; long nock. Presently very scarce.

VAM type I-B1. Not to be confused with next. VAM 70. Part

of reported mintage included Group III coins. The nock is the end of shaft between arrow feather tips; VAM p. 68 miscalls it "center arrow feather."

5510 1878 Doubled obv.; long nock.

VAM type II/I-B1. Doubling usually on LIBERTY. VAM 79–84, others.

5511 1878 Normal, thin LIBERTY; short nock. Presently very scarce.

VAM type I-B2. VAM 100.

5512 1878 Doubled obv.; short nock.

VAM type II/I-B2. At least 31 vars.

5513 1878 Normal, thick LIBERTY; short nock.

VAM type II-B2. At least 12 vars.: VAM 130–33, 146, 185–97. Proofs (ill.): See Breen {1977}, p. 161; many were melted as unsold. Auction 80:1737, $9,750. The proofs are thought to have been among the 200 delivered March 26. Julian [1986].

V. SEVEN TAIL FEATHERS, SLANTING TOP ARROW FEATHER
Issue of June 28–Dec. 31
[4,300,000− + 50−P]

5514   1878 No lines in wheat leaves; normal obv.
VAM type II-C. Rounded breast, unlike any foregoing. VAM 210, 221, 223. Part of reported mintage included Group IV coins.

5515   1878 Same, doubled obv. die.
VAM type II/I-C. VAM 200, 201, 220.

5516   1878 Lines in wheat leaves.
VAM type III-C. Top obv. leaf point just above r. cotton blossom points at S (in VAM types I, II it points to pellet following S); this obv. hub continues through 1904. VAM 202–3, 222, 230. Proofs (VAM 215) are Ex. rare: of 50 delivered Nov. 8, 34 were sold, the rest "released into circulation" in Jan. 1879 (Julian [1986]); fewer than 7 seen to date. 1980 NY Met (NERCA 4/80):730, $16,000. In all, Groups II–V, 129 obvs., 132 revs.

VI. BRANCH MINT ISSUES
(As Group IV Above)

5517   1878 S [all kinds 9,774,000] Long nock. Presently Ex. rare.
Not in VAM; their type II-B1. 2 vars. Discovered Dec. 1979. Compare detail ill. of **5509.** Ten pairs of dies shipped April 8, of which 3 obvs. and 8 revs. were condemned by the San Francisco Coiner as unusable. Mintage began April 18 from the 2 usable revs. All seen to date are circulated.

5518   1878 S Short nock.
VAM type II-B2. Compare detail ill. of **5511.** In June, 36 pairs of dies shipped; some held over for 1879 use. At least 9 obvs. show minor doubling. At least 17 minor vars.

5519   1878 CC [all kinds 2,212,000] Long nock; close CC.
VAM type II-B1; see detail ill. of **5509.** Ten pairs of dies shipped April 8, received April 16, on which day a few "samples" were struck (proofs? presentation coins?): Carson City *Morning Appeal* 4/17/1878. VAM 1, 1A, 2, 4, 5, others. The Treasury released nearly 70,000 UNCS. 1963–64; Wall Street investors got many of them. Some 60,993 remained in GSA holdings (1975). Compare next 3.

5520   1878 CC Same; doubled obv. die. Presently very scarce. VAM 18.

5521   1878 CC Long nock, wide C C.
VAM 3, 16, 17. C's almost full width of a C apart. Compare next.

5522   1878 CC Doubled obv. die; long nock, wide C C. Presently very scarce.
VAM 6. Doubling on cotton leaves and stars. Repunched date.

5523   1878 CC Short nock, close CC.
VAM type II-B2. In all, 30 pairs of dies shipped in June; at least one rev. held over for 1880 use. VAM 7–11, 14–15.

5524   1878 CC Doubled obv. die; short nock, close CC. Presently very scarce.
VAM 13. Doubling on all stars. Repunched date.

5525   1878 CC Short nock, wide C C.
VAM 12. Mintmark as **5521.**

Issues of 1879–1904
As Group V Above Unless Otherwise Noted

5526   1879 [14,806,000 + 650P]
At least 11 minor vars., mostly partly repunched dates. These come with "open" or "closed" 9; in the latter, knob joins

loop, probably heavier impression from same logotype. Specimens without full breast feathers bring less. In all, 129 obvs., 86 revs.

5527 1879 O [all kinds 2,887,000 + 12P] Medium roundish O.
Same comments. Many "sliders" and heavily bag-marked UNCS.

5528 1879 O Triple O. Presently very rare.
VAM 4, originally believed over horizontal O; RPM 1 calls it triple O, earlier punched north and south of final position. This also has repunched 9.

5529 1879 O Tall O.
Same comments as to **5526.** At least 9 vars. The 12 proofs (ill.) were struck Feb. 20, 1879, on reopening of the New Orleans branch as a coining facility. 1) N.O. Superintendent, Mint Cabinet, SI. Clain-Stefanelli {1970}, fig. 36. 2) Leo A. Young, Auction 80:1743, $36,000, Wayne Miller. 3) 1973 CSNS, Auction 79:1046, $14,500, Barker, Burdick, Wayne Miller, Bruce Amspacher. Impaired. 4) Kagin 11/73:1342, Wayne Miller. Breen {1977}, p. 235. Authentication of any purported specimen is mandatory.

5530 1879 S [all kinds 9,110,000] Rev. of 1878.
Parallel arrow feathers; short nock; small s. VAM 4–10, representing at least 4 revs. held over from 1878. Most UNCS. are from the 3,000 in the Redfield hoard. Usually heavily bag-marked.

5531 1879 S Rev. of 1879.
Slanting top arrow feather; taller S. Same comment as to **5526.** Often prooflike.

5532 1879 CC [all kinds 756,000] Normal CC.
4 minor vars. Compare next.

5533 1879 CC Large over small CC.
VAM 3; RPM 1. Repunched date; severe die rust at CC. This is the least rare single var. of the date. Some 4,123 were in GSA holdings (1975); several hundred others (bag-marked) in Redfield hoard.

5534 1880 [all kinds 12,600,000 + 1,355P] 1880/79. Presently rare.
VAM 23 (1977 Supplement). Traces of crossbar and knob on thick parts of 80; tiny corner of 7 at upper r. of 8. Compare next 2. Discovered by Anthony J. and Dazelle Morano, *NSM* 12/64, p. 3273.

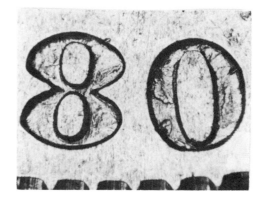

5535 1880 8/7. Presently rare.
At least 5 vars., none obvious. Price for VAM 6 (ill.). VAM 7 (part of crossbar of 7 within upper loop of second 8) is rarest, bringing possibly double price of others, which typically show only traces of top serifs of 7 on upper edges of 8.

5536 1880/9. Presently rare.
VAM 25 (1977 Supplement). Part of upper loop of 9 within very top of 0; faint trace of knob on thick lower l. part of 0. Other vars. probable.

5537 1880 Normal.
At least 18 minor vars., mostly with minor repunching on date. A bag of 1,000 prooflike specimens was dispersed in 1971. Proofs (VAM 13) have minute repunching on base of 1. In all, 91 obvs., 77 revs.

5538 1880 O [all kinds 5,305,000] 80/79; small round o mintmark.
VAM 4. Part of crossbar of 7 within loop of 8. Compare next 2. A few hundred prooflike UNCs. were in the Donovan hoard (Superior Galleries, 1977).

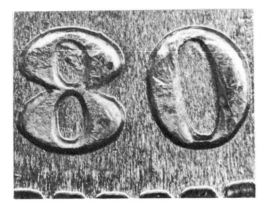

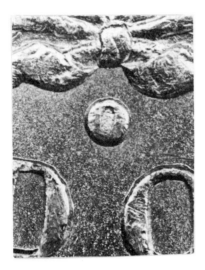

5539 1880 O 8/7; small round o mintmark.
VAM 6, 6A, 6B, 16. First 3 have serif of 7 at upper l. of second 8; last has l. end of crossbar of 7 within thick part of upper loop of 8 (VAM 1977 Supplement).

5540 1880 O 8/7; medium oval O mintmark.
VAM 5, 17. First like **5538** obv.; second has obv. of VAM 16 in **5539**.

5541 1880 O Normal date; small round o mintmark.
At least 9 vars., many with partly repunched dates. "Sliders" are plentiful.

5542 1880 O Normal date; medium oval O mintmark.
At least 5 vars. "Sliders" are plentiful. Compare next.

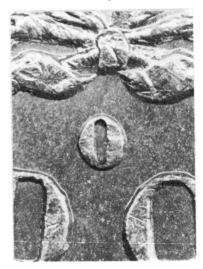

5543 1880 O Same, "Impaled Eagle." Rare.
VAM 2A. One of the most pronounced die chisel marks ever seen on a U.S. coin, across eagle's neck, nearly joining wings. Usually in low grades.

5544 1880 S [all kinds 8,900,000] 80/79, medium S.
VAM 8, 12. Price for VAM 8, with parts of crossbar and top loop of 9 in 80; other var. is less obvious. Medium S as in 1881–99.

5545 1880/79 S Largest S.
VAM 9. Same obv. as VAM 8 preceding. Lower serif of S away from middle.

5546 1880/9 S Medium S.
VAM 11. Die file marks in 0, attempting to efface 9.

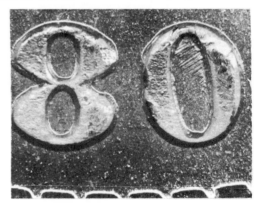

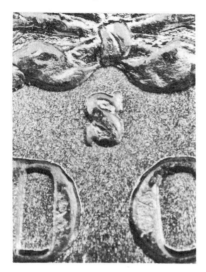

5547 1880 S 8/7, largest S. Presently very rare.
VAM 10. Both edges of crossbar of 7 within loop of second 8. S as in **5545.**

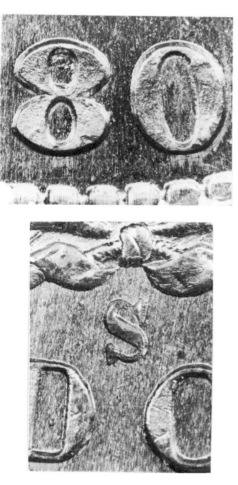

5548 1880 S Normal. Medium S.
At least 20 vars., many with minor partial repunching on dates. Often prooflike. Gems are plentiful but have nevertheless sometimes commanded four-figure prices. Many bags released by the Treasury late in 1938: *NSM* 1/55, p. 1. Over 5,000 in Redfield hoard. Compare **5550.**

5549 1880 S Normal. Largest S.
At least 11 vars.; same comments as to last.

5550 1880/1 S Medium S. Presently Ex. rare.
Upper half of upright of 1 within 0. Made late fall 1880 when dies were being prepared for 1880 and 1881 (cf. **3991).** Discovered by Art Moyano.

5551 1880 CC [all kinds 591,000] 80/79, parallel feathers. Presently very scarce.
VAM 4. Rev. of 1878, short nock, small round cc. Probably the clearest overdate in the series; compare next. Discovered by this writer among Treasury-hoard coins at the 1964 ANA Convention. Rarely found prooflike.

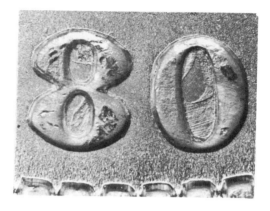

5552 1880 CC Parallel arrow feathers.
VAM 7. Rev. as preceding. Obv. began as 8/7 but most traces of overdate effaced by repolishing.

5553 1880 CC "8/high 7," small cc. Presently very scarce.
VAM 5. Slanted top arrow feather henceforth. Serifs of 7 atop second 8.

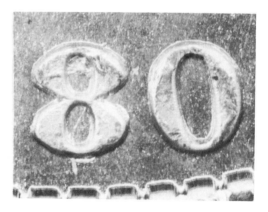

5554 1880 CC "8/low 7," small cc. Presently rare.
VAM 6. Most of 7 shows within second 8.

5555   1880 CC Small cc.
   VAM 5A, 8. Same comment as to **5552** except slanted top
   arrow feather.

5556   1880 CC Large CC.
   VAM 3, 9. Same comment as to **5555.** Many released by
   Treasury, 1938 *(NSM* 1/55, p. 1); some 131,529 remained in
   GSA stocks, 1975.

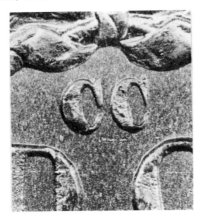

5557   1881 [all kinds 9,163,000 + 984P] Normal date.
   At least 10 minor vars., most with minor traces of repunching on date. Compare next. In all, 59 obvs., 47 revs.

5558   1881 8/7. Presently very scarce.
   Trace of 7 in lower loop of second 8. Discovered by Art
   Moyano, 1969.

5559   1881 O [all kinds 5,708,000]
   Same comment as to **5557.** Medium O only. "Sliders" are
   plentiful. In all, 55 obvs., 40 revs.

5560   1881 O over S. Presently very rare.
   Similar to **5567.** Discovered by Art Moyano.

5561   1881 S [all kinds 12,760,000]
   At least 22 minor vars., most with minor traces of repunching on date and/or S. Medium S only henceforth through
   1899. Gems are plentiful. The Treasury released many bags
   in 1938 *(NSM* 1/55, p. 1) plus over 40,000 more UNCs. about
   1960–61; possibly 10,000 more in Redfield hoard. In all, 85
   obvs., 85 revs.

5562   1881 S Second 8/7. Presently scarce.
   At least 11 obvs. "Horn" (serif of 7) at upper l. of 8; traces of
   shaft of 7 in lower loop. Some show traces of 9 within final l.
   Discovered by Art Moyano, 1971.

5563   1881 CC [all kinds 296,000] Normal.
   At least 3 vars., without or with minute traces of repunching
   on date. Large CC henceforth. GSA (1975) held 147,485
   UNCs. Compare next. In all, 25 pairs of dies, not all used.

5564   1881 CC Second 8/7.
   Earliest state of VAM 2; crossbar of 7 within upper loop of
   second 8. Independently discovered by this writer and Art
   Moyano. Later states, with most of 7 gone, will price as preceding; VAM (p. 256) estimated that these comprised 40% of
   total mintage.

5565   1882 [11,100,000 + 1,101 + P]
   At least 15 minor vars., many with traces of repunching on
   date. Often with partly or completely filled 2 (not an overdate). Knob of 2 touches or barely free of middle stroke; we
   are not convinced these are different logotypes. Business
   strikes are from 58 obvs., 60 revs.; proofs from 2 pairs of dies.

5566   1882 O [all kinds 6,090,000] Normal O.
   Same comments except 17+ vars. Many are prooflike. In all,
   33 pairs of dies.

5567   1882 O over S.
   VAM 3–6, 17, 23 (1977 Supplement); OMM 1–3. Those with
   less of the S visible at O command smaller premiums or will
   price as preceding. Very rarely prooflike.

5568   1882 S [9,250,000]
   Same comments as to **5565.** Possibly 5,000 UNCs. were in
   Redfield hoard. In all, 55 pairs of dies.

5569   1882 CC [1,133,000]
   Same comments as to **5565** except about 5 minor vars. Treasury released the first bags in late 1938; GSA held over
   605,000 (1975), mostly UNC. Large CC henceforth. In all, 15
   pairs of dies.

5570   1882 CC Doubled rev. die. Presently rare.
   Not in VAM. Doubling plainest on legend.

5571   1883 [12,290,000 + 1,039P]
   Many minor vars., some with traces of repunching on 3 or
   83. That with low 3 (VAM 6, not rare) may represent hand
   reworking or a different logotype; the difference is difficult to
   see. Treasury released several bags (different vars.) in 1938.
   Proofs (one pair of dies made) have a minute wart on cheek.
   Business strikes are from 62 obvs., 59 revs.

5572   1883 O [8,725,000 + 12P]
   At least 16 minor vars., some with minor repunching on
   parts of date or O. Most survivors are UNC., from Treasury
   bags (1938) or GSA holdings. Gems are common. Proofs: See
   Breen {1977}, p. 235; authentication is mandatory. In all, 40
   obvs., 36 revs.

5573   1883 S [6,250,000]
   Minor vars., without or with dash below 8, from 40 pairs of
   dies. "Sliders" are plentiful; hundreds of bag-marked UNCs.
   came from the Redfield hoard.

5574   1883 CC [1,204,000]
   At least 4 minor vars. from 10 pairs of dies, one (VAM 4)
   with repunching on date. UNCs. are from Treasury bags
   (1938, 1961–63) and GSA holdings (755,000).

5575   1884 [all kinds 14,070,000 + 875P] Normal.
   Minor vars., one (VAM 5) with repunching on 18; compare
   next. Much hoarded. In all, 60 pairs of dies, plus one pair for
   proofs.

5576 1884 Dot. Scarce.

Raised dot adjacent to Morgan's initial M on obv. and rev. 2 obvs., VAM 3 with large dot, VAM 4 with small; deliberately done, purpose unknown despite conjectures in VAM. First reported by Francis X. Klaes, *NSM* 5/62.

5577 1884 O [all kinds 9,730,000] Oval O, slit opening.

Mintmark as in 1879–83. At least 17 minor vars. from 10 pairs of dies (and leftover revs.), many with repunching on date or mintmark; some look almost as though O is over S or C (not confirmed). Most survivors are from Treasury bags (1938, 1960–2); many are weakly struck.

5578 1884 O Round O, wide opening.

Mintmark as in 1885–1904; VAM 2, 18. Forms a minority of survivors.

5579 1884 S [3,200,000]

At least 4 minor vars. from 20 pairs of dies. "Sliders" are plentiful (and usually overgraded); real UNCs. are rare enough to have attracted forgers' attention: Many fakes have S added to genuine Philadelphia coins. Authentication is mandatory! Auction 82:807, UNC., $4,500. Very rarely prooflike.

5580 1884 CC [1,136,000]

At least 9 minor vars. from 10 pairs of dies, some with light repunching on date and/or CC. UNCs. are plentiful, from Treasury bags (1938, 1961–63) and GSA holdings (962,000).

5581 1885 [all kinds 17,786,837 + 930P] Normal.

At least 10 minor vars. from 89 obvs., 88 revs., some with traces of repunching on 5 or 85. UNCs. are largely from Treasury bags released in Dec. 1954. Compare next. Proofs are from 2 obvs., 1 rev.

5582 1885 Obvious double date. Very scarce.

VAM 6. Doubling plainest at tops of all digits.

5583 1885 O [9,185,000]

Same comment as to **5581** except that the Treasury releases began 1938. In all, 10 pairs of dies.

5584 1885 S [1,497,000]

At least 6 minor vars. from 20 pairs of dies, some with partial repunching on date or mintmark. Flat strikings are common.

5585 1885 CC [228,000]

4 vars. from 10 pairs of dies. Most survivors are UNC., including about 148,000 from GSA holdings. The fourth var. (in 1977 VAM Supplement) has obvious bar of 7 emerging from base of second 8, but no other trace of overdate; scarce.

5586 1886 [all kinds 19,963,000 + 886P] Even 6.

Top and base of 6 on same arc line as 188: see enl. ill. at VAM 7. Found with open 6 (knob free of loop) or closed 6 (knob touches loop); latter may be heavier impressions of same logotype: Compare next 2. Many minor vars. from 63 obvs., 60 revs., some with traces of repunching on date or filled 6. Many UNCs. from Treasury bags released Dec. 1954.

5587 1886 Obvious double date. [Incl. in 886P] Proofs only.

Not in VAM; date first entered too low, slanting up to r., then corrected higher and level. Apparently even 6. 1974 GENA:110, others.

5588 1886 High 6.

Top and base of 6 well above arc line of 188: see enl. ills. at VAM 6, 8. Closed 6. I have not seen the 1886/5 reported by Ted Clark.

5589 1886 O [all kinds 10,710,000] Even 6.

Same comments as to **5586,** except no quantities of UNCs. released. Usually in low grades; "sliders" plentiful; choice UNCs. seldom seen, rarely prooflike.

5590 1886 O High 6.

Same comments. Date as **5588** (VAM 2, others).

5591 1886 S [750,000]

3 minor vars., one with repunching on S. Many UNCs. from the Redfield hoard.

5592 1887 [all kinds 20,290,000 + 710P] Normal date.

At least 13 minor vars. from 55 obvs., 54 revs., many with partial repunching on date; at least 2 doubled obv. dies, neither obvious (VAM 12, 13). Treasury holdings yielded many UNC. bags.

5593 1887/6

VAM 2. Discovered by Ted Clark, 11/71; LM 10/72:878. The 1886 date was from the High 6 logotype. Price for early states as ill.; later states show progressively less traces of 6, finally only microscopic fragments. These bring lower premiums and are apt to pass unnoticed.

5594 1887 Obvious double date. Very scarce.

VAM 5. Doubling plainest below tops of 87.

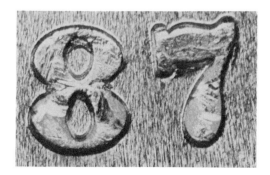

5595 1887 O [all kinds 11,550,000] Normal date.
Many minor vars. Treasury bags (March 1964) include many weak strikes.
5596 1887 O Obvious double date. Rare.
VAM 2.

5597 1887/6 O
VAM 3. Always flat strikes. Considered rare until 400 turned up at the 1977 ANA Convention. Overdate never much clearer than that ill. Discovered by Bob Riethe, late 1972.

5598 1887 S [1,771,000]
At least 5 minor vars. from 20 obvs., 13 revs. Several thousand UNCs. in Redfield hoard.
5599 1888 [19,183,000 + 800P] Normal.
Several minor positional vars. from 64 obvs., 54 revs. Proofs have date slanting up to r.
5600 1888 Obvious double date. [Incl. in 800P] Proofs only. Very rare.
Not in VAM. Date first punched to l. of final position. Forms a tiny minority of proofs. Discovery coin, "Anderson Dupont":2586.
5601 1888 O [all kinds 12,150,000] Oval O, slit opening.
Mintmark as in 1879–84. VAM 2, 5, 6. Forms a minority of survivors.
5602 1888 O Round O, wide opening.
VAM 1, 3, 7, 8, 9, others. Miller {1982}, p. 9, alludes to examining 24 mint bags (24,000 pieces) in eastern Montana, 1971–78. Some with repunching on date; VAM 9 (rarer) has slight doubling on wreath and arrows.

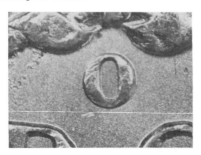

5603 1888 O Double lips. Very rare.
VAM 4; mintmark as last. Also called "Hot Lips." Doubled obv. die, plainest on lips, chin, upper eyelid, cotton leaves, and blossoms. Usually in low grades. Discovered by Chester M. Bryk, *NSM* 6/62, p. 1011.

5604 1888 S [657,000]
Without or with minor repunching on date or S. Over 3,000 UNCs. in the Redfield hoard, including over 1,000 prooflikes.
5605 1889 [21,726,000 + 711P]
At least 12 minor vars. from 57 obvs., 50 revs., 6 with partly repunched dates. "Open 9" coins have knob free of loop, "closed 9" have knob touching loop; we are not convinced these are different logotypes, as both have high 9. Many Treasury bags appeared in Dec. 1954.
5606 1889 O [all kinds 11,875,000] Oval O, slit opening.
VAM 2. Forms a minority of survivors. Flat strikings are frequent.
5607 1889 O Round O, wide opening.
At least 13 minor vars., some with repunching on date or O. Flat strikings are frequent; "sliders" numerous. Compare next.
5608 1889 O Same, wide date. Presently scarce.
VAM 10, 11. Different logotype, not seen on other mints: 8 9 much farther apart than other digits, 9 not high.
5609 1889 S [700,000]
At least 6 minor vars., some with repunching on 9 or S. High 9 logotype as usual. Several UNC. bags were retrieved from San Francisco Mint vaults, 1937; at least 1,000 bag-marked UNCs. in the Redfield hoard.
5610 1889 CC [350,000]
High 9. Three minor vars. from 2 pairs of dies out of 10 obvs. and 7 revs. made. VAM 1 (middle of second 8 centrally above a dentil) usually shows faint crack joining 89; VAM 2 (middle of second 8 above space between dentils) does not. Both revs. have second C minutely low and leaning minutely l. Usually in low grades; rare enough EF to UNC. that forgers have affixed CC mintmarks to genuine Philadelphia coins. Authentication is mandatory. Many true mint-state survivors are prooflike, e.g., 1982 ANA:2979, $17,000. At least 1,000 and possibly as many as 3,000 were in Treasury holdings, 1964.

5611 1890 [16,802,000 + 590P] Even date.

At least 9 minor vars. from 48 obvs., 49 revs., some with partial repunching on date. We are not sure if the open 9 (VAM 2, knob free of loop) represents a different logotype rather than a lighter impression or a repolished die.

5612 1890 High zero.

Base and top of 0 above arc line of 189. Minor vars. exist. VAM 7, others.

5613 1890 O [10,710,000] Even date.

At least 9 minor vars. Many UNCs. from Treasury holdings.

5614 1890 O High zero.

As **5612.** VAM 7, others.

5615 1890 S [8,230,373]

At least 12 minor vars., some with repunching on mintmark. Many UNCs. from Treasury holdings; several thousand in Redfield hoard.

5616 1890 S Obvious doubled date. Very scarce.

VAM 12 (ill. in VAM is mislabeled 11). Date first entered slanting up to r., then corrected.

5617 1890 CC [2,309,041]

At least 7 minor vars., some with partly repunched dates or CC. Mintmarks lean r. or l. or are sometimes irregularly placed. Probably comes with both even date and high 0 logotypes. A little over 3,900 were in the Treasury/GSA holdings; hundreds of others in Redfield hoard. Many of the best are prooflike. Compare next.

5618 1890 CC "Tail bar." Rare.

VAM 4. Heavy die gouge. Usually in low grades.

5619 1891 Closed 9. [8,693,556 + 650P] Normal.

UNCs. are usually heavily bag-marked. May exist with Open 9 (see **5621**).

5620 1891 Closed 9. Doubled Ear. Presently rare.

VAM 2. Doubled obv. die, plainest at earlobe, outer edge of ear, and hair above ear.

5621 1891 O [7,954,529]

At least 9 minor vars. from 30 obvs., 29 revs., some with repunched mintmark. UNCs. are usually heavily bag-marked. We are not certain if Open and Closed 9's represent different logotypes (knob touches loop or free of it).

5622 1891 S [5,296,000]

At least 6 minor vars. from 27 pairs of dies, some with minor repunchings on mintmark. At least 5,000 UNCs. were in Redfield hoard, many of them spotty prooflike strikings. "Sliders" are plentiful.

5623 1891 S Doubled obv. die. Very scarce.

VAM 3. Doubling plainest at l. stars and eyelid.

5624 1891 CC [1,618,000]

At least 4 minor vars. from 24 obvs., 23 revs., including "Spitting Eagle" (die chip just below opening of beak: common). Treasury/GSA holdings included over 5,600; others in Redfield hoard.

5625 1892 [1,036,000 + 1,245P]

Usually in low grades. UNCs. are mostly weak strikes or heavily bag-marked, including those in Redfield hoard. In all, 9 pairs of dies.

5626 1892 O [2,744,000]

At least 5 minor vars. Usually in low grades. Gems are mostly from a single bag discovered in 1977. Very rarely prooflike.

5627 1892 S [1,200,000] Normal.

At least 3 minor vars. Usually in low grades. UNCs. are rare enough to have attracted the attention of forgers who affixed mintmarks to genuine Philadelphia coins; authentication is mandatory. Many of the genuine UNCs. are prooflike. Carter:358, $14,300. See next.

5628 1892 S Double date. Very scarce.

VAM 2. Date first punched too low, then corrected; plainest within 892, knob of original 2 remains as triangular patch. Usually in low grades.

5629 1892 CC [1,352,000]

At least 7 minor vars., with CC tilted or variously spaced; VAM 6 has second C too low, others repunched 2 or CC. Reportedly none in Treasury holdings, but at least 1,000 in Redfield hoard.

5630 1893 [389,000 + 792P]

At least 5 minor vars. from 7 pairs of dies, 2 with 3 repunched (plainest at top). UNCs. are usually notably bag-marked, from Treasury and Redfield hoards. Very rarely prooflike.

5631 1893 O [300,000]

Usually in low grades. Most UNCs. are heavily bag-marked, many prooflike. In all, 10 obv. dies; revs. were left over from previous years.

5632 1893 S [100,000]

Usually in low grades. Many forgeries exist, most made by affixing S mintmark to genuine 1893 Philadelphia dollars; authentication is mandatory. All genuine specimens to date show raised line up from upper l. edge of T(Y) through crossbar; cf. *NUM* 7/78, p. 1388. Probably over half the UNC. survivors come from the 20 found in a bag of 1894 S's discovered about 1952 in Great Falls, Mont. Leo A. Young, Auction 80:1795, $48,000; Jerome Kern, Carter:364, $57,750. Apparently only one pair of dies was used out of 10 obvs. and 2 revs. shipped.

5633 1893 CC [677,000 + 12?P]

The proofs (ill.) were made for closing ceremonies, being the last issues from this branch mint. 1) Carter:365, $26,400. 2) 1973 FUN, Auction 79:1099, $39,000. Though no quantities turned up in Treasury holdings, at least 1,000 were in the Redfield hoard; hundreds of these show scrapes on cheek or breast feathers from a coin counting machine. Many of the best are prooflike but not well struck. They

come normal, or with CC leaning r. (these often with chip between outer loops of 3), or with top of 3 repunched similar to 1893 Philadelphia. In all, 10 obvs., 5 revs. shipped; some of these were remintmarked for 1900 O. See **5671, 5673.**

5634 1894 [110,000 + 972P]

Beware removed mintmark; authentication of high-grade specimens is necessary. UNCS. are mostly from a bag of 1,000 found in Great Falls, Mont., about 1961. In all, 7 obvs., 5 revs.

5635 1894 O [1,723,000]

At least 6 minor vars. from 10 obvs., 7 revs. Usually in low grades. UNCS. (from Treasury releases, 1963) are mostly weak. "Sliders" are plentiful.

5636 1894 S [1,260,000]

UNCS. are mostly from Treasury bags released before 1953. In all, 18 obvs., 13 revs.

5637 1895 [12,000 + 880P]

No business strikes known, though they were struck from at least one of the 5 obvs. and 4 revs. made for this mintage. All circulated survivors examined to date (possibly 10) are from one or other of the 2 vars. of proofs; both ill. in Breen {1977}, p. 197. Authentication of any nonproof is mandatory because many forgeries have been created by removing mintmarks from O or S coins. Carter:369, Proof, $22,000.

5638 1895 O [450,000]

At least 3 minor vars. from 5 pairs of dies. Usually in low grades; many in or near UNC. are weak strikes.

5639 1895 S [400,000] Normal.

Same comments. About 1,000 heavily bag-marked UNCS. were in Redfield hoard; about these the same comments apply as to 1893 CC. In all, 10 obvs., 6 revs.

5640 1895 S Double S. Presently rare.

VAM 3; RPM 1. Mintmark first punched high and leaning crazily to l., then lower and leaning r.

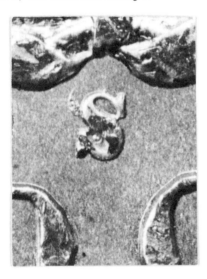

5641 1895 S S over horizontal S. Very rare.

RPM 2. "VAM 4" (not in original book).

5642 1896 [9,976,000 + 762P]

Over 16,000 were in Redfield hoard including hundreds of prooflikes.

5643 1896 Doubled obv. die. Presently rare.

VAM 4. Doubling plainest on stars.

5644 1896 Double date. Presently rare.

VAM 5. Repunching plainest on 1 and atop 6.

5645 1896/4 Rare.

Earliest state of VAM 1A. Part of upright of 4 within and above loop of 6.

5646 1896 O [4,900,000] Medium round O, wide opening.

Mintmark as 1884–95 and later years. At least 7 vars., some with repunching on numerals. Usually in low grades; UNCS. from Treasury bags (about 1963) are often weak and dull, few are choice or prooflike.

5647 1896 O Medium oval O, slit opening. Rare.

VAM 8. Mintmark as in 1879–84, 1888–89. Leftover die? Usually in low grades.

5648 1896 O Small round o. Rare.

VAM 4. Probably from the quarter-dollar mintmark punch. Usually in low grades, very rare above VF.

5649 1896 S [5,000,000]

Many minor positional vars., some with repunching on numerals or S. Most UNCS., including several hundred from the Redfield hoard, are heavily bag-marked. Very rarely prooflike.

5650 1897 [2,822,000 + 731P]

At least 6 minor vars. from 13 obvs., 12 revs., most with repunched numerals. The Redfield hoard contained over 16,000 UNCS.

5651 1897 O [4,004,000]

Usually in low grades; "sliders" are plentiful, UNCS. are often weak and very rare in gem state or prooflike. Many minor vars. from 22 pairs of dies.

5652 1897 S [5,285,000]

Many minor vars. from 38 pairs of dies. Several thousand UNCS. in Redfield hoard, including at least 1,000 prooflike.

5653 1898 [5,884,000 + 735P]

Open or closed 9 (knob free of loop or touching); we are not sure these are different logotypes. Over 16,000 UNCS. in Redfield hoard. In all, 30 pairs of dies, plus 3 obvs., 2 revs. for proofs.

5654 1898 O [4,440,000]

Many minor vars. from 30 pairs of dies, half of them with repunched final 8. Most of the dozens of Treasury bags (1,000 each) released Nov. 1962 went to Wall Street investors.

5655 1898 S [4,102,000]

At least 6 minor vars. from 20 obvs., 15 revs. Many "sliders," including the Redfield group, though the latter also contained several hundred UNCS.

5656 1899 [330,000 + 846P] Open 9's.

Small knob away from loop. Business strikes and proofs. Thousands of UNCS. survive from Treasury holdings. Only 3 pairs of dies, plus a fourth pair for proofs.

5657 1899 Closed 9's.

Larger knob joins loop. Business strikes only; same comment.

5658 1899 O [12,290,000] Open 9's, large O.

As **5656.** At least 8 minor vars. from 85 pairs of dies, some with partly repunched dates. Many bags from Treasury releases before Dec. 1962 went to Wall Street investors.

5659 1899 O Closed 9's, large O.

As **5657.** VAM 2, 8, 9, 10, others. Same comment.

5660 1899 O Closed 9's, small round o.

VAM 4, 5, 6. Mintmark as in 1880 and 1896: quarter-dollar punch? Usually in low grades; very scarce choice.

5661 1899 S [2,562,000] Open 9's, medium narrow S.

As **5656.** S as in 1879–98, serifs almost touch middle curve. At least 8 minor vars. from 20 pairs of dies, some with repunching on mintmark. Usually in low grades, except for about 1,000 UNCs. in Redfield hoard.

5662 1899 S Open 9's, large wide S.

As **5656.** S as in 1900–4, serifs away from middle curve. VAM 2, 8. Usually in low grades.

5663 1899 S Closed 9's, large wide S.

As **5657.** S as preceding. VAM 9. Usually in low grades. Forms a minority of survivors.

5664 1900 [all kinds 8,830,000 + 912P] Old rev. hub; open 9.

Old rev. hub (1879–1900) has small stars; space between wing and back of neck forms a narrow V. Open 9 has knob away from loop. VAM 5, 9, 10, others. Compare next 4. Business strikes from 66 obvs., 61 revs. + leftover dies; proofs from 2 pairs of dies.

5665 1900 Old rev. hub; closed 9.

As preceding; knob of 9 touches loop. Many minor vars. Treasury bags went to Wall Street investors before 1963.

5666 1900 New rev. hub; closed 9.

New rev. hub (1900–4) has large stars; space between wing and back of neck forms a wider U than on **5664.** VAM 2, others. But compare next 2.

5667 1900 New rev. hub; doubled rev. die. Rare.

VAM 11. Doubling plainest on eagle. Compare next.

5668 1900 New over old rev. hub. Presently rare.

Not in VAM. This working die received one blow from each hub by error. Note double olive immediately l. of claw.

5669 1900 O Old hub. [all kinds 12,590,000] Open 9; small o. Presently rare.

Knob away from loop; mintmark as in 1880, 1896, 1900, and quarter dollars. VAM 5. Usually in low grades.

5670 1900 O Open 9; large O, normal.

Many minor vars., some with partly repunched dates.

5671 1900 O Open 9; large O over CC.

OMM 3, 4; VAM 9, 11. During removal of the CC Assay Office (ex-Mint) furnishings, 6 working revs. were found, sent to Philadelphia, and remintmarked for New Orleans use. Compare **5673.** No prooflikes found.

5672 1900 O Closed 9; large O, normal.

Many minor vars., some with repunching on numerals.

5673 1900 O Closed 9; large O over CC.

OMM 1, 2, 5; VAM 7, 8, 10, 12. Explanation as **5671.** Not found prooflike.

5674 1900 S [all kinds 3,540,000] Open 9. Old rev. hub; narrow S.

VAM 1, 3. Mintmark as in 1879–98, serifs almost touch middle curve. "Sliders" are plentiful; thousands of UNCs. from Redfield hoard. Compare next 3. In all, 35 pairs of dies.

5675 1900 S Old rev. hub; narrow triple S. Presently rare.

VAM 3A, called "wide over narrow S."

5676 1900 S Old rev. hub; large wide S.

VAM 2, 4. Mintmark as in 1901–4, serifs away from middle curve. Same comments as to **5674.**

5677 1900 S New rev. hub; large wide S. Presently scarce.

VAM 5.

5678 1901 [all kinds 6,962,000 + 813P] Old rev. hub.
VAM 1. Business strikes only. Usually in low grades; many "sliders," not many real UNCs., almost no gems or prooflikes. Beware removed mintmarks; authentication recommended. In all, 43 obvs., 44 revs. plus leftovers.

5679 1901 New rev. hub.
VAM 2 (business strikes) and 4 (proofs); latter with minor doubling in rev. die. Beware removed mintmark. Leo A. Young, Auction 80:1818, UNC., $8,250.

5680 1901 New rev. hub; doubled eagle. Rare.
VAM 3. Doubled rev. die, plainest at tail (14 feathers show), arrows, lower parts of wings, and beak. Usually in low grades, none seen UNC.

5681 1901 New over old hub. Presently rare.
Not in VAM. As **5668**; double olive l. of claw.

5682 1901 O [all kinds 13,320,000] Old rev. hub.
VAM 1. Compare next 2. Prooflike coins are often weak.

5683 1901 O New rev. hub.
Many minor vars. Weak strikes are common. Wall Street investors bought large quantities from Treasury releases, 1962–63. Compare next.

5684 1901 O New over old rev. hub. Presently rare.
Not in VAM. As **5668**; double olive l. of claw.

5685 1901 S [all kinds 2,848,000] Old rev. hub.
VAM 1, 3, others. Often weak; almost never prooflike.

5686 1901 S New rev. hub.
VAM 2, 4, others. Often better struck than preceding. Almost never prooflike.

5687 1901 S New over old rev. hub. Presently rare.
Not in VAM. As **5668**; double olive l. of claw.

5688 1902 [all kinds 7,994,000 + 777P] New rev. hub. Normal.
"Sliders" are plentiful. In all, 80 obvs., 67 revs.

5689 1902 New over old rev. hub. Presently rare.
Not in VAM. As **5668**; double olive l. of claw.

5690 1902 O [all kinds 8,636,000] Old rev. hub, small round o. Presently rare.
VAM 3. Mintmark as in 1880, 1896, 1900, and quarter dollars. Usually in low grades.

5691 1902 O New rev. hub, large O.
Many minor vars. from 140 obvs., 107 revs., some with filled 2 (not an overdate), repunching on 1 or mintmark. The Treasury released several hundred thousand UNCs. in Nov. 1962.

5692 1902 O New over old rev. hub. Presently very scarce.
Not in VAM. At least 6 rev. dies. As **5668**; double olive l. of claw.

5693 1902 S [all kinds 1,530,000] New rev. hub. Normal.
Minor vars., some with partly filled 2 (not an overdate) or repunching on 02. Weak strikings are common; UNCs. often

heavily striated, including several thousand from Redfield hoard.

5694 1902 S New over old rev. hub. Presently rare.
Not in VAM. At least 2 rev. dies. As **5668**; double olive l. of claw.

5695 1903 New rev. hub. [4,652,000 + 755P]
Open and closed 9's claimed for this date; we are not sure that these represent different logotypes. Several hoards including possibly a few hundred prooflikes (not gems) from Redfield. In all, 46 obvs., 40 revs.

5696 1903 O New rev. hub. [4,450,000]
Usually in mint state; minor positional vars. Before the Treasury released nearly 100,000 in Nov. 1962, this was a rarity. VAM 2 is claimed to be a taller mintmark with narrow slit as in 1879, but the photograph in the VAM book does not confirm this, and I have not seen one with the 1879 punch.

5697 1903 S [all kinds 1,241,000] New rev. hub. Small s. Presently rare.
VAM 2. Apparently from the quarter-dollar punch. Usually in low grades. Ex. rare UNC.

5698 1903 S Large S.
Usually in low grades; very rare UNC. 1978 ANA:1261, $3,000. UNCs. are mostly from a tiny group released by the Treasury in Nov. 1953: *NSM* 1/55, p. 1. Beware forgeries made by affixing S mintmark to genuine Philadelphia coins. Authentication is mandatory.

5699 1903 S New over old rev. hub. Presently rare.
Not in VAM. As **5668**; double olive l. of claw.

5700 1904 New rev. hub. [2,788,000 + 650P]
"Sliders" are plentiful; most real UNCs. are dull or heavily nicked, from a bag dispersed early in 1979. There are several small hoards of proofs.

5701 1904 O New rev. hub. [3,720,000]
At least 9 minor vars., of which at least 5 have one or more digits repunched. Wall Street investors bought tens of thousands from Treasury releases of Nov. 1962 (compare **5696**). Prooflikes are plentiful.

5702 1904 S New rev. hub. Normal. [2,304,000]
Usually in low grades; UNCs. are weak or heavily bag-marked, gems rare.

5703 1904 S New over old rev. hub. Presently rare.
Not in VAM. As **5668**; double olive l. of claw.

5704 1921 [all kinds 44,690,000 + 10+P] Redesigned. Rev., 17 berries.
Parallel arrow feathers, flat breast. The seventeenth berry is within r. wreath at top, opposite stand of R. Business strikes and Zerbe strikes. For the Zerbe strikes see Breen {1977}, p. 220; these are usually poorly cleaned, and have die file mark up to r. from l. tip of l. serif of second U in UNUM; business strikes exist from this obv.

5705 1921 Rev., 16 berries.
Lacks the seventeenth berry described above. Business strikes and Chapman proofs (ill.). Some business strikes have only 157 edge reeds (about 34 to the linear inch)—"Infrequent Reeding"—instead of the usual 188–89. Chapman proofs (very brilliant) have hollow obv. area (die polish) around Morgan's initial M, and faint scattered die striations around UN AM RICA. Leo A. Young, Auction 80:1832, $19,000. See introductory text.

5706 1921 Same, raised round dot in field.
Location varies; size varies, usually from half the size of a berry to full berry size. At least 35 vars. Discovery reported by Frank Spadone, 1963; confirmed by Steve Sabella and Leroy C. Van Allen, June 1979. *CW* 10/17/79, p. 54. Significance unknown, possibly hardness testing on individual working dies.

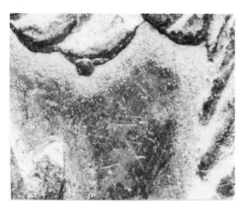

5707 1921 S 16 berries. [21,695,000]
Micro s. Coinage began May 9. Usually badly nicked. Proofs exist; see Breen {1977}, p. 238. Authentication of proofs is mandatory.

5708 1921 S Same, raised round dot in field.
As **5706**. At least 9 vars. Discovered by Steve Sabella, June 1979.

5709 1921 D 16 berries. [20,345,000]
Micro D. Minute positional vars. Compare next.

5710 1921 D Same, raised round dot in field.
As **5706**. At least 11 vars. Discovered by Steve Sabella, June 1979.

5711 1921 D Officially engraved presentation specimen. [100]
The first 100 struck, May 9, were engraved in obv. fields in small capitals: 9TH (or other serial number) DOLLAR RELEASED FROM 1ST 100 EVER COINED AT DENVER MINT THOMAS ANNEAR, SUPT. No. 1 is in Colorado Historical Society; no. 2 is untraced; nos. 3 through 12 were in Mehl's MBS, Dec. 18, 1923. *NNW* 9/9/78, p. 15. These are not proofs. As this engraving could be imitated, authentication is essential.

ix. FRANCISCI'S PEACE DESIGN (1921–35)

Born in war, the United States has reflected the fact in its coinage ever since 1796, when Robert Scot's mistake (or Mint Director Boudinot's militant chauvinism?) placed the warlike arrows in the eagle's dexter claw (the place of honor) on all silver and gold denominations, relegating the olive branch of peace to the sinister or less honorable side. In 1872, William Barber's "Amazonian" silver pattern coins (Judd 1195, 1200, 1205) omitted both LIBERTY and olive branch (in the year of the Peace Jubilee celebrations, at that!), featuring instead two eagles, two shields, and a sword in addition to the arrows, with IN (This) GOD WE TRUST across one of the shields. (Generations later, the folkloric equivalent was "Trust in God but keep your powder dry"; in WW II, it became "Praise the Lord and pass the ammunition.") And in 1916, Weinman's new dime rev. showed the lictor's fasces of rods and axes (the power of corporal or capital punishment) far more prominently than the almost unrecognizable olive branch. Not until 1921 did our country get around to celebrating peace on a coin, and even then only over strong Congressional opposition!

We owe the idea of a coin commemorating peace (specifically the Treaty of Versailles, ending WW I) to Farran Zerbe, late Historian of the American Numismatic Association, and founder of the Chase Manhattan Bank Money Museum. Apparently this was the first time that a coin collector ever wielded enough political clout to influence not only the Bureau of the Mint but Congress as well.

At the ANA Convention (Chicago, Aug. 25, 1920), Zerbe presented a paper, "Commemorate the Peace with a Coin for Circulation," proposing a new design for the half dollar or—should silver-dollar coinage be resumed pursuant to the Pittman Act—then that denomination instead. This paper appeared in *NUM* 10/20, p. 443, incorporated into an account of convention proceedings: an all but unprecedented honor. The ANA's enthusiasm was so great that it created a committee to prepare a bill for Congress. Chaired by Judson Brenner, this group comprised Rep. William A. Ashbrook (D.-Ohio), Dr. J. M. Henderson, Howland Wood, and Zerbe himself. At a meeting in Dec. 1920, the committee converted Rep. Albert Henry Vestal (R.-Ind.) to support of the project. Vestal was then Chairman of the House Committee on Coinage, Weights, and Measures, and his backing was believed essential.

On May 9, 1921, Morgan dollar coinage resumed at the San Francisco branch: to Zerbe's acute disappointment, as he had hoped instead for adoption of a Peace design. On the same day, Rep. Vestal introduced the Peace dollar coinage bill as a joint resolution. However, when Vestal (seeking immediate passage) tried to place this resolution onto the unanimous consent calendar, a single objection occurred, and the ensuing debate lasted until adjournment without a vote. (It developed that the Peace dollar could be issued without Congressional approval: The Morgan design had been current for well over its statutory 25-year tenure.)

The federal Commission of Fine Arts announced another design competition, Nov. 23, 1921, inviting the nation's eight leading sculptors to submit models. The winner was Anthony de Francisci (pronounced fran-chee-shee), who portrayed his then 23-year-old wife, née Teresa Cafarelli, as Ms. Liberty, with a "radiate" crown somewhat like that on certain ancient Roman coins, though more explicitly intended to recall that on the Statue of Liberty. Six days after the Commission had approved his sketches, Francisci submitted preliminary relief models, whose rev. showed the eagle breaking a sword, for disarmament. Isaiah 2:4. This device was publicized on Dec. 19, the same day the Commission approved his models—only to meet with howls of raging protest from hawkish officials: They insisted that this design would be interpreted as defeat rather than as negotiated peace! Because of these objections, the Mint Bureau ordered changes, and Mint Engraver George Morgan (in the first of a series of alterations done without Francisci's consent) remodeled the eagle, minus sword or arrows but with olive branch, atop an isolated mountain peak inscribed PEACE, in lettering of a style very different from that elsewhere on the coin. Hastily approved, it was even more hastily translated into working hubs and dies, and some 1,006,473 were struck Dec. 26–31, 1921, in high relief. A messenger delivered the first one to Pres. Harding, Jan. 3, 1922; others went the same day to the Secretary of Treasury and the Director of the Mint. Some of these are likely to have been among the matte-finish and satin-finish 1921 proofs (below).

Unfortunately, approval of the design must have come from the first proofs, not from production coins. The latter (mostly struck under reduced pressure to minimize unexpectedly rapid die breakage) were weak and vague in centers. Morgan, whose own design had been superseded, lowered the relief on the electroplate model—by hammering it with a flat board!—and made numerous niggling changes, while Francisci was forced to travel to the Mint, ostensibly to supervise necessary revisions, but in actuality to stand by and helplessly watch his original concept trivialized. Taxay {1966}, pp. 354–59.

Except for the matte proofs of 1922 Type of 1921, all subsequent Peace dollars are from the modified design; letters are often hard to read even on perfect mint-state survivors.

There are actually four different Peace proof issues, all of them discoveries of recent decades.

1. 1921 Matte. Fine-grain matte surface, similar to that found on 1913–16 proof Buffalo nickels. Central hair and all feathers sharp, as in ill. of **5712**. Possibly 6–8 known.

2. 1921 Satin Finish. No trace of mint frost; central hair and feathers as sharp as on the matte proofs; scattered obv. die file marks slant up and down, crossing one another in upper l. fields and through and around upper parts of letters in LIBERTY (mostly parallel to horizontal elements of letters), others in arcs of approximately concentric circles. Triangular pellet after TRVST is in unusually high relief, as are rays on rev.; this die has similar relief marks in fields, notably at S OF. Possibly 7–10 known, though business strikes exist from one or both of these dies; the latter have only ordinary striking quality (flat in central hair and on many feathers, notably leg and forward

parts of wing, where rays meet them). Discovered at the 1975 ANA Convention.

3. 1922 Type of '21. High relief, concave fields as in 1921; design modified, two short rays added to coronet (making 11 in all), lettering redrawn (especially noticeable at L and WE TRVST), all hair details stronger, mountain entirely redrawn, feathers strengthened. Matte surfaces like the first 1921's; the only 1922 high-relief dollars. Ill. **5713**. 6–8 known. First described in Breen {1961}.

4. 1922 Regular design. Low relief, flat fields, thinner letters and numerals, long, thin curved tail to R in TRVST, thin rays in coronet (13 tall, 12 short), four large berries in branch, leaves larger and heavier, mountain range again entirely different. The working dies used for making the few proofs have die file marks slanting slightly up to r. from either side of talons; it is unknown if these were later used for business strikes, but the design continues unaltered into 1935. On the proofs, rims are much sharper than on business strikes; inner coronet line exceptionally strong; full central hair, full feathers, letters (especially in mottoes) far sharper than on business strikes; satin finish, a little nearer that on "Roman finish" gold proofs of 1909–10 than anything else. Ill. **5714**. Only 3 proofs known.

These must not be confused with the seemingly prooflike processed coins, first reported about 1965 in the Los Angeles area. The latter have artificial mirrorlike fields (from polishing) and consequent loss of detail on letters.

On the other hand, a very few rare specimens of later years show prooflike surfaces (mirror finish, in fields only, not on letters or devices); these are doubtless from dies which had been hastily repolished to efface clash marks.

Regular business strikes are from the same hubs as no. 4 above. No date or mintmark can be called rare, though the 1928 has proved to be hard enough to find choice that fakers have simulated it by removing mintmarks from 1928 S. Most Peace dollars saw little circulation except in Nevada gambling casinos. In other states, they tended to remain in banks as part of their legally required cash reserves, being paid out around Christmas time for gift purposes, then returning in January.

Coinage was halted in 1928 after the bullion purchased from Western silver mine owners was exhausted. (The Pittman Act, as amended, required such purchases in enough quantity to replace the 270,232,322 melted Morgan dollars.) We have been unable to trace, or completely understand, the notation "Struck for cornerstone purposes" affixed to 1928 in many old catalogs.

Predictably, the Western silver mine owners even took advantage of the 1929–37 Great Depression to enrich themselves further with still more publicly subsidized federal purchases. Their first act was the "Thomas Amendment" to the Agricultural Adjustment Act (May 12, 1933). This empowered the government to accept silver on war debt accounts at 50¢ per oz., the total not to exceed $200 million; silver certificates (Series of 1933, 1934, 1935) were to be issued against the amounts paid in, and the bullion would be coined into silver dollars and lower denominations. Yielding to further pressure from the congressional friends of silver, Pres. Roosevelt issued a proclamation, Dec. 21, 1933, requiring that the mints coin silver dollars from bullion newly purchased from Western mine owners. However, even this was apparently not enough for the latter, as the Silver Purchase Act of June 18, 1934 ordered the Treasury to buy silver at home and abroad until its market price reached $1.2929 per oz. (equivalent to the monetary value of the silver in dollar coins) or until the monetary value of the Treasury's silver holdings reached 1/3 of that of its gold stock. Additional silver dollars were to be coined to redeem silver certificates.

Under these various authorizations, slightly over seven million silver dollars were coined from 1934–35. These were of the Peace design but from modified dies; lettering of IN GOD WE

TRVST was thinner, tail of R in TRVST almost straight. Some dated 1935 S are from a further modified rev.; on these, below tail a seventh ray shows, its upper extension (making four in all above tail) pointing at mintmark. Thomas W. Voetter {1940} discovered this modification.

The final appearance, or rather the final abortive use, of the Peace Dollar design occurred in 1965, creating one of the legendary vanished rarities of U.S. coinage. The Act of Aug. 3, 1964 provided for mintage of 45 million silver dollars, pursuant to previous authorizing acts. Various numismatic columnists (this writer among them) publicized the fact that (as usual with silver dollars) this mintage would benefit only a small special interest group, this time perhaps less the owners of Western silver mines than the owners of Nevada gambling casinos, while doing nothing whatever to lessen the tightness in supplies of lower-denomination coins. For once, pressure from critics outweighed pressure from beneficiary groups, and after the Denver Mint had coined 316,076 (dated 1964), May 15–24, 1965, the Treasury (with Pres. Johnson's approval) countermanded the authorization and ordered all recalled and melted. Fern Miller, of the Denver Mint, told the local coin dealer Dan Brown that as usual various employees had purchased two new dollars apiece, but that when the recall order came in, nobody kept any record either of the numbers sold to employees or the numbers turned in. It is therefore entirely possible that a few specimens survive. Paranoid Treasury officials, desperately fearing that any such coins would reach collectors and generate profits, most likely would attempt to seize and destroy them all before any court decision. Let us at least hope that a specimen will be preserved in the Smithsonian Institution.

FRANCISCI'S PEACE DESIGN

Designer, Anthony de Francisci. Engraver, George T. Morgan, after Francisci. Mints, Philadelphia (no mintmark), San Francisco (mintmark S), Denver (D). Mintmarks below ON(E). Physical Specifications, as before, except that official weight tolerance for 1964 D is ± 6 grs. = ± 0.39 gms. Authorizing Acts, as before, but see introductory text.

Grade range, GOOD to UNC. GOOD: Date legible, all devices complete in outline, all letters legible (see EXCEPTIONS). VERY GOOD: PEACE at least partly legible; rim complete; lower parts of wings demarcated; major hair contours show. FINE: Individual locks demarcated; tail feathers and lower third of neck feathers show. VERY FINE: Some single hair strands clear; three lowest wing feathers demarcated. EXTREMELY FINE: Most of finest hair strands clear; isolated tiny rubbed spots (forelock, around face, back of eagle's head, etc.); partial mint luster. UNCIRCULATED: *No* trace of wear. NOTE: "Sliders" are common. EXCEPTIONS: On 1922–28, parts of IN GOD, PEACE, and PLURIBUS may be blurry even in VF.; on 1921, central details will be weak even in mint state, but mint luster will show on the weak areas.

5712 1921 High relief. [1,006,473 + ?P]
Mintage began Dec. 26, 1921. Normally weak in centers except on proofs (like the matte proof ill.); see introductory text.

5713 1922 High relief, type of 1921. [?P] Proofs only. Ex. rare.
See introductory text. Auction 85:1277, $37,400; "Four Memorable Colls.": 652, $38,500.

5714 1922 Low relief, regular type. [51,737,000 + ?P]
First ill. is one of the three satin-finish proofs; business strikes (also ill.) are normally weak in centers and on rev. letters. Alleged doubled obv. dies have proved to be strike doubling, no 2 identical.

5715 1922 S [17,475,000]
Minor positional vars. of mintmark on this and all S and D coins to follow. Rims often weak on this and later S mints. The Redfield hoard yielded many nicked UNCS. of this and all later S mints (except 1934 S).

5716 1922 D [15,063,000]
"Sliders" are plentiful; most UNCS. are heavily bag-marked.

5717 1923 [30,800,000]
The Treasury released many bags in Nov. 1945. One var. has minor doubled rev. die. Occasionally mistaken for the much scarcer 1928.

5718 1923 S [19,020,000]
Rarely found choice. "Sliders" are plentiful. Occasionally mistaken for 1928 S.

5719 1923 D [6,811,000]
Same comments as to **5716**.

5720 1924 [11,811,000]

5721 1924 S [1,728,000]
Same comments as to **5716**.

5722 1925 [10,198,000]
Same comments as to **5716.** The Treasury released many in 1945.

5723 1925 S [1,610,000]
Not often found choice. The Redfield hoard contained about 5,000 weakly struck UNCS.

5724 1926 [1,939,000]
The Treasury released many in 1944. "Sliders" are plentiful.

5725 1926 S [6,980,000]
"Sliders" are plentiful. The Redfield hoard yielded thousands of nicked UNCS.

5726 1926 D [2,348,700]

5727 1927 [848,000]

5728 1927 S [866,000]
The Redfield hoard yielded several thousand UNCS.

5729 1927 D [1,268,900]
UNCS. are rarely choice.

5730 1928 [360,649]
"Sliders" are always available for a price. Beware specimens fabricated by removing S mintmark. See introductory text.

5731 1928 S [all kinds 1,632,000] Very small s.
Rarely well struck or choice. Many in the Redfield hoard were scratched by a coin-counting machine.

5732 1928 S Larger S. Presently very rare.
Mintmark as in some lower denominations: boldface (thick middle stroke), sharp vertical serifs.

5733 1934 Modified design. [954,057]
See introductory text. "Sliders" are plentiful.

5734 1934 S Modified design. [1,011,000]
UNCS. are mostly from a hoard found in San Francisco about 1962, though 35 turned up at the 1978 F.U.N. convention, and at least one other hoard is reported. Auction 82:828, $3,000. Usually in low grades. "Sliders" are available for a price. Beware of forgeries made by affixing S mintmarks to genuine Philadelphia coins; authentication recommended.

5735 1934 D [all kinds 1,569,500] Modified design. Minute D. VAM 1. Mintmark from same punch as formerly. Seldom choice; "sliders" are plentiful. None in Treasury or Redfield hoards.

5736 1934 D Same. Doubled obv. die. Presently rare.
Similar to **5738.**

5737 1934 D Larger D.
VAM 2. Mintmark heavy, as on the quarter dollar. Same comments as to **5735.** Compare next.

5738 1934 D Larger D; doubled obv. die. Presently rare.
Doubling plainest on motto and profile. *NUM* 8/82, p. 2037.

5739 1935 [1,576,000]
"Sliders" are plentiful.

5740 1935 S [all kinds 1,964,000] Old rev. hub.
3 rays below ONE. Choice UNCS. are plentiful both from

Redfield and from the hoard that yielded most UNC. 1934 S's. See introductory text.

5741 1935 S New rev. hub.
4 rays below ONE. Discovered by Thomas W. Voetter. See introductory text.

5742 1964 D [316,076] Untraced.
See introductory text.

x. GASPARRO'S EISENHOWER DESIGN (1971–74)

When the Mint Bureau decided to honor Neil Armstrong and "Buzz" Aldrin for planting mankind's first footprints on the Moon, a problem arose: on which denomination? Cent, nickel, dime, quarter, all seemed too unimpressive; the Kennedy half dollar would have required an Act of Congress, thanks to the Act of Sept. 25, 1890 which gave any current design 25 years' tenure. As several successive Mint Directors, fearing collectors and counterfeiters, had repeatedly declared commemorative half dollars a no-no, officialdom decided to revive the dollar coin. Ambivalently, the coins for circulation were to be in the regular nickel-clad "sandwich metal" composition decreed by the Coinage Act of July 23, 1965, but those earmarked for collectors were silver-clad like the half dollars.

Mint Engraver Frank Gasparro chose to represent the historic message, "The Eagle Has Landed," with the Eagle about to drop his olive branch into the Plain of Tranquility (fortunately he brought no arrows). Spaceship Earth is visible near the restored New Constellation of 1783 (13 stars in a circular arc). Alas, Gasparro's Earth shows neither the beautiful swirling clouds actually seen from the Moon, nor an accurate outline of the continents, but contours vaguely like parts of the USA, Mexico, Central America, and northern South America, with a grossly exaggerated West Indies. Gasparro adapted his device from the Apollo IX insignia designed by Michael Collins and James Cooper for NASA.

Because Pres. Dwight D. "Ike" Eisenhower had died four months before the Moon landing, authorities chose his portrait for obv. Gasparro eased his task by using the same layout as on the current quarter dollar. Both designs had to be modified several times, reportedly to improve striking quality.

The coins early received the sobriquet of "Ike" dollars, though a few careless promoters called the nickel-clad issue "silver" dollars and got into trouble with federal authorities.

Nickel-clad "Ikes" were struck at 170 tons force, 110 per minute; die life averaged between 100,000 and 200,000 pieces.

The rarest coins of this design are the 1974 D's struck on heavy silver-clad blanks. On Oct. 10, 1974, a Las Vegas black-jack dealer brought the first one to *Coin World*. The Mint Bureau confirmed that an unknown number of silver-clad blanks were accidentally included among nickel-clad blanks rejected as unfit for proof coinage and shipped from San Francisco to the Denver Mint. *CWA*, p. 181.

To distinguish silver-clad from nickel-clad coins, first look at the core (on edge): white on former, reddish (copper) on latter; silver-clad is heavier; ring test (see Glossary) differs.

No information is yet available about the degree of scarcity of the various minor vars. However, two of these have already been publicized as rarities, and may well remain so: the 1971 S "Peg Leg" proofs (serifs off foot of R in LIBERTY due to excessive die polishing), and the 1972 Philadelphia "Type II." This latter is from the master die used for proofs: indented outline around continental shore; West Indies as a single mega-island; FG free of tail.

Public Law 93-541 (Dec. 26, 1974) authorized 1975 strikings to continue the 1974 date, lest collectors hoard the coins. Coinage was halted so that the entire 1975–76 mintage would bear the Bicentennial design, affording collectors no chance to promote anything as scarce.

Over widespread protests, Congress donated $9 million (proceeds of sales of silver-clad "Ike" proofs) to Eisenhower College, Seneca Falls, N.Y. (Acts of 10/11/74, 12/27/74; PL 93-441, 554.) The school lost most of its students and closed July 22, 1982.

For similar coins dated 1977–78, see Sect. xiii.

GASPARRO'S EISENHOWER DESIGN

Designer, Frank Gasparro, after Michael Collins and James Cooper. Engraver, Gasparro. Mints, Philadelphia (no mint-mark), San Francisco (mintmark S), Denver (D). Mintmarks in field below truncation. Composition, silver-clad, outer layers silver 800 Fine, bonded to inner core of 21% silver, 79% copper; nickel-clad, outer layers 25% nickel, 75% copper, bonded to inner core of pure copper. Weight, silver-clad, 379.512 ± 15.18 grs. = 24.592 ± 0.984 gms.; nickel-clad, 350 ± 14 grs. = 22.68 ± 0.9 gms. (Tolerance legally defined as 4% of standard weight.) Diameter, Edge, as before. Authorizing Act, Dec. 31, 1970.

Grade range, VERY FINE to UNC. EXTREMELY FINE: Isolated tiny spots of wear, principally on cheek, jawbone, high points at edge of neck, eagle's head, legs, and parts of edges of wings; central feathers clear; partial mint luster. NOTE: Generally collected only in mint state.

5743 1971 Nickel-clad. "Type I." [47,799,000]

Low relief. 2 prototypes struck Jan. 25, then destroyed. Regular coinage released Nov. 1, 1971. Ills. of **5744**.

5744 1971 S Silver-clad. "Type I." [6,868,530]
Issue began March 31. Ills. above **5743**.

5745 1971 S Silver-clad. "Type II." [4,265,234P] Proofs only. High relief, round Earth, weakly defined continents; see introductory text. Sold separately from the proof sets. Average die life 3,500 impressions.

5746 1971 S Same. "Peg Leg." [Incl. above] Proofs only. Presently rare.
Footless R in LIBERTY. From overpolished die.

5747 1971 D Nickel-clad. "Type I." [68,587,424]
Coinage began Feb. 3. *CWA* p. 179.

5748 1972 [all kinds 75,890,000] Nickel-clad. "Type I."
Low relief, as **5743**. Compare next.

5749 1972 Nickel-clad. "Type II." Presently rare.
As **5745**; see introductory text. Compare next.

5750   1972 Nickel-clad. "Type III."
  Modified high relief as in 1973–74. No incuse outline behind
  lower r. crater; 3 distinct Caribbean islands l. of Florida.

5751   1972 S Silver-clad. "Type II." [2,193,056 + 1,811,631P]
  Sold separately from the proof sets.
5752   1972 D Nickel-clad. "Type I." [92,548,511]
  Reported in silver-clad, but the only one seen to date is a
  forgery.
5753   1973 Nickel-clad. [Net 1,769,258]
  Modified high relief obv. and rev. hereafter, as in **5750.** In
  actuality, 2,000,056 were struck, the "net mintage" figure issued in mint sets, the rest melted. None made for circulation.
5754   1973 S Nickel-clad. [2,760,339P] Proofs only.
  Included in the proof sets, unlike previous years.
5755   1973 S Silver-clad. [1,883,140 + 1,013,646P]
  Proofs sold separately from the proof sets.
5756   1973 D Nickel-clad. [Net 1,769,258]
  In actuality 2 million were minted; net mintage figure represents those sold in mint sets, remainder melted. None made
  for circulation.
5757   1974 Nickel-clad. [27,366,000]
  Mintage continued into 1975: See introductory text.
5758   1974 S Nickel-clad. [2,612,568P] Proofs only.
  Included in the proof sets.
5759   1974 S Silver-clad. [1,900,000 + 1,306,579P]
  Proofs sold separately from the proof sets. See introductory
  text.
5760   1974 D Nickel-clad. [45,517,000]
  Same comment as to **5757.** Compare next.
5761   1974 D Silver-clad. Very rare, about 30 known.
  Discovered by a Las Vegas blackjack dealer. See introductory
  text.

xi. WILLIAMS'S BICENTENNIAL DESIGN (1975–76)

On Oct. 6, 1973, the Treasury Department announced an
open contest for new rev. designs for the Bicentennial coinages.
The story behind this issue has been told in full in Chap. 27,
Sect. xix, introductory text. After the judges winnowed nearly
1,000 entries down to a dozen semifinalists, they finally chose
22-year-old Dennis R. Williams's rev. for the dollar, March 6,
1974. This depicts the Liberty Bell (as on the 1926 Sesquicentennial half dollar) superimposed on the Moon. Williams's initials DRW are just r. of the clapper.

Obvs. of all Bicentennial coins were the same as the previous
designs for their denominations, except that the date was 1776–
1976 for the entire coinage of both years, lest coin collectors
hoard quantities of either 1975 or 1976.

Despite vast publicity, these dollar coins rarely reached circulation. They were no substitute for either dollar bills or
smaller denominations. They were acceptable in almost no
vending machines except those in Nevada that sell dreams of
wealth. (Many of the one-armed bandits prefer the casinos' own
specially minted gaming tokens.)

As usual, when a new design is introduced, it must be de-
bugged; the Bicentennial dollars were no more an exception to
this rule than were the original "Ikes." As a result, early in
1975 the designs were modified. Var. I has tail of final S extending up to middle of E in STATES, and tail of R in DOL-
LAR is straight; on Var. II, tail of final S extends only minutely
above lower serif of E, and tail of R in DOLLAR is curved.
There are many other minor changes in letters and other details, but those just named permit instant unambiguous identification.

The obv. modifications are much more difficult to spot without examples of both types for comparison. On Var. I, center
bar of E in WE is about the same length as top and base; on
Var. II, this bar is much shorter. To date no transitional coins
(obv. Var. I, rev. Var. II, or vice versa) are reported, though
either or both combinations may exist.

Silver-clad coins were released in driblets through 1982,
when the rise in silver prices induced the Mint Bureau to end
issue.

Amazingly for so brief a mintage, and despite the Mint Bureau's extreme care to guard against making or releasing anything collectors could call a rarity, the Bicentennials have so far
yielded two extreme rarities: the two types of proof dollars
without mintmark S. The first (Issue of Aug. 1974) showed up
in the set exhibited under armed guard at the 1974 ANA Convention; supposedly all were destroyed, but considering their
original recipients, it is entirely possible that destruction was
not total. One hopes that a set reaches the Smithsonian Institution. The Var. II silver-clad proof without S was reportedly
found in a Washington, D.C., department store cash register,
early 1977; later via Devonshire Galleries to Andy Lustig.

WILLIAMS'S BICENTENNIAL DESIGN

Designers, obv., Frank Gasparro; rev., Dennis R. Williams.
Engraver, Gasparro. Mints, Physical Specifications, Authorizing Acts, as before, plus Bicentennial Act, Oct. 18, 1973.

No grade range or standards established. Business strikes are
collected only in mint state.

VARIETY I

5762   1776–1976 Issue of Aug. 12, 1974. [3+P] Proofs only.
  Possibly survives.
  Without mintmark. Probably silver-clad. Included in 3-piece
  sets with **4447, 5300.** Ill. *NNW* 8/27/74.   1) Pres. Gerald R.
  Ford.   2) Ford's appointment secretary.   3) Mint Bureau,
  exhibited at 1974 ANA Convention, Bal Harbour, Fla.; ill.
  1976 Yeoman Guide Book. Reputedly all destroyed. Any
  purported survivor must be authenticated, as specimens
  might be simulated by removal of S mintmark or by buffing
  or plating regular Philadelphia coins.
5763   1776–1976 Issue of 1975. Nickel-clad. [4,019,000]
  See introductory text. Release began July 7, 1975.

5764 1776–1976 S Silver-clad. [4,294,081 + 3,262,970P]
Sold in 3-piece proof and business-strike sets with quarter and half dollar. Release ended 1982.

5765 1776–1976 S Nickel-clad. [2,845,450P] Proofs only.
Included in 6-piece proof sets.

5766 1776–1976 D Nickel-clad. [21,048,710]

VARIETY II

5767 1776–1976 Issue of 1976. Nickel-clad. [113,318,000]
See introductory text.

5768 1776–1976 Silver-clad proof. Ex. rare.
Only one traced. See introductory text.

5769 1776–1976 S Nickel-clad. [4,194,730P] Proofs only.
Release ended July 22, 1976. Included in 6-piece proof sets.

5770 1776-1976 D Nickel-clad. [82,179,564]
A silver-clad specimen turned up about 1978.

xii. EAGLE REVERSE RESUMED (1977–78)

After the Bicentennial celebrations ended, the Mint Bureau resumed manufacture of regular "Ikes" as in 1974. No reason was given for so doing; the coins, like their older siblings, accumulated in bank vaults, rarely appearing in circulation.

The very rare 1977 D silver-clad coins were struck on blanks intended for S-Mint Bicentennials but erroneously sent to Denver, in parallel with the 1974 D silver-clad. Only about 15 survivors are traced.

After the Mint Bureau's Dr. Alan Goldman decided on issuing a new smaller dollar coin (the Susan B. Anthony Mini-Dollar), further coinage of "Ikes" ended. Regrets have not been noticeable.

EAGLE REVERSE RESUMED

Designer, Engraver, Mints, Physical Specifications, Authorizing Acts, as before except that no silver-clad coins were officially made.

Grade range and standards, as before. NOTE: Collected only in mint state, except for the silver-clad coin.

5771 1977 Nickel-clad. [12,596,000]

5772 1977 S Nickel-clad. [3,251,152P] Proofs only.
Issued with the proof sets.

5773 1977 D Nickel-clad. [32,983,000]
Compare next.

5774 1977 D Silver-clad. Very rare, about 15 known.
Struck on blanks intended for S-Mint Bicentennials; see introductory text. *CW* 2/22/78; *NNW* 2/25/78.

5775 1978 Nickel-clad. [25,702,000]

5776 1978 S Nickel-clad. [3,127,781P] Proofs only.
Issued with the proof sets.

5777 1978 D [33,012,890]

CHAPTER 30

WILLIAM BARBER'S TRADE DOLLARS
(1873–85)

The issue of this coin was an expensive mistake—its motivation mere greed, its design a triumph of dullness, its domestic circulation and legal-tender status a disastrous provision of law leading only to ghastly abuses, its repudiation a source of hardship for Pennsylvania coal miners and other laborers held in virtual peonage by company stores, its recall a long overdue but very mixed blessing, and its collection a source of decades of frustration.

Chinese port merchants, during the mid- and late 19th century, refused to accept any foreign silver coins except oldstyle Mexican pesos. American importers trading with Chinese dealers had to pay premiums of up to 15% for these coins in order to pay for any goods they ordered; and often pesos were unavailable, so that only the few merchants who had them could buy anything. About 1870, the importers' friends in the California legislature petitioned Congress to make special overweight dollars for the China trade, 420 grs. each at 900 Fine. This weight supposedly matched that of the Mexican peso; it was 1.8% heavier than standard dollars.

The new coins at first were to be known as "Commercial Dollars," after a letter by John Jay Knox, Comptroller of the Currency, to Secretary of Treasury George S. Boutwell (quoted in Judd, p. 126). Two pattern designs of 1871 and three of 1872 accordingly bore a rev. die with that title. However, when the Act of Feb. 12, 1873 authorized the denomination, it renamed the coins "Trade Dollars." Accordingly, the regular six-piece sets of patterns for this denomination (1873, Judd 1276, 1281, 1293, 1310, 1315, and 1322) used the new name, as did the rarer ones outside the sets. A completely different design was finally adopted. For the full historical background of design and issue, see Willem {1965}.

When the first trade dollars reached Hong Kong and Canton (Kwangtung province, now Guangdong), Oct. 1873, official assays proved the coins to be good silver of higher weight than pesos, and proclamations ordered their acceptance in trade, tax payments, and tariff payments. Nearly the entire 1873 issue from all mints (except proofs) went to China, where merchants chopmarked them with characters representing names or personal trademarks. Top grade 1873's of any mint are now rare. Chopmarked specimens exist of all dates and mintmarks 1873–78, including 1875 S/CC; a complete set was exhibited at the 1985 ANA Convention.

A last-minute rider, hastily tacked on to the 1873 Mint Act to benefit the silver lobby, gave trade dollars domestic legal-tender status in all payments up to $5; this led to disastrous abuses. In 1876, a fall in silver prices resulted in millions of trade dollars suddenly appearing in change in California: Their face value was considerably above their bullion value. On July 22, 1876, Congress revoked their legal-tender status, but mintage for the China trade continued for two more years. In 1877–78, over 8.6 million went into circulation in the Eastern states; employers bought them up in quantity at slightly over bullion value (80–83¢ each), and then put them into pay envelopes at face value. In communities where company stores were the sole retail sources for goods, storekeepers either accepted them only at the lower values, or more often raised prices; elsewhere merchants and banks either accepted them only at bullion value or refused the coins altogether: Revocation of legal-tender status left this option open. Many petitions reached Congress seeking recall of the coins; other petitions sought restoration of legal-tender status at $1 apiece. (PL 89-81, the Coinage Act of July 23, 1965, has apparently restored legal tender to the coins, though now their bullion value and numismatic value make the question irrelevant.) Mintage for circulation ended in 1878; proofs continued to appear in the regular proof sets (with a few yearly extras) through 1883.

The proofs dated 1884, however, were clandestine concoctions for William Idler, who had been for over two decades the Mint's appropriately named fence for restrikes and fantasy coins. They first came to the attention of the numismatic world in 1908 when Capt. John W. Haseltine offered six proofs from Idler's holdings. The following roster is the most nearly complete one yet attempted:

1. Adolphe Menjou, King Farouk, W. G. Baldenhofer, Ben Koenig ("Fairbanks"), Samuel Wolfson, Dan Messer, Jack Klausen, Joel Rettew, QS 11/76:426 (ill.).

2. W. F. Dunham, Floyd Starr estate.

3. J. H. Clapp, Louis Eliasberg estate.

4. Col. E. H. R. Green, Burdette G. Johnson, Jack Roe, Jerome Kern, Carter:440, $45,100.

5. "Anderson Dupont":2652.

6. William Cutler Atwater, Will W. Neil, R. C. Pelletreau,

Jerry Cohen, Julian Leidman, Jim Halperin, NERCA 11/9/75:639, $39,000, Mulford B. Simons, pvt. coll.

7. James Kelly, pvt. coll.

8. Fred Olsen, G. S. Ewalt, Dr. Calvert Emmons, Western Numismatics, 1980 ANA:2643, $30,000. Cleaned.

9. "Pvt. coll., late 1940s," 1976 ANA:723 in assembled proof set.

10. Chicago estate, RARCOA, World-Wide, Steve Ivy, R. Marks, Bowers, Herstal:734, $30,000, D. Apte, Mulford B. Simons, pvt. coll.

These cannot be directly connected to the original inventory which included Andrew Madsen Smith's coin, Idler's six, the eighth in a private coll., and two others of which Farran Zerbe had lost track. Stephen K. Nagy sold three of Idler's to Virgil Brand. (Smith, who also had a copper proof, was the Mint's major public relations agent for decades.) There are also two silver-plated copper strikings, both of which have been offered as regular silver proofs:

a) Kreisberg 9/18/61:1213, Kreisberg 11/29/65:5123, KS 5/66:1302, 1975 ANA:1218, Bowers, J. Vernon Epps.

b) Dr. Calvert L. Emmons:813, Delp:761, pvt. coll.

The 1885's reached the attention of the numismatic world on the same occasion as the 1884's. The current roster:

1. Idler, Haseltine, H. O. Granberg, W. H. Woodin, Col. E. H. R. Green, B. G. Johnson, Jack Roe, Jerome Kern, Carter:441, $110,000, Auction 84:192, $90,750.

2. Idler, Haseltine, pvt. coll., W. C. Atwater, Mrs. R. Henry Norweb.

3. Idler, Haseltine, pvt. coll., Edgar Adams, Virgil Brand, Adolphe Menjou, King Farouk, W. G. Baldenhofer, Jim Halperin, "Forecaster."

4. Idler, Haseltine, J. H. Clapp, Eliasberg estate.

5. Idler, Haseltine, pvt. coll., Fred Olsen, G. S. Ewalt:43, $11,000, Leo A. Young, Auction 80:1626, $110,000, pvt. coll., Auction 84:1810, $16,250. Badly cleaned.

A bona fide offer of $250,000 was made in 1974 in my presence for no. 3, and refused; Halperin later offered it for $300,000, but sold it at a reported $165,000.

After the mid-1880s, trade dollars began returning to this country from China, mostly with chopmarks, sometimes dozens or hundreds of them. For many years these coins' anomalous legal status meant that chopmarked pieces were deemed noncollectible (because mutilated), and many collectors and dealers turned them in at bullion value. Changes in the law have abolished this limitation. Willem {1965} discusses chopmarks at length; certain types, in particular those in which the characters are in relief, are rare.

Jewelers made many (without chopmarks) into lockets, alias "box dollars." These are internally hinged, sometimes containing photographs. They have a hidden circumferential gap between rim or beaded border and field (usually rev.); they open to thumbnail pressure within beaded border near U, TES, CA, or DO.

A piquant public commentary on the "Liberty as beachcomber" design (and on the company store abuses?): Artists altered many trade dollars to show Ms. Liberty denuded and sitting on a chamberpot: Ill. Dr. Clark:3170. No other 19th-century coin was ever so unpopular. Every specimen is a memento of one of the most controversial American issues between Reconstruction and the Sherman Silver Purchase Act.

WILLIAM BARBER'S TRADE DOLLARS

Designer, Engraver, William Barber. Mints, Philadelphia (no mintmark), San Francisco (mintmark S), Carson City (CC). Mintmarks, below NS. Composition, 90% silver, 10% copper. Diameter, 1.5″ = 38.1 mm. Weight, 420 ± 1.5 grs. = 27.22 ± 0.1 gms. Authorizing Act, Feb. 12, 1873.

Grade range, POOR TO UNC. GOOD: Date and all inscriptions legible except for LIBERTY and the two mottoes; devices completely outlined; eye visible as a spot. VERY GOOD: Garment line shows at shoulder; hair shows at back of lower neck and over shoulder; partial wheat stems, mottoes, and wing feathers. FINE: Coronet and hair knot show partial details; most wheat stems separated; full mottoes and LIBERTY (usually weak); eagle's eye and nostril show. VERY FINE: Points of both knees clear; drapery at l. breast (observer's r.) partly visible; at least half head feathers and ¾ wing feathers. EXTREMELY FINE: Isolated tiny rubbed spots only (above ear, l. breast, leg, foot, wheat heads, breast feathers; partial mint luster. UNCIRCULATED: *No* trace of wear. NOTE: Cleaned "sliders" are common. EXCEPTIONS: Even coins near mint state sometimes show chopmarks. Grade as though these were absent, then mention them. Rubber-stamped chopmarks (rare) are not impairments; relief chopmarks within depressed ovals or circles (scarce) and the common incuse chopmarks lower values according to how much design detail is lost, but far less than random mutilations.

5778   1873 [397,000 + 865P] Normal serifs.
Coinage began July 11; first release [40,000] July 14. Auction 82:1777, UNC., $3,000. The majority of survivors are chopmarked; see introductory text.

5779   1873 Broken serifs.
Early damage to the hub, at E(S) and (O)F. Willem:693. Usually chopmarked.
5780   1873 S [703,000]
Coinage began in July. Auction 82:1778, UNC., $2,500. Usually in low grades and/or chopmarked.
5781   1873 CC [124,500]
First release, [4,500] July 23. CC central or low: "Gilhousen":1452–53. Usually in low grades and/or chopmarked. Douglas Winter reports one with repunched 73; Bortin:1201. I have not seen the wide C C var. claimed in Carson:108.
5782   1874 [987,100 + 700P]
Minute positional vars. Often chopmarked. Broken serifs are partly repaired by hand on some dies of 1874–75 "Type I," all mints (see **5788**).
5783   1874 S [all kinds 2,549,000] Minute s. Very scarce.
Mintmark .033 ± .001″ = 0.84 mm. Willem:710, as "micro" s; 1984 Midwinter ANA:1496; others.

5784 1874 S Medium S.
Mintmark .042″ = 1.1 mm. Several positional vars.
5785 1874 S Large S. Rare.
Mintmark .046″ = 1.17 mm. Serifs far from middle curve.
"Gilhousen": 1458; Willem:711.
5786 1874 CC [all kinds 1,373,000] "Micro" cc. Rare.
C's .029″ = 0.74 mm., as on 1873–4 half dollars.
5787 1874 CC Tall boldface CC.
C's .042″ = 1.1 mm. Positional vars. exist. "Gilhousen":1456–57.
5788 1875 [all kinds 218,200 + 700P] "Type I" rev. Rare.
"Type I" revs. (1873–76) have berry under claw. Business
strikes (e.g., Willem:715) are rare, a small minority of
[149,200] delivered April–May 1875. Proofs (under 12 seen,
e.g., Willem:712; Phoenix:1474, $2,000; 1982 ANA:2478)
form a tiny minority of [300P], Jan. 1875. Proofs discovered
by John M. Willem, *NSM* 10/67, p. 1750. See ills. of **5778**,
5798.
5789 1875 "Type II" rev.
"Type II" revs. (1875–85) have no berry below claw; berry
stems thinner; leaves differ in shape. Design change discovered by Elliot Landau, Dec. 9, 1952; cf. *NUM* 6/53. Forms
the majority of business strikes and over 90% of proofs, but
1875 "Type II" business strikes are rarer than 1878 CC. See
ill. of **5799**.
5790 1875 S [all kinds 4,487,000] "Type I" rev. Minute s.
Mintmark 0.84 mm as **5783**.
5791 1875 S "Type I" rev. Large S.
Mintmark 1.17 mm as **5785**.
5792 1875 S Same. S over CC. Rare.
OMM 1. Elbow of branch arm has small rust pit; almost
always cracked through letters. 2 rev. vars., differing in pattern of cracks. On later states, with cracks heavy, the CC
fades. Usually EF to UNC. Discovered by C. H. Farrar, *NSM*
2/65. Auction 82:1228, UNC., $1,350.

5793 1875 S "Type II" rev. Tall S.
Mintmark 1.17 mm. as in **5785**.
5794 1875 S Same. "Punctuated" motto. Rare.
Plain, round relief pellet between IN.GOD
5795 1875 S "Type II" rev. Minute s. Very rare.
Mintmark 0.84 mm as in **5783**. "Gilhousen":1462.
5796 1875 CC [all kinds 1,573,700] "Type I" rev. Tall CC.
C's 1.1 mm, as **5787**. CC wider or closer: 1984 Midwinter
ANA:1509–11.
5797 1875 CC "Type II" rev. Tall CC. Very rare.
C's as preceding. Possibly part of [61,000], Dec. 1875.
NERCA 3/77:531; Willem:720.
5798 1876 "Type I" obv. and rev. [145,000 + ?P] Scarce.
"Type I" obv. (1873–76) has ends of Ms. Liberty's scroll
pointing l. (On "Type II," ends point down.) Business strikes
(ill.) have still more broken serifs, probably explaining aban-

donment of rev. hub. Not over 4 proofs reported, e.g., Wil-
lem:729 (broken serifs as in **5779**).
5799 1876 "Type I" obv., "Type II" rev. [310,000 + ?P]
8 pairs of dies; minted June–Sept. 1876. Proof mintage of
both types included in dubious report of [1,150P]: Breen
{1977}, p. 155. May exist with "Type II" obv.

5800 1876 S "Type I" obv. and rev. [1,843,000] Large S.
S 1.17 mm as in **5785**. Willem:737, others.
5801 1876 S Same. Minute s. Very rare.
Mintmark 0.84 mm as in **5783**. Willem:738.
5802 1876 S "Type I" obv., "Type II" rev. [3,384,000] Minute
s.
Auction 80:1372, UNC., $3,500; many others. The alleged
1876/5 (Auction 86:1234, UNC., $2,310) is unconfirmed.

5803 1876 S "Type II" obv. and rev. Very rare.
"Type II" obv. (1876–85) has ends of Ms. Liberty's scroll pointing down, R T apart, drapery simplified.

5804 1876 CC "Type I" obv. and rev. "Micro" cc. Ex. rare.
C's 0.74 mm as in **5786**. Leftover 1874 die? Mintage included in **5806**. Willem:735.

5805 1876 CC "Type I" obv. and rev. Tall CC. Very rare.
C's 1.1 mm as in **5787**. Mintage included in **5806**. 1975 ANA:1203; Willem:734. Jack Beymer discovered a doubled rev. die, plainest on feathers and branch; enl. ill.

5806 1876 CC [all kinds 509,000] "Type I" obv., "Type II" rev. Tall CC.
Usually in low grades.

5807 1877 [all kinds 3,039,200 + ?P] Heavy date, 18 touch.
Obv. and rev. "Type II" henceforth. 29 obvs., 30 revs. Positional vars. exist. Cf. 1974 GENA:1167. Proof mintage unknown; Mint report [510P] unconfirmed by Archives data, true quantity probably smaller.

5808 1877 Similar. Double-punched date. Proofs only.
1974 GENA:1165–66. Business strikes may exist.

5809 1877 Light date, bases of 1 8 apart.
Positional vars. exist. 1974 GENA:1168.

5810 1877 S [all kinds 9,519,000] 18 touch; large S.
Mintmark 1.17 mm, as **5785**. Positional vars. exist. 1984 Midwinter ANA:1524; others.

5811 1877 S Same, blunt tail to R. Rare.
Upturned pointed tip to (DOLLA)R broken off; mintmark leans crazily to l. 1974 GENA:1174; Willem:750; 1984 Midwinter ANA:1528.

5812 1877 S 18 touch; large S; doubled rev. die. Very rare.
Normal R. Doubling plain on most letters.

5813 1877 S 1 8 free; large S.
As **5810**. 1984 Midwinter ANA:1523, 1527; others. Positional vars. exist.

5814 1877 S 1 8 free; minute s. Very rare.
Mintmark 0.84 mm, as **5783**. 1974 GENA:1169; Willem:751; others.

5815 1877 CC [all kinds 534,000–] Heavy date, 18 touch.
Tall CC as in **5787**. Usually in low grades. Part of reported mintage probably included in the 44,148 melted at Carson City Mint, July 19, 1878.

5816 1877 CC Light date, 1 8 apart.
Same comments.

5817 1877 CC Same, repunched date.
Same comments. 1974 GENA:1175.

5818 1878 [900P] Proofs only.
Rarer than mintage figure suggests. Only 683 sold; 217 were "released into circulation" in 1879. Julian [1986].

5819 1878 S [all kinds 4,162,000] Medium, filled S.
S 1.1 mm. 1984 Midwinter ANA:1532; others. Positional vars. exist.

5820 1878 S Large clear S.
S 1.17 mm, as **5785**. 1984 Midwinter ANA:1533–35; others. Positional vars. exist.

5821 1878 S Doubled rev. die. Rare.
Doubling plainest at 420 GRAINS. Willem:756. ANACS enl. ill. in *NUM* 8/82, p. 2037.

5822 1878 CC [all kinds 97,000–] Normal 8 and CC. Rare.
Deliveries [56,000] Jan., and [41,000] Feb., most of latter probably included among 44,148 melted at Carson City Mint, July 19, 1878. Rev. of 1877, first C too low. Usually in low grades. 1974 GENA:1179; Lamborn, "Fairfield":1415, UNC., $3,200; Auction 80:1376, UNC., $5,750. The alleged "Type I" coin proved to be a cast counterfeit.

5823 1878 CC Repunched 8 and CC. Rare.
CC about even. 1974 GENA:1180. Usually in low grades.

5824 1878 CC Repunched 8; misplaced CC. Rare.
Same obv.; CC far to r., above DO. MHS I:708; "Fairfield":1416, UNC., $3,000; 1982 ANA:884.

5825 1879 [1,541P] Proofs only.
Top of 8 imperfect. 2 minor rev. vars.: normal or incomplete
feathers. "Gilhousen":1477–78. On latter, rev. heavily repolished, many feathers in legs and lower belly fragmentary.

5826 1880 [1,987P] Proofs only.
2 minor obv. vars.: top of 1 below G or below GO.

5827 1881 [960P] Proofs only.
Usually with flat head and stars. Breen {1977}, p. 169.

5828 1882 [1,097P] Proofs only.
Same comments.

5829 1883 [979–P] Proofs only.
Rarer than 1881–82; probably some were melted as unsold.
Many survivors are impaired.

5830 1884 Proofs only. 10 known.
Clandestine issue. See introductory text for history and roster.

5831 1885 Proofs only. 5 known.
Same comments.

CHAPTER 31

GASPARRO'S SUSAN B. ANTHONY MINI-DOLLARS (1979–81)

As early as 1977, the fate of dollar coinage was in doubt owing to a combination of factors, any of which might have jeopardized it: 1) Never in this country's history has the general public willingly circulated silver dollars on a large scale; 2) since the first $1 notes began circulating in 1862, the public has always preferred to spend paper and hoard silver; 3) aside from saving Bicentennial souvenir coins, the public has shown little interest in "Ike" dollars; 4) Nevada gambling casinos (which formerly played a large role in silver-dollar circulation) have, since 1965, increasingly adopted dollar-size gaming tokens redeemable in paper only at the issuing establishment (partly following suggestions by this writer); 5) increasing concern for reducing nonmilitary federal expenditures suggested that the Treasury could save millions by abolishing the denomination. This last would save costs of dies, planchet manufacture, striking, equipment maintenance, and distribution. The Mint Bureau consulted the Research Triangle Institute, which in its 9/15/76 report recommended either abolishing dollar coinage, or issuing coins of smaller size and lower weight. Both the Mint people and the general public (other than some coin collectors) favored abolition.

At this point the Bureau of Engraving and Printing released figures indicating that the manufacture of $1 notes accounted for a large proportion of the Bureau's total costs, that unprecedented need for astronomical quantities of these notes required ordering extremely expensive new printing equipment, and that costs of plates, paper, and inks were rising, while the effective life of a $1 note remained short. The Bureau recommended against abolishing dollar coinage because so doing would supposedly increase demand for $1 notes; whereas extensive circulation of dollar coins might relieve the Bureau of some pressure and long-term costs. A $1 note costs 3¢ to make, but lasts possibly 18 months; a $1 coin costs perhaps 15¢ to make, but lasts decades.

In line with this ivory-tower theorizing, the Mint Bureau's Dr. Alan Goldman devised a dollar coin project conforming closely to the Research Triangle Institute's recommendations. Bicentennial publicity had indicated some public interest in portraying a woman on paper currency. Some public officials and many politicians felt that this would be a favor to the Women's Liberation movement, productive of goodwill and extra votes, despite such portrayal having no effect on the living conditions of housewives, women secretaries, or other female workers. Goldman apparently believed that both smaller coin size and portraying a woman would increase the smaller dollar coins' potential circulation. Nominations ranged from Sacajawea to Sojourner Truth to Carrie Nation (complete with hatchet). Goldman chose Susan B. Anthony (who had after all been in the top 10 in almost all the straw polls), and decided to retain the reverse's "Eagle Has Landed" motif. Adoption of any smaller diameter meant that vending machines might be victimized by use of low-value foreign coins of similar size. Goldman determined that this problem would be minimal at a diameter of $1.043'' = 26.5$ mm, and a weight of 125 grs. = 8.1 gms. Unfortunately, this meant that the coins would be readily mistaken for quarter dollars. To minimize this problem, Goldman directed that the inner border on both sides be a regular 11-sided polygon, and launched a media campaign (at taxpayer expense) to educate the public about the new coins. His recommendations were incorporated into the Act of Oct. 10, 1978. This Act was based on a bill introduced 5/15/78 by Rep. Mary Rose Oakar (D.-Oh.) with various cosponsors.

During Nov. 1978 the Philadelphia Mint made almost one million test strikings. How these differed from the production coins of 1979 (if at all) has not been revealed. The Bureau negotiated a contract with Olin Brass Co. for nickel-clad strip in unprecedented quantity; production began at the Philadelphia Mint on Dec. 13, 1978.

As the Mint bureaucracy has feared and loathed coin collectors since the Civil War, despite making proof sets to sell to them at increasingly higher prices, certain officials voiced concern lest speculators (whom they could not distinguish from dealers or collectors) "withhold the new dollars from circulation." Goldman accordingly ordered that the coins be stockpiled until at least 500 million specimens (from all three mints) were on hand, setting a target date of July 2, 1979, for release. As if to prove that such antinumismatic tactics were futile, someone displayed and sold coins from several bags of the new mini-dollars at a convention in spring 1979. Treasury authorities expressed shock and horror, and began an investigation, vowing criminal prosecution. The results, if any, have not been published.

However, Goldman need not have worried about coin collectors' alleged effect on public supply or demand. When the coins were finally released on July 2, public demand was minimal, adverse criticism all but unanimous: The coins were condemned as too near in size to the quarter dollar. Some objected to Ms. Anthony's portrait as ugly; others found it unrealistically prettified, and all denounced as outrageous the notion of having a dollar coin smaller and lighter than a half dollar. Worse, many change-making machines and vending machines accepted "Susies" only as quarter dollars, or rejected them as counterfeits. Nor did the Treasury's expensive teach-the-public campaign improve matters; storekeepers nationwide adopted a policy of refusing the coins wherever possible, and discouraging their use at any cost. An even more expensive postal promotion died within two weeks.

Only a tiny fraction of the 800 million plus coined ever reached circulation, and fewer stayed there. Most of the 14 million lbs. of "Susies" still languish in Treasury vaults; the rest are mostly in banks. Nothing could force their circulation short of abolition of the $1 note. This was in fact tried experimentally during late fall 1980; victims were armed forces personnel overseas. For a while they were paid only in "Susies" and $2 bills, and all PX's (Post Exchange: military company stores) rounded their prices up to the nearest 5¢, to eliminate use of one-cent coins. But in Dec. 1980 the Deutsche Bank (West Germany) valued "Susies" at only 1 DM (Deutschmark) apiece, while paper dollars traded regularly at 1.75 DM: a 43% discount, equivalent to a major pay cut for those soldiers who could not trade in their "Susies" for paper! Responding to protests on both sides of the Atlantic, the Treasury abandoned this experiment in Jan. 1981 *(CW* 11/19/80, p. 1).

Mintages dwindled. The 1981 issues did not circulate; none have been made since, nobody has voiced regrets. The Mint Bureau recently ran a promotion campaign which sold about 1 million 6-piece sets at a premium to the general public. These sets contained **5832, 5835, 5838–39, 5841–42.**

GASPARRO'S SUSAN B. ANTHONY MINI-DOLLARS

Designer, Frank Gasparro (rev. after Michael Collins and James Cooper). Engraver, Gasparro. Mints, Philadelphia (mintmark P), San Francisco (S), Denver (D). Mintmarks behind shoulder. Composition, outer layers 25% nickel, 75% copper, bonded to inner core of pure copper. Weight standard, 125 ± 5 grs. = 8.1 ± 0.3 gms. = 56 to the lb. avoir. Diameter, 1.043″ = 26.5 mm. Authorizing Acts, Oct. 10, 1978; Title 31, U.S. Code, § 5112.

No grading standards established; collected only in mint state. NOTE: Business strikes of 1979 from all mints are apt to show weakness at mouth and nose.

5832   1979 P "Type I." [About 199,472,000] Thick numerals. Date far from rim. Coinage began Dec. 13, 1978. Compare next 2. Cast counterfeits are overweight (about 135.2 grs. = 8.76 gms.); they show raised bubble marks. Ill. *CW* 5/28/86, p. 82.

5833   1979 P "Type I." Thin numerals. Date still farther from rim.

5834   1979 P "Type II." [About 160,750,000] Date nearly touches rim. Base of 1 and tail of 9 less than either digit's thickness away from rim. (Rim enlarged, date unchanged.) Mintage figures from George E. Hunter, Assistant Director for Technology, in a letter to John A. Wexler. *EVN* 4/83, p. 17, specifying 643 "Type II" obv. dies. On some obvs., date apparently touches rim; this was unintentional. No S or D coins of "Type II" are reported.

5835   1979 S [all kinds 109,576,000 + 2,735,031P] Mintmark with straight sides. Business strikes Feb. 2 through October; proofs July–October.

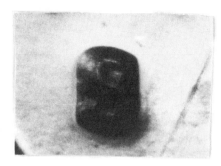

5836   1979 S Same, third star much too small. Presently very scarce. A die polishing problem, found on a minority of proofs. Discovered by Lyle Haakenson, Davenport, Ia. *CW* 1/23/80, p. 56.

5837   1979 S Block S. [425,000P] Sans-serif mintmark. Found only on coins issued Nov.–Dec. Lighter and heavier impressions differ as ill. Repunched mintmarks are known. Mintage figures from Alan Herbert.

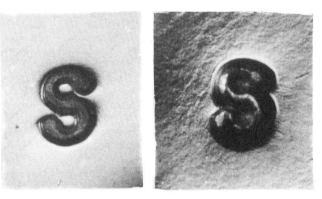

5838   1979 D [288,015,744] Mintage began Jan. 9.

5839   1980 P [27,610,000] Date very close to rim, as on **5834.** May exist with date farther from rim.

5840   1980 S Old-type S. Reported. S as **5835.** From a die made in fall 1979 during the change to the new mintmark punch.

5841   1980 S [all kinds 20,422,000 + 3,554,806P] Block S.

5842   1980 D [41,628,708]

5843   1981 P [3,000,000]

5844   1981 S [all kinds 3,492,000 + 3,733,083P] Mintmark like 8. This is the worn "block S" punch of 1979.

5845   1981 S Open S. [330,000P] Proofs only. Round serifs away from middle stroke.

5846   1981 S Third star too small. Proofs only. As **5836.** *CW* 9/23/81, p. 106.

5847   1981 D [3,250,000]

5848–5999   Reserved for any future dollar coins intended to replace $1 bills, and for any nongold coins of higher face value. For the Olympic dollars, see Chap. 39.

Part Four

FEDERAL
GOLD COINAGES

CHAPTER 32

LONGACRE'S GOLD DOLLARS

i. SMALL SIZE OR "TYPE I" (1849–54)

Though a gold coin of the denomination of one dollar had been an integral part of Alexander Hamilton's original scheme for our national coinage (1791), no design for an actual coin of this kind was talked of until about 1831, and then private interests made the first move.

Alt Christoph Bechtler (who later anglicized his name to Christopher, Sr.), head of a family of immigrants from Baden (Germany), opened a jewelry shop in Rutherfordton, N.C., in 1830. Discovering gold on his lands, and learning that the main local medium of exchange was gold dust and nuggets from nearby mines, Bechtler decided to take advantage of the situation. Owing to bandits and hostile Indians, transporting gold to the Philadelphia Mint through 500+ miles of wilderness was risky. Only driblets of Carolina gold bullion reached the Mint, despite Rutherford County's then being one of the major gold-producing areas in the country.

Accordingly, Bechtler advertised in the North Carolina *Spectator and Western Advertiser* for several weeks, beginning July 2, 1831, that he would coin gold dust and nuggets for nominal fees. No law forbade the practice; only debased fraudulent imitations of federal gold and silver were outlawed. From then through 1840, the Bechtler family's output of coins exceeded $2,241,000, probably half of it in gold dollars (Ill. Chap. 42, Sect. i). Production from 1841–46 was still larger, but amounts are not exactly known. Many of Bechtler's earliest gold dollars, issued 1832–34, reading C. BECHTLER. RUTHERF: 30 G(rains)./* N. CAROLINA GOLD ONE DOLLAR, began to reach the Philadelphia Mint during the immense meltings of old-tenor gold beginning Aug. 1, 1834. The Mint's assayers found that Bechtler's coins were worth within a few cents each of stated values. Compensating for variable bullion fineness, each dollar weighed about 15% above federal standard, i.e., totaling well over 1/5 of the legal weight of a half eagle. This official vote of confidence was repeatedly published, helping natives to feel that Bechtler's gold was as good as the federal product, and actually preferable because made by a local family everyone trusted. As late as the Civil War, many contracts were specified as payable in Bechtler gold; and for decades after that, many Southerners never saw any other kind.

Public attention to Bechtler's gold coins had two consequences: Beginning in 1835, the Treasury began making plans to build branch mints in Charlotte, N.C., and Dahlonega, Ga., exclusively to coin gold (which mints duly opened in 1838); and from 1836 on there was talk of making federal gold coins of $1 denomination. Congressmen, especially from the southeastern seaboard states, doubtless realized that the Bechtlers were prospering from this enterprise. Apparently ignoring this fact, and instead alleging a proposal for an international gold coinage (the gold dollar was, not coincidentally, close in value to a dozen European monetary units, and might be usable in international trade), they interpolated a clause authorizing mintage of gold dollars into an 1836 bill. Mint Director Robert Maskell Patterson adamantly opposed it; and all that remains of this proposal is a tiny handful of patterns designed by Christian Gobrecht, dated 1836, showing a liberty cap in rays (echoing a Mexican motif). These have dies aligned head-to-toe as usual with U.S. coins; edges are plain, weight standard 25.8 grs. (proportionately to the larger gold denominations).

Gobrecht's Pattern Gold Dollar
Ex J. W. Garrett: 1074. Courtesy Bowers & Ruddy Galleries, Inc.

Alt Christoph Bechtler continued to coin gold in $1, $2.50, and $5 denominations, assisted by his son August and his nephew Christopher, Jr., until 1842, when the old man died. August continued the business, at first for a year or so in his own name, then succeeded 1843–46 by Christopher, Jr., who went on using August's dies. Output was enormous. Most of their later coins were gold dollars reading A.BECHTLER. 1 DOL.*/CAROLINA GOLD. 27 G(rains). 21 C(arats). Thousands of these survive, in all grades of preservation; ill. Chap. 42, Sect. ii. They were promptly counterfeited in brass, and both the genuine and the fakes began finding their way to the Mint among foreign coins deposited for conversion into federal issues. Assays determined that August and Christopher, Jr.'s, gold dollars were much more variable and of generally lower value than Alt Christoph's earlier coins. Christopher, Jr.'s, alcoholism doubtless contributed to the collapse of his enterprise; but his coins stayed in circulation.

Again not coincidentally, the House Ways and Means Committee reintroduced a proposal to make gold dollars, Jan. 1844. Patterson, still vehemently opposed, furnished a few more patterns (from the 1836 dies but with rev. turned the other way), and told the congressmen that these could be readily counterfeited in gilt silver. For evidence, Patterson went so far as to furnish gold-plated samples struck in silver from the 1836 dies. This was deliberately misleading; gold coins passed only by weight, worn ones being accepted only at a discount, if at all. No storekeeper would be so trusting as to accept unfamiliar gold coins from a stranger without tests somewhat more rigorous than those today demanded of strangers' out-of-state checks! Patterson's denunciation alleged falsely that no public demand existed for such coins, as the Spanish and Colombian half escudos of similar value had not been made for over 20 years; he deliberately ignored the large domestic circulation of Bechtler dollars. His dishonest tactics quashed the 1844 bill.

Nevertheless, five years later a similar proposal again came up. During the "Hard Times" period of 1837–44 (much like the Great Depression of 1929–37), coins of all kinds were hoarded, and pay envelopes—if one was so lucky as to have any during the massive unemployment—were stuffed instead with private scrip and "wildcat" bank notes, many acceptable only at a discount, if at all. But beginning in 1848, immense supplies of gold bullion from the newly opened California mines started to reach world markets, lowering the value of gold in terms of silver dollars—conversely raising the price of silver reckoned in terms of gold eagles. This trend escalated enough to induce bullion dealers to buy up silver dollars and half dollars (eventually smaller silver as well) for melting and export, exactly as would occur in 1965 and later years: Silver coins were worth more than face value as bullion. Rep. James Iver McKay (D.-N.C.) introduced a bill on Jan. 25, 1849, to authorize mintage of gold dollars; in February, he amended it to authorize $20 coins as well. Over continuing opposition from Mint Director Patterson, Congress passed the bill, and it became law on March 3, 1849.

Patterson's opposition proved to be for reasons partly political, partly venal. After Gobrecht's death in 1844, James Barton Longacre obtained the Mint engravership through his friend John C. Calhoun—a name anathema to the Pennsylvania dynasties then running the Mint. Patterson wanted no Engraver at all, lest such an outsider interfere with the lucrative medal-making business then operated within the Mint by his crony Franklin Peale. So long as no new denominations were needed, working dies could continue to be reproduced mechanically; Longacre's job was a sinecure and might have been abolished. But Congress would not be deterred. Something had to take the place of the vanished silver and the dishonest paper currency; the only logical candidate was the gold dollar.

Longacre's Hand-engraved Pattern Dollars
Ex J. W. Garrett: 1075. Courtesy Bowers & Ruddy Galleries, Inc.

Despite Peale's officious opposition and attempted sabotage, Longacre (with the help of an assistant, Peter F. Cross) managed to complete master dies for the gold dollar on May 7, 1849. On May 8, a few proofs and some 1,000 business strikes were coined, the first of over 11,719,000 of this design to be

issued from Philadelphia and four branch mints through June 17, 1854. During most of that period, gold dollars formed the bulk of the nation's *legal* circulating medium between the 3¢ and the $2.50 denominations, managing to replace a few drops of the flood of worthless bank notes and scrip.

After the issue of larger, thinner ("Type II") gold dollars began in Aug. 1854, banks were under orders to return the small-size dollars to the Mint or the New York Subtreasury. By 1861, some eight million of the original 11 million coined had reached the Subtreasury. Mint Director James Ross Snowden ordered them shipped to the Philadelphia Mint, where they were melted down and recoined into "Type III" gold dollars, quarter eagles, and double eagles.

Many of the survivors have been converted into jewelry or included in later meltings. Possibly 1% of the original mintage remains today in numismatically acceptable condition. (Numismatists normally reject gold coins with any traces of solder; look on edges for any discoloration, any lump or other interruption of edge reeding, or any indication that reeding has been simulated by hand tooling. Local porosity is also grounds for suspicion.) It follows that many of the lower mintages from Charlotte and Dahlonega have become rarities; some of the C- and D-Mint coins are almost unobtainable in or near mint state. Data on striking characteristics of C-Mint coins derive partly from unpublished researches by Douglas Winter.

The rarest coin of this design is 1849 C Open Wreath. Only one genuine var.: short r. point to star opposite tip of nose; hollow leaf below 1 of date, partly detached leaf tip below 9, incomplete ribbons (lapped die), and a tiny die chip or file mark above RI (this last fades out). These criteria will instantly enable rejection of forgeries made by affixing C mintmarks to genuine Philadelphia coins or by scraping top leaf groups off genuine C-Mint dollars. The roster is the most complete yet attempted:

1. Waldo Newcomer (before 1933), Belden Roach:1083 (as "UNC."), Charles M. Williams, Robert F. Schermerhorn, 1956 ANA:1571, $6,000, D.N., Midwest pvt. coll., Auction 79:749, $90,000, "Orchard Hills" (1982 F.U.N.):1350, $50,000. Discovery coin, ill. *NUM* 3/51, p. 301. EF, lint mark near ear.

2. McReynolds (before 1956), Leo A. Young, C. Southwick, 1974 GENA:1952, $35,000, Midwest pvt. coll., S 5/2/86:1330, $25,850. VF–EF, scratched, somewhat impaired.

3. New Netherlands (over the counter), Tex. specialist. Nearly UNC.

4. Donald Lumabue, NERCG, 7/78; *CW* 8/16/78, p. 10, offered at $95,000; ANACS E9196A. EF (ill.).

5. Pvt. coll., also discovered 1978.

Note that on most branch-mint dollars through 1854, obvs. normally show varying degrees of extra outlines on stars and central devices. This is less often true of Philadelphia coins, whose dies had these extra outlines removed through polishing. Their presence depended on how many blows from the hub were needed to sink a working die; such coins are not Mint errors.

Cast and struck counterfeits have been made in quantity since WW II, in (among other locales) Italy, Lebanon, and most Middle Eastern nations. Their intended buyers included troops, tourists, jewelers, bullion hoarders, and naive collectors; dates are primarily 1850–54 without mintmark. They are in gold of legal weight or near it, unlike the more easily identified earlier counterfeits made to spend, which were mostly in base metals. Authentication recommended.

Director's Reports long claimed that four 1854 C gold dollars were struck: a dummy bookkeeping entry covering four dollars and eight half eagles of 1853 that were stolen by bandits, in transit to Assay Commission, Feb. 1854. Beware 1854 Philadelphia dollars with C mintmark fraudulently affixed.

LONGACRE'S SMALL SIZE OR "TYPE I"

Designer, James Barton Longacre. Engraver, Longacre, with help of P. F. Cross. Mints, Philadelphia (no mintmark), New Orleans (mintmark O), Charlotte, N.C. (C), Dahlonega, Ga. (D), San Francisco (S). Mintmark below wreath. Composition, gold 0.900, silver not over 0.050, rest copper. Weight, 25.8 ± 0.25 grs. = 1.672 ± 0.016 gms., containing 0.04837 oz. pure gold. Diameter 1/2″ = 12.7 mm. Reeded edge. Authorizing Act, March 3, 1849; composition conformable to Act of Jan. 18, 1837.

Grade range, POOR to UNC.; not collected in low grades. FINE: Half hair details; about half coronet beads. VERY FINE: Partial details on roll of hair above ear to above brow; most coronet beads clear; partial internal leaf details. EXTREMELY FINE: Tiny isolated rubbed spots only, mostly just above and behind ear, at bun behind head, at lowest edges of curls just above truncation, and on some leaf tips. Partial mint luster. Mint State: *No* trace of wear. NOTE: Beware coins with local porosity, rim discolorations, interrupted edge reeding, or other traces of solder mounts. EXCEPTIONS: Many C- and D-Mint coins show central weakness; sharp strikings are unusual and on rarer dates may suggest fraudulently affixed mintmarks; authentication strongly recommended. Cast counterfeits of 1850–54 were made in quantity since 1950 for investors, dealers, and the public.

6000   1849 "Type I." Open wreath. Small head, no L initial. [1,000 + ?P]
Struck May 8. Coronet point midway between stars; 2 stars below truncation obviously repunched. 2 minor rev. vars. for business strikes; at least 7 proofs known from one of these. Auction 84:795. Many UNCS. survive, saved as first of their kind. Auction 81:1311, UNC., $3,000. Enl. photos.

6001   1849 "Type II." Small head, with L. Flat obv. fields. Coronet point midway between 2 stars; L on truncation. At least 3 vars. Enl. photos.

6002   1849 "Type II." Small head, with L. Concave obv. fields. Coronet point as preceding. Obv. field saucer-like (not merely banked). Heavy stars, that at 5:00 double-punched showing 9 points, that below bust very close to it and almost touching a dentil.

6003   1849 "Type III." Large head. ["Types II–III," 255,039+] Heavy date.
Coronet point nearer star at r. Mintage (May 9–June 7) may include some "Type IV" coins. Many minor vars. Enl. photos.

6004   1849 "Type III." Large head, thin numerals. Rare.
Same but hair-thin serifs and horizontal elements as on **6006**.
6005   1849 "Type IV." Closed wreath. [326,028−] Heavy date.
Head as in "Type III." Mintage represents final delivery; this may have included some "Type III" coins. Closed wreath dies were sunk from a hub raised from an Open Wreath rev. altered by punching in an extra group of leaves at top of each branch, plus 2 new pairs of berries. Many minor vars.; date often blurry or partly repunched. Enl. photos.

6006   1849 "Type IV." Closed Wreath. Thin numerals. Very rare.
2 minor vars. At least 3 proofs known. Enl. photos.

6007   1849 C Open Wreath. 5 known.

2 pairs of dies shipped June 10 and 13; only one used for this type, which matches Philadelphia "Type III." Discovered by Waldo Newcomer in the 1920s. Only the one var. (enl. photos). See introductory text for die characteristics and roster.

6008   1849 C Closed Wreath. Small c. [11,634] Very scarce.

2 revs. shipped July 10; all deliveries came long after. Matches Philadelphia "Type IV." Mintage figure includes preceding. 2 obv. vars. Usually VF or worse; prohibitively rare choice.

6009   1849 D Open Wreath. Small D. [21,588]

Matches Philadelphia "Type III." 2 pairs of dies shipped June 2–4, received June 16. Two minor rev. vars.; commoner (normal D) die cracked up, other (minutely repunched D) rusted. Both vars. often weakly struck. Amato, Auction 81:1316, UNC., $7,500.; Eliasberg:4, UNC., $2,750. Enl. photos.

6010   1849 O Open wreath. Small o. [215,000]

3 pairs of dies shipped June 2. Matches Philadelphia "Type III." Usually VF–EF. Auction 82:319, UNC., $4,000.

6011   1850 [481,953 + 1+P]

Many minute vars.; lighter and heavier dates. One proof was in the set made up for the Congressional Committee on the Library, per letter of Mint Director Patterson, Sept. 26, 1850; untraced. Many fakes exist.

6012   1850 C Small c. [6,966] Rare.

2 pairs of dies, both with Closed Wreath; heavier or lighter date. Borders usually weak; flans often defective. Ex. rare in mint state. Auction 81:1319, UNC., $3,400.

6013   1850 D Small D. [8,382] Rare.

3 pairs of dies shipped, Dec. 11, 1849, a fourth to Charlotte in error, forwarded April 3, 1850. Only one var. seen. Ex. rare in mint state.

6014   1850 O Small o. [14,000]

6 pairs of dies shipped; only one var. known. Rarest O-Mint dollar.

6015   1851 [3,317,671]

28 obvs., 20 revs.; minute positional vars.; date lighter or heavier, high, low, or slanting down to r. Sometimes with

extra outlines on stars like many C- and D-Mint coins: See introductory text. 2 proofs were in the J. B. Longacre estate (1870); these remain unlocated. Many fakes exist.

6016   1851 C Small c. [41,267]

3 pairs of dies; leftover 1850 obvs. may also have been used. The only C-Mint dollar available UNC. Carter:457, $8,250.

6017   1851 D Small D. [9,882] Rare.

5 revs. shipped, at least 2 used till both cracked; 3 leftover obvs. One rev. has repunching below central base of 1 and l. of 5; the other, repunching at r. foot of first 1. These may correspond to deliveries of [3,147] Feb., and [6,735] June.

6018   1851 O Large O. [290,000]

4 pairs of dies shipped; heavy or light stars, positional vars.

6019   1852 [2,043,531] Normal date.

Numerous minute vars. from 18 obv. and 13 rev. dies. Many fakes exist. See introductory text.

6020   1852 Repunched 18. Rare.

Doubling at tops of 18. NN 54:934.

6021   1852 Repunched 52. Very rare.

Repunching above base of 5 and middle stroke of 2.

6022   1852 C Large C. [9,434] Rare.

3 pairs of dies shipped. Without or with part of base of extra 1 below 1 in date, latter often from rusty dies. Not quite as rare in UNC. as 1850 C. Often weak at LA and base of large 1, from foreign matter adhering to die, e.g., Auction 81:1328–29, UNC., $27,000 and $3,500.

6023   1852 D Large D. [6,360] Rare.

2 revs. shipped Dec. 1851, apparently only one used. Usually with heavy obv. clash marks; usually VF, prohibitively rare UNC. Carter:452, $6,050.

6024   1852 O Large O. [140,000]

6 pairs of dies shipped, at least 4 pairs used, one with light repunching on base of 1 in date.

6025   1853 [4,076,051]

Many minor positional vars. Fakes are plentiful; see introductory text. Crude cast copies were offered in Acre (Israel) souvenir stores in 1969. *NSM* 5/69, p. 801.

6026   1853 C Large C. [11,515] Normal C.

3 revs. shipped; obvs. were leftovers from 1852. Two minor vars. with normal C. Planchets often defective, showing splits or chips.

6027   1853 C Double-punched C. Rare.

Date less heavy than on preceding; obv. die increasingly rusty.

6028   1853 D Large D. [6,583] Rare.

3 revs. shipped; obvs. were leftovers from 1852. Only one var. seen: die file mark from rim through base of star about 9:00. Usually poorly struck. Ex. rare in mint state. Auction 81:1332, sharp UNC., $8,200.

6029   1853 O Large O. [290,000]

6 revs. shipped; obvs. were leftovers from 1852. At least 4 minor positional vars.

6030   1854 [855,502 + 1+P] Normal date.

Many positional vars. Final delivery June 17. One proof, from the set the Mint shipped to Bremen, Germany, in exchange for "cabinet coins," was "liberated" during WW II and turned up at the 1975 ANA Convention; later, Auction 85:1874, $68,750. Wayte Raymond had seen another before 1951; untraced. Fakes are plentiful; see introductory text.

6031   1854 Partly repunched date.

Repunching plainest on bases of 85; on later die states this fades. A rarer var. shows top of 4 repunched. For "1854 C" coins see introductory text.

6032   1854 D Small D. [2,935] Very rare.

3 revs. shipped, apparently only one used; obvs. were leftovers from 1852. Prohibitively rare choice: Auction 81:1335, $15,000. The 8 obvs. and 5 revs. shipped to New Orleans remained unused.

6033 1854 S Medium S. [14,632]
5 pairs of dies shipped. Minute positional vars. H. P. Smith, Clapp, Eliasberg:24, UNC., $5,280.

ii. LARGE SIZE, NARROW HEAD
(Aug. 1854–56)

Shortly after Col. James Ross Snowden became Mint Director in 1853, he decided that our national coinage needed refurbishing. One of his prime targets was the gold dollar, which was proportionately smaller and thicker for its weight than he felt it should be. At Snowden's request, Longacre made the original dies of the $3 piece broader than originally planned to minimize any chance that the new coins could be mistaken for either quarter eagles or half eagles. The result was technically satisfactory enough that Snowden then requested Longacre to follow the same proportions in redesigning the gold dollars. This meant increasing the diameters from 1/2″ = 12.7 mm (the 1849–54 standard) to 9/16″ = 14.3 mm.

Obv. was an inexact copy of the $3 head: "narrow Indian Princess head," in higher relief than usual (a blunder), statutory inscription replacing stars. Actually, this head did not represent any Native American; it was another of Longacre's numerous copies of the *Venus Accroupie*, or 'Crouching Venus,' a Roman marble in one of the Philadelphia museums. Longacre used this head in over a dozen different contexts, altering headdress according to fancy. It first appears on the gold dollar and double eagle of 1849, then on the $3, later on the "Indian head" cent, still later on the 1865 nickel 3¢ and a variety of pattern 5¢ coins, finally on the pattern eagles of 1868 only a few months before Longacre's death.

For rev., Longacre copied the device originally chosen for the $3 coin but more familiar on the Flying Eagle cents: a wreath of corn, cotton, maple, and possibly tobacco leaves enclosing value and date. Dies were completely hubbed except for dates and mintmarks, which had to be entered by hand as usual. Treasury Secretary Guthrie approved the design on Aug. 18, and coinage began the next day.

Issues were brief and limited: 1854–55 Philadelphia, 1855 from three Southern branch mints, 1856 San Francisco—after the device had been condemned. The 1856 S dies were shipped west in 1855 before Snowden's decision to redesign the obv. In all, only 1,704,985 were issued for circulation: about 1/7 the mintage of small-size dollars.

The coins proved unsatisfactory from the beginning. Longacre had miscalculated, overestimating the power of coining presses then in use. This error most of all affected the C- and D-Mint issues: These branches were using presses installed in 1838, some of them much older even then. Inevitably, few "Type II" gold dollars were well enough struck to bring out full central details; most are weak on central hair, with 8 and LL (and sometimes the whole date) blurry or illegible. (This could not have been anticipated from the five Philadelphia proofs.) Even Longacre's L initial on truncation is hard to see and often unnoticed.

Most of the limited mintages wore down quickly to illegibility, and went back to Philadelphia for recoinage. Survivors (many of these also weak or low grades) number fewer than 16,000 from all mints: a survival rate of about 0.9%. Many also show traces of solder: See Sect. i, introductory text. High-grade specimens stimulate vigorous type-collector demand—a pressure which did not diminish even after discovery of a hoard of UNC. 1855's.

LARGE SIZE, NARROW HEAD DOLLARS

Designer, Engraver, James Barton Longacre. Mints, Philadelphia (no mintmark), Charlotte (mintmark C), Dahlonega (D), New Orleans (O), San Francisco (S). Mintmark below knot. Physical Specifications, Authorizing Acts, as before, except Diameter now 9/16″ = 14.3 mm.

Grade range, POOR to UNC. Not collected in low grades. FINE: Earlobe clear; TY barely legible, LIBER clear; partial hair and feather details; bow knot, leaves, and cotton bolls completely outlined but mostly without internal details. VERY FINE: LIBERTY complete; some hair details above forehead and around neck; partial internal details in knot, leaves, and bolls. EXTREMELY FINE: Isolated tiny rubbed spots at feather tips, forelock, hair above and below ear, cheek, leaf tips, knot, corn husks, and cotton bolls; partial mint luster. NOTE: Beware coins with any trace of solder; see introductory text, Sect. i. EXCEPTIONS: Many have weak central hair and dates, most of all 1855 C, D; grade by surface.

6034 1854 [all kinds 783,943 + 5+P] Thin obv. letters.
Thin sharp serifs to obv. letters (normal); compare all following. Mintage covers Aug. 19–Dec. 31. Minor positional vars.: date high, low, placed to l. or r. of center, or slanting down to r. One of the 5 proofs of Aug. 17 went from Mint Director Snowden to Treasury Secretary Guthrie for design approval. 1) Mint, SI. 2) Brock, J. P. Morgan, ANS. 3) Cohen, Parmelee, Woodin, Starr estate. 4) Newlin 10/31/ 1884, T. H. Garrett, J. W. Garrett:403, $90,000, Auction 83:761. 5) "Melish":1742, N.Y. State specialist. Enl. photos.

Ex J. W. Garrett: 403. Courtesy Bowers & Ruddy Galleries, Inc.

6035 1854 Double-punched date. Very rare.
On one var., date was first entered slanting up to r., then corrected level. Discovered by E. J. Black about 1973. On a second, date was first punched well to r. of final position, plainest at 54. ANACS, *NUM* 4/80, p. 827.
6036 1854 Date slants crazily down to r. Ex. rare.
Discovery coin, NN 54:940. The effect is grotesquely lopsided.
6037 1854 Triple row of beads above LIBERTY. Ex. rare.
Doubled obv. die. Discovered by this writer in winter 1967–68; discovery coin, LM 3/68:395. Compare 1973 GENA:375.
6038 1854 Heavy obv. letters. Very rare.
Thick blunt serifs; extra outlines on U ICA; low date. Usually, heavy clash marks both sides; later, cracks from 4 to rim and through D S and TES to top feather. Usually in low grades, only one UNC. seen. Discovery coin, NN 49:706.
6039 1855 [all kinds 758,269 + ?P] Normal date, closed 5's.
Many minor vars. from 21 obv., 28 revs.; 8 and LL usually weak. Knob of 5's touch cusp. This and next are common in UNC. from a hoard discovered about 1972.
6040 1855 Thin letters and date; open 5's.
Knob distant from cusp. Proofs and business strikes; minor positional vars. of latter. Possibly 9 proofs reported: Sears, Clapp, Eliasberg:26, $62,700, Jay Miller.

6041 1855 C Small c. [9,803] Rare.

3 pairs of dies shipped; only one rev. apparently used, 2 minor obv. vars. Untraced UNC.; prohibitively rare AU, Ex. rare EF, usually comes VF or worse with weak 8 and LL. Bullowa, Bareford:30, "UNC.," $7,500. Often with heavy clash marks on both sides.

6042 1855 D Small D. [1,811] Very rare.

3 pairs of dies shipped; only one used. D r. of center; often with heavy rev. clash marks, later a vertical crack from rim to wreath grazing mintmark at r. Possibly 3 UNCs., including Miles, Ullmer:340, $7,500 (1974). Ex. rare in EF or better; usually weak VF or worse with weak 8 and LL. Enl. photos.

6043 1855 O Large O. [55,000]

6 pairs of dies shipped; 4 minor vars. seen.

6044 1856 S [all kinds 24,600] Upright 5, small s. Normal s.

6 pairs of dies shipped, March 1856 (probably made late 1855). 2 minor vars.: Date normal or weak, latter from a lapped die which cracks up. Bareford:32, UNC., $3,800. Compare next.

6045 1856 S Double s.

RPM 1. Price only for early die state (ill.) with nearly half of extra S plain. Later shattered die states with most of extra S gone will price as preceding. Discovered by this writer, 1959; discovery coin, NN 54:944.

iii. LARGE SIZE, BROAD HEAD DOLLARS (1856–89)

Less than a year after the "Type II" or Narrow Head dollars went into circulation, all concerned knew that the design must be changed: Specimens were already coming back to the Mint for recoinage, some with dates hardly legible. And many coins hot out of press had the same fault, adjust the presses as you will: weakness in centers so that obvs. looked worn, dates blurry.

As soon as Longacre could be spared from completing the experimental dies for the 1855 bronze pattern cents, Mint Director James Ross Snowden ordered him to begin work on a modified design for the gold dollar. Diameter would remain the same: Snowden, only a few years later, referred to the "evident evil" of simultaneously having in circulation two coins of the same denomination but different sizes. But the obv. head not only had to be of lower relief, it had to be arranged differently to avoid placing relief areas opposite rev. relief details wherever possible. (This same technical requirement necessitated the shift in 1858 from Flying Eagle to "Indian" cents.) Longacre's solu-

tion was to adapt the $3 coin design. On the new dies, legend was nearer border, head farther from letters and different in plumes' shapes, locations, and proportions. No impressions remain of experimental dies of this design. The new design was adopted Jan. 1, 1856, remaining unchanged through the end of 1889, when the denomination was abolished.

Mintage began with a small group using the half-dime date logotype with upright 5. For unknown reasons, the next two dozen revs. all had dates from the quarter-eagle logotype with slanting 5. Those of 1857–60 were smaller in quantity owing to a financial panic, which caused bank failures, business closures, mortgage foreclosures, mass unemployment, and hoarding of all forms of bullion. Large mintages of 1861–62 came partly from melted worn double eagles, but largely from among eight million melted small-size gold dollars: See Sect. i, introductory text.

The outbreak of the Civil War rendered gold scarce. Associated New York City banks voted in Clearing House, Dec. 28, 1861, to suspend specie payments for the duration; from then until about 1879 gold was hoarded as worth more than face value in greenbacks. During the war, silver and even nickel cents were hoarded; people quickly came to realize that four quarters or 100 cents would buy more groceries than a greenback dollar or any bank note whatever. What little gold was coined mostly went to holders of certain bonds and to whichever overseas creditors would accept nothing else. From the collector's perspective, this means that most gold coins, 1863–87, were scarce (many even rare) from the day of mintage, being limited issues destined mostly for export and probable melting —aside from the tiny handfuls of proofs for collectors. The exported coins began showing up in British, French, and Swiss banks after WW II; for which reason most surviving gold dollars of this period are in or near mint state.

The major exception is moderately large mintages of gold dollars between Nov. 1873 and Dec. 1874, made from melted, outworn, or uncurrent gold coins of earlier decades.

On Jan. 18, 1873, Chief Coiner Archibald Loudon Snowden complained that date logotypes featured a peculiar 3 ("Closed 3") which could be readily mistaken for an 8. Punchmakers in the Engraving Department had to furnish a complete set of new date logotypes for all denominations ("Open 3"). The Coiner's fears proved well founded: As recently as 1961, several years after Harry Boosel publicized this document, I saw 1873 Closed 3 gold dollars, 3¢ nickels, and shield nickels being misdescribed in auction as "1878"!

Both 1873 and 1874 dollars come with full or partial LIBERTY on headband (sometimes only LIB, LI, or even a solitary L visible), or with no LIBERTY at all—a result of wear on the hub. William Barber in 1874 raised another obv. hub from the master die of 1856, indistinguishable in detail from its predecessors. This served for the remaining low-mintage years through 1889, probably fewer than 50 working obvs. in all.

Numerous counterfeits of 1873–74, mostly with only L or LI on headband, have come to light since the 1960s. Most are high-quality gold of full weight, being aimed at bullion dealers, investors, and speculators. The most dangerous, and one of the commonest, has an irregular lump obscuring the individual dots which normally make up the l. terminal tassel of wreath (about 11:00): See ill. in Akers {1975A}, p. 84. Their legal status is moot; they are freely bought and sold as "bullion coins" overseas and among nonnumismatic gold dealers in the USA. From the collector's perspective, the best fate for them is melting.

Dangerous fakes, also in good gold, exist for many of the rarer dates between about 1868 and 1878. Authentication is urgently recommended!

Despite limited mintages of the Broad Head dollars 1879–89, mint-state survivors are plentiful. Most of the [1,600] of 1880 went to hoarders; during the 1950s and '60s, the holdings of

Horace L. P. Brand, Charles E. Green, and others yielded hundreds of choice examples. Smaller hoards turned up of other dates in the period; all are available for a price. Worn survivors are very unusual, and apparently nonexistent for 1880, which almost always comes prooflike UNC. Type collectors have snapped up many of these, especially as the coins are attractive sharp strikings.

This denomination is also notable for unprecedentedly large mintages of proofs 1884–89. More proof gold dollars were minted than silver minor proof sets; in 1889, [1,779P] gold dollars, compared with [711P] sets from cent to silver dollar. Many proofs of the mid-1880s are routinely found nicked and scratched owing to incompetent handling by the Coin and Medal Clerk at the Philadelphia Mint. Breen {1977}, p. 182, quotes the original complaint, which resulted in this clerk's dismissal.

For reasons never clearly explained, the Act of Sept. 25, 1890 abolished the denomination. But as the Coinage Act of July 23, 1965 (PL 89-81), Sect. 392, says "All coins and currencies of the United States, regardless of when coined or issued . . . shall be legal tender for all debts," one might argue that this act restores the original legal-tender status to gold dollars, superseding the 1934 regulations which had demonetized gold.

Previous warnings about coins with traces of solder apply.

LARGE SIZE, BROAD HEAD DOLLARS

Designer, Engraver, James Barton Longacre. Mints, Philadelphia (no mintmark), Charlotte (mintmark C), Dahlonega (D), San Francisco (S). Mintmark below knot. Physical Specifications, Authorizing Acts, as preceding.

Grade range, POOR to UNC. Not collected in low grades. FINE: Earlobe visible; traces of detail in forelock and hair above and below ear; few internal details to leaves, knot, and cotton bolls. VERY FINE: Traces of detail on curled ends of feathers; partial internal details in major locks of hair, leaves, knot, and bolls. EXTREMELY FINE: Tiny isolated rubbed spots only; partial mint luster. UNCIRCULATED: *No* trace of wear. NOTE: Beware counterfeits and coins with traces of solder (see introductory text). EXCEPTIONS: C- and D-Mint coins through 1861 show characteristic local weaknesses; 1873–74 may lack part or all of LIBERTY. When in doubt, grade by surface.

6046 1856 Upright 5. [33,660− + ?P]
Half-dime date logotype. 3 minor vars., believed included in initial delivery, Feb. 17. Enl. photos. The unique (?) proof, believed first one struck, is in Starr estate, ex 1941 ANA:586.

6047 1856 Slanting 5. [1,729,276+ + ?P] Heavy closed 6.
Quarter-eagle date logotype. Many minor vars. from 27 obvs., 28 revs. (incl. preceding). Often weakly struck. Dates vary: high to low, l. or r. of center, level or slanting up or

down to r. In the Beck estate was one with date very low, 5 touching bow. Proofs (8 known?) have date low and slanting up to r.: Stickney, Clapp, Eliasberg:31, $10,450; Auction 85:1367, $12,650. Enl. photos.

6048 1856 Slanting 5; thin open 6. Rare.
The 6 is thinner and shallower than 185; knob well away from loop. Date is low in field. Often with heavy clash marks on both sides. No dies were sent to Charlotte (reason unknown); 2 pairs of dies went to New Orleans, but remained unused.

6049 1856 D Upright 5, large D. [1,460] Very rare.
3 pairs of dies shipped March 11, received April 5, 1856; only one used. U always weak; O(LLAR) normally filled; 85 usually weak, as are high points of hair and tops of plumes. Usually worn. Grade by surface. Jay:219, UNC., $2,000 (1967); Auction 81:1343, AU, $11,000, Auction 84:1302, $9,900; Eliasberg:33, AU, $6,600, Hancock & Harwell. Enl. photos.

6050 1857 [744,780 + ?P]
Minute positional vars. Often weakly struck. Proofs (possibly 10 survive) have thin obv. letters; date low, slanting up to r.: D. S. Wilson, Clapp, Eliasberg:34, $8,800.

6051 1857 C Large C. [13,280]
3 minor vars. Always unevenly struck on defective planchets; grade by surface. Ex. rare in mint state.

6052 1857 D Large D. [3,533] Rare.
2 pairs of dies. Weak at upper rev. and on hair and plumes; grade by surface. Prohibitively rare UNC.: Rawson, Clapp, Eliasberg:36, $3,520.

6053 1857 S Medium S. [10,000] Very scarce.
2 minor vars.: date a little above center or well below. Very rare in mint state.

6054 1858 [all kinds 117,995 + ?P] Normal date.
With or without double punching with lower loop of second 8, former rare; discovery coin, NN 54:954. Proofs have unusually thin letters and low date; possibly 10–12 are known. H. P. Smith, Clapp, Eliasberg:38, $13,750. Enl. photos.

6055 1858/7 Ex. rare.
Serif and tiny part of crossbar of 7 show at upper l. of final 8; interiors of loops of this 8 irregular at r. Date low and heavy. Tex. pvt. coll.

6056 1858 Large letters. Proof only. Unique?
Judd 224. ANS, ex a gold proof set in Cogan 3/29/1882:472, J. Colvin Randall, J. Pierpont Morgan. Dies by Anthony C. Paquet. Possibly 3 copper strikings survive. Enl. photos.

6057 1858 D Large D. [3,477] Rare.
2 pairs of dies received Jan. 6; 3 minor vars., without or with minute repunching on D. Almost always weak at 85 and on parts of hair and plumes; often with incuse mark (foreign matter adhering to die) near ED. Ex. rare in mint state: Ullmer:342, $8,500 (1974).

6058 1858 S Medium S. [10,000]
2 minor positional vars., from 3 obvs., 10 revs. shipped. Ex. rare in mint state: Bell, "Memorable," Bareford:36, $4,750.

6059 1859 Broad numerals, normal date. [168,244]
In all, 9 obvs., 10 revs. made; to date at least 5 minor vars. May exist with narrow numerals like **6062–64**. The broad-numerals logotype is like those used on half dimes, probably by Anthony C. Paquet.

6060 1859 Repunched 9. Rare.

6061 1859 Repunched date. [80–P] Proofs only.
Earlier specimens show repunching on entire date, plainest on 18; later strikings (repolished die) show repunching only on 18. Most were melted as unsold; possibly 12–15 survive. Earle, Clapp, Eliasberg:41, $5,775.

6062 1859 C Narrow numerals, large C. [5,235] Rare.
Same comments as to **6051**. Grade by surface. Ex. rare UNC.

6063 1859 D Narrow numerals, large D. [4,952] Rare.
2 pairs of dies received after Jan. 6. Usually poorly struck, weakest at 85, plumes and parts of hair; sometimes with heavy clash marks. Neil, Bareford:38, UNC., $5,500. Carter:490, UNC., $6,050.

6064 1859 S Narrow numerals, medium S. [15,000]
8 revs. shipped; obvs. left over from 1858. Two minor vars., one with minutely repunched S (NN 54:959). Prohibitively rare UNC.

6065 1860 [36,514 + 154–P]
At least 4 minor positional vars. Proofs (struck April 5) have low date; possibly 20–30 survive, the rest melted as unsold. Date numerals through 1865 smaller than formerly.

6066 1860 D Large D. [1,566] Very rare.
2 pairs of dies. Only one var.; U blurry, borders weak, flans defective; sometimes with fourfold clash marks. Usually VF to EF. Miles, Ullmer, $8,500, Auction 81:1353, $11,500, Auction 84:1306, $19,800. UNC. Enl. photos.

6067 1860 S Medium S. [13,000] Normal.
4 pairs of dies shipped Dec. 2, 1859. Compare next.

6068 1860 S Inverted S. Rare.
Lower curve of S smaller than upper. If in doubt, invert the coin and recheck. Discovery coin, NN 51:787. Compare **3316.**

6069 1861 [527,150 + 349–P]
Many minor vars. from 31 obvs., 36 revs. Date varies from thin to heavy, latter with bases of 18 almost or quite touching. Rarely with traces of repunching on final 1: 1982 ANA:978, UNC., $1,000. Proofs have low date, no extra outlines on DOLLAR, but the same remark holds for some business strikes. Most proofs were melted as unsold; probably fewer than 25 survive, some impaired.

6070 1861 D Small D. [CSA issue, mintage unrecorded] Very rare.
2 pairs of dies shipped Dec. 10, 1860, arriving Jan. 7. No gold dollars coined under Union authority. In April 1861, after the Confederacy seized the Mint, rebel authorities coined an unknown quantity of gold dollars, using an obv. of 1860 and one of the 2 new revs. U weak; ICA often weak; details on hair and plumes generally weak; rev. dentils, part of r. ribbon, and outermost parts of wreath incomplete and weak (lapped die). Grade by surface. At least 4 UNCS. survive: Clapp, Eliasberg:49, $16,500; Pierce, Miles, Ullmer:343, $19,500, Vincennes:375, $42,000 (Paramount 9/14/81), Auction 84:1307, $44,000; Auction 81:1356, $27,000; pvt. coll. Possibly the most coveted of all gold dollars because of its Confederate origin. 2 revs. shipped to Charlotte, 2 to New Orleans, 4 to San Francisco, but all apparently remained unused. Enl. photos.

6071 1862 [all kinds 1,361,365 + 35P] Normal date.
Many minor vars. from 53 obvs., 47 revs. Proofs (Feb. 16) have polish in topmost feather, heavy low date, some hollow leaves; possibly 15–20 survive. Dates 1861–63 have the smallest numerals used in U.S. coins, like the 3¢ silver of these years.

6072 1862 Boldly repunched 1. Rare.
1976 EAC:1512; others.

6073 1862 Double date. Very rare.
Date first punched too high, then corrected lower. See next.

6074 1862 Doubled obv. die. Very rare.
Discovered by George Schultheis, 1975. Rev. as preceding; also exists with normal date, discovered by Ted Clark. Kagin 332:3023 (Long Beach 2/2–4/84).

6075 1863 [6,200 + 50P] Very rare.

Proofs (March 23) have die polish below ear; date to r., tip of serif of 1 below L. Carter:498, $7,150. Business strikes (June 24–Nov. 30) come from proof dies or from a rev. with date further l., tip of serif of 1 below O. Most survivors are AU to UNC. Auction 81:1358, UNC., $4,200. Most UNC. business strikes, 1863–66, show field striations.

6076 1864 Heavy date, 64 touch. [50P] Proofs only. Very rare.

Minted Feb. 11; repolished obv. of 1863, die polish in topmost feather and below ear. About as rare as 1863 proofs.

6077 1864 Thin numerals, 6 4 apart. [5,950] Rare.

Date slightly lower than preceding; dies often clashed, rarely cracked from rim between A T to top feather. Usually EF to AU; gold varies greatly in color. Clapp, Eliasberg:52, UNC., $6,600; Brand I:30, $15,400. The 2 deliveries, [2,400] Feb. 23 and [3,500] Dec. 6, cannot be told apart.

6078 1865 Original. Low date, almost level. [3,700 + 25P] Rare.

Business strikes (Jan. 27) come usually AU to UNC., without or with clash marks; Auction 81:1360, UNC., $11,500. Proofs (March 8) are from the same rev., after repolishing; Clapp, Eliasberg:53, $7,700. The very last proofs show massive die buckling; entire area from TA across head to F A is convex. This die state is Ex. rare; discovery coin was from Jerome Kern, Rawls, Heim colls. 2 obvs., one rev. for business strikes.

6079 1865 Restrike. Date slants sharply up to r. [?P] Proofs only. 2 known.

Similar to the restrike $3 of this date, Judd 440, and probably made at the same time (1872?). 2 seen, a third reported.

6080 1866 [7,100 + 30P] Very scarce.

Proofs have tops of wreath joined; possibly 15 survive. Clapp, Eliasberg:54, $5,500. The 2 deliveries are indistinguishable: [25P] with sets Jan. 15; [5P] with sets June 8. Business strikes (mostly AU to UNC.) have tops of wreath separate, many with clash marks. The 2 deliveries are indistinguishable: [1,100] Jan. 27; [6,000] Feb. 9.

6081 1867 [5,200 + 50P] Very scarce.

Business strikes (Jan. 24) have date level or slanting slightly down to r.; survivors are mostly EF to UNC., many with clash marks. Auction 81:1364, UNC., $4,800. Proofs have date slanting slightly up to r.; possibly 15–18 survive. The [25P] each of March 5 and July 2 cannot be distinguished. Carter:502, $6,875.

6082 1868 [10,500 + 25P] Scarce.

Proofs (Feb. 20) have wreath tops attenuated; often, though not always, with rev. die 180° from normal alignment. Possibly 15–18 survive. Business strikes (Feb. 25) have lower date; 2 minor vars., both with normal date. Auction 81:1365, UNC., $9,000. Double-date coins seen to date are all counterfeits of the 1950s.

6083 1869 [5,900 + 25P] Very scarce.

Business strikes (Feb. 15) have extra outlines on obv. letters; "teardrop" chip below r. corner of eye, die file mark through ear; low date, wreath weak at r. (lapped die). Survivors are mostly AU to UNC.: Auction 81:1366, UNC., $1,900; Arnold-Romisa:50, $6,600. Proofs (Feb. 19) have date central, with field striations below AR and r. of large 1; possibly 12–15 survive. Clapp, Eliasberg:57, $6,050.

6084 1870 [6,300 + 35P] Very scarce.

Business strikes (Jan. 20) have obv. of 1869, low date (traces of repunching on 0), small dot just above l. foot of (DOL-LA)R. Most survivors are AU to UNC. Auction 81:1367, $5,000. Proofs have centered date; die polish around ERT and top feather. H. P. Smith, Clapp, Eliasberg:58, $5,500. The [25] of Feb. 3 cannot be told from the [10] of June 1.

6085 1870 S Small s. [3,000] Rare.

Early states show repunching on S, bulge within it; on later

states, repunching fades and S looks filled. Possibly 40–50 survive, mostly EF to UNC. (a tiny hoard?) except for ex-jewelry items. McNally, Auction 81:1369, UNC., $6,700. Two rev. dies shipped after May 14, received May 28, replacing 2 earlier dies (sent Dec. 1869) which lacked mintmark. Enl. photos.

6086 1871 [3,900 + 30P] Rare.

Proofs (Feb. 20) have thin obv. letters; 12–15 survive. H. P. Smith, Clapp, Eliasberg:60, $6,875. Business strikes (Feb. 15) have extra outlines on obv. letters, die file marks at DOL; usually EF to UNC., a little weak in centers. Auction 81:1370, UNC., $6,000. Two pairs of dies, received at San Francisco Dec. 16, 1870, remained unused.

6087 1872 [3,500 + 30P] Rare.

Proofs (Feb. 3) have obv. of 1871 proofs; 7 wholly below L, date about centered; 13–17 survive. Business strikes have lower date, 2 often partly filled; extra outlines on U RICA. Survivors are mostly EF to UNC.: Mills, Clapp, Eliasberg:61, $4,400; Auction 81:1372, UNC., $10,400. The 3 deliveries cannot be told apart: [1,000] March 18; [500] Oct. 21; [2,000] Dec. 18.

6088 1873 Closed 3. [1,800 + 25P] Very rare.

Proofs (ill., Feb. 18) have incomplete feather below T(ES); most of the 15–18 survivors are lintmarked. Clapp, Eliasberg:62, $6,600. Business strikes (July 28) have IBERT and 87 weak; only one pair of dies. Discovery coin, NN *Numisma* 7–8/56:4168. Survivors are mostly EF to AU.: Auction 80:319, almost UNC., $5,000. Mint-state specimens are rare. See introductory text. Enl. photos.

Ex J. W. Garrett: 410. Courtesy Bowers & Ruddy Galleries, Inc.

6089 1873 Open 3. [123,300] Full LIBERTY.

In all, 5 obvs., 6 revs. with open 3. Two possible proofs seen from drastically repolished dies; enl. photos.

6090 1873 Open 3. Partial LIBERTY.

Several vars. Often with long vertical die file mark on neck.

6091 1873 Open 3. Without LIBERTY.

See introductory text.

6092 1874 [all kinds 198,800] Full LIBERTY.

Many minor vars. The prooflike UNC. in LM 9/67:287 with incomplete 4 (diagonal missing) may be from a clogged die; no other has become available for checking. Compare next 3.

6093 1874 Partial LIBERTY. [? + 20P]

Several vars. of business strikes. Proofs (Feb. 14) have date low, too far r.; possibly 12 survive: Eliasberg:63, $7,700. Beware counterfeits, seemingly UNC. See introductory text.

6094 1874 Only L on headband. Those with large lump forming triangular terminal tassel at l. top of wreath, instead of the normal disconnected dots as at r. tassel, are counterfeits made in the 1960s. See introductory text.

6095 1874 No LIBERTY.

Early strikings show repunched 1; on later ones, this fades out, and heavy clash marks appear. Beware of counterfeits.

6096 1875 [400 + 20P] Very rare.

Proofs (Feb. 13) have polish in ERT and topmost feather; no spine down from chin; bows clear; heavy extra outlines on wreath and DOLLAR; corner of 5 minutely l. of tip of A. Possibly 15 survive. Garrett (1976):457, $14,000. Gilt copper examples are lightweight. Business strikes have spine below chin, parallel to neckline and close to it; bows filled; corner of 5 in line with l. tip of A. UNC. survivors are prooflike and have often been sold as proofs; they outnumber proofs nearly 2 to 1: Auction 80:878, $21,000; Auction 81:1378, $12,500; Dr. Green, Bareford:60, $11,500; Carter:511, $14,300.

6097 1876 [3,200 + 45P] Very scarce.

Proofs have die file mark through base of A toward M; no rust pit on neck; date slants minutely down to r. Possibly 25–28 survive, many cleaned or impaired. The [20] of Feb. 19 cannot be told from the [25] of June 13. Carter:512, $4,950. Business strikes (2 obvs., 3 revs.) usually have minute rust pit on neck; date level or slants slightly up to r. Survivors are usually EF to UNC., often prooflike, often porous, usually weak in centers and on some plumes. The Nygren coll. had 50 with loops removed. H. P. Smith, Clapp, Eliasberg:65, UNC., $5,225.

6098 1877 [3,900 + 20P] Rare.

Proofs [10 each Feb. 24, May 31] have date slanting up to r., no lump on cheek or jaw; 12–14 survive. Eliasberg:66, $6,875. Business strikes (at least 2 vars., 3 pairs of dies made) have lump on jaw or on cheek near ear; survivors are EF to UNC., usually prooflike. Auction 81:1380, UNC., $4,000.

6099 1878 [3,000 + 20P] Rare.

Proofs (Feb. 9) have extra outlines on all of DOLLAR, normal date; 12–15 survive. D. S. Wilson, Clapp, Eliasberg:67, $7,150. Business strikes (2 vars.) come with or without extra outlines on DOLL; final 8 often filled. Survivors are usually AU to UNC., bag-marked, often prooflike. Auction 81:1381, UNC., $2,700.

6100 1879 [3,000 + 30P] Very scarce.

Proofs have no clash marks; [20], Jan. 25, State I, have crisscross lines in l. bow; [10], Nov. 22, State II (from drastically repolished dies) lack them. Possibly 15–18 survive of both. Carter:515, State I, $3,575. Same dies (BER weak) apparently used on them and on business strikes, which normally come AU to UNC., often deceptively prooflike, many with clash marks.

6101 1880 [1,600 + 36P]

Proofs have no die file marks at ATE; wreath tops join; top serif of 1 below adjacent leaf tip. Other vars. are possible. The [20] of Feb. 14 cannot be told from the [16] of late Sept. Possibly 24–28 survive in all. Proofs and some UNCS. show faint traces of extra 8's within 88; these fade out. Prooflike business strikes from the hoards are often hard to tell from proofs, but normally proofs show porosity neither at ends of plumes nor at borders, nor have they clash marks. For the hoards, see introductory text.

6102 1881 [7,620 + 87P] Partly repunched date.

Parts of extra 8's within 88. Two obv. vars. Proofs have heavy letters with partial extra outlines, but so do some business strikes (mostly UNC. with a minority of AU's; often hard to tell from proofs); see preceding. In date 1 and second 8 centered below O and L; compare next.

6103 1881 Normal date.

Date farther to r.; 1 below r. curve of O, r. edge of 8's slightly beyond ends of L's. Prooflike business strikes; proofs may exist.

6104 1882 [5,000 + 125P]

Proofs have clear 2; this die may also occur on business strikes, which are almost always UNC. and prooflike. Other UNCS. have partly or wholly filled 2.

6105 1883 [10,800 + 207P]

3 vars., business strikes (usually prooflike UNC.) and proofs both coming without or with traces of repunching and filling in 8's.

6106 1884 [all kinds 5,230 + 1,006P] Normal date.

Business strikes are nearly always UNC. and prooflike. 4 vars., 2 showing minute traces of repunching on date; some proofs with it, some without.

6107 1884 Double date. Proofs only. Very rare.

Date first punched in much too low and slanting up to r., then corrected higher and level. Later die states show only bases of extra 18 and top of extra 4; still later ones only traces of top of extra 4. These later states will price as preceding. Discovery coin, NN 51:813.

6108 1885 [11,156 + 1,105P]

5 vars. of business strikes, 4 of them also known in proof state. Most business strikes 1885–87 are prooflike UNC., usually with granular borders.

6109 1886 [5,000 + 1,016P]

Proofs have 6 and leaf l. of date normal, neither attenuated nor with extra outlines. At least 3 vars. of business strikes; the "recut 6" is actually clashmarked from TY, and it forms about 1/8 the population of business strikes, which are nearly always prooflike UNC.

6110 1887 [7,500 + 1,043P]

Proofs have top of wreath closed, 7 wholly below A; other vars. may exist. Most business strikes are prooflike UNC., sometimes with clash marks from ERTY. Some counterfeits have very thin obv. letters.

6111 1888 [15,623 + 957P]

At least 5 vars. of business strikes, 2 of them found also on proofs; ERT normal or weak. Most survivors are UNC., prooflike or frosty.

6112 1889 [28,950 + 1,779−P]

Proofs have ERT weak, date low, like some UNCS. Many melted as unsold. UNCS. are plentiful, saved as last of their kind. Dates higher or lower, normally slanting down to r. See ills. in Auction 82:1333–36. Counterfeits are common.

CHAPTER 33

QUARTER EAGLES

i. SCOT'S HERALDIC DESIGN, NO STARS (1796)

This coin has three distinctions: It is the first precious-metal coin without stars issued for circulation by the USA prior to 1836; it is the first ever to show the heraldic eagle, which would become standard on all silver and gold denominations 1798–1807; it is the earliest made showing 16 rev. stars honoring Tennessee's admission. The dies show evidence of careless haste, suggesting time pressure. Though documentation is lacking, quarter eagles may have been included in presentation sets commemorating the admission, June 1, 1796. Prooflike presentation coins of this date are known of all other denominations above the cent except the half eagle.

Dies are by Robert Scot (possibly with John Smith Gardner's help, as Hilt {1980} believes). The obv. copies the 1795 half eagle, rev. the Great Seal of the United States (1782; compare the version on the back of the current $1 bill). We do not know the obv.'s ultimate prototype; conjecturally, it was adapted from some Roman copy of a Hellenistic goddess, her hair altered, a big soft cap added. This was long mistaken for the *pilleus,* alias Phrygian cap or liberty cap. The latter was a close-fitting felt cap, ceremonially placed on slaves' heads when they gained their freedom (partly to conceal the short haircuts which instantly identified slaves); it was also worn by freemen after release from the status of prisoners of war (for similar reasons, slaves were originally prisoners of war and their progeny), and by victorious gladiators whose prizes included release from the arena. The liberty cap had the shape of a half eggshell, symbolizing its wearer as a chick emerged from captivity. However, Mint Director Moore identified the cap on the gold coins as a high-fashion headdress of the 1790s: see Chap. 36, Sect. iii, introductory text. Its nearest familiar relative is the mobcap in some portraits of Martha Washington.

On the other hand, all Scot's versions of the heraldic eagle (no less than 10 different device punches) share what is either a heraldic blunder or a piece of stupid saber-rattling bravado: The warlike arrows are in eagle's dexter or more honorable claw (observer's l.), whereas the olive branch of peace is relegated to his sinister or less honorable claw: heraldically committing this country to a martial posture in excess of even modern hawks' demands. Compare Chap. 24, Sect. iii, introductory text. The eagle-and-clouds punch used in 1796–97 has 16 stripes to shield, representing red by eight solid bars (raised on coin), rather than vertically shaded as later.

Presentation pieces aside, the first batches for circulation come from one obv. and two rev. dies. Pursuant to Warrants 75 and 77, the [66] of Sept. 22 and the [897] of Dec. 8 went to the Bank of the United States. Hilt says the first batch are his var.

2-A (four known): arrows extend well beyond N, first S and F very close to wings, indentations between clouds are directly below upright of T(A) and l. curve of O; always with vertical crack from rim through E(S) down through head, shield, and tail. Discovered by Harry Bass. The others (Hilt 2-B) have lump at wingtip almost touching F, and the cloud indentations are l. of upright of T(A) and well to r. of center of O; obv. develops a crack from rim at 9:00. Presentation pieces are thought to have this latter rev., uncracked obv.: Mougey:1144; Lusk:93 (?).

Survivors (usually F to EF) are usually unevenly struck: hair near ear, near temple, and at lower part of cap; eagle's neck, breast feathers, and lower part of shield. Border dentils are often weak or incomplete, most of all at lower l. and lower r. obv. Later impressions are often weak at E(RTY), possibly a problem with die alignment as this letter is directly opposite another relief area—eagle's tail. Real UNCs. are prohibitively rare.

SCOT'S HERALDIC DESIGN, NO STARS

Designer, Engraver, Robert Scot. Mint, Philadelphia. Composition, gold 11/12, rest copper with traces of silver. Weight standard, 67.5 grs. = 4.37 gms. Diameter, about 13/16″ = 20.6 mm. Edge, vertically reeded. Authorizing act, April 2, 1792.

Grade range, VERY GOOD to UNC. FINE: Partial detail to eye, nose, mouth, wing feathers, horizontal shield lines; only outlines of drapery and outermost curls; motto complete but weak. VERY FINE: Partial folds of cap and drapery; all major outlines of locks show; partial detail to leaves and tail feathers. EXTREMELY FINE: Isolated tiny rubbed spots only; generally traces of prooflike surface. UNCIRCULATED: *No* trace of wear. NOTES, EXCEPTIONS: See introductory text.

6113 1796 [963] Very rare.
2 rev. vars.; see introductory text. Garrett:732, AU, $125,000, Ed Hipps; Dunham, Eliasberg:79, EF, $26,400. Real presentation strikings have brilliant prooflike surfaces and are better struck than that ill. Enl. photo.

Ex J. W. Garrett: 732. Courtesy Bowers & Ruddy Galleries, Inc.

ii. SCOT'S HERALDIC DESIGN, WITH STARS (1796–1807)

During this whole decade, quarter eagles were coined only in isolated driblets of a few hundred or at most a few thousand pieces. In most of these years, each date represented a new design modification—creating instant rarities and type coins. The problem is less why the coins are rare, why so few were made to begin with, but why any were struck at all! To judge from available Archives records, they were ordered on whim by a few local banks (principally the Bank of Pennsylvania and the Bank of the United States); to judge from the condition of survivors, they spent most of their time in vaults. Between 1803 and 1833, the Mint's major output consisted of cents, half dollars, and half eagles; all other denominations had a kind of poor-relative status—seldom called for, few made, little welcome.

Design modifications in this group have mostly to do with number and arrangement of stars in obv. field and above eagle. To understand the sequence, recall that on coins intended for general circulation from 1783–92 the number of stars was normally 13 for the Original 13 United Colonies: the "New Constellation" echoing the flag of 1777 (see Chap. 10, introductory text), later echoing the Great Seal of 1782. Vermont's copper coins at first used a circle of 14 stars with STELLA QUARTA DECIMA, 'The Fourteenth Star,' for local desire to join the Union, which became a reality in 1791. Kentucky became the fifteenth state in 1792, and Peter Getz's pattern half dollars continued the concept by showing 15 stars above eagle: Chap. 16, introductory text. Silver coins in 1794 and gold coins in 1795 followed suit save that the 15 stars were in obv. field. But on Tennessee's admission to the Union, June 1, 1796, Mint Director Elias Boudinot became aware that no law prevented other territories from subsequent admission as new states; which meant that the number of stars on coins had to be frozen, rather than increasing indefinitely. At some unrecorded date in 1797, Boudinot therefore ordered Scot to limit the number of stars on new dies to the original 13; but he left their arrangement to Scot's taste, or lack of it.

The final batch of quarter eagles of 1796 [432], coined at the end of December but delivered Jan. 14, 1797, showed 16 stars, divided 8 + 8 (i.e., 8 l., 8 r., copying the $10 die of June 1796). This is, of course, not an alteration of the old No Stars die, which had broken; E R T Y are spaced much farther apart. Rev. shows 16 stars, but differs from either die found with the No Stars obv. (previous section) or from the 1797. Possibly five prooflike presentation strikings survive; Winter:495, $33,000 (1974); Auction 84:1365, $74,250. Probably fewer than 30 business strikes survive. Hilt thinks the [98] delivered Feb. 28, 1797, per Warrant 82, were from these dies, making [530] in all; this is impossible to prove. Most survivors are VF to EF; mint-state ones show some prooflike surface but lack the exceptional detail sharpness of the presentation coins.

Quarter eagles of 1797 have obv. stars 7 + 6, reflecting Boudinot's order; obv. always shows a heavy crack from Y through field to last star. Rev. must have been made in 1796, as it shows 16 stars randomly scattered above head. Hilt thinks the [585] between 3/14/1797 and 1/11/1798 bore this date (Warrants 83, 93, and 102). Possibly 20 survive, mostly VF; prohibitively rare in mint state, and the numerous auction records for coins called AU represent possibly four specimens playing Musical Chairs, with another two or three optimistically graded.

Those of 1798 have a new rev. device punch: 13 stripes on shield, six vertically shaded for gules (heraldic red), seven blank for argent (heraldic silver or white). Both vars. have the rev.

"arc" arrangement discussed under dismes (Chap. 25, Sect. ii) and dollars (Chap. 29, Sect. iii): a row of six stars just below clouds, a row of five below that, plus one each at beak and behind head. In the 1950s, possibly seven or eight examples from the dies with close date and four berries continually showed up at auctions and in dealers' cases at major conventions. Four are UNC., including "Melish":1102 with the "fatal" obv. break; a fifth (ex Leo A. Young, 1959 ANA:956, Bell II:78) is a prooflike presentation piece. Repeated sightings of these same few coins gave the date briefly a reputation for being over-rated in rarity, and this var. was believed the commoner of the two. In recent years these coins have all mysteriously vanished; we have been unable to locate a usable photograph! The other var., with wider date and five berries, was originally believed of the highest rarity, as for many years only four were known, and only one of these (ill.) qualified as UNC. Since about 1968, others have shown up in lower grades; today, when a 1798 is offered at auction, it is likely to be one of the eight to 10 with five berries, of which three or four qualify as UNC. The delivery of [480], 12/28/1799, was long believed to comprise the Five Berries coins; none with date 1799 has ever been rumored.

Beginning in 1802, obvs. show stars 8 + 5, copying the half eagles of 1798–1806. The single 1802 obv. is generally called an overdate, 1802/1, a perception possibly influenced by the 1802/1 half-eagle dies. Any trace of 1 within 2 on the quarter eagles requires a microscope. This obv. comes with four rev. dies, two of them also used on dismes; the rarest has leaf wholly free of I, the two least rare respectively with first star (farthest l., below first cloud) obviously double-punched, or with A away from wing. Most survivors are VF to EF.

Because annual Director's Reports showed a delivery of 423 quarter eagles for 1803, for long this date was believed to exist as a rarity, though nobody ever managed to find a specimen. Adams-Woodin {1913} managed to compound the confusion by listing alleged copper trial pieces from regular dies of this date, and specifying that these should not be confused with the brass British gambling counters of vaguely similar design with KETTLE r. of date. The Kettle counters come also—very rarely—in silver; and some brass specimens have had the name scraped away, possibly to simulate gold coins or trial pieces. But the workmanship is so different from Scot's that no collector who has seen a Kettle counter side by side with a quarter eagle of this design is likely to mistake either for the other. The 1803 delivery is now acknowledged to comprise coins dated 1802.

Two rev. types exist for 1804: The rarer one shows 13 rev. stars in the "arc" arrangement (above), the less rare 14 rev. stars in the old (1798) "cross" arrangement (intersecting straight lines forming diamond-shaped patterns). This latter die was also used on dismes of 1804; it is believed a leftover from 1798–99 when the cross arrangement occurred on dismes, dollars, and half eagles. Possibly nine survive with 13 stars, none above EF; three times as many with 14 stars, in all grades.

The single var. of 1805 has stars 7 + 6; this obv. die was softened at year's end and a 6 punched over the 5, as with one each of the quarter-dollar and half-dollar obvs. of this date—an emergency measure not again repeated, as the redated dies did not hold up long. Other overdates are normally from dies not earlier used and probably not given initial hardening with their earlier dates; reuse of 1805 dies after overdating testifies to Scot's running out of die steel: See introductory texts to Chap. 17, Sect. iv, Chap. 27, Sect. ii, and Chap. 28, Sect. iii. Survivors are mostly VF or EF with a few AU's and "sliders," uncandidly upgraded; prohibitively rare in mint state. However, the 1806/4 is from an unused 1804 die (stars 8 + 5).

Most survivors of this design are dated 1807, with stars again 7 + 6; most are better struck than their elders, survivors better preserved.

From poor relations and odd little souvenirs, these coins have become great prizes. The usual warning (Chap. 32, Sect. i) about solder marks applies; but the coins are rare enough to command collector attention even when mutilated.

SCOT'S HERALDIC EAGLE DESIGN, WITH STARS

Designer, Engraver, Mints, Physical Specifications, Authorizing Acts, as before.
Grade range and standards, as before.

I. 16 STRIPES ON SHIELD

6114 1796 Stars 8 + 8. [432] Very rare.
Hilt 1-C. Delivered Jan. 14, 1797. Enl. photos. Clapp, Eliasberg:80, AU, $26,400. See introductory text.

Ex J. W. Garrett: 733. Courtesy Bowers & Ruddy Galleries, Inc.

6115 1797 Stars 7 + 6. [427] Very rare.
Hilt 5-D. Rev. reused on 1798/7 disme. Obv. break varies in intensity. Usually VF; Spedding, Clapp, Eliasberg:81, EF, $12,100; Auction 80:886, AU, $34,000. Bell II:77, "gem UNC." (unseen), and 1970 ANA:1424, said to be prooflike, may be finest. Mintage figure comprises the [98], [128], and [201] of Feb. 28, March 14, and June 29, 1797; Hilt thinks the first were dated 1796, the other 2 deliveries plus [256] of Jan. 11, 1798, were all the 1797's. See introductory text.

Ex J. W. Garrett: 737. Courtesy Bowers & Ruddy Galleries, Inc.

II. 13 STRIPES ON SHIELD

6116 1798 [All kinds 1,094] Stars 6 + 7. Close date, 4 berries. Ex. rare.
Hilt 4-B. See introductory text. "Melish":1102 has a "cud" rim break obliterating most of 1, first 3 stars, and part of fourth: "fatal break."

6117 1798 Wide date, 5 berries. Very rare.
Hilt 3-I, who identifies these as the [358] struck May–Aug. 1798. Rev. of 1798–1800 dismes with narrow A's. Spedding, Clapp, Eliasberg:82, AU, $8,250. See introductory text.

6118 1802 Stars 8 + 5. [3,035]
4 vars.; see introductory text. Mintage figure includes [423] coined in 1803 from 1802-dated dies.

6119 1804 Rev., 14 stars, cross arrangement. [2,324+] Rare.
Hilt 7-F. Rev. left over from 1798, used also on dismes. Auction 82:900, UNC., $15,000. Enl. photos.

6120 1804 Rev., 13 stars, arc arrangement. [1,003−] Ex. rare.
Possibly 9 known. Usually in low grades. Charlotte:1672 (S 3/17/79), EF, $20,000; Carter:533, EF, $27,500, M. Brownlee.

6121 1805 Stars 7 + 6. [1,781] Very scarce.
See introductory text. 1980 ANA:66, UNC., $14,000.

6122 1806/4 Stars 8 + 5. [1,136] Rare.
See introductory text. Auction 82:902, UNC., $9,250.

6123   1806/5 Stars 7 + 6. [480] Very rare.
Obv. and rev. of **6121**, altered by Scot: See introductory text. Always with some stage of break at LIB. Usually in low grades. Newlin, Garrett:740, $22,000, Robison:825, AU, $12,000.

6124   1807 Stars 7 + 6. [6,812]
See introductory text. Usually cracked through base of date and l. stars.

iii. REICH'S CAPPED DRAPED BUST (1808)

John Reich, the German immigrant who sold himself into indentured service to get to the United States during the Napoleonic Wars, and was rescued to become Assistant Engraver of the Mint (1807–17), received orders from Mint Director Patterson to provide improved designs for all denominations: a slap at Scot, his superior in office. Reich's sole contribution to the quarter-eagle denomination is a single pair of dies for a single-year type coin of a tiny mintage: an instant rarity. On Feb. 26, 1808, came the single delivery, [2,710], using date and letter punches reused on 1809 dismes, and bust and device punches not later resurrected. Obv. bears Reich's usual "signature": thirteenth (lower r.) star is notched. Fewer than 50 survivors are traceable, the true number possibly between 35 and 40.

The reason for this tiny issue is unknown, though early die breakage may have had something to do with it. Only one coin has been reported with unbroken obv. die (unverified); all seen to date show a crack extending from cap through all stars at r. All survivors, including the three UNCS., show excessively narrow borders, usually incomplete. This must have been seen as a design flaw conducive to rapid wear on both sides, as on the half-dollar revs. of 1836–37 and the 1861 S Paquet double eagles. Predictably, survivors are in lower grade range than those of earlier dates lacking this problem. The distribution includes three UNCS., possibly six AU's, 15 or more in VF-EF, perhaps a dozen in VG to F. Most are weak on wingtips and tops of letters; all are weak on parts of borders; all have some stars flat; most show rim dents or bruises, as though the entire issue had been spilled on a floor at the Mint.

But even in worn condition, this date has always been subject to unusual demand, much of it representing pressure from type collectors who want one of each major design. Many survivors have accordingly spent decades in museums, estates, or permanent collections; any that shows up at auction will attract fierce competition.

No Archives documentation explains the small mintage, abandonment of the design, or noncoinage of quarter eagles for the dozen years to follow. All we have is conjectures; mine follow.

The tiny mintage may reflect early die breakage and/or quick filling of bank orders for quarter eagles. Banks normally specified the denomination into which they wanted their deposits of foreign coins or native bullion coined, and over 90% of the time they wanted most or all their gold deposits coined into half eagles. Except for 1816–17, when a fire in the Mint's outbuilding housing rolling mills prevented conversion of gold or silver ingots into strip or planchets, coinages of half eagles remained

large. The Mint Director may have believed that until more banks ordered quarter eagles, there would be no point in making more dies for them. A more appropriate question is why quarter-eagle coinage was resumed at all; Archives documents fail to provide a reply.

Abandonment of the design may reflect Scot's personal pique. Note that in 1813, Scot replaced Reich's perfectly good half-eagle design with his own capped-head type, and that in 1816 he replaced Reich's beautiful though eccentric "Classic Head" cent obv. with one of the ugliest conceptions ever to misrepresent Ms. Liberty: Possibly Scot's sight was by then failing. Compare introductory texts to Chap. 18, Sects. ix, x, and Chap. 36, Sects. iii, iv.

Whatever the causes, the 1808 is a highly coveted rarity. Survivors are under 2% of original mintage (earlier figure was 4%), possibly from the weak borders' exposing the coins to undue wear.

REICH'S CAPPED DRAPED BUST

Designer, Engraver, John Reich. Mints, Physical Specifications, Authorizing Acts, as before.

Grade range, VERY GOOD to UNC. FINE: Eye complete, ear half visible, LIBERTY and motto legible but weak, eagle's eye visible. VERY FINE: Partial cap, hair, and claw details; over half wing feathers visible at least as outlines. EXTREMELY FINE: Isolated tiny rubbed spots only; partial Mint luster. UNCIRCULATED: *No* trace of wear. NOTES, EXCEPTIONS: See introductory text.

6125   1808 [2,710] Very rare.
Struck Feb. 26. For peculiarities of striking and grade, see introductory text. David S. Wilson, Clapp, Eliasberg:89, AU, $26,400, Kevin Lipton; Col. Green, Jerome Kern, Dr. Judd, Dr. Ketterman, Jimmy Hayes, Auction 84:1372, $99,000, D. Akers. UNC.

iv. SCOT'S CAPPED HEAD (1821–27)

After over a dozen years of noncoinage of this denomination, apparently a few banks specified that parts of their deposits of gold bullion and foreign coins should be coined into quarter eagles—possibly as Christmas presents or souvenirs. Accordingly, Robert Scot (then 77 years old and with failing sight, but secure in his life tenure as Engraver) devised crude copies of his 1813 half-eagle design, and hastily translated them into one working device punch for head and another for eagle with scroll, thence into working dies. The coins were smaller (19 mm as against the former 20.6), but minutely thicker to preserve their weight unchanged. Letter punches were by Henry Starr.

Only a single obv. die was used in each year, though a second was made for 1821 which remained unused until 1824, when its final 1 was altered to a 4. Reportedly a second 1825 obv. was altered at the Mint by Kneass to 1826—so effectively that at most a microscopic corner of 5 shows at upper l. of 6 and often not even that; its overdate status has been disputed. It must have been made long after its brother of 1825, as it has larger stars as in 1827.

Only a single rev. die exists for each year except 1825. The first rev. of that year is the die of 1821–24: [3,324] Feb. 16–June 30; the second is that of 1826–27: [1,110] Oct.–Dec. 1825. This second var., discovered about 1915 by Waldo Newcomer, has larger denominator, large 2 close to leaf, fraction bar opposite a point a little above center of 2, stem end directly above curve of D rather than above its upright. It remains very rare despite decades of examination of 1825's; possibly 8–10 survive.

Mintages remained of the same order of size as in previous years. Generally, from 30–50 survive of each date, except for 1825 close fraction and 1826. Survivors are mostly VF to UNC., though mint-state examples of 1821, 1826, and 1827 are seldom offered; beware "sliders."

The same warning applies as formerly about coins showing traces of solder.

SCOT'S CAPPED HEAD

Designer, Robert Scot, rev. after Reich. Engraver, Scot. Mint, Physical Specifications, Authorizing Acts, as before, except Diameter approximately 3/4″ = 19 mm.

Grade range and standards, as 1808, though without the peculiar weaknesses of that date.

6126 1821 [6,448 + ?P] Rare.
Small stars, 1821–25. Proofs and earliest business strikes show guide lines (arcs) between words; on later ones these are effaced. Some (proofs and business strikes) have a tiny depression on cheek from foreign matter adhering to die. To date 7 proofs are traced, one in SI: Clain-Stefanelli {1970}, fig. 20. Garrett:743, Proof, $120,000; Parmelee, Mills, Clapp, Eliasberg:90, Proof, $46,200, Auction 84:1373, $71,500; Carter:536, UNC., $12,650. Enl. photos.

6127 1824/1 [2,600 + ?P] Rare.
Date differently spaced from preceding. Serif of 1 within top triangle of 4, and faintly on upper diagonal. Business strikes (Jan. 30) are normally weaker on head and parts of shield and adjacent wing and leg feathers. Spedding, Clapp, Eliasberg:91, AU, $7,700; Auction 79:1665, UNC., $25,000. Proofs: 1) Mint, SI (cleaned). 2) Cleneay, Woodin, "onesided" (mirror obv. field, frosty rev. field). 3), 4) Pvt. colls. Enl. photos.

Ex J. W. Garrett: 744. Courtesy Bowers & Ruddy Galleries, Inc.

6128 1825 Distant fraction. [3,324] Rare.
Rev. of 1821–24. Often weak on head. See introductory text. Carter:538, UNC., $17,600, R. L. Hughes.

6129 1825 Close fraction. [1,110 + ?P] Very rare.
Rev. of 1826–27. See introductory text. One proof in SI, 2 others reported; possibly 8–10 business strikes, coined Oct.–Dec. 1825. Enl. photos.

Ex J. W. Garrett: 746. Courtesy Bowers & Ruddy Galleries, Inc.

6130 1826 Larger stars. [760 + ?P] Very rare.
Business strikes coined March 31; generally cataloged as overdate: See introductory text. Pierce, Miles, Ullmer:359, UNC., $14,500 (1974); Auction 79:225, UNC., $31,000. Possibly 3 proofs survive.

6131 1827 [2,800 + ?P] Rare.
Business strikes coined Feb. 19. Usually weak on head. Carter:540, UNC., $17,600. One proof reported.

v. KNEASS'S MODIFIED CAPPED HEAD (1829–34)

After Robert Scot died in 1823, the Mint hired William Kneass, a local engraver of bank-note plates, as his successor. Kneass's special assignment was not to create new designs but to improve existing designs of all series in his spare time, by mechanically multiplying working dies from current device punches. This project yielded modified designs for dismes in 1828, followed in 1829 by similar improved versions of half dismes, quarter eagles, and half eagles, and in 1831 by their counterparts in half cents and quarter dollars. Cents and half dollars would not be attempted for several years; there was still too much demand for coinage in these denominations to afford time to create new device punches.

Kneass's modified designs were notable for smaller stars and letters (from punches by Christian Gobrecht), redrawn heads and eagles (with a more professionally finished look than Scot's frequently crude conceptions), but most of all for beaded borders surrounded by high, plain raised rims produced by a "close collar." This new invention consisted of a heavy block of steel containing a hole the same diameter as the finished coin, grooved to impart the reeded edge; this resisted edgewise expansion of planchets at the moment of striking, furnishing "a mathematical equality to their diameters," according to Mint Director Samuel Moore.

Mintages remained of roughly the same quantities as before; survivors are slightly rarer, and occur in about the same grade range, with perhaps a few more UNCs. Die life was potentially much longer; a single rev. of 1830 stayed in use for proofs and business strikes through 1834—but there was too little bank demand for quarter eagles in any one year to exhaust the effective life of any one obv. die, so that for each year there is only one var.

Proofs exist for each year in this group, but most survivors are impaired; probably most were spent during the 1837–44 "Hard Times" period.

The most famous of these years, and one of the most illustrious of all American gold rarities, is 1834 with motto. Most of the [4,000] coined before May 30 remained in the Mint, to be melted after Aug. 1, when the new law became effective, reducing standard weight enough to render each old-tenor quarter eagle worth $2.665 (+ silver content of alloy). Several survivors originated as proofs, and not impossibly all did; no mint-state business strike is known, and all the best ones have proof surface. Mint Director J. R. Snowden (1860) could find no record that any business strikes of 1834 old-tenor were released. The roster is as nearly complete as possible, though quality of illustrations in some auction catalogs precludes positive identification.

1. Adam Eckfeldt (1838), Mint Cabinet, SI. Proof.

2. J. Colvin Randall (Dec. 1895), John H. Clapp, Louis Eliasberg:100, $20,900, Kevin Lipton. Lightly rubbed Proof.

3. Harold Newlin (12/31/1884), T. Harrison Garrett, J. W. Garrett:753, $60,000, Auction 82:1860, $30,000. AU, ex-Proof.

4. A. J. Allen, Ira Reed, Thomas L. Gaskill, NN 48:201. EF, ex-Proof.

5. James Ten Eyck, Belden Roach, Louis Eliasberg, NN 49:575, Grant Pierce, R. L. Miles:100, $6,600, Nathan Shapero:750, $4,200. AU.

6. John Story Jenks, William Cutler Atwater, Clinton Hester, 1949 ANA, Chadwick-Darnell:158. EF. Possibly same as no. 13 below?

7. Hillyer Ryder, F. C. C. Boyd, WGC, "J. F. Bell," "Memorable":94, pvt. colls., Mocatta Metals, 1979 ANA:57, $32,000. AU, ex-Proof?

8. Charles M. Williams, Adolphe Menjou:1180, H. P. Graves. EF. Possibly same as no. 11 or 12?

9. Waldo C. Newcomer, Col. E. H. R. Green, Jerome Kern:22, Carter:546. EF, nicked and scratched, $12,650.

10. James Lawson estate (before 1880), Mabel Sandford, 1947 ANA. VF+.

11. Mackenzie, Nicholson Family:53. VF. Possibly same as one of above.

12. "Alto":71. Same comment.

13. Arthur Lamborn, "Fairfield":1461, $19,000, Auction 80:888, EF, $33,000. Same comment.

14. Shuford:1723. Possibly same as one of above; quality of photographic reproduction prevents certainty.

15. 1973 ANA:820. Same comment.

KNEASS'S MODIFIED CAPPED HEADS

Designer, Engraver, William Kneass, after Scot and Reich. Mint, Philadelphia. Physical Specifications, Authorizing Acts, as before, except Diameter 0.7″ = 18.2 mm.

Grade range, F to UNC., most often VF–AU. Grade standards, as before, but without the peculiarities of 1808.

6132   1829 [3,403 + ?P] Rare.
Business strikes coined Feb. 9. Most survivors are EF. At least 8 proofs, possibly 12, mostly nicked and scratched. Enl.

photos. Auction 79:765, UNC., $17,000; Carter:541, UNC., $14,300; Garrett:1980, Proof, $105,000.

6133   1830 [4,540 + ?P] Rare.
U(NITED) plainly repunched; this rev. continued through **6137**, repeatedly repolished. Apparently 5 proofs, one each in SI and OCL. Auction 86:893, UNC., $11,000.

6134   1831 [4,520 + ?P] Rare.
Business strikes mostly EF–AU or better. At least 8 proofs, 4 with minor impairment; Stickney, Clapp, Eliasberg:97, $30,800, D. Kagin.

6135   1832 Modified head. [4,400 + ?P] Rare.
Higher apparent relief; different contours to curls, especially below LIBE and above date. This new head punch continues into 1834. Business strikes are not as well struck as 1829–31. Clapp, Eliasberg:98, UNC., $14,300. Proofs: 1) Cohen, Winslow Lewis, Maris, choice. 2) Davis, Woodin, nicked. 3) Bell, "Memorable," Chadwick-Darnell:157, nicked on cheek. Enl. photos.

Ex J. W. Garrett: 751. Courtesy Bowers & Ruddy Galleries, Inc.

6136   1833 [4,160 + ?P] Rare.
Rarer in all grades than 1829–32; much rarer UNC. Proofs: 1) Mint, SI. 2) Parmelee, Mills, Clapp, Eliasberg:99, $50,600. 3) Hall, Graves. 4) Woodin, Newcomer, Col. Green, "Bell," "Memorable," impaired. 5) Pvt. coll.

6137   1834 [4,000− + ?P] Ex. rare.
See introductory text for discussion and roster. Enl. photos.

Ex J. W. Garrett: 753. Courtesy Bowers & Ruddy Galleries, Inc.

vi. THE REICH-KNEASS "CLASSIC HEADS" (1834–39)

For several decades, the effect of enormous quantities of Mexican, Peruvian, and other Latin American silver reaching world markets had been increasingly to lower the price of silver in terms of gold, or in effect to raise the price of gold bullion (reckoned in Mexican dollars) to a point where U.S. old-tenor gold coins became worth more than face value. During the 1820s and early '30s, most Philadelphia gold coins went to bullion dealers, who promptly shipped them out for melting.

Archives documents of this period mention mass assays in Europe, in one of which (Paris, 1831) no less than 40,000 U.S. half eagles perished in a single melt. Something had to be done, and quickly. The expedient which finally managed to become law was a bill lowering the official weight of the gold eagle from 270 to 258 grs., and its quality from 11/12 (916.7 Fine) to 232/258 (899.225 Fine), with the half eagle and quarter eagle in proportion. This became law as the Act of June 28, 1834, effective Aug. 1. Mint Director Samuel Moore correctly anticipated that enormous numbers of old-tenor gold coins (1795–1834) of all kinds would be brought in for recoinage, as the difference in bullion content made enough profit available to induce the public and the bullion dealers to bring the coins to the Mint rather than ship them overseas. In preparation for this flood of recoinage orders, Moore instructed William Kneass to prepare a large surplus of working dies for half eagles and quarter eagles, omitting the motto E PLURIBUS UNUM to enable instant identification: All old-tenor gold coins bore this motto, none of the new ones would show it.

Kneass, for reasons which may have had to do with uniformity of design in all denominations, chose to copy the old John Reich "Classic Head," first seen on cents 1808–14, later on half cents 1825–36. His eagle was a somewhat sharpened-up version of one Reich had designed for gold coins in 1807.

We may take it as more than coincidence that both the half cents and the new gold pieces bore this head rather than any other. Scot had replaced the Reich "Classic Head" on cents in 1816 by the "Matron Head," probably the ugliest head of Ms. Liberty ever to appear on a U.S. coin. Though his reason is undocumented, we can make some plausible guesses. Recall first that Scot had been a bank-note-plate engraver in the 1780s, on the basis of which irrelevant skill he received the Mint engravership, Nov. 1793. During the decades following, he had to learn to make device punches copying others' designs; but whenever he had to create his own, the results occupied a narrow range between banality and crudity. Whenever Mint authorities hired an Assistant Engraver, the appointees found themselves professionally hampered, their best designs replaced by Scot's inferior ones as soon as possible. As early as 1807, Mint Director Patterson regarded as urgent the appointment of an Assistant Engraver to improve on Scot's designs because Scot's advancing age made his capacity to do his own work increasingly dubious. For this very reason the Treasury approved hiring John Reich, who had been for six years vainly knocking at the Mint's door, despite two successive Directors regarding him as the best diesinker in the United States. We may assume, then, that when Reich became Assistant Engraver and began creating new coin designs, Scot took this as an insult. This may have been why Reich received no raise in salary during 10 years of service; it may also explain why Scot replaced Reich's half-eagle design in 1813 and his cent design in 1816: professional jealousy. In introductory texts to Chap. 17, Sect. v, Chap. 18, Sects. ix and x, I speculated that one possible ground alleged for replacing the "Classic Head" design was its peculiarly androgynous concept: Ms. Liberty's hairdo is masculine by ancient Greek standards, and its fillet was primarily a prize worn by boy athletes for winning town games, never by women. Reich quit the Mint on the tenth anniversary of his appointment, ostensibly because of inadequate salary; but these personal rebuffs almost certainly loomed large in his decision, especially considering why Reich had been hired in the first place! After Scot died in 1823, the next half cents to be issued bore not any new design (which they well might have), but Reich's old "Classic Head" portrait.

And so this androgynous effigy was honored in 1834 by Kneass's choosing it for the new quarter eagles and half eagles. The flood of gold deposits anticipated by Mint Director Moore began that summer and increased during the next two years;

issues of quarter eagles (beginning officially as of Aug. 1) exceeded all expectations. From then through 1839, over 910,000 came from Philadelphia bearing this design, plus some 57,475 from the newly built Southern branches at Charlotte, N.C., Dahlonega, Ga., and New Orleans, La., all with mintmark above date (1838–39). The Philadelphia total for 1834–36 alone is over 10 times the total old-tenor quarter-eagle coinage.

With such large mintages, one would expect the coins to be relatively common. And in ordinary grades they are always available for a price; but any "Classic Head" gold coin in mint state is a rarity. These coins went into circulation at once and stayed there, few being saved as souvenirs. Even the hoards discovered after WW II yielded virtually none in mint state.

Several design modifications followed. Coins of 1834 come with two entirely different heads; the first, called "Small Head," is instantly recognizable by the date's distance from lowest curls. The later one, called "Booby Head" by John H. Clapp before 1942, has 4 almost touching curl; its effigy is no credit to Reich or Kneass: thick lips, jaw jutting forward, eye very deeply set. Coins of 1835 show a taller head with narrower bust, upper ribbon end almost concealed by a curl. In 1835, Kneass suffered a stroke, and Christian Gobrecht made later dies. Presumably the 1836's with Head of 1834 and Head of 1835 were from dies completed earlier but with final digit omitted, whereas the Head of 1837 is Gobrecht's own modification. On this last, hair above brow slopes far back, very distant from sixth star. In 1838, Gobrecht replaced this head by a still cruder one imitating the "Booby Head," but larger with tiny stars; nor was his new version of 1839 any improvement.

However, with adoption in 1839 of the new Coronet Head concept (extended to quarter eagles in 1840), Gobrecht was to standardize the design: 67 years of stereotypy would follow five years of experiment.

THE REICH-KNEASS "CLASSIC HEADS"

Designer, William Kneass, after Reich. Engravers, Kneass, Christian Gobrecht. Mints, Philadelphia (no mintmark), Charlotte (mintmark C), Dahlonega (D), New Orleans (O). Mintmarks above date, 1838–39. Composition, 1834–36, gold 232/258 = 899.225 Fine, remainder copper with traces of silver; 1837–39, gold 90% (900 Fine), silver not over 5%, rest copper. Weight, 1834–36, 64.5 ± 0.129 grs. = 4.18 ± 0.0084 gms.; 1837–39, 64.5 ± 0.25 grs. = 4.18 ± 0.0162 gms. Diameter, $11/16'' = 17.5$ mm. Edge, vertically reeded. Authorizing Acts, 1834–36, Act of June 28, 1834; 1837–39, Act of Jan. 18, 1837.

Grade range, GOOD to UNC.; not collected in lowest grades. FINE: Ear and all major hair contours visible; partial wing and neck feathers; partial shield lines. VERY FINE: At least half hair and wing-feather details clear; about half azure (nearly horizontal lines in shield). EXTREMELY FINE: Tiny isolated rubbed spots only; partial mint luster. UNCIRCULATED: *No* trace of wear. EXCEPTIONS: Weakly struck coins, especially from branch mints, may not show full azure, adjacent wing feathers, nor hair details above ear even in mint state; grade by surface, look for mint luster on the weak areas. Beware specimens with any trace of solder from former use as jewelry; look for interruption or repairs to edge reeding at 12:00 and 6:00, any local porous discoloration, or any traces of hand tooling to efface such treatment.

6138　1834 [all kinds 112,234 + 4+P] Small head, large arrowheads.

Date far from curls; roll of curls on back of head almost straight. This obv. type discovered by Waldo Newcomer, described in John H. Clapp's notebooks, and first published by B. Max Mehl in the 1940s. Proofs (enl. photos) have bases of

E(S) and O repunched; at least 8 survive, mostly impaired (spent during the Hard Times?). On business strikes, repunching fades out.

Ex J. W. Garrett: 754. Courtesy Bowers & Ruddy Galleries, Inc.

6139 1834 Small head, small arrowheads. Very rare.
Same obv.; arrowheads distant from CA. Discovered by Newcomer about 1926.

6140 1834 Large or "Booby" head. 6 rev. vars.
Large 4 very close to curl; deep indentation in curls at 2:30; thick lips, jutting jaw, eye more deeply set. Price for var. with split berry in branch, A M well apart (enl. photos); others are rarer. One proof known.

6141 1835 Taller head. [131,402— + ?P] 4 rev. vars.
Most of reported mintage was dated 1834. Some 1835's precede 1834's with same revs. Price for split-berry rev. of **6140**; at least 5 proofs from these dies, incl. Earle, Clapp, Eliasberg:102, $30,800. Enl. photos.

Ex J. W. Garrett: 755. Courtesy Bowers & Ruddy Galleries, Inc.

6142 1836 [all kinds 547,986+ + ?P] Head of 1834. 3 rev. vars. Rare.
Both ribbon ends plain (device punch of **6140**); date spaced 183 6. At least 4 proofs known. Part of mintage may have borne date 1835. Most of the gold for this year's output came from melted old-tenor coins; part was from French Indemnity payments.

6143 1836 Head of 1835.
Tall head; only tip of upper ribbon shows; tiny forelock close to sixth star. Forms the majority of survivors of this date. Often weak in centers. One proof known (Breen {1977}, p. 65). Device punch by Kneass; dies completed and dated by Gobrecht after Kneass's stroke. Enl. photos.

TRANSITIONAL HEADS, 1836–39

6144 1836 Head of 1837. Very rare.
Hair slopes back directly from fillet, far from sixth star. Device punch by Gobrecht. Usually weak above ear. Parmelee, Mills, Clapp, Eliasberg:103, Proof, $35,200.

6145 1837 Same type. [45,080— + ?P] Very scarce.
Much of reported mintage was dated 1836. Usually weak above ear. One var. shows repunching on 8 7 and eighth through tenth stars, the other does not. Possibly 3 proofs known; Parmelee, Mills, Clapp, Eliasberg:104, $39,600.

6146 1838 Modified head, smaller stars. [47,030+]
Rude imitation of **6140**; 2 revs. of 1837 reused. Obv. border broader than formerly. No proofs reported. In VF or EF, less rare than 1837 or 1839; in choice UNC., Ex. rare. Eliasberg:105, UNC., $13,200.

6147 1838 C Double-punched C. [7,880] Very scarce.
Heavy double obv. rim. Mintmark first entered touching 3, then corrected higher; 2 obvs., 3 revs. shipped, only one pair used, all defaced in 1843. Often shows depression on cheek, from foreign matter adhering to die; this varies in position. Usually in low grades.

6148 1839/8 New head. [27,021− + ?P]
Rev. of 1836. Head redesigned: Back curls and upper curls differ; longer obv. dentils, larger stars. Usually in low grades; prohibitively rare UNC. 3 proofs known. Part of mintage probably bore date 1838. First published as overdate in Green {1936}.

6149 1839/8 C [10,740+] 3 rev. vars.
2 obvs. shipped Jan. 10 including overdate. First 2 vars. from 2 revs. shipped for 1838 C; first [5,880, March 16] is from 1838 rev.: weak elongated berry, leaves have stems, arrows barely free of CA, later cracked vertically from rim through E(S). Second [4,860, May 16] has no berry, leaves stemless, arrows merge into CA. Third (mintage incl. in next) has same obv., new rev. shipped May 3; stemless hook-shaped berry, final S repunched. All Ex. rare UNC.

6150 1839 C Repunched 39. [7,400−]
3 first punched too low, then corrected; second obv. from Jan. 10 shipment. Rev. as third die of preceding, one of 2 revs. shipped May 3. Both dies later shattered. Mintage figure comprises deliveries July 30–Dec. 9, and includes third var. of preceding. Ex. rare UNC. Enl. photos.

6151 1839/8 D Head of 1838 C. [13,674]
2 pairs of dies shipped Jan. 10, only one obv. used; one rev. has small thin claws, letters spaced apart (heavily lapped die, ill. Akers {1975B}, p. 41); the other (ill.) has normal (heavy) claws, letters more closely spaced. Both vars. are prohibitively rare UNC.; neither can be correlated to delivery figures: [5,487] Feb., [4,026] March, [4,161] April.

6152 1839 O [all kinds 17,781] Wide fraction, small arrows.
Date high and curved; no berry, disconnected arrow shafts. Struck from one of 2 pairs of dies shipped March 14. Device punch imitates **6140**. Ill. in Akers {1975B}, p. 42. Enl. photos.

6153 1839 O Close fraction, large arrows.
Date low and straight; third, fourth, and fifth stars repunched; with disconnected berry. Struck from the second pair of dies shipped March 14. Scarcer than preceding. Occasionally comes with rev. aligned 180° from normal. Enl. photos.

vii. GOBRECHT'S CORONET HEAD DESIGN (1840–1907)

Even Christian Gobrecht probably never suspected that his final version of the quarter-eagle design would outlive him by over 60 years, becoming one of the most familiar and unchanging national concepts since the Spanish Pillar Dollar. Ever since late 1834, first William Kneass and then Gobrecht had been experimenting with designs of all U.S. coin denominations, trying to reach a version of each which would remain satisfactory for ensuing decades. The head Gobrecht adopted for eagles in 1839 was reduced and modified for half eagles and quarter eagles, in the latter requiring no noticeable changes. Not even the adoption of the motto IN GOD WE TRUST (1866) was to affect quarter eagles, which looked in 1907 very much as in 1840. The rev. may have been by Robert Ball Hughes.

Actually, Longacre modified the rev. in 1859, later Philadelphia coins ("Type II" rev.) having smaller arrowheads spaced apart; but San Francisco quarter-eagle mintages continued to use leftover 1854–57 revs. until 1876.

To minimize variation, as an anticounterfeiting device, quarter-eagle dies were completely hubbed—comparable to portraits and border elements on current dollar bills, which are mechanically reproduced for the same reason. The only exceptions were dates and mintmarks. First Gobrecht, then Longacre (or, sometimes, workmen in the Engraving Dept.) entered dates by hand, using four-digit logotypes; variations occur by erroneous choice or misplacement of a logotype. Dates were very small 1840–43, changing later that year to a larger size; some later dates would be larger or smaller, but only in 1873 did another change occur within the year. This followed the Chief Coiner's complaint, Jan. 18, 1873, about the "closed 3's" readily mistaken for 8's; William Barber, Longacre's successor in the engravership, had to furnish a new set of date logotypes ("Open 3"). Mintmarks vary markedly in size and shape through 1878; 1880–1907 coins are all from Philadelphia, without mintmarks.

In 1848, some 230 oz. of native bullion from the new California bonanzas came to the Philadelphia Mint from Secretary of War William L. Marcy, who had received them from Col. R. B. Mason, then Military Governor of California. Marcy instructed Mint Director Robert Maskell Patterson to have the gold coined into specially marked quarter eagles, over and above the amount needed for the Congressional medals just authorized for Gens. Zachary Taylor and Winfield "Old Fuss and Feathers" Scott. These orders yielded some [1,389], Dec. 1848, each one counterstamped CAL. above eagle; survivors have become highly coveted rarities.

However, rarities in this denomination are mostly either low-mintage Charlotte or Dahlonega coins before the Civil War, or low-mintage Philadelphia coins 1863–72, 1874–77, while specie payments were still suspended and little gold bullion reached the Mint. Several of these dates have become very famous; possibly the most famous of all is the 1841, of which no mintage record survives. No specimen was known to exist outside the Mint Cabinet Collection until 1909; at present possibly a dozen proofs and ex-proofs are traced, mostly impaired. Only a single pair of dies was used (enl. ill.); all specimens have fine narrow edge reeding, entirely unlike the 1841 C and 1841 D coins from which mintmarks have been removed to make fraudulent imitations. Aside from their edges, 1841 C's tend to be weak on ERTY, adjacent hair, bun, locks below LIBE, stars, claws, and lower feathers; the tiny mintmark c overlaps end of arrow feather, and removal affects feather even aside from leaving telltale evidence of monkey business below it; most show a knife-rim at upper r. obv. and l. rev. On the other hand, 1841 D's tend to be weak on locks just above and below ear, and on bun, claws, and neck feathers. The slightest doubt is grounds for authentication of any alleged 1841 Philadelphia quarter eagle.

The following roster is the most nearly complete ever attempted; doubts remain owing to quality of illustrations in some auction catalogs.

1. Mint Cabinet Collection, SI. Proof. Clain-Stefanelli {1970}, fig. 22.

2. J. C. Mitchelson, CSL. Impaired.

3. Waldo Newcomer, Col. E. H. R. Green, Charles M. Williams, "J. F. Bell," Clifford T. Weihman, Cardinal Spellman, Archdiocese of N.Y. Proof.

4. Adolphe Menjou, R. F. Schermerhorn, Robert Friedberg, H. P. Graves, Grant Pierce, 1976 ANA:2787, $41,000. Proof, rubbed in fields.

5. A. H. Baldwin set, Burdette G. Johnson, Wayte Raymond, Waldo Newcomer, Col. E. H. R. Green, F. C. C. Boyd, "J. F. Bell," "Memorable," Eliasberg:117, $82,500. Proof.

6. Samuel Wolfson:114, $15,000, Alex Shuford:1731, $18,000, Herstal:734A, $26,000. Impaired.

7. William Forrester Dunham, "J. F. Bell" (1945), Bell II:108, $13,000 (1963), RARCOA, unidentified thieves at GENA Convention, N.Y., Dec. 6, 1964; *CW* 12/28/64. *VF,* field marks l. of eighth star, before lower lip, between wing and base of D, etc. Not recovered.

8. Upper N.Y. State noncollector accumulation (1958), Bowers, pvt. coll., Arthur Lamborn (duplicate), Herdman:6406, $17,500. VF+.

9. LM 2/72, "Terrell," Robison:115, $13,000. VF+.

10. Stephen Baer, Q. David Bowers, Arthur Lamborn,

"Fairfield":1481, $19,000, Windsor:254, $19,500. EF, rim nicks upper obv. Ill. at **6154.**

11. 1973 ANA:821. VF or better, $26,000.

12. Mehl 3/26/40, Kreisberg 6/70. F. Not verified.

Others are reported, mostly VF to EF.

The other date famous enough and rare enough to require a roster is 1854 S, the initial issue from the San Francisco Mint [246]. Most of that branch mint's scanty supply of parting acids had to be reserved for making double eagles; coinage of half eagles and quarter eagles was suspended after the initial deliveries. Again, as with 1841, the roster is the most nearly complete yet attempted, and uncertainties in it arise from the same source.

1. Davis-Graves:825, Harry Bass? VF+, horizontal abrasion above eagle.

2. Atwater, Grant Pierce, Miles, 1973 ANA:826, $9,000, 1974 MANA:1547, $24,000, Arthur Lamborn, "Fairfield":1544, $10,000 (1977), Scott-Kinnear:13, $9,900. VF, nick above thirteenth star, rough on upper l. obv., lower l. rev. Enl. photos.

3. F. C. C. Boyd, WGC, "Bell," "Memorable," Clinton Hester or C. M. Williams, Menjou:1326, NN 51:837, pvt. colls., "Rio Rancho":89, $31,000. VF+, scratch from arrow to M.

4. Waldo Newcomer, Col. E. H. R. Green, "Bell," Farouk:278, Gilhousen:184, "Rio Rancho":90, $13,000, Dr. Altany, Windsor:307, $24,000. F to VF.

5. Roach, Wolfson, S. Hallock duPont:85, 1983 Grand Central:2762, $10,000. F, scratch above eagle's head, another (parallel upper wing) to rim close to F.

6. Kreisberg/Schulman 2/60:2592, 1979 ANA:82, $8,750. Auction 81:1405. VG–F, $9,200.

7. "Western bank," B. Max Mehl, 1910, H. O. Granberg, Mehl, Elmer Sears, John H. Clapp, Eliasberg:170, $7,150. VG/G.

8. Tex. pvt. coll. Loop removed, traces of solder.

9. Tex. pvt. coll. Obv. VF, scratched; rev. shank removed, affecting NITE and MERI.

There are probably at least two others around.

Data on striking quality of C mint coins partly follow unpublished researches by Douglas Winter.

With the single exception of 1862/1, overdates in this series have remained obscure and controversial. Some 1846's, under strong magnification, show traces of what seems to be a 4 within 6; most 1849's show some repunching on date, and an 1849/8 has been repeatedly claimed but remains unconfirmed. The 1853/2 remains of extreme rarity.

Specimens of the later years 1878–1907 are always available for a price, partly because British, French, and Swiss banks yielded numerous UNCs. during the two decades following WW II. This has had the unexpected side effect of making rare dates like 1881 and 1885 easier to locate than some larger mintages of earlier years. Type collectors have absorbed most of these later dates.

GOBRECHT'S CORONET HEAD DESIGN

Designer, Christian Gobrecht, obv. after Benjamin West ("Venus" in *Omnia Vincit Amor*, 1839); rev. after Reich and Kneass. Engravers, Gobrecht for obv. master die and both hubs, Longacre for 1859–1907 rev. hub. Mints, Philadelphia (no mintmark), Charlotte (mintmark C), Dahlonega (D), New Orleans (O), San Francisco (S). Mintmarks below eagle. Physical Specifications, as 1837–39, except diameter nearer to 17/24" or 18 mm. Pure gold content, 3.7611 gms. = 0.1209 oz. troy. Authorizing Acts, as 1837–39.

Grade range, POOR to UNC.; not collected below FINE except

for rarities. FINE: Partial hair detail, coronet line blurry, few wing feathers outlined, no internal detail to leaves or shield lines. VERY FINE: All major hair contours visible, with partial detail of individual locks; coronet line clear; at least half wing feathers clear, at least half azure and gules (horizontal and nearly vertical shield lines) intact. EXTREMELY FINE: Isolated rubbed spots only; partial mint luster. UNCIRCULATED: *No* trace of wear. EXCEPTIONS: Some mintmarked coins before 1877 may be weakly struck in centers; grade by surface. NOTE: Beware coins with traces of solder or evidence of its removal; look for interruption or repairs of edge reeding at 12:00 or 6:00, local discoloration, porosity, or retooling to obliterate any of these.

6154   1840 [18,859 + ?P]
Normally weak in centers; usually in low grades, prohibitively rare above EF. 3 proofs known, 2 impaired. Enl. photos.

Ex J. W. Garrett: 757. Courtesy Bowers & Ruddy Galleries, Inc.

6155   1840 C Small c. [12,822]
3 minor vars., from 2 pairs of dies shipped Feb. 5–6; usually better struck than other mints of this date. Normally shows partial knife-rims. Very rare above EF. Neil, Bareford:85, UNC, $6,500.

6156   1840 D Small D. [3,532] Rare.
Coined Nov. 23. Only one var.; 2 pairs of dies shipped Feb. 6. Usually VF; unknown UNC, prohibitively rare AU. Bareford:86, AU, $6,750.

6157   1840 O Large O. [22,800 −] Very rare.
Struck March–April 1840 from one pair of dies shipped March 17. Possibly much of this delivery comprised coins dated 1839. Mintmark above bar and numerator. The only UNC known is Pierce:1102, in a Tex. pvt. coll.

6158   1840 O Small o. [10,780+]
Some [7,200] delivered in several batches July–Dec. 1840, plus [3,580] Aug. 1841, which must have been made before the 2 pairs of 1840 dies were destroyed Feb. 27, 1841. For long this isolated 1841 delivery was thought to represent 1841 O coins; none are known. Mintmark further r.; obv. shows vertical die file marks near first 2 stars. Usually VF–EF, weak on hair above and below ear, and on neck and leg feathers; Ex. rare UNC. Eliasberg:115, UNC, $7,425, Harry Bass.

6159   1841 Fine edge reeding. [No record] Proofs only. Ex. rare.
Authentication urgently recommended. First published in Eckfeldt & DuBois {1842}; miscalled "patterns" in Snowden

{1860}; remained unknown to collectors outside the Mint Cabinet until Edgar Adams publicized the date in 1909. See introductory text for warnings and roster.

6160   1841 C Small c, coarse edge reeding. [10,281]
See introductory text. 2 rev. vars., one from an 1840 C rev., one from a die shipped Feb. 18, 1841. Ex. rare in UNC. Bareford:87, AU, $2,600.

6161   1841 D Small D, coarse edge reeding. [4,164] Rare.
Coined April 30. Three obvs., 4 revs. shipped; only one var. Usually VF; prohibitively rare AU. See introductory text.

6162   1842 [2,823 + ?P] Rare.
Long believed of extreme rarity, but after WW I several low-grade survivors turned up; still prohibitively rare AU, unknown UNC. One proof in SI, 2 others (impaired) in pvt. colls.

6163   1842 C Small c. [6,729] Rare.
Only one var. seen: Date slants up to r., rev. of 1841 C. One obv. shipped Dec. 22, 1841; the second, March 11, 1842, is not identified. Striking quality like 1841 C; see introductory text for latter. Always weak; usually F or VF, prohibitively rare in EF.

6164   1842 D Repunched 18; small D. [4,643] Rare.
Only one var. Striking qualities like 1841 D (in introductory text). Usually in low grades; prohibitively rare above EF.

6165   1842 O Small o. [19,800]
One pair of dies shipped Dec. 23, 1841; last impressions have break through bases of AMERIC to rim above C. Striking quality like **6158**. Unknown in UNC.; prohibitively rare above EF.

6166   1843 Larger date. [100,546 + ?P]
Date logotype as on dime. Available in all grades for a price. At least 5 proofs known, 2 in cased complete sets.

6167   1843 C Small date, crosslet 4, small c. [2,988] Rare.
Delivered April 28, from a single pair of dies shipped Dec. 23, 1842. Most survivors are EF, with knife-rims at l. obv., field bulge at end of bust, and usually a crack from latter to rim. Dealers often exaggerate this date's rarity; at the 1974 ANA Convention, at least 8 different ones were in the bourse. Mitchelson, Clapp, Eliasberg:125, AU, $4,675.

6168   1843 C Large date, plain 4, large C. [23,076]
Delivered in 5 batches between June 30 and Dec. 30. Date originally slanted up to r., then corrected, so that early states have plain doubling at 18, later fading. Usually VF; very rare EF.

6169   1843 D Small date only. Small D. [32,672]
Mintmark as 1840–42. Better struck than previous D mints but apt to show some weakness in hair. Minor positional

vars., from 2 obvs., 5 revs., shipped between Dec. 22, 1842 and Jan. 17, 1843. Coined March 17–Sept. 30.

6170   1843 D Large D. [3,537] Very rare.
Coined Oct. 7. Mintmark as 1844–59. Only the one die, shipped July 15. Discovery coin, Wilharm, Clapp, Eliasberg: 127, AU, $1,540.

6171   1843 O Small date, large O. [288,002] Normal stars.
In all, 6 obvs., 10 revs. shipped, probably not all used; 6 vars. from 2 obvs., 5 revs. including following.

6172   1843 O Same, tiny stars. Rare.
Stars thin, attenuated; either the hub was weakly impressed, or obv. die reground. Rev. as next; base of mintmark repunched. Discovery coin, "Melish":1154.

6173   1843 O Large date and O. [76,000]
Much scarcer than the small-date type; very rare UNC. Always with base of mintmark repunched.

6174   1844 [6,784 + ?P] Rare.
Struck Aug. 31. Usually in low grades; prohibitively rare AU. 3 proofs known, including one in SI, one in Dr. Judd's cased proof set, and the former Newcomer, Boyd, Bell, "Memorable" specimen.

6175   1844 C Large C. [11,622]
In Dec. 1843, 3 obvs., 5 revs. shipped; probably only one pair used. Large C mintmark continues through 1860. Usually F–VF, centers weak; prohibitively rare AU. Mintage interrupted because a burglar raided and burned down the Mint Building during the night of July 27, 1844; Mint operations resumed early 1846.

6176   1844 D Large D. [17,332]
3 pairs of dies; 4 minor vars. Large D continues through 1859. Even UNCs. are usually weak in centers.

6177   1845 [91,051 + ?P]
Date from the dime logotype. At least 7 minor vars., distinguishable by their die breaks. Proofs: 1) Mint, SI. 2) Cased complete proof set. 3) Col. Green, "Bell," "Memorable." 4) Set of 3 gold denominations in Paul Williams:1818, $127,500.

6178   1845 D [19,460]
2 pairs of dies shipped; only one var. seen, rev. of 1844. Usually VF to EF; prohibitively rare UNC.

6179   1845 O Repunched 18. [4,000] Rare.
Delivered Jan. 22, 1846, two days before the first shipment of 1846 O dies arrived. Only one var.; the other 3 pairs of 1845 O dies remained unused, like the 6 pairs of 1844 O dies. The large O continues through 1857. Usually in low grades; Ex. rare EF, prohibitively rare above. Clapp, Eliasberg:135, AU, $2,640; Brand I:110, UNC., $8,800. Most show a depressed mark between a curl on back of neck and thirteenth star (foreign matter on die). First publicized by B. Max Mehl; famous because omitted in annual Mint reports; believed Ex. rare until worn ones began showing up in the 1950s.

6180●   1846 [all kinds 21,598 + ?P] Normal date.
Usually in low grades; prohibitively rare UNC. Date as on dime. Proofs: 1) Mint, SI. 2) ANS. 3) Cased proof set. 4) Wetmore, Jenks, Clapp, Eliasberg:136, $28,600.

6181   1846 "Overdate."
Traces of repunching on all 4 digits, triple outlines on 4; 6 apparently over 4. First brought to my attention about 1965 by Sam Jillette.

6182   1846 C [4,808] Rare.
2 pairs of dies shipped, only one used? Only the rare earliest state shows plain extra base of 1 below 1 in date. Usually VF–EF; a few "seawater UNCs." reported. D. S. Wilson, Clapp, Eliasberg:137, UNC., $10,450. C-Mint coins henceforth have finer edge reeding than formerly.

6183   1846 D Double D. [2,360] Very rare.
Coined Jan. 22, from the first pair of dies, received Jan. 11. Mintmark first entered far to l. of final position. Discovered by Harry Bass.

6184   1846 D Normal D. [16,943]
Coined after March 23, from the second pair of dies, received March 11. Faint double outlines on 846; die file marks above NITE. Ex. rare above AU.

6185   1846 O [62,000]
2 vars. from 4 obvs., 2 revs. shipped; the revs. differ in position of O. Usually VF and weak on claws, leg, and neck feathers. Very rare in higher grades. Mills, Clapp, Eliasberg:139, $1,650.

6186   1846 O "Overdate."
Repunched 4; microscopic traces of 4 within 6, like 6181. Robison:137.

6187   1847 [all kinds 29,814 + ?P] Normal date.
Very rare above EF; usually VF. The only proof traced is in SI.

6188   1847 Heavily repunched 18. Very rare.
Discovery coin, NN 51:825.

6189   1847 C [23,226]
3 pairs of dies shipped. Even UNCs. show weakness on feathers nearest shield: Cowell, Clapp, Eliasberg:141, UNC., $5,060. Later strikings show rev. die plainly rusted.

6190   1847 D [15,874] Normal date.
3 pairs of dies shipped. Usually better struck than previous D-mints.

6191   1847 D "Overdate." Rare.
Strong repunching at bases of 47, not matching curves of 7. On the earliest die state this looks like 47/46 but remnants of final digit are too blurry for certainty. Discovery coin, Eliasberg, Ivy. 2 rev. vars.; in the second, date repunching partly effaced. Latter will price as 6190.

6192   1847 O [all kinds 124,000] Normal date and O.
In all, 3 obvs., 5 revs. shipped Dec. 1846. Some show period joined to large D. Despite large mintage, rare EF, Ex. rare AU.

6193   1847 O Double O. Rare.
Mintmark first too low, touching bar, then corrected. Discovery coin, "Melish":1180.

6194   1847 O Double date. Rare.
Doubling plainest at 18; 2 rev. vars. Discovery coin, Gaskill, NN 48:249; other var., Ruby:1720.

6195   1848 [7,497 + ?P] Rare.
Touted as a rarity since about 1958, when "J. F. Bell" circulated want lists including this date; dealers found none in stock, and the hunt was on. Survivors are usually VF to EF, Ex. rare AU. Proofs have tiny die chip on neck, final 8 midway between truncation and border; business strikes, final 8 nearer truncation, and a line slants up to l. from l. foot of 1 in date. Proofs: 1) Mint, SI. 2) Woodin, Boyd, "Melish," pvt. coll. 3) Davis-Graves, Tex. coll., Davies-Niewoehner:495, $60,000. 4) Pvt. coll., impaired.

6196   1848 CAL [1,389 + ?P] Rare.
See introductory text. Forgeries exist, made by privately punching CAL. into regular 1848's; note enlarged details of genuine. Position of CAL. in field varies, but not shapes of letters and period, nor their mutual positions. In the James F. Lindsay coll., 1978 GENA:1839, one showed triple-punching on CAL. Most survivors are VF to EF; some UNCs. are prooflike and have been sold as proofs: Clapp, Eliasberg:145, $41,800, Auction 85:923, $46,200. The 3 proofs in the Long-

acre estate (1870) have not been identified; check description at **6195** for proof dies. Authentication recommended. Enl. photos.

6197 1848 C [16,788]
4 obvs. shipped; revs. of 1847. Usually uneven strikes, very rare above EF, prohibitively rare UNC. Rarely with buckled obv. die.

6198 1848 D [13,771]
3 pairs of dies; 2 vars. In Dec. 1847, 4 obvs., 6 revs. sent to New Orleans, but no 1848 O coinage followed.

6199 1849 [all kinds 23,294] Normal date.
Sometimes with minute repunchings. The "1849/8" has not been confirmed. Openings within 49 are almost never completely clear.

6200 1849 Double date south. Rare.
Date first punched low, then corrected.

6201 1849 Double date west. Very rare.
Date first punched l. of final position. "Unicorn" var.: spine up from bust.

6202 1849 C [10,220] Very scarce.
3 pairs of dies. Borders often weak; many survivors are weak on feathers around shield, and show a knife-rim at r. on either side. Usually VF or EF; prohibitively rare AU. One die shows minute repunching on 49.

6203 1849 D [10,945]
3 pairs of dies. Borders often weak.

6204 1850 [252,923 + 1+P] Heavy date.
Lowest arrowhead touches CA, unlike next. Proofs untraced, but one was in the set made up for the Library Committee.

6205 1850 Thin numerals. Rare.
Hair-thin serifs. Rev. lapped die: lowest arrowhead free of CA.

6206 1850 C [9,148] Very scarce.
3 pairs of dies. Normally weak on leg and neck feathers. Ex. rare in AU or above.

6207 1850 D [12,148]
3 pairs of dies. Usually weak on borders, claws, and leg feathers. Ex. rare in AU. S 3/85:885, UNC., $3,740.

6208 1850 O [84,000]
4 obvs., 18 leftover revs. from 1845–47. Always weak in centers; Ex. rare in AU.

6209 1851 [all kinds 1,372,748] Normal date.
In all, 10 obvs., 9 revs. Minute positional vars.

6210 1851 Double date. 2 vars. Scarce.

6211 1851 C [14,923]
3 pairs of dies; only one var. seen, rusty rev. of 1849–50. Normally weak on hair just above ear; Ex. rare in EF. Finest: LM 4/70:665, UNC.

6212 1851 D [11,264]
3 obvs., leftover revs. Normally weak at dentils, claws, and leg feathers. Ex. rare AU or above; Roach, Eliasberg:158, UNC., $6,325.

6213 1851 O [all kinds 148,000] Normal date.
In all, 8 obvs., 4 revs. Very rare in mint state.

6214 1851 O Double date.
Date first punched slanting down to r., then corrected level. Price for earlier die states, with parts of extra 51 plain in field. Later die states (after obv. reground), showing only traces of extra 1, will price as preceding. Discovery coin, Gaskill, NN 48:267. Doug Winter describes a different double date (first punched too high) in Charmont:4030.

6215 1852 [1,159,681]
In all, 11 obvs., 10 revs. Date varies greatly in position: high, close to bust; centered; low, close to border; or slanting down to r. (ill. Akers {1975B}). Some have numerals more heavily punched than others.

6216 1852 C [9,772] Rare.
3 pairs of dies shipped, apparently only one used; this has traces of repunching on 18, which fade. Often with knife-rim at l. obv.; normally weak in centers. Very rare above EF; Ex. rare UNC. Most UNCs. are from a hoard of 5 discovered in May 1986.

6217 1852 D [4,078] Very rare.
3 obvs. shipped, apparently only one used. Normally weak on dentils. Very rare above EF. Deliveries [2,061] Jan., [2,017] April. Low mintages reflect tokenism: Depositors preferred half eagles only. Julian {1966B}.

6218 1852 O [140,000] Normal O.
6 obvs. shipped; leftover revs. from 1851. Date usually slants down to r. Ex. rare above EF.

6219 1852 O Extra heavy O. Very rare.
Mintmark in unusually high relief, base and top thick; heavier at r. than at l. Except for size, this recalls the 1854 O "Huge O" quarter dollar: Mintmarked at New Orleans? Phoenix:1660.

6220 1853 [all kinds 1,404,668] Normal date.
Many positional vars., like 1852. Some show minute traces of repunching on date. Often weak. Common UNC. from a hoard said to number at least 500.

6221 1853/2 Ex. rare.
Upper and lower edges of base stroke of 2 plain between 53. Discovery coin, NN 54:873, Dr. Sloss.

6222 1853 Heavily doubled base of 1. Very rare.
NN 51:834; Hirt:1380. Three obvs. were shipped to Charlotte, 6 to New Orleans, and 5 pairs to the San Francisco Provisional Branch, but all remained unused.

6223 1853 D [3,178] Very rare.
3 obvs. shipped, apparently only one used; rev. of 1852. Weak at dentils, hair above ear and below LIBE, leg feathers, and claws. Usually VF, rarely better, prohibitively rare UNC. Bareford:98, UNC., $4,000.

6224 1854 [596,258]
Many minor positional vars.; 54 normally touch.

6225 1854 Heaviest date. Proofs only. [1+P] Unique?
Date exceptionally heavily punched into die, thick serifs; base of 1 double. 1) Mint, City of Bremen (in 1854 set), "liberated" during WW II, found in a bag of ordinary quarter eagles in a Zurich bank, pvt. coll., $35,000 (1974), Mocatta Metals, 1976 ANA:2804, $8,000, Harry Bass.

6226   1854 C [7,295] Very rare.

3 obvs. shipped, apparently only one used. Weak in centers; partial knife-rim at upper obv., lower rev. Ex. rare in EF.

6227   1854 D [1,760] Very rare.

Identical comments to **6223** except prohibitively rare above EF. Roach, Eliasberg:168, EF, $4,180.

6228   1854 O [all kinds 153,000] Strong date, 54 touch or about touch.

6 obv. dies in all. Ex. rare in UNC.

6229   1854 O Thin numerals, 5 4 apart. Rare.

Enl. photos.

6230   1854 S [246] Ex. rare.

5 pairs of dies shipped; only one used (enl. photos). Beware forgeries made by adding mintmarks to Philadelphia coins; in these, position of date or S will differ from those on the piece ill. For history and roster see introductory text.

6231   1855 [235,480 + ?P]

In all, 5 obvs., 6 revs. Date varies greatly in position. One described as proof and off center was stolen from Yale Univ. and remains untraced. Dr. Conway Bolt's alleged proof remains unverified.

6232   1855 C [3,677] Very rare.

3 pairs of dies shipped; only one var., rev. of 1854, small obv. rim break. Partial knife-rim at lower obv. and rev.; centers weakly struck. Usually VF; Ex. rare above. Lamborn, "Fairfield":1547, UNC., $5,500.

6233   1855 D [1,123] Very rare.

3 pairs of dies shipped; only one var., rev. of 1852. Always weak on dentils, claws, leg, and neck feathers. Usually F or VF; Ex. rare above, unverified to exist UNC. Roach, Eliasberg:173, EF, $4,180. Two pairs of dies were shipped to New Orleans, 6 obvs. and 2 revs. to San Francisco, but all remained unused.

6234   1856 Slanting 5. [384,240 + ?P]

Date from dime logotype; 15 pairs of dies, minor positional

vars. Often weakly struck. The large-date coin reported in G. H. Hall coll. (1945) has never shown up. Proofs: 1) Mills, Mitchelson, Clapp, Eliasberg:174, $24,200. 2) Reimers, Newcomer, Boyd, "Bell," "Memorable," Wolfson, Ullmer:363, $30,000 (1974).

6235   1856 C [7,913] Very rare.

3 pairs of dies shipped; only one var., minute traces of repunching at C (which fade). Usually VF; Ex. rare above AU, only one seen UNC. Generally weak on parts of hair; planchets almost always defective.

6236   1856 D [874] Very rare.

3 pairs of dies; only one var. That ill. (enl.) is typical for striking quality, enabling instant identification of forgeries made by affixing D mintmark to Philadelphia coins. Usually VF; possibly 4 AU's, 2 UNCs. Miles, Ullmer:364, $15,000 (1974), Auction 82:1861, $19,000.

6237   1856 O [21,000]

4 obvs., leftover revs. Much scarcer than mintage figure suggests. Very rare in EF. Mintmark partly hidden by feather (ill. Akers {1975B}) or fully visible, the latter rarer.

6238   1856 S [71,120]

In all, 10 obvs., 6 revs. shipped Nov. 1855–March 1856. Minor positional vars. Scarcer than mintage figure suggests; Ex. rare UNC. Lamborn, "Fairfield":1555, UNC., $3,500.

6239   1857 [214,130 + ?P]

Minor positional vars.; one with traces of repunching on 1, and round hollow atop second shield stripe (center punch in hub?): Walton:2815. Proofs: 1) Woodin, Gaskill, Kagin. 2) Reported.

6240   1857 D [2,364] Rare.

2 pairs of dies shipped. Only one var.; rev. of 1856. Usually VF to EF; possibly 4–6 AU's, at least 3 or 4 UNCs.

6241   1857 O [34,000]

Minor positional vars. Weaker in center than previous O mints. Usually VF or EF, rare above.

6242   1857 S [69,200]

Minor positional vars.; about as rare as 1856 S. Usually F to nearly EF; Ex. rare above EF. Flat strikes are the rule. Mintage includes [1,200], Jan. 19, 1858; the 10 obvs. later shipped for 1858 S remained unused.

6243   1858 [47,377 + ?P]

Much scarcer than mintage figure suggests; rare UNC. Proofs: 1) Mint, SI. 2) J. P. Morgan, ANS. 3) Mills, Clapp, Eliasberg:184, $16,500. 4) Parmelee, Woodin, Brand, Ira Reed, Gaskill, LM 3/67. 5) Ten Eyck:91 (rev. rim stains), Ullmer:365, $22,000. 6) Pvt. coll., impaired.

6244   1858 C [9,056]

Only one var.; rev. of 1856. Weak in centers. Prohibitively rare UNC.

6245   1859 [all kinds 39,444 + 80−P] "Type I" rev., long arrowheads.

Hub of 1840–58: Lowest arrowhead almost touches CA, talons closed. See ill. of **6248.** One obv., 2 revs.; centered date. Auction 79:233, UNC., $3,600. "Type I" possibly [24,518] = [12,000] Feb. 12 + [12,518] Feb. 18. Most proofs were melted; they have low date to l.   1) Mint, SI.   2) J. P. Morgan, ANS.   3) Boyd, "Bell," Wolfson.   4) Atwater, Carter:553, $13,750.   5) D. S. Wilson, Clapp, Eliasberg:186, $15,400.   6),   7) Pvt. colls.

6246   1859 "Type II" rev., short arrowheads.
Hub of 1859–1907: Open talons, small arrowheads spaced apart, lowest far from CA. See ill. of **6263.** Business strikes incl. in [39,444] above: possibly [14,926] = [10,356] May 24 + [4,570] Aug. 19. Discovery coins 1977 ANA:4796–97.

6247   1859 D "Type I" rev. [2,244]
2 pairs of dies shipped. Only one var.; rev. of 1857. Sharper struck than former D mints, but still usually weak on dentils. Very rare UNC.

6248   1859 S "Type I" rev. [15,200] Very scarce.
6 obvs. shipped Nov. 1858; revs. left over from 1856. Minor positional vars.; S normal (lighter or heavier) or partly filled. Often weakly struck. Ex. rare above EF. Auction 80:894, UNC., $1,600. Enl. photos.

6249   1859 S "Small s." Rare.
Mintmark extremely thin, weakly punched into die.

6250   1860 "Type I" rev. Possibly exists.

6251   1860 "Type II" rev. [22,675 + 112−P]
Scarcer than mintage figure suggests. Proofs (April 5) have very thin central stripes; most were melted, possibly 30 survive; Mills, Clapp, Eliasberg:190, $7,700; Carter:554, $11,550, G. Holloway.

6252   1860 Plainly repunched 1. Rare.
Repunching obvious at base. Rhodes:2694, others.

6253   1860 C "Type I" rev. [7,469] Rare.
One var.; rev. of 1856–58. Always weak on hair and ERTY, shield and adjacent feathers; grade by surface. Prohibitively rare in UNC.

6254   1860 S "Type I" rev. [35,600] Normal date.
4 obvs. shipped; revs. left over from 1856. Some show die crumbling between mintmark and stem. Usually VF to EF; prohibitively rare in AU. Clapp, Eliasberg:192, UNC., $5,775.

6255   1860 S Partly repunched date. Rare.
Parts of other digits between 86 and 60.

6256   1861 "Type I" rev. Ex. rare.
Business strikes only. Discovered by Doug Winter, CW 10/19/83, p. 46. From a die of 1859 or earlier. Auction 86:1352, UNC., $3,190.

6257   1861 [all kinds 1,272,518 + 90−P] "Type II" rev. Normal date.
In all, 21 obvs., 24 revs. Many minor positional vars. Proofs (April 5) have date far to l.; most were melted as unsold, and survivors are a little rarer than 1860; Carter:556, Proof, $10,450. Much of the bullion for business strikes came from melted "Type I" gold dollars stored at the N.Y. Subtreasury. All later Philadelphia quarter eagles are "Type II."

6258   1861 Double date. Very rare.
Doubling plainest at 18; two minor positional vars. Discovery coin, "Melish":1251.

6259   1861 S "Type I" rev. [24,000] Very scarce.
One obv. shipped Nov. 1860, one June 1861; leftover revs.

from 1856. Much rarer in all grades than mintage figure suggests; usually weak VF, Ex. rare in EF, unknown UNC. Dies also went to New Orleans (4 obvs.), Charlotte, and Dahlonega (2 pairs each); the Union coined nothing from them, but the Confederacy might conceivably have done so.

6260   1862 [all kinds 112,353 + 35−P] Normal date.
8 pairs of dies. Mostly made from melted "Type I" gold dollars. Minor positional vars. Many proofs melted; survivors (12–18?) have very low date, partly filled 2 (effaced overdate?), and rev. of 1861 proofs. Mills, Clapp, Eliasberg:195, $8,800.

6261   1862/1 Very rare.
Discovered by Aubrey E. Bebee, 1962. *NSM* 1/63, p. 28. Possibly 12 known, none UNC. 1976 ANA:2818, EF, $2,000.

6262   1862 S "Type I" rev. [8,000] Very rare.
2 obvs. shipped Nov. 1861; revs. of 1856. Usually weak VF; Ex. rare above, only 2 reported UNC. S-Mint coins continue to have "Type I" rev. through 1876.

6263   1863 [30P] Proofs only. Very rare.
All coined March 23, from one pair of dies. Forgeries exist, altered from 1868 (much broader numerals), or by removing mintmark from 1863 S (which has "Type I" rev.); these are readily detectable. Of possibly 18 survivors, at least 6–9 are impaired. Enl. photos. Miles, Ullmer:369, $50,000 (1974); Ely, Garrett (1976):408, $52,500; Mills, Clapp, Eliasberg:197, $39,600.

6264   1863 S [10,800] Rare.
Identical comments as to 1862 S, though not quite as rare in lower grades. Sears, Clapp, Eliasberg:198, UNC., $5,720.

6265   1864 [2,824 + 50P] Very rare.
Business strikes (low date, ear filled) are rarer than proofs, unknown UNC.; the [424] of Feb. 25 cannot be told from the [2,400] of Dec. 6. Proofs (Feb. 11) have date slanting down to r.; rarer than 1863. Ullmer:370, $11,000 (1974); Spedding, Clapp, Eliasberg:199, $8,250.

6266   1865 [1,520 + 25P] Very rare.
Business strikes (Jan. 27) from one obv., 2 revs.; end of curl

above 6 (date to r.), rarer than proofs, unknown UNC. Proofs (March 8) have end of curl above 5, rust pits on neck, rarer than 1860–64; of possibly 12 survivors, at least 5 are impaired. Wolfson, Ullmer:371, $10,000 (1974); Garrett (1976):415, $47,500; Mills, Clapp, Eliasberg:200, $10,450.

6267   1865 S [23,376]
2 vars. (normal or with traces of repunching on date), from 3 obvs. shipped Nov. 1865; rev. of 1863 S. Same comments as to **6262.**

6268   1866 [3,780 + 30P] Rare.
Business strikes have light repunching on base of 1, date slanting down to r.; most are VF, prohibitively rare above EF. Proofs (possibly as rare as 1863) have date centered and level. Clapp, Eliasberg:202, $7,700.

6269   1866 S [38,960]
6 obvs. (2 shipped Nov. 1865, 4 in May 1866); revs. of 1856. High or low dates. Arrowheads smaller than usual (lapped dies?). Usually VF; prohibitively rare in AU. The 4 obvs. of May 1866 proved brittle and were most likely not used.

6270   1867 [3,200 + 50P] Rare.
Usually EF; prohibitively rare AU or above. Proofs (almost as rare as 1863) show faint crack through 67; Carter:558, $12,100. Business strikes (Jan. 22) have hollows (polished areas) below BE and in and below ear. Auction 79, Auction 80:895, UNC., $4,800.

6271   1867 S [28,000] Normal rev.
Ex. rare above EF. Often weak.

6272   1867 S Doubled rev. die.
Doubling plainest on wing tip at l. and UNITED STATES OF. Discovery coin, NN 49:631. Same comments as to preceding.

6273   1868 [3,600 + 25P] Very scarce.
Business strikes (Jan. 20) have 2 rust pits on neck; usually EF to AU, rare in UNC. Proofs (Feb. 20) have no rust pits; possibly 15–17 survive; Carter:559, $14,850.

6274   1868 S [34,000] Normal rev.
Usually VF, but there are possibly 10 UNCs. Compare next.

6275   1868 S Doubled rev. die.
Doubling plainest on denomination and STATES OF AMERICA. 2 obvs. (cited in Mint records as revs. in error) shipped Feb. 1868.

6276   1869 [4,320 + 25P] Very scarce.
Business strikes (Feb. 5) have date high, close to bust. Proofs (Feb. 19) have low date and a line above base of L; possibly 15 survive. Turner, Clapp, Eliasberg:208, $7,150.

6277   1869 S [29,500]
Weak in centers; rev. of **6274.** Usually VF; Ex. rare in AU. Auction 80:896, UNC., $4,750. Six obvs. shipped Oct. 1868; only one var. seen.

6278   1870 [4,520 + 35P] Very scarce.
Business strikes (Jan. 17) have date slanting down to r.; most survivors are EF, higher-grade coins Ex. rare. Proofs have date high and nearly level; possibly 15–20 survive. Earle, Clapp, Eliasberg:210, $5,775.

6279   1870 S [16,000]
4 obvs. shipped Dec. 1869; only one var. seen, its rev. a leftover "Type I" die from 1856. Usually weak, especially in centers; usually VF, prohibitively rare UNC.

6280   1871 [5,300 + 30P] Very scarce.
Business strikes (Feb. 9) have neckline blurry, date slanting up to r. (tops of both 1's almost equidistant from bust), usually EF. Proofs (Feb. 20) have date to l., final 1 farther from bust, tiny rust pit on neck. Fewer than 15 survive. H. P. Smith, Clapp, Eliasberg:212, $7,700.

6281   1871 S [22,000]
4 obvs. received Dec. 16, 1870. Very rare UNC. Lamborn, "Fairfield":1601, UNC., $2,100; Auction 79:239, UNC. $3,300. Douglas Winter reports one with triple-punched final 1.

6282   1872 [3,000 + 30P] Rare.
Business strikes (Jan. 22) have low date to r.; Ex. rare UNC. Proofs (Feb. 3) have date high, close to bust; possibly 16 survive: Carter:560, $12,650.

6283   1872 S [18,000]
4 obvs. shipped Nov. 1871; old revs. of 1856. Two minor positional vars. Ex. rare above AU.

6284   1873 Closed 3. [55,200− + 25P]
Knobs of 3 very close together; see introductory text. Business strikes are usually VF or EF, rarely UNC. Auction 79:1186, UNC., $5,500. Mintage comprises [1,600] Jan. + [53,600] Feb., which figure may have included some with open 3. Proofs (Feb. 18) have low date; possibly 19 survive, some impaired. Carter:561, $8,250. Enl. photos.

Ex J. W. Garrett: 768. Courtesy Bowers & Ruddy Galleries, Inc.

6285   1873 Open 3. [122,800+]
Knobs of 3 smaller, far apart; see introductory text. Mintage figure includes all those struck after Feb.: See comment to preceding.

6286   1873 S Closed 3. [27,000]
4 obvs. shipped Nov. 1872. Usually VF, weak in centers; prohibitively rare in UNC.

6287   1874 [3,920 + 20P] Very scarce.
Business strikes have a rust pit at earlobe. Proofs (Feb. 14) lack it; 2 dentils flanking fifth star are defective. Possibly 14 survive: Woodin, Clapp, Eliasberg:218, $9,350; Carter:562, $10,450.

6288   1875 [400 + 20P] Very rare.
Business strikes have date to l., 5 far from truncation; prooflike surfaces. At least 2 UNCs. (one in Tex. pvt. coll., another ex 1973 ANA, Davies-Niewoehner:497, $9,500), 4 AU's, 7 EF's. Few others VF or worse. Often offered as proof or impaired proof. Proofs (Feb. 13, ill.) have date to r., 5 nearly touching truncation near r. corner; possibly 12–15 survive. Ely, Garrett (1976):456, $21,000; Auction 80:897, $31,000; Mills, Clapp, Eliasberg:219, $18,700, Auction 85:927, $19,250. Forgeries made by removing mintmarks from genuine 1875 S coins are easily detected by having "Type I" rev. (arrowhead nearly touching A), unlike the genuine, which has "Type II" rev.

6289   1875 S [11,600]
4 obvs. shipped Sept. 1874; revs. left over from 1856; only one var. seen. Usually VF, weak in centers; very rare in higher grades. Coarser edge reeding than on Philadelphia coins (see preceding).

6290 1876 [4,176 + 45P] Rare.
One pair of dies for business strikes; raised bar at neck next to jaw (foreign matter adhering to the hub when this obv. was sunk from it). Usually VF; very rare above. Proofs have no neck bar; possibly 24 survive. Woodin, Clapp, Eliasberg:221, $7,700.

6291 1876 S [5,000] Very rare.
One pair of dies; bar at neck, similar to preceding (same cause), date higher. Always weak on hair and central feathers. Usually VF; Ex. rare in AU. Final "Type I" rev. David, Clapp, Eliasberg:222, UNC., $1,430.

6292 1877 [1,632 + 20P] Rare.
Business strikes from one obv. and 2 revs.; date well to r. Most are EF or better, many prooflike. Proofs have date about centered below bust; possibly 12–15 survive, several impaired: Clapp, Eliasberg:223, $12,100.

6293 1877 S "Type II" rev. Small s. [35,400]
4 pairs of dies, minor positional vars. May exist with "Type I" rev. as formerly.

6294 1878 [286,240 + 20P]
3 pairs of dies for business strikes. Proofs (Feb. 9) have date slanting up to r.; of possibly 12 survivors, at least 3 are impaired. D. S. Wilson, Clapp, Eliasberg:225, $8,250.

6295 1878 S [all kinds 178,000] Small narrow s.
4 pairs of dies, of which 3 have this style S (as in 1877); they vary notably in positions of S and date.

6296 1878 S Wide squat S.
Mintmark as in 1879.

6297 1879 [88,960 + 30P]
Minor positional vars.; one die of business strikes has minute repunching on bases of 1 9. Proofs have date high, close to bust; possibly 15–18 survive. Mills, Clapp, Eliasberg:227, $10,450.

6298 1879 S Wide squat S. [43,500]
4 pairs of dies; mintmarks vary in position.

6299 1880 [2,960 + 36P]
Business strikes are usually EF to UNC., often prooflike; many offered as impaired proofs. Possibly 24 proofs survive, some impaired. Clapp, Eliasberg:229, $9,350.

6300 1881 [640 + 51P] Very rare.
Proofs are more often seen than business strikes; they have hollows (areas of excess die polish) at BER, in and below ear; forelock away from brow; r. base of final 1 left of center of dentil. Earle, Clapp, Eliasberg:230, $8,800; Auction 82:1870, $10,500. Business strikes have none of the above features; r. base of final 1 about over space between dentils. Most survivors are EF to AU, often offered as impaired proofs (sometimes vice versa). Prohibitively rare UNC.

6301 1882 [4,000 + 67P]
Proofs have low date; polish in and below ear and around BERTY; l. base of 1 left of center of dentil. Carter:567, $9,075. Business strikes (mostly EF to UNC., many prooflike) have faint traces of repunching within first 8 and above 2 (which fade); l. base of 1 nearly over r. edge of dentil.

6302 1883 [1,920 + 82P] Rare.
Proofs (Feb. 10) come with high or low date; latter Clapp, Eliasberg:232, $4,950; Auction 82:1872, $6,500. Business strikes (mostly EF to UNC., prooflike) are apparently from the low-date proof obv. Authentication of alleged proofs is recommended.

6303 1884 [1,950 + 73P] Rare.
Proofs have r. base of 4 about over space between dentils; later ones (after die was repolished) have a hollow at BER. Clapp, Eliasberg:233, $4,675. Business strikes (mostly EF to prooflike UNC.) have r. base of 4 l. of center of dentil, and a die file mark through MER, which fades.

6304 1885 [800 + 87P] Rare.
Proofs have nearly horizontal die file marks near tops of

white stripes in shield. Carter:571, $11,000, G. Holloway. Business strikes (mostly EF to AU, many prooflike) lack these marks, but have tiny raised center dot within circle in ear. Authentication of alleged proofs is recommended.

6305 1886 [4,000 + 88P]
Proofs have l. base of 1 about over r. edge of dentil, and no polish in white stripes. Garrett (1976):498, $2,700. Business strikes (mostly EF to UNC., the best ones prooflike) have base of 1 minutely repunched (fades), its l. point a little r. of center of dentil, and polish within white stripes.

6306 1887 [6,160 + 122P]
Proofs have date high, almost touching truncation; Carter:572, $7,425, G. Holloway. Business strikes have date lower, farther from bust. Most are EF to UNC. but rarer choice than 1882 or 1886.

6307 1888 [16,006 + 92P]
2 positional vars. of date in business strikes.

6308 1889 [17,600 + 48P]
Prooflike business strikes have date low, 9 close to border, unlike proofs. Clapp, Eliasberg:238, Proof, $5,225.

6309 1890 [8,720 + 93P]
Usually EF to UNC. Mills, Clapp, Eliasberg:239, Proof, $8,250.

6310 1891 Doubled rev. die. [10,860]
Doubling obvious on OF AMERICA. Most are EF to UNC., largely UNC.

6311 1891 Normal rev. [80P] Proofs only.
Date high and on earliest impressions shows faint traces of repunching on bases of 891. Clapp, Eliasberg:240, $6,050.

6312 1892 [2,440 + 105P]
Proofs have date to l.; left base of 1 about touches center of dentil. Eliasberg:241, $4,950. Business strikes (EF to UNC., mostly AU or better, many prooflike) have date to r., 2 close to edge of truncation, l. base of 1 a little r. of l. edge of dentil. Bareford:106, UNC., $4,800.

6313 1893 Normal date. [30,000]
Most survivors are UNC.

6314 1893 Partly double-punched date. [106P]
Lower knobs of extra 93 just l. of 93. Mint, Clapp, Eliasberg:242, $6,050.

6315 1894 [4,000 + 122P]
Proofs have date to l., left base of 1 very close to r. edge of dentil, minute wart on chin, scattered die file marks around periphery of shield. Mint, Clapp, Eliasberg:243, $4,675. Business strikes (mostly AU or UNC., many prooflike) lack these marks; date higher, l. base of 1 left of center of dentil.

6316 1895 [6,000 + 119P]
Proofs have minute point down from lower part of bun: Mint, Clapp, Eliasberg:244, $6,600; Carter:576, $10,725. Two vars. of business strikes, one from the proof obv.; mostly UNC., often prooflike. Authentication of alleged proofs recommended.

6317 1896 [19,070 + 132P]
Proofs have date far to r.: Mint, Clapp, Eliasberg:245, $7,150; Carter:577, $9,900. Minor positional vars. of business strikes, mostly UNC.

6318 1897 [29,768 + 136P]
Proofs have 2 minute dots in center of ear: Mint, Clapp, Eliasberg:246, $8,800. Most business strikes are UNC.

6319 1898 [24,000 + 165P]
Most business strikes are UNC. Mint, Clapp, Eliasberg:247, Proof, $5,775; Carter:578, Proof, $12,650, G. Holloway.

6320 1899 [27,200 + 150P]
Same comment. Mint, Clapp, Eliasberg:248, Proof, $4,675.

6321 1900 [67,000 + 205P]
Proofs have faint repunching on bases of 19, die file mark down from T(Y). Eliasberg:249, $7,700. Most business strikes are UNC.

6322 1901 [91,100 + 223P]

Proofs have scattered crisscross marks within shield; these fade. Mint, Clapp, Eliasberg:250, $5,775; Carter:579, $11,000, G. Holloway. Most business strikes are UNC.; some have traces of repunching on base of final 1. Phoenix:1939.

6323 1902 [133,500 + 193P]

Proofs 1902–7 are semibrilliant on devices, not frosty like those of earlier dates. Mint, Clapp, Eliasberg:251, $7,150. Most business strikes are UNC.; minor positional vars.

6324 1903 [201,060 + 197P]

Same comments. Mint, Clapp, Eliasberg:252, $4,675.

6325 1904 [160,790 + 170P]

One of the 2 minor vars. of proofs has repunching on base of 4; both have tiny center dot at ear. Mint, Clapp, Eliasberg:253, $4,675. Most business strikes are UNC. Pieces with tiny raised lump within 0 of date are counterfeits.

6326 1905 [217,800 + 144P]

Same comments about proofs as to 1901. Mint, Clapp, Eliasberg:254, $5,775. Pieces dated 1905 S are counterfeits.

6327 1906 [176,330 + 160P]

Most business strikes are UNC. Mint, Clapp, Eliasberg:255, Proof, $6,325; Carter:582, Proof, $9,350.

6328 1907 [all kinds 336,294 + 154P] Normal date.

Proofs have date to r., low, slanting up to r.: Mint, Clapp, Eliasberg:256, $6,600; Carter:583, $8,250. Minor positional vars. of business strikes, which are normally UNC. Compare next.

6329 1907 Repunched date.

Early impressions (rare) have repunching at top of 9, within 0, and at base of 7: date first entered slanting down to r., then corrected. "Charmont":4069. Later states (less rare) have repunching obvious only at base of 7. Discovery coin, Straus, NN 53:497.

viii. PRATT'S INDIAN HEAD DESIGN (1908–29)

Around New Year's Day, 1908, Dr. William Sturgis Bigelow, an intimate friend of Pres. Theodore Roosevelt, got the idea of making coins with devices sunk beneath the fields—not true intaglio, but rather with relief designs depressed so that the highest points would not be at once worn away, somewhat in the manner of certain Egyptian Fourth Dynasty stelae. The late Augustus St. Gaudens had just bequeathed the nation two coin designs of unprecedented magnificence for the double eagles and eagles; so hard was this act to follow that a totally new approach was needed for the smaller gold coins to have any public impact. Nobody expected Mint Engraver Charles E. Barber to produce anything but banality, or to cooperate with any outside designer; the latter would have to work in secrecy and present a fait accompli so that Barber could not abort his project.

Obtaining a go-ahead from Roosevelt, Bigelow persuaded the Boston sculptor Bela Lyon Pratt to submit models in this technique. Pratt's Native American chieftain model remains unnamed, his tribe unknown. This was simultaneously an "impression emblematic of Liberty" as the Mint Act of 1792 specifies (for after all the Indians were free peoples until white men's laws made them third-class citizens), a compliment to Theodore Roosevelt, and a continuation of a trend begun in 1899 with G. F. C. Smillie's magnificent portrait of Sioux chief Ta-to-ka-inyanka ('Running Antelope') on the $5 silver certificate. Pratt's eagle was a deliberate bow to St. Gaudens, and an equally deliberate tweak at Barber (who had in 1892 revived the heraldically encumbered Great Seal eagle for the overcrowded revs. of the then current quarter dollar and half dollar). In its original version it must have been worthy of J. J. Audubon. Pres. Roosevelt enthusiastically approved the designs, and ordered that Pratt's models go at once to the Mint for translation into master dies, hubs, and working dies so that coins of the new designs could reach the public as soon as possible. Defying presidential orders, Barber held up production for months by insisting on reworking the Pratt models. In a diluted form they finally reached the Coiner's Department, and on Oct. 9, 1908, the first Indian Head quarter eagles left the Mint, reaching the public during the next few weeks.

Pratt's designs at once came under attack, probably because of their unfamiliar conception. One of their severest critics was the Philadelphia coin dealer Samuel Hudson Chapman, who falsely alleged that the designs were antinaturalistic, unhygienic, incapable of stacking, and too easily counterfeited. (Chapman's major objection to the eagle was well founded, but the blame is on Barber, not Pratt; Pratt knew what a bald eagle looked like from working with models and photographs—otherwise Roosevelt would not have approved his design!— whereas Barber evidently did not.) Despite these objections, the design remained without further modification through 1929. After the stock market, the land boom, the whole Roaring Twenties life-style, and the accompanying Social Darwinism collapsed in Oct. 1929, little gold reached the Mint, and most of it was coined into double eagles for international payments; no more quarter eagles were ordered by banks or federal agencies. Regulations of 1934, demonetizing gold, ended that metal's legal-tender status; the Coinage Act of July 23, 1965 (PL 89-81), Sect. 392, has apparently restored it.

All 15 date-mintmark combinations of this design were coined in large enough quantities to insure their permanent availability at a price, the only difficult one being 1911 D. This last has accordingly been touted as a "key coin"—one the collector must reach for if (s)he wishes to complete a set. Quantities of counterfeits reached the United States from Hong Kong in 1960; on the commoner sort, mintmark is too large, flat, in high relief, tilted to r., and too close to arrow; on the other, the D is more like the genuine. Both have abnormal edge reeding (lens-shaped indentations); both have shiny spots on Indian's feathers below and r. of center, and/or minute bubbles or cavities. Genuine examples have a knife-rim as ill., and edge reeding consists of parallel bars and grooves extending the coin's full thickness. If your coin does not identically match that ill. in mintmark shape, size, position, and in location and extent of knife-rims, authentication is mandatory.

The only real rarities of this design are the matte proofs, which were issued in very limited quantities. They were unpopular because they are darker and duller than business strikes. Many were melted in 1916 as unsold. Forgers have simulated these too, deceiving only those unfamiliar with the genuine article; real matte proofs have much more sharpness on all feathers and other relief details than do normal mint-state business strikes, something untrue of the imitations.

This design is overall one of the more aesthetically satisfying among 20th-century American coinages, fortunately easily available—for a price—in perfect preservation.

PRATT'S INDIAN HEAD DESIGN

Designer, Bela Lyon Pratt. Engraver, Charles E. Barber, after Pratt. Mints, Philadelphia (no mintmark), Denver (mintmark D). Mintmark l. of arrowheads. Physical Specifications, Authorizing Acts, as previously.

Grade range, VERY GOOD to UNC. FINE: Lettering and stars complete in outlines; knot of hair cord visible; partial feathers near end of wing. VERY FINE: Partial headband detail; small feathers clear, partial detail on larger feathers; second layer of wing feathers shows; some detail on breast and leg feathers.

EXTREMELY FINE: Tiny rubbed spots only on isolated high points; full leg feathers; stars have sharp centers; partial mint luster. NOTE: Not collected below VF, except for 1911 D. Beware coins with traces of solder or evidence of its removal: look for interruption or repairs of edge reeding at 12:00 or 6:00, local discoloration, porosity, or retooling to obliterate any of these.

6330   1908 [564,821 + 236−P]
Business strikes are weak on eagle. Proofs (ill., enl.) have dark matte surface and nearly complete knife-rims on both sides. Many reportedly melted, Jan. 2, 1909. Mint, Clapp, Eliasberg:257, $9,900; Carter:584, $14,850.

6331   1909 [441,760 + 139P]
Difficult to find choice UNC. Proofs (twice as rare as 1908) have light satiny ("Roman Gold") finish halfway between matte and mirrored; they normally show knife-rims. Mint, Clapp, Eliasberg:258, $7,150.

6332   1910 [492,000 + 682P]
Business strikes are often weak in centers. Proofs normally have same finish as 1909. Mint, Clapp, Eliasberg:259, $7,700; Auction 82:1897, $9,250. Hirt:1440 has light matte finish, like 1908 and 1911 but much lighter in color. One other is reported with dark matte finish like 1911. The "Roman Gold" proofs are rarer than other dates 1908–13; probably many were spent or melted as unsold. Many believe the 682 mintage figure is a typographical error.

6333   1911 [704,000 + 191P]
Proofs have dark matte finish similar to 1908. Clapp, Eliasberg:260, $7,150.

6334   1911 D [55,680]
2 pairs of dies; only one var. known (the other die-pair yielded only 70 impressions, according to Denver Mint records consulted by Alan Craig). Mintmark on the genuine

is normally weak; knife-rim as ill., though this last detail is less obvious on lower-grade survivors. Usually VF to AU. UNCs.: Auction 79:1205, $12,000; Auction 80:369, $11,000; Auction 82:1900, $8,500. See introductory text for description of counterfeits. Authentication is urgently recommended.

6335   1912 [616,000 + 197P]
Proofs have fine sandblast finish, unlike 1908–11. Clapp, Eliasberg:262, $7,425; Auction 82:1902, $9,000.

6336   1913 [722,000 + 165P]
Proofs have the same finish as 1912, but are minutely less rare. Potts, Clapp, Eliasberg:263, $8,800; Auction 82:1903, $10,000.

6337   1914 [240,000 + 117P]
Proofs have coarser sandblast finish, darker than 1912–13; they are rarer than 1908–13. Potts, Clapp, Eliasberg:264, $11,000; Auction 80:364, $19,500. UNC. business strikes are scarcer than previous Philadelphia issues since about 1896.

6338   1914 D [448,000]
UNC. survivors are usually soft on wing and leg, and often also on head feathers; look for mint luster on the weak areas.

6339   1915 [606,100 + 100−P]
Proofs have the same finish as those of 1914; they are Ex. rare, mostly melted unsold in 1916. Potts, Clapp, Eliasberg:266, $7,150; Auction 80:365, $19,500.

6340   1925 D [578,000]
Occasional specimens are very weak on D; we have heard of, but not seen, one on which the D does not show. This and following dates are always available choice UNC.

6341   1926 [446,000]
6342   1927 [388,000]
6343   1928 [416,000]
6344   1929 [532,000]

CHAPTER 34

LONGACRE'S THREE-DOLLAR PIECES
(1854–89)

The first proposal for a $3 coin dates back to June 1832, when Rep. Campbell P. White (D.-N.Y.), chairman of a Select Committee, presented a report (HR Report 496, 22nd Congress, 1st Session) condemning bimetallism and introducing a bill, HR 603, which would have authorized coinage of a $3 piece at 75 grs., along with $2.50 and $5 gold coins of proportionate weights. This bill never reached a vote, though a modified version (minus the $3) became the Mint Act of June 28, 1834.

When the Act of March 3, 1845 authorized issue of postage stamps, it fixed the local prepaid letter rate at 5¢. The very same Act of March 3, 1851 which authorized Sen. D. S. Dickinson's base silver 3¢ as part of the currency also reduced the letter rate to 3¢. Congressmen appeared to believe (following the faulty reasoning of Mint Director Robert Maskell Patterson) that the main purpose of the new 3¢ piece would be to buy postage stamps without using the unpopular, heavy, and often filthy copper cents. Accordingly, the Mint Act of Feb. 21, 1853, best known for authorizing lightweight silver coinage with arrows at date, also included a fine-print clause authorizing issue of a $3 gold coin, to weigh 77.4 grs. at 900 Fine, for uniformity with other current gold pieces. Congressmen believed that this coin would be convenient for exchange for rolls or small bags of silver 3¢ pieces, and for buying sheets of 3¢ stamps—always bypassing use of copper cents.

Longacre submitted two designs to Mint Director Pettit; relief models of the approved one followed shortly. Its so-called "Indian Princess" head, so far from attempting to depict any Native American, is still another avatar of the Greco-Roman *Venus Accroupie* profile which had already served Longacre for the gold dollar and double eagle, though with a feathered headdress supposed to emphasize "national character." Taxay {1966}, p. 213, reproduces several Longacre drawings illustrating this conception.

The first 15 proofs appeared on April 28, 1854; regular coinage began May 1, the first delivery being [23,140] on May 8. Curiosity seekers and the general public saved many as souvenirs; the 1854 (with the largest mintage of all) is accordingly one of the few dates always available for a price even in mint state (the others are 1874 and 1878). Many others circulated only briefly and ended their travels as watch fobs, cufflinks, or other jewelry, a circumstance which drastically reduces their desirability to collectors. (Check top and bottom edges for traces of discoloration, porosity, retooling, interruption of reeding, or remnants of solder.)

Only the one date 1854 (from all mints) has small letters in

DOLLARS; others 1855–89 have large DOLLARS, making two types in all for this denomination. Oddly, the die used for 1856 proofs shows large DOLLARS superimposed on small DOLLARS. Evidently it received a blow from each hub in fall 1854 but was withheld as a closet skeleton, resurrected, dated, and repolished later for proof use without further inspection. Harry Bass first reported this corrected blunder, about 1972.

Limited mintages were the rule from 1854 until the denomination was abolished by the Act of Sept. 25, 1890 (coinage had actually ended in 1889). For many of these years the majority of survivors originated as proofs for collectors, though many were either spent or kept as pocket pieces by later owners so that their proof status is obscured. But the result was a large number of coveted rarities and heavy collector demand for proofs of some years, followed by limited issues of restrikes of 1865, 1873, 1875, and possibly other dates.

The 1873 deserves special mention here. Dies with closed 3 were prepared in late fall 1872 for all denominations. These occasioned a complaint by Chief Coiner Archibald Loudon Snowden, Jan. 18, 1873, alleging that the final digit (especially on smaller coins) could be readily mistaken for an 8. The Director ordered William Barber's Engraving Dept. to prepare a new set of date logotypes with open 3; working dies for all denominations (except the 3¢ silver, half dime, and silver dollar, abolished by the new Mint Act of Feb. 12, 1873) followed shortly. Original gold proof sets obtained from the Coiner in 1873 show that the $3—unlike any other denomination—had open 3. Paradoxically, closed 3's are known, rarely in proof state, usually in F to EF grades; there is no Mint record of their coinage, and as some of these pieces have obv. dies identified as dating from 1879, they have been characterized as restrikes. However, preservation of other closed 3's does not permit positive identification of their obv. dies with coins of any other date, and the suggestion has lately been advanced that these latter may represent a delivery of a few hundred original 1873's, probably in January, mostly for circulation, omitted from Mint records in error.

On the other hand, some proof restrikes of 1873 are rarer than originals, most notably the "dished" coins, which have the appearance of convex obv., concave rev., as though they had been laterally compressed. Were they given reeded edges *after* striking?

The rarest $3 coin of all, however, has not been restruck. On May 14, 1870, Gen. O. H. LaGrange, superintendent of the San Francisco Mint, wired Mint Director Pollock in Philadelphia to the effect that he had just discovered that the $1 (silver or gold?) and $3 dies (shipped in Dec. 1869) lacked the mintmark S, that 2,000 pieces (of which denomination?) had been struck but not released, and that he needed instructions on how to handle the situation. Pollock's unlocated reply evidently ordered return of the dies to Philadelphia for replacement by properly mintmarked ones. On May 26, LaGrange shipped the S-less dies back via Wells Fargo, adding that Coiner J. B. Harmstead had cut an S into the $3 die to strike a single piece for the cornerstone of the new Mint Building. (This is the "Granite Lady" building, now the Old Mint Museum, at Fifth and Mint Sts., between Market and Mission Sts., San Francisco.) Harmstead, it seems, also made a duplicate for his own use; it went onto a watch fob or the like. When Thomas L. Elder auctioned one of the collections assembled by William H. Woodin (later Secretary of Treasury) in March 1911, this coin (from which the loop had in the meantime been skilfully removed) was offered, along with a piece of paper reading, "This is a duplicate of the coin struck for the cornerstone of the San Francisco Mint and the only one in existence. J. B. Harmstead." Seventy years later, while TV cameras whirred, this coin brought $687,500 in the Eliasberg estate sale. Millions saw it featured on "CBS Morning News," Oct. 27, 1982, in an interview with Q. David Bowers; *CW* reprinted that interview, 11/10/82, p. 22. Even before that, the 1870 S had already become one of the three most famous American gold coins, side by side with the Brasher doubloon and the 1849 double eagle.

The usual story has it that $3 gold coins were made only so long as the letter rate remained 3¢, being discontinued when it was changed again, and perhaps in part because of the letter-rate change. Whether or not this was the intention of Congress, nevertheless $3's saw little postal use in the West and South, as they were minted in Dahlonega and New Orleans only in 1854, and in San Francisco for circulation only 1855–57 and 1860. Threes thus represent relics of an interesting but abortive experiment; today they are among the most highly coveted of American gold coins. No specific reason was advanced for their discontinuance, though low mintages 1879–89 (testifying to little public demand) may have had something to do with it.

The Coinage Act of July 23, 1965, PL 89-81, Sect. 392, apparently restored their legal-tender status, though nobody is likely to make a test case.

LONGACRE'S THREE-DOLLAR PIECES

Designer, Engraver, James Barton Longacre. Mints, Philadelphia (no mintmark), Dahlonega (mintmark D), New Orleans (O), San Francisco (S). Mintmarks below wreath. Composition, 90% gold, not over 5% silver, rest copper. Weight 77.4 ± 0.25 grs. = 5.015 ± 0.0162 gms. (Tolerance per 1873 act, apparently confirming earlier figure as it remains uniform with other denominations.) Reeded edge. Diameter 13/16″ = 20.6 mm. Authorizing Act, Feb. 21, 1853.

Grade range, POOR TO UNC. FINE: Partial hair detail, beads partly intact, LIBERTY weak but complete, partial wreath details. VERY FINE: Partial details in curled tops of feathers; beads complete; partial internal details in cotton bolls. EXTREMELY FINE: Isolated tiny rubbed spots only; partial mint luster or prooflike surface. UNCIRCULATED: *No* trace of wear. NOTE: Not collected below VF except for great rarities. Beware ex-jewelry coins (see introductory text). EXCEPTIONS: Certain dates show weaknesses as noted; mint-state examples will show luster on weak areas.

"TYPE I": SMALL *DOLLARS* (1854)

6345 1854 Heavy obv. letters. [15+P] Proofs only.
Struck April 28, 1854 (others later?). Enl. photos. Garrett:417, $45,000; Jenks, Clapp, Eliasberg:272, $39,600; others.

Ex J. W. Garrett: 417. Courtesy Bowers & Ruddy Galleries, Inc.

6346 1854 Normal letters. 5 4 free. [138,618]
First delivery May 8; final delivery Nov. 10. At least 2 positional vars. of date. Hair often weak below LIBERTY. The single pair of dies shipped to Charlotte remained unused.
6347 1854 D Large D; 54 touch. [1,120] Rare.
Coined July 1854 from one pair of dies, shipped June 19. Bold D from half-eagle mintmark punch. Note distinctive striking characteristics (enl. ill.): weak concave dentils at upper obv. and rev., incomplete leaf l. of date, etc.; these will detect forgeries made by affixing D to Philadelphia coins. Usually in F or VF; possibly 5 or 6 AU's. Auction 81:386, UNC., $72,500.

6348 1854 O [all kinds 24,000] Strong letters, date, and O. Rare.
3 pairs of dies shipped. Light doubling on UNITED (fades); full JBL on truncation; date slants slightly down to r.; later, dies heavily clashed. Prohibitively rare UNC.
6349 1854 O Weak letters, date, and O.
Only upper half of JBL on truncation; incomplete ribbon and wreath (lapped die); later, cracked through mintmark, ribbons, and AMERICA. Ill. Akers {1976}. Prohibitively rare UNC.

"TYPE II": LARGE *DOLLARS*

6350 1855 Slanting 5's. [50,555 + ?P]
One pair of dies for business strikes (normal wreath, traces of repunching at and l. of knob of final 5). Plentiful in VF to AU, rare UNC. Proofs have hollows (polished areas) within wreath at 2:00–2:30, below maple leaf and between corn leaves.   1) Woodin, Clapp, Eliasberg:275, $28,600, Auction 85:934, $31,900. 2) McCoy:1987, Ely, Garrett (1976):393, $35,000, H. Bass. 3) Boyd, Kern, pvt. coll. Others reported. Leba-

nese forgeries of the 1950s are apparently EF–AU and have unnaturally thick letters. 6 "obvs." (evidently meaning dated revs.) were shipped to New Orleans, but no 1855 O coins followed.

6351   1855 S Slanting 5's, large S. [6,000 + ?P] Scarce.
3 obvs., 7 revs. (date sides) shipped, only one var. of business strikes; later, clash mark through S. Often weakly struck; Ex. rare in EF, prohibitively rare AU, only 2 or 3 UNCs. reported. Bareford:126, $11,000. Proofs: 1) "Sierra foothills estate," David Stagg, John Dannreuther, Auction 84:881.   2) Pvt. coll.

6352   1856 Upright 5. Normal DOLLARS. [26,010]
4 pairs of dies made; 2 vars., scarcer with date to left (1 centered below O) and heavy 6, commoner with date higher, farther r., and slanting minutely up to r. Very rare UNC.

6353   1856 Large over small DOLLARS. [?P] Proofs only. Ex. rare.
Polish below ear and on throat. See introductory text.   1) Boyd, WGC.   2) Garrett (1976):394, $21,000.   3) Auction 81:391, $20,500, Dennis With, slightly impaired.   4) H. Bass.   5) M. Brownlee.

6354   1856 S [all kinds 34,500] Large S. Ex. rare.
S 1.7 mm as in half dollars. Cf. Charmont:4153. The only one I have seen since 1954 has S grossly repunched, all elements thick. In all, 10 pairs of dies shipped: 4 pairs Nov. 1855, 2 pairs Dec. 1855, 4 pairs March 1856, most remaining unused.

6355   1856 S Medium S. 2 vars.
S 1.3 mm as on later half dollars and dimes. Price for var. ill., with break from base of L; very rare UNC. The other var. (much rarer) has date farther r., no break at L; S lower, leans l. Both come weakly struck.

6356   1856 S Small s. Very scarce.
S about 1 mm. Usually weak and in low grades; prohibitively rare UNC.

6357   1857 [all kinds 20,891 + ?P] Normal I's.
2 minor vars. of business strikes, without and with doubling on r. side of final A, which may reflect the first 2 deliveries: [7,832] June 19, and [11,050] Aug. 7. Date slants down to r.; rust pit at D(OLLAR). Recent counterfeits have surfaces unlike the genuine, and though seemingly UNC. are weaker in details than the genuine (which is normally well struck). Compare next. Proofs have obv. of **6353**, repolished (large hollow in throat). 1) Mint, SI. 2) Parmelee, Woodin, Clapp, Eliasberg:280, $20,900.   3) Boyd, Grant Pierce, Jay, Ullmer:411, $21,000, Auction 82:1368, $12,000. Tiny flan chip below truncation.   4) Kern, Wolfson.   5) W. J. Jenks, Garrett (1976), Auction 81:394, $30,000.

6358   1857 Broken I's. Rare.
Upper l. serif missing on I(TED) and I(CA). Low date, no rust pit at D. Possibly represents the final delivery, [2,009] Dec. 28. Counterfeiters used one of these for making a copy obv. die with revs. of many dates.

6359   1857 S Large S. [14,000] Scarce.
Only one var. seen; date normally weak. Usually in low grades; almost unobtainable above EF. Auction 81:395, UNC., $20,000.

6360   1858 [2,133 + ?P] Very scarce.
Business strikes coined Aug. 26; normal feathers. Date slants up to r. on these and proofs. Usually VF to EF; very rare above AU. Proofs (9–12 survive) have incomplete feather on forward edge of headdress, 3 minute die file marks from back of head. Woodin, Clapp, Eliasberg:282, $15,400. Between Nov. 1857 and July 1858, 3 obvs. and 10 revs. were shipped to San Francisco, but no 1858 S coins followed.

6361   1859 Repunched 1 9. [6,391 + 80–P]
Oddly shaped numerals attributed to Anthony C. Paquet. Business strikes coined Feb. 25. Dies later clashed—rev. showing 2 marks (from within ear) above second L—then repolished (repunching on 1 now faint). Early state, with obviously repunched 1, is rarer. Usually VF to EF, very rare in AU or better. Proofs have same rev., repolished, with the 1858 obv.; at least 35 sold at Mint, rest melted. Auction 79:265, $19,000; Auction 81:398, $29,500; Jewett, Clapp, Eliasberg:283, $14,300.

6362 1859 Tops of 18 repunched. [6,247]

Coined Oct. 10. Mintage may include some late-state specimens of **6361.** No mint-state example seen in many years. The 2 revs. shipped to New Orleans and the 4 to San Francisco remained unused.

6363 1860 [7,036 + 119−P]

Business strikes coined Jan. 31; only one var. seen, very rare UNC. Bareford:129, UNC., $12,000. Most proofs were melted as unsold. Mougey, Clapp, Eliasberg:284, $9,900.

6364 1860 S Small s. [Net 4,408] Very scarce.

In all, [7,000], of which 2,592 were found lightweight and remained unissued until Dec. 1869, when they were melted for recoinage into other denominations. 4 revs. shipped Nov. 2, 1859; only one var. seen. Usually in low grades; rare EF, very rare AU, only 3–5 UNC.: Dickinson-Lindsay, Clapp, Eliasberg:285, $20,900.

6365 1861 [5,959 + 113−P]

3 pairs of dies made; only one var. seen on business strikes (delivered March 26), with thin letters and field striations on obv. Usually EF or worse, very rare above. Most proofs (April 5) were melted as unsold; possibly 9 or 10 survive. Mougey, Clapp, Eliasberg:286, $9,350. Two revs. shipped to San Francisco Nov. 1860, unused.

6366 1862 [5,750 + 35P] Normal neckline.

3 vars. of business strikes (Feb. 6), from one obv. and 2 revs. plus one 1861 obv. left over. Most have field striations. Usually EF or worse; rare above, very rare UNC. Auction 80:906, $14,000. Proofs (Feb. 16) have obv. of 1861, date to l., 6 not beyond L; possibly 15–20 survive. Auction 79:268, $26,000; Clapp, Eliasberg:287, $13,200.

6367 1862 Without distinct neckline. Very rare.

Forward edge of neck blurred into field (die repolishing). Discovery coin, "Cicero":229. The 2 revs. shipped to San Francisco in Nov. 1861 remained unused.

6368 1863 [5,000 + 39−P] Rare.

Business strikes (Nov. 21) usually have field striations, and often show triple clash marks; most are VF or EF. Most UNCs. are from a tiny group from Europe, ca. 1968. Mocatta, 1979 ANA:127, $24,000. Proofs (March 23) are much rarer than 1862, possibly 10–15 extant. Woodin, Clapp, Eliasberg:288, $14,300; Auction 82:1372, $11,000. The 2 revs. shipped to San Francisco Nov. 1862 remained unused.

6369 1864 Normal date. [50−P] Proofs only. Very rare.

All coined Feb. 11; date slants up to r. Fewer than 20 survive, some impaired. Garrett (1976):413, $10,000.

6370 1864 Repunched 18. [2,630] Rare.

The 2 deliveries, [440] Feb. 25 and [2,190] Dec. 6, cannot be told apart. Usually VF to EF; very rare above, Ex. rare UNC. Auction 81:406, $27,000. The 4 revs. shipped to San Francisco Nov. 1863 remained unused.

6371 1865 Original. Low, level date. [1,140 + 25P] Very rare.

Business strikes (Feb. 27) are usually in low grades, Ex. rare in AU, prohibitively rare UNC.; Auction 81:407, $26,000. All are from one pair of dies, its rev. used on proofs (March 8); possibly 12 proofs survive from it. A second var. of proofs with date nearly centered, placed farther to r. (tip of 5 well beyond r. foot of A), has obv. of some 1867–68 proofs (hence a restrike?); it is nearly as rare as originals. Garrett:422, $40,000; Clapp, Eliasberg:290, $17,600. The 2 revs. shipped to San Francisco Nov. 1864 remained unused.

6372 1865 Restrike. Date slants up to r. Proofs only. Ex. rare.

Judd 440. Obv. of 1872. Strikings exist in silver and copper. In date, 18 weaker, 5 heavy, its crossbar unusually long. 1) Woodin, Newcomer, Boyd, Judd, Dr. Wilkison. 2) Brand, Farouk.

6373 1866 [4,000 + 30P]

Business strikes (Feb. 7) have heavy 1; usually EF; very rare UNC. (less so than 1864–65). Proofs have normal 1, upper part of final 6 filled (unlike business strikes); some have obv. of 1865 original proofs, others have obv. of 1867 (see Breen {1977}, p. 131), with a single rev. Woodin, Clapp, Eliasberg:291, $13,200. The 2 revs. shipped to San Francisco Nov. 1865 remained unused.

6374 1867 [2,600 + 50P]

Business strikes (Jan. 24) have very low date; usually VF to EF. The few prooflike UNCs. are from a tiny hoard dispersed in the 1960s. Coins with very heavy letters, thick serifs, are counterfeits. Proofs have higher date, heavy 7 (ill. Akers {1976}); possibly 15–20 survive. H. P. Smith, Clapp, Eliasberg:292, $12,100.

6375 1868 [4,850 + 25P]

Business strikes (Feb. 18, low date) are usually EF. Brand I:235, UNC., $9,900. Proofs (Feb. 20, high date) usually have rev. 180° from normal alignment; earliest ones (Garrett:425, $9,000) have traces of 7 within 8, later ones lack it (the majority). Clapp, Eliasberg:293, $9,900.

6376 1869 Overdate. [2,500]

Earliest states (Feb. 11) show traces of 8 within 9; later, dies clashed, repolished to remove clash marks, thereafter with traces of extra outlines at 9 but the 8 mostly gone. Usually VF to EF, very rare above.

6377 1869 Normal date. [25P] Proofs only. Ex. rare.

Date low, to l.; 2 obv. dies. Possibly 12 survive. Clapp, Eliasberg:294, $14,300. Business strikes so called are later states of preceding. The 4 revs. shipped to San Francisco Oct. 1868 remained unused.

6378 1870 [3,500 + 35P]

Business strikes (Jan. 18) are mostly EF; leaf l. of date is an isolated fragment. Some UNCs. are deceptively prooflike. Proofs (possibly 15–20 survive) have date much lower, barely above bow; leaf l. of date intact. Ullmer:419, $8,500 (1974).

6379 1870 S [2]

2 rev. dies shipped to San Francisco Dec. 1869 both lacked mintmark. See introductory text. 1) Cornerstone, San Francisco Mint. 2) Coiner J. B. Harmstead, H. T. Van Camp, William H. Woodin:1160, $1,450, Waldo Newcomer, Celina Coin Co. (Ted and Carl Brandts, NUM 12/45), $11,500, Eliasberg:296, $687,500, H. Stack, pvt. coll. Loop removed; s small, atypical in form.

6380 1871 71 about touch. [1,300 + 30P] Rare.

Business strikes (Jan. 6, date very low, 7 nearly touching bow) are usually EF to AU; most UNCs. are prooflike: Carter:605, $15,400. Proofs (2 obvs.) have date nearly central; about a dozen survive. H. P. Smith, Clapp, Eliasberg:297, $13,200. Two pairs of dies received in San Francisco Dec. 16, 1870, remained unused.

6381 1872 [2,000 + 30P]

Business strikes (Feb. 2) are usually EF to UNC., often prooflike. At least 2 vars. of proofs (date lower than on business

strikes); Breen {1977}, pp. 143–44. Clapp, Eliasberg:298, $5,500. Two revs. shipped to San Francisco Nov. 1871 remained unused.

6382   1873 Open 3. Original. [25P] Proofs only. Ex. rare.
Delivered Feb. 18; possibly 10–14 survive. Enl. photos. Ely, Garrett:424, $44,000; Auction 82:1377, $15,000. Coins with rusted dies are restrikes and much rarer than originals. Breen {1977}, p. 147.

Ex J. W. Garrett: 424. Courtesy Bowers & Ruddy Galleries, Inc.

6383   1873 Closed 3. Normal field. [No record] Rare.
See introductory text. Most survivors are VF to EF; none seen UNC. Proofs are very rare. Breen {1977}, p. 264. Compare following. 2 closed 3 dies shipped to San Francisco Nov. 1872 remained unused. Enl. photo.

6384   1873 Closed 3. "Dished" restrike. 6–8 known? Proofs only.
Obv. appears convex, rev. concave; see introductory text. Auction 81:416, $40,000; Eliasberg:299, $30,800, Auction 84:885.

6385   1874 [41,800 + 20P]
3 minor positional vars. of business strikes. UNCs. are usually frosty, rarely prooflike. Proofs have obv. of **6382**, bases of F extra thin; uprights of 1 and 4 centered below O and A. About 12 survive, some impaired. Auction 82:1378, $13,000; Mougey, Clapp, Eliasberg:300, $13,200.

6386   1875 Original. [20P] Proofs only. Very rare.
Struck Feb. 13 for the proof sets. Obv. of 1874 proofs; heavy point on bottom of upper serif of (DOLLAR)S, microscopic lump on curve of that S just below the point, die scratch near dentils at upper r. above 2 maple leaves, no pronounced extra outlines on r. wreath or ribbons. Possibly 10–12 survive; beware lightweight gilt-copper or gilt-aluminum strikings (Judd 1436, 1437). Pierce, Jay, Ullmer:421, $150,000, Auction 81:418, $125,000; Ely, Garrett (1976):455, $91,000; Carter:610, $121,000, Auction 85:936, $99,000.

6387   1875 Restrike. Proofs only. Very rare.
Prominent rust marks on OL; extra outlines on r. ribbon and much of r. wreath. Possibly 12–15 known; usually not distinguished in price from originals. Wilcox, Clapp, Eliasberg:301, $110,000. Breen {1977}, pp. 153–54, 264–65.

6388   1876 [45P] Proofs only. Very rare.
Possibly 25–30 survive, at least 7 or 8 of them impaired. Breen {1977}, p. 156. Garrett (1976):456, $27,000, Auction 82:379, $16,000; Auction 81:419, $37,500; Carter:611, $35,200.

6389   1877 [1,468 + 20P] Rare.
Business strikes are from 2 obvs., 1 rev., date minutely below center; usually EF to AU, UNCs. prooflike and sometimes offered as proofs. Proofs have very low date; obv. develops rust pits on neck. Auction 79:278, $19,000; Auction 81:421, $32,000; Clapp, Eliasberg:303, $16,500. Forgeries include altered dates (look for tool marks in that area) and pieces struck from false dies; authentication recommended.

6390   1878 [82,304 + 20P]
3 vars. of business strikes with normal date; compare next. UNCs. are plentiful; hoards existed until recent years (over 30 in the J. A. Beck estate, and I have seen what was claimed to be an original roll of 20). Proofs have the 1877 obv. with rust pits on neck; possibly 12 survive. Auction 81:423, $41,000; D. S. Wilson, Clapp, Eliasberg:304, $13,200.

6391   1878 Overdate. Rare.
Centered date, curved line (not matching top of 8) within upper loop of final 8. Discovery coin, "Cicero":243. Later die states, with this line mostly faded, will price as preceding.

6392   1879 [3,000 + 30P]
Business strikes (Dec. 20), usually prooflike UNC. from hoards, have clear 9. Auction 82:1917, $3,250; Carter:614–15, $4,070, $5,225. Proofs have the rusty 1877–78 proof obv.; lower part of 9 filled. Possibly 15–18 survive. Eliasberg:305, $11,000.

6393   1880 [1,000 + 36P] Rare.
Business strikes (Dec. 4) are mostly prooflike UNC. from hoards; low date, bows complete, tops of wreath joined. Auction 82:1919, $6,250. Proofs have the rusted 1877–79 obv., with line through dentils l. of OF; bow incomplete within. Possibly 20 survive. Clapp, Eliasberg:306, $14,300.

6394   1881 [500 + 54P] Rare.
Business strikes (June 4) are mostly in low grades. Several prooflike UNCs. and EF–AU's turned up in Europe after 1965. JBL weak; mark between RT; recutting below r. end of crossbar of A(TES); rust parallels inner edge of wreath. Bortiglio, Bareford:141, UNC., $9,500. Proofs (possibly 25 survive) lack

the above stigmata; date slants minutely up to r. Clapp, Elias-berg:307, $16,500.

6395   1882 [1,500 + 76P]

Business strikes (Dec. 23) have extra outlines to ribbon. Most are AU to UNC. Those with missing serifs to I(TED) and I(CA) are counterfeits. Compare next. Proofs have obv. of 1881; leaf l. of date detached; no extra outlines to ribbon. Clapp, Eliasberg:308, $8,800.

6396   1882 over high 2.

Business strikes only; line nearly vertically up from 2. Later die states have rust marks in feathers. Counterfeits of this var. have been plentiful since about 1975; some have obv. I's missing serifs, others show minute capital omega within loop of R(TY), the maker's signature.

6397   1883 [900 + 89P]

Business strikes (Dec. 15) have level centered date, tops of wreath joined. Usually in low grades; most EF to UNC. survivors (prooflike, nicked, and scratched) are from a tiny hoard found about 1968. Auction 81:430, UNC., $5,000. Proofs have low date slanting down to r.; tops of wreath apart. Eliasberg:309, $14,300.

6398   1884 [1,000 + 106P]

Business strikes (Dec. 13) are mostly bag-marked UNCs., often prooflike but without the stigmata of proofs. Proofs have faint extra outlines at RICA, traces of extra outlines around terminal tassels atop wreath. Clapp, Eliasberg:310, $16,500.

6399   1885 [800 + 110P]

Business strikes (March) have leaf l. of date incomplete; most are prooflike UNCs., without the stigmata of proofs though often sold as such. Auction 81:432, $4,250; Auction 82:1921, $1,950. Proofs have extra outlines on AM and 3; leaf l. of date normal. Eliasberg:311, $15,400.

6400   1886 [1,000 + 142P]

Business strikes (Dec.) are mostly AU to UNC. For stigmata of proofs (2 vars.) see Breen {1977}, p. 182. Eliasberg:312, $14,300.

6401   1887 Doubled obv. die. [6,000]

Doubling plainest on RICA, less so on B RTY; other letters heavy. Most survivors are AU to UNC., some deceptively prooflike.

6402   1887 Normal. [160P] Proofs only.

RICA normal, not doubled. Usually normal die alignment; rarely with rev. 180° from normal, e.g., 1971 CSNS:433. Compare next. Eliasberg:313, $13,200.

6403   1887 Overstruck. 3 known.

Undertypes are specimens of **6402** with rev. rotated 180°. Look for traces of extra date between OLLAR and 3, extra DOLLARS between DOLLARS and date. 1) LM 11/65:346, Russell Heim. 2) LM 9/68:541, 10/69:420, 6/71:847, 1975 CSNS (RARCOA):279, choice, lint mark l. of 3. 3) LM 10/73:479, Breen I:132, nicked.

6404   1888 Doubled obv. die. [5,000]

Doubling plainest on UNITED. Business strikes (April), mostly AU to UNC. A few proofs known (mintage incl. in next).

6405   1888 Normal letters. [291P] Proofs only. Very scarce.

Big rust patch on neck. H. P. Smith, Clapp, Eliasberg:314, $12,100.

6406   1889 [2,300− + 129−P]

Business strikes (Dec.) are mostly EF to UNC.; many melted in 1890 at abolition of denomination. UNC. survivors include 50 bought by Virgil M. Brand from the Mint. Proofs are much rarer than other dates 1882–88; leaf l. of date complete, extra outlines on l. ribbon and l. top wreath. Auction 81:436, $15,000; Clapp, Eliasberg:315, $10,450.

CHAPTER 35

BARBER'S "STELLAS" OR FOUR-DOLLAR PIECES (1879–80)

During the 1870s two international problems (both based on deceit and deliberate confusion) agitated both Congress and the Mint. One was the "rivalry" between silver and gold, an issue nobody understood until Carothers {1930} and few even today; the other was an alleged need for international trade coins, on the precedent of medieval Florentine florins, later ducats, escudos, and pesos. (Compare Chap. 30, 32, Sects. i, introductory texts.) In a period of universal obscurantism and systematic evasion, the proposals made by (or to) Congress, the Treasury and the Mint were even more obscure than most and satisfied nobody, leading only to a few hundreds of sample coins and a few millions of lines of political rhetoric. The $4 gold coins or "Stellas" attempted to solve both international problems simultaneously, and their fate became the most ridiculous of all.

This silver/gold "rivalry" was to become subject matter for thousands of learned papers and books exhibiting mostly their authors' ignorance, reams of futile congressional debates, and eventually the main issue in the 1896 and 1900 presidential campaigns, inspiring William Jennings Bryan's obfuscatory "Cross of Gold" speech. Underlying all the rhetoric were official policies only partly concealing the real issue, which was subsidies to wealthy mine owners while people starved in the streets. (See Chap. 29, Sect. ix, introductory text.) Its source goes back to Jan. 24, 1848, when one James Marshall found gold at Sutter's Mill on the American River near Coloma, Calif., failed to keep his mouth shut about it, and consequently died in poverty. Through about 1856, the amounts of gold shipped east from California (eventually to reach European bullion markets) were so vast as to affect world price structures. Compared with silver or Treasury notes or bank notes, gold in such oversupply began to depreciate, commanding less and less in terms of silver dollars, meaning that silver prices soared (reckoned in gold eagles, pounds sterling, etc.). Silver coins became profitable to melt, and vanished from circulation in the USA before 1852. Official reduction in weights of silver coins helped, but the bank panic of 1857 (worsened by crop failures) ultimately resulted in New York banks' suspending specie payments, Dec. 28, 1861. This meant that banks would not even redeem Treasury notes, let alone their own paper, in anything, and all coins vanished from circulation, not to reappear until the late 1870s. (What circulated instead was scrip, private tokens, and fractional currency.) During the early 1870s, the Comstock Lode and other Nevada silver discoveries created the converse situation to 1849–53: silver fell in terms of gold dollars or greenbacks. The German Empire under Bismarck adopted a gold standard and dumped some 8,000 tons of silver onto the market, worsening the problem. Silver then had few industrial

uses except coinage, and the mine owners' congressional friends (Reps. Richard P. "Silver Dick" Bland, John Adam Kasson, and William Darrah Kelley) did all they could to propose new issues of silver coin (the Trade Dollars and Morgan Dollars among them) as a captive market for silver bullion at artificially inflated prices. This unholy trinity also became instrumental in various proposals (1868–80) for international coinage, aimed at creating a larger foreign market for domestic silver. This explains in part their adoption of metric weights of U.S. silver coins 1873–1964, as well as for the "goloid" and "metric" coins, including the Stellas.

In 1879, Rep. Kasson dreamed up still another new coinage proposal which would allegedly solve the "rivalry" and be internationally acceptable: $20's and $4's or "Stella" coins of "metric gold" (containing 10% silver), and dollars of Dr. Wheeler W. Hubbell's "goloid" alloy (silver containing about 4% gold, not enough to change its color). There were two designs of Stellas, the flowing hair type by Barber, the coiled hair obv. by Morgan; their name comes from the large five-pointed star on rev.

Only a few original proof sets (Stella, goloid, and "goloid metric" dollars) were made in Dec. 1879 from the Barber designs; those with the Morgan obvs. were clandestine issues. At least 425 additional sets followed in 1880 from the 1879 Barber dies, by order of Congress: 25 in Jan., 100 in early April, 300 in mid-May. After even the congressmen noticed that metric gold looked just like the ordinary coin gold, and that goloid was indistinguishable from standard silver, they killed the authorizing bill: Julian {1984}.

As the same dies were used for original Stellas and official restrikes, distinguishing between them has been a difficult problem. Coiled hair or Morgan Stellas of 1879 are not known to have been restruck; they normally lack the central striations (on the strip from which these planchets were cut) found on most 1879 Flowing Hair Stellas and all the 1880 issues. Presumably the very rare 1879 Flowing Hair coins without central striations are the originals. None has been auctioned in many years, though many restrikes have been marketed as originals owing to their having correct weights. An element of confusion was introduced in the early 1950s because the first few restrikes weighed proved lightweight, whereas Coiled Hair coins weigh the 108 grs. = 7 gms. called for by the authorizing bill. Later researches have shown that restrikes range from 103.2 to 109 grs., which fact makes weight no longer a usable test, whether for the usual ones or the final batch with rusty dies. We are unable as yet to devise a test more reliable than the planchet striations.

Though extremely popular today, and much exaggerated in rarity, Stellas in their own day provided a juicy scandal resulting in amusing newspaper copy for several years—and many laughs at the expense of the congressmen who had ordered the restrikes. The story broke that while no coin collector could obtain a Stella from the Mint Bureau at any price, looped specimens commonly adorned the bosoms of Washington's most famous madams, who owned the bordellos favored by those same congressmen. Today there are several dozen 1879 Flowing Hair Stellas with telltale traces of removal of those same loops, whose owners probably sometimes wish the coins could talk.

BARBER'S "STELLAS" or FOUR-DOLLAR PIECES

Designers, Engravers, Charles E. Barber (rev. and Flowing Hair obvs.), George T. Morgan (Coiled Hair obvs.). Mint, Philadelphia. Composition, gold $^{60}/_{70}$ = 857.142 Fine, silver $^{3}/_{70}$ = .0428, copper $^{7}/_{70}$ = .100. Weight 108.03 grs. = 7 gms.; restrikes vary. Reeded edge. Diameter 22 mm.

Proofs only; see introductory text.

6407 1879 Flowing hair. Original. [?P] Ex. rare.
Judd 1635. Issue of Dec. 1879. Without central striations on either side; often confused with next. None offered in many years. See introductory text. Ill. of **6408.**

6408 1879 Flowing hair. Official restrike of 1880. [425+P]
Judd 1635. With central striations. 103.2–109 grs. = 6.67–7.06 gms. Eliasberg:316, $39,600; Kern, Carter:631, $57,750. Late impressions (rare) show rusted dies. Actual mintage from R. W. Julian {1984}, though estimated at 400 by Adams {1913}, at 450 in *NUM* 2/06, p. 59, and at "about 500" by R. E. Preston of the Mint Bureau (in a memorandum accompanying Dunham:2062), or 600 by W. Elliot Woodward in various 1880s auction catalogs. More than half the survivors show traces of cleaning or improper handling; many are frankly impaired; several dozen show solder residues from earlier use as jewelry (see introductory text), but their scandalous history keeps them in demand.

6409 1879 Coiled hair. [?P] Very rare.
Judd 1638. At least 10 known; estimated 15 survive. H. P. Smith, Garrett:431, $115,000; Auction 80:385, $175,000; Eliasberg:317, $101,750; Kern, Carter:632, $88,000. Always weak in hair above ear. As "Rio Rancho":133 shows central striations, unlike other survivors, it may be a restrike.

6410 1880 Flowing hair. [?P] Very rare.
Judd 1657. Small date, partly repunched (over 1879?). Always with central striations. Possibly 18–25 survive. Garrett:432, $65,000; Auction 80:386, $105,000; Eliasberg:318, $55,000; Kern, Carter:633, $68,750, G. Holloway.

6411 1880 Coiled hair. [?P] Ex. rare.
Judd 1660. To date 9 traced, 5 with frosty devices (incl. those in SI and 1976 ANA), 4 with semimirrorlike devices (incl. Wilkison's and one ex Davies/Niewoehner). Eliasberg:319, $99,000; Kern, Carter:634, $72,250, R. Hughes. Always weak in hair above ear, showing central striations.

CHAPTER 36

HALF EAGLES

i. SCOT'S SMALL EAGLE DESIGN (1795–98)

One of the first acts of the new Mint Director, Henry William DeSaussure, after Washington had appointed him (1795) over his own protests, was to announce his two major ambitions for the Mint. The first of these was to place gold into circulation; the second, to improve all current coin designs. His predecessor, David Rittenhouse, about May 1795, had already ordered Robert Scot to prepare dies for half-eagle coinage. DeSaussure publicized the Mint's readiness to coin deposits of gold, and on July 31 he proudly signed his first delivery warrant, authorizing the Coiner to transfer to the Treasurer of the Mint a batch of 744 half eagles. Between then and Sept. 16 the Mint released [8,707], thought to comprise [2,749] Wide Dates (six vars. from three obvs. and four revs., July 31–Aug. 22) and [5,958] Close Dates (six vars. from four obvs. and five revs., Sept. 1–16): excessively short die life. The Director interrupted coinage, apparently not from lack of dies (see below) but because he wished the Coiner's Dept. to begin issue of eagles, or $10 coins; the first duly followed six days later.

Scot's ultimate source for his obv. design is unknown. Probably he copied some unlocated contemporaneous engraving of a Roman copy of a Hellenistic goddess, altering the hair, adding drapery and an oversize soft cap. (This is not the pilleus or liberty cap: See introductory texts to Sect. iii below and Chap. 33, sect. i above.) We are a little more certain of the origin of the rev.: It is Scot's adaptation of a sketch or engraving of a first-century A.D. Roman onyx cameo, no. 4 in the Eichler-Kris catalog of these cameos in the Kunsthistorisches Museum in Vienna, a lesser relative of the Gemma Augustea and possibly by the same master. The eagle's attributes (wreath in beak, palm branch in claws) are the same, though Scot turned him from a profile view to a front view. However, on coins not sharply enough struck (or too worn) to show legs and claws in full detail, it is sometimes difficult to tell if the eagle's abdomen or back faces us. Scot's eagle is copied on U.S. Official and Diplomatic Service uniform buttons, Albert {1974} OD 1.

The four Wide Date obvs. all have first star entirely below lowest curl, and L touching cap. Two of them come with a rev. showing final S corrected from a D. The five Close Date obvs. all have numerals crowded together, first star entirely l. of lowest curl, L usually free of cap, and (with one exception) final star well away from drapery: evidently an intentional change of layout. There were originally at least seven dies of this Close Date type, but one was altered in date to 1796, another to 1797. Three others remained unaltered and were used (still dated 1795) in either Dec. 1798 or Dec. 1799 with Heraldic revs.: See Sect. ii below. As the Wide and Close Date types are so distinc-

tively different, collectors would do well to obtain one of each. Price aside, this is not nearly so difficult a task as it might sound. Col. E. H. R. Green's hoard included several dozen, dispersed about 1942–44. Many survivors are in or near mint state, saved as souvenirs, first of their kind.

At least two revs. remained usable in 1796; one was combined with the 1796/5 die in five deliveries, total [6,196], June 28–Dec. 22, 1796. Probably the [434] of Jan. 4, 1797, bore date 1796; possibly also the [278] of March 14 and even the [345] of March 25, 1797. That might make the total of 1796-dated coins as high as 7,253. But whatever its true mintage, 1796 is rarer as a date than 1795, though without the additional popular interest shared by coins of the first year of issue.

The remaining [2,552], delivered May 2 through Aug. 28, 1797, are thought to have been Small Eagle vars. dated 1797: two obvs. with 15 stars (from dies made in 1795 or early 1796 but with final digit omitted) and one with 16. The latter must have been completed after Tennessee's admission as sixteenth state, June 1, 1796, and likewise left without final digit, this being then a common Mint practice when it was uncertain in what year a die would go to press. All three vars. are of great rarity, probably fewer than 35 surviving in all grades. I conjecture [1,162] May 2 with 15 stars; [1,390] June 7–Aug. 28 with 16 stars. Robert Hilt's different hypothetical figures appear in main text.

This design ends with one of the major American rarities: the 1798 Small Eagle, which has one of the revs. earlier used with a Close Date die of 1795. We can only conjecture why only seven are known; possibly the rev. broke at once. The roster of survivors includes some of the most honored names in American numismatics:

1. Joseph J. Mickley (before 1867), William Sumner Appleton, W. Elliot Woodward, Jan. 18, 1883, T. Harrison Garrett, John Work Garrett, JHU, Garrett:437, $110,000, Auction 83:367, $71,500. EF, rim dent above E(D). Possibly the discovery coin, Bache I:2752, "Very good, only a little circulated." (March 1865) Ill. at **6421.**

2. Lorin G. Parmelee, George Woodside, Mint Cabinet Coll., SI. VF, rev. scratched.

3. James Ten Eyck, Waldo Newcomer, Col. E. H. R. Green, King Farouk, P. H. Wittlin, W. G. Baldenhofer, believed Josiah Lilly, SI. EF.

4. B. Max Mehl (1924), John H. Clapp, Eliasberg:330, $77,000, pvt. coll. VF.

5. John Butler (Burlington, N.J., pharmacist, ca. 1900), his son — Butler, George H. Earle, Col. James W. Ellsworth, Wayte Raymond, William Cutler Atwater, pvt. coll. VF, scratched above RI. Ill. in Adams {1935} and *SC.*

6. Raymond L. Caldwell (florist, Highland Ave.· Lancaster,

Pa.), Col. James W. Flanagan:1063, James Aloysius Stack estate. VF. Ill. *NUM* 4/35 p. 212.

7. Rev. Foster Ely:17 (11/17/1886), R. Coulton Davis (?), H. P. Graves, Clifford T. Weihman, pvt. coll. Nearly VF, obvious rev. digs and scratches.

Obv. is the Large Close Date var. of 1798, in an early die state, before it developed the rim break over fourth star or the two cracks from rim through first star into field (one of them reaching hair). For several reasons (spelled out in Breen {1966}, pp. 15–17), the Small Eagle coin precedes the Heraldic (Breen 1-B) with the same obv. This suggests that the Small Eagle coins might have comprised the [691] of Jan. 4, 1798. However, if this delivery actually represents coins prepared as part of the emergency issue of Dec. 1797, following the Mint's reopening after the yellow fever epidemic, these 691 must have borne date 1797, and the Small Eagle 1798's would have been included in the [1,856] released Feb. 28, 1798. We are unlikely to have a definitive answer to this question. However, what is much more important here is how many survive. There is no rumor of an eighth specimen; discovery of a new one would unquestionably reach the front pages of all the coin-trade papers.

SCOT'S SMALL EAGLE DESIGN

Designer, Engraver, Robert Scot. Mint, Philadelphia. Composition, gold 11/12 = 917 Fine. Weight 135 grs. = 8.75 gms. Diameter approx. 1″ = 25.4 mm. Reeded edge. Authorizing Act, April 2, 1792.

Grade range, POOR to UNC.; not generally collected in low grades. VERY GOOD: Date and all letters clear, devices completely outlined, but only traces of internal details in curls, hair, wing feathers, and leaves. FINE: Major drapery contours intact; partial detail in hair above drapery and on cap; partial separation of lower feathers in wings. VERY FINE: Partial details in upper part of cap; all major contours of drapery, hair, curls, wing feathers, tail feathers show, though breast and leg feathers will usually be flat. EXTREMELY FINE: Isolated rubbed spots only—typically behind ear, on cheekbone, shoulder, end of drapery, eagle's breast, and legs; partial mint luster. UNCIRCULATED: *No* trace of wear. NOTE: In all grades, specimens often show file marks; these are adjustment marks, made on planchets before striking, to reduce weight to legal standard. They are not impairments, but should be mentioned in any description of grade.

6412 1795 [all kinds 8,707] Wide date, first star low, 4 berries.
Breen 1-B, 1-C, 2-C = Hilt 4D, 4B, 3B. Conjecturally [2,749]; Hilt thinks 3,885. Wide-date coins normally have numerals no closer than on that ill.; see introductory text. Garrett:433, AU, $60,000. See comments in 1982 ANA:2662.

6413 1795 Wide date, first star low, 3 berries.
Breen 1-A = Hilt 4C, who thinks these were the [2,684] of Sept. 1–3, 1795. No berry inside l. branch of wreath. Earle, Clapp, Eliasberg:320, EF, $11,000.

6414 1795 Wide date, first star low; STATES over STATED. Breen 3-D, 4-D = Hilt 1A, 2A, who thinks these were [744] + [520] = 1,264, July 31 and Aug. 11, 1795. The spurs from dentils occur on several dies of this date; they apparently represent Scot's tool slipping, not cracks. Breen 3-D: Earle, Clapp, Eliasberg:323, AU, $12,100; 4-D, Sears, Clapp, Eliasberg:324, EF, $8,800.

6415 1795 Close date, 4 berries, normally placed.
First star well to l.; [5,958?]: See introductory text. Normal berry placement means one berry each on inside and outside edges of both branches. Breen 5-E, 6-E, 6-F = Hilt 5E, 6E, 6G. Hilt identifies these with [870], Sept. 16, 1795, + [780], June 28, 1796, + [2,460], Dec. 8, 1796. Price for Breen 6-E; the 6-F (very scarce) has D repunched, the 5-E (very rare) has 5 repunched. Both obvs. were resurrected for use with heraldic revs.: See next section. Compare next 2.

6416 1795 Close date, 3 berries. Rare.
No berry inside l. branch. Breen 6-G = Hilt 6F, who thinks these are the [2,346] of July 27, 1796. Rev. reused on **6421.** Ill. Akers {1979}. Garrett (1976):366, AU, $8,500; Auction 81:859, EF, $10,500.

6417 1795 Close date, 4 berries, none inside l. branch. Ex. rare.
2 berries outside l. branch; r. branch normal. Breen 8-I = Hilt 8I (ill.) has "apostrophe" (part of extra E) between tops of BE, rev. of 1796; Breen 7-H (Hilt 7H) has (S)T lacking l. base. Hilt thinks these were respectively [337] and [273] of Dec. 22, 1796 and Sept. 21, 1796. For the Heraldic Eagle coins of this date see next section.

6418 1796/5 [6,916+]

Breen 9-I = Hilt 9I. Mintage possibly [7,253]: See introductory text. Hilt thinks these are the [1,057] of Jan. 14, March 14, and March 25, 1797. Usually VF–EF; Ex. rare UNC. Mickley, Appleton, Garrett:434, EF, $14,000; Auction 82:924, $36,000; Sears, Clapp, Eliasberg:327, AU, $16,500.

6419 1797 15 stars. [1,162?] Very rare.

Mint report, this and next, [3,609]: See introductory text. Breen 10-J, 11-J = Hilt 11L, 12L, who thinks these are the [545] + [113] of June 7–19, 1797. Only one berry in wreath. Breen 10-J: Clapp, Eliasberg:328, EF, impaired, $12,100; 11-J (ill. Akers {1979}), W. J. Jenks, Garrett:435, EF, $20,000.

6420 1797 16 stars, small eagle. [1,390?] Very rare.

Breen 12-K and new var. = Hilt 13K, 13J, who thinks them part of [1,162], May 2, 1797. See introductory text. Only 2 berries in wreath. Price for former, with both berries outside branches. Miles, Ullmer:438, $21,000, Newlin, Garrett:436, EF, $17,000; Carter:638, AU, $16,500. On the other var., r. berry is inside branch; this was originally known only in a defaced copper striking ex Woodside, Brand, NN 41, Rothert:1266, Pine Tree Auctions; Robert Hilt discovered the unique (?) gold impression in 1972. Obv. reused in **6424.**

6421 1798 Small eagle. 7 known.

Breen 1-A = Hilt 14F. Always with inner circle below date, to guide Scot in making dentilated border. See introductory text for roster. Discovered by W. Elliot Woodward (Bache I:2752), March 1865. Enl. photos. Obv. reappears in **6426.**

ii. SCOT'S HERALDIC DESIGN (1798–1807)

For this denomination more than any other, the beginnings of this design are shrouded in mystery. The Heraldic rev. appears on half eagles dated 1795, which could never have been issued in that year; it appears on coins dated 1797, probably released in Dec. 1798 or Dec. 1799, following one of the then annual yellow fever epidemics. Quantities made of these anomalous emergency coinages are unknown but evidently very small. Nor do we know Scot's immediate prototype for the obv. (see preceding section); nor whether the heraldic revs. were made in summer 1796 or 1797, let alone when they first went into use. All we have is educated guesses, based on what can be deduced from scanty Archives records and from the coins themselves. But then numismatics, ancient and modern, must always depend on similar droplets of direct evidence and similar deluges of Holmesian deduction to reach its conclusions.

The heraldic eagle design is Scot's inaccurate adaptation of the Great Seal of the United States (1782), with the blunder (or ill-timed militaristic bravado, which was a blunder of another kind) of placing the warlike arrows in the eagle's dexter claw (observer's l.), the more honorable position, while relegating the olive branch of peace to his sinister claw. This design first appeared in 1796, on quarter eagles, probably in connection with Tennessee's admission to the Union as sixteenth state: Its earliest coin versions all show 16 stars above eagle, including the anachronistic half eagles dated 1795. Compare Chap. 24, Sect. iii, introductory text.

The following attempt to account for the five anomalous vars. dated 1795, 1797, and 1797/5 derives from Breen {1966} with additional data and corrections.

On the "1795" coins we find three obvs. earlier seen on Small Eagle coins, dies 5, 6, and 7 of nos. **6415–17** (die combinations 5-E, 6-E, 6-F, 6-G, and 7-H in that order). I have labeled the three Heraldic "1795" coins 5-W, 6-W, and 7-X; but 6-W preceded 5-W, as the rev. die comes unbroken with obv. 6, heavily broken with obv. 5. Obvs. 5 and 7, when combined with Heraldic revs., are always rusted. In addition, 7-X evidently followed the 1797-dated coin with the same Heraldic rev., as rev. X is unbroken with the 1797, but cracked or heavily broken with 1795 obv. 7. The circumstance of obvious rust on these dies suggests careless storage for months or years. Ordinarily, when dies had to be stockpiled, they were picked up in tongs and dipped in a tub of hot (liquid) fat, as a sealant against moisture, to retard rusting. Because gold coins, then as later, were a major public relations item for the Mint and the federal government, the coiners normally treated these dies more carefully than those of lower denominations. Why, then, didn't anyone seal these half-eagle dies against rust? Why were they nevertheless put into use, rusted and broken, in what must have been singularly limited press runs?

We begin with Julian's hypothesis {1963, 1974, etc.} that Mint Director DeSaussure personally halted half-eagle coinage early Sept. 1795 so that issue of eagles could begin without further delay. This left several Close Date dies still fit for coinage: obvs. 5, 6, 7 (previously used), 9 (later altered to 1796), and 13 (later overdated to 1797), with obvs. 10, 11, and 12 possibly complete except for final digit of date. (We do not know what happened to obv. 8. Presumably it broke; survivors are exceedingly rare: See **6417.**) Evidently all these usable dies were properly sealed and stored. Then, in early 1796, obv. 9 was overdated to read 1796/5 and sent to press. During fall 1796, the annual yellow fever epidemic made Philadelphia a no-man's land; while the Mint prepared for closure, dies were sealed and stored in a vault in the Bank of the United States. When coinage resumed, Dec. 1796, at least one of the dies lacking final digit was dated 1797 and hardened for use. Between Jan. 4 and Aug. 28, 1797, the [3,609] half eagles delivered surely were of the Small Eagle type, dated 1796 and 1797. Immediately thereafter, word came of another yellow-fever epidemic, and the Mint closed Sept. 1, not to reopen until Nov. 9. Dies again went to storage in the Bank of the United States, but this time the closure was much more hasty than in 1796, and there may not have been enough time to seal all the dies in hot fat before carting them over to the bank. No half-eagle coinage followed reopening. In 1798, Scot made new obvs., three of them using the old Large 8 punch (which broke), three using the Small 8 from the new set of numeral punches completed in February. From Jan. 4 through Aug. 15 the Coiner delivered [21,641] half eagles: [691] Jan. 4 (Small Eagle?), [12,303] Feb. 28–May 5 (Heraldic, Large 8?), and [8,647], June 23–Aug. 15 (Heraldic, Small 8?). From Aug. 20 through Nov. 1, the Mint was again closed for the epidemic. On Dec. 5 followed [3,226], emergency issues, possibly comprising some or all of these: 1795 Heraldic, 1797/5, 1798 Rusted Dies. Other issues attributed to Dec. 1798, made in haste in various denominations to fill back orders, also show severe die rust and breakage: Evidently any dies that would stand up even briefly were used, no matter how haphazard or anachronistic their combinations.

The date 1798 is also remarkable for two types of rev. star layouts, called "cross" and "arc." In the former, stars above eagle form intersecting straight lines which create diamond-shaped patterns; in the latter, the 13 stars are in a curved row of six below clouds, a concentric arc under those, with the twelfth and thirteenth stars, respectively, at beak and behind head. The cross pattern appears on over a dozen dies of 1797–99 (including at least five half-eagle revs.) and recurs on quarter-eagle and disme revs. of 1804–5, thought to be leftovers from 1798. Compare introductory texts to Chap. 25, Sect. ii; Chap. 29, Sect. iii; Chap. 33, Sect. ii.

As one of the 1798 half-eagle revs. also shows 14 stars, this presents another problem: Why 14, not 13, 15, or 16? In 1792, when the Mint began operations, there were 15 states: the Original Thirteen plus Vermont and Kentucky; in June 1796, the "Territory South of Ohio River" became the sixteenth state under the name of Tennessee; and coin dies thereafter bore 16 stars rather than 15. There was already talk of admitting part or all of the Northwest Territory (including the present Ohio, Indiana, Illinois, Michigan, Wisconsin, and eastern Minnesota) into the Union. Coin dies could not make room for indefinitely increasing numbers of stars. Mint Director Boudinot, sometime in 1797, ordered that henceforth Scot's dies should bear only 13 stars. Exceptions to this rule thereafter (aside from the 1836 Gobrecht dollar rev., the St. Gaudens double eagles, and certain commemorative coins) result from error or emergency reuse of obsolete dies. The errors include the 14-star 1798 half-eagle rev., the 1817 cent obv. with 15 stars, and the 1832 half-eagle obv. with 12; the emergency issues include the "1795" Heraldic Eagle coin with 16 rev. stars.

The date 1799 is much rarer than its mintage figure suggests. Coins delivered during this year almost certainly include many dated 1798, though some few half eagles delivered in 1800 may have borne date 1799. Large stars on the last three revs. made for this year reflect manufacture of a new star punch which continued through the next few years. The emergency delivery of [760], Dec. 28, 1799, probably includes backdated pieces from cracked and rusted dies.

Except for the 1800 with M corrected from a much larger M (probably that from the font used for eagles or silver dollars), vars. of 1800–3 are mostly minor, with the peculiarity that each obv. outlasted many minutely differing revs. The mintage figure for 1800 includes [26,006] minted in 1801 from dies of 1800. As

long ago as 1860, Dr. Dickeson reported seeing half eagles dated 1801, and collectors long hunted them in vain. To date all six "1801" coins met with have proved to be forgeries, made by removing the 2 from 1802/1.

Many coins delivered in 1804 bore date 1803. The commonest var. dated 1803 (Breen 1-D) shows crack through shield, branch, and E(RICA), evidently following the two least rare 1804's, which have this same rev. uncracked or with less of the crack developed. "Large date" coins (alias "large 8") of 1804 are from a blundered die: Scot first punched 180 into the die blank, using the extra-large numeral punches intended for the $10 coins. When he positioned the 4 for hammering in next to the 0, he noticed that there was not enough room for it. The next step was to have this die blank reground to efface part of the large 180, and to enter the date from smaller punches, from the font in use for cent dies.

In 1805, the mintage figures given for Wide Date, Imperfect 1 and Close Date, Perfect 1 are conjectural but fit the relative scarcity of these types. The former, [8,083], comprises the six deliveries of March 12–June 13; the latter, [25,100], the six deliveries of Sept. 11–Dec. 21. We know that the Perfect 1 came into use to replace the broken punch of 1800–5.

Coins of 1806 generally listed as pointed and knobbed 6's actually constitute two major types. Pointed 6 coins all have stars 8 + 5 (i.e., 8 l., 5 r.); the [9,676] figure represents those minted in the first half year. Those with Knobbed 6 have stars 7 + 6. More survive from this single die-pair than of all other 1805–6 half-eagle vars. together; it is the commonest single var. of the Heraldic design in all grades including mint state. There may have been a hoard of UNCs.

Some uncertainty remains about the mintage of 1807. All official sources give [84,093] as total for the year; quarterly reports (in *American State Papers—Finance* and elsewhere) are plagued with typographical errors. Snowden {1860}, using documents not in the National Archives the last time I was there, claimed that the change to the new Reich design occurred on Sept. 30, 1807, and quoted [33,496] as mintage of the Heraldic design. He must have assumed that the seven deliveries of Feb. 5 through June 27 contained all the Heraldic coins. But either he made errors in addition, or typographical errors made hash of his discoveries. The true total seems to be [32,488].

Most collectors have been content with one of the design, or at best with one of each date 1798–1807. However, the vars. are so marked, and so fascinating, that in lower denominations their counterparts would have been in extreme demand as major type coins.

SCOT'S HERALDIC DESIGN

Designer, Engraver, Mint, Physical Specifications, as before.

Grade range and standards, as before, except that in addition, for VERY GOOD expect partial motto; for FINE, motto complete though some letters are weak; for VERY FINE, much of azure (horizontal shading in shield) and most wing feathers are intact.

I. BACKDATED ISSUES: 16 STRIPES, 16 REV. STARS

6422 "1795" Large rev. stars, 5 berries. Ex. rare.
Breen 5-W, 6-W = Hilt 5O, 6O, who thinks these respectively [238] + [24], Aug. 12–28, 1797. See introductory text. The former, Mickley, Appleton, Garrett:438, AU, $27,500.
6423 "1795" Small rev. stars, 4 berries. Very rare.
Breen 7-X = Hilt 7M, who thinks this was included in [1,162] May 1797. Struck after following. See introductory

text. Eliasberg:331, EF, $28,600; Miles, Ullmer:437, $16,000, 1976 ANA:2921, $16,500, Robison:328, $16,500, EF; Baldenhofer, Auction 84:1414, UNC., $46,200.

6424 "1797" 16 obv. stars, normal date. Unique?
Breen 12-X = Hilt 13M, who thinks this was included in [1,162] as above. Struck before preceding, from same rev., with obv. of **6420.** 1) Woodin, Newcomer, Col. Green, Farouk, W. G. Baldenhofer, Josiah Lilly, SI. Ill. Akers {1979}; ill. (from the Col. Green photographic inventory) in Flanagan, Bell (1944), and Hall catalogs, but not sold with those collections.

6425 1797/5 Ex. rare.
Breen 13-Y = Hilt 10N, who thinks these were the [470] of July 8, 1797. The other vars. listed in John H. Clapp's notebooks (Eliasberg estate) are untraced; Adams's new var. (14-Z) proved to be a drastically rusted die state of 13-Y. 1) Mickley, Appleton, Garrett:329, EF, $15,000. 2) Earle, Clapp, Eliasberg:332, VF/EF, $12,100. 3) Baldenhofer, Naftzger, Auction 82:1926, EF, $15,000. 4) Carter:640, EF, $12,100. A few others.

II. 13 FIVE-LINE STRIPES

6426 1798 Large 8 [12,303+]. Close date, 4 berries.
Breen 1-B. Obv. of **6421.** Six pales gules (vertical stripes), each shaded with 5 lines; 7 white stripes (standard henceforth). "Cross" star arrangement (see introductory text). Later with badly cracked obv. die. Mintage figure includes group III below.

III. 13 THREE-LINE STRIPES, LARGE DATE

6427 1798 "Arc" arrangement, 14 rev. stars. Very rare.
Breen 2-C. On late impressions with shattered die, eleventh star (next to r. in second row) is weak. This new device punch with 3 lines per stripe continues through 1807. Auction 82:925, EF, $3,700.

6428 1798 Arc arrangement, 13 stars.
Breen 2-D. Usually with 2 lumpy breaks at ES O; later states (ill.) have others at TE(D) and AT. These may have been part of the Dec. 5 emergency delivery. Mougey, Clapp, Eliasberg:334, AU, $4,290.

6429 1798 Cross arrangement. Ex. rare.
Breen 3-E. Wide date, 4 berries. Not to be confused with **6426** or **6431.**

IV. SMALL DATES

6430 1798 [all kinds 8,647+] Small 8. Arc arrangement.
Breen 4-F. Mintage figure includes next; see introductory text. Earle, Clapp, Eliasberg:335, AU, $3,520.

6431 1798 Small 8. Cross arrangement.
Breen 6-H (ill.), 5-G. Price for former; Eliasberg:336, EF/AU,

$3,300. Breen 5-G (Ex. rare) has first star much farther from curl, rev. stars squeezed together, claw and 2 top leaves smaller, thinner (lapped die).

6432 1799 [all kinds 7,451+] Small 9's; small stars, arc pattern. Ex. rare.
Breen 2-C, 4-I. But compare **6435**. The former, H. P. Smith, Clapp, Eliasberg:339, AU, $4,400.

6433 1799 Small 9's; small stars, cross pattern, 5 berries.
Breen 1-A. Rev. ill. at **6431**.

6434 1799 Small 9's; small stars, cross pattern, 4 berries. Rare.
Breen 2-B. Rev. ill. at **6429**. Earle, Clapp, Eliasberg:338, AU, $5,720.

6435 1799 Last 9 repunched; small stars, arc pattern.
Breen 3-D, 3-E. Price for latter (ill.); Earle, Clapp, Eliasberg:341, UNC., $16,500. Former (Ex. rare) has S and F much closer to wings; Clapp, Eliasberg:340, EF, $3,520.

6436 1799 Same obv.; large rev. stars. Rare.
Breen 3-F. Stars wider than base of either T in STATES. Ill. Akers {1979}. Clapp, Eliasberg:342, EF, $3,520.

Ex J. W. Garrett: 441. Courtesy Bowers & Ruddy Galleries, Inc.

6437 1799 Small 9's; large rev. stars. Very rare.
Breen 4-G, 4-H. Latter Clapp, Eliasberg:343, EF, $3,080.

6438 1800 [37,628+] Normal M.
See introductory text. At least 3 rev. vars. Adams 5 (Breen 2-E), with final star about touching drapery, remains untraced; on the usual obv., final star is well away from drapery. The McCoy, French, Flanagan, Webb, Baldenhofer:1206 prooflike coin may qualify as a presentation striking; it has not been available for examination.

6439 1800 Blundered M. Rare.
Breen 1-C. M over much larger M; note extra upright at r. Enl. photos.

6440 1802/1 [53,176+]
Obvious overdate. First obv. has 1 centered in 2, with 7 revs. (including one of 1800 and one of 1803); second obv. has 1 in l. part of 2, with 2 touching drapery; 4 revs.

6441 1803/2 [32,506+]
All 3 revs. have l. base of T's broken off; many coined in 1804. See introductory text.

6442 1804 [all kinds 30,476−] Small over large date.
Breen 1-A, 1-B. Blundered obv., also called "large 8," "large date," and "small over large 8." See introductory text.

6443 1804 Small date. 3 vars.
Price for either var. with crack through shield and E(RICA): Breen 2-E, 3-E (ill.); latter ill. in Akers {1979}, former lacks repunching on 4. Carter:646, UNC., $8,250.

6444 1805 Wide date, imperfect 1. [8,083?] Very rare.
Breen 1-A, 2-B (ill.); price for latter. Zug, Clapp, Eliasberg:352, AU, $3,960; Carter:647, AU, $5,500. Breen 1-A (much rarer) has evenly spaced date, star almost touching curl. See introductory text.

6445 1805 Close date. [25,100?] Rare. 3 vars.

6446 1806 Stars 8 + 5; pointed 6. [9,676] Small D and A. Rare.

Breen 1-A. Enl. photos. The small A is most noticeable in STATES. Auction 79:296, UNC., $8,000.

6447 1806 Similar; large D and A. Very rare.

5 vars. Always weak in centers. The large D and A are as in next.

6448 1806 Stars 7 + 6; knobbed 6. [54,417]

Breen 5-E. See introductory text.

6449 1807 [all kinds 32,488] Small date and stars; small rev. stars.

Breen 1-A. Date spaced 1 807. Usually weak in centers.

6450 1807 Small date and stars; large rev. stars. Rare.
Breen 1-B, 2-B, 2-C (ill.). Usually weak in centers.

6451 1807 Small date, large stars; large rev. stars. Ex. rare.
Breen 3-C. Date spaced 1 8 07. Usually weak in centers.

6452 1807 Large date and stars; large rev. stars. Rare.
Breen 4-C. Usually weak in centers. Clapp, Eliasberg:357, UNC., $9,900.

iii. REICH'S CAPPED BUST LEFT DESIGN (1807–12)

Almost six months to the day after John Reich became Assistant Engraver of the Mint, assigned to produce improved designs on all denominations, his new half eagles appeared; Mint Director J. R. Snowden {1860} said the date was Sept. 30, 1807. They promptly met with adverse criticism, some newspaper accounts characterizing Reich's new effigy of Ms. Liberty on half eagles and half dollars as "the artist's fat mistress."

Almost all obvs. by John Reich, 1807–17 inclusive, on every denomination from dismes through half eagles, show lowest star at r. with one point notched: his "signature." On some dies this notched point faces border; on others (no half eagles) it faces curl. Don Taxay apparently first called the notched star a signature, before 1963; Stewart Witham {1967}, following Overton, called these notched stars "scallops." On coins dated 1818 and later these notched points no longer occur; Reich left the Mint March 31, 1817, after exactly 10 years without a pay raise and with much professional jealousy from the superannuated Robert Scot, his superior in office but not in talent.

This series is notable for changes in numerals: two different overdates for 1808, the entire 1809 mintage from an overdate die, the 1810's with four different combinations of large and small dates with large and small letters, the 1811's with two different sizes of 5. Placing the denomination on gold and silver coins was a Reich innovation; earlier U.S. coins (except for half cents, cents, and 1796–97 half dollars) lacked any denomination, because they passed by weight and fineness rather than "by tale" (by count, with each coin assumed to contain full face value).

Unlike later gold coins, the vast majority of specimens of this design will grade EXTREMELY FINE or ABOUT UNC., few (mostly pocket pieces) lower. This circumstance does not spell out discovery of hoards; more likely the survivors (possibly 1% of original mintages, a figure not far from that found for other denominations of the period) were put away early as souvenirs or heirlooms, or kept in banks' cash reserves. In their own day they formed only an infinitesimal fraction of circulating gold, most of it foreign trade coins and all legal tender: Portuguese escudos and 4,000 Reis coins, French 20 and 40 francs, British guineas, Spanish and Mexican 8 Escudos and fractions, Dutch ducats, etc.: Solomon {1976}. Among these, a federal half eagle stood out like a sea gull among crows, apt to be saved as a curiosity. After Aug. 1, 1834, when federal gold-weight standards were lowered, old-tenor gold coins became worth well over face value; the worn ones went to the melting pots, the higher-grade ones were increasingly cherished as quaint old-fashioned heirlooms, eventually as antiques and rarities. Cambists valued them at $5.33 each, but the bankers and bullion dealers who bought them so cheaply later found a ready market among coin dealers and collectors. Enough were made that even at a 1% survival ratio most collectors can eventually hope to own at least one.

Much controversy has developed to little purpose over whether the mobcap Reich placed on Ms. Liberty's head was intended to represent the *pilleus,* or Phrygian liberty cap. The following correspondence appears to settle the matter. Bracketed remarks are mine.

Mint of the United States, Philada., Feb. 14, 1825
Thomas Jefferson Esqr
Monticello
Sir,
It is not without hesitation and reluctance that I prefer a

request, which will be the occasion of any inconvenience to one who has acquired so high a claim to be exempted from intrusion; but I know not to whom I can address myself with the hope of obtaining information so accurate, as you, I doubt not, possess, on a subject to which I respectfully solicit your attention.

The character of the "impression emblematic of Liberty" on our coins, does not appear, from any record I have seen, to have been determined by specific instruction from the government; nor has it been settled by any uniform practice here. The journals of the Senate, and other notices of the proceedings of Congress, show that the head of the President was at first intended as the device for one side of our coins [introductory text, Chap. 16]; and that the House of Representatives substituted the words now in the Law. [Mint Act, April 2, 1792, quoted above, quotation marks supplied.] But, neither the journals, nor the brief notices which the papers contain of the debates of that period, give any indication of the precise emblem intended.

The first coins struck were cents of 1793, on which the emblem adopted was a female head, with hair wildly flying behind. In 1795 [actually Sept. 1793: Chap. 18, Sect. iii] the cap of Liberty was introduced supported on a wand projected behind the head. In 1796 or '97 the cap was discarded and has not since been restored. [For cents, June 1796; for half cents, June 1800.]

In 1794 the first silver coins were struck. The head of Liberty was here also adopted with flowing hair, without the accompaniment of a cap. This style was retained on the silver coins, with slight modification, until about the year 1808 [actually Sept. 1807], when Mr. Patterson [then Mint Director] procured a more pleasing head of Liberty, and ornamented it with a dress [the cap]; not intended, as I learn from the Officers of the Mint, to represent the cap of Liberty, nor approaching it in form, but taken from life, and considered a model in good taste of the fashion of the time. The inscription of the word LIBERTY was, at the same period, transferred from the margin of the coin to the band of the cap. This head dress continues to the present day on the Silver Coins since issued, but has never been adopted on the dollar; none having been struck, nor any new dies of that denomination made since 1805. [Actually 1804 for striking, 1803 for diemaking.]

The first Gold Coins were struck in 1795. The head on them was, from the first, ornamented with a cap head dress; not the Liberty cap in form, but probably conforming to the fashionable dress of the day. This continued until 1808 [again, Sept. 1807], when the headdress of the gold coins was conformed to that adopted on the silver. . . . I have recited the above detail of facts, familiar, probably, to your notice at the time, if not in some instance emanating from your authority, in order to lessen the trouble of recalling them to your recollection.

It seems expedient, if indeed there is not an official obligation, to complete the series [of denominations] of our dies, and the unsettled question of what is the proper emblem of Liberty, for our coins, is entitled to consideration before a new original die of our money is prepared. Permit me therefore to request information on the following points, as having a fair relation to the subject:

1. What figure or device may be considered as intended by Congress, or the administration of the mint, by the words in the Law, "an impression emblematic of Liberty."

2. Was the cap of Liberty adopted or alluded to as the fit emblem by any act of the confederation, or of any of the states, or by popular usage, during the revolution, or previously to 1792, so that this device may be supposed to have been intended?

3. When emblems or representations of Liberty were in those times resorted to, on public occasions, of what descriptions were they?

4. If the Liberty cap can be the emblem intended in the Law, or if it be deemed an Americanized and suitable emblem, is it proper to place it on the head of the figure personifying Liberty?

Such information or suggestions as you may find it convenient to favour me with, will be thankfully received. When I am satisfied as to the impression emblematic of Liberty which can be sustained on the best ground, a few pattern pieces will be struck, to be submitted to the consideration of the government, which if approved, or with such modifications as shall be directed, may fix the character of our coins. [Unknown.]

Supposing the female head to be an appropriate figure, three views in relation to it present themselves. To adhere to the present dress cap, or copy it so nearly as not to exhibit the appearance of any specific change. —To exclude the cap and adopt an easy disposition of the hair, with no ornament but the band of Liberty. —To adopt the classic style of cap, which though resembling the cap of Liberty in form, would, nevertheless, be distinguished from it by being worn on the head of the figure, if it be true that the cap of Liberty is out of place there. —The first would be the easiest, being a style familiar to the Engraver of the Mint [William Kneass]. —The second, if happily executed, would perhaps be most pleasing as being more true to life and nature. —The third has the advantage of a permanent standard in the exquisite models of art derived from classic times.

I am with great respect
Your Obdt Sert
Samuel Moore
Director

Omitted passages dealt principally with the copper coins' never having worn the Liberty cap per se. No patterns date from Moore's time; but his "three views" all were in production at different times: the "present dress cap" (1813–29), the head with band but no cap (1834–38), and the "classic style of cap" (1795–1807).

Jefferson's reply was brief and noncommittal, saying only that the liberty cap is not proper to be worn on the head of the goddess, as we were never slaves, and that he did not recall any common, let alone official, impression of liberty prior to 1792. In actuality, the commonest Revolutionary emblems of liberty, as found on newspaper mastheads and paper currency, included such devices as a bird escaping its cage, a horse without bridle or reins, a Minuteman with sword, a Native American, a liberty cap on pole, a frontiersman with musket, and the goddess (Bellona?) with sword and spear, trampling a king with SIC SEMPER TYRANNIS. Still commoner were dreary allegorical females, mostly combining the scales of Justice with the cap of liberty and bales, boxes, or barrels for Commerce, i.e., Mammon. (Eighty years later, Augustus St. Gaudens said his concept of liberty was "a leaping boy": *NUM* 3/13, p. 131.) Presidential portraits qualify no better as "impressions emblematic of liberty" now than in 1792: See Chap. 16, introductory text.

Despite all this controversy raised by Reich's inoffensive design, Ms. Liberty continued to wear her cap until June 1834 on gold, until mid-1839 on half dollars, and until 1837–38 on smaller silver; to carry it on a pole until 1891 on silver below the dollar; and again to wear it on half dollars as recently as 1947.

REICH'S CAPPED BUST LEFT DESIGN

Designer, Engraver, John Reich. Mint, Philadelphia. Physical Specifications, Authorizing Acts, as before.

Grade range, VERY GOOD to UNC.; rarely collected below VERY FINE, usually found EXTREMELY FINE or better. FINE: Major folds of cap show; eye complete, ear partly intact, motto weak but complete, partial wing-feather details. VERY FINE: Over half hair and wing-feather details; most shield lines clear; partial leg- and neck-feather details. EXTREMELY FINE: Isolated tiny spots of wear only; partial mint luster. UNCIRCULATED: *No* trace of wear. NOTE: Dangerous counterfeits exist; authentication recommended.

6453   1807 [51,605]
2 rev. vars. Price for that ill. (rev. of 1808). The other die (Ex. rare) has D nearer wing, 5 much farther from leaf, and a crack through E(S) to eagle's head.

6454   1808/7 [all kinds 55,578] Wide date. Very rare.
Breen 1-A. Ill. Akers {1979}. Serif of 7 mostly l. of 8; shaft in l. parts of loops. Compare next.

6455   1808/7 Close date.
Breen 2-A. Crossbar of 7 within 8, shaft mostly gone.
6456   1808 Normal 8, close 5D. Very rare.
Breen 3-A, 4-A (ill.). Price for latter; 3-A has stars much closer to dentils, and date is spaced 1 8 08. Obvs. hereafter have coarser dentils.

6457   1808 Normal 8, wide 5 D.
Breen 4-B.

6458   1809/8 [33,875]
Only one var.; overdate later fades out.

6459   1810 [all kinds 100,287+] Large date and 5.
Many UNC. survivors, probably from an old hoard.

6460   1810 Large date, small 5. Ex. rare.
Breen 1-B. Fewer than 6 seen, none UNC.

6461   1810 Small date, small 5. Ex. rare.
Breen 2-B. Fewer than 8 seen, none UNC. 1) Pierce, Miles:347. 2) "Cicero," KS 4/67, Auction 81:1426, $20,000, R. E. Naftzger, Auction 82:1927, $4,250. This was originally UNC. with initials MIC in field, "repaired" in the 1950s; ill. Akers {1979}.

6462   1810 Small date, tall 5. Rare.
Breen 2-C, 2-D, 3-D. Many struck in 1811: See next.

6463   1811 [99,851−] Tall 5. Very scarce.
Breen 1-A. Rev. of **6462**, but struck before many 1810's with this rev., as the 1810's often show signs of rust above eagle's head and neck. Over half the reported mintage of this year was dated 1810.
6464   1811 Small 5.
Breen 1-B. This style 5 continues into 1812.

6465 1812 [58,087+] Close 5D. Very scarce.

Breen 1-A. Leftward-leaning numerals on many denominations, 1810–12, suggest a left-handed apprentice in the Engraving Dept. for these years only.

6466 1812 Wide 5 D.

Breen 1-B. Many UNCs., apparently from an old hoard. Probably formed the majority of deliveries reported for 1813.

iv. SCOT'S CAPPED HEAD LEFT DESIGN (1813–29)

This and the following (Kneass's Modified Capped Heads, 1829–34) are by far the most difficult of all half-eagle designs to obtain. The reason is not low mintage, but high meltage: a by-product of the colossal influx of silver from Mexican and Peruvian mines. This immense increase in the supply of silver on world markets compared with gold lowered the price of silver reckoned in gold, appearing as an inexorable rise in the value of gold reckoned in Mexican dollars. This is the reality behind the numerous statements about the world ratio rising from Alexander Hamilton's original 1791–92 estimate (15 to 1) to nearly 18 to 1. Its major side effects included hoarding and melting of older gold coins when their bullion value exceeded their face value by enough to afford a profit over the cost of melting. In the National Archives is a reference to public assays (Paris, 1831), at one of which some 40,000 U.S. half eagles of "recent mintage" (the elusive 1815–30) were melted and found to be of full weight and fineness. This was doubtless only one among many such holocausts, and more were to come through 1837.

Virtually the entire mintages were melted, survivors amounting to minute fractions of 1%: for 1814, possibly 0.2%; for 1821, about 0.1%; for 1827–28, under 0.05%; for 1822 and 1829, possibly 0.02%. No date in the period 1821–29 can be called less than rare; most are very rare, and the vast majority of survivors range from EF to UNC.

Only the dates 1813–15 are by Reich; these bear his usual signature, a notch on one point of thirteenth (lowest r.) star. Reich left the Mint March 31, 1817, after 10 years of service without a salary raise. When half eagles were next coined (1818), they bore Scot's crude copy of the Reich device punch, and the notched star no longer appears. On the Scot device punch, hair is coarser, cap more obviously wrinkled.

No gold was coined 1816–17 because on Jan. 11, 1816, a fire in the Mint's rear outbuilding damaged the machines for rolling strip and cutting planchets. This prevented any further coinage

of gold or silver until completion of extensive repairs and installation of improved machinery.

Some dates in this period have become extremely famous. Of 1815, only [635] were minted, Nov. 3, for Thomas Parker, Charles Kalkman, and the Bank of Pennsylvania (depositors of the bullion made into these coins). About a dozen survive today, mostly UNC., and appearance of one at auction is front-page news in coin fandom. The following roster is as nearly complete as possible:

1. Pvt. coll., Dec. 4, 1885, Mint Cabinet, SI. UNC. Clain-Stefanelli {1970}, fig. 25.
2. Swedish Mint Museum, Stockholm. From the King of Sweden (which one?).
3. W. Elliot Woodward, Harold P. Newlin, Thomas Harrison Garrett, John Work Garrett, JHU, Garrett:460, $150,000, Auction 84:901, $79,750. Borderline UNC. Enl. photos.
4. J. C. Mitchelson estate, CSL. Loop removed.
5. W. J. Jenks, Heman Ely, H. P. Smith:204, "VF," $1,050 (1906), pvt. coll.
6. Stickney:660, $2,000 (1907). EF.
7. Col. Mendes I. Cohen, Parmelee, Chapman (ca. 1909), John H. Clapp, Louis Eliasberg (duplicate), "H. R. Lee," pvt. coll. Borderline UNC.
8. B. Max Mehl (1912), H. O. Granberg, William H. Woodin, Col. James W. Ellsworth, Knoedler Galleries, Wayte Raymond, Waldo C. Newcomer, William Cutler Atwater, Carter:655, $57,750. AU.
9. H. P. Smith, John H. Clapp, Eliasberg:370, $71,500. UNC.
10. Waldo Newcomer, Col. E. H. R. Green, Farouk, Spink, W. G. Baldenhofer. AU.
11. H. P. Graves, Dr. Clifford Smith, George Walton estate, 1976 ANA:2935, $75,000, Stanley Kesselman, R. E. Naftzger, Brent Pogue. UNC., rim nick opposite second leaf group.
12. James Ten Eyck, Col. James W. Flanagan, "J. F. Bell," "Memorable":314, Clinton Hester, pvt. coll. AU+, rim nick just l. of 5 in value.

Kagin 111:1819 (Dec. 31, 1951), and Menjou:1460, both called UNC., may be the same as others listed above, possibly nos. 7, 11, or 12.

As forgeries of the 1815 have been created by altering the final digit of genuine 1813's, authentication is recommended. Examination of the rev. die is no help: The same rev. was used on most 1813's and all 1814–15 coins. Your best procedure is to look for any monkey business around date. Star positions provide a check: on the 1813, second and fifth (clockwise, counting lower l. star as first), respectively, aim at above center of dentil and between dentils; on the genuine 1815, these stars, respectively, aim at bottom and center of dentils.

A crude die-struck forgery of the 1815 exists; this is oversize (26 mm), head larger than the genuine, stars smaller, numerals in ruder style, border dentils and edge reeding much finer than the genuine; leaves are blunt, letters crude (especially the R), and eagle is without lower beak. I saw this in 1958; present location unknown.

Even more famous than the 1815, however, is the 1822. Only three survive, though a fourth was long rumored (probably the Seavey-Parmelee counterfeit). The following roster is up to date as of 1983:

1. Adam Eckfeldt, Mint Cabinet, Smithsonian Inst. VF. Clain-Stefanelli {1970}, fig. 27.
2. Joseph J. Mickley (privately), W. S. Appleton, W. E. Woodward, M. David (1899), Virgil Brand, Horace Louis Philip Brand, A. Kosoff, $14,000 (1945), Eliasberg:378, $687,500, David W. Akers (Paramount), Brent Pogue. EF. Ill. in brochure describing Eliasberg's collection, *An Exhibition*

{1952}. Earliest part of pedigree deduced by Carl W. A. Carlson, *CW* 8/7/85, p. 57.

3. Harlan P. Smith (bought over the counter as ordinary old-tenor gold for $6.50, ca. 1884), placed in Parmelee:938 (1890) to replace Parmelee's counterfeit, and bought in at $900, H. P. Smith:210, William Forrester Dunham:2095, $11,575, Charles M. Williams, Kosoff & Kaplan, B. Max Mehl, Amon Carter, Sr., & Jr., Josiah Lilly, SI. VF–EF, tiny dent in fourth red stripe. Ill. in Akers {1979}. Dunham refused an offer of $35,000 from J. Pierpont Morgan for this coin.

The Parmelee counterfeit (ex George F. Seavey coll., 1873) is thought to be the one which eventually went via the David Proskey estate to a N.Y. dealer's reference collection of forgeries. It is grossly oversize and crude, as is a similar piece shown me in Boston about 1958; either of these may be the one mentioned in Edgar H. Adams's notebooks as owned by one "Wiatt."

In almost the same level of fame as the 1815, though rarer, is 1829 "Type I," commonly known as the Large Date for comparison with the later style (see Sect. v below). For a variety of reasons I assume that the first three deliveries of this denomination were of this older design: [7,781] March 31, [5,584] May 1, [12,010] June 30, total [25,375]. Whatever the actual mintage, only seven survivors are traced:

1. Parmelee:988, Byron Reed estate, OCL. UNC.
2. Joseph J. Mickley (pvt. sale), William Sumner Appleton, W. Elliot Woodward (1/23/1883), T. Harrison Garrett, John Work Garrett, JHU, Garrett:471, $165,000. Prooflike UNC. Ill.
3. H. P. Smith:218, John H. Clapp, Eliasberg:387, $82,500. UNC. Ill. in *SC* and Guide Book.
4. Mougey:1075, William H. Woodin, Waldo Newcomer, Col. E. H. R. Green, King Farouk, Dr. Clifford Smith:1691, $11,000, 1976 ANA:2945, $65,000, Harry Bass. UNC.
5. Randall:934, William Cutler Atwater:1646, pvt. coll. UNC., obv. prooflike.
6. David S. Wilson:79, Brand I:280, $88,000, Auction 85:941, $104,500. Proof obv., UNC. rev.
7. Unidentified old lady, Messer & Coen, William Fox Steinberg, Edwin Shapiro, 1964 ANA:2863, Berube's "Greater Houston":552 (1/66), Paramount's Grand Central sale (11/66), Kagin, 1974 MANA:1617, $19,000, 1986 FUN:2029, $10,000. F, rev. mutilated (parts of wings and shield reengraved to restore detail obliterated by solder).

SCOT'S CAPPED HEAD LEFT DESIGN

Designer, obv., Robert Scot; rev., John Reich. Engravers, Reich 1813–15, Scot 1818–29 (device punches posthumously used). Mint, Philadelphia. Physical Specifications, Authorizing Act, as before.

Grade range and standards, as before.

I. BY JOHN REICH

6467   1813 [95,428–]
2 minor rev. vars. Most delivered this year bore date 1812.

6468   1814/3 [15,454–] Rare.
Overdate gradually fades. Rev. of second var. of 1813. Rarer as a date than 1813 or 1818.

6469   1815 [635–] Very rare.
See introductory text for history and roster. Rev. of second var. of 1813. Enl. photos. Beware alterations from 1813 and struck counterfeits.

Ex J. W. Garrett: 460. Courtesy Bowers & Ruddy Galleries, Inc.

II. BY ROBERT SCOT

6470   1818 [all kinds 48,588–]   S T A T E S O F   one word. Very rare.
Breen 2-B. Note position of final star; this layout copies 1813–15. Garrett:461, UNC., $22,000; Randall, Clapp, Eliasberg:372, AU+, $6,325.

6471   1818 Normal spacing, wide 5 D. Very rare.
Breen 1-A. Rarer than preceding. Note position of last star; this layout continues. Clapp, Eliasberg:371, AU, $5,225.

6472   1818 5D/50. Very rare.
Breen 3-C. Discovery coin, H. P. Smith (1906), Clapp, Eliasberg:373, UNC., $39,600; rediscovered, NN 54:748.

6473 1819 [all kinds 51,723—] 5D/50. Ex. rare.

Breen 1-A. Rev. of preceding. Possibly 7 known. Enl. photos. 1) Mint, SI. Clain-Stefanelli {1970}, fig. 26. 2) Mickley, Appleton, Garrett:462, $85,000, R. E. Naftzger, Brent Pogue. UNC. 3) H. P. Smith, Clapp, Eliasberg:374, $37,400, UNC. 4) Carter:656, VF, $23,100. 5) Brand, Auction 85:1914, UNC., $66,000.

6474 1819 Wide date, normal 5 D. Ex. rare.

Breen 1-B. Possibly 6 or 7 known. Obv. as preceding, rev. as next.

6475 1819 Close date. Ex. rare.

Breen 2-B. Date spaced 1 81 9, 81 very close at tops. 1) Ten Eyck:185. 2) 1976 ANA:2936, $34,000, UNC. 3) Auction 79:1230, $31,000, impaired. Enl. photos.

6476 1820 [all kinds 263,806— + ?P] Flat-based 2, large letters. Rare.

At least 3 minor vars. Letter and numeral punches in this period were made by Henry Starr. Enl. photos. Dohrmann, Garrett:463, $13,000, AU; Spedding, Clapp, Eliasberg:375, $9,900, UNC.; Carter:658, UNC., $17,600.

6477 1820 Curve-based 2, large letters. Very rare.

Note letters ATE, the T taller; compare following. At least 2 minor vars. Enl. photos. Mocatta, 1979 ANA:149, $27,000, Proof; Auction 82:1928, $14,500, UNC.

6478 1820 Curve-based 2, small letters. Very rare.

Note letters ATE. Enl. photos. Eliasberg:376, $26,400, UNC. Rarer than the large-letters vars.

6479 1821 [34,641— + ?P] Very rare.

3 minor obv. vars. H. P. Smith, Clapp, Eliasberg:377, UNC. $28,600.

6480 1822 [17,796—] 3 known.

See introductory text. Beware struck counterfeits.

6481 1823 [14,485—] Rare.

Survivors are F to UNC. Garrett:465, $10,000, AU.

6482 1824 [17,340—] Very rare.

Possibly 14–18 survive, mostly UNC. Letter and numeral punches hereafter made by Christian Gobrecht. Garrett:466, $47,500, UNC.

6483 1825/1 [All kinds 29,060— + ?P] Very rare.

Breen 1-A. F to UNC., mostly EF. Garrett:467, $19,500, UNC. Proofs: 1) Mint, SI. 2) Parmelee, Steigerwalt, Woodin, Newcomer, Green, Flanagan, "Bell," Eliasberg, Farouk, Wilkison, Mocatta Metals, pvt. coll. The mutilated "1825/23" in 1947 ANA has not been verified.

6484 1825/4 2 known.
1) Cohen (1875):145, Earle:2394, John H. Clapp, Eliasberg:381, $220,000, S. Kesselman. Ex-proof. 2) N. M. Kaufmann, $140,000, Kagin, ill.

6489 1829 "Type I." [25,375 − ?] 7 known.
Large planchet as preceding; large date, stars, and letters; radial border dentils. See introductory text; compare **6490.** Enl. photos.

Ex J. W. Garrett: 470. Courtesy Bowers & Ruddy Galleries, Inc.

6485 1826 [18,069 − + ?P] Rare.
Most survivors are UNC. Garrett:468, UNC., $23,000. Proofs: 1) Mint, SI. 2) Randall, Parmelee, Steigerwalt, Woodin, Newcomer, Col. Green, Farouk, pvt. coll.

6486 1827 [24,913 − + ?P] Ex. rare.
Possibly 12–15 survive, mostly UNC. Garrett:469, $60,000, R. E. Naftzger, Auction 81:441, $48,500; Wolfson, R. E. Naftzger, Auction 82:1931, UNC., $17,500. Proofs: 1) Mint, SI. 2) H. P. Smith, Clapp, Eliasberg:384, $22,000, impaired, now AU.

6487 1828/7 [all kinds 28,029 − + ?P] 4 or 5 known.
"Horns" (serifs of 7) atop 8. Possibly [12,299] March 31–June 30. 1) Newcomer, Col. Green, Farouk, Clifford Smith, 1976 ANA:2944, $25,000, R. E. Naftzger, Auction 82:1932, $42,500, UNC. 2) Eliasberg, "H. R. Lee," Josiah Lilly, SI. UNC. 3) "Bell," Flanagan, "Anderson Dupont," W. G. Baldenhofer, Samuel Wolfson, J. H. Murrell, Auction 80:927, $55,000, AU+. 4) H. P. Smith, Clapp, Eliasberg:385, $44,000, S. Kesselman. Ex-proof.

6488 1828 Ex. rare.
Always weak in centers. Possibly [15,730] late in year. 2 vars.: first star distant from bust, Bell II, Auction 81:442, $40,000, AU; first star close to bust (ill., enl.). 1) Mint, SI, proof. 2) Mrs. Norweb, proof. 3) Garrett:470, $70,000, AU. 4) H. P. Smith, Clapp, Eliasberg:386, $26,400, AU. 5) "Dupont," Baldenhofer, Wolfson, Naftzger, Auction 82:1933, $40,000, UNC. 6) Davies-Niewoehner:561, $92,500, Auction 79:817, $110,000, UNC. 7) Atwater, Carter:663, initials in field, $8,250. 8) Auction 79:1234, EF, impaired, $14,000.

v. KNEASS'S MODIFIED CAPPED HEAD LEFT DESIGN (1829–May 1834)

Between 1828 and 1834, Robert Scot's successor William Kneass made many successive unobtrusive modifications in all denominations except the half dollar—all in the direction of a more finished, slick appearance. These were in conjunction with technological improvements then being introduced at the Philadelphia Mint.

That most relevant to the present group of half eagles is the "close collar" (Newman calls it the "collar die"), a then recent invention to equalize coin diameters and simultaneously to improve striking quality. Earlier coins had been struck in an open collar, which is a flat metal plate with a hole somewhat larger than the diameter of a finished coin, serving to position a planchet atop the lower die for striking, but not to restrain its expansion. Edge lettering, reeding, or other ornamentation were imparted in a separate operation by the Castaing machine (parallel bars) before the blanks went to press; the open collar did not affect them. Because centering was not always exact, dies were normally of much greater diameter than the finished coins, and included long radial-line dentilated borders so that any unstamped areas might not tempt the ungodly to clip or shave off precious metal before spending the coins.

With the new close collar, all this was changed, including border design and die diameters, and the principle remains in use to the present day. A close collar is a heavy steel block with a hole the diameter of the finished coin, into which the face and part of the neck of the lower die must fit; the hole may be plain or vertically grooved to impart a reeded edge, but cannot have other ornamentation as this would either prevent ejection of the finished coin or be sheared off in the process. During the striking, a flywheel at the press first retracts both dies, then the hopper releases a planchet, which feeder fingers (the "layer-on") move to drop into the coining chamber (the cylindrical space between lower die face and close collar). As the flywheel continues to move, the lower die stays where it is but the upper die descends with a force of 40 to 75 or more tons (depending on diameter), causing metal of the planchet to flow into all crevices and corners, creating the raised protective rim and bringing up peripheral details. The flywheel's further rotation causes the upper die to withdraw, the lower die to rise through the close collar, ejecting the hot, newly struck coin, after which feeder fingers brush it into the receiving bin, and the process repeats.

Kneass accordingly produced new dies with plain rims sur-

Ex J. W. Garrett: 471. Courtesy Bowers & Ruddy Galleries, Inc.

rounding beaded borders; this feature, essential to the new technology, was specially mentioned in Mint correspondence of the period, and it is still in use, though the beaded borders were abandoned in 1930 except for the New Rochelle commemorative half dollar. The illusion of higher relief in Kneass's dies (and many later ones) is partly from the way relief details were distributed, partly from basining (imparting variable radius of curvature to fields).

Vars. of the half eagles, 1829–34, are fewer and more minor. Mintages were larger, because considerable quantities of gold began reaching the Mint from Georgia and North Carolina. Bechtler's extensive coinages (introductory texts, Chaps. 32 and 42, Sect. i) are one reason why federal mintages in the early 1830s were not larger still; many preferred to have their nuggets and granules locally coined rather than risk shipment to Philadelphia with the hazards of bandits and hostile Indians.

However, most of the coins continued to be melted as worth over face for reasons detailed in previous sections; and this melting was why the 1834 Mint Act lowered official weight (causing even more melting of old-tenor gold). The change of design to the "Classic Head" (see next section) was to enable everyone instantly to tell new from older standard coins.

Because of these extensive meltings, all dates of the Reich-Kneass design are rare, some Ex. rare. The very first of these, 1829 "Type II," is one of the most famous of all half-eagle rarities. Date, stars, letters, and diameters are all smaller than "Type I." The proofs are thought to have been made in celebration of the new design, as with the half dismes and dismes of the year. Of possibly [32,076] minted plus an unknown number of proofs, only the following survivors are traceable today:

1. Mint Cabinet Coll., SI. Proof.
2. McCoy:1958, J. O. Emery, Woodward 27:1013 (Emery, Taylor & Loomis colls., March 9, 1880), Byron Reed estate, OCL. Proof.
3. Col. Mendes I. Cohen:149 (1875), Lorin G. Parmelee, Lyman Low, James Ten Eyck:194, Waldo Newcomer, Col. E. H. R. Green, King Farouk, Spink's, Mrs. R. Henry Norweb. Proof.
4. Harold P. Newlin, Oct. 31, 1884, T. Harrison Garrett, John Work Garrett, JHU, Garrett:472, $65,000, Stanley Kesselman. AU+. Ill.
5. Rev. Foster Ely, Cleneay:574, H. P. Smith:219, Dunham:2102, Flanagan:1105, 1963 FUN:4187, $21,500, Superior Galleries 9/24/70:574, $23,500, RARCOA 2/72:871, $20,000, pvt. coll. Borderline UNC.
6. Ben G. Green 5/25/06:443, John H. Clapp, Eliasberg:388, $28,600, Kevin Lipton. EF, cleaned.
7. Matthew Adams Stickney, Earle:2397 (?), Bell I:351, Adolphe Menjou, "Melish":1953, various Kagin sales, 1974 MANA:1618, $100,000. EF–AU, nicked.
8. Yorktown (Indiana) estate, Leon Hendrickson, 1967 Grand Central:806, Pradeau-Bothamley:574, $23,500, Davies-Niewoehner:562, $70,000, J. C. Burnheimer:1079, $50,000. AU, rim nick between ER.

Akers {1979} claims that others exist including at least one more proof.

Nearly as famous as the 1829 is the 1832 blundered die with only 12 stars. Apparently only six are traceable:

1. Pvt. coll., Feb. 24, 1883, Mint Cabinet, SI.
2. Parmelee:1013, Byron Reed estate, OCL. UNC.
3. H. O. Granberg (1913):1023, William H. Woodin, Waldo Newcomer, Col. E. H. R. Green, King Farouk, pvt. coll. Ill. ANS {1914}, plate XV, and SC.
4. Stickney:674, Jenks:5772, Col. Green, Josiah Lilly, SI. Holed between seventh and eighth stars, later plugged.

5. Mehl 12/12/22, Atwater:1650, Eliasberg:393, $44,000, EF, flat stars. Ill. Akers {1979}.
6. C. Varner, discovered at 1977 ANA, EF, $26,000.

The 1833 with small date is almost equally rare but far less publicized.

Mintage of this design, [74,709−], ended May 30, 1834. Of these only [50,141] left the Mint; the rest were melted as soon as it became apparent that the new Mint Bill would become law, which it did June 28, effective Aug. 1. The Aug. 1 date began the Great Meltings of old-tenor gold: See following section.

KNEASS'S MODIFIED CAPPED HEAD LEFT DESIGN

Designer, William Kneass, after Scot, after Reich. Engraver, Kneass. Mint, Philadelphia. Physical Specifications, as before, except Diameter 15/16″ = 23.8 mm. Authorizing Act, as before.
Grade range, VG–UNC., mostly EF–AU. Grade standards, as before.

6490   1829 "Type II." [32,076?− + ?P] Ex. rare.
See introductory text for discussion and roster.

Ex J. W. Garrett: 472. Courtesy Bowers & Ruddy Galleries, Inc.

6491   1830 [all kinds 126,351− + ?P] Large 5 D. Very rare.
Rev. of **6490**. In date, 0 usually shows traces of repunching. Mumford, Clapp, Eliasberg:389, UNC., $18,700. One proof reported long ago, untraced.
6492   1830 Small 5 D. Rare.
Rev. of next. Obv. as **6491**, before or after repolishing; on later states, 0 no longer shows repunching. Dohrmann, Garrett:473, UNC., $23,000. Proofs: 1) OCL.   2) Earle, Clapp, Eliasberg:390, $19,800.

6493   1831 [all kinds 140,594− + ?P] Small 5 D. Very rare.
Rev. of **6492**. Newlin, Garrett:474, $16,000, AU; Eliasberg:391, $45,000, UNC. Proofs: 1) Parmelee:1003, H. P. Smith, pvt. coll.
6494   1831 Large 5 D. Rare.
Rev. different from **6490–91**. Obv. as last, sometimes cracked from rim to fifth star to forelock. Randall, Clapp, Eliasberg:392, AU, $16,500. Two proofs reported.

6495 1832 [all kinds 157,487—] 13 stars, flat-based 2. Very rare.

Fourth star repunched. Usually AU to UNC. Population estimates range from 6 (manifestly too low) to 25 (too high); mine is 14–18. Garrett:475, $15,000, AU; Miles, Delp, Naftzger, Auction 82:1935, $18,000, UNC.; Chatlin, Brand I:281, "proof," $39,600, pvt. coll.

Ex J. W. Garrett: 475. Courtesy Bowers & Ruddy Galleries, Inc.

6496 1832 12 stars, curve-based 2. Ex. rare.

Rev. of **6495**, period distant from small D. See introductory text for roster.

6497 1833 [all kinds 193,620— + ?P] Small close date. Ex. rare.

Price for var. ill. 1) S 3/10/81, $29,000, Hancock & Harwell, 1982 ANA:2670, $13,000, UNC. 2) Auction 82:1936, $18,000, UNC.; others. Another reported var. (unique?) has period close to D.

6498 1833 Large wide date. Rare.

Many states of cracks, rust marks, and eventually a rim break above TED. Emery, Garrett:476, $15,000, AU; Frossard, Clapp, Eliasberg:395, $12,100, AU. Proofs: 1) Mint Cabinet, SI. 2) Randall, Parmelee, Farouk, N.Y. State specialist. 3) Nicholas Petry:314, unlocated.

6499 1834 [all kinds net 50,141— + ?P] Plain 4. Rare.
Coined March 31. Most are EF. Price for var. ill. (enl.) with 4

leaning slightly r. Eliasberg:396, $16,500, UNC.; Carter:669, UNC., $20,900. That with closer date, 4 leaning l., is Ex. rare. Roach:555–56.

6500 1834 Crosslet 4. Very rare.

Estimated population 14–18. Late impressions show cracks through last 5 stars. Survivors are F to UNC., mostly EF. Enl. photos. W. J. Jenks, Garrett:477, $34,000, UNC.; Auction 82:1937, $12,000, UNC.

vi. THE REICH-KNEASS "CLASSIC HEADS" (Aug. 1834–38)

Ever since regular coinage began in 1793, the Mint's principal output tended to consist of one denomination in each metal: copper cents, silver half dollars, gold half eagles. During the institution's first 50 years, it made more dies for any one of these denominations than for all the remaining denominations put together. The problem created by increasing coinage output in the 1820s and '30s was always to multiply working dies identical in principal devices: Stereotypy was wrongly believed a deterrent against counterfeiting.

This problem became acute after Congress passed the Mint Act of June 28, 1834, reducing the weight of all gold coins. As soon as it became apparent that this bill had a good chance of passage, the [24,568] half eagles with motto held in the Mint since manufacture, May 30, went back to the Melter and Refiner (see previous section). Anticipating floods of old-tenor (1795–1834 heavier-standard) gold for recoinage, Mint Director Samuel Moore ordered Engraver William Kneass to prepare new dies in quantity. Instead of following the original congressional recommendation to distinguish the new dies by adding AUGUST 1, 1834 to the date, Moore ordered Kneass to redesign them omitting the Great Seal's motto, E PLURIBUS UNUM. Moore had been trying to phase out this motto since 1831: See Chap. 27, Sect. iv, introductory text. Partly to save time, partly through personal preference, Kneass always chose to adapt older designs, and this time the honor went to John Reich's "Classic Head" effigy, as seen on half cents 1809–11, 1825–34, and cents 1808–14. The eagle was an adaptation of one Reich had put on half eagles in 1807. This time nobody fussed about the design's androgynous quality. (Earlier, some such objection, multiplied by jealousy, had induced Scot to replace the design in 1816 with his own ugly "Matron Head" cent obv.: Chap. 18, Sects. ix, x.) But for one or another reason, Kneass and later Gobrecht made at least eight modifications of it before abandoning it for the "Coronet" concept: See next section.

Kneass had his work cut out for him: Many dies had to be completed in a few weeks so quantities of gold coins could be on hand to pay the first long lines of depositors on Aug. 1, the effective date of the new Mint Act. Each working obv. required no less than 17 design elements (13 stars and date) to be added by hand, plus probably 80-odd blows from a twin-pellet punch to make the border, over and above the head punch. Each rev. was still worse: 22 letters and the numeral 5, plus the border, in addition to the eagle punch. Every die needed hand strengthening, basining, and polishing. This experience sufficiently explains why the new experiments of this period culminated in a design whose entirety could be hubbed except for date and mintmark (1839).

The anticipated flood of older coins did materialize; it has been estimated that over 99% of the original pre-1834 mintage was melted, 1834–43, much of it being turned into Classic Head half eagles. Supplies were augmented by a variety of other sources: the Smithson bequest (1838), which created the Smithsonian Institution; French Indemnity coins (1836–37), paid by the "Citizen King" for some forgotten incident, representing a triumph for Pres. Andrew Jackson; and, most tragic of all, bullion from parts of Georgia owned by the Cherokee Nation under perpetual treaty with the U.S. government. As always, the Native Americans had honored the treaty, but the white men did not, and when gold was discovered on Cherokee lands, the whites dispossessed the natives (Dec. 20, 1835) and forced them to relocate via the "Trail of Tears." Hazards of shipping gold to Philadelphia (largely shipwrecks, poor roads, bandits, and understandably hostile Indians) induced the government to build branch mints at Charlotte, N.C., and Dahlonega, Ga., to compete with the Bechtler family in coining locally mined gold: See introductory texts to Chaps. 32 and 42, Sect. i.

Coinages of the new design far exceeded even the Mint's most optimistic expectations. The coins went at once into circulation and stayed there, few being saved as souvenirs. As a result, mint-state survivors are very rare, though F to EF specimens are plentiful. They are mementos of a period of rapid change, expansion, and experimentation at the Mint, immediately succeeded by decades of stereotypy (the Coronet Design). We are only at the beginning of knowledge about the numerous vars. of this series. Unlisted ones almost certainly exist; we would appreciate seeing them.

THE REICH-KNEASS "CLASSIC HEADS"

Designer, William Kneass, after Reich. Engravers, Kneass 1834–35; Christian Gobrecht, 1836–38. Mints, Philadelphia (no mintmark), Charlotte, N.C. (mintmark C), Dahlonega, Ga. (mintmark D). Mintmark above date. Composition, 1834–36, gold 232/258 = 899.225 Fine, remainder copper with traces of silver; 1837–38, gold 90%, silver not over 5%, rest copper. Weight, 129 ± 0.0258 grs. = 8.24 ± 0.0168 gms. Reeded edge. Diameter, 15/16″ = 23.8 mm. Authorizing Acts, June 28, 1834; Jan. 18, 1837.

Grade range, VERY GOOD to UNC.; not collected in low grades. FINE: Partial hair detail, ear outlined, headband edges worn, partial wing and neck feathers, partial shield details. VERY FINE: All major hair contours show; over half wing and neck feathers. EXTREMELY FINE: Isolated tiny rubbed spots only; partial mint luster. NOTE: Beware specimens with traces of solder removal. Centers often weak, 1836–38.

I. KNEASS'S HEADS, 1834–35

6501   1834 [all kinds 658,028 + 4+P] First head; large plain 4.
Truncation markedly curved, its end broad and rounded. Center stroke of 8 thick; large knobs to 3. Four vars. Enl.

photos. Ill. Akers {1979}. Proofs: Eliasberg:400, $11,000; others. In Walton:2265, ex Morse, Renz, was one counterstamped C. BECHTLER N.C. 22 [= Carats].

6502   1834 Second head; small plain 4.
Truncation nearly straight, its end narrow; curl below eighth star more elaborate. Center stroke of 8 thin; large knobs to 3. Five vars. Enl. photos.

6503   1834 Second head; crosslet 4, smaller arrows. Rare. Center stroke of 8 thick; smaller knobs to 3. Discovered by J. H. Clapp. Discovery coin, Clapp, Eliasberg:401, $1,650, EF; 1980 ANA:229, $11,500, AU.

6504   1835 [all kinds 371,534 + ?P] First head, small date. Truncation nearly straight; forelock single; center stroke of 8 thin; open 3. Enl. photos. Ill. Akers {1979}. Randall, Garrett:368, $2,100, UNC.

6505 1835 Second head, small date.
Truncation much curved, its end rounded; center stroke of 8 thick; "closed" 3 (upper knob about touches cusp). Enl. photos.

6506 1835 Third head, large date. Very rare.
Truncation curved, its end narrower; center stroke of 8 thin; open 3. Ill. is of a proof, one of 3 traced. Stickney:680, "large letters," is untraced.

II. GOBRECHT'S TRANSITIONAL HEADS, 1836–38

6507 1836 [all kinds 553,147+ + ?P] First head, small 5.
Similar to last but top ribbon end horizontally ribbed; single forelock. Slender arrowheads, small 5. Many of this date delivered in 1837.

6508 1836 Second head, small wide date, large 5.
Wide rounded end to truncation, top ribbon end plain, double forelock; 1 shorter than 8, knobs of 3 closer to cusp, 6 narrow.
6509 1836 Second head, large close date, large 5.
As last but tall 1, knobs of 3 far apart, tall broad 6. Ill. Akers {1979}. Randall, Garrett (1976):369, $4,500, UNC.

6510 1836 Third head; shorter talons, large 5.
Similar, but truncation less curved, its end broader than on first head; curls above LIB differ from both; single forelock. Talons shorter, sharper, and less curved; no berry in branch. 2 proofs known.

6511 1837 [all kinds 207,121− + ?P] Large date, small 5. Very scarce.
Mintage includes many dated 1836. Double forelock; berry in branch. Ill. Akers {1979}. Enl. photos.

6512 1837 Large date, large 5. Scarce.
Single forelock; berry in branch. Proofs: 1) Mint Cabinet, SI.
6513 1837 Small date. Very rare.
Single forelock; no berry. In date 1 less tall than 8; knobs of 3 close together; small 7; date high, closely spaced. Discovered by John H. Clapp; first published by David M. Bullowa, *NUM* 10/49, p. 612. Usually in low grades; only 2 UNCS. seen.

6514 1838 [all kinds 286,538− + ?P] Large arrows, small 5.
TES closely spaced. Ill. Akers {1979}. W. J. Jenks, Garrett

(1976):371, $7,500 UNC. Proofs: 1) OCL. Much of reported mintage bore dates 1836–37.

6515 1838 Small arrows, large 5. Rare.
T E S widely spaced; talons shorter, thinner. Enl. photos.

6516 1838 C Repunched 5. [10,959]
5 first punched too high, then corrected; this fades, later states often showing break from rim through leaves, leg, shield, wingtip, r. rim. (ill.) Mintage began March 27, 1838. Usually VF; prohibitively rare AU.

6517 1838 C Normal 5. [6,220] Rare.
ST below A; break, rim through U, feathers, shield, r. rim near wingtip. "Melish":1982. Struck 2/19–4/16/1839, before the 1839 dies were shipped from Philadelphia. Usually VF; prohibitively rare AU.

6518 1838 D [20,583]
Only one var., from dies brought by coiner David H. Mason from Philadelphia, Jan. 26, 1838; a second pair rusted unused. First delivery [80], April 17, 1838; a specimen went to Mint Director Robert Maskell Patterson. Usually VF to EF; very rare UNC. Auction 82:1938, $8,250, UNC.

vii. GOBRECHT'S CORONET HEADS, NO MOTTO (1839–66)

When it became apparent that Mint Engraver William Kneass would be unable to resume duties after his stroke, the new Assistant Engraver Christian Gobrecht had to take over Kneass's full duties (though without the title or salary). One of his assignments was another new half-eagle design. Mint Director Robert Maskell Patterson wanted the smaller gold coins to be uniform with the eagle or $10 of Dec. 1838; and so the 1839 half eagles show the first version of a Coronet Head portrait to become as familiar as the Pillar Dollar or the Athenian Owl.

Despite these half eagles being for many years the Mint's major product, despite their being for generations familiar in trade, bulky in bank holdings, and welcome in Christmas stockings, our knowledge of their vars. is still in its infancy. The general outlines are known: head changed in 1840, diameter enlarged in 1840, dates and letters enlarged 1842–43, all dies completely hubbed except for dates and mintmarks, which had to be entered by hand. But Longacre's timidity at this blacksmith's chore (for most of 1844–48 his sole duty as Engraver after Gobrecht's death), resulted in numerous repunched or blundered dies. Most of these were discoveries of recent years; a few herein are published for the first time. The large-letter design may have been by Robert Ball Hughes.

As on other denominations, in 1859 the rev. was modified. Later Philadelphia coins 1860–65 (but not those from branch mints) are from the new hub ("Type II" rev.): Eagle's claws are smaller, shorter, sharper, and end farther from branch or arrows than formerly. Old hub coins may exist for 1859–61 from Philadelphia but we have seen none. An injury to the obv. hub (1863) left a notch on topmost point of seventh star (at 12:00) on all 1863–78 half eagle obvs. from all mints.

Rarities in this series are mostly either low-mintage branch-mint issues before the Civil War, or low-mintage Philadelphia issues during it, while specie payments were suspended and little bullion reached the Mint. See introductory text, Chap. 32, Sect. iii.

Many survivors from Southern branch mints (notably 1843 O, 1853–55 C, 1852–55 D) show full mint sharpness but dull matte surfaces; these are known as "seawater UNCs." They were retrieved from a wrecked ship, said to be a Confederate transport, sometime before 1974. Details have not yet become available, but the hoard also included double eagles and probably other denominations. "Seawater UNCs." sell for EF or AU prices, but in some instances no finer specimens are available.

Data on the Charlotte branch are from the National Archives. Pursuant to resolutions of the Secession Convention, Dec. 1860, rebel authorities seized the branch, April 20, 1861, hoisting a Confederate flag over the building, hauling down the Union flag. They required all officials and employees to take oaths of allegiance to the CSA; they fired all who refused. Operations continued as usual, including [887] half eagles delivered in May; the branch closed in October. At closure, someone shipped to Philadelphia a parcel of 12 half eagles reserved for assay from the Feb.–April coinages under Union control. The Assay Commission tested them, Feb. 1862, and found them all within legal limits of weight and fineness.

Data on the Dahlonega Mint are from Julian {1966}. This branch was plagued from the start by continual political infighting, and in later years by lack of gold bullion. Rebel authorities seized it April 8, 1861, in much the same manner as the Charlotte and New Orleans branches (for the latter, see introductory texts to Chap. 28, Sect. x, Chap. 38, Sect. i, and Chap. 47). Records of the Dahlonega Mint under the Confederacy are untraced; the rebels coined gold dollars and half eagles, quantities unknown. On March 31, 1861, this branch held at least $13,345 in uncoined bullion (much of it apparently as planchets ready for press). This implies ballpark figures of about 1,000 gold dollars and 2,469 half eagles, but the actual mintages were probably smaller. On the night of the evacuation of Richmond, April 9, 1865, Confederate authorities shipped their treasury records and all the gold and silver held by the CSA and Richmond banks by train (under guard of the Midshipman Corps, Capt. William H. Parker, CSN, in charge) to the Charlotte branch for storage. When Stoneman's Union Cavalry Raiders approached Charlotte, the whole consignment was rushed first to Augusta, Ga., then to Abbeville, S.C., where the gold and silver coins were distributed to Confederate troops: Irvine {1939}. Many of the Confederate records reached the National

Archives; the Dahlonega Mint records are rumored to be in private hands in the South.

The San Francisco branch began in 1852 as a provisional mint under the evasive title of "United States Assay Office of Gold" (see Chap. 40). It could not function as a regular branch mint in quite the same way as those in New Orleans, Charlotte, or Dahlonega for reasons amounting to a combination of legal quibble, greed, and political jealousy. The Act of Jan. 18, 1837 had specified that gold coins must contain 900 parts gold, not over 50 silver, the rest copper; this act's original intention was to give gold coins better color and durability, ternary alloys being preferred to the old-tenor gold ($11/12$ gold, $1/12$ copper) or to the impossibly soft pure gold. However, California native ore proved to average about 888 parts gold, the rest silver; and though foreign gold coins remained legal tender nationwide at bullion value, and though private gold coins circulated at face value in the Southeast (Bechtler's) and the West Coast (Moffat's, Wass Molitor's, and Kellogg's), nevertheless they were not receivable for taxes or at the San Francisco Custom House unless they conformed to the 1837 Act. Some of the more short-sighted congressmen opposed the cost of a full-scale branch mint (which would have to either include, or sponsor construction of, a plant for making the concentrated acids used in parting silver from gold to make coins of legal fineness). They preferred that gold bullion be shipped east, despite the hazards of bandits and hostile Indians in overland travel, or the equal hazards of shipwreck "round the Horn," so that local bullion dealers could make higher profits. Though the Philadelphia Mint shipped regular half-eagle dies to Augustus Humbert at the provisional mint, no 1853 S coins were struck from them, and only [268] 1854 S half eagles when the long-awaited regular branch finally opened. In months to follow, local manufacturers began synthesizing the necessary acids, and the new San Francisco Mint (no longer "provisional") recoined millions of private gold coins into federal issues, which could be used for back taxes and for retrieving necessary supplies from the Custom House where they had been rotting for months and years.

In 1860, a peculiar form of counterfeiting began to drive Mint authorities, bankers, and bullion dealers into panic. Unknown makers sawed genuine gold coins in halves edgewise, scooped out most of their interiors, replaced the gold by platinum disks of proper weight, joining the gold shells to the disk and fabricating a reeded edge of very thin gold to conceal their work. These coins had proper weight, produced a proper color on a touchstone, rang well, and became detectable only by being pried apart or tested for specific gravity ($21+$ gms./cc instead of the normal $17.3+$). No immediate solution was forthcoming. Mint officials revived the eccentric experiments (1836–56) of one Dr. J. T. Barclay: lettering edges, increasing diameters of larger denominations, basining dies more to make fields double-concave. Though the Civil War shelved the problem (by driving gold out of circulation), a permanent answer came only when the market price of platinum rose above that of gold. Occasional specimens still turn up, as do crudely gilt platinum fakes of various dates; all are valuable today for their metallic content.

Mintage ended because the Mint Act of March 3, 1865 mandated addition of IN GOD WE TRUST. The 1866 S coins without motto were made before new dies arrived.

GOBRECHT'S CORONET HEADS, NO MOTTO

Designer, Christian Gobrecht, obv. after Benjamin West, rev. after John Reich and William Kneass. Engravers, Gobrecht and James Barton Longacre. Mints, Philadelphia (no mintmark),

New Orleans (mintmark O), Charlotte (C), Dahlonega (D), San Francisco (S). Mintmark above date, 1839; later below eagle. Composition, gold 90%, silver not over 5%, rest copper. Weight, 129 ± 0.025 grs. $= 8.24 \pm 0.016$ gms., containing 7.522 gms. or 0.2418 troy oz. pure gold. Reeded edge. Diameter, 1839–40, $7/8'' = 22.5$ mm; later, $17/20'' = 21.65$ mm. Authorizing Act, Jan. 18, 1837.

Grade range, POOR to UNC.; not collected in low grades except for extreme rarities. FINE: LIBERTY fully legible; partial hair details; partial wing details near shield; all pales gules clear but shading may be blurry; at least one claw clearly outlined. VERY FINE: Top coronet line must have no more than one tiny blurred segment; all major hair details visible (end of lovelock may be weak); at least half wing-feather details; partial neck-and leg-feather details; at least half shading on shield clear. EXTREMELY FINE: Isolated tiny rubbed spots only; partial mint luster. UNCIRCULATED: *No* trace of wear. NOTE: Beware coins showing traces of solder removal.

I. FIRST HEAD; MINTMARK ABOVE DATE

6519   1839 [118,143 + 2 + P]
Earliest state, including proofs, shows traces of 8 within 9; this fades quickly. Rust pit on neck. Usually VF to EF. Enl. photos. D. S. Wilson, Clapp, Eliasberg:408, $10,450, UNC. Proofs: 1) Woodin, Newcomer, Col. Green, Farouk. 2) "Melish":1983, Kagin, cleaned.   3) East German pvt. coll., late 1981, NERCG, in a proof set with quarter eagle and eagle.

6520   1839 C [17,205]
One pair of dies shipped May 3; mintage began June 17. Ex. rare in AU.
6521   1839 D [18,939–]
2 pairs of dies: D above 3 (ill.) or above 39 (ill. Akers {1979}). Very rare in AU. Uncertainty in mintage figure is because this quantity is known to include assay coins, possibly as many as 34. Dies shipped March 22, received April 25; mintage began at once.

II. SECOND HEAD, MINTMARK BELOW EAGLE

6522 1840 [all kinds 137,382 + ?P] "Broad mill." Very scarce.

Very fine edge reeding; 22.5 mm as in 1839. Very rare above EF. Mitchelson, Clapp, Eliasberg:411, UNC., $3,575. Proofs: 1) Mint, SI. 2) Woodin, Newcomer, Green, Farouk. Enl. photos.

6523 1840 "Narrow mill."

Coarse edge reeding; 21.65 mm. Minor vars. exist. Very rare above EF. Garrett (1976):372, $1,000, UNC.

6524 1840 C [all kinds 18,956] Medium C. "Broad mill."

22.5 mm. 2 pairs of dies shipped Jan. 24. Notice about the change of diameter followed Feb. 6, but there is doubt that Charlotte authorities acted on it. Usually weak in centers, much more on obv. than rev.

6525 1840 C "Narrow mill."

21.65 mm. Possibly exists. Compare preceding.

6526 1840 D "Broad mill." Medium D. [4,439] Very rare.

22.5 mm. 2 pairs of dies shipped Jan. 24, received Feb. 3; two deliveries Feb. 22, [2,528] and [1,909], before new collar was made. Unobtainable choice.

6527 1840 D "Narrow mill." Medium D. [18,459]

21.65 mm. Mintmark above V or VE. A third pair of dies shipped Oct. 20, received Oct. 30; [4,594] Dec. 10–30.

6528 1840 O "Broad mill." Small o. [4,620] Very rare.

22.5 mm. One pair of dies shipped Jan. 21; mintage continued through March. Unobtainable choice.

6529 1840 O "Narrow mill." [35,500] Small round o.

21.65 mm. This and next minted Aug. through Feb. 1841; see **6535**.

6530 1840 O "Narrow mill," medium oval O.

21.65 mm. Ill. Akers {1979}. From one pair of dies shipped May 29. Obvs. destroyed Feb. 27, 1841.

6531 1841 [15,833 + ?P] Rare.

Coarser reeding, 21.65 mm henceforth. A tiny hoard of UNCs. turned up about 1953, but the date remains rare in all grades. S 3/85:804, $30,800, Manfra Tordella & Brookes, UNC. Proofs: 1) Mint, SI. 2) Clapp, Eliasberg:416, $30,800. 3) Reported.

6532 1841 C Small c. [21,467]

2 pairs of dies. About 6 UNCs. known. Gehring, Ryder, Naftzger, "Melish":1991, Bareford:165, $5,750, Auction 79:1237, UNC., $6,250.

6533 1841 D Medium D. [4,105] Rare.

Rev. of 1840. Deliveries [1,131] Jan. 18 and [2,974] Feb. 22. Ex. rare in AU.

6534 1841 D Small D. [25,287]

2 revs. received Feb. 13; mintage May 31–Dec. 24. Ill. Akers {1979}. Obv. shows minute repunching on date (later fades). Ex. rare AU. Auction 81:444, $15,000, UNC.

6535 1841 O [50] Unlocated.

Director's Report says [8,350]; Archives records establish that this comprises [6,300] Jan. 1841 + [2,000] Feb., from 1840 dies which were not destroyed until Feb. 27. The single 1841 obv. die was shipped Dec. 21, 1840; [50] Aug. 1841. Rev. will be same as **6529** or **6530**; authentication is mandatory!

6536 1842 Small date, small letters. [12,682 + ?P]

First delivery, April 30, 1842. Ex. rare above EF; usually badly nicked. Eliasberg:419, $2,860, AU+. Proofs: 1) Mint, SI. 2) Cleneay, Woodin, Farouk, N.Y. State specialist.

6537 1842 Small date, large letters. [14,896]

Minted Aug.–Oct. 31. Some are from obv. of **6536**. Usually VF, Ex. rare above. Auction 82:929, $2,200, AU. Enl. photos.

6538 1842 C Small date and c. [4,595−] Very rare.

Obv. die broke March 22; last coins show "cud" break at 12:00. Mintage includes a small number of assay pieces. Usually F–VF; prohibitively rare above EF. 1982 F.U.N.:1407, UNC., $15,400.

6539 1842 C Large date, small c. [23,589−]

One obv. die shipped March 11; leftover revs. Knife-rims at r. obv. and rev. Mintage includes a small number of assay pieces. Very rare in AU; 3–5 UNCs. reported. Enl. photos. Sears, Clapp, Eliasberg:421, $17,600, UNC.

6540 1842 D Small date, letters, and D. [37,917]

One pair of dies shipped Dec. 20, 1841, received about Jan. 1. Very rare above EF. Eliasberg:422, $3,520, AU.

6541 1842 D Large date and letters, small D. [21,691] Very rare.

One pair of dies shipped Sept. 29, received Oct. 7; mintage from then through Dec. 29. Prohibitively rare above EF. Eliasberg:423, $24,200, Auction 84:1333, AU, $23,100, H. Bass.

6542 1842 O Small date, letters, and o. [16,400]
One pair of dies shipped Dec. 20, 1841. Ex. rare in EF. Earle, Clapp, Eliasberg:424, $3,850, AU.

6543 1843 Large letters. [611,205 + ?P] Normal stars.
Large-letters hub, adopted Sept. 1842, continues. Minor positional vars. At least 4 proofs known including 2 in the cased sets (N.Y. State specialist; Carter:630, $132,000, D. Drykerman).

6544 1843 Small thin stars. Rare.
Either from a drastically lapped die or from one hubbed with insufficient force: curls delicate, stars have small thin points internally separated. NN 49:405; NN 55:393.

6545 1843 C Large date, small rev. letters, small c. [44,201]
One obv. shipped Dec. 23, 1842; 2 old revs. Occasional specimens are on broader flans (resurrected 1840 collar?). Very rare in EF. The sharpest survivors are "seawater UNCs.": See introductory text.

6546 1843 D Large date and letters. [98,452] Small D.
4 obvs., 2 revs. (arrived March 14) plus 4 old revs. Mintmark as in 1840–42. Very rare above EF.

6547 1843 D Same, large D. Very scarce.
Obv. of preceding, with rust marks from 3 to truncation. Ill. Akers {1979}.

6548 1843 O Large date, small letters, small o. [19,075]
Leftover 1842 revs.; 2 (of 3) obvs. shipped Dec. 19–27, 1842. Very rare in EF, Ex. rare above. A few "seawater UNCs." (see introductory text); prohibitively rare full UNC.

6549 1843 O Large date, large letters, large O. [82,000]
Obvs. as above; 2 revs. shipped March 2. (A third rev., sent July 1, was held for 1844 use.) Same comments for grade.

6550 1844 [340,330 + ?P]
Minor positional vars. of date. Rare in UNC. Proofs have date far to l. 1) Mint, SI. 2) Newcomer, Boyd, WGC, "Bell," "Memorable":345. 3) Cased set, Dr. Judd, N.Y. State specialist.

6551 1844 C Large C. [23,631]
Large letters and mintmark henceforth. 3 obvs., 4 revs. shipped. Usually weak on legs. Prohibitively rare above EF. Eliasberg, "Lee," Bareford:166, $4,750, UNC. Mintage interrupted because a burglar burned down the Mint, July 27, 1844; rebuilding was completed only in 1846.

6552 1844 D Large D. [88,982]
Large letters and mintmark henceforth. 3 pairs of dies.

6553 1844 O Large O. [364,600] Normal stars.
Large letters and mintmark henceforth. 8 pairs of dies. 1982 ANA:1053, $5,100, prooflike UNC. Proofs: 1) Parmelee:1152, Woodin. 2) Reported.

6554 1844 O Small thin stars. Rare.
Similar to **6544**, probably from same cause. NN 49:408; shattered rev. die state, "Melish":2010.

6555 1845 [417,099 + ?P] Heavy date.
Minor vars., all with 84 touching or about touching. Rare above AU. Mitchelson, Clapp, Eliasberg:436, $3,080 UNC. Proofs have date low, to l. 1) Mint, SI. 2) Parmelee, Woodin, Newcomer, Col. Green, Burdette G. Johnson, "Bell," "Memorable":347. Ill. 3) Cased set, N.Y. State specialist. 4) Set, Paul D. Williams:1818, with quarter eagle and eagle, $127,500.

6556 1845 Partly repunched date. Rare.
NN 50:846; others.

6557 1845 Thin numerals. Very scarce.
8 4 well apart. Very rare above EF. Discovery coin, Clapp, Eliasberg:435, $2,420, UNC.

6558 1845 D [90,629]
2 pairs of dies shipped Dec. 1, 1844, received Dec. 21. Date well to l. or well to r., former ill. Akers {1979}. Both vars. rare AU. Clapp, Eliasberg:437, $10,450, UNC.

6559 1845 O [41,000] Normal date. Very scarce.
4 pairs of dies plus leftover revs. from 1844. Very rare above EF, prohibitively rare UNC.

6560 1845 O Plainly repunched 18. Rare.
Twice as rare as preceding. In later die states repunching fades; these will price as **6559**. Discovery coin (early state), NN 46:366. Prohibitively rare choice.

6561 1846 [all kinds 395,942 + ?P] Large date.
Note spacing 1 846. Positional vars.: date centered or well to l.; see ill. (different var.) in Akers {1979}. Very rare UNC. At least 4 proofs known.

6562 1846 Small date. Rare.
Note spacing 184 6. Discovered by William H. Woodin before 1914. Prohibitively rare above VF.

6563 1846 C Large date. [12,995] Rare.
2 obvs., leftover revs. from 1844. Only one var. seen; base of 1 shows light repunching. Ex. rare above EF. D. S. Wilson, Clapp, Eliasberg:440, $13,200, UNC.

6564 1846 D [all kinds 80,294] Large date. Normal D.
One pair of dies received Jan. 11, a second March 11; 2 more obvs. July 8. At least 2 vars. with normal D, date low or centered. Usually VF–EF, rare above, very rare UNC.

6565 1846 D Large date, blundered rev., double D.
Mintmark first punched far too high, buried in device, then corrected. Date low or centered. Same comment as to grade range. Prohibitively rare UNC.: 1) Hancock & Harwell (enl. ill.). 2) Eliasberg:441, UNC., $2,420.

6566	1846 O Large date. [58,000]

In all, 5 obvs., 3 revs. plus leftover revs. Ex. rare above EF, prohibitively rare UNC.

6567	1847 [all kinds 915,981 + ?P] Normal date.

Many minor positional vars. Proofs: 1) Mint, SI. No duplicate reported.

6568	1847 Double 18. Very rare.

Breen 1; Hirt:1516. Discovery coin, 1963 FUN:4220.

6569	1847 Double 1. Rare.

Breen 2. Date very high in field; part of extra 1 below and r. of final position. "Melish":2027. Bill Fivaz discovered another with part of base and upright of inverted 1 (rotated 180°) protruding from throat.

6570	1847 Double 7. Rare.

At least 3 vars., differing in rev. cracks; one minutely differs in date position. Sometimes called "7 over smaller 7" as in cents, but apparently the same logotype was used, date partly effaced before correction. NN 50:849.

6571	1847 Blundered die, extra 7 in border. Ex. rare.

Top of extra 7 below space between 47. Discovery coin, NN 55:999. Not over 4 reported to date.

6572	1847 C [84,151]

3 pairs of dies; 7 touching truncation (ill. Akers {1979}) or lower date (scarcer). Prohibitively rare AU.

6573	1847 D [64,405]

3 pairs of dies shipped Dec. 2, 1846. One obv. shows minute traces of extra bases of 1 and 4 left of those digits. Very rare in AU.

6574	1847 O [12,000] Rare.

5 obvs., 7 revs. Prohibitively rare above EF. Only 2 vars., normal or weak O.

6575	1848 Large date. [260,775 + ?P]

Date from half-cent logotype, all mints. Minor vars., mostly notable for cracked dies. Rarer than mintage figure suggests; very rare EF. Proofs: 1) Mint, SI. 2) Farouk:251.

6576	1848 C [64,472]

3 pairs of dies. Prohibitively rare in AU. Usually weak in central obv.

6577	1848 D [47,465] Normal date and stars.

3 pairs of dies shipped Jan. 17–18; 2 more revs. in summer. At least 3 rev. vars.; see also next 2. Prohibitively rare above EF.

6578	1848 D Small thin stars. Rare.

Rev. normally aligned or 180° away. Explanation apparently as in **6544.** Discovery coins, "Melish":2046–47.

6579	1848 D "Large 1." Ex. rare.

Date unevenly logotyped, 1 exceptionally heavy, 848 progressively less so. Discovered by W. H. Woodin before 1914 but not again seen until 1968. The 6 pairs of 1848 O dies shipped remained unused.

6580	1849 [133,070] Normal date.

Large date, all mints, as on half cents. Minor positional vars. Ex. rare in AU.

6581	1849 Very thin numerals. Very rare.

Hairlike serifs and horizontal elements. From drastically repolished obv.

6582	1849 Doubled 49. Ex. rare.

Date high; 49 first punched too low, then corrected. Discovery coin, 1963 FUN:4224.

6583	1849 "Overdate." Ex. rare.

Discovered by W. H. Woodin, who called it "1849/47." Extremely heavy 9, first punched at an angle, then corrected. Discovery coin, Woodin, Boyd, WGC:402, UNC., $100 (1946). Mint tolerance henceforth ± 0.5 grs. = ± 0.032 gms.

6584	1849 C [64,823]

3 pairs of dies. Date high (ill. Akers {1979}) or low. Ex. rare UNC.

6585	1849 D [39,036] Rare.

3 pairs of dies shipped Sept. 20, 1848, received Oct. 1, plus 3 leftover revs. Minor positional vars. Ex. rare AU. The 6 1849 O obvs. shipped remained unused.

6586	1850 Large date. [64,491 + 1+P] Very scarce.

Open 5; may exist with closed 5 (knob touching cusp). Ex. rare above EF. For the proof see **6011, 6204.**

6587	1850 C [63,591]

3 pairs of dies plus leftovers. C weak or normal; at least 5 minor vars. Very rare AU. Seawater UNCs. exist.

6588	1850 D [43,984] Very scarce.

Mintage figure from Julian {1966B}. 3 pairs of dies received Dec. 22, 1849, one more Oct. 31, 1850. D weak or normal. Prohibitively rare above EF. The 4 1850 O obvs. shipped to New Orleans remained unused.

6589	1851 [377,505] Normal date.

Very large date, all mints. 6 obvs., 5 revs. Minor positional vars. Ex. rare above AU.

6590	1851 First 1 heavily repunched. Very rare.

6591	1851 C [49,176] Very scarce.

3 obvs., leftover revs. from 1849–50. Date high or central. Usually weak in centers. Very rare above EF; prohibitively rare UNC.

6592	1851 D [62,710] Normal date.

4 obvs., 5 old revs. Usually weak in centers. Ex. rare AU, prohibitively rare UNC.

6593	1851 D Mintmark far to r. Rare.

Mintmark above E and space to r. Discovered by W. H. Woodin. "Melish":2061; 1976 ANA:2972, $1,600.

6594	1851 D First 1 plainly repunched; D far to r.

Same comments as to **6592.** Rev. of **6593.**

6595	1851 D First 1 plainly repunched; normal rev.

Same comments as to **6592.**

6596	1851 O [41,000] Rare.

4 obvs., 2 revs. plus leftover dies from 1847–48. Prohibitively rare AU, unknown UNC.

6597	1852 [573,901]

Dates from half-cent logotype, all mints; 9 obvs., 5 revs. Several positional vars. exist. Auction 82:377, UNC., $1,650.

6598	1852 Thin numerals. Very scarce.

Hairlike serifs and horizontal elements.

6599	1852 C [72,574]

3 pairs of dies: 1 heavily imbedded in bust, barely touching, or well clear (logotype farther l. than usual). Ex. rare UNC. Seawater UNCs. from a ship salvaged about 1972.

6600	1852 D [91,452]

6 pairs of dies received Jan. 1; 3 obvs., 1 rev. shipped June 7. Minor positional vars., 1 touching or free of bust. Always weak in centers. Ex. rare UNC.; less rare in "seawater UNC."

(see introductory text). The 2 1852 O obvs. shipped remained unused.

6601 1853 [305,770]

Dates from half-cent logotype, all mints. Positional vars.; compare next 2. Very rare AU.

6602 1853 Doubled obv. die. Rare.

Doubling plainest on seventh through thirteenth stars.

6603 1853 Thin numerals. Very scarce.

Serifs and horizontal elements hairlike.

6604 1853 C [65,571]

3 obvs., leftover revs. Positional vars. only: 1 about touching bust or distant, with strong C; latter obv. also with very weak C. All scarcer than mintage figure suggests. Same comment as to **6599** about "seawater UNCs." "Bell," "Memorable," Bareford:173, $7,500, UNC.

6605 1853 D [89,678]

3 obvs. received Dec. 24, 1852, one pair Oct. 8, 1853, 2 revs. Nov. 1, 1853. Positional vars. only; rare earliest state of one rev. shows repunching on base of D. Usually weak in centers. Same comment as to **6599** about "seawater UNCs." "Bell," "Memorable," Bareford:174, $17,000, UNC. The 4 1853 O obvs. and the 6 pairs of 1853 S dies remained unused; for the latter, see introductory text.

6606 1854 [160,675 + 1+P] 54 about touch.

May exist with 5 4 apart. Several positional vars. Very rare above EF. The proof, from the set made for the City of Bremen, remains untraced. See **6610**.

6607 1854 C Open 5. [39,283] 54 about touch.

3 obvs., leftover revs. Ex. rare in EF. Weak C above E, or strong C above V or IV. Same comment as to **6599** about seawater UNCs. Director's Annual Report mintage figure [29,391] includes 8 assay coins of 1853 C lost in transit to the Assay Commission, Feb. 1854, from the same mixup that produced the purported mintage of 4 1854 C dollars: See introductory text, Chap. 32, Sect. i.

6608 1854 D Open 5. [All kinds 56,413] 54 about touch, strong D.

3 obvs. received about Jan. 1, 2 more June 30; leftover revs. Normally weak in centers and dentilated borders. Very rare above AU except as "seawater UNCs."

6609 1854 D 5 4 apart, strong D.

Obv. die sometimes rusty. Same comments on grade and striking.

6610 1854 D 5 4 apart, faint D.

Same obv., rusty. Specimens have been cherrypicked as Philadelphia coins. See WGC:518; "Melish":2076. Same comments as to **6608**.

6611 1854 O Open 5. [46,000] 5 4 free.

6 obvs., leftover revs. Often weakly struck. Very rare above AU.

6612 1854 S Closed 5. [268] 3 known.

Date low, 54 almost touch; knob of 5 touches cusp, unlike C, D, O coins; large (1.7 mm) S above E. 5 pairs of dies shipped, only one used; mintage limited owing to shortage of parting acids. Forgeries were reportedly created by joining split

halves (obv. of 1854, rev. of 1855 or '56 S), and may be made by affixing S mintmark to genuine Philadelphia coins. Authentication is mandatory. Survivors: 1) Pvt. coll., NYC, 1919, Waldo Newcomer, Col. Green, King Farouk, Josiah Lilly, SI. EF, rim nicks and scrapes. 2) Western coll. before 1941, Col. Green, Samuel W. Wolfson:448, $16,500, Mrs. R. Henry Norweb. EF. 3) F. C. C. Boyd, WGC:543, Eliasberg:471, $187,000, Stanley Kesselman. AU, ill.

6613 1855 Slanting 5's. [117,098 + ?P]

7 pairs of dies; positional vars. Very rare above AU. The proof reported by Wayte Raymond (before 1951) remains untraced.

6614 1855 Blundered date. Very rare.

Top of extra 1 in border below space between 18. Clashed dies.

6615 1855 Date slants crazily up to r. Rare.

Final 5 about touches truncation very close to corner. Ill. Akers {1979}.

6616 1855 C Slanting 5's. [39,788] Very scarce.

3 pairs of dies. Ex. rare in AU or above except as seawater UNCs. from the source of those of **6599**: See introductory text.

6617 1855 D Slanting 5's. [22,432] Very scarce.

3 pairs of dies, shipped Nov. 24, 1854. Same comments as to **6616**. To date 2 obv. vars., one with vertical crack from rim to bust grazing knob of first 5, the other with dot (chip?) between bases of 18.

6618 1855 O Slanting 5's. [11,100] Rare.

6 obvs. shipped, leftover revs.; to date 2 rev. vars., without or with small round hollow area atop second stripe. Often weakly struck. Usually in low grades; prohibitively rare above EF.

6619 1855 S Large S. [61,000] Very scarce.

7 obvs., 3 revs. plus leftovers. 3 vars.; date weaker or stronger. Prohibitively rare above EF.

6620 1856 Large date, upright 5. [197,900 + ?P]

15 pairs of dies. Positional vars.: date high, central, or lower; but see next. Very rare UNC. The proof reported by Wayte Raymond (before 1951) remains untraced.

6621 1856 Doubled rev. die. Rare.

Doubling plainest on UNITED and MERI. High date, 1 close to bust.

6622 1856 C Large date, upright 5. [28,457] Very scarce.

3 pairs of dies. Usually unevenly struck. Prohibitively rare AU. Seawater UNCs. exist.

6623 1856 D Large date, upright 5. [19,786] Very scarce.

3 pairs of dies, received Dec. 28, 1855, plus leftover revs. Rounded, beveled rims on all D mints 1855–61. Very rare above EF.

6624 1856 O Large date, upright 5. [10,000] Rare.

4 obvs., 2 revs. Without or with slight repunching on 1. Prohibitively rare above EF. 1980 ANA:252, AU, $1,400.

6625 1856 S Large date, upright 5. [All kinds 105,100] Large S. Very rare.

S 1.7 mm as 1854–55. Four obvs., 2 revs. received Dec. 1855, plus leftover revs. 2 minor vars. Discovered by William H. Woodin. Compare next.

6626 1856 S Medium S. Very scarce.

S 1.3 mm. 6 obvs., 4 revs. shipped March 1856. Several minor positional vars. Prohibitively rare above EF.

6627 1857 [98,188 + ?P]

Date from half-cent logotype on all mints. Scarcer than mintage figure suggests; very rare above AU. Minor positional vars.; date level or slanting up to r. Proofs (date slants sharply up to r.): 1) Ten Eyck, Clapp, Eliasberg:482, $39,600. 2) S 4/11/78:866, $23,000, S. Kesselman.

6628 1857 Repunched 185. Rare.

Discovery coin, NN 54:762. Late states with repunching faded out will price as preceding.

6629 1857 C [31,360] Very scarce.
Very rare in AU, prohibitively rare UNC. Usually weak in centers.

6630 1857 D [17,046] Very scarce.
2 pairs of dies received Jan. 4, 1857, plus leftovers; 3 rev. vars. Weakly struck in centers; beveled rims. Very rare UNC.

6631 1857 O [13,000] Rare.
Prohibitively rare above EF.

6632 1857 S Large S. [47,000]
S 1.7 mm, as in 1854–56. At least 2 positional vars. Prohibitively rare above EF.

6633 1857 S Small s. [40,000]
S 1 mm as in later years. Same grade comments as preceding.

6634 1858 [15,136 + ?P] Rare.
Ex. rare above EF. Auction 79:310, UNC., $9,000. Proofs have high date, die polish in all but rightmost stripe: 1) Mint, SI. 2) Cogan 3/29/1882:422 set, Randall, Morgan, ANS. 3) Ten Eyck, Clapp, Eliasberg:488, $39,600. 4) Parmelee, Woodin, Newcomer, Boyd, "Bell," Farouk, Ullmer:446, $60,000, Mocatta Metals, 1979 ANA:176, $44,000.

6635 1858 C [38,856]
2 rev. vars., the rarer one with over half of C above E. Very rare above EF; prohibitively rare UNC. Auction 79:311, UNC., $2,700.

6636 1858 D [all kinds 15,362] Large D. Very scarce.
Mintmark as previously; struck from leftover revs. Ill. Akers {1979}. Weak in centers; rims beveled, stars usually flat. Usually in low grades; Ex. rare above EF. Barnet, Auction 82:1408, UNC., $4,400. See next.

6637 1858 D Smaller D. Very rare.
Mintmark as in 1859–61, broader than it is tall. From 2 pairs of dies received Jan. 6. Same grade comments as preceding.

6638 1858 S Small s. [18,600] Rare.
S about 1 mm. 4 obvs. shipped Oct. 1857, 2 more March 1858; leftover revs. from 1857. Ex. rare above VF; unobtainable UNC.

6639 1859 "Type II" rev. [16,814 + 80–P] Rare.
Smaller date. New rev. hub: claws shorter, end farther from branch. 2 pairs of dies for business strikes. May exist with "Type I" rev. (old rev. hub of 1840–58). Ex. rare above EF. Most proofs were melted; fewer than 8 traced, including 1) Mint, SI. 2) Brock, Morgan, ANS. 3), 4) Royal Mint. 5) Mumford, Clapp, Eliasberg:492, $35,200.

6640 1859 C "Type I" rev. [31,847]
Old rev. hub of 1840–58. 2 vars.; rev. always weak, and on the less rare var. it is badly rusted (die of 1860–61). Very rare above EF; grade by obv. and surface. Sears, Clapp, Eliasberg:493, UNC., $8,800.

6641 1859 D "Type I" rev. [10,366] Very scarce.
Old rev. hub of 1840–58. Two pairs of dies received after Jan. 6. Weak in centers; rims beveled. Very rare above EF. 1980 ANA:256, UNC., $3,600.

6642 1859 S "Type I" rev. Small s. [13,220] Very rare.
4 obvs. shipped Nov. 1858, 2 more May 1859; leftover revs. of 1857. Only one var. seen. Usually in low grades, prohibitively rare above VF. 4 1859 O obvs. remained unused.

6643 1860 "Type II" rev. [19,763 + 62–P] Rare.
Smaller dates through 1863. May exist with "Type I" rev. Only one var. of business strikes seen; prohibitively rare above EF. Of proofs (April 5) at least 30 sold at Mint, rest melted Jan. 1862 as unsold. 1) Mint, SI. 2) Brock, Morgan, ANS. 3) Ely, Garrett:482, $18,000. 4) Ten Eyck, Clapp, Eliasberg:496, $17,600. 5) Carter:678, $10,450; others.

6644 1860 C "Type I" rev. [14,813] Normal date. Very scarce.
Rev. of **6640,** rusty, flat, weak; grade by surface and obv. detail. Ex. rare above EF.

6645 1860 C Double-punched date. Ex. rare.
Date first entered to l. of final position. Discovery coin, NN 49:441.

6646 1860 D "Type I" rev. [14,635] Very scarce.
2 pairs of dies plus leftovers; 3 minor vars. Very rare UNC.

6647 1860 S "Type I" rev. Small s. [21,200] Rare.
4 obvs. shipped Nov. 2, 1859; leftover revs. from 1857. Only one var. seen. Ex. rare EF, unobtainable above.

6648 1861 "Type II" rev. Heavy numerals. [695,864 + 66–P]
Many minor positional vars., most distinctive (very scarce) with date far to l., serifs of first 1 nearly lined up with end of truncation. At least 10 proofs melted Jan. 1862 as unsold; survivors have attenuated spiny tail feathers. Ten Eyck, Clapp, Eliasberg:500, $14,300.

6649 1861 Thin numerals. Rare.
Hairlike serifs and horizontal elements.

6650 1861 C "Type I" rev. Union issue. [5,992] Rare.
Low date; die file marks above UNITED and RICA. Usually unevenly struck. Prohibitively rare above AU. The 3 deliveries, [1,700] Feb. 28, [2,248] March 31, and [2,044] April 18, from one of the 2 obvs. and a leftover rev., cannot be told apart. Compare next.

6651 1861 C CSA issue. [887] Ex. rare.
Delivered May 1861. Same dies, rusted and cracked through tops of AMERI. Prohibitively rare choice.

6652 1861 D "Type I" rev. [1,597+] Very rare.
2 obvs. shipped Dec. 19, 1860, received Jan. 7, 1861, one put to press before Feb. 28 with an 1860 rev. Quantity coined by CSA after April 8 is unknown; see introductory text. Ex. rare above EF. Apparently always flat on claws, arrow butts, and arrowheads, and sometimes also on upper r. stars and parts of hair. Beveled rims. Clapp, Eliasberg:502, UNC., $37,400, Auction 84:1353, $41,800; Miles, Ullmer:448, $12,500, Auction 83:856, UNC., $30,800.

6653 1861 S "Type I" rev., small s. [18,000] Very rare.
2 obvs. shipped Nov. 1860, another June 1861; revs. left over from 1857. Only var. known has rev. of **6647.** Prohibitively rare above VF, unknown AU. Auction 80:935, EF+, $2,200.

6654 1862 "Type II" rev. [4,430 + 35P] Very rare.
3 pairs of dies for business strikes, apparently only one used, Sept. 15; almost all are VF–EF, prohibitively rare above. Proofs struck Feb. 16, low "center dot" on third pale gules; fewer than 12 traceable: Wilcox, Clapp, Eliasberg:504, $9,350, Kagin.

6655 1862 S "Type I" rev. Small s. [9,500] Very rare.
2 obvs. shipped in April, only one used; rev. of 1857. Prohibitively rare above VF, unknown above EF. Mitchelson, Clapp, Eliasberg:505, EF, $2,200.

6656 1863 "Type II" rev. [2,442 + 30P] Very rare.
Business strikes (April 20) are mostly VF–EF; prohibitively rare above EF. Of proofs (March 23) possibly 12 survive, including Clapp, Eliasberg:506, $13,200, and Carter:680, $17,600.

6657 1863 S "Type I" rev. Large S. [17,000] Very rare.
2 obvs. shipped Nov. 1862; leftover revs. Only one var. seen, rev. of 1856. S 1.7 mm. Prohibitively rare above VF.

6658 1864 "Type II" rev. [4,170 + 50P] Very rare.
Larger date, high, level, well to l., no die scratch below ear.

The [250] of Feb. 25 cannot be told from the [3,920] of Dec. 6. Usually VF to EF, Ex. rare in AU. Auction 79:313, UNC., $3,100. Possibly 12–15 proofs survive, all with horizontal die scratch below ear, including Auction 80:397, $29,000; Clapp, Eliasberg:508, $10,450.

6659 1864 S "Type I" rev. Large S. [3,888] Very rare.
4 obvs. shipped Oct. 1863; only one used (chip below ear), rev. of 1856. S 1.7 mm. Prohibitively rare above VF. Auction 79:314, EF, $3,900; Atwater, Eliasberg:509, EF/VF, $2,530.

6660 1865 "Type II" rev. [1,270 + 25P] Ex. rare.
One pair of dies for business strikes (Jan. 27): date centered, level, placed to l., chip between 65; usually VF to EF, prohibitively rare above. Proofs (March 8) lack the die chip; date slants down to r. About 8–10 survive, including Ullmer:450, $17,000; Garrett:483, $21,000; Wilcox, Clapp, Eliasberg:510, $17,600.

6661 1865 S [all kinds 27,612] "Type I" rev. Large S. Very rare.
3 obvs. shipped Nov. 1864; rev. of 1856. S 1.7 mm and always weak. Prohibitively rare above VF; unknown above EF. Roach, Eliasberg:511, EF, $1,210.

6662 1865 S Medium S. Ex. rare.
Discovery coin, Bolt:1021, Tex. pvt. coll. Rev. left over from 1857. Same grade comments.

6663 1866 S No motto. "Type I" rev. Large S. [9,000] Very rare.
3 obvs. shipped Nov. 1865, rev. of 1856. S 1.7 mm. Usually in low grades; prohibitively rare above VF. Eliasberg:512, VF+, $825.

viii. MOTTO ADDED (1866–1908)

The Act of March 3, 1865, which authorized coinage of shield nickels and issue of certain classes of interest-bearing Treasury notes, also ordered that henceforth all U.S. coins large enough to provide room for the motto IN GOD WE TRUST should bear those words. The Mint took this to mean the half eagle, eagle, double eagle, and all silver denominations larger than the dime. Two prototype (?) proof sets of the gold denominations were coined with motto and date 1865, possibly for Mint Director Linderman in 1867–68. Regular coinage followed in 1866 after the Secretary of Treasury approved Longacre's layout.

When collectors and dealers speak of "Liberty head half eagles" or "common gold fives" without other designation, they invariably mean only this type with motto. Most familiar of all U.S. gold below the $20 denomination, coins of this type were issued in enormous quantities (larger overall than all previous designs together). A common display item is a set of half eagles from all seven mints (the only denomination struck by them all); the three Southern coins will normally be of Coronet design without motto, the other four of the present type. So large were the mintages that even the Dahlonega and Carson City coins will not provide major difficulty unless one wishes mint-state examples. (But the vast majority from any mint, before 1879, will grade VF; some S- and CC-Mint coins are unknown in mint state.)

Except for 1873, even Philadelphia coins are rare prior to 1878. Until that year, specie payments were still suspended, gold was hoarded, and paper currency circulated instead, with the same goods or services on a two-tier pricing system: Prices were always quoted higher in greenbacks than in gold. Mintages in 1873 were large because the Treasury deposited quantities of worn-out and obsolete gold pieces for recoinage. Some dates are more often seen in proof state (generally impaired) than as business strikes, notably 1869, 1875, 1876, and possibly 1877. Later years 1878–1907 (except for the proof-only 1887 Philadelphia) constitute much of the bulk of "common gold," which is more often hoarded than collected, irrespective of date and mintmark. This hoarding practice delayed discovery of the obvious 1881/0 overdate for generations, because until recent years nobody had bothered to examine common gold more closely than sufficed to establish its genuineness.

San Francisco issued much more gold than Philadelphia for much of the period 1866–77. Nevertheless these early S-Mint coins are all scarce, some rare, and all very rare in mint state.

Carson City issues were limited for political reasons by orders from Mint Director Henry R. Linderman; Nevada bullion preferentially went to San Francisco. The excuse of limited output in turn was urged as reason to close the Carson branch, in 1885–88 and again for good in 1893. Because in 1872–73 it made some debased lightweight coins, Superintendent H. F. Rice was fired; he could have been executed. Distrust of CC coins led to routine testing; many survivors show edge test marks.

Limited New Orleans issues [136,600 total] reflect economic conditions in the postwar South: Little gold reached this branch mint for coinage of any denomination.

After the official resumption of specie payments (1878), the Treasury paid out immense numbers of half eagles to redeem worn-out greenbacks, National Bank notes, and interest-bearing notes. The coins eventually found their way into banks' cash reserves, many overseas; Lentex Corporation and other importers in the 1950s and '60s retrieved many from French and Swiss banks. With occasional exceptions like 1887–90 Philadelphia and 1892 O, most dates 1880–1907 are available for a price in or near mint state with the usual bag marks; business strikes free of nicks and scratches are rare.

Proofs 1866–1907 are rarer than their mintages suggest; many survivors are impaired. Those of 1880–86 are often nicked and scratched because the Medal Clerk at the Philadelphia Mint mishandled them (Breen {1977}, p. 182). Later ones were spent in depression years (1893, 1904, 1921, 1929–33) prior to the 1934 recall of gold.

The 1908 has long been rumored to exist in brilliant proof state, but this coin has remained unavailable for examination. In the ANS 1914 Exhibition, William H. Woodin displayed a group of proof Liberty head half eagles 1866–1908 inclusive. This might have been a typographical error, but then Morgenthau 382:300 (11/16/37) specifically described a 1908 "old type" in brilliant proof, as did Farouk:264. Considering in what haste the "Palace Collections of Egypt" had to be cataloged, it is entirely possible that a regular UNC. 1908 was mistakenly included with a group of proofs; but it is also possible that Farouk had the Woodin and/or Morgenthau coin.

MOTTO ADDED

Designer, Christian Gobrecht, obv. after Benjamin West, rev. after John Reich and William Kneass; motto scroll by James Barton Longacre. Engravers, Longacre, William Barber, Charles E. Barber. Mints, Philadelphia (no mintmark), New Orleans (mintmark O), San Francisco (S), Carson City (CC), Denver (D). Mintmark below eagle. Composition, gold 90%, silver not over 5%, rest copper. Weight 129 ± 0.5 grs. = 8.24 ± 0.032 gms. Reeded edge. Diameter, $^{17}/_{20}'' = 21.65$ mm. Authorizing Acts, Jan. 18, 1837; March 3, 1865; Feb. 12, 1873.

Grade range, POOR to UNC.; not collected below VERY FINE except for some extreme rarities. Grade standards, as before, except that for FINE expect complete but barely legible motto; for VERY FINE, full clear motto. These standards are in addition to those for 1839–66, not instead of them. NOTE: Beware coins showing any traces of solder removal.

6664 1865 Prototype. [2P] Proofs only.
Judd 445. Obv. of **6660** proof; rev. apparently as next.   1) Mint, SI. Clain-Stefanelli {1970}, fig. 40.   2) Mason & Co., 6/17/70:422 (in set with $10, $20), Woodin, Newcomer, Boyd, Farouk, pvt. coll. Ill. of **6665.**

6665 1866 [6,700 + 30P] Very rare.
Business strikes (Feb. 5) have date about central under bust; usually VF–EF, prohibitively rare above EF. Warning: Well-worn examples may be S-Mint coins with S faint: See next. Proofs (enl. ill. at **6664**) have date well to l.; the [25] of Jan. 15 cannot be told from the [5] of June 8. About 10–12 survive. Ely, Garrett:484, $23,000.

6666 1866 S Motto. Very small s. [34,920] Rare.
6 revs. shipped March 16, received April 14; obvs. were the 3 dies shipped Nov. 1865. This mintmark punch continues through 1879. Prohibitively rare in EF. On lower-grade examples, S is often faint and apt to be missed.

6667 1867 [6,870 + 50P] Very rare.
Business strikes have date central; prohibitively rare above EF. The [3,270] of Jan. 18 cannot be told from the [3,600] of June 8. Warning: Well-worn examples may be S-Mint coins with S faint: See next. Proofs have date high and to l. (ill. Akers {1979}); [25] each March 5 and July 2. Possibly 10 survive. H. P. Smith, Clapp, Eliasberg:515, $11,550; Carter:681, $16,500, D. Akers.

6668 1867 S [29,000] Very rare.
Usually in low grades; prohibitively rare above VF. Mitchelson, Clapp, Eliasberg:516, EF+, $1,210. Lower half of rev. usually weak. Specimens with weak S have been offered as Philadelphia coins.

6669 1868 [5,700 + 25P] Very rare.
Business strikes (Jan. 16) have date high (1 close to bust) and slanting down to r. Prohibitively rare above EF. Auction 80:936, UNC., $3,000. Proofs (Feb. 20) have 1 about centered between bust and border, date slanting down to r., rust above truncation, reversed C-shaped mark in hair l. of ear. About 10–12 survive; Carter:682, $11,000.

6670 1868 S [52,000] Very scarce.
Bottom of scroll weak, S sometimes weak. Prohibitively rare in EF.

6671 1869 [1,760 + 25P] Ex. rare.
Business strikes (Feb. 5) are usually EF to AU, partly proof-like; unobtainable UNC. Proofs (Feb. 19) have scroll incomplete below WE; about 10–12 survive. Eliasberg:519, $9,900.

6672 1869 S [31,000] Rare.
6 obvs. shipped Oct. 1868, not all used; leftover revs. 2 minor positional vars., both with weak S. Weakly struck; usually in low grades, prohibitively rare above VF.

6673 1870 [4,000 + 35P] Very rare.
Business strikes (Jan. 17) are nearly as rare as 1869; prohibitively rare above EF. Date slightly below center. Proofs have high date, slanting down to r.; the [25] of Feb. 3 cannot be told from the [10] of June 1. About 12 survive; Carter:683, $13,200, R. Hughes.

6674 1870 S [17,000] Rare.
The 3 deliveries cannot be told apart: [3,000] August; [6,000] September; [8,000] December. 2 minor positional vars. from 4 pairs of dies shipped Dec. 1869. Usually in low grades; prohibitively rare EF.

6675 1870 CC [7,675] Very rare.
Mintage began March 1 [400]. Usually in low grades; prohibitively rare above VF, only 2 AU's reported: 1) Auction 79:1248, $7,250, 1982 ANA:2675, $2,300.   2) 1979 ANA:182, $6,300. Because a CC mintmark could be affixed to genuine Philadelphia coins, or onto S mints from which S had been removed, authentication is necessary.

6676 1871 71 nearly touch. [3,200 + 30P] Very rare.
Business strikes are almost all VF–EF; prohibitively rare above EF. The 2 deliveries cannot be told apart: [2,800] Feb. 6; [400] Dec. 21. Proofs have minute repunching on first 1 (fades); possibly 8–10 survive, including 1980 ANA:259, $27,000; H. P. Smith, Clapp, Eliasberg:524, $18,700.

6677 1871 S 71 about touch. [25,000] Very scarce.
4 obvs. received 12/16/1870. Usually VF–EF; prohibitively rare above, unknown UNC. Eliasberg:526, AU+, $2,420. Compare next.

6678 1871 S Double-punched date. Very rare.
Date first entered low, then corrected higher (about central). Discovery coin, "Bell," Eliasberg, "H. R. Lee," NN 49:448.

6679 1871 CC 71 about touch. [20,770] Rare.
Date slants down to r.; rev. of **6675**. Usually in low grades; prohibitively rare EF. Auction 79:1249, $9,000, Auction 80:937, $6,000, UNC.

6680 1872 [1,660 + 30P] Very rare.
Business strikes (Jan. 13) are usually EF; UNCs. are from a tiny hoard (possibly 10) which turned up about 1958, all somewhat prooflike. High date to l., scroll incomplete, scattered faint die file marks above TED and TES. Auction 79:316, UNC., $4,500. Proofs (Feb. 3) have date a little below center, normal scroll. Possibly 12 survive; Clapp, Eliasberg:527, $11,000; Carter:684, $14,850.

6681 1872 S [36,400] Rare.
4 obvs. shipped Nov. 1871; leftover revs., not all used. Most survivors are F to VF; prohibitively rare EF.

6682 1872 CC [16,980] Rare.
2 obvs. shipped. Usually in low grades; prohibitively rare EF.

6683 1873 Closed 3. [49,280? + 25P]
Mintage figures from Harry X Boosel, including [1,800] Jan. 29, and [48,200] Nov. 5–8; these batches not distinguishable. Usually VF or EF; Ex. rare above. Warning: Low-grade examples may be S-Mint with weak S. Proofs (Feb. 18) have date to l., slanting slightly down to r. About 9–12 survive, some impaired. Ely, Garrett:455, $21,000; Carter:685, $14,300. Enl. photo. Mint tolerance hereafter ± 0.25 grs. = ± 0.016 gms.

6684   1873 Open 3. [63,200]
Mintage figure from Boosel, comprising coins delivered Nov. 19–29. Same grade range and comments. Enl. photo.

6685   1873 S Closed 3. [31,000] Very rare.
4 obvs. shipped Nov. 1872; not all used. Usually in low grades; Ex. rare above VF, unknown AU. Mintmark weak and may escape notice.

6686   1873 CC Closed 3. [7,416] Very rare.
3 obvs. shipped; only one var. seen, date low and slanting up to r. Weakly struck, usually in low grades; prohibitively rare above VF, unknown UNC. 1976 ANA:2998, AU, $2,700.

6687   1874 Normal rev. [20P] Proofs only. Ex. rare.
Delivered Feb. 14; date well to l. Not over 10 survive. Ely, Garrett:486, $26,000; Clapp, Eliasberg:533, $15,400; Carter:686, $18,700.

6688   1874 Doubled rev. die. [3,488] Very rare.
Date slants down to r.; doubling on UNITED STATES. Usually VF to EF; prohibitively rare above.

6689   1874 S [16,000] Very rare.
Date well to l.; weak S. Usually in low grades; prohibitively rare above VF, unknown AU.

6690   1874 CC [21,198] Very scarce.
CC wide (ill. Akers {1979}) or closer with second C higher. Usually in low grades; Ex. rare in EF. Robison I:498, UNC., $19,000.

6691   1875 [200 + 20P] Ex. rare.
Business strikes have l. base of 1 left of center of dentil; fewer than 5 known. 1) Wolfson, 74ANA:884, AU; 2) Boyd, WGC:429, VF. Authentication mandatory; compare descriptions of next 3. Proofs (Feb. 13) have l. base of 1 r. of center of dentil; possibly 8–10 survive. Garrett (1976):454, $81,000; Mumford, Clapp, Eliasberg:536, $60,500.

6692   1875 S [9,000] Very rare.
4 obvs. shipped Sept. 1874. Only one var. seen: thin stars, much of scroll incomplete (especially at TRUST). Prohibitively rare EF, unknown UNC.

6693   1875 CC [all kinds 11,828] Normal rev., close CC. Very rare.
Usually, plain rust pits around UNITED and eagle, one very prominent below E(D). Ill. Akers {1979}. Always in low grades, obv. weak.

6694   1875 CC Doubled rev. die, wider C C. Very rare.
Second C low; doubling at FIVE D. Same grade comments.

6695   1876 [1,432 + 45P] Very rare.
Business strikes (ill. Akers {1979}) have low date, lump on cheek vertically below pupil (on level with earlobe). Most are EF, a few UNC. Auction 80:938, $5,000. Proofs have lump on neck just below jaw, vertically above 1. The [20] of Feb. 19 cannot be told from the [25] of June 13. Possibly 14–18 survive. Clapp, Eliasberg:539, $11,000; Carter:687, $15,400.

6696   1876 S [4,000] Very rare.
Incuse center punch in earlobe; S always weak. Usually in low grades; prohibitively rare above VF. W. J. Jenks, Garrett (1976):487, $34,000.

6697   1876 CC [6,887] Rare.
Lump on neck below jaw. Without or with doubling on UNITED FIVE D., but in available grades this is almost indistinguishable. Prohibitively rare above EF. Clapp, Eliasberg:540, UNC., $26,400.

6698   1877 [1,132 + 20P] Very rare.
Business strikes (1 obv., 2 revs. made) have centered date, rust pits on neck; most are EF. Carter:688, AU, $2,860. Authentication is necessary to exclude removed mintmarks. Proofs have low date, rust pits on chin; the [10] each of Feb. 24 and May 31 cannot be told apart. Garrett (1976):488, $21,000; Auction 80:939, $27,000; D. S. Wilson, Clapp, Eliasberg:542, $20,900.

6699   1877 S [26,700] Very scarce.
S usually weak. Usually in low grades; prohibitively rare above EF.

6700   1877 CC [8,680] Rare.
Usually in low grades; prohibitively rare above EF.

6701   1878 [131,720 + 20P] Thin numerals.
Business strikes have hair-thin serifs and tops and bases of 8's; but compare next 2. Proofs (Feb. 9) have open mouth (inner lip details gone), polished area at ERT. Not over 9 survive; D. S. Wilson, Clapp, Eliasberg:545, $14,300.

6702   1878 Heavy numerals.
Thick base and serif to 1; thick tops and bases of 8's. Positional vars. exist.

6703   1878 Partly repunched date. Rare.
Junction of upper and lower loops of a low 8 within lower loop of 8. Gilhousen:1503; discovery coin, Tex. pvt. coll.

6704   1878 S [144,700]
Minor positional vars. Rare in UNC.

6705   1878 CC [9,054] Very rare.
Always in low grades; prohibitively rare in EF, unknown AU. Auction 80:398, EF, $3,100; Eliasberg:546, EF, $2,200.

6706   1879 New obv. hub. [301,920 + 30P]
Light dent on top point of seventh star, rather than the notch seen there 1864–78. Minor positional vars. The [20] proofs of Jan. 25 cannot be told from the [10] of Nov. 22; die polish at ERT, eye, ear, and WE ST. Mint, Garrett:489, $16,000.

6707   1879 S New obv. hub. [426,200]
Minor positional vars. of date and S, some with traces of repunching. Final appearance of the tiny S common since 1866.

6708   1879 CC New obv. hub. [17,281] Scarce.
Usually in low grades.

6709   1880 [all kinds 3,166,400 + 36P] Normal date.
Many positional vars. of business strikes; compare next. The [20] proofs of Feb. 14 cannot be told from the [16] of Oct. 2. Possibly fewer than 10 survive. Mint, Garrett:490, $18,000; Clapp, Eliasberg:551, $12,100.

6710   1880/9. Very rare.
Knob of 9 within lower part of 0. Discovery coin, "Gilhousen":509.

6711   1880 S Taller S. [1,348,900]
The new S punch continues through 1906. Many positional vars., some with minor traces of repunching.

6712   1880 CC [51,017]
At least 3 positional vars. Very rare in AU.

6713   1881 [all kinds 5,708,760 + 42P] Normal date.
Many positional vars.; compare next 2. Probably fewer than 15 proofs survive, some impaired. Eliasberg:554, $11,000; Carter:693, $13,200.

6714 1881 Double date. Rare.

At least 4 vars.; price for either ill. Those with more of initial date position visible command higher premiums.

6715 1881/0 Very scarce.

2 vars. That ill. was discovered in 1969. Base of scroll, attenuated above eagle's eye, fades out on later states. The other var. has the 1880 date low, slanting up to r., the 1881 date higher and level; discovered about 1979.

6716 1881 S [969,000] Normal S.

Many positional vars., some with light repunching on S. Compare next.

6717 1881 S over O. Presently very rare.

The small o is clear at center of S; not to be confused with filled mintmark. Discovered by Jay Miller, Jan. 1982.

6718 1881 CC Taller CC. [13,886] Rare.

Taller CC continues through 1893 except as noted. Usually in low grades; prohibitively rare above EF.

6719 1882 [2,514,520 + 48P]

Many minor positional vars. Probably fewer than 15 proofs survive, some impaired; Clapp, Eliasberg:557, $12,100.

6720 1882 S [969,000] Tall filled S.

Many positional vars., some with minor repunching on S. Revs. returned to Philadelphia Mint for inspection and reuse; some showed alterations to outer edge of tail and branch, and "added stems." The altered dies are unidentified, but may occur on S-Mint coins of later dates.

6721 1882 S Tall clear S. Very scarce.

No trace of filling, especially in "holes" above and below middle stroke of S. 2 vars., one with traces of repunching. NN 55:1029.

6722 1882 CC Tall CC. [82,817]

6723 1883 [233,400 + 61P]

Several minor positional vars.; scarcer UNC. than mintage figure suggests. Proofs have date slanting sharply up to r. (ill. Akers {1979}); fewer than 20 survive, some impaired. Clapp, Eliasberg:560, $11,000.

6724 1883 S [83,200] Very scarce.

Usually in low grades; very rare above VF. Same comment as to **6720** about returned dies.

6725 1883 CC Small roundish cc. [12,958] Very scarce.

From a leftover die of 1880 or earlier. Usually in low grades; prohibitively rare above EF. The usual tall CC, reported long ago, remains unverified.

6726 1884 [191,030 + 48P] 8 4 apart.

Business strikes and proofs; latter have heavy 1 with a rust pit on lower part of its upright. Fewer than 12 proofs survive, some impaired; Auction 79:319, $8,000; Clapp, Eliasberg:563, $8,250.

6727 1884 84 touch.

Positional vars. exist. Probably the same date logotype, more heavily entered.

6728 1884 S [177,000] 84 touch.

Several positional vars.; compare next. Usually in low grades; Ex. rare in AU.

6729 1884 S 8 4 apart. Rare.

6730 1884 CC Tall CC. [16,402] 84 touch. Very scarce.

Prohibitively rare in AU. Often weakly struck. Only one var.; line through RTY.

6731 1885 [601,440 + 66P] Closed 5.

Knob touches cusp; positional vars. exist. Business strikes may exist with "open 5" (knob away from cusp): compare **6733.** Sometimes shows traces of repunching atop 5. Probably under 25 proofs survive, some impaired; Clapp, Eliasberg:566, $9,900.

6732 1885 S [1,211,500] Closed 5.

Knob touches cusp. Many minor positional vars., often with filled S.

6733 1885 S Open 5.

Knob free of cusp; thin date; clear S. Uncertain if different logotype, light impression from regular one, or lapped dies.

6734 1886 [388,360 + 72P]

Minor positional vars. Possibly only 20–24 proofs survive, some impaired. Clapp, Eliasberg:568, $9,350.

6735 1886 S [all kinds 3,268,000] Normal S.

Many minor positional vars.; S usually filled, sometimes showing traces of repunching.

6736 1886 S Triple S. Very rare.

Parts of extra S's l. and r. of final position.

6737 1887 [87P] Proofs only. Very rare.

Possibly 30 survive, many impaired. Ullmer:460, $18,000 (1974); Eliasberg:570, $22,000; Carter:699, $16,500. Coins offered in lower grade must be authenticated because many forgeries were made by removing S from 1887 S coins, and some of these have date position same as the proof. Enl. photos.

6738   1887 S [1,912,000]

Same comment as to **6735**. A hoard of at least 25 UNCs. turned up in Long Beach, Calif., 1985.

6739   1888 [18,202 + 94P] Very scarce.

Business strikes have low date to r.; usually EF to AU, very rare AU or above. Proofs have low date to l. Possibly 30–35 survive, some impaired. Clapp, Eliasberg:572, $5,500.

6740   1888 S [293,900]

Minor positional vars. Usually VF; very rare above.

6741   1889 [7,520 + 45P] Rare.

Business strikes have date slightly below center of space, die file marks across white stripes of shield. Usually EF–AU; very rare UNC. Proofs have low date slanting slightly up to r.; under 20 survive. Earle, Clapp, Eliasberg:574, $12,100.

6742   1890 [4,240 + 88P] Very rare.

Business strikes have date well to r., low with chip below B; top curl on back of neck severed. Usually EF to AU; prohibitively rare UNC. Proofs have date well to l.; fewer than 30 survive. Walters, Clapp, Eliasberg:575, $12,100.

6743   1890 CC [53,800]

6744   1891 [61,360 + 53P] Scarce.

Business strikes are usually EF to AU; Ex. rare UNC. Proofs have attenuated tail feathers just above leaf; possibly 25–30 survive. Mougey, Clapp, Eliasberg:577, $9,900.

6745   1891 CC [208,000]

6746   1892 [753,480 + 92P]

Minor positional vars. of business strikes. Proofs have date low, to l. (like some UNCs.); under 30 survive, some not well struck up in centers. Mint, Clapp, Eliasberg:579, $7,700; Carter:703, $9,350.

6747   1892 O [10,000] Rare.

Medium roundish O, narrow slit opening. Usually EF–AU; unobtainable choice. Authentication recommended to exclude affixed mintmarks. Eliasberg:581, AU, $2,640.

6748   1892 S [298,400]

Minor positional vars. Usually in low grades; Ex. rare in AU.

6749   1892 CC [82,968] Normal CC.

Rarely from drastically repolished die: scroll broken, WE in field. Positional vars. are possible. Compare next.

6750   1892 CC Double-punched CC. Very rare.

Discovery coin, Eliasberg, "H. R. Lee," NN 49:487.

6751   1893 [1,528,120 + 77P]

Minor positional vars. Proofs have date well to l. Mint, Clapp, Eliasberg:583, $8,250, Kagin; Carter:705, $8,250.

6752   1893 O [110,000]

Larger mintmark than **6747**. Centered or low date, latter sometimes with shattered dies. Usually EF or AU, rare UNC.

6753   1893 S [224,000]

At least 3 positional vars. Same grade comment.

6754   1893 CC [60,000]

Date central or low to l.; latter ill. Akers {1979}. First C low. Usually VF to EF, scarce AU, rare UNC.

6755   1894 [957,882 + 75P]

Minor positional vars. Proofs have date high to l., slanting up to r., 4 close to truncation (ill. Akers {1979}); rarer than mintage suggests. Eliasberg:587, $8,250; Carter:706, $8,250.

6756   1894 O [16,600] Scarce.

Mintmark as in **6752**, slightly asymmetrical, l. part thicker. 4 positional vars. Usually EF to AU; very scarce UNC., rare choice.

6757   1894 S [55,900] Very scarce.

Mintmark normal or with traces of repunching. Usually VF; prohibitively rare above AU.

6758   1895 [1,345,855 + 81P]

Date varies greatly in position: central; low and level; low and slanting up to r.; far to l. Proofs have low date to l. Eliasberg:590, $8,250; Carter:707, $9,350.

6759   1895 S [112,000] Scarce.

Same grade comment as to **6754.**

6760   1896 [58,960 + 103P] Normal rev. Scarce.

2 positional vars. of date. Usually EF to AU, rarely choice. Proofs have date low to l. Mint, Clapp, Eliasberg:592, $9,350.

6761   1896 Doubled rev. die. Very rare.

Doubling plain on legend. Same grade comments.

6762   1896 S [155,400] Scarce.

Minor positional vars. Same grade comment as to **6757**.

6763   1897 [867,000 + 83P]

Minor positional vars. Proofs have date low to l., slanting up to r. Mint, Clapp, Eliasberg:594, $8,250.

6764   1897 S [354,000]

Minor positional vars. Very rare above AU, Ex. rare in UNC. Mint, Clapp, Eliasberg:595, $13,200.

6765   1898 [633,420 + 75P]

Minor positional vars. Possibly 25 proofs survive; Mint, Clapp, Eliasberg:596, $11,000; Carter:713, $22,000.

6766   1898 S [1,397,400]

Minor positional vars.; S clear, partly filled, or minutely doubled.

6767   1899 [all kinds 1,710,630 + 99P] Normal date, open 9's. Knob of 9 away from loop. Minor positional vars. Proofs have low date to l. Mint, Clapp, Eliasberg:598, $6,050; Carter:714, $22,000.

6768   1899 Normal date, closed 9's.

Knob of 9 joins loop. Minor positional vars.

6769   1899 Repunched 99. Rare.

Parts of extra 9's show at l. of loops. 1983 Midwinter ANA:1637, others.

6770   1899/8 Open 9's. Ex. rare.

Lower loop of 8 plain within lower part of 9 and between knob and loop of 9. Discovery coin, Miles:557, Tex. pvt. coll.

6771   1899 S [1,545,000] Open 9's.

Minor positional vars. May exist with closed 9's. 2 proofs reported: 1) Col. Green proof set (other coins Philadelphia), Ronnie Carr. 2) Dr. Green:473.

6772   1900 [1,405,500 + 230P] Normal date and stars.

Minor positional vars. Proofs have low date. Mint, Clapp, Eliasberg:600, $7,150; Carter:715, $14,300.

6773   1900 Double-punched date. Very rare.

Discovery coin, NN 49:502.

6774 1900 Doubled obv. die. Proofs only. Very rare.
Doubling plainest on stars. Forms a minority of proofs. Discovery coin, NN 51:991.

6775 1900 S [329,000] Normal date.
Very rare in UNC. Beware prooflike oversize forgeries with edge reeding unusually widely spaced. Any prooflike coin offered should be authenticated.

6776 1900 S Double-punched date. Very rare.
Parts of extra zeros plain within upper parts of 00. Discovery coin, Miles:560, Tex. pvt. coll.

6777 1901 [615,900 + 140P] Normal date.
Minor positional vars. Proofs have low date to l. Carter:716, $20,900.

6778 1901 Partly repunched date. Very scarce.
One var. has first 1 double at base, and spine from dentils near eleventh star; the other has final 1 repunched (NN 49:504).

6779 1901 S [3,648,000] Normal date.
Many minor positional vars. Plentiful in choice UNC. from old hoards. Brand I: 368, AU, has S/smaller s (25¢ punch?).

6780 1901/0 S Very scarce.
Discovered by Ted Clark, Feb. 1973. 1980 ANA:276, UNC., $1,100. Later die states with less of the zero showing on either side of final 1 command less premium.

6781 1902 [172,400 + 162P]
Minor positional vars. Proofs have low date to l.; Carter:717, $13,750. All proofs 1902–07 have devices semibrilliant rather than frosty as heretofore.

6782 1902 S [939,000]
Minor positional vars.; without or with light repunching on S.

6783 1903 [226,870 + 154P]
Minor positional vars. Many proofs are impaired; choice: Eliasberg:606, $10,450; Carter:718, $15,400.

6784 1903 S [1,855,000]
Minor positional vars.

6785 1904 [392,000 + 136P]
Minor positional vars. Proofs have spine down from toe of L, outer leaf in upper group short, thin; top outer berry claw-like; hollow in wing below (I)N. Eliasberg:608, $7,700.

6786 1904 S [97,000] Scarce.
With (rarely) or without light repunching at top of 9; sometimes with cracks through first 6 stars. Usually VF; rare above EF, very rare UNC. Mint, Clapp, Eliasberg:609, $12,100.

6787 1905 Normal date. [302,200]
Date high, low, or central.

6788 1905 Repunched 5. [108P] Proofs only.
Date well to l.; top of 5 plainly double. Mint, Clapp, Eliasberg:610, $7,700.

6789 1905 S [880,700]
At least 5 minor positional vars.

6790 1906 [all kinds 348,735 + 85P] Normal date, open 6. Scarce.
Knob away from loop. Minor positional vars.

6791 1906 Normal date, closed 6.
Knob joined to loop. Proofs have high date. Mint, Clapp, Eliasberg:612, $9,350.

6792 1906 Overdate. Ex. rare.
Heavy repunched date, closed 6, part of another digit within loop, its curvature not matching that of 6. Hirt:1578; others. Not over 6 seen.

6793 1906 S [598,000] Open 6.
As **6790.**

6794 1906 S Closed 6.
As **6791.**

6795 1906 D [320,000] Open 6.
Minor positional vars. This may exist in proof state celebrating the beginning of coinage at this branch.

6796 1906 D Closed 6.
Positional vars., some with repunching on D. One var. has D leaning crazily to l. Nothing is known about respective rarity of these.

6797 1907 [626,100 + 92P] Normal date.
Minor positional vars. Zug, Clapp, Eliasberg:615, Proof, $9,350.

6798 1907 Partly repunched date.
Repunching plainest at base of 1 and top of 7. 1982 ANA:2683, others. On earlier die states, repunching also shows above base of 0.

6799 1907 D [888,000]
Minor positional vars.

6800 1907 D Repunched 7. Presently rare.
The 7 first punched to r. of final position. 1982 ANA:2684, others.

6801 1908 [421,874 + ?P]
Minor positional vars. Proofs untraced; see introductory text.

ix. PRATT'S INDIAN HEAD DESIGN (1908–29)

One of the fulfillments of Pres. Theodore Roosevelt's "pet crime" plan—improving coinage designs, bypassing the stupefying mediocrity of Mint Engraver Barber—was issue of gold coins in the new design by Bela Lyon Pratt. The story behind this design is in Chap. 33, Sect. viii, introductory text. To this same "pet crime" project we owe the magnificent St. Gaudens eagles and double eagles, and ultimately also the Lincoln cent and buffalo nickel, undisputedly making this period the zenith of American coinage art, at least for sheer numbers of excellent designs introduced to circulation. (Barber got his revenge by watering down the designs.)

Nevertheless, hardly were the first Pratt half eagles out of the Mint before traditionalists began attacking the design on flimsy grounds. Earlier I cited S. Hudson Chapman's objections. A more serious criticism which could have been raised is that Barber ordered mintmarks to be placed just l. of arrowheads, failing to notice that the O, S, or D will be weakly struck and wear down in that location more quickly than any other detail.

As a result, some of the rarer dates like 1908 S and 1909 O come so weak that mintmarks are difficult to read with certainty, and occasionally the ungodly either affix an O to a genuine Philadelphia coin or alter 1909 D to simulate the rarer mintmark.

A consequence of a different kind is the 1916 without mintmark S. Though the Philadelphia Mint issued no half eagles in 1916, at least two survivors lack the mintmark. These are generally thought to be 1916 S's weakly struck so that S does not show. The only one I have examined is strong enough to make that conclusion dubious. Alternative possibilities include foreign matter in the die clogging the mintmark, lapping to remove clash marks, and inadvertent omission of mintmark. As neither specimen reported is uncirculated, the question remains undecidable.

Aside from this var., the rarest Pratt half eagles in mint state are 1909 O, 1915 S, 1911 D, and most other S-Mint issues. In other grades, 1929 is unquestionably rarest. It remained unrecognized until March 1944, when a specimen estimated at a routine $25 at auction brought nine times that figure. During ensuing decades, at least 60 specimens (mostly mint state with varying amounts of bag marks) were dispersed from original rolls; a fourth roll of 20 remained in private hands in 1978. Dispersal has been slow to avoid depressing the market.

Proofs 1908–15 are much rarer than those of the preceding decade, rarer than their reported mintages suggest. Doubtless heirs mistakenly spent some, and turned in others during the Great Recall of 1934. Reportedly, many of the [75P] of 1915, with some unsold 1914's, went to the Mint's melting pots in Jan. 1917. These proofs use several variants of the matte, sandblast, and satin finishes. The list herein (as in Breen {1977}) is doubtless incomplete, but any authentic proof of an unlisted finish will be an extreme rarity. Fraud artists have simulated proofs by sandblasting business strikes; but the real proofs have much more sharpness of detail (especially on feathers). Edges are much sharper than on business strikes. Some of these fraudulently altered coins aroused suspicion because the sandblast finish covered nicks and scratches. Authentication is recommended.

The Coinage Act of July 23, 1965 (PL 89-81), Sect. 392, has apparently restored legal-tender status to half eagles.

PRATT'S INDIAN HEAD DESIGN

Designer, Bela Lyon Pratt. Engraver, Charles E. Barber, after Pratt. Mints, Philadelphia (no mintmark), New Orleans (mintmark O), San Francisco (S), Denver (D). Mintmarks l. of arrowheads. Physical Specifications, Authorizing Acts, as before.

Grade range, VERY GOOD to UNC.; not collected below VERY FINE. FINE: Knot of hair cord visible; partial feather contours both sides; full date, letters, and stars, but no central details. VERY FINE: Over half headband details; hair-cord knot clear; partial internal details to Indian's feathers; partial details on breast and leg feathers, over half wing-feather details. EXTREMELY FINE: Isolated tiny rubbed spots only; partial mint luster. UNCIRCULATED: *No* trace of wear; look on cheekbone, headdress below BE, and shoulder of wing (below back of eagle's neck). NOTE: Mintmarked coins are often weak in centers and at mintmarks.

6802   1908 [577,845 + 167–P]
Proofs (enl. photos) have dark matte finish. Green {1936}, p. 139, claims that fewer than 100 gold proof sets were issued, the rest melted, Jan. 2, 1909; unconfirmed but probable: Garrett:496, $24,000; Mitchelson, Clapp, Eliasberg:618, $7,150.

6803   1908 S [82,000] Very scarce.
Usually in low grades. The Brand estate contained many UNCS., and others turned up since 1968. Auction 82:1948, UNC., $5,500.

6804   1908 D [148,000]
A hoard of at least 50 UNCS. turned up in 1976.

6805   1909 [627,060 + 78P]
Available in all grades short of gem mint state, rarely then. Proofs (except for next number) are of the "Roman gold" finish: semibrilliant, satiny. Garrett:497, $23,000; Auction 80:413, $30,000; Mint, Clapp, Eliasberg:621, $12,100.

6806   1909 Dark matte proof. Ex. rare.
DiBello:1004, Auction 81:1868, $17,000. Authentication recommended.

6807   1909 O [34,200] Very scarce.
Usually VF to EF, weakly struck; Ex. rare in mint state. Enl. photos. 2 vars.: Mintmark double-punched, or normal and weakly punched. Authentication recommended; l. side of mintmark must be clear and free of monkey business. Mitchelson, Clapp, Eliasberg:623, UNC., $30,800, Auction 83:404; Johnson-Meyer:1315, Auction 79:1279, UNC., $33,000.

6808   1909 S [297,200]
The peculiar die marks on Indian's neck (ill. Akers {1979}) are probably clash marks. Very rare in mint state; Auction 79:1280, UNC., $4,200.

6809   1909 D [3,423,560] Normal D.
Over 1,000 UNCS. turned up in South America about 1955; a smaller hoard surfaced in 1976.

6810   1909 D Solid D.
No opening within mintmark. Many of these were in the hoards.

6811   1910 [604,000 + 250P]
Plentiful except in gem UNC., then rare. Proofs have "Roman gold" finish, like 1909; claims of dark matte proofs like 1908 or 1911 remain unverified. Garrett:498, $19,000; Mint, Clapp, Eliasberg:625, $12,100; Carter:724, $22,550.

6812   1910 S [770,200]
Often weakly struck. Usually VF to EF; very rare UNC.

6813   1910 D [193,600] Normal D.
Usually VF to EF; formerly rare UNC., but a hoard of 283 showed up in 1980. Some of these may have had the **6814** rev.

6814   1910 D Solid D.
Same comments.

6815   1911 [915,000 + 139P]
Proofs have dark matte finish like 1908 but differing slightly in texture of grain: Garrett:499, $18,000; Pena, Clapp, Eliasberg:628, $13,200; Carter:725, $24,200. Dangerous forgeries exist: 13th star incomplete, top of (E)D rough. Ill. *CW* 4/30/86, p. 82.

6816   1911 S [1,416,000]
S often weak or blobby; positional vars. exist. Common in VF or EF, rare in UNC.

6817   1911 D [72,500] Very scarce.
Only one pair of dies. Ex. rare UNC.; beware "sliders."

6818   1912 [790,000 + 144P]
Proofs have fine sandblast finish, like 1913. Under a microscope they show millions of minute shiny facets: Garrett:500, $26,000; Auction 80:416, $30,000; Clapp, Eliasberg:631, $13,200.

6819   1912 S [392,000]
Same comment as to **6816.** Often weakly struck.

6820   1913 [916,000 + 99P]
Proofs have same finish as 1912: Garrett:501, $19,000; Potts, Clapp, Eliasberg:633, $14,300.

6821   1913 S [408,000]
Same comment as to **6816.**

6822   1914 [247,000 + 125P]
Proofs have coarser sandblast finish than 1912–13; under a microscope they show larger facets: Garrett:502, $24,000; Eliasberg:635, $10,450. Hard to find choice UNC.

6823   1914 S [263,000]
Same comment as to **6816.** Very rare UNC.

6824   1914 D [247,000]
Mintmark often blurry. Many bag-marked UNCs. from an old hoard.

6825   1915 [588,000 + 75 – P]
Proofs have same finish as 1914; Ex. rare, some reportedly melted in Jan. 1917: Garrett:503, $27,000; Potts, Clapp, Eliasberg:638, $11,000, Kagin.

6826   1915 S [164,000] Very scarce.
Same comment as to **6816.** Often weakly struck. Usually F to EF. Pieces dated 1915 D are counterfeits made in the 1950s.

6827   1916 S [240,000]
Mintmark usually rather weak or blobby. Usually VF to AU, though many UNCs. turned up in El Salvador fairly recently. Auction 79:1288, UNC., $10,000.

6828   1916 No S. 2 known.
See introductory text. 1) Discovery coin, Morgenthau 382:311 (11/16/37), probably later F. C. C. Boyd, WGC:471, VF.   2) Richard DeMers, found about 1963.

6829   1929 [662,000 –] Very scarce.
Usually AU to UNC., unevenly struck, from original rolls; see introductory text. Dr. Clifford Smith, Auction 79:1289, $29,000; Eliasberg:641, $6,380; Auction 81:1857, $10,000. Most believed melted in 1934.

CHAPTER 37

EAGLES OR TEN-DOLLAR PIECES

i. SCOT'S SMALL EAGLE DESIGN (1795–97)

Mintage of only three denominations—the disme, the silver dollar, and the 10-dollar coin officially called the eagle—sufficed to commit American coinage firmly to the decimal system; and for years it seemed that coinage of these denominations had no other purpose, as they enjoyed little demand and less circulation. As we have seen, for decades the Mint's principal output consisted of one denomination in each metal: gold half eagles, silver half dollars, and copper cents. The half eagle seems to have been favored because its bullion value was conveniently close to that of many foreign coins of the period (British guineas and sovereigns, French louis d'or and 24 Livres coins, Portuguese/Brazilian 4,000 Reis and 2 Escudos, etc.); the half dollar because of its size; cents primarily as an alternative to privately made copper tokens.

However, the eagle, though specially named as our nation's gold monetary unit, was for various reasons inconvenient for international trade. It came near in value only to the French double louis and the British double guinea, neither commonly seen in commerce; it was too large for small transactions (in which guineas or louis d'or would be favored), but too small for convenient transportation or storage of large sums (compared to doubloons, five-guinea coins, or 12,800 Reis pieces). As all these foreign coins were legal tender in the United States, bankers preferred them over less familiar types, and accordingly they ordered far fewer eagles than half eagles coined from their deposits of bullion. During its entire history, 1795–1933, the eagle was coined in smaller quantities: just under 57.7 million pieces, compared to just under 79 million half eagles.

Some such advice from banker friends may have influenced Mint Director Henry William DeSaussure to order that half eagles be coined first: See Chap. 36, Sect. i, introductory text. Robert Scot's dies followed the half-eagle design exactly, the same sketches or engravings of some Roman goddess and that first-century Roman onyx cameo serving for both. He completed four pairs of dies for 1795 coins, but only three revs. went into use, the fourth being saved for 1796–97 issues. Their palm branch was an oblique heraldic reference to the southern homeland of Mint Director DeSaussure (possibly also to Gen. Washington?). Most survivors show 13 leaves on the branch; the third rev. (very rare) has only nine, the fourth (the 1796–97 die) 11. Out of the [5,583] coined between Sept. 22, 1795, and March 30, 1796, approximately 3% survive, mostly VF to AU with possibly a couple of dozen somewhat prooflike UNCs. saved as first of their kind. One of these went to Gen. Washington at Mount Vernon.

Coinage dated 1796 has 16 stars, rather than 15, alluding to

the admission of Tennessee to the Union as sixteenth state, June 1, 1796. The first eagles with 16 stars for circulation were delivered on June 2, probably preceded by prooflike presentation strikings in connection with the Tennessee celebrations (as with other denominations). Stars are divided 8 + 8 as on the quarter eagle. Of [4,146] made, just under 2% survive; this date is distinctly rarer than 1795 in all grades, though unappreciated because lacking the extra appeal of the first year of issue.

The final year is also the rarest. Its single var. has stars awkwardly arranged 12 + 4; this die broke at once. I have reconstructed its mintage as [3,615] March 25–May 2, 1797; if this is the correct period of issue, fewer than 1.5% survive.

In all, only six obvs. and four revs. were used in seven combinations, only one Ex. rare (1795 Nine Leaves), compared to the 11 pairs of dies for half eagles of this design. Completeness is possible for a price, and the set of seven would make an extremely impressive display.

SCOT'S SMALL EAGLE DESIGN

Designer, Engraver, Robert Scot. Mint, Philadelphia. Composition, gold $11/12 = 917$ Fine, rest copper with traces of silver. Weight standard 270 grs. = 17.496 gms. Diameter, about $2^{1}/16'' = 33.33$ mm. Reeded edge. Authorizing Act, April 2, 1792.

Grade range, GOOD to UNC.; rarely collected in low grades. FINE: Major contours of cap, hair, and drapery intact; leaves in palm branch and wreath can be counted and show partial internal detail. VERY FINE: Most folds clear in drapery and cap; partial detail on hair on cap, below ear, and behind head; all wing feathers separated except at tips, partial detail on leg, breast, and neck feathers. EXTREMELY FINE: Few isolated tiny rubbed spots; partial mint luster. UNCIRCULATED: *No* trace of wear. NOTE: Many specimens show adjustment marks = file marks inflicted on planchets before striking to reduce weight to standard. These are not impairments but must be mentioned in grading. Beware specimens showing traces of solder; look on top and bottom edges for discoloration, tool marks, interruption of edge reeding, repairs, or discoloration with local porosity.

6830 1795 [all kinds 5,583] Stars 10 + 5, 13 leaves in branch. 4 vars., Sept. 27, 1795–March 30, 1796. Usually VF to AU

with perhaps 20–30 prooflike UNCs., of which possibly 4 or 5 qualify as presentation strikings; these are from Breen 1-A = Hilt 1A dies, ill., least rare var. Earle, Clapp, Eliasberg:642, UNC., $39,600; Eliasberg:643, UNC., $57,200. The rarest var., Breen 3-B = Hilt 3C, has tenth star touching cap: Garrett:1655, UNC., $130,000.

6831 1795 9 leaves in branch. Ex. rare.

Breen 4-C = Hilt 2B. Possibly [116] March 30, 1796, + part of [1,169] March 19, 1796; Hilt thinks they comprised about 210 of the June 21, 1796 delivery. Usually with flan chips (foreign matter adhering to dies?). 1) Dr. Angus Black (ill.), UNC. 2) Kagin, Breen II:198, $11,000, 1977 ANA:5020, AU, $9,000. 3) "Cicero":61, Kagin 305:925 (1/3–4/75), EF, $16,000. 4) Manfra Tordella & Brookes "over the counter," EF. 5) Andrew M. Watson:1863, VF, scrubbed. 6) S 9/13/68:372, $2,300, "AU". 7) Granberg, Woodin, Newcomer, discovery coin, VF, unlocated, possibly same as one of preceding.

6832 1796 Stars 8 + 8. [4,146] Rare.

Breen 1-A = Hilt 4D, who thinks [3,615] of March 25–May 2, 1797; my figures represent deliveries June 2, 1796–Dec. 22, 1796. Eleven leaves in branch. Usually VF to AU, possibly 35–50 survivors; few lower grades; possibly 5–8 prooflike UNCs. Often weak in centers. Dohrmann, Garrett:1656, AU, $40,000; Pierce, Auction 82:941, UNC., $29,000.

6833 1797 Stars 12 + 4. [3,615] Very rare.

Breen 1-A = Hilt 5D, who thinks [1,907], June 7, 1797. Only one seen with unbroken dies; all others show break as ill., on last stages extending into neck and jaw. Possibly 25–30 VF to AU, 5 or 6 UNC. Mickley, Appleton, Garrett:1657, AU, $39,000; Carter:730, UNC., $30,250.

Ex J. W. Garrett: 1657. Courtesy Bowers & Ruddy Galleries, Inc.

ii. SCOT'S HERALDIC DESIGN
(1797–1804)

Robert Scot's designs for this denomination copied those of the quarter eagle. Ms. Liberty's buxom draped and capped effigy continued from 1795–97; the heraldic eagle derived from that of the Great Seal of the United States, but with the same blunder or ill-timed piece of saber rattling as on the smaller denominations: The warlike arrows are in the dexter or more honorable claw, outranking the olive branch for peace. Compare Chap. 24, Sect. iii, introductory text.

If the conjectured and reconstructed mintage figures of the previous section are correct, then eagle coinage of the new design must have begun with [10,840] between June 7, 1797, and Jan. 30, 1798. These coins have only 13 rev. stars, evidently immediately following Mint Director Boudinot's decision to stop adding a new star for every new state. (See introductory sections, Chap. 25, Sect. ii; Chap. 33, Sect. ii; Chap. 36, Sect. ii.) Their single obv. has 16 stars divided 10 + 6, evidently completed before that decision. Possibly 2% survive, mostly VF to EF.

Two of the three revs. have "cross" star arrangement (stars are in intersecting straight lines forming diamond-shaped patterns), as described in the introductory texts just cited; the third has the "arc" arrangement: a row of six paralleling clouds, a row of five under them, and the twelfth and thirteenth flanking beak and neck. The "cross" revs. are probably the earliest completed by whichever assistant or apprentice worked in 1798–99; if later research in pay records locates his name and inclusive dates, we may be able to deduce time of manufacture and use of these dies, and more accurate mintage figures.

The great rarities of this period are the two vars. dated 1798/7. The two deliveries of [900] and [842], Feb. 17 and 28, 1798, are believed to comprise, respectively, **6836** with stars 9 + 4, and **6837** with stars 7 + 6. Coinage of eagles was interrupted thereafter until May 14, 1799. Early breakage of both obv. dies may have been why.

In extreme contrast, the date 1799 (stars 8 + 5 henceforth) is one of the two most often seen of this design, the other being 1801. Between May 14, 1799, and Sept. 4, 1800, [37,449] were struck, all believed dated 1799. Of the five obvs. and seven revs. in 10 combinations, two are plentiful (Breen 4-E and 5-G, in **6840–41**), forming the majority of survivors of this date; with the 1801, they comprise the majority of this design. About 2% survive, including many UNCs. Some of these revs. 1799–1803 may be half-dollar dies.

Again in contrast, the single var. dated 1800 (believed to comprise only the [5,999] of Nov. 18–25, 1800) is rare, especially in mint state; its limited mintage is doubtless relevant to early breakage of obv. die. Possibly 2% or slightly less survive in all grades.

And in still greater contrast, the date 1801 exists in two vars., one (close date, eighth star far from cap: Breen 1-A, rev. of 1799–1800) Ex. rare; the other (wide date, eighth star very close to cap, rev. of 1803) commonest of all, 1795–1804. Mintage figure [44,344] includes [15,090] delivered in 1802 from 1801-dated dies. At a survival ratio of about 2%, nearly 1,000 are around, many UNC.

Eagles of 1803 share a peculiarity with half eagles 1800–3: A single obv. die is combined with several very similar revs. Unlike the half eagles, but like the half dollars, the eagles fall into two naked-eye rev. types: small and large rev. stars, the small as in 1797–1801, the large as in 1804. Large stars are as wide as either S in STATES. The first of the two large stars revs. has traces of a small star within the rightmost cloud; the other die reappears with the single 1804 obv. Mintages include [8,979] Aug. 19–Oct. 19, 1803 (Small Stars?) plus [6,038] June 1–Dec. 11, 1804 (Large Stars?); less than 2% survived the melting pots.

The final date, 1804, is rarer than its mintage suggests, particularly choice. Of the single var., only a little over 1% survive out of [3,757] delivered Dec. 28–31, 1804.

On Dec. 31, 1804, coinage of this denomination halted, pursuant to verbal orders from Pres. Thomas Jefferson. The reason was extensive meltings by bullion dealers, exactly as with the silver dollars; neither denomination would reappear in circulation for over 30 years. But as with the dollars, a proof-only 1804 with plain 4 and beaded borders was a mysterious addition to the series.

This final var. remained unexplained until 1962. It was first pictured—without special comment—in a photographic plate of Liberty heads in 1869 *AJN;* its rare auction appearances were notable largely because all specimens seen were proofs. Only with the discovery of the King of Siam's original cased proof set of 1834, which contained both this and the 1804 "Class I" proof dollar, was the mystery solved. Four proofs were made in Nov. 1834 for inclusion in the four cased proof sets intended for diplomatic presentation: See Chap. 29, Sect. iv, introductory text. They are rarer than the 1907 Rolled Edge with Periods or the 1933, and twice as rare as the 1804 dollar, but have not had the publicity of those. There are also at least five silver impressions from these dies; I have not yet had opportunity to study these to ascertain if they were made in 1834 or restruck in 1858–60. If they are on half-dollar planchets, weights will establish the time of issue as with the 1838–39 half-dollar patterns: Half-dollar blanks 1794–1836 weigh 208 grs. = 13.48 gms.; 1853–73, 192 grs. = 12.44 gms.

Even without the 1804 backdated proofs, the set of Heraldic eagles has become difficult to complete, partly because of high floor prices on even the least rare vars., partly because type-collector pressure has made the 1798/7 Stars 7 + 6 seem much rarer than it is.

SCOT'S HERALDIC DESIGN

Designer, Engraver, Robert Scot (except as noted). Mint, Physical Specifications, Authorizing Act, as before.

Grade range and standards, as before; in addition, for FINE expect motto complete but weak, partial shading on shield, few wing feathers separated; for VERY FINE expect full motto, over half wing feathers clear, partial tail feathers. NOTES, EXCEPTIONS: As before.

I. SHIELD WITH SEVEN PALES GULES

6834 1797 Stars 10 + 6. [10,940] Rev. "Cross" star arrangement.
Breen 2-B, 2-C = Hilt 6E, 6F. Hilt thinks these are [4,449] + [2,561] of June 29, 1797–Jan. 23, 1798. See introductory text. Price for Breen 2-B, with straight branch; Zug, Clapp, Eliasberg:648, AU/UNC., $15,400. The var. ill. (2-C) is much rarer, especially with break between ER to leaf.

6835 1797 Same obv.; "arc" star arrangement.
Breen 2-D = Hilt 6G. Rev. of 1798. Obv. always with crack through final 7 to drapery. Available for a price in VF to AU; Garrett:1658, EF, $12,000. Prohibitively rare in mint state.

6836 1798/7 Stars 9 + 4. [900]
Breen 1-A. Feb. 17, 1798. Of possibly 18–20 known, 6 are UNC., 3 mutilated, the others VF to AU. Various states of die breaks. Enl. photos. Newlin, Garrett:1659, $52,500; Eliasberg:649, AU/UNC., $33,000, Stanley Kesselman.

6837 1798/7 Stars 7 + 6. [842]
Breen 1-A. Feb. 28, 1798. Of 13 known, 5 are at least border-

line UNC., one has loop removed, the rest VF to AU, usually weak in centers. Various states of die breaks. Newlin, Garrett:1660, AU, $120,000; Rutherford, Clapp, Eliasberg:650, $50,600, EF/AU, M. Brownlee. Enl. photos.

II. SHIELD WITH SIX PALES GULES

6838 1799 [all kinds 37,449] Stars 8 + 5. Small obv. stars, close date. Rare.
4 vars. Not to be confused with any to follow!

6839 1799 Small stars, wide date. Ex. rare.
Breen 1-A and new obv.; latter LM 2/72:433 and Breen II:201. Berry below center of final A (hold coin so that this A is upright); space between clouds l. of center of E; rust pit between UN. Neither obv. is to be confused with next or **6841.** Wayman:4, UNC., $11,500; Auction 82:944, UNC., $15,500.

6840 1799 Small stars, irregular date.
Breen 4-D, 4-E (ill.); price for latter. Former (Ex. rare) has jagged die defect within C(A). Note date configuration: 1 very far from curl, first 9 below 7 9.

6841 1799 Large obv. stars.
Breen 5-F, 5-G (ill.); price for latter. Former (prohibitively rare) has berry beyond r. tip of r. foot of final A (hold coin so

that this A is upright); corner of F about touches border. Obv. might be mistaken for **6838–39,** but all stars are crowded together, eighth and thirteenth distinctively rotated. Large obv. stars continue through 1804.

6842 1800 [5,999] Rare.
Nov. 18–25, 1800. Rev. = 1799 5-G. See introductory text. Almost always with die breaks through LIBERTY and stars. Very rare UNC. Taylor, Garrett:1662, AU, $11,000; Mills, Clapp, Eliasberg:655, AU/UNC., $20,900.

6843 1801 [44,344]
Jan. 19, 1801–Dec. 30, 1802. See introductory text. Price for var. ill. (Breen 2-B), with wide date, eighth star close to cap., rev. of 1803; this often shows spines in cap. The other var. (Breen 1-A), with close date, eighth star away from cap, and rev. of **6842,** is Ex. rare; Auction 82:946, UNC., $12,500; Akers {1980} ill.

6844 1803 Small rev. stars. [8,979]
Believed to comprise [4,816] Aug. 19 plus [4,163] Nov. 19. Date from half-dollar punches ("small 3" type); 4 revs. Mickley, Appleton, Garrett:1664, AU, $12,000; Eliasberg:657, UNC., $27,500.

6845 1803 Large rev. stars. [6,038] Extra star in cloud.
Breen 1-E. See introductory text. Small star entirely within cloud below F, not always clear; discovered by Harry Bass at 1966 ANA. Very rare UNC. Wayman:7, UNC., $15,000.

6846 1803 Large rev. stars, no extra star. Ex. rare.
Breen 1-F. Rev. of next. Leaf point between RI. Einstein:444 (struck after next).
6847 1804 Crosslet 4. [3,757] Rare.
Rev. of **6846.** Both dies come with various states of cracks. Possibly 6 UNCs. known. Eliasberg:659; UNC., $35,200. Altered dates from 1801 (and possibly other years) are reported; these are instantly identifiable by the revs., because Large Stars revs. occur only 1803–4, and the 1804 die differs in leaf position from the 1803.

6848 1804 Plain 4. [4+P] Proof only. Ex. rare.
Judd 33. By William Kneass. Beaded borders; plain 4 with flat top, style of various 1834 denominations. Struck Nov. 1834 for diplomatic presentation sets; see introductory text and Newman-Bressett {1962}. 1) Parmelee, Steigerwalt, Woodin, Clapp, Eliasberg:660, $33,000. 2) Col. Green, Eliasberg, "H. R. Lee," Baldenhofer:1459, pvt. coll. 3) Virgil Brand, C. E. Green, pvt. coll. 4) Mint, State Dept., King of Siam proof set (about $1 million), pvt. coll.

iii. GOBRECHT'S CORONET DESIGN, NO MOTTO (1838–66)

Verbal orders of Pres. Jefferson had stopped mintage of eagles as of Dec. 31, 1804. But in July 1838, after two different acts altering the weight and fineness standard of U.S. gold coins, the Secretary of Treasury instructed Mint Director Robert Maskell Patterson to resume coinage of this denomination at once. Acting Engraver Christian Gobrecht prepared new dies, and on Dec. 6, four "specimens" (proofs?) went to the Secretary of Treasury, followed by 7,200 business strikes. Gobrecht copied the head of Venus in Benjamin West's recent painting *Omnia Vincit Amor,* with slightly changed headdress but with the same triple-beaded cord on her bun, and the same coronet (here inscribed LIBERTY); this is the same prototype used for the latest style of cents in 1839, differently modified. A slicked-up version of the old John Reich eagle served for rev.; on 1839 "Type I" (Type of 1838) this is called large letters.
This same design continued into late June 1839, this "Head of 1838" being highly prized as an ephemeral type. In Oct. 1839, Gobrecht's redesigned head appeared, continuing essen-

tially unchanged until 1907. Revs. of 1839 "Type II" through 1865 have smaller letters.
Issues remained very limited; only a few years had mintages in excess of 200,000, and even some of these are rare. In mint state, all are rare, most unobtainable. Dates 1840–42 are in small numerals, from the logotypes used for cents; thereafter larger, though large and small dates exist for 1850 and 1854 O, evidently from wrong choice of date logotype. Longacre succeeded to the Mint engravership in 1844 on Gobrecht's death; because of the recent mechanization whereby all dies were completely hubbed except for dates and mintmarks, his job through 1848 as Engraver consisted largely of the blacksmith's chore of punching those elements into working dies. His timidity resulted in some spectacular repunchings and a few overdates and corrected blunders; the most extraordinary of these are beyond doubt the 1845/44 O, 1846/5 O, 1849/8, and 1865/981 S. This last originally had the three-digit logotype, 186_ entered inverted (rotated 180°), then corrected.
Part of the reason for limited mintages 1838–44 was the Hard Times, years of unemployment and starvation; after 1850, another reason was that for ordinary transactions half eagles were preferable, whereas for enormous interbank and international payments double eagles were much preferred. After New York banks suspended specie payments, Dec. 28, 1861, little gold reached the mints for coinage, and most of that was earmarked for international payments.
In 1859, Longacre prepared a new rev. hub, found on Philadelphia coins through 1865. This differs from the old 1840–58 hub in having shorter, thinner claws. It does not occur on branch-mint coins because their revs. through 1865 were all dies left over from 1857–58.
The very last issue without motto consisted of [8,500] from San Francisco, minted in Feb. 1866 before the new revs. with motto arrived.

GOBRECHT'S CORONET DESIGN, NO MOTTO

Designer, Christian Gobrecht, after West and Reich. Engravers, Gobrecht (1838–44), Longacre (1844–65). Mints, Philadelphia (no mintmark), New Orleans (mintmark O), San Francisco (S). Mintmark under eagle. Composition, gold 90%, silver not over 5%, rest copper. Weight, 258 ± 0.25 grs. = 16.718 ± 0.016 gms., containing 15.0444 gms. or 0.4837 troy oz. pure gold. Diameter, 18/16″ = 26.8 mm. Reeded edge. Authorizing Act, Jan. 18, 1837.
Grade range, GOOD to UNC.; not collected in low grades except for extreme rarities. FINE: Full LIBERTY; major hair contours; few feathers separated; one claw outlined; all shield stripes countable, shading may be blurry. VERY FINE: Top line of coronet broken above not over 3 letters of LIBERTY; all major hair lines show; most feathers separated except near ends of wings; shield lines partly clear. EXTREMELY FINE: Few tiny isolated rubbed spots only; partial mint luster. UNCIRCULATED No trace of wear. NOTE: Beware specimens with solder residues, as before. EXCEPTIONS: Many O and S coins are weak in centers.

I. FIRST HEAD, LARGE LETTERS

6849 1838 [7,200 + ?P] Rare.
Dec. 6, 1838. Prohibitively rare above EF. Wilharm, Clapp Eliasberg:661, AU/UNC., $30,800. Proofs: 1) Mint, SI, rev scratched. Clain-Stefanelli {1970}, fig. 23. 2) Parmelee, Woodin, Newcomer, Col. Green, B. G. Johnson, "Bell," Fa

rouk:166, N.Y. State pvt. coll. 3) Low, Brand, Cardinal Spellman, Davies-Niewoehner:612, $105,000. One other reported. Enl. photos.

6850 1839/8 [all kinds 25,801] "Type I." Head of 1838.
March 30–June 29, 1839; commonly "1839 large letters." Earliest state with obvious overdate is very rare: "N.Y. Coll.":244. Later, traces of 8 (l. of knob and at upper and lower r. outer curves of 9) fade; these later states will price as next. Usually VF–EF; unobtainable UNC.

6851 1839 Normal date, "Type I."
Usually VF–EF; prohibitively rare. UNC. Carter:741, UNC., $12,100. Proofs: 1) Mint, SI. 2) Parmelee, Jenks, Clapp, Eliasberg:1662, $121,000, M. Brownlee. 3) East European pvt. coll., 1981, Mark Emory for NERCG, in a proof set including $2½ and $5.

II. SECOND HEAD, SMALL LETTERS

6852 1839 "Type II." [12,447]
Oct. 30–Dec. 31. Coronet point near sixth star. This type difference discovered by B. Max Mehl, who miscalled it a "pattern" in *Mehl's Numismatic Monthly,* 12/10. Usually in

low grades; prohibitively rare AU. 1976 ANA:3057, UNC., $15,000. Enl. photos.

6853 1840 Modified head. [47,338 + ?P]
Coronet point almost midway between stars; curls behind neck and base of bun altered, as 1840–47. Date in straight line henceforth. Prohibitively rare AU. Proofs: 1) Mint, SI.

6854 1841 [63,131 + ?P]
Prohibitively rare UNC. Proofs: 1) Mint, SI.

6855 1841 O [2,500]
Tall oval O. One pair of dies shipped Jan. 1, 1841. Often weakly struck. Usually F to VF, Ex. rare EF, prohibitively rare AU, unknown UNC. Clapp, Eliasberg:665, AU, $4,400.

6856 1842 Small date. [18,623 + ?P]
Jan.–April 30 (see Breen {1967}, p. 28). Date as in 1840–41, and as on Small Date coins of lower denominations. Only one var. seen; usually F to EF, prohibitively rare AU. Wayman:14, UNC., $5,500; Clapp, Eliasberg:666, AU, $1,650. Proofs: 1) Mint, SI.

6857 1842 Large date. [62,884]
May–Dec. 31. Prohibitively rare AU.

6858 1842 O Large date. [27,400]
2 rev. vars.; one pair of dies shipped Oct. 22, 1842, the other var. having the 1841 O rev. Prohibitively rare AU.

6859 1843 [75,462 + ?P] Normal date.
Varies in position and heaviness. Prohibitively rare AU; more proofs (6) are traceable than full UNCs.! Compare next 2.

6860 1843 Double date. Rare.
Not to be confused with next. Coins with less repunching visible will price as preceding. Prohibitively rare AU.

6861 1843 Triple date. Very rare.
Low heavy date, all digits doubled, 4 triple-punched; use a strong glass. Best seen is the AU in a Tex. pvt. coll., ex Grant Pierce.

6862 1843 O [175,162] Very thin numerals.
Serifs and bases of 8 3 hairlike; 2 rev. vars. Ex. rare UNC.

6863 1843 O Heavy numerals.
3 vars. In all, 4 obvs., 5 revs. Ex. rare UNC. Wayman:13, UNC., $2,900.

6864 1844 [6,361 + ?P] Rare.
The [4,600] of Nov. 20 cannot be told from the [1,761] of Dec. 31. Prohibitively rare EF. Wayman:19, EF, $1,550. Proofs have low date slanting up to r.: 1) Mint, SI. 2)

Newcomer, Boyd, WGC, "Bell," "Memorable":547.   3)
Cased proof set ex Dr. Judd.

6865   1844 O [118,700]
6 pairs of dies; positional vars. of date and O. Often weakly
struck. Prohibitively rare AU. Proofs: 1) Parmelee:1151,
Woodin.

6866   1845 [26,153 + ?P] Normal heavy date.
Interiors of 845 crude enough to suggest repunching. Not to
be confused with either of next 2. Prohibitively rare above EF.
Proofs have date far to l.:   1) Mint, SI.   2) Cased proof set,
N.Y. State pvt. coll.   3) Garrett:1667, $38,000.   4) British
estate, Paul D. Williams:1818, in set with $2½ and $5,
$127,500.

6867   1845 Thin numerals. Rare.
Hairlike serifs, bases of 85. Apparently unknown UNC.

6868   1845 O [all kinds 47,500] Normal date.
84 touch. In all, 5 pairs of dies plus leftover 1844 O revs.
Prohibitively rare AU. Cleneay, Ten Eyck, Clapp, Elias-
berg:674, UNC., $28,600.

6869   1845 O Repunched 84. Rare.
Breen 2, 3. 8 4 free; 2 rev. vars. Same grade comment.

6870   1845 O Double date. Very rare.
3 vars. All 4 digits repunched. Discovery coin, NN 49:241.
Same grade comment. Wayman:22, UNC., $5,250.

6871   1845/44 O Ex. rare.
Date 1844 first cut well to l. of final position for 1845. Up-
right of 4 within lower part of 5. Discovery coin, Pierce:1454,
Tex. pvt. coll.

6872   1846 [20,095 + ?P]
Date as on small date cents. 4 minor vars. Prohibitively rare
above EF. Proofs have no die file marks in shield: 1) Mint,
SI.   2) Cased set, N.Y. State pvt. coll.   3) Clapp, Elias-
berg:675, $46,200, D. Kagin.

6873   1846 O [all kinds 81,780] Normal date.
Medium date, as on half dollars. 6 obvs., 4 revs. shipped, plus
5 revs. left over from 1844–45. O normal or partly
repunched. Prohibitively rare UNC.; Cleneay, Ten Eyck,
Clapp, Eliasberg:676, $30,800.

6874   1846 O Double-punched 6. Very rare.
Not to be confused with preceding or following. Unknown
UNC.

6875   1846/5 O Rare.
2 obvs., probably those shipped Dec. 12, 1845 and Jan. 24,
1846. One has knob of 5 within loop of 6, other parts higher:
NN 55:1089; 1976 ANA:3064, UNC., $3,500. The other has
trace of curve of 5 within loop of 6, part of top of 5 (including
point) within and at r. of top of 6. Unknown UNC. Discovery
coin, NN 54:691.

6876   1846 O Small thin stars. Very rare.
Die weakly hubbed and/or drastically lapped. Mintmark far
to r., over space between N D, as on one var. of **6875**. Unknown UNC. Discovery coin, Mumford, Clapp, Elias-
berg:677, AU, $6,050.

6877   1847 [862,258 + ?P] Thin numerals.
Hairlike serifs; top and base of 8 very thin. At least 3 vars.
Scarcer than next. Ex. rare UNC.

6878   1847 Heavy numerals.
At least 5 vars. Plentiful VF; very rare UNC. Clapp, Elias-
berg:678, UNC., $15,400. Proof: 1) Mint, SI.

6879   1847 Extra-heavy 7. Rare.
Rounded contour within angle of 7 (die crumbling?); TEN D
extra heavy. Discovery coin, KS 2/60:2776. The coin with
repunched date remains unverified.

6880   1847 O [571,500] Normal date.
6 pairs of dies, some with minute traces of repunching at 1 or
4. Often weakly struck. Plentiful in VF; Ex. rare UNC.: Way-
man:26, $6,500. Rarely with rev. rotated 180°.

6881   1847 O Double 18. Very rare.
Discovery coin, Neumoyer:2578. Prohibitively rare UNC.;
1976 ANA:3067, UNC., $2,800.

6882   1848 New obv. hub. [145,484 + ?P] Open 4; normal
date.
Minor changes in back curls; tenth star points to upper part
of dentil (formerly lower part); curve of truncation slightly
more pronounced at r. The "open 4" date logotype has crosslet of 4 small and distant from base, as on some cents and half
dollars. May exist with closed 4, as in **6884**. See ill. in Akers
{1980}. Prohibitively rare UNC.; 1980 ANA:324, $11,000;
Auction 82:392, $3,100. Possibly 5 proofs; ill. Breen {1977},
p. 88.

6883   1848 Open 4. Thin numerals. Rare.
Hairlike serifs, bases and tops of 8's. NN 55:1093;
Holmes:3718; Carter:749, UNC., $4,180.

6884   1848 O New hub. Closed 4. [35,850] Rare.
6 pairs of dies shipped before Dec. 31, 1847. Crosslet of 4
long, almost touching base, as on some cents and half dollars;
ill. Akers {1980}. Often weakly struck. Prohibitively rare
UNC.

6885   1849 [all kinds 653,618] Normal date.
At least 8 vars. Weight tolerance henceforth ± 0.5 grs. = ±
0.032 gms. Plentiful VF; Ex. rare UNC. Eliasberg:682, UNC.,
$11,550.

6886   1849 Double 1. Rare.
Base of extra 1 crosses upright. Martin Field:960; others.
Later states with this line faded will price as preceding.

6887   1849 Double date. Very rare.
Breen 7. Parts of all 4 digits show within and around date;
part of loop of extra 9 shows through l. side of circle of 9.
Later, cracked through first 9 stars. Not to be confused with
next. Prohibitively rare AU.

6888   1849/1848 Very rare.
Breen 8. Date 1848 first punched very high, slanting up to r.,
then repunched with 1849 logotype; at l. of 9 is much of *lower*
loop of 8. Later, cracked through 4 to neck. Discovery coin,
KS 2/60:2779. Apparently unknown UNC.

6889   1849 O [23,900] Rare.
6 obvs.; 12 leftover dies from 1844–48, not all used. Ex. rare
EF; unknown UNC.

6890   1850 [all kinds 291,451 + 1+P] Large date.
Date as on cents; see ill. in Akers {1980}. Closed 5 (knob
touches cusp); may exist with open 5. Positional vars. exist.
Ex. rare UNC.; Clapp, Eliasberg:685, UNC., $4,400. One proof
made, in set for Congressional Committee on the Library;
untraced. Compare next 2.

6891   1850 Large date, double 1. Very rare.
Breen II-3. Date high; closed 5; base of 1 double to naked
eye.

6892 1850 Small date. Very rare.

Date smaller than on cents or previous eagles since 1842, from logotype intended for half eagles. Positional vars. exist: NN 55:1096; "Melish":2410–11. Discovery coin, NN 46:136.

6893 1850 O Large date. [57,500]

Closed 5. Eight obvs., 2 revs. plus leftovers from 1844–48. Prohibitively rare AU. Earle, Clapp, Eliasberg:686, UNC., $37,400.

6894 1851 [176,328] Heavy numerals.

5 obvs., 8 revs. Thick serifs. Positional vars. exist. Ex. rare UNC.

6895 1851 Base of first 1 double.

Breen 4. Similar to **6891.**

6896 1851 Thin numerals. Scarce.

Hairlike serifs, bases of 85, top of 8.

6897 1851 O [263,000] Normal shield.

7 obvs., 5 revs. Minor positional vars. Often weakly struck. Prohibitively rare UNC.; the best one is probably ex Cleneay:505. Compare next.

6898 1851 O Hollow ring atop second stripe.

Apparently a center punch on rev. hub; this circle is slightly wider than the pale gules it surmounts. See ill. in Akers {1980}. This feature recurs on some later O mints (different working dies). 3 obv. dies. Often weakly struck. Ex. rare UNC.; best may be Grant Pierce:1465 and Clapp, Eliasberg:688, $24,200, H. Bass.

6899 1852 [263,106] Thin numerals.

8 obvs., 12 revs. Date as in cents. Positional vars. exist. Ex. rare AU. Wayman:35, UNC., $1,500; Auction 82:393, UNC., $1,150.

6900 1852 Heavy numerals. Very rare.

"Gilhousen":155. Ex. rare AU.

6901 1852 O [all kinds 18,000] Normal shield. Rare.

6 obvs., leftover revs. At least 2 positional vars. Often weakly struck. Prohibitively rare AU; only one seen UNC.

6902 1852 O Hollow ring atop second stripe. Very rare.

As on **6898,** different working die. See ill. in Akers {1980}. Often weakly struck. Prohibitively rare AU.

6903 1853 [all kinds 201,253] Normal.

Positional vars. exist; date generally below center of space between bust and border. One obv. has minute repunching above base of 1. Compare next 2. The few UNCs. known are mostly from a hoard found in North Carolina before 1973.

6904 1853 Doubled rev. die. Very rare.

Ivy Cambridge:2066. Doubling on many letters.

6905 1853/2 Ex. rare.

Date very low, very heavy; plain thin traces of middle stroke

Courtesy
Ted Clark

of 2 within 3. Possibly 8–10 known, none UNC. Discovery coin, Neumoyer:2583, Breen, Kagin, Tex. pvt. coll.

6906 1853 O [all kinds 51,000] Normal.

6 obvs. shipped; leftover revs. from 1851. Minor positional vars. Prohibitively rare UNC.

6907 1853 O Double-punched date. Very rare.

Breen 1. Discovery coin, Pierce:1468; cf. "Gilhousen":655.

6908 1853 O Normal date; hollow ring atop second stripe. Rare.

Breen 5. As in **6898, 6902,** different working die. One proof known, ex LM 3/69:421, Auction 79:1303, $17,500, ill. here and in Breen {1977}, p. 235.

6909 1853 O Repunched 53; hollow ring atop second stripe. Very rare.

Rev. similar to last. The 5 pairs of dies shipped to the San Francisco Provisional Branch Mint remained unused.

6910 1854 Small date. [54,250 + 1+P] Heavy date, 54 touch.

On lighter strikings 5 4 may be barely free. Positional vars. exist. Compare next 2. Prohibitively rare UNC. The proof, from the set the Mint gave the City of Bremen, has not been located.

6911 1854 Blundered date. Very rare.

Base and part of upright of extra 1 on dentilated border below 18. First star about touches border. Date otherwise as preceding.

6912 1854 Thin numerals, 5 4 apart. Rare.

Date as on most cents.

6913 1854 O [all kinds 52,500] Small date.

Date as on Philadelphia coin ill. in Akers {1980}. At least 8 obvs. shipped; leftover revs. Positional vars.; 5 4 apart, but may exist with 54 touching. Often weak in centers. Prohibitively rare UNC.

6914 1854 O Large date. Rare.

2 vars. Discovery piece, Atwater:1529, possibly reappearing as Dr. Green:609. Almost always weak in centers. Usually in low grades, unknown UNC.

6915 1854 S Small date, large S. [123,826]

6 pairs of dies (and leftover revs. from 1853?); 5 4 apart. S 1.7 mm. Minute positional vars. Rare AU, Ex. rare UNC.

6916 1855 [121,701 + ?P] Thin numerals.

Hairline serifs, very thin bases of 855. In all, 3 pairs of dies. Very rare UNC.; the few known are from a tiny hoard. The solitary proof Wayte Raymond recorded before 1949 remains untraced.

6917 1855 Heavy numerals. Rare.

2 vars. Thick serifs to 1, thick bases to 855. Wayman:42, UNC., $2,100.

6918 1855 O Thin numerals. [18,000] Rare.

4 obvs.; leftover revs. Prohibitively rare above EF. Clapp, Eliasberg:697, AU, $1,430. The only UNC. seen is ex Miles, Scanlon colls.

6919 1855 S Medium S. [9,000] Rare.

6 obvs. shipped; leftover revs. S 1.3 mm. Prohibitively rare above EF; no full AU seen. Roach, Eliasberg:698, EF+, $1,760.

6920 1856 [60,490 + ?P]

All mints, large date, upright 5 only; see ill. in Akers {1980}. 5 pairs of dies; 3 positional vars. Ex. rare AU, prohibitively rare UNC. The single proof reported by Wayte Raymond remains untraced.

6921 1856 O [14,500] Rare.

4 obvs., 2 revs. Prohibitively rare above AU. Wayman:46, AU, $2,500.

6922 1856 S [all kinds 68,000] Medium S. Very scarce.

9 obvs., 2 revs., both shipped Dec. 1855; leftover revs. from 1854–55. At least 2 positional vars. of mintmark. S 1.3 mm. Prohibitively rare UNC.

6923 1856 S Large S. Very rare.

S 1.7 mm. Possibly represents the last of the 3 deliveries: [14,000] Jan., [55,500] Sept., [2,500] Dec. Discovered by John H. Clapp before 1942. Unknown UNC. Wayman:47, AU, $750.

6924 1857 [all kinds 16,606 + ?P] Normal date. Rare.

The 2 deliveries, [2,916] in first half year, [13,690] in second, cannot be told apart. 2 rev. vars. Prohibitively rare above AU. Proofs: 1) Ten Eyck, Clapp, Eliasberg:702, $77,000, S. Kesselman, Auction 85:948, $41,800.

6925 1857 Overdate. Ex. rare.

Curve of another digit between 57, touching curve of 5 and serif of 7. It is uncertain if this is part of another 5, another 7, or a 6. Discovery coin, Lester Merkin, March 1969.

6926 1857 O [5,500] Very rare.

2 pairs of dies; 3 minor vars. Prohibitively rare above EF.

6927 1857 S Medium S. [26,000]

S 1.3 mm. Date centered or low; latter ill. Akers {1980}. Prohibitively rare AU. Wayman:50 (centered date), AU, $1,700.

6928 1858 [2,521 + ?P] Very rare.

Business strikes (Nov. 23): "floating" (incomplete) curls behind neck (lapped die); 1 minutely above center of space between bust and border; TEN D. heavier than other letters, faint field striations slant south-southeast. Beware forgeries made by removing O or S mintmark. Possibly 12–15 survive, mostly F to EF (heavily bag-marked). Atwater, Eliasberg:705, AU, $7,150; Manfra, Tordella & Brookes, Bohren Trust Fund, Auction 80:954, UNC., $115,000. Proofs: curls behind neck normal; date far r. 1) Mint, SI. Clain-Stefanelli {1970}, fig. 24. 2) Cogan 3/29/1882:422 set, Randall, Morgan,

ANS. 3) Mint, Parmelee, Woodin, Newcomer, Boyd, Dr. Green, Carter:759, $121,000, D. Akers. 4) Jewett:847, Low, Brand, pvt. coll.

6929 1858 O [20,000] Rare.

Low date, normal neck curls (unlike preceding); earliest state shows traces of another 8 within both loops of second 8 (fades). Later states, after die relapped, have thinner numerals. Usually VF to EF; very rare AU, Ex. rare UNC.: Cleneay:513, believed later Clapp, Eliasberg:706, UNC., $4,950; others from the Jackson, Tenn., hoard.

6930 1858 S Medium S. [11,800] Rare.

4 obvs. shipped Oct. 1857; old revs. The [800] of first quarter cannot be told from the [11,000] of second. S 1.3 mm, normal or with light traces of repunching. Date high in field (1 very close to bust), upper curls partly disconnected behind neck, lower curls firmly attached, unlike 1858 Philadelphia. Ex. rare above VF. Wayman:53, AU, $2,200.

6931 1859 "Type II" rev. [16,093 + 80–P] Rare.

New hub: claws thinner, more open than formerly. One pair of dies for business strikes; low heavy date. Prohibitively rare AU. Most of the 80 proofs (low thin date) were melted in 1860 as unsold; about 10 survive: 1) Mint, SI. 2) Brock, Morgan, ANS. 3), 4) Royal Mint (Llantrisant). 5) Ten Eyck, Clapp, Eliasberg:708, $41,800, Stack. 6) Atwater, Carter:760, $35,200. 7) Kern, Rapoport, Wolfson, Kreisberg 6/16/69:1072, harshly cleaned. Others in pvt. colls. Enl. photos.

6932 1859 O "Type I" rev. [2,300] Ex. rare.
3 obvs. shipped, apparently only one used; leftover rev. of **6929.** Fewer than 12 survive. Usually in low grades; prohibitively rare EF. Wayman:55, EF, $4,200; Mitchelson, Clapp, Eliasberg:709, EF, $3,080.

6933 1859 S "Type I" rev. Large S. [7,000] Very rare.
6 obvs. shipped; 2 leftover revs. S 1.7 mm. Usually in low grades; prohibitively rare EF. Wayman:56, EF, $1,700.

6934 1860 "Type II" rev. [15,055 + 50–P] Rare.
Prohibitively rare above AU. Ten Eyck, Clapp, Eliasberg:711, UNC., $24,200, Auction 85:959, $25,300. At least 30 proofs sold in sets, rest melted Jan. 1862 as unsold; not over 10 traceable. 1) Mint, SI. 2) Brock, Morgan, ANS. 3) Ely, Garrett:1688, $39,000. 4) Atwater, Carter:761, $28,600. Others in pvt. colls.

6935 1860 O "Type I" rev. [11,100] Rare.
Only one var.; rev. of **6929.** Ex. rare EF; Wayman:58, AU, $3,200; Auction 84:411, UNC.

6936 1860 S "Type I" rev. Large S. [5,000] Very rare.
4 obvs. shipped; 2 leftover revs. of **6933.** S 1.7 mm. Prohibitively rare EF. Wayman:59, EF, $2,200.

6937 1861 "Type II" rev. [113,164 + 69–P]
8 obvs., 10 revs., at least 7 positional vars. Mostly made from melted 1849–54 gold dollars. Prohibitively rare UNC. Some proofs melted Jan. 1862 as unsold; probably fewer than 10 survive. Ten Eyck, Clapp, Eliasberg:714, $25,300; Carter:762, $28,600. The 2 obvs. shipped to New Orleans remained unused.

6938 1861 S "Type I" rev. Large S. [15,500] Rare.
3 obvs. shipped; leftover revs. 2 vars. S 1.7 mm. Often weakly struck. Prohibitively rare EF. Wayman:61, EF, $1,000.

6939 1862 "Type II" rev. [10,960 + 35P]
2 pairs of dies. The [980] of March 25 cannot be told from the [2,410] of Sept. 15 or the [7,570] of Nov. 18. Prohibitively rare in AU. Possibly 12–15 proofs survive. Ten Eyck, Clapp, Eliasberg:716, $20,900; Carter:763, $26,400.

6940 1862 S "Type I" rev. Large S. [12,500] Rare.
4 obvs. shipped; leftover revs. 3 minor positional vars. S 1.7 mm. Often weakly struck. Prohibitively rare above EF.

6941 1863 "Type II" rev. [1,218 + 30P] Ex. rare.
Business strikes (April 20) are mostly VF to EF, heavily nicked. Miles:668 is possibly the only UNC.; Wayman:64, EF, $4,600. Proofs (March 23) have partly filled 3; possibly 8–10 survive: Auction 79:334, $28,000; Randall, Clapp, Eliasberg:718, $30,800, Hugh Sconyers; Geiss, Carter:764, $25,300.

6942 1863 S "Type I" rev. Medium S. [10,000] Very rare.
4 obvs. shipped Nov. 62; leftover revs. Only one var.: low date nearly central below truncation, unlike Philadelphia coins (on which date is far r.); ill. Akers {1980}. S 1.3 mm. Usually in low grades; prohibitively rare EF. Dunham, Eliasberg:719, EF+, $1,430; Auction 84:412, UNC.

6943 1864 "Type II" rev. [3,530 + 50P] Very rare.
Date slants minutely up to r. The [160] of Feb. 25 cannot be told from the [3,370] of March 14. Prohibitively rare in AU. Proofs (Feb. 11) have date well to l., slanting down to r.; 12–15 survive. Ullmer:490, $37,500 (1974); Garrett (1976):411, $16,000; Walton, Jay, Dines, Delp, Wayman:66, $17,000; Mumford, Clapp, Eliasberg:720, $18,700.

6944 1864 S "Type I" rev. Medium S. [2,500] Ex. rare.
3 obvs. shipped Oct. 1863. Possibly 10–12 known; usually weakly struck and in low grades; unknown above EF. Wayman:67, EF, $3,200.

6945 1865 "Type II" rev. Doubled rev. die. [3,980] Very rare.
Doubling plainest on S OF AMERICA and adjacent wingtip. The [650] of Jan. 27 cannot be told from the [3,330] of March 14. Prohibitively rare above EF. Wayman:68, EF, $2,200.

6946 1865 Normal "Type II" rev. [25P] Proofs only.
Coined March 8; possibly 8–10 survive. Garrett:1669, $37,000; 1980 ANA:328, $37,000; Wilcox, Clapp, Eliasberg:733, $30,800.

6947 1865 S [all kinds 16,700] "Type I" rev. Large S. Doubled rev. Very rare.
3 obvs. shipped Nov. 1864; leftover revs. S 1.7 mm. Doubling plainest at TEN, UNITED, adjacent wingtip, leaves, feathers. Prohibitively rare above VF. Wayman:69, EF, $1,700; Roach, Eliasberg:723, EF, $1,650. In all grades slightly rarer than next.

6948 1865/981 S "Type I" rev. Large S. Very rare.
See introductory text. The ill. is of one of the earlier die states; later states show less of extra digits. Prohibitively rare above EF. Wayman:70, EF, $1,800. Discovered by R. J. Salisbury about 1958.

6949 1866 S No motto. "Type I" rev. Medium S. [8,500] Very rare.
3 obvs. shipped Nov. 1865; these continued on **6953.** One var.; date slants down to r. Coined Feb. 1866. Prohibitively rare above VF. Wayman:71, EF (scratched), $2,400; Eliasberg:724, EF, $2,090.

iv. MOTTO ADDED (1866–1907)

Ultimately because of the Rev. M. R. Watkinson's insistence that this country must recognize God on its coins (no matter what they might be spent for), Treasury Secretary Salmon P. Chase ordered that the motto IN GOD WE TRUST be added to the larger gold and silver denominations, approving Longacre's scroll design. The Act of March 3, 1865 included a clause mandating the motto. Two gold prototype proof sets were made with motto revs., dated 1865; regular coinage followed in 1866.

From 1866 through 1878, mintages remained small, producing some of the most famous rarities of the series: 1872, 1873, 1875–77 at Philadelphia; 1870 and 1873 at Carson City. The former reflect banks' failure to resume specie payments (redemption in gold or silver of even federal paper); the latter, political pressure: official orders limiting mintages, the limitations being used as an excuse to close the Mint: See Chap. 36, Sect. viii, introductory text. Most of the mints' scanty output went to melting pots; probably not much over 1% survives of any one date or mintmark to this period, except for proofs, where the survival ratio is about 30% to 60%, reflecting that they were meant to be saved.

No complete set in uncirculated condition of all dates and mintmarks of this period has ever been assembled. For many, no mint-state survivors are known; F to VF is the usual grade range for most S mints 1866–77 and all Carson City coins 1870–79. Many Philadelphia business strikes, 1866–77, are known only in VF to EF.

After the Specie Resumption Act of 1878, mintages increased, enough so that when the average collector mentions "Liberty head eagles" or "common date eagles" without other designation, hearers automatically understand the meaning as Philadelphia or S mints 1880–1907.

In those years, most vars. consist of minute differences in position of date or mintmark (the only elements still entered by hand). Because most have been accumulated for their bullion content, owners have seldom studied them. Closer attention to them, as with the half eagles, may reveal more remarkable vars., in particular more overdates besides those of 1879, 1899, and 1906 D, these last all being discoveries of recent decades.

Coinage was interrupted pending preparation of the new St. Gaudens design; see following section.

MOTTO ADDED

Designer, Christian Gobrecht, obv. after Benjamin West, rev. after John Reich; motto by Longacre. Engravers, Longacre 1866–68, William Barber 1869–79, later Charles E. Barber. Mints, Philadelphia (no mintmark), New Orleans (mintmark O), San Francisco (S), Carson City (CC), Denver (D). Mintmark below eagle. Physical Specifications, as before. Authorizing Acts, Jan. 18, 1837; March 3, 1865; Feb 12, 1873.

Grade range, FAIR to UNC.; not collected below VF except for some extreme rarities. Grade standards, as before, except that for FINE expect in addition barely legible but complete motto; for VERY FINE, expect full clear motto. Beware of coins showing traces of solder.

6950 1865 Prototype. [2P] Proofs only.
Judd 449. Obv. as **6946**; rev. as next. 1) Mint, SI. Clain-Stefanelli {1970}, fig. 40. 2) Mason 6/17/1870:422, Woodin, Newcomer, Boyd, Farouk, in set with $5, $20. Copper strikings may come gilt; standard weight of gold, 258 grs. = 16.718 gms., or nearly double the weight of copper.

6951 1866 Normal date. [30P] Proofs only. Ex. rare.
The [25P] of Jan. 15 cannot be told from the [5P] of June 8. Date well to l. Possibly 8–10 survive. Ely, Garrett:1670, $37,000; Carter:765, $30,800.

6952 1866 Double date. [3,750] Very rare.
All minted Feb. 1. Date first entered to r. of final position; parts of all 4 extra digits show. Earlier states have die file mark through wingtip and ST; this fades, as do traces of extra digits. Prohibitively rare above EF. Wayman:72, EF, $1,050.

6953 1866 S Minute s. [11,500] Rare.
6 revs. shipped March 26, received April 14; 3 old obvs. used. The [5,500] of April cannot be told from the [6,000] of June. Usually in low grades; prohibitively rare in EF. Wayman:73, EF, $1,200.

6954 1867 [3,090 + 50P] Very rare.
Proofs have high date (ill. Breen {1977}, p. 135); possibly 8–12 survive, the 2 batches [25P each] of March 5 and July 2 indistinguishable. Ullmer:491, $15,000 (1974); Clapp, Eliasberg:727, $17,600. Business strikes have lower date (2 vars., Jan. 11). Prohibitively rare AU. Wayman:74, $2,200, Auction 82:395, $1,450, AU; Carter:766, EF, $2,090.

6955 1867 S [9,000] Very rare.
Ill. Akers {1980}. Prohibitively rare above VF. Wayman:75, EF, $2,050.

6956 1868 [10,630 + 25P] Rare.
Date above center, slanting down to r.; the [3,000] of Jan. 14 cannot be told from the [7,630] of Aug. 21. Prohibitively rare above EF. Wayman:76, AU, $1,100. Proofs (Feb. 20) have date about central, level, placed far to l.; ill. Breen {1977}, p. 137. Possibly 8–10 survive. Ullmer:492, $21,000 (1974); Carter:767, $30,000.

6957 1868 S [13,500] Very rare.
Date high, slants down to r. Usually weakly struck; prohibitively rare above VF. Wayman:77, EF, $1,200.

6958 1869 [1,830 + 25P] Very rare.
Business strikes (Feb. 1) have low date, eleventh star with extra outlines, scroll incomplete around IN. Prohibitively rare in EF. Wayman:78, EF, $1,700. Warning: Well-worn specimens may be 1869 S with weak mintmark; see next. Proofs (Feb. 19) have thin date to l., tenth star with extra outlines; scroll normal, minutely doubled rev. Ill. Breen {1977}, p. 138. Possibly 8–10 survive. Wilcox, Clapp, Eliasberg:731, $33,000.

6959 1869 S [6,430] Very rare.
6 obvs. shipped Oct. 1868; 2 minor rev. vars, minute s faint (usual) or bolder. Date higher than on **6958**. See ill. in Akers {1980}. Usually in low grades; prohibitively rare EF. Lamborn, "Fairfield":1814, UNC., $6,500.

6960 1870 Normal 0. [35P] Proofs only. Ex. rare.
Date high, well to l., slanting minutely down to r. Ill. Breen {1977}, p. 140. The [25P] of Feb. 3 cannot be told from the [10P] of June 1; possibly 10–12 survive. Clapp, Eliasberg:733, $15,400.

6961 1870 Repunched 0. [3,990] Very rare.
The [2,500] of Jan. 17 cannot be told from the [1,490] of Aug. 15. Date slants down a little more to r. than **6960.** Ex. rare above EF. Wayman:80, AU, $1,800.

6962 1870 S [9,000] Very rare.
Coined Dec. 1870, from 4 pairs of dies shipped Dec. 1869 (apparently only one used). Spur from tail of R(ICA); minute weak s as in **6959**. Prohibitively rare above VF; Wayman:82, UNC., $5,000; Clapp, Eliasberg:735, AU, $4,675.

6963 1870 CC [5,908] Ex. rare.
Small roundish cc through 1877. Centered date, thin stripes, IN ST in field (scroll edges incomplete especially at r.). Mintage began with [1,644] Feb. 15; prohibitively rare above VF, possibly only 10–12 survive. Auction 79:1307, AU, $7,750; Clapp, Eliasberg:734, VF, $3,575.

6964 1871 71 very close. [1,790 + 30P] Very rare.
Business strikes have centered date, 1 about equidistant between bust and border. Prohibitively rare above VF. Proofs (Feb. 20) have low date; possibly 10–12 survive. Ill. Breen {1977}, p. 142. H. P. Smith, Clapp, Eliasberg:736, $33,000.

6965 1871 S 71 very close. [16,500] Very rare.
4 obvs. received Dec. 16, 1870. Prohibitively rare above VF. Wayman:84, AU, $2,700.

6966 1871 CC [all kinds 8,085] 71 very close. Normal rev. Very rare.
Usually weakly struck. Prohibitively rare above VF. Eliasberg:737, EF, $2,420. Compare next.

6967 1871 CC 71 very close. Doubled rev. die. Very rare.
Same comments; minutely less rare. These vars. cannot as yet

be correlated with the deliveries: [900] February, [3,325] March, [1,160] August, [1,800] November, [900] Feb. 1872 from 1871 dies.

6968   1872 [1,620 + 30P] Ex. rare.

Business strikes (Jan. 11) have l. base of 1 r. of center of dentil; possibly 10–12 survive, mostly in low grades. 1976 ANA:3097, UNC., $4,250. Possibly could be simulated by 1872 S with mintmark removed; die peculiarities in latter afford immediate identification (see next). Proofs (Feb. 3) have l. base of 1 left of center of dentil; 10–12 survive. Auction 80:424, $33,000; Ten Eyck, Clapp, Eliasberg:739, $23,100.

6969   1872 S [17,300] Very rare.

Centered date to r. (unlike preceding); die file mark from eighth star to head; chips between upper points of third and fourth stars; extra line in shield below lower edge of azure. Ex. rare above EF; Wayman:87, AU, $1,600.

6970   1872 CC [all kinds 4,600] Normal rev. Very rare.

2 obvs. shipped. Often weakly struck. Prohibitively rare above VF. Wayman:86, EF, $1,800. See next.

6971   1872 CC Doubled rev. die. Ex. rare.

Doubling plainest at STA and adjacent wingtip. Same grade comments. These vars. cannot yet be correlated with deliveries: [1,100] July, [1,600] September, [1,900] December.

6972   1873 Closed 3. [800 + 25P] Ex. rare.

Business strikes (Jan. 25) have date lower in field than proofs; possibly 8–10 survive, F to EF. Wayman:88, $7,000, Auction 82:396, $4,800, EF; Eliasberg:742, VF, $4,400. They could be simulated by 1873 S coins with mintmark removed; authentication is mandatory. Proofs (Feb. 18, ill.) have date below center; possibly 10–12 survive, some impaired. Ely, Garrett:1671, $40,000; Auction 79:336, $36,000; Atwater, Carter:770, $20,900. Gilt copper strikings weigh far less than standard.

6973   1873 S Closed 3. [12,000] Very rare.

4 obvs. shipped Nov. 1872; only one var. seen. Usually weakly struck, unlike the Philadelphia coins. Prohibitively rare EF. Wayman:90, UNC., $2,800.

6974   1873 CC [all kinds 4,543] Closed 3. Normal. Ex. rare.

Breen 1. Usually in low grades. Wayman:89, EF, $2,300. Compare next 2.

6975   1873 CC Repunched 18, normal rev. Ex. rare.

Breen 3. Bases of 18, upper serif of 1 repunched. Usually in low grades. Compare next.

6976   1873 CC Repunched 18, doubled rev. die. Ex. rare.

Breen 2. Same obv.; doubling plainest at TEN D. and AMERICA. Usually in low grades.

6977   1874 [53,140 + 20P] Rare.

4 minor vars. of business strikes; Ex. rare above EF. Most were recoined from obsolete gold dollars and quarter eagles. Of proofs (Feb. 14) about 8–10 survive. Ely, Garrett:1672, $49,000; Atwater, Carter:771, $28,600.

6978   1874 S [10,000] Very rare.

2 minute positional vars. Usually weakly struck; prohibitively rare above VF.

6979   1874 CC [16,767] Rare.

CC usually weak and faint. See ill. in Akers {1980}. Often

weakly struck; prohibitively rare above VF. Clapp, Eliasberg:746, UNC., $17,600.

6980   1875 [100 + 20P] Ex. rare.

Business strikes (ill., enl.) have low date, l. base of 1 r. of center of dentil; dentils narrow and well separated from about 10:00 to 1:00; no lump atop Y (unlike 1875 CC). Possibly 4–6 survive. Mocatta, 1979 ANA:313, EF, $62,000; Atwater, Carter:772, VG, $27,500. Proofs (Feb. 13) have low date, farther to l., l. base of 1 over l. edge of dentil; top of second stripe weak. Ill. Akers {1980}. Possibly 8–10 survive, some impaired. 1) Mint, SI. 2) Brock, Morgan, ANS. 3) Parmelee, Woodin, Boyd, WGC, "Bell," "Memorable":573, Farouk, Kosoff. 4) Garrett (1976):453, $91,000. 5) Clapp, Eliasberg:748, $104,500, H. Sconyers. 6) H. P. Smith set, Dunham:2245. Same comment as to 1873 about underweight gilt copper strikings.

6981   1875 CC [7,715] Very rare.

Centered date; lump atop r. arm of Y; 2 minor positional vars. of rev. Ill. Akers {1980}. Usually weakly struck, F to VF, prohibitively rare above. Wayman:94, AU, $1,700; Clapp, Eliasberg:749, EF, $1,980.

6982   1876 [687 + 45P] Ex. rare.

Business strikes have low date, no rust pits on neck; die file marks below LIB and through ERTY; l. base of 1 almost over r. edge of dentil. Possibly 12–15 survive, mostly in low grades. 1976 ANA:3049, AU, $3,800. Proofs have rust pits on neck near jaw; the [20] of Feb. 19 cannot be told from the [25] of June 13. Possibly 14–18 survive, some impaired. Garrett:1673, $21,000; Clapp, Eliasberg:750, $15,400; Carter:773, triple-struck (other strikings rotated 5° and 10° from final one), $17,600.

6983   1876 S [5,000] Very rare.

Date about central, unlike **6982.** Ex. rare above VF. Wayman:97, EF, $1,200.

6984   1876 CC [4,696] Very rare.

Same comments. Usually weak in centers. 1976 ANA:3100, UNC., $2,000.

6985   1877 [797 + 20P] Ex. rare.

Business strikes (2 obvs., 1 rev. made, only one die-pair used) have date about centered, l. base of 1 r. of center of dentil, weak outlines to scroll, IN ST in field; minutely doubled rev., plainest on UNITED STATES and adjacent wingtip; top and base of second stripe weak, its l. line detached. Ahwash, Auction 80:955, UNC., $17,500, Auction 84:949, $9,900; Carter:774, AU, $5,775. Beware forgeries made by removing mintmark from 1877 S. Authentication mandatory. Proofs have low date, l. base of 1 about over l. edge of dentil, rev. of 1876 proofs with polish above space over IN in scroll. Ill. Breen {1977}, p. 159. The 2 batches, [10 each] Feb. 24 and May 31, cannot be told apart. Possibly 10–12 survive. Garrett:1674, $31,000.

6986   1877 S Taller S. [17,000] Rare.

3 minor vars. Prohibitively rare above EF.

6987 1877 CC [3,332] Very rare.
2 vars., low or centered date. Weak in centers. Prohibitively rare in EF. Wayman:99, EF, $1,900.

6988 1878 [73,780 + 20P]
Business strikes have date low or central. Proofs (Feb. 9) have low date, l. base of 1 slightly r. of center of dentil, repolished rev. of 1876–77 proofs; ill. Breen {1977}, p. 162. Possibly 8–10 survive: Auction 79:338, $13,000; D. S. Wilson, Clapp, Eliasberg:756, $18,700.

6989 1878 S Very small s. [26,100] Rare.
Prohibitively rare above VF.

6990 1878 CC Taller CC. [3,244] Very rare.
This taller mintmark continues through 1893 except as noted. Usually in low grades; prohibitively rare above VF. Wayman:102, EF, $3,200.

6991 1879 [all kinds 384,740 + 30P] Normal.
Several minor positional vars. Ex. rare in mint state. Proofs have date low to l.; detached "floating" curls behind neck. Possibly 10 survive. Mint, Garrett:1675, $34,000.

6992 1879 Doubled rev. die. Rare.
Doubling plainest on arrows and shafts; 2 obv. vars.

6993 1879/8 Ex. rare.
Part of lower r. loop of 8 within loop of 9. Discovery coin, Bell I:644. Only 2 UNCs.: 1) 1973 MANA:1698, Breen II:257, $1,250 (1975). 2) 1982 ANA:2694.

6994 1879 O [1,500] Very rare.
Possibly 12–15 survive. Prohibitively rare above EF. Lamborn, "Fairfield":1823, AU, $5,750; 1980 ANA:333, EF, $3,000.

6995 1879 S Taller S. [224,000]
Filled mintmark; minute positional vars. Very rare UNC.

6996 1879 CC [1,762] Ex. rare.
Usually in low grades; prohibitively rare above VF. Possibly 10–12 survive. Auction 79:1321, EF, $5,400; Clapp, Eliasberg:760, VF+, $3,575.

6997 1880 [1,644,840 + 36P]
Minute positional vars. Probably fewer than 10 proofs survive. Mint, Garrett:1676, $27,000.

6998 1880 O [9,200] Rare.
Always with lightly doubled stars; 2 minor rev. vars. Prohibitively rare in AU.

6999 1880 S [all kinds 506,250] Tiny s.
Minor positional vars. Mintmark as in previous years; see ill. of 1878 S in Akers {1980} for type. Often weakly struck.

7000 1880 S Taller S.
Same comment; this mintmark as in 1881–99. Ill. Akers {1980}. Often weak.

7001 1880 CC [11,190]
2 minor vars. Prohibitively rare UNC.

7002 1881 [3,877,220 + 42P] Normal rev.
Many minor vars., including the "nut var." (something held in eagle's beak) and one with raised round dot within upper loop of second 8. Proofs (March 19) have date to r., incomplete curls behind neck. Clapp, Eliasberg:767, $13,200; Carter:776, $19,800.

7003 1881 Doubled rev. die. Rare.
Price for that with obvious doubling on most of legend, extra outlines mostly to r. of final position. Other vars. with less noticeable doubling will price as preceding.

7004 1881 O [8,350] Rare.
Low date slanting up to r. Prohibitively rare in AU. Wayman:114, AU, $1,600.

7005 1881 S [970,000]
Minor positional vars.

7006 1881 CC [24,015]
2 minor positional vars. Very rare above AU. Clapp, Eliasberg:768, UNC., $3,850.

7007 1882 [2,324,440 + 44P]
Minor positional vars. Proofs have slanting die file marks through T(Y); thin shallow stripes. Probably fewer than 15 survive. Carter:777, $24,200.

7008 1882 O [10,820] Rare.
Prohibitively rare in AU. Wayman:118, UNC., $2,800.

7009 1882 S [132,000]
Ex. rare in AU. Revs. returned to Philadelphia Mint for inspection and reuse; some (not identified) showed alterations to outer edge of tail and branch, and "added stems." These may reappear with obvs. of later date.

7010 1882 CC [6,764] Very rare.
Prohibitively rare above EF. Eliasberg:772, AU, $3,080.

7011 1883 [208,700 + 49P]
Minor positional vars. Proofs have low date slanting up to r., incomplete feathers below shield. Mocatta, 1979 ANA:320, $10,500; Carter:778, $11,000.

7012 1883 O [800] Ex. rare.
Low date slants up slightly to r.; l. base of 1 above l. edge of dentil; narrow mintmark as in 1879–82, high, equally close to claw and feather; later, cracked through tops of UNIT and OF to adjacent wingtip. Usually VF; prohibitively rare in AU. Eliasberg:777, EF, $3,575; Carter:779, AU, $6,875.

7013 1883 S [38,000] Very scarce.
Usually weakly struck; very rare above EF. Eliasberg:778, UNC., $1,870. Same comment as to **7009.**

7014 1883 CC [all kinds 12,000] Small wide cc.
2 positional vars. Very rare above EF. Wayman:121, AU, $1,800.

7015 1883 CC Tall close CC. Very rare.
Doubled rev. die, doubling plainest at upper legend, beak, and wing near OF. Ex. rare above EF.

7016 1884 [76,890 + 45P] Very scarce.
Ex. rare in AU. Auction 82:1955, UNC., $3,500. Proofs have low date slanting up to r., incomplete curls behind neck, l. base of 1 left of center of dentil, r. base of 4 about over r. edge of dentil; possibly 8–10 survive. Garrett (1976):483, $15,000; Clapp, Eliasberg:779, $25,300; Carter:780, $23,100.

7017 1884 S [124,250]
Filled S, minute positional vars.; one with S leaning well to l. Ex. rare above EF.

7018 1884 CC [9,925] Normal obv., close tall CC. Rare.
Prohibitively rare in EF.

7019 1884 CC Canceled obv., wide C C. Rare.
Chisel marks on bust, neck, hair below ear, and at LI(BER)T; ill. Akers {1980}. These marks are raised on the coin; an unsuccessful attempt was made to efface them from the die before it went to press. Same grade comment as preceding. Discovery coin, Wolfson:746, Tex. pvt. coll.

7020 1885 [253,462 + 67P]
Very rare in AU. Minute positional vars. Proofs have incomplete feathers below second white stripe, die file marks within first 2 white stripes near top; possibly 14–18 survive. Clapp, Eliasberg:782, $14,300; Carter:781, $16,500.

7021 1885 S [228,000]
Minute positional vars. The 5 pairs of dies shipped to Carson City remained unused owing to closure of that branch.

7022 1886 [236,100 + 60P]
Minute positional vars. Ex. rare in AU. Possibly 15–20 proofs survive; Carter:782, $17,600.

7023 1886 S [826,000]

7024 1887 [53,600 + 80P] Scarce.
Business strikes have level date. Proofs have date high and slanting up to r.; 4 red stripes thin, feathers attenuated below second. Possibly 15–20 survive; Eliasberg:786, $14,300; Carter:783, $18,700.

7025 1887 S [817,000]

7026 1888 [132,924 + 72P]
Ex. rare above AU. Proofs have low date, rev. of 1887; ill. Breen {1977}, p. 188. Possibly 20–25 survive. Eliasberg:788, $12,100.

7027 1888 O [21,335] Very scarce.
4 pairs of dies; 2 minor positional vars. seen. Mintmark has wider opening than in previous O mints. Extremely rare UNC.: Wayman:134, $1,350.

7028 1888 S [648,700]
3 minor vars., the most marked with lump between outer r. loops of final 8. Often weakly struck.

7029 1889 [4,440 + 45P] Very rare.
Beware forgeries made by removing S from genuine 1889 S coins. Authentication mandatory. Usually EF to AU. Proofs have date high to r.; possibly 12 survive: Carter:785, $17,600.

7030 1889 S [425,400]
At least 4 minor vars.; S usually filled, in one die with traces of repunching.

7031 1890 [57,980 + 63P] Very scarce.
Proofs have date to r., slanting up to r.; incomplete curls behind neck; polish at ear, eye, and usually TY; possibly 20–25 survive.

7032 1890 CC [17,500] Very scarce.
Tall heavy CC through 1893. Very rare in mint state.

7033 1891 [91,820 + 48P] Scarce.
Proofs have date to r., slanting up to r.; incomplete curls behind neck. Possibly 15 survive. Garrett:1677, $20,000; Carter:786, $16,500.

7034 1891 CC [103,732] Normal CC.
At least 3 positional vars. of date and mintmark; not to be confused with next.

7035 1891 CC Second C double-punched. Rare.
RPM 1. Second C first punched well to r. of final position, then corrected; overlapping parts of both are clear. Spine below chin; various states of cracks through stars. Phoenix:1731; 1982 ANA:2695.

7036 1892 [797,480 + 72P]
Business strikes come with clear 2 or lower half of 2 filled (r. of angle, above base); this is not an overdate. Clear-2 coins sometimes have extensive cracks through legend. Proofs have low date; possibly 25–30 survive. Carter:787, $10,175.

7037 1892 O Round O. [28,688] Very scarce.
Various stages of cracks through legend. UNCs. are from a hoard of 25 found in 1979.

7038 1892 S [115,500]
Minute positional vars. UNCs. are from a tiny hoard found about 1977.

7039 1892 CC [40,000] Very scarce.
Earliest impressions show traces of repunching on 89; later, these fade, and cracks develop through stars. Very rare in mint state. Clapp, Eliasberg:798, UNC., $9,900.

7040 1893 [1,840,840 + 55P]
Minor positional vars. Proofs have low date slanting up to r.; disconnected curls behind neck; missing feather below second red stripe. Possibly 15–20 survive. Mint, Clapp, Eliasberg:801, $14,300; Carter:788, $16,500.

7041 1893 O [17,000] Rare.
Without or with die polish below ear.

7042 1893 S [141,350] Normal S.
Positional vars. exist; compare next. Often weakly struck. Over 2/3 of surviving UNCs. are from a small hoard discovered in 1977.

7043 1893 S Double S. Very rare.
Entire top of extra S shows r. of top of mintmark. Later states showing less of the extra S will price as preceding.

7044 1893 CC [14,000] Rare.
Very rare in AU.

7045 1894 [2,470,735 + 43P]
Minor positional vars., some with extensive cracks through stars or legend, one with traces of repunching on base of 1. Proofs have low date slanting up to r., rev. of 1893 proofs; possibly 15–20 survive. Mint, Clapp, Eliasberg:805, $10,450.

7046 1894 O [107,500]
Minor positional vars.; curls behind neck normal or disconnected. Rare in mint state.

7047 1894 S [25,000] Very scarce.
Generally somewhat prooflike. Ex. rare AU. Wayman:152, UNC., $2,600.

7048 1895 [567,770 + 56P]
Minor positional vars.; curls behind neck normal or disconnected. Proofs have low date slanting up to r.; die polish at eye and IB(ERT)Y; "floating" curls behind neck. Possibly 18–20 survive. Carter:789, $20,900.

7049 1895 O [98,000]
At least 2 minor rev. vars., both minutely doubled dies. Very rare UNC.

7050 1895 S [49,000] Normal filled S. Rare.
Usually VF to EF; prohibitively rare AU. Mint, Clapp, Eliasberg:810, UNC., $14,300.

7051 1895 S Double-punched S. Rare.
Same comments. Rarer than preceding.

7052 1896 [76,270 + 78P]
Business strikes sometimes show obv. die cracks. Possibly 20–25 proofs survive. Mint, Clapp, Eliasberg:811, $8,800; Carter:790, $20,350.

7053 1896 S [123,750]
S normal or a shapeless blob. Minor positional vars. Often weakly struck. Prohibitively rare AU. Mint, Clapp, Eliasberg:812, UNC., $10,450.

7054 1897 [1,000,090 + 69P] Normal date.
Minor positional vars., one with traces of repunching on 18. See next. Proofs have low date slanting up to r., light repunching on base of 1; possibly 35–40 survive. Mint, Clapp, Eliasberg:813, $9,350.

7055 1897 Heavily repunched 1. Rare.
Extremely heavy 1, obvious double base. Obv. quickly shattered. Discovery coin, "Melish":2553.

7056 1897 O [42,500]
Very rare UNC. Mint, Clapp, Eliasberg:814, UNC., $10,450.

7057 1897 S [234,750]
Very rare AU. Mint, Clapp, Eliasberg:815, UNC., $8,800.

7058 1898 [812,130 + 67P]
Minor positional vars. Proofs have low date slanting sharply up to r.; possibly 35–40 survive, some cleaned or impaired. Mint, Clapp, Eliasberg:816, $12,100; Carter:792, $20,900.

7059 1898 S [473,600]
Several positional vars., one with mintmark leaning far to r.: NN 49:313. UNCs. (rare) are from a tiny hoard found in 1977.

7060 1899 [all kinds 1,262,219 + 86P] Normal date.
Minor positional vars., including one with top of final 9 faintly repunched, another with light repunching within tops of 99. Rhodes:2915. Proofs have faint traces of repunching on bases of 18. Possibly 25–30 survive. Mint, Clapp, Eliasberg:818, $14,300; Carter:793, $16,500.

7061 1899 Overdate. Very rare.
Plain traces of other digits within upper loops of 899, differing in curvature. Discovery coin, Breen I:260, Hirt:1642.

7062 1899 O [37,047]
Very rare in mint state. Mint, Clapp, Eliasberg:819, $24,200.

7063 1899 S [841,000] Medium S, filled.
Several positional vars. "Melish":2564.

7064 1899 S Squat S.
Mintmark broader, less tall, not filled. Positional vars. exist. "Melish":2561–63.

7065 1900 [293,840 + 120P]
Many minor positional vars. Proofs have low date to r.; possibly 35–40 survive. Mint, Clapp, Eliasberg:821, $14,300; Carter:794, $16,500.

7066 1900 S [81,000] Medium filled S.
All vars. very rare in EF. Compare next 2.

7067 1900 S Open S. Normal date. Scarce.
Serifs of S farther from middle stroke. Ill. Akers {1980}.

7068 1900 S Open S; repunched 90. Rare.
Parts of extra 90 within upper halves of 90; same S.

7069 1901 [1,718,740] Normal date.
A hoard of hundreds of UNCs. showed up in the 1950s.

7070 1901 Repunched 190. Proofs only. [85P]
Bases of 19, inner top of 0 plainly repunched. Possibly 30–40 survive. Mint, Clapp, Eliasberg:823, $11,000; Carter:795, $19,800.

7071 1901 O [72,041] Normal mintmark.
Rare UNC.

7072 1901 O Double-punched mintmark. Very scarce.
Very rare UNC.

7073 1901 S [2,812,750] Normal.
Common in mint state from one or several hoards, totaling over 1,000; many minute positional vars. Compare next 2.

7074 1901 S Doubled rev. die. Rare.
Doubling plainest on UNITED STATES OF, wings, beak, branch.

7075 1901 S Repunched date. Very scarce.
Doubling obvious on bases of 19, top of 0. 1984 Midwinter ANA:338.

7076 1902 [82,400 + 113P] Scarce.
Rare in mint state. Possibly 35–40 proofs survive; Mint, Clapp, Eliasberg:826, $12,100.

7077 1902 S [469,500]
UNCs. are mostly from 2 hoards discovered after 1970, over 1,000 in all.

7078 1903 [125,860 + 96P]
Possibly 35–40 proofs survive. Mint, Clapp, Eliasberg:826, $12,100.

7079 1903 O [112,771]
Minor positional vars., at least 2 with minutely repunched mintmark.

7080 1903 S [538,000]
Positional vars., several with heavily cracked dies. UNCs. are from the 2 hoards mentioned at **7077.**

7081 1904 [161,930 + 108P]
Proofs have high date slanting down to r.; possibly 35–40 survive. Mint, Clapp, Eliasberg:831, $11,000; Carter:796, $16,500.

7082 1904 O [108,950]

7083 1905 [200,992 + 86P]
Proofs have date far to l.; missing feathers below second white stripe; possibly 30–35 survive. Mint, Clapp, Eliasberg:833, $11,000.

7084 1905 S [369,250]
Minor positional vars., one with light repunching on mintmark. Very rare in mint state.

7085 1906 [165,420 + 77P]
Proofs have date high, far to l.; possibly 30–35 survive. Ill.

Akers {1980}. Mint, Clapp, Eliasberg:835, Proof, $10,450; Carter:799, $15,400.

7086 1906 O [86,895]
Very rare in mint state. Clapp, Eliasberg:837, $2,860.

7087 1906 S [457,000]
Minor positional vars., some with heavily cracked dies. Often weakly struck. Rare in mint state.

7088 1906 D [all kinds 981,000 + 12?P]
Many positional vars. of date and mintmark. Many UNCs. were saved as first of their kind. The proofs were supposedly struck March 12, 1906, to celebrate inception of coinage. Cf. Breen II:288.

7089 1906/5 D Ex. rare.
Crossbar of 5 visible within top of 6. Die doubtless prepared fall 1905, not yet assigned to a mint, given one blow from a 1905 logotype while dies for 1905 coins were still being made, then heavier corrections from a 1906 logotype, only later shipped to Denver. Date central, heavily impressed, possibly to divert attention from the overdate.

7090 1907 [1,203,900 + 74P]
Minor positional vars. of business strikes. There may have been a hoard of UNCs. Proofs have high date to l., die polish at IBERTY, end of scroll below ST vague; possibly 30–35 survive: Mint, Clapp, Eliasberg:839, $12,650.

7091 1907/7 Rare.
Base of 7 obviously repunched.

7092 1907 S Smaller s. [210,500]
Minor positional vars. Very rare UNC.

7093 1907 D [1,030,000]
Minor positional vars. Much more difficult to find UNC. than 1906 D. At least one proof reportedly struck.

v. ST. GAUDENS'S DESIGN, NO MOTTO (1907–8)

For the new eagle design, Augustus St. Gaudens (in consultation with Pres. Theodore Roosevelt) decided to use not a standing figure but a head, feeling that the heroic effect of any standing figure, as chosen for the double eagle, would be lost in smaller diameter. The President, disgusted beyond measure at what he called our "atrociously hideous" coinage, had asked St. Gaudens to design replacements. The profile St. Gaudens chose originated in a figure of Nikē ('Victory'), part of his Gen. Sherman Monument (1905), ultimately inspired by a Hellenistic Wingless Victory on the temple of Zeus Sōtēr ('Father Jove who saves us') at Pergamon. Tharp ({1969}, p. 357) says his model was Alice Butler. At Pres. Roosevelt's insistence, and for no other reason, St. Gaudens gave this head a nationalistic character by the absurd addition of a feathered warbonnet, such as neither Ms. Liberty nor any Native American woman would ever have worn. And so this new design acquired the misleading sobriquet of "Indian head," properly applicable only to Pratt's 1908–29 half eagles and quarter eagles. Possibly the warbonnet also served to conceal any connection with the Sherman monument, to minimize protests in the South.

On the other hand, St. Gaudens's standing-eagle device is splendid in its original form, reminiscent of late Egyptian and early Roman work at its best, though it is seen in untampered form only in the rare experimental pieces **7094–96.**

The very first of these ("Type I") are the only available gold $10's showing the St. Gaudens conceptions in anywhere near their pristine splendor. Commonly called "wire edge with periods," these have raised triangular dots before UNITED, after AMERICA, before TEN and after DOLLARS. Their distinctive rim (miscalled "wire edge," properly "knife-rim"—in Mint parlance a "fin") is a nearly uniform, extremely narrow extra rim outside the plain border, caused by metal being forced between dies and collar at striking. It is poorly adapted to coins for circulation, as it may interfere with ejection of coins from dies and later with stacking, quite aside from being a potentially irritating dirt catcher; the next dies lacked this feature. Central details differ from all subsequent designs. With a single unique exception, all have 46 stars on edge—a device replacing the old reeded edge and continued through 1911. This edge was imparted by a segmented collar which withdrew after the blow imparting the design to allow the newly struck coin to eject.

Almost all of the 50 matte- or satin-finish proofs of this type have vanished, or remain unrecognized. They should be needle sharp in central details on both sides, which the 400-odd regularly seen specimens are not. The latter have a peculiar surface entirely unlike that of ordinary production coins of other dates, with millions of irregular random striations in fields.

Then followed a second version ("Type II"), retaining the triangular dots, but with a high raised lip or protective rim, similar to that on proof Lincoln cents; this is usually miscalled "rolled edge." The mintage is uncertain: Most reference books say 20,000; Mint Director Frank Leach, 34,100; Philadelphia Mint Superintendent John H. Landis, [31,550]. As Landis was there at the time, whereas Leach was in Washington, I tend to credit Landis's figure. But whatever the correct original figure, for unspecified reasons all were melted except 42, of which three are ensconced in SI, others in various museums and estates. The documented first specimen struck, Sept. 13, 1907, a matte proof, was bid up to $11,000 in 1972 ANA:2585 to Harry Bass; this piece was stolen in 1983 and has not yet been recovered. It differs notably in surface from the usual UNCs. The most probable reason for meltage was Mint Engraver Charles E. Barber's complaints; Barber had objected to every outsider's design since 1879, as he would continue to complain until his death in 1917.

Whatever the reason, the design finally put into circulation is not by St. Gaudens at all, but is instead Barber's inferior copy of the St. Gaudens models. Not only is the relief less bold, but the triangular dots are omitted, the branch is differently shaped, a curl encroaches on IBE, some letters are differently shaped, and feather ends are clearer—though central hair and feathers are not. This type continued through part of 1908, and is commonly miscalled "Indian, no motto."

Unlike later years, Denver coins of 1908–10, without and with motto, show a very broad boldface D, like that on the 1906–7 $20's. This mintmark, like the corresponding smaller one for San Francisco, is tilted so as to follow the curve of border.

Many borderline UNC. specimens survive of the 1907, saved as first year of design; but pristine coins are very difficult to find of this year, and more so of 1908 without motto.

ST. GAUDENS'S DESIGN, NO MOTTO

Designer, Augustus St. Gaudens. Engraver, St. Gaudens (1907 "Type I, II"); Barber (1907–8 "Type III"). Mints, Philadelphia (no mintmark), Denver (mintmark D). Mintmark above leaves. Physical Specifications, as before, except raised stars on edge. Authorizing Acts, as before.

Grade range, FINE to UNC. Not collected in low grades. FINE: Partial contours on neck hair; most feathers separated but their junction with headband cannot be seen; "shoulder" of wing (below and l. of motto) blurs into neck and breast but some feathers near its end and on tail are separated. VERY FINE: At least half hair details; most feathers clearly touch headband; about half feathers separated on wing below motto. EXTREMELY FINE: Isolated tiny rubbed spots on eyebrow, cheekbone, hair below LIB, and at center, forward edges of wings; partial mint luster. UNCIRCULATED: *No* trace of wear. EXCEP-

TIONS: Regular 1907's are often weak even in mint state; look for mint frost on the weak areas.

7094 1907 "Type I," starred edge. [Net 448− + 50−P]
Judd 1774. Triangular dots; knife-rim. Mintage originally [500], including the proofs, less 2 officially melted. One proof was in the Capt. North cased set. See introductory text and Breen {1977}, pp. 207–8. Not intended for circulation. Almost all survivors are UNCS. distributed to officials and VIPs. Mint, Garrett:1682, UNC., $20,000; Mitchelson, Clapp, Eliasberg:842, $26,000. See introductory text.

7095 1907 "Type I," plain edge. Unique? Reported.
Judd 1774a.
7096 1907 "Type II." [Net 42− + 1+P]
Judd 1775. Triangular dots; flat border. Original mintage uncertain, most likely [31,550−]; see introductory text. First coined Sept. 13, 1907. Besides the documented first specimen, there are possibly 3 or 4 other proofs, one in the Capt. North set. Most other survivors are UNC. S 12/11/80:751, UNC., $56,000; Mint, Garrett:1683, UNC., $60,000; Mitchelson, Clapp, Eliasberg:843, $38,500; Carter:801, $44,000; Auction 85:968, $41,800.

7097 1907 "Type III." No periods. [239,406]
By Barber after St. Gaudens. Without or with minute doubling on obv. stars. Usually weak in centers. Many UNCs. were saved of the new design; many of these are nicked, scratched, or cleaned. The 2 apparently experimental proofs in DiBello:1170, later Auction 81:1869–70, have not become available for verification.

7098 1908 No motto. [33,500]
Similar to preceding. Only one var.: thick letters in LIBERTY, low relief, very faint die lines at date, minute dot on l. edge of 1 in date. Usually weak in centers.
7099 1908 D No motto. [210,000]
As last. Minute positional differences of mintmark. Weak in centers; often dull.

vi. THE BARBER-ST. GAUDENS DESIGN, WITH MOTTO (1908–33)

Less than a year after adoption of the St. Gaudens design, an outraged and furious Congress (probably goaded by vociferous clergy) ordered that the motto IN GOD WE TRUST be forthwith restored to the coinage, as mandated by the Act of March 3, 1865. The 1907 issues and the first ones of 1908 had lacked this motto because Pres. Theodore Roosevelt, on religious grounds (Dutch Reformed Church and Freemasonry), believed that placing the name of God on currency was a debasement amounting to blasphemy. After all, these coins bearing the name of God were likely too often to be dropped, stepped on, used in rigged gambling or for hiring assassins or buying murder weapons.

Congressmen, of course, had forgotten about the jeers which greeted the original addition of this motto to our coins. Many even in the 1860s recognized that it was likely to be misread or satirically rendered, as in fact happened; "In Gold We Trust" and "In God We Trust—All Others Must Pay Cash" became mock slogans heard to the present day. Others assumed that the proper name of the god worshipped by the owners—and possibly some of the makers—was Mammon.

Nevertheless, Congress insisted on flinging this particular lump of incense onto the altar, even as—in one of the weirder coincidences—the British Parliament was to do three years later when George V's new 1911 Canadian "Godless" coins omitted the traditional initials D.G. (= DEI GRATIA, 'By the grace of God'). Possibly the congressmen were more concerned with proving that they were not atheists than with preserving separation of church and state.

The new design with motto is by Charles E. Barber, after St. Gaudens. Aside from the addition of the motto, none of Barber's niggling changes are defensible as improvements unless one insists that more of the first U of UNUM *had* to show. Nor is striking quality improved.

Denver Mint coins 1908–10 continue the extra broad mintmark, tilted so as to follow the curve of border, as on **7099;** later dates show a much smaller mintmark. S mintmarks are always small, also following the curve of border.

Coins dated 1908–11 have 46 stars on edge as before; 1912–33, 48 stars, the extra two being added to honor the admission of Arizona and New Mexico. Edges continued to be imparted by segmented (tripartite) collars.

All proofs 1908–15 are much rarer than their mintage figures suggest; notably rarer than most dates 1897–1907. Many were melted in 1917 as unsold, others spent during the 1921 and 1929–33 financial crises. These proofs have finishes differing from one year to another; see Breen {1977}, pp. 207–16. Dangerous forgeries exist; authentication strongly recommended.

Before 1920 no dates or mintmarks are rare in ordinary grades, though some are Ex. rare choice. Thereafter, only two dates are readily obtainable: 1926 and 1932. In my experience, 1920 S is rarer than 1930 S or 1933. For some decades one 1930 S turned up in the San Francisco area every three years, probably from a single roll. The 1933 is usually considered rarest, only a few dozen at most legally released in Jan.–Feb. 1933. About 1952 a small hoard, possibly 20–30 in all, probably the majority of the coins issued, showed up on the East Coast. (I studied eight of them on a single tray in 1953: gem mint-state beauties.) A few others turned up later, from French and Swiss banks. No hoard of 1920 S ever appeared, though since 1980 possibly four or five have returned from Europe, and reportedly 10 more were found in upper New York State. Most of these late dates only come UNC. with varying amounts of bag marks, testifying to their long residence in bank cash reserves.

The Coinage Act of July 23, 1965 (PL 89-81), Sect. 392, has apparently restored their legal-tender status.

THE BARBER-ST. GAUDENS DESIGN, WITH MOTTO

Designer, Engraver, Charles E. Barber, after St. Gaudens. Mints, Philadelphia (no mintmark), San Francisco (mintmark S), Denver (D). Mintmark opposite or below arrow points. Physical Specifications, Authorizing Acts, as before.

Grade range and standards, as before. NOTE: Not collected in low grades.

7100   1908 Motto. [341,486 + 116P]
Proofs have dark matte finish, between khaki and olive color, like half eagles and quarter eagles of this year. Of over 25 examined, nearly half show nicks or shiny spots from careless handling. Garrett:1685, $32,500; Mitchelson, Clapp, Eliasberg:847, $11,000. Compare next.

Ex J. W. Garrett: 1685. Courtesy Bowers & Ruddy Galleries, Inc.

7101   1908 Motto. "Roman Finish" proof. Ex. rare.
Same finish as 1909–10 proofs: satiny, semibrilliant, pale lemon color. 1) BMFA, 1976 ANA:3151, $7,500, Robert Kruthoffer. Authentication mandatory.

7102   1908 S [59,850] Normal S.
S below arrow points, about parallel to upright of T(EN). UNCS. are from 2 small hoards, one (of at least 20) found in the 1940s, the other (fewer, choice) from Europe in the 1970s. Mint, Clapp, Eliasberg:849, $14,300.

7103   1908 S Double S. Very rare.
RPM 1.

7104   1908 D Motto. [836,500]
Broad D, parallel to upright of T(EN), partly or wholly below arrow points. Slightly harder to find choice than 1908 S, though much less rare in lower grades.

7105   1909 [184,789 + 74P]
Difficult to find in mint state. Proofs normally have "Roman" finish: satiny, semibrilliant, pale lemon color: Garrett:1686, $28,000; Mint, Clapp, Eliasberg:850, $19,250.

7106   1909 Dark matte proof. Ex. rare.
Similar to 1908 proofs. 1) DiBello:1177, Auction 81:1871, $19,000. 2) Beck I:548. Authentication is mandatory.

7107   1909 S [293,250] Normal S.
Mintmark opposite or slightly below arrow points. UNCS.

(about 70–90 in all?) are mostly from a small hoard found in South America about 1977.

7108 1909 S Double-punched S. Very rare.
RPM 1.

7109 1909 D [121,540] D opposite arrow points.
Broad D, parallel upright of T(EN), directly l. of arrow points. Minor positional vars. Very scarce UNC. Compare next.

7110 1909 D Mintmark below arrow points.
Apparently an intentional change of position to give a less cramped effect. Less scarce UNC. than preceding.

7111 1910 [318,500 + 204 – P]
Proofs of this number have "Roman" finish, as **7105**. Most were evidently melted; they are much rarer than mintage figure suggests. Authentication is necessary. Mint, Garrett:1682, $35,000; Mint, Clapp, Eliasberg:853, $24,200. Compare next.

7112 1910 Satin finish proof. Ex. rare.
Finish similar to **7094–96**. 1) Breen I:276. 2) 1974 GENA:2100. 3) Discovered at a 1982 Long Beach convention.

7113 1910 S [811,000]
Mintmark as in **7107**. Very scarce in mint state. Wayman:199, UNC., $2,000.

7114 1910 S Triple S. Ex. rare.
RPM 1.

7115 1910 D [2,356,640] D below arrow points.
Broad mintmark as in **7110**. Minute positional vars. UNCs. are from an old hoard.

7116 1910 D Mintmark partly above arrow points. Rare.
As **7109**. Probably a leftover die.

7117 1911 [505,500 + 95P]
Proofs have dark matte finish like 1908, or "mustard colored" (Akers {1980}) sandblast finish like 1912. These are difficult to identify without having both at hand for comparison; it is unknown which is rarer. Authentication is necessary. Mint, Garrett:1688, $39,000; Clapp, Eliasberg:856, $17,600. Many forgeries exist of choice business strikes, 1911–15; these often have ditch-like indentation between DO and leaves.

7118 1911 S [51,000]
Mintmark as in **7107**. UNCs. are mostly from a small hoard, said to number 60 pieces, found in the Philippines ca. 1976, thence to NERCG via Spain.

7119 1911 D Small D. [30,100]
The tiny mintmark is below a point opposite central arrow point; this position becomes standard on S- and D-Mint coins henceforth. Very rare UNC. Wayman:201, UNC., $3,300. Authentication is necessary.

7120 1912 48 stars on edge. [405,000 + 83P]
Proofs (very rare) have fine sandblast finish, showing millions of sparkling facets under a magnifier. Authentication is mandatory. Mint, Garrett:1689, $22,000; Clapp, Eliasberg:859, $20,900, Kagin.

7121 1912 S 48 stars on edge. [300,000]
Squat S henceforth. Rare in mint state. Wayman:204, $2,400.

7122 1913 [442,000 + 71P]
Proofs are as in 1912; same comments. Mint, Garrett:1694, $22,000; Clapp, Eliasberg:861, $22,000.

7123 1913 S [66,000]
S slightly smaller. Very rare in mint state. 1980 ANA:379, UNC., $31,000.

7124 1914 [151,000 + 50P]
Proofs have coarse sandblast finish; under a strong glass, the facets are slightly larger than in 1912. Authentication is mandatory. Mint, Garrett:1691, $36,000; Clapp, Eliasberg:863, $24,200.

7125 1914 S [208,000]
Very scarce in mint state. Auction 79:361, $8,750. Compare next.

7126 1914 S Double S. Rare.
RPM 1.

7127 1914 D Small D. [343,500]

7128 1915 [351,000 + 75 – P]
Proofs are as in 1914; authentication is mandatory. Mint, Garrett:1692, $28,000; Clapp, Eliasberg:866, $18,700.

7129 1915 S [59,000]
Usually VF to EF; rare in mint state. Auction 80:964, UNC., $6,250.

7130 1916 S [138,500]
UNCs. are from 2 small hoards found about 1976–77. Many forgeries have raised marks in space between upper l. stars and rim, and a raised dot below fourth star (clockwise from l.).

7131 1920 S Larger S. [126,500 –] Very rare.
Mostly melted; see introductory text. Usually UNC. with bag marks; centers often weak, especially at RTY. Auction 80:457, $50,000; G. S. Godard, Auction 82:404, UNC., $27,000; Comparette, Clapp, Eliasberg:869, $40,700.

7132 1926 [1,014,000]
Usually found UNC. Plentiful from old hoards.

7133 1930 S Larger S. [96,000 –] Rare.
S as in 1920. Mostly melted; see introductory text. Usually UNC. with bag marks: 1980 ANA:394, $27,000; Wayman:215, $14,500; Auction 85:1953, $18,150.

7134 1932 [4,463,000] Normal dies.
Almost always UNC. Plentiful from old hoards.

7135 1932 Doubled obv. die. Rare.
Doubling plainest on 32.

7136 1932 Doubled rev. die. Rare.
Doubling plainest on letters at l., particularly UN, G, and TE(N).

7137 1933 [312,500 –] Very rare.
Minted Jan.–Feb. 1933; mostly melted. Enl. photos. See introductory text. Always UNC. Roach, Eliasberg:873, UNC., $93,500, H. Sconyers. Ludicrous prooflike forgeries turned up about 1960: high relief, extra-concave fields, unevenly spaced stars (last 3 join rim), long straight tails to R's in mottoes, dot joins N D in denomination, feathers hide top of S.

CHAPTER 38

DOUBLE EAGLES

i. LONGACRE'S LIBERTY HEAD DESIGN, NO MOTTO (1849–66)

One of the consequences of the immense discoveries of gold in California was an inordinate increase in gold bullion coming to the Philadelphia Mint for coinage. Authorities felt that large-scale domestic or international transactions payable in gold should be made in more compact form than eagles or smaller denominations. Accordingly, Rep. James Iver McKay (D.–N.C.) was persuaded to introduce an amendment to his Gold Dollar bill, Feb. 1849, which would authorize coinage also of $20's, to be called Double Eagles. These were to weigh 516 grs. = 33.436 gms., a little over a troy oz. each, and be roughly comparable in value to several Latin American denominations.

Mint Director Robert Maskell Patterson, aided at every turn by his brilliant, officious, and unscrupulous friend Franklin Peale (then Chief Coiner), seized on this as an opportunity to oust Longacre from the Mint engravership. His rationalization was ostensibly technical: Longacre, like Scot and Gobrecht before him, was by training a portrait engraver on copper plate, not a diesinker. But the real reasons were venal and political: On the one hand, Longacre's presence as Engraver might interfere with Peale's lucrative business of making medals; on the other, Longacre had obtained his post through John C. Calhoun, a name anathema to the Patterson dynasty at the Mint. Peale, with Patterson's tacit approval, began harassment. After Longacre completed the original dies for the gold dollar (despite attempted sabotage: Chap. 32, Sect. i, introductory text), he used the same prototype, the *Venus Accroupie,* 'Crouching Venus,' for the $20 obv., only to find that Peale immediately condemned it as in too high relief. He then started over, late fall 1849, with the help of Peter F. Cross (ca. 1820–56), working under Peale's policy of pinpricks. This time the work got as far as a master die, when Peale announced that it broke on the first trial. On his third attempt, Longacre finished a pair of working dies dated 1849. At least two proofs were coined on Dec. 22; one of these is in the Smithsonian Institution, the other went to Treasury Secretary William M. Meredith. At some later date, probably 1859 or 1860, Mint Director Snowden gave a gilt brass striking from these dies to R. Coulton Davis, the Mint's friendly neighborhood druggist; this was most likely part of Davis's reward for helping Snowden recover the plain-edged 1804 dollars in the 1858 scandal. (See Chap. 29, Sect. iv, introductory text.) However, this brass striking has long since vanished, along with Meredith's gold proof and any others Peale may have made for himself and his cronies. Longacre vainly tried to buy one of the gold impressions (dated 1849 or from the undated master die?), but Peale refused, and Patterson would not overrule him; Longacre had to content himself with one of the two or three undated silver strikings.

On Christmas Day, 1849, Patterson clandestinely offered the engravership to the illustrious Charles Cushing Wright, who accepted, effective whatever day they could get rid of Longacre. However, Longacre somehow heard about this, and went to Calhoun for help in retaining his position.

About Jan. 26, 1850, the first production coins appeared. Many were saved as first of their kind; other mint-state specimens came from the Baltimore hoard, mostly thoroughly bagmarked. All double eagles, 1850–58, are from a master die in which LIB was corrected from LLI: a condition publicized by Carl W. A. Carlson, "NY Coll.," p. 19.

The Baltimore hoard coins were found in a copper receptacle in the cellar of 132 South Eden St., Baltimore, Aug. 31, 1934. A court decision awarded the coins to the two boys who found them (Theodore Jones and Henry Grob); Perry Fuller wrote the catalog for the auction, which dispersed everything on May 2, 1935. This hoard is the source for many of the surviving high-grade coins from this epoch, particularly many of the best early dates of double eagles. There were at least 317 double eagles (92 of them dated 1850, and one of the rare 1856 O's), 81 eagles, 257 half eagles, 78 quarter eagles, and 2,903 gold dollars. Most were EF to UNC.; all were dated 1834 to 1856.

No design changes occurred on rev., which is in low enough relief that even Peale could not fault it. Its double scroll was Longacre's deliberate allusion to the denomination of double eagle, its glory (stars in rays) recalled the Great Seal of the United States.

The new obv. hub of 1859 was part of Longacre's refurbishing assignment of 1859–60, affecting every denomination with the possible exception of the gold dollar and $3 coin. Changes are minor: Truncation is differently shaped, initials JBL differently located on it, and position of Ms. Liberty's name on her coronet is minutely shifted.

Proofs were made 1858–65 in extremely small numbers; few collectors could afford them even then. The first piece made at San Francisco, April 1854, went to the Mint Cabinet; it is a brilliant proof.

In an abortive attempt to improve the design, Assistant Engraver Anthony C. Paquet (1814–82) produced a modified rev. with taller narrower letters in 1859–60. This was accepted, but as soon as the Philadelphia coins went into production, Jan. 5, 1861, a technical error came to light: The border was much too narrow, without protective raised rim outside, exposing the coins to excessive abrasion. Mint Director Snowden telegraphed the San Francisco branch to use the old leftover revs. rather than the new Paquet dies, but by the time his wire arrived, some [19,250] had already been issued. These first came to notice in *NUM* 3/37, p. 199, where A. J. Fecht illustrated the discovery coin, identifying it as having a pattern rev.; until 1951, nobody saw the Archives documents explaining how a San Francisco coin could have this rev. Paul H. Wittlin turned up 25–30 in

French and Swiss banks in the mid-1950s, mostly VF to EF with plenty of bag marks. Only three Philadelphia coins are reported with this type rev. In Cohen:1314 (1875), Edward Cogan said, "All but two were remelted—this one and one in the possession of Mr. W. J. Jenks of Philadelphia."

New Orleans coinages were limited, especially after 1853. Most of the final date, 1861 O, was made under the Confederacy. As the same dies were used before and after the rebels seized the branch mint, it is impossible to tell with certainty whether any given coin was made under the Union or the rebels. But as the Union made only [5,000] out of [17,741], the chances are 71% (or 7 to 3 odds) that your specimen left the press while rebel flags flew over the building. Compare Chap. 28, Sect. x, introductory text, and Chap. 47.

Philadelphia issues made during the Civil War are all much rarer than their mintage figures suggest. As with lower denominations, most were probably exported and melted.

The last coins issued without motto were 1866 S's, coined before the new dies arrived. Aside from the abortive Paquet issue, they are the rarest double eagles of this design from the San Francisco Mint.

LONGACRE'S LIBERTY HEAD DESIGN, NO MOTTO

Designer, Engraver, James Barton Longacre, with assistance of Peter F. Cross. Mints, Philadelphia (no mintmark), New Orleans (mintmark O), San Francisco (S). Mintmark below tail. Composition, gold 90%, silver not over 5%, rest copper. Weight, 516 ± 0.5 grs. $= 33.436 \pm 0.032$ gms., containing 30.0888 gms. or 0.9074 troy oz. pure gold. Diameter $1\frac{1}{3}'' = 34$ mm. Authorizing Act, March 3, 1849; composition and weight conform to Act of Jan. 18, 1837.

Grade range, GOOD to UNC.; not collected in low grades. FINE: Major hair contours intact; LIBERTY legible; about ¼ of coronet beads show; eagle's eye visible, partial wing details, part of motto on scroll readable. VERY FINE: Partial hair detail below LIBERTY; most coronet beads show in outline; over half wing details; partial tail-feather details; partially separated lines (shading) in chief azure of shield; Latin motto clear. EXTREMELY FINE: Isolated tiny rubbed spots only; partial mint luster. UNCIRCULATED: *No* trace of wear. NOTE: Many branch-mint coins are weakly struck; uncirculated survivors have mint luster on weak areas. Coins too heavily nicked and scratched from bank sacks will not bring UNC. prices. In general, if bag marks obscure much hair or feather details, the coin will price lower than UNC.

7138   1849 [2+P] Proofs only.
Judd 117. Coined Dec. 22, 1849. See introductory text.   1) Franklin Peale, Mint Director Robert Maskell Patterson, Mint Cabinet, SI. Clain-Stefanelli {1970}, fig. 33. Enl. photos. J. Pierpont Morgan vainly offered the Mint Bureau $35,000 for this coin.   2) Peale, Patterson, Secretary of Treasury William M. Meredith, Meredith estate, Stephen K. Nagy, pvt. coll. Photographs indicate that this piece lacks the nicks of the Smithsonian coin. Others may exist. The unique gilt-brass striking (Judd 118, ex Snowden, R. Coulton Davis,

Courtesy Krause Publications

Woodside coll., 1892) remains unlocated; it will weigh much less than the gold.

7139   1850 [all kinds 1,170,261 + 1+P] Closed 5, normal A's. Knob of 5 touches cusp. Several minor positional vars. of date. Some 92 UNCS. were in the Baltimore hoard; see introductory text. Wayman:217, UNC., $8,500. Proofs: 1) Part of set for Congressional Committee on the Library. 2), 3) J. B. Longacre estate, 1870. All remain untraced.

7140   1850 Closed 5, broken A in STATES.
L. half of crossbar missing (dent on hub, repaired by hand on many working dies).
7141   1850 Open 5, thin numerals, normal A. Rare.
Knob of 5 away from cusp.
7142   1850 Open 5, thin numerals, broken A. Rare.
Obv. as 7141, rev. as 7140. Auction 81:944, UNC., $4,050, others.
7143   1850 O [141,000] Closed 5, heavy date.
Knob of 5 touches cusp. 2 pairs of dies shipped; 2 rev. vars. 5 UNCS. in Baltimore hoard.
7144   1850 O Open 5, thin date. Rare.
1975 ANA:1582. Rev. as one var. of preceding.
7145   1851 [2,087,155] Heavy date.
Thick serifs. 13 obvs., 33 revs., not all revs. necessarily used. Minor positional vars. The Baltimore hoard contained 79, mostly UNC.
7146   1851 Thin numerals.
Hairlike serifs. Minor positional vars. Auction 81:466, UNC., $7,750.
7147   1851 O [315,000] Heavy date.
As 7143. 9 pairs of dies. Often weakly struck. 10 satiny UNCS. were in the Baltimore hoard.
7148   1851 O Thin numerals.
As 7144. Often weakly struck. 1976 ANA, Auction 81:1908, UNC., $8,000; Carter:835, UNC., $8,250.
7149   1852 [all kinds 2,053,026] Thin numerals, normal A. Hairlike serifs and horizontal elements of 8 and 2. Minor positional vars. from 15 obvs., 29 revs. The Baltimore hoard contained 47. Probably exists with broken A, as 7140. Wayman:221, UNC., $4,200.
7150   1852 Heavy numerals, normal A.
Thick serifs. Positional vars.
7151   1852 Heavy numerals, broken A.
Obv. as preceding, rev. as 7140.
7152   1852 Obvious double date. Scarce.
Heavy numerals.
7153   1852/1 Untraced.
Cleneay:444. We cannot see how the Chapman brothers could have confused this with any of preceding.
7154   1852 O [190,000]
6 obvs., 4 revs. Minor positional vars. Often weakly struck. Only 2 choice ones in the Baltimore hoard, but other UNCS. exist, finest possibly ex Dunham, Holmes:3909. Wayman:222, UNC., $4,200.
7155   1853 [all kinds 1,261,326] Normal heavy date and A. Minor positional vars. Rare in mint state. The Baltimore

hoard contained 27 (possibly including some of next 6 vars.), many of which may have been AU rather than UNC.

7156 1853 Normal heavy date, broken A.
Obv. as last, rev. as **7140**. Wayman:223, UNC., $2,700.

7157 1853 Normal thin numerals, normal A.
Hairlike serifs and horizontal elements.

7158 1853 Normal thin numerals, broken A.
Obv. as last, rev. like **7156**.

7159 1853 Obviously repunched 1. Scarce.
Repunching plainest at base. Discovery coin, LM 10/66:368.

7160 1853 Obviously repunched 3. Rare.
Plain extra outlines 1. of inner curves of 3. Discovery coin, 1975 ANA:1592. Other vars. exist. Compare next 2.

7161 1853 Blundered date. Rare.
Base of another 3 between 53, a little above bases. Base of extra 1 below and l. of 1. Evidently began as a double date, first slanting up to r., then mostly effaced and corrected. NN 54:662, 55:1190; others.

7162 1853/2. Ex. rare.
Lower l. quarter of 2 between lower knob, cusp, and lower inner r. curve of 3. Part of differently shaped 5 (from 1852 logotype) overlapped by 5 of 1853. Dot below R(TY); repunching around base of 1; broken rev. A, corrected by hand. Later these fade. Discovered by this writer, Jacksonville, Fla., Jan. 1959. Publicized by Ted Clark, "Will the Real 1853/2 $20 Please Stand Up?", *CW* 1/7/81, p. 1. The 5 pairs of dies shipped to the San Francisco Provisional Branch Mint Sept. 22, 1853, remained unused; revs. may have been held over for 1854 use.

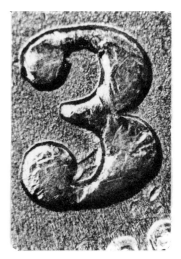

Courtesy Ted Clark

7163 1853 O [71,000] Heavy date, broken A.
6 obvs. shipped; leftover revs. from 1850–52. May exist with normal A. Rare UNC. 1976 ANA:3171, $3,400, Auction 81:1911, $4,600, UNC.

7164 1853 O Doubled obv. die. Rare.
Doubling plain on all stars. Discovery coin, LM 10/66:369.

7165 1854 [757,899 + 1+P] Normal small date, 5 4 free, normal A.
Positional vars.; may exist with 54 touching. Rare UNC.; 12 in Baltimore hoard. Wayman:225, UNC., $3,000. Proofs: 1) Mint, City of Bremen set, unretrieved. 2) Morgenthau 416:5 (6/12/40).

7166 1854 Normal small date, 5 4 free, broken A. Rare.

7167 1854 Repunched small date, normal A. Very scarce.
Date first punched too high, then corrected. Tops of 1 54 obviously double, 8 normal; 54 about touch.

7168 1854 Large date, normal A. Rare.
From the logotype used for silver dollars. May exist with broken A. Usually VF to EF; Ex. rare UNC.

7169 1854 O Small date. [3,250] Ex. rare.
Date slants down to r.; 5 4 free. In all, 8 obvs. shipped, probably only one used (die file marks at TY); leftover rev. from 1852. Usually weakly struck, VF to EF. Auction 79:934, EF, $45,000; Eliasberg:883, AU, $44,000, Stack; Carter:841, VF, $19,800. Forgeries could be made by affixing O mintmarks to genuine Philadelphia coins; authentication recommended.

7170 1854 S Large S. Small heavy date, 54 touch, normal A. [1+P] Unique?
1) First piece struck, April 3, 1854; Superintendent Robert Aiken Birdsall, Mint Director Snowden, Mint Cabinet, SI. Proof. Clain-Stefanelli {1970}, fig. 34. Ill. No business strike yet reported from these dies. S 1.7 mm.

Courtesy Krause Publications

7171 1854 S Small date, 5 4 apart. [141,468] Normal A.
8 pairs of dies. S 1.7 mm. Usually S touches tail, though on one die it is free, and on another it is embedded: Roach 197–98. Most UNCs. are from a hoard discovered in July 1977, at least 100 pieces. Auction 82:1447, $2,600. Many more porous "seawater UNCs." came from a wreck (allegedly the *Yankee Blade),* some still encrusted; compare Chap. 36, Sect. vii, introductory text. An encrusted UNC. brought $2,700 in Auction 82:1446.

7172 1854 S Small date, 5 4 apart, broken A.
Many are from the same hoards. Wayman:226, UNC., $5,750.

7173 1854 S As last but extra-thin numerals and letters. Rare.

7174 1855 Slanting 5's only. [364,666] Normal date.
5 pairs of dies. Positional vars. of date. May exist with broken A. Very rare UNC.; 6 (possibly not mint state) were in the Baltimore hoard.

7175 1855 Extra heavy date.
Serifs, horizontal elements, and slants of 5's very thick.

7176 1855 Thin numerals.
Same elements hair-thin. Wayman:227, UNC., $3,000.

7177 1855 O Slanting 5's. [8,000] Very rare.
4 obvs. shipped; revs. left over from 1852. Usually weakly struck, VF to EF. Auction 81:467, EF–AU, $7,000; Carter:844, AU, $9,900.

7178 1855 S Slanting 5's. Medium S. [879,675] Normal A.
S 1.3 mm, sometimes faint. In all, 12 obvs., 6 revs. May exist with large S (1.7 mm) as in 1854. A dozen UNCs. in Baltimore hoard; many "seawater UNCs.": compare **7171.** Eliasberg:887, UNC., $4,125.

7179 1855 S Medium S, broken A. Scarce.
As last and **7140.** Carter:845, UNC., $5,225.

7180 1856 Upright 5. [329,878]
Positional vars. from 10 pairs of dies. "Seawater UNCs." from same wreck as **7178.**

7181 1856 O Upright 5. [2,250] Ex. rare.
In all, 4 obvs., 2 revs.; only one var. (ill.), possibly 10–12 known. Finest is probably ex Larry Demerer, 1979 ANA, *CW* 9/24/80, p. 1, *NUM* 1/81, UNC., $312,500, private sale. Carter:847, prooflike AU, $46,200; Eliasberg:889, EF–AU, $49,500, Manfra Tordella & Brookes (possibly ex Baltimore hoard). Others are F to EF, weak strikes. Forgeries could be made by adding O mintmark to genuine Philadelphia coins; if yours differs in dies or striking quality from that ill., have it authenticated.

7182 1856 S Upright 5. Medium S. [1,189,750] Normal date and A.
S 1.3 mm; 17 obvs., 10 revs. Minor positional vars.; may exist with large S (1.7 mm). The Baltimore hoard contained 23. Several choice UNCs. from a Northern California estate ca. 1973; Auction 82:1448, $2,900. "Seawater UNCs." exist from same source as **7171.**

7183 1856 S Normal date, broken A.
Carter:848, cleaned UNC., $7,700.

7184 1856 S Double-punched 56. Scarce.
Usually EF.

7185 1857 [439,375]
Dates as in large-date cents, all mints. Minor positional vars. Rare UNC.

7186 1857 O [30,000] Rare.
Thin shallow mintmark; often with die rust before ear, weakly struck. Ex. rare UNC.

7187 1857 S [970,500] Medium S. Normal A.
S 1.3 mm. Minor positional vars. A few UNCs. from a Northern California estate ca. 1973. Eliasberg:893, UNC., $4,675.

7188 1857 S Medium S. Broken A.
As **7140, 7179.**

7189 1857 S Large S. Very rare.
S 1.7 mm, as 1854. Discovery coin, "Melish":894.

7190 1858 [211,714 + ?P] Normal A.
Minor positional vars. Wayman:235 UNC., $4,800. May exist with broken A. Proofs: 1) Mint, SI. 2) Cogan 3/29/1882:422 set, Randall, Morgan, ANS. 3) Mint, Parmelee, Woodin, Newcomer, Boyd, WGC:861, "Bell," "Memorable":684. 4) Low, Brand, Morgenthau 416:9 (6/40), unlocated.

7191 1858 O [35,250] Normal. Rare.
Thin weak O. Often weakly struck. Ex. rare UNC. Atwater, Eliasberg:895, AU, $2,640. Compare next.

7192 1858 O Blundered die. Very rare.
Part of a third 8 protrudes from lower curl into field.

7193 1858 S Medium S. [846,710] Normal A.
S 1.3 mm; 12 obvs., 6 revs. Minor positional vars. May exist with broken A. Few UNCS. from the Northern California estate. Wayman:237, UNC., $2,300.

7194 1859 New obv. hub. [43,597 + 80−P] Normal date.
New hub, 1859–76: JBL farther l. on truncation, not below curls; modified curls; truncation more markedly curved. See ill. at **7200.** Two pairs of dies; often with crack through stars. Wayman:238, AU, $2,600. Most proofs melted as unsold. 1) Mint, SI. 2) Mint, Brock, Morgan, ANS. 3) Ten Eyck, Clapp, Eliasberg:897, $71,500. 4) Parmelee, Boyd, WGC, "Bell," "Memorable":685. 5) Bell I, Eliasberg, "H. R. Lee":1703. 6) Atwater:1251, Chadwick-Darnell:814. 7) N.Y. State pvt. coll. in set. Others probably exist.

7195 1859 Double-punched 18.
Repunching plainest at tops of 18; this fades ("Gilhousen":868). Discovery coin, LM 10/66:384. Late die states with repunching almost invisible will price as preceding.

7196 1859 O [9,100] Thin numerals. Very rare.
Thin mintmark: Carter:856, EF, $4,400; heavy mintmark: Roach, Eliasberg:898, VF, $3,850. In all, 9 obvs., 6 revs., mostly unused. Often weakly struck.

7197 1859 O Heavy numerals. Very rare.
Prohibitively rare UNC. "Gilhousen":869. Lamborn, "Fairfield":2572, UNC., $6,250.

7198 1859 S Medium S. [636,445] Normal dies.
10 obvs. shipped Nov. 1858; leftover revs. Few UNCs. from Northern California estate. Compare next.

7199 1859 S Double LIBERTY. Very rare.
Doubled obv. die.

7200 1860 Regular Longacre rev. [577,670 + 59−P]
Minor positional vars. Very rare UNC. Clapp, Eliasberg:900, $12,100. Proofs have date slanting down to r., 0 nearer border than 1. Fewer than 10 survive. Ely, Garrett:789, $80,000. Compare **7203–6.**

Ex J. W. Garrett: 789. Courtesy Bowers & Ruddy Galleries, Inc.

7201 1860 O [6,600] Very rare.

Often weakly struck. Prohibitively rare UNC. Atwater, Eliasberg:901, AU/UNC., $15,400, Manfra Tordella & Brookes.

7202 1860 S Medium S. [544,950]

S 1.3 mm. 6 obvs. shipped Nov. 2, 1859; leftover revs. from 1858. Few UNCS. from same Northern California source as **7182.**

PAQUET REV., Nov. 1860–Jan. 1861

7203 1860 Prototype. [1+P] Unique?

Judd 272a. Mint Cabinet, SI. Clain-Stefanelli {1970}, fig. 39.

7204 1861 [3+] Ex. rare.

Adams-Woodin 334. Jan. 5, 1861. See introductory text. All survivors are UNC. business strikes, not proofs. 1) Bache I:2818, $37 ("said to be unique"), Seavey (?), Parmelee, Woodin, Newcomer, Boyd, Farouk, Spink, pvt. coll. 2) Col. Cohen, R. Coulton Davis, M. A. Brown:53, Brand, Norweb. 3) W. J. Jenks (?), European pvt. coll., Wittlin, $20,000 (1968), Kosoff, RARCOA, pvt. coll.

7205 1861 S [19,250] Plain period after TWENTY D. Very rare.

Small s. 4 pairs of dies shipped Nov. 1860. 2 minor positional vars. with period. Discovery coin, A. J. Fecht, ANS, ill. *NUM* 3/37, p. 199. Others are mostly F to EF, revs. severely bag-marked; possibly 30 turned up by P. H. Wittlin in French and Swiss banks in mid-1950s: See introductory text. Unknown UNC. MHS II:1115, AU+; Auction 79:941, AU, $20,000.

7206 1861 S No period after TWENTY D Very rare.
Probably a filled die. Mintmark lower than on **7205.**

NORMAL DESIGN RESUMED, Jan. 1861–Feb. 1866

7207 1861 [2,976,453 + 66−P] Normal date.

Date varies, heavy to fairly thin, high to low. Mintage figure may include **7204.** In all, 118 obvs., 114 revs., which may include the Paquet dies. Many bag-marked UNCS. Carter:862, gem, $10,450. Mostly coined from melted "Type I" gold dollars. Proofs (April 5) mostly melted Jan. 1862 as unsold. Carter:861, $46,750.

7208 1861 Partly repunched date. Rare.
Repunching plainest below top serif of 8 and within top of 8.

7209 1861 O [17,741]

3 pairs of dies shipped Dec. 10, 1860; only one used. Mintage includes [5,000] for Union, [9,750] for State of Louisiana after rebels took over the branch mint, and [2,991] for the CSA. These cannot be told apart with certainty; possibly the rebel strikings are those with greatest weakness at base of date.

7210 1861 S Medium S. [748,750] Heavy date.
8 obvs., 4 revs.: 4 obvs. shipped Nov. 1860 for use with Paquet revs., 4 pairs of dies June 1861. Ex. rare UNC. 1976 ANA:3205, UNC., $2,000.

7211 1861 S Thin numerals. Rare.
Hairline serifs to 1's and horizontal elements of 86.

7212 1862 [92,133 + 35−P] Rare.
7 obvs., 4 revs. Possibly 12–15 proofs known, some impaired. Auction 82:1963, $31,000; Graves, Bareford:229, $26,000.

7213 1862 S Medium S. [854,173] Normal date.
10 obvs. shipped (4, Nov. 1861; 6, April 1862); old revs. Prohibitively rare UNC.; 1976 ANA:3207, $2,600; Wayman:249, $3,000, S 6/83:747, $4,100.

7214 1862 S Plainly repunched 86. Rare.

7215 1863 [142,790 + 30P] Rare.
Ex. rare UNC. About 12–15 proofs known, some impaired. Eliasberg:909, Proof, $37,400.

7216 1863 S [all kinds 966,570] Medium S. Very scarce.
10 obvs. (4, Nov. 1862; 6, March 1863); old revs. Ex. rare UNC.

7217 1863 S Small s. Rare.
4 revs. shipped March 1863. Ex. rare UNC. Wayman:251, UNC., $2,000.

7218 1864 Large date. [204,235 + 50P] Rare.
Ex. rare UNC.; Auction 80:1982, $5,500. Possibly 12–15 proofs known: Eliasberg:911, $44,000.

7219 1864 S Small s. [793,660] Very scarce.
11 obvs., 6 revs. (5 obvs. Oct. 1863; rest, May 1864). Ex. rare UNC.

7220 1865 [351,175 + 25P] Very scarce.
13 obvs., 9 revs. Minute positional vars. Very rare UNC. Wayman:254, $1,800. Possibly 6–8 proofs: Garrett:790, $80,000; Ten Eyck, Clapp, Eliasberg:913, $39,600.

7221 1865 S Small s. [1,042,500]
14 obvs., 8 revs. (6 obvs. Nov. 1864, rest May 1865). Usually EF; UNCs. are from a tiny hoard discovered about 1967.

7222 1866 S Small s. [120,000] Rare.
Feb. 1866. 6 obvs. shipped Nov. 1865; old revs. 2 minor positional vars. Usually F to VF. Prohibitively rare AU.

ii. MOTTO ADDED (1866–76)

Unlike the design spacing on lower denominations, adding the motto IN GOD WE TRUST to the double eagle did not result in undue crowding of the design. Longacre, to fulfill the demands of Congress and Treasury Secretary Salmon P. Chase (but ultimately of the Rev. M. R. Watkinson, of Ridleyville, Pa., progenitor of the idea), slightly enlarged the oval of stars above eagle's head, inserting the motto within. This was, however, not the only alteration. The shield, formerly with straight sides, now has rococo borders; the double scroll has smaller but more elaborate finials encroaching less on IBUS; leaves are differently shaped and there are nine rather than the former eight; wings are closer to both E's (in some dies appearing to touch, or joined by a pseudo-border); tail closer to NT, requiring smaller mintmarks.

Most dates in this period show up oftenest in VF with S mintmarks. Philadelphia issues 1866–72 are mostly scarce, except for the 1867 UNCs. from a hoard (possibly 2,000, found in Europe about 1966, distributed in the USA beginning about 1973). For political reasons, official orders limited the Carson City issues 1870–73. Authorities and bankers preferred to ship bullion to San Francisco, alleging lower cost. Claims (partly verified) that the CC Mint issued some lightweight and/or debased coins, 1871–73, led to dismissal of the Superintendent, H. F. Rice, and to the frequently seen edge test marks on Carson City gold pieces of this period. This discovery gave ammunition to the Carson Mint's official attackers, and rationale to many who sought to have this branch abolished; but their real reasons had to do with who would get the coveted contracts for transporting ores and finished coins. The only readily available Carson City issues are dated 1874–76, coined from local bonanzas. Other CC dates are all rare, and in mint state all but unknown.

Philadelphia issues of 1873 were larger because coined from melted obsolete issues; San Francisco issues 1874–76 still larger from abundant bullion from the same bonanzas that swelled the CC-Mint output. Though EF's are plentiful, UNCs. are rare. How rare depends less on amounts coined than on the numbers recovered ca. 1953–64 from French and Swiss banks.

There are two date logotypes for 1871—the same two as for silver dollars. On the earlier, 71 practically touch, with long serifs to 1's; on the later, 7 1 are spaced apart, with shorter serifs. We know that the former came first because it appears on obvs. shipped to branch mints in the fall of 1870, whereas that with 7 1 apart comes only on Philadelphia coins. Reason for the change remains unknown.

On the other hand, reason for the change from "closed" to "open" 3 in 1873 is well documented. William Barber, Mint Engraver, furnished a set of date logotypes for 1873 working dies, early Nov. 1872. On the smaller denominations, the large knobs on 3's are so close together that these 3's are readily mistaken for 8's (as has repeatedly happened on shield nickels and gold dollars). Chief Coiner Archibald Loudon Snowden filed a formal complaint to Mint Director James Pollock, Jan. 18, 1873; Pollock ordered Barber to make a new set without this fault. On the double eagles, the distinction is fairly difficult: Closed 3 obvs. have knobs approximately equal in size, spaced closer together than the width of either knob; open 3 dies have upper knob noticeably smaller than lower, and they are farther apart than the width of lower knob. The closed 3 logotype is as on silver dollars; open 3 as on trade dollars. The 25 proofs and a minority of Philadelphia business strikes have closed 3; these latter were formerly considered rare, but collectors learned how to identify them and retrieved many in all grades. Carson City coins all have closed 3, as do most San Francisco 1873's; the 1873 S open 3 remains rare.

In 1876, William Barber wished to improve on his predecessor's designs, but his project went only far enough to make two obvs. with repositioned head. The first of these was combined with a regular rev. die; the second with a new rev. reading TWENTY DOLLARS (see following section). Only one specimen of each is known. The First Transitional (regular rev.) first came to collector attention when the unscrupulous dealer John W. Haseltine published both of them in *NUM* 6/09, pp. 133–34. It is not absolutely certain whether he found them among the holdings of his father-in-law William Idler (the Mint's fence since the 1860s) or in the trunkful of pattern, experimental, and other nonstandard coins held by former Chief Coiner A. Loudon Snowden. This enormous group went from Snowden to Haseltine for William H. Woodin, as part of the price for Woodin's returning two 1877 gold $50 pattern pieces to the Mint Cabinet Collection; he had bought them from Snowden for $10,000 apiece. This 1876 First Transitional went successively to Stephen K. Nagy (Haseltine's agent and son-in-law), Woodin, Waldo Newcomer, F. C. C. Boyd, King Farouk, and Spink's for a private collector. Other specimens may exist, mistaken for ordinary 1876's, or may be simulated by gilt copper strikings. The latter will necessarily be lightweight, probably less than half the 516 grs. = 33.436 gms. of a gold specimen.

MOTTO ADDED

Designer, James Barton Longacre. Engravers, Longacre 1866–68, William Barber 1869–76. Mints, Philadelphia (no mintmark), San Francisco (mintmark S), Carson City (CC). Mintmarks below tail. Physical Specifications, Authorizing Acts, as before.

Grade range, FINE to UNC.; not collected in low grades except for a few extreme rarities. Grade standards, as before.

7223 1865 Prototype [2P] Proofs only.
Judd 452. Included in 2 gold proof sets which contained the $10 and $5 with motto. Types exactly as **7224.**   1) Mint Cabinet, SI. Clain-Stefanelli {1970}, fig. 40.   2) Mason & Co. 6/17/1870:422, Woodin, Newcomer, Boyd, Farouk. Beware gilt copper proofs; these are grossly underweight compared to any double eagle. Ill. of **7225.**

7224 1866 Normal date. [698,745]
Minor positional vars. Very rare in mint state. Carter:875, UNC., $2,860.
7225 1866 Top of extra 1 in rim. [30P] Proofs only. Ex. rare. Breen {1977}, p. 132. The misplaced digit is outside beaded border; use a strong glass. Ill. at **7223.** Possibly 10–12 survive, some impaired. Ely, Garrett:791, $80,000; Woodin, Clapp, Eliasberg:916, $39,600, H. Sconyers.
7226 1866 S Very small s. [722,250]
6 revs. shipped March 1866 for use with the 6 obvs. on hand since Nov. 1865; 8 obvs., 6 revs. shipped in May 1866, which proved brittle and were replaced by 8 more revs. Sept. 1866. The minute s continues to about 1879. Very rare UNC.: Wayman:257, $3,000, S 6/15/83:757, $4,700.
7227 1867 [251,015 + 50P]
Available for a price in UNC. (with many bag marks), from a hoard of possibly 2,000 discovered in Europe about 1966; see introductory text. Possibly 10–12 proofs survive; Wetmore, Clapp, Eliasberg:918, $44,000; Carter:877, $30,800.
7228 1867 S [920,750]
Ex. rare UNC.
7229 1868 [98,575 + 25P] Rare.
Some business strikes (like some proofs) show dentils plainly clashmarked l. and r. of tail to scroll. Ex. rare UNC. Possibly

10–12 proofs survive: Mocatta, 79 ANA:450, $27,000; Elias-berg:920, $26,400; Carter:880, $26,400.

7230 1868 S [837,500]

Very rare UNC. Wayman:261, $1,100.

7231 1869 [175,130 + 25P]

Very rare UNC. Carter:884, $7,425. Possibly 10–12 proofs: Clapp, Eliasberg:992, $33,000; Carter:883, $37,400.

7232 1869 S [686,750] Normal rev.

8 obvs. shipped Oct. 1868; old revs. Very rare UNC. Clapp, Eliasberg:923, $3,740. Compare next.

7233 1869 S Doubled rev. die. Rare.

LM 10/66:409. Doubling plainest at TES OF and oval of stars.

7234 1870 [155,150 + 35P]

Very rare in mint state. Possibly 10–12 proofs: Clapp, Elias-berg:924, $28,600.

7235 1870 S [982,000]

10 obvs., 6 revs. shipped Dec. 1869. Very rare in mint state; 1979 ANA:451, $7,000, 1982 ANA:2732, $2,600.

7236 1870 CC [3,789] Ex. rare.

Mintage began with [1,332] March 10. Usually in low grades; unknown UNC. Bryant-Mathey, Allen, Robison I:894, AU, $28,500; Kagin 305:931 (1/3–4/75), EF, $32,000; Carter:887, VF, $24,200. Authentication recommended.

7237 1871 [all kinds 80,120 + 30P] 71 almost touch. Very rare.

Long serifs to l's; see introductory text. Unobtainable UNC. Carter:889, AU, $2,090. Possibly 8–10 proofs survive: Elias-berg:927, $26,400; Garrett, Auction 79:371, $21,500; Atwater, Dr. Green, Amon Carter, Sr. & Jr., 1980 ANA:400, $33,000, 1982 ANA:2733, $12,500.

7238 1871 7 1 apart. Very rare.

Short serifs to l's; see introductory text. Same logotype as the later silver dollars.

7239 1871 S 71 almost touch. [928,000]

10 obvs., 8 revs. received Dec. 16, 1870. Minor positional vars. Auction 79:946, UNC., $5,250. May exist with 7 1 apart.

7240 1871 CC 71 almost touch. [17,387] Rare.

Very rare above EF. Wayman:267, EF, $3,000; Carter:890, VF, $3,960.

7241 1872 [251,850 + 30P]

Minor positional vars. Normally, bases of 18 very close; on heavier impressions they may touch, on lighter ones (re-lapped dies?) they are apart. Very rare in mint state: Way-man:269, $1,150. Possibly 8–10 proofs survive: Ten Eyck, Clapp, Eliasberg:930, $18,700.

7242 1872 S [780,000]

10 pairs of dies shipped Nov. 1871. Usually with fairly thin numerals, bases of 1 8 apart; see preceding. Wayman:271, UNC., $850.

7243 1872 CC [26,900] Rare.

4 obvs., 2 revs. shipped, possibly more. C C vary in spacing. Very rare above EF. Wayman:270, EF, $1,150.

7244 1873 [all kinds 1,709,800 + 25P] Closed 3. Scarce.

See ill. and introductory text. First publicized by Harry X Boosel. Minor positional vars. Rare UNC.: Wayman:272, UNC., $3,000. Possibly 12–15 proofs survive: Ely, Gar-rett:792, $65,000; Carter:895, $37,400 (nicks).

7245 1873 Open 3.

Business strikes only. Minor positional vars. See introductory text. UNCs. are usually heavily bag-marked.

7246 1873 S [all kinds 1,040,600] Closed 3.

See introductory text. Same comments as to **7244.** 10 pairs of dies shipped Nov. 1872.

7247 1873 S Open 3. Very rare.

See introductory text. Discovered by Harry X Boosel. No record of die shipments for this issue. Bryant-Mathey, Robi-son I:906, VF.

7248 1873 CC Closed 3. [22,410] Rare.

Usually in low grades. Very rare above EF. Auction 80:968, AU, $3,100; Carter:897, AU, $2,860.

7249 1874 [366,780 + 20P]

Minor positional vars. UNCs. are usually heavily bag-marked. Possibly 7–9 proofs survive (coined Feb. 14); Ely, Gar-rett:793, $70,000; Carter:899, $39,600.

7250 1874 S [1,214,000]

Minor positional vars. UNCs. are usually severely bag-marked. Compare next.

7251 1874 S Double S. Rare.

Mintmark first punched too low, then corrected. NN 49:127.

7252 1874 CC [115,085]

Usually with small thin arrowheads (lapped die). Same com-ment as to **7250.**

7253 1875 [295,700 + 20P] Normal.

Same comment as to **7250.** Possibly 8–10 proofs survive (coined Feb. 13). Weigh any candidate: Gold proofs weigh about 516 grs. = 33.4 gms., copper or aluminum gilt strik-ings are much lighter. Clapp, Eliasberg:939, $60,500, Hugh Sconyers, Auction 85:978, $46,200; Carter:903, $31,900.

7254 1875 Canceled JBL. Rare.

Heavy die file mark obliterates Longacre's initials: petty spite?

7255 1875 S [1,230,000]

Many minor positional vars. UNCs. are usually severely bag-marked.

7256 1875 CC [111,151] Close CC.

CC less than a C's width apart. Same comments as to preced-ing.

7257 1875 CC Wide C C.

CC about the width of a C apart, or more. Same comments.

7258   1875 CC Wide C C, doubled rev. die.
Doubling plainest on ERICA and TWENTY D. 1974 GENA:1250; 1982 ANA:2739. Same comments.
7259   1876 [583,860 + 45P]
15 obvs., 13 revs. Possibly 8–10 proofs survive: Newlin, Garrett:794, $52,500; Ullmer:524, $45,000, Groves:595, $42,000; Carter:907, $25,300 (cleaned).
7260   1876 S [1,597,000]
Same comments as to **7255.**
7261   1876 CC [138,441] Close CC.
Same comments as to **7256.**
7262   1876 CC Wide C C, doubled rev. die. Rare.
"Melish":959. Rev. of **7258.**

TRANSITIONAL ISSUE: REPOSITIONED HEAD

7263   1876 Unique?
Judd 1488. Coronet markedly divides first 6 from last 7 stars, similar to **7264** (see next section). Regular rev. See introductory text for details and pedigree. Ill. Breen {1977}, p. 156; obv. proof, rev. UNC.

iii. THE LONGACRE-BARBER DESIGN, *TWENTY DOLLARS* (1877–1907)

This is the type represented most often in type collections, hoards, and dealers' stocks as generic "Liberty head twenties." It is by far the most durable production of the forgettable William Barber. (Barber succeeded to the Engravership at Longacre's death on Jan. 1, 1869.) At least Barber had the courtesy to retain Longacre's initials J.B.L. on truncation of neck.

The only noticeable design change during this period was the rev. hub of 1900–7, in which back of eagle's neck is smooth. This is by Charles E. Barber, William Barber's son and equally forgettable successor. Explanation for the change remains unknown. Conjecturally, it was part of Barber's attempt to refurbish most current designs; note the comparable niggling changes on obvs. of quarters and halves, rev. of dollars. To date, all double eagles of 1900–7 from Philadelphia or San Francisco have the new rev., though coins of either Mint may exist with old revs. left over from 1899, and—on the precedent of the Morgan dollars—"doubled" working revs. may exist showing impressions from both old and new hubs.

Issues were unprecedentedly large. Annual output from San Francisco 1877–83 exceeded anything earlier in this denomination; but even these figures were dwarfed in 1894–1907. In 1904, the Philadelphia Mint coined over 6¼ million double eagles, the largest gold emission of any date or mint except for 1928: the archetype of "common gold." Mint-state specimens of many of these dates (usually with many bag marks) turned up in quantity in French and Swiss banks in the 1950s and '60s. Speculators and investors seeking a hedge against inflation habitually chose this design as until recent years it was an economical way of hoarding gold so long as federal law prohibited hoarding the metal in ingot form. After PL 93-373, Sect. 2, rescinded the prohibition in 1974, double eagles remained a favorite hoarder item, albeit a more expensive one. At least these pieces offer the advantage of being legitimate coins made for circulation, without the taint of racism associated with their chief rivals and successors the krugerrands.

In simultaneous extreme contrast, this design is also notable for some of the most famous of American gold rarities. Unlike their St. Gaudens counterparts, these result less from extensive meltage than from low mintage. This remark applies to 1879 O, 1879 CC, and several Philadelphia dates in the '80s, where the

minuscule quantities of business strikes have mostly vanished. Such dates as 1881, 1882, and 1885 Philadelphia can be readily simulated by removing mintmarks from the common S-Mint coins; authentication is essential to exclude such frauds and to distinguish prooflike business strikes from carelessly made and/ or impaired proofs. The dates whose sales reach the front pages of coin-trade papers, however, are 1883 and 1884, with respective mintages of [92P] and [71P]; the former was long considered much rarer because the annual Director's Reports misquoted its mintage as [40].

Nor is that error the only one. Proof mintage figures from that source contain many others. Corrected figures herein come from the National Archives, based on Breen {1977}. Many dates are rarer in proof state than their mintage figures suggest; this is sometimes because unsold proofs were melted, more often because proofs were spent, especially during the panics of 1893, 1921, and 1929–33.

No reason has been advanced for the 1879 O mintage; possibly the New Orleans Mint Superintendent anticipated a local demand for this denomination. However, even before the Civil War, $20's were seldom in demand in that area; Southerners were used to the Bechtler coins, and tolerated their Union counterparts, but never took to $10's and $20's. New Orleans banking houses could take care of any local needs for $20's by using Philadelphia and S-Mint coins on hand, rather than insisting on the local product.

Overdates in this series are all of recent discovery. They are at present all very rare, but others are likely to turn up as more dealers examine their common gold holdings, exactly as with the 1881/0 and 1901/0 S half eagles.

Proofs of 1902–7 have devices satiny or semibrilliant rather than frosty as formerly; the texture in those areas is much less granular, but short of actual examination, only high-resolution macrophotographs could exhibit the difference. Nothing has come to light about either the change in manufacturing method or its rationale.

Proofs of 1906 D and 1907 D were reportedly made for local celebrations, the former on the official opening of the Denver branch mint for coinage after 44 years during which it had functioned only as an assay office: See Chap. 46.

THE LONGACRE-BARBER DESIGN

Designer, William Barber, after Longacre. Engravers, William Barber 1877–79, Charles E. Barber 1879–1907. Mints, Philadelphia (no mintmark), New Orleans 1879 (mintmark O), San Francisco (S), Carson City (CC), Denver (D). Mintmarks below tail. Physical Specifications, as before.

Grade range and standards, as before. NOTE: Many specimens occur without discernible wear but with some hair and feather details obscured by bag marks. These usually price as ABOUT UNC., not as UNC. Price spread between ordinary UNCS. and those free of bag marks is from 50% to 500% or more.

7264   1876 Prototype. Proof only. Unique?
Judd 1490. Date farther l. than on **7263**, LIBERTY differently positioned on coronet. 1) Haseltine (with **7263**), Nagy, Woodin, Newcomer, Boyd, Farouk:292, New Netherlands, Dr. Wilkison, Paramount, A-Mark, Larry Whitlow, Auction 86:1451, $99,000. Ill. *NUM* 6/09, pp. 133–34. May

be simulated by gilt copper strikings; any such coin will be grossly lightweight.

7265 1877 [397,650 + 20P]

10 obvs., 14 revs. Minor positional vars. Possibly 6–8 proofs survive; Garrett:795, $47,500.

7266 1877 S [1,735,000]

Minor positional vars. of this and all later S mints.

7267 1877 CC Taller CC. [42,565]

Very rare UNC. Auction 79:1384, UNC., $2,200.

7268 1878 [all kinds 543,625 + 20P] Normal date.

Minor positional vars.; but compare next. Often weakly struck. Carter:914, gem, $6,600. Possibly 8–10 proofs survive.

7269 1878/7 Very rare.

Part of shaft of 7 plain within lower loop of 8.

7270 1878 Doubled rev. die. Very rare.

Doubling most obvious on letters. First reported by Ed Fleischman of ANACS.

7271 1878 S [1,739,000]

Minor positional vars. Often heavily bag-marked.

7272 1878 CC [13,180] Rare.

Ex. rare UNC.; Auction 80:1984, $3,500; Wayman:289, $5,250.

7273 1879 [207,600 + 30P]

Possibly 8–10 proofs survive: Mint, Garrett:796, $65,000.

7274 1879 O [2,325] Very rare.

Usually in low grades or heavily bag-marked; prohibitively rare UNC. Wayman:292, EF, $4,600; Mocatta, 1979 ANA:465, UNC., $23,000. Authentication recommended.

7275 1879 S [all kinds 1,223,800] Normal date. Tall S.

Same comment as to **7271**. Mintmark as in silver dollars.

7276 1879 S Overdate. Presently Ex. rare.

As ill. Possibly 9 over 7? Discovered at the 1979 ANA Convention.

7277 1879 CC [10,708] Very rare.

Usually in low grades; prohibitively rare UNC.: Auction 79:1385, $3,200; Wayman:293, choice, $4,600.

7278 1880 [51,400 + 36P] Very rare.

Much rarer in business-strike form than mintage suggests; usually found EF or ex-proof. Possibly 8–10 proofs survive: Mint, Garrett:797, $65,000; Carter:922, $30,800.

7279 1880 S Small squat s. [836,000]

Same comment as to **7268**. May exist with taller S as on silver dollars.

7280 1881 [2,220 + 61P] Ex. rare.

Business strikes have l. base of first 1 about over r. edge of dentil, r. base of final 1 about over center of dentil; possibly 12 known, mostly EF or AU with bag marks. Auction 80:971, AU, $12,000; Wayman:297, AU, $5,750; Carter:924, AU, $8,250. Authentication recommended to avoid deception by S-Mint coins with mintmark removed. Proofs have l. base of first 1 over center of dentil, r. base of final 1 nearly over r. edge. (The broken r. tail feather occurs on both proofs and business strikes.) Possibly 16–20 survive, some impaired. Ullmer:529, $40,000 (1974); Clapp, Eliasberg:957, $30,800, Kagin.

7281 1881 S Taller S. [727,000]

May exist with small squat s as **7279** (leftover rev.).

7282 1882 [590 + 59P] Ex. rare.

Same dies apparently used for proofs and business strikes. Very low date, l. base of 1 minutely r. of l. edge of dentil; feathers behind neck lapped away, not touching scroll; both scrolls and 2 rightmost pales gules thin. Fewer than 8 business strikes reported; Wayman:299, AU, $10,000; Auction 82:1964, AU, $11,000; Carter:927, EF, $12,100. Authentication recommended for same reason as **7280**. Possibly 15–20 proofs survive: Miles, Ullmer:527, $42,500; Garrett (1976):470, $25,000; Clapp, Eliasberg:959, $34,100, Kagin; Carter:926, $37,400.

7283 1882 S [all kinds 1,125,000] Small squat s. Rare.

Mintmark as **7279**; leftover rev.? "Melish":988.

7284 1882 S Tall S.

Mintmark as **7275, 7281**. Minor positional vars.; forms vast majority of the date.

7285 1882 CC [39,140]

7286 1883 [92P] Proofs only. Very rare.

In date, 1 about centered between bust and border; l. base of 1 about over r. edge of dentil; r. edge of 3 about in line with r. side of lowest curl; back of eagle's neck rough, fleur de lys below beak fragmented. Possibly 18–24 survive, several impaired. Garrett (1976):476, $72,500; Clapp, Eliasberg:962, $88,000, Hugh Sconyers, Auction 85:980, $68,200.

7287 1883 S [1,189,000]

Same comment as to **7271**. Tall S as on silver dollars henceforth through 1899.

7288 1883 CC [59,962] Normal.

7289 1883 CC Dot r. of 3. Rare.

The dot is raised, round, and about in line with middle of 3. Compare the 1884 silver dollars with raised dot at Morgan's initial M.

7290 1884 [71P] Proofs only. Very rare.

The peculiar color discontinuity is always present on neck and cheek; it does not occur on S or CC coins. Rev. apparently same as **7286.** Possibly 16–20 survive, some impaired. Miles, Ullmer:528, $110,000 (1974); Mint, Garrett (1976):482, $72,500; Clapp, Eliasberg:965, $82,500, Hugh Sconyers, Auction 85:981, $55,000.

7291 1884 S [916,000]
7292 1884 CC [81,139]
7293 1885 [751 + 78P] Very rare.

Business strikes have usual notch in truncation minutely l. of 5; date a little below center, l. base of 1 nearly over r. edge of dentil; l. line of sixth (rightmost) pale gules partly thin. Possibly 12–15 survive; authentication recommended for same reason as **7280.** Most are EF to AU. Auction 79:955, UNC., $38,000; Mocatta, 1979 ANA:469, UNC., $28,000; Carter:936, UNC., $24,200. Proofs have date farther r., notch on truncation above r. edge of second 8, l. base of 1 above l. of center of dentil, rust on neck above first 8; r. tail feather broken, first 3 pales gules heavier than rest. Possibly 14–18 survive, some impaired. Ullmer:529, $40,000 (1974); Clapp, Eliasberg:968, $39,600, H. Sconyers.

7294 1885 S [683,500]

Minor positional vars. All seen to date have closed 5 (knob touches cusp); may exist with open 5 like some other denominations.

7295 1885 CC [9,450] Rare.

Same comments. Always weakly struck, rev. rim beveled. Usually VF; prohibitively rare AU. Groves:606, UNC., $3,100; Carter:937, UNC., $3,300.

7296 1886 [1,000 + 106P] Very rare.

Business strikes have 1 almost centered between bust and border; notch in truncation almost above inner l. curve of 6. Possibly 8–10 survive. Robison:940, UNC., $10,000; Carter:940, EF, $10,450. Proofs have low date, notch above l. edge of 6 and minutely to l.; possibly 20–24 survive, some impaired or worn down to EF, e.g., Wayman:309, $9,000. Eliasberg:971, $38,500; Carter:939, $37,400.

7297 1887 [121P] Proofs only. Very rare.

Rev. of 1886 proofs, tiny break in r. tail feathers just below arrow (less than in some other dates), l. petal of fleur de lys below beak disconnected. Alleged circulated proofs must be authenticated to rule out removed S mintmark. Possibly 20–25 survive, some impaired. Wayman:310, $41,000; Eliasberg:972, $46,750; Carter:941, $34,100.

7298 1887 S [283,000]
7299 1888 [226,164 + 102P]

Often weakly struck. Possibly 35–40 proofs survive, many nicked. Clapp, Eliasberg:974, $24,200.

7300 1888 S [859,600]
7301 1889 [44,070 + 41P] Rare.

Business strikes are much rarer than mintage figure suggests. Possibly 12–15 proofs survive. Woodin, Clapp, Eliasberg:976, $24,200; Carter:945, $37,400.

7302 1889 S [774,700]
7303 1889 CC [30,945]

Positional vars. exist, one with part of base of extra 1 below center of base of 1 in date. Very rare AU, Ex. rare UNC.: Auction 79:957, $2,000; Wayman:315, $1,800.

7304 1890 [75,940 + 55P]

Business strikes have top of 1 repunched; this fades out. Eliasberg:979, UNC., $1,760. Proofs have low date slanting up to r., heavy ray below E incomplete; double punching on third star (above N G) unusually obvious (it is in the hub and weakly present on most issues 1877–99). Possibly 14–18 survive, some impaired. 1982 ANA:754, $12,000; Carter:949, $38,500.

7305 1890 S [802,750]
7306 1890 CC [91,209]
7307 1891 [1,390 + 52P] Very rare.

Possibly 12 business strikes survive, of which 4 are AU to UNC., the rest VF to EF. Auction 79:959, AU, $4,250; Wayman:320, AU, $4,200; Carter:954, EF, $4,180. Authentication recommended. Proofs have rays below TE thin; possibly 15–18 survive. Garrett:798, $90,000; Carter:953, $26,400.

7308 1891 S [1,288,125]
7309 1891 CC [5,000] Very rare.

Auction 82:1454, UNC., $3,100; Wayman:321, AU, $3,600; Carter:955, AU, $3,850.

7310 1892 [4,410 + 93P] Very rare.

Possibly 16–20 business strikes survive, of which 3 or 4 are UNC.; authentication recommended to exclude removed S mintmarks. 1976 ANA:3273, UNC., $4,200; Wayman:323, AU, $3,300; Carter:957, UNC., $8,525. Possibly 18–22 proofs survive: Garrett:799, $65,000; Mint, Clapp, Eliasberg:985, $42,000.

7311 1892 S [all kinds 930,150] Normal date.
7312 1892/1 S Presently very rare.

Top of 1 plain within top of 2. Discovered by Robert Emmer, April 20, 1978. On later impressions this fades.

7313 1892 CC [27,265]

Very rare in mint state. Wayman:324, UNC., $1,900.

7314 1893 [344,280 + 59P]

Probably fewer than 30 proofs survive, in 2 positional vars.; Breen {1977}, p. 195. Mint, Clapp, Eliasberg:988, $24,200.

7315 1893 S [996,175]
7316 1893 CC [18,402]

Popular final year of issue. Rare UNC.: Auction 79:960, $2,600; Wayman:327, $2,200; Carter:961, $2,310.

7317 1894 [1,368,940 + 50P]

Possibly 20–25 proofs survive, some impaired. Mint, Clapp, Eliasberg:991, $18,700; Carter:964, $23,100.

7318 1894 S [1,048,550]

Douglas Winter discovered a repunched mintmark: Bortin:232.

7319 1895 [1,114,605 + 51P]

Possibly 25–30 proofs survive. Mint, Clapp, Eliasberg:993, $20,900.

7320 1895 S [1,143,500]
7321 1896 [792,535 + 128P] Normal date.

Possibly 20–25 proofs survive, some impaired. Mint, Clapp, Eliasberg:995, $22,000.

7322 1896 Double date. Very rare.

Discovered by E. M. Seneca. All 4 digits show repunching at top, even to naked eye. Later, cracked through base of date. "Charmont":4410.

7323 1896 S [1,403,925]
7324 1897 [1,383,175 + 86P] Normal date.

Possibly 18–24 proofs survive, some impaired. Mint, Clapp, Eliasberg:997, $26,400.

7325   1897 Repunched 89. Very rare.

These digits first entered to l. of final position, then corrected. "N.Y. Coll.":285. Later states have only lower half of extra 9 remaining (die relapped), overlapping base and knob; these are nearly as rare. Still later states showing less traces of extra 9 price as preceding.

7326   1897 S [1,470,250]

7327   1897 S Obviously repunched 1. Very rare.

1984 Midwinter ANA:418. Visible to the naked eye.

7328   1898 [170,395 + 75P]

Much scarcer than mintage figure suggests, especially UNC. Possibly 30–36 proofs survive; Mint, Clapp, Eliasberg:999, $19,800.

7329   1898 S [2,575,175]

Douglas Winter discovered a repunched date, plainest at base of 1. Bortin:237.

7330   1899 [all kinds 1,669,300 + 84P] Normal date, closed 9's.

Knobs of 9's touch loops. May exist with open 9's, as **7333**. Compare next. Probably 35–40 proofs survive, some impaired. Mint, Clapp, Eliasberg:1001, $27,500.

7331   1899/8 Closed 9's. Very rare.

Part of l. lower loop of 8 left of knob of final 9; part of r. lower loop of 8 between knob and inner curve.

7332   1899 S [all kinds 2,010,300] Closed 9's.

As **7330**.

7333   1899 S Open 9's.

Knobs away from loops of 9's.

7334   1900 New rev. hub. [1,874,460 + 124P]

Back of eagle's neck smooth, as in 1901–7. Possibly 40–45 proofs survive, many impaired. Mint, Clapp, Eliasberg:1003, $26,400. Ill. of **7351**. May exist with old rev. hub.

7335   1900 S New rev. hub. [2,459,500] Clear S.

May exist with old rev. hub (1899 rev.). The new S punch, with serifs farther from middle stroke, continues through 1907. Common UNC. from at least one bag of 1,000 recently discovered in El Salvador.

7336   1901 [111,430 + 96P]

Very scarce in mint state. Possibly 36–40 proofs survive, many impaired. Garrett:800, $60,000; Mint, Clapp, Eliasberg:1005, $19,800. May exist with old rev. hub.

7337   1901 Base of first 1 obviously double. Scarce.

7338   1901 S [1,596,000]

Same grade comment as to **7335**. May exist with old rev. hub.

7339   1902 [31,140 + 114P] Scarce.

Usually weak VF to EF, rare UNC. Wayman:345, $1,400. Possibly 40–45 proofs survive, some impaired. Garrett:801, $57,500; Carter:983, $20,900.

7340   1902 S [1,753,625]

Same grade comment as to **7335**.

7341   1903 [287,270 + 158P]

Dangerous forgeries exist, gem UNCs., made in the late 1970s for investors. Possibly 40–45 proofs survive, many cleaned or impaired. Mint, Clapp, Eliasberg:1009, $17,600; Carter:986, $17,600.

7342   1903 S [954,000]

Same grade comment as to **7335**.

7343   1904 [6,256,699 + 98P]

Same comments as to **7341**, including proofs: Myers, Wayman:349, $14,500; Mint, Clapp, Eliasberg:1011, $23,100; Carter:989, $19,800 (rim dents).

7344   1904 S [5,134,175]

Same grade comment as to **7335**.

7345   1905 [58,919 + 92P] Scarce.

Often weak, infrequently UNC. Possibly 40–45 proofs survive, many cleaned or impaired: Mint, Clapp, Eliasberg:1013, $20,900.

7346   1905 S [1,813,000]

Same grade comment as to **7335**.

7347   1906 [69,596 + 94P] Scarce.

Often weak, infrequently UNC.: Wayman:353, $2,000. Possibly 50–60 proofs survive, many cleaned or impaired. Mint, Clapp, Eliasberg:1015, $17,600; Carter:994, $14,300.

7348   1906 S [2,065,750]

Same grade comment as to **7335**.

7349   1906 D [620,250 + 12P] Normal D.

Proofs were struck for presentation purposes, celebrating inception of coinage of this denomination, April 4, 1906. Breen {1977}, p. 238.

7350   1906 D Obviously double-punched D. Rare.

7351   1907 [1,451,786 + 78P]

Possibly 40–45 proofs survive, many cleaned or impaired: Garrett:802, $65,000; Clapp, Eliasberg:1018, $20,900. Ill. at **7334**.

7352   1907 S [2,165,800] Normal date.

Same grade comment as to **7335**.

7353   1907 S Double-punched 18. Rare.

Tops of extra digits above and r. of 18.

7354   1907 D [842,250 + ?P]

Proofs reportedly coined Sept. 30, 1907; Farouk:154. Breen {1977}, p. 238. At least one bag of UNCs. turned up.

iv. ST. GAUDENS'S *MCMVII* PROTOTYPES

Prudery and political infighting delayed for many years, and almost prevented altogether, the part Augustus St. Gaudens was destined to play in improving American gold-coin design. In 1891, St. Gaudens sat on the judging committee evaluating designs submitted for the new issue of silver coins, only to find none satisfactory (the best artists had boycotted the competition, as the prize was too small to be worthwhile)—and to see Mint Engraver Charles E. Barber foist off a mirror image of the Morgan dollar head (with hair cropped and vegetable matter removed) as an "improvement" on any of the submissions. Shortly afterward, St. Gaudens received a commission to design the official medal for the 1892 World's Columbian Exposition. The models he submitted featured a magnificent portrait of Columbus, "transfigured as he sets foot on the New World," and for rev. a Grecian youth, unashamedly naked, holding torch and wreaths to crown the victors (the medal's recipients): ill. Dryfhout {1982}, Pl. 151.3. The Board of Gentlemen Managers of the Exposition accepted his models, but when they publicized this design, Anthony Comstock (with what George Bernard Shaw and H. L. Mencken called his usual "comstockery") decided to Do Something. Comstock (1844–1916), founder of the Society for the Suppression of Vice, the terror of pornographers but the owner of the reputedly second largest pornography collection in the world, and able to wield immense power through his friends in Congress, at once denounced the St. Gaudens rev. as "obscene," beginning a torrent of verbal abuse at the sculptor and the Exposition. Afraid to stand up to this fanatic, or to defend St. Gaudens from fundamentalist prudery, the Exposition people withdrew the rev. and asked Charles E. Barber to design a replacement; predictably, this was notable only for banality. Understandably infuriated, St. Gaudens swore that he would go to his grave before having anything further to do with the Mint Bureau. And for 14 years he refused any further commissions which might involve him with that institution.

But in 1905 came the "offer he could not refuse." Pres. Theodore Roosevelt, his personal friend for years, asked St. Gaudens to design his official inaugural medal, which he did, choosing Adolph Alexander Weinman (designer of the 1916 dime and half dollar) to complete the modeling. Roosevelt used this as an opening wedge to induce St. Gaudens to design coins to replace Barber's; on Nov. 27, 1904, he had written to Treasury Secretary L. M. Shaw about the possibility of hiring someone like St. Gaudens to improve our "atrociously hideous" coinage. (Letter formerly in possession of Harry Bass, stolen with the documented first specimen of **7096.**) The President was so pleased with the medal that he began confiding to St. Gaudens details of his "pet crime"—his longtime dream, now feasible from within the White House, of freeing our national coinage from its unbearable dullness of design, and trying to restore to it some of the beauty and dignity of ancient Greek coins. St. Gaudens replied on Jan. 9, 1906: "Whatever I produce cannot be worse than the inanities now displayed on our coins." But as his models approached their magnificent completion, the sculptor's health declined, and he was forced to rely more and more on his pupil Henry Hering to deal with the Mint Bureau. On May 29, St. Gaudens wrote to Roosevelt: "If you succeed in getting the best of the polite Mr. Barber . . . or the others in charge, you will have done a greater work than putting through the Panama Canal. Nevertheless, I shall stick at it, even unto death." (Prophetic words: He died Aug. 3, 1907, never seeing even one of his coins in circulation.) Trying to bypass Barber's jealous opposition (and possible sabotage?), Hering had some of the necessary reductions (from foot-tall bas-reliefs to coin size) made in Paris, producing them barely in time to silence Barber's "It can't be done: I told you so."

Pres. Roosevelt personally chose from among St. Gaudens's proposed designs the standing Liberty (said to have been modeled by Alice Butler, like his $10 coin) and the flying eagle, this latter originally meant for the cent and admittedly inspired by the Gobrecht/Longacre flying eagle of the 1856–58 cents. It took all Hering's persistence—and presidential orders—to force Barber to complete the mechanical processes of making the "Ultrahigh Relief" MCMVII dies **(7355).**

Accordingly, during Feb. and March 1907, some 24 proof specimens were made of this incredible design, each nearly double the thickness at edge of the regular double eagle. Each required nine impressions at 172 tons apiece in a hydraulic press. Only these faithfully represent St. Gaudens's conception, cherished as the stunning climax of American coin design. The art expert Cornelius Vermeule has justly compared it to the Nikē of Samothrace! Two were melted, two remain in the Smithsonian Institution, one is in the ANS museum, and one (featured on "CBS Morning News," 10/27/82) brought $242,000 in the Eliasberg estate sale.

After St. Gaudens's death, Hering attempted to put the modified design or "regular High Relief Roman Numerals" coinage into production at the Philadelphia Mint, but Barber overruled him at every possible turn. Barber was convinced that neither St. Gaudens nor Hering nor any other outsiders knew anything about minting processes, especially about supervising reduction of relief models for making master dies, and that the whole project should be aborted as quickly as possible, even if it had to be sabotaged.

Over Barber's objections, and only at the direct orders of Pres. Roosevelt ("Begin the new issue even if it takes you all day to strike one piece!"), the second set of experimental master dies **(7358)** went into production about Nov. 18, 1907. There were apparently six pairs of working dies made from the complete hubs raised from these master dies; two different segmented edge collars were in use, each with the Latin motto and stars. On Collar I, bases of M in UNUM are level; on Collar II, they slant. The working dies differ only in patterns of irregular curved raised lines in fields. Some reports give the total issue as [11,250], others as 12,153; the former figure is better attested, but to it must be added an unknown quantity of satin-finish proofs. Each normal striking required five blows from the press to bring the design up to acceptable clarity of relief detail. These are the "regular" Roman Numerals type, arguably the finest American coin design ever to reach circulation, if among the most impractical. Predictably, they met with vociferous protests from bankers, who kept insisting that "the new coins won't stack." Few circulated; most were kept as souvenirs, and the most worn ones apparently were pocket pieces. The actor Adolphe Menjou had a weakness for this issue; his hoard of 250 was not dispersed until the 1970s.

Barber claimed that only five proofs were made "on the medal press," evidently requiring six or seven impressions apiece from the dies. This claim has proved to be a lie; Barber's estate, which came to light some years after his death (1917), yielded at least six. His widow had a seventh, and others cannot be traced to him. Satin-finish MCMVII proofs are extremely difficult to identify short of physical comparison with one known to be from the original Barber group. In general, a possible proof will differ from ordinary (!) MCMVII coins in having inner borders sharp on both sides, relief details fully brought up, all berries rounded, all Capitol pillars countable, all tail feathers with clear ends; edge letters are bolder than on normal strikings in the same collar, with horizontal striations between them. Proofs ordinarily do not have more than a trace of knife-rim, unlike the normal strikings of **7359–60.** See Breen {1977}, p. 209, for extended discussion.

There are two variants generally collected as major vars.: "flat rim" and "knife-rim," generally known by the misnomers "flat edge" and "wire edge." (The edge shows motto and stars; the rim is the boundary between border and edge.) Many estimates agree that the approximately 3,000 of Nov. 1907 had flat rims, the 8,250-odd of December showed knife-rims. This detail consists of a thin raised flange around half or more than half circumference on either side (usually both), manifestly from metal being squeezed between the collar and dies on successive blows at striking. It is irregular enough to have been most likely unintentional, unlike that on the "Type I" St. Gaudens $10's of 1907; it may have caused difficulties in ejecting coins from the dies, and doubtless made Barber feel all the more justified in opposing the design as an impractical presidential whim.

Dangerous forgeries have been appearing since about 1973–74. The least deceptive of these is so weak at eagle's head that eye and beak are partly blurred; Ms. Liberty has no mouth. Far more dangerous are the "Omega" pieces, which show a capital omega incised into the coin (or rather into the positive from which the rev. die was made) within the space bounded by eagle's claw. This suggests that they are by the maker of the fake 1882 $3 coins with the same omega signature within R of LIBERTY. There is at least one other equally dangerous forgery around. Authentication is mandatory!

ST. GAUDENS'S MCMVII PROTOTYPES

Designer, Augustus St. Gaudens. Engravers, St. Gaudens, Henry Hering. Mint, Philadelphia (no mintmark). Physical Specifications, Authorizing Acts, as before, but edge E * PLURIBUS * UNUM* * * * * * * * * *

Grade range, for **7358–60,** VERY GOOD to UNC., usually EF to UNC.; other numbers UNC. or Proof. FINE: Over half drapery lines and feathers. VERY FINE: Partial garment lines immediately above and below bosom; remaining garment lines almost complete except at upraised knee; feathers separated except at breast and upper edge of l. wing (that nearer observer). EXTREMELY FINE: Full mint sharpness except at tiny isolated rubbed spots: nose, l. breast, upraised knee, etc.; drapery lines on bosom complete; partial mint surface. UNCIRCULATED: *No* trace of wear. EXCEPTIONS: Possibly the commonest grade is "slider," marketed as "commercial UNC." or too often as plain UNC.; look for the telltale rubbed spot on knee.

7355 MCMVII Ultrahigh Relief. [24—P?] Proofs only. Ex. rare.

Judd 1778. No border, only sharp rim continuous with deeply basined field. MCMVII far from drapery; tiny Capitol; star above l. arm of Y; rev. 14 rays in sunburst. Nearly double thickness at edge; large edge letters, curved tops to U's, reading with rev. up. 1) Mint, SI. 2) C. E. Barber, ANS. Enl. photos. 3) Theodore Roosevelt, Ullmer:546, $200,000, Manfra, Tordella & Brookes. 4) Theodore Roosevelt Museum. 5) 1956 ANA:1773, Dr. Wilkison, Paramount, A-Mark, Auction 80:977, $230,000. 6) Clapp, Eliasberg:1021, $242,000, M. Brownlee. 7) Col. Green, Bell I:867A. 8) Kern:626. 9) Farouk:296. 10) KS 2/61:1417. 11) Lilly, SI, probably one of nos. 7)–10). 12) St. Gaudens, Pres. Roosevelt, Cornelius Van Schaak Roosevelt, 1967 to SI. Compare next 2.

7356 MCMVII Ultrahigh Relief. Inverted edge letters. Proofs only. 2 known.

Edge reads with obv. up. 1) "Mint employee," St. Gaudens family, Capt. Andrew North (in cased set), Stack's, exhibited at 1956 ANA Convention, dispersed ca. 1980, NERCG, Boston Jubilee:323, $175,000, Manfra, Tordella & Brookes, Auction 85:983, $286,000. "The Rarest" {1980}. 2) Kosoff Estate:848, $264,000.

7357 MCMVII Ultrahigh Relief. Plain edge. Unique?

Complete extra knife-rim; rev. cracked, rim at 8:30 through long ray to adjacent long ray. 1) Cased set as **7356,** John Dannreuther, pvt. coll. "The Rarest" {1980}.

7358 MCMVII Regular High Relief. [All kinds 11,250 + ?P] Flat rim, Collar I.

No knife-rim. MCMVII close to drapery; large Capitol; star nearly central above Y; rev. 13 rays in sunburst. On edge, bases of M level. Allegedly [3,000] Nov. 1907. Usually with local softness on some details of hair, drapery, face, oak leaves, sunburst, or tail feathers; proofs are sharp on these details. All proofs and some few of the best normal strikings show recutting at inner r. of first U in UNUM. Wayman:360, UNC., $23,000; Eliasberg:1023, UNC., $17,600. Eliasberg:1022, Proof, $50,600. Another proof was in the Capt. North cased set. See Breen {1977}, p. 209. Authentication is mandatory.

7359 MCMVII Regular High Relief. Knife-rim, Collar I.

Knife-rim is outside the raised flat rim; see introductory text. Allegedly 8,250 coined Dec. 1907 of this and next; probably close to the true figure, as about 3 knife-rim coins show up for every one of **7358.** Authentication is mandatory.

7360 MCMVII Knife-rim, Collar II.

Bases of M in UNUM not level. Mintage included in preceding. For satin-finish proofs see Breen {1977}, p. 209. Matte proofs: 1) Capt. North set (minute traces of knife-rim). 2) DiBello:1317, Auction 81:1872, $34,000. Authentication is mandatory.

7361 MCMVII Plain edge. Unique?

515.8 grs. = 33.42 gms. 34.3 mm. Ben M. Douglas, "Numismatic Notes," Washington (D.C.) Sunday *Star,* 7/13/69; Collectors' Clearinghouse, *CW* 8/6/69. 1) Victor H. Weill, Weill:80, $43,500, pvt. coll., Ron Gillio.

v. THE BARBER-ST. GAUDENS DESIGN, NO MOTTO (1907–8)

After Augustus St. Gaudens died in Aug. 1907, Mint Engraver Charles E. Barber prepared his own copy dies in low relief, in the expectation that coinage would have to proceed with some practical modification of the MCMVII design. Originally these copy dies were to have been made by mechanical reduction from St. Gaudens's higher-relief models. In actuality, Barber produced some perfunctory reductions on one of the Mint's portrait lathes, pronounced them unfit for coinage, and used this as an excuse to make his own imitations. The master dies and hubs made from them bore the date in ordinary numerals 1907 rather than the Roman MCMVII. They are routinely miscalled "Arabic numerals," this name manifestly bestowed by persons who had never seen coins with actual Arabic inscriptions or dates.

By Presidential orders, the motto IN GOD WE TRUST was omitted, even as from the MCMVII design. Theodore Roosevelt, a deeply religious man and a Freemason, believed that inscribing the deity's name on coins which might be used for criminal purposes was blasphemy: See Chap. 37, Sect. vi, introductory text.

Barber's dies were completely unsatisfactory—a travesty of St. Gaudens's original concept. Henry Hering, St. Gaudens's pupil and collaborator (as well as the artist's principal liaison with the Mint Bureau), refused to approve them. This created difficulties because St. Gaudens's widow could not be paid without such approval.

Finally, in spring 1908, Hering visited the Philadelphia Mint with the widow's son and their attorney, and denounced the poor quality of Barber's version of the design. When Barber attempted to blame St. Gaudens's original design, Hering produced the far superior reductions he had privately obtained in France against this exact contingency as evidence that the fault lay instead with Barber's bungling obstructionism. Mrs. St. Gaudens was eventually paid after negotiations. We may connect this event with the change from Short Rays to Long Rays.

This particular variation has never been publicized, though it is obvious to the naked eye. A Short Rays obv. is shown as 1907 "Arabic," a Long Rays as obv. of 1908 No Motto in the Yeoman Guide Book, though without mention that both types occur on No Motto coins of 1908 and 1908 D. I discovered these about 1965 but was unable to locate enough 1908's and 1908 D's for a frequency count until May 1980, when (through the courtesy of Gerald Bauman and Paul Nugget, of Manfra, Tordella & Brookes) I had opportunity to check through their extensive holdings. These yielded, for 1908 Philadelphia, 24 with Short Rays and 29 with Long Rays; for 1908 D, four of each.

I had earlier an impression that 1908 Short Rays was scarcer than the Long Rays; this has continued to be confirmed. What surprised me was that 1908 D turned up so infrequently. Actually, the quantities found in MTB's stock are closely proportional to the mintages of 1908 and 1908 D, evidently representing a random sample (mostly housed in rolls simply as "St. Gaudens" without segregation into dates and mintmarks). We may conjecture, then, that the actual mintage breakdown into Short Rays and Long Rays coins will prove to be in approximately the proportion 5:6 for 1908 Philadelphia, and roughly 1:1 for 1908 D: roughly 1.9 million 1908 Short Rays as against 2.3 million 1908 Long Rays; somewhat over 330,000 of each type from Denver. Monthly coinage figures for this period have remained unavailable, nor have we any information about the date of change of type.

A note on edge lettering is in order. The Ultrahigh Relief MCMVII had the largest edge lettering of all, followed by MCMVII Collars I and II. Collar I was reused (in error or experiment?) on a unique matte proof of 1907, then promptly replaced by the new Small Edge Letters collar. To avert any confusion, we give the lettering on each segment of the tripartite collars: Large Edge Letters: I * * * * * * * E * I P L U R I B U S I * U N U M * * * * I Small Edge Letters: I * * * * * * E I * P L U R I B U S * I U N U M * * * * * I

On the latter, the E is notably smaller than formerly. There are several minor variants, but this layout remained in use through 1933.

The Barber-St. Gaudens Design, No Motto

Designer, Engraver, Charles E. Barber, loosely after St. Gaudens. Mints, Philadelphia (no mintmark), Denver (mintmark D). Mintmark above date. Physical Specifications, Authorizing Acts, as before.

Grade range, FINE to UNC.; seldom collected below EXTREMELY FINE. FINE: Forelock not visible; garment smooth, nearly half wing details intact, partial breast feathers. VERY FINE: Some garment lines near bosom; partial leg details; forelock shows; at least half feathers on wings and breast. EXTREMELY FINE: Isolated tiny rubbed spots only: brow, nose, breast, upraised knee, few breast feathers; other details complete; partial mint luster. UNCIRCULATED: *No* trace of wear. NOTE: Uncirculated coins normally show bag marks. If these nicks and scratches obscure significant details of drapery or feathers, the coin will price as of lower grade.

7362 1907 Large edge letters. [?P] Proofs only.
Collar I of MCMVII coins: See introductory text and previous section. 1) Capt. North cased set, NERCG, Ken Goldman, Hatie:2855, matte proof, $71,500. "The Rarest" {1980}. Ill. of **7363.**

7363 1907 Small edge letters. [361,667 + ?P]
See introductory text. Minor vars. of edge. UNCS. are often weak. Matte proofs: 1) Wayte Raymond (ill. at **7362**). 2) James Kelly, Nov. 1957. 3) Mehl, Kern:629, Mehl estate, 1958 ANA:2052. One of these recently showed up in California.

7364 1908 [all kinds, no motto, 4,271,551] Short rays.
Nearest ray ends about 1 mm from branch, as in 1907. Often weakly struck. Probably over 1.9 million made. See introductory text.

7365 1908 Long rays.
Nearest ray about touches branch; modified drapery. Obv.

master die reused through 1911. Probably over 2.3 million made. Often weak. See introductory text.

7366 1908 D [all kinds, no motto, 663,750] Short rays.
As **7364.** Probably 331,000+ made. See introductory text.

7367 1908 D Long rays.
As **7365.** Probably 331,000+ made. See introductory text.

vi. MOTTO ADDED (1908–33)

Though Pres. Theodore Roosevelt was devoutly religious and a Freemason, he disagreed with Congress and the average citizen on the need—or the desirability—of having God's name placed on coins. Ever since the Rev. M. R. Watkinson had come up with the idea (1861), officialdom and the general public approved of keeping IN GOD WE TRUST on the coins; possibly some dimly remembered the line from one of the later stanzas of Francis Scott Key's "The Battle of Fort McHenry" (later renamed "The Star-Spangled Banner"): "And this be our motto, In God is our trust." Roosevelt's objection to the motto is more consonant with the First Amendment principle of separation of church and state; his line of reasoning is discussed in Chap. 37, Sect. vi, introductory text.

Though there is much to be said for Roosevelt's view, Congress disagreed, feeling (like much of the general public) that anyone opposing the use of God's name on coins was of necessity an atheist and probably an anarchist or even a Bolshevik. Congress therefore ordered that henceforth all coins large enough to accommodate the motto should do so, in compliance with the Act of March 3, 1865.

Barber reworked the double eagle rev. to carry this motto. His revision had nine tail feathers instead of the former eight, and 33 rays instead of 34, but the location of rays remained unaltered. Barber omitted one at extreme l., and made the heavy rays thinner and some of them longer.

Until Pres. Franklin Delano Roosevelt abolished gold coinage in 1933, there was only one more design change. Coins of 1912–33 show 48 obv. stars instead of the former 46, commemorating the admission of New Mexico and Arizona as forty-seventh and forty-eighth states, Jan. 6 and Feb. 14, 1912. The two extra stars were added to the end of the curved row at lower r., about 5:00, among oak leaves below date, but without other design modification. Barber evidently did this by sinking a master die from a 1908–11 hub and punching in the stars by hand, thereafter in turn raising working hubs from it and sinking working dies.

Relative rarity of the later dates, unlike those of earlier years, owes less to limited mintages than to extensive meltages and random survival of specimens in French and Swiss banks during the decades after the Great Recall of 1933–34. Secrecy about some of the rarer dates, on both sides of the Atlantic, has obscured the picture: Thanks to the unlamented Leland Howard and his Office of Domestic Gold and Silver Operations (ODGSO), federal interference with imports of numismatic material increased during the 1950s and '60s side by side with official paranoia about collectors, and with collectors' fears that Treasury snoops would search, seize, and destroy first, before any legal actions for recovery could be instituted. In more recent years, now that Howard and the ODGSO are as dead as the Volstead Act and one no longer needs a license to import gold coins, the picture has become clearer—and the gold coins costlier. However, exact numbers rediscovered have remained elusive, partly because many dealers irrationally fear that such information might lower prices.

Wholesale meltage destroyed the majority of the dates 1912–33. This has not significantly affected 1928, which has the largest mintage of any gold coin of any denomination in American history. In a few instances (1920 S, 1921, 1927 D, 1930 S, 1931 D) low mintage aggravated the problem, so that fewer specimens reached Europe. A few dates (1913 S, 1924 S, 1926 D) were virtually unknown to American collectors until the 1950s, when handfuls were recovered in France.

As a result, when specimens of the rarer years are offered at all, they are normally uncirculated with the usual bag marks; but the same remark also applies to many of the commoner dates.

There is one important var. in this group, the overdate 1909/8. As with the 1918/7 D nickel and S quarter, this resulted from use of both 1909 and 1908 hubs on a single working die blank, probably during fall 1908 when working dies were being prepared for both years. This var. was discovered by Edgar H. Adams in 1910, then forgotten until its rediscovery about 1943. It is less scarce than the normal date except in mint state.

Mintmark D is from a wide punch (boldface extended, in typographical language) through 1910, as on the eagles. This was difficult to fit between rays above date, so that on many specimens the D leans l. Coins of 1911 and later years from Denver show a tiny mintmark similar to that on cents. It is barely possible that coins of 1910 D or 1911 D may exist with both styles of mintmark; if so, the 1910 Small D and/or the 1911 Large D would be great rarities.

In March 1933, Presidential Order 6260 prevented any further release of gold coins from the mints. Though eagles had been legally issued in January and February from Philadelphia, double eagles were not. Nevertheless, an unknown quantity managed to leave the Mint Bureau, allegedly obtained by clandestine exchange for other double eagles in unissued stocks at the Philadelphia Mint. B. Max Mehl, in the Roach sale (1944), admitted to having sold two of the 8–10 then known. The first one to appear at auction (Col. Flanagan's, also in 1944) was seized by the Treasury Department, as have all others to come to federal attention since then: *NumRev* 13, p. 17 (1/47). King Farouk's (Farouk:185) was withdrawn but not returned to the Treasury; whereabouts unknown. At least one other was reportedly flung into the ocean to avoid seizure, prior to 1956. The only chance anyone has to see what these legendary coins look like is to view the exhibit at the Smithsonian Institution.

What the first Roosevelt began in 1907, the second ended in 1933; and the date 1933 forms as rare an end to the double-eagle series as 1849 did to its beginning.

The Coinage Act of July 23, 1965 (PL 89-81), Sect. 392, has apparently restored legal-tender status to the double eagle.

MOTTO ADDED

Designer, Engraver, as before. Mints, Philadelphia (no mintmark), San Francisco (mintmark S), Denver (D). Mintmarks above date. Physical Specifications, Authorizing Acts, as before.

Grade range, VERY FINE to UNC.; not collected below EXTREMELY FINE except for extreme rarities. Later dates are almost always UNC. with varying degrees of bag marks. Grade standards, as before.

Obv. 46 Stars

7368 1908 [156,258 + 101P]

Obv. as **7365**; this Long Rays design continues through 1911. Ill. of **7372**. Two different finishes on proofs: light matte (3 known), dark matte (usual, ill.); but compare next. Light matte proofs are pale orange-yellow to light khaki; Breen {1977}, p. 211. Dark matte proofs are nearly olive-drab, like the smaller denominations. Mint, Garrett:805, $60,000; Mitchelson, Clapp, Eliasberg:1027, $28,600, Kagin.

7369 1908 "Roman Finish" proof. Unique?

As in 1909–10; pale lemon color, semibrilliant fields. 1) BMFA, 1976 ANA:3302, $10,000.

7370 1908 S [22,000]

Usually EF to AU. Eliasberg:1029, UNC., $17,600. The report of a bag of 1,000 found in Central America has not yet been confirmed.

7371 1908 D Wide D. [349,500]

Mintmark often leans l.; minor positional vars. of this and later D mints. UNCs. are mostly from a hoard of 100 found about 1979.

7372 1909 [all kinds 161,215 + 67P] Normal date.

Scarcer than next. Proofs have "Roman" finish (ill.); they may exist with matte or other finish. Garrett:806, $85,000; 1980 ANA:448, $43,000; Eliasberg:1031, $30,800.

7373 1909/8

See introductory text. Discovered by Edgar H. Adams. Usually EF to AU, seldom mint state. Auction 79:388, $3,200, Auction 81:1472, $4,200, UNC.

7374 1909 S Normal S. [2,774,925]

Minor positional vars. of this and later S mints. A hoard of at least 1,000 UNCs. turned up about 1983.

7375 1909 S Double S. Very rare.

"Cicero":50. Mintmark first punched weakly in normal position, then more heavily far too high and leaning l.

7376 1909 D Wide D. [52,500] Rare.

Usually in EF. Very rare in mint state. Eliasberg:1032, UNC., $37,400. Sometimes with minor repunching on D; this remark holds for many later D mints.

7377 1910 [482,000 + 167P]

A hoard of 15 UNCs. turned up in 1981. Proofs have "Roman" finish, like 1909, but may exist matte. Mint, Garrett:807, $90,000; Eliasberg:1034, $33,000.

7378 1910 S [2,128,250]

A hoard of about 100 UNCs. turned up in a Swiss bank about 1981; and a bag of 1,000 was discovered about 1983 in Central America.

7379 1910 D Wide D. [429,000]

May exist with small D; see introductory text.

7380 1911 [197,250 + 100P]

Proofs have dark matte finish, similar to 1908. Probably fewer than 20 survive. Mint, Garrett:808, $72,500; 1980 ANA:454, $43,000; Clapp, Eliasberg:1037, $33,000.

7381 1911 S [775,750]

7382 1911 D [846,500] Small normal D.

May possibly exist with Wide D as in 1910; see introductory text.

7383 1911 D Double D. Rare.

1982 ANA:2798, UNC., $800.

Obv. 48 Stars

7384 1912 [149,750 + 74P]

See introductory text. Often EF to AU; UNCs. are often weakly struck or extensively bag-marked, seldom choice. Auction 79:1409, UNC., $4,000. Proofs (ill.) are about as rare as those of 1911. Mint, Garrett:809, $75,000; Clapp, Eliasberg:1040, $26,400.

7385 1913 [168,780 + 58P]

Same grade comments. Proofs have the same finish as 1912, but are rarer still. Mint, Garrett:810, $77,500; Clapp, Eliasberg:1041, $35,200.

7386 1913 S [34,000]

Most are UNC. with extensive bag marks, from French banks ca. 1953–56. The report of a bag of 1,000 from Central America, 1983, remains unconfirmed.

7387 1913 D [393,500]

7388 1914 [95,250 + 70P]

Same grade comments as to 1912. Proofs (Ex. rare) have coarse sandblast finish; Breen {1977}, p. 216. Mint, Garrett:811, $85,000; Clapp, Eliasberg:1044, $28,600.

7389 1914 S [1,498,000]

A hoard of at least 2,000 UNCs. turned up in 1978, others in 1983.

7390 1914 D [453,000]

7391 1915 [152,000 + 50P]

Possibly less than 12 proofs survive; they have the same finish as 1914. Breen {1977}, p. 216. Mint, Garrett:812, $60,000; Clapp, Eliasberg:1047, $28,600.

7392 1915 S [567,500]

A hoard of over 50 UNCs. turned up in 1980. A bag of 1,000 was recovered in Central America, 1983.

7393   1916 S [796,000]

UNCs. are mostly from a hoard of at least 3,000 discovered in 1983.

7394   1920 [228,250]

7395   1920 S [558,000] Ex. rare.

Possibly 8–12 survive, mostly weakly struck UNC. Eliasberg:1051, UNC., $30,800.

7396   1921 [528,500] Very rare.

Most survivors are EF to AU, possibly 15–18 in all, including about 5 from European sources since 1981. Auction 79:1416, UNC., $28,000; G. S. Godard, Auction 82:447, UNC., $32,000; Eliasberg:1052, AU+, $28,600. European forgeries made before 1953 have all numerals leaning r., and lettering differs from the genuine. Authentication recommended.

7397   1922 [1,375,500]

Many UNCs. are from a hoard of possibly 150 discovered in 1983. Some have prooflike revs.

7398   1922 S [2,658,000]

At least 7,000 UNCs. turned up in Central America, 1983.

7399   1923 [566,000]

7400   1923 D [1,702,250]

Manfra, Tordella & Brookes handled a hoard of over 1,000 UNCs., including many from the Brand estate, 1981–82.

7401   1924 [4,323,500]

7402   1924 S [2,927,500] Very scarce.

Almost all survivors came from French banks ca. 1953–56; most are UNC. with extensive bag marks. Mintmark varies from upright to leaning sharply r., and from light to heavy.

7403   1924 D [3,049,500] Very scarce.

Same comments. Often weakly struck. Another UNC. hoard, possibly 30 pieces, turned up in summer 1983.

7404   1925 [2,831,750]

7405   1925 S [3,776,500] Very scarce.

Same comment as to **7402.**

7406   1925 D [2,938,500] Rare.

Same comment. In all, 24 obvs., 28 revs. In LM 10/66:536 was a var. from weakly hubbed and/or heavily lapped obv.: branch unusually thin, arm shallow.

7407   1926 [816,750]

Bill Fivaz discovered a minor doubled obv. die: *CW* 5/9/84, p. 70.

7408   1926 S [2,041,500] Rare.

Same comment as to **7402.** About 7 positional vars. of mintmark. Eliasberg:1065, UNC., $5,500. The report of a bag of 1,000 UNCs. from Central America remains unconfirmed.

7409   1926 D [481,000] Rare.

Same comment as to **7402.**

7410   1927 [2,946,750]

7411   1927 S [3,107,000] Very rare.

Possibly 15 known. Same comment as to **7402.** Often weakly struck. Eliasberg:1068, UNC., $5,225.

7412   1927 D [180,000] Ex. rare.

4 pairs of dies, 2 edge collars. Most are UNC. See introductory text. 1), 2) Denver Mint, SI. 3) Schermerhorn, Lilly, SI. 4) Boyd, WGC, Eliasberg:1067, $176,000, D. Kagin, $250,000 *(CW* 8/3/83, p. 1), Manfra, Tordella & Brookes, $290,000, Dr. William Crawford. 5) "Bell," S 12/81:1252, $220,000. 6) LM 10/69:526, "Gilhousen":1041, $60,000 (1973). 7) Dr. Green:917. 8) J. W. Schmandt:1072. 9) Kagin 51:192, EF, unverified. 10) James Kelly (late 1940s), Auction 84:999, $198,000. Mark on ninth ray from l. 11) S 10/22/85:868, $275,000, probably same as one of preceding. No. 7) may duplicate 3); 8) may duplicate 6). Dangerous forgeries exist, made by affixing D mintmark onto genuine Philadelphia coins. Authentication is mandatory!

7413   1928 [8,816,000]

7414   1929 [1,779,750] Rare.

Estimates range from 60 survivors (reasonable) to "a few hundred" (most likely too high); almost all are UNC., including the 40 discovered in England, 1984. Eliasberg:1070, AU, $6,050; Wayman:404, UNC., $11,000; Carter:1078, UNC., $12,650.

7415   1930 S [74,000] Very rare.

Possibly 25 survive, almost all UNC. with bag marks; most came from European banks about 1960. Wayman:405, $25,000; Eliasberg:1071, $18,700; Carter:1079, AU, $19,250.

7416   1931 [2,938,250] Very rare.

Possibly 18–20 survive, all UNC. Auction 80:1998, $57,500; Wayman:406, $21,000; Eliasberg:1072, $17,600; Carter:1080, $24,750.

7417   1931 D [106,500] Rare.

Possibly 30–35 survive, almost all UNC.; a hoard of 20 turned up in the Midwest, 1984. Wayman:407, $21,000; Auction 82:455, $16,500; 1982 ANA:2834, $16,000; Carter:1081, $26,400.

7418   1932 [1,101,750] Very rare.

Possibly 22–25 survive, almost all UNC. Eliasberg:1074, AU, $10,450; Wayman:408, UNC., $26,000; Carter:1082, UNC., $26,400.

7419   1933 [445,500–] Ex. rare.

Cannot be legally held. Specimens are in SI. See introductory text.

Part Five

COMMEMORATIVE
COINAGES

CHAPTER 39

OVERVIEW

Originally there was little distinction between "regular" and commemorative coinages, the latter by definition having devices alluding to some specific locality, event, or important personage, aside from the ruler who authorized its issue. Ancient Greek coins routinely commemorated anything from totem animals (the Athenian owl, the Ephesian stag, the Thracian ithyphallic satyr) to local industry (the anchor on coins of Apollonia, the grapevine on those of Maroneia, the ship's prow on those of Samos, etc.) to battles and even athletic victories. Sometimes they displayed city badges whose devices' names punned on the city name: *selinos,* 'celery leaf,' for Selinos; *rhodos,* 'rose,' for Rhodes. Similar practices abounded in Roman and medieval coinages. Only in the last couple of centuries have sharp boundaries been made between commemorative coinages and any other kind; and in recent years the greatest difference is that commemoratives are increasingly often NCLT's (noncirculating legal-tender coins) sold at a premium to coin collectors or the general public, though theoretically able to circulate.

Among United States coins, arguably the 1848 CAL quarter eagle **(6196)** is a commemorative issue, memorializing the discovery of gold in California, parallel to the Elephant, VIGO, and LIMA silver coins of England. One could equally argue that the Lincoln cent of 1909 and the Washington quarter of 1932 were commemoratives (respectively of a centennial and a bicentennial), except that these were distributed as regular issues rather than being sold at a premium. Similar considerations apply to the 1946 Roosevelt dime, 1964 Kennedy half dollar, and 1971 Ike dollar (commemorating deaths), and to the 1776–1976 Bicentennial issues.

Properly speaking, however, the United States commemorative series consists only of NCLT coins made for special celebrations, sold at premiums to collectors and the general public, allegedly to raise funds for the event or locality being celebrated. When a proposal for such an issue passes both houses of Congress and becomes law, the sponsoring commission recommends designs to the Mint Bureau. In most instances, artists outside the Mint have created the models, which must be reduced to coin size. The Mint delivers the coins to the commission at face value; the promoters market them at whatever the traffic will bear. Sometimes commissions work with local coin dealers, sometimes on their own. Unsold coins have sometimes been spent, in other instances wholesaled to coin dealers, in still others returned to the Mint for melting.

During the 1930s, the commissions in charge of the Boone, Arkansas, Oregon, and Texas issues took advantage of legal loopholes, obtaining numerous small issues of coins identical except for date and mintmark, sometimes in driblets over several years. This practice sometimes meant that speculators could obtain particular dates when nobody else could.

Dealers and collectors denounced it as an abuse, and their protests reached Congress, ultimately leading to the Act of Aug. 5, 1939 forbidding any further issue of pre-1939 designs of commemorative coins: "the end of an era." However, in Aug. 1946 Pres. Truman approved commemorative issues for Iowa and for Booker T. Washington's birthplace. The latter was a ghastly blunder, as the promoter, one S. J. Phillips, revived the old abuses and mishandled the distribution so badly that years later some of his coins were found in circulation while others were being peddled in drugstores, and Phillips was defaulting on his $140,000 debts.

For another 30 years, the Phillips fiasco served as justification for the Mint Bureau's adamant opposition to all attempts to restore commemorative coinages; and successive administrations followed the Treasury line as gospel. The official arguments against their issuance, apparently prepared by Treasury Dept. legal counsel about 1930, stress "creating confusion among the public and encouraging counterfeiting" (Ganz {1976}, p. 29). These have been blindly repeated ever since, despite their manifest irrelevancy to the real issue, which was market manipulation and profiteering. Various coin columnists, including this writer, have advocated resumption of commemorative coinage, honoring events of national (not merely local) importance, and distribution by federal agencies. These recommendations bore fruit in the 1982 Washington commemorative half dollars. However, the controversial 1983–84 Olympics coins represent weaknesses in even the current system, and the controversy's end is not in sight.

Order of listing is chronological, determined by dates of authorizing acts and/or initial release. Alphabetic order has been tried in other books, but contains a built-in weakness: Many coins are known by varying popular names other than their official titles. Chronological order has the advantage of illustrating shifts and developments of style—an important aspect of the history of art in and out of coinage.

Previously unavailable historical information derives from Swiatek-Breen {1981}, which contains much more details, especially of the scandalous (and sometimes even criminal) actions connected with authorizing bills and distribution of the coins. These range from venality to outright fraud; and in one notorious instance (1924 Huguenot) the Federal Council of Churches of Christ in America used the coins as a fund-raising project in flagrant violation of the First Amendment. The scandals attached to these coins make them, if anything, a more attractive proposition to collectors: memorabilia of some events which in their own day were considered comparable to Jay Gould's attempt to corner the gold market, to the Whiskey Ring, to the Tweed Ring, or to Teapot Dome.

Commemorative coins (gold and silver alike) are normally collected only in mint state, as befits NCLT coins. However, distributors and in a few instances banks spent quantities of them rather than returning them to the Mint for melting after the original issue period had expired; in addition, the general public has a way of mistreating coins even bought at a premium as souvenirs. This has made some issues very difficult to locate in choice mint state. "First Points of Wear" for each issue derive from grading standards adopted in Swiatek-Breen {1981}, pp. 325–54, ultimately from Gettys-Catich {1958}.

If a coin is offered to you as UNCIRCULATED, check the "First Points of Wear": a truly mint-state specimen has *no* trace of rubbing on it; a weakly struck UNCIRCULATED piece will show mint luster on these spots, but no wear. For ABOUT UNCIRCULATED, expect some few of these spots to show minute traces of rubbing, nearly complete mint luster. Many such are routinely offered as anything from "sliders" to "MS-63." For EXTREMELY FINE, expect most of these spots to show rubbing, partial mint luster. Beware of pieces which have been cleaned and recolored; rubbed spots can be obscured by the sulfide coating. If in doubt, insist on a coin without even potential sources of this kind of uncertainty. Even if *you* are certain that the coin is as represented, its next purchaser may be harder to convince.

Proofs are known of many issues; all are rare, many were made for Mint Engraver John R. Sinnock and other VIPs rather than for public sale, and the roster is probably incomplete.

Commemorative silver coins match the 1873–1963 issues in physical specifications: Lafayette dollar, 412.5 grs. = 26.73 gms., 1.5″ = 38.1 mm; half dollars, all kinds, 192.9 grs. = 12.5 gms., 1.205″ = 30.6 mm; Isabella quarter, 96.45 grs. = 6.25 gms., 0.955″ = 24.3 mm; Pan-Pacific fifties, 1,290 grs. = 83.59 gms., round 1.75″ = 43.2 mm, octagonal, side to side 1¹³/₁₆″ = 46 mm, diagonally 1¾″ = 44.5 mm; quarter eagles, 64.5 grs. = 4.18 gms., ¹⁷/₂₄″ = 18 mm; gold dollars, 25.8 grs. = 1.672 gms., ⁹/₁₆″ = 14.3 mm. Edges always reeded. Philadelphia coins have no mintmark; Denver D, San Francisco S.

INDIVIDUAL DESIGNS

WORLD'S COLUMBIAN EXPOSITION HALF DOLLARS

Alias: Columbians 1892, 1893.

Occasion: Fund-raising for the Exposition (Jackson Park, Chicago, May 1–Oct. 30, 1893), originally scheduled to open Oct. 12, 1892, for the 400th anniversary of Christopher Columbus's discovery of the Caribbean islands which he mistook for India.

Designs: Obv. is Charles E. Barber's fictitious head of Columbus, after a plaster model by Olin Levi Warner (1844–96) in the Chicago Historical Society, allegedly after a photograph of Jerónimo Suñel's statue in Madrid, this in turn based on Charles Legrand's fanciful portrait in the Madrid Naval Museum. Rev. is George T. Morgan's copy (from a photograph) of the replica of the *Santa María* made in Spain for the Exposition; his initial M is concealed in the rigging. Two hemispheres represent those on the *Dos Mundos*, 'Two Worlds,' pillar dollars or Pieces of Eight, which had bulked large in legal-tender circulating silver in the USA until May 1857.

Authorizing Act: Aug. 5, 1892.

Mintage: Authorized, 5 million both dates; struck, Nov. 19– Dec. 31, 1892, [949,896 + 103P]; struck, dated 1893, [4,050,000 + 2,105 for assay].

Proofs: 1892—nos. 1–100, 400, 1492, 1892, but later owners discarded most of the tattered envelopes. The #1 coin was sold to the Remington typewriter firm for $10,000 as a publicity stunt; see Swiatek-Breen, pp. 65–73.

Grades: VG up, most often VF to EF. "Sliders" are far commoner than mint-state survivors.

First Wear Points: Eyebrow, cheek, hair behind forehead and jaw; top of sail nearest stern, sails at mainmast and foremast, r. side of Eastern Hemisphere.

7420   1892 [Net 949,896 + 103P]
Ill. (enl.) is of the first proof made, Nov. 19; Swiatek-Breen, p. 62. First proof auctioned, Woodin I:248. 1982 ANA:2510, "Proof," $1,375.

7421   1893 [Net 1,548,300 incl. 1+P]
The #1 proof (Jan. 3) is in the Chicago Historical Society. Others are reported, e.g., Woodin I:249, "an unmistakable proof." These are unverified. I have not seen 1982 ANA:2511, "Proof," $1,900.

THE ISABELLA QUARTER

Alias: Isabella.

Occasion: As preceding. The Exposition's Board of Lady Managers (organized after Susan B. Anthony lobbied for it in Congress) desired the coins for fund-raising.

Designs: Both sides by Charles E. Barber. Obv. is a fictitious portrait of Queen Isabella, Columbus's patron. Rev. depicts an idealized spinner with distaff and spindle, symbolic of what was thought to be woman's major industry 1492–1892.

Authorizing Act: March 3, 1893.

Mintage: Authorized, 40,000; coined June 13, 1893, [39,877 + 103P + 23 assay]; melted, aside from assay coins, 15,809.

Proofs: First 100, plus nos. 400, 1492, 1892. As with the 1892 halves, most original numbered envelopes perished; see Swiatek-Breen, pp. 114–15. Die file marks around MB; knife-rims, obv. clockwise 10:00 to 4:00, rev. almost complete.

Grades: Mostly EF to UNC., principally "sliders."

First Wear Points: Cheekbone, center of lower part of crown, strand of wool crossing thigh, knees, shoulder, hair.

7422   1893 [Net 24,088 + 103P]
Ill. (enl.) is of an impaired proof. 1982 ANA:2490, "Proof," $2,200. Auction 86:1296, Proof, $5,250.

THE LAFAYETTE SILVER DOLLAR

Alias: Lafayette.

Occasion: Participation in 1900 Paris Exposition; fund-raising to defray part of cost of Paul Wayland Bartlett's equestrian statue of Lafayette at Exposition, to which the USA had pledged $50,000, which was coordinated by the Lafayette Memorial Commission, Robert J. Thompson, secretary.

Designs: By Charles E. Barber. Jugate heads of Washington (after Houdon) and Lafayette (after the Caunois medal of 1824); layout copied from Peter L. Krider's Yorktown medal of 1881. Rev. is from an early sketch of Bartlett's statue; inscription alludes to cents contributed by schoolchildren.

Authorizing Act: March 3, 1899.

Mintage: Authorized, 50,000; struck, [50,000 + 26 assay], Dec. 14, 1899; melted, 14,000 (1945).

Proofs: One reported by Swiatek, said to be brilliant.

Grades: Usually VF to AU and "sliders," rarely mint state.

First Wear Points: Washington's cheekbone, Lafayette's lower curls; boot, thigh, rear leg, blinder. These areas, especially on rev., are often weak even on mint-state survivors.

7423 1900 [Net 36,000 + ?P]
5 die vars.; Swiatek-Breen, pp. 129–30. Forgeries exist; authentication is strongly recommended.

THE LOUISIANA PURCHASE GOLD DOLLARS

Alias: Jefferson 1903 and McKinley 1903.

Occasion: Fund-raising for the Louisiana Purchase Exposition, Forest Park, St. Louis, April 30–Dec. 1, 1904.

Designs: By Charles E. Barber. Jefferson obv. (recognizable by cravat and periwig) unintentionally resembles Napoleon; crudely copied from John Reich's Indian Peace medal (1801). McKinley obv. (recognizable by bow tie) probably added because of his assassination in office; copied from Barber's inaugural medal, ultimately from life.

Authorizing Act: June 28, 1902 (rider to an appropriations bill).

Mintage: Authorized, coined, [125,000] of each type; about 107,625 of each type melted, which probably includes assay coins.

Proofs: First 100 of each type.

Grades: Many were mishandled or used as jewelry, not spent.

First Wear Points: Cheekbones, sideburns, both types.

7424 1903 Jefferson [Net 17,275 + 100P]
Moderately dangerous forgeries exist; authentication recommended. Auction 80:1497, Proof, $7,000. Enl. photos.

7425 1903 Jefferson in original holder. [Incl. in 100P] Ex. rare.
The holder is a mounted framed affidavit certifying the within coin to be one of the first 100 struck, signed by Superintendent John H. Landis and by Chief Coiner Rhine R. Freed. All [100P] were originally so issued, but most of the coins have long since been removed from them. Ill. Swiatek-Breen, p. 119. Some holders still show tissue paper covering the coins. Cf. Dr. J. M. Henderson:108 (framed pair); 1983 ANA:4519, $11,550. Ill. reduced.

7426 1903 McKinley [Net 17,275 + 100P]
Same comment and rev. as **7424**. Enl. photo.

7427 1903 McKinley in original holder. [Incl. in 100P] Ex. rare.
Same comment as **7425**. 1983 ANA:4522, $10,450.

THE LEWIS & CLARK EXPOSITION GOLD DOLLARS

Alias: Lewis & Clark 1904, 1905.
Occasion: Fund-raising for the Exposition, Portland, Ore. June 1–Oct. 14, 1905.
Designs: By Charles E. Barber. Date side portrays Meriwether Lewis, other side Capt. William Clark. Barber copied Charles Willson Peale's portraits in Independence Hall, Philadelphia. The 1904 and 1905 differ only in date.
Authorizing Act: April 13, 1904, creating the Exposition.
Mintage: Authorized, 250,000; coined, Sept. 1904, [25,000 + 28 assay]; March and June 1905, [35,000 + 41 assay]; melted, 1904: 15,003; 1905: 25,000.
Proofs: Possibly 5–7 each known.
Grades: These did not circulate, but the general public mishandled many.
First Wear Points: Temples, hair near ear, both sides.

7428 1904 [Net 9,997 incl. ?P]
Forgeries exist; authentication recommended. Proofs: 1) Mint, SI. 2) ANS. Enl. photos.

7429 1905 [Net 10,000 incl. ?P]
Same comment.

THE PANAMA-PACIFIC INTERNATIONAL EXPOSITION HALF DOLLAR

Alias: Pan-Pac Half.
Occasion: Fund-raising for the Exposition, Feb. 20–Dec. 4, 1915, near the Marina in San Francisco, celebrating opening of the Panama Canal, Aug. 15, 1914.
Designs: By Charles E. Barber. Ms. Liberty scatters flowers from her ill-proportioned child's cornucopia; beyond, sunset over the Golden Gate. Rev., oak and olive branches (unexplained) flank an eagle imitating that on Morgan's dollars.
Authorizing Act: Jan. 16, 1915.
Mintage: Authorized, 200,000; coined, [60,000 + 30 assay]; melted, 32,866.
Proofs: 2 rumored to exist, satin finish, with S mintmark. This is aside from the gold [2], silver [6+?], and copper [4] strikings without mintmark, made in Philadelphia. One of the two gold strikings—ex Brand, B. G. Johnson, Celina, Adolph Friedman, Kosoff, Newport Balboa S&L—was 1979 ANA:1365, $27,000; the other, Farouk, Norweb.
Grades: Many sold to the general public, which mishandled them. Rarely choice; usually banged up, cleaned, or worn.
First Wear Points: Liberty's shoulder, child's shoulders and hips, eagle's breast.

7430 1915 Prototype. No mintmark. Silver. [6+P?] Ex. rare. 1979 ANA:1364, $15,000. At least one of these was purchased as a normal S-Mint coin. See Swiatek-Breen, p. 190.

7431 1915 S [all kinds, net 27,134] Normal S. First coined June 29, 1915. Enl. photos.

7432 1915 S Double S.
Price for that with 2 S's vertically overlapping. On a rarer but less spectacular var., S was first punched to r. of final position. 1984 Midwinter ANA:2111.

PANAMA-PACIFIC INTERNATIONAL EXPOSITION GOLD DOLLAR

Alias: Pan-Pac Dollar.
Occasion: As preceding.
Designs: By Charles Keck. The man wearing a cap, often mistaken for a baseball player, is meant for one of the laborers who helped build the Panama Canal. Rev., two dolphins sym-

bolize the meeting of the Atlantic and Pacific Oceans. S mintmark is below space between DO.

Authorizing Act: Jan. 16, 1915.

Mintage: Authorized, 25,000; coined, [25,000 + 34 assay] May–July 1915; melted, 10,000 after Nov. 1, 1916.

Proofs: See below for prototypes without mintmark. One brilliant proof with mintmark is reported, unverified.

Grades: These did not circulate, but the general public mishandled many.

First Wear Points: Peak of cap, heads of dolphins.

7433 1915 Prototype, no mintmark, reeded edge. [?6+P] Ex. rare.

Survivors are from a single original set showing different stages of breakage of dies; others may exist, bought as normal S-Mint coins.

7434 1915 Prototype, no mintmark, plain edge. [?2+P] Ex. rare.

Same comments.

7435 1915 S [Net 15,000] Normal S.

First coined June 29, 1915. Forgeries exist; authentication recommended. Enl. photos.

7436 1915 S Double S. Very rare.

RPM 1. S first punched below and to r. of its final position.

PAN-PACIFIC INTERNATIONAL EXPOSITION GOLD QUARTER EAGLE

Alias: Pan-Pac 2½.

Occasion: As preceding.

Designs: Obv. by Charles E. Barber, rev. by George T. Morgan. Columbia (?) rides sidesaddle and facing backward, on a hippocampus (alluding to the Canal as enabling transportation of landbased goods?); she holds a caduceus, reportedly alluding to Col. Gorgas's medical triumph over the malaria and yellowfever epidemics. Mintmark S in exergue, far r. of date. Rev. suggests a Roman legionary standard, possibly alluding to the necessity of keeping the Canal open during the war.

Authorizing Act: Jan. 16, 1915.

Mintage: Authorized, 10,000; coined, [10,000 + 17 assay]; melted, 3,251.

Proofs: One reported without S mintmark; unverified.

Grades: Rarely choice; usually rubbed or mishandled.

First Wear Points: Head, breast, knee, hippocampus's head and shoulder; eagle's neck, legs, and torch band.

7437 1915 No mintmark. Prototype. Unverified.

7438 1915 S [Net 6,749]

First coined June 29, 1915. Forgeries exist; authentication recommended. Enl. photos.

PANAMA-PACIFIC INTERNATIONAL EXPOSITION FIFTY-DOLLAR GOLD PIECES

Alias: Pan-Pac fifties, round and octagonal.

Occasion: As preceding.

Designs: Athena, in Athenian helmet, Roman date MCMXV on shield; her owl sits on branch of ponderosa (?) pine. S mintmark in field between rightmost cone and inner border. Initials RA below branch = Robert Aitken, designer. On both sides of octagonal coin, but not the round, is an extra border of dolphins, friendly companions of boats throughout the continuous water route completed by the Canal.

Authorizing Act: Jan. 16, 1915.

Mintage: Authorized, 1,500 each; coined, octagonal, [1,500 + 9 assay], round, [1,500 + 10 assay]. First piece of each type struck June 29, 1915, at a ceremony (see Swiatek-Breen, p. 206); melted, octagonal, 855, round, 1,017.

Proofs: Unknown.

Grades: Rarely choice; usually mishandled by the general public. Most often with edge dents.

First Wear Points: Cheek, hair, upper parts of helmet, wreath, owl's legs, upper parts of wings, brows, and beak.

7439 1915 S Octagonal. [Net 645]

Carter:1117, UNC., $31,900.

7440 1915 S Round. [Net 483]

Carter:1118, UNC., $38,500.

7441   1915 S Five-piece set in lined case of issue. Rare. Comprises **7431, 7435, 7438–40.** For the #1 set see Swiatek-Breen, p. 206.

7442   1915 S Five-piece set in copper frame of issue. Very rare. As preceding. Ibid., p. 203.

7443   1915 S Ten-piece set in copper frame of issue. Ex. rare. 2 each of same numbers as **7441.** Possibly 4 sets survive. Ibid., p. 205. Ill. below (reduced).

THE McKINLEY MEMORIAL GOLD DOLLARS

Alias: McKinley 1916, 1917.

Occasion: Fund-raising for construction of the McKinley Birthplace Memorial, Niles, Ohio, probably in time for the 75th anniversary of his birth.

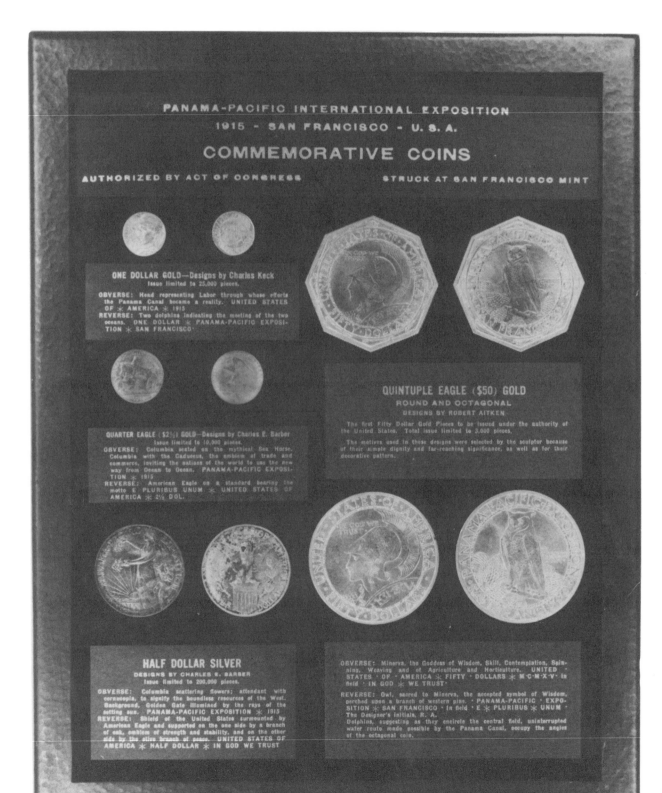

Designs: Portrait by Charles E. Barber. Morgan's rev. inaccurately depicts the Memorial.

Authorizing Act: Feb. 23, 1916.

Mintage: Authorized, 100,000 maximum; coined, Aug. and Oct. 1916, [20,000 + 26 assay], Feb. 1917, [10,000 + 14 assay]; melted, 10,023 of the 1916 issue only.

Proofs: 1916, at least 6; 1917, at least 5. See Breen {1977}, pp. 217–19, and Swiatek-Breen, p. 159.

Grades: These did not circulate; some were mishandled by the public.

First Wear Points: Temple, hair above ear, pillar above second 1 of date, base of flagpole.

7444 1916 [Net 9,977 incl. ?P]
Several die vars., date differently spaced. Often weakly struck at First Wear Points.

7445 1917 [Net 10,000 incl. ?P]
Same comments. Forgeries exist; authentication recommended. Enl. photos.

ILLINOIS CENTENNIAL HALF DOLLAR

Alias: Illinois; Lincoln.

Occasion: To help finance county celebrations statewide.

Designs: Beardless bust of Lincoln is George T. Morgan's translation of Andrew O'Conner's heroic statue, unveiled at Springfield, Aug. 1918, as part of centennial ceremonies. John R. Sinnock's eagle turns away from the rising sun, i.e., westward like the immigrants into Illinois; scroll bears state motto STATE SOVEREIGNTY NATIONAL UNION.

Authorizing Act: June 1, 1918.

Mintage: Authorized, 100,000; coined, [100,000 + 58 assay], Aug. 1918.

Proofs: At least 2 in satin finish, reportedly others in matte finish.

Grades: VF to UNC. The public mishandled many, spent many others.

First Wear Points: Hair above ear, cheekbones, brow, jaw, grass, eagle's breast.

7446 1918 [100,000]

THE MAINE CENTENNIAL HALF DOLLAR

Alias: Maine.

Occasion: To help defray cost of Maine Centennial Celebration, Portland.

Designs: State arms: moose couchant, behind him a pine tree; supporters, Agriculture with scythe, Commerce with anchor; crest, the Blazing Star with motto DIRIGO, 'I lead.' Rev., wreath of some kind of long-leaf pine; Maine = "Pine Tree State." The moose apparently alludes to the fur trade, the pine tree the lumber industry; the scythe suggests some aboveground crops (potatoes would have been harder to emblematize), the anchor Maine's fisheries and lobster trappers. Devices were apparently prescribed by the Centennial Commission, modeled by Anthony de Francisci, altered by Morgan and/or Sinnock.

Authorizing Act: May 10, 1920.

Mintage: Authorized, 100,000; coined, [50,000 + 28 assay]. They were sold through much of 1921, by the State Treasurer, long after the celebration ended.

Proofs: Matte finish; forgeries exist, authentication mandatory.

Grades: F to UNC. The public spent many, mishandled many others. Central details on moose and pine tree were flat in the original model, no better even on proofs (Swiatek-Breen, p. 150). Faces are always weak.

First Wear Points: Hands adjacent to shield; bow knot.

7447 1920 [50,000 incl. ?P]

PILGRIM TERCENTENARY HALF DOLLARS

Alias: Pilgrim 1920, 1921.

Occasion: Various local celebrations throughout New England, honoring the Pilgrim Fathers' arrivals at Provincetown and Plymouth Rock (1620); the coins presumably helped raise funds for these.

Designs: Imaginary portrait of Gov. William Bradford (1590–1675, author of *History of Plimmoth Plantations)* holding a bible. Initial D below his elbow is that of the designer, Cyrus E. Dallin. Rev. is intended for the *Mayflower* in full sail, though it has an anachronistic flying jib (from bowsprit to a stay extending from foremast).

Authorizing Act: May 12, 1920.

Mintage: Authorized, 300,000 total; coined, Oct. 1920, [200,000 + 112 assay], July 1921, [100,000]; melted, 1920, 48,000, 1921, 80,000.

Proofs: 1920, two matte, respectively ex J. R. Sinnock and Ira Reed; 1921, one seen by Wayte Raymond, reportedly matte, untraced.

Grades: F to UNC. Many spent or mishandled by the general public.

First Wear Points: Cheekbone, hair above ear, crow's nest, stern.

7448   1920 [Net 152,000 + ?P]
No obv. date, unlike next.

7449   1921 [Net 20,000 + ?P]

THE MISSOURI CENTENNIAL
HALF DOLLARS

Alias: Missouri 2★4 or Missouri 2-by-4; Missouri Plain.

Occasion: Fund-raising for the Missouri Centennial Exposition and State Fair, Sedalia, Aug. 8–20, 1921, commemorating statehood, Aug. 10, 1820.

Designs: The frontiersman was originally intended to represent Daniel Boone (1734–1820), possibly after the Albin Polasek bust of Boone in the NYU Hall of Fame. On **7450,** the 2★4 means "twenty-fourth State." On rev., a frontiersman is sending an Indian away, symbolic of the white settlers' expelling Native Americans from Missouri Territory; the 24 stars represent the Union upon admission of Missouri. Monogram RA = Robert Aitken, designer.

Authorizing Act: March 4, 1921.

Mintage: Authorized, 250,000; coined, 2★4, [5,000], plain, [45,000 + 28 assay], July 1921; melted, plain, 29,500.

Proofs: One matte proof 2★4 reported, probably for John R. Sinnock.

Grades: F to UNC. Many were mishandled or spent.

First Wear Points: Hair behind Boone's ear; frontiersman's shoulder and arm.

7450   1921 2★4. [5,000 + ?P]

7451   1921 Plain. [Net 15,400]

THE ALABAMA CENTENNIAL
HALF DOLLARS

Alias: Alabama 2x2, Alabama 2-by-2; Alabama Plain.

Occasion: Local pride of the lame-duck Alabama Centennial Commission (1919–20, for statehood, Dec. 14, 1819), under Mrs. Marie Bankhead Owen; profits were to go to unidentified "historical and monumental" projects.

Designs: BIBB = William Wyatt Bibb (1780–1820), Alabama's first governor (1816–20). KILBY = Thomas E. Kilby, state governor at time of mintage (in violation of the 1866 law forbidding portrayal of living persons on coins). The 22 stars and, on **7452,** the 2x2, refer to Alabama's status as twenty-second state; the x alludes to the red St. Andrew's cross on the state flag. The warlike eagle (no olive branch) is from the state seal, as is the motto HERE WE REST. Initials LGF = Laura Gardin Fraser, designer.

Authorizing Act: May 10, 1920.

Mintage: Authorized, 100,000 maximum; coined, 2x2, Oct. 1921, [6,000 + 6 assay], plain, Dec., [64,000 + 38 assay]; melted, plain, 5,000.

Proofs: One matte 2x2 reported, unverified, probably made for John R. Sinnock.

Grades: F to UNC. Many were spent, others mishandled.

First Wear Points: Kilby's forehead, cheek, and jaw l. of earlobe; eagle's lower neck and top of wings. Eagle's feet are usually weak; mint-state survivors show mint luster there.

7452   1921 2x2. [6,000 + ?P]

7453   1921 Plain. [59,000 + ?P]

THE GRANT MEMORIAL HALF DOLLARS

Alias: Grant Star; Grant Plain.

Occasion: Fund-raising to finance construction of memorial buildings in Georgetown and Bethel, and a 5-mile highway from New Richmond to Point Pleasant (all Ohio locales associated with Grant before the Civil War); all on behalf of the Ulysses S. Grant Centenary Memorial Commission, celebrating Grant's birthday, April 27, 1822, Point Pleasant.

Designs: Grant's bust is after a Mathew Brady photograph; rev. depicts Grant's birth house. Monogram LGF = Laura Gardin Fraser, designer. The star on **7454** has no specified meaning; possibly one of the General's uniform stars?

Authorizing Act: Feb. 2, 1922.

Mintage: Authorized, 250,000 maximum; coined, with star, [5,000 + 6 assay], plain, [95,000 + 55 assay], March 1922; melted, 750 with star, 27,650 plain.

Proofs: With star, at least four matte or sandblast (surface differs from earlier examples of both), one from the J. R. Sinnock estate. Without star, four matte or sandblast proofs reported, unverified.

Grades: The general public spent many and mishandled others.

First Wear Points: Cheekbone, leaves below U. Flatness on hair above ear is usual; true UNCs. should show mint luster in the area.

7454   1922 With star. [Net 4,250 + ?P]

Lower l. point of incuse star thin and narrow, lower r. point wide and rounded, odd internal detail. Almost always with clash marks between chin and G, and in field just r. of tie. Forgeries exist, including many fabricated by punching a star into genuine Grant Plain coins: See details in Swiatek-Breen, pp. 89–93. Authentication recommended.

7455   1922 Plain. [Net 67,350]

THE GRANT MEMORIAL GOLD DOLLARS

Alias: Grant Star Dollar; Grant Plain Dollar.
Occasion, Design, Authorizing Act: As preceding.
Mintage: Authorized, 10,000 maximum; coined, each type, [5,000 + 8 assay], March 1922.
Proofs: Rumored to exist with star, unverified.
Grades: Generally UNC., occasionally mishandled.
First Wear Points: As preceding.

7456   1922 With star. [5,000]

7457   1922 Plain. [5,000]
Cast forgeries exist; ill. Swiatek-Breen, p. 92.

THE MONROE DOCTRINE CENTENNIAL HALF DOLLAR

Alias: Monroe.
Occasion: Publicity for the American Historical Revue and Motion Picture Historical Exposition, Los Angeles, June 1923, sponsored by the motion picture industry.
Designs: Personified continents (a motif derived from Ralph Beck's 1901 Pan-American Exposition seal); ocean currents, probably representing unending flow of imports and exports. Monogram CB = Chester Beach, designer. MONROE = James Monroe; ADAMS = John Quincy Adams, author of the "Monroe Doctrine" proclamation included in Monroe's presidential message, Dec. 2, 1823. (See introductory text, Chap. 43.) Below date, S = San Francisco mintmark.
Authorizing Act: Jan. 24, 1923.
Mintage: Authorized, 500,000; coined, [274,000 + 77 assay].
Proofs: Two reported, unverified, supposedly matte; one probably for John R. Sinnock.
Grades: Mostly VG to EF. Probably over 90% were spent by local banks, or by inheritors during the 1929–37 Depression. Always weak; most "UNCs." have been cleaned or qualify only as "sliders."
First Wear Points: Adams's cheekbone, Ms. North America below CT.

7458   1923 S [274,000]

THE HUGUENOT-WALLOON
TERCENTENARY HALF DOLLAR

Alias: Huguenot.

Occasion: The Huguenot-Walloon New Netherland Commission (Rev. John Baer Stoudt, chairman) promoted this as an undercover fund-raiser for the Federal Council of Churches of Christ in America, blatantly violating the First Amendment principle of separation of church and state. Stoudt (artist and coin collector) devised the concept. Allegedly, the events commemorated are the arrival of 110 Lowlands Huguenots (Calvinists) aboard the *Nieuw Nederlandt* on the Hudson River in upstate New York, and other Dutch Calvinist settlements in New York and New Jersey, 1621–24. Swiatek-Breen, pp. 105–6.

Designs: By Rev. John Baer Stoudt. COLIGNY = Admiral Gaspard de Coligny (1519–72), killed during the St. Bartholomew's Day Massacre; WILLIAM THE SILENT = Willem I (1533–84), prince of Orange, assassinated by pro-Spanish extremists in The Netherlands. Neither man was relevant to the coin's alleged occasion; both were dubiously venerated as Protestant martyrs. The ship is Stoudt's equally fanciful rendition of the *Nieuw Nederlandt.* NEW NETHERLAND = the Dutch settlements. M on Coligny's shoulder = Mint Engraver George T. Morgan, who fumblingly made the models with help from James Earle Fraser.

Authorizing Act: Feb. 26, 1923.

Mintage: Authorized, 300,000; coined, [142,000 + 80 assay], Feb. and April 1924. Of these, 87,000 were sold to the public under pressure from the Federal Council of Churches of Christ in America; the other 55,000 were spent.

Proofs: One matte proof reported, probably for John R. Sinnock; untraced.

Grades: VF to UNC. The general public mishandled many even aside from those they spent.

First Wear Points: Coligny's cheekbone, center of stern, lower mainsail.

7459   1924 [142,000]

THE STONE MOUNTAIN HALF DOLLAR

Alias: Stone Mountain.

Occasion: Celebrating commencement June 18, 1923, of heroic carving of Confederate leaders and soldiers on Stone Mountain, Ga. (completed 1970); and in memory of Warren G. Harding (mainly why the authorizing act passed).

Designs: The equestrian figures resembling Marx and Freud respectively represent "Stonewall" Jackson and Robert E. Lee (in hat); these are part of an enormous procession carved into the mountain by Gutzon Borglum (who sculpted Mount Rushmore). Borglum's initials GB are near horse's tail. The 35 stars = Union and Confederate states together as of 1865. Rev. inscription originally also mentioned Harding, but because Pres. Coolidge objected, the coins omitted Harding's name.

Authorizing Act: March 17, 1924. See Swiatek-Breen, pp. 227–28,

Mintage: Authorized, 5,000,000; coined, [2,310,000 + 4,709 assay], Jan. 21–March 1925; melted, 1,000,000.

Proofs: One matte proof reported, probably for John R. Sinnock; untraced.

Grades: Probably more than half were spent, especially among those bought for promotional purposes by the B&O Railroad, the Coca-Cola Bottling Co. in Atlanta, the Southern Fireman's Fund Insurance Co., and numerous southern banks. Survivors come F to UNC. Part of Harvey Hill's publicity projects for these coins included having some counterstamped to produce "unique" items for auction, some on behalf of statewide "Great Harvest Campaign" promotions, others on behalf of the United Daughters of the Confederacy. Counterstamped pieces could be faked; acceptable proof of genuine counterstamps is either documentation or proven punch linkage to documented specimens: Swiatek-Breen, pp. 228–30. Counterstamps generally include a state abbreviation and a number.

First Wear Points: Lee's elbow, eagle's breast.

7460   1925 [Net 1,310,000] Normal.

7461   1925 Doubled obv. die. Very rare.
Doubling plainest at date.

THE LEXINGTON-CONCORD
SESQUICENTENNIAL HALF DOLLAR

Alias: Lexington; Minute Man.

Occasion: Memorializing the two battles which began the Revolutionary War, April 19, 1775; publicity and fund-raising for two local celebrations.

Designs: The Minute Man, awaiting the Call to Arms sounded by the bells in the Old Belfry at Lexington, is a close copy of Daniel Chester French's *Grand Concord Man* statue (erected April 1875). PATRIOT refers partly to the statue, partly to the celebration (April 19 is Patriot Day, a Massachusetts holiday). Chester Beach, designer, used drawings by the

Concord artist Philip Holden for layout, and a photograph of the Old Belfry.

Authorizing Act: Jan. 14, 1925.

Mintage: Authorized, 300,000 maximum; coined, [162,000 + 99 assay]; melted, 86.

Proofs: One matte proof reported, from the John R. Sinnock estate; as yet unavailable for examination.

Grades: VF to UNC. The public mishandled many.

First Wear Points: Thighs and top edge of belfry. Even mint-state coins are sometimes weak on these points and on hat, chin, and musket; check for presence of mint luster.

7462   1925 [161,914 + ?P]

THE FORT VANCOUVER CENTENNIAL HALF DOLLAR

Alias: Vancouver.

Occasion: Fund-raising for local celebration on behalf of Fort Vancouver (Washington) Centennial Corporation, Aug. 17–24, 1925.

Designs: Bust of Dr. John McLoughlin (1784–1857), builder of Fort Vancouver and Oregon City, and Hudson's Bay Company chief administrator in Oregon Territory. A frontiersman defends stockaded settlement; Mount Hood and the Columbia River are in background. LGF = Laura Gardin Fraser, designer, after sketches by John T. Urquhart and models by Sydney Bell. McClure {1984}.

Authorizing Act: Feb. 24, 1925.

Mintage: Authorized, 300,000 maximum; coined, [50,000 + 28 assay], Aug. 1, 1925, San Francisco Mint (S mintmark omitted); melted, 35,034.

Proofs: One matte proof seen, two others reported. Forgeries have been made by sandblasting or pickling ordinary business strikes; authentication is recommended.

Grades: VF to UNC. Several hundred were gilt; many others spent, kept as pocket pieces, or mishandled.

First Wear Points: Cheekbone and nearby hair above ear; up-raised knee.

7463   1925 [S] [Net 14,966]
Q. David Bowers dispersed a hoard of over 300 UNCs., found in 1982. Counterfeits (some prooflike) often have depressed area within D(OLLAR); authentication recommended.

THE CALIFORNIA DIAMOND JUBILEE HALF DOLLAR

Alias: California. (Mint's original title: "Jubilee Souvenir Half Dollar.")

Occasion: Fund-raising for local celebrations in San Francisco and Los Angeles, Sept. 1925, honoring 75th anniversary of statehood (Sept. 9, 1850, part of Compromise of 1850); sponsored by San Francisco Citizens' Committee, Angelo J. Rossi, chairman.

Designs: By Jo Mora. A gold miner inspects gravel from a stream for gold flakes or nuggets—the ancient technique used by the "Forty-Niners." The grizzly bear alludes to the California Republic's bear flag under Gen. John C. Frémont, 1846–50. S mintmark below D(OLLAR).

Authorizing Act: Feb. 16, 1925.

Mintage: Authorized, 300,000 maximum; coined, Aug. 1–26, [150,000 + 20 assay]; melted, 63,606.

Proofs: Satin-finish proofs with S reported, unverified.

Grades: VF to UNC. The general public mishandled many, spent others.

First Wear Points: Sleeve folds; bear's shoulder.

7464   1925 Prototype. No mintmark. Proof only. [?P] Ex. rare.
1) Ex J. R. Sinnock estate, matte proof.
7465   1925 S [Net 86,394]

THE SESQUICENTENNIAL OF AMERICAN INDEPENDENCE HALF DOLLAR

Alias: Sesqui Half.

Occasion: Souvenirs at Sesquicentennial Exposition, Philadelphia, June 1–Nov. 30, 1926, on behalf of National Sesquicentennial Commission, created by Congress.

Designs: Busts of Pres. Washington and Pres. Calvin Coolidge, the latter portrayal violating the 1866 Act of Congress forbidding depiction of living persons on coins; the Liberty Bell. JRS = John R. Sinnock, Mint Engraver, who copied designs by John Frederick Lewis. Taxay {1967}, p. 115; Swiatek-Breen {1981}, p. 222. The low relief doubtless pleased Mint people but nobody else.

Authorizing Act: March 3, 1925.

Mintage: Authorized, 1,000,000 maximum; coined, [1,000,000 + 528 assay]; melted, 859,408.

Proofs: Matte finish; more detail than normal on hair, elmwood yoke, and bell. These could readily be forged by pickling or sandblasting business strikes; authentication recommended.

Grades: VF to UNC. The public mishandled many and spent many others.

First Wear Points: Washington's cheekbone; lower part of bell. Always weak; look for mint luster on the weak areas.

7466 1926 [Net 140,592 + ?P]
Proofs: 1) Farouk, Hydeman, Cox:2124. 2) Ex J. R. Sinnock estate. 3), 4) Reported.

THE SESQUICENTENNIAL
GOLD QUARTER EAGLE

Alias: Sesqui 2½.

Occasion: As preceding.

Designs: Ms. Liberty (with cap) holds Declaration of Independence; sun behind Independence Hall, Philadelphia. JRS = John R. Sinnock, Mint Engraver, designer.

Authorizing Act: As preceding.

Mintage: Authorized, 200,000 maximum; coined, May–June, [200,000 + 226 assay]; melted, 154,207.

Proofs: Matte finish, with more detail sharpness than normal. Readily simulated by pickling or sandblasting business strikes. Authentication recommended.

Grades: VF to UNC. The general public spent or mishandled many.

First Wear Points: Bottom of scroll, central tower above roof.

7467 1926 [Net 45,793 + ?P]
Forgeries exist; authentication recommended. Proofs: 1) Ira S. Reed, David M. Bullowa, Swiatek. 2) J. R. Sinnock estate, pvt. coll. Others reported.

THE OREGON TRAIL MEMORIAL
HALF DOLLARS

Alias: Oregon (+ date).

Occasion: Fund-raising for the Oregon Trail Memorial Association, Inc. (of New York), erecting monuments at various important points along the Trail. Date 1926 was 75th anniversary of Ezra Meeker's (1830–1928) explorations.

Designs: The Indian, without peace pipe, warns, "So far and no farther!" Behind him, a line of Conestoga covered wagons heads west along the Trail on a U.S. map. D or S (for Denver or San Francisco) mintmark r. of HALF. By Laura Gardin Fraser. Rev., Conestoga covered wagon takes a pioneer family westward. By James Earle Fraser. Mint reports call the wagon side the obv. Fuljenz [1986].

Authorizing Act: May 17, 1926; repealed by Act of Aug. 5, 1939. See introductory text and Swiatek-Breen, pp. 181–83.

Mintage: Authorized, 6 million maximum; coined, total, [264,245 + 174 assay]; melted (aside from assay coins), 61,317: 75 of 1926, 17,000 of 1926 S, 44,000 of 1928, 242 of 1933 D. Net mintage figures below exclude these.

Proofs: Matte finish, 1926 only.

Grades: Some of the 1926 and 1926 S coins were spent or mishandled by the general public. Later dates did not circulate, mostly going to speculators, normally UNC. in three-piece sets, sometimes with bag marks.

First Wear Points: Indian's hand holding bow; hip of ox; top rear of wagon. On 1926 Philadelphia, hand holding bow normally will not show thumb or index finger; other issues generally will.

7468 1926 [Net 47,925 + ?P]
"Ezra Meeker Issue." Struck Sept. 1926. Ill. of **7470.** Proofs: 1) J. R. Sinnock, Bebee, Swiatek. 2) Pvt. coll. For the names given this and later Oregons, see Swiatek-Breen.

7469 1926 S [Net 83,000]
Struck Oct.–Nov. 1926. Issued at $1 each. Gems are plentiful.

7470 1928 [Net 6,000]
"Jedediah Smith Issue." Released July 1933 at $2, mostly to speculators. Ill. at **7468.**

7471 1933 D [Net 4,998]
"Century of Progress Issue."

7472 1934 D [7,000]
"Fort Hall, Fort Laramie, and Jason Lee Issue." Usually well struck.

7473 1936 [10,000]
Marketed by American Pioneer Trails Association as late as 1943, and by the Oregon Trail Memorial Association through 1945. Swiatek-Breen, pp. 183–87.

7474 1936 S [5,000]
"Whitman Mission Coins" or "Marcus Whitman Issue." Speculators got most.

7475 1937 D [12,000]
Same comment as to **7473.**

7476 1938 [6,000]
Mostly marketed in 3-piece sets, **7476–78,** at $6.25/set.

7477 1938 S [6,000]
Same comment.

7478 1938 D [6,000]
Same comment.

7479 1939 [3,000]
Marketed in 3-piece sets, **7479–81,** at $7.50/set; protests followed.

7480 1939 S [3,000]
Same comment.

7481 1939 D [3,000]
Same comment.

THE VERMONT SESQUICENTENNIAL HALF DOLLAR

Alias: Vermont.

Occasion: Fund-raising for the Vermont Historical Trust to aid the Bennington Museum (and other local museums and historical societies) and to celebrate the sesquicentennial of the Battle of Bennington (Aug. 16, 1777). Distributor was the Bennington Battle Monument and Historical Association, John Spargo, president.

Designs: Idealized portrait of Ira Allen, co-founder of the Green Mountain Boys, founder of the Univ. of Vermont, leader of the 1775–77 Provincial Conventions resulting in Vermont's becoming an independent republic, 1778–91. Rev. was originally to show the Battle Monument, then Fay's "Catamount" Tavern (where much Revolutionary planning took place); but the federal Fine Arts Commission insisted on replacing this with what was supposed to be a Vermont catamount *(Felis lynx canadensis* = the short-tailed Canada lynx); the coin shows a generic wildcat of unidentifiable species. CK = Charles Keck, designer.

Authorizing Act: Feb. 24, 1925.

Mintage: Authorized, 40,000 maximum; coined, Jan.–Feb. 1927, [40,000 + 34 assay]; melted, 11,892.

Proofs: One matte proof reported, from John R. Sinnock estate.

Grades: VF to UNC. The public mishandled many and spent others.

First Wear Points: Hair at and above ear and temple; wildcat's upper shoulder. Many are weakly struck in these areas and cheek; look for mint luster on weak areas.

7482   1927 [Net 28,108 + ?P]

THE HAWAIIAN SESQUICENTENNIAL HALF DOLLAR

Alias: Hawaii; Capt. Cook.

Occasion: Fund-raising by the Capt. Cook Sesquicentennial Commission, to establish the Capt. Cook Memorial Collection (now at the Bernice Pauahi Bishop Museum, Honolulu), in conjunction with local celebrations throughout the Islands.

Designs: Bust of Capt. James Cook, discoverer of the Islands, Jan. 18, 1778. After CAPT. is a compass. Eight triangles in lower field represent the 8 largest islands. CB = Chester Beach, engraver. Landscape represents part of Waikiki Beach at Mamala Bay, Diamond Head beyond. Native warrior chief extends hand in welcome. Original designs by Juliette Mae Frazer of Honolulu, partly after sketches by Bruce Cartwright, Jr., of the Commission. Commander Victor Stewart Kaleoaloha Houston (Territorial Delegate to Congress) demanded and got dozens of niggling changes; Taxay {1967}, pp. 127–31. The

Cook portrait is after a Josiah Wedgwood cameo, allegedly in turn from a painting by Dance in the gallery of Greenwich Hospital, London; the warrior design is influenced by the statue of King Kamehameha I near the Royal Palace in Honolulu.

Authorizing Act: March 7, 1928.

Mintage: Authorized, 10,000; coined, [10,000 + 8 assay], June 1928.

Proofs: See Swiatek-Breen, p. 97, for list of recipients of the [50] sandblast proofs; nine are in museums, at least 12 others traced are in private hands. Forgeries exist; authentication urgently recommended.

Grades: These did not circulate, but the public mishandled many.

First Wear Points: Cheek, roll of hair above ear, hair above temple, shoulder above truncation; warrior's fingers and knees.

7483   1928 [9,950 + 50P]

Above figure includes 200 withheld for presentation; 4,975 offered in the Islands, and 4,975 on the mainland. Proofs: Pres. Coolidge, Auction 79:673, $11,000; Bauer, H. Krause, McAfee, 1979 ANA:1378, $12,500.

THE MARYLAND TERCENTENARY HALF DOLLAR

Alias: Maryland.

Occasion: Fund-raising for celebrations sponsored by the Maryland Tercentenary Commission, honoring anniversary of arrival of colonists aboard the ships *Ark* and *Dove,* 1634, at St. Mary's, the first group of settlers in what had become Lord Baltimore's land grant.

Designs: Bust of Cecil Calvert, second Lord Baltimore (1609–75): See Chap. 1, Sect. iii, introductory text. His coat of arms (quartered with Lady Baltimore's) are crested and mantled, with supporters Labor (with spade) and Fisheries (with fish). HS = Hans Schuler, designer. Motto (seldom legible) is the sexist one of the State of Maryland: FATTI MASCHII PAROLE FEMINE, 'Deeds [are] manly, words womanly.' Portrait is after Gerard Soes's inaccurate likeness (Baltimore's coins would have been a better source), with a Puritan collar which Baltimore would never have worn.

Authorizing Act: May 9, 1934.

Mintage: Authorized, 25,000; coined, [25,000 + 15 assay], July 1934.

Proofs: Three matte proofs seen, others reported. Forgeries are easily made by sandblasting or pickling business strikes; authentication is essential.

Grades: EF to UNC. The public mishandled many, circulated fewer.

First Wear Points: Calvert's nose; top coronet (with flags) and adjacent mantling. Even gem mint-state survivors are often weak at cheekbone and eyebrows; see ill. in Swiatek-Breen, p. 154.

7484   1934 [25,000 + ?P]

7489   1935 Small 1934. [Net 10,000]
The small 1934 above PIONEER persists through 1938 from all mints. Struck Oct. 1935. Ill. of **7495.**

THE DANIEL BOONE BICENTENNIAL HALF DOLLARS

Alias: Boone.

Occasion: Fund-raising to finance restoration of four historic sites, in celebration of the 200th birthday of Chief Big Turtle, né Daniel Boone (1734–1820). Sponsored by the Daniel Boone Bicentennial Commission, Lexington, Ky., C. Frank Dunn, chairman.

Designs: Fictitious portrait of Boone, based on frontispiece in Collins's *History of Kentucky* (1847, 1878 eds.). On rev., Boone is in a historically impossible palaver with the Shawnee Chief Black Fish, allegedly discussing the treaty which was to end the nine-day siege of Fort Boonesboro, in Transylvania (!), part of what is now Kentucky. Mintmark D or S (if any) will be behind Black Fish's heel. Devices specified by the Commission to Augustus Lukeman, designer.

Authorizing Acts: May 26, 1934; 1935–38 with small 1934 above PIONEER YEAR, Act of Aug. 26, 1935. Both abolished by Act of Aug. 5, 1939.

Mintage: Authorized, 600,000; coined, total, [108,000 + 103 assay]; melted, 1937–38, aside from assay coins, 21,400; these are deducted for net mintages below.

Proofs: Controversial; see Swiatek-Breen, p. 31.

Grades: The public mishandled the Philadelphia issues 1934–37; scarcer branch mints normally come choice.

First Wear Points: Hair behind Boone's ear; rev., Black Fish's shoulder.

7485   1934 [Net 10,000]
Struck Oct. 1934; sold for $1.10 each. Ill. of **7486.**

7486   1935 Plain. [Net 10,000]
Ill. at **7485.** Struck March 1935, sold at same price.
7487   1935 S Plain. [Net 5,000]
Struck May 1935; originally sold for $1.60 each.
7488   1935 D Plain. [Net 5,000]
Same comment.

7490   1935 S Small 1934. [Net 2,000]
Struck Nov. 1935; sold with next at $3.70/pair, mostly to speculators, who called these the "Rare Boones" and kited prices, beginning the controversy which led to abolition of commemorative coinage.
7491   1935 D Small 1934. [Net 2,000]
See preceding.
7492   1936 [Net 12,000]
Originally sold for $1.10 each.
7493   1936 S [Net 5,000]
Originally sold for $1.60 each.
7494   1936 D [Net 5,000]
Same comment.
7495   1937 [Net 9,800]
Originally sold at $1.60; after May 1937, available only in a pair with **7497,** at $7.25. Ill. at **7489.**
7496   1937 S [Net 2,500]
Originally sold at $5.15; a few weeks later, only available in 3-piece sets with **7495** and **7497** at $12.40. Rarely with brilliant prooflike obv.
7497   1937 D [Net 2,500]
Originally sold only with **7495** at $7.25 per pair; later in sets as preceding. The Commission falsely announced that this would end the Boone Issue: Swiatek-Breen, p. 30.
7498   1938 [Net 2,100]
Only sold in 3-piece sets (**7498–7500**) at $6.50. Speculators got most.
7499   1938 S [Net 2,100]
Same comment.
7500   1938 D [Net 2,100]
Same comment.

THE TEXAS CENTENNIAL HALF DOLLARS

Alias: Texas.

Occasion: Preliminary fund-raising for the Texas Centennial Exposition, Dallas, 1936, sponsored by the American Legion Texas Centennial Committee.

Designs: Eagle superimposed on star, for Texas as Lone Star State; meaning of oversize oak branch unknown. The six stars flanking HALF DOLLAR probably allude to the six flags on rev. Winged Victory holds in her dexter hand an olive branch for peace (?) while her sinister hand rests on a miniature replica of the Alamo (the historic burnt-out church in Alamo Plaza, San Antonio), where Gen. Santa Ana besieged 187 revolutionaries including Jim Bowie and Davy Crockett, Feb. 24–March 6, 1836. Above her wings are the six flags which have flown over Texas (Spain, France, Mexico, the Republic, the USA, and the Confederacy); at sides, two medallions representing Gen. Sam Houston (at observer's left) and Stephen F. Austin; below the Alamo, centennial dates; below her l. knee, above T(HE), may occur mintmark D or S for Denver or San Francisco. At r. of the Alamo, PC = Pompeo Coppini, designer.

Authorizing Act: June 15, 1933; repealed by Act of Aug. 5, 1939.

Mintage: Authorized, 1,500,000 maximum; coined, total, [304,000 + 193 assay]; melted, aside from assay coins, 154,522; these figures deducted for net mintages below. Meltages were to induce the Mint to make later dates, mostly going to speculators.

Proofs: Unverified to exist.

Grades: VF to UNC. The public spent many of 1934, mishandled many of this and later dates. Over 60% of all dates, even gem UNCS., come weak in centers, notably on Ms. Victory's breasts (unequally flat), branch hand, and drapery below it: See ill. in Swiatek-Breen, p. 236.

First Wear Points: Eagle's upper leg and upper breast; Ms. Victory's brow and knee.

7501 1934 [Net 61,350]
Coined Oct.–Nov. 1934. Originally sold at $1 each. Ill. of **7504.**

7502 1935 [Net 9,988]
Coined Nov. Originally sold at $1.50, like **7503–4.**
7503 1935 S [Net 10,000]
7504 1935 D [Net 10,000]
Rarely prooflike, from brilliantly polished dies; ill. at **7501.**
7505 1936 [Net 8,903]
Issued in 3-piece sets, **7505–7,** at $4.50 per set.
7506 1936 S [Net 9,057]
7507 1936 D [Net 9,032]
7508 1937 [Net 6,566]
Issued in 3-piece sets, **7508–10,** at $4.50 per set.
7509 1937 S [Net 6,630]
Same comment.
7510 1937 D [Net 6,599]
Same comment.
7511 1938 [Net 3,775]
Issued in 3-piece sets, **7511–13,** at $6 per set.
7512 1938 S [Net 3,808]
Same comment.
7513 1938 D [Net 3,770]
Same comment.

THE CONNECTICUT TERCENTENARY HALF DOLLAR

Alias: Connecticut; Charter Oak.

Occasion: To aid in financing statewide celebrations, 1935, sponsored by the Connecticut Tercentenary Commission, Samuel Fisher, chairman.

Designs: The Charter Oak (felled at age 1,000 by lightning, Aug. 21, 1856), with the cavity in trunk in which Joseph Wadsworth hid the royal charter when Sir Edmund Andros came to seize it, Oct. 31, 1687; symbol of Connecticut's colonial independence. By Henry Kreis, obv. vaguely after one of C. D. W.

Brownell's four paintings of the Charter Oak (1855–56) in the Connecticut Historical Society. Date 1635 is of beginning of first formally organized central government under John Winthrop. Mint reports call the eagle side the obv. Fuljenz [1986].

Authorizing Act: June 21, 1934.

Mintage: Authorized, 25,000; coined, April–May 1935, [25,000 + 18 assay].

Proofs: Possibly five or six matte proofs reported; see ill. in Swiatek-Breen, p. 76. Forgeries can be easily made; authentication urgently recommended.

Grades: EF to UNC. The general public spent few but mishandled many.

First Wear Points: Base of tree, upper part of wing. Even choice UNCs. often come weak on upper wing, legs, and claw pads; look for mint luster on weak areas.

7514 1935 [25,000 + ?P]

THE CITY OF HUDSON, N.Y., SESQUICENTENNIAL HALF DOLLAR

Alias: Hudson.

Occasion: Local celebration, sponsored by Hudson Sesquicentennial Committee.

Designs: Henry Hudson's ship *Half Moon* at full sail; crescent moon for ship's name; CB = Chester Beach, designer. Rev., city seal (ca. 1785), showing King Neptune riding backward on spouting whale, triton behind. City motto ET DECUS ET PRETIUM RECTI, 'Both an ornament and a reward of the righteous man.' Date 1785 is for incorporation of Hudson, originally Claverack Landing.

Authorizing Act: May 2, 1935.

Mintage: Authorized, 10,000; coined, [10,000 + 8 assay].

Proofs: Matte finish, two reported; authentication mandatory.

Grades: Not circulated, but the general public mishandled many.

First Wear Points: Central obv.; city motto. Even gem UNCs. are often weak on hull, central sails, Neptune's face, leg, motto.

7515 1935 [10,000 + ?P]
Coined and delivered June 28, sold out at $1 each by July 2. Extensively hoarded. Forgeries exist; authentication recommended.

THE CALIFORNIA-PACIFIC INTERNATIONAL EXPOSITION HALF DOLLAR

Alias: San Diego.

Occasion: Souvenir sales at San Diego World's Fair, Balboa Park, 1935–36.

Designs: Adaptation of state seal: Minerva with spear and shield (surrogate for the aegis) on which is the head of the Gorgon Medusa, with miners' slogan EUREKA (pronounced Hew-RAY-ka), 'I found it!' Cornucopia alludes to the state's natural resources; grizzly bear is the state animal; behind all, square-rigged schooner, miner, and mountains. RA = Robert Aitken, designer. Rev., Chapel of St. Francis (with dome) and California Tower, at Balboa Park, within tressure. Mintmark S (1935) or (1936) below T(RUST).

Authorizing Acts: May 3, 1935; Recoinage Act, May 6, 1936, specifying that the unsold 1935 coins were to be melted and recoined into a new var. dated 1936.

Mintage: Authorized, 250,000 maximum; coined, 1935, [250,000 + 132 assay]; melted, recoined, 1936, [180,000 + 92 assay]; remelted, 150,000.

Proofs: Two "matte" proofs reported, one seen by Wayte Raymond, the other ex John R. Sinnock estate; the only one examined is satin finish and far sharper than business strikes. Authentication is essential.

Grades: These did not circulate, but the general public mishandled some.

First Wear Points: Knees and upper r. part of California Tower. Even gem UNCs. of 1936 D are uniformly weak on tower (much more than 1935 S); look for mint luster on weak areas.

7516   1935 S [Net 70,000 + ?P]

Originally sold at $1 each; many UNCs. are from a hoard of 31,050 dispersed in 1966. Usually, S is blurry. Proofs: 1) Brian Hendelson, "Charmont":931, $1,600. Satin finish.

7517   1936 D [Net 30,000]

Originally sold at $1.50; Exposition Treasurer Emil Klicka withheld many and raised the price to $3 in 1937. Almost never shows detail in upper r. part of California Tower.

THE OLD SPANISH TRAIL HALF DOLLAR

Alias: Spanish Trail.

Occasion: Fund-raising for El Paso Museum at quatrocentennial celebrations, El Paso, Tex., L. W. Hoffecker, chairman, later ANA President.

Designs: Cow's head is a punning device for Alvar Núñez Cabeza de Vaca, explorer, treasurer of Panfilo de Narváez's expedition (1527–42), author of *Los Naufragios,* 'The Shipwrecked Men,' 1542, grisly chronicle of catastrophe and heroism. Yucca tree in bloom, probably for design purposes and because it is common to the area; stylized map attempting to represent the overland part of Núñez's westbound expedition,

from San Agustín (St. Augustine, Fla.) to what is now El Paso; the actual terminus is unknown and may have been as far west as California. LWH = L. W. Hoffecker, designer; models by Edmund J. Senn, local sculptor.

Authorizing Act: June 5, 1935.

Mintage: Authorized, 10,000; coined, [10,000 + 8 assay], Sept. 1935.

Proofs: Matte finish, one seen by Wayte Raymond, the other from J. R. Sinnock estate. Authentication mandatory.

Grades: EF to UNC. The general public spent few but mishandled many.

First Wear Points: Top of cow's head, central part of yucca, upper rev. inscription.

7518   1935 [10,000 + ?P]

Offered at $2 each, sold out immediately. Forgeries exist; authentication recommended.

THE ARKANSAS CENTENNIAL HALF DOLLARS

Alias: Arkansas.

Occasion: Local statewide centennial celebrations, the most important one in Little Rock; date 1836 alludes to Arkansas's admission to the Union (June 15), though 1936 is likely to have been taken locally as meaning also the 75th anniversary of Arkansas's joining the Confederacy.

Designs: Female head in Phrygian cap presumably means Ms. Liberty; her garland might ambiguously represent any of the state's produce. The male head is intended for a Quapaw Indian chief. Diamond-shaped emblem alludes to the diamond mine in Pike County; its 13 stars mean not the 13 original colonies but the upper half of the 25-star array in the state flag (Arkansas was the twenty-fifth state admitted), and covertly also the 13 seceding states. Within the diamond, three small stars represent the three flags (Spain, France, and USA) which had flown over Arkansaw Territory; the large one above represents the state's participation in the Confederacy: "The South Will Rise Again." Behind the eagle and diamond, the rising sun was locally taken to mean the Rising South. Its seven longest rays (above the diamond) would then stand for the seven original seceding states (South Carolina, Mississippi, Florida, Alabama, Georgia, Louisiana, and Texas) while the six shorter ones flanking the eagle mean the six which joined the CSA later (Virginia, Arkansas, North Carolina, Tennessee, Missouri, and Kentucky). Mintmark D or S r. of sun. Designs by Edward Everett Burr; models by Emily Bates, both local talent. (Burr spelled out most of the complicated symbolism in correspondence with H. P. Caemmerer, of the federal Commission of Fine Arts. Taxay {1967}, p. 146; Swiatek-Breen, pp. 13–14.) Date below HALF DOLLAR is that of issue of the individual coins.

Authorizing Act: May 14, 1934; abolished Aug. 5, 1939.

Mintage: Authorized, 500,000; coined, total, [95,300 + 101 assay]; melted, 9,600; these figures deducted for net mintage figures below.

Proofs: One dated 1935, matte, reported to Wayte Raymond before 1950, untraced.

Grades: Many of 1935, fewer of 1936, went to the general public and were mishandled; later dates mostly UNC.

First Wear Points: Cheek; headband behind eye; eagle's head and top of dexter wing. Often weakly struck in centers; look for mint luster on weak areas.

7519 1935 [Net 13,000]
The [10,000] of May cannot be told from the [3,000] of Oct. Both sold at $1 each; entire later batch promoted by B. Max Mehl, who doubled the price after Jan. 1, 1936. Ill. of **7527**.

7520 1935 S [Net 5,500]
Coined Nov., all sold to B. Max Mehl, who raised price to $2.75 after Jan. 1, 1936, selling many in pairs (**7520–21**) at $5.

7521 1935 D [Net 5,500]
Same comment as to **7520**.

7522 1936 [Net 9,650]
At first sold for $1.50, later that year in sets (**7522–24**) at $6.75; most went to dealers outside Arkansas. Locals called these sets "Orphan Issue."

7523 1936 S [Net 9,650]
Same comment.

7524 1936 D [Net 9,650]
Same comment.

7525 1937 [Net 5,500]
Stack's (highest bidder for the retail concession) marketed this in cased sets (**7525–27**) at $8.75.

7526 1937 S [Net 5,500]
Same comment.

7527 1937 D [Net 5,500]
Same comment. Ill. at **7519**.

7528 1938 [Net 3,150]
Stack's marketed this in cased sets (**7528–30**) at $8.75.

7529 1938 S [Net 3,150]
Same comment.

7530 1938 D [Net 3,150]
Same comment.

7531 1939 [Net 2,100]
Stack's marketed this in sets (**7531–33**) at $10. Speculators got most. Collectors, dealers, and locals protested the Arkansas Commission's marketing tactics; Congress passed the Act of Aug. 5, 1939 revoking all previous authority to make commemoratives.

7532 1939 S [Net 2,100]
Same comment.

7533 1939 [Net 2,100]
Same comment.

THE FOUNDING OF PROVIDENCE, R.I., TERCENTENARY HALF DOLLARS

Alias: Rhode Island.

Occasion: Statewide celebrations, the biggest in Providence, of the 300th anniversary of Roger Williams's landing and agreement to purchase land from local Indians, June 24, 1636; coordinated by the Rhode Island and Providence Plantations Tercentenary Committee, Judge Letts, chairman.

Designs: Obv. remotely adapted from Providence city arms: a Narragansett Indian welcomes Roger Williams, who stands (bible in hand) in canoe with musket. Behind the Indian is a stylized corn plant; below latter may occur D or S mintmark. Mingling sun's rays with LIBERTY symbolized religious freedom, a major theme of the coin and celebrations. Rev. loosely copies state arms except that the state motto IN TE DOMINE SPERAMUS, 'In Thee, O Lord, We Hope,' is replaced by HOPE. Designs and models by John Howard Benson and A. Graham Carey, of the Rhode Island School of Design.

Authorizing Act: May 2, 1935.

Mintage: Authorized, 50,000; coined, total, [50,000 + 34 assay].

Proofs: Unconfirmed.

Grades: Some Philadelphia coins went to the general public and were mishandled.

First Wear Points: Indian's r. shoulder; center of anchor.

7534 1936 [Net 20,000]
Coined Jan.; all sold March 5, 1936 and between 9 A.M. and 3 P.M., many by mail order through Horace M. Grant of Grant's Hobby Shop, approx. 5,000 as singles, rest in sets with **7535–36**: see Swiatek-Breen, pp. 214–15. Ill. of **7536**. Rarely prooflike.

7535 1936 S [Net 15,000]
Normally in sets (**7534–36**).

7536 1936 D [Net 15,000]
Same comment. Ill. at **7534**.

THE WISCONSIN TERRITORIAL CENTENNIAL HALF DOLLAR

Alias: Wisconsin.

Occasion: Statewide local celebrations.

Designs: Stylized pile of lead ore and soil with pickaxe, alluding to the lead mines which attracted many immigrants in the 1820s. Date "4th Day of July Anno Domini 1836" is when Henry Dodge became first Territorial Governor. The whole copies the Territorial Seal. The badger is state animal and heraldic supporter in the state's Great Seal. Three arrows symbolize the Black Hawk War of the 1830s; the olive branch represents the peace (massacre and expulsion of the Indians) that made the area safe for white settlers. Initial H below = Benjamin Hawkins, designer, who used devices specified by the Coinage Committee of the Wisconsin Centennial Commission. Mint reports call the badger side the obv. Fuljenz [1986].

Authorizing Act: May 15, 1936.

Mintage: Authorized, no maximum; coined, [25,000 + 15 assay].

Proofs: Unconfirmed to exist.

Grades: EF to UNC. The general public mishandled many.

First Wear Points: Miner's hand, badger's shoulder.

7537 1936 [Net 25,000]

THE CLEVELAND CENTENNIAL/GREAT LAKES EXPOSITION HALF DOLLAR

Alias: Cleveland.

Occasion: Sales at the Exposition (June 27–Oct. 4, 1936, on the lakefront), promoted by the Cleveland Centennial Commemorative Coin Association, Thomas G. Melish, treasurer (see Cincinnati, below).

Designs: Bust of Gen. Moses Cleaveland (1754–1806), one of the directors and surveyors for the Connecticut Land Company, which bought 3,267,000 acres of what was later called northeastern Ohio, including the city site which Gen. Cleaveland laid out and which was later named for him (with changed spelling). BP = designer Brenda Putnam. The nine rev. stars mark nine principal cities (Duluth, Milwaukee, Chicago, Detroit, Toledo, Toronto, Buffalo, and Rochester are the other eight) on the five Great Lakes; the compass symbolizes Cleveland as a center of industry for an area with a 900-mile radius.

Authorizing Act: May 5, 1936.

Mintage: Authorized, 25,000 to 50,000; coined, two indistinguishable batches, July 1936 and Feb. 1937, each [25,000 + 15 assay].

Proofs: None reported.

Grades: EF to UNC. The general public mishandled many.

First Wear Points: Hair behind Cleaveland's ear, cheekbone, top of compass.

7538 1936 [Net 50,000]
Mintage includes next 3.

7539 1936. In numbered notarized holders. [200, incl. in above]
These were the first 200 struck; they are the best strikings, without bag marks. Notarized statement on back of holder (ill. Swiatek-Breen, pp. 49–50) is signed by Thomas G. Melish.

7540 1936 With 1941 counterstamp. [100, incl. in above] Very scarce.
Small round counterstamp die portraying Gen. Cleaveland,

artist unknown; impressed by Western Reserve Numismatic Club during its 20th anniversary celebration.

7541 1936 With 1971 counterstamp. [20?, incl. in above] Very rare.
Small round counterstamp die portraying Gen. Cleveland, name below, FIFTY YEARS 1971 in field, artist unknown. At least 13, possibly 20, impressed by Western Reserve Numismatic Club during its Golden Jubilee celebration.

THE CINCINNATI HALF DOLLARS

Alias: Cincinnati.

Occasion: None. The "Cincinnati Musical Center Commemorative Coin Association" (Thomas G. Melish, chairman) promoted this issue for pure greed. No 1886 event could be found for commemoration, nor did Stephen Foster have anything to do with Cincinnati's undeniably great contribution to American musical life. See Swiatek-Breen, pp. 41–42.

Designs: Idealized portrait of Stephen Foster. Monogrammed CO = Constance Ortmayer, designer. Female with lyre is a personification of Music. Mintmark D or S, if any, below 1936 date; 1886 date is fictitious.

Authorizing Act: March 31, 1936.

Mintage: Authorized, 15,000; coined, total, [15,000 + 16 assay], July 1936.

Proofs: Unconfirmed.

Grades: Except for the 200 presentation sets, these normally have many bag marks. Initials CO are normally weak.

First Wear Points: Hair nearest Foster's temple; bosom.

7542 1936 [Net 5,000]
Mintage includes **7545**. First sold, Aug. 1936, in sets (**7542–**

44), at $7.75/set, mostly to speculators, who promptly raised the price to $45, later the same year to $75. Numerous protests followed. Beware cast counterfeits; see ill. in Swiatek-Breen, pp. 43–44. Authentication urgently recommended. Ill. of **7544.**

7543   1936 S [Net 5,000]
Same comments.
7544   1936 D [Net 5,000]
Same comments. Ill. at **7542.**
7545   1936 Set in numbered notarized holder. [200]
First 200 sets made, similar to **7539;** Melish signed notarized statement on holder. Most surviving pristine gems originated in these sets.

THE LONG ISLAND TERCENTENARY HALF DOLLAR

Alias: Long Island.
Occasion: Local celebrations, May 1936, of the 300th anniversary of the first settlement on the Island (Breuckelin on Jamaica Bay, later spelled Brooklyn), sponsored by the L.I. Tercentenary Celebration Committee, Louis C. Wills, chairman.
Designs: Accolated busts representing a Dutch settler and an Algonquin Indian, latter alluding to the 13 tribes living in the area when Henry Hudson discovered it. Monogram HKW = Howard Kenneth Weinman, designer, son of the A. A. Weinman who had designed the new dime and half dollar in 1916. The ship is meant for one of those that brought over the settlers.
Authorizing Act: April 13, 1936.
Mintage: Authorized, 100,000 maximum, to be struck and issued no later than April 13, 1937, but dated 1936; struck, [100,000 + 53 assay], Aug. 1936; melted, 18,227.
Proofs: Unknown.
Grades: The general public mishandled many; heavy nicks and scratches are common.
First Wear Points: Dutchman's cheekbone; mainsail.

7546   1936 [Net 81,773]

THE YORK COUNTY, ME., TERCENTENARY HALF DOLLAR

Alias: York.
Occasion: Local celebration sponsored by the York County Tercentenary Commission, through the York County Tercentenary Commemorative Coin Association, Walter P. Nichols, secretary-treasurer.
Designs: Stockade, representing Brown's Garrison on the Saco River. WHR = Walter H. Rich, designer, after an anonymous woodcut published in Frank C. Deering, *The Proprietors of Saco,* 1931. Rev. depicts the county seal.
Authorizing Act: June 26, 1936.
Mintage: Authorized, 30,000; coined, [25,000 + 15 assay], of which 10,000 were reserved for Maine residents, who in fact bought over half the total.
Proofs: Unknown.
Grades: EF to UNC. The general public mishandled many.
First Wear Points: Mounted sentry, rims, pine tree in shield.

7547   1936 [Net 25,000]

THE COLUMBIA, S.C., SESQUICENTENNIAL HALF DOLLARS

Alias: Columbia, S.C.
Occasion: Local celebration, March 22–29, 1936, sponsored by the Columbia Sesqui-Centennial Commission. Its chairman, the Hon. James H. Hammond, wanted nationwide distribution "to keep these coins out of the hands of speculators."
Designs: Justice, unblindfolded, stands in city plaza, Old and New State Houses behind. Behind base of the stylized palmetto tree are two bunches of arrows in saltire; before it, lopped oak branch. This device alludes to the British attempt to besiege Fort Moultrie (on Sullivan's Island, Charleston Harbor), June 28, 1776. This fort was constructed of palmetto logs, in which the British projectiles harmlessly buried themselves, while those from Fort Moultrie wrecked the redcoats' oaken ships. Thirteen stars ostensibly connote the Original 13 Colonies, but may covertly allude to the 13 seceding states of the Confederacy. Mintmark D or S may occur below Ms. Justice's foot. By A. Wolfe Davidson; devices probably prescribed by the Commission.
Authorizing Act: March 18, 1936.
Mintage: Authorized, 25,000; coined, total, [25,000 + 23 assay], Sept. 1936, received October.
Proofs: Unknown.
Grades: The extra Philadelphia coins largely went to local residents (who had the first 24 hours after the coins went on sale to place orders); they mishandled many.
First Wear Points: Bosom, top of palmetto.

7548   1936 [Net 9,000]
Offered at $2.15. Preference given to orders for sets **(7548–50)** at $6.45, limit of 10 sets per customer.

7549   1936 S [Net 8,000]
   Normally comes in set **(7548–50),** originally offered at $6.45.
7550   1936 D [Net 8,000]
   Same comments.

THE BRIDGEPORT, CONN., CENTENNIAL HALF DOLLAR

Alias: Bridgeport; P. T. Barnum.
Occasion: Local celebrations of centennial of city incorporation, sponsored by Bridgeport Centennial, Inc.
Designs: Head of Phineas Taylor Barnum (1810–91), showman, city planner, philanthropist. Initial K (below RT of LIBERTY) = Henry Kreis, designer. His ultramodern eagle, inverted, unintentionally suggests a shark with open mouth, tongue, and two dorsal fins.
Authorizing Act: May 15, 1936.
Mintage: Authorized, minimum 25,000, no maximum; date 1936 to continue indefinitely regardless of year of mintage; repealed, Act of Aug. 5, 1939; coined, [25,000 + 15 assay], Sept. 1936.
Proofs: Unknown.
Grades: EF to UNC. The general public mishandled many.
First Wear Points: Cheekbone, parts of wing.

7551   1936 [Net 25,000]
   Sold at $2 each, limit of 5 per customer. Nearly 1,000 remained unsold, but were hoarded rather than melted; the hoard was dispersed in the 1970s.

THE LYNCHBURG, VA., SESQUICENTENNIAL HALF DOLLAR

Alias: Lynchburg; Carter Glass.
Occasion: Local celebration, "Lynchburg in Old Virginia Celebrates Its 150th Birthday," Oct. 12–16, 1936.
Designs: By Charles Keck. Bust of Sen. Carter Glass (1858–1936), one of the founders of the Federal Reserve System, creator of the FDIC, Wilson's Secretary of Treasury, etc.; the only man portrayed on a U.S. coin who also signed paper currency. This device was over his protest and violated the April 7, 1866 Act banning portrayal of living persons on coins or currency. Ms. Liberty stands in Monument Terrace, with the Confederate Monument (above 19 of 1936) and the Old Courthouse.
Authorizing Act: May 28, 1936.
Mintage: Authorized, 20,000; coined, [20,000 + 13 assay], Sept. 1–20.
Proofs: Unknown.
Grades: EF to UNC. The general public mishandled many.
First Wear Points: Hair above Glass's ear; bosom and head.

7552   1936 [Net 20,000]
   Sold during the celebration at $1 each (limit of 10 per customer); $1.25 through mail orders.

THE ELGIN CENTENNIAL HALF DOLLAR

Alias: Elgin; Pioneer.
Occasion: To finance construction of the Pioneer Memorial, a sculptural group by Trygve Rovelstad (begun 1934, still incomplete!), at Davidson Park, Elgin, Ill., on the site of the log cabin of James and Hezekiah Gifford, who settled there about 1834 and founded Elgin. On the statue's base is a dedication TO THE MEN WHO HAVE BLAZED THE TRAILS, WHO HAVE CONQUERED THE SOIL, AND WHO HAVE BUILT AN EMPIRE IN THE LAND OF THE ILLINI, which may have (with Rovelstad's 1935 medal for the actual Elgin Centennial) inspired introduction of the bill to authorize this coinage.
Designs: By Trygve Rovelstad. Head copies his statue *Head of a Pioneer,* ill. Taxay {1967}, p. 217. His initials TR are below the beard. Date 1673 was stupidly substituted (by whose orders?) for the original model's 1835; Elgin did not exist in 1673, which was the year Joliet and Marquette entered the territory as missionaries. Rev. vaguely represents a model of the Memorial: frontiersman with rifle, wife with infant, and two grown sons. The original statues are to be bronze, 12 feet high, on the 8-foot granite base.
Authorizing Act: June 16, 1936.
Mintage: Authorized, 25,000 maximum; coined, [25,000 + 15 assay], Oct. 1936; melted, 5,000, to keep speculators from getting them.
Proofs: One seen, satin finish. San Diego Sale, 9/27–8/85:824, $5,500, Brian Hendelson.
Grades: EF to UNC. The general public mishandled many. Most are weakly struck, especially on rev. faces. The infant is normally a blur.
First Wear Points: Pioneer's cheekbone; rifleman's l. shoulder.

7553   1936 [Net 20,000]
   Sold Oct.–Dec. 1936 by L. W. Hoffecker at $1.50.

THE ALBANY CHARTER HALF DOLLAR

Alias: Albany.

Occasion: Local celebrations, sponsored by the Albany Dongan Charter Committee, honoring the 250th anniversary of the Albany (N.Y.) City Charter, July 22, 1686.

Designs: American beaver *(Castor canadensis),* because in 1686 trapping them for pelts was a main industry: whence this animal's depiction in the city seal. Maple keys for punctuation, and maple branch in beaver's mouth and paws, signalize the maple as the New York State tree. On rev., Gov. Dongan (l.) bids farewell to Robert Livingston and Peter Schuyler (later Albany's first mayor, holding charter). Near Dongan's foot, GKL = Gertrude K. Lathrop, designer. Behind Dongan is a pine tree; this and the twin pine cones for punctuation allude to local pine forests, symbolic of fertility—and of nearby paper mills. Above all, an eagle with LIBERTY in some of the smallest letters ever seen on a U.S. coin (below CH).

Authorizing Act: June 16, 1936.

Mintage: Authorized, 25,000; coined, Oct.–Nov. 1936, [25,000 + 13 assay]; melted, 7,342 (1943).

Proofs: Unverified, though forgeries have been so offered.

Grades: The public mishandled some, circulated few.

First Wear Points: Beaver's hip; Dongan's sleeve.

7554   1936 [Net 17,658]

THE SAN FRANCISCO-
OAKLAND BAY BRIDGE HALF DOLLAR

Alias: Bay Bridge.

Occasion: Opening of the bridge to traffic, Nov. 12–14, 1936. Specimens were distributed by the San Francisco-Oakland Bay Bridge Celebration and San Francisco Citizen's Celebration Committee (Frank R. Havenner, chairman), some via Clearing House Association, others at kiosks near the toll plazas so that motorists could buy without getting out of their cars.

Designs: California grizzly *(Ursus arctos horribilis),* modeled by Monarch II, "last of the grizzlies," for 26 years resident of a cage in Golden Gate Park; appropriately, LIBERTY is underfoot. Monogram JS = Jacques Schnier, designer. No significance has been established for the four stars. S mintmark near foot, above A(LF). Rev. The Bay Bridge; in foreground, the Ferry Tower on the Embarcadero; upper l., Yerba Buena Island; beyond, remainder of bridge sketched toward Oakland and Berkeley; behind, the Berkeley Hills.

Authorizing Act: June 26, 1936.

Mintage: Authorized, 200,000 maximum; coined, [100,000 + 55 assay]; melted, 28,631 (1937).

Proofs: Unknown.

Grades: EF to UNC. The general public mishandled many.

First Wear Points: Monarch's l. shoulder; Berkeley Hills.

THE DELAWARE SWEDISH
TERCENTENARY HALF DOLLAR

Alias: Delaware.

Occasion: Local celebrations statewide (and in New Jersey and Pennsylvania), honoring the 300th anniversary of the landing of the ships *Kalmar Nyckel,* 'Key of Kalmar,' and *Fogel Grip* with the first Swedish settlers at Delaware Bay, March 1638. They built Fort Christina (now a Wilmington park) and Holy Trinity Church (1698–99), now Old Swedes Church, allegedly the oldest Protestant church in the USA still in use.

Designs: The ship *Kalmar Nyckel,* after a scale model at the Swedish Naval Museum; three diamonds for punctuation, alluding to the three counties (Kent, New Castle, and Sussex), approximately to their shape, and to the state's fertility (from the "acres of diamonds" symbolism common in the 1930s). Date 1638 is of the ship's arrival. CLS = Carl L. Schmitz, designer. Rev., the sun shines through clouds at the Old Swedes Church, with the side arch (1750) and belfry (1802). Date 1936 on rev. is that of authorization, not striking. Mint reports call the church side the obv. Fuljenz {1986}.

Authorizing Act: May 15, 1936; repealed, Aug. 5, 1939.

Mintage: Authorized, minimum 25,000 (no maximum); coined, [25,000 + 15 assay], March 1937; melted, 4,022.

Proofs: Unverified.

Grades: The general public mishandled many. Most are weakly struck at centers (mainsail and gable above arch), often with minute granularity at the weak areas.

First Wear Points: Mainsail and gable above arch.

7556   1936/1938 (i.e., 1937) [Net 20,978]

THE ROBINSON-ARKANSAS
HALF DOLLAR

Alias: Robinson; Arkansas-Robinson.

Occasion: Competitive greed. When the Texas Centennial Commission sponsored a bill in Congress (1936) to authorize five new revs. for the Texas half dollars, the Arkansas Centennial Commission did likewise, seeking three. When the Texas bill failed, the Arkansas bill (amended to specify one rev. alteration) passed.

Designs: Bust of Sen. Joseph T. Robinson (D.-Ark.), then Senate Majority Leader, earlier Governor (1913) and nominee for Vice President under Al Smith (1928). This violated the 1866 law forbidding portrayal of living persons on coins. K below B(INSON) = Henry Kreis, designer. Rev. as regular 1936 Arkansas (**7522**), symbolism explained at **7518**. Mint reports call the eagle side the obv. Fuljenz {1986}.

Authorizing Act: June 26, 1936.

Mintage: Authorized, at least 25,000 but not over 50,000; coined, [25,250 + 15 assay].

Proofs: At least nine satin-finish proofs known: first struck, ill. in Swiatek-Breen, p. 23. These have exceptionally clear detail on Robinson's hair near ear, central feathers, scroll where it passes over feathers, and ridges on claws.

Grades: EF to UNC. The general public mishandled some.

First Wear Points: Cheekbone, eagle's head, top of wing below SAS.

7557   1936 [Net 25,250 + ?P]

Marketed by Stack's at $1.85 each. The proofs went directly to the Arkansas Centennial Commission; Wayte Raymond had four, one of them in NN 61:572, one sold privately (1979) at $8,900.

THE ROANOKE ISLAND HALF DOLLAR

Alias: Roanoke; Sir Walter Ralegh; Virginia Dare-Sir Walter Ralegh, etc.

Occasion: Celebration at Old Fort Raleigh on Roanoke Island, Aug. 1937, of the 350th anniversary of the colony and of the birth of Virginia Dare (Aug. 15, 1587); sponsored by the Roanoke Colony Memorial Association and various other local civic and "historical associations."

Designs: Errol Flynn posing as Sir Walter Ralegh. (Misspelled RALEIGH on the coin because the federal Commission of Fine Arts insisted that the obv. die must follow the spelling in the authorizing act.) Monogram WMS = William Marks Simpson, designer. Flanked by two ships intended to be "similar to those in which the Colonists crossed the ocean," Eleanor Dare holds the infant Virginia Dare; behind them, a sapling of mountain pine (?).

Authorizing Act: June 24, 1936. This specified the date 1937 no matter when the coins were to be struck, prior to July 1, 1937.

Mintage: Authorized, minimum 25,000, no maximum; coined, [50,000 + 30 assay], half each in Jan. and June 1937; these two batches cannot be told apart; melted, 21,000.

Proofs: Possibly as many as 50 satin finish (ill.); these have clarity of detail unknown on business strikes, especially at mustache, upper beard, hair adjacent to ear, Eleanor Dare's hair, sleeve, cuff, lower bodice (below cuff and hand), and gathered draperies below that. Note also the differing granular textures of face and coat. Fields are nearly but not quite mirrorlike.

Grades: EF to UNC. The general public mishandled many; UNCs. often have noticeable nicks and scratches.

First Wear Points: Hat brim, Eleanor Dare's head and upper l. arm.

7558   1937 [Net 29,000 + ?P]

THE BATTLE OF GETTYSBURG HALF DOLLAR

Alias: Gettysburg.

Occasion: The Blue and Gray Reunion, July 1–3, 1938, the exact 75th anniversary of the battle, where tens of thousands of surviving Union and Confederate veterans gathered, and Pres. Roosevelt dedicated the Eternal Light Peace Memorial. Sponsored by the Pennsylvania State Commission of Gettysburg.

Designs: Union and Confederate soldiers, looking like brothers—in a war which in fact did pit brother against brother: a duality concept echoed on rev., where the fasces (= power of life and death, sovereignty of the state) divides Union and Confederate arms. Oak and olive branches, ostensibly for war and peace, actually connote authority and victory: the Union triumph followed by Reconstruction. Date 1936 is that of the authorizing act. By Frank Vittor.

Authorizing Act: June 16, 1936.

Mintage: Authorized, 50,000; coined, [50,000 + 28 assay], June 1937; melted, 23,100.

Proofs: Unknown.

Grades: EF to UNC. The veterans and the general public mishandled many; even UNCs. are often heavily nicked and scratched.

First Wear Points: Cheekbones of both soldiers; three ribbons binding fasces.

7559   1936 [Net 26,900]

THE BATTLE OF ANTIETAM HALF DOLLAR

Alias: Antietam.

Occasion: Celebration at the battlefield, Sept. 4–17, 1937, honoring the 75th anniversary of the battle, Sept. 17, 1862; sponsored by the Washington County (Md.) Historical Society and the U.S. Antietam Celebration Commission (Park W. T. Loy, chairman of former, secretary of latter).

Designs: Maj. Gen. George B. McClellan (two stars before him alluding to his Army rank), and Gen. Robert E. Lee (three stars behind him denoting his Confederate Army rank). Monogram WMS = William Marks Simpson, designer. The bridge is that over Antietam Creek (key to strategic high ground overlooking Sharpsburg), a bitterly contested object of the battle; it was later renamed Burnside Bridge after the inept Gen. Ambrose E. Burnside.

Authorizing Act: June 24, 1937.

Mintage: Authorized, 50,000 maximum; coined, [50,000 + 28 assay]; melted, 32,000.

Proofs: Reported but unconfirmed.

Grades: EF to UNC. The general public mishandled many.

First Wear Points: Lee's cheekbone, leaves, rims. Even pristine gems are often weakly struck at top central area of bridge.

7560 1937 [Net 18,000]
The first specimen went to Pres. Roosevelt on Aug. 12. The Commission sold these at $1.65.

THE NORFOLK, VA., TERCENTENARY HALF DOLLAR

Alias: Norfolk.

Occasion: Originally for local celebration (1936) sponsored by the Norfolk Advertising Board and Norfolk Association of Commerce, but the Senate would only pass the authorizing act with the word "coins" changed to "medals." Sen. Carter Glass promised the promoters a second chance, and pushed a new bill through Congress in 1937, creating another lame-duck issue like the Alabama and the Stone Mountain.

Designs: Norfolk city seal. The young plants near plough are possibly peanuts (an important local crop); below them are three stylized wheat sheaves. The cable borders separating seal from outermost legend may allude to ships' ropes (suiting this naval city); the scallop shells continue the maritime theme. Mottoes ET TERRA ET MARE DIVITIAE TUAE = 'Both land and sea are your riches'; CRESCAS = 'May you grow' or 'May you prosper.' Rev., Norfolk's Royal Mace, presented to the Borough of Norfolk by Lt. Gov. Robert Dinwiddie (1753) —the only such historic treasure ever presented to an American city. Date 1636 is that of the original Norfolk Land Grant; flanking it are two dogwood sprigs. Monogram WM+MES = William Marks Simpson and his wife Marjorie Emory Simpson, designers.

Authorizing Act: June 28, 1937.

Mintage: Authorized, 25,000 maximum; coined, [25,000 + 13 assay]; melted, 8,077.

Proofs: Unverified.

Grades: EF to UNC. The general public mishandled many.

First Wear Points: Lower l. sails; high points of Royal Mace.

7561 1936 (i.e., 1937) [Net 16,923]
Originally sold at $1.50 each, limit of 20 per customer.

THE NEW ROCHELLE, N.Y., HALF DOLLAR

Alias: New Rochelle.

Occasion: Local celebration, June 10–20, 1938, sponsored by the New Rochelle Commemorative Coin Committee (Mayor Harry Scott, honorary chairman; Pitt M. Skipton, chairman) and Westchester County Coin Club, commemorating the settlement of this area (1688) by Huguenots from La Rochelle, who bought the 6,000-acre tract (present city site) from John Pell of Pelham Manor via Jacob Leisler: Skipton {1939}.

Designs: One of Jacob Leisler's people (on behalf of the settlers) delivers a fatted calf (to John Pell or his heirs) every June 24, from an eccentric clause in the original deed of grant. GKL = Gertrude K. Lathrop, designer. The fleur de lys (a symbol of France since 1180) appears on the arms of both La Rochelle and New Rochelle.

Authorizing Act: May 5, 1936.

Mintage: Authorized, 25,000; coined, [25,000 + 15 assay], April 1937; melted, 9,749.

Proofs: Reportedly 50 presentation coins on polished blanks, plus 10–14 matte proofs. Forgeries exist; authentication urgently recommended.

Grades: EF to UNC. The general public mishandled many.

First Wear Points: Calf's hip; high points of fleur de lys.

7562 1938 (i.e., 1937) [Net 15,251 + ?P]
The documented #1 specimen is a brilliant prooflike presentation coin, ex Pitt M. Skipton, Anthony Swiatek, Rick Sear, Dennis Brown. Another (unnumbered), 1982 ANA:2538, $1,250; Auction 86:1774, $6,050. No sale record for matte proofs.

THE IOWA STATEHOOD CENTENNIAL HALF DOLLAR

Alias: Iowa.

Occasion: Statewide celebrations, sponsored by the Iowa State Centennial Committee under Gov. Blue.

Designs: Adaptation of state arms, the 29 stars alluding to Iowa's being the twenty-ninth state to enter the Union. The state motto (blurry on many specimens) is OUR LIBERTIES WE PRIZE AND OUR RIGHTS WE WILL MAINTAIN. The Old Stone Capitol in Iowa City is without the building's sidewise stairs, plaza, or outbuildings. AP (r. of DOLLAR) = Adam Pietz, Assistant Engraver of the Mint. Mint reports call the eagle side the obv. Fuljenz {1986}.

Authorizing Act: Aug. 7, 1946.

Mintage: Authorized, 100,000; struck, [100,000 + 57 assay], Nov. 1946.

Proofs: Unknown.

Grades: EF to UNC. The general public mishandled many; UNCs. are often notably bag-marked.

First Wear Points: Eagle's neck and head; central pillars.

7563 1946 [Net 100,000]

Comprises 94,000 sold to Iowans at $2.50 each, 5,000 to outsiders at $3 each; 500 are reserved for the state sesquicentennial (1996), 500 for the bicentennial (2046).

THE BOOKER T. WASHINGTON HALF DOLLARS

Alias: BTW; B.(ooker) T. Washington; and various derogatory epithets.

Occasion: Fund-raising for the Booker T. Washington Birthplace Memorial, Rocky Mount, Franklin County, Va.; ostensibly "to perpetuate the ideals and teachings of Booker T. Washington and to construct memorials to his memory," actually to enrich the promoter, one S. J. Phillips.

Designs: Isaac Scott Hathaway's effigy of the illustrious educator is from a life mask; the two stylized buildings are intended for the Hall of Fame at New York Univ. and the slave cabin where Booker T. Washington was born. Mintmark D or S may occur below cabin, above R(TY).

Authorizing Act: Aug. 7, 1946. For details see Swiatek-Breen, pp. 249–54.

Mintage: Authorized, 5 million; struck, Philadelphia, [1,654,000 + 589 assay], San Francisco, [856,000 + 239 assay], Denver, [656,000 + 313 assay], total, [3,166,000 + 1,205 assay]; melted, exclusive of assay coins, 1,581,631; net mintages, as reconstructed in Swiatek-Breen, p. 251, below.

Proofs: Unknown.

Grades: VF to UNC. Many went to the general public (sold in drugstores in the mid-1950s); others were spent. Gems are scarce; most UNCs. are nicked and scratched. Many are weak at brows, cheekbones, part of nose, central inscription, and upper part of cabin.

First Wear Points: Cheekbone, central inscription.

7564 1946 [Net 500,000]

Coined in December. Distributed by the Commission. Many were spent. Ill. of **7571**.

7565 1946 S [Net 200,000]

Same comments.

7566 1946 D [Net 100,000]

Same comments.

7567 1947 [Net 50,000]

Coined November. Distributed by Stack's, at $6 per set (**7567–69**).

7568 1947 S [Net 50,000]

Same comment, except coined in December.

7569 1947 D [Net 50,000]

Same comment as to **7566**.

7570 1948 [Net 8,000]

Coined in May. Distributed by Bebee's, at $7.50 per set (**7570–72**).

7571 1948 S [Net 8,000]

Same comment. Ill. at **7564**.

7572 1948 D [Net 8,000]

Same comment.

7573 1949 [Net 6,000]

Coined January. Same comment, except issue price $8.50 per set (**7573–75**).

7574 1949 S [Net 6,000]

Same comment.

7575 1949 D [Net 6,000]

Same comment.

7576 1950 [Net 6,000]

Distributed by Bebee's. Issue price $8.50 per set (**7576–78**).

7577 1950 S [Net 256,000]

Extras sold singly as type coins, like **7564–65**, probably at $3. Sets coined in January, singles Jan.–Feb. Many were spent.

7578 1950 D [Net 6,000]

Same comment as to **7576**. Coined in January.

7579 1951 [Net 255,000]

Bebee's sold extra singles (coined Aug. 1–6) at $3. Many spent.

7580 1951 S [Net 7,000]

Bebee's sold sets (**7579–81**), coined January, at $10.

7581 1951 D [Net 7,000]

Same comments. Of the 1,581,631 melted, 87,000 were unsold sets, the remainder unsold singles. Bullion from these went to make the Washington-Carver issue (see next).

THE BOOKER T. WASHINGTON/ GEORGE WASHINGTON CARVER HALF DOLLARS

Alias: Carver; Washington/Carver; and various derogatory epithets.

Occasion: Fund-raising for the Booker T. Washington Birthplace Memorial (as preceding) and the George Washington Carver National Monument Foundation (Diamond, Mo.), and "to oppose the spread of communism among Negroes in the interest of National Defense," this last a chimera intended to pressure Congress (under the influence of the reprehensible Sen. Joseph R. McCarthy) to pass the authorizing bill. The real reason was to help the promoter, S. J. Phillips, pay off his creditors and avoid lawsuits over broken contracts and misappropriated funds. (In actuality, black people were suspicious of Communism, and there were then almost no black radical groups; they ignored these coins as they had ignored the BTWs.)

Designs: Accolated busts of Dr. Carver and B. T. Washington, by Isaac Scott Hathaway, the former probably from photographs, the latter from the same life mask used for the BTWs. The map and superfluous U.S.A. inscription substituted for the original design, which the State Department had vetoed; this latter (ill. Taxay {1967}, p. 252) showed the American Legion badge with UNITED AGAINST THE SPREAD OF COMMUNISM . NATIONAL AMERICANISM COMMISSION . around. Mintmark D or S may occur above IC(ANISM).

Authorizing Act: Sept. 21, 1951. Bullion for these was to come from melted and unsold BTWs.

Mintage: Authorized, 3,415,631 = 1,834,000 uncoined BTWs + 1,581,631 melted; coined, Philadelphia, [2,136,000 + 319 assay], San Francisco, [248,000 + 54 assay], Denver, [38,000 + 19 assay], total, [2,422,000 + 392 assay]; melted, 1,091,198. Net mintages below are from the reconstruction in Swiatek-Breen, p. 259.

Proofs: Unknown.

Grades: EF to UNC. Many were spent, mostly of the extras earmarked for sale as singles. Even gem UNCs. are usually weak at Carver's cheekbone.

First Wear Points: Carver's cheekbone; U.S.A. on map.

7582 1951 [Net 50,000]
Coined in December. Single type coins offered at $5.50; many remained unsold and were later peddled at lower prices, down to 60¢ each, finally spent. Ill. of **7588.**

7583 1951 S [Net 10,000]
Coined in December. Sold in sets **(7582–84)** at $10, later discounted to $6.50.

7584 1951 D [Net 10,000]
Same comments.

7585 1952 [Net 634,000]
Same comment as to **7582,** except coined in March.

7586 1952 S [Net 8,000]
Sold in sets **(7585–87)** at $10, later discounted to $6.50.

7587 1952 D [Net 8,000]
Same comment.

7588 1953 [Net 7,200]
Coined in January; sold in sets **(7588–90)** at $10, later discounted to $6.50. Ill. at **7582.**

7589 1953 S [Net 48,000]
Same comment. Singles offered at $5.50, later discounted, many spent.

7590 1953 D [Net 7,200]
Same comment as to **7588.**

7591 1954 [Net 8,000]
Coined in Jan. and Feb.; offered in sets at $10, price briefly raised to $12, later discounted to $6.50.

7592 1954 S [Net 42,000]
Coined for sets as preceding; extra singles Aug. 1–6, many spent.

7593 1954 D [Net 8,000]
Coined for sets as **7591–93.** The debacle of this and the BTWs reinforced official opposition to further proposals for commemorative coins for over 25 years. This is partly why the Bicentennial coins were made for circulation, not for private-sector promotion.

THE GEORGE WASHINGTON HALF DOLLARS

Alias: Washingtons.

Occasion: His 250th birthday.

Designs: Equestrian Washington; Mount Vernon. EJ = Elizabeth Jones, Engraver of the Mint; MP (in shrubbery) = Michael Peloso, assistant. Head after Gilbert Stuart; garments after a John Trumbull painting. Mintmark S (on proofs) or D (on UNCS.) r. of mane. Silver 900 Fine, 12.5 gms., as previously.

Authorizing Act: Dec. 23, 1981. Promoted by Reps. Doug Barnard (D.-Ga.) and Frank Annunzio (D.-Ill.); passed House May 19, Senate Dec. 9.

Mintage: Authorized, not over 10 million (all dated 1982), to be coined no later than Dec. 31, 1983. *CWA,* p. 184, says production ended Jan. 11, 1984. Final mintage figures from *NNW* 8/5/86, p. 3. Coins authorized but unsold were melted at San Francisco.

Proofs: Included in above.

Grades: Not circulated.

First Wear Points: Button on bridle across nose; horse's face.

7594 1982 No mintmark. Possibly survives.
Trial strikings only, supposedly all destroyed.

7595 1982 S Proofs only. [4,894,044P] Normal date.
The [3,307,645P] struck Aug.–Dec. 1982 cannot be told from the [1,586,399P] struck in 1983. Offered at $10.50.

7596 1982 S Open 8 like S.
Die polish completely disconnects strokes from intersection. Discovered by Dwight Stuckey, *CW* 1/26/83, p. 70.

7597 1982 D [2,210,458]
The [695,698] struck Oct.–Dec. 1982 cannot be told from the [1,514,804] coined in 1983. First 5 were coined at Denver Mint ceremonies, July 1, 1982, by Donna Pope, Mint Director; Nora Hussey, Denver Mint Superintendent; William H. McNichols, Jr., Mayor of Denver; Adna G. Wilde, Jr., ANA president; and Anthony Swiatek: *CW* 2/15/84, p. 3; 8/6/8, p. 3.

THE 1983 OLYMPIC SILVER DOLLARS

Alias: Discus Dollars.

Occasion: Fund-raising for the Los Angeles Olympic Organizing Committee. Originally intended to be part of a set of 28 coins, to be marketed by Lazard Frères (France) at exorbitant prices. After much public protest, the present denominations and types were adopted instead.

Designs: Discus throwers in unison, like so many Rockettes; pose vaguely after Myron's *Diskobolos,* but the incuse muscular definition, eyebrows, and nose owe more to comic strips; no eyes or mouth. The linked rings have for decades symbolized the modern Olympics; the "moving star" emblem was for the 1984 Summer Games. Mintmark P, S, or D below date. EJ below feet = Elizabeth Jones; EJ JM on rev. = Elizabeth Jones and John Mercanti, of the Engraving Department of the Mint. Anachronistic standards: Silver 900 Fine, 412.5 grs. = 26.730 gms., 1.5″ = 38.1 mm, as 1837–1964.

Authorizing Act: PL 97-220, 97th Congress, July 22, 1982.

Mintage: Authorized, not over 50 million of these and the 1984 dollars. Coined, as below. Net mintage figures are from the Mint Bureau, published in *CW* 12/25/85, p. 3, with corrections in *CW* 1/8/86, p. 3. The +'s reflect possible additional sales "from U.S. Postal Service philatelic outlets and credit card chargebacks." Coins authorized but unsold are to be melted.

Proofs: As below. First struck Feb. 10, 1983, 11:30 A.M. The 13 ceremonial strikings were destroyed. All coined during the first week (quantity unknown) required three blows from the dies; later strikings only two. To date these remain indistinguishable.

Grades: These did not circulate. Special packaging has minimized public mishandling.

7598   1983 No mintmark. Possibly survives.
Trial strikings, allegedly all destroyed. Ill. of **7600**.

7599   1983 P [Net 294,543+]
First public sale, June 28, noon, Independence Hall, Philadelphia. Sold in 4 "package options": a) [29,974] in what the Mint called "Three-piece UNC. sets" (with **7602, 7605**), at $395 until Aug. 15, 1983, only to the earliest orderers of the "Three-piece Proof sets" described at **7600**; b) [174,014] in "1983 Uncirculated Dollar sets" (with **7600–1**), at $89, beginning late 1983; c) [81,629] individually at $28; d) [8,926+] in specially cased "Six-coin sets" (with **7600, 7602, 7603, 7605** UNC., **7606** Proof), at $850. This last option was revealed by Mint Director Donna Pope before a House Coinage subcommittee: *CW* 1/8/86, p. 3. The coins are indistinguishable.

7600   1983 S [Net 174,014 + 1,577,025+P]
Sold in 7 "package options": a) [174,014] in what the Mint called "1983 Uncirculated dollar sets" described at **7599**; b) [260,083P] in "Three-piece proof sets" (with **7603, 7605**), at $352 from Oct. 15, 1982 to Jan. 25, 1983, at $416 from Jan. 26 to June 5, 1983; c) [4,000P] in similar sets with **7603, 7607,** at the Olympic site; d) [386,809P] in "Proof silver dollar sets" (with **7603**), at $48 from Oct. 15, 1982 to Jan. 25, 1983, at $58 to June 5, 1983; e) [140,361P] in "1983-S Prestige Proof sets," at $59, beginning fall 1983 (the dollar added to repackaged regular proof sets); f) [8,926+P] in specially cased "Six-coin sets" (described at **7599**); g) [776,846P] individually, at $24.95 from Oct. 15, 1982 to Jan. 25, 1983, $29 through June 5, 1983, thereafter $32. This last figure includes [290P] numbered PNCs (special postal cachets), postmarked Benjamin Franklin Station, Philadelphia, June 28, 1983, and

sold at $35.18 each over the counter only that one day. Nos. 1–21 went to VIPs, 22–290 to the public, according to Philip Scott Rubin (eyewitness). Proofs with dies aligned 180° from normal were destroyed at the Mint; a few may have escaped.

7601   1983 D [Net 174,014]
Sold only in "1983 Uncirculated dollar sets" described at **7599**.

THE 1984 OLYMPIC SILVER DOLLARS

Alias: "Gateway" Dollars, and various derogatory epithets.
Occasion: As preceding.

Designs: The "Gateway" sculpture before the Los Angeles Coliseum: Two columns support a lintel, on which are headless male and female figures, "all brawn, no brains," unintentionally symbolizing the Orwellian motto "Ignorance is strength." Between them, the flame's configuration suggests that someone is making a rude gesture with the middle finger. The federal Fine Arts Commission had condemned the design as "a loser"; the Mint ignored all such objections. Large mintmark P, S, or D at lower l., above (ANGEL)ES. Eagle on rock holds an olive branch for peace, but no arrows. Initials RG = Robert Graham, designer of sculpture and coin. See Ed Reiter's column, New York *Times,* 3/4/84, p. H33; and Reiter {1984}. Composition, weight and diameter as preceding.

Authorizing Act: As preceding.

Mintage: Authorized, as preceding. Coined, as below. Net mintage figures are from same sources as preceding.

Proofs: As below.

Grades: These did not circulate. Special packaging has minimized public mishandling.

7602   1984 P [217,954]
Ill. of **7603**. Sold in 4 "package options": a) [29,974] in what the Mint called "Three-piece Uncirculated sets," described at **7599**; b) [116,675] in "1984 Uncirculated dollar sets" (with **7603–4**), at $89; c) [62,379] individually at $28; d) [8,926+] in "Six-coin sets," described at **7599**. The coins are indistinguishable.

7603   1984 S [116,675 + 1,801,210P]
Ill. above **7602**. Sold in 7 "package options": a) [116,675] in what the Mint called "1984 Uncirculated dollar sets," described at **7602**; b) [260,083P] in "Three-piece proof sets," described at **7600**; c) [4,000P] in similar sets at the Olympic site, with **7600** and **7607**; d) [386,809P] in "Proof silver dollar sets," with **7600**; e) [824,712P] individually, beginning at 1984 F.U.N. convention, Jan. 4–7, 1984, at $32; f) [316,680+P] in "1984-S Prestige Proof sets" (dollar added to repackaged regular proof sets), at $59, beginning early March 1984; g) [8,926+P] in "Six-coin sets," described at **7599**.

7604   1984 D [116,675]
Sold in "1984 Uncirculated dollar sets," described at **7602**. Minor doubled rev. dies have been reported. *NNW* 7/14/84, p. 1.

THE 1984 OLYMPIC GOLD TEN DOLLARS

Alias: Torchbearers Gold Eagle; Dick and Jane.

Occasion: As preceding.

Designs: Male and female runners with torch (based on the relay racers, though in the ancient games these were all male); linked Olympics rings. JM JP at lower l. = John Mercanti and James M. Peed, designers, of the Engraving Department of the Mint. Mintmark below date; these are the first coins to bear the W mintmark for West Point. Rev., eagle loosely copying that of the Great Seal, differing from Scot's and Barber's treatments by having the glory of stars in rows of 5, 4, 3, and 1. Below tail, Mercanti's initial JM. Anachronistic 1837–1933 standard, 258 grs. = 16.718 gms., except lacking silver alloy: 90% gold, 10% copper. 1.06″ = 27 mm. Planchets by Johnson Matthey Co. *CW* 8/3/83, p. 6.

Authorizing Act: As preceding.

Mintage: Authorized, not over 2 million. Coined, as below. Net mintage figures from same sources as preceding.

Proofs: As below.

Grades: These do not circulate. Special packaging has minimized public mishandling.

7605   1984 W [75,886 + 381,085P]

First piece struck at West Point Bullion Depository, Sept. 13, 1983, by Treasury Secretary Donald T. Regan. Sold in 5 "package options": a) [29,974] in what the Mint called "Three-piece Uncirculated sets," described at **7599;** b) [36,986] individually at $339, in Europe beginning Jan. 1984, in the USA beginning June 1984; c) [8,926+] UNC. and [8,926+P] Proof in "Six-coin sets," described at **7599;** d) [260,083P] in "Three-piece proof sets," described at **7600;** e) [112,076+P] individually at $352, beginning March 1, 1984.

7606   1984 P [33,309P]

Sold individually at $352, beginning spring 1984.

7607   1984 S [48,551P]

2 "package options": a) [4,000P] in what the Mint called "Three-piece proof sets" (described at **7600**) sold at the Olympic site; b) [44,551] individually at $352, beginning spring 1984. Enl. photos.

7608   1984 D [34,533P]

Sold individually at $352, beginning spring 1984.

IMMIGRANT HALF DOLLAR

Alias: Immigrant.

Occasion: Centenary of the Statue of Liberty. Mint price includes $2 surcharge per coin for restoration.

Designs: Statue of Liberty, side view, welcomes an ocean liner

of 1885–1920 period (common carrier of immigrants); behind, sunset and New York City skyline of ca. 1913. Mintmark in r. field near (S)T. Rev., rear view of immigrant family with baggage on Ellis Island pier, facing distant New York City skyline. Obv. by Edgar Z. Steever, IV; rev. by Sherl J. Winter. Copper core clad with 75% copper, 25% nickel, as current half dollars of regular design. 175 grs. = 11.34 gms. Diameter, 1.205″ = 30.61 mm. 2.18 mm thick.

Authorizing Act: PL 99-61, 99th Congress, July 9, 1985.

Mintage: Authorized, maximum 25 million including proofs.

Proofs: As below.

Grades: These did not circulate. Special packaging has minimized public mishandling.

7609   1986 S Proof. [?P]

First struck at a ceremony Oct. 18, 1985, simultaneously with **7612,** moments after **7613,** while the West Point and San Francisco "coining facilities" were linked by special telephone hookups. First piece coined by Thomas Miller, officer in charge. *CW* 10/30/85, p. 1. Mint price $7.50. Ill., U.S. Mint.

7610   1986 D Nickel-clad.

First coined at a ceremony, Dec. 6, 1985. First 5 coins struck by Denver Mint Superintendent Nora Hussey, Kenneth E. Bressett (ANA Director of Education), Dan Brown, Charles Davenport, and Hazel Whisett. *CW* 12/25/85, p. 3. Mint price $6.

ELLIS ISLAND SILVER DOLLAR

Alias: Ellis Island.

Occasion: As preceding. Mint price includes $7 surcharge per coin for restoration of the Statue of Liberty.

Designs: Front view of Statue of Liberty; behind, the Ellis Island immigration building. Mintmark below U(ST). Rev., her torch divides the first couplet of Emma Lazarus's poem, "Give me your tired, your poor,/Your huddled masses yearning to breathe free." By John Mercanti; poem inscription by Matthew Peloso. Silver 900 Fine, 412.5 grs. = 26.73 gms. Diameter 1.5″ = 38.1 mm. 2.84 mm thick. *CW* 10/30/85, pp. 1, 10, 18.

Authorizing Act: As preceding.

Mintage: Authorized, maximum 10 million.

Proofs: The first ones received 3 blows from the dies apiece, 500 coins per die; die and press failures followed. Survivors, if any, are not yet distinguishable from later strikings. Mintmark is in the master die.

Grades: These did not circulate. Special packaging has minimized public mishandling.

7611   1986 P [?]
Mint price $22.

7612   1986 S Proof. [?P]
First coined at a ceremony, Oct. 18, 1985, by Deputy Mint Director Eugene Essner. Others coined then by John Mercanti and various dignitaries. Mint price $24. Ill., U.S. Mint.

STATUE OF LIBERTY HALF EAGLE

Alias: [?]

Occasion: As preceding. Mint price includes $35 surcharge per coin for restoration of the Statue of Liberty.

Designs: Low-angle view of head of Statue of Liberty. Mintmark W in field near jaw. Rev., pouncing eagle. By Elizabeth Jones. Gold 90%, silver 6%, copper 4%. 129 grs. = 8.359 gms. Diameter 0.85″ = 21.59 mm. 1.75 mm thick. EY of LIBERTY incuse for contrast with embossed rays of radiate crown. The design has been praised as of exceptional merit and originality.

Authorizing Act: As preceding.

Mintage: Authorized, maximum 500,000.

Proofs: As below.

Grades: These do not circulate. Special packaging has discouraged public mishandling.

7613   1986 W [95,198 + 404,802P]
First two proofs coined at a ceremony Oct. 18, 1985, by Treasury Secretary James A. Baker, III, moments before the first strikings of **7609** and **7612.** Third specimen coined by Lee A. Iacocca, then chairman of the Statue of Liberty-Ellis Island Centennial Commission; others by Treasury Secretary Katherine Ortega, Mint Director Donna Pope, Chief Sculptor/Engraver Elizabeth Jones, Rep. Frank D'Annunzio (D.-Ill.), sponsor of the authorizing bill, Reps. Benjamin A. Gilman and Hamilton Fish Jr. (both R.-N.Y.), West Point Bullion Depository Superintendent Clifford Barber, and ANA president Florence Schook. Mint price $175 Proof, $165 UNC. Entire issue sold out by mail, Jan. 1986. The [48,000 + 108,000P] struck in Jan. 1986 cannot be distinguished from those made in Dec. 1985. The Mint sold [21,958P] as singles, [342,995P] in 3-coin sets with **7609** and **7612,** [48,876] in 3-coin sets with **7610** and **7611,** and [38,893 + 38,893P] in 6-coin sets with **7609–12** inclusive. These "package option" figures are incomplete and subject to revision. *CW* 3/12/86, p. 3; 4/9/86, p. 58; 4/16/86, p. 95; 5/21/86, p.1.

Courtesy of Coin World

7614–7699   Reserved for future commemorative issues.

Part Six

THE UNITED STATES PROVISIONAL BRANCH MINT AT SAN FRANCISCO (1851-53)

CHAPTER 40

OVERVIEW

Less than a year after James Marshall had discovered gold in northern California, hundreds of outraged San Francisco merchants, miners flagrantly underpaid for their ores, and the general public were already petitioning the Military Governor, R. B. Mason, to set up a State Assay Office. This would issue ingots officially stamped with fineness, weight, and value, in a single stroke ridding the public of a variety of abuses. Opposition predictably came from those who stood to lose the most by the measure: gold-dust dealers, certain bankers, makers of light-weight or debased gold coins, and certain politicians. The gold-dust dealers normally bought gold dust, granules, and nuggets at $6 to $8 per oz., smelted it, and resold it at $16 to $18 per oz.; the others made similar profits. Despite the outraged protests from these quarters, the legislature on April 20, 1850, voted the State Assay Office into existence. (See Chap. 43, Sect. ii.) At once the gold-dust dealers persuaded some of their banker friends to boycott the Assay Office ingots. To weaken the effect of the boycott, respected merchants publicly announced that they would continue to accept the ingots at par. However, everyone knew that this would remain only a stopgap measure—quite aside from the legal issue: If these ingots passed as money, they violated the Constitution, which forbids states coining money. The only answer was to establish a federal branch mint.

Accordingly, Sen. Thomas Hart Benton (D.-Mo.) and William McKendree Gwin (D.-Ca.) began pushing a bill to authorize a branch mint in San Francisco. In a degree of shortsighted stupidity unusual even for Congress at the time, delegations from New York opposed the measure because they wanted a branch mint for their own state; those from Georgia and Louisiana opposed any new branch mint in either California or New York as "unfair competition" for the Dahlonega and New Orleans branches; and representatives from Pennsylvania deludedly opposed the bill as a possible threat to the Philadelphia Mint! The result was a compromise act, Sept. 30, 1850, establishing not a branch mint but a federal Assay Office of Gold in San Francisco, authorizing issue of ingots of $50 to $10,000 value, "to be struck of refined gold, of uniform fineness, and with appropriate legends and devices, similar to those on our smaller coins [!] with their value conspicuously marked, and the inscriptions LIBERTY and UNITED STATES OF AMERICA." This weasel wording concealed what the California authorities and Mint Director R. M. Patterson well knew: The ingots would circulate as money, with inscriptions conformable to the Mint Act of April 2, 1792, differing primarily in denomination from normal federal coins.

Reasons for this subterfuge were partly legal, partly technological. Native California ores ranged from about $850/1{,}000$ to $925/1{,}000$ gold, the rest $75–150/1{,}000$ silver. Federal gold coins had to contain $900/1{,}000$ gold, not over $50/1{,}000$ silver, the rest copper,

pursuant to the Act of Jan. 18, 1837. To bring California gold to the federal standard required copper (very scarce) and parting acids (concentrated nitric, sulfuric, and hydrochloric acids), which were not locally made, and could not be safely shipped either overland or via Panama or Cape Horn. The new Mint Director, George N. Eckert, wrote to Treasury Secretary Corwin that some 150,000 lbs. of parting acids would be necessary for each year's operations in San Francisco. In practice, substandard gold was brought to stated fineness (880, 884, 887, or 900) by adding measured weights of proofing pieces (small bars of 999+ Fine gold) to each melt, and deducting their cost from the value of the finished coins; but parting acids were necessary to make proofing pieces. Calling the new coins "ingots" and the new provisional branch mint "U.S. Assay Office of Gold" was a neat solution, evading any possible legal penalties. But the Philadelphia Mint officials treated Augustus Humbert as a branch-mint superintendent, requiring him to report monthly gold and unparted ingot manufactures on the same kinds of forms used by all branch mints; they supervised manufacture of master dies and hubs for the ingots; and, just in case someone began manufacturing enough parting acids that Humbert and his subcontractors (Moffat & Co.) could make coins of legal fineness, the Engraving Department shipped regular 1853 S dies (half dime to double eagle) to the Assay Office.

The $50 ingots or "slugs" or "Californians" did pass as money; for most of 1851–53 they were the principal accepted currency in California. Earlier dies gave the issuer's name as AUGUSTUS HUMBERT U.S.ASSAYER OF GOLD; later ones as UNITED STATES ASSAY OFFICE OF GOLD; but it was the same provisional branch mint, located at first on Montgomery St. between Commercial and Clay, later at 608–10 Commercial St. Humbert arrived in San Francisco on Jan. 30, 1851, bringing master dies or hubs, and on Jan. 31 he struck his first octagonal ingots. Quantity issue began Feb. 14. Anticipating Humbert's arrival, Collector of Customs T. Butler King was authorized by Pres. Fillmore, Dec. 2, 1850, to receive any or all issues of the new Assay Office in payment of tariffs: a de facto recognition that they passed as federal money, effective from the first day of issue.

Opposition to the new provisional branch mint arose from the same people who had boycotted the former State Assay Office ingots. Bankers could no longer buy gold dust for $6 to $8 per oz. while Humbert's federal operation paid miners $16 per oz., less 2.75% manufacturing charges; nor could they sell gold dust to private coiners at high profits.

Worse, nearly all private gold coins vanished, most being melted for recoinage into Humbert $50's. This created a coin shortage: Articles priced below $50 could not be bought without smaller coins for change; the State Constitution excluded paper currency of any kind, and coins of $5 to $20 (let alone anything smaller) became scarce enough to command premiums. The obvious answer was for the Assay Office to issue smaller denominations. However, federal authorities back east, callous or at best unaware of how damaging the coin shortage's effects were becoming to the California general public, yielded to political pressure from the Assay Office's opponents, and forbade Humbert to make any "ingots" of lower denomination than $50. Foreign coins came in by ship and reached circulation at inflated valuations; eventually, bankers discounted the Humbert ingots to below bullion value. This led to a business slump in Nov.–Dec. 1851, attributable almost entirely to the shortage of small coin: Nobody could buy or sell without enormous difficulty making change. In the meantime, the state legislature had repealed an earlier act, so that once again private gold coiners could legally issue gold coins of the essential $5, $10, and $20 denominations. Doubtless the Assay Office's enemies rejoiced: Every piece made by the private sector meant a loss in revenue to Humbert and the Moffat firm. Federal small change commanded a 3% premium when available at all, which was not often. Because the Treasury continued to refuse permission to Humbert to make ingots of smaller denominations, Moffat & Co. resumed private coinage, issuing $10's and $20's beginning about Jan. 12, 1852.

On Dec. 9, 1851, Treasury Secretary Corwin yielded to pressure from Humbert and his friends in Congress, and authorized the Assay Office to issue $10's and $20's. The letter of authorization arrived on Jan. 10, 1852—only to be followed two days later by a cancellation, allegedly on account of the introduction into Congress of a bill concerning a "Mint and Assay Office in San Francisco." After further protests—including the remarkable claims that the private coins of Wass, Molitor & Co. were passing at 2% above those of the federal Assay Office, and that owing to federal inaction on this issue, their firm had been unable to pay expenses for a month—Secretary Corwin again yielded. A letter dated Jan. 7, 1852 (received Feb. 11) finally authorized federal issue of $10 and $20 ingots, which began the next day. Two days later, John Little Moffat retired from the operation, which continued, under the remaining partners Joseph R. Curtis, Philo H. Perry, and Samuel H. Ward, to use the title "Moffat & Co." (the most trusted name in California assaying and coining) and to retain their federal subcontract with Humbert.

Political opposition intensified. A law of Aug. 31, 1852 required that all gold coins acceptable at the Custom House must conform to the 1837 Mint Act in fineness. On Sept. 4, Assistant Secretary of Treasury William L. Hodge wrote to T. Butler King, Collector of Customs, that this law would be enforced against the Humbert ingots. This turned out to be Sen. Gwin's attempt to destroy the Assay Office as the only remaining obstacle to establishment of a regular branch mint. When Hodge's notification arrived on Oct. 8, the news created panic. Almost all business halted; coins of legal fineness could not be had even at a premium, copper was scarce, parting acids unobtainable. Public demonstrations followed, nearly amounting to riots. T. Butler King appeared at the biggest, Oct. 9, offering to accept any Humbert ingots at 900 Fine (even without the legal copper content) if he could be indemnified against any loss in so doing. A committee of local merchants agreed to cooperate, and Humbert began to issue $50's at 900 Fine. King notified Congress of this arrangement; fortunately nobody filed charges against him for violating the Aug. 31 act or Hodge's directive. Humbert's new 900 Fine ingots continued in use even after the Assay Office closed for good, Dec. 14, 1853, as part of the transfer to the official federal branch mint. The latter took over operations in the same building, using much of the same equipment. A plaque marks the spot today, though without mention of Humbert's provisional mint. Issue of regular federal coins began on April 15, 1854; in the meantime, private coiners remained at work.

Despite the high prices Assay Office ingots have lately brought, they have always been among the most plentiful of California's pioneer gold coins. Enormous hoards have been amassed from time to time. The late George Walton and the late John A. Beck each simultaneously owned over 100 "slugs"; I have seen as many as 120 on display in a single convention.

In addition to the normal Humbert issues, a large number of irregular and apparently experimental pieces surfaced during the 1950s, many as a result of advertising campaigns mounted by John J. Ford, Jr., circularizing banks, antiques dealers, bullion dealers, newspapers, and other establishments in cities and small towns throughout the mining districts in California, Nevada, Oregon, Idaho, Colorado, Wyoming, Utah, Arizona, and New Mexico. These were attacked in 1966 on insufficient evidence; the controversy has long since died down unresolved.

Original models for the $50 ingot obvs. were made by the illustrious sculptor/medallist Charles Cushing Wright under subcontract from the Philadelphia Mint. Humbert, who had been a watchmaker in New York, created the engine-turned revs. Later dies, as well as individual device punches, word and numeral logotypes or gang-punches, and single-letter punches, were the work of Georg Albrecht Ferdinand ("Albert") Küner.

Standard weights for $50 ingots varied according to fineness: At 880 Fine, 1,319.3 grs. = 85.49 gms.; at 887, 1,308.9 grs. = 84.82 gms.; at 900, 1,290 grs. = 83.59 gms. Twenties and $10 were proportionate: A $20 at 884 Fine weighed 525.34 grs. = 34.042 gms.; at 900, 516 grs. = 33.436 gms. A $10 at 884, 262.67 grs. = 17.021 gms.; at 900, 258 grs. = 16.718 gms. Actual weights are very close to the theoretical figures, which neglect the few cents extra provided by the silver alloy in each coin.

The ____D____C on earlier 1851 Humbert ingots was to provide space for stamping in 50, 100, or whatever higher denomination, and if necessary, for stamping in amounts in dollars D and cents C for bullion storage ingots of odd amount. Most likely those with 50 in central rev. came first of all, that number briefly representing one superfluous extra stamping per piece.

The series of $50's with edges lettered AUGUSTUS | HUMBERT | UNITED | STATES | ASSAYER | OF GOLD | CALIFORNIA | 1851 were made by hand-stamping each complete word onto one segment of edge: again, time-consuming extra operations which proved unnecessary. The individual words differ in position, sometimes slanting or double-punched, and occasionally with one or more words inverted (logotype rotated 180°). Normally, edge reads when rev. is upward. Because the digits 880 or 887 on the earlier ingots were also hand-stamped, these vary in position and spacing: Compare Beck I:660–66; Carter:1119–24. On later issues they were punched into the die instead.

K numbers are from Kagin {1981}; KM (= Krause-Mishler), from SCWC; Adams, from Adams {1913}.

THE U.S. PROVISIONAL BRANCH MINT, SAN FRANCISCO

Designers, Charles Cushing Wright (obv.), Augustus Humbert (rev.). Engravers, Wright, Humbert (1851 $50's); Albert Küner (1852); Longacre (1853)? Mints, Moffat's (Clay & Dupont); U.S. Assay Office, Montgomery St., later 608–10 Commercial St. Composition, Weights, see introductory text. Diameters, $50: 26/16" = 41 mm (side to side), 28/16" = 44 mm (corner to corner); $20: 23/16" = 35 mm; $10: 17.5/16" = 28 mm. Edges, as below. Authorizing Act, Sept. 30, 1850.

Grade range, GOOD to UNC., usually VF to EF; seldom collected below FINE. GOOD: Partial wing feathers; enough rev. detail to identify type. VERY GOOD: Over half wing feathers. FINE: Wing feathers intact except at top 2 to 3 rows; partial LIBERTY on scroll; partial breast feathers. VERY FINE: At least half breast feathers; LIBERTY intact, though RT will be weak. EXTREMELY FINE: Isolated tiny rubbed spots on breast and top edge of wing; full LIBERTY. UNCIRCULATED: *No* trace of wear; original mint luster. NOTE: Nearly all $50's show rim or edge dents; many have fields retooled or polished. Grade as if these defects were absent, then specify as to severity. EXCEPTIONS: $50's are normally weak on arrow butts, upper shield, and claw holding branch; usually also on l. part of rock below base point of shield.

i. AUGUSTUS HUMBERT,
U.S. ASSAYER (1851–52)

1. LETTERED EDGE $50's

7700   1851 50 D. 887 THOUS. Large 7. With 50 on rev. Very rare.
Kagin 4; KM 31.1a; not in Adams. Top of 50 on rev. may point to top or bottom of coin measured from obv. Large 7 is at least as tall as 8's; compare next. Gibson:168; Beck I:664, 666; Carter:1120, AU, $26,400. Date on edge through **7705.**

7701   1851 50 D. 887 THOUS. Small 7. With 50 on rev. Very rare.
Same dies; 7 shorter than 8's. Gibson:169; Beck I:665; Ellsworth, Garrett:896, AU, $37,500; Grinnell, Carter:1121; others.
7702   1851 50 D. 887 THOUS. No 50 on rev. Unverified.
Kagin 4a; KM 31.2a; Adams 12. Supposedly same dies. Inadvertent omission?
7703   1851 50 D. 880 THOUS. With 50 on rev. 10–12 known.
Kagin 1; KM 31.1; Adams 11. Same dies.   1) ANS.   2) Lilly, SI.   3) Auction 82:488, EF, $22,000. Others in pvt. colls.

7704   1851 50 D. 880 THOUS. No 50 on rev. Rare.
Kagin 2; KM 31.2; not in Adams. Same dies, usually with

various states of rust and repolishing. Rust plainest at eagle's ribbon. Kagin 2a, with ASSAYER inverted on edge, is untraced (cf. HR 11/69:596); for explanation see introductory text. Ellsworth, Garrett:894, AU, $50,000; Beck I:660, Auction 79:995, UNC., $51,000.
7705   1851 50 D. 880 THOUS. "Rays from central star." Unique?
Kagin 3; KM 31.4; not in Adams.   1) Peltzer, MacAllister, Clarke I:701, Kagin. Obv. polished.

2. REEDED EDGE ISSUES;
OBV. NAME AND DATE

7706   1851 FIFTY DOLLS. 880 THOUS. in relief.
Kagin 5; KM 32.1. Two obv. dies, first (heavy rust differently located from var. ill.; return on scroll—below US—strong, feathers intact: Beck I:674) very rare, second as ill. Rev., target 15 mm, of 20 circles. State I: Return on scroll strong; no die rust. Beck I:668, 672, others. State II: Both dies lightly rusted. State III: Worn die, return on scroll weak, incomplete feathers above and l. of shield; light rust. Beck I:667, 669–71, others. State IV: Same, heavy rust (ill.). State V: Return on scroll gone, feathers weaker, heavier rust. Auction 82:979, ABOUT EF, $7,500; Carter:1127, EF, $11,000; Ellsworth, Garrett:895, EF, $21,000.

7707   1851 FIFTY DOLLS 887 THOUS. in relief; large central target.
Kagin 6; KM 32.1a. Target almost 16 mm; 22 circles. Broad blank margin (about 2 mm) between rev. device and separate border within octagon. Rust varies from almost none (Humbert, Zabriskie, Ellsworth, Garrett:897, Proof, $500,000, ill.; Beck I:679, 684; Carter:1133) to slight (Beck I:681;

Ex J. W. Garrett: 897. Courtesy Bowers & Ruddy Galleries, Inc.

Carter:1130, EF, $10,450) to heavy (Beck I:678, 685; Wayman:419, EF, $10,450).

7708 1851 FIFTY DOLLS 887 THOUS. in relief; small central target.
Kagin 7; KM 32.2 Target 14.5 mm; 19 circles. Narrow margin (about 1.2 mm) between rev. device and separate border within octagon. Obv. always heavily rusted; rev. varies in severity of rust. Beck I:677, 680, 682–83; Grinnell, Carter:1131, EF (polished), $11,000.

7709 1852 FIFTY DOLLS. 887 THOUS. in relief. Rare.
Kagin 11; KM 32.2. Redesigned eagle by Küner; ends of scroll point outward; smaller date. Rev., as **7708,** heavily rusted. Zabriskie, Ellsworth, Garrett:898, AU, $42,500. For other $50's see **7714–16.**

7710 1852/1 TWENTY DOLS. 884 THOUS: [7,500] Very rare.
Kagin 9; KM 30. Struck in a single day between March 5 and April 2, 1852. Usually cracked through bases of most obv. letters except value. Geiss, Carter:1136, EF, $7,150; Auction 79:1458, AU, $14,000. Proofs: 1) Humbert, Zabriskie, Ellsworth, Garrett:890, $325,000. "407.6 grs." (i.e., 507.6?) 2) Bell I:1058, Maj. Alfred Walter, NN 60:577. 3) Reported, impaired.

Ex J. W. Garrett: 890. Courtesy Bowers & Ruddy Galleries, Inc.

7711 1852/1 TEN DOLS. 884 THOUS: Rare.
Kagin 8. I(FORNIA) repunched; always with diagonal rev. break. All struck Feb. 11–14, 1852. Specimens from different ore deposits differ in color. Usually VF, rarely choice. Ellsworth, Garrett:889, AU, $17,000; Auction 82:982, UNC., $3,500. Kagin 8a, "IINITED," is unverified: Die break at base of U? compare next. Enl. photos.

7712 1852 TEN DOLS. 884 THOUS: Close date. Rare.
Kagin 10; KM 29.1. A(SSAYER) above F, unlike next. Obv. later cracked through bases of UNITED: Kagin 10a; KM 29.2, "IINITED." Clifford:26, EF, $3,250; Mickley, Garrett:888, AU, $13,000.

Ex J. W. Garrett: 888. Courtesy Bowers & Ruddy Galleries, Inc.

7713 1852 TEN DOLS. 884 THOUS: Wide date. Rare.
2 rev. vars.: A(SSAYER) above O or above space between FO (ill.).

ii. UNITED STATES ASSAY OFFICE OF GOLD (1852–53)

Designer, Wright. Engravers, Küner; Longacre (1853 $20). Mint, reorganized Moffat & Co., Montgomery St. between Clay and Commercial. Other specifications, as before.
Grade range and standards, as before.

7714 1852 FIFTY DOLLS. 887 THOUS. Medium target.
Kagin 13; KM 54. Target 15 mm, 20 circles, similar to **7706.** Without and with various stages of die break at rim above

O(RNIA), eventually touching O (ill.). Issue of March–Oct. 1852. Ellsworth, Garrett:904, EF, $30,000; Waltman, Carter:1138, AU, $29,700.

7715 1852 FIFTY DOLLS. 900 THOUS. Medium target. Very rare.
Rev. as preceding. Beck I:697, others. Issue of Oct.–Dec. 1852; probably included in [13,800] Jan. 1853.

7716 1852 FIFTY DOLLS. 900 THOUS. Small target. Very rare.
Kagin 14; KM 54a. Target 14.5 mm, 19 circles, like **7708.** Beck I:694–96; Nygren, Garrett:905, EF, $27,500. Probably comprises rest of [13,800] Jan. 1853, and [10,000] Feb. 1853.

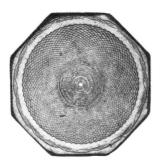

7717 1852 TEN DOLS. 884 THOUS Rev., incomplete upper frame line. Ex. rare.
Kagin 12; KM 50.1 var. O(FFICE) below I(TED). Rawson, Garrett:900, UNC., $18,000, Kagin.

7718 1852 TEN DOLS. 884 THOUS Rev., normal frame line. Rare.
Same obv., cracked. O(FFICE) below N(ITED). Rev. border beads strong (Kagin 12a1; KM 51.2) or weak (Kagin 12a2; KM 51.3, ill.). The former, Auction 82:985, UNC., $4,500.

7719 1853 TEN D. 884/0 THOUS Ex. rare.
Kagin 15; KM 52. Break develops from Y to border. 1)"Bell," Geiss, Walton, Lilly, SI. 2) Nygren, Lawrence, Bell I, 1973 ANA, VF. 3) Clifford, Kagin, EF. 4) Zabriskie:364, Ronnie Carr. 5) DiBello:1391, 78 ANA:1681, VF. 6) Auction 79:1463, EF, $19,000. 7) S 12/5/75:1006, EF. 8) Beck III:442, EF. 9) Sup. 9/30/85:2938, Kagin, midwest coll., VF.

7720 1853 TEN D. 900THOUS Very rare.
Kagin 16; KM 52a. Struck March–April 1853. Gibson:181; Woodward (7/5/1882), Garrett:901, UNC., $35,000.

7721 1853 TWENTY D. 884/0 THOUS. Ex. rare.
Kagin 17; KM 53. Struck Feb. 23–March 1, 1853. 1) Mint, SI. 2) Lilly, SI. 3) Garrett:902, EF, $23,000. 4) Geiss, Carter:1147, UNC., $22,000. 5) NN 8/69, 78 GENA:2224, Auction 79:1465, EF, $9,000. 6) Walton, DiBello:1392, 83 ANA:3614, AU. 7) Bell I:1044, NN60:577, Clifford, Kagin, VF.

7722 1853 TWENTY D. Narrow 900T HOUS. Very rare.
KM 53a var. Rev. as **7721,** often with crack from r. frame

line to border. Later die states (lapped obv.) show barless A's, missing ribbon between lower beak and adjacent wing. Mintage included in next.

7723 1853 TWENTY D. Wide 900/880T HOUS. [2,500,000+]
Kagin 18; KM 53a. At least 20 minor vars., struck March–Oct. 30, 1853. These vars. do not differ positionally (all dies hubbed); they show different patterns of die breaks and/or rust, normal or barless A's, normal or missing serifs on I's and some other letters. Brand, Auction 82:987, $10,500 UNC. One very rare var. with lump in final 0 of 880 has been claimed as 900/884, but no other traces of 4 show. Proofs: 1) Bache I:2816, Seavey, Parmelee, Ulex, Proskey, Newcomer, Mehl, Raymond, Col. Green, "Bell," Kosoff, Farouk, Kosoff, pvt. coll. 2) Mint, SI. Both suspected of being clandestine Philadelphia Mint strikings ca. 1858–63. The 16–20 controversial proofs (Kagin 12, p. 328) have 170 edge reeds, barless A's, dent on (UN)I; they vary in alloy: Clifford:30, $7,000. For the 1853 $20 with MOFFAT & CO., see **7789** below.

iii. CONTROVERSIAL COIN INGOTS (1853)

Thought to have been made during preparation of dies for **7719–23**. Unlike bullion storage ingots, these have no serial numbers, and are in even denominations; unlike proofing pieces, they have standard fineness rather than 999 or 9999. All turned up during the 1950s; all are controversial; all are exceedingly rare.

7724 1853 1 Ounce Disk. Unique?
Kagin 20. 900 = Fineness; 1 = 1 oz. Embodies a suggestion

made at the Philadelphia Mint, 1850. 1) Franklin, Ford, Murrell, Rowe, Clifford:47, $18,500. 479.9 grs. = 31.09 gms.

7725 1853 20.00 DOLS. 900 THOUS. Ex. rare.
Kagin 21a. Die vars. exist. Usually 516 grs. = 33.4 gms.; one was clipped to 496.85 grs. = 32.195 gms.

7726 1853 20 DOLS. 900 THOUS. Counterstamped 3 516. 2 known.
Kagin 21. 3 = March 1853? 516 = grs. 1) Ford, Lilly, SI. 2) Pvt. coll. Similar ingots in odd denominations (one each) are thought to be bullion storage ingots, alias "assay bars."

7727 1853 TWENTY D. 900/800 THOUS. Octagonal. Unique?
Kagin 15, p. 329. 1) Franklin, $22,000 (1958), Murrell, Clifford:33, $9,000. 421.3 grs. = 27.3 gms.

7728 1853 50 D. 900T HOUS. Reeded edge. 3 or 4 known? Kagin 17, p. 330. 1) Franklin, Lilly, SI, 1,281.25 grs. = 83.024 gms. 2) Franklin, Murrell, Clifford:36, $19,000, 1,315.75 grs. = 85.259 gms. 3) Franklin, Murrell, Clifford:37, $22,000. Broad flan. 1,286.3 grs. = 83.351 gms. 4) Kagin 17a. Smaller thicker flan, about 2,080 grs. = 134.8 gms. Pvt. coll.

7729 1853 200 D. Unique? Kagin 23. Eagle die from same hub as **7727,** blank space left for denomination; GRS. and blank space for weight. On the cut-off edge are initials A.H. for Augustus Humbert, suggesting adjustment of weight to stated figure. 1) Ford, Bank of California. Stated weight 5,162 grs. = 334.5 gms.; actual weight?

Part Seven

PRIVATE, PIONEER, AND TERRITORIAL GOLD COINS

CHAPTER 41

GEORGIA ISSUES (1830, 1849)

The first major gold rush in the history of the United States occurred in Georgia and North Carolina in 1828, with smaller discoveries in Alabama and South Carolina. Small quantities of gold had been turning up in Mecklenburg County, N.C., off and on since 1799; but publicity about the 1828 finds brought thousands of victims of "gold fever" to that area and to various other Southern Appalachian locales. About $2 million from these regions had trickled to the Philadelphia Mint in preceding decades, but this figure is known to be small compared to what went into local use or was shipped to Europe. Overland travel between the Southern gold districts and Philadelphia was extremely hazardous, between lack of usable roads and an oversupply of bandits and understandably hostile Indians. It was this gold rush which occasioned the tragic "Trail of Tears": After gold was discovered on Cherokee lands, there was no way to prevent white men from moving in and forcibly relocating the natives.

On July 24, 1830, Templeton Reid (1789–1851), metalworker, jeweler, gunsmith, watchmaker, and general factotum, received publicity in the Milledgeville *Georgia Journal* as making coins of $10, $5, and $2½ out of locally mined bullion without alloy; reportedly about $1,500 face. Shortly afterward, he moved to West Washington St., Gainesville, to be at the center of the gold mining district. His coinage operation continued there from about Aug. 1 to Oct. 18, 1830, despite attacks from local rivals claiming that Reid's coins were worth less than face value and that private coinage was illegal even when not debased. In actuality, Reid made his coins very slightly lighter than federal standard, but his gold was about 942 Fine rather than the federal 917, so that if anything his coins were worth a little more than face value as bullion. Though the Constitution forbade states to coin money, it did not forbid individuals to do so. Reid coined only small amounts (estimated mintages herein are modified from Dr. Dexter Seymour's researches), and the vast majority of Reid's coins were melted at the Philadelphia Mint. Reid spent his last 15 years as inventor and manufacturer of new types of cotton gins in Columbus, Ga. A full account of his activities is in Seymour {1974, 1977}. A plaque marking the approximate location of the Gainesville mint was unveiled Sept. 9, 1979. *CW* 10/17/79, p. 1.

The obscure coins with Reid's name and CALIFORNIA GOLD were not made in California, as in 1849 Reid was not in physical condition to travel west, even if he could have raised the necessary funds. Almost certainly he made them in Columbus, Ga., from a tiny sample of California ore which had somehow reached him rather than the Dahlonega Mint. Eckfeldt & Dubois {1851} valued one of his new $10 coins at $9.75, adding the notation "(Georgia)". The weight standard suggests that Reid estimated this ore at about 893 Fine, the Mint at 871.

Only one authentic $10 is known; this has DO(LLAR) touching, TEN DOLLAR double-punched (without final S). Stephen K. Nagy made, or ordered made, forgeries from copy dies, about 1900–10. These have D O spaced apart, and TEN DOLLAR normal. Impressions come in gold (Ex. rare), silver, copper (some overstruck on large cents and other coins), and various base metals.

Only one $25 coin was ever reported; this piece was in the Mint Cabinet Collection, from which it was stolen on Aug. 16, 1858, and never recovered. Weight was reported as 649 grs. = 42.1 gms. Engraved ills. indicate that the period after AS-SAYER is nearly midway between R and D of REID. Should another piece from these dies ever show up, it would be unsafe to assume without proof that it is the stolen example; most likely the thief melted the ex-Mint coin to sell as bullion, rather than expose himself and his descendants to prosecution by keeping it in a collection.

Nagy's forgeries of this denomination have period much nearer to R than to D. They come in various metals, and are rarer than his $10's.

TEMPLETON REID, 1830, 1849

Designer, Engraver, Reid. Mints, Reid's, Milledgeville (July 1830), Gainesville (Aug.–Oct. 1830), Columbus, Ga. (1849). Composition (1830), gold unalloyed, approx. .942 ± .01 gold, remainder silver and tin; (1849), same but about .871 gold. Weights, Diameters, variable, as noted.

No grading standards established; grades below are Dexter Seymour's and auctioneers'.

7730   1830 $2.50 [About 1,056] Very rare.
Kagin 1; KM 79. About $11/16'' = 18$ mm. About 60.5 grs. = 3.92 gms. Seymour estimates approximately 24 survivors, most showing a tiny drill point (secret mark) near top of upright of R(GIA). Wayman:409, EF, $40,000; Zabriskie, Ellsworth, Garrett:504, $47,500, Wayman:410, VF, $25,000, 86 ANA:2180. 62.1 grs. = 4.02 gms., $35,200.

7731 1830 $5 [About 310] Ex. rare.

Kagin 2; KM 80. About ¹⁵·⁵/₁₆″ = 25 mm. About 123 grs. = 7.98 gms. 1) Comparette, SI, AU. 2) Col. Green, Smith & Sons, Josiah Lilly, SI, EF. 3) Howland Wood, Plumezer, Granberg, Newcomer, Boyd, Kosoff, Williams, "Melish":2339, Willis I. duPont, EF–AU, nicks. Ill. ANS {1914}, Pl. 34. 4) Nygren, Garrett:505, $200,000, 1983 ANA:3572, EF, rim dent. 5) W. P. Brown, Hidden, Brand, Morgenthau 311:237 (11/33), pvt. coll, EF. 6) Unknown provenance, ill. Guide Book, AU. 7) Tourrès:263 (Vinchon 3/68), Clifford, Kagin, ill. AU. 8) Unknown provenance, ill. *SC,* EF, dented. Possibly same as 3). 9) Low (1905), pvt. coll., "ABOUT FINE." 10) DeWitt Smith (1908), Brand II:1536, Auction 85:1992, $31,900, VF–EF, 125.1 grs. = 8.106 gms.

7732 1830 TEN DOLLARS [About 250, this and next] Ex. rare.

Kagin 3; KM 81. About ²¹/₁₆″ = 33.7 mm. 244.2–251 grs. = 15.82–16.17 gms. Enl. photos. 1) Granberg, Newcomer, Col. Green, Smith & Sons, Lilly, SI, EF. Ill. ANS {1914}, Pl. 34. 2) Unknown provenance, ill. Guide Book, AU. 3) KS 4/67:601, Irving Moskowitz:1485, $41,000, Kagin, VG, edge test mark. 4) "Bell," "Memorable":940, Norweb, ANS, ill. 5) G. D. Case (Milledgeville), Samuel Guthman, T. E. Leon, Brand II:1537, EF, 247.8 grs. = 16.06 gms.

7733 n.d. (1830) TEN DOLLARS 40 stars. Ex. rare.

Kagin 4; KM 82. Same diameter. 246–248 grs. = 15.97–16.07 gms. 1) Comparette, SI, AU, ill. Clain-Stefanelli {1970}, fig. 49. 2) G. D. Case, Samuel Guthman, T. E. Leon, Virgil Brand, C. E. Green, Smith & Sons, Lilly, SI, EF. Ill. Yeoman Guide Book, 1947–70 eds. 3) Henrick, Todd, Dubose, Mertes, Ball, KS 5/66:1514, AU, cleaned. Brass counterfeits are rumored; these would be grossly underweight.

7734 1849 TEN DOLLAR (sic). Original. Unique.

Kagin 1, p. 303; KM 47. 1.11″ = 28.1 mm. 260 grs. = 16.88

7736   1849 TWENTY-FIVE DOLLARS Original. Unlocated. Kagin 2, p. 303; KM 48. The Mint Coll. specimen weighed 649 grs. = 42.1 gms. See introductory text.

7737   1849 TWENTY-FIVE DOLLARS Nagy "restrike." Ex. rare.
See introductory text.

gms.   1) Mint, SI. Clain-Stefanelli {1970}, fig. 50. See introductory text. Enl. photos.

7735   1849 TEN DOLLAR (sic). Nagy "restrike." Ex. rare.
See introductory text.

CHAPTER 42

NORTH CAROLINA ISSUES (1831–50)

Alt Christoph Bechtler (1782–1842), born in Pforzheim (Grand Duchy of Baden), served apprenticeship there as goldsmith, silversmith, and gunsmith, and in 1829 emigrated to New York with his sons August and Karl and a nephew Christoph, arriving Oct. 12. Two weeks later they applied for citizenship, and shortly afterward opened a clock and watch repair shop in Philadelphia. Sometime in March or April 1830 they moved to Rutherfordton, N.C., where this family would long have the only local jewelry and watchmaking business. They bought a tract of land between Mountain Creek and Catheys Creek, about 3½ miles north of the center of town, and began their enterprise on July 30, according to advertisements in the North Carolina *Spectator and Western Advertiser.* By this time they had anglicized their names to Christopher, Augustus, and Charles, though they continued to be known by their original German names. Portraits of Alt Christoph, August, and four other Bechtlers are illustrated in the Walton sale, p. 157, where it was announced they would be given to the Smithsonian.

The coincidence of a tight money supply, a shortage of specie, large local discoveries of gold dust and nuggets, Alt Christoph's metallurgical skill, the virtual impossibility of safe shipment of bullion to the Philadelphia Mint, and no laws against private coinage made the next move obvious. When Congress ignored a petition by local miners and merchants, praying for establishment of a branch mint in the gold district, the Rutherford County people turned to Bechtler, asking him to assay and stamp their gold. Accordingly, he advertised on and after July 2, 1831, that he would do so, specifying $2.50 and $5 denominations. An editorial in the July 2 edition of the *Spectator* described both coins, evidently Series I pieces, quoting Bechtler as saying he was already planning to improve the dies (evidently for Series II). His operation continued for nearly 20 years.

Bechtler made his own dies, punches, presses, and other equipment; his output was of honest weight, and its variations from stated fineness were entirely from limitations in available technology. Between then and about 1846 his establishment coined over $2.2 million; federal mint officials made no attempt to interfere, knowing that the Constitution was on Bechtler's side. For decades even after the Civil War, many people in the South never saw any other gold than Bechtler's, and contracts were frequently made payable in the latter: Featherstonhaugh {1906}; Griffin {1929}; Kagin {1981}.

Counterfeiters promptly imitated several Bechtler issues; some of their output consisted of cast copies in low-grade gold or baser metals, others were crude imitations from false dies.

(Specimens differing in lettering from vars. illustrated herein are automatically suspect; authentication is recommended.)

The date AUGUST 1, 1834 on some $5 coins alludes to the original text of the bill which later became the Mint Act of 1834. This had proposed to identify new-tenor or reduced-weight coins by affixing the effective date. At the last moment, officials changed their minds, and Kneass's dies for the new federal coins omitted the motto (Classic Heads: Chap. 33, Sect. vi; Chap. 36, Sect. vi). But in the meantime, Bechtler had already made his dies and begun coining at the new standard, 28 grs. per dollar rather than the former 30.

Three different wordings thereafter appeared on Bechtler's coins: NORTH CAROLINA GOLD, CAROLINA GOLD, and GEORGIA GOLD. These "location stamps" (as they were then called) apparently designated three average finenesses of gold even if the particular ores could not be traced to those locations. These were respectively 20, 21, and 22 Carats, at 140, 134, and 128 grs. per $5. Actual weights are generally within a grain or two of those stated on the coins. Most likely they were issued concurrently; which vars. were struck depended on the fineness of ores brought in to be coined.

Issues diminished after the Charlotte and Dahlonega Mints opened in 1838. Alt Christoph gave his coining business to his son August in 1840. August moved to midtown Rutherfordton, at the corner of what is now Sixth and North Washington Sts. There he issued enormous quantities of gold dollars between 1842 and his death in July 1846.

Christopher Jr. inherited August's business, but developed a drinking problem, which doubtless contributed to the claims that some of his gold dollars (which continued the A.BECHTLER title, using August's old 27 G. 21 C. dies, now rusted) were below proper weight or fineness. He abandoned his coining enterprise in either 1849 or early 1850, after which he continued only as a jeweler. It is probably no coincidence that this was immediately after the Philadelphia, Charlotte, New Orleans, and Dahlonega Mints began giving him competition by coining gold dollars in quantity—discouraging a business in which the Bechtler family had enjoyed a monopoly for over 18 years. Bullion thereafter went preferentially to the federal branch mints; but Bechtler's coins continued to circulate side by side with the government's product.

About 1921–22, Henry Chapman located three Bechtler $5 dies, one with A.BECHTLER, one with C.BECHTLER, and a rev. (Earlier reports say he had these as early as 1908, but this is unconfirmed.) He took the dies to the Philadelphia Mint to make proof strikings. I have seen (courtesy of George Frederick Kolbe) a receipt to Chapman, March 22, 1922, signed by Ada C. Williams, Medal Clerk, "for Ten (10) Gold Bechtler Medals, .999 Fine, at $20.6718, 4.30 ozs. Gold $88.89, Labor $10.80, total $99.69." The document did not specify whether A.Bechtler or C. Bechtler, but the fabric of both types is the same. I conjecture that he had five struck of each in March 1922, possibly others later. Far from coincidentally, one of each appeared in Reimers:856–57 (July 25, 1922).

THE BECHTLERS, RUTHERFORDTON, N.C. (1831–50)

i. ALT CHRISTOPH BECHTLER (1831–40)

Designer, Engraver, Alt Christoph Bechtler. Mint, Bechtler's, 3½ miles N. of Rutherfordton. Composition, native gold, 20 Carats = .833 gold (Series I–V); 21 Carats = 0.875 gold (Series VI); 22 Carats = 0.917 gold (Series VII), rest silver and tin. Weight standards, per dollar, at 20 Carats, 30 grs. = 1.94 gms.; at 21 Carats, 26.8 grs. = 1.73 gms.; at 22 Carats, 25.6 grs. = 1.65 gms. $2.50 coins, at same finenesses, respectively 75 grs. = 4.86 gms.; 67 grs. = 4.34 gms.; 64 grs. = 4.14 gms. $5's, at same finenesses, respectively 150 grs. = 9.72 gms.; 134 grs. = 8.68 gms.; 128 grs. = 8.28 gms. Diameters, dollars, about 2/3″ = 17 mm; $2.50, 4/5″ = 20 mm; $5, 21/20″ = about 26 mm.

Grade range, POOR to UNC.; no standards agreed on. We suggest VERY FINE: fully bold lettering; EXTREMELY FINE: partial mint surface. Most survivors fall within this range. Beware coins with traces of solder or other mutilation.

SERIES I: "WEIGHTLESS," 20 CARATS, July–Sept. 1831
All with ASSAYER and NORTH CAROLINA GOLD

Finely Reeded Edges

7738 n.d. (1831) $2.50. Coarse beads both sides. 5 or 6 known. Kagin 6; KM 42.2. 57 beads obv., 50 rev. Barless A's; Y like a V with added serif. Walton, Gibson:160, UNC., $3,200 (1974); Zabriskie, Ellsworth, Garrett:514, 72.1 grs. = 4.73 gms., VF, $4,500. Enl. photos. I have not seen Lusk:712, "plain edge," VF. Shuford:2575 is an early counterfeit.

7739 n.d. (1831) $2.50. Fine beads obv., coarse rev. 6 known? Kagin 5; KM 92.3. 79 beads obv., 63 rev. 71.8 grs. = 4.65 gms.

7740 n.d. (1831) $2.50. CAROLINA above 2.50. Unique? Kagin 7; KM 93.1. Obv. of **7738**. Rev., 88 beads; heavily broken from rim through OR to 50. 73.3 grs. = 4.75 gms. 1) Morris, Jenks, Nygren, Walton:2249.

7741 n.d. (1831) 5 DOLLARS. RUTHERFORD COUNTY. 2 or 3 known. Kagin 14; KM 99.2. Not to be confused with **7743**. 1) Walton:2259, EF. 2) Newcomer, Boyd, Bolt:1181, UNC., 148 grs. = 9.59 gms., ill. Kagin. Enl. photos. 3) Reported.

SERIES II: WEIGHTS ADDED TO SERIES I DIES
Fall 1831

Finely Reeded Edges

7742 n.d. (1831) $2.50. 75.G. below 20.C. 8–10 known. Kagin 8; KM 92.1. Garrett:513, EF, 73.8 grs. = 4.78 gms., $6,750; Stiekney, Hidden, Newcomer, Walton, Beck, Klausen, Ketterman, Auction 82:970, UNC., $9,250.

7743 n.d. (1831) 5 DOLLARS. 150.C. below 20.C. 10–12 known. Kagin 15; KM 99.1. Zabriskie, Ellsworth, Garrett:520, AU, 148.9 grs. = 9.649 gms., $11,500. The C. in 150 C. is an error for G(rains). Enl. photos.

SERIES III: NEW DIES, *N. CAROLINA GOLD*
Winter 1831/2 Through July 1834

Finely Reeded Edges

7744 n.d. ONE DOLLAR. 30.G.
Kagin 1; KM 89. Finely serrated borders. Average 29.8 grs. = 1.93 gms. The most plentiful of all C.Bechtler coins; George Walton's hoard included 13. Often found imperfectly centered, parts of borders missing. Die buckles, weakening 30.G. side. First type of gold dollar coined in the USA. Hesslein, Garrett:508, $1,600, Wayman:411, EF, $1,500.

7745 n.d. $2.50. 75.G. obv., 20.C. rev. 4 known.
Kagin 9; KM 93.2. Borders as **7744**. Edge reeding wider than on **7738–40, 7742.** 1) Walton:2250, Clifford, Kagin, EF, ill. 2) Walton:2299, VanRoden:891, VF. 3) Bolt:1173, EF. 4) H. P. Smith, DeWitt Smith, Brand II:1538, 73.3 grs. = 4.75 gms., buckled obv.; discovery coin, *NUM* 12/12, p. 478. 5) Lilly, SI, ill. Taxay-Scott. 6) Newcomer, Boyd, ill. ANS {1914}, Guide Book.

SERIES IV: 20 C. 28 GRAINS PER DOLLAR
August 1, 1834 on $5's

Aug. 1834–1840

7746 n.d. ONE DOLLAR. :CBECHTLER. 28.G high. 10–12 known.
Kagin 2; KM 88.2. Rev. of **7744**. Finely reeded edge. 27.6 grs. = 1.79 gms. Steig:1784, VF, $1,525. Compare next and **7761.**

7747 n.d. ONE DOLLAR. C:BECHTLER. 28.G centered. Very rare.
Kagin 3; KM 88.1. Same edge; about same weight. Rosborough, Gaylord, Gibson:155, UNC., $1,900 (1974); Ellsworth, Garrett:507, VF, 27.2 grs. = 1.76 gms., $1,700. But compare **7761.**

7748 n.d. 5 DOLLARS. No period after RUTHERFORD Reeded edge. Ex. rare.
Kagin 16; KM 96.2. 1) Walton:2251, ill. Kagin. 137.5 grs. = 8.91 gms. 2) Walton:2300, VF. 3) Shuford:2579, VF. Compare next. 4) Zabriskie, Newcomer, Boyd, Williams, Smith, Willis duPont. Walton:2522, said to have plain edge, is unverified.

7749 n.d. 5 DOLLARS. Similar, no C before BECHTLER. Plain edge. Unique?
Kagin 15a, d begins opposite top stroke of 5. 138.7 grs. = 8.99 gms. 1) Fla. jeweler, N.C. pvt. coll.

7750 n.d. 5 DOLLARS. Period after RUTHERFORD. Plain edge. Rare.
Kagin 17; KM 96.1. Barless A's. 139.8 grs. = 9.059 gms. Auction 82:971, UNC., $4,500. Similar pieces with error AUCUST, ATRUTHERFORD one word, O's too large, D too small, tailless R's, are old counterfeits.

7751 n.d. 5 DOLLARS. RUTHERF: CARATS close to 20. Plain edge. Ex. rare.
Kagin 18; KM 97.1. Barless A's. 1) Walton:2254, QS 9/73:1371, AU. 2) Walton:2307, EF. 3) Garrett (1976):389, EF. 138 grs. = 8.942 gms. 4) Bolt:1176, mounted.

7752 n.d. 5 DOLLARS. RUTHERF: CARATS far from 20. Plain edge. Very rare.
Kagin 19; KM 97.2. Normal A's. 137.7 grs. = 8.923 gms. Walton:2253; Ellsworth, Garrett:516, EF, 140 grs. = 9.072 gms., $5,000. Obv. recurs on proof restrike **7769.**

SERIES V: CAROLINA GOLD. 21 CARATS
26.8 Grains per Dollar

Plain Edges Henceforth Except as Noted

7753 n.d. 2.50 [Dollars]. 67.G. Rare.
Kagin 10; KM 90. Barless A's. Bement, Ellsworth, Garrett:510, EF, 66.5 grs. = 4.31 gms., $2,900.

7754 n.d. 5 DOLLARS. RUTHERF: Star below 134.G.
Kagin 20; KM 94. Normal A's. Average 134.4 grs. = 8.709 gms. Usually with adjustment marks. Last impressions have die broken through IN. Dies aligned either way (head to toe or head to head). Wayman:412, EF, $3,600; Auction 82:972, UNC, $3,900. One known with lump of gold added in center: Kagin 20A, ex a North Carolina museum, Klausen, Kagin, Crouch. 131.9 grs. = 8.547 gms.

7755 n.d. 5 DOLLARS. RUTHERF: No star below 134.G: Reeded edge. 2 known.
Kagin 26. Rev. like **7766.** Usually listed as a transitional issue, ca. 1842. 1) Kelley, Lilly, SI. 2) MacFarland I:2055, $7,500, Brownlee.

SERIES VI: GEORGIA GOLD. 22 CARATS
25.6 Grains per Dollar

7756 n.d. 2.50 [DOLLARS]. 64.G. Uneven 22 above CARATS Very rare.
Kagin 11; KM 76.1. Barless A's. Dies shatter. 63.6 grs. = 4.12 gms.

7757 n.d. 2.50 [DOLLARS]. 64.G. Even 22 above CARATS 10–12 known?
Kagin 12; KM 76.2. Barless A's. Dies shatter. About same weight. Walton:2246, AU, others.

7758 n.d. 5 DOLLARS. RUTHERFORD. 128.G: Colon at :GEORGIA 3 known?
Kagin 21; KM 78.2. 1) Ex Boyd estate. 2) Gaylord, Gibson:162, Wayman:413, AU, $11,500. 3) Walton:2256, EF. Compare next.

7759 n.d. 5 DOLLARS. Same, no colon at GEORGIA Very rare.
Kagin 22; KM 78.1. Periods in legends. Ellsworth, Garrett:518, EF, 127.3 grs. = 8.249 gms., $4,000.

7760 n.d. 5 DOLLARS. RUTHERF: Very rare.
Kagin 23. Die of **7751.** 126.6–127.7 grs. = 8.204–8.274 gms. Ellsworth, Garrett:519, VF, $3,600.

SERIES VII: No Initial Before BECHTLER
20 C., 28 Grains per Dollar

C. & A. Bechtler, 1840–42

7761 n.d. ONE DOLLAR. Reversed N.
Kagin 4; KM 87. Dies shatter. For similar coins with C.BECHTLER see **7746–47.** Similar pieces with normal N, from Newcomer coll. and in ANS (without punctuation), are almost certainly early counterfeits.

7762 n.d. 2.50 [DOLLARS]. 70.G: Very rare.
Kagin 13; KM 91. Dies buckle and shatter. Zabriskie, Ellsworth, Garrett:511, 68.7 grs. = 4.45 gms., EF, $3,200; Clifford:5, AU, $4,200; Auction 82:969, $4,750.

ii. AUGUST BECHTLER (1842–46)
Coinage Continued by Christopher Jr., 1846–50

CAROLINA GOLD

7763 n.d. (1842) 1 DOL: 27.G. 21.C. Reeded edge. Ex. rare.
Kagin 25; KM 83.2. Early die state. 1) Bolt:1183, Clifford, Kagin. But compare next. Ill. of **7764.**

7764 n.d. (1842–50) 1 DOLLAR. Same dies. Plain edge.
Kagin 24; KM 83.1. Average 21.8 grs. = 1.41 gms. Earlier
states, before die rusted, are nearer correct weight; later ones
lighter, occasioning claims of debasement. Dentils first blur,
then fade out; light die cracks develop; dies become increasingly rusty. Rusted-die coins include many struck by Christopher Jr. Walton's hoard contained 98 specimens, early and
late states. Survivors are believed to number over 400, by far
the most plentiful single var. of private gold coins. Ill. at
7763. Brass counterfeits are numerous; they weigh much less
than the gold.

7765 n.d. (1842–46) 5 DOLLARS. 128.G. 22. CARATS. 8
known.
Kagin 28; KM 85. 1) Ellsworth, Garrett:523, $2,500,
Coles:1212, $4,400, VF, 126.7 grs. = 8.21 gms., $2,500. 2)
Walton:2262, said to have reeded edge. 3) Lilly, SI. 4)
Mitchelson, CSL. 5) Proskey, Granberg, Newcomer, Wil-
liams, duPont. 6) Clifford, Kagin. 7) Moskowitz, Kagin,
midwest coll. 8) Pvt. coll.

7766 n.d. (1842–46) 5 DOLLARS. 134.G: 21. CARATS.
Rare.
Kagin 27; KM 84. Hebbeard, Garrett:522, 133.7 grs. =
8.664 gms., AU, $6,600; Walton:2261 reportedly has reeded
edge. Rev. die survives in a museum.

7767 n.d. (1842–46) 5 DOLLARS. 141.G: 20. CARATS. 8–10
known.
Kagin 29; KM 86. Ellsworth, Garrett:524, F, 138.8 grs. =
8.994 gms., $2,400; Walton:2263, AU, said to have reeded
edge.

Chapman Restrikes (1922)

Proofs Only, 999 Fine, Plain Edge

7768 n.d. 5 DOLLARS. A.BECHTLER. [5+P] Ex. rare.
Kagin 30. Dies of **7767.** See introductory text. Always with
the die break and rust marks. Auction 79:1448, $8,000.

7769 n.d. 5 DOLLARS. C.BECHTLER. Same rev. [5+P] Ex.
rare.
Kagin 31; KM 98. Obv. of **7751–52.** Always with the die
break and rust marks. No originals of this die combination.
See introductory text.

CHAPTER 43

CALIFORNIA GOLD RUSH ISSUES (1849–56)

Overview

We owe the existence of such coinages by private U.S. citizens to a coincidence. Washington's Farewell Address warned our government to avoid "foreign entanglements," and this was taken to mean (among other things) involvement with European territorial disputes in this hemisphere. By 1822–23 most of the Latin American colonies had overthrown Spanish rule, while the so-called Holy Alliance nations were plotting to restore it on behalf of the divine right of kings. At this point, Pres. James Monroe and Secretary of State John Quincy Adams, alluding to the Washington warning, worked out a declaration (the "Monroe Doctrine"), without legal force, intended to serve as notice to the Holy Alliance that the USA would resist any efforts of European powers to take over any territories in North or South America. Though largely ignored, this declaration remained the basis of U.S. foreign policy for generations, and it was a specific rationalization for the Mexican war (1846–48). To avoid any possible British or Hudson's Bay Company seizure of California, Commodore Stockton took possession of that territory for the USA early in the war. On Feb. 2, 1848, the Treaty of Guadalupe Hidalgo forced the Mexican government to cede California—legalizing this immense land grab. The coincidence: On Jan. 24, 1848, James Marshall had discovered gold in the American River at Sutter's Mill in the Coloma area, near Sacramento.

Sometime in the following May, the Mormon Sam Brannan rode horseback through San Francisco streets yelling "Gold! Gold! Gold on the American River!", with results that might have been compared to yelling "Fire!" in a crowded theater. In the next 18 months, over 75,000 gold seekers arrived from the East Coast, creating a frontier lifestyle, sending prices of all kinds of goods and services skyrocketing, flooding world markets with gold bullion so that its value in terms of silver dollars shrank—or, what is the same thing, silver coins' value rose in terms of gold until they became worth more melted down as bullion than their face value, and a coin shortage developed. Dozens of coining companies also undertook the hazardous journey to the gold fields, overland via St. Joseph, Mo., or around Cape Horn, or via steamer to Chagres (on the Isthmus of Panama), up the Chagres River and overland to Panama City, thence by steamer to San Francisco. They braved shipwreck, epidemics, vitamin-deficiency diseases, sunstroke, tropical infections, starvation, hostile Indians, and sometimes even battle: A chronic cold war repeatedly heated up between Panama and Colombian authorities. Small wonder, then, that many of the companies which had intended to make coins from native gold had to spend their cash and abandon their heavier equipment en route. Once in California, they were not automatically better off. Bullion dealers paid $6 to $8 per oz. for gold ore,

shipping much of it back to the Philadelphia Mint at $16 to $18 per oz. Frauds and swindles were numerous. The Custom House (source of almost all necessary goods other than the few locally made) would release nothing except in exchange for treasury notes, legal-tender foreign gold coins, or federal silver or gold—siphoning off most of the specie that managed to enter the area. Neither gold dust, nuggets, nor privately made ingots or coins were acceptable for customs duties.

Nevertheless, in response to acute public need, many local firms somehow managed to make dies and stamp locally mined bullion, at first into rectangular ingots, then—as more heavy machinery arrived or could be locally built—into coins. Public concern with ingots and coins was always whether they contained their face value in bullion. Native gold ranged from about 850–925 Fine, averaging close to 880, the remainder being silver and trace elements. Most firms made no attempt to refine the gold, other than bringing substandard melts up to 880 or so by using proofing pieces (Chap. 40, final section). Usually they made their coins a little heavier than federal standard, expecting that this would compensate for any deviation in fineness—at least enough to avoid denunciation for debasement. This procedure allowed many coins to circulate that otherwise might not have. A few firms alloyed their coins with copper, but this practice (which was rare, as copper was scarce) was frowned on. Nevertheless, abuses were frequent, and scandals followed, together with recurrent public disapproval of private coins. The consistent exception was the issues of Moffat & Co., which firm enjoyed a reputation so unimpeachable that its coins always passed at par everywhere except the Custom House.

The very first private coiner's name is uncertain. We know him only as "Dr. M.," originally from Baltimore. He worked around the end of Dec. 1848, and is thought to have been responsible for the anonymous $10 ingot of 1849, no. **7770**. (Baltimore *Sun,* Feb. 19, 1849, cited in Kagin {1981}.) The first firm whose members' names are known was Norris, Gregg & Norris, i.e., Thomas H. Norris, Charles Gregg, and Hiram A. Norris, originally of 62 Gold St., New York City. This firm coined $5's at Benicia City in May 1849, similar to federal issues in design except for the SAN FRANCISCO imprint and initials N G & N. These have not survived, though later coins made by the same firm survive in quantity.

By the end of 1849, some 18 coining firms were in action in California, most though not all in the San Francisco area. The federal government took no action against them, aside from ruling that their output could not be used in payment of customs duties. No law then existed against private coinage so long as it neither defrauded the public nor fraudulently misrepresented itself as federal issue (i.e., counterfeited U.S. gold or silver coins). This loophole remained open long after the Gold Rush, only being closed by the Act of June 8, 1864 (aimed at makers of Civil War tokens), which forbade manufacture of coins of original design or imitating those of any country to pass current as money. Conceivably, the wording of this statute (as of Title 18, U.S. Code, Sect. 486) might be interpreted to ban the output of any private mint (e.g., the Franklin Mint) engaged in making coins to circulate in other countries; in practice, contracts with governments of those other countries have been held to constitute legal authority exempting private mints from such prohibition.

There were three major periods of private gold issue in California:

I. *Winter 1848/9 through April 1850.* Unofficially ended, about Jan. 1850, by public disclosure of debasement of the Pacific Co. and Mormon gold coins, among other issues. Thereafter, private gold (except that of Moffat & Co.) traded only at 8% discount. Officially ended by Acts of April 8 and 20, 1850: The April 8 act (a dead letter) forbade issue of any gold piece of under 4 oz. weight (about $64), the April 20 act required all private coiners to redeem their product at face value on demand (unenforceable, as federal coins were unavailable).

II. *May 1850 through March 1851.* The State Assay Office under O. P. Sutton and Frederick D. Kohler set up branches in San Francisco and Sacramento, authorized to issue rectangular ingots of at least 2 oz. weight, officially stamped with weight, fineness, and value. They made $50 ingots in quantity, which passed as money, and odd denominations like $37.31, the latter theoretically for bullion storage. In practice, any State Assay ingots freely circulated in the gambling casinos and wherever else anyone would accept them in payments. For reasons not altogether clear, the State Assay Office ended its own operations Jan. 29, 1851, just before the arrival of Augustus Humbert as United States Assayer. Possibly legal counsel had reminded the State Assay Office directors that California's admission to the Union as a state made any further issues unconstitutional: No state could coin money.

Period II saw the rise and fall of a few private coiners, competitors to Moffat & Co., issuing enormous quantities of gold coins, reaping immense profits. Late in March 1851, the banker-turned-muckraker James King of William saw his chance for a coup: He sent samples of his rivals' coins to Augustus Humbert, United States Assayer, to reveal any deficiencies in weight or fineness. Humbert rated them at from 97% to 99% of face value, not from fraud but from problems in technology. King gleefully sent these results to local newspapers, correctly anticipating that his fellow muckrakers would denounce the coins (except Moffat's) as debased: Kagin {1981}, pp. 127–30; Breen {1983}, p. 6. When the newspapers began their smear campaign against Baldwin & Co. (until then the biggest private issuer of all), the legislature passed the Act of April 21, 1851, requiring all private coiners to redeem their product in federal coins or go to prison for five years or pay fines of $500 to $5,000. King and his fellow bankers then began posing as public benefactors: They generously offered to take the coins off holders' hands at discounts of only 20% below face value, and made millions by reselling them to Humbert for recoinage into octagonal $50's. This created a coin shortage, which worsened into 1852: See discussion in Chap. 40, introductory text. For political reasons, Humbert's provisional mint was forbidden to issue coins of lower denominations, and later the Custom House was forbidden to accept even Humbert ingots; the coin shortage became severe enough to create hardship, arguably creating and certainly worsening a business panic. Many firms collapsed, many citizens lost jobs and went hungry; meanwhile James King of William and his fellow bankers amassed large fortunes.

III. *Jan. 1852 through 1856.* Where Humbert as U.S. Assayer could do nothing to alleviate the coin shortage, private coiners stepped in. Moffat & Co. briefly coined $10's and $20's (until federal authorization finally enabled Humbert to make them); Wass, Molitor & Co. made $5's in quantity and smaller amounts of $10's and $20's, which federal authorities rated as so close to face value that James King of William and his cronies could do nothing against them. Federal silver coins passed at 3% premium when available at all, which was seldom; most regular United States coins went on a one-way trip to the Custom House.

Beginning about July or Aug. 1852, local manufacturing jewelers in San Francisco began issuing fractional gold coins: 25¢, 50¢, and $1 denominations. These were frankly token issues, suitable for small change ($1 then bought a bowl of soup at the cheapest restaurants), and containing about 75% to 80% of face value in bullion. This disadvantage was small compared to the 1848–49 use of pinches of gold dust, which had resumed during the coin shortage. Cambists of 1855 listed "California Dollars" at 98¢ each, "California Gold Half Dollars" at 48¢, side by side with 1849 N G & N $5's at $4.75 and (1849) Miner's Bank $10's at $9.75. (See ill. in Breen {1983}, p. 50.) Issues of gold fractional coins continued through 1856.

Closure of the U.S. Assay Office in Dec. 1853 was expected to lead to immediate opening of the federal branch mint in San Francisco. But the latter establishment did not begin to issue coins until April 1854, and then only in quantities too small to alleviate the coin shortage. On the same day that the Assay Office closed, Kellogg & Co. opened; in response to urgent requests from local bankers, they began issuing $20's in quantity beginning Feb. 9, 1854, and through the end of 1855.

All these private coinage operations ended in 1856, possibly on official request, after the San Francisco branch mint obtained enough parting acids to issue enough legal coins to alleviate the coin shortage. But by then the Gold Rush was over.

California private coinages herein are arranged in a sequence unlike any previously attempted: Within each of the three periods, order is alphabetic. No strict chronological sequence is possible because on the one hand many coiners were working simultaneously during fall 1849, and on the other the actual time of issue of some pieces is unknown. Moffat & Co., which overlapped all three periods, is placed in Period I because its continuous issue began in 1849. The State Assay Office ingots are at the beginning of Period II. Humbert's United States Assay Office, which otherwise would occupy most of Period II and III, has Chap. 40 to itself. The fractional gold coins occupy a large segment of Period III, grouped together for convenience by denomination and shape. The present study makes no attempt to describe bullion storage ingots, or patterns known to exist only in base metals. Research here is ongoing, but the most recent discoveries in all these lines—including the most controversial specimens—are described in detail in Kagin {1981}. Kagin numbers are from the latter; KM numbers from *SCWC;* BG numbers (on fractionals) from Breen {1983}.

i. PERIOD I: 1849–APRIL 1850

1. ANONYMOUS

7770   1849 Ten Dollars. Rectangular. Unique?
    Kagin 2, p. 312. Specie ingot, CAL/49/GOLD. Rev., TEN/ DOLLARS. Not punchlinked to anything else. Conjecturally attributed to "Dr. M.," of Baltimore, winter 1848–49; see

introductory text. Authentication of this or any similar item is mandatory.   1) Kagin coll.

2. J. H. BOWIE

Joseph Haskins Bowie (1818–79), of the Maryland Bowies, departed for California on the frigate *St. Andrews,* March 12, 1849, with his cousins Hyde Ray and Hamilton Bowie, arriving sometime that summer to join his other cousin, Dr. Augustus Bowie, Navy surgeon, who set up his practice at Clay and Dupont Sts., San Francisco, across from the Moffat & Co. office. Nothing is known of the actual coinage, which must have been very limited as local newspapers never mentioned it. Don Kagin, who discovered what little is known about the issuer, conjectures that Broderick & Kohler may have done the actual striking on Bowie's behalf (see *Miners Bank* below), and that most of the output would have been melted early for profit. The low stated fineness discouraged circulation; the high bullion value would have encouraged buying up for recoinage. Stated weight 137 grs. at 879 Fine = 120.4 grs. fine gold per $5 as against 116.1 per federal $5 = $5.168 each. Until the comparatively recent discovery of the $5, this firm was known only by a copper pattern dollar, marked 24 G. 24 C. If any gold specimens were struck of the latter, they vanished even more quickly for the same reason, entirely aside from the softness of 24-carat gold which makes it impractical for coinage.

7771   1849 5 DOLLARS. 2 known.
Kagin 1, p. 282; KM 22. Pine tree, CAL GOLD above, 1849 below. Rev., name, denomination 879/137 GRS.   1) Ford, Bank of California. 132.7 grs. = 8.599 gms.   2) Colorado coll., Don Kagin, Texas pvt. coll.

3. CINCINNATI MINING & TRADING CO.

Originally known as the California Mining & Trading Co. of Cincinnati, this firm was organized on or about Jan. 1, 1849, with J. H. Levering, president, W. B. Norman, vice president, David Kinsey, treasurer, and Samuel T. Jones, secretary, among 50 members in all, each of whom subscribed $500 for expenses of the journey to California. Don Kagin has provided evidence that the dies were made by H. & W. Johnson (later known for Civil War token dies) at Nixon & Co.'s paper mill in Cincinnati, and that Broderick & Kohler (who also coined for the Pacific Co. and the Miners Bank) struck them sometime between Aug. and Dec. 1849. After the discredit of Broderick & Kohler, the Cincinnati coins were most likely melted in quantity as of too low fineness. Survivors are so rare that grade is irrelevant.

7772   1849 FIVE DOLLARS, Plain edge. Unique?
Kagin 1, p. 283; KM 23. Similar to the $10's.   1) Lilly, SI. Clain-Stefanelli {1970}, fig. 52. 132.5 grs. = 8.586 gms. Enl. photos.

7773   1849 TEN DOLLARS. Reeded edge. Ex. rare.
Kagin 3, p. 283; KM 24. Die break from lower beak to F(ORNIA). Beware of white-metal forgeries, some misspelled TRACING CO.   1) Woodward (1884), Zabriskie, Ellsworth, Garrett:885, EF, 257.6 grs. = 16.69 gms., $270,000.   2) Spink 8/14, Brand II:1539, $104,500, struck over a J.S.O. $10 (**7796**), EF, 256.7 grs. = 16.63 gms.   3) Fishel, Brand, Kosoff, VF, 258.2 grs. = 16.73 gms.

Ex J. W. Garrett: 885. Courtesy Bowers & Ruddy Galleries, Inc.

7774   1849 TEN DOLLARS. Same dies, plain edge. Unique?
Kagin 2, p. 283. Die broken as preceding.   1) Chapman, Brand, Newcomer, Lilly, SI. 257.9 grs. = 16.71 gms. Clain-Stefanelli {1970}, fig. 52.

4. MASSACHUSETTS & CALIFORNIA CO.

The most probable issuer of the speculative coins bearing this title was the Massachusetts & California Gold Co., of Northampton, Mass.: Josiah Hayden (manufacturer of gold pens), president; Annis Merrill, cashier; William H. Hayden, assayer; Rev. Frederick P. Tracy, company agent. Organized Jan. 15, 1849, capitalized eventually at $50,000, the firm met annually in Northampton until Jan. 1854, while Merrill, William H. Hayden, Tracy, and some others left for California, May 26, 1849. Apparently their coining press and other heavy equipment, though shipped May 21 aboard the *Alice Tarlton,* never reached California. Most likely the extant coins were produced as samples in Massachusetts; they reportedly have enough copper alloy to make this probable. The only var. accepted as a genuine 1849 product is **7775**. Other vars.—in gold, silver, nickel, copper, and various other metals, without denomination, or with 5 DOLLARS, or with FIVE D. and more modern letters—are concoctions produced by or for Stephen K. Nagy early in the present century. No complete catalog of these has been made to date; all are Ex. rare. In Clifford:58–70, 13 different Nagy vars. are described and illustrated.

7775   1849 FIVE D. Reeded edge. Ex. rare.
Kagin 1, p. 292; KM 35. Clain-Stefanelli {1970}, fig. 53. Arms, vaquero throwing lasso, proper; supporters, bear (dexter) and stag; crest, arm holding arrow, on torse; motto ALTA, 'Upper' (the part of California which joined the Union, as distinct from *Baja,* 'Lower [California],' the Mexican peninsula). Note 8 berries on each branch, and denomination FIVE D. rather than any other form. Kagin gives weight as 115.5 grs. = 7.484 gms., impossibly low unless at 999+ Fine.

5. MEYERS & CO.

Nothing is known of this firm, not even its location. The fabric strongly suggests deliberate emulation of the Moffat & Co. $16 ingots of July 1849, which is why this piece is assigned to Period I.

7776 n.d. (1849) $18.00, 1 Oz. Troy. Unique?

Kagin 1, p. 292. Rectangular specie ingot, the 1 before OZ.TROY and the value $18.00 stamped separately into the finished piece, as are U.S. STANDARD/WARRANTED on rev. 1) Levick, Murrell, Clifford:73, $21,000. Theoretical weight 480 grs. = 31.1 gms.; actual weight ?.

6. MINERS BANK

Stephen A. Wright and Samuel Haight, respectively president and cashier of Miners Bank, Portsmouth Square, San Francisco (corner of Washington and Kearny Sts.), vainly attempted to issue paper currency ($1 bills dated March 1, 1849). On Aug. 7, they petitioned the Collector of Customs to receive their proposed $5 and $10 coins—again in vain. Nevertheless, they had the firm of Broderick & Kohler strike $10's in quantity, Oct.–Nov. 1849, at the Kohler & Co. mint in the City Hotel or Jones Building, Clay St. on the south side of Portsmouth Plaza. David C. Broderick did the actual striking, using the ancient hammer method as coining presses were unavailable (James C. L. Wadsworth, Testimony in California Supreme Court, Aug. 20, 1852. Transcript on Appeal, 4th District Court, San Francisco, Case File: Harvey Sparks v. F. D. Kohler and David C. Broderick, #129, State Archives No. 1407, California State Archives, Sacramento, Sect. 10, cited in Kagin {1981}). They stopped coining for Miners Bank on Jan. 1, 1850; the latter firm dissolved Jan. 14.

Because official assays rated these coins at 866 Fine (some even with copper alloy), valued at about $9.65, they became unpopular; brokers valued them at $8 apiece (San Francisco *Daily Alta California,* April 11, 1850, p. 2).

7777 n.d. (1849) TEN. D. Very rare.

Kagin 1, p. 293; KM 36. Mostly EF to UNC. 257.2–259 grs. = 16.67–16.78 gms. Earlier strikings are in orange-colored gold (copper alloy), on broad flans with full border dentils. A hoard of at least 10 UNCs. turned up in Texas in the 1950s, being quietly dispersed to avoid adversely affecting the market. Ellsworth, Garrett:916, UNC., $135,000; Auction 82:989, UNC., $24,000. Dangerous counterfeits exist; authentication is mandatory! Later strikings, from the same dies, are in greenish gold (silver alloy), on narrower flans with almost no border dentils; edge reeding coarser. Kagin 1, p. 293. 1) Clifford:75, $8,250.

7. MOFFAT & CO.

This firm originally comprised four partners: John Little Moffat (1788–18??), Joseph R. Curtis, Philo H. Perry, and Samuel H. Ward. They left New York City on the *Guilford,* Feb. 15, 1849, arriving shortly before June 21, on which date they began advertising in San Francisco papers as "Moffat & Co., Assayers." They had the highest recommendations from such worthies as Robert J. Walker, then Secretary of Treasury, and Beebee, Ludlow & Co., then the largest bullion-dealer firm in the United States. During their four years in business, their repute remained unimpeachable.

They first issued rectangular specie ingots in July 1849, mostly in the denomination $16 **(7778).** Odd denominations such as the $9.43 and $14.25 **(7779–80)** were originally bullion storage ingots (others ranged as high as $256.24), but in the absence of coins they passed at face value in casinos and any other establishments which had accepted gold dust by weight; most were later melted for recoinage.

Beginning in early Aug. 1849, they issued $10 coins; the $5's followed a few weeks later. Dies were by the Bavarian goldsmith Albert Küner (b. Georg Albrecht Ferdinand Küner), who had arrived July 22, becoming Moffat's chief engraver, though he also made dies for many other coiners. Moffat & Co. consistently offered to redeem any of its coins in federal specie at par, with the result that they passed at face value with never a discount, alone among the products of California private mints.

On Jan. 31, 1851, Moffat & Co. received a federal subcontract to make $50 ingots under supervision of Augustus Humbert. Humbert's establishment, later officially "United States Assay Office of Gold," was actually a provisional federal branch mint; for its history and issues see Chap. 40.

Before that date, Moffat & Co. had issued $5's dated 1850, the final batch [17,800] during Jan. 1851; these are believed to be impressions of **7786** from rusted and shattered dies.

The $10's of 1852 **(7787–88)** were coined in response to local petitions, after the Treasury Department had disallowed Humbert's request for authority to issue "ingots" of $10 and $20 denominations. Moffat promptly retired from the firm to work with the San Joaquin Diving Bell Co.

The final issue bearing the MOFFAT & CO. title appeared in July 1853; why these $20's **(7789)** were made simultaneously with the immense output of Assay Office coins of the same denomination **(7723)** is unknown.

On Dec. 14, 1853, Moffat & Co. and the U.S. Assay Office closed for good, all its equipment being bought out by the new federal branch mint. Most of its coins were later melted for recoinage into regular S-Mint gold.

7778 n.d. (July 1849) $16. Very rare.

Kagin 3, p. 294. Standard rectangular specie ingot, approx. 35 × 15 × 3.8 mm. All show a stem spot on blank r. edge. Denomination corresponded to Latin American doubloons then current. Stated weight at 20¾ carats, 436.5 grs. = 28.28 gms.; observed, 432–460 grs. = 27.99–29.81 gms. Eckfeldt & DuBois {1850}. Clifford:83, EF, $13,000; Ellsworth, Garrett:927, VF, $20,000; Auction 82:976, EF, $14,000. Counterfeits exist; authentication recommended.

7779 n.d. (July 1849) $14.25. Unique?

Kagin 2, p. 294. Possibly intended as a bullion-storage ingot, but certainly circulated as money at the time. Stated weight at 21¾ carats: 366 grs. = 23.72 gms. 1) Mehl (1932), Wayte Raymond, F. C. C. Boyd, King Farouk, 1956 ANA:1835, Josiah Lilly, SI.

7780 n.d. (July 1849) $9.43. Unique?

Kagin 1, p. 294. As preceding. 21⁷/₁₆ CARAT. On blank back is punched 10 DWT. 6 GRS. in one line. = 246 grs.; recorded weight, 245.2 grs. = 15.89 gms. 1) Mint, SI. Clain-Stefanelli {1970}, fig. 51. Others formerly existed in higher denominations up to $256.24.

7781 1849 TEN D. Very rare.

Kagin 5, 5a, p. 295; KM 38.3–4. 2 minor vars. Usually weak on central curls; 8 repunched (fades); die buckles at date. Issued Aug. 1849. 257 grs. = 16.65 gms. S.M.V. = "Standard Mint Value." Not to be confused with either of next 2. Usually in low grades. Gibson:194; Beck I:658; Garrett (1976):390, VG, $1,300.

7782 1849 TEN DOL. Large letters. Very rare.

Kagin 6a, p. 296; KM 38.1. Small fine border dentils on both sides; large O's in legend; middle arrow point aims well below period. 258.1 grs. = 16.72 gms. Compare next. Gibson:193, EF; Beck I:657; Clifford:82, F, $1,700; Adams, Garrett:924, ABOUT EF, $4,500.

7783 1849 TEN DOL. Small letters. Very rare.

Kagin 6, p. 296; KM 38.2. Coarser dentils; small o's; straight tail to R (unlike **7781–82**); middle arrow point aims just above period. 257.5 grs. = 16.69 gms. Ellsworth, Garrett:925, ABOUT EF, $5,000.

Ex J. W. Garrett: 925. Courtesy Bowers & Ruddy Galleries, Inc.

7784 1849 FIVE DOL.

Kagin 4, 4a, 4b, pp. 294–95. KM 37.1–3. Several minor vars., differing largely in patterns of die breaks and/or rust. Issued through fall and winter 1849 and probably early 1850. Average weight given as 130.2 grs. = 8.437 gms. Often in low grades. Zabriskie, Ellsworth, Garrett:922, AU, $10,000.

7785 1850 FIVE DOL. Small eagle and branch.

Kagin 7, p. 296; KM 37.4. Minor vars. exist. To distinguish from next, note that branch does not reach M, and eagle's neck is not so curved; its head looks at AL. 129–129.9 grs. = 8.359–8.417 gms. Garrett (1976):391; Gibson:196, $1,600, Wayman:423, AU, $3,200; Auction 82:977, UNC., $6,750. One seen countermarked W.W. LIGHT DENTIST; see J. S. Ormsby, below.

7786 1850 FIVE DOL. Large eagle and branch.

Kagin 7a, p. 296; KM 37.5. Minor vars. exist. Branch lies along base of M; eagle's neck much curved; its head looks at wing. Weight as last. Hesslein, Garrett:923, UNC., $21,000. Rusted-die coins are believed to be issue of Jan. 1851 [17,800].

7787 1852 TEN D. [all kinds 8,590+] Close date, small 880. Very rare.

Kagin 8, p. 297; KM 39.2. Date evenly spaced; NIA much nearer scroll than on next. Issue of Jan. 12, 1852. Stated weight corresponds to standard 263.86 grs. = 17.098 gms. at 880 Fine. Other accounts say [8,650]. Geiss, Carter:1150, EF, $8,800.

7788 1852 TEN D. Wide date, larger 880. Very rare.

Kagin 9, p. 297; KM 39.1. Date irregularly spaced, 85 leaning away from 2. Zabriskie, Ellsworth, Garrett:926, EF, 262.9 grs. = 17.04 gms., $7,000; "Bell," "Memorable":970, Auction 82:981, "Proof(?)," $16,000.

7789 1853 TWENTY D. [75,000+] Rare.

Kagin 19 (under USAOG); KM 40. 512.3–516.1 grs. = 33.2–33.44 gms. Other accounts say [75,636]. Issued July–Oct. 1853. Rev. die reused by Kellogg & Co., 1854 (**7917**). W. J. Jenks, Garrett:928, VF, $4,000; Auction 82:988, UNC., $7,500.

8. NORRIS, GREGG & NORRIS

The firm of this name manufactured ironmongery at 62 Gold (!) St., between Beekman and Fulton Sts., New York City, as late as 1849. Its three members, Thomas H. Norris, Charles Gregg, and Hiram A. Norris, left for the California goldfields early in 1849; neither departure nor arrival dates were recorded. In May 1849 they manufactured half eagles at Benicia City, of a design unknown today. The notice in the *Daily Alta California,* May 31, 1849, indicates that their coins almost certainly bore the usual imitation federal Liberty head and eagle, like the later Moffat & Co. coins, but with N G & N on coronet, and SAN FRANCISCO CAL. around eagle. Later in the year, the firm obtained new dies from Albert Küner, of a design unlike any others, and issued large quantities of **7790–93.** Philadelphia Mint assays rated three of their coins at 870, 880, and 892 Fine, bullion value $4.83, $4.89 and $4.95 plus about 2½¢ extra in

each for the silver content. Possibly the four known 1849 vars. may signal different finenesses. Weights on all cluster closely around 129 grs. = 8.36 gms.

Before April 6, 1850, they moved out of Benicia City to Stockton, where they coined the type with STOCKTON below date 1850. Establishment of the State Assay Office in the same month may have occasioned their discontinuance.

No grading standards are established; we suggest EXTREMELY FINE: Full 5 on shield. UNCIRCULATED: *No* trace of wear.

7790 1849 HALF EAGLE. Period after ALLOY. Reeded edge.

Kagin 4, p. 299; KM 41.3. Auction 82:975, UNC., $10,000.

7791 1849 HALF EAGLE. Period after ALLOY. Plain edge. Rare.

Kagin 2, p. 299; KM 41.1. Ellsworth, Garrett:931, UNC., $37,500; Auction 82:974, UNC., $6,750; Carter:1151, AU, $10,450.

7792 1849 HALF EAGLE. No period after ALLOY Reeded edge. Very rare.

Kagin 3, p. 299; KM 41.4. Auction 82:484, EF, $3,750.

7793 1849 HALF EAGLE. No period after ALLOY Plain edge.

Kagin 1, p. 299; KM 41.2.

7794 1850 STOCKTON. Plain edge. Unique?

Kagin 5, p. 299; KM 42. STOCKTON instead of SAN FRANCISCO; 16 stars, unlike the 22 on 1849's. Discovered in Stockton, early 1958. 1) Stockton jeweler, Earl Parker, duPont, Golden I:3004, 1967 KS:605, plugged, $18,500.

9. J. S. ORMSBY

Dr. John S. Ormsby, his brother Maj. William M. Ormsby, and their clerk O. H. Pierson, left Pennsylvania overland in spring 1849, departing St. Joseph, Mo., on April 14, arriving in Sacramento (the nearest large trade center to the goldfields) in late Sept. or early Oct. 1849. They opened a gold-smelting and -coining establishment at 140 K St., beneath the Golden Eagle Saloon, near Front St. They coined native gold without any attempt to refine it. Blanks were imperfectly annealed, which meant that many cracked, laminated, or split, others were "dumb" (failing to ring owing to occluded gas bubbles) or porous. They struck 5 DOLLS. and 10 DOLLS. pieces that fall, charging a high seignorage (close to 6%). To improve their coins' physical quality, they briefly hired a leading dental surgeon, Dr. William W. Light, assigning him the task of refining the bullion at $50 per day, but Dr. Light promptly quit to try mining on his own. Issue was extensive, but independent assays showed that the coins were debased (bullion value of a $10 was only $9.37), and public denunciations immediately followed. Most of the coins were melted.

Dr. Ormsby went back to Pennsylvania, but—evidently unafraid of showing his face in the gold districts after his coins' repudiation—returned to California with his wife. He set up medical practice in Sonoma County, eventually being elected to the state legislature. His former clerk Pierson went into partnership with Dr. Light in a Sacramento dental clinic. Maj. W. M. Ormsby became an auctioneer, stock and carriage dealer, afterward establishing a stage line and a real estate business. A few years later, he laid out the town of Carson City, Nev., built a hotel there in 1858, and died in battle against the Paiute Indians near Winnemucca, May 12, 1860. Ormsby County in Nevada is named for him.

The coins are so rare that grade is irrelevant. All are weakly and unevenly struck, presumably by sledgehammer.

7795 n.d. (fall 1849) 5 DOLLS. Unique?
Kagin 1, p. 300; KM 43. Similar to next, but 13 stars above DOLLS., 7 below. Discovery, *NUM* 7/11, p. 248. 129.1 grs. = 8.366 gms. 1) Jacob B. Moore, Sr. (first postmaster), Jacob B. Moore, Jr., Edgar H. Adams, J. W. Scott, Frank Smith, Waldo Newcomer, F. C. C. Boyd, Josiah Lilly, SI.

7796 n.d. (fall 1849) 10 DOLLS. Ex. rare.
Kagin 2, p. 300; KM 44. 1) Mint, SI. 258.5 grs. = 16.75 gms. Clain-Stefanelli {1970}, fig. 54. 2) Reimers, Cartwright, DeWitt Smith, Brand II:1540, F, 256 grs. = 16.59 gms. 3) A. Humbert, Zabriskie, Ellsworth, Garrett:933, F, $100,000. Enl. photos. 4) B.G. Johnson, Pointer, Leo A. Young, Klausen, 1973 ANA:1000, VF, $37,500. 5) Reimers, Smith, Cartwright, Brand, Boyd, duPont. VF.

Ex J. W. Garrett: 933. Courtesy Bowers & Ruddy Galleries, Inc.

10. PACIFIC COMPANY

Of the four firms using this or any similar title, the chronology best fits the Pacific Company, founded Jan. 8, 1849, by John W. Cartwright, 32 India St., Boston, with eventually 37 other subscribers. Each member contributed $1,000 toward the journey to California. They bought the ship *York,* and departed April 1, 1849, arriving in San Francisco Sept. 16. The group then headed for the goldfields nearest to Benicia City and disbanded, Oct. 8–20. Kagin has conjectured that they sold their dies (one pair each for $1, $2½, $5, and $10 denominations) to Broderick & Kohler (see Miners Bank above), who struck $5's and $10's by sledgehammer. Early assays valued them at $4.48 per $5 coin, $7.86 per $10. Most were melted in the general discredit of Period I private gold, the bullion going into either State Assay Office ingots or Humbert $50's. Of the $1, only silver and tin trial pieces survive (there is no proof any gold strikings were ever made); of the $2½, four silver trial pieces (e.g., Garrett:934), none in other metals: Kagin {1981}.

All denominations are so rare that grade is irrelevant.

7797 1849 5 DOLLARS. Reeded edge. Ex. rare.
Kagin 1, p. 301; KM 45. 1) Mint, SI. Clain-Stefanelli {1970}, fig. 55. 2) DeWitt Smith, Cartwright, Virgil Brand, Horace L. P. Brand, Robert Friedberg, Brand-Lichtenfels:2211, Gibson:200, $90,000 (1974), Wayman:417, "AU," $85,000, Coles:252, 157, 750. Nearly UNC., scratches above eagle's head. 3) Garrett:935, VF, $180,000. 129.7 grs. = 8.404 gms. Enl. photos. 4) Charles M. Williams, 1951, $5,000, Willis duPont.

Ex J. W. Garrett: 935. Courtesy Bowers & Ruddy Galleries, Inc.

7798 1849 10 DOLLARS. Reeded edge. Ex. rare.
Kagin 3, p. 301; KM 46.2. 1) Virgil Brand, Horace L. P.

Brand, Robert Friedberg, Brand-Lichtenfels:2210, $24,000 (1964), Josiah Lilly, SI, EF, 228.4 grs. = 14.8 gms. Clain-Stefanelli {1970}, fig. 55.   2) Newcomer, $8,000, Charles M. Williams, 1951, $12,500, Willis duPont.   3) DeWitt Smith, Brand II:1544, AU, $132,000. 256.8 grs. = 16.64 gms.

7799 1849 10 DOLLARS. Same dies. Plain edge. Ex. rare.
Kagin 2, p. 301; KM 46.1. Kagin gives weight as 229 grs. = 14.84 gms.

ii. PERIOD II:
May 1850–March 1851

1. STATE ASSAY OFFICE (May 13, 1850– Jan. 29, 1851)

The Act of April 20, 1850 established this as an alternative to any more lightweight private gold coins. Gov. Peter Burnett appointed O. P. Sutton as director and, of all unlikely choices, Frederick D. Kohler (maker of the lightweight Pacific Co. and Cincinnati Mining & Trading Co. coins) as assayer. Possibly Burnett believed that the circumstances of the job would keep Kohler honest. The Assay Office's mandate was to issue rectangular ingots weighing at least 2 oz. each, officially stamped with weight, fineness, and value. As the Act of April 8, 1850 had forbidden issue of any gold piece of less than 4 oz. (about $64), most likely the authorities believed that the Assay Office would be melting all the discredited private gold coins and issuing ingots instead. Doubtless this law did dispose of many of the lightweight Period I coins, explaining their rarity. However, it proved a dead letter. Moffat's 1850 $5's were mostly struck before the Act went into effect, but this firm also made others in early 1851 from 1850-dated dies **(7786)**. Presumably public confidence in Moffat & Co. encouraged continued circulation of their coins.

Sutton began operations at the San Francisco office, May 13, 1850, through Jan. 29, 1851. For most of that time he did the melting, assaying, and stamping at the Baldwin & Co. building on the south side of Clay St., at Portsmouth Square. Kohler opened the Sacramento office at Third and J Sts., July 1, 1850; it apparently closed at the same time as the San Francisco office, in anticipation of arrival of Augustus Humbert as federal assayer. Because many of these State Assay Office ingots (particularly those in the convenient $50 denomination) were acceptable in the gambling casinos and in most places which had formerly accepted gold dust, they formed an important part of circulating money of the time. However, their issue was illegal for that very reason: The federal Constitution forbids states to issue money, and California's admission to the Union in Sept. 1850 required adherence to constitutional law. There is no evidence that anyone attempted to suppress State Assay Office operations because of this technicality; to do so would have been to create a worse coin shortage than already existed.

All State Assay Office ingots are of similar appearance, bearing punched-in logotypes or gang punches naming F.D.KOHLER as STATE ASSAYER, CAL., with individually punched numerals for CARAT, weight in DWT. and GRS., value in $ and CT.S, with date 1850. Those from the Sacramento office also have SAC. on front and Kohler's name and title on blank back. Some have STATE ASSAYER, with or without Kohler's name, logotyped on edges. At present all survivors are of different denominations, each being technically unique. Bowers (at Garrett:911) quotes an article from the *Daily Alta California,* Nov. 20, 1868, to the effect that the Kohler ingots were known as "slugs," that the largest ones were cut down to about the size herein illustrated, that the $50 denomination was issued in quantity, that all passed as money in

the casinos, and that the Philadelphia Mint assays valued a Kohler $50 at $52.

a. SAN FRANCISCO OFFICE

7800 1850 $37.31. Unique?
Kagin 1, p. 290. 22 CARAT. 40 DWT. Stated weight = 960 grs. = 62.2 gms.   1) Farouk:345, Ford, Lilly, SI.

7801 1850 $40.07. Unique? Unlocated.
Kagin 2, p. 290. 21⅛ CARAT. 44¾ DWT. Stated weight = 1,074 grs. = 69.59 gms. Stolen from the Mint Cabinet Collection, Aug. 16, 1858; never recovered, almost certainly melted down.

7802 1850 $41.68 Unique?
Kagin 3, p. 290. 21⅜ CARAT. 46 DWT. Stated weight = 1,104 grs. = 71.53 gms.   1) New Netherlands, Lilly, SI. In 46, 6 corrected from 1.

7803 1850 $45.34. Unique?
Kagin 4, p. 291. 21½ CARAT. 49¾ DWT. Edge, STATE (west) ASSAYER (east). Stated weight = 1,194 grs. = 77.37 gms.   1) Bruce Cartwright (1907), Virgil Brand, B. G. Johnson, King Farouk, New Netherlands (1956), Lilly, SI.

7804 1850 $50.00. Unique?
Kagin 5, p. 291. 20¹⁵⁄₁₆ CARAT. 56⅕ DWT. All 4 edges

Ex J. W. Garrett: 911. Courtesy Bowers & Ruddy Galleries, Inc.

show STATE ASSAYER. 1,348.9 grs. = 87.41 gms. 1) Dr. Spiers, Society of California Pioneers (ca. 1877), Fred Huddart, Waldo Newcomer, Mehl (1931), Garrett:911, $200,000.

7805 1850 $54.09. Unique? Unlocated.
Kagin 6, p. 291. 21 CARAT. 60¾ DWT. Edge not described but likely to be as preceding. Stated weight = 1,458 grs. = 94.48 gms. Known from description in Richardson {1867}.

b. SACRAMENTO OFFICE

7806 1850 $36.55. Unique?
Kagin 7, p. 291. 20 CARAT. 42 DWT. 12 GRS. SAC°. Rev., F.D.KOHLER/STATE ASSAYER. Stated weight = 1,020 grs. = 66.09 gms. 1) H. L. Taylor (1908), Virgil Brand, F. C. C. Boyd, Farouk:346, Lilly, SI.

7807 1850 $47.71. Unique?
Kagin 8, p. 292. 21 CARAT. 51 DWT. 2 GRS. Rev., similar to preceding. West and east edges (short edges) logotyped F.D.KOHLER; north and south (long) edges, STATE ASSAYER. Stated weight = 1,226 grs. = 79.44 gms. 1) New Netherlands (1956). Other denominations certainly existed and may still survive. Authentication is mandatory.

2. ADAMS & CO.

This was a Boston "express and forwarding agency" which opened a San Francisco branch in Oct. 1849 on the east side of Montgomery St., north of California St., under D. H. Haskell, manager. The firm diversified, like its competitor Wells Fargo & Co., entering the banking business. Between Oct. and Dec. 1851 it accumulated enough odd bullion to place an order with its near neighbor Wass Molitor & Co. to assay it and form it into ingots to be stamped with ADAMS & CO. and value. One of the two known specimens is a bullion-storage ingot reading ADAMS & C°/N° 934/881 THOUS/$54.33 at l.; DWT/57¹/₁₂ at r.; below, SMV/DOLS CTS./54.33. Shorter edges read 1851 and CAL; longer, W.M. & Co. ASSRS and SAN FRANCISCO (Kagin 1, p. 272). On the other (below), absence of serial number or stated weight suggests that it was intended as a specie ingot. Certainly it would have circulated in the gambling casinos. The piece is controversial; no alloy tests have been performed, no punch linkage with other ingots demonstrated. Use of individual punches instead of logotypes argues against a large issue.

7808 n.d. (1851) 5 D. Unique?
Letters individually punched. 1) Ford, Lilly, SI.

3. BALDWIN & CO.

George C. Baldwin and Thomas S. Holman had a jewelry, watchmaking, and later assaying and coining business on Clay St. on the south side of Portsmouth Plaza. On March 15, 1850, the partners bought out F. D. Kohler's assaying and coining apparatus (as Kohler was then anticipating appointment to the office of State Assayer, which duly occurred six weeks later). On May 1, Baldwin & Co. began advertising in the *Pacific News* (p. 4) as "Successors to F.D.KOHLER & Co./Assayers, refiners and coiners/Manufacturers of jewelry, etc./George C. Baldwin and Thos. S. Holman./All kinds of engraving. Our coins redeemable on presentation." Their operation was evidently successful, as during the first three months of 1851 alone they coined at least $590,000 face value—$60,000 more than Humbert's federal Assay Office! Part of the reason for this volume of coinage was that melting of many of the Period I coiners' $5, $10, and $20 pieces left a coin shortage, and Moffat & Co. instead issued octagonal $50's under their subcontract with

Humbert, failing to relieve the shortage of smaller denominations. Local banks and merchants (including Edward E. Dunbar's California Bank, Tucker & Reeve, etc.) advertised that they would accept Baldwin's coins at face value.

However, in March 1851, the muckraker James King of William, allegedly in the interest of public morality, submitted specimens of various current gold coins to Augustus Humbert for assay, and sent the results to all the local newspapers, in the hope of discrediting all the private coiners. Humbert's assays described the Baldwin $20's as averaging 516^{10}/$_{32}$ grs. at 871 Fine, value $19.40; $10's, 259.5 grs. at 872 Fine, value $9.74; $5's, 130^{11}/$_{14}$ grs. at 871 Fine, value $4.91. (A few months later, Eckfeldt & DuBois {1851} quoted Philadelphia Mint assays of Baldwin $10's at $9.96 true value, or only 1¢ less than Moffat's; but by then the damage was done.) Newspapers blew this roughly 3% discount into a resounding scandal, enhancing King's reputation as a purported defender of the public interest, but forcing Baldwin and his later partner (a Mr. Bagley) to leave California for good on April 15. James King of William and fellow bankers thereafter bought up Baldwin's $10's and $20's at $8 and $16, respectively, and enriched themselves by reselling them in quantity at much higher figures as bullion to Augustus Humbert for recoinage into octagonal $50's. By Dec. 1851, Baldwin's coins were seldom seen at all; today all are rare, the 1851 $10 and $20 Ex. rare.

No grading standards are established. All Baldwin dies are by Küner.

7809   1850 FIVE DOL. Rare.

2 minor vars.: heavy date, Kagin 2, p. 279; thin date and stars (same obv. reground?); KM 17 ill.; cf. Beck I:712–13. Reeded edge. SM.V. = "Standard Mint Value." Final A in CALIFORNIA first punched inverted (rotated 180°), then corrected. Color varies: The more orange specimens apparently contain some copper alloy, the more greenish only the native silver. 130.2–132.5 grs. = 8.437–8.586 gms. On the coins with thin date and stars, die breaks develop: from rim through M.V. to wing (Garrett:877); later, from rim below date to twelfth star; finally, through last 5 stars, heavily out to border above ninth star: S 6/83:826. Stickney, Zabriskie, Ellsworth, Garrett:877, EF, $10,000, Ron Gillo.

7810   1850 TEN DOLLARS. Very rare.

Kagin 3, p. 279; KM 18. *Vaquero,* 'Cowboy' or 'Horseman' design, signed A.KUNER on ground below horse. Reeded edge. The small s in DOLLARs represents an awkward solution to a layout problem. 263.1–263.8 grs. = 17.04–17.09 gms. The distinctive design contributes to its extreme popularity. Beck I:714, UNC., $62,500 (1975); Auction 79:1470, UNC., $50,000; Zabriskie, Raymond, Garrett:878, AU, $77,500. "Restrikes" from copy dies (ca. 1906–10?) have modern letters; see ill. at Garrett:879.

7811   1851 TEN D. 8–10 known.

Kagin 4, p. 280; KM 19. Reeded edge. Later strikings, e.g., Kaufman:50, S 6/83:829, have rim break over fourth star. 259.5–259.9 grs. = 16.82–16.84 gms. Beck I:716, cleaned EF, $12,500 (1975); Auction 79:1471, AU, $16,500; Nygren, Garrett:880, EF, $32,500.

7812   1851 TWENTY D. Possibly 4 known.

Kagin 5, p. 280; KM 20. Reeded edge. BALDWIN&C on coronet (a spacing problem).   1) Nygren, Garrett:881, VF, $110,000.   2) Charles M. Williams, "Melish":2331, Lilly, SI.   3) Clifford, Kagin.   4) Clifford, Bank of California.

4. DIANA GAMBLING HOUSE

This was one of the largest of the San Francisco casinos. It fronted the entire north side of Portsmouth Square, from Clay St. to Commercial St. Like its Las Vegas successors, it also provided drinks and various kinds of entertainment in an atmosphere of luxury. Proprietors were James William, D. Webster, and Stephen Whipple. Though all casinos accepted rectangular ingots as well as octagonal ones and round coins, apparently at least this one (again like its Las Vegas imitators) saw the advertising possibilities in stamping its own tokens, perhaps for use as counters within its walls.

7813   n.d. (1851?) TWENTY DOLLARS. 2 known.

Kagin 1, p. 284; KM 25. 35 mm. Reeded edge.   1) Ford, Lilly, SI.   2) Kagin, Ford. Enl. photos.

5. DUBOSQ & CO.

Theodore Dubosq, Sr. (jeweler, of North Second St., Philadelphia), Theodore Dubosq, Jr. (of Baltimore), and Henry A. Dubosq, left Philadelphia for San Francisco aboard the *Grey Eagle,* on or about Jan. 18, 1849, bringing along machinery for melting and coining native gold. They arrived on May 18. The senior Dubosq took in another partner, a Mr. Goodwin, in 1850. During Period I they apparently coined little or no gold; none has survived, nor have we seen references to such coins in newspapers of the time. However, in 1850–51 the firm struck immense quantities of $5 and $10 pieces, from dies dated 1850: some $150,000 during the first quarter of 1851 alone, which would mean ballpark figures of 10,000 of each denomination. As James Barton Longacre had patterns for these coins in his estate, some students have claimed that this artist jeopardized his already precarious Mint engravership to make dies for his old friends the Dubosqs. At least equally likely: Longacre may have contemplated a move to California as a diesinker if his enemies in the Mint (Director Robert Maskell Patterson and Coiner Franklin Peale) managed to oust him.

Dubosq's coins were widely circulated and accepted at par. Even the assays obtained by James King of William did not manage to discredit them: The $5's weighed 131 grs. each at 880 Fine = $4.96; the $10's, 262 grs. each at 880 Fine = $9.93, while Eckfeldt & DuBois {1851} rated them at 100% par value, or above even those of Moffat & Co.! Nevertheless, in the wake of the scandal that King's machinations began, Dubosq's coins were melted down in quantity along with other private mints' output. Dubosq sold his $10 rev. die to Wass, Molitor & Co. for the latter firm's 1852 coinage (**7924**). Survivors are of the highest rarity. No grading standards are established.

7814 1850 FIVE D. 3 known.
Kagin 1, p. 284; KM 26. T.DUBOSQ on coronet. S.M.V. = "Standard Mint Value." Ills. of white metal "splashers" (trial die impressions). 1) Byron Reed, OCL. 2) DeWitt Smith, Brand, Lilly, SI. 3) Bell I:1048, Maj. Alfred Walter (1951), plugged.

7815 1850 TEN D. Ex. rare. 8 known.
Kagin 2, p. 284; KM 27. Reeded edge. 1) Mehl, Brand, Lilly, SI. 2) Brock, Univ. of Pa., Ward, Mehl, Carter:1153, F, $38,500. 3) Lawrence:1357, Newcomer, Mehl, F. 4) Mehl (1914), Newcomer, "Bell," Williams, Willis duPont. Loop removed. Stolen in 1967. 5) Bank of California. 6) Henry Chapman, 1983 ANA:3625, F–VF, $27,500. 7) Allan Pankey, 86 ANA:5456, AU, scratched, $46,200, 259.88 grs. = 16.84 gms. *NNW* 8/5/86, p. 3. 8) Found in a Placerville creek bed, early 1985, sold to Ron Gillio. AU+, brilliant, nicked.

6. DUNBAR & CO.

Edward E. Dunbar left New York Dec. 23, 1848, on the *Crescent City,* arriving in Chagres on Jan. 2; he walked across the Isthmus of Panama in nine days and took the steamer *California* for San Francisco, arriving Feb. 28, 1849. He set up a business as a commission merchant and auctioneer, on Washington St. near the foot of Sacramento St., diversifying to wholesale operations. In Nov. 1849 he opened the "Merchants' Exchange and Reading Room" in Washington St., apparently in his auction warehouse. Less than a month later one of the "Great Fires" broke out, and stored gunpowder demolished the building. By Sept. 1850, Dunbar had managed to recoup enough of his losses to set up Dunbar's California Bank, in the Howard & Green building on Montgomery St. Two months later he diversified from buying, selling, shipping, and insuring gold dust by adding an exchange office dealing in city, county, and state scrip. (This paper currency violated the state constitution, but there was then no other way civil servants could be paid.) From Dec. 3, 1850, through mid-Jan. 1851, notices in the California *Courier* repeated that Dunbar would redeem Baldwin's gold coins at par. By March 1851, Dunbar was issuing his own half eagles, apparently from Küner's dies.

For unknown reasons, James King of William included no Dunbar coin in the group he sent to Augustus Humbert for assay; later, Humbert refused to test any of them! However, F. D. Kohler as State Assayer valued one of Dunbar's $5 coins at $5.13, while Philadelphia Mint assays quoted in Eckfeldt & DuBois {1851} valued one at $4.98. Even these favorable reports failed to exempt Dunbar's coinage from discounts and mass melting during the scandal over Baldwin & Co. Dunbar later returned to New York, where he was instrumental in founding the Continental Bank Note Company, which later became part of the American Bank Note Company conglomerate.

7816 1851 FIVE D. Ex. rare.
Kagin 1, p. 285; KM 28. DUNBAR &C on coronet: another spacing problem. S.M.V. = "Standard Mint Value." Kagin gives weight as 131 grs. = 8.489 gms. 1) Cleneay, Newcomer, Williams, Lilly, SI. 2) Bell I:1050, Maj. Alfred Walter, Carter:1152, EF, $60,500. 3) DeWitt Smith, Brand, Walton, Leo A. Young, 1973 ANA:1010, $37,500, Klausen, Auction 79:1472, $72,500, Kagin. Nearly EF, initials removed. Ill.

7. JAMES KING OF WILLIAM & CO.

James King of William (1822–56) gave himself the eccentric suffix (a patronymic?) to distinguish himself from several others named James King in the Washington, D.C., area. He became a muckraking political journalist, connected for some time with the Washington *Daily Globe*. On Nov. 10, 1848, he reached Yerba Buena Cove (later the port of San Francisco), bound for Hangtown, the center of the mining district. However, on the biblical precedent "To dig I am not able; to beg I am ashamed," he quickly decided that he would rather buy, sell, and lend gold dust than hunt for it. He became one of the partners of the banker Samuel J. Hensley in several successive firms, buying gold dust to resell to coiners at high profits, at first at Sutter's Fort, then at Sacramento, later still on his own in San Francisco as King's Exchange and Deposit Office, Montgomery St. between Clay and Merchant Sts. After his bank manager embezzled everything, leaving him penniless, King went back with Hensley, but in early 1851 he was again on his own as James King of William & Co., 131 Montgomery St., at the corner of Commercial St. His issue of $20 ingots appears to date from this period.

Envious of the profits being made by Baldwin & Co. and other big Period II private coiners, King concocted a plot which would at once discredit them and enrich himself. He knew, as did everyone else, that private coiners' output tended to run slightly below full bullion value; unlike everyone else, he chose to define this as dishonesty rather than either seignorage or technological limitations. Accordingly, on March 21, 1851, King sent a parcel of Baldwin, Schultz, and Dubosq coins to his friend Augustus Humbert, United States Assayer, for testing. Predictably, the assays rated them at from 97% to 99% of face value. On March 28, King sent the figures to all local newspapers, creating one of the biggest scandals of that period, occasioning corrosive attacks on these firms (most of all Baldwin & Co.) and on private gold coins of all kinds. Thereafter, bankers, brokers, and bullion dealers refused to accept the coins at any higher figure than 80¢ on the dollar, at which manifestly absurd discount they bought them in quantity from panicked holders, to resell at a high profit to Humbert for recoinage into octagonal $50's. This action unquestionably worsened the economic depression which immediately followed, and may even have caused it, by creating an instant coin shortage and destroying public confidence. Not that King's action brought him the vast wealth he craved: He continued in the banking business only to fail again and again. He resumed what Kagin called "crusading journalism," beginning the San Francisco *Daily Evening Bulletin* on Oct. 8, 1855, as a vehicle for muckraking attacks on "immorality and corruption." One of his more illustrious victims was Sen. David C. Broderick, formerly of Broderick & Kohler (above, Period I, at Pacific Co.). His last one was County Supervisor James P. Casey, who shot him to death on May 14, 1856, because King had exposed Casey's closet skeleton (a previous term in Sing Sing Prison). King died May 20, occasioning formation of the Second Vigilance Committee (eventually comprising 25,000 members!); on the day of King's funeral, the Committee stormed the police station to where Casey had fled, and hanged the murderer from the nearest tree.

7817 n.d. (1851?) 20 DOLLARS. Rectangular ingot. Unique?
Kagin 1, p. 289. In tablet, JAS. KING/OF [between leaves]/ WILLIAM & CO. Rev., in tablet, CALIFORNIA/GOLD [between leaves]/20 DOLLARS. Used as a watch fob; retains loop at one corner.   1) Bank of California.

8. H. M. NAGLEE & CO.

Capt. Henry M. Naglee, a West Point graduate from Philadelphia, arrived in California as an officer in Col. Jonathan D. Stevenson's "New York Volunteers" regiment, March 10, 1847. After he was mustered out following the end of the Mexican War, Naglee opened the banking house of Naglee & Sinton on the first floor of the then Parker House (the site is now occupied by the Hall of Justice). His partner, Richard H. Sinton, promptly quit to form the firm of Bagley & Sinton; Bagley is not identified with certainty but may have been the man who later became a partner in Baldwin & Co. (above). Naglee continued to operate his bank as Naglee & Co. After the 1849 Great Fire destroyed the Parker House, Naglee relocated to the corner of Montgomery and Merchant Sts., where he issued his ingots until a run on his bank forced him out of business in Sept. 1850: Cross {1927}, I, pp. 48–51.

7818 1850 $100. Rectangular ingot. Unique?
Kagin 1, p. 298. H.M.NAGLEE [curved]/&/CO./$100. Rev., 100.DOLL./IN CAL.M./COIN 880/2640GR.THO. Date on edge. Rev. legend = "100 Dollars in California Moffat Coin. 880 Thousandths [Fine]. 2,640 Grains." All letters individually punched into ingot.   1) Lilly, SI.

9. SCHULTZ & CO.

Judge G. W. Schultz and William Thompson Garratt set up a foundry and metalworking establishment on Clay St., behind Baldwin's mint, about Sept. or Oct. 1850. Garratt built the machinery to forge, turn, and harden dies for Albert Küner, at $100 per day. Eventually the firm worked with most of the private mints of the area, making dies on its own account for both Burgoyne & Co. and Argenti & Co., local bankers. Between Jan. and March 1851, Schultz & Garratt had accumulated enough of their own gold dust to come up with the idea of making their own coins. Küner obligingly made a pair of $5 dies, misspelled SHULTS & CO. on coronet. (As Don Kagin points out, more than one biographer avers that the firm also coined $10 pieces, but none have survived. Because no newspapers of the period mentioned this denomination as among Schultz's issues, and no other evidence confirms such issue, the alleged $10 is omitted below.) Garratt claimed that the firm's coins contained 10% copper alloy but that this did not reduce their value: The coins were, as usual, made a few grains heavier to compensate. Nevertheless, when James King of William had Augustus Humbert assay a batch of Schultz $5's, the result (129 14/15 grs. average at 875.25 Fine) represented them as worth only $4.87 apiece. Most perished during the general discrediting and melting of private gold coins: See Baldwin & Co. and James King of William & Co., above. By the time Eckfeldt & DuBois {1851} published the Philadelphia Mint's assays rating the Schultz coins at $4.97 apiece, King was already enjoying his victory. Schultz & Co. dissolved in April 1851.

7819   1851 FIVE D. 10–12 known.

Kagin 1, p. 302; KM 49. 122.6–128.8 grs. = 7.944–8.346 gms. Usually in low grades. Early strikings have thirteenth star touching truncation; later impressions, from reground obv., have this star free of device. Obv. die later rusts; rev. develops a heavy crack from wingtip through GOL to rim. Auction 79:1472, EF, $30,000; Slack, Garrett:941, VG, $26,000.

iii. PERIOD III: 1852–56

ANONYMOUS FRACTIONAL ISSUES

For generations these were among the most mysterious of all issues thought to be associated with the California Gold Rush. Collectors kept them as curiosities, making no distinctions among them except between "genuine" coins that bore the word DOLLAR (in full or abbreviated) or CENTS, and "charms" or "tokens," which did not. Mistaken theories abounded; some students believed all or nearly all, dated 1852–82, to have circulated as money, whereas others thought all or nearly all to be souvenirs of 1870–1915 made by jewelers in New York City, Leavenworth, Kan., and elsewhere. The truth has finally become available; the summary herein follows Breen {1983}.

The San Francisco *Daily Alta California,* Aug. 25, 1852, quoted the following story from the New Orleans *Picayune:* "We were shown this morning a gold half dollar, California money, which is so much like the United States gold dollar piece, that the best judges would be completely deceived [!] at a first glance. The half dollar piece is lighter in color, and somewhat smaller in diameter, than the dollar. They are of a private issue, and have stamped on them, HALF-DOLLAR CALIFORNIA GOLD 1852." This description most closely matches round half dollar BG 427 **(7879).** We may therefore take Aug. 1852 as an approximate beginning point for the series of fractionals; die- and punch-linkage evidence shows that some undated vars. also date to 1852. (The only alleged "1851" fractional coin is a manifest forgery of recent decades.)

Scuba divers Glenn E. Miller, Pete Greenwood, Dick Ander-

son, and Mark Williams, 1963–76, recovered many specimens (undated and dated 1852–53) from the wreck of the 1,291-ton sidewheel steamer *Winfield Scott.* She departed San Francisco Dec. 1, 1853, for Panama, only to smash into rocks off the north side of Anacapa Island (about 30 miles off Santa Barbara), sometime after 11:30 P.M. Dec. 2: See full account in Breen {1983}, pp. 5–6. These fractional pieces were found with other California coins including Moffat $5's of 1849 and 1850, an 1852 Humbert $10, and seven gold nuggets. The vars. (listed in Breen {1983}) are die-linked and punch-linked with many others, absolutely establishing them as of the 1852–53 period.

During 1851–52, a coin shortage developed in California, partly because James King of William had managed to discredit his rival private coiners, inducing panicked holders to turn in their coins of $20 and lower denominations at 20% discount for conversion into Humbert $50 ingots. For political reasons, Humbert was long forbidden to issue anything of lower denomination. Scarcity of any kind of reliable coin in denominations below $10 severely handicapped and eventually almost halted all ordinary business in the San Francisco area: Federal coins (which commanded a 3% premium) mostly went to the Custom House and stayed there; and not enough of the overvalued foreign silver coins were available to enable most grocers or clothing stores to make change. There was talk of resuming the detested 1848–49 practice of using gold dust for small change—an invitation to the dishonest to adulterate the gold granules with brass filings. Where neither private coiners nor the federal assayer could do anything, local jewelers stepped in. Jay Roe has made chemical analyses of various types of these 1852–56 fractionals, establishing that they were struck from unalloyed native California gold, at about 75% to 80% of "standard" weight. (At 880 Fine, a "standard" 25¢ would weigh 6.6 grs. = 0.428 gms.; 50¢, 13.2 grs. = 0.855 gms.; $1, 26.4 grs. = 1.71 gms.) This amount of underweight was doubtless ignored in token small change; anyone who might have objected most likely received some such answer as "better honest gold than adulterated dust."

Proof that these coins circulated, rather than merely being jewelers' souvenirs like later issues of 1859–82, is found in cambists of 1855–58. Breen {1983}, p. 50, reproduces the cover of *Dye's Gold and Silver Coin Chart Manual,* "Containing Fac Similies [sic] of All the Various Pieces of Ancient and Modern Times," published by John S. Dye, Broker, 172 Broadway, New York, 1855. This was one of a series of such books giving bullion values of domestic and foreign coins to help bankers and other financial houses. The cover shows a Norris Gregg & Norris $5 **(7792** or **7793)** as "Cal. Gold, $4.75."; a Miners Bank $10 **(7777)** as "California Gold, $9.75."; a round 1853 half dollar (apparently Nouizillet's, **7880),** as "California Gold Half Dollar, 48 cts."; and an octagonal Frontier & Deviercy 1854 dollar **(7889)** as "California Dollar, 98 cts.," side by side with an 1854 $3 as "U.S.Coin, $3.00," an 1854 "Type II" federal gold dollar as "United States (new) Gold Dollar, $1.00," and an 1851 silver 3¢ as "3 cts." Similar cambists of 1858–59 are cited in Breen {1983}, pp. 5, 51. In no way were the California fractionals distinguished from other circulating coins of the period.

Makers of nearly all the 1852–56 fractionals included their initials on the dies. Unsigned dies are, with very few exceptions ("mavericks"), linked by device punches and/or letters to the signed ones. Makers' initials have been identified through extensive circumstantial evidence; their full names and addresses have turned up in city directories and newspapers of the period. All were manufacturing jewelers in San Francisco (except Deriberpe); oddly, most were Frenchmen. (Contrary to some earlier conjectures, there is no evidence that either Albert Küner or Ferdinand Gruner made any of the dies.) All are listed below; for any apparently not listed, see Breen {1983}.

D, DERI, DERIB = M. Deriberpe or Deriberpie (both

spellings recur), engraver, 58 Kearny St., 1852–53. At first he made dies for other firms, but left for the goldfields in 1853, coining large quantities of octagonal dollars 1853–54 on his own.

D.N. = M. Deriberpe & Antoine Louis Nouizillet, doing business as "Nouizillet & Co.," out of Nouizillet's store in 58 Kearny St., from about Aug. 1852 through early 1853.

F.D. = Frontier, Deviercy & Co., i.e., Pierre Frontier and Eugène Deviercy or Diviercy (both spellings recur), 81 Bush St. near Montgomery St., 1852–56. Frontier resumed issue 1859–73 of lighter weight "coin charms," some using his old undated obvs. from 1856; these later pieces are outside the scope of this study and are fully dealt with in Breen {1983}, "Period Two." Some directories anglicize his name to Peter. Frontier & Deviercy made dies for other firms, as detailed in main text. Cf. A. Reimers, *NUM* 7/16, p. 329.

G.G. = H. Gaime, Guillemot & Co., 103 Montgomery St., 1853. This was the San Francisco branch of a New York jewelry firm; Frontier & Deviercy made their dies.

G.L. = Either G. Lange, 212 Dupont St., 1853–54, or G. H. Loring & Co., 156 Sacramento St., third floor, 1854. Frontier & Deviercy made their dies too.

N. = Antoine Louis Nouizillet, 58 Kearny St., 1852–54, before and after his period with Deriberpe. Some directories spell the name Nouzillet; some give the first name as "Antonio"; some list him as having Isadore (or F.) Routhier as partner. The very rare backdated "1856" half dollar with this initial, BG 916, has a G obv. (below) first used in 1864 (BG 917), hence it falls outside the present study.

N.R. = Nouizillet & Routhier, 175 Commercial St., 1854–56; their coins are dated 1855.

Coins with the single initial G are by Robert B. Gray & Co., 616 Merchant St., 1859–71, successors to Nouizillet & Routhier; the undated quarter BG 834 (small Liberty head, 13 stars around, G below; ¼/DOLLAR/CAL. in wreath, no berries) is a very rare muling of two of Gray's dies, both used with other dies dated 1870 and 1871, which is why it is omitted from the present study.

Those with initial K are by Herman Kroll; all were made in the 1880s or later and backdated. They were struck in 9-carat gold with plain edges; in the 1960s, parties unknown found his dies and made restrikes in 22-carat gold with reeded edges: Breen {1983}, pp. 149–51.

a. OCTAGONAL QUARTERS

Designers, Engravers, Mints, as below. Diameters, 6/16″ = 9.5+ mm side to side, 10 mm corner to corner. Composition, gold about 870–880 Fine. Weights, 5–5.28 grs. = 0.32–0.342 gms.

Grade range, FINE to UNC. No grade standards established. Beware coins with traces of solder on edges. All photos of **7820–7913** inclusive are enlargements; those marked "Enl. photos" are further enlarged.

FRONTIER & DEVIERCY

Beaded Circle Revs.

7820 1853 Narrow head, 9 stars. Rare.
BG 101. This head earlier appeared on this firm's round quarters. One was in the *Winfield Scott* treasure.

7821 1853 Broad head, 4 stars, same rev. Rare.
BG 102. Less rare than preceding; 6-pointed stars.

7822 1854 Same obv.; ¼ DOLLA blunder. Unique?
BG 103. Kenneth W. Lee estate. Beaded circle was unduly small to accommodate CALIFORNIA. GOID. [sic!], creating spacing problems. Note double D in DOLLA. Enl. photos.

7823 1854 Same obv.; normal DOLLAR. Rare.
BG 104. Repunched A and 4. Obv. quickly cracked, rev. rusted.

7824 1854 Same head, 5 5-pointed stars.
BG 105. DOLLAR too far l.

7825 1855/4 Same head, 4 5-pointed stars.
BG 106. Same rev., drastically reground and overdated. Rare.

7826 1856 FD on coronet; 8 5-pointed stars.
BG 107. Obv. reused in 1859, BG 701.

A.L.NOUIZILLET

Small Heads, Wreaths

7827 1854 11 stars; ¼ DOL. Rare.
BG 108. Head loosely copies that of Longacre's gold dollars 1849–54.

7828 1854 Same obv.; ¼ DOLLAR.
BG 109.
7829 1855 Same head, 12 stars around. Rare.
BG 110. Rev. shattered early.

7830 1856 Same obv.
BG 111. Rarely with heavy clash marks; dies drastically re-polished to remove them. Obv. reused by Gray with 1860-dated rev., BG 729.

b. ROUND QUARTERS

Designers, Engravers, Mints, as below. Diameters, 6–6.5/16″ = 9.5–10 mm. Composition, Weights, as Octagonal Quarters.

Grade range, FINE to UNC.; no grade standards established. Beware coins with traces of solder on edges. NOTE: Edges reeded by file; adjustment marks are common at borders.

FRONTIER & DEVIERCY

Narrow Heads, Wreaths

7831 n.d. (1852–53) 13 stars; 25 CENTS. Ex. rare.
BG 201, 202, respectively with very large triangular bow and small flat bow; price for latter (ill.). Garrett:2154, AU, $1,300.

7832 n.d. (1852–53) 12 stars; beaded ring. Very rare.
BG 203. Beaded circle between wreath and plain raised rim.

7833 n.d. (1852–53) Same obv.; ¼ D O L L . Very rare.
BG 204. Discovered by Elmer Sears about 1914.

7834 n.d. (1852–53) 12 stars, * ¼ DOLLAR *. Ex. rare.
BG 205. Star crowded into base of truncation.

7835 n.d. (1853) 10 stars, same rev. Very rare.
BG 207.

7836 n.d. (1853) Same obv./No star below DOLLAR. Very rare.
BG 206. One was in the *Winfield Scott* treasure.

7837 1853 Same obv.; flat-top 3. 3 or 4 known.
BG 208. Struck before **7835–36.**

7838 1853 Similar; round-top 3, reversed 4 in ¼. Ex. rare.
BG 209. One was in the *Winfield Scott* treasure.

Broad Heads, Wreaths

7839 1853 F.D., 11 stars; same rev. 2 or 3 known.
BG 210. Discovered by David Proskey.

7840 1853 FD., 13 large hollow stars; same rev. Unique? Unlocated.
BG 211. 1) Nygren:261.

7841 1853 Same obv.; flat-top 3, normal 4 in ¼. 3 or 4 known.
BG 212. Rev. of **7837**. FD punched over 2 lowest stars.

7842 1853 Same head, plain border. Unique?
BG 213. All but one of the 13 small stars touch border; small straight date, close to DOLLAR, die of **7845** (BG 217). 1) Edward M. Lee, Kenneth W. Lee.

7843 1853 Largest head, widest curved date. Ex. rare.
BG 214–15. Date follows curve of wreath, 8 free of bow (enl. photos) or touching it. Head as on **7853–59**. Discovered by David Proskey, 1884. Respectively Brand I:640–41, UNC., $600, AU, $300.

7844 1854 Same obv.; fragmented wreath. 4 known.
BG 216. Obv. reground, stars small and grossly unequal, one just r. of coronet hardly visible.

GAIME, GUILLEMOT & CO.

G G. Below Broad Head, Plain Rim

7845 1853. Ex. rare.
BG 217–19. Positional vars., 3 or 4 known of each. Brand I: 642, AU, $750.

M. JORDAN

7846 1854. Possibly 8–10 known.
BG 220. Attribution to Jordan is based on his use of the same device (defiant eagle on torse) in his advertisement in the 1854 San Francisco directory. Thought to commemorate the opening of his jewelry store, 130½ Montgomery St.

A.L. NOUIZILLET

Small Heads, Wreaths

7847 n.d. (1852–54) 11 stars.
BG 221.

7848 n.d. (1852–54) 12 stars; ¼ DOLLAR *.
BG 222–23. Often with break joining tops of wreath and numerator.

7849 n.d. (1852–54) 12 stars; no star below DOLLAR.
BG 224.

7850 1855 10 stars. Rare.
BG 225–27. All 3 positional vars. are very rare.

7851 1856 10 stars. Rare.
BG 228–29. Price for latter (normal R); former, with R first punched too high, then corrected, is Ex. rare.

7852 1856 12 stars.
BG 230.

c. OCTAGONAL HALVES

Designers, Engravers, Mints, as below. Diameters, 7/16″ = 11+ mm side to side, 12 mm corner to corner. Composition, gold 870–880 Fine. Weights, 9.9–10.6 grs. = 0.64–0.684 gms.

Grade range, FINE to UNC. No grading standards established. Beware coins showing traces of solder.

FRONTIER & DEVIERCY

Largest Heads; Eagles

7853 1853 Largest head, F.D. below; eagle with scroll. Ex. rare.
BG 301. Eagle copies that on Humbert $50's. 1) Bill O'Connor, UNC., ill. in Doering {1982}. 2) Garrett:2168; AU, $5,400. 3) Clarke:547, cleaned AU. 4) Kosoff Estate:937, AU+, $2,310. 5) Jay Roe, Harmer Rooke 9/76:136, AU. 6) Dr. French, Kagin 1979 FPL, EF. 7) Kenneth W. Lee estate, pierced, ill. here and Breen {1983}.

7854 1853 Same head, F.D. behind; eagle with rays. Rare.
BG 302. At least 3 were in *Winfield Scott* treasure. Rays may allude to the new 1853 federal quarters and halves. Later develops "cud" rim break at r. obv., obliterating a star. Compare next.

7855 1853 Same but FD and date below, 10 stars. Ex. rare.
BG 303. Obv. as next; rev. as preceding. Possibly 6 known.

Largest Heads; Beaded Circles

7856 1853 Same obv.; 2 stars below beads.
BG 304. One was reportedly in the *Winfield Scott* treasure.

7857 1854 Similar, date below, 9 stars; same rev.
BG 305.
7858 1854 Similar but 10 5-pointed stars; FD * below beads.
BG 306.

7859 1856 Similar, 13 large 5-pointed stars. Very rare.
BG 307. Star below date. Ill. as current money in *Petersons' Complete Coin Book,* Philadelphia: T. B. Peterson & Bros., 306 Chestnut St., 1859 (another cambist: Compare introductory text): Breen {1983}, p. 5.

A.L.NOUIZILLET

Date in Wreath

7860 1854 Small head. Very rare.
BG 308. Head as on this firm's quarters and round halves. Star in opening of wreath; N. follows GOLD.
7861 1855 Large head.
BG 309. Head as on this firm's round halves and octagonal dollars 1855–56 only; N. follows GOLD.

7862 1856 Same obv.; N. below wreath.
BG 310–11. Price for latter (ill.) with 4 pairs of berries on each branch; former, with 5 pairs of berries on r. branch, is Ex. rare.

d. ROUND HALVES

Designers, Engravers, Mints, as below. Diameters about $^7/_{16}'' = 11+$ mm. Composition, Weights, as Octagonal Halves. Grade range and standards, as Octagonal Halves. NOTE: Beware of coins with traces of solder on edges.

FRONTIER & DEVIERCY

Narrow Head, Wreath

7863　1852 Date in center of wreath; no D.N.
BG 401. Rev. of **7867.**

Broad Heads

7864　1853 Rev., small eagle; no G.G. Unique?
BG 402.　1) Bill O'Connor. Compare **7870.**
7865　1854 FD Ex. rare.
BG 403–4. Part of extra F hangs from lower r. star below D.
BG 404 has long dash following date.

7866　1855 FD::: on coronet. Very rare.
BG 405–6. Price for former; latter (much rarer) has second L low: Garrett:2188, AU, $550.

"D.N."

7867　1852 D.N. below head; date in center. Rare.
BG 407. Rusted dies; coined after **7868–69.** D.N. = Deriberpe & Nouizillet; partnership broken up by Deriberpe's departure for goldfields? Device punch reappears on dies Deriberpe made for Frontier & Deviercy before Frontier made the Broad Head hub. Compare **7879.**

7868　1853 D.N. Same obv.; flat top to 3. Ex. rare.
BG 408. Rev. reappears on **7872.** Brand I:811, AU, $350.

7869　1853/2 D.N. Same obv.; round top to 3, no star below wreath.
BG 409. Compare **7880.**

GAIME, GUILLEMOT & CO.

Broad Heads

7870　1853 GG. below head; small eagle. Ex. rare.
BG 410–13. One of these has rev. of **7864.** Dies by Frontier.

7871　1853 G.G. below head; divided date below wreath. Very rare.
BG 414. A similar coin without G.G. is unconfirmed.

M. DERIBERPE

"DERI Dollars" Head; Date in Center

7872　1853 HALF D. at l. Very rare.
BG 415–16. Very rare. Price for former (rev. of **7868**); on latter (much rarer) bust point joins star just below it.

7873 1853 No D below head; HALF D at r. Ex. rare.
BG 417–19. Compare next 2. Enl. photos.

7874 1853 D below head; same rev. Rare.
BG 420–21. Price for latter (period within D, star almost touches above bun, ill.). Former (no period, star touches bun below top) is Ex. rare. D = Deriberpe.

7875 1853 D below head; star above date. Ex. rare.
BG 422. Discovered by F. C. C. Boyd. Obv. of BG 421 (preceding), period within D. Enl. photos.

7876 1854 D below head; star above date. Ex. rare.
BG 423. Discovered by Elmer Sears about 1914. Another var. has obv. of **7875:** Brand I:819, UNC., $1,000.

7877 1854 14 stars; date divides star and D. 2 known.
BG 424. 1) E. M. Lee, Kenneth W. Lee estate. 2) Comstock:1197, unlocated.

7878 1854 Same obv.; date without star or D. 3 known.
BG 425. 1) Doering. 2) Pvt. coll. 3) Brand I:821, EF, $385.

ANTOINE LOUIS NOUIZILLET

Small Heads; Date in Center

7879 1852 No D.N. Ex. rare.
BG 426–27. Possibly the first fractionals made, Aug. 1852: See introductory text. Only 2 or 3 known of either var. Compare **7867.** Brand I:773, AU+, $1,300.

7880 1853 No D.N. Round-top 3; star below wreath.
BG 428–30. Compare **7869.** One ill. on cover of Dye's 1855 cambist, valued at 48¢: See introductory text.

7881 1854 Date below head; empty wreath. Rare.
BG 431. Rev. usually cracked. Compare next.

Large Heads

7882 1855 Same rev., date added within wreath. Very rare.
BG 432–33. One of the few instances of a die altered after use. Head as on octagonal halves **7861–62,** octagonal dollars **7905–8.** Price for former (stars close to bun and lowest curl). BG 433 (ill.), with stars very close to border, one about touching bust point, is Ex. rare; discovered by A. C. Nygren. Star below wreath, unlike next.

7883 1856 Similar, N. below wreath.
BG 434.

UNCERTAIN MAKER (JOSEPH BROS.?)

7884 1853 State arms; eagle. Possibly 25–30 known.
BG 435. Attributed to Joseph Bros. (J. B. and L. B. Joseph), 175 Clay St., formerly of Liverpool, partly because this firm's successor, Nathan Joseph (a younger brother), made many imitations of it in later years, advertising his continuity with Joseph Bros. Grafton:536, EF, $21,000; Auction 80:1887, UNC., $10,500; Garrett:2185, bent, $1,800; Auction 86:1499–1500, UNC., $3,740, $2,640; Brand I:815, UNC., $7,150.

UNKNOWN MAKER

7885 1854 Eagle with shield, no scroll. 10–12 known.
BG 436. By the maker of octagonal dollar **7909**. Design copies **7889**. Garrett:2187, EF+, $1,400; Kosoff Estate:945, AU, $2,200.

e. OCTAGONAL DOLLARS

Designers, Engravers, Mints, as below. Diameters, 1/2" = 12.5 mm side to side, 13.55 mm corner to corner. Composition, gold 870–880 Fine. Weights, 19.8–21.1 grs. = 1.28–1.37 gms.
Grade range, VERY GOOD to UNC. No grading standards established.

FRONTIER & DEVIERCY

Largest Heads, Eagles

7886 n.d. (1853). Rev., ONE.DOL. Very rare.
BG 501. Struck after next 2. Edge reeded by file. At least rev. is by Deriberpe, possibly both dies. Obv. reappears on **7897**. Brand I:879, AU, $2,000.

7887 1853 Same obv., crude eagle, inverted 53. Unique?
BG 502. Elongated feathers, ONE DOL far apart, R LD too low, resting on wingtips; in date, 53 inverted (rotated 180°). O in COLD (!) filled. Probably Frontier's first dollar.   1) J. J. Teaparty, Doering.
7888 1853 Same obv., crude eagle, normal date. 5 known.
BG 503. Similar but C in COLD (!) too low; 53 normal.

7889 1854 Same obv.; 2 stars in legend. Very rare.
BG 504. Usually in low grades. Later (ill.), cracked through l. star to scroll. Ill. on cover of Dye's cambist (1855), valued at 98¢: See introductory text. Brand I:912, EF, $935.

Large Heads, Beaded Circles, FD

7890 1853 10 stars; * F D below beads.
BG 505. Same head as **7853–59**.

7891 1854 Same obv.; 4 small 6-pointed stars in legend. 3 known.
BG 506. Compare next.   1) Jay Roe, AU.   2) Doering ill., apparently EF.   3) Bill O'Connor, F.
7892 1854 Same obv.; 4 large 5-pointed stars in legend. 4 known.
BG 507.   1) Kenneth W. Lee estate, UNC.   2) O'Connor.   3) Roe.   4) Pvt. coll.

7893   1854 Same obv.; 2 large 5-pointed stars in legend. Very rare.
BG 508–9. Price for former, rev. stars at corners; latter (ill.), with upper star vertically above circle, is much rarer.

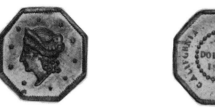

7894   1854 Same obv.; only one 5-pointed star in legend.
BG 510. Successive die repolishings make obv. stars minute.

7895   1855/4 Similar, large obv. stars.
BG 511. Same rev., overdated, final 5 heavily repunched.

7896   1856 Same obv.; 2 small 5-pointed stars in legend, no FD. Ex. rare.
BG 512.   1) Garrett:2208, UNC., $6,000, Jay Roe.   2) E. M. Lee, Kenneth W. Lee estate, UNC., ill.   3) Clarke:666, UNC.   4) Doering ill.

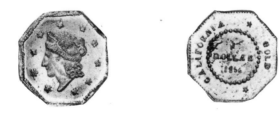

UNCERTAIN ISSUER G.L.

7897   1854 Largest head; 1 DOLLARD (!). 2 known.
BG 513. Obv. of **7886–89.** Rev., 1/DOLLARD/.1854. in wreath; CALIFORNIA GOLD . G.L. FD above, 5 stars below. The FD mostly effaced.   1) Matt DeRoma, Doering {1982} ill. at 414½.   2) Harry Bass. Doubtless rejected for the blunder. Struck before **7889.**

M. DERIBERPE

DERI(B) Below Beaded Circle

7898   1853 No stars flank DERI. Very rare.
BG 514–15. Price for former (ill.), with head tilted back, coronet point nearly midway between stars; one was in *Winfield Scott* treasure. BG 515, with coronet point almost touching a star, is much rarer.

7899   1853 Stars flank DERI; GOID. Ex. rare.
BG 516–17. "Microscopic" obv. stars (die drastically overpolished). Broken L's look like I's.
7900   1853 Stars flank DERI; GOLD.
BG 518–24.

7901   1853 Stars flank DERIB. Very rare.
BG 525–26. One of each was in *Winfield Scott* treasure.

7902   1854 Two stars in legend; GOLD. 3 or 4 known.
BG 527. Wide date, legend far from beaded circle, some letters touch octagonal borders. Compare next.
7903   1854 Similar, GOID. Very rare.
BG 528. Close date, legend close to beaded circle.

7904   1854 Similar, 2 stars between DERI and GOLD. Unique?
BG 529. Legend midway between sides and beaded circle; DOLLAR aims between (GOL)D and star.   1) Jay Roe.

A.L.NOUIZILLET

N *Below Beaded Circle*

7905 1853 Stars 6 + 7.
BG 530. At least 10 were in the *Winfield Scott* treasure. Often in low grades. This head recurs on **7861–62.**

7906 1853 Stars 6 + 1 + 6, same rev.
BG 531. Obv. of next.

Wreath, Multi-Dot Ornaments

7907 1854 Same obv.
BG 532. No initial, but obv. requires attribution to Nouizillet. Usually in VF to AU, rare in mint state.

NOUIZILLET & ROUTHIER

7908 1855 Same obv.; N. R. follows GOLD.
BG 533. Usually VF to AU, rare in mint state.

UNKNOWN MAKER

7909 1854 Eagle without scroll. 7 or 8 known.
BG 534. By the maker of **7885.** Rude imitation of **7889.** Discovered by David Proskey, 1884. Brand I:911, EF, $2,970.

f. ROUND DOLLARS

Designers, Engravers, Mints, as below. Diameters, about $9/16'' = 14$ mm. Composition, Weights, as octagonal dollars. Grade range, FAIR to UNC. No grading standards established.

FRONTIER & DEVIERCY

7910 1854 Small head, no FD. 2 known.
BG 601. Head as on **7890–96.** 1) E. M. Lee, Kenneth W. Lee estate, discovery coin, VG. 2) Bill O'Connor, ill. Doering {1982}, VG. The Roe coin with apparently same obv. and date 1857 is too rough to enable authentication, but rev. is entirely unlike **7910.**

7911 1854 FD below broad bust. Very rare.
BG 602–3. Latter (ill., star divides F D) discovered by A. C. Nygren.

GAIME, GUILLEMOT & CO.

7912 1853 Large head, G.G.; eagle on rock. 2 known.
BG 604. Dies by Frontier & Deviercy. Discovered by David Proskey. 1) Newcomer, Clarke:683, Donald R. Hyink, VF (ill.). 2) F. C. C. Boyd, NN *Numisma*:5194, EF, unlocated.

UNCERTAIN ISSUER G.L.

7913 1854 Different large head, G L flank large ribbon. 7 or 8 known.
BG 605. Dies by Frontier & Deviercy; see introductory text. Clarke:685, same dies but lacking G at l., had been made into a hinged locket.

NAMED ISSUERS

1. BLAKE & AGRELL

Gorham Blake (1829–97), sometime Superintendent of iron mines in Vermont, reached California in 1852, working for Adams & Co. in Placerville, later becoming a buyer of gold dust for Wells Fargo & Co. In 1854 he moved to Sacramento and set up an assay office. From Nov. 12, 1855, through Dec. 27, he was in partnership with John Agrell, assaying ores and stamping ingots, at 52 J St., between Second and Third Sts., Sacramento. The partnership then dissolved; Don Kagin {1981} says Agrell died. Blake continued in Sacramento into 1856 as "Blake & Co.," the "Co." evidently his new associate W. R. Waters. Copper strikings of their 1856 $20 bear this latter title; no gold impressions are known. Recurrent coin shortages resulting from repeated closures of the San Francisco branch mint doubtless occasioned Blake's short-lived enterprise. It came well recommended: Blake's assayer was David Lundblom, formerly of the U.S. Assay Office (Sept.–Dec. 1853) and of Kellogg & Co. (below).

There are two major unsolved problems about the controversial surviving issues of Blake & Agrell and Blake & Co. Though local newspapers described Blake & Agrell as one of the largest assayers in the area, they never mentioned this firm's coins. Worse, all surviving coins and ingots have the singular misspelling AGNELL. This spelling first became known to the numismatic world from Adams {1913}, p. 108. As Adams's source was the Sacramento *Union,* Nov. 12, 1855, and later issues, he certainly knew the correct spelling, so that "Agnell" was a typographical error. Strange indeed to find it on the coins, which were unknown until the 1950s! Against the first objection there is an obvious reply: San Francisco newspapers ignored many genuine coins of Periods I and II. Against the second objection, Don Kagin has called attention to a comparable error on the coins of Schultz & Co., all misspelled SHULTS. Since only two Blake dies are involved, both manifestly by a single unidentified engraver, it is possible that the latter worked from some other location and under handwritten orders, in which a lower-case n might be mistaken for a lower-case r.

The surviving pieces, if authentic, must have been issued during less than six weeks in all. Rectangular dies for the $25 specie ingot were also used for bullion-storage ingots in other denominations, including an uncut strip of three (ill. reduced). No grading standards exist.

7914 1855 BLAKE & AGNELL (sic)/(25) DOLLS. Unique? Kagin 1, p. 281. Denomination and fineness punched into ingot, not die.   1) Ford, Bank of California. 626.7 grs. = 40.61 gms. = $24.29; standard at 900 Fine would have been 645 grs. = 41.8 gms.

7915 1855 (50) DOLLS. Unique? Kagin 3, p. 281. Denomination punched into ingot.   1) Ford, Bank of California. 1,284.6 grs. = 83.241 gms. (Standard 1,290 grs. = 83.591 gms.)

7916 1855 Same obv., (20) DOLLS.; BLAKE & CO. Unique? Kagin 4, p. 282. Reeded edge.   1) Ford, Bank of California. 507.7 grs. = 32.9 gms. = $19.68 at 900 Fine. Double-struck.

2. KELLOGG & CO.

John Glover Kellogg and G. F. Richter were, respectively, cashier and assayer of Moffat & Co., before and during the subcontract linking that firm with Augustus Humbert's U.S. Assay Office (the Provisional Branch Mint). On the same day that the latter dissolved, Dec. 14, 1853, Kellogg and Richter opened their own assaying establishment in response to urgent requests from local bankers. Because the federal branch mint delayed opening, bankers requested them to make gold coins under their own imprint. Kellogg & Co. began coining $20's on Feb. 9, 1854, at first at the rate of 1,000 pieces per day. Their dies have been dubiously attributed to Albert Küner, though Ferdinand Gruner (who made the dies for the 1855 pattern $50's) is an equally likely candidate. Alonzo Phelps {1882} said that Kellogg & Co. made in all about $6 million, i.e., about 300,000 $20's. The proportion of 1854's to 1855's is about 5 to 3, which suggests ballpark figures of about 180,000 1854's to about 120,000 1855's. The true figures are probably a little lower for 1854, a little higher for 1855. Kagin says Humbert succeeded to Richter's post as assayer in 1855, which circumstance explains Humbert's owning proofs of both the 1854 $20 and the 1855 $50.

Many uncirculated survivors dated 1854 come from the Thayer County hoard: Breen {1952}. This consisted of 58 pieces found by two boys in the woods near Alexandria, Neb., in 1907. Supposedly two ranchers, Bennett and Abernathy, hid them there in 1867 while vainly trying to escape hostile Indians.

Plans to issue a $50 coin went as far as striking about 12 proof samples. The roster is as nearly complete as possible:

1. Augustus Humbert, Capt. Andrew C. Zabriskie, Col. James W. Ellsworth, Garrett:910, $300,000, Kagin, Auction 85:975, $79,750. Ill.

2. Kellogg family, "J. F. Bell," "Memorable":967, Don Keefer, Fuad K. Saab, Gibson:189, $110,000 (1974), Auction 79:996, $140,000, S 10/27/83:239, $110,500.

3. George W. Rice, DeWitt Smith, Virgil Brand, W. F. Dunham, Waltman:37, Carter:1149, $154,000, Harlan White.

4. Fred Huddart, George H. Earle, Judge C. W. Slack, Col. E. H. R. Green, Amon Carter, Sr. & Jr., Josiah Lilly, SI. Impaired.

5. H. O. Granberg, William H. Woodin, Willis duPont. Stolen in Oct. 1967; recovered Aug. 1978. *CW* 8/9/78, p. 1.

6. John A. Beck I:729, Dr. Ketterman, Arnold-Romisa:330, B&M 6/10/85:24.

7. N. M. Kaufman:66, $115,000, Auction 80:982, $130,000, Stack's, Auction 84:2000. Ill. Yeoman Guide Book.

8. C. W. Cowell, Waldo Newcomer, Amon Carter, Sr. & Jr., 1962 N.Y. Metropolitan sale, 1973 ANA:1030, Breen I:455, West Coast pvt. coll. Impaired, fields buffed.

9. John Story Jenks, Reuting, A. C. Nygren, George Alfred Lawrence, John H. Clapp, Eliasberg estate.

10. J. W. Schmandt, Dan Brown, John Herhold Murrell, Henry H. Clifford, Kagin, 83 ANA:3630. Rim dent below first 5; field cut between eighth and ninth stars.

11. British pvt. coll., 1984 Greater NY:784 (S 5/3–4/84), $180,400.

Two others are supposed to have been in the Kellogg family, including one held by John Glover Kellogg's son Karl. These may be included in the above list. The dies were still extant in 1970.

KELLOGG & CO.

Designers, Engravers, Ferdinand Gruner, others (?), the $20 after Longacre. Mint, Kellogg's, 104–6 Montgomery St., San Francisco. Diameter, $20, as federal issue; $50, 27/16″ = 42.9 mm. Reeded edge. Composition, $20, gold 900 Fine; $50, gold 887 Fine.

Grade range, $20, FINE to UNC.; $50, proof only. VERY FINE: All major hair locks clearly demarcated, over half individual strands visible, over half wing feathers separated. EXTREMELY FINE: Isolated tiny rubbed spots only; partial mint luster.

7917   1854 TWENTY D. Short arrowheads.
Kagin 1, 1a, 1b, pp. 286–87; KM 33.1–3. Arrowheads distant from scroll; rev. of **7789.** 513.9–515.7 grs. = 33.3–33.42 gms. Date thin (ill.) or heavy, latter with larger coronet beads. Auction 82:991, thin date, UNC., $28,000. That ill. is a proof, ex Humbert, Zabriskie, Ellsworth, Garrett:908, $230,000, Midwest dealer, 1982 ANA:2928, $58,000. Enl. photos.

Ex J. W. Garrett: 908. Courtesy Bowers & Ruddy Galleries, Inc.

7918   1854 TWENTY D. Long arrowheads.
Kagin 2, p. 287; KM 33.4. Uppermost arrowhead almost or quite touches ornament above. 2 obv. vars., thin date (very rare) and heavy date (ill.), both dies of **7917.**

7919   1855 TWENTY D. Long arrowheads.
Kagin 3, p. 287; KM 33.4. Same rev. Rarer UNC. than preceding.

7920   1855 TWENTY D. Short arrowheads.
Kagin 3a, 3b, p. 288; KM 33.5–6. Date heavier or weaker; rev. of **7917.**

7921   1855 FIFTY DOLLS. Proofs only. Ex. rare.
Kagin 4, p. 288; KM 34. Stated weight 1,309 grs. = 84.82 gms. For roster see introductory text.

Ex J. W. Garrett: 910. Courtesy Bowers & Ruddy Galleries, Inc.

3. WASS, MOLITOR & CO.

Counts S. C. Wass and A. P. Molitor, freedom fighters in the Hungarian War of Independence, set up an assay office on Montgomery St. below Bush St., in 1851. Among the firms for which they made bullion-storage ingots was Adams & Co., Wells Fargo's rival, the largest express company then in business. In November, Wass, Molitor & Co. moved to larger quarters in Naglee & Co.'s building at the corner of Montgomery and Merchant Sts. The firm achieved a reputation for total honesty side by side with Moffat & Co., paying off depositors within 48 hours (instead of the usual eight days) at the U.S. Assay Office in Humbert ingots. An editorial in the Nov. 25, 1851, San Francisco *Herald* (the same issue in which the firm announced this 48-hour service) regretted that this firm did not mint its own smaller coins as an urgently needed alternative to Humbert $50's. Accordingly, late in Dec. 1851, Wass, Molitor & Co. prepared obv. dies, buying at least one $10 rev. from Dubosq & Co. (**7815**). On Jan. 6, 1852, the first Wass, Molitor $5's appeared, $10's following about a week later. An editorial in the *Herald,* Jan. 8, 1852, evaluated the new $5's as 880 Fine but enough heavier than the federal issue to be worth $5.04 apiece. Six days later, the same newspaper reported that this firm was coining from $7,000 to $8,000 daily: a modest amount, either 1,400 to 1,600 $5's or 700 to 800 $10's, or some combination thereof. Most likely production stepped up later. The firm charged the same 2.75% seignorage as the United States Assay Office.

Reuse of the old Dubosq $10 rev., and probably other old dies, explains the weak appearance of revs. of almost all Wass, Molitor $5's and $10's. (Don Kagin first pointed out their reuse of the Dubosq rev.) Weakness of their $20's has other causes, which may mean use of a press not meant for coins of this size and developing insufficient force. We do not know on what press they coined their $50's.

After the U.S. Assay Office began coining its own $10's and $20's, Wass, Molitor & Co. halted issues; this is why none of their coins bear date 1853 or 1854. However, after the Assay Office closed in Dec. 1853, the new federal branch mint delayed opening until April 1854 and even then had to shut down several times in 1854–55 for lack of parting acids, copper for alloying gold, or other technological problems. By then most private coiners were out of business, their coins already melted by either the Assay Office or its federal successor. The result was a coin shortage, with severe difficulties in conducting business, paying wages, tariffs, or taxes, even buying groceries. In March 1855, local bankers again petitioned Wass, Molitor & Co. to resume coinage. The firm did so, issuing $10's and $20's around the beginning of April 1855, and $50's on May 16. As the final 5 on some of these dies is on a raised disk, apparently the dies were originally dated 1852 and the final digit drilled out to avoid overdates. The *Daily Alta California* reported on May 16 that the firm was coining $38,000 per day in $20's and $50's: again, a very modest amount—1,900 $20's or 760 $50's daily, and most likely output increased later. However, when the federal branch mint resumed full-scale operations, this time supposedly for good, Wass, Molitor & Co. abandoned coinage. Molitor departed for London in 1856; Wass sought other occupations. Tests by the San Francisco branch mint rated the coins at full face value. Nevertheless, most were eventually melted for conversion into federal coins.

WASS, MOLITOR & CO.

Designers, Engravers, various. Mint, Wass, Molitor & Co., Montgomery and Merchant Sts. Composition, 1852, gold 880 Fine; 1855, gold 900 Fine. Weight standards, 1852, $5, 131.93

grs. = 8.549 gms.; $10, 263.86 grs. = 17.098 gms.; 1855, $10, 258 grs. = 16.718 gms.; $20, 516 grs. = 33.436 gms.; $50, 1,290 grs. = 83.591 gms. Diameters, as federal coins, except $50 = 27/16″ = 42.9 mm.

Grade range, VERY GOOD to UNC. VERY FINE: Over half hair details intact. EXTREMELY FINE: Isolated tiny rubbed spots only; partial mint luster. UNCIRCULATED: *No* trace of wear. EXCEPTIONS: All $5's and $10's have rev. weaker than obv.; sometimes a coin with full EF obv. sharpness will show few or no distinct feathers. Twenties are a little better struck but also weaker on rev. than obv. NOTE: Many $50's have fields tooled to remove unsightly nicks, dents, or scratches. Grade as though these defects were not present, then describe the impairments.

7922 1852 FIVE DOLLARS. Small head, rounded bust. Very rare.
Kagin 1, p. 304; KM 55.1. End of bust rounded, directly above 1 of date. Always weakly and unevenly struck, date weak, surfaces granular. Ellsworth, Garrett:942, VF, $5,000. Enl. photos. A single specimen (Kagin 1a; KM 55.2) is known struck on a "wrong stock" blank cut from strip intended for $10's; 169.8 grs. = 11 gms.

Ex J. W. Garrett: 942. Courtesy Bowers & Ruddy Galleries, Inc.

7923 1852 FIVE DOLLARS. Large head, pointed bust. Very rare.
Kagin 2, p. 304; KM 56. End of bust pointed, closer to first star than to 1. Two periods below O in CO on coronet. Gibson:206, VF-EF, $3,400 (1974); Garrett:943, F, $3,400; Bell I:1034, Maj. Alfred Walter, Carter:1156, AU, $9,350.

7924 1852 TEN D. Long neck, large close date. Ex. rare.
Kagin 3, p. 305; KM 57. Rev. of **7815**, always weak; 2 on slightly raised disk (die originally dated 1851?). S.M.V. = "Standard Mint Value." Called by all earlier students "small head." Raymond, Garrett:944, F, 261.9 grs. = 16.97 gms., $5,000; Geiss, Carter:1155, VF, $4,675. Enl. photos.

7925 1852 TEN D. Short neck, pointed bust, wide uneven date. Rare.

Kagin 4, p. 305; KM 58. Same rev.; shattered dies. Rev. always weak. Called "large head" by all previous reference works. Auction 82:990, UNC., $8,250; Geiss, Carter:1154, VF/VG, $2,310.

7926 1852 TEN D. Short neck, blunt bust, small close date. Unique?

Kagin 5, p. 306; KM 59.1. Head of 1855. Same rev., still worse cracked. Discovered by Jack Klausen, about 1973. 1) Klausen, 1973 ANA:1019, 1983 ANA:3652, $11,000. Enl. photos.

7927 1855 TEN D. Ex. rare.

Kagin 6, p. 306; KM 59.2. Final 5 on raised disk (unused 1852 die). Rev. always weak. 1) Humbert, Cartwright, Smith, Slack, Lawrence, Morris, 1973 ANA:1020, F. 2) Wilcox, Renz, F. 3) Bourquin, Zabriskie, Geiss, Walton:2217, VF. 4) Garrett:945, VF, 254.5 grs. = 16.49 gms., $11,000. 5) Lusk, Clapp, Eliasberg, ABOUT F. 6) Lilly, SI. 7) Clifford:114, VF, $5,200. 8) Clifford, Bank of California.

7928 1855 TWENTY DOL. Small head. Rare.

Kagin 7, p. 306; KM 61. Head very similar to preceding, possibly from same device punch? W.M.& C°. on coronet. Note 900 THOUS. on scroll. Wings and neck usually weak. Nygren, Garrett:946, EF, $16,000.

7929 1855 TWENTY DOL. Large head. 3 known.

Kagin 8, p. 307; KM 60. Device punch apparently same as **7930,** producing a crowded appearance. Head copies federal $20, but W.M.& C°. on coronet. Rev. as preceding. Reason for rarity unknown.   1) Mehl (1929), Midwest coll., Lilly, SI, ill. 2) Newcomer, Brand, Roach, Geiss, Carter:1161, F–VF, $40,700.   3) Lawrence:1406, UNC., $7,000 (1929), Yale Univ., unidentified thieves.

7930 1855 50 DOLLARS. Rare.

Kagin 9, p. 307; KM 62. Head as preceding except no initials on coronet. Average weight 1,287.9 grs. = 83.455 gms. Issued in quantity beginning May 16, 1855. Probably 60–75 known. Usually heavily dented, nicked, and scratched; often with fields retooled or polished to minimize other damage. Auction 79:1478, UNC., $37,500; Ellsworth, Garrett:947, UNC., $275,000. Enl. photos.

Ex J. W. Garrett: 947. Courtesy Bowers & Ruddy Galleries, Inc.

CHAPTER 44

MORMON ISSUES (Dec. 1848–60)

The history of the Gold Rush is inextricably intertwined with that of the Church of Jesus Christ of Latter Day Saints, more familiarly known as the Mormon Church. As Don Taxay has pointed out, Mormon "Forty-Niners" included both James Marshall (who made the actual discovery of gold, Jan. 24, 1848) and Sam Brannan (who galloped through San Francisco streets shouting about it), as well as many of the earliest miners. One of the richest deposits was on Mormon Island, downstream from Sutter's Mill at Coloma on the American River.

When Mormon miners began bringing gold dust back in quantity to Deseret ('Honeybee') Territory (the Salt Lake City area), Brigham Young conceived the idea of creating a distinctive local coinage. On Nov. 25, 1848, Young and John Taylor conferred with John Mobourn Kay, formerly connected with one of the Birmingham (England) private mints, to determine procedures for smelting and coining California gold ores. Between them they determined the devices and inscriptions. Kay and Alfred B. Lambson forged the die blanks; Robert L. Campbell and Kay engraved them. Rust {1984}, pp. 38–45; Kagin {1981}.

These devices and inscriptions require explanation. Obvs. depict the Emblem of Mormon Priesthood, the "three-pointed Phrygian Crown," above the All-Seeing Eye. HOLINESS TO THE LORD is the King James Version's rendering of Exodus 28:36, originally intended for engraving on the Hebrews' sacred jewels. The clasped hands device stands for friendship. G.S.L.C.P.G. = "Great Salt Lake City Pure Gold," though the bullion all came from California except for the 1860 mintage, which was from Colorado gold. On the $10, instead of the initials, was PURE GOLD. Both labels were misnomers: Not only was California gold naturally alloyed, the Salt Lake City coiners admixed it still further. The Latter Day Saints' own term for their gold pieces was "Valley Coins."

The very first issue was of $10 denomination. Kay struck [46] $10's in Dec. 1848: 25 on Dec. 12, 21 more on Dec. 19. Apparently the dies were dated 1849 in anticipation of coinage continuing into the next year. Immediately afterward, the crucibles broke, so that no more ore could be smelted, no ingots formed. As the need for a circulating medium was severe, Brigham Young (with others of the Mormon Church's 12 Apostles) signed and circulated handwritten paper currency dated between Dec. 29, 1848, and Jan. 5, 1849. These (along with several later issues of 1849) were recalled and burned after the Church managed to buy new crucibles, Sept. 1849.

Coinage resumed on Sept. 12, at the Deseret Mint, actually the home of Dr. William Sharp, South Temple Ave., Salt Lake City, now the site of the Hotel Utah garage (Rust {1984}, p. 43). Kay and Campbell made dies for $2½, $5, and $20 coins. Any more $10's must have been from the old dies. They struck many thousands of specimens of $2½'s and $5's, which found enthusiastic acceptance among the Saints as an improvement over gold dust.

However, as soon as any Valley Coins reached "Gentile" (non-Mormon) territories, assayers tested them and at once recalled the line from Daniel 5:27: "weighed in the balance and found wanting." All were lightweight and of low fineness. The Mormon coins became the object of scorn and contempt exceeding even that heaped later on Baldwin's issues: San Francisco newspapers' commoner epithets for them included "spurious," "debased," and "vile falsehoods." Nor did the Philadelphia Mint's own assays help: Eckfeldt & DuBois {1850} quoted the average fineness at 866, weights and bullion values correspondingly low—a circumstance which doubtless contributed nearly as much as the polygamy issue to federal opposition to the Mormons. According to the Mint's assayers, Mormon $20's ranged from 436 to 453 grs. (28.3–29.4 gms.), value $16.90 to $17.53; $10's, 219–224 grs. (14.2–14.5 gms.), value $8.50 to $8.70; $5's, about 111 grs. = 7.19 gms., value $4.30; $2½'s, about 58 grs. = 3.76 gms., value $2.25. The fineness, notably lower than the normal range for California gold, strongly suggested either incompetence or fraud, strange for a church labeling its own coins as "Pure Gold." Most of the Mormon coins that found their way to California perished in the mass meltings (1851–52) following James King of William's smear campaign against Baldwin & Co. In the meantime, bankers had accepted them only at 25% discount, if at all, while other discredited coins passed at 20% off face value.

By Brigham Young's orders, the new coins of 1850 were alloyed with silver and struck from redesigned dies. Mintage of 1850-dated $5's continued through June 19, 1851. Not that it helped: These shared in the ill repute of the 1849 issues, and perished similarly. Mass meltings made rarities of them all.

In 1852–53, Enoch and John Reek brought Nevada gold ore for coinage. It proved so low grade ($11.50/oz) that the church redeemed all the coins struck from it: Rust {1984}, p. 46.

The Saints' final coins were struck from Colorado gold, reportedly about 917 Fine, with only its natural silver alloy. Obv. depicts the Lion of Judah; rev., a straw skep beehive protected by the American eagle. The beehive was a holy symbol of industriousness. DESERET ASSAY OFFICE on rev. was actually the jewelry shop of J. M. Barlow, at which place Barlow and Douglas Brown struck the coins with the help of David McKenzie. According to Kagin, Barlow made the dies; others have attributed them to Albert Küner. The inscription in the Deseret alphabet (only in use during 1852–69) is in English, a phonetic rendering of HOLINESS TO THE LORD. The [202] coined July 27 through Dec. 12, 1859, from 1860-dated dies, cannot be distinguished from the [587] struck between Jan. 14, 1860 and March 8, 1861: Rust {1984}, pp. 86–87. The Gentile Territorial Gov. Alfred Cummings prohibited them in 1861. The *Deseret*

News, March 5, 1862, says that Mormon gold coins became uncurrent as of that date.

Estimated mintages herein are ballpark figures based on Mc-Garry {1950}, who gave the total as $75,000 for all 1849–51 issues; this amount is partitioned according to known relative frequencies of occurrence. The actual numbers of $10's and $20's were probably a little larger, those of the 1849 $2½'s and $5's probably slightly smaller.

No grading standards are established. We suggest that for VERY FINE over half the fingers should be separated; for EXTREMELY FINE, all should be. The grading problem is complicated by early progressive die failure: Despite Kay's experience with a Birmingham mint, neither he nor any of the other Saints knew how to harden a die properly, and several obvs. began buckling, the $2½ by far the worst. So convex are most coins of this denomination, that even on pieces with mint luster, details of eye and bases of some letters are blurred.

LATTER DAY SAINTS, STATE OF DESERET.

Issue of Dec. 1848: "PURE GOLD."

7931 1849 TEN. DOLLARS [46+] 8–10 known.
Kagin 3, p. 313; KM 106. Plain edge. Usually in low grades. See introductory text.   1) Mint, SI.   2) Brand, Lilly, SI.   3) Leavitt (1884), Dietrich, Brown, Zabriskie, Slack, Lawrence, Waltman, Morris, 1973 ANA:1038, VG.   4) Bolt:1148, F.   5) Ex Charles M. Williams.   6) Sheppard, Granberg, Brand, Clifford, Kagin, 221.5 grs. = 14.35 gms.   7) Knoop, Walton, Gibson, Leo A. Young, 1983 ANA:3659, F, planchet defect below cap.   8) Col. Green, Jerome Kern, Carter:1163, AU, $132,000, R. L. Hughes.   9),10) Mormon Temple, Salt Lake City.

Issue of Sept. 1849–1851: "G.S.L.C.P.G."

7932 1849 TWO.AND.HALF.DO. [Estimated 3,560] Rare.
Kagin 1, p. 313; KM 102. Plain edge. Obv. normally convex, affecting eye, "Phrygian crown," and lower parts of all letters; 1 in date weak. Very rare with all letters legible. 56.5–58.5 grs. = 3.66–3.79 gms. Bangs & Co. (1881), Garrett:950, VF, $9,000; Auction 82:993, UNC., $6,750.

7933 1849 FIVE.DOLLARS [Estimated 5,340] Rare.
Kagin 2, p. 313; KM 103. Plain edge. Similar; weak at parts of eye, hand, 8, and borders. Usually in low grades. 111.2–113.5 grs. = 7.206–7.354 gms. Mehl (1921), Garrett:951, VF, $7,500; Auction 82:994, VF, $3,650.

7934 1849 TWENTY.DOLLARS [Estimated 1,080] Very rare.
Kagin 4, p. 313; KM 107. Plain edge. 444.5–445.7 grs. = 28.8–28.89 gms. Usually in low grades, scraped, or otherwise impaired. Hands always weak. Auction 79:1489, EF, $37,500; Zabriskie, Ellsworth, Garrett:954, EF, $50,000.

7935 1850 FIVE DOLLARS [Estimated 3,560] Rare.
Kagin 5, p. 314; KM 104. Plain edge. Above eye is halo; base of "Phrygian crown" is always indistinct. Significance of 9 stars is uncertain. 109.3–111 grs. = 7.083–7.19 gms. Hesslein, Garrett:952, VF, $6,000; Auction 82:995, UNC., $8,500.

"DESERET ASSAY OFFICE," UTAH TERRITORY

Issue of 1860–61

7936 1860 5.D. [789] Rare.
Kagin 6, p. 314; KM 105. Reeded edge. 121.9 grs. = 7.9 gms. See introductory text. Ten Eyck, Garrett:953, EF, $16,000; Auction 82:996, UNC., $10,000.

CHAPTER 45

OREGON TERRITORIAL ISSUES
(March–Sept. 1849)

During the generations before the California Gold Rush, the inhabitants of the Willamette Valley, like those of the entire Pacific Northwest, managed to survive on a barter economy. The primary media of exchange were beaver pelts and wheat; the latter became legal tender by act of the Provisional Government of 1843. By the spring of 1848, the area's population had grown to 13,000, its largest settlement being Oregon City, population 800. On Aug. 9, 1848, gold dust from California arrived aboard the brig *Henry,* and within two months an estimated 2/3 of the Territory's male population had left for the California mining district, where they founded Hangtown (later called Placerville). By mid-Jan. 1849, some $400,000 in gold dust reached Oregon, with the usual results: perpetual disputes over its weight and fineness, the necessity of weighing and testing, and petitions by the citizenry for a local mint. One of these petitions, dated Feb. 7, 1849, reached the legislature; on Feb. 16 it passed a law 16 to 2, setting up such a mint at Oregon City, 15 miles north of Portland. The act named James Taylor as Director, Truman Powers as Treasurer, George L. Curry as Assayer, and W. H. Willson as Melter and Coiner. Gold coins (reckoned at $16.50 per oz.) were to be struck in $5 and $10 denominations, to depict the territorial arms, and to read OREGON TERRITORY 1849. Profits were to pay the cost of dealing with a local Indian uprising known as the Cayuse War.

However, before any coin dies could be made, the first Territorial Governor (Joseph Lane) arrived, declared the area a Territory of the United States, and on March 3 nullified the coinage act as being in violation of the United States Constitution: an action of dubious legality, as this forbids the states to issue money, but says nothing of territories.

What a state (or, presumably, a territorial government) could not legally do, private citizens could and did. Eight prominent businessmen met in the counting room of Campbell & Smith, in Oregon City, and formed the Oregon Exchange Company, intending to make coins out of gold dust. Some of these men were the same ones named in the former mint act. James Taylor was Director, W. H. Willson Assayer. William H. Rector supervised manufacture of dies, irons, and press. James Gill Campbell sketched designs for the coins. The functions of George Abernethy (formerly Provisional Governor of the Territory), William K. Kilborne, Theophilus Magruder, and Noyes Smith were not spelled out, but most likely included raising funds for equipment. These eight partners' initials appeared on the $5 coins as issuing authority.

Rector hired Thomas Powell to construct the press and other ironmongery (including die blanks) from scrap wagon wheel rims. Both men helped with "turning" (lathe work on dies). Rev. Hamilton Campbell, Methodist missionary, assisted by Rector, engraved the $5 dies from James Gill Campbell's drawings.

These dies contained a couple of anomalies: T.O. for "Territory of Oregon" instead of O.T. for "Oregon Territory"; and among the eight partners, James Gill Campbell's initial appeared as G for his middle name (was he known as Gill Campbell?), perhaps to avoid confusion with the Rev. Campbell, the engraver, who was not one of the partners. Hence the coins' initials K. M. T. A. W. R. G. S. should be read respectively as Kilborne, Magruder, Taylor, Abernethy, Willson, Rector, Gill Campbell, and Smith. Owing to lack of time, the company voted to put the dies into use despite these apparent errors. Brown {1892}, p. 414, says that they struck [6,000].

The $10 dies, engraved by Victor Wallace, gave the location as O.T., rendered Gill Campbell's initial as C, and omitted the initials of Abernethy and Willson as these men did not put up extra funds for purchasing new equipment. Brown gives the mintage as [2,850].

All the "Beaver Money" coins were made from unalloyed California gold without attempt at assay or standardization. To make up for any possible deficiencies in fineness, the partners set the coins' weight at well above federal standards. Philadelphia Mint assays valued them at $5.50 and $11; California bankers, at $4 and $8, doubtless to make profit on melting, and contributing to their rarity. Coinage operations ended about Sept. 1, 1849, when both crucibles broke, following less than six months' use. By 1850, California gold coins were becoming available to supplement the Beavers, and the emergency which had led to the latter was over.

Both denominations are unusually soft, commonly with nicks, dents, scratches, and planchet chips or flakes; they also vary greatly in color. No grading standards are established. We suggest VERY FINE: Beaver's eye, about half fur, and nearby vegetation should be clear. EXTREMELY FINE: More than half fur must be intact; only a few tiny rubbed spots. On the $10, die buckling weakens beaver and central rev.: grade by surface.

OREGON EXCHANGE CO.

7937   1849 5 D. [6,000] Rare.
   Kagin 1, p. 315; KM 100. Plain edge. Stated weight 130
   G(rains) = 8.42 gms.; observed, 128–132 grs. = 8.29–8.55
   gms. (The reeded-edge coin reported by Farran Zerbe is un-
   confirmed to exist.) Usually in low grades, banged up, and
   sometimes tooled in fields. Auction 79:1485, AU, $14,500;
   Jenks, Garrett:948, VF, $20,000; LM 9/67, Auction 82:992,
   UNC., $29,000. Enl. photos.

Ex J. W. Garrett: 948. Courtesy Bowers & Ruddy Galleries, Inc.

7938   1849 TEN.D. [2,850] 13–16 known.
   Kagin 2, p. 315; KM 101. Plain edge. Stated weight 10.D. 20
   G. = 10 dwt 20 grs. = 260 grs. = 16.85 gms.; observed,
   257.3–262 grs. = 16.67–17 gms. Usually in low grades as
   preceding; always weak in centers. Auction 79:1486, AU,
   $57,500; Garrett:949, F, $40,000. Enl. photos.

CHAPTER 46

JEFFERSON TERRITORY/COLORADO ISSUES (1860–61)

1. CLARK, GRUBER & CO.

Though reports recurred for generations of small finds of gold nuggets in the wilderness near the South Platte River, only in 1858 did these stimulate anything comparable to the California Gold Rush. Its effective beginning date was Aug. 26, 1858, when the Kansas City *Journal of Commerce* reported success on the part of two groups of prospectors on the South Platte, about eight miles above Cherry Creek: about 1/2 to 2/3 oz. of gold per man per day. At the junction of these streams, other groups of prospectors in Oct. 1858 founded a new town named Auraria. This name, from Latin *aurum,* 'gold,' repeated that of the Georgia hometown of one of the leaders, William Green Russell. On Nov. 16, yet another group, from Leavenworth and Lecompton, Kans., settled on the east side of the South Platte and founded another town, which they named Denver City after the then Governor of Kansas Territory, John W. Denver (nominally in charge of the whole area). Denver City grew rapidly, especially after May 6, 1859, when John Gregory discovered enormous quantities of gold near Central City, and the story reached newspapers in all the larger eastern cities; by April 1860, Denver City absorbed Auraria.

Local leaders found that food was scarce, housing minimal, some supplies could not be purchased at any price nearer than Omaha, Neb., or St. Joseph, Mo., theft and violence were common, and law enforcement nonexistent. Normally they would have gone to the territorial authorities in Kansas City, but Kansas Territory was then embroiled in the "Bleeding Kansas" carnage that erupted into civil war, and no help could be expected. Later in 1859, the authorities took the only remaining course: They set up their own government, calling the region Territory of Jefferson. It would not be renamed Colorado until 1861.

Gold dust and nuggets became the ubiquitous media of exchange, exactly as in California 10 years earlier. Gold-dust brokers set up a profitable business of buying the unrefined ore at $12 to $16 per oz., paying in Eastern bank drafts or occasionally in federal coins, and the less scrupulous ones created abuses similar to those common in California. But even the most honest among the brokers had to pay surcharges for insuring and transporting the bullion under armed guard; the risk of loss was very great, coins minted from it in Philadelphia took a minimum of three months to get back to the Denver City area, and the risk of robbery of stagecoaches was maximal when their payload contained gold coins. Only one satisfactory answer remained: a local mint—and it did not matter if this was federally or privately operated.

Into this acute necessity came Clark, Gruber & Co., bankers, brokers, assayers, and minters. It has been well said that the history of the beginning of commerce in Colorado Territory is the history of this firm. Its partners were Austin M. Clark, his brother Milton Edward Clark (the firm's attorney), and Emanuel H. Gruber. In Dec. 1859, Milton Clark traveled to Philadelphia to buy dies and presses, and to New York to buy other minting equipment; on Jan. 18, 1860, the firm bought three lots in Denver City on which they built their mint; and on March 30, one L. L. Todd arrived to help set up the "Assay and Coinage Office." This was a two-story brick building on the corner of McGaa and G Sts. (the present 16th and Market). Trial strikings of the four denominations ($2.50, $5, $10, and $20) were ready on July 11, one day after the building actually opened, and on July 20 the firm invited local VIPs and newspaper people in to witness the first coinage of $10's, about 100 pieces *(Rocky Mountain News,* 7/20/1860). Clark, Gruber & Co. began advertising in the same paper on Aug. 8, and in the *Western Mountaineer* on Aug. 9, specifying that "The native gold is coined as it is found alloyed with silver. The weight will be greater, but the value the same as the United States coin of like denominations."

Coinage totaled some $120,000 between July and Oct. 1860, continuing into the winter until heavy snows made further prospecting impractical, and resuming at the spring thaw. The firm discovered quickly that its issues of 1860 were too soft to wear well. Accordingly, its redesigned issues dated 1861 (coined through 1862) contained a little extra alloy in the interest of durability, but their gold content remained at 1% over the federal standard so that nobody could accuse the firm of debasement or other dishonesty. They were Colorado Territory's exact counterpart of California's Moffat & Co., even to a federal takeover for conversion into a branch mint.

The phrase PIKES PEAK GOLD DENVER has to do more with mint location than with bullion sources; though the whole area was known as the "Pike's Peak District," most of the nuggets and dust actually came from the Central City area and other mining towns west of Denver. The image of Pike's Peak is fictitious, suggesting a volcanic cone rather than merely one massif in a mountain range longer than Colorado Territory. (On the copper strikings from the first or rejected die, it is stylized into an equilateral triangle.) The engraver is unknown, believed to be someone under contract with Bailey & Co., Philadelphia: one of the Lovetts? The mountain die of the $10, worn and rusted, lately turned up in Philadelphia.

Mintages are not precisely known. The firm provided approximate totals in the *Weekly Commonwealth & Republican,* Jan. 8, 1863, as follows: Coined, July 1860 to Jan. 1, 1861, $131,220.50; calendar 1861, $240,165; calendar 1862, $222,919.50. Given these figures and Kagin's rarity ratings for the eight date-denomination vars., we can arrive at ballpark estimates of the original mintages. These assume that the rarity ratings are accurate and that the survivors are a random sample, no one denomination or date being too heavily favored for saving, nor selectively melted. This procedure indicates that about 1/68 of the 1860 mintage survives, but only about 1/159 of that dated 1861, suggesting that many of the latter were converted into ingots. These ballpark estimates are included in the main text, below.

During 1862, for reasons never made clear (but likely to have included federal pressure), Clark, Gruber & Co. switched from coining gold dust to forming it into rectangular ingots. These ingots were accepted at stamped value nationwide and as far off as Europe and Australia. Though issued in immense quantities (Kagin says over $828,000!), no specimen is traced today. Most likely all were converted into coin at one or another federal mint, or used in industry.

On April 16, 1863, the federal government bought out the firm at a pittance, on the pretense of setting up a branch mint. However, much to the discomfiture of locals, no coinage followed until 1906; the Denver "Mint" functioned only as an assay office during its first 40 years.

The above account derives from Kagin {1981}, Clifford {1961}, Mumey {1950}, Hall {1890}, Smiley {1901}, Stone {1918}, Spring {1963}, and Adams et al. {1984}.

CLARK, GRUBER & CO.

Designer, Engraver, unknown (L. L. Todd? George W. Mc-Clure?). Mint, Clark's, McGaa and G Sts., Denver City. Composition, native Colorado gold, about 828.5 Fine, without (1860) or with (1861) unspecified alloy. Weight standard, $20, 560 grs. = 36.3 gms.; $10, 280 grs. = 18.1 gms.; $5, 140 grs. = 9.07 gms.; $2½, 70 grs. = 4.54 gms.; $20 and $10 up to 5% heavier, $5 and $2½ up to 10% heavier. Diameters, respectively, 22/16" = 35 mm; 11/10" = 28 mm; 7/8" = 22 mm; 7/10" = 18 mm. Reeded edges.

Grade range, VG to UNC., normally VF to AU. VERY FINE: Over half hair or feather details intact; most trees on mountain clear. EXTREMELY FINE: Tiny isolated rubbed spots only; partial mint luster. EXCEPTIONS: Some are weak in centers as noted below.

7939   1860 2½ D. [About 15,096] Very scarce.
Kagin 1, p. 316; KM 63. Omission of Gruber's name from coronet represents spacing problems on this and next. Centers always weak (relief too high). Earliest strikings (Aug. 1860) have prooflike fields; later ones develop cracks at l. and upper stars. Many were saved as first of their kind. 69.4–74 grs. = 4.5–4.8 gms. Aulick, Garrett:526, UNC., $12,000; Clifford:189, EF, $2,000; Beck, Auction 82:997, UNC., $4,750.

7940   1860 FIVE D. [About 6,920] Very scarce.
Kagin 2, p. 317; KM 65. Central obv. usually weak. Gruber's name omitted for same reason as preceding. 138.8–140.9 grs. = 8.994–9.13 gms. Die later cracked from rim to C(LARK): Clifford:191, EF, $2,200. Wayman:429, AU, $2,800; Ellsworth, Garrett:531, UNC., $9,000; Auction 82:998, UNC., $5,500.

7941   1860 TEN D. [About 3,500] Rare.
Kagin 3, p. 317; KM 67. First denomination struck, July 20, 1860. Fictitious view of Pike's Peak: See introductory text. 275.7–280 grs. = 17.87–18.1 gms. Many were saved as first of their kind. Later strikings have die cracks through many letters. Aulick, Garrett:536, AU, $6,400; Wayman:428, EF, $6,500; Auction 82:999, UNC., $9,250.

7942   1860 TWENTY D. [About 1,020] 11–14 known.
Kagin 4, p. 317; KM 69. Fictitious view of Pike's Peak as preceding. 566.5–568 grs. = 36.71–36.81 gms. Shield almost always weak. Auction 79:1494, EF, $30,000; Mehl (1922), Garrett:542, AU, $40,000; Wayman:427, EF, $22,000.

7943   1861 2½ D. [About 31,800] Very scarce.
Kagin 5, p. 318; KM 64. PIKES PEAK on coronet on all denominations. 73.8–74 grs. = 4.78–4.8 gms. Always weak in centers. Coarser or finer edge reeding, latter (Kagin 5a) very rare. Ellsworth, Garrett:529, EF, $1,600; Wayman:434, EF, $1,800; Clifford:189, EF, $2,000.

Ex J. W. Garrett: 529. Courtesy Bowers & Ruddy Galleries, Inc.

7944   1861 FIVE D. [About 19,192] Very scarce.
Kagin 6, p. 318; KM 66. Usually weak in centers. Later, cracks from rim to C(LARK), VE(R). 140–143.4 grs. = 9.07–9.292 gms. Ellsworth, Garrett:534, VF, $1,600; Wayman:433, EF, $2,400.

7945   1861 TEN D. [About 15,900] Very scarce.
Kagin 7, p. 318; KM 68. Usually weak at eagle's neck, shield, claws, and stem. Later, die cracked through date and upper letters. One is overstruck on an 1849 $10. Weight range (excluding the overstrike), 287.7–295.4 grs. = 18.64–19.14 gms. Ellsworth, Garrett:539, EF, $3,600; Wayman:432, EF, $2,300.

7946   1861 TWENTY D. [About 6,360] Very rare.
Kagin 8, p. 319; KM 70. V(ER) corrected from erroneous N. Usually weak on hair below PIKES PEAK and r. of ear, shield and scrolls l. and r. of chief azure. One is overstruck on an 1857 S $20: Ford (1961), Kagin, Colorado pvt. coll., 1983 ANA:3724. Weight range (excluding overstrike), 580–588.4 grs. = 37.6–38.18 gms. Gibson:211, AU, $21,000 (1974); Clifford:202, EF, $14,000; Wayman:431, AU, $15,000.

2. JOHN J. CONWAY & CO.

Following immense discoveries of gold at Georgia Gulch, near Parkville, Summit County, traders visited the mining camps selling whiskey and other "necessary supplies" at inflated prices, reckoning gold dust at $14 to $16 per oz. The miners began refusing to buy anything unless their gold dust was valued at $18 per oz.: It was after all considerably finer than its California counterpart. At this juncture, John J. Conway & Co., Parkville jewelers and bankers, offered to coin gold dust into $2½, $5, and $10 pieces: Hall {1890}, p. 328.

On Aug. 13, 1861, the Denver *Rocky Mountain News* denounced Conway's coins as lightweight, debased, and worth less than face value, citing assays in Denver which had rated them at 772.5 Fine, the $5's worth only $4.26 apiece. Eight days later, the same paper printed a retraction—the often-quoted lines about the "mint in Georgia Gulch, conducted by J. J. Conway & Co., jewelers and bankers. Their machinery seems to be as fine as that of Clark, Gruber & Co., and their five- and ten-dollar gold pieces look as nice and rich as Uncle Sam himself could get up." But even this was not enough, and Conway had another assay of a $5 made in Denver, by one T. G. Perrenaud, which gave weight as 140.3 grs. (= 9.091 gms.), 0.822 gold, 0.078 silver, 0.100 presumably copper, and value $5.01. The same newspaper published these results on Sept. 24, 1861. Nevertheless, despite this vindication, Conway's mint closed shortly afterward; the main reason seems to have been that gold production in Georgia Gulch dwindled. Parkville, once the county seat, became a ghost town. Conway's dies eventually went to the Colorado Historical Society, which issued some 200

sets of "goldine" (brass) restrikes in 1956: See Clifford:206–8. Kagin pictures the dies: {1981}, p. 320.

Conway's original coins are so rare that grading is irrelevant. Nothing is known of their designer, engraver, or weight standards.

7947   n.d. (Aug.–Sept. 1861) 2½ DOLL'S Ex. rare.
Kagin 1, p. 321; KM 71. 1) Virgil Brand, H. L. P. Brand, Robert Friedberg, KS 3/64, Gibson:215, $39,000 (1974), Wayman:435, AU, $42,000, S 10/27/83:270. 2) Powell, RARCOA, NN, Batchelder, Gibson:216, EF, scratched, $19,000. 3) Williams, Lilly, SI. 4) Clifford, Kagin. 68.5 grs. = 4.44 gms. 5) SI. 6) Clifford, Bank of California. 7) Clemens, Granberg, Newcomer, Green, Williams, duPont.

7948   n.d. (Aug.–Sept. 1861) FIVE DOLLARS Ornate 5 in center. Ex. rare.
Kagin 2a, p. 321; KM 72.1. 1) SI. 2) Granberg, Woodin, Newcomer, Mehl (1925), Garrett:550, EF, 140.8 grs. = 9.124 gms., $100,000, Kagin. Enl. photos. 3) Brand, Williams, EF. 4) Taylor-Windle:506, Granberg, Newcomer, Green, duPont, VF, 141.19 grs. = 9.149 gms. 5) Elmer Sears (9/12), Brand II:1555, EF, 134.1 grs. = 8.69 gms. 6) Smith & Sons, Lilly, SI.

Ex J. W. Garrett: 550. Courtesy Bowers & Ruddy Galleries, Inc.

7949   n.d. (Aug. 1861?) FIVE DOLLARS. Without ornate 5. Unique?
Kagin 2, p. 321; KM 72.2. Unfinished die of preceding? 1) Overstruck on an 1845 half eagle, 129 grs. = 8.36 gms. Kreisberg (1965):25a, $28,750, Marks:1145, $36,000 (1972).

7950   n.d. (Aug.–Sept. 1861) TEN DOLLARS. Ex. rare.
Kagin 3, p. 321; KM 73. 1) Mint, SI. Clain-Stefanelli {1970}, fig. 56. 2) Lilly, SI. 3) Clifford, Kagin, 260 grs. = 16.84 gms., ill.

3. PARSONS & CO.

Dr. John D. Parsons, a native of Indiana with a metallurgical background, arrived in Denver City about July 23, 1858, and headed for Oro City with his assaying equipment. He formed a real estate partnership with a Mr. Black in Denver, but set up his equipment at Tarryall Mines, "near the mouth of the canyon northwest of Como where the railway now passes up to cross the range to Breckenridge," midway between the towns of Tarryall and Hamilton: Smiley {1901}. The Denver *Rocky Mountain News,* June 27, 1861, described the Parsons mint as in Hamilton, and mentioned sight of "facsimiles" (evidently the rare copper trial strikings) of his $2½ and $5 coins; the *Miners Record* of Sept. 7 refers to seeing Parsons's first gold $2½ a few days earlier.

Lyman Low claimed in Winslow J. Howard:315 (June 3, 1886, quoted in NN 60:603) that Dr. Parsons's brief operation yielded under $500 in coins during its final month, because the Phillips Lode (his major ore source) was exhausted. That would have meant something like 84 $2½'s and 56 $5's: surely only a small fraction of his total output, because the survivors of those denominations number 1/14 of the named figures—many times higher than the survival ratios for all other pioneer gold for which even approximate mintages are known.

The controversial $20 ingot, if genuine, must have preceded arrival of Parsons's dies and presses. All this needed was letter and numeral punches, a crucible for melting the gold, and an ingot mold for forming it. At its stated weight in 18½-carat (771 Fine) gold, it purports to contain 473.6 grs. pure gold = $20.40; it is slightly lighter, and its fineness remains untested.

Most of Parsons's output must have gone to Clark, Gruber & Co. for conversion into ingots, especially if the coins were heavily debased. This accusation is in Whiteley {1958}; I have been unable to find confirmation. The coins are heavier than federal standard and were probably made from unrefined native gold, like Clark Gruber & Co. coins of 1860.

An unsolved problem is why the final S is omitted from Parsons's name in both $2½ and $5 dies. Kagin suggests that this was a spacing problem, which might make sense on the $2½ die but not on the $5: PARSON is spread out enough that had the engraver known the correct spelling he could have made room for the S. Others have attributed it to the medical man's handwriting—a problem notorious among physicians ever since they began writing prescriptions.

The word ORO (Spanish: 'gold') on the dies refers to Oro City in California Gulch, near Leadville, Colo., where Dr. Parsons settled before beginning to work his claims in Buckskin Joe and Tarryall following exhaustion of local gold placers. Apparently Parsons had ordered his dies months earlier, while preparing to move to Oro City from Denver. Their obv. device inaccurately represents a quartz-reduction mill, for extracting gold from crushed ore.

There is no evidence that Dr. Parsons made any more coins after 1861. A few years later he was back in Denver, writing a handbook on mining; he also did some exploration, managed a boardinghouse for invalids, and started the Denver Woolen Mills (1870) and the ill-fated Denver Aqueduct Company (1873), blocked by political manipulation. He died in 1881: Young {1983}.

7951 1860 TWENTY DOL.S Specie ingot. Unique?
Kagin 1, p. 322. As ill. Letters individually punched into

ingot, S's all rotated 180° from normal. Stated weight = 614.4 grs. = 39.81 gms.; actual weight 610 grs. = 39.53 gms. See introductory text. 1) Lilly, SI. Warning: Numerous base-metal forgeries exist, many of them made by Curtin & Pease for promotional purposes during the 1960s; all are much lighter in weight than the original. Authentication is mandatory.

7952 n.d. (1861) 2½ D. 6 known.
Kagin 2, p. 322; KM 74. 1) Mint, SI. 73.5 grs. = 4.763 gms. 2) C. S. Wilcox:1084, DeWitt Smith, Virgil Brand, B. Max Mehl, Charles M. Williams, 1956 ANA:1858, John Herhold Murrell, 1958 ANA:2016B, Henry H. Clifford, Kagin, ill. 71 grs. = 4.6 gms. 3) Gregory:2413, S. H. Chapman, Garrett:547, $85,000, Coles, Auction 84:1498. 73.2 grs. = 4.74 gms. 4) Slack:48, Bell I:1052, Maj. Alfred Walter, NN 60:603, Lester Merkin, Wayman:436, $48,000. 72.5 grs. = 4.714 gms. 5) W. H. Smith (1885), Waldo Newcomer, B. Max Mehl, Wayte Raymond (1933), Lammot duPont, Willis H. duPont, unidentified thieves, Oct. 5, 1967. "F," weight unknown. 6) F. C. C. Boyd, Frank Smith, Smith & Son (Wheaton, Ill.), Josiah K. Lilly, SI, weight unknown. The first 4 have all been graded VF at one time or another; all are similarly weak on wings, neck, and shield.

7953 n.d. (1861) FIVE D. 3 known.
Kagin 3, p. 322; KM 75. 1) Mint, SI, weight unknown. 2) Mehl (1922), Garrett:549, $100,000, S 10/27/83:268. 130.7 grs. = 8.469 gms. 3) A. C. Gies, F. C. C. Boyd, Charles M. Williams, John Rowe, J. H. Murrell, 1956 ANA:1857, KS 4/67:622, H. Clifford, Kagin, ill., 128.3 grs. = 8.314 gms. 4) Boyd, Kelly, Lilly, SI. 5) Granberg, Newcomer, Green, duPont.

7954–7999 Reserved for future discoveries in Pioneer Gold.

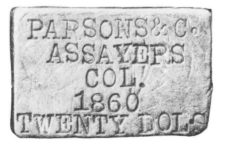

Part Eight

OTHER AUTHORIZED
LOCAL ISSUES

CHAPTER 47

COINAGES OF THE SOUTHERN CONFEDERACY (1861)

In Dec. 1860, the Secession Convention resolved that the New Orleans branch mint should be "taken into trust" on behalf of the Confederacy. The actual transfer took place Feb. 28, 1861. Incumbent officers were confirmed in their positions on swearing allegiance to the Confederate States of America. These included William A. Elmore, Superintendent; A. J. Guirot, Treasurer; Howard Millspaugh, Assayer; M. F. Bonzano, M.D., Melter and Refiner. Bonzano remained on duty as a Union spy; his reports to the Union Treasury are in the National Archives: Compare Chap. 28, Sect. x, introductory text, and Breen {1977}, p. 239. Dr. B. F. Taylor was appointed Chief Coiner. There was no Engraver, as the Philadelphia Mint had supplied dies since the beginning of branch-mint coinage in 1838.

Through Feb. 27, the establishment had delivered [330,000] half dollars (**4903–5**) and [5,000] double eagles (**7209**) under the Union. After the seizure by rebel authorities, operations continued, using Union dies. Deliveries in March were recorded as for the State of Louisiana: [1,240,000] half dollars, [9,750] double eagles; in April, for the CSA, [962,633] half dollars, [2,991] double eagles. Except for a single half-dollar var. (**4906**), these are in general indistinguishable from the Union issue.

During April 1861, CSA Treasury Secretary C. G. Memminger solicited designs for half-dollar dies. The one he approved combined the Union obv. type with the Confederate arms, as used on the four Confederate proofs. A. H. M. Patterson, engraver and diesinker of Commercial Place, New Orleans, received the assignment to make working dies of the new design, but apparently went no further than a single rev. This could have been used in the dollar press opposite another die blank to raise a hub, but apparently either he did not know the technique, or proper die steel was in too short supply: Available documentation does not reveal which. Conrad Schmidt, foreman of the coining room, prepared the Confederate die for press, burnishing it and a Union obv. to create proofs, not noticing that this die was already cracked from rim to bridge of nose, almost touching seventh star.

On some unspecified day in the last half of April 1861, the New Orleans branch mint struck four proofs, which went to VIPs as detailed below. Pending Memminger's approval and orders to proceed with production coinage, the project was suspended. In the meantime, this cracked Union obv. remained in press, and one of the regular revs. was inserted, producing **4905**, the "Cracked Confederate Obv." var.; the obv. cracked further between foot, rim, and adjacent stars, the rev. through bases of HALF DOL. We owe this discovery to Martin Luther Beistle {1929}, who called the var. 5-D, or with cracked dies 5a-Da.

During the remainder of the month, production of half dollars continued from these and other Union dies.

However, instead of the expected go-ahead, Memminger ordered suspension of all further coinage operations. His reason has not been published; as the New Orleans branch mint had ample uncoined bullion on hand, the most probable explanation was difficulty in obtaining enough high-quality steel to make dies. The institution closed on April 30, 1861. Dr. Bonzano generously offered to stand guard; he did so until Union troops arrived, but was unable to prevent them from indulging in vandalism. Confederate authorities took the remaining gold and silver (coined and uncoined) to safety on the rebel transport *Star of the West.*

Dr. Taylor, as Chief Coiner, retained the rev. die and one of the four proofs, but maintained secrecy for over a decade after the war, lest he be prosecuted for treason in having supervised manufacture of the rebel coins. He broke the story in the New Orleans *Picayune,* April 9, 1879, publishing correspondence between himself and the Hon. Marcus J. Wright, of the Adjutant General's Office. The coin dealer Ebenezer Locke Mason, Jr., promptly contacted Dr. Taylor and bought the coin and die, reselling both to J. W. Scott. The coin's century of later history is detailed at **8000.**

Scott found that the Confederate die was extensively rusted and that a piece had chipped out of border near ER(ICA). He proposed to make and promote restrikes, but was understandably dubious that the die would last long enough to complete even a few dozen impressions. With the help of David Proskey, he repolished it to minimize rust, and struck 500 "white metal" (probably tin) tokens (**8003**). As the die suffered no further deterioration during this limited run, Scott went ahead with his original plan, which was oddly ingenious and guaranteed to prevent confusion between his restrikes and the original proofs. He obtained 500 1861 half dollars, probably many coming from circulation, supposedly all O-Mint coins, though this is impossible to prove or disprove. Proskey, under his supervision, placed the first few on a brass block, obv. down, probably within some kind of plain collar to prevent undue spreading under pressure, and overstruck their Union revs. with the Confederate die (**8001**): *CW* 7/14/82. As the Union rev. impressions mingled too obviously with the Confederate, Proskey planed off the revs. of the remainder of the 500 before overstriking them. The result is immediately identifiable: Obvs. and edges are flattened, revs. are unevenly struck (most often with local weaknesses in legend), weight range is about 185–188 grs. = 11.99–12.18 gms., compared with the standard 192 grs. = 12.44 gms. After striking his full 500 specimens **(8002)**, Scott allegedly annealed the Confederate die and defaced it with chisel marks, striking a few brass splashers, and finally selling the die (with Taylor's original proof) to the Hon. J. Sanford Saltus, after several vain attempts to move it at auction. The last report of a brass splasher was in the Elliott Smith collection, about 1923. Supposedly Saltus gave the die to the Louisiana Historical Society, but inquiries made there during the 1950s revealed that they had no record of it nor any idea of its location. Part of Scott's promotion was circulars dated Oct. 17, 1879 *(NUM* 12/11, p. 422; Beistle {1929}, pp. 255–56), falsely claiming that the entire issue had sold out, that he had received 67 extra orders he was unable to fill, and offering $2.50 each to anyone who would resell his restrikes to Scott. Proskey claimed that for many years Scott had specimens on hand. The above account follows Evans {1885}, Beistle {1929}, Philpott {1950, 1951}, and Breen {1977}, pp. 239–40.

For the half eagles minted under the Confederacy in 1861 at the Charlotte and Dahlonega branch mints, see Chap. 36, Sect. vii, introductory text.

Less is known about the Confederate pattern cent of 1861, and that little derives from Capt. John W. Haseltine, whose memory was at best unreliable, and whose honesty has been justly questioned. At least this much is reasonably certain: During early 1861, agents of the CSA approached the Philadelphia engraver and diesinker Robert Lovett, Jr., through their liaison in the Philadelphia jewelry firm of Bailey, Banks & Biddle, proposing a contract coinage of cents. These were to be of original design, and of copper-nickel. No weight standard was cited; most likely the rebels (or Lovett) had in mind something uniform with the Union issue, 72 grs. = 4.67 gms., of the same size as the copper-nickel Indian cents. Lovett went far enough with the project to make a pair of dies and strike a dozen specimens. Obv. derives from one of his advertising pieces of 1860; rev. wreath shows corn, cotton, maple, tobacco, wheat (?), two barrels, and a cotton bale signed L. After making these, Lovett became terrified that Union authorities would locate him and sentence him to death for treason. Making coins for the rebels was surely construable as "giving aid and comfort to the Enemy in time of war." He hid the coins and dies in his cellar, except for one which he kept as a pocket piece, apparently to remind himself of his vanished chance at glory had the Confederacy won, and attempted to drown his anxieties in drink; why he did not merely destroy the evidence is unclear. Nobody knew anything about this until late 1873, when he inadvertently spent his pocket piece at a bar in West Philadelphia. When the startled bartender read the coin's inscription, he told some unnamed third party, who told both J. Colvin Randall and Capt. John W. Haseltine. Haseltine bought the coin and over the ensuing months repeatedly visited Lovett to try to extract information and buy the dies and any other Confederate cents. Lovett, despite the obvious evidence, continued to deny having made them, until eventually, drunk and goaded beyond endurance, he confessed all, selling Haseltine the dies and all remaining impressions. Haseltine told two different stories of the discovery (both are reproduced at Garrett:1995–96); in one of these he bought 11 cents from Lovett, in the other only 10. Haseltine then made restrikes in gold, silver, and copper, again telling inconsistent stories about how many were struck: either three or seven in gold, five or 12 in silver, 55 or 56 in copper, apparently all in March 1874, claiming falsely that "after the fifty-fifth impression the collar burst and the dies were badly broken." His advertisement of the copper restrikes, dated April 2, 1874, is quoted at Garrett:1996; his earliest notice of the original is in the Haseltine Sale, 1/13–15/1874:665.

Henry Chapman bought the dies and struck a unique (?) mule combining the rev. with a Lovett Washington obv. (of Baker 209); this was later in the G. M. Parsons and Edmond A.

Rice colls. Judson Brenner exhibited the CSA cent dies at the 1911 ANA convention. *Mehl's Numismatic Monthly* 9–10/11, p. 106; Ford [1951A].

Subsequent history and location of the dies remained unknown until 1961, when Robert Bashlow obtained them, found that the obv. was unbroken, the rev. in the act of cracking at l. edge, both dies defaced (by whom?) with chisel marks and hammer blows, but still marginally fit for use. Bashlow (later of Williams Trading Co., New York, a wholesale importer of foreign coins) had the Philadelphia medalist firm August C. Frank Co. make transfer dies from them (lest the original Lovett dies break), and struck large quantities of "second restrikes" in 1961–62 for the Confederate centenary. These coins, also called "Bashlow restrikes," are instantly identifiable by the raised lumps and ridges resulting from use of defaced dies. The original rev. finally did break at l. edge; Bashlow presented both Lovett dies to the Smithsonian Institution. Clain-Stefanelli {1970}, fig. 85.

Various small silver medalets have been claimed as Confederate dimes and half dimes, largely from a combination of wishful thinking and greed. Nothing is known of their origin. The only reason to believe that they might have circulated as money is their worn state. All are of extreme rarity, but hardly fall within the scope of this study. They are described here so that those unfamiliar with them will know what they are being offered.

a. Flag, cantoned with 13 stars, A UNITED SOUTH 1861. Rev., cotton (?) branch, 13 stars. Silver. About 9/16″ = 14 mm. Weight ?. Always pierced. 8–12 known. DeWitt C1861-2. Maris, Jenks, Garrett:1998, $3,100. This has been called a "Confederate half dime," but the size is nearest the 3¢ silver. First reported by P. Sid Jones, who received one in Kentucky, Oct. 9, 1862. *CCJ* 4/1878, p. 63.

b. Head l., dividing JEFFERSON DAVIS; below, unidentified signature C.R. Rev., date 1861 within wreath, OUR FIRST PRESIDENT around upper half. Silver, reeded edge. About 7/10″ = 18 mm. Weight ?. Always looped or with loop removed from top edge. About 12 known, some gilt. DeWitt C1861-1. Garrett:1999–2000, $700 each. Called the "Jefferson Davis dime," from the size.

c. Head l., G.T.BEAUREGARD. BRG.GEN. CSA. around; below, signature C.R. Rev., within wreath, MANASSAS/21/JULY/1861. Silver, reeded edge, same size. Weight ?. Always looped or with loop removed. Probably equally rare. Garrett:2002–3, $900, $1,600. Called the "Beauregard dime," from the size.

THE CONFEDERATE HALF DOLLARS

Designer, Engraver, obv., Longacre, after Gobrecht, after Sully; rev., A. H. M. Patterson. Mint, New Orleans. Composition, 90% silver, as Union issue. Diameter, 1.2″ = 30+ mm. Weight standard, originals, 192 grs. = 12.44 gms.; restrikes, as noted.

Grade range, originals, as noted; restrikes, grade moot, obv. and edge reeding always flattened (unlike originals); rev. generally EF to UNC.: See introductory text.

8000   1861 Original. Proofs and ex-proofs only. [4P] 4 known. See introductory text for history. 1) New Orleans Mint, Chief Coiner Dr. B. F. Taylor, Ebenezer Locke Mason, Jr., J. W. Scott, J. Sanford Saltus, ANS, Proof. 2) New Orleans Mint, Dr. E. Ames, his son, Ames family, pvt. coll. (Rondout, N.Y., 1910), Thomas L. Elder (1912), H. O. Granberg, William H. Woodin, Waldo Newcomer, Col. E. H. R. Green, Burdette G. Johnson, Eric P. Newman. EF, formerly proof. 190.5 grs. = 12.34 gms. 3) New Orleans Mint, Prof. Biddle (Tulane Univ.), Biddle family, pvt. coll. (New Orleans, 1960s), James Cohen, Lester Merkin, pvt. coll. (enl.

ill.) EF+, formerly proof. 190 grs. = 12.3 gms. First published, Breen {1977}, p. 239.   4) New Orleans Mint, C. G. Memminger, Jefferson Davis, pvt. colls., Bream, his son Mark Bream (Cashtown, Pa.), "his sister in Ohio," T. L. Schnur, Paul Franklin, John J. Ford, Jr. Worn, but edge and obv. are normal, not flattened. Taxay {1963}; Breen {1977}, p. 240. Supposedly Davis's pocket piece, confiscated when Union soldiers captured him (in female garments) and confined him in Fort Monroe.

8001   1861 (i.e., 1879) Prototype restrike. [Incl. in next] 2 known.
Overstruck on regular 1861 half dollar, traces of Union rev. visible around the CSA die. Obv. flattened as next; normal weight, unlike next. NYPL:2891–92, $1,122, $852, respectively, with CSA die normally aligned (as current U.S. coins) or rotated 180° with respect to the Union obv.
8002   1861 (i.e., 1879) Regular restrike. [500]
Overstruck on regular 1861 half dollar, rev. ground down. Obv. flattened; see introductory text. Rev. rusted, bulging in center, and chipping at dentils above ER(ICA), unlike originals. 185–188 grs. = 11.99–12.18 gms. One specimen shows obv. remarkably double-struck, dates at top and bottom: Scott, Levick, Woodward 67:2468 (5/26/1884), pvt. colls., W. A. Philpott, Kagin 277:754A (5/6/68). 185 grs. Philpott {1950}. One is known with obv. of **4906**. Kosoff Estate:4243, UNC., $1,870.

8003   1861 (i.e., 1879) Scott token. White metal. [500]
See introductory text. Inscription reads in this order: 4 ORIGINALS STRUCK BY ORDER OF C.S.A. IN NEW ORLEANS 1861. * * * * * * * REV. [sic!] SAME AS U.S. (FROM ORIGINAL DIE : SCOTT). Original price, 50¢, Oct. 1879. Other medals with revs. of this design are fabrications of the 1960s.

8004   n.d. (1879) Rev. of **8000**, uniface, brass. [2+]
Said to be from the CSA die after the latter was canceled with a chisel mark.   1) J. Sanford Saltus, Louisiana Historical Society (with the die), later untraced.   2) Elliott Smith, F. C. C. Boyd estate. Philpott {1950}.

THE CONFEDERATE CENTS

Designer, Engraver, Robert Lovett, Jr. Mint, originals, Lovett's, Philadelphia; Haseltine restrikes, Peter L. Krider's, Philadelphia; Bashlow restrikes, August Frank's, Philadelphia. Composition, originals, copper-nickel, probably federal standard; both types of restrikes, as noted. Diameter, 3/4" = 19 mm. Weight standard unknown.
These did not circulate.
8005   1861 Original. Copper-nickel. [12] Ex. rare.
Steigerwalt, Garrett:1995, "EF," $12,500, possibly the piece Lovett spent at the West Philadelphia bar (discovery coin): See introductory text.

HASELTINE RESTRIKES

8006   1861 (i.e., 1874) Gold. [7?] Ex. rare.
See introductory text.   1) SI.   2) Steinberg (1948), Eliasberg estate.   3) Farouk, C. Ramsey Bartlett.   4) Brand, KS 3/64, LM 10/73, Groves:467 ($6,000), Robison:325, Steig:2013, impaired, $4,000.
8007   1861 (i.e., 1874) Silver. [12?] Ex. rare.
Garrett:1897, Proof, $3,900.
8008   1861 (i.e., 1874) Copper. [55+?] Rare.
See introductory text. Garrett:1896, Proof, $2,400.

BASHLOW RESTRIKES, Defaced Dies

8009   1861 (i.e., 1961–62) Platinum. [3] Ex. rare.
8010   1861 (i.e., 1961–62) Gold. [3] Ex. rare.
8011   1861 (i.e., 1961–62) Silver. [5,000]
Entire batch sold out at $7.50 each before April 1962.
8012   1861 (i.e., 1961–62) "Nickel silver." [50] Rare.
Alloy specifications unstated.
8013   1861 (i.e., 1961–62) Bronze. [20,000]
Sold at $2.50 each, 1962.
8014   1861 (i.e., 1961–62) "Goldine." [5,000]
Brassy alloy, composition unspecified. Sold at $4.50 each, 1962.
8015   1861 (i.e., 1961–62) Lead. [50] Rare.
8016   1861 (i.e., 1961–62) Aluminum. [50] Rare.
8017   1861 (i.e., 1961–62) Tin. [50] Rare.
8018   1861 (i.e., 1961–62) Zinc. [50] Rare.
8019   1861 (i.e., 1961–62) Red fiber. [50] Rare.
May exist in other metals. There are also uniface impressions in gold and silver (probably 2 or 3 each of obv. and rev.), reversed (hub) impressions, and a few other fancy productions, all Ex. rare. No detailed catalog exists.

CHAPTER 48

FEDERAL EMERGENCY COINAGES FOR ALASKA (1935–36)

In 1935, the Alaska Rural Rehabilitation Corporation (A.R.R.C., an agency of the federal government, created to help locals during the Great Depression) struck some $20,300 in "bingles"—trade tokens ranging in face value from 1¢ to $10. These were for use in the Matanuska Valley Colonization Project, in the Palmer area, about 50 miles from Anchorage. The Project had imported 204 Midwestern families to run marginal 40-acre farms, beside earlier settlers' descendants. For uncertain reasons, federal coins were scarce and the settlers were largely on a barter economy; the A.R.R.C. bingles were federal competition with private tokens. Unlike the latter, the bingles were made legal tender; their extreme light weight (the 10¢ weighs less than 1/3 of a silver dime) made them easy to lose.

Local stores began accepting them, luring the colonists' trade away from the A.R.R.C. company store in Palmer: a consequence the authorities had not foreseen. They stopped further issue in 1937 and began redeeming the A.R.R.C. bingles in ordinary federal coins; in 1938 they revoked the bingles' legal-tender status and melted most of them. Over half the transplanted settlers returned to the Midwest, and the government abandoned the project.

About 1958–59, Ms. Laura Lawrence investigated the issues, discovered the above facts, and learned that exactly 200 sets, 1¢ through $10, had been reserved out of the original mintage for presentation purposes. These sets are uncirculated, the aluminum pieces more or less prooflike, the brass ones less so. It is generally safe to assume that any really choice survivors come from broken presentation sets; those found singly are normally dull, discolored, nicked, and scratched. No grading standards are agreed on.

Nothing is known about mint location, designer, diesinker, or federal specifications as to weight standards (if any). Weights given below are of the coins pictured, from this writer's presentation set; others may differ. All have plain edges. Only one die var. is known of each denomination. Obv. and rev. differ only in minor positional details. The $5 and $10 (especially the latter) are much rarer than their mintage figures might suggest. ARRC {1955}; Fernald & McDowell {1965}; GBD {1965}, pp. 103–5; Bolotin {1982}.

8020 n.d. (1935) ONE CENT. Aluminum. Octagonal. [5,000] GBD 8, p. 105. 12.5/16″ = 20 mm side to side; 22 mm corner to corner. 16.5 grs. = 1.07 gms. Enl. photos.

8021 n.d. (1935) FIVE CENTS. Aluminum. [5,000] GBD 7, p. 105. 13/16″ = 22 mm. 19 grs. = 1.2 gms. Enl. photos.

8022 n.d. (1935) TEN CENTS. Aluminum. [5,000]
GBD 6, p. 105. 11.5/16″ = 18 mm. 11.4 grs. = 0.74 gms. Enl.
photos.

8023 n.d. (1935) TWENTY-FIVE CENTS. Aluminum.
[3,000]
GBD 5, p. 104. 15/16″ = 24 mm. 24.5 grs. = 1.59 gms. Enl.
photos.

8025 n.d. (1935) ONE DOLLAR. Aluminum. [2,500]
GBD 3, p. 104. 1½″ = 38 mm. 50.8 grs. = 3.29 gms. Enl.
photos.

8024 n.d. (1935) FIFTY CENTS. Aluminum. [2,500]
GBD 4, p. 104. 20.5/16″ = 33 mm. 41.8 grs. = 2.71 gms. Enl.
photos.

8026 n.d. (1935) FIVE DOLLARS. Brass. [1,000] Rare. GBD 2, p. 104. 1″ = 25.4 mm. 80.4 grs. = 5.21 gms. Enl. photos.

8027 n.d. (1935) TEN DOLLARS. Brass. [1,000] Rare. GBD 1, p. 103. 20.5/16″ = 33 mm. 148.6 grs. = 9.63 gms. Enl. photos.

CHAPTER 49

COINAGE OF THE KINGDOM OF HAWAII

i. THE COPPER *KENETA* OF 1847

Among all the issues attributed to Hawaii before the Kingdom became a Territory of the United States, the only ones with reasonable claim to relevance to the present study are those authorized by the Kingdom itself, which coincidentally happen also to be the only ones coined by known makers in the continental United States: the 1847 *keneta* (= 'cent(s)') and the 1883 silver issues.

A decade after the senseless murder of Capt. Cook, King Kamehameha I (also known as "Kamehameha the Great"), originally one among many petty kings in the Islands, conquered his rivals and forcibly unified the area, ending uncounted generations of civil war. Among his various innovations was the recognition of gold and silver as primary media of exchange; this had the side effect of making him very wealthy, as on his death (1819) he reportedly left some $200,000 in foreign gold and silver coins—having a purchasing power of at least 50 times that amount reckoned in 1984 dollars. After his day, natives began to think in terms of *dala* ('dollar(s)') and *keneta* rather than of pounds, shillings, and pence, or of any of the other foreign moneys of account. This was partly because of the decimal system, partly from the ubiquitous and frequently regrettable influence of American missionaries. The latter induced the new King Kamehameha II (Liholiho, reigned 1819–24) to abolish the old religion and make some form of capitalist Christianity official, much to the detriment of natives' health: Where they had formerly fished and gathered and farmed their own food as free people, thereafter they labored for unscrupulous white men from the mainland. Among the obvious by-products were competitive greed, exploitation, poverty, epidemics, and a currency shortage. William Hooper, manager of the Koloa Plantation (Kauai, 1836), introduced an abuse widespread even in recent decades: He paid his laborers only in scrip which could be spent only at the company store, where everything was deliberately overpriced to create insurmountable debt and prevent workers from leaving; its more familiar name is peonage. His scrip (overprinted on French theater tickets) was in the same denominations which had been introduced by the New England missionaries (and which would be made official by laws introduced nine years later): $1, 50¢, 25¢, 12½¢, 6¼¢, and 3⅛¢, based alike on the United States coinage system and (for the three smallest denominations) on the Spanish and Mexican fractional silver bits, medios, and cuartillas, all legal tender in the United States and more familiar even than federal dimes or half dimes.

By the mid-1840s, natives were increasingly dissatisfied with barter economy (and, one suspects, with having to sing the local equivalent of "I owe my soul to the company store"). Coined money was in incessant demand and chronic shortage. King

Kamehameha III (Kauikeaouli, reigned 1825–54) devoted Chapter 4, Section 1, of his new legal code of 1846 to the official monetary system of the Islands, explicitly tying it to that of the United States. In translation: "The currency of the Hawaiian Islands shall consist of the *Dala,* valuing 100 Keneta American currency; the *Hapalua* ['Moiety of 2' = Half], valuing 50 Keneta; the *Hapaha* ['Moiety of 4' = Quarter], valuing 25 Keneta; the *Hapawalu* ['Moiety of 8'], valuing 12½ Keneta; the 16th of a Dala, valuing 6¼ Keneta; and a copper coin [Keneta] impressed with the head of His Majesty, surrounded by the words KAMEHAMEHA III KA MOI ['. . . The King'], and on the reverse, AUPUNI HAWAII ['Kingdom Hawaii']. The Minister of Finance shall cause to be minted for circulation, a copper coin as described in the preceding section; and with the advice of ⅔ of the Privy Council and approbation of His Majesty, he may also cause to be minted any small silver coins of such description and quantity as the said Council shall direct" (Hawaiian {1846}, key words rechecked and retranslated).

Pursuant to this new law, the Hawaiian government made a contract with the private mint of H. M. & E. I. Richards, Attleboro, Mass. The royal agent was James Jackson Jarvis, editor of the newspaper *Polynesian,* friend of the diesinker Edward Hulseman. The first and only order was for 100,000 Keneta or *Hapa Hanele* ('Moiety of 100') costing $869.56. When the coins arrived in Honolulu harbor on board the *Montreal,* Jan. 14, 1847, they proved an extreme disappointment. Not only was the King's portrait almost unrecognizable, the denomination was misspelled as HAPA HANERI. Stories are told that many natives threw them into the ocean rather than accept them in payments or spend them. Governors of the other islands nevertheless ordered quantities of them from the Central Treasury in Honolulu, giving them out in change from tax collections, and presumably as small change in other transactions. By 1862, only 11,595 were still outstanding, this being the last year recorded in which the Treasury disbursed them. They remained legal tender in the Islands until 1884, and circulated long afterward for convenience, being valued at one keneta apiece at the Treasury in exchange for the 1883 silver coinage.

There were two obv. dies and five regular revs., a sixth being known only in pewter trial strikings. Revs. differ primarily in numbers of berries on each branch.

Besides the 100,000 shipped to Hawaii, samples remained with the Richards firm in Massachusetts. Wayte Raymond used to travel to Belmont, Mass., to buy them from the original makers' descendants: *NNW* 1/1/63. This source must have been exhausted before 1956; it is the origin of most pristine UNCIRCULATED survivors. Those recovered from the Islands are generally worn; the best ones are discolored, probably from bilge water aboard the *Montreal,* in whose hold they had spent many months.

In 1947, centennial copies of the 1847 Keneta were made for

the tourist trade; issues continued into recent years, retaining the 1847 date. (They sold in 1967 at 25¢ each at Waikiki souvenir stands.) There are many minor vars.; normally they come in brass and have below wreath SOUVENIR ALII OF HAWAII. This is a fun-loving businessmen's group, though originally *alii* meant 'caste of warrior nobility,' like the Kshatriya in India, ranking just below the *kahuna* or 'priestly caste, shamans,' like the Brahmins.

THE **COPPER KENETA** OF 1847

Designer, Engraver, Edward Hulseman. Mint, Richards's, Attleboro, Mass. Composition, copper. Weight standard, uncertain, possibly 50 to the lb. Diameter, 17/16″ = 27 mm. Plain edge.

Grade range, VERY GOOD to UNC. FINE: Partial hair and epaulet details; partial internal detail to leaves. VERY FINE: Nearly full details at epaulet, hair, and leaves; intact collar ornaments. EXTREMELY FINE: Few tiny isolated rubbed spots. UNCIRCULATED: *No* trace of wear; usually spotted or stained: See introductory text.

8028 1847 HAPA HANERI (Keneta). [Net 11,595+] Large bust and letters.
KM 1d, 1e; Medcalf-Fong C1Ab, C1A, respectively, with 15 and 18 berries; price for former, latter rare. The crosslet 4 is taller than the 7.

8029 1847 Same. Small bust and letters.
KM 1c, 1a, 1b; Medcalf-Fong C1Aa, C1Ad, C1Ac. Price for second, with 13 berries; others are scarcer. Plain 4, not taller than 7. The 3 pewter strikings (same obv., 24 berries) are controversial and believed of much later origin.

ii. **BARBER'S SILVER COINAGE OF 1883**

When King Lunalilo died on Feb. 3, 1874, without naming a successor, the Hawaiian legislature began deliberations, and nine days later elected one David Kalakaua to the throne, where he reigned as King Kalakaua I. Whatever else may be said about him (and "fun-loving" is one of the more charitable epithets: he revived the hula), Kalakaua attempted to bring his kingdom into the 19th century. He created four new royal orders; he traveled round the world to meet VIPs from here, there, and everywhere; he talked of a national coinage (a dead letter since the unpopular 1847 Keneta). During his Grand Tour, 1881, the King met officials from the national mints at Vienna, Brussels, and Paris, all of whom had proposals for contract coinages for Hawaii. One of these proposals (from Paris, on behalf of a New Caledonia mine owner) went far enough that His Majesty ordered a sample of pattern 5-Keneta coins to be submitted for royal approval. These were struck on thin German silver flans [200]; MAILLECHORT on edge = French name for this metal. They portrayed him as KALAKAUA KING OF SANDWICH ISLANDS, and their rev. depicts a garter, crowned and inscribed with the royal (later territorial and state) motto UA MAU KE EA O KA AINA I KA PONO, 'The Life of the Land is Perpetuated in Righteousness.' Within the garter is a large ornate 5; a cross surmounts the crown. The King may have approved of his flattering portrait, but he certainly disapproved of the misspelling of the motto (the coins show it as AU MAU . . .), and he dropped the project. Similar pieces with small ball atop crown are Canadian copies made in the early 1900s; they come in nickel and aluminum on thick flans (2.7–3.1 mm), and in nickel, aluminum, and copper on thin flans (1.4–1.7 mm).

During the same year, the King conferred with American officials. Secretary of State James G. Blaine publicly announced that Hawaii was of such importance to the safety of the United States that no nation could be allowed to have her. Thereafter, U.S. foreign policy increased a friendly presence and economic links with the Islands.

Unsurprisingly, in 1883 Claus Spreckels (banker, sugar tycoon, and power behind the throne) came to the King with a proposal to have the United States strike silver coins for the Islands. Conveniently, an Act of Jan. 29, 1874 had already authorized the federal mints to strike coins for foreign countries. Under its terms, the royal government formally applied to have 1 million Dala coined in silver. Spreckels submitted sketches indicating what was wanted in design; Mint Director Horatio C. Burchard modified them, and Charles E. Barber created the master dies and hubs. Five pairs of working dies for each denomination were sunk from the latter. The original application had specified the denominations Dala, Hapalua, Hapaha, and Hapawalu, or 1/8 Dala, but between then and the manufacture of working dies this was changed to call for the *Umi* ('Ten') Keneta instead of the Hapawalu. This alteration explicitly tied the Hawaiian silver issue to that of the United States in denominations, even as in standards of weight, composition, and size— greatly lowering the cost of the operation, as there was now no need to make special planchets: Normal United States dollar, half, quarter, and dime blanks could be used instead. Perhaps more significantly still, the Umi Keneta shows the words ONE DIME in center in larger lettering than the Hawaiian denomination.

Coinage began with six proof sets, Sept. 1883, at Philadelphia. Production coinage (1,950,000 pieces) followed at San Francisco from Nov. 17, 1883, through June 1884, all dated 1883. Some 20 additional proof sets were made in 1884 from the original 1883 proof dies; these were intended only for presentation to Hawaiian dignitaries, not for public sale. This later batch included both the Umi Keneta and the Hapawalu; the only original sets seen in both silver and copper included both denominations. No production coins were made from the Hapawalu dies; all the authentic proofs are from a single pair of dies with upright 8's in date.

After June 1884, the working dies were defaced at the San Francisco Mint; they are said to remain in the Hawaiian State Archives, while the original hubs supposedly remain in the Philadelphia Mint: Medcalf-Fong, p. 12.

Sets of alleged "patterns" from rusty dies came to collector attention after dispersal of King Farouk's collections (1954). These include a Hapawalu with italic 8's in date 1883, and Dala, Hapalua, and Hapaha dated 1884. They occur in platinum, gold, bronze, and "oroide" or other brassy composition. They are not legal issues by or for Hawaii. Their workmanship leaves no alternative to the conclusion that they are clandestine concoctions of later date; some (all?) gold impressions are overstruck on U.S. coins, one of the Hapawalu being stamped on an

1880 quarter eagle. (See list in *SCWC* {1985}, p. 2364, which source also describes the private patterns of 1891–95.)

After Hawaii became a Territory of the United States, the Treasury decided that thereafter the Islands should use United States coins of the normal designs and denominations. Accordingly, orders went out to banks and other establishments in the Islands, ordering withdrawal of all the 1883 Hawaiian coins from circulation; as soon as any were deposited, they were to be shipped back to the mainland for melting. This made the Dala a scarce coin, especially in choice condition; the Hapalua is also difficult to find in top grade. On the other hand, the Hapaha is plentiful in mint state owing to discovery of many rolls of UN-CIRCULATED specimens after WW II; these reached coin dealers instead of Treasury melting pots.

BARBER'S SILVER COINAGE OF 1883

Designer, Charles E. Barber, after Claus Spreckels. Engraver, Barber. Mint, proofs, Philadelphia; business strikes, San Francisco. Diameters, Dala, 1½″ = 38.1 mm; Hapalua, 1.2″ = 30.5 mm; Hapaha, 0.95″ = 24.3 mm; Hapawalu, ¹³/₁₆″ = 20.6 mm; Umi Keneta, 0.7″ = 17.9 mm. Composition, silver 900 Fine. Weights, Dala, 412.5 grs. = 26.73 gms.; Hapalua, 192.9 grs. = 12.5 gms.; Hapaha, 96.45 grs. = 6.25 gms.; Hapawalu, 48.23 grs. = 3.125 gms.; Umi Keneta, 38.58 grs. = 2.5 gms.

Grade range, VERY GOOD to UNC. FINE: Partial details on ear, hair, and crown; over half details on arms. VERY FINE: Over half hair and ear details; minor wear on principal outlines of arms. EXTREMELY FINE: Few tiny isolated rubbed spots only; on the Dala, expect almost completely intact mantling; partial mint luster. NOTE: Many specimens of the Dala have been poorly cleaned.

8030 1883 UMI KENETA or ONE DIME. [Net 249,921 + 26+P]
KM 3; Medcalf-Fong C4E. Original mintage [250,000] less 79 melted.

8031 1883 HAPAWALU or EIGHTH DOL. Proofs only. [20+P] Very rare.
KM 4; Medcalf-Fong C4D. Upright 8's. See introductory text. Bortin:334.

8032 1883 HAPAHA or ¼ D(ala). [Net 242,600 + 26+P] Normal date.
KM 5; Medcalf-Fong C4C. Original mintage [500,000] less 257,400 melted.

8033 1883/1383 HAPAHA.
Corrected blunder. *SCWC* {1985}, p. 2364, estimates 40,000 minted, incl. above.

8034 1883 HAPALUA or ½ D(ala). [Net 87,755 + 26+P]
KM 6; Medcalf-Fong C4B. Original mintage [700,000] less 612,245 melted.

8035 1883 AKAHI ['One'] DALA. [Net 46,348 + 26+P]
KM 7; Medcalf-Fong C4A. Original mintage [500,000] less 453,622 melted.

BIBLIOGRAPHY, ABBREVIATIONS, TYPOGRAPHIC CONVENTIONS

Abbreviations of bibliographic items are explained in their proper alphabetic places. A few catalogs referred to only once in main text may not be cited hereinbelow. Auction catalog listings are condensed thus: "Jenks, John Story, coll., A, HC 12/7–17/1921. C-S 2320. (Plate reps.) [60 with orig. plates]" = "Catalog of the John Story Jenks collection, auction, Henry Chapman, Dec. 7–17, 1921. Clain-Stefanelli, *Select Numismatic Bibliography,* no. 2320. Reprints exist of the photographic plates. Only 60 copies originally contained photographic plates." Firm name following date is that of the auction house where the sale was held, if different from cataloger's firm.

Boldface numbers mean exclusively guide numbers **1–8035** from main text.

Italics designate book or magazine titles.

SMALL CAPITALS are reserved for grade designations.

, in coin pedigree enumerations separates names of successive owners of the same specimen. Usually, lot number and price are given only for the coin's latest appearance.

; in coin auction citations separates different specimens.

: A colon preceding a number = 'lot number in the designated auction, mail bid sale, or fixed price list.' Thus Garrett:1197 = J. W. Garrett auction, lot 1197. In this Bibliography, a colon separates city and publisher's name.

1), 2), etc., in coin pedigree enumerations, indicates an attempted census of reported examples.

* Affixed to C-S entries, e.g., C-S 3923*, designates titles so marked in Dr. Elvira Clain-Stefanelli's bibliography as recommendations.

+ 'Plus unknown quantity of extra impressions.'

− 'Less unknown quantity melted' or 'Less unknown quantity of other date(s) included in mintage herein cited.' Which one is always clear from context.

' ' Single quotation marks designate translations or interpretations.

" " Double quotation marks enclose verbatim quotations or titles of articles or chapters of books.

[ ] Square brackets containing a number = 'Quantity issued, normally from official records.' These are often combined with +, −, and/or P[roofs], to make such combinations as [160,000− + ?P] = '160,000 business strikes, some melted at the time, plus an unknown number of proofs'; [587,200+ + 600−P] = 'At least 587,200 business strikes, plus 600 proofs, some of them officially melted'; [? + ?P] = 'Quantities officially struck unknown, but include both business strikes and proofs'; [?P] = 'No business strikes; proofs only, quantity made unknown'; [4+P] = 'No business strikes; 4 or more proofs made.' In this Bibliography, [500] = 'Only 500 copies printed.'

{ } Curved brackets (not parentheses) enclose date of biblio-graphic item cited to distinguish it from others by the same author.

A

A = Auction (hereinbelow), contrasted with FPL, MBS.

Adams {1909} = Adams, Edgar Holmes, *Official Premium List of U.S. and Territorial Gold Coins.* N.Y.: Willetts, 1909.

Adams {1913} = ———, *Private Gold Coinage of California 1849–55, Its History and Its Issues.* Brooklyn, N.Y.: the author, 1913 (reprint from *AJN* 1912); reps., incl. Stackpole, 1975. C-S 3420. Superseded by Kagin {1981}.

Adams {1920} = ———, *United States Store Cards.* N.Y.: Edgar H. Adams and Wayte Raymond, 1920; reps., including Miller {1962}. Adams numbers are kept in Rulau-E, below.

Adams {1934A} = ———, "Early United States Gold Coins: Eagles," serial in *CCJ,* May 1934–July 1934. Covers 1795–1804 only.

Adams {1934B} = ———, "Early Half Eagles and Their Varieties," serial in *CCJ,* Sept. 1934–March 1935, unfinished; covers 1795–1803. Later Adams numbers in this series have been retrieved from copies of Adams's notebooks, several of which are in ANS and pvt. colls. This and preceding largely superseded by Breen {1966}, {1967A}, {1967B}.

Adams, Eugene H.; Dorsett, Lyle W.; and Pulcipher, Robert S., *The Pioneer Western Bank—First of Denver: 1860–1980.* Denver: First Interstate Bank of Denver and State Historical Society, 1984. Extensively ill. history, including many details about Clark, Gruber & Co.

Adams-Woodin = ——— and Woodin, William Hartman, *U.S. Pattern, Trial and Experimental Pieces.* N.Y.: ANS, 1913; reps., James Kelly, 1940, 1959. C-S 3421. Largely superseded by Judd.

Ahwash, Kamal, *Encyclopedia of U.S. Liberty Seated Dimes, 1837–91.* Media, Pa.: Kamah Press, 1977 [500]; rep., 1981. With collaboration of Dr. John W. McCloskey. Die-var. study.

AJN = *American Journal of Numismatics.* N.Y.: ANS. Vols. I–LIII = May 1866 through 1919. C-S 106.

Akers {1975A} = Akers, David W., *U.S. Gold Dollars 1849–1889.* Englewood, Ohio: Paramount Publications, 1975. Largely auction records, as are next 5; all contain high-quality enlarged ills., useful for distinguishing striking quality of branch-mint coins from that of Philadelphia coins of the same date, for detecting pieces fraudulently altered by adding or effacing mintmarks.

Akers {1975B} = ———, *U.S. Quarter Eagles, 1796–1929.* Same publisher, 1975.

Akers {1976} = ———, *U.S. Three Dollar Gold Pieces 1854–1889, U.S. Four Dollar Gold Pieces 1879–1880.* Same publisher, 1976.

Akers {1979} = ———, *U.S. Half Eagles 1795–1929.* Same publisher, 1979.

Akers {1980} = ———, *U.S. Eagles 1795–1933.* Same publisher, 1980.

Akers {1982} = ———, *U.S. Double Eagles 1849–1933.* Same publisher, 1982.

Albert {1949} = Albert, Alphaeus W., *Washington Historical Buttons.* Hightstown, N.J.: the author, 1949. C-S 3924.

Albert {1966} = ———, *Political Campaign and Commemorative Buttons.* Same publisher, 1966.

Albert {1973} = ———, *Record of American Uniform and Historical Buttons, with Supplement.* Same publisher, 1973; 2nd printing, Sept. 1974.

Albright, Leonard, "Matte Proof Lincoln Cents 1909–1917," *NUM* 10/83, pp. 2051–62. Valuable for photographic identification marks.

Allenburger, Dr. Christian A., coll., MBS, in Mehl "Royal Sale," 3/23/48. Early U.S. proofs.

Altman-Haffner, colls., A, in PT 4/28–30/75. Cat. mostly by Breen.

Alvord, F. R., coll., A, S. H. Chapman 6/9/24 [24 with plates]; reps. Half cents.

An Exhibition of the World's Greatest Collection . . . Presented by the Baltimore National Bank, Baltimore and Light Sts., Baltimore 3, Md. 1952. Brochure about the Eliasberg collection.

ANA = American Numismatic Association. Citations with ANA preceded by a date refer to annual ANA Convention auctions, generally held in July or August. In the following listings, cities are those in which the auction was held, not necessarily the city where the auctioneer had his offices.

1941 ANA. Philadelphia. Ira S. Reed. In convention program booklet.

1947 ANA. Buffalo. Numismatic Galleries = A. Kosoff, Abner Kreisberg. Prann's colonials; Ernest Henderson's cents ("Sheraton Coll.").

1949 ANA. San Francisco. Ibid. Floyd Starr's duplicate large cents.

1951 ANA. Phoenix, Ariz. James Kelly.

1952 ANA. New York City. New Netherlands, Edward Gans, Hans M. F. Schulman, Henry Grunthal. Homer Downing's large cents. Rare colonials.

1954 ANA. Cleveland, Ohio. Federal Coin Exchange = Michael Kolman, Jr.

1956 ANA. Chicago. James Kelly. Rare gold.

1957 ANA. Philadelphia. Federal Coin Exchange, as 1954 ANA.

1958 ANA. Los Angeles. A. Kosoff. Lenox Lohr's patterns.

1959 ANA. Portland, Ore. Leo A. Young.

1962 ANA. Detroit, Mich. James Kelly and James E. Charlton.

1964 ANA. Cleveland, Ohio. Federal Brand Enterprises = Michael Kolman, Jr.

1971 ANA. Washington, D.C. Stack's. W. C. Blaisdell's pattern cents; rare gold.

1973 ANA. Boston. Jess Peters. Pioneer gold.

1975 ANA. Los Angeles. Sup. Ostheimer's silver dollars; Harry Glassenberg's half dollars.

1976 ANA. New York City. S. Colonials, cents, gold, etc., from colls. of MHS, BMFA.

1977 ANA. Atlanta, Ga. Hollinbeck-Kagin. 5 vols. in boxed set.

1978 ANA. Houston. B&R. Robert E. Branigan estate, etc.

1979 ANA. St. Louis. NERCA.

1980 ANA. Cincinnati. Ivy.

1981 ANA. New Orleans. B&R.

1982 ANA. Boston. Ivy. William R. Sieck coll., etc.

1983 ANA. San Diego. Kagin. Notable for its Peter Max cover.

1986 ANA. Milwaukee. Kagin.

ANACS = ANA Certification Service.

ANACS {1983} = *Counterfeit Detection: A Reprint from* The Numismatist. Colorado Springs: ANA 1983. (Box 2366, Colorado Springs, Colo. 80901.) Essential.

ANS = Museum of the American Numismatic Society, Broadway between 155 and 156 Sts., New York, N.Y. 10032. Source of many volumes cited herein.

ANS {1914} = ———, *Exhibition of U.S. and Colonial Coins,* Jan. 17–Feb. 18, 1914. N.Y.: ANS, 1914. C-S 3367. Extensively illustrated, documenting the then current ownership of many extreme rarities.

ANS {1958} = ———, *Centennial Publication of the ANS.* Ed., Harald Ingholt. N.Y.: ANS, 1958. Festschrift, largely on ancient and foreign coins, here cited as containing Breen {1958C}, Newman {1958}.

ANS {1976} = ———, *Studies on Money in Early America.* Eds., Eric P. Newman, Richard G. Doty. N.Y.: ANS, 1976. Bicentennial Festschrift, largely on colonial coins, paper, and economics. One of the most important collections this museum has ever published.

ANS {1985} = ———, *America's Copper Coinage 1783–1857.* N.Y.: ANS, 1985. Papers presented to Coinage of the Americas Conference, Nov. 30–Dec. 2, 1984.

Anthon Part V = Prof. Charles Anthon, coll., A, George W. Cogan, 10/20–2/1884; N.Y., Bangs & Co.

Appleton [+ roman numerals] = Appleton, William Sumner, *A Description of Medals of Washington in the Collection of W. S. Appleton.* Boston: T. R. Marvin & Son, 1873. Rep. from *AJN* serial, 1873. Supplementary numbers are in *AJN,* 1876. There is some overlap with what are called coins or tokens.

Arnold-Romisa = Danny Arnold and Romisa, et al., colls., A, B&M 9/17–19/84.

ARRC {1955} = Alaska Rural Rehabilitation Commission, *20 Years of Progress in the Matanuska Valley.* Anniversary Booklet. Palmer, Ak.: ARRC, 1955. Cited by Prosper E. DeVos in *NSM* 9/59, pp. 2137–40.

ASPF = American State Papers: Finance: Documents, legislative and executive, of the Congress of the United States. Selected and edited under the authority of Congress. 5 vols. Washington, D.C.: Gales & Seaton, 1832–61.

Atkins, James, *Coins and Tokens of the Possessions and Colonies of the British Empire.* London: Bernard Quaritch, 1889. C-S 2826*.

Atwater = Atwater, William Cutler, coll., MBS, BMM, 6/11/46.

Attinelli, Emmanuel Joseph, *Numisgraphics.* N.Y.: the author, 1876. Rep., retitled *A Bibliography of American Numismatic Auction Catalogues 1828–1875,* Lawrence, Mass.: Quarterman Publications, 1976. Orig. ed. is Ex. rare; rep. has explanatory foreword and price guide by John W. Adams.

AU = the grade ABOUT UNCIRCULATED, between EXTREMELY FINE and UNCIRCULATED.

Auction 79, colls., A, Para, S, RARCOA, Sup., 7/26–7/79.

Auction 80, colls., A, same firms, 8/14–15/80.

Auction 81, colls., A, same firms, 7/23–4/81.

Auction 82, colls., A, same firms, 8/13–14/82.

Auction 84, colls., A, same firms, 7/25–6/84.

Auction 85, colls., A, same firms, 7/26–7/85.

"Austin," colls., A, B&R (as "Amer. Auction Assoc."), 5/31–6/1/74.

"Autumn," colls., A, S, 9/8–9/78.

avg. = average

B

B&M = Bowers & Merena Galleries, Wolfeboro, N.H., auctioneers, publishers. Successors to next.

B&R = Bowers & Ruddy Galleries, Hollywood, Calif., auctioneers, publishers. B&R RCR = their Rare Coin Review house organ (largely FPL).

Bache I = colls., A, William Elliot Woodward, assembled from holdings of Messrs. Bache, Bertsch, Finotti, Colburn, etc. 3/20–24/1865. N.Y.: George A. Leavitt.

Bache II = colls., A, Woodward, as preceding, 12/19–23/1865. [Title page says Bach; we follow Attinelli, {1876}, pp. 42–43, for spelling.]

Baker = numbers in Baker, William Spohn, *Medallic Portraits of Washington*. Philadelphia: Robert M. Lindsay, 1885; here used, rep. with additions, marginal notes, and ills., Ed., George Fuld. Iola, Wis.: Krause Pubs., 1965. C-S 4178*. Rosichan 1035. Includes many circulating coins.

Baldenhofer, W. G., coll., in Farish-Baldenhofer, A, S, 11/11/55. Early gold.

Bancroft, Hubert Howe, *History of California*. 7 vols. San Francisco: The History Co., 1884–90. Quotes otherwise unavailable primary sources on the "Forty-Niners."

———, *History of Utah 1540–1886*. In *Works*, vol. XXVI. Same publisher, 1889. The only early historian to give the Mormons' side as part of a balanced presentation.

Bank of Bermuda, *"Hogge Money": The Bank of Bermuda Coin Collection: a Short History of Coins Used for Trading in Bermuda from the 16th Century to the Present Date*. Foreword by Sir Henry J. Tucker. Ills. from the Bank Collection. Published by the Bank, 2nd ed., revised. London: Robert Stockwell, 1972. Relevant to the 1615/6 Sommer Islands coinages.

Bareford I = Harold S. Bareford, coll., gold, A, S, 12/1/78.

Bareford II = ———, coll., silver and copper, A, S, 10/22–3/81.

Barton, William, *Memoirs of the Life of David Rittenhouse, LL.D., F.R.S.* Philadelphia: Edward Parker, No. 178 Market St., 1813.

Bascom, George Jonathan, coll., A, HC, 1/16/15.

"Bazaar Notes" = Anonymous, "Provincial Copper Coins or Tokens of the 18th and 19th Centuries," in *The Bazaar, the Exchange and Mart*, London, 7/5/1882, p. 18. One of D&H's sources.

Beck I = John A. Beck estate, coll., A, QS, 1/27–29/75. Gold.

Beck II = ibid., A, QS, 2/12–13/76. More gold.

Beck III = ibid., A, QS, 2/14/77.

Behrens, Kathryn L., *Paper Money In Maryland 1727–1789*. Baltimore: Johns Hopkins Univ. Press, 1923. C-S 3639. Economic history and social context.

Beistle, Martin Luther, *A Register of U.S. Half Dollar Die Varieties and Sub-Varieties*. Shippensburg, Pa.: the author, 1929 (reps.). C-S 3424. Rosichan 816. [135 with glossy photographic plates.] The sections covering 1794–1836 are superseded by Overton {1970}.

Bell {1963} = Bell, Robert Charles, *Commercial Coins, 1787–1804*. Newcastle upon Tyne: Corbitt & Hunter, 1963. C-S 2891a. Rosichan 954. British token coinage intended for circulation, not for collectors, advertising (and supposedly redeemable by) their makers. Supplements D&H.

Bell {1968} = ———, *Specious Tokens and Those Struck For General Circulation*. Same publisher, 1968. Rosichan 956. Similar tokens intended for small change, circulated by merchants who did not expect to redeem them; odd and rare vars. intended for collectors. Also supplements D&H.

Bell I = 'J. F. Bell' (pseudonym of Jacob F. Shapero), coll., gold, A, S, 12/7–9/44. See also "Memorable" and next.

Bell II = ibid., A, RARCOA, 4/26–28/63.

Bement, Clarence S., coll., A., HC, 5/29/16.

Berry, M., *Étude et Recherches Historiques sur les Monnaies de France*. Paris: chez Dumoulin, 1853. Includes some coins now classed as belonging to Canada/Louisiana.

Betts {1886} = Betts, Charles Wyllys, *Counterfeit Half Pence Current in the American Colonies, and Their Issue from the Mints of Connecticut and Vermont*. Speech delivered before ANS. N.Y.: Quick Print, 1886. (rep.) C-S 4542. Early deductions about Machin's Mills and Bungtown issuers.

Betts {1894} = ———, *American Colonial History Illustrated by Contemporary Medals*. [Posthumous; completed by his brother, Frederic H. Betts, eds., William Theophilus Rogers Marvin and Lyman Haines Low.] N.Y.: Scott Stamp & Coin Co. [i.e., Boston: Marvin], 1894. C-S 4183*. Rosichan 1037. (Reps., that here used: Boston: Quarterman, 1972.) Betts classed as medals some items generally collected as coins.

Betts {1897} = Betts, Benjamin, "Some Undescribed Proclamation Medals," *AJN* 10/1897; rep., N.Y., 1898, supplement 1900.

Biographical Directory of the American Congress 1774–1971. Senate Document 92-8, 92nd Congress, 1st Session. Washington: Government Printing Office, 1971.

[Birchall, Samuel,] *An Alphabetical List of Provincial Copper Coins or Tokens, issued between the years 1786 and 1796*. Leeds: Printed by Thomas Gill, 1796. Author's name omitted from cover and title page, but recovered from text.

Black, Dr. Angus, coll., A, in NN61.

BM = British Museum. Here credited as owner of rare colonial coins.

BMFA = Boston Museum of Fine Arts. Part of coll. in 1976 ANA.

BMM = B. Max Mehl, Fort Worth, Tex., dealer responsible for many MBS, 1908–55. Most are herein cited by consignors' names or cover titles.

Bodine, Walt, "Varieties of the 1840-O Quarter," *Gobrecht Journal* 36, pp. 6–9 (7/86). Enl. ills.

Bogert, Henry, coll., A, Augustus B. Sage, 2/28–3/5/1859; Bangs, Merwin & Co., N.Y.

Bolender, Milford Henry, *The United States Early Silver Dollars from 1794 to 1803*. Freeport, Ill.: the author, 1950 (rep.). C-S 3425. Die-var. study, following Haseltine's "Type Table" A, 11/28/81.

Bolotin, Norm, "A Spendable History of Alaska," *NUM* 11/82, pp. 2703–7.

Bolt, Dr. Conway A., coll., A, S, 4/21–3/66. Pioneer and other gold.

Boosel, Harry X, *1873–1873*. Chicago: Hewitt Bros., 1960. The title includes a typographic representation of the "closed" and "open" 3's on U.S coins of that year. Historical background of the diverse and often puzzling issues of 1873.

Bortin, Lee, et al., colls., A, Heritage, 7/18–20/84.

Bowers {1979} = Bowers, Q. David, *The History of United States Coinage as Illustrated by the Garrett Collection*. Hollywood: Bowers & Ruddy Galleries, 1979. Issued in connection with this firm's 4 auctions of the Garrett coll. on behalf of Johns Hopkins Univ. Other auctions by B&R are cited under titles or cover names.

Bowers {1983} = ———, *Virgil Brand: The Man and His Era*. Wolfeboro, N.H.: Bowers & Merena Galleries, 1983. Issued in connection with this firm's auctions of material from the Brand estate. Other auctions by B&M are cited under titles or cover names.

Boyd, Frederick C. C., estate, Ringoes, N.J., privately dispersed after 1956, many coins still held by John J. Ford, Jr.

Brady, J. D., "Rediscovery of Joseph Wright's Medal of Washington," *Museum Notes* No. 22, p. 256. N.Y.: ANS, 1977.

Brand, Virgil, beer tycoon, legendary hoarder; estate privately dispersed ca. 1928– , parts via his heirs Armin W. Brand and Horace Louis Philip Brand, other groups via BMM, Burdette G. Johnson (St. Louis Stamp & Coin Co.), Wayte Raymond, Charles Elmore Green, Arthur M. Kelley, Robert Friedberg, Hans M. F. Schulman, NN, etc., etc. See next 2.

Brand I = ———, coll., A, B&M, 11/7–8/83. Largely early gold.

Brand II = ———, coll., A, B&M, 6/18–9/84. Colonials and pioneer gold.

Breen {1951A} = Breen, Walter, "Coinage of the New Orleans Mint in 1861," *NUM* 4/51, pp. 387–394. On the Confederate takeover.

Breen {1951B} = ———, "Trial Piece Designed for U.S. Cent," *NUM* 12/51, pp. 1310–13. On the mislabeled Dickeson restrikes from the Eckfeldt revenue-stamp dies.

Breen {1952} = ———, "Survey of American Coin Hoards," *NUM* 1/52, pp. 7–24; 10/52, pp. 1005–10. C-S 3343. Describes many treasure troves and ill. specimens therefrom.

Breen {1954A} = ———, "Notes on Early Quarter Dollars," *NSM* 2/54, pp. 137–46. Update of Browning {1925}.

Breen {1954B} = ———, "The United States Patterns of 1792," *CCJ* 154. C-S 3420. One of a series of monographs issued by Wayte Raymond continuing *CCJ*. Deductions about these coins' makers, timing, historical circumstances, etc. One of the sources of Chap. 16 supra.

Breen {1954C} = ———, "The United States Minor Coinages, 1793–1916," *CCJ* 155. C-S 3429. Part of the same series of monographs.

Breen {1954D} = ———, "Secret History of the Gobrecht Coinages," *CCJ* 157–58. C-S 3428. Same comment. Largely drawn from National Archives documents.

Breen {1957} = ———, "The Rarest American Colonial and U.S. Gold Coins," *NSM* 6/57, pp. 1065–71.

Breen {1958A} = ———, "Silver Coinages of the Philadelphia Mint, 1794–1916," *CCJ* 159. C-S 3431. As Breen {1954C, D}.

Breen {1958B} = ———, "Valentine's 'U.S. Half Dimes': A Supplement," *CCJ* 160. C-S 3432. Rep. in Valentine {1975}.

Breen {1958C} = ———, "Brasher & Bailey: Pioneer N.Y. Coiners, 1787–1792," in ANS {1958}, pp. 137–45. C-S 3371.

Breen {1960} = ———, "Varieties of the GLORIAM REGNI Coins," in NN54:1, 4/22/60.

Breen {1961} = ———, "The 1922 Type of 1921 Peace Dollar," *NSM* 7/61, pp. 1721–28.

Breen {1962A} = ———, *Dies and Coinage.* N.Y.: Robert Bashlow, 1962; rep. Chicago, Hewitt Bros., 1965. Pamphlet monograph surveying mintage methods ancient and modern.

Breen {1962B} = ———, "The Hundred Year Vendetta," *NSM* 8/62, pp. 2177–89. History of the feud between the Philadelphia Mint and coin collectors, which generated an adversary relation between the Mint Bureau and its best customers that has continued into recent years, long after officialdom had forgotten why. It began in 1858; for details see Chap. 29, Sect. iv. Other details are in Newman-Bressett {1962}, Taxay {1966}, Breen {1977}.

Breen {1964A} = ———, *Major Varieties of U.S. Gold Dollars.* Chicago: Hewitt Bros., 1964 (reps.). C-S 3432a. Rep. from *NSM* 10–11/63.

Breen {1964B} = ———, *Varieties of U.S. Quarter Eagles.* Same publisher, 1964 (reps.). C-S 3432c. Rep. from *NSM* 4–10/64.

Breen {1965} = ———, *Major Varieties of U.S. Three-Dollar Pieces.* Same publisher, 1965. (rep.)

Breen {1966} = ———, *Early U.S. Half Eagles, 1795–1838.* Same publisher, 1966. (rep.)

Breen {1967A} = ———, *U.S. Half Eagles 1839–1929.* Same publisher, 1967 (rep.).

Breen {1967B} = ———, *U.S. Eagles 1795–1933.* Same publisher, 1967 (rep.).

Breen {1968} = ———, *New Varieties of U.S. Gold Coins.* Same publisher, 1968. Supplement to last 6.

Breen {1971A} = ———, "Hancock's Revenge," serial in *NNW*, 1971. On Washington coins, specially referring to the "Roman Head" cent of 1792.

Breen {1971B} = ———, "*Le Chameau* Treasure." Historical commentaries in the Parke-Bernet Galleries A, 12/10–11/71.

Breen {1972A} = ———, "Federal Shinplasters," serial in *NNW* beginning 7/18/72; deals with fractional currency. Part of overall longer serial *New Looks at Old Notes, NNW* ca. 1971–74.

Breen {1972B} = ———, "The Money Censors," *Coinage* 8/72, pp. 70ff. On prudish alterations in U.S. coin designs, dictated by such moralists as Anthony Comstock.

Breen {1972C} = ———, "Paper Coins," *Coinage* 9/72, pp. 42ff. On nickel 3¢ and 5¢ coins, created to retire paper fractional currency.

Breen {1974} = ———, "From Fish Scales To Forgotten Sleepers," *Coins* 8/74, pp. 55ff. On silver 3¢ pieces, alias trimes.

Breen {1976A} = ———, "North American Colonial Coinages Under the French Regime, 1640–1763," in ANS {1976}, pp. 43–74. A complete revision of the earlier serial in *WNJ*. Superseded by Chap. 5 supra.

Breen {1976B} = ———, "Legal and Illegal Connecticut Mints 1785–1789," in ANS {1976}, pp. 105–33. Revision of conclusions reached in EAC {1975}. Historical background for Chap. 6, Sect. iv, supra.

Breen {1977} = ———, *A Coiner's Caviar: Walter Breen's Encyclopedia of U.S. and Colonial Proof Coins, 1722–1977.* Albertson, N.Y.: FCI Press, July 1977.

Breen {1979} = ———, "The 'New York' IMMUNIS: A Mystery Unraveled," *CNL* 54, pp. 667–76 (4/79). Basis for Chap. 11, Sect. v, supra.

Breen {1983} = ———, *California Pioneer Fractional Gold.* With collaboration of Ron Gillio. Santa Barbara: Pacific Coast Auction Galleries, 1983. Originally a catalog of the Kenneth W. Lee estate; owing to publicity, a syndicate which had originally planned to buy the collection (but had not been heard from in some time) returned and bought it intact for $400,000. The completed catalog was converted into a text, superseding Lee {1979}, and Doering {1982}. The historical background to "Period One" is the basis for Chap. 43, Sect. iii, supra.

Breen {1984} = ———, *Walter Breen's Encyclopedia of United States Half Cents.* South Gate, Calif.: American Institute of Numismatic Research, 1984. Photography by Jack Collins. Basis for Chap. 17, supra. Supersedes Gilbert {1916}, CMM {1971}, Cohen {1982}.

Breen {1985} = ———, "Robert Scot's Earliest Device Punches," in ANS {1985}, pp. 10–29. The heads on 1794 cents used device punches but each working die had hair extensively modified by hand.

Breen I, colls., A, PT, 3/4/74. (No coins therein were property of this writer.)

Breen II, colls., A, PT, 6/25/75. Gold. Same comment.

Breen III, colls., A, PT, 6/19–20/76. Same comment.

Breen-Swiatek: See Swiatek-Breen.

Breen-Turoff = ——— and Turoff, Michael, "The Mysterious Miss Liberty," *Coins* 10/71, p. 62ff. On Miss Anna Willess Williams, Morgan's model for his silver dollar of 1878.

Breisland, W. L., coll., colonials, A, in S, 6/20–22/73.

Bressett {1960} = Bressett, Kenneth E., "The HIBERNIA VOCE POPULI Coinage of 1760," *CNL* 10/60.

Bressett {1976} = ———, "Vermont Copper Coinage," in ANS {1976}, pp. 173–98. Revised from the order established in his photographic plates of 1957. Mint assignments were developed in collaboration with Breen.

Breton, Pierre Napoléon, *Histoire Illustrée des Monnaies et Jetons du Canada.* Montreal, 1894 (reps.). C-S 2473*. A revision using the same numbers is his *Popular Illustrated Guide,* Montreal, 1912 (reps.), C-S 2474*.

Brock, Leslie Van Horn, *The Currency of the American Colonies 1700–1764: A Study in Colonial Finance and Imperial Relations.* Ph.D. dissertation, Univ. of Michigan, 1941; rep., N.Y., 1975.

Brogdon, H. C., "Notes on the Maryland, Annapolis and Baltimore Coins," *NUM* 11/38, pp. 954–56. Historical details about the silversmiths Chalmers and Standish Barry.

Brooks-Colburn-Finotti, et al., colls., W. Elliot Woodward, 4/28/1863; Bangs, Merwin & Co., N.Y.

Brown, Joseph Henry, *Brown's Political History of Oregon.* Portland, Ore.: W. B. Allen, 1892.

Brown Library = John Carter Brown Library of Brown Univ., coll., part I, A, PT, 5/20–22/76. (Part II comprised paper currency only.)

Browning, Ard W., *Early Quarter Dollars of the United States, 1796–1838.* N.Y.: Wayte Raymond, 1925. [50] (reps.) C-S 3433. Some of the reprints use remainders of original text plus new contact prints from the original negatives. Use with Breen {1954A} pending appearance of the George Frederick Kolbe annotated reprint.

Burnheimer, J. C., coll., A, Para, 5/6–8/76.

Burnie, Robert Harry, *Small California and Territorial Gold Coins: Quarter Dollars, Half Dollars, Dollars.* Pascagoula, Miss.: the author, 1955. C-S 3435. Rosichan 821. For California fractionals, superseded by Breen {1983}; for later regional and exposition souvenirs, it is the only available text, though desperately in need of replacement.

Bushnell {1858} = Bushnell, Charles Ira, *An Arrangement of Tradesmen's Cards, Political Tokens,* (etc., etc.), N.Y.: the author, 1858.

Bushnell {1859A} = ———, *Early American Coinage, Vol. 1,* bound ms. vol. in ANS, latest entries ca. 1859. Sourcebook compilation of data from old newspaper stories, historical texts, etc.

Bushnell {1859B} = ———, *An Historical Account of the First Three Business Tokens Issued in the City of New York.* N.Y.: pvt. ptd. [the author], 1859. On the 1789 Mott's and 1794–95 Talbot, Allum & Lee tokens. Preface dated July 1, 1859. Rep. in next.

Bushnell {1864} = ———, *Crumbs for Antiquarians.* N.Y.: pvt. ptd. (the author), 1864. [50] Bound collection of his pamphlets, including Bushnell {1859B}. Bushnell's credibility is suspect, but he is our earliest source for some material on early New York issues, and for some data our only source.

Bushnell, Charles Ira, estate, A, SH&HC, 6/20–24/1882. [400 + 100 with plates] Early American coins, medals, and tokens. Lorin G. Parmelee had bought the collection intact from Bushnell's estate, consigned it to the Chapman brothers, and attended the auction to buy in everything he wished to keep, without alerting other buyers to his strategy. The catalog's format (large quarto), factual errors, and repetitions of some of Bushnell's lies led to denunciations in the numismatic press—and to notoriety for the Chapmans. See John J. Ford, Jr., "The Bushnell Sale," *CCJ* 3–4/51.

Buss, Jerry, coll., A, Sup, 1/28–30/85.

Byrne, Ray, coll., "Coins and Tokens of the Caribees" [sic], A, Jess Peters, 6/13–15/75.

C

C = mintmark of Charlotte, N.C., branch mint, 1838–61, gold coins only.

"Cambridge," coll., A, NERCA, 12/3–4/76.

"Capitol City," colls., A, MARCA, 2/15–16/85.

Carlson, Carl W. A., "Birch and the Patterns of '92," *NUM* 3/82, pp. 628–45.

Carnegie, David K., coll., A, NERCA, 11/13–15/80. Your copy should include the errata sheet.

Carnegie Institute, coll., A, Spink & Son, 3/24–26/83.

Carothers, Neil, *Fractional Money.* N.Y.: John Wiley & Sons, 1930. Original edition rare because a warehouse fire destroyed most copies. Rep., N.Y.: A. M. Kelley, 1967. C-S 3345. Rosichan 833. The first text ever to make monetary theory intelligible. Should have been asterisked in C-S.

Carson, E. A., coll., CC-Mint issues, incl. in Willing, A (1976).

Carter = Amon G. Carter, Jr., Family, coll., A, S, 1/18–21/84. Federal and pioneer gold.

cat. = catalog.

Cauffman, Emil, coll., A, Edward Cogan, 5/3/1871.

CC = mintmark of Carson City branch mint, gold and silver coins only, 1870–85, 1889–93.

CCJ = Coin Collector's Journal. I. N.Y.: John Walter Scott, 12/1875–12/1888; II. N.Y.: Scott Stamp & Coin Co., continuous with III. N.Y.: Wayte Raymond, Inc., 4/34–58. The last dozen or so numbers were separate monographs in pamphlet format of same size as the magazine of 1934–51; those of 1958 were issued after Raymond's death.

"Century," coll. (i.e., A. Buol Hinman), A, Para, 4/30–5/1/65.

Chadwick-Darnell, colls. (i.e., I. E. Chadwick and C. A. Darnell), MBS, Kosoff, 5/2/52.

Chamberlain {1954} = Chamberlain, Georgia Stamm, "Joseph Wright: First Draughtsman and Diesinker to the U.S. Mint," *NUM* 12/54, pp. 1282–87. C-S 3478.

Chamberlain {1955} = ———, "John Reich, Assistant Engraver to the U.S. Mint," *NUM* 3/55, pp. 242–49. C-S 3479.

Chamberlain {1958} = ———, "Robert Ball Hughes, Sculptor, and the U.S. Coinage of 1840," *NUM* 8/58, pp. 928–32. C-S 3480.

Chambers, Robert B., coll., A, Woodward, 2/27/1866; G. A. Leavitt, N.Y.

Champa, Armand, coll., A, B&R as Amer. Auction Assoc., 5/19–20/72.

Charlton, James E., *Standard Catalogue of Canadian Coins, Tokens and Paper Money.* Racine, Wis.: Whitman Publishing Co., var. eds. C-S 2477.

"Charmont," colls., A, Ivy, 8/11–14/83.

Christmas, Rev. Henry, *Irish Coins of Copper and Billon.* London, 1862, 1863. 2 vol. in 1.

Chubbuck, Samuel W., coll., A, Haseltine, 2/25/1873; Thomas Birch & Sons, Philadelphia.

Ciani, Luigi (Louis), *Les Monnaies Royales Françaises de Hugues Capet à Louis XVI.* 2 vols. in 1. Paris: Florange et Ciani 1926–31. (reps.)

"Cicero," Midwestern coll., A, in NN55. Gold coins.

Clain-Stefanelli, Vladimir, "History of the National Numismatic Collection," in SI, U.S. National Museum, *Bulletin 229: Contributions from the Museum of History and Technology:* Papers 31–33. Washington, D.C.: SI, 1970. Orig., 1968.

Clapp, George H., ALCOA founder-president, conchologist; his large-cent coll. is housed in ANS.

Clapp, John H., of Washington, D.C., var. coll., sold July 1942 to Louis Eliasberg.

Clark, Dr. Glenn M., et al., colls., A, HIM, 2/17–8/84.

Clarke, Dr. E. Yale, coll., A, S, 10/25/75.

Clarke, T. James, cardboard box tycoon, coll., sold piecemeal, some gold privately by BMM before 1954, cents partly via R. E. Naftzger; see next 3 entries.

Clarke I = ———, part of coll., A, Kosoff, 4/27/56.

Clarke II = ———, parts of coll., A, scattered in NN47 and NN48.

Clarke III = ———, parts of coll., A, NASCA, 6/26–29/78.

Clay, Dr. Charles, of Manchester, England, coll., A, W. H. Strobridge, 12/5–7/1871; G. A. Leavitt, N.Y. Colonial coins, including some forgeries and other controversial items.

Clement, John, *First Settlers in Newton Township, N.J.* Camden: Camden County Historical Society, 1974. Relevant to Mark Newby and his coinage.

Cleneay, Thomas, coll., A, SH&HC, 12/9–13/1890.

Cleveland, Edmund J., coll., A, Edward Cogan, 5/7/1872; Bangs, Merwin & Co., N.Y.

Clifford, Henry H., *Pioneer Gold Coinage of the West, 1848–61.* Los Angeles: pvt. ptd., 1961. Rep. from *The Western Brand Book,* Book 9.

Clifford, Henry H., coll., A, B&R, 3/18–20/82. Pioneer gold.

Cline, J. H., *Liberty Standing Quarters.* n.d., n.p., i.e., Dayton, Ohio: the author, Sept. 1976. [600 hardcover; 10,000 paperback.] Rev. ed., 1986.

CMM = Cohen, Roger S., Jr., Munson, Paul, Jr., and Munde, Ray, *American Half Cents, the Little Half Sisters.* Bethesda, Md.: the authors, 1971. [2,000] Rosichan 810. Superseded by Cohen {1982} and Breen {1984}.

CNJ = Canadian Numismatic Journal, 1956–

CNL = Colonial Newsletter, 1960– , current ed. James C. Spilman, Box 4411, Huntsville, Ala. 35802. C-S 197; Rosichan 1656. Research papers, announcements of discoveries, reprints of inaccessible primary sources; extremely important to specialists.

Coffey, G., *National Museum of Science and Art, Dublin: Guide to the Collection of Irish Antiquities (Royal Irish Academy Collection).* Dublin: Printed for H.M. Stationery Office by Cahill & Co., 1895; rev. ed., 1911. Based on the Dr. Aquilla Smith gift.

Cogan, Edward, coll., A, 4/7/1863; Bangs, Merwin & Co., N.Y.

Cohen, David H., "The Randall Hoard," in ANS {1985}, pp. 41–51.

Cohen, Col. Mendes I. (1796–1879), of Baltimore, coll., A, E. Cogan, 10/25–27/1875; Bangs, Merwin & Co., N.Y. Owner of the keg of Virginia halfpence, gradually dispersed 1861–1929: Newman {1962}, p. 139.

Cohen, Roger S., *American Half Cents, the Little Half Sisters.* Arlington: "Wigglesworth & Ghatt," i.e., the author, 1982. Revision of CMM, some few numbers changed.

COINage, monthly, Encino, Calif.: Behn-Miller Publishers. Rosichan 1648.

COINS, monthly, Iola, Wis.: Krause Publications, 1962– Rosichan 1649. Earlier continuous antecedents: *Flying Eaglet,* 1955–59; *Coin News,* 1959; *Coin Press,* East Orange, N.J.: Frank Spadone, 1959–61. Many good papers.

Colburn, Jeremiah, coll., A, Woodward, 10/20–24/1863; Bangs, Merwin & Co., N.Y.

Collins, Jack, *Catalogue I,* numismatic books (library of Jerry Cohen and Abner Kreisberg), A, 10/1/83. Source for some corrections in this Bibliography, here gratefully acknowledged. Collins is the photographer of many coins in this *Encyclopedia,* and the publisher of Breen {1984}.

"Coll. of a Prominent American": see Granberg.

coll(s). = collection(s).

"Commonwealth," coll., A, NERCA, 7/29–30/77.

Comstock, Samuel W., coll., in Comstock-Gunther, A, Elder, 1/25–6/35. Fractional pioneer gold.

Conbrouse, Guillaume, *Catalogue Raisonnée des Monnaies de France.* Paris: A. Rollin, 1839.

Copeland, Bernard L., coll., A, S 4/27/67.

Cornell-Oglethorpe, colls., A, S, 5/30–31/75.

Cox, R. E., coll., A, S, 4/26–28/62. Half dollars. In 1962 NYMet convention sale.

Craig, Alan D., "Sleuthing the 1922 D Cents," *WNJ* 7/64, pp. 44–50. Update of his articles in *NSM* 11/62, 4/63.

Craig, Sir John, *The Mint: a History of the London Mint from A.D. 287 to 1948.* Cambridge (England): University Press 1953. C-S 2805. From the Tower Mint's archival sources. Relevant to both William Wood and the Virginia halfpence, and to our knowledge of developments in minting technology over the centuries. Extremely important; scholarly and readable.

Craig, William D., *Coins of the World 1750–1850.* Racine, Wis.: Western, 3 eds. 1966, 1971, 1976. His numbers are also used in *SCWC.*

Crosby {1875} = Crosby, Sylvester Sage, *The Early Coins of America; and the Laws Governing their Issue.* Boston: the author, 1875. [500] Partly rep. from *AJN* 1873–75. Actually printed in part by Charles Chaplin, in part by T. R. Marvin. C-S 3375*. Rosichan 826. Reps.: Boston: Estes & Lauriat, 1878 (i.e., binding of unsold fascicles from original 500 copies); Chicago: R. Green (i.e., Charles Elmore Green), 1945 [500]; N.Y.: Burt Franklin, 1970; Boston: Quarterman, 1981. This is the book which induced the ANS to place Crosby's name on the museum architrave. "All later writings on American numismatics are a series of footnotes to Crosby." —Sydney P. Noe.

Crosby {1897} = ————, *The United States Coinage of 1793, Cents and Half Cents.* Boston: the author, 1897 [200], rep. from *AJN* 1896; reps., 1933, 1962, others. C-S 3438. Numerical sequence largely superseded by Sheldon {1949, 1958}; var. descriptions and other text remain worthwhile.

Cross, Ira Brown, *Financing an Empire: History of Banking in California.* 4 vols. Chicago: S. J. Clarke, 1927. C-S 3439. Vol. I contains material relevant to pioneer gold coinage.

Crouch, Dr. Walter Lee, coll., A, Sup, 9/13–16/77.

C-S = Clain-Stefanelli, Elvira Eliza, *Select Numismatic Bibliography,* N.Y.: Stack's, 1965. Largely supersedes Grierson's and earlier bibliographies.

CSL = Connecticut State Library, Hartford, home of the John C. Mitchelson coll.: colonial coppers, gold, etc.

CSNA = California State Numismatic Association.

CSNS = Central States Numismatic Society.

Curto, James J., *Indian and Post Trader Tokens: Our Frontier Coinage.* Colorado Springs: ANA, 1962, rep. from *NUM* 1951, 1956, 1957 serials. C-S 3927. Relevant to the 1820 NORTH WEST COMPANY tokens.

CW = Coin World, weekly, Sidney, Ohio, 1960–

CWA = Coin World Almanac. 4th ed. Sidney, Ohio: Amos Press Inc., 1984.

cwt = hundredweight. One cwt = 112 lbs. avoir. = 1,792 oz. avoir. = 784,000 grs. = 50.802 kg.

D

D = a) mintmark of Dahlonega, Ga., branch mint, 1838–61 (gold only); b) mintmark of Denver, Colo., branch mint, 1906– .

D&H = Dalton, R., and Hamer, S. H., *English Provincial Token Coinage of the 18th Century.* London 1910–22 (14 parts + addenda). Reps., London: Seaby 1967; Chicago: Argonaut, 1967; that here used, Boston: Quarterman, 1972. C-S 3896*. Rosichan 959. Includes many relevant to America, and much information about designers, engravers, and mints of origin.

Davenport, coll., A, Sup, 2/21–22/77.

Davies-Niewoehner, colls., A, Para, 2/14–15/75. Early gold.

Davis, David J.; Logan, Russell J.; Lovejoy, Allen F.; McCloskey, John W.; and Subjack, William L., *Early United States Dimes 1796–1837.* Ypsilanti, Mich.: John Reich Collectors Society, 1984. Die-var. study.

Davis, R. Coulton, coll., A, N.Y. Coin & Stamp Co. (David Proskey and Harlan P. Smith), 1/20–24/1890. Patterns and other rarities from the Mint.

Davis, W. J., *The 19th Century Token Coinage of Great Britain,*

Ireland, the Channel Islands, and the Isle of Man. London, 1904. C-S 1897.

———— and Waters, A. W., *Tickets and Passes of Great Britain and Ireland, Struck or Engraved on Metal, Ivory, etc., for use at Theatres, Public Gardens, Shows, Exhibitions, Clubs, Societies, Schools, and Colleges* [etc., etc.] Leamington Spa, England: Courier Press, 1922.

Davis-Graves = George L. Davis and Henry P. Graves, colls., A, S, 4/8–10/54. Some material is from R. Coulton Davis estate (1890). Catalog partly by C. Douglas Smith (large cents).

Decatur, Stephen, "Ephraim Brasher, Silversmith of New York," *American Collector,* VII, 5, pp. 8–9 (6/38).

Delp, Winner F., coll., A, S, 11/17–18/72.

"Devonshire," colls., A, NERCA, 11/14–15/77.

DeWitt, J. Doyle, *A Century of Campaign Buttons, 1789–1889.* Hartford, Conn.: the author, 1959. C-S 3933. Rosichan 484. Includes many political tokens that circulated as money.

DF = Dowle, Anthony, and Finn, Patrick, *The Guidebook to the Coinage of Ireland from 995 A.D. to the Present Day.* London: Spink, 1969. Rosichan 484. Relevant to the 1760 VOCE POPULI coppers.

DiBello, Gaston, Part II, coll., A, S, 5/14–16/70. Gold. (Part I was foreign coins.)

Dickeson, Montroville W., M.D., *The American Numismatic Manual.* Philadelphia: Lippincott, 1859; 2nd ed., 1860; 3rd ed., 1865. C-S 3446. A pioneering effort to cover the same material as this Encyclopedia, before the necessary comparison methods were developed.

Dickinson, H. W., *Matthew Boulton.* Cambridge, England: University Press, 1937. Standard biography.

Dieffenbacher, Alfred, *Counterfeit Gold Coins, 19th and 20th Centuries, Fully Illustrated.* Montreal: Dieffenbacher Coin Ltd., 1963. C-S 4551. Looseleaf binder, greatly enlarged ills.; extremely comprehensive, and the methods used therein are still of value for detecting suspicious pieces.

Director's Reports = *Annual Reports of the Director of the Mint . . . 1795–1983,* (titles and imprints vary), Philadelphia; later issues, Washington: Government Printing Office. Early issues are in *ASPF.*

Doering, David, *California Fractional Gold.* First ed., n.p., n.d. (= Santa Monica, Calif.: the authors, April 1980), listing Susan Doering as coauthor [1,000]; second ed., drastically revised, without mention of coauthor, n.p. (= Santa Monica: the author), (June) 1982. Of value for ills. of rare vars.; prices are wishful thinking.

Dolnick, Michael M., "Design Changes on the Liberty Standing Quarter," *NUM* 10/54, pp. 980–82.

Donovan, R. A., coll., A, Ivy, 7/28–9/78.

Douglas, Damon G., "The Original Mint of the New Jersey Coppers," *Proc.* [Proceedings] *N.J. Historical Society* 69, pp. 223–230 (7/51). C-S 3376. On Rahway Mills.

Dryfhout, John H., *The Work of Augustus St. Gaudens.* Hanover & London: University Press of New England, 1982. Extensively illustrated catalogue raisonné, including the medallic work leading to the St. Gaudens coinage dies of 1907. Illustrations are of extraordinary quality.

DuBois, William Ewing, *Pledges of History: A Brief Account of the Collection of Coins Belonging to the Mint of the United States.* Philadelphia: pvt. ptd., 1846. [150] C-S 3481. A predecessor of Snowden {1860}; rep. in Eckfeldt & DuBois {1850}.

Dunham, William Forrester, coll., MBS, BMM 6/3/41.

Dunlap, William, *A History of the Rise and Progress of the Arts of Design in the United States.* Eds., Frank William Bayley and Charles Eliot Goodspeed. 3 vols. Boston: C. E. Goodspeed & Co., 1918; rep., N.Y.: B. Blom, 1965. Orig. ed., 2 vols., N.Y.: George P. Scott & Co., 1834.

"Dupont" I = "The Anderson Dupont Catalogue, Part I" (a Massachusetts estate; the names are those of Charles Anderson and Charles Dupont, intermediaries), coll., A, large cents, S, 9/24–25/54. Catalog partly by Dr. William H. Sheldon, partly by Breen.

"Dupont" II = ————, Part II, coll., A, S, 11/11–13/54. Catalog partly by Breen.

dwt = pennyweight(s). 1 dwt = 24 grs. = 1.56 gms.

Dyer, Graham P., and Gaspar, Peter P., "A Virginia Numismatic Discovery," *Museum Notes* 27, pp. 231–37 (1982). N.Y.: ANS, 1982.

                              E

EAC as book title = Sheldon {1949}. As group title = Early American Coppers, Inc., specialist society, publisher of *Penny Wise;* founded by Herbert A. Silberman. Direct inquiries to Rod Burress, Box 15782, Cincinnati, Ohio 45215.

1975 EAC, colls., A, PT, 2/15/75. Colonial coppers (many from Theodore L. Craige coll.) and large cents. Cat. partly by Breen. Precursor of Breen {1976B} and presupposed in latter.

1976 EAC, colls., A, PT, 2/27–28/76; cat. incl. 1976 Sub. Wash. (Dr. Clifton Brakensiek et al.), A, PT, 3/5–6/76. Cat. partly by Breen.

Earle, George H., coll., A, HC, 6/25–29/12.

Eavenson, George [et al.], colls., A, SH&HC, 4/16–17/03. Relevant portions are from a coll. deduced to be that of Patterson DuBois, Mint Cabinet curator.

Eckfeldt & DuBois {1842} = Eckfeldt, Jacob Reese, and DuBois, William Ewing, *A Manual of Gold and Silver Coins of All Nations, Struck Within the Past Century.* Philadelphia: Assay Office of the Mint, 1842; supplements, 1849, 1851, latter Philadelphia: A. Hart. C-S 2291.

Eckfeldt & DuBois {1850, 51, 52} = ————, *New Varieties of Gold and Silver Coins, Counterfeit Coins and Bullion: with Mint Values.* Philadelphia: the authors, 1850; rev. eds., N.Y.: G. P. Putnam, 1851, 1852. The revisions largely have to do with pioneer gold. Includes rep. of DuBois {1846}. C-S 3348.

EF = the grade EXTREMELY FINE, defined for each series and design in corresponding section of main text.

Egolf, Howard D., coll., A, S, 5/5/61.

Einstein, Harry ("Parkyakarkus"), et al., colls., A, B&M 6/23–25/86.

Elder, Thomas L., series of A, cited by dates; publisher of several books cited herein.

Eliasberg, Louis, Sr., estate, largely from the John H. Clapp coll. (Washington, D.C., July 1942); cited as the most nearly complete coll. of U.S. coins ever assembled; duplicates sold in "H. R. Lee" and NN 49. Main gold coll., A, as "The United States Gold Coll.," B&R, 10/27–29/82. Discussed on "CBS Morning News," 10/27–28/82; interview text in *CW* 11/10/82, p. 22.

Ellsworth, Col. James W., coll., privately sold via Knoedler Galleries and Wayte Raymond, 1923.

Ely, Hon. Heman, coll., A, Woodward, 1/8–10/1884.

Emery & Nichols, colls., A, B&M, 11/12–14/84.

Emmons, Dr. Calvert L., coll., A, S, 9/19–20/69.

"Empire" [i.e., Charles A. Cass], coll., A, S, 11/12–15/57.

Empire Review (1960–65), *Empire Topics* (1958–59), house organs of Q. David Bowers, precursors of B&R RCR. Mostly FPLs, MBSs, some editorial material, incl. occasional contributions by Breen.

Engel {1970A} = Engel, Sydney C., "Engel's Expertise," *CW* 7/15/70. Former Philadelphia Mint coiner's reminiscences.

Engel {1970B} = ————, *CW* 8/19/70. More of the same.

Enl. = enlarged.

Ernst, Joseph Albert, *Money and Politics in America 1755–1775.* Chapel Hill, N.C.: Univ. of North Carolina Press, 1973. Economic abuses leading to the Revolution; revisionism giving unsuspected meanings to the usual history-classroom platitudes.

ESC = Seaby, Herbert A., and Rayner, Peter Alan, *English Silver Coins, 1649–1949.* London: B. A. Seaby Ltd., various eds., 1957– . C-S 2798. Rosichan 419. Standard reference.

Essex Institute, coll., A, S, 2/6–8/75. Not to be confused with Essex Numismatic Properties, a New England coin firm.

ETCM = Error Trends Collectors Magazine, Oceanside, L.I., N.Y., 1969– .

"European Coll.", A, Woodward, 7/20/1884.

Evans, George G., *Illustrated History of the United States Mint and a Complete Description of the American Coinage* [!]. Philadelphia: George G. Evans, 1314 Filbert St., 1885, various eds. through 1901. (That for 1892, "Centennial Edition," is prized by collectors.) Largely superseded by Taxay {1966}; still of occasional value as a supplement to the latter.

EVN = Error-Variety News Magazine, Quakertown, Pa., 1977–

Ewalt, George Sealy, coll., A, S, 11/22–23/65.

Ewing, George E., Jr., "Origins of Edge Lettering on Early American Coinage," in ANS {1985}, pp. 59–72.

F

F The grade FINE, defined in many sections of main text, for issues collected in this grade.

F Short for FECIT = 'he made it.'

"Fairbanks," coll. (i.e., Ben H. Koenig), said to be from Fairbanks, Ak., A, S, 12/10/60.

"Fairfield," coll. (i.e., Arthur Lamborn), A, B&R, 10/6–8/77.

Farouk I, king of Egypt, colls.: duplicates, "A Royal Sale," MBS, BMM, 3/23/48; main coll., "Palace Colls. of Egypt," expropriated by the Nasser government, A, Sotheby's, Cairo, 2/24–3/6/54 (rep.). C-S 2323. Warning: The latter catalog was prepared in extreme haste. Many important coins were lumped into large lots without grading, var. identification, or pedigree; most ills. are too blurry to be usable. Many of the coins were poorly cleaned and lacquered.

Featherstonhaugh, Dr. Martin, "A Private Mint in North Carolina," *Publications of the Southern History Association,* 3/06 (rep.). Partly quoted in Kagin {1981} and at Garrett:115.

Fecht, A. J., "A $20 Gold Coin With Pattern Reverse," *NUM* 3/37, p. 199. On discovery of the 1861 S double eagle with Paquet rev.

Fernald, Kay, and McDowell, Kay, *Rubles to Statehood.* Anchorage, Ak.: the authors, 1965. On Alaskan bingles; the ARRC issue is at pp. 82–84.

Fewsmith, William, coll., A, Ebenezer Locke Mason, Jr., 10/4–7/1870; Leavitt, Strebeigh & Co., N.Y.

Field, Martin, coll., A, PT, 9/26–27/78.

Finotti, Rev. Joseph M., coll., A, Woodward, 11/11–14/1862; Bangs, Merwin & Co., N.Y.

Flanagan, Col. James W., coll., A, S, 3/23–25/44.

Fleischer, Donald S., coll., A, S, 9/7–8/79.

Fonrobert, Jules, coll., A, Adolph Weyl, 2/18/1878, C-S 3185.

Ford {1950} = John Jay Ford, Jr., with Kenney, Richard D., "Authentication of Colonial Coins: The Clinton Cent," in *CCJ* 132, 9–10/50.

Ford {1951A} = ———, "Numismatica Americana: The Confederate Cent," in *CCJ* 134, 1–2/51. C-S 3441.

Ford {1951B} = ———, "Numismatica Americana: The Copper Company of Upper Canada," in *CCJ* 136, 5–6/51. C-S 2482.

Ford {1975} = ———, "Newly Discovered Washington Pattern Coins," *NUM* 9/75, pp. 1939–48.

Forman-Taxay Associates [= Harry Forman and Don Taxay], colls., A, 12/6–7/74. For Philadelphia Metropolitan Convention. Cat. by Don Taxay.

Forrer, Leonard S., *Biographical Dictionary of Medallists.* 6 vols. + 2 supplements. London: Spink, 1904–30 (rep.).

Forrest, S. S., coll., A, S, 9/15–16/72.

"Four Memorable Colls." (i.e., James Murray, S. R. Swope, W. C. Young, Roy H. Van Ormer), colls., A, B&M, 9/9–11/85.

FPL = Fixed Price List. Contrast A, MBS.

Frank, B., coll., A, S, 11/23/56.

Friedberg, Robert P., *Gold Coins of the World: Complete from A.D. 600 to the Present.* Rev. and ed. by Jack Friedberg. N.Y.: Coin & Currency Inst., 1971. (Replaces orig. ed., 1958, C-S 2294.)

Friesner, William M., coll., A, Frossard, 6/7/1894. Contained the 1838 O half dollar with the documentation from the New Orleans Mint's coiner, Rufus Tyler, establishing the number struck.

Frossard, Édouard, *Monograph of United States Cents and Half Cents Issued Between the Years 1793 and 1857.* Irvington-on-Hudson, N.Y.: the author [i.e., Boston: T. R. Marvin], 1879. [300] (rep.) C-S 3442. Based largely on the Merritt coll. Pioneer attempt to cover the subject matter of Chapts. 17 and 18 hereinabove.

Frossard, coll., A, Édouard Frossard, 10/2–3/1884; Bangs & Co., N.Y. Other auctions cataloged or offered by Frossard are cited by name herein, or individually in main text by dates.

Fuld {1956} = Fuld, George and Melvin, "The Talbot, Allum & Lee Cents," *NSM* 9/56:1474–82.

Fuld {1964} = ——— and ———, "The Origin of the Washington 1783 Cents," speech presented to the 1964 ANA Convention, Cleveland, Ohio, 8/20/64, following briefer account in *CNL* 6/64, pp. 53–58; rep. as ditto'd pamphlet; revised version, *NUM* 11/64, pp. 1475–81.

Fuljenz, Mike, "Research in Mint Records Reveals Intended Obverses." N.N.W. 9/9/86, 10ff.

F.U.N. = Florida United Numismatists, regional group holding conventions in Florida every January. Auctions cited below:

1963 F.U.N. = "Million Dollar Auction at the Fontainebleau, Miami Beach," colls., A, Federal Brand Enterprises (= Michael Kolman, Jr.), 1/3–7/63.

1977 F.U.N., colls., A, PT, 1/8/77. Catalog misdated 1976 on cover.

1978 F.U.N., colls, A, PT, 1/6–7/78.

G

G = the grade GOOD, defined for individual series in main text (largely Colonials and earliest types of each U.S. denomination).

Gable, William F., coll., A, SHC, 5/27/14.

Gadoury, Victor, and Droulers, Frédéric, *Monnaies Royales Françaises, 1610–1792.* Monte Carlo: Gadoury, 1978. Source of many mintage figures for French Régime (Canada/Louisiana) coins. Herein cited as GD.

Gadoury, Victor, and Cousinie, Georges, *Monnaies Coloniales Françaises, 1670–1980.* Monte Carlo: Gadoury, 1979.

G&R = Grellman, John R., Jr., and Reiver, Jules, *Attribution Guide for United States Large Cents 1840–1857.* Vol. I (1840–48). Montgomery, Ala.: J. R. Grellman, 1986. Looseleaf notebook, ill. by line drawings, updating Newcomb {1944}. Vol. II (1849–57) is scheduled for 1987. Regrettably ignores proof dies.

Ganz, David L., *14 Bits: The Story of America's Bicentennial*

Coinage, 1976. Washington, D.C.: Three Continents Press, 1976. Partly rep. and rev. from his serial in *NUM* 3–6/75.

Garrett 1976 = John Work Garrett, part of coll., A, S, 3/12–13/76. Compare next 4.

Garrett I = ———, part of coll., A, B&R, 11/28–29/79. Colonial coppers (Vermont, Massachusetts, New York), Brasher Doubloon, CONSTELLATIO NOVA silver, half cents, cents, minors, patterns, U.S. gold (except $2½, $10, $20), pioneer gold other than California. Lots 1–622. Numbering continuous with next 3 so that in main text the I, II, III are often omitted. "For the Johns Hopkins University."

Garrett II = ———, part of coll., A, B&R 3/26–27/80. Quarters, silver dollars, trade dollars, $2½, $20, commemoratives, pioneer gold (California, Oregon, Mormon), patterns, Hard Times tokens. Lots 623–1195.

Garrett III = ———, part of coll., A, B&R, 10/1–2/80. Colonials, U.S. nickel and small-silver issues, proof sets, $10. Lots 1196–1692.

Garrett IV = ———, part of coll., A, B&R, 3/25–26/81. Machin's Mills coppers, Washington items, Brasher Doubloons, Patterns of 1792, California fractional gold, bullion storage ingots, Confederate and Hawaiian issues, medals, currency. Lots 1693–2354.

Gaylord, Emerson, coll., A, Mayflower, 5/18/63, Boston.

GBD = Gould, Maurice, Bressett, Kenneth E., and Dethridge, Nancy and Kaye, *Alaska's Coinage Through the Years*. Racine, Wis.: Western, 1965. C-S 3446. Rosichan 987. Supersedes 1960 ed.

GD = Gadoury and Droulers, above.

Geiss, Frederic W., coll., MBS, BMM, 2/18/47.

GENA = Great Eastern Numismatic Assoc., regional group holding conventions each autumn; see following citations.

1973 GENA, colls., A, PT, 9/22/73. Catalog partly by Breen. Originally a pullout section of *CW* 8/29/73, separately rep.

1974 GENA, colls., A, PT, 9/18–21/74. Same comment. Rep., hard covers [8], Feb. 1975.

1978 GENA, colls., A, Kagin, 9/29–30/78. Also cited as Kagin 313th sale.

Gerry Nelson, et al., colls., A, B&R, 4/30/82.

Getty, coll., A, B&R, 5/5–6/77. Here cited primarily for the McClurg coll. of bust half dollars.

Gettys-Catich = Gettys, Loyd B., and Catich, Edward M., "AU or BU?," serial on grading regular coins, *NUM* 5/56, pp. 515–21; 6/56, pp. 633–37; 7/56, pp. 747–52; on grading commemoratives, *NUM* 8/58, pp. 899–915. Rep., Colorado Springs: ANA, n.d.; rep. also in Bagg, Richard, and Jelinski, James J., *Grading Coins: A Collection of Readings*. Portsmouth, N.H.: Essex Publications, 1977. Ancestral to the current ANA grading system, before the powers that be decided to affix unstandardized Sheldon numbers to the verbal descriptions.

Gibbons II, coll., A, NASCA, 12/81.

Gibbs, William T., "Liberty Head 5 Cents Centenarian," *CW* 2/9/83, p. 70.

Gibson, coll., A, S, 11/11/74. Pioneer gold.

Gies, A. C., coll., FPL, S, 1940. Half dollars. Did not include Gies's hoards of other denominations.

Gilbert, Ebenezer, *The United States Half Cents. From the First Year of Issue, in 1793, to the Year When Discontinued, 1857*. N.Y.: Elder Numismatic Press, 1916, reps. C-S 3443. The original has matte photographic plates; reps. (not generally so identified) have glossy plates of poorer quality. Rarely comes with a supplemental plate (3¼" × 7") ill. 1831 "Gilbert 1-A" and an accompanying descriptive slip; both ill. (reduced) as lot 265, Jack Collins A ("An Important Numismatic Library"), 10/1/83. Mostly superseded by CMM, Cohen, and Breen {1984}, though many collectors still habitually use Gilbert numbers.

Gilhousen, Clarke E., et al., colls., A, Sup., 2/19/73. Gold coins.

"Gilhousen," colls. (largely property of Dr. Charles L. Ruby), A, Sup, 10/1–4/73. Catalog mostly by Breen.

Gladfelter, David D., "Mark Newby: Quaker Pioneer," *TAMS Journal* 14.5, pp. 166–76 (11/74). Corrects earlier biographic data.

Glaser {1962} = Glaser, C. Lynn, "Art in American Coinage," *NSM* serial, pp. 2462–74, 2792–2800, 3092–3101. C-S 3444. Independent of Vermeule {1971} and in some ways supplementary thereto.

Glaser {1968} = ———, *Counterfeiting in America*. N.Y.: Clarkson Potter, 1968. Rosichan 107. History at once scholarly, scandalous, and hilarious.

Glendining & Co., colls., A, 3/21/35. London. Other colls. auctioned by this firm are cited in main text by date or owner's name.

gm(s). = gram(s). The conversion factor here used: 1 gm. = 15.432356 grs. troy or avoir. Rounding off avoids conflict with the other conversion factor 15.4323478 cited in older sources.

Gobrecht Journal, house organ of Liberty Seated Collectors Club, 12/1974– , ed., Dr. J. R. McCloskey, 5718 King Arthur Drive, Kettering, Ohio.

Golden I = "Golden Sale of the Century, Part I," colls., A, KS, 3/21/62.

Golden II = ———, Part II, colls., A, KS, 1/17–19/63.

"Golden Jubilee" = Jerome Kern (the composer), et al., colls., MBS, BMM, 5/23/50.

Goodman, Leon, colls., A, HIM, 7/29–30/82.

Gould, Maurice, and Bressett, Kenneth E., *Hawaiian Coins, Tokens and Paper Money*. Racine, Wis.: Whitman 1961. Rosichan 836. Overlaps Medcalf-Fong {1967}.

Gould-Bressett-Dethridge: See GBD above.

gr(s). = grain(s), troy or avoir. Conversion factor here used: 1 gr. = 0.0647989 gm. Weights in grs. are cited because authorizing acts past and present have specified them.

Grafton, coll., in Numismatics of Wisconsin convention A, Kurt R. Krueger, 5/10–11/80. Fractional California gold.

Granberg, H. O., colls., sold piecemeal, largely through William Hartman Woodin, later Secretary of Treasury: MBS, BMM, 7/14/13, 7/16/19, 11/19/19; A, U.S. Coin Co. (= Wayte Raymond and others), 5/19–21/15 (as "Coll. of a Prominent American"). Part of Granberg's colls. were ill. in ANS {1914}.

"Grand Central," colls., A, HIM, 11/4–6/83.

Grand, Theodore, et al., colls., A, S, 12/11/47.

Green, Charles Elmore, *Mint Record and Type Table*. Chicago: Swift, 1936 (reps.).

Green, Dr. Charles W., coll., MBS, BMM, 4/26/49. Gold coins.

Green, Col. Edward Howland Robinson, son of Hetty Green (the multimillionaire "Witch of Wall Street"), collector/hoarder of coins, stamps, pornographic films, railroad cars, etc.; colls. sold privately ca. 1936–45, via F. C. C. Boyd, Burdette G. Johnson, Art Kelley, BMM, Wayte Raymond, S, etc.

Gregory, Charles, coll., A, SHC, 6/19–20/16.

Griffin, Clarence, *The Bechtlers and Bechtler Coinage, and Gold Mining in North Carolina, 1814–1830*. Forest City, N.C.: Forest City Courier, 1929; rep. *NUM* 1929, pp. 549–58, 808. C-S 3447.

Groce, George C., and Wallace, David H., *New-York Historical Society's Dictionary of Artists in America, 1564–1860*. New Haven: Yale Univ. Press, 1964.

Grove, Frank W., *The Medals of Mexico*, vol. 1: *Medals of the Spanish Kings*. Guadalajara, Mexico: the author (i.e., San José, Calif.: Prune Tree Graphics), 1970. [1,000] Rosichan

1018. Here cited for the 1760 and 1789 Florida proclamation pieces. Vols. 2 and 3 are not relevant.

Groves, Donald, coll., A, S, 11/11–12/74.

Grueber, Herbert A., *Handbook of Coins of Great Britain and Ireland in the British Museum.* London: Bernard Quaritch, 1899. C-S 2870*. Here cited for coins shipped to the American colonies.

Gschwend, Peter, coll., A, Elder, 6/15–16/08. William H. Woodin bought the coll., cherrypicked it, and consigned the remainder to Elder.

Guggenheimer, F. S., coll., A, S, 1/22/53.

H

H = Haseltine var. numbers, in "[Capt. John W.] Haseltine Type Table Catalogue," coll., A, Haseltine, 11/28/1881 (reps.). C-S 3449. Dollars, halves, and quarters. Research by J. Colvin Randall, but Haseltine (for unknown reasons) deliberately omitted any mention of Randall's name, and Randall's later colls. went at A through George W. Cogan, William Elliot Woodward, etc. Haseltine was a Philadelphia coin dealer, son-in-law of William Idler; father-in-law of Stephen K. Nagy; first employer of SH&HC.

Haines, Benjamin, coll., A, William H. Strobridge and Edward Cogan, 1/19–23/1863; Bangs, Merwin & Co., N.Y.

Haines (1880) = Haines, Ferguson, coll., A, Woodward, 10/13–16/1880.

Haines (1888) = ———, coll., A, SH&HC, 10/17–18/1888.

Hall, Frank, *History of Colorado.* Chicago: Blakely, 1890.

Halsell, John Glenn, coll., A, S 3/21/84.

Harsche, Bert, *Detecting Altered Coins.* 5th ed., with revs. by staff of *NNW* and *Coins Magazine;* mint-error forgery section by Alan Herbert. Florence, Ala. 35630: ANCO [= Anderson News Co.], 1973.

Harte I = Roy Harte, et al., colls., A, B&R, 11/16–18/77.

Harte II = ———, et al., colls., A, B&R, 3/27/81.

Harte III = ———, et al., colls., A, B&R, 1/25–27/83.

"Haseltine Sale," colls., A, Haseltine, 1/13–15/1874; Thomas Birch & Sons, Philadelphia. Herein cited for the first mention in print of the Confederate cent.

Haseltine {1909} = Haseltine, Capt. John W., "Two Unique Double Eagle Varieties, Previously Unpublished," *NUM* 6/09, pp. 173–74. First mention of the 1876 transitionals.

Hatie, George D., coll., A, B&M, 8/3/83.

Hawaiian {1846} = Hawaiian Islands. *Statute Laws of His Majesty King Kamehameha III, passed by the houses of nobles and representatives during the 21st year of his reign. . . .* A.D. 1845 and 1846. . . . Honolulu, Oahu: C. E. Hitchcock, 1846. Transl. of *Kanawai i kauia e ka moi, e Kamehameha III,* 2 vols. Honolulu: Mea pai palapala a na misionari Amerika, 1846–47.

Hawn I = Hawn, Reed, coll., A, S, 8/28–29/73.

Hawn II = ———, coll., A, S, 3/11–12/77.

Haxby-Willey = Haxby, J. A., and Willey, Robert C., *Coins of Canada.* 2nd ed. Racine, Wis.: Western, 1972. Rosichan 714. Research by Willey; photography by Haxby. Here cited for scholarly French Régime material.

HC = Henry Chapman, Philadelphia dealer, holding numerous auctions 1906–32 after the split with his brother Samuel Hudson Chapman.

Heaton, Augustus Goodyear, *Mint Marks,* i.e., *A Treatise on the Coinage of the United States Branch Mints.* Washington, D.C.: the author, 1893. C-S 3483. This one book created the modern collector interest in the subject.

Heifetz, Jascha [the violinist], coll., A, Wayte Raymond and J. G. MacAllister, 3/15–16/38; J. C. Morgenthau, N.Y., 388th Sale.

Heim, Russell, coll., A, S, 6/15/72.

Hellwig, colls., A, B&R, 2/7/79.

Hemstreet, Charles, *The Story of Manhattan,* N.Y.: Charles Scribner's Sons, 1901. Overlaps with the same author's *Nooks and Corners of Old New York,* N.Y.: same pub., 1899, 1909; and his *When Old New York Was Young,* N.Y.: same pub., 1902, 1910.

Henderson, C. W., coll., A, Ivy, 1/27/78.

Henderson, Dr. J. M., coll., A, SHC, 5/27/21. Mostly large cents; very limited ed., few copies survive.

Herdman, Donald F., coll., A, B&R, 12/8–9/77.

Hering, Henry, "History of the $10 and $20 Gold Coins of 1907 Issue," *NUM* 8/49, pp. 455–58. (Orig. 1920.) Hering was assistant to the coins' designer Augustus St. Gaudens.

Herrera y Chiesanova, Adolfo, *Medallas de Proclamación y Juras de los Reyes de España.* Madrid: Imprenta de Manuel Giner Hernández, Calle de la Libertad numero 16, 1882 (reps.). C-S 4166. Here cited for the Florida pieces.

Herstal, Stanislaw, et al., colls., A, B&R (as "Amer. Auction Assoc."), 2/7–9/74.

Hetherington, John J., coll., A, Wayte Raymond and James G. MacAllister, 6/10/33; J. C. Morgenthau, N.Y., 310th Sale.

Hickson, Howard, *Mintmark CC—History of the United States Mint at Carson City, Nevada.* Carson City: Nevada State Museum, 1972. Rosichan 805.

Hilt, Robert P., II, *Die Varieties of Early United States Coins.* Omaha, Neb.: RTS Publishing Co., 1980. Controversial in-depth analysis of Archives documents, relevant to federal gold and silver coins 1794–98.

HIM = Herbert I. Melnick, Inc., auctioneers.

Hindle, Brooke, *David Rittenhouse.* Princeton, N.J.: Princeton Univ. Press, 1964. Standard biography.

Hirt, David L., et al., colls., A, PT, 11/20–22/75.

Hobson-Jobson = Yule, Henry, and Burnell, Arthur Coke, *Hobson-Jobson: A Glossary of Colloquial Anglo-Indian Words and Phrases.* New ed., ed., William Crooke. 2nd ed. Delhi: Munshiram Manoharlal, 1968 (orig. 1903). Etymology and historical contexts of many common English words whose Anglo-Indian origins were long forgotten; of anthropological and sociological interest.

Hocking {1906} = Hocking, W. J., *Catalogue of the Coins and Tokens in the Museum of the Royal Mint.* London: Ptd. for His Majesty's Stationery Office by Darling & Son, 1906.

Hocking {1910} = ———, *Catalogue of the Dies, Medals and Seals in the Museum of the Royal Mint.* London: same pub., 1910.

Hoffman, Francis S., coll., A, Woodward, 4/24–27/1866; Leavitt, Strebeigh & Co., N.Y.

Hoffman, Henri, *Les Monnaies Royales de France depuis Hugues Capet jusqu'à Louis XVI.* Paris, 1878. C-S 2598.

Hofstadter, Richard, "Free Silver and the Mind of 'Coin' Harvey," in *The Paranoid Style in American Politics,* N.Y.: Vintage 1967, pp. 238–315. Essential for understanding the silver/gold "rivalry" of 1870–1900.

Holmes, Milton, coll., A, S, 10/5–8/60. Vars. of early federal coins.

Hoober, Richard T., "Financial History of Colonial Maryland," *NUM* 8/62; reps., Colorado Springs: ANA, n.d. C-S 3659.

Howard, Winslow J., coll., A, Lyman Low, 6/3/1886.

Howe, Octavius Thorndike, *Argonauts of '49: History and Adventures of the Emigrant Companies from Massachusetts, 1849–50.* Cambridge, Mass.: Harvard Univ. Press, 1923.

HR = Harmer Rooke Numismatics, auctioneers. Herein cited: A of 11/17/69, 12/5/72.

Humbert, Augustus, coll., A, SH&HC, 5/1–2/02. Generally known as Weeks-Humbert sale; Humbert was head of the San Francisco Provisional Branch Mint, aka United States Assay Office of Gold.

Hydeman, Edwin, coll., A, Kosoff, 3/3/61.

I

Idler, William, Philadelphia coin dealer, fence for the Philadelphia Mint's irregular and clandestine "cabinet coins," ca. 1859–87; father-in-law of Capt. John W. Haseltine.

"Ill. Hist." = *Illustrated History of U.S. Coins,* coll. (i.e., Dr. J. Hewitt Judd et al.), FPL, A. Kosoff, 1962; Encino, Calif.

Irvine, Dallas D., "The Fate of the Confederate Archives," *Amer. Hist. Rev.* XLIV, 4, pp. 83ff (7/39).

Ivy = Steve Ivy Rare Coins, auction firm, herein cited by cover title.

Ivy Cambridge, coll., A, Ivy, 12/12–13/82. Not to be confused with NERCA's Cambridge sale.

J

J = Judd numbers (patterns, experimental coins, etc.), from Judd, below.

Jackman, Allison W., coll., A, HC, 6/28–29/18.

Jackson, Malcolm N., coll., U.S. Coin Co. (Wayte Raymond, et al.), 5/20–22/13.

Jay, Charles, coll., A, S, 10/27–28/67.

JCC = *Journals of* [Continental] *Congress: containing their Proceedings from September 5, 1774* (to Nov. 3, 1788). Published by Authority. 13 vols. Philadelphia: Falwell's press, 1800–1. Rep., 4 vols., Washington, D.C.: Way & Gideon, 1823; rep., 34 vols., Washington: Government Printing Office, 1904–16.

Jefferson, Thomas, *The Papers of Thomas Jefferson.* Ed., Julian Parks Boyd. Princeton, N.J.: Princeton Univ. Press, 1950–61. Relevant material is in vol. VII.

Jencks-Paine = A. V. Jencks and G. T. Paine, colls., A, Woodward, 12/10–12/1866; Leavitt, Strebeigh & Co., N.Y.

Jenks, John Story, coll., A, HC, 12/7–17/21. C-S 2320. (plate reps.) [60 with orig. plates.]

Jenks (1880) = Jenks, William J., coll., A, Woodward, 9/1–3/1880.

Jenks (1883) = ———, coll., A, Woodward, 6/25–26/1883.

Jenning, coll., A, in S, 6/26/58.

JHU = Johns Hopkins University, repository of the Garrett colls. 1942–79.

Johnson, Burdette G., dealer, aka St. Louis Stamp & Coin Co.; handled much of the Virgil Brand and Col. Green estates in the 1940s. Part of Johnson's estate appeared in Schulman (1951).

Johnson, Mary Coffin, *The Higleys And Their Ancestry,* N.Y., 1896.

Johnson-Meyer, colls., i.e., Charles M. Johnson and Dr. Ivan H. Meyer, A, B&R, 2/9–11/78.

Judd, Dr. J. Hewitt, *United States Pattern, Experimental and Trial Pieces.* Racine, Wis.: Whitman/Western, 6 eds., 1959–77. Based in part on researches of Breen and of the late William Guild. The 4th ed. (1970) totally rewritten by Breen; the 6th (1977) rewritten by A. Kosoff, with irrelevant additions (mint errors of Eisenhower dollars).

Julian {1962A} = Robert W. Julian, "The Patterns of 1792," *NSM* 6/62, pp. 1836–42.

Julian {1962B} = ———, "The Digges Letters," *Seaby's Coin & Medal Bulletin,* 10–11/62. On Hancock's Washington cents.

Julian {1963} = ———, "The Beginnings of Coinage—1793," *NSM* 5/63, pp. 1357–64. Revised version is in *NSM* 12/74, p. 60ff.

Julian {1964} = ———, "The Harper Cents," *NSM* 9/64, pp. 2370–74.

Julian {1965} = ———, "The 1796 Copper Coinage," *NSM* 10/65, pp. 2714–22.

Julian {1966A} = ———, "Notes on U.S. Proof Coinage: Silver and Minor," *NSM* 3/66, pp. 513–17.

Julian {1966B} = ———, "The Dahlonega Mint," serial, *NSM* 4/66, 5/66, 7/67, 8/67, 11/67, 11/68.

Julian {1969} = ———, "Coiner Snowden's Trial Coins Bring Rebuke From Mint Director," *NSM* 5/69, pp. 758–760.

Julian {1972A} = ———, "New York Coiners Plague Hobby With Bogus 1848, 1849 Cents," *NSM* 6/72, pp. 528–30.

Julian {1972B} = ———, "U.S. Half Cent Thrives Despite Second Rate Treatment," *NSM* 10/72, pp. 886–904.

Julian {1974} = ———, serial on Mint history, various titles, beginning "New Nation: Brave but Broke," *Coins Magazine* 4/74, p. 82ff, and 4 later installments that year.

Julian {1975A} = ———, "Cent Coinage 1794–95," *NSM* 1/75, p. 6ff.

Julian {1975B} = ———, "British Planchets and Yellow Fever," *NSM* 6/75, pp. 36–44.

Julian {1975C} = ———, "From Shortage to Surfeit: The Cent Coinage of 1799," *NSM* 8/75.

Julian {1977} = ———, "First Years of the New Orleans Mint," *Coins* 11/77, pp. 62–67.

Julian {1978} = ———, "The Illegal Dollars of 1794–1795," *Coins* 3/78, pp. 46–52.

Julian {1982} = ———, "Most Gobrecht Dollars Not Patterns," *CW* 11/24/82, p. 81. Last installment of a serial; earlier installments 7/21, 8/4, 10/20.

Julian {1984} = ———, "How Many Half Cents? Old Documents Dispute Today's Accepted Figures for 1832 to 1835," *NNW* 6/9/84, p. 6.

Julian {1986} = ———, "The Silver Proof Coinage of 1878," *NUM* 12/86, pp. 2493–98.

Other citations to Julian without date are from personal communication.

K

Kagin {1957} = Kagin, Arthur M., "Spanish-American Style Doubloon," *NSM* 11/57, pp. 2097, 2103. On Brasher's Doubloon of Lima type.

Kagin {1961} = ———, "The Most Notorious U.S. Coin," *NSM* 10/61, pp. 2587–89. On the 1838 restrike dollar overstruck on an 1859 dollar.

Kagin (other dates except next) = series of MBS 1940–73, A 1973–84, earlier ones under style of Hollinbeck-Kagin Coin Co., Des Moines, Ia.

Kagin, Donald, *Private Gold Coins and Patterns of the United States.* N.Y.: Arco 1981. Originally a Ph.D. dissertation, Union Graduate Schools, 1978.

Kaufman, Nathan M., estate, coll., A, RARCOA, 8/4–5/78.

KB = Bressett {1976}, q.v.

Kelly, James (various dates) = series of A's under either his own name or the firm name World Numismatiques.

Kenney, Richard D., *Struck Copies of Early American Coins,* publ. by *CCJ,* 1952. C-S 3386. Covers mid-19th century die-struck imitations by Idler, Robinson, Bolen, Merriam, Dickeson, Elder, Wuesthoff, etc., with tests to distinguish them from originals. Most of the salient tests are enumerated in Part One above.

Kensington, colls., A, B&R, 12/12–13/75.

Kern, Jerome (the composer), coll., MBS, in "Golden Jubilee Sale," BMM 5/23/50.

Kessler, Alan, *The FUGIO Cents.* Newtonville, Mass.: Colony Coin Co. 02160, 1976. Supersedes Newman {1952A}, but uses Newman numbers. A die var. study, valuable for visual grading standards.

Klein, G. M., coll., "Vicksburg Cabinet," A, Woodward, 5/21/1888.

Kliman, Myron, *The Two-Cent Piece and Varieties.* South Laguna, Calif.: Numismatic Enterprises, 1977.

KM = Krause-Mishler numbers in *SCWC.*

Knapp, William A., coll., MBS, BMM, 3/13/45.

Kosoff Estate, coll., A, B&M 11/4–6/85.

Kramer, Albert, *Identification and Classification of the Double D Lincoln Cent Varieties.* Chicago: Hewitt Bros., n.d. (ca. 1968), rep. from *NSM* serial 1965–68.

Krugjohann, C. W., coll., A, B&R, 5/14–15/76.

KS = Kreisberg, Abner, and Schulman, Hans M. F., joint A, held annually 1957–67 at the Waldorf-Astoria Hotel, N.Y. Herein cited by dates.

Kurth, Howard H., "The AUCTORI PLEBIS Coppers," *NumRev* v1n2, pp. 54–56 and plate IX (1943).

L

l. = left (side, edge).

Lafaurie, Jean, "Les Pièces de XXX et XV Deniers Frappées en 1709–13," *Bulletin de la Société Française Numismatique,* 1968, pp. 279–283.

Landau, Elliot, coll., A, in NN52.

Lang, Carole Ann, "Mark Newbie: The Courage of Collingswood," *NUM* 9/77, pp. 1817–23.

Lauder, Loye L., coll., A, William Doyle Galleries, 12/15–16/83. Colonials.

Lawrence, Dr. George Alfred, coll., A, Elder, 6/26–28/29. Pioneer gold.

Lee {1932} = Lee, Edward Melvin, *California Gold Quarters, Halves, Dollars.* Glendale, Calif.: Tower-Lee, 1932. C-S 3455. Superseded by Breen {1983}. Describes as "Reported" some pieces which still remain unlocated.

Lee {1970} = Lee, Kenneth W., *California Gold Dollars, Half Dollars, Quarter Dollars.* Los Angeles: University Press, 1970. Rosichan 822. Superseded by Breen {1983}.

Lee {1979} = ———, ———. Santa Ana, Calif.: George Frederick Kolbe Publications, 1979. [1,600] Same comment. Contains a loose price supplement. Photography by Jack Collins, who graciously furnished enlargements used herein.

"Lee, H. R.," coll., A, S, 10/2–4/47. Duplicates from the Louis Eliasberg coll.

Lefroy {1872} = Lefroy, Maj. Gen. Sir John Henry, *Memorial of the Discovery and Early Settlement of the Bermudas or Somers Islands.* London 1872. Relevant material is in Vol. I, pp. 59–113.

Lefroy {1876} = ———, "The Hog Money of the Sommer Islands," *Num. Chronicle* (New Series) 16, pp. 153–57 (1876).

Lefroy {1877} = ———, "On a New Piece of Bermuda Hog Money of the Value of Twopence," *AJN* 12, pp. 16–18 (7/1877); *Num. Chronicle* (New Series) 18, pp. 166–68 (1878).

Lefroy {1882} = ———, *The Historye of the Bermudaes or Summer Islands.* Ed. from a ms. in the Sloane coll., British Museum. London: Printed for the Hakluyt Society, 1882.

Lefroy {1883} = ———, "On a New Piece of Bermuda Hog Money of the Current Value of IIId," *Num. Chronicle* (3rd Series) 3, pp. 117–18 (1883).

Lermann, I. M. A., coll., A, Woodward, 12/29–31/1884.

LeRoux, Joseph, M.D., *Le Médaillier du Canada/Canadian Coin Cabinet.* Montreal: Beauchemin, 1888, 1892; rep., Winnipeg, Manitoba: Canadian Numismatic Publishing Institute (Division of Regency Coin & Stamp), 1964, [1,000]. C-S 2484. Rosichan 716, 1006.

Levick, Joseph N. T. (1859), coll., A, E. Cogan, 12/19/1859. Bangs, Merwin & Co., N.Y.

Levick (1864) = ———, et al., coll., A, Woodward, 10/18–22/1864. G. A. Leavitt, N.Y.

Levick (1865) = ———, coll., A, E. Cogan, 5/29–31/1865. Bangs, Merwin & Co., N.Y. Postponed from 4/27–29 owing to Lincoln's assassination.

Lightbody, Colin, coll., A, E. Cogan, 12/6/1866; Bangs, Merwin & Co., N.Y.

Lilliendahl, William A. (1862), coll., A, W. H. Strobridge, 5/26–28/1862. Bangs, Merwin & Co., N.Y.

Lilliendahl (1863), ———, coll., A, Strobridge, 12/15/1863. Bangs, Merwin & Co., N.Y.

Linderman, Henry R., sometime Director of the Mint, later Superintendent of the Philadelphia Mint, coll., A, J. W. Scott, 2/28/1888.

LM = Lester Merkin auctions, cited by date as follows; catalogs mostly by Breen, 1964–72.

LM 8/64 = Louis Helfenstein large cents, 8/14/64. Rep., "Library Edition," [100].

LM 11/65, colonials, rare silver and gold, Arnold Perl colonial paper, 11/5–6/65.

LM 4/66, early proof half dimes, early dimes, George Fuld's WEALTH OF THE SOUTH mulings, 4/1/66.

LM 10/66, colonials, Arthur Fritz large cents, early silver, $20 vars., 10/19/66.

LM 3/67, colonials, half cents, cents, bust halves, rare gold, 3/15/67.

LM 9/67, colonials, half cents, cents, silver, gold, pioneer items, patterns, 9/20/67.

LM 3/68, colonial coins and currency, Helfenstein and Judd half cents, silver, original proof sets (as obtained from the Mint) 1877–1916, 3/6–7/68.

LM 6/68, currency, colonials, cents to dollars, gold vars., 6/12/68.

LM 9/68, half cents, half dimes, silver dollars incl. A. J. Ostheimer duplicates and patterns, gold vars., 9/18/68.

LM 11/68, George J. Bauer colonials, cents, dollars, Hawaiian items, mint errors, 11/20/68.

LM 3/69, half cents, cents, gold, Hawaiian material, 3/28–29/69.

LM 10/69, quarter dollars, bust halves, gold vars., 10/4/69.

LM 4/70, cents to dollars, gold, currency, Lilly's encased postage, 4/17–18/70.

LM 6/70, colonials, patterns, miscellany, 6/26–27/70.

LM 9/70, cents, silver, half dollar vars., gold, pioneer items, patterns, 9/25–26/70.

LM 2/71, currency, half-dollar vars. (Burton Krouner coll.), patterns, 2/12–13/71.

LM 6/71, half cents, cents, silver, patterns, 6/4–5/71.

LM 2/72, colonials, Washington medals, half cents, cents, silver, bust halves (Wayne G. Slife coll.), gold, currency, 2/12/72.

LM 6/72, cents, silver, gold, currency, 6/24/72.

LM 10/72 = 1972 GENA, colonials, cents (Wayne G. Slife coll.), quarter dollars, currency, 10/6–7/72.

LM 10/73, colonials, cents, silver, gold (some from Dr. Katz coll.), including gold Confederate cent, 10/31/73.

LM 9/74, colonials, cents, silver, gold, patterns, fractional currency; catalog partly by Richard Picker, 9/11/74.

Lohr, Maj. Lenox R., part of coll., A, S, 10/24/56; another part was in 1958 ANA, others privately sold.

Longacre, James Barton, Mint Engraver, estate, coll., A, Ebenezer Locke Mason, Jr., 1/21/1870, Moses Thomas & Sons, Philadelphia.

Lord, Thomas R., & Co., *Supplement to the Cincinnati Detector and Bank Note Report, Containing Facsimiles of Various Gold and Silver Coins Most Generally Found in Circulation.* Cincinnati, Thomas R. Lord & Co., 1853. One of a series of cambists, giving trade (bullion) values for foreign coins which were then (until 1857) legal tender.

Loubat, Joseph Florimond, duc de, *The Medallic History of the United States of America 1776–1876.* 2 vols. N.Y.: the author, 1878. C-S 4203*.

Low, Lyman H., *Hard Times Tokens.* Boston: W. T. R. Marvin, 1886; second ed., 1900; supplement, 1906; reps., including that by Charles V. Kappen, with plates by Edgar H. Adams, San Jose, 1955; largely superseded by Rulau {1980}.

Lyman, John P., coll., A, SHC, 11/7/13.

M

M = Maris {1881} numbers for New Jersey coppers; Miller {1920} numbers for Connecticut coppers.

MacFarland, Part I, colls., A, B&R, 1/14–16/81.

McClure, Dudley L., "The Good Dr. McLoughlin," *NNW* 6/23/84, p. 6ff.

McCoy, John F., coll., A, Woodward, 5/17–21/1864; George A. Leavitt, N.Y.

McCoye, Frank, coll., A, SH&HC, 5/5/1887.

McGarry, Sheridan, *Mormon Money, NUM* 1950, pp. 591–604; rep., Colorado Springs: ANA, n.d. (ca. 1962). C-S 3711. Rosichan 931.

McKean, Frederick G., coll., A, HC, 5/9/29.

MANA = Middle Atlantic Numismatic Assoc., regional group holding annual conventions. See next.

1973 MANA = "Sale of the 70s," colls., A, Kagin, 11/2–3/73 = Kagin 301st sale.

Manning, J. L., coll., MBS, BMM, 5/17/21.

MARCA = Mid-American Rare Coin Auctions.

Maris {1869} = Maris, Edward, M.D., *Varieties of the Copper Issues of the United States in the Year 1794.* Philadelphia: William K. Bellows, 1869. [100]; 2nd ed., 1870 [100?]. C-S 3456. First var. study of 1794 cents and half cents; gave each var. a mnemonic title.

Maris {1881} = ———, *Historical Sketch of the Coins of New Jersey.* Philadelphia: William K. Bellows, S.W. Corner 4th & Appletree Sts., 1881. Elephant folio. [50], reps., that here used: Lawrence, Mass.: Quarterman Publications, 1974, retitled *The Coins of New Jersey,* with new foreword and price guide by Breen. C-S 3387*.

Maris {1886} = ———, coll., A, H. P. Smith (i.e., Maris), 6/21/1886, Stanislaus V. Henkels, Philadelphia. [50] Colonials. The New Jersey cents went as a group to Garrett, and reappeared in Garrett III. Maris put H. P. Smith's name on his catalog reportedly for modesty's sake.

Marks, Robert, et al., colls., A, B&R (as Amer. Auction Assoc.), 11/10–11/72.

Mason & Co., colls., A, Ebenezer Locke Mason, Jr., 6/17/1870; Leavitt, Strebeigh & Co., N.Y.

Mason's Coin and Stamp Collector's Magazine, Philadelphia: Ebenezer Locke Mason, Jr., 1867–72; 1882–91. C-S 259.

Massey, J. Earl, "Early Money Substitutes," in ANS {1976}, pp. 15–24.

Matthews, A. W., coll., A, Woodward, 12/16–19/1885.

Mazard, Jean, *Histoire Monétaire et Numismatique des Colonies et de l'Union Française,* 1670–1952. Paris: Émile Bourgey, 1953. C-S 2602.

MBS = Mail Bid Sale (contrast A, FPL).

Medcalf-Fong = Medcalf, Gordon G., and Fong, Robert B. T., *Hawaiian Money and Medals.* Kailua, Hawaii: Numismatics Hawaii, Inc., 1967.

Medina, José Toribio, *Medallas de Proclamaciones y Juras de los Reyes de España en América.* Santiago de Chile: the author, 1917. [150] Rep., Lawrence, Mass.: Quarterman 1977. C-S 4159*.

Mehl, B. Max, Fort Worth, Tex., dealer (116 MBS, 1906–55), cited as BMM.

"Melish" = colls., A, Kosoff, 4/27/56 = 1956 CSNS sale. Actually property of R. E. Naftzger, Clinton W. Hester, and others, though catalog was named after the estate of Thomas G. Melish, while containing nothing therefrom. Melish was the promoter of the Cincinnati and Cleveland commemorative half dollars.

"Memorable," coll., A, Numismatic Gallery, 3/1–2/48. Title reads *A Memorable Sale of United States and Territorial Gold Coins.* Actually property of "Jacob F. Bell," i.e., Jacob Shapero. Auctioneer firm = Abe Kosoff and Abner Kreisberg, partnership 1943–54.

Menjou I = Menjou, Adolphe (the actor), colls., A, Numismatic Gallery, 6/15/50. Part of the coins belonged to Charles M. Williams (a Cincinnati executive).

Menjou II = ———, coll., KS, 1/25/57. Other parts privately sold.

Merkin, Lester, New York specialist dealer, possibly most famous for handling the sale of the King of Siam's cased 1834 proof set for approximately $1 million; cited as LM, above.

MHS = Massachusetts Historical Society, repository of the William Sumner Appleton colls. See next 2.

MHS I = ———, part of coll., A, S, 10/23/70.

MHS II = ———, part of coll., A, S, 3/29/73.

Mickley, Joseph J., "Father of American Coin Collecting," coll., A, Woodward, 10/28–11/2/1867; Leavitt, Strebeigh & Co., N.Y.

Mickley Estate, coll., A, Moses Thomas & Sons, Philadelphia, 11/5–6/1878. Incl. the broken and rusted dies Joseph J. Mickley had retrieved from scrap metal sold by the Mint in 1816, though descriptions are too vague to be helpful.

1983 Midwinter ANA, colls., A, Ivy, 2/24–26/83.

1984 Midwinter ANA, colls., A, Ivy/Heritage, 2/23–26/84.

Miles, Dr. B. B., coll., A, G. W. Massamore, 5/18–19/1881.

Miles, R. L., Jr., coll., A, S, 10/25–26/68. Gold coins.

Miles, R. L., Jr., coll., A, S, 4/10–12/69. Silver and minor coins.

Miller, Donald M., *The Money of the Merchants: a Catalogue of U.S. Store Cards or Merchants Tokens.* Indiana, Pa.: the author, 1962. C-S 3943. Largely a rev. of Adams {1920} with additions and prices. Superseded by Rulau {1980–83}.

Miller, Henry Clay, with Ryder, Hillyer, *State Coinages of New England,* comprising Miller's "The State Coinages of Connecticut," Ryder's "The Colonial Coins of Vermont," and Ryder's "The Copper Coins of Massachusetts." N.Y.: ANS, 1920 [200], rep. from *AJN,* Vol. LIII, pp. 1–76 (1919). C-S 3388*, 3411*, 3412*. Usually cited as Miller-Ryder.

Miller, Wayne, *Analysis of Morgan and Peace Dollars.* Helena, Mont.: the author, 1976.

———, *The Morgan and Peace Dollar Textbook.* Metairie, La.: Adam Smith Publishing Co., 1982. Revision of preceding.

Miller-Ryder: See Miller, Henry Clay, above.

Mills, John G., coll., A, SH&HC, 4/27–29/04.

Mint Cabinet Accounts and Memoranda, 1857–1904. Ms. vol., compiled by successive Curators and Assistant Curators of the Mint Cabinet, largely William Ewing DuBois and Patterson DuBois. Primary source for Mint Cabinet accession data. Now in SI Dept. of Numismatics.

mm = millimeters.

Montagu, Hyman, *The Copper, Tin and Bronze Coinage and Patterns for Coins of England.* 2nd ed. London: Bernard Quaritch, 1893. C-S 2787.

Montgomery, Dr. D. C., Jr., coll., A, B&R, 2/20–22/76.

Moore, Richard D., and Hawley, Cyril H., "The Higley Coppers 1737–39," *Bulletin of the Connecticut Historical Society,* 7/55; rep. in *AUCTORI CONNEC and Other Emissions,* published by Hartford Numismatic Society. Richardson, Tex.: The Hobby Press, 1959.

More, Philip, coll., A, B&R, 4/6–8/78.

Morgan, J. Pierpont, coll., bequest to ANS, incl. gold and silver proof sets 1858–1908 with some few earlier ones, obtained from Robert C. W. Brock.

Morgenthau, J. C., & Co., auctioneers; catalogs mostly prepared by Wayte Raymond and James G. MacAllister, cited herein by dates of individual sales.

Morin, Victor, "Castorland," *Bulletin des Recherches Histo-*

riques, 8/38; transl. by John Myers O'Hara, *NUM* 10/42, pp. 717–20.

"Morton, Elizabeth," coll., A, PT, 10/18/75. Colonials.

Moser, David C., "The Remarkable World War II Cents," *NUM* 8/82, pp. 1965–68.

Mosher, Stuart, "Notes on 1895 Morgan Dollars," *NUM* 7/55:726–28. The material on Farran Zerbe's proof 1921 S dollars (p. 727) came to Mosher from Zerbe himself (personal communication, 1945). Mosher was Editor of *NUM,* and Curator of Numismatics at SI.

Moskowitz, Irving, coll., A, Kreisberg & Cohen, 2/15–16/77. Gold.

[Mott, James, Treasurer,] New Jersey, *Treasurer Receipt Books, 1783–1799. James Mott, Treasr to the State of New Jersey, Dr On account of Cash received from sundry persons.* Ms. vol., Princeton Univ. Library. Primary source for quantities of New Jersey coppers legally issued.

Mougey, Peter, coll., A, Elder, 9/1–3/10. [50 with plates]

"Mount Vernon," coll., A, Sup, 11/15–18/76.

m.p. = melting point.

MTB = Manfra, Tordella & Brookes. NYC dealers.

Mull, R. H., coll., A, Parke-Bernet Galleries, 5/11/50. Included an 1804 dollar.

Mumey, Nolie, *Clark, Gruber & Co. (1860–65): A Pioneer Denver Mint. History of Their Operations and Coinage.* Denver: Artcraft Press, 1950 [800], reps. C-S 3458.

Muñoz IV = Miguel Muñoz, et al., Part IV, colls., A, Sup, 6/7/82.

Munro, John James, ed., *The London Shakespeare.* 6 vols. N.Y.: Simon & Schuster, 1957; London: Eyre & Spottiswood, 1958. Material relevant to the Sommer Islands is in Vol. II, p. 1396.

Murdoch, John G., coll., A, Sotheby, Wilkinson & Hodge, London. In 8 parts, 3/31/03–12/14/04. Relevant coins are in the part sold 7/21–30/03.

MWANA = Midwinter ANA, annual convention; 1983–84 A are cited above at Midwinter.

MWNA = Metropolitan Washington Numismatic Association, regional group holding conventions.

1978 MWNA = Kagin's 312th sale, A, 7/14–15/78.

N

N = Newcomb numbers, from Newcomb {1944}, q.v.

Nagengast, Bernard, *The Jefferson Nickel Analyst.* Sidney, Ohio: the author, 1979.

NCLT = Non-Circulating Legal Tender. Coins of authorized design which could legally circulate but in practice are sold at a premium instead, e.g., proofs and commemorative issues.

n.d. = no date.

Neil, Will W., coll., MBS, BMM, 6/17/47.

Neil {1927} = ———, "U.S. Half Dimes," serial in 1927 *NUM,* rep. in Valentine {1975}.

Nelson, Gerry, et al., colls., A, B&R 4/30/82.

Nelson {1903} = Nelson, Philip, M.D., *The Coinage of William Wood 1722–33.* Brighton: W. C. Weight, 1903; rep., London: Spink, 1959. C-S 2810.

Nelson {1904} = ———, *The Coinage of Ireland in Copper, Tin and Pewter.* Liverpool, 1904, 1905, rep. from *British Numismatic Journal* 1903–4, pp. 169–264; rep., London: Spink, 1959. C-S 2889.

Nelson {1905} = ———, *The Coinage of William Wood for the American Colonies.* London, 1905, rep. from *British Numismatic Journal* 1903–4, pp. 265–86; rep., London: Spink, 1959. C-S 3389.

NERCA = New England Rare Coin Auctions. Division of next.

NERCG = New England Rare Coin Galleries.

Nettels, Curtis Putnam, *The Money Supply of the American Colonies Before 1720.* "Univ. of Wisconsin Studies in the Social Sciences and History, no. 20." Madison: Univ. of Wisconsin Press, 1934; rep., N.Y.: A. M. Kelley, 1964. C-S 3390.

Neumoyer, Charles W., coll., "A History of Money Through the Ages," A, S, 5/4–7/60.

Newcomb, Howard Rounds, *The United States Copper Cents of the Years 1816–1857.* N.Y.: Numismatic Review [i.e., Stack's], 1944 [750]; reps., 1956, 1963, 1981. C-S 3459.

———, Part I, coll., A, James G. MacAllister and Wayte Raymond, 2/7–8/45 = J. C. Morgenthau 458th Sale. Cents 1793–1814; silver vars.

———, Part II, coll., A, ———, 5/16/45 = J. C. Morgenthau 461st Sale. Cents 1816–57; coll. sold intact to Floyd Starr, q.v.

Newcomer, Waldo, coll., privately sold piecemeal ca. 1933–45, parts by Wayte Raymond, F. C. C. Boyd, BMM, others; other parts in J. C. Morgenthau 336, 345, 348, 394, 430, others; much went to Col. Green, q.v.

Newlin, Harold P., *A Classification of the Early Half Dimes of the United States.* Philadelphia: J. W. Haseltine, 1883 [60 + 40 with plates]; reps., 1933 and others, including Valentine {1975}. C-S 3460.

———, coll., A, J. W. Haseltine 66th Sale, 4/10/1883.

Newman {1952A} = Newman, Eric P., "Varieties of the FUGIO Cent." In *CCJ* 144, 7–8/52. Revision of his article in *CCJ* 122, 1–2/49. Mostly superseded by Kessler.

Newman {1952B} = ———, "The 1776 Continental Currency Coinage." In *CCJ* 144, 7–8/52. C-S 3391, where misdated 1957. Should be used with supplement, Newman {1959B}.

Newman {1955} = ———, "First Documentary Evidence on the American Colonial Pewter 1/24 Real." *NUM* 7/55, pp. 713–17.

Newman {1956} = ———, *Coinage for Colonial Virginia.* N.Y.: ANS, 1956. NN&M 135. C-S 3392*. History and vars. Use with supplement, Newman {1962}.

Newman {1958A} = ———, "A Recently Discovered Coin Solves a Vermont Numismatic Enigma." In ANS {1958}, pp. 531–542. C-S 3393. On the 1776 small-date Tory copper by Machin's Mills. The enigma was Vermont coppers' consistent use of British shield and occasional mulings with dies for Tory coppers.

Newman {1959A} = ———, *Secret of the Good Samaritan Shilling.* ANS, 1959. NN&M 142. C-S 3395*. Abridged rep. in Noe {1973}.

Newman {1959B} = ———, "The Continental Dollar Meets Its Maker." *NUM* 8/59, pp. 915–26. C-S 3394. On Elisha Gallaudet, who made plates for Continental Currency Feb. 1776 fractional notes, and who signed one die of the Continental tin coins E G FECIT.

Newman {1962} = ———, "Additions to Coinage for Colonial Virginia." In *Museum Notes* X, pp. 137–43. N.Y.: ANS, 1962. C-S 3397.

Newman {1976A} = ———, *The Early Paper Money of America.* "Bicentennial Edition." Racine, Wis.: Western, 1976. Rosichan 917. Rev. of original 1967 ed. An epochal breakthrough, worthy to stand beside Crosby {1875}; beyond question Newman's finest achievement.

Newman {1976B} = ———, "American Circulation of English and Bungtown Halfpence." In ANS {1976}, pp. 134–172. Rev. of a speech made earlier at ANS. Origin and meaning of "bungtown" and "bungtown coppers" (see Glossary); incidentally elucidates the obscure Shakespearean epithet "bung"; demolishes any claim that evasion coppers (other than the AUCTORI PLEBIS and Washington NORTH WALES) ever circulated in America.

Newman {1983} = ———, "Benjamin Franklin and the Chain Design," *NUM* 11/83, pp. 2271–81.

Newman-Bressett = ———and Bressett, Kenneth E., with collaboration of Walter Breen and C. Lynn Glaser ("Associates in Research"), *The Fantastic 1804 Dollar*. Racine, Wis.: Whitman/Western, 1962. C-S 3461. Rosichan 818. Amazing detective work; definitive history. The true first edition [16] was being run off during the 1962 ANA Convention, when James C. Risk revealed the story of the King of Siam's 1834 proof set containing an original 1804 dollar. Bressett phoned a stop press order to Racine so that corrections could be made. Copies generally available are a second edition though not so marked; the rare first edition has a chapter entitled "The Diplomatic Gift Delusion," which was necessarily replaced.

"Newport," coll., A, B&R (as "Amer. Auction Assoc."), 1/30–2/1/75.

NJHS = New Jersey Historical Society, coll., A, Parke-Bernet Galleries, 9/24–25/69.

NN = New Netherlands Coin Co. (Charles M. Wormser). Notable for series of A's, through 1960 mostly cataloged by Walter Breen and rewritten by John Jay Ford, Jr., later as noted below. The following are cited herein:

NN33, 4/13–14/51. D. C. Wismer estate, Part I, etc.

NN35, 11/10/51. D. C. Wismer estate, Part III; material from Ryder estate, Wayte Raymond, etc.

NN36, 1/26/52. More of the same.

NN38 = their sections of 1952 ANA, q.v.

NN39, 11/22/52. John Pawling and Earl M. Skinner colls. Half cents, cents.

NN40, 5/9/53. George Manley Kendall coll.

NN41, 9/26/53. Hillyer Ryder cents, etc., consigned by Wayte Raymond.

NN44, 6/23/54. Hillyer Ryder half cents, consigned by Wayte Raymond; parts of R. J. Kissner, J. J. Gambert, O. K. Rumbel colls., etc.

NN45, 4/22/55. Parts of J. J. Gambert, Ralph J. Lathrop, T. James Clarke colls.

NN46, 6/17/55. Clarence W. Peake, Earl E. Odal colls.

NN47, 4/19–20/56. Part of T. James Clarke and Harry Pedersen colls.

NN48, 11/24/56. Judge Thomas L. Gaskill's quarter eagles; parts of T. James Clarke and John Zug colls.

NN49, 6/12–13/57. Eliasberg duplicates; Mai C. B. Evans coll.

NN50, 12/6–7/57. Cents from F. C. C. Boyd and Thomas L. Gaskill colls.; Wayte Raymond duplicates.

NN51, 6/19–20/58. "Maryland Consignment"; remnant of Brand estate colonials.

NN52, 12/13/58. Elliot Landau coll. (A condition perfectionist.)

NN53, 6/16–18/59. Part of Philip G. Straus estate.

NN54, 4/22–23/60. "European Gentleman" (a British dealer?), Jonathan Glogower coll. (consigned by Robert Bashlow), Frank Hussey cents (as "Old North Carolina coll.").

NN55, 12/7–8/60. Gold coins incl. "Cicero" coll.

NN56, 6/27–28/62. Colonials, cents, other U.S. coins from a British source. Cataloged largely by Ford.

NN57, 12/10–11/63. Three Pennsylvania colls., cents to dollars. Cat. largely by Don Taxay. Later catalogs partly by Ford, partly by Breen, partly by G. Jon Hanson.

NN59, 6/13–15/67. Parts of F. C. C. Boyd, George Roebling, and Wayte Raymond estates.

NN60, 12/3–4/68. Maj. Alfred Walter estate; material from Boyd, Brand, Lathrop, Wayte Raymond estates, others.

NN61, 6/30/70. Jesse Taylor and Dr. Angus Black estates.

NN/Seaby I, 11/6/70. Colonial coins.

NN/Seaby II, 11/14–15/73. Extraordinary large cents from the R. E. Naftzger coll.

NN&M = "Numismatic Notes and Monographs," series of paperback studies published by ANS, 1920–

NNW = *Numismatic News Weekly,* Iola, Wis.: Krause Publications, 1955– . Rosichan 1651.

Noe {1942} = Noe, Sydney P., *The Castine Deposit: an American Hoard*. NN&M 100. N.Y.: ANS, 1942. C-S 3398. On a hoard buried about 1704 in Castine, Me.

Noe {1943} = ———, *The New England and Willow Tree Coinages of Massachusetts*. NN&M 102. N.Y.: ANS, 1943. C-S 3399*. Rep. in Noe {1973}. History and var. study; notable for use of transparencies to elucidate original appearance of Willow Tree dies from multiple-struck survivors.

Noe {1947} = ———, *The Oak Tree Coinage of Massachusetts*. NN&M 110. N.Y.: ANS, 1947. C-S 3400*. Rep. in Noe {1973}.

Noe {1950} = ———, "The Coinage of Massachusetts Bay Colony." *Proc. American Antiquarian Society*. Worcester, Mass.: the Society, 4/50, pp. 11–20. Reps. C-S 3401.

Noe {1952} = ———, *The Pine Tree Coinage of Massachusetts*. NN&M 125. N.Y.: ANS, 1952. C-S 3402. Rep. in Noe {1973}. Should have been asterisked in C-S.

Noe {1973} = ———, *The Silver Coinage of Massachusetts*. Ed., Alfred Hoch. Lawrence, Mass.: Quarterman Publications, 1973. Incl. reps. of Noe {1943, 1947, 1952}; part of Newman {1959A}; foreword by Eric P. Newman; chronology and price guide by Walter Breen; biographical sketch by Ruth Noe Pistolese. Essential reference in this series.

NSM = *Numismatic Scrapbook Magazine,* Chicago: Hewitt Bros., monthly, 1935–75. C-S 331; Rosichan 1652.

NUM = *The Numismatist*. Official organ of ANA, monthly, 1888– . Various publication offices incl. Monroe, Mich.; Cedar Rapids, Ia.; Federalsburg, Md.; now Colorado Springs. C-S 360; Rosichan 1653.

Numisma = title of several periodicals. The 2 cited here: (I) Irvington, N.Y.: Édouard Frossard, 1877–91. C-S 309. (II) Ed., John Jay Ford, Jr., N.Y.: New Netherlands, 1954–60. C-S 310.

Numismatic Gallery = Abe Kosoff and Abner Kreisberg, partnership, N.Y., series of A, MBS, and FPL, individually cited, 1942–54.

NumRev = *Numismatic Review*. Ed., Thomas Ollive Mabbott. Irregular publication, 16 issues, 6/43–10/47. N.Y.: Stack's. C-S 329.

NV = Nelson-Vlack numbers, on Robert A. Vlack's photographic plates of 1760 VOCE POPULI/HIBERNIA coppers, after Nelson {1904} with additions.

"N.Y. Coll.", A, HIM, 7/31/83.

Nygren, Arthur C., coll., A, HC, 4/29/24. Pioneer gold.

NYMet = New York Metropolitan Convention (annual), with auctions. Herein cited:

1956 NYMet = S, 5/4–6/56.

1962 NYMet = same cat. as R. E. Cox, q.v.

NYPL = N.Y. Public Library, coll., A, B&R, 10/30/82.

O

O = mintmark of New Orleans Mint, gold and silver only, 1838–61, 1879–1909.

obv(s). = obverse(s), "heads" side of coins.

OCL = Omaha City Library, repository of the Byron Reed estate.

Olsen, Fred E., coll., MBS, BMM, 11/7/44.

OMM = overmintmark numbers in Wexler-Miller {1983}, pp. 247–65.

OMS = off metal striking: See Glossary.

orig(s). = original(s).

O.S. = Old Style dating, from Julian Calendar. Its New Years Day was March 25. The change to New Style or Gregorian Calendar occurred in Britain and the American Colonies in 1752.

Osina, Neil, *Variety Coin Center Error Catalogue.* 3rd ed. Alhambra, Calif.: the author, n.d. (1982).

Overton, Al C., *Early Half Dollar Die Varieties, 1794–1836.* 2nd ed. Colorado Springs: the author, 1970 (rep.). Rosichan 817. Completely supersedes his first edition (1963); total rewriting was necessary to incorporate John Cobb's (uncredited) researches. Replaces Beistle and Haseltine Type Table descriptions and numbers for those years.

Oviedo, colls., A, S, 9/14–15/83.

P

P = mintmark of Philadelphia Mint, on wartime 5¢ 1942–45, Susan B. Anthony dollars, and since 1980 on all denominations from 5¢ up.

Page, Alfred, *Numismatique des Colonies Françaises.* FPL #18. Paris: Page, 1931.

"Palace Collections of Egypt": See Farouk.

Para = Paramount International Coin Corp., Englewood, Ohio; series of A's cited herein by names or dates.

"Paris," coll., A, J. W. Scott, 12/12–13/1894.

Park, Laird U., coll., A, S, 5/26/76. Colonials.

"Park Forest," colls., A, B&R, 10/3/80.

Parmelee, Lorin G., coll., A, N.Y. Coin & Stamp Co. [= David Proskey and Harlan P. Smith], 6/25–27/1890. [100 with plates] Rep., 1975.

Parsons, George M., coll., A, HC, 6/24–27/14.

Patterson, Richard S., and Dougall, Richardson, *The Eagle and the Shield.* Washington, D.C.: Govt. Printing Office, 1978.

Paxman, Dr. Curtis R., coll., A, B&R (as "Amer. Auction Assoc."), 11/4–6/74.

Peck, C. Wilson, *English Copper, Tin and Bronze Coins in the British Museum, 1558–1958.* London: Trustees of the BM [i.e., Oxford Univ. Press], 1960, 2nd ed. 1964. C-S 2790*. Rosichan 416. Epochal contribution.

Pelletreau, Robert C., coll., A, S, 3/6–7/59.

Peltzer, Richard F., coll., A, London, Glendining & Co., 6/20/37. C-S 3235.

Perlitz, William F., "John Chalmers, Issuer of the Annapolis Coinage," *NUM* 11/48, p. 721. Don Taxay and associates later located what they believed to be the actual site.

Petry, Nicholas, coll., A, SH&HC, 5/10/1893.

Phelps, Alonzo, ed., *Contemporary Biography of California's Representative Men.* 2 vols. San Francisco: A. Bancroft & Co., 1881–82.

Phelps, Noah Amherst, *History of Simsbury, Granby and Canton, from 1642 to 1845.* Hartford, Conn.: Press of Case, Tiffany & Burnham, 1845.

Phelps, Richard Harvey, *History of Newgate of Connecticut, at Simsbury, now East Granby.* Albany, N.Y.: J. Munsell, 1860. Primary source for the Higley material in Crosby {1875}. Story of the infamous prison near the Higley copper mines.

———, *Newgate of Connecticut: Its Origin and Early History.* Hartford, Conn.: American Publishing Co., 1876, 1892, other eds. Revision of Phelps {1860}.

Philpott {1950} = Philpott, W. A., Jr., "A Unique (?) Confederate Half Dollar Restrike," *NUM* 4/50, pp. 189–93. This is the double-struck specimen, later identified as from J. N. T. Levick.

Philpott {1951} = ———, "More About the Confederate Half Dollar," *NUM* 1/51, p. 61.

Philpott {1970} = ———, "Early Research Proves Variations, Not Uniformity, Prevailed in Notes," *CW* 8/5/70, p. 32. Interview with a Treasury official, with commentaries. Here cited for first publication in numismatic circles of Anthony Comstock's inducing the Treasury to recall over 35 million 1896 $5 silver certificates as "obscene." Compare Breen {1972B}.

"Phoenix," colls., A, Ivy, 6/11–12/82.

PHS = Pennsylvania Historical Society, repository of the W. S. Baker coll. of Washington coins and medals, from which he compiled his book.

Picker, Richard, "Variations of the Die Varieties of the Massachusetts Oak and Pine Tree Coinage," in ANS {1976}, pp. 75–90. Supplement to Noe {1973}.

Picker, Richard, coll., A, S, 10/24/84. Colonial coins.

Pierce, Grant, coll., A, S, 5/6–8/65.

PNC = Philatelic-numismatic combination. Special commemorative postal cachet (printed envelope), housing a coin or bill, postmarked at the date and city of the celebration.

Pratt, George W., coll., A, Woodward, 9/29–10/1/1879.

Prattent, Thomas, *The Virtuoso's Companion and Coin Collectors Guide.* 8 vols. in 4. London: For the Proprietor by M. Denton, 1795–97. (Date of Vol. 1 changed in ms. on all copies seen, from 1796 to 1795; all plates in Vol. 1 dated 1795 by engraver.) Illustrations and index of the then current copper token coinages. Here cited for identifying the AUCTORI PLEBIS as "American" and providing a terminal date.

Pridmore, Maj. Fred, *The Coins of the British Commonwealth of Nations to the End of the Reign of George VI.* 4 vols. London: Spink & Son, 1960– . C-S 2834 (Vol. I only). Rosichan 488. An attempt to complete Atkins {1889}; relevant material is in Vol. III.

Prieur, P., "Contribution à l'Étude de la Monnaie de Reims," *Revue de Numismatique,* 1950, pp. 71–132.

Prime, William Cowper, *Coins, Medals and Seals, Ancient and Modern.* Franklin Square, N.Y.: Harper & Bros., 1861. Originally aimed at children; here cited for first publication of the Bank of New York hoard of FUGIOs.

"Prominent American": see Granberg.

"Promised Lands," colls., A, PT, 4/30–5/1/74. The title refers to Colonial America and Palestine/Israel, the coinage series there offered. Rep., hard covers [10], late 1974.

"Prudential," colls., A, NERCA, 5/19–20/78.

PT = Pine Tree Auctions, division of First Coinvestors Inc., Albertson, L.I., N.Y. 11507. Auctions largely cataloged by Walter Breen; cited by owner or title.

PW = Penny-Wise, publication of EAC, 1969–

Pye, Charles, *A Correct and Complete Representation of all* [!] *the Provincial Copper Coins, Tokens of Trade, and Cards of Address, On Copper, Which were circulated as such between the Years 1787 and 1801, when they were entirely superseded* [etc., etc.]. 2nd ed. London: Issued by Matthew Young, also by Sherwood, Neely, and Jones, and in Birmingham by R. Jabet, Beilby and Knotts, 1801. Revision of next.

———, *Provincial Copper Coins or Tokens Issued Between the Years 1787 and 1796*[!], *engraved by Charles Pye of Birmingham from the Originals in His Own Possession.* London: John Nichols & T. Egerton; Birmingham: Thomas Pearson, 1795.

Q

qr = quarter cwt = 28 lbs. avoir. = 196,000 grains = 12.7 kilograms.

QS = "Quality Sales," i.e., Jerry Cohen and Abner Kreisberg, series of A's 1973– cited by date or name. Catalogs partly by Jack Collins (the coin photographer).

q.v., qq.v. = 'which see.'

R

r. = right (side, edge).

R (followed by a number) = Rarity, using the 8-point Sheldon scale: See Glossary at Rarity.

Ralston, Wallace, colls., A, Ivy, 5/30/83.

Randall, J. Colvin, colls., A, G. W. Cogan, 3/28/1882.

———, A, Woodward, 6/29–30/1885, 9/15/1885. See also Haseltine.

RARCOA = Rare Coin Co. of America, Chicago; series of A's cited by dates.

Rawls, James C., coll., A, S, 6/12/70.

Raymond, John T., coll., A, Lyman H. Low, 6/27/1887.

Raymond, Wayte, inventor of coin albums, publisher, compiler (*SC*, q.v.), sponsor of major numismatic research by Walter Breen and others; owner, Hillyer Ryder coll.; cataloger, J. C. Morgenthau auctions, with James G. MacAllister; colls., see NN.

Reakirt, Lt. Jay P., coll., inherited from J. P. Reichardt, largely from the Mickley coll. and others of the 1860s; MBS, Columbus (Ga.) Stamp & Coin Co., 3/26/63. The entire coll. was reportedly bought intact by an unidentified institution.

Redbook = Yeoman Guide Book, below.

Reiter, Ed, "Arts Commission Never Approved 1984 Dollar," *NNW* 6/2/84, p. 10.

Reiver, Jules, *Variety Identification Manual for United States Half Dimes, 1794–1837.* [Wilmington, Del.: the author,] 1984. Essential updating of Valentine {1975}.

rep(s). = reprint(s).

rev(s). = reverse(s), "tails" side of coins; herein also = revised.

Rhodes, E. M., colls., A, Heritage (Ivy & Halperin), 12/17–18/83.

RIA = Royal Irish Academy. See inventory in Coffey {1911}.

Richardson, Albert Deane, *Beyond the Mississippi.* Hartford: American Publishing Co., 1867. Herein cited for description of an 1850 State Assay Office ingot.

Richardson, John M., "The Copper Coins of Vermont," *NUM* 5/47, pp. 331–54; reps., Colorado Springs: ANA, n.d. C-S 3408. Extends the Ryder descriptions and numbers to cover vars. discovered after 1920; often cited as RR = Ryder-Richardson. Superseded by Bressett {1976}.

"Rio Rancho," coll., A, Sup, 10/15/74, gold coins.

Roach, Belden E., coll., MBS, BMM, 2/8/44.

Robison, Ellis, coll., Part I, A, S, 2/2–3/79, gold coins.

——, Part II, coll., A, S, 2/10–13/82.

——, Part III, coll., A, S, 12/2–3/82.

Roe, Jack, coll., MBS, in Waltman-Roe-Ryan sale, BMM, 6/12/45.

Roper, John L., II, coll., A, S, 12/8–9/83. Extraordinary colonials.

Rosichan, Richard, *Stamps and Coins. Spare Time Guides: Information Source for Hobbies and Recreations, no. 5.* Littleton, Colo.: Libraries Unlimited, 1974. A major bibliography, actually a catalogue raisonné. Rosichan numbers are cited herein beside C-S numbers as they overlap.

Rothert, Matt, coll., A, B&R (as "Amer. Auction Assoc."), 11/16–17/73.

Rousseau, M. J., *Catalogue des Monnaies Nationales de France.* Paris: Rollin et Feuardent, 1861.

Rovensky, J.; Hoffecker, L. W.; Futter, Oliver Eaton, colls., MBS, BMM, 11/30/54.

RPM = repunched mintmark numbers in Wexler-Miller {1983}.

RR = Ryder-Richardson numbers, in Richardson {1947} above.

Rubin, Philip Scott, "Auction Appearances and Pedigrees of the 1792 Silver Center Cents," in ANS {1985}, pp. 132–148.

Ruby, Dr. Charles L., coll., Part I, A, Sup, 2/11–13/74. Colonials, half cents, cents; cat. partly by Breen, partly by Denis Loring.

——, Part III, A, Sup, 2/10/75. (Part II comprised foreign coins; other silver incl. in "Gilhousen," above.)

Rulau, Russell, *Hard Times Tokens.* Iola, Wis.: Krause Publications, 1980. A revision of Low, above, assigning additional numbers for tokens not in the original list. This and next two are essential tools for specialists.

Rulau-E = ——, *Early American Tokens,* 2nd ed. Iola: Krause, 1983. Merchants' issues before the middle 1830s.

—— and Fuld, George, *Medallic Portraits of Washington.* "Centennial Edition." Iola:Krause, 1985. Illustrated revision of Baker {1885}.

Rust, Alvin E., *Mormon and Utah Coin and Currency.* Salt Lake City: Rust Rare Coin Co., 1984. Definitive. Illustrates hitherto unpublished material from Mormon Church archives.

Ryan, Maurice, coll., MBS, in Waltman-Roe-Ryan sale, BMM, 6/12/45. Half dollars.

Ryder, Hillyer {1919A}, "The Colonial Coins of Vermont," *AJN* LIII, pp. 63–68, 1919, rep. in Miller-Ryder. C-S 3412. Superseded by Richardson {1947} and Bressett {1976}.

—— {1919B}, "The Copper Coins of Massachusetts," *AJN* LIII, pp. 69–76, 1919, rep. in Miller-Ryder. C-S 3411. The numbering system follows Crosby {1875}.

Ryder-Richardson or RR numbers: See Richardson {1947} above.

S

S = mintmark of San Francisco, 1854–1955, 1968–   .

S (as publisher or auctioneer) = Stack's, N.Y., A and FPL cited by date or owners' names.

Sanford, E. Harrison, coll., A, E. Cogan, 11/12/1874; Bangs, Merwin & Co., N.Y.

[San Francisco.] *City Directory, 1852.* San Francisco: A. W. Morgan & Co. Ptd. by F. A. Bonnard at the Dispatch Printing Office, corner Commercial and Leidesdorff Sts., Sept. 1852. Copies of this and next 2 are in Bancroft Library, Univ. of California, Berkeley.

——. *Lecount & Strong's City Directory of San Francisco for 1854.* San Francisco: Lecount & Strong, Montgomery St., copyright 1853.

San Francisco Business Directory for the Year Commencing Jan. 1, 1856. San Francisco: Baggett, Joseph & Co. Steam Press of Monson & Valentine, 127–129 Sansome St., copyright 1855.

sc. *scilicet* 'supply [omitted word].'

SC = Standard Catalogue of United States Coins. 19 eds. New York: Wayte Raymond, 1934–57. Originally compiled by Wayte Raymond; last 3 eds. partly by John Jay Ford, Jr., historical sections by Walter Breen.

Scanlon, George F., coll., A, S, 10/24–27/73.

Schab, Henry W., "The Life and Coins of John Chalmers," *NUM* 11/84, pp. 2293–2312. Rep., "Researcher delves into life, coins of John Chalmers," *CW* 8/21/85, pp. 68ff.

Schulman, Hans Morits Friedrich, A, 4/26/51. Comprises material from J. Pierpont Morgan, Howard D. Gibbs, Burdette G. Johnson, et al. Later Schulman sales are cited by title or as KS + date.

Schwarz, Ted, "Miss Liberty Veils 'Lewd' Representation," *NSM* 1/74, pp. 18–24. On the design change in 1917 quarters.

Scott, Stanley, coll., A, B&R (as "Amer. Auction Assoc."), 6/5–7/75.

Scott-Kinnear, colls., A, Sotheby's, N.Y., 10/14/82.

SCWC = Standard Catalogue of World Coins. Iola, Wis.: Krause Publications, 1983– . Uses KM numbers (= Krause-Mishler). Page refs. are to the 1986 ed., c1985.

Seaby, Herbert A., ed., *British Copper Coins and Their Values.* London: Seaby's Numismatic Publications, 1961.

Seavey, George F., coll., A, W. H. Strobridge, 9/22/1863; Bangs, Merwin & Co., N.Y.

——, coll., A, W. H. Strobridge, 6/18/1873; George A. Leavitt, N.Y. The coll. was by then property of Lorin G. Parmelee. Not to be confused with W. H. Strobridge, *Descriptive Catalogue of the Seavey Collection,* Cambridge, Mass.: Harvard University Press, 1873.

Seymour, Dexter C., "Templeton Reid, First of the Pioneer Coiners," *Museum Notes* 19, pp. 225–266. N.Y.: ANS, 1974.

——, "The 1830 Coinage of Templeton Reid," *Museum Notes* 22, pp. 267–310. N.Y.: ANS, 1977. Updating of foregoing.

SH&HC = Samuel Hudson Chapman and Henry Chapman, brothers, dealers, partners 1877–1906; series of A's (1879–1906) cited by owners' names.

SHC = Samuel Hudson Chapman, series of A's (1907–24) after the dissolution of the partnership; cited by owners' names.

Sheldon {1949} = Sheldon, Dr. William H.; Downing, Homer K.; Sheldon, M[ilancie?]. H., *Early American Cents.* N.Y.: Harper & Bros., 1949. [2,500] C-S 3465. Dr. Sheldon (my mentor) was the constitutional psychologist who gave the language the terms "endomorph, mesomorph, ectomorph." He here propounded the basic "equation" of a "science of cent values," "Market Value = Basal Value × Numerical Grade." Superseded by following.

Sheldon {1958} = ——; Breen, Walter; Paschal, Dorothy Iselin, *Penny Whimsy.* N.Y.: Harper & Bros., 1958. C-S 3466. [2,500] + reps., incl. Florence, Ala.: Anderson News Co., and Lawrence, Mass.: Quarterman, 1976. Revision of foregoing; rendered obsolete by subsequent discoveries of new vars., and by evidence that his basic equation (above) could not be made to work despite various ad hoc manipulations. Use with caution. A new encyclopedic study of this series is in preparation.

Shinkle, C. H., coll., A, Wayte Raymond and James G. MacAllister, 4/26/32 = J. C. Morgenthau 278th Sale.

Shortt, Adam, *Archives du Canada: Le Change et les Finances./Documents Relating to Canadian Currency, Exchange and Finance During the French Period.* 2 vols. Ottawa: Bureau des Publications Historiques/Board of Historical Publications, Canadian Archives, 1925. C-S 2492. Primary sources in French and English translation, with bilingual commentaries and ills.; fundamental for knowledge of French Régime coinages for Canada and Louisiana Territory. Should have been asterisked in C-S.

SI = Smithsonian Institution, Washington, D.C., repository of Mint Cabinet and Josiah K. Lilly Estate colls.

Sieck-Harte = Sieck, Rudy, and Harte, Roy, colls., A, B&M, 3/26–28/84.

Simms, Jeptha Root, *History of Schoharie County, and Border Wars of New York.* Albany: Munsell & Tanner, 1845. Chap. XIX, pp. 540–646, deals with Capt. Thomas Machin, proprietor of Machin's Mills mint; Simms's primary sources (the Machin family papers) remain unlocated.

Sipsey, Everett T., "New Facts and Ideas of the State Coinage," *CNL* 10/64, pp. 65–70; partly rep. in *PW* XI, pp. 294–96 (1978). The facts include some not earlier recorded; the ideas are controversial.

Skipton, Amy C., *"One Fatt Calfe."* New Rochelle, N.Y.: New Rochelle Commemorative Coin Association, 1939. [200] History of the commemorative issue; the title quotes the clause in the deed of grant from which the coin's designer Gertrude K. Lathrop derived the obv. device.

Slabaugh, Arlie, *U.S. Commemorative Coins.* Rev. ed. Racine, Wis.: Western, 1976. (Orig. ed., 1962.) C-S 3467. Rosichan 824. Overlaps only partly with Taxay {1967} and Swiatek-Breen; recommended supplement.

Slack, Judge Charles W., coll., "The Romance of the Pioneers," MBS, BMM, 5/5/25. Pioneer gold.

Sleicher, William, coll., A, SHC, 10/9–10/19.

Smiley, Jerome Constant, *History of Denver, with Outlines of the Earlier History of the Rocky Mountain Country.* Denver: The Denver *Times*/The Times-Sun Publishing Co., 1901.

Smith, Aquilla, M.D., M.R.I.A., "On the Copper Coin Commonly Called Saint Patrick's," *Proc. and Trans. of the Kilkenny and Southeastern Archaeological Society,* March 15, 1854 (rep.). Cited from the pamphlet rep. in ANS. This was one of the primary sources for the chapter on Mark Newby in Crosby {1875}.

Smith, Dr. Clifford, coll., A, S, 5/6–8/55.

Smith, Harlan P., coll., A, SH&HC, 5/8–11/06. The Chapman brothers broke up their partnership following this auction. Smith had been David Proskey's partner in N.Y. Coin & Stamp Co., auctioneers of the Parmelee, R. Coulton Davis, George Woodside, E. W. Ropes, and other extraordinary collections.

Smith, Henry A., coll., A, Woodward and Strobridge, 3/24–26/1863; Bangs, Merwin & Co., N.Y.

Smith, Capt. John, *Generall Historie of Virginia, New England, and the Summer Isles, with the Names of the Adventurers, Planters, and Governours from their first Beginning, Ano. 1584, to this Present 1624.* London: Printed by I. D[awson]. and I. H[aviland]. for Michael Sparkes, 1624; many later eds. and reps.

Smith, Thomas L., estate, coll., A, S, 6/15/57.

Smith, W. H., coll., A, Haseltine, 1/19–22/1885.

SMS = Special Mint Sets (see Glossary).

Snelling {1762} = Snelling, Thomas, *A View of the Silver Coin and Coinage of England from the Norman Conquest to the Present Time* [etc., etc.]. London: Printed for Thomas Snelling, near the Horn Tavern, in Fleet St., 1762. This and next were 2 of the primary sources for Crosby {1875}.

Snelling {1769} = ——, *Miscellaneous Views of the Coins Struck by English Princes in France, Counterfeit Sterlings, Coin Struck by the East India Company, Those in the West India Colonies* [etc., etc.]. London: Printed for T. Snelling, (No. 163) next the Horn Tavern, in Fleet St., 1769. The relevant section is Part V: "Pattern Pieces."

Snelling {1776} = ——, *Thirty-Three Plates of English Medals. By the late Mr. Thomas Snelling.* London: Sold by Thomas Snelling, Printseller in Fleet St., 1776. Here cited for the earliest appearance of William Wood's Crowned Rose device.

Snider = Estate of Marvin S. and Ruby L. Snider, colls., A, Sup, 6/4–7/84.

Snowden {1860} = Snowden, James Ross, *"Mint Manual,"* i.e., *A Description of Ancient and Modern Coins in the Cabinet Collection of the Mint of the United States.* Philadelphia: J. B. Lippincott, 1860. C-S 3488. Actually prepared by George Bull and William Ewing DuBois.

Snowden {1861} = ——, *"Washington and National Medals,"* i.e., *A Description of the Medals of Washington: The Medallic Memorials of Washington in the Mint of the United States.* Philadelphia: J. B. Lippincott, 1861. C-S 4209.

Sobin, George, Jr., *The Silver Crowns of France, 1641–1973.* Teaneck, N.J.: Richard Margolis, 1974. Relevant to the *Chameau* Treasure.

Solomon, Raphael E., "Foreign Specie Coins in the American Colonies," in ANS {1976}, pp. 25–42.

Speir, H. Philip, et al., colls., A, S, 3/8–9/74. The relevant material is not Speir's gold but an anonymous coll. of early quarter dollars.

Spence, Dr. David L., coll., A, S, 3/15/75. Colonials; TAD's half cents.

Spiro, Jacob N., coll., A, in Schulman 3/18–19/55. New Jersey coppers.

Spring, Agnes Wright, *The First National Bank of Denver: The Formative Years 1860–65.* Denver: Bradford-Robinson Printing Co., n.d. (i.e., 1963). C-S 3849. Relevant to Clark, Gruber & Co.

Stack, James Aloysius, estate, part of coll., A, S, 3/13–15/75.

Steckler, S. G., estate, coll., A, S, 9/13/74.

Steig, Michael, colls., A, B&R, 9/21–23/82.

Steiner, Phillip, and Zimpfer, Michael, *Modern Mint Mistakes.* 4th ed. Wanatah, Ind.: the authors, 1974.

Stevin {1585} = Stevin van Brugghe, Simon, called Simon Stevinus, *De Thiende. Leerende door onghehoorde lichticheydt alle rekeninghen onder den menschen noodigh vallende, atverdighen door heele ghetalen sonder gebrokenen.* Tot Leyden: By Christoffel Plantijn 1585. = *La Disme: enseignant facilement expédier par Nombres Entiers sans rompus tous Comptes se rencontrant aux Affaires des Hommes.* À Leyde: De l'imprimerie de Christophe Plantin, 1585. Title = 'The Decimal System: Easy instructions for simplifying all arithmetical calculations found in business, by using whole numbers without fractions.' The French transl. reappears in the same publisher's *L'Arithmétique de Simon Stevin de Bruges,* 1585. Describes Stevin's invention of the decimal system; earliest source of the term *disme,* ancestor of *dime.* See next 2.

Stevin {1608} = ――――, *Disme: the art of tenths, or, Decimall arithmeticke,* transl., Robert Norton. Imprinted at London by S. S[tafford]. for Hugh Astley, 1608. (reps.) First English translation of preceding.

Stevin {1634} *Les Oeuvres Mathematiques de Simon Stevin de Bruges.* Transl. and ed., Albert Girard. Leyde: chez B. & A. Elsevier, 1634. This is the edition that became familiar to the French Encyclopedists and thence to the founders of the U.S. coinage system.

Stewart {1924} = Stewart, Frank H., *History of the First United States Mint, Its People and Its Operations.* Camden, N.J.: the author, 1924 (reps.). C-S 3489. Most of the original edition perished in a fire. By the founder of the Stewart Electric Co., which firm owned the land on which the First Mint (1792–1833) stood, but was unable to generate any public support for preserving the historic building; excavations at its demolition (1909) yielded planchets and other artifacts preserved in Congress Hall, Philadelphia. This rambling, anecdotal study quotes early Mint documents not elsewhere seen, and constitutes one of the primary sources for Taxay {1966}.

Stewart {1947} = ――――, *Mark Newby, the First Banker in New Jersey, and His Patrick Half Pence* [etc., etc.]. Woodbridge, N.J.: Gloucester County Historical Society, 1947.

Stickney, Matthew Adams, estate, coll., A, HC, 6/25–29/07.

Stone, Wilbur Fiske, et al., *History of Colorado.* 4 vols. Chicago: S. J. Clarke Publishing Co., 1918–19.

Straus, Philip G., estate, part of coll., A, S, 5/1–3/59. The remainder went in NN53.

1975 Sub. Wash. = 1975 Suburban Washington Convention sale ("The Washington, D.C., Sale"), colls., A, PT, 2/21–22/75.

Sup = Superior Galleries, Los Angeles and Beverly Hills, auctioneers.

Swiatek-Breen = Swiatek, Anthony, and Breen, Walter, *Encyclopedia of United States Gold and Silver Commemorative Coins.* N.Y.: FCI/Arco, April 1981.

Swift, Jonathan, *The Drapier's Letters to the People of Ireland Against Receiving Wood's Halfpence.* Dublin, anonymous letters serially published, 1724; many eds., that here used: ed., Herbert Davis, Oxford: The Clarendon Press, 1935 (rep. 1965).

T

TAD [initials?], part of coll., A, S, 2/4–6/76. Large cents, many from S auctions in the 1950s, where the buyer representing TAD was one Dorothy Nelson, bidding as D.N. Half cents from the same coll. went with the Dr. Spence coll.

Taxay {1963} = Taxay, Don, *Counterfeit, Misstruck, and Unofficial U.S. Coins.* N.Y.: Arco, 1963; rep., London: Garnstone, 1971. C-S 3361. Rosichan 832. Of value for learning to distinguish fakes from genuine coins, real from spurious mint errors, originals from restrikes.

Taxay {1966} = ――――, *United States Mint and Coinage.* N.Y.: Arco, 1966; rep., London: Garnstone, 1971. Rosichan 802. Supersedes all previous Mint histories. Beyond doubt Taxay's masterpiece.

Taxay {1967} = ――――, *Illustrated History of United States Commemorative Coinage.* N.Y.: Arco, 1967. Rosichan 825. Overlaps Swiatek-Breen and Slabaugh; valuable supplement.

Taxay {1968} = ――――, "The FUGIO Cents," *Coins* 10/68, pp. 30–33.

Taxay-Scott = ――――, *Scott's Comprehensive Catalogue and Encyclopedia of U.S. Coins.* N.Y.: Scott Publications, 1971; rev. ed., 1976 (ed., J. Rose and H. Hazelcorn). Rosichan 796. Intended as a counterpart to the Scott *Specialized Catalogue of U.S. Stamps.* Cited herein largely for instances of disagreement with conclusions independently reached; obsolete, use with caution.

Ten Eyck, James, estate, coll., MBS, BMM, 5/2/22.

"Terrell," coll., A, B&R, 5/18–19/73.

Tharp, Louise Hall, *St. Gaudens and the Gilded Era.* Boston: Little Brown & Co., 1969. Anecdotal biography; the material on St. Gaudens's coin designs is fragmentary. Necessary supplements include Hering {1949} and Dryfhout {1982}.

"The Rarest Set of Gold Coins in the World," n.p., n.d. [i.e., N.Y.: Stack's, 2/80]. Brochure offering the cased Capt. Andrew North set of St. Gaudens gold at $1 million. The set was later broken up; individual pieces are cited herein at **7094, 7096, 7355–7, 7359, 7361.** The others were regular UNC. 1907 and 1908 Motto $10 and $20 coins.

Thompson {1848} = *Thompson's Coin Chart Manual,* N.Y.: Thompson, 1848. Annual editions as early as 1836. One of a series of cambists, like Lord {1853}.

Thompson {1949} = Thompson, J. D. A., "Evasions," *Seaby's Coin & Medal Bulletin,* 6/49. On British imitation halfpence with evasive inscriptions meant to deceive illiterates, long erroneously believed to circulate in America. Many of the inscriptions are topical, alluding to events of 1789–1805.

Tingstroem, Bertel, *Swedish Coins 1521–1968.* Stockholm: Numismatiska Bokförlaget, 1969. Transl. by Nigel Rollison of *Svensk Numismatisk Uppslagsbok,* same publisher, 1968. Here cited for details about the Swedish "Copper Mountain."

Trudgen, Gary A., "Thomas Machin—Patriot," *CNL* 11/83, pp. 832–48.

Twining, J. S., coll., A, Woodward, 4/27/1886.

U

Ullmer, Theodore, coll., A, S, 5/23–24/74. Gold coins, mostly proofs.

UNC. = the grade UNCIRCULATED. To qualify, a coin must be free of any visible trace of wear.

V

Valentine {1931} = Valentine, D[aniel]. W[ebster]., *The United States Half Dimes.* N.Y.: ANS, 1931. NN&M 48. C-S 3470. Superseded by next.

Valentine {1975} = ――――, ――――, *with Additional Material by Kamal M. Ahwash, Walter Breen, David J. Davis, Will W. Neil, Harold P. Newlin.* Lawrence, Mass.: Quarterman, 1975. Includes reps. of Breen {1958B}, Newlin {1883}, Neil {1927}. Use with Reiver {1984}.

VAM = Van Allen, Leroy C., and Mallis, A. George, *The Comprehensive Catalogue and Encyclopedia of U.S. Morgan and Peace Dollars.* N.Y.: FCI/Arco, 1976. Of major importance for its historical and technical material, largely from the National Archives. There are several mimeographed and offset supplements, that here used dated 1977.

var(s). = variety, varieties.

Vattemare, Alexandre, *Collection de Monnaies et de Médailles de l'Amérique du Nord de 1652 à 1858, Offerte à la Bibliothèque Impériale.* Paris: Imprimerie de Ad. Lainé et J. Havard, rue Jacob, 56, 1861. C-S 3363, which says published by the Bibliothèque Nationale (unconfirmed).

Vermeule, Cornelius, *Numismatic Art in America: Aesthetics of U.S. Coinage.* Cambridge, Mass.: Harvard Univ. Press, 1971. Rosichan 786. Of major importance as a history of coin motifs and designs.

VF = the grade VERY FINE, defined in each section of main text.

VG = the grade VERY GOOD (next below FINE), defined in each section of main text in which the series is collected in that grade.

Vlack, Robert A., *Early American Coins.* 2nd ed. Johnson City, N.Y.: Windsor Research Publications [i.e., Q. David Bowers], 1965.

Vlack Plates = ———, glossy photographic plates of Colonial coins, n.d. (1960s–'70s, reps.), incl. 1760 VOCE POPULI, "18th Century Counterfeit Halfpence Made In America" (i.e., Machin's Mills and Mould-Atlee Tory Coppers), and Washington 1783 Coins.

Voetter, Thomas W., "The 1935 S Peace Dollar Die Variety," *NUM* 10/40, p. 695.

W

W = mintmark of West Point, first used on 1984 Olympic $10.

Wagner, Dick, "Delay Despoils Denver Dime Debut," *NSM* 9/73, pp. 788–96.

Wallace, E. V., *A Numismatography of the Lincoln Cent.* Chicago: Hewitt Bros., n.d. (1954). Originated the term "fidos" for mint errors.

Waltman-Roe-Ryan sale, colls., MBS, BMM, 6/12/45.

Walton, George O., estate, coll., A, S, 10/2–5/63. Notable gold: Charlotte, Dahlonega, Bechtler, and California pioneer material.

Warner, Thomas, *Communion Tokens: a Descriptive Catalogue.* Boston: Marvin, 1888, rep. from *AJN* XX (1887–88). C-S 3867.

Watson, Andrew M., coll., A, S, 10/28–9/66.

Watson, Richard (bishop of LLandaff, 1737–1816), *Chemical Essays.* 5 vols. London: Printed for J. Dodsley, 1782–88; 5th ed., London: Printed for T. Evans, sold by J. Evans, 1789–91. Preface dated Feb. 9, 1786. Here cited as first source to mention the 1776 Continental Currency tin patterns.

Watters, C. A., coll., A, Glendining & Co., 6/14/17.

Wayman, Raymond J., coll., A, S, 9/10/81. Gold.

Weill, Victor H., coll., A, Schulman, 4/26–8/72.

Wetmore, Maj. William Boerum, coll., A, SH&HC, 6/27–8/06.

Wexler, John A., *The Lincoln Cent Doubled Die.* n.p., n.d. [i.e., the author, 1984]. Extensive photographic var. study.

Wexler-Miller = Wexler, John A., and Miller, Tom, *The RPM Book: A Comprehensive Listing and Price Guide to Repunched Mint Marks and Over Mint Marks.* Newbury Park, Calif.: Lonesome John Publishing Co., 1983. Cited as RPM.

Weyl, Adolph, colls., A, Weyl, Berlin, 10/13/1884. This is the auction to which someone (either Capt. John W. Haseltine, Idler, or the Chapman brothers) had consigned an 1804 dollar to give it a European pedigree.

WGC = "World's Greatest Collection" (i.e., F. C. C. Boyd), A, Numismatic Gallery, (= A. Kosoff, Abner Kreisberg), 6 parts in 5: I, 1/20/45; II, 3/3/45; III, 4/14/45; IV–V, 5/12/45; VI (gold coins only), 1/25–26/46.

White, Lewis, coll., A, E. Cogan, 4/17–18/1876.

Whiteley, Dr. Philip, "Colorado Specie," *NUM* 7/58, p. 783.

Whitman, C. T., coll., A, SH&HC, 8/10–11/1893.

Wilcox, C. S., coll., A, SH&HC, 11/6–7/01.

Wild, William J., *Six Over Twelve.* Brooklyn, N.Y.: the author, 1966. Pamphlet incl. photocopy of typescript and 2 photographic prints. Documents the Oak Tree sixpences overstruck on cutdown shillings.

Willem, John M., *The United States Trade Dollar: America's Only Unwanted, Unhonored Coin.* N.Y.: Marchbanks Press, 1959 [500]; 2nd ed., Racine, Wis.: Western, 1965. C-S 3473. Rosichan 820. Thorough historical study.

———, estate, coll., MBS, Henry Christensen, 9/5/80. Incl. vars. of trade dollars.

Willey, Robert C., "The Colonial Coinage of Canada," serial, *CNJ,* 1969–83. The Canadian counterpart of Crosby {1875}, superseding all previous writings in this field.

Williams, Paul D., coll., A, B&R, 9/27–29/79.

Williamson, Raymond H., *The Franklin Press Token of 1794.* n.d. (ca. 1958), dittoed pamphlet.

Willing, Dr. Edward B., coll., A, B&R, 6/24–25/76. Compare Carson.

Wilson, David S., coll., A, SHC, 3/13–14/07.

Wilson, James B., coll., A, Elder, 10/5–7/08.

Wilson, W. W. C., coll., A, Wayte Raymond, 3 parts: I, 11/16–18/1925; II, 11/3–4/26; III, 11/21/27.

"Windsor," colls., A, Abner Kreisberg, 11/13–14/81.

Winsor, Richard B., coll., A, SH&HC, 12/16–17/1895.

"Winter," coll, A, S, 1/31/74.

Winter {1978} = Winter, Douglas A., "The North American Token," *NUM* 3/78, pp. 490–95; revised from "The North American Token: A Study," *PW* 9/77, pp. 209–13.

Winter {1983} = ———, "Brasher Half Doubloon Still Baffling," *CW* 8/17/83, p. 108.

Winthrop, coll., A, B&R, 9/19–20/75.

Witham, Stewart A., "John Reich's 'Scallops,'" *NSM* 11/67, pp. 1934–35. On the notched point "signature" on Reich's working obvs.

WNJ = *Whitman Numismatic Journal.* Mount Morris, Ill., 1964–68. C-S 412. Notable for articles embodying outstanding numismatic scholarship.

Wolfson, Samuel W., coll., A, S, 10/12–13/62. Gold coins.

———, coll., A, S, 5/3–4/63. Silver coins.

Wood, Howland, *The Gold Dollars of 1858.* N.Y.: ANS, 1922. NN&M 12. First study of the unique Large Letters proof.

———, "The Sou Marqué." In "The Coinage of the West Indies," *AJN* XLVIII, pp. 129–36, 1914.

Wood, Isaac F., coll., A, SH&HC, 7/11–12/1894.

Woodin, William H., colls., A, Part I, Edgar H. Adams 2/10–11/11; Part II, Elder, 3/2–4/11. Other parts privately to Waldo Newcomer, Col. Green, Virgil Brand, Wayte Raymond, others. Woodin was later Secretary of Treasury.

Woodside, George D., coll., A, N.Y. Coin & Stamp Co., 4/23/1892. Extraordinary patterns.

Woodward, W. Elliot, of Roxbury, Mass., series of 111 A, many cited herein by dates or former owners' names.

Woodworth, John, *Reminiscences of Troy From Its Settlement in 1790 to 1807,* Albany, N.Y.: Joel Munsell, 1853; 2nd ed., 1860. Earliest printed mention of the Albany Church Pennies.

Wright, Dr. Benjamin P., *The American Store or Business Cards.* Serial in *NUM* 1898–1901; rep., TAMS, 1963; rep., Boston: Quarterman, 1972. C-S 3944a.

Wroth, Lawrence, *Abel Buell of Connecticut: Silversmith, Type Founder and Engineer.* Middletown, Conn.: Wesleyan Univ. Press, 1958. C-S 3419. Rosichan 788.

X Y

Yeoman, Richard S., compiler, *A Guide Book of United States Coins.* Racine, Wis.: Whitman/Western, annually, 1947–

C-S 3366. Rosichan 797. More valuable for the historical overview than for the prices; immense amounts of information amazingly condensed.

————, "The 1848 Quarter Eagle With CAL." *NUM* 1953, pp. 674–86. Rep. in *Selections from* The Numismatist, vol. 1, pp. 193–205, Colorado Springs: ANA, 1960; rep. in Yeoman *Guide Book* (above), 1977 ed., pp. 241–46. C-S 3475.

Young, Edwin L., "Dr. John D. Parsons: A Colorado Pioneer," *NUM* 9/1983, pp. 1841–48.

Z

Zabriskie, Capt. Andrew C., coll., A, HC, 6/3/09.

Zay, Ernest, *Histoire Monétaire des Colonies Françoises, d'après les Documents Officiels.* Paris: J. Montorier, 1892; reps. C-S 2609.

Zelinka, Jerry, "The enigmatic VOCE POPULI Halfpenny of 1760." *CNL* 47, pp. 556–65 (10/76). Zelinka numbers are used herein by permission.

GLOSSARY

Boldface terms *within* a definition constitute cross-references to other entries. A few terms used only about a single issue or series are defined in the main text.

A

ABOUT UNC. Grade level between **EXTREMELY FINE** and **UNCIRCULATED;** usually cited as **AU**. Typically, either has full mint sharpness without mint bloom, or has nearly full mint luster with traces of rubbing or enough bag marks to interfere with design details.

addorsed [Heraldry] Placed back to back.

adjustment marks File marks, inflicted on a **planchet** before **striking**, to reduce weight to mint standard; they do not constitute impairment to the coin. In the Philadelphia Mint, gold or silver **blanks** were weighed after being cut from **strip;** lightweight ones were melted, normal ones cleaned and **upset** before going to press, heavy ones went to the adjusters (women with files and leather aprons). Weighing and adjusting sometimes had to be repeated. Every few hours, the contents of the leather aprons went back to the melting pots. In the 1850s, the 50-odd female adjusters worked in a room called the "Canary Cage." Adjusting was done only on edges after the early 1800s.

aigrette [Heraldry] Headdress of tufted feathers, originally egret plumes.

alignment In the striking press, **working dies** are normally placed so that their central axes coincide, and the top of obv. is nearest to bottom rev. (unlike medals). Deviations may be rotational (top of obv. is nearest to some other part of rev.), lateral (axes of dies are parallel but do not coincide: Typically, one side of the coin is normally centered, the other side apparently off center), or axial (axes of dies and therefore die faces are not parallel). Axial displacement is rarest because striking force disproportionately affects one edge of a die more than the other, causing prompt breakage; typically, one side of the coin is normal, the other unusually strong at one **rim,** weakening to illegibility at the opposite.

aliquot [Arithmetic] Common or proper fractional part.

alloy 1. Legally fixed proportion of metals in a coin. 2. More loosely, the baser metal(s) in a coin, as the copper and/or silver in a gold coin.

alteration 1. Intentional change in a die, producing an **overdate** or **overmintmark** or a corrected blunder. 2. Fraudulent change of one or more letters or numerals or other elements on a finished coin, including insertion or removal of mintmark, etc. The context always eliminates any possible ambiguity.

anneal Soften metal by heating. **Die blanks** are annealed before handwork with engraving tools, and before and/or between blows from the **hub,** the former to make fine detail work possible, the latter to avoid stress-hardening and brittleness. **Planchets** are annealed before striking, to save wear and tear on dies.

annular In the shape of a ring or washer.

annulet [Heraldry] A small ring.

arc arrangement On the Scot heraldic revs., 1796–1807, stars are normally placed in a curved row or arc of 6 just below clouds, another arc of 5 below them, with the 2 other stars at beak and behind head. Contrasted with **cross arrangement.**

argent 1. [Heraldry] Silver, corresponding to white; the **arms** of the United States are **blazoned** as "Argent, 6 **pales gules,** a **chief azure,"** meaning "On a white background, 6 vertical red stripes, top third of total area blue," but the rule forbidding color on color or metal on metal requires that the white be represented as silver ('argent') rather than as color ('blanc'). 2. Generic term for money in France and French colonies.

argentan, argenton Vars. of **German silver** containing varying proportions of copper, nickel, tin, zinc, antimony, etc., but no silver.

arms [Heraldry] Shield, charged with a pattern or design identified with the individual or corporation entitled thereto: Compare **blazon.**

assay n. Quantitative analysis of metallic content. v. To perform and report such analysis.

assay bar Old term for **bullion-storage ingot.**

assayer Official whose task is to **assay** gold and/or silver.

assembled set A **proof set** completed by buying individual coins; antonym, **original set.**

attributes [Iconography] Objects worn or held by a god(dess) or other mythological figure or personification, enabling identification. Examples: the scales of Justice, the cap of Liberty, the trident of Neptune, etc.

attribution 1. Assignment to a designer, engraver, mint, and/ or other source. 2. Assignment of var. number from one of the specialized reference books on a series.

authentic As represented; genuine, made when and where the coin purports to have been made.

avoirdupois Old weight standard, 1 lb. avoir. = 16 oz. avoir. = 7,000 grs. Used for everything except silver, gold, and platinum; eventually to be replaced by metric weights. Included herein because authorizing acts specified weights in this standard.

azure [Heraldry] Blue. Represented on coins by horizontal shading.

B

backdated Said of dies given a date earlier than that in which they were actually made.

baquette (French dialect) Small emblem representing a standing cow; dialect term meaning 'little cow.' Found on coins from Pau en Béarn.

barbed [Heraldry] With feathers (and usually claws) depicted.

barter economy That in which wages and prices are measured in terms of commodities rather than coins or paper currency.

base metal Any except silver, gold, or platinum (the "noble" metals).

base point [Heraldry] The pointed bottom of a shield.

basin v. To impart a convex curvature to the face of a die. In general, this produces not a spherical surface, but one in which the radius of curvature varies, being greatest near center, least near edge.

Bath metal Brass of 75% copper, 24.7% zinc, with 0.3% silver added; used in William Wood's ROSA AMERICANA coins.

Bay Shilling Old term for Pine Tree shilling; Bay = Massachusetts Bay.

beaded Said of a border consisting of round beads rather than radial lines, **dentils,** etc.

bend [Heraldry] A stripe diagonally from **dexter chief point** (observer's upper l.) to lower **sinister** border (observer's lower r.).

bill of exchange 18th-century document authorizing transfer of funds without subjecting precious metal to the risk of overseas travel.

billon Any mixture of copper and silver in which the copper predominates.

billon-neuf adj. Said of French or French Colonial **billon** coins made on new **blanks** rather than **overstruck** on earlier coins.

bit 1. Any coin valued at 1/8 dollar; typically, a Spanish or Mexican **real.** 2. The 100 Unit coin in Morris's 1783 scheme, Chap. 10 supra.

bitt Caribbean term for any coin current at 6 Doggs or 1 Escalin.

black dogg Caribbean term for any coin current at 1 **Stampee** = 1/6 Bitt = 1/6 **Escalin** = 2/3 Penny. 'Black' most likely alludes to discolored **billon,** which looks like silver when new, but like lead after brief circulation.

blank An unstruck **planchet.**

blank cutter Machine for shearing **blanks** out of **strip;** same principle as a cookie cutter. Rolled strip of proper thickness is passed through it; what comes out is **first-process planchets** and the perforated residue variously known as **scissel, shruf(f), clippings,** or **web.**

blazon v. [Heraldry] To describe the designs on a shield according to correct heraldic conventions; this procedure is terse and completely unambiguous. See example at **argent;** others abound in main text.

blundered die One containing an error in entry of one or more letter or numeral punches; most often the error is corrected but remains visible.

booby head 1. Ebenezer Mason's name for the cent head of 1839 immediately preceding the 1840 head. 2. John H. Clapp's name for the second quarter-eagle head of 1834 without motto.

border Raised circle whose outer circumference is the **rim** of a die or coin. Before 1836, normally **dentilated** or **serrated;** ca. 1836–1916, **beaded;** later, normally a plain raised lip or shelf.

Boston Shilling Old term for Pine Tree shilling.

botony See **cross.**

bourse Hall at a convention, where dealers display material for sale.

branch mint Any federal coining facility except the Philadelphia Mint. See **mintmark.**

brass 1. Obsolete term for any copper coinage. 2. Alloy of copper and zinc, sometimes containing tin or other minor components; proportions vary.

brilliant proof One with mirrorlike **fields** and unpolished **devices.**

britannia A var. of **German silver;** compare **argentan.**

brockage If a newly struck coin fails to be ejected, each **blank** thereafter fed into the **coining chamber** will receive an impression on one side from the die, on the other (**incuse and reversed**) from the trapped coin, becoming brockages. The trapped coin (capped die coin or brockage maker) spreads, and may wrap itself around the die, becoming cup-shaped.

bronze Alloy of copper and tin; proportions vary. In the periods 1864–1942, 1947–1962, cent metal was legally "French bronze" comprising 95% copper, 5% tin and zinc (proportions to be fixed by the Mint Director).

bronzed Said of a coin or medal given a protective coating or artificial patina by coating it with bronzing powder and baking it. The process was invented in Boulton & Watt's Soho Mint ca. 1788, experimentally used in the Philadelphia Mint ca. 1830–1880, at first on cent and half-cent proofs, later on medals. The composition of bronzing powder remains unknown.

bubble marks Raised blebs, from cavitations in the mold in which something was cast. Their presence on tin, pewter, or lead coins—or on porous copper coins—is grounds for suspicion that the pieces were cast **counterfeits** rather than struck. They most often occur at letters, numerals, or fine details of devices, rather than in fields.

buckled die One failing because improperly hardened; some area is caved in, showing as an abnormal bulge on coins struck from it. Sometimes simulated by gas bubbles in a **dumb blank.**

bullion Uncoined precious metal.

bullion-storage ingot Cast bar of gold, silver, or some mixture of the two, stamped with weight, composition, and assayer's and/or owner's identification; sometimes with an odd denomination like $36.55 rather than an even one like $50. Gambling casinos accepted these as money, but in later years such ingots stopped circulating. The date of a given ingot may be deducible only from the recorded years of the assayer's operations; that of ingots from Philadelphia or branch mints only from the style of their stamps. Knowledge in this area is only fragmentary.

Bungtown 1. Insulting 18th-century epithet for any filthy backwoods town; from *bung,* 'arse'. 2. Lightweight copper coin attributed to makers in such a town, especially North Swansea/Rehoboth, Mass., and possibly Westerly, R.I.; particularly to imitation British halfpence. Only the more prudish folk etymology attempted to derive it from Birmingham or its dialect form Brummagem, after the city where private mints exported coppers to New York and Philadelphia merchants. 3. Misnomer for **evasion copper,** from S. K. Harzfeld and Charles N. Schmall.

burnished Given a glossy surface by a buffing wheel. Strip intended for making proof planchets was burnished; working dies (especially proof dies) were initially burnished. But a coin burnished after striking is legitimately salable only as impaired: The process interferes with original surfaces, lessening sharpness of devices.

business strike A coin given only one blow from the dies, intended for normal circulation or commercial use; same as **production coin,** opposite of **proof.**

bust Device including head, neck, and some part of shoulder or chest; German, *Brustbild.*

buzzard dollars Early nickname for Morgan dollars.

C

caduceus [Iconography] Hermes's winged staff with twin serpents (sometimes depicted as ribbons). Originally a herald's emblem; later identified as medical.

cambist Paperback book (magazine format), prior to 1865, recording current **bullion** prices of foreign coins in circulation; some also listed current bank notes, genuine and counterfeit.

cameo Devices in relief or embossed, like our present coins; opposite of **incuse** or **intaglio.**

canton [Heraldry]   1. One of the four quarters of a shield, flag, or banner, contrasted with the rest by color or device, as the starry blue canton on the U.S. flag.   2. One of the four areas separated by arms of a cross.

cantoned Having devices placed in one or more **cantons** (either sense).

card money Canadian currency, 1685–1760, originally consisting of playing cards with written values, dates, and official signatures.

cartwheel coppers British twopence and pennies of 1797, made by Boulton & Watt; so called from their unusually large rims.

cartwheel effect Mint bloom on an uncirculated **production coin,** consisting of minute radial corrugations; these vanish rapidly after even brief circulation, accordingly becoming a test for the grade (except on prooflike strikings). "Tilt a frosty uncirculated piece back and forth in the light and radial lines of light rotate in fields somewhat like the blurry lines on moving cartwheels or carriage wheels in a Western movie." Breen {1977}, p. 298.

cast v. Pour liquid metal into a mold to impart shape and sometimes devices. Antonym: **strike.** n. Anything so made. Antonyms: **struck, die-struck.** Compare next two.

cast blank A planchet made in a mold the size and shape of the intended coin. Copper coins were in the 18th century sometimes made on cast blanks, though the practice was disapproved as easing the counterfeiters' task. Genuine copper coins were normally struck on blanks cut from rolled **strip.** Cast blanks have rounded edges (without shear marks from the **blank cutter**) and will show porosity in protected areas, but under high magnification, edges of devices show the same kind of striations as other struck coins. Examples include some 1760 VOCE POPULI coppers.

cast copy One made in a mold taken from a normal (die-struck) coin. Look for porous surfaces and edges, a slick greasy feel, and **bubble marks.**

Castaing machine Named for Jean Castaing, the engineer who perfected it, this imparted edge ornamentation and/or edge lettering to **planchets** before striking. Mounted onto a bench were two parallel bars, each containing half the edge device, set apart minutely less than the **blank's** diameter, one fixed, the other spring-mounted and set to move forward at the pull of a long handle. Each blank passed through the machine, rolling enough to receive the complete edge device. In practice, slippage sometimes produced blundered edge inscriptions (parts missing or overlapping); more rarely, a blank might be run through a second time. Mint personnel commonly called the operation "rounding and edge marking." The machine went into use in the mid-17th century, becoming obsolete with the invention of the **close collar.** Until well into the 19th century, its details (though long since published) were protected by oaths of secrecy exacted from workmen and Mint officers: Craig {1953}; Breen {1962A}; Ewing {1985}.

celator Artist who engraved a design in **intaglio** directly onto a **die blank,** in a technique close kin to engraving sealstone gems. Later synonyms include **die engraver, diesinker.** The engraver in any official mint eventually had to become enough of a sculptor to create **device punches.** Since the late 19th century, the engraver's tasks in the Philadelphia Mint have included making relief models suitable for conversion into **galvanos** which the **portrait lathe** would mechanically copy into **matrixes** or **master dies,** these in turn eventually used to **raise hubs** from which **working dies** would be sunk.

Here the idea is to multiply identical coins in unprecedented quantity.

cent   1. Massachusetts copper coin equated to $1/100$ of a Spanish dollar.   2. Alternative term for Morris's 1783 **Bit** or silver 100 Unit coin.   3. Federal coin equated to $1/100$ dollar.

cent stock Copper intended for cents but cut into **planchets** for some other denomination, notably half cents 1795–1803; compare **spoiled cent stock.**

center dot Raised dot at geometric center of a coin, from the compass used on a working die to lay out circular arcs for positioning lettering, stars, date, or other peripheral elements. Rarely found after 1839.

center-grained Said of an edge impressed with short diagonal marks which occupy less than half the cylindrical surface; contrasted with diagonal reeding, which extends over its entirety. One of the forms of **safety edge.**

center punch Unlike **center dot,** a round **incuse** mark at geometric center of a coin, apparently from a compass point on the hub. Found on a minority of mid-19th-century coins, mostly eagles and half dollars.

chatter Unwanted vibratory movement of a **die,** producing minor double striking.

cherrypick To recognize and buy a rare var. which had been offered as common. More often said of specialists buying from dealers, than of dealers buying from the general public. So fearful are some dealers of cherrypickers that they attempt to refuse to show their wares to collectors known or suspected to be specialists, e.g., members of EAC.

chief [Heraldry] Upper third of a shield, contrasting with the remainder in color or device.

chief points [Heraldry] Upper corners of a shield: dexter, at observer's upper l.; sinister, at observer's upper r. On some shields, a middle chief point is between them: Chap. 6, Sect. v.

cinquefoil [Heraldry] Small ornament in shape of a five-petaled flower seen from vertically above.

circulated   1. Released to the general public.   2. Showing signs of wear from being passed from hand to hand. Antonym: UNCIRCULATED.

clad metal Any **strip** fabricated by bonding both sides of a central core to thinner layers ("cladding") of a different metal. Synonym: **Sandwich metal.** Two kinds are in common use in federal coinage (1965–   ):   1. Copper core bonded to nickel alloy.   2. **Billon** core bonded to higher-grade silver alloy.

clash marks Impressions of part of a **device** or **legend** of one **die** onto field of the die facing it in press. From the dies striking each other at normal coining force without a **planchet** between them. Earlier this was from the moneyer's failure to feed a planchet; later, from failure of the mechanical feeder to release a planchet into the **coining chamber,** or because the press continued to run after the hopper was empty of blanks.

Classic Head Ebenezer Mason's term for the John Reich head found on half cents 1809–29, cents 1808–14, gold coins 1834–39: short curly hair with long lovelock, bound by a **fillet** inscribed LIBERTY, after numerous ancient Greek statues of boy athletes.

cléchée See **cross.**

clipped   1. Said of a thin silver or gold coin from which some part of the edge has been shaved or sheared.   2. Said of a **planchet** of which some part is missing owing to a misplaced blow from the **blank cutter** ("curved clip") or which is incomplete because cut from the end of the **strip** ("straight clip").

clippings Perforated metal **strip** from which **planchets** had been cut by the **blank cutter.** Synonyms: **scissel, shruf(f), web.**

close collar Heavy steel plate, perforated to the exact size of the finished coin, fitting around and above the neck of the lower die, defining the cylindrical space (**coining chamber**) in which the **planchet** is struck. It insures that the coins will all be of equal diameter; if grooved, it imparts vertical **edge reeding.** After striking, the upper die retracts, and the lower die rises through the collar, ejecting the finished coin so that feeder fingers or **layer-on** can brush it into the receiving bin with its fellows, while another planchet is fed to await striking. A flywheel governs all these motions. Newman-Bressett {1962} calls the contrivance a **collar die,** but the term "close collar" appears in Mint correspondence as early as 1829, when it was introduced for use on half dimes and gold coins, rendering the **Castaing machine** obsolete. Compare **open collar.**

closed 3 Style of numeral 3 found on the earliest dies of 1873, on the smaller denominations having knobs so close together as to be readily mistaken for an 8. Subject of a formal complaint from the Chief Coiner, Jan. 18, 1873: Boosel {1960}. Compare **open 3.** Similarly for closed 5, 6, or 9, in which knob touches cusp or loop, though without documentation.

clover leaf cent Earliest name (1869) for the 1793 var. with sprig of **trefoils** above date; apparently bestowed by its discoverer, Richard B. Winsor. Later called **strawberry leaf** or **cotton leaf cent.**

cob Latin American coin struck by hammer on crude irregular **planchet,** sheared off the end of a rolled silver or gold bar; authorized by Philip III at Madrid, Aug. 9, 1598, for mints at México, Lima, Potosí, Santa Fé de Bogotá (Colombia), and Santo Domingo on Ysla Española; coined ca. 1652–1772, and in Guatemala more briefly. Proper name is *macuquina.*

coin n.   1. Originally, **bullion** formed into pellets or disks of standardized weight and stamped to enable circulation as **money.**   2. Later, similar items in any metal purportedly intended for circulation as money.   3. Later, similar items in any metal which could theoretically circulate but which were sold at a premium (**proofs, commemoratives,** other **NCLT** items). Compare **medals, patterns, tokens, counters.**

coin v.   1. Generally, to make **bullion** into circulating **money.**   2. Specifically, to impart designs onto **planchets.**

coiner The mint official in charge of stamping **planchets** into **money.**

coining chamber The cylindrical space bounded by lower die, upper die, and **close collar.** Each **planchet** is fed into it, receiving one blow from the upper die (two or more for **proofs**), then ejected to make room for the next.

collar Metal plate with a coin-size perforation to position the **planchet** for striking: See **open collar, close collar.**

collar die Term in Newman-Bressett {1962} for **close collar.**

collot French colonial copper sol or 12 Deniers coin, counterstamped RF (1793) for Guadeloupe, and thereafter valued throughout the Caribbean at 3 Sols 9 Deniers = 2¼ Pence = ¼ Bitt = ¼ Escalin = 1½ Stampees = 1½ Doggs. Named after Gov. Georges Henri Victor Collot, who signed the proclamation authorizing their issue, 10/2/1793. Pridmore III, pp. 228, 339–40.

colonials Generic term for coins made in or for America before the federal Mint began regular operations. In practice, a few later items are included.

commemoratives Generic **NCLT** items whose designs memorialize the occasion for which they were struck.

common gold Large mintage half eagles, eagles, and double eagles, ca. 1878–1907, and later dates, mostly saved by bullion speculators.

complete hub One containing all details of an obv. or rev. design except for date or mintmark. Since 1907 these have also included dates.

contract coinage   1. Any made by private parties under franchise granted by a local, state, or national government. The contractors normally paid the authorities the equivalent of 10% or 15% of their gross output for the privilege, circulating the rest or selling it (often at discounts) to merchants, who spent the individual coins. Examples include state copper coinages of Vermont, Connecticut, and New Jersey.   2. Any made by private mints for other governments, paid for by the latter; the output was shipped to the ordering authority for distribution. Examples include the Hawaiian copper coinage of 1847, and more recently some issues by the Franklin Mint.   3. Any made by a national mint for a foreign government, as the Philadelphia Mint has done since the 1870s. These last groups are outside the scope of this Encyclopedia.

copperheads 1860s term for copper or bronze cent-size (rarely 2¢ size) tokens made and circulated by private parties; later called Civil War tokens. The bronze Philadelphia Mint cents of 1864 and later years were briefly known as "Government copperheads" because made in similar composition and of about the same weight.

copper panic Sudden mass refusal by NYC merchants, July 20, 1789, to accept any kind of copper coins at their former rate (14 to the shilling); the price collapsed to 60 to the shilling. Thereafter, for some years, paper scrip circulated instead.

coppers Generic late 18th-century term for copper coins of halfpenny size of any origin, whether official or **bungtowns.**

copy Generic imitation of a genuine coin. Includes **counterfeits, forgeries, electrotypes, cast copies, struck copies.**

copy dies Dies imitating some earlier issue, made later to simulate it, most often for clandestine purposes. Examples include the "Second Restrike" rev. found on half cents dated 1831, 1836, 1840–48, 1852; the rev. of 1804 "restrike" dollars, dies of the 1804 plain 4 eagle, Nagy's $10 and $25 Templeton Reid dies, and the 1884 dies of Hawaiian type.

cotton leaf cent One from the 1793 obv. showing a sprig of **trefoils** above date, interpreted by S. S. Crosby as cotton leaves. Formerly called **"clover leaf," "strawberry leaf,"** or **"strawberry sprig."**

couchant [Heraldry] Said of an animal depicted as lying down.

coulter Pointed blade on a plow, hanging below plowbeam, ahead of the share, for cutting clods; later called "hanging colter." Only the first nine obv. dies of New Jersey coppers lack it, explaining their name of "Coulterless" or "No Coulter." Urban children knew the term mostly from Robert Burns's poem "To a Mouse."

counter   1. Anything used for tallying; French, **jeton.**   2. Specifically, anything of the size and general appearance of a coin, used in gambling to represent the latter; ancestral to poker chips. Examples include the brass pieces vaguely resembling 1803 $5 and $2½, signed KETTLE.

counterchanged [Heraldry] Vice versa: said of a supplementary device whose colors are those previously mentioned but transposed. Example: Lord Baltimore's arms, "**paly** of six, **sable** and **or,** a **bend** counterchanged," as on his coins, nos. **64–75,** where the colors on the bend are or and sable.

counterfeit Unauthorized imitation of a coin, generally distinguishable from the genuine by differences in manufacturing methods. Herein specifically refers to pieces falsely made to circulate as money, or more recently to gold coins falsely imitating genuine ones, made to sell to bullion dealers, jewelers, speculators, gold hoarders, etc. Numismatic fakes, made to deceive coin collectors and dealers, are instead called **forgeries.**

countermark, counterstamp Any letters, numerals, or devices stamped onto a finished coin. The two terms are traditionally interchangeable, though some students have attempted to use one to mean official stamps (e.g., the CAL on some 1848 quarter eagles, the 1640 fleur de lys in oval or 1763 crowned C on French billon coins, the RF on 1767 copper sous, the Danish West Indian crowned FR VII on American coins ca. 1849), the other only for private markings. Official countermarks are not counted as an impairment of the host coin, and the countermarked device is graded separately. The status of unofficial countermarks varies according to their origin: The Bechtler countermark on a federal half eagle is apt to be highly prized, the WOOD'S MINSTRELS or HOUCK'S PANACEA BALTIMORE or other documented (dated and located) commercial announcement will attract many specialists, whereas the jeweler's hallmark or unidentified device, name, or initials will attract fewer.

Coyning Engine Archaic term for a **screw press.**

crenelated Having the top edge furnished with rectangular depressions, as in a fort, where concealed archers or gunmen could fire down on attackers.

crest [Heraldry] A device surmounting the **arms,** and **blazoned** separately; examples herein include the coronet on Lord Baltimore's coins, the eagle and demiglobe on **torse** above New York arms on the EXCELSIOR and GEORGE CLINTON coppers, the eagle above arms on the Washington LIBERTY AND SECURITY pence, the arm and arrow on torse on the MASSACHUSETTS and CALIFORNIA gold coins. Crests have sometimes been made into complete devices independent of the arms; examples herein include the eagle on demiglobe on New York pattern coppers, and the nag's head on torse on New Jersey coppers.

croisette potencée [Heraldry] **Crosslet** whose arms end in elaborate Y shapes, said to represent crutch heads.

cross arrangement That found on some silver and gold coins 1797–99, 1804–5; the stars above eagle form parallel straight lines intersecting in diamond patterns. Antonym: **arc arrangement.**

cross botony [Heraldry] Cross whose arms end in groups of three joined disks. The name indicates that these were thought of as buttons.

cross cléchée [Heraldry] Cross whose arms spread out, ending in Y shapes; like the Maltese cross except that the points are cut off.

cross fichée [Heraldry] Cross whose upright is extended at bottom into a long point for driving into the ground. Also spelled "fitchy."

cross pointée [Heraldry] Cross whose arms end in pointed wedges.

crosslet 1. [Heraldry] A tiny cross, usually Greek (equalarmed) and without ornamented arms. Herein found mostly as punctuation in legends. 2. The serif on r. end of crossbar of a 4, as on some coins of 1804 and 1834; "plain 4" coins lack this serif.

crown 1. Any silver coin of about the size of a silver dollar. 2. British name for a 5-shillings coin.

cuartilla Silver coin of the value of 1/4 real = 1/32 Spanish or Mexican dollar.

cud Lump on a coin struck from a die from which a piece has broken off. The term is attributed to Del Ford.

cuirassed Said of a bust furnished with armor.

cupro-nickel Alloy of copper with more nickel than in the 1857–64 cents; the common proportion in the USA is 25% nickel, 75% copper, in other countries 20% nickel, 80% copper.

currency 1. Paper circulating as money. Antonym: **specie,** hard money. 2. Current money of all kinds. 3. Condition of being **current.**

current 1. In circulation in a given place and time; antonym: obsolete. 2. Authorized to circulate at a given place and time; antonyms: **uncurrent,** retired, withdrawn, recalled.

cut 1. Border device on paper currency, imparted by woodcut or copper plate or in general any method except typesetting. 2. Short for halftone cut.

cut money Spanish or Latin American dollars chopped into quarters or eighths for small change; often lightweight, sometimes counterfeit.

cwt = **hundredweight** = 112 lbs. avoirdupois = 50.802 kg.

D

dala Hawaiian money of account = U.S., Spanish, or Mexican dollar.

debased Said of coins underweight or of precious-metal content inferior to legal standards, or to those claimed on the coin's face. Not always **counterfeit:** genuine examples include the later gold dollars by Christopher Bechtler, Jr., from dies reading A.BECHTLER, and the Mormon gold coins with PURE GOLD or P.G. which were nevertheless heavily alloyed.

debasement 1. Issue of lightweight coins. 2. Issue of coins below legal standard in precious-metal content. A crime formerly equivalent to counterfeiting; conviction of a mintmaster on this charge formerly rated a death penalty.

decad Continental Congress's name for a proposed copper coin (1785–86).

demi écu (French) Silver coin of half the weight of an **écu.**

demi sol (French) Coin of half the value of a **sol,** usually **billon.**

demiglobe Upper segment (properly, upper half) of a globe, generally rendered with latitude and longitude lines.

denarium 'Tenfold' or 'decimal.' Herein found only as legend on Lord Baltimore's pattern copper, where short for *aes denarium,* interpreted as 'penny.' From Latin *denarius,* 'piece of 10 asses = of the value of 10 standard coppers.'

denier Old French money of account, originally 1/12 **sol.**

denomination Multiple or fraction of a monetary unit. Sometimes but not always an official name of a coin; authorizing acts always named the 2½-dollar coins "quarter eagles."

dentilated Said of a **border** furnished with **dentils.** Contrasted with **beaded** and **serrated.**

dentils Ornaments shaped like small teeth; ends may be rectangular, rounded, or with dull points.

device Principal design element.

device punch Steel bas-relief, used for sinking a **device** into a **die;** like a **hub** but without **legends.** Generally raised from a **matrix.**

dexter [Heraldry] R. side of shield, from the bearer's point of view; observer's l.; the more honorable side. Antonym, **sinister.**

die That which stamps a design into a **planchet.** So that the devices and inscriptions will be in relief and readable, the die is **incuse** or **intaglio** and retrograde.

die blank Steel cylinder ready to be made into a **die** by being impressed with **devices, inscriptions,** etc. Between successive blows from a **device punch** or **hub,** the die blank must be **annealed** to prevent brittleness; later it is cleaned and hardened.

die-linked Said of 2 or more vars. of coins sharing the same **die.**

diesinker One who impresses designs and inscriptions into a **die blank.** The older terms **engraver** or **celator** suggest freehand work; **diesinker** instead suggests one who uses letter punches and/or **device punches.** In practice there was much overlap.

die state Discrete stage in the life history of a die, from new (intact and generally with initial polish) to worn, clashed, cracked, chipped, broken, and/or rusted. The appearance of a new crack or set of **clash marks** represents a distinct die state; mere lengthening of an existing crack is not always so counted.

différent French term for small device identifying mintmaster or engraver. Cf. **privymark.**

dime Official legal name for the federal coin of 10 cents or 1/10 dollar; a later spelling of **disme.**

disme (French) 1. Simon Stevin's neologism {1585} for decimal reckoning. 2. In the Mint Act of 1792, official name for the federal coin of 10 cents or 1/10 dollar. Originally must have rhymed with steam; later with time.

dogg Caribbean term for any coin valued at 1 **Stampee** or ⅙ **Bitt.** Originally short for **black dogg.**

dollar 1. Anglicization of **thaler** = Central European coin containing somewhere near an ounce of silver. 2. Common name for the Spanish silver peso of 8 Reales. 3. Common name for any Latin American silver coin of about the same weight. 4. Federal money of account, intended to match preceding; legally defined by the 1792 Mint Act as 416 grs. silver of fineness 892.43+ (= ¹,⁴⁸⁵/₁,₆₆₄, i.e., 371.25 grs. = 24.057 gms. pure silver. 5. Federal money of account, legally defined by the 1837 Mint Act as 412.5 grs. silver at 900 Fine = 371.25 grs. pure silver. 6. Federal money of account, defined by the 1792 Mint Act as 27 grs. gold at ¹¹/₁₂ or 22 carats Fine = 24.75 grs. or 1.604 gms. pure gold. 7. Federal money of account, defined by the 1837 Mint Act as 25.8 grs. gold at 900 Fine = 23.22 grs. or 1.5046 gms. pure gold. 8. Federal money of account, defined by Pres. Roosevelt (Jan. 31, 1934) and again by the Bretton Woods Agreement (July 1944) as ¹/₃₅ oz. gold. 9. Federal money of account, defined by Pres. Nixon (Dec. 18, 1971) as ¹/₃₈.₈ oz. gold. 10. Federal money of account, defined by Nixon (Feb. 1973) as ¹/₄₂.₂₂ oz. gold. 11. Current Federal **fiat money** unit, without legally fixed equivalent in gold or silver; its purchasing power depends, loosely, on fluctuations in the gold market.

double Any French coin of 2 deniers; originally, *double tournois,* 'double denier coin of Tours standard.'

double eagle Official name for the federal $20 gold coin.

double stripes Said of any die in which the U.S. shield represents **pales gules** by two lines for shading (rather than three or four or more).

double-struck Said of any coin which has received two impressions from the **working dies** in accidentally imperfect alignment. **Proofs** normally receive such extra blows in perfect alignment.

doubled die One which received one of its several blows from **hub** or **device punch** in accidentally imperfect alignment: Wexler {1984}, following Alan Herbert, distinguishes seven types, which comprise three classes:

A. Displaced extra blows from same or indistinguishable hubs. (Herbert-Wexler Types I, IV, V, respectively "Rotated," "Offset," and "Pivoted.") The most famous example: 1955 cent, **2214.**

B. Displaced extra blows from same or indistinguishable hubs which have worn, chipped, or otherwise deteriorated between blows. (Herbert-Wexler Types II, VI, respectively "Distorted" and "Distended.") Often hard to tell from class A.

C. Displaced extra blows from two distinguishable hubs: "dual hub vars." (Herbert-Wexler Types III, VII, respectively "Design" and "Modified.") Famous examples include the cent obvs. **2229, 2232, 2257, 5251,** all post-1916 overdates; and the 1909/8 double eagle **7373.**

doubloon 1. Spanish or Latin American gold 8 Escudos, standard weight 417.75 grs. = 27.07 gms. 2. Either of Ephraim Brasher's gold coins of similar weight.

douzain French 17th-century name for **billon** coin of 12 deniers.

draped bust Any coin on which the bust is depicted as showing any kind of loose cloth rather than a uniform. The term is used for certain Connecticut coppers, Washington token cents, and federal coinage series.

dumb blank A **planchet** which fails the **ring test** because of **occluded gas** bubbles or cracks.

E

eagle 1. Any **device** thought to represent one of the larger predatory birds, especially American. 2. Official name for the $10 gold coin.

écu French dollar-size coin; the name (French: 'shield') is from the Bourbon arms prominent on the earliest designs.

edge The cylindrical boundary of a coin. Not to be confused with **border** or **rim.** May be plain, lettered, reeded, or ornamented. "The third side of a coin," imparted by **blank cutter, Castaing machine, close collar,** or **virole brisée.**

edge device Pattern of letters and/or ornaments on edge.

edging, edge marking Old terms for imparting edge lettering or ornamentation by the **Castaing machine.**

edge reeding Ribs on edge, imparted by **Castaing machine** or **close collar.**

electrotype A **copy** of a coin or token or medal made by electrodeposition of copper or silver onto molds made from the original. The 2 shells so produced are usually filled with lead or **fusible alloy** and cemented together. More rarely, the shells are built up by continued deposition of copper or silver instead ("solid electrotypes"). The process was common in the 1850–1870 period when coin photographs were unavailable, and had its uses in educating collectors as to the approximate appearance of original rarities. It acquired evil repute in later decades when some unscrupulous dealers sold such copies as genuine coins. Electrotyping is used today to create **galvanos.**

emission sequence Chronological order of die vars. Steps in determining it include 1) grouping vars. sharing a single obv. die; 2) grouping vars. sharing a single rev. die; 3) arranging those in each group according to **die states.** Where changes in **edge device** or type of **planchet** occur, further modifications may be necessary.

engrailed [Heraldry] Festooned with joined arcs. A misnomer for various kinds of edge or border ornamentation, most often for diagonally reeded edge.

engraver 1. Later name for **celator** or **diesinker.** 2. Short for Engraver of the Mint, the official in charge of manufacture of dies at the Philadelphia Mint. 3. In the preliminary headings for each section of main text, refers to whoever completed the working dies, as distinct from who designed them.

erased [Heraldry] With jagged edge. The antonym is couped, "cut off (cleanly)," though this term does not occur in main text (**truncation** is commoner usage).

escalin (Caribbean Creole: 'shilling') Caribbean money of account = 1 **Bitt** = 6 **Doggs.**

escudo Spanish gold coin, about 52.22 grs. = 3.384 gms. = ⅛ **doubloon.**

estoile [Heraldry] Ornament representing a star; normally with six (sometimes eight) long wavy points, probably representing its flickering. Not to be confused with the **molet.**

estoppel Legal impediment, a by-product of some previous contract or enactment. The corresponding verb form: estopped.

evasion copper Lightweight coin rudely imitating British or Irish halfpence of George II or III but with fictitious dates and irrelevant or fanciful **legends** which could deceive only the illiterate; e.g., GEORGE RULES for GEORGIUS III REX, or BRITONS ISLES for BRITANNIA, or HISPANIOLA for HIBERNIA: Thompson {1949}. Many types came from William Lutwyche's mint in Birmingham. Not to be confused with **bungtown copper.**

ex Designating a coin's numismatic source; Latin, 'out of.'

exergue Lower segment of a coin's circular area, generally set off from the remainder by a straight line; may contain date or designer's initials. Examples in federal coins occur on Liberty-seated designs, Standing Liberty quarters, Walking Liberty half dollars.

experimental coin Test of a new circulating medium: new metal or **alloy,** denomination, or manufacturing method.

EXTREMELY FINE Grade level defined for each series in main text. A century ago, the equivalent was "barely circulated."

F

face value 1. Exchange value defined by some **inscription** on a coin ("mark of value"). 2. Nominal value based on weight standard.

FAIR Grade level below **GOOD**; typically, identifiable but without complete inscriptions. Collectible only for extreme rarities.

fantasy piece A coin designed on whim or to create a rarity, not out of any urgency for a circulating medium. Examples in federal coinage include the 1866 Philadelphia silver without motto, 1859–60 half dimes and dimes without UNITED STATES OF AMERICA, 1868 large cent of 1857 type.

farthing Coin passing as ¼ penny = ¹⁄₄₈ shilling. Farthings did not circulate in the American colonies after the Revolution.

fasces [Iconography] Roman emblem: an axe, its handle surrounded by lictors' rods and bound to them by thongs. It symbolized the power to kill mercifully by the blade or mercilessly by the rods. Later generations softened this to mean "the power of life and death."

fecit (Latin:) 'He made it.' Affixed to an artist's signature, as E G FECIT on one obv. of Continental Currency tin patterns; often abbreviated to F. as in C.GOBRECHT F. on the 1836 dollar obvs.

Festschrift (German:) 'Festival writing.' Booklength collection of learned papers in celebration of some event or personage.

fiat money [Economics] That which circulates because a government decrees it, without any reference to convertibility into precious metal.

fido Old term for mint error; acronym for Freaks, Imperfections, Defects, Oddities: Wallace {1954}.

field Plain background around **devices** on a **die**; space for **inscriptions.**

fillet Old term for a hair ribbon, awarded to athletes as a prize for winning town games (ancestral to the blue ribbons awarded to exhibitors, etc.).

fillet head Old term for **draped-bust** cent (1796–1807).

fimbriated Properly, fringed; alludes to the bordered stripes on the Union Jack.

fin Mint term for **knife-rim.**

FINE Grade designation defined for each series in main text.

Fine 1. Parts per thousand of principal metal; sterling silver is 925 Fine, federal coin gold 900, etc. 2. In such legal phrases as "fine gold" or "fine troy oz.," pure, unalloyed.

finial An ornament at the very top or upper corner(s) of a device.

first-process planchet One not yet given the **upset rim.**

fish scales Common term for federal **billon** or silver 3¢ coins while they were still **current,** 1851–73: Breen {1974}.

Five Finger Word The cheerleader's chant says it all: "Gimme a G!—Gimme an R!—Gimme an E!—Gimme another E!—Gimme a D!—What do they spell?" Often alluded to by a spread-fingers gesture: Jack Collins.

flan Alternate term for **planchet** or especially **blank.**

fleur de lys [Heraldry] Stylized lily. Appears on French **arms,** and on British coins because of English kings' centuries-long claim to the throne of France. Sometimes shortened to **lys.**

fleuron [Heraldry] Small stylized ornament representing an oversimplified **fleur de lys.** Often drawn like the Greek character for *psi* on its side.

florin Coin of the value of 2 shillings.

font [Typography] Matched set of letters (properly, upper and lower case) representing a single design concept. Letters on coins are mostly upper case; many were designed and made into punches by typefounders. The distinctions of **oldstyle, modern, sans-serif,** text or "Gothic," boldface, condensed, extended, italic, and script are exactly as in typography.

forgery Fraudulent imitation aimed at collectors or dealers; herein distinguished from circulating **counterfeits.**

fraction 1. Short for **fractional coin,** including **cut money;** e.g., Spanish fractions. 2. Numerical denomination on some early federal coins: ½ on half dollars of 1796–97, ¹⁄₁₀₀ on cents 1792–1807, ¹⁄₂₀₀ on half cents 1793–1808.

fractional coin 1. Spanish or Latin American small silver coins, reckoned in halves, quarters, eighths or sixteenths of a dollar; **legal tender** in the United States until 1857. 2. Federal coins of denominations between the silver 3¢ and the half dollar inclusive. Both meanings come from reckoning these as **aliquot** parts of dollars.

fractional currency and **notes** 1. Any circulating paper of denomination below $1. Before 1864 this was most often banknotes or **scrip.** 2. Federal notes of denomination between 3¢ and 50¢, issued 1862–76.

French bronze Mint Director Pollock's official name for cent metal 1864–1942, 95% copper, 5% tin and zinc in proportions to be determined by the Director. See **bronze.**

fusible alloy [Metallurgy] Any metal mixture with a low melting point. Formerly often used for making **splashers.** A common example is Wood's metal, 50% bismuth, 25% lead, 12.5% each tin and cadmium, m.p. 71° C. = 159.8° F. Not to be confused with **Wood's coinage metal,** which is **Bath metal.**

G

galvano Impression of a plaster relief model created by electrodeposition; a preliminary stage in creation of original dies for medals or coins.

gangpunch Alternate term for **logotype;** a punch bearing several letters or numerals.

gem Applied to an **UNCIRCULATED** or **Proof** coin, denotes "flawless" and connotes "high aesthetic quality."

German silver Dr. Lewis Feuchtwanger's term (ca. 1837–64) for any of several white alloys of copper, nickel, tin, zinc, antimony, etc. His other term "American silver" quickly became obsolete; "Feuchtwanger's metal" refers to the alloy he used for his sample coins. Other alloys in the same family are known as **argentan, argenton, britannia,** maillechort, packtong, etc. None contain any silver. *NUM* 6/13, pp. 297–302.

glaive Weapon whose head has an axelike blade opposite a sharp point; related to the halbert.

glory [Heraldry] Stars or other device or inscription represented as in the sky or luminous, generally by proximity of clouds or rays or both.

gnomon The pointer on a sundial, whose shadow indicates the hour.

Godless Epithet for any coin omitting a reference to God which had been standard on its predecessors. Examples include the British 1849 florins and Canadian 1911 coins omitting D[ei] G[ratia], 'By the grace of God,' and the federal $10 and $20 of 1907–8 omitting IN GOD WE TRUST.

goloid Either of Dr. Wheeler W. Hubbell's proposed coinage metals: silver with a small percentage of gold, supposedly enough to end the "rivalry," but actually not enough to change the color. Found in federal pattern coins, 1878–80.

GOOD 1. Grade level defined for each series in main text; typically, with date and all inscriptions legible, with complete outlines of devices but no internal details. 2. Genuine.

grade, grading "An excuse for price."—John D. Wright. Rating of a coin's place on a scale whose lower extreme is illegible wear (**POOR**), and whose upper extreme is perfect preservation (superb pristine **UNCIRCULATED** or superb pristine **Proof**). See **numerical grading.**

grading standard Verbal descriptions of the various stages on the scale mentioned under **grade.** That here used is substantially identical to that of ANACS = ANA Certification Service, but without the anachronistic numbers. See **numerical grading.**

grain A weight (troy or avoirdupois) = 0.06479891 gram. Herein used because authorizing acts specified coin weights in this unit.

gram Standard metric system unit of mass = 0.001 that of the platinum-iridium cylinder at the National Bureau of Standards or its twin at the International Bureau of Weights and Measures, Paris.

greenback 1. Any federal Demand Note of 1861 ($5, $10, or $20, with "on demand" in inscription, and without Treasury seal); so called because these were the first Treasury notes to use green ink for back designs. 2. Any federal Legal Tender Note of 1862 or 1863.

Gresham's law When two kinds of money are simultaneously in circulation, the overvalued kind will drive the undervalued out of circulation. People saved gold and heavier silver, spent lightweight silver and paper.

groat Silver coin of 4 pence denomination.

guide lines Circular arcs, whose center is at the **center dot,** put onto a **die blank** to guide the workman (**engraver,** letterer, or apprentice) in entering letters, numerals, or stars. Normally they are polished off before the die is sent to press; occasional traces remained on some dies as late as the mid-1830s. They became obsolete with the introduction of **complete hubs.**

guinea British gold coin, named after the West African source of the bullion for its first coinage, 1663. At first 20 **shillings,** later 30 (1694), thereafter revalued lower, eventually down to 21 shillings (1813).

guinea pig principle Named because neither a pig nor from Guinea. Catchphrase for ridiculous folk etymologies: compare **lucus a non lucendo.**

gules [Heraldry] The color red, from French *gueules,* 'fur neckpiece dyed red,' represented by vertical shading. See the **blazoning** at **argent;** compare **double stripes, triple stripes.**

H

half cent 1. Massachusetts copper coin, 1787–88, of half the value of a **cent.** 2. Federal copper coin, 1793–1857, of 1/200 dollar denomination.

half crown British silver coin of the value of 2 shillings 6 pence.

half dime Federal silver coin of 1/20 dollar denomination, 1837–73.

half disme Federal silver coin of 1/20 dollar denomination, 1792–1837.

half eagle Official name for Federal gold $5 coin, 1795–1929.

half pence [Also spelled as one word] 1. Collective name for British copper coins of the value of 1/2 penny = 1/24 shilling each. 2. Collective name for privately minted copper coins of roughly the same size; the lightweight sort came to be known as **coppers.**

hallmark Maker's identification mark, comparable to a signature, found on pewter, silver, and gold utensils and jewelry. Occasionally found as countermarks on coins, the most famous being Ephraim Brasher's roman E.B in oval.

hammer method Technique for making coins since the 8th century B.C., superseded in the 17th and 18th centuries by the **screw press.** A **coiner** or moneyer held the upper die atop the **blank** which rested on the lower die, while a workman (originally a slave) struck the upper die's flat end with a sledgehammer. If the first blow did not bring up the design clearly enough, a second or third blow might be necessary. The method was fast but hazardous to the coiner's fingers.

Hard Ware British 18th-century euphemism for privately made **coppers,** especially in ships' bills of lading.

HIBERNIA coins 1. Generic Irish coins; from Latin Hibernia, 'Ireland.' 2. William Wood's copper coins for Ireland, 1722–24, later exported to the American colonies. 3.

Roche's 1760 VOCE POPULI halfpence and farthings, also later exported to America.

hippocampus Mythological beast, generally represented as with forequarters of a horse, hindquarters and tail of a fish. Probably from drawings attempting to make sense out of travelers' descriptions of fur seals or other warm-blooded sea beasts.

Hogge Money Lightweight token copper coins current in Bermuda, 1616, so called from their obv. hog device.

howdah (Hindi) Ornamental seat in which one rides atop an elephant.

hub A specialized die used not for striking coins but for imparting designs to **working dies.** So that the coins will be in relief and readable, dies are **intaglio** and reversed; the hubs are therefore in relief. Earlier hubs were **device punches,** later ones included partial inscriptions; still later came **complete hubs.** Several blows ("entries") from the hub are necessary to impart the design; an occasional by-product is **doubled dies.**

hundredweight Anglo-American weight = 1/20 long ton = 112 lbs. avoirdupois = 784,000 grs. = 50.802 kilograms. Abbreviation, cwt.

I

incuse Said of letters or devices sunk below neighboring surfaces. Antonyms: embossed, in relief.

inescutcheon [Heraldry] Small shield superimposed on center of a larger one.

ingot 1. Long, flat rectangular solid of metal, produced by pouring the melted ore or bullion into a mold where it cools and solidifies; the largest ones made in mints are rolled into **strip** for cutting into **planchets.** 2. Short for **bullion-storage ingot.** 3. Short for **specie ingot.** 4. Official evasive name for the octagonal $50 coins made by Augustus Humbert's United States Assay Office of Gold under federal contract.

inscription Words, numerals, and abbreviations on a coin, other than dates, mintmarks, and engravers' or designers' signatures. Compare **legend.**

intaglio Said of devices sunk below neighboring surfaces. Antonyms: in cameo, in relief.

J

Janvier lathe Type of reducing lathe or three-dimensional pantograph used for making reduced-size copies of **galvanos** in creating master dies and hubs.

"Jefferson head" Ebenezer Mason's name for the John Harper sample cents of 1795; from a fancied resemblance to Jefferson's profile.

joe Generic term for various Portuguese eighteenth-century gold coins. From the king's name IOANNES or IOSEPHUS.

jola (Mexican Spanish dialect) 'small copper coin.' Probably from Spanish *joya,* 'trinket'. Compare **sou.**

jugate 'Yoked together,' directly from Latin *jugati.* Said of adjoined busts on a coin, facing the same way, depicted in such a perspective as makes them look joined.

jumbo [Philately] On an extraordinarily broad **flan.**

K

keneta Hawaiian money of account = U.S. cent.

knife-rim Thin raised extension of edge, at outermost rim of a coin, from where metal was forced between die and close collar at striking. Mint personnel call it a **fin** and object to its presence on coins because it can create problems in ejecting the finished coin. It is usually a cue to replace a collar which has stretched with prolonged use. Not diagnostic of proofs. Neither a flaw nor a specially desirable trait of a coin.

L

langued [Heraldry] Depicted with tongue exposed.

lapped Smoothed on a lapstone, to remove minor irregularities.

large cent Federal copper cent, 1793–1857; later term to distinguish any of these from cents of the current size. In its own day, merely "cent."

Lawful Money 18th-century exchange rate equating the Spanish dollar to 6 shillings. This made 1 penny = 1/72 dollar = 1/9 bit.

layer-on Mechanical feeder, shuttling back and forth above the **coining chamber,** alternately to receive a new blank, drop it atop the lower die, and push out each newly struck coin. Ill. *CW* 10/8/86, p. 84.

leaved edge One ornamented with an indefinitely repeated device of twin leaves; common to Latin American dollars, 1776 CONTINENTAL CURRENCY tin coins, Morris's 1783 CONSTELLATIO NOVA silver patterns, and one var. of 1792 Washington half dollars.

legal tender Anything that may be legally offered in payment of a debt or other financial obligation. The creditor or other party to whom the sum is payable must then accept it rather than demanding any other form of payment. The U.S. Constitution debars any state from making anything but gold and silver legal tender; which led to generations of controversy over whether cents or nickel coins could qualify, and (after the Civil War) reams of Supreme Court opinions and reversals over whether federal paper currency could qualify. (Framers of the Constitution intended to forbid paper currency of any kind, under the name "bills of credit.") Half cents and large cents were never legal tender; trade dollars lost their legal-tender status in 1876; but the Coinage Act of July 23, 1965 has made all U.S. coins, current or obsolete, of all denominations and metals, into legal tender. Compare **NCLT.**

legend That part of a coin's or medal's **inscription** placed in a circular arc parallel to the border.

letter punch Steel **punch** for imparting a letter to a die; formerly made by typefounders in matched sets called **fonts.** Contrasted with **logotype.**

letters of marque and reprisal Documents commissioning their grantees as legal pirates in international waters. The federal government retains the right to issue these: U.S. Constitution, Article I, section 8, paragraph 11, and section 10, paragraph 1.

liard French copper coin of 3 (later 2) **deniers** value.

liberty 1. Legal status of anyone either born outside of slavery or lucky enough to avoid being captured for sale or taken prisoner of war. 2. Legal status of one who had been released from slavery or prison by any method except escape. 3. Either of these personified as a goddess. 4. 18th-century buzzword for economic autonomy: legal entitlement to buy and sell produce and other commodities without official interference. 5. Any of the female personifications on U.S. coins. 6. Paradoxically, any of the presidential heads on U.S. coins is legally an "impression emblematic of liberty" (Act of April 2, 1792; 31 U.S.C. 324, Sect. 3517) despite George Washington's objection to coin portraiture as "monarchical."

liberty cap 1. The **pilleus** or Phrygian cap, shaped like half an eggshell, in ancient Rome placed on the head of an ex-slave at manumission, partly to symbolize emergence from confinement (as the chick from the eggshell), partly to conceal the ultrashort haircut which marked slave status. 2. [Iconography] The conical cap used in the 18th century to symbolize **liberty** (senses 3, 4). 3. Any representation of this last, as a device on coins or medals.

lightweight Said of a coin noticeably below legal weight standard; "weighed in the balance and found wanting," as in Daniel 5:27. While coins still represented a legally prescribed amount of precious metal, any weight deficiency was grounds for suspicion.

linck Name for zinc in the Royal Patent for Wood's ROSA AMERICANA coins. Compare **tutanaigne.**

livres (tournois) French money of account; 1 livre = 20 **sols.**

logotype A single punch containing a word or two, three, or four digits of a date.

long ton English weight = 2,240 pounds avoirdupois = 1,016.047 kilograms.

louis d'argent Generic term for a French silver coin with a Bourbon portrait.

louis d'or Generic term for a French gold coin with a Bourbon portrait, 1640–1793. Weight varied from about 6.5 to 8.6 gms.

Louis Mirliton Nickname for the **louis d'or** coined at 27 livres by Edict of Aug. 1723. Quantities officially shipped to Canada went instead to the ocean floor in the wreck of the *Chameau* off Cape Breton, Nova Scotia, Aug. 26, 1725, and were retrieved in 1965 by a salvage team. The name Mirliton, 'reed flute,' apparently alludes to a popular song ridiculing the Prime Minister at the time of the coins' issue.

lucus a non lucendo (Latin:) '[It's called] a grove because it's not luminous.' Old catchphrase for ridiculous folk etymologies; compare **guinea pig principle.**

Lyon dollar Generic name for any Dutch **crown;** so called from the prominent lions as principal device on Frisian lion daalders and many others.

lys [Heraldry] Ornament representing a **fleur de lys.**

M

macaronic Said of verses or inscriptions containing words or phrases from different languages.

mailed bust Same as **cuirassed.**

main de justice (French) Device like a scepter but surmounted with a hand; supposedly an emblem of French law courts.

major variety One differing from others of the same type, date, and mintmark (if any) in a change of at least one design element, or an intentional change of layout. The changed element may be a single letter, numeral, or star, or anything larger. Compare **minor variety.**

mantling [Heraldry] Drapery or fur depicted as surrounding a shield.

maravedí Small Spanish copper coin = 1/34 real.

marc French unit of weight = 244.7529 gms. French coins were struck at weight standards of so many to the marc.

Mark Name of Morris's 1783 silver pattern 1,000-Unit coin.

marqué See **sol marqué.**

martlet [Heraldry] Emblem representing a swallow, depicted as a bird without feet; from the legend that these birds flew lifelong without touching ground.

Masonic punctuation Three dots in an equilateral triangle, vertex up.

master coin Pre-1858 term for **proof.**

master die Same as **matrix.**

master hub In modern minting practice, one raised from a **matrix** to sink negatives from which **working hubs** are raised.

matrix Original **die,** used not for striking **coins** but for raising **device punches** or **hubs.** Normally engraved intaglio on a **die blank,** which is thereafter hardened and put in a press opposite another die blank with a conical face. Repeated blows impart the relief details.

Matron Head Euphemism for Robert Scot's ugly cent head of 1816–35.

matronymic Surname of mother's family, affixed after regular surname (patronymic).

matte proof One given its uniformly granular or dull surface at the Mint by pickling in acid; a European 1890s technique adopted at the Philadelphia Mint in 1907, but abandoned before 1936.

maverick Coin or token of undetermined origin.

medal Commemorative item differing from a coin in neither being made to a recognized coinage weight standard nor intended to circulate. Some pieces are of ambiguous status; herein, this remark applies most of all to the Pitt, Rhode Island, and certain Washingtons. Decision to list them among coins has come less from tradition than from recognition that many in fact did circulate and some were struck to known weight standards.

medalet Diminutive **medal.**

medallist A designer and/or diesinker of **medals.**

medio (Spanish) Short for **medio real,** Spanish or Latin American silver coin of ½ real = 1/16 dollar, nearest in value to the half disme or half dime.

mercantilism Political/economic philosophy based on the notion that a nation's wealth consists not in land but in the amount of gold and silver held within its borders. See Part One, Overview, supra.

metric gold Dr. Wheeler W. Hubbell's proposed coinage metal, used for the $4 or Stella coins of 1879–80.

metrology Scientific study of weight and measurement standards; essential adjunct to numismatics.

milled Said of coins struck on **blanks** cut from rolled strip. The term "milled edge" is an obsolete misnomer for **reeded edge.**

mills 1. Rollers to make **ingots** into **strip** from which **blanks** are cut. 2. Hence, part of the title of a mint: Rahway Mills, Machin's Mills. The original was Monnaie du Moulin, 'Mill Mint,' Paris, beginning in 1553 when royal authorities bought the Augsburg mills and presses.

mini-dollar The Susan B. Anthony dollar coin, so called because of its small diameter compared with all previous dollar coins of silver or **sandwich metal.**

minor variety 1. One differing from others only in minor repunchings, repairs, etc. 2. A **positional variety.** Contrast **major variety.**

mint n. 1. Any coining establishment. 2. Capitalized, any of the branches of the federal mint system, or of any royal or other national mint.

mint v. To strike coins.

mint bloom Pristine surface of a freshly minted coin, produced by cold flow under the dies: Compare **cartwheel effect.** Cannot be effectively simulated (compare **whizzing);** cannot be restored to a coin which has lost it from wear or cleaning.

mint state Same as UNCIRCULATED: Free of any trace of wear. See **slider.**

mintage 1. Process of striking coins. 2. Quantity coined.

mintmark Letter or symbol identifying the mint of origin of a coin. On federal coins, mintmarks are normally punched by hand into each working die at the Philadelphia mint. On proof dies, 1985– , the S or W mintmark is in the master obverse.

Mirliton (French) Reed flute: See **Louis Mirliton;** explanation for the coin's sobriquet is in Chap. 5.

modern letters [Typography] Those with vertical and horizontal serifs and marked contrast between thick and thin elements; antonym, **oldstyle.** The change dates to about 1800–20.

moidore Generic term for Portuguese/Brazilian gold coin, properly *moeda de ouro* or 4,000 reis.

molet [Heraldry] Spur rowel, in shape of pentagram or five-pointed star, often **voided.**

moneyer In **mintage** by **hammer method,** the man who positioned each **blank** onto the lower **die** and inspected the **coin** after each blow; the **coiner.**

motto Aphorism, often set off from **legends** or other inscriptions on a **coin** or **medal,** often included in **blazoning** of **arms.**

American examples before the current "In God We Trust" and "E Pluribus Unum" include many listed in "Inscriptions on Colonial Coins: Translations and Index" above. In some, e.g., "Immunis Columbia/Constellatio Nova" and "Liberty Parent of Science and Industry," distinctions between motto and legend are obscured or obliterated. How seriously mottoes were taken is shown by the furor over presidential orders omitting "In God We Trust" from 1907–8 $10 and $20.

mousquetaire 1. (French) Musketeer, royal soldier, as in the Dumas stories. 2. **Billon** coin bearing **voided** Greek crosses like those on the soldiers' tabards.

mule v. To make a coin by combining two dies not meant to go together. n. Any coin so made.

multiple striking Visible evidence of a coin's receiving more than one blow from the dies. Common on coins made by the **hammer method.**

Muttonhead Derisive name for one type of Connecticut copper.

N

NCLT "Non-Circulating Legal Tender." Term for coins (**commemoratives** and/or **proofs**) struck to legal weight and composition standards which could theoretically circulate but in practice do not because sold at a premium over face value.

new-tenor Coins made at a new weight standard; specifically, gold made on and after Aug. 1, 1834, silver after the 1837 or 1853 weight changes. The term was earlier used by the Massachusetts Generall Court about certain issues of the colony's paper currency. Antonym: **old-tenor.**

nickel 1. Any cent, 1857–64, of the 88% copper, 12% nickel **alloy** then official. 2. Any 5¢ piece, 1866– , of the legal **cupro-nickel** alloy. 3. Popular solecism for that alloy. 4. The element (magnetic when pure); from the old German name for its ore, Kupfer-Nickel, 'devil's copper,' requiring the very fires of hell to melt, and notorious for causing allergies.

nickel-clad See **sandwich metal.**

nimbus [Iconography] A halo, traditionally represented as rays or a disk around a saint's head or other object thought to be sacred.

nock [Archery] End of an arrow shaft, behind the feathers, notched to fit against the bowstring.

numerical grading Obsolescent practice of affixing numerals to each **grade** designation: Basal State (= barely identifiable and unmutilated) 1; FAIR 2; ABOUT GOOD 3; GOOD 4, 5, 6; VERY GOOD 7, 8; ABOUT FINE 10; FINE 12, 15; VERY FINE 20, 25, 30, 35; EXTREMELY FINE 40, 45; ABOUT UNCIRCULATED 50, 55; Mint State 60, 65, 70. Other numerical grade designations were never authorized by Sheldon. He devised this scale after noticing that auction and fixed price sales of 1794 cents (ca. 1925–45) exhibited fairly consistent relations between price and grade: A GOOD sold at twice a FAIR; a VERY GOOD almost twice a GOOD; a FINE three times a GOOD; a VERY FINE five times a GOOD or almost double a FINE; an EXTREMELY FINE eight times a GOOD or about five times a VERY GOOD; an ABOUT UNCIRCULATED about seven times a GOOD or two and one half times a VERY FINE; a Mint State about 12 times a GOOD or five times a FINE or three times a VERY FINE; and an original blazing mint-red piece would then bring about 15% more than a toned one. From these observations Sheldon made the mental leap to an equation which he believed fundamental to a "science of cent values": Market Price = Numerical Grade × Basal Value (value in Basal State). However, publication of his books {1949, 1958} permanently affected the market enough to destroy this relationship between price and grade, and with it both his hypothetical "science of cent values" and any remaining rationale for these numbers. Because Sheldon standardized descriptions of each grade level for large cents, the numbers remain in use in

EAC; but because they have not been so standardized for other series, despite the ANA Grading Guide, they are not used herein. They have become a focus of the very same abuses, primarily overgrading, which Sheldon had devised them to combat; among the most flagrant instances are those involving alleged grades between 58 and 67, which represent distinctions nowhere precisely described, and about which disagreement has become both frequent and acrimonious. See **slider.**

O

obsessive date One officially continued after the actual year. Examples include the Massachusetts silver coins, which bore the date 1652 for 30 years; various state coppers which bore the date 1787 until July 1789; and the 1964–65 federal coins pursuant to Section 204, Coinage Act of July 23, 1965.

obverse The "heads" side of a coin; antonym: **reverse.** Which side is which is not always obvious; decisions about such ambiguous coins are explained in the introductory sections of text.

occluded gas Gas bubbles trapped in the **ingot** at cooling and solidifying. Most will escape when the ingot is rolled into **strip; blanks** cut from such metal will show lamination defects from the bubbles' breaking, but occasionally bubbles too small or too deeply buried to escape that way will remain, producing a **dumb blank.**

off center Said of a coin only partly resting within the **coining chamber** at striking. Typically, it will have a crescent-shaped blank area opposite one in which border or even design is incomplete.

old-tenor Coin struck before a new weight standard became official. Antonym: **new-tenor.** Examples: gold coins issued before Aug. 1, 1834; silver coins issued before the weight changes of 1837 or 1853.

oldstyle [Typography] Said of letters characterized by wedge-shaped serifs, not all horizontal or vertical; thick elements not heavily contrasted with thin (and in curves, as upper case B, C, D, G, O, P, R, often canted to l., not vertical). Antonym: **modern letters.**

OMS "Off Metal Striking." Impression from regular dies on a **blank** of other than the authorized metal.

one-sided proof A coin minted by normal proofing techniques except that the rev. die remained unpolished; obv. has mirrorlike field, rev. hasn't. Such coins occur occasionally 1817–36 and more rarely later.

open collar Thin plate with a perforation a little larger than the finished coin, placed above the lower die and serving to position the blank atop the latter but without restraining expansion at striking. This was to protect the edge device and ease ejection of the finished coin. Replaced in various denominations during 1829–36 by the **close collar.**

open 3 Style of 3 found on later dies of 1873, with the knobs far apart. Produced in response to the Coiner's complaint, Jan. 18, 1873, about the **closed 3.** Similarly for other open digits, in which knob of 5, 6, or 9 is free of cusp or loop; but no documentation survives for these changes.

or [Heraldry] Gold; a metal, not a color (compare **argent**).

original 1. Said of an issue actually made in the year of its date; antonym: **restrike.** 2. Said of the "Class I" 1804 dollars, made in Nov. 1834 for diplomatic presentation purposes; contrasted with the restrikes of 1858–59.

original die 1. A **matrix.** 2. A die made for and used in the year of its date; antonyms: **restrike die, copy die.** 3. Said of the rev. of the "Class I" 1804 dollars, as preceding entry.

original (proof) set One containing the identical specimens received together from the mint in the year of issue; antonym: **assembled set.**

oroide Brassy **alloy** used for costume jewelry; named after its superficial resemblance to gold. Sometimes spelled without the final *e.*

overdate 1. Var. in which at least one digit of a date has been changed, either for mint economy or to correct a blunder. 2. Loosely, similar var. in which a rotated (misplaced) digit is corrected. 3. To make any such alteration in a die.

overmintmark Var. in which a **mintmark** is overpunched in the die with a different one, generally for mint economy; famous examples include the 1900 O/CC dollars and the 1938 D/S nickels.

overstrike 1. To use an earlier coin as a planchet for a different one. 2. Any coin so made. The practice was common in the French mints; famous American examples include Vermont coppers overstruck on CONSTELLATIO NOVA coins, New Jersey coppers overstruck on many other types of coppers, and federal cents and half cents overstruck on Talbot, Allum & Lee tokens.

P

pale [Heraldry] A vertical stripe.

pale gules [Heraldry] Vertical red stripe; herein specifically on the U.S. shield, where represented on coins by vertical shading. See next.

paly [Heraldry] Having the field divided into vertical stripes. See the blazoning at **argent.**

pan To search gravel in a stream for granules, flakes, or lumps of gold or gold-bearing quartz.

par 1. 100% of face value. 2. Equal current value (with a named **specie** unit).

parting Separating silver from gold: a necessary stage in refining gold bullion.

parting acids Concentrated nitric, sulfuric, and hydrochloric acids used in **parting.**

passant [Heraldry] Said of an animal depicted as walking, normally toward observer's l., usually with r. forepaw raised.

passant gardant [Heraldry] Said of an animal **passant** with his face turned toward the observer.

pattern Proposed coin design not adopted. Compare **prototype, experimental piece.** Patterns often come in other than the proposed metals; many patterns for both federal and pioneer gold coins are unknown in gold: See, respectively, Judd and Kagin {1981}.

peage New England Puritan abbreviation of **wanpanpiag;** compare **wampum.**

pedigree Sequence of owners of a coin. Ideally, equivalent to the legal term "chain of title." In practice, often contains gaps because many dealers discard, falsify, or suppress pedigree data to prevent collectors from deciphering their cost codes or learning their markup; some even clean coins lest they be recognized at subsequent auction appearance. This has the unwanted side effect of making some coins appear to be commoner than they actually are.

pence Collective plural of **penny.**

penny 1. Old British monetary unit = $1/12$ shilling = $1/240$ pound sterling. 2. William Wood's name for his middle-size ROSA AMERICANA coins. 3. Common error for **cent.**

peso Spanish or Latin American silver **dollar** or 8 Reales coin.

pewter Generic term for alloys of tin and lead with various trace elements.

pheon [Heraldry] Ornament representing a stylized arrowhead or javelin head; often more resembles a bird's footprint.

picayune (Cajun Creole) 1. Louisiana term for a **medio;** from French *picaillon,* 'small copper coin,' Provençal *picaioun* 'small change.' 2. After 1838, a half dime, because those newly released from the New Orleans Mint passed at par with medios.

pièce de caprice (French) Same as **fantasy piece.**

piedfort (French) Coin struck on a blank several times normal thickness; not a mint error but a **pièce de caprice.**

pilleus Latin name for the Phrygian **liberty cap.**

plain edge One without reeding, lettering, or ornamentation, as on our current cents and nickels.

planchet Disk on which a design is stamped to make a **coin, medal,** or **token.** An unstruck one is called a **blank.**

planchet defects Those present on the **blank** before striking. **Occluded gas** in the **ingot** produces laminations and splits when the bubbles break during rolling into **strip.** Inhomogeneities or inclusions of foreign matter in the ingot produce discolored streaks (formerly called "drift marks"), or sometimes granular cavitations or cracks. Because these all preceded striking, they do not count as damage to the coin.

plated coins Generally, coated with some other metal after striking, often for fraudulent purposes. The few rare exceptions are noted in the main text.

plug To fill a hole with metal. Repairs of this kind may mitigate the damage caused by piercing, but cannot abolish it.

portrait 1. Representation of an individual as such, as of George Washington on many Early American coins. 2. Representation of an individual as a personification, as Teresa Cafarelli de Francisci on the Peace dollar. Composite portraits, such as the Indian on the buffalo nickel, fit in here. However, the presidential effigies on current U.S. coins are legally "impression(s) emblematic of **liberty**" rather than portraits! 31 U.S.C. 324, Sect. 3517.

portrait lathe Three-dimensional pantograph for reducing large relief models to coin size; the modern version is the **Janvier lathe.**

positional variety Any **minor variety** differing from others only in positions of hand-entered **punches** or **logotypes** with respect to each other or to devices. In practice, when lettering or dates differ greatly in spacing, suggesting either an intentional change of layout or a blunder, such dies are listed as **major varieties.**

presentation pieces Coins minted with unusual care, from new dies on carefully selected blanks, generally prooflike, intended for visiting dignitaries or other VIPs, either before the Philadelphia Mint standardized the proofing process in 1817, or at branch mints.

presently In the main text, affixed to a rarity rating, indicates that the var. is too recent a discovery to permit a reasonable estimate of the quantity available. This usage is generally restricted to modern series where many roll lots remain unchecked.

press 1. Engine for stamping **dies** onto **blanks;** also called striking press or coining press. Includes both the **screw press** and its successors. 2. Engine for stamping **hubs** onto **die blanks,** usually "hubbing press." 3. Same as **blank cutter;** in this sense, usually "cutting press."

pristine Said of a **mint state** or proof coin with original surfaces intact, never cleaned, or at least without any visible evidence of cleaning.

privymark 1. British numismatic term for **différent.** 2. Any similar unexplained symbol, generally at beginning or end of legend, or (in the Mark Newby coins) below the king. Both meanings may allude to the local mintmaster, engraver, provincial mint, or even the group ordering that particular batch of coins. The peculiar ornaments on some Connecticut coppers may function similarly or for quality control.

proclamation money Official exchange rate conforming to Queen Anne's Proclamation of June 18, 1704, effective Jan. 1, 1704/5, valuing the Spanish or Mexican dollar at not over 6 shillings. Compare Crosby {1875}, p. 117.

proclamation piece A commemorative item struck in any of the Spanish dominions to celebrate a coronation.

production coin Same as **business strike;** one made to circulate, normally given only one blow from the dies. Antonyms: **pattern, presentation piece, pièce de caprice, proof, prototype,** etc.

proof Specially minted coin, normally given two or more blows from the dies to bring up the designs more sharply than on **production coins.** Normally minted on burnished blanks from burnished dies; exceptions include **matte proof, sandblast proof, satin-finish proof.**

proof dies Those specially burnished and otherwise prepared for making **proof** coins. Because the coins are not **annealed** between impressions, they become stress-hardened and wear down the dies more rapidly than do **production coins.** The Mint Bureau gave average die life (1971) for cent proof dies at 2,300 obv., 2,900 rev.; nickels, 2,500 obv., 2,300 rev.; dimes, 2,600 obv., 2,700 rev.; quarters, 1,500 (i.e., 2,500?) obv., 2,200 rev.; half dollars, 2,400 obv., 3,200 rev.; Eisenhower dollars, 2,500 obv., 3,500 rev. The corresponding figures for dies for **business strikes:** cents, 1,000,000 obv., 1,200,000 rev.; nickels, 170,000 obv., 185,000 rev.; dimes, 150,000 obv., 165,000 rev.; quarters, 155,000 obv., 170,000 rev.; half dollars, 150,000 obv., 180,000 rev.; Eisenhower dollars, 100,000 obv., 200,000 rev. (*NSM* 9/72, pp. 842–43.) Earlier figures were lower; at least as recently as 1888, some proof dies were used also for making production coins.

proof set Group of **proof** coins of one date, as sold by a mint in the year of issue. Compare **assembled set, original set.**

proofing 1. The process of making **proof** coins. 2. See next.

proofing piece Small bar of 999+ Fine gold, used for bringing low-grade melts up to mint standard; formerly commonly used in federal mints and in the San Francisco Provisional Branch Mint (Augustus Humbert's U.S. Assay Office of Gold).

prooflike Said of a **presentation piece** or an exceptional **production coin,** struck from brilliantly polished dies on a **blank** which may or may not also have been polished before striking. The "depth" of prooflike finish is measured by the distance at which the coin will clearly and readably reflect print. Sometimes the dies were polished to remove **clash marks** or other defects; clues to this condition include incompleteness of relief details and/or traces of clash marks in protected areas.

proper 1. [Heraldry] Of its own natural colors. 2. Said of a die intended for a particular combination; other combinations using it or its partner are **mules.**

prototype 1. A design adopted in the subsequent year. Examples: 1856 Flying Eagle cent, 1858 "Indian" cent of type of 1859, 1882 nickel without CENTS, 1876 $20 of type of 1877 (repositioned head, TWENTY DOLLARS). 2. A design of which one side is current, the other later adopted, though the combination may not appear on later production coins. Examples: 1858 "Indian" cent with regular rev. of 1857; 1876 $20 with head of 1877 and regular TWENTY D. rev.: also called **transitional.** 3. A proposed design which differs only in minor details from that later adopted. Examples: 1875 20¢ coin with small date and overlapping leaves; 1878 dollar without designer's initial M. Coins thought to be prototypes may in fact be **restrikes** or afterthoughts, **pièces de caprice.** Examples include the 1863–65 coins with motto IN GOD WE TRUST.

punch 1. Tool for impressing a design element into a die. Compare **device punch, letter punch, logotype, hub.** 2. Use such a tool on a die.

punchlinked Said of dies sharing one or more **letter punches** or numeral punches from the same **font.** Punch linkage constitutes evidence that the same diesinker worked on all dies sharing these punches.

Q

quarter 1. Weight of 1/4 **hundredweight** = 28 lbs. avoirdupois = 196,000 grains = 12.7 kilograms. 2. Abbreviation for **quarter dollar.**

quarter dollar Legal name for the 25¢ coin.

quarter eagle Legal name for the $2.50 gold coin.

quatrefoil [Heraldry] Ornament representing a four-petaled flower, seen from vertically above.

quincunx [Heraldry] Arrangement of five elements (pellets, small ornaments, etc.) with four at corners of a square, the fifth within, as on each 5-spot on dice or dominoes.

Quint Morris's term (1783) for the 500-Unit coin.

R

raise To emboss devices on a hub or device punch, not by relief carving but by placing it in press opposite an original die or other suitable negative.

rare Said of a coin of which only a limited number exist in collectors' hands. Where this number is in the thousands, the term becomes a misnomer. See next.

rarity scale Estimate of surviving population of a coin, originally in impressionistic terms (R = Rare, RR = Very Rare, RRR = Extremely Rare, etc., up to RRRRRR = unique: older European usage), more recently attempting to be quantitative. The scale most commonly used today was adapted by Dr. Sheldon {1949, 1958} from Noel Humphreys (about 1853):

R-8 = Estimated 1–3 known, "Unique or Nearly Unique."
R-7 = Estimated 4–12 known, "Extremely Rare."
R-6 = Estimated 13–30 known, "Very Rare."
R-5 = Estimated 31–75 known, "Rare."
R-4 = Estimated 76–200 known, "Very Scarce."
R-3 = Estimated 201–500 known, "Scarce."
R-2 = Estimated 501–1,250 known, "Uncommon."
R-1 = Over 1,251 known; "Common." (Used by permission.)

These designations were originally standardized only for large cents 1793–1814. They do not discriminate properly among coins with larger overall populations, where a coin of which 2,000 or even 5,000 survive brings many times the price of its cousin of which 10,000 survive. And in other series, a coin of which 4–6 survive may bring many times the price of its relation of which 8–10 survive. Worse still, any honest rarity rating must be understood as "known to the writer at this time," and possibly obsolete by the time the book reaches print! See **presently.** But as nearly as possible, a "Very Rare" herein will rate at least Rarity 6, Sheldon scale, and similarly for other ratings.

real Spanish monetary unit = 1/8 **peso** = 1 **bit** = about 12 1/2¢. Plural, **reales.**

rebus Message encoded in symbols, readable by combining their successive names or meanings. The device of the 1776 Continental Currency tin patterns is an elementary example.

reduction 1. The process of mechanically producing a master **die** or **hub** the size of a coin from a much larger **galvano,** using a **portrait lathe.** 2. Any die or hub so made. In practice, each reduction needs much hand-finishing work. This process is a stage in translating new designs into coins, not of using current designs.

red stripes Alternative term for **pales gules,** represented on coins by vertical shading.

reeded Said of an edge with vertical ribs, as on our current dimes, quarters, and higher-denomination coins. A diagonally reeded edge has these ribs parallel but all slanting in the one direction rather than vertical.

reeding The ribs in a **reeded** edge. Different **close collars** are recognizable by distinctive thickness and spacing of these ribs.

relief Degree to which devices protrude outward from fields. In general, the higher the relief, the more blows from the **hub** necessary to make a **working die,** and the more blows from the working die necessary to bring up the design on the finished coin or medal. This is why **production coins** are in low enough relief to show all essential details from a single blow from the dies.

remedy Permitted deviation of weight. Herein, the figure following the ± sign in "Weight Standard" for each series. The figures cited are from authorizing acts or from *CWA*, pp. 346–48, which quotes the Director of the Mint.

renard [Heraldry] Emblem representing a fox.

replica Properly, a **copy** made by the same institution which made the **original.** Loosely, any copy or reproduction.

restrike Generic term for any coin minted after the year of its date. In practice, the term is not applied to **production coins** (e.g., the 1802- and 1803-dated silver dollars struck in 1804, the 1845 O quarter eagles made in Jan. 1846, etc.), where mint economy or unavailability of new dies dictated the policy, but to **proofs** struck later to accommodate favored parties. The label has unjustly become a stigma, avoided as a designation of many coins lest auction prices fall; in actuality, many restrikes are rarer than originals, and some have no original counterparts (e.g., 1838–39 Gobrecht dollars with starry rev.).

reverse The "tails" side of a coin; antonym: **obverse.** Which side is which is not always obvious; decisions about such ambiguous coins are explained in introductory texts.

rim Circular circumference where **edge** meets **border.** On **proofs** this is usually "squared" (having a rectangular cross-section); on **production coins** it is normally beveled. See **knife-rim.**

ring test Procedure for distinguishing a struck coin from an **electrotype** or **cast copy;** or for telling if two coins of the same kind are of the same metal. Balance the coin on a fingertip and gently tap it on the **rim** with another coin. A struck coin will produce a prolonged tone; anything else, a brief "tink" or a dull thud. (Exceptions: A struck coin on a **dumb blank** or with a **planchet** crack will ring briefly or not at all; a coin unusually thick for its diameter will ring more briefly than a thinner one of the same metal and diameter.) Two coins of the same diameter, thickness, and alloy will produce the same note; small changes in alloy produce large changes in pitch of the note. The test, while not necessarily conclusive of genuineness in itself, has heuristic value: After hearing a dull thud, one scrutinizes the edge for the seam characterizing electrotypes, and other areas for porosity, **bubble marks, stem spot,** or other evidence of casting.

rolled blank A **planchet** cut from rolled **strip.** Antonym: **cast blank.**

rolled edge Misnomer for the second prototype St. Gaudens $10 of 1907.

rolled stock Generic term for half-cent **planchets** rolled from **strip** 1796–1800, contrasted with those cut down from misstruck cents (**spoiled cent stock**) or from Talbot, Allum & Lee tokens (**token stock**).

roller dies Those mounted on rollers; **strip** was passed between them and only later cut into **planchets** and given **reeded edges.** This coining technique was briefly in use in the 17th century; see examples and illustrations in Peck {1964}. Some Mark Newby coins may have been made this way.

rolling mills Pairs of heavy cylinders for squeezing **ingots** into **strip.**

"Roman Gold" finish That regularly found on proof gold 1909–10, more mirrorlike than **satin finish,** less so than the fields of

brilliant proofs. A. Kosoff popularized the term in the 1940s, but it may have earlier origins.

"Roman Head" John Gregory Hancock's satirical cent of 1792, portraying Washington as a degenerate, effeminate Roman emperor, in allusion to the President's labeling portrait coinage as "monarchical," and in revenge for his sabotaging any prospect of contract coinage.

roundel [Heraldry] A small disk, originally representing a coin.

S

sable [Heraldry] The color black, represented on coins by crosshatching.

safety edge Any of several alternatives to ordinary **reeded edge** or edge lettering; includes various types of **center-grained edges,** curved reeding, reeding with a raised line bisecting all ribs, etc.

Saints 1. Mormons; short for Latter-Day Saints. 2. Colloquial abbreviation of St. Gaudens gold coins, especially $20's in bullion transactions.

saltire [Heraldry] X-shaped formation, as crossed spears or scepters.

sandblast proof One made by sandblasting coins given the normal multiple blows from polished dies; compare **matte proof.** Several variants of this finish appear on federal gold coins 1908–9, 1911–15.

sandwich metal Derogatory epithet for **clad metal,** especially **nickel-clad,** as in current federal dimes and quarters; the root image is of red meat (core) between two thin layers of white bread (cladding). Objections arose early because the coins are lightweight, have a slick, almost greasy feel, and on the **ring test** yield only a brief note—in all, three criteria resembling those of **cast copies,** abandoning anticounterfeiting tests in use for over 2,000 years.

sans-serif [Typography] Said of letters without serifs (short ornamental cross-strokes at tops, bales, or ends). Formerly, horizontal, vertical, and curved elements were equally thick; occasional exceptions exist after the early 1930s. Examples of the former include **7600, 7772–73, 7932–35, 7947–48;** of the latter, **7607.**

satin-finish proof One with a surface a little nearer to **"Roman Gold"** than to matte; sometimes a little nearer to **brilliant-proof** finish than to either. Details of manufacture unknown, except that the coins were given extra blows from the dies; they do not show the **cartwheel effect** of **business strikes.** Examples include some 1921 and 1922 Peace dollars and certain commemoratives.

scarce In short supply, but with more survivors accessible than of a coin properly labeled as **rare.**

scissel Same as **clippings.**

screw press Engine for stamping **blanks** to make coins. The lower die is fixed into an anvil, generally wedged or fastened with set screws, to discourage loosening and rotation or **chatter. Blanks** are positioned atop it by **open collar** (prior to 1829) or in the **coining chamber** by **close collar** (beginning in 1829). The upper die is mounted at the end of what is essentially a rotating pile driver: a column fitted with screw threads, caused to descend rapidly with great force by rotating two weighted arms attached to the upper end of the column. The arms are attached to ropes pulled by workmen or horses, depending on press size; only the smallest presses could be operated by two laborers plus the **moneyer.** Larger presses could serve not only for larger coins but for stamping **hubs** into **working dies,** or raising hubs from **matrixes.** The inventors were Renaissance medallists attempting to rediscover how the ancient Romans made coins in high relief. Some features of the screw press are credited to Leonardo da Vinci; others to Boulton & Watt, including the automatic feed and safety devices in use at the Philadelphia Mint since 1793.

scrip Privately issued promissory notes payable in bank notes rather than in coin.

seawater UNCS. Epithet for gold coins recovered from wrecked ships; these typically show no wear but surfaces are granular or porous.

second-process planchet One which has been given a raised **rim;** contrast **first-process planchet.**

security edge Same as **safety edge.**

seeded [Heraldry] Said of a flower depicted with central dots representing stamens and pistils.

seignorage Difference between a coin's **face value** and its net cost; the latter is reckoned as sum of bullion value and manufacturing cost.

semester Half year. French mints routinely distinguished coins struck in the second semester from those made in the first, by placing a dot below one letter of legend.

serrated Formed like saw teeth; said of border elements shaped like sharply pointed wedges.

set up trial Impression, generally made weaker than normal, made during preparation of a press to test whether the dies are positioned to come together at the proper distance (thickness of finished coin).

Sheldon scale 1. His 8-point **rarity scale.** 2. His **numerical grading** scale.

shell-case bronze Alloy of 95% copper, 5% zinc, used for shell cases during WW II, which cases were retrieved by official orders and eventually used for cent metal, 1944–46.

shilling 1. British monetary unit = 12 **pence** = 1/20 pound sterling; 92.9 (later 87.27) grs. troy of silver 925 Fine. 2. Massachusetts Bay Colony monetary unit = 72 grs. troy of silver at same fineness. 3. Maryland monetary unit = 55.7 grs. troy of silver at probably same fineness. Other colonies and states defined the unit differently but made no silver coins exemplifying their standards.

shinplaster Derogatory epithet for paper currency, especially depreciated or of low face value; from the common military practice of using such notes to stanch leg wounds or sores. The term dates back to the War of 1812 and possibly to the Revolution; it became obsolete only with the retirement of fractional currency in the late 1870s. Some copper tokens of the late 1830s ("Hard Times tokens") actually read SUBSTITUTE FOR SHIN PLASTERS, parallel to the Canadian motto PURE COPPER PREFERABLE TO PAPER.

shooting thaler Swiss commemorative coin struck for local marksmanship exhibitions; from German, *Schützenfestthaler.*

shruf(f) Late 18th-century term for **clippings;** both spellings recur.

signature 1. Initials or name of a designer or engraver. 2. A **privymark;** those most familiar in federal coins include the notched star used by John Reich 1807–17 and the dot in field below wreath found on John Gardner's 1795 half dollar revs.

silver-clad The kind of **sandwich metal** with a core of **billon** (21% silver) and outer layers of higher-grade (80%) silver.

Silly Head Ebenezer Mason's name (6/1868) for one of the 1839 cent heads.

sinister [Heraldry] User's l. side = observer's r. side; the less honorable side of a shield or of a device on it. Its dishonorable or even evil connotations date to ancient Greece, where *aristerós*—'left, clumsy, ill-omened'—was a word so dreaded as to be replaced by the euphemism *euónymos*—'well-named'; where your l. foot was never to be set on a friend's threshold (soldiers still start marching with Left!). Throughout the Middle East, one's l. hand is reserved for toilet paper; to eat with it insults all present. Dozens of languages' words for left-handed connote clumsiness, treachery, or malevolence.

sink To impart **intaglio** design elements onto a **die blank.** Originally done by hand carving (the **celator's** art); later, by hammering in **letter punches** and/or placing the die blank in **press** opposite a **hub** or **device punch.** Antonym: **raise.**

Sivil Dollar Spanish (not Mexican) silver dollar: from the common 18th-century English spelling of Seville, one of the major mint sites in Spain.

sixfoil [Heraldry] Ornament representing a flower with six petals, seen from vertically above.

sixpence Half a **shilling.**

sizain (French) **Billon** coin of 6 **deniers;** half a **douzain.**

slider Current slang for a coin objectively EXTREMELY FINE or ABOUT UNCIRCULATED but salable as Mint State, particularly after cleaning and possibly recoloring. Many silver and gold coins offered as "Mint State 60" or "Mint State 63" are in fact sliders. You have been warned.

slippage Malfunction of the **Castaing machine:** a **blank** run through it sticks or slips instead of rolling normally, accordingly missing some edge letters or receiving some overlapping ones.

slipped [Heraldry] Said of a flower represented as with stem showing.

slipped and leaved [Heraldry] Said of a flower represented as with stem and leaves.

sol French money of account = 1/20 livre. Its weight and silver content varied, as did the number of **deniers** into which it was divided.

sol marqué (French) 1. Any **billon** coin given the 1640 **countermark** of **fleur de lys** in beaded oval. 2. Any billon coin overstruck with the 1692–93 recoinage dies: Chap. 5 above. 3. The larger size billon coin of the 1738–64 issue. 4. French, Canadian, and other French colonial money of account equated to preceding.

sol tampé (Caribbean Creole) Any **billon** coin given the (1763) **countermark** of crowned C. Later anglicized to **stampee.**

soleil [Heraldry] Personified sun, depicted as with face and rays.

sou (French) 1. A coin of 2 **sols** value. 2. Generic term for small coin or small change; compare Mexican Spanish **jola.**

spark erosion Electrodeposition technique for making a false die from a coin. Dies so made show millions of microcavities, which can be polished off fields but not off devices or inscriptions. Coins struck from such dies show micropimples on relief details, which are less well defined than in the genuine.

Special Mint Sets Substitute for proof sets, minted 1965–67. Apparently each coin received a single blow from polished dies on planchets cut from burnished strip.

specie Gold or silver, "hard money," as contrasted with paper **currency.**

specie ingot Rectangular **ingot** in an even denomination, intended to circulate as money when no proper coining machinery was available. Examples include the Moffat & Co. $16's and the Kohler/State Assay Office $50's. Compare **bullion-storage ingot.**

specie payments Redemption of paper currency in **specie,** 1815–May 10, 1837; ca. 1845–Dec. 28, 1861; 1877–1968. Compare next.

specie payments suspended Official or interbank agreement to refuse to make **specie payments,** May 10, 1837–ca. 1845; Dec. 28, 1861–1877; June 24, 1968, after which date silver certificates would no longer be redeemed in silver bullion.

speculative issue Said of 18th-century **coppers** made to circulate on their own authority, or of sample coppers proposed for a **contract coinage.**

spelter 18th-century name for zinc.

splasher 1. Droplet of brass, bonded to a copper **blank,** representing gold at the crown on the St. Patrick (Mark Newby) coins and some other copper issues of the time of Charles I. 2. Impression of a die in fusible alloy, thin brass, or some other soft metal requiring little force; 18th- and 19th-century splashers often show ragged edges and traces of old newspapers adhering to blank backs, suggesting that the liquid metal was poured onto the papers, the latter used both to position it atop the die (while a rolling pin produced the impression) and to ease prying it off afterward. The French term is *cliché.*

spoiled cent stock Said of half cents, spring 1796–1803, struck on **blanks** made by cutting down misstruck cents. Contrast **rolled stock, token stock.**

stampee 1. Anglicization of **sol tampé.** 2. Caribbean money of account = **dogg** = 1/6 **bitt.**

standard 1. Legally or officially designated weight. 2. Legally or officially designated **fineness.**

Standard Mint Value Common legend on pioneer California gold (generally abbreviated S.M.V.), claiming that the coin so designated was of high enough weight and fineness to pass at par with federally minted coins of the same denomination.

standard silver 1. In the USA, silver 900 Fine. 2. Legend on pattern coins of 1869, proposing a lightweight issue to redeem fractional currency.

star 1. Symbol or ornament representing a heavenly body other than sun, moon, planet, or comet; rays proceeding from around a central point. The heraldic **estoile** has six or sometimes eight wavy lines. 2. Symbol of pentagram shape, properly a heraldic **molet** or spur rowel; mistaken for an estoile from the appearance of such ornaments in the arms of George Washington, and so represented in the arms and flag of the United States.

statutory legend Any **legend** specified by the act authorizing a coinage, particularly naming the issuing authority. Examples: AUCTORI VERMON, AUCTORI CONNEC, and UNITED STATES OF AMERICA. Required on all federal coins by Act of April 2, 1792 and 31 U.S.C. 324, Sect. 3517.

steelies Slang for 1943 cents of zinc-coated steel.

stella Name of the proposed $4 gold coin of 1879–80; from the large **star** device on rev. (Latin: *stella* = 'star').

stem spot Round area on a **cast** piece where molten metal entered the mold and was broken away at cooling. Normal on Moffat & Co. ingots.

sterling 1. Silver 925 Fine; the British **standard.** 2. Generic British **specie.**

stock 1. **Strip** rolled to thickness of a particular denomination. 2. **Blanks** cut from such strip.

stock die One usable in any number of different combinations, not exclusively referring to the firm ordering **tokens** struck from it.

stop 1. British term for a period or colon marking an abbreviation or end of an inscription. 2. A pellet or small ornament separating words (in full or abbreviated) in an inscription.

store card Any **token** advertising the issuing firm; sometimes given out as business cards now are, formerly often circulated as small change.

strawberry leaf, strawberry sprig Old misnomers for **cotton-leaf cent;** see discussion in Crosby {1897}.

stria(e) (Latin) "Line(s), generally straight, in relief on a coin, often in parallel groups or randomly scattered" (Breen {1977}, p. 306). Parallel striae occur most often in fields on 19th-century coins, generally from a file, lapstone, grinding wheel, or buffing wheel applied to the die; scattered striae are a feature of St. Gaudens's prototype $10 and $20 coins of 1907, but occur also on some 1921 Peace dollars and some commemoratives. They are not a guarantee of genuineness, let alone of proof status. Their configuration is distinctive for each working die.

strike 1. To stamp a coin design onto a **blank.** 2. Impression of relief detail: shallow (weak) or bold (strong, sharp).

striking 1. Batch of coins from a single source, delivered together. 2. Process of stamping coins. 3. As sense 2 of **strike.**

strip 1. What an **ingot** is rolled into; **blanks** are cut from it. 2. Chemically remove toning, tarnish, spots, atmospheric contaminants, corrosion, patina, etc., from a coin; drastically clean.

struck Made by stamping onto a blank. Antonym: **cast.**

struck copy An imitation made from **copy dies.** Antonyms: **cast, electrotype.** Many pre-1890 instances, by Bolen and others, have become collectibles in their own right: Kenney {1952}.

supporter [Heraldry] Either of a pair of figures depicted as holding the shield (with its crest, mantling, etc.) between them. They may be human, animal, or mythological figures.

swingletree T-shaped attachment to a plow, at or near end of beam, to which the beasts of burden are roped or chained for pulling it. Dr. Maris {1881} spelled it "singletree."

T

tale Physical count. Usually in the phrase "by tale," meaning that the coins are each reckoned at face value, rather than separately weighed to ascertain bullion value.

taler Phonetic respelling of **thaler.** Rhymes with pallor or valor.

tenor Standard weight/fineness/exchange rate: See **new-tenor, old-tenor.**

thaler Generic term for any European silver-dollar-sized coin. (Silent h; rhymes with valor.) Originally, German for 'from the valley,' short for Joachimsthaler, name of one of the earliest (Bohemian) coins of this size. Ancestor of the modern term **dollar.**

three cents 1. **Billon** coin of this value, 1851–53; see **fish scale.** 2. Silver coin of this value, 1854–73; officially **trime.** 3. Cupro-nickel coin of this value, 1865–89, issued to retire fractional notes of this denomination.

three-dollar piece, three-dollar(s) gold Coin of this value, 1854–89.

threepence Coin valued at 1/4 **shilling.**

tin pests Localized corrosion (discoloration, crumbling) on tin coins, where metallic tin (beta-tin) has changed to powdery alpha-tin. A result of exposure to cold weather, especially in presence of even a single particle of alpha-tin.

togate Said of a bust draped in a toga.

token 1. Item presentable as evidence of membership. 2. **Store card.** 3. Anything locally usable as substitute for a coin, e.g., on public transit or for paid admission.

token stock Said of half cents, spring 1796–97, struck on cut-down Talbot, Allum & Lee tokens.

torse [Heraldry] A twisted wreath, seen edge on; a heraldic crest often rests on one, as if on a cushion.

Tory Conservative royalist. Compare next.

Tory copper Imitation British halfpenny, circulating in the USA after the Revolution; herein are listed only those made in America, not imported from Birmingham. In the 1780s the domestic and imported vars. were both called **Bungtown coppers.**

tour [Heraldry] Emblem representing a chess rook or small castle tower.

Tower Mint That housed in the Tower of London.

Tower Standard Weight and fineness standards in use at the **Tower Mint.** See "Metrology" tables at the beginning of Part One.

trade dollar Denomination coined 1873–85, 1.8% heavier than the standard silver dollar, and intended for use between American trading ships and Chinese port merchants.

transfer die A **copy die** fabricated by raising a **hub** from an old die and sinking this hub into a new **die blank.** Examples of **restrikes** so made include the Albert Collis WASHINGTON

BORN VIRGINIA pieces and Bashlow's "second restrike" Confederate cents.

transitional design Same as **prototype,** sense 2.

transposed arrows Said of any heraldic eagle design in which the arrows are in **dexter** claw rather than normally in **sinister** claw. (However, in the Scot heraldic eagle designs of 1796–1807, arrows are normally in dexter claw.)

trefoil [Heraldry] Emblem or ornament representing either a three-petaled flower, a clover leaf, or the club suit.

tressure Supplementary inner border of arches joined at cusps by ornaments or angles.

trial of the pyx Annual test of coins by the Assay Commission (or its local counterpart) to ascertain if the mintmaster had issued any **debased** ones. The pyx was an official receptacle for samples of each batch; named after the receptacle for transporting consecrated wafers.

trial piece Any **OMS** in baser metal than the intended coin. Typically, trial pieces of copper coins are in brass, tin, "white metal," or lead; trial pieces of silver or gold coins are in any of the above or in copper. Between about 1863 and 1885, U.S. proof sets were struck from regular dies in copper, nickel, and aluminum; these are commonly classed as trial pieces, though a more accurate designation is **pièces de caprice.**

trime James Ross Snowden's name for the **billon** and silver **three-cents** coins. Not publicly used while the coins were current.

triple stripes Said of **pales gules** with three lines of vertical shading per stripe.

triplet head Abel Buell's device punch for Connecticut coppers, used by his son Benjamin (April 1789) and later sold to Machin's Mills, recognizable by a wreath whose leaves are in groups of three.

troy ounce Weight = 1/12 **troy pound** = 480 grs. = 31.1 gms.

troy pound Weight = 5,760 grs. = 373.24 gms. Troy weights were used only for gold and silver, later also platinum.

truncation The lower cutoff edge of a head or bust.

Tudor rose The double rose (five inner petals within five outer), symbolizing the union in the Tudor dynasty of the white and red roses of the Yorkists and Lancastrians in the Wars of the Roses. (It became the Royal Badge of England in 1486, at the marriage of Henry VII to Elizabeth of York.) Used as a device in William Wood's ROSA AMERICANA coins, though its meaning may not have been known to King George I at whom this iconographic flattery was aimed.

"Turban Head" 1. Misnomer for John Reich's "Classic Head" design. 2. Misnomer for Gobrecht's 1836–39 half-dollar bust. Both senses originated with ignorant people who had never seen a real turban.

turn Impart roundness (cylindrical contours) to a **die blank** by lathe.

tutanaigne Crosby's misreading of next, in the Royal Patent for Wood's ROSA AMERICANA coins.

tutenag(ue) Zinc ore or impure zinc metal; from Portuguese *tutanaga,* Mahratti and Gujarati *tuttināga,* ultimately Skr. *tuttha* 'blue vitriol, sulfate' + *nāga* 'lead, tin, base metal.' Hobson-Jobson, s.v. Tootnague; OED s.v. tutenag.

two-cent piece Bronze coin of this value, issued 1864–73.

type Major subdivision of a design: 1883 nickels without and with CENTS are different types of the same design, as are 1853 and 1873 silver coins without and with arrows. Compare **major variety.**

U

UNCIRCULATED 1. **Mint state,** contrasted with **circulated;** free of any trace of wear. 2. Unworn **business strike,** contrasted with **proof.**

uncurrent No longer legal to **circulate.**

undertype Struck coin used as a **planchet** to be **overstruck** with other dies.

uniface With a design on only one side, the other side blank. Said of **splashers** and other die trials; of several vars. of AUCTORI PLEBIS coppers struck on one side only; and of mint errors resulting from two **blanks** simultaneously reaching the **coining chamber.**

union 1. The starry blue **canton** in the American flag. 2. Federal government comprising only those states which did not secede at the Civil War.

unique 1. One of a kind; the only one made. 2. The only survivor of its kind; a dangerous claim to make about any coin.

Unit Morris's hypothetical money of account (1783) = $1/1{,}440$ Spanish dollar = 1/4 gr. silver (actually 0.01742 gm.).

upset To compress a **first-process planchet** edgewise in order to insure roundness and impart raised **rims,** making it into a **second-process planchet.**

V

variety Any coin recognizably different in dies from another of the same **design, type,** date, and mint. Compare **major variety, minor variety.** Herein normally abbreviated var.

VERY GOOD Grade level defined in main text for each series collectible in that grade; typically, with complete inscriptions but only partial interior details.

VERY FINE Grade level defined for each series in main text; typically, complete in even the most minute details with minor signs of wear.

virole brisée (French) Segmented collar for imparting **edge devices** as on some of Droz's patterns for Boulton (1788), and as on St. Gaudens gold coins beginning in 1907.

voided [Heraldry] With interiors absent or hollowed out.

W

wampum Worn-down abbreviation for next.

wanpanpiag (Algonquin) Native American money: strings of handmade shell beads, which derived their value from the time required to make them. Legal currency in Massachusetts Bay Colony after 1627. See Chap. 1, Sect. ii, introductory text.

warrant Written authorization; in the First Mint, written orders (dated and serially numbered) by the Director authorizing transfer of newly struck coins from the Coiner to the Treasurer of the Mint or other authorized recipients.

wartime silver Coinage metal for 5¢ pieces, Oct. 1942–Dec. 1945, consisting of 35% silver, 56% copper, 9% manganese.

web Modern term for **scissel;** perforated remains of **strip** after **blanks** were cut from it. See **blank cutter.**

weight standard Weight authorized by law, which coins struck under such authority must neither exceed nor fall short of. In practice, for reasons of technological limitation, minor deviations are permitted; their limits are called the **remedy.**

whizzing Giving a coin a false surface fraudulently simulating **mint bloom,** generally by wire brush or the like. Whizzed coins are technically mutilated. See *CW* 5/21/86, p. 42, for ills.

wire edge 1. Misnomer for a **knife-rim.** 2. Misnomer for the first **prototype** St. Gaudens $10 of 1907.

witch piece, witch token Thin silver coin, generally a Massachusetts silver coin, bent (often showing teethmarks) and carried as a charm to protect the user against alleged baleful influence of witches during the Salem witchcraft delusion of 1692. Noe {1952} called attention to a possible relationship between such bent silver pieces and the Mother Goose rhyme about the crooked man who walked a crooked mile, "And found a crooked sixpence/Against a crooked stile."

Wood's coinages 1. The ROSA AMERICANA coins: above, Chap. 2, Sect. ii. 2. The 1722–24 HIBERNIA coins: above, Chap. 2, Sect. iii.

Wood's coinage metal Same as **Bath metal.**

working die One used for striking coins, rather than for making **hubs.**

working hub One used for making **working dies.**

INDEX OF NAMES

Boldface numbers are as in main text; individuals so cited may be named or portrayed on coins, or former owners or designers, etc., alluded to thereunder. Initials known or believed to represent names are indexed by first letter; for others see Bibliography or Index of Subjects. Names of firms, institutions, cities, counties, states, countries, etc. appear in Index of Subjects. Initials DM following a name = Director of the Mint; MCC = Member of Continental Congress; SM = Superintendent of the named Mint; SS = Secretary of State; ST = Secretary of Treasury.

INDEX OF SUBJECTS

Boldface numbers are as in main text; lightface numbers are page numbers. For unidentified initials see Index of Names.